MW00717658

American Casebook Series
Hornbook Series and Basic Legal Texts
Black Letter Series and Nutshell Series

of

WEST PUBLISHING
P.O. Box 64526
St. Paul, Minnesota 55164–0526

Accounting

FARIS' ACCOUNTING AND LAW IN A NUTSHELL, 377 pages, 1984. Softcover. (Text)

FIFLIS' ACCOUNTING ISSUES FOR LAWYERS, TEACHING MATERIALS, Fourth Edition, 706 pages, 1991. Teacher's Manual available. (Casebook)

SIEGEL AND SIEGEL'S ACCOUNTING AND FINANCIAL DISCLOSURE: A GUIDE TO BASIC CONCEPTS, 259 pages, 1983. Softcover. (Text)

Administrative Law

AMAN AND MAYTON'S HORNBOOK ON ADMINISTRATIVE LAW, 917 pages, 1993. (Text)

BONFIELD AND ASIMOW'S STATE AND FEDERAL ADMINISTRATIVE LAW, 826 pages, 1989. Teacher's Manual available. (Casebook) 1993 Supplement.

GELLHORN AND LEVIN'S ADMINISTRATIVE LAW AND PROCESS IN A NUTSHELL, Third Edition, 479 pages, 1990. Softcover. (Text)

MASHAW, MERRILL, AND SHANE'S CASES AND MATERIALS ON ADMINISTRATIVE LAW—THE AMERICAN PUBLIC LAW SYSTEM, Third Edition, 1187 pages, 1992. Teacher's Manual available. (Casebook)

ROBINSON, GELLHORN AND BRUFF'S THE ADMINISTRATIVE PROCESS, Fourth Edition, approximately 1000 pages, 1993. (Casebook)

Admiralty

HEALY AND SHARPE'S CASES AND MATERIALS ON ADMIRALTY, Second Edition, 876 pages, 1986. (Casebook)

MARAIST'S ADMIRALTY IN A NUTSHELL, Second Edition, 379 pages, 1988. Softcover. (Text)

SCHOENBAUM'S HORNBOOK ON ADMIRALTY AND MARITIME LAW, Student Edition, 692 pages, 1987 with 1992 pocket part. (Text)

Agency—Partnership

DEMOTT'S FIDUCIARY OBLIGATION, AGENCY AND PARTNERSHIP: DUTIES IN ONGOING BUSINESS RELATIONSHIPS, 740 pages, 1991. Teacher's Manual available. (Casebook)

FESSLER'S ALTERNATIVES TO INCORPORATION FOR PERSONS IN QUEST OF PROFIT, Third Edition, 339 pages, 1991. Softcover. (Casebook)

HENN'S CASES AND MATERIALS ON AGENCY, PARTNERSHIP AND OTHER UNINCORPORATED BUSINESS ENTERPRISES, Second Edition, 733 pages, 1985. Teacher's Manual available. (Casebook)

REUSCHLEIN AND GREGORY'S HORNBOOK ON THE LAW OF AGENCY AND PARTNERSHIP, Second Edition, 683 pages, 1990. (Text)

SELECTED CORPORATION AND PARTNERSHIP STATUTES, RULES AND FORMS. 1993 Edition, approximately 975 pages. Softcover.

STEFFEN AND KERR'S CASES ON AGENCY-PARTNERSHIP, Fourth Edition, 859 pages, 1980. (Casebook)

STEFFEN'S AGENCY-PARTNERSHIP IN A NUTSHELL, 364 pages, 1977. Softcover. (Text)

Alternative Dispute Resolution

NOLAN–HALEY'S ALTERNATIVE DISPUTE RESOLUTION IN A NUTSHELL, 298 pages, 1992.

List current as of July, 1993

Alternative Dispute Resolution—Cont'd

Softcover. (Text)

RISKIN AND WESTBROOK'S DISPUTE RESOLUTION AND LAWYERS, 468 pages, 1987. Teacher's Manual available. (Casebook) 1993 Supplement.

RISKIN AND WESTBROOK'S DISPUTE RESOLUTION AND LAWYERS. Abridged Edition, 223 pages, 1987. Softcover. Teacher's Manual available. (Casebook) 1993 Supplement.

RISKIN'S DISPUTE RESOLUTION FOR LAWYERS VIDEO TAPES, 1992. (Available for purchase by schools and libraries.)

American Indian Law

CANBY'S AMERICAN INDIAN LAW IN A NUTSHELL, Second Edition, 336 pages, 1988. Softcover. (Text)

GETCHES, WILKINSON AND WILLIAMS' CASES AND MATERIALS ON FEDERAL INDIAN LAW, Third Edition, approximately 900 pages, 1993. Teacher's Manual expected. (Casebook)

Antitrust—see also Regulated Industries, Trade Regulation

BARNES AND STOUT'S ECONOMIC FOUNDATIONS OF REGULATION AND ANTITRUST LAW, 102 pages, 1992. Softcover. Teacher's Manual available. (Casebook)

FOX AND SULLIVAN'S CASES AND MATERIALS ON ANTITRUST, 935 pages, 1989. Teacher's Manual available. (Casebook) 1993 Supplement.

GELLHORN AND KOVACIC'S ANTITRUST LAW AND ECONOMICS IN A NUTSHELL, Fourth Edition, approximately 475 pages, 1993. Softcover. (Text)

HOVENKAMP'S BLACK LETTER ON ANTITRUST, Second Edition, 347 pages, 1993. Softcover. (Review)

HOVENKAMP'S HORNBOOK ON ECONOMICS AND FEDERAL ANTITRUST LAW, Student Edition, 414 pages, 1985. (Text)

POSNER AND EASTERBROOK'S CASES AND ECONOMIC NOTES ON ANTITRUST, Second Edition, 1077 pages, 1981. (Casebook) 1984–85 Supplement.

SULLIVAN'S HORNBOOK OF THE LAW OF ANTITRUST, 886 pages, 1977. (Text)

Appellate Advocacy—see Trial and Appellate Advocacy

Architecture and Engineering Law

SWEET'S LEGAL ASPECTS OF ARCHITECTURE, ENGINEERING AND THE CONSTRUCTION PROCESS, Fourth Edition, 889 pages, 1989. Teacher's Manual available. (Casebook)

Art Law

DUBOFF'S ART LAW IN A NUTSHELL, Second Edition, 350 pages, 1993. Softcover. (Text)

Banking Law

BANKING LAW: SELECTED STATUTES AND REGULATIONS. Softcover. 263 pages, 1991.

LOVETT'S BANKING AND FINANCIAL INSTITUTIONS LAW IN A NUTSHELL, Third Edition, 470 pages, 1992. Softcover. (Text)

SYMONS AND WHITE'S BANKING LAW: TEACHING MATERIALS, Third Edition, 818 pages, 1991. Teacher's Manual available. (Casebook)

Statutory Supplement. *See Banking Law: Selected Statutes*

Bankruptcy—see Creditors' Rights

Business Planning—see also Corporate Finance

PAINTER'S PROBLEMS AND MATERIALS IN BUSINESS PLANNING, Second Edition, 1008 pages, 1984. (Casebook) 1990 Supplement.

Statutory Supplement. *See Selected Corporation and Partnership*

Civil Procedure—see also Federal Jurisdiction and Procedure

AMERICAN BAR ASSOCIATION SECTION OF LITIGATION—READINGS ON ADVERSARIAL JUSTICE: THE AMERICAN APPROACH TO ADJUDICATION, 217 pages, 1988. Softcover. (Coursebook)

CLERMONT'S BLACK LETTER ON CIVIL PROCEDURE, Third Edition, 318 pages, 1993. Softcover. (Review)

COUND, FRIEDENTHAL, MILLER AND SEXTON'S CASES AND MATERIALS ON CIVIL PROCEDURE, Sixth Edition, approximately 1300 pages, 1993. Teacher's Manual available. (Casebook)

COUND, FRIEDENTHAL, MILLER AND SEXTON'S

Civil Procedure—Cont'd

CIVIL PROCEDURE SUPPLEMENT. Approximately 475 pages, 1993. Softcover. (Casebook Supplement)

FEDERAL RULES OF CIVIL PROCEDURE—1993–94 EDUCATIONAL EDITION. Softcover. Approximately 1200 pages, 1993.

FRIEDENTHAL, KANE AND MILLER'S HORNBOOK ON CIVIL PROCEDURE, Second Edition, approximately 1000 pages, 1993. (Text)

KANE AND LEVINE'S CIVIL PROCEDURE IN CALIFORNIA: STATE AND FEDERAL 1992 Edition, 551 pages. Softcover. (Casebook Supplement)

KANE'S CIVIL PROCEDURE IN A NUTSHELL, Third Edition, 303 pages, 1991. Softcover. (Text)

LEVINE, SLOMANSON AND WINGATE'S CALIFORNIA CIVIL PROCEDURE, CASES AND MATERIALS, 546 pages, 1991. Teacher's Manual available. (Casebook)

MARCUS, REDISH AND SHERMAN'S CIVIL PROCEDURE: A MODERN APPROACH, 1027 pages, 1989. Teacher's Manual available. (Casebook) 1991 Supplement.

MARCUS AND SHERMAN'S COMPLEX LITIGATION–CASES AND MATERIALS ON ADVANCED CIVIL PROCEDURE, Second Edition, 1035 pages, 1992. Teacher's Manual available. (Casebook)

PARK AND MCFARLAND'S COMPUTER-AIDED EXERCISES ON CIVIL PROCEDURE, Third Edition, 210 pages, 1991. Softcover. (Coursebook)

SIEGEL'S HORNBOOK ON NEW YORK PRACTICE, Second Edition, Student Edition, 1068 pages, 1991. Softcover. (Text) 1993–94 Supplement.

SLOMANSON AND WINGATE'S CALIFORNIA CIVIL PROCEDURE IN A NUTSHELL, 230 pages, 1992. Softcover. (Text)

Commercial Law

ALCES AND BENFIELD'S PAYMENT SYSTEMS: CASES, MATERIALS, AND PROBLEMS, 569 pages, 1993. Teacher's Manual available. (Casebook)

BAILEY AND HAGEDORN'S SECURED TRANSACTIONS IN A NUTSHELL, Third Edition, 390 pages, 1988. Softcover. (Text)

EPSTEIN, MARTIN, HENNING AND NICKLES' BASIC UNIFORM COMMERCIAL CODE TEACHING MATERIALS, Third Edition, 704 pages, 1988. Teacher's Manual available. (Casebook)

HENSON'S HORNBOOK ON SECURED TRANSACTIONS UNDER THE U.C.C., Second Edition, 504 pages, 1979, with 1979 pocket part. (Text)

MEYER AND SPEIDEL'S BLACK LETTER ON SALES AND LEASES OF GOODS, 317 pages, 1993. Softcover. (Review)

MURRAY AND FLECHTNER'S SALES AND LEASES: PROBLEMS AND MATERIALS ON NATIONAL AND INTERNATIONAL TRANSACTIONS, Approximately 650 pages, September, 1993 pub. Teacher's Manual available. (Casebook)

NICKLES' BLACK LETTER ON NEGOTIABLE INSTRUMENTS (AND OTHER RELATED COMMERCIAL PAPER), Second Edition, 574 pages, 1993. Softcover. (Review)

NICKLES, MATHESON AND DOLAN'S MATERIALS FOR UNDERSTANDING CREDIT AND PAYMENT SYSTEMS, 923 pages, 1987. Teacher's Manual available. (Casebook)

NORDSTROM, MURRAY AND CLOVIS' PROBLEMS AND MATERIALS ON SALES, 515 pages, 1982. (Casebook)

RUBIN AND COOTER'S THE PAYMENT SYSTEM: CASES, MATERIALS AND ISSUES, 885 pages, 1989. Teacher's Manual Available. (Casebook)

SELECTED COMMERCIAL STATUTES. Softcover. Approximately 1900 pages, 1993.

SPEIDEL AND NICKLES' NEGOTIABLE INSTRUMENTS AND CHECK COLLECTION IN A NUTSHELL, Fourth Edition, 544 pages, 1993. Softcover. (Text)

SPEIDEL, SUMMERS AND WHITE'S PAYMENT SYSTEMS: TEACHING MATERIALS, Fifth Edition, approximately 575 pages, 1993. Softcover. Teacher's Manual available. (Casebook)

SPEIDEL, SUMMERS AND WHITE'S SALES AND SECURED TRANSACTIONS: TEACHING MATERIALS, Fifth Edition, approximately 1150 pages, 1993. Teacher's Manual available. (Casebook)

SPEIDEL, SUMMERS AND WHITE'S SECURED TRANSACTIONS: TEACHING MATERIALS, Fifth

Commercial Law—Cont'd

Edition, approximately 500 pages, October, 1993 pub. Reprint from Speidel et al., Sales and Secured Transactions, Fifth Edition. Softcover. Teacher's Manual available. (Casebook)

STOCKTON AND MILLER'S SALES AND LEASES OF GOODS IN A NUTSHELL, Third Edition, 441 pages, 1992. Softcover. (Text)

STONE'S UNIFORM COMMERCIAL CODE IN A NUTSHELL, Third Edition, 580 pages, 1989. Softcover. (Text)

WHITE AND SUMMERS' HORNBOOK ON THE UNIFORM COMMERCIAL CODE, Third Edition, Student Edition, 1386 pages, 1988 with 1993 pocket part (covering Rev. Arts. 3, 4, new 2A, 4A). (Text)

Community Property

MENNELL AND BOYKOFF'S COMMUNITY PROPERTY IN A NUTSHELL, Second Edition, 432 pages, 1988. Softcover. (Text)

VERRALL AND BIRD'S CASES AND MATERIALS ON CALIFORNIA COMMUNITY PROPERTY, Fifth Edition, 604 pages, 1988. (Casebook)

Comparative Law

BARTON, GIBBS, LI AND MERRYMAN'S LAW IN RADICALLY DIFFERENT CULTURES, 960 pages, 1983. (Casebook)

GLENDON, GORDON AND OSAKWE'S COMPARATIVE LEGAL TRADITIONS: TEXT, MATERIALS AND CASES ON THE CIVIL LAW, COMMON LAW AND SOCIALIST LAW TRADITIONS, 1091 pages, 1985. (Casebook)

GLENDON, GORDON AND OSAKWE'S COMPARATIVE LEGAL TRADITIONS IN A NUTSHELL. 402 pages, 1982. Softcover. (Text)

Computers and Law

MAGGS, SOMA AND SPROWL'S COMPUTER LAW—CASES, COMMENTS, AND QUESTIONS, 731 pages, 1992. Teacher's Manual available. (Casebook)

MASON'S USING COMPUTERS IN THE LAW: AN INTRODUCTION AND PRACTICAL GUIDE, Second Edition, 288 pages, 1988. Softcover. (Coursebook)

Conflict of Laws

CRAMTON, CURRIE, KAY AND KRAMER'S CASES—COMMENTS—QUESTIONS ON CONFLICT OF LAWS, Fifth Edition, approximately 750 pages, 1993. (Casebook)

HAY'S BLACK LETTER ON CONFLICT OF LAWS, 330 pages, 1989. Softcover. (Review)

SCOLES AND HAY'S HORNBOOK ON CONFLICT OF LAWS, Student Edition, 1160 pages, 1992. (Text)

SIEGEL'S CONFLICTS IN A NUTSHELL, 470 pages, 1982. Softcover. (Text)

Constitutional Law—Civil Rights—see also First Amendment and Foreign Relations and National Security Law

ABERNATHY'S CIVIL RIGHTS AND CONSTITUTIONAL LITIGATION, CASES AND MATERIALS, Second Edition, 753 pages, 1992. (Casebook)

BARNES AND STOUT'S THE ECONOMICS OF CONSTITUTIONAL LAW AND PUBLIC CHOICE, 127 pages, 1992. Softcover. Teacher's Manual available. (Casebook)

BARRON AND DIENES' BLACK LETTER ON CONSTITUTIONAL LAW, Third Edition, 440 pages, 1991. Softcover. (Review)

BARRON AND DIENES' CONSTITUTIONAL LAW IN A NUTSHELL, Second Edition, 483 pages, 1991. Softcover. (Text)

ENGDAHL'S CONSTITUTIONAL FEDERALISM IN A NUTSHELL, Second Edition, 411 pages, 1987. Softcover. (Text)

FARBER, ESKRIDGE AND FRICKEY'S CONSTITUTIONAL LAW: THEMES FOR THE CONSTITUTION'S THIRD CENTURY, 1127 pages, 1993. Teacher's Manual available. (Casebook) 1993 Supplement.

FARBER AND SHERRY'S HISTORY OF THE AMERICAN CONSTITUTION, 458 pages, 1990. Softcover. Teacher's Manual available. (Text)

FISHER AND DEVINS' POLITICAL DYNAMICS OF CONSTITUTIONAL LAW, 333 pages, 1992. Softcover. (Casebook Supplement)

GARVEY AND ALEINIKOFF'S MODERN CONSTITUTIONAL THEORY: A READER, Second Edition, 559 pages, 1991. Softcover. (Reader)

LOCKHART, KAMISAR, CHOPER AND SHIFFRIN'S CONSTITUTIONAL LAW: CASES—COMMENTS—QUESTIONS, Seventh Edition, 1643 pages, 1991. (Casebook) 1993 Supplement.

LOCKHART, KAMISAR, CHOPER AND SHIFFRIN'S

Constitutional Law—Civil Rights—Cont'd

THE AMERICAN CONSTITUTION: CASES AND MATERIALS, Seventh Edition, 1255 pages, 1991. Abridged version of Lockhart, et al., Constitutional Law: Cases–Comments–Questions, Seventh Edition. (Casebook) 1993 Supplement.

LOCKHART, KAMISAR, CHOPER AND SHIFFRIN'S CONSTITUTIONAL RIGHTS AND LIBERTIES: CASES AND MATERIALS, Seventh Edition, 1333 pages, 1991. Reprint from Lockhart, et al., Constitutional Law: Cases–Comments–Questions, Seventh Edition. (Casebook) 1993 Supplement.

MARKS AND COOPER'S STATE CONSTITUTIONAL LAW IN A NUTSHELL, 329 pages, 1988. Softcover. (Text)

NOWAK AND ROTUNDA'S HORNBOOK ON CONSTITUTIONAL LAW, Fourth Edition, 1357 pages, 1991. (Text)

ROTUNDA'S MODERN CONSTITUTIONAL LAW: CASES AND NOTES, Fourth Edition, 1137 pages, 1993. (Casebook) 1993 Supplement.

VIEIRA'S CONSTITUTIONAL CIVIL RIGHTS IN A NUTSHELL, Second Edition, 322 pages, 1990. Softcover. (Text)

WILLIAMS' CONSTITUTIONAL ANALYSIS IN A NUTSHELL, 388 pages, 1979. Softcover. (Text)

Consumer Law—see also Commercial Law

EPSTEIN AND NICKLES' CONSUMER LAW IN A NUTSHELL, Second Edition, 418 pages, 1981. Softcover. (Text)

SELECTED COMMERCIAL STATUTES. Softcover. Approximately 1900 pages, 1993.

SPANOGLE, ROHNER, PRIDGEN AND RASOR'S CASES AND MATERIALS ON CONSUMER LAW, Second Edition, 916 pages, 1991. Teacher's Manual available. (Casebook)

Contracts

BARNES AND STOUT'S THE ECONOMICS OF CONTRACT LAW, 127 pages, 1992. Softcover. Teacher's Manual available. (Casebook)

CALAMARI AND PERILLO'S BLACK LETTER ON CONTRACTS, Second Edition, 462 pages, 1990. Softcover. (Review)

CALAMARI AND PERILLO'S HORNBOOK ON CONTRACTS, Third Edition, 1049 pages, 1987. (Text)

CALAMARI, PERILLO AND BENDER'S CASES AND PROBLEMS ON CONTRACTS, Second Edition, 905 pages, 1989. Teacher's Manual Available. (Casebook)

CORBIN'S TEXT ON CONTRACTS, One Volume Student Edition, 1224 pages, 1952. (Text)

FRIEDMAN'S CONTRACT REMEDIES IN A NUTSHELL, 323 pages, 1981. Softcover. (Text)

FULLER AND EISENBERG'S CASES ON BASIC CONTRACT LAW, Fifth Edition, 1037 pages, 1990. (Casebook)

HAMILTON, RAU AND WEINTRAUB'S CASES AND MATERIALS ON CONTRACTS, Second Edition, 916 pages, 1992. Teacher's Manual available. (Casebook)

KEYES' GOVERNMENT CONTRACTS IN A NUTSHELL, Second Edition, 557 pages, 1990. Softcover. (Text)

SCHABER AND ROHWER'S CONTRACTS IN A NUTSHELL, Third Edition, 457 pages, 1990. Softcover. (Text)

SUMMERS AND HILLMAN'S CONTRACT AND RELATED OBLIGATION: THEORY, DOCTRINE AND PRACTICE, Second Edition, 1037 pages, 1992. Teacher's Manual available. (Casebook)

Copyright—see Intellectual Property

Corporate Finance—see also Business Planning

HAMILTON'S CASES AND MATERIALS ON CORPORATION FINANCE, Second Edition, 1221 pages, 1989. (Casebook)

OESTERLE'S THE LAW OF MERGERS, ACQUISITIONS AND REORGANIZATIONS, 1096 pages, 1991. (Casebook) 1992 Supplement.

Corporations

HAMILTON'S BLACK LETTER ON CORPORATIONS, Third Edition, 732 pages, 1992. Softcover. (Review)

HAMILTON'S CASES AND MATERIALS ON CORPORATIONS—INCLUDING PARTNERSHIPS AND LIMITED PARTNERSHIPS, Fourth Edition, 1248 pages, 1990. Teacher's Manual available. (Casebook) 1990 Statutory Supplement.

HAMILTON'S THE LAW OF CORPORATIONS IN A NUTSHELL, Third Edition, 518 pages, 1991. Softcover. (Text)

Corporations—Cont'd

HENN AND ALEXANDER'S HORNBOOK ON LAWS OF CORPORATIONS, Third Edition, Student Edition, 1371 pages, 1983, with 1986 pocket part. (Text)

SELECTED CORPORATION AND PARTNERSHIP STATUTES, RULES AND FORMS. 1993 Edition, approximately 975 pages. Softcover.

SOLOMON, SCHWARTZ AND BAUMAN'S MATERIALS AND PROBLEMS ON CORPORATIONS: LAW AND POLICY, Second Edition, 1391 pages, 1988. Teacher's Manual available. (Casebook) 1992 Supplement.

Statutory Supplement. *See Selected Corporation and Partnership*

Corrections

KRANTZ' THE LAW OF CORRECTIONS AND PRISONERS' RIGHTS IN A NUTSHELL, Third Edition, 407 pages, 1988. Softcover. (Text)

KRANTZ AND BRANHAM'S CASES AND MATERIALS ON THE LAW OF SENTENCING, CORRECTIONS AND PRISONERS' RIGHTS, Fourth Edition, 619 pages, 1991. Teacher's Manual available. (Casebook) 1993 Supplement.

Creditors' Rights

BANKRUPTCY CODE, RULES AND OFFICIAL FORMS, LAW SCHOOL EDITION. Approximately 925 pages, 1993. Softcover.

EPSTEIN'S DEBTOR-CREDITOR LAW IN A NUTSHELL, Fourth Edition, 401 pages, 1991. Softcover. (Text)

EPSTEIN, LANDERS AND NICKLES' CASES AND MATERIALS ON DEBTORS AND CREDITORS, Third Edition, 1059 pages, 1987. Teacher's Manual available. (Casebook)

EPSTEIN, NICKLES AND WHITE'S HORNBOOK ON BANKRUPTCY, 1077 pages, 1992. (Text)

LOPUCKI'S PLAYER'S MANUAL FOR THE DEBTOR-CREDITOR GAME, 123 pages, 1985. Softcover. (Coursebook)

NICKLES AND EPSTEIN'S BLACK LETTER ON CREDITORS' RIGHTS AND BANKRUPTCY, 576 pages, 1989. (Review)

RIESENFELD'S CASES AND MATERIALS ON CREDITORS' REMEDIES AND DEBTORS' PROTECTION, Fourth Edition, 914 pages, 1987. (Casebook) 1990 Supplement.

WHITE AND NIMMER'S CASES AND MATERIALS ON BANKRUPTCY, Second Edition, 764 pages, 1992. Teacher's Manual available. (Casebook)

Criminal Law and Criminal Procedure—see also Corrections, Juvenile Justice

ABRAMS AND BEALE'S FEDERAL CRIMINAL LAW AND ITS ENFORCEMENT, Second Edition, approximately 990 pages, 1993. (Casebook)

BUCY'S WHITE COLLAR CRIME, CASES AND MATERIALS, 688 pages, 1992. Teacher's Manual available. (Casebook)

DIX AND SHARLOT'S CASES AND MATERIALS ON CRIMINAL LAW, Third Edition, 846 pages, 1987. (Casebook)

GRANO'S PROBLEMS IN CRIMINAL PROCEDURE, Second Edition, 176 pages, 1981. Teacher's Manual available. Softcover. (Coursebook)

HEYMANN AND KENETY'S THE MURDER TRIAL OF WILBUR JACKSON: A HOMICIDE IN THE FAMILY, Second Edition, 347 pages, 1985. (Coursebook)

ISRAEL, KAMISAR AND LAFAVE'S CRIMINAL PROCEDURE AND THE CONSTITUTION: LEADING SUPREME COURT CASES AND INTRODUCTORY TEXT. Approximately 825 pages, 1993 Edition. Softcover. (Casebook)

ISRAEL AND LAFAVE'S CRIMINAL PROCEDURE—CONSTITUTIONAL LIMITATIONS IN A NUTSHELL, Fifth Edition, 475 pages, 1993. Softcover. (Text)

JOHNSON'S CASES, MATERIALS AND TEXT ON CRIMINAL LAW, Fourth Edition, 759 pages, 1990. Teacher's Manual available. (Casebook)

JOHNSON'S CASES AND MATERIALS ON CRIMINAL PROCEDURE, 859 pages, 1988. (Casebook) 1993 Supplement.

KAMISAR, LAFAVE AND ISRAEL'S MODERN CRIMINAL PROCEDURE: CASES, COMMENTS AND QUESTIONS, Seventh Edition, 1593 pages, 1990. (Casebook) 1993 Supplement.

KAMISAR, LAFAVE AND ISRAEL'S BASIC CRIMINAL PROCEDURE: CASES, COMMENTS AND QUESTIONS, Seventh Edition, 792 pages, 1990. Softcover reprint from Kamisar, et al., Modern Criminal Procedure: Cases, Comments and Questions, Seventh Edition. (Casebook) 1993 Supplement.

Criminal Law and Criminal Procedure—Cont'd

LaFave's Modern Criminal Law: Cases, Comments and Questions, Second Edition, 903 pages, 1988. (Casebook)

LaFave and Israel's Hornbook on Criminal Procedure, Second Edition, 1309 pages, 1992 with 1992 pocket part. (Text)

LaFave and Scott's Hornbook on Criminal Law, Second Edition, 918 pages, 1986 with 1993 pocket part. (Text)

Loewy's Criminal Law in a Nutshell, Second Edition, 321 pages, 1987. Softcover. (Text)

Low's Black Letter on Criminal Law, Revised First Edition, 443 pages, 1990. Softcover. (Review)

Podgor's White Collar Crime in a Nutshell, Approximately 300 pages, 1993. Softcover. (Text)

Saltzburg and Capra's Cases and Commentary on American Criminal Procedure, Fourth Edition, 1341 pages, 1992. Teacher's Manual available. (Casebook) 1993 Supplement.

Subin, Mirsky and Weinstein's The Criminal Process: Prosecution and Defense Functions, 470 pages, 1993. Softcover. Teacher's Manual available. (Text)

Vorenberg's Cases on Criminal Law and Procedure, Second Edition, 1088 pages, 1981. Teacher's Manual available. (Casebook) 1993 Supplement.

Domestic Relations

Clark's Hornbook on Domestic Relations, Second Edition, Student Edition, 1050 pages, 1988. (Text)

Clark and Glowinsky's Cases and Problems on Domestic Relations, Fourth Edition. 1150 pages, 1990. Teacher's Manual available. (Casebook) 1992 Supplement.

Krause's Black Letter on Family Law, 314 pages, 1988. Softcover. (Review)

Krause's Cases, Comments and Questions on Family Law, Third Edition, 1433 pages, 1990. (Casebook) 1993 Supplement.

Krause's Family Law in a Nutshell, Second Edition, 444 pages, 1986. Softcover. (Text)

Economics, Law and—see also Antitrust, Regulated Industries

Barnes and Stout's Cases and Materials on Law and Economics, 538 pages, 1992. Teacher's Manual available. (Casebook)

Malloy's Law and Economics: A Comparative Approach to Theory and Practice, 166 pages, 1990. Softcover. (Text)

Education Law

Alexander and Alexander's The Law of Schools, Students and Teachers in a Nutshell, 409 pages, 1984. Softcover. (Text)

Yudof, Kirp and Levin's Educational Policy and the Law, Third Edition, 860 pages, 1992. (Casebook)

Employment Discrimination—see also Gender Discrimination

Estreicher and Harper's Cases and Materials on the Law Governing the Employment Relationship, Second Edition, 966 pages, 1992. (Casebook) 1992 Statutory Supplement.

Jones, Murphy and Belton's Cases and Materials on Discrimination in Employment, (The Labor Law Group). Fifth Edition, 1116 pages, 1987. (Casebook) 1990 Supplement.

Player's Federal Law of Employment Discrimination in a Nutshell, Third Edition, 338 pages, 1992. Softcover. (Text)

Player's Hornbook on Employment Discrimination Law, Student Edition, 708 pages, 1988. (Text)

Player, Shoben and Lieberwitz' Cases and Materials on Employment Discrimination Law, 827 pages, 1990. Teacher's Manual available. (Casebook) 1992 Supplement.

Energy and Natural Resources Law—see also Oil and Gas

Laitos' Cases and Materials on Natural Resources Law, 938 pages, 1985. Teacher's Manual available. (Casebook)

Laitos and Tomain's Energy and Natural Resources Law in a Nutshell, 554 pages, 1992. Softcover. (Text)

Selected Environmental Law Statutes—1993–94 Educational Edition. Softcover. Approximately 1300 pages, 1993.

Environmental Law—see also Energy and Natural Resources Law; Sea, Law of

CAMPBELL-MOHN, BREEN AND FUTRELL'S ENVIRONMENTAL LAW: FROM RESOURCES TO RECOVERY, (Environmental Law Institute) Approximately 975 pages, 1993. (Text)

BONINE AND MCGARITY'S THE LAW OF ENVIRONMENTAL PROTECTION: CASES—LEGISLATION—POLICIES, Second Edition, 1042 pages, 1992. (Casebook)

FINDLEY AND FARBER'S CASES AND MATERIALS ON ENVIRONMENTAL LAW, Third Edition, 763 pages, 1991. Teacher's Manual available. (Casebook) 1993 Supplement.

FINDLEY AND FARBER'S ENVIRONMENTAL LAW IN A NUTSHELL, Third Edition, 355 pages, 1992. Softcover. (Text)

PLATER, ABRAMS AND GOLDFARB'S ENVIRONMENTAL LAW AND POLICY: NATURE, LAW AND SOCIETY, 1039 pages, 1992. Teacher's Manual available. (Casebook)

RODGERS' HORNBOOK ON ENVIRONMENTAL LAW, 956 pages, 1977, with 1984 pocket part. (Text)

SELECTED ENVIRONMENTAL LAW STATUTES—1993-94 EDUCATIONAL EDITION. Softcover. Approximately 1300 pages, 1993.

Equity—see Remedies

Estate Planning—see also Trusts and Estates; Taxation—Estate and Gift

LYNN'S INTRODUCTION TO ESTATE PLANNING IN A NUTSHELL, Fourth Edition, 352 pages, 1992. Softcover. (Text)

Evidence

BERGMAN'S TRANSCRIPT EXERCISES FOR LEARNING EVIDENCE, 273 pages, 1992. Softcover. Teacher's Manual available. (Coursebook)

BROUN AND BLAKEY'S BLACK LETTER ON EVIDENCE, 269 pages, 1984. Softcover. (Review)

BROUN, MEISENHOLDER, STRONG AND MOSTELLER'S PROBLEMS IN EVIDENCE, Third Edition, 238 pages, 1988. Softcover. Teacher's Manual available. (Coursebook)

CLEARY, STRONG, BROUN AND MOSTELLER'S CASES AND MATERIALS ON EVIDENCE, Fourth Edition, 1060 pages, 1988. (Casebook)

FEDERAL RULES OF EVIDENCE FOR UNITED STATES COURTS. Softcover. Approximately 575 pages, 1993.

FRIEDMAN'S THE ELEMENTS OF EVIDENCE, 315 pages, 1991. Teacher's Manual available. (Coursebook)

GRAHAM'S FEDERAL RULES OF EVIDENCE IN A NUTSHELL, Third Edition, 486 pages, 1992. Softcover. (Text)

LEMPERT AND SALTZBURG'S A MODERN APPROACH TO EVIDENCE: TEXT, PROBLEMS, TRANSCRIPTS AND CASES, Second Edition, 1232 pages, 1983. Teacher's Manual available. (Casebook)

LILLY'S AN INTRODUCTION TO THE LAW OF EVIDENCE, Second Edition, 585 pages, 1987. (Text)

MCCORMICK, SUTTON AND WELLBORN'S CASES AND MATERIALS ON EVIDENCE, Seventh Edition, 932 pages, 1992. Teacher's Manual available. (Casebook)

MCCORMICK'S HORNBOOK ON EVIDENCE, Fourth Edition, Student Edition, 672 pages, 1992. (Text)

ROTHSTEIN'S EVIDENCE IN A NUTSHELL: STATE AND FEDERAL RULES, Second Edition, 514 pages, 1981. Softcover. (Text)

Federal Jurisdiction and Procedure

CURRIE'S CASES AND MATERIALS ON FEDERAL COURTS, Fourth Edition, 783 pages, 1990. (Casebook)

CURRIE'S FEDERAL JURISDICTION IN A NUTSHELL, Third Edition, 242 pages, 1990. Softcover. (Text)

FEDERAL RULES OF CIVIL PROCEDURE—1993-94 EDUCATIONAL EDITION. Softcover. Approximately 775 pages, 1993.

REDISH'S BLACK LETTER ON FEDERAL JURISDICTION, Second Edition, 234 pages, 1991. Softcover. (Review)

REDISH'S CASES, COMMENTS AND QUESTIONS ON FEDERAL COURTS, Second Edition, 1122 pages, 1989. (Casebook) 1992 Supplement.

WRIGHT'S HORNBOOK ON FEDERAL COURTS, Fourth Edition, Student Edition, 870 pages, 1983. (Text)

First Amendment

BARRON AND DIENES' FIRST AMENDMENT LAW IN A NUTSHELL, Approximately 450

First Amendment—Cont'd

pages, September, 1993 pub. Softcover. (Text)

GARVEY AND SCHAUER'S THE FIRST AMENDMENT: A READER, 527 pages, 1992. Softcover. (Reader)

SHIFFRIN AND CHOPER'S FIRST AMENDMENT, CASES—COMMENTS—QUESTIONS, 759 pages, 1991. Softcover. (Casebook) 1993 Supplement.

Foreign Relations and National Security Law

FRANCK AND GLENNON'S FOREIGN RELATIONS AND NATIONAL SECURITY LAW, Second Edition, approximately 1150 pages, 1993. (Casebook)

Future Interests—see Trusts and Estates

Gender Discrimination—see also Employment Discrimination

KAY'S TEXT, CASES AND MATERIALS ON SEX–BASED DISCRIMINATION, Third Edition, 1001 pages, 1988. (Casebook) 1992 Supplement.

THOMAS' SEX DISCRIMINATION IN A NUTSHELL, Second Edition, 395 pages, 1991. Softcover. (Text)

Health Law—see Medicine, Law and

Human Rights—see International Law

Immigration Law

ALEINIKOFF AND MARTIN'S IMMIGRATION: PROCESS AND POLICY, Second Edition, 1056 pages, 1991. (Casebook)

Statutory Supplement. *See Immigration and Nationality Laws*

IMMIGRATION AND NATIONALITY LAWS OF THE UNITED STATES: SELECTED STATUTES, REGULATIONS AND FORMS. Softcover. 519 pages, 1992.

WEISSBRODT'S IMMIGRATION LAW AND PROCEDURE IN A NUTSHELL, Third Edition, 497 pages, 1992. Softcover. (Text)

Indian Law—see American Indian Law

Insurance Law

DEVINE AND TERRY'S PROBLEMS IN INSURANCE LAW, 240 pages, 1989. Softcover. Teacher's Manual available. (Coursebook)

DOBBYN'S INSURANCE LAW IN A NUTSHELL, Second Edition, 316 pages, 1989. Softcover. (Text)

KEETON'S COMPUTER-AIDED AND WORKBOOK EXERCISES ON INSURANCE LAW, 255 pages, 1990. Softcover. (Coursebook)

KEETON AND WIDISS' INSURANCE LAW, Student Edition, 1359 pages, 1988. (Text)

WIDISS AND KEETON'S COURSE SUPPLEMENT TO KEETON AND WIDISS' INSURANCE LAW, 502 pages, 1988. Softcover. Teacher's Manual available. (Casebook)

WIDISS' INSURANCE: MATERIALS ON FUNDAMENTAL PRINCIPLES, LEGAL DOCTRINES AND REGULATORY ACTS, 1186 pages, 1989. Teacher's Manual available. (Casebook)

YORK AND WHELAN'S CASES, MATERIALS AND PROBLEMS ON GENERAL PRACTICE INSURANCE LAW, Second Edition, 787 pages, 1988. Teacher's Manual available. (Casebook)

Intellectual Property Law—see also Trade Regulation

CHOATE, FRANCIS AND COLLINS' CASES AND MATERIALS ON PATENT LAW, INCLUDING TRADE SECRETS, COPYRIGHTS, TRADEMARKS, Third Edition, 1009 pages, 1987. (Casebook)

HALPERN, SHIPLEY AND ABRAMS' CASES AND MATERIALS ON COPYRIGHT, 663 pages, 1992. (Casebook)

MILLER AND DAVIS' INTELLECTUAL PROPERTY—PATENTS, TRADEMARKS AND COPYRIGHT IN A NUTSHELL, Second Edition, 437 pages, 1990. Softcover. (Text)

NIMMER, MARCUS, MYERS AND NIMMER'S CASES AND MATERIALS ON COPYRIGHT AND OTHER ASPECTS OF ENTERTAINMENT LITIGATION—INCLUDING UNFAIR COMPETITION, DEFAMATION, PRIVACY, ILLUSTRATED, Fourth Edition, 1177 pages, 1991. (Casebook) Statutory Supplement. See *Selected Intellectual Property Statutes*

SELECTED INTELLECTUAL PROPERTY AND UNFAIR COMPETITION STATUTES, REGULATIONS AND TREATIES. Softcover.

International Law—see also Sea, Law of

BERMANN, DAVEY, FOX AND GOEBEL'S CASES AND MATERIALS ON EUROPEAN COMMUNITY LAW, 1218 pages, 1993. (Casebook) Statutory Supplement. *See European Economic Community: Selected Documents*

International Law—Cont'd

BUERGENTHAL'S INTERNATIONAL HUMAN RIGHTS IN A NUTSHELL, 283 pages, 1988. Softcover. (Text)

BUERGENTHAL AND MAIER'S PUBLIC INTERNATIONAL LAW IN A NUTSHELL, Second Edition, 275 pages, 1990. Softcover. (Text)

EUROPEAN COMMUNITY LAW: SELECTED DOCUMENTS. 687 pages, 1993. Softcover

FOLSOM'S EUROPEAN COMMUNITY LAW IN A NUTSHELL, 423 pages, 1992. Softcover. (Text)

FOLSOM, GORDON AND SPANOGLE'S INTERNATIONAL BUSINESS TRANSACTIONS—A PROBLEM-ORIENTED COURSEBOOK, Second Edition, 1237 pages, 1991. Teacher's Manual available. (Casebook) 1991 Documents Supplement.

FOLSOM, GORDON AND SPANOGLE'S INTERNATIONAL BUSINESS TRANSACTIONS IN A NUTSHELL, Fourth Edition, 548 pages, 1992. Softcover. (Text)

HENKIN, PUGH, SCHACHTER AND SMIT'S CASES AND MATERIALS ON INTERNATIONAL LAW, Third Edition, approximately 1500 pages, 1993. (Casebook) 1993 Documents Supplement.

INTERNATIONAL LITIGATION AND ARBITRATION: SELECTED TREATIES, STATUTES AND RULES. 277 pages, 1993. Softcover

INTERNATIONAL ORGANIZATIONS IN THEIR LEGAL SETTING: SELECTED DOCUMENTS. 371 pages, 1993. Softcover

JACKSON AND DAVEY'S CASES, MATERIALS AND TEXT ON LEGAL PROBLEMS OF INTERNATIONAL ECONOMIC RELATIONS, Second Edition, 1269 pages, 1986. (Casebook) 1989 Documents Supplement.

KIRGIS' INTERNATIONAL ORGANIZATIONS IN THEIR LEGAL SETTING, Second Edition, 1119 pages, 1993. Teacher's Manual available. (Casebook) Statutory Supplement.

LOWENFELD'S INTERNATIONAL LITIGATION AND ARBITRATION, 869 pages, 1993. Teacher's Manual available. (Casebook) Statutory Supplement. *See International Litigation: Selected Documents*

WESTON, FALK AND D'AMATO'S INTERNATIONAL LAW AND WORLD ORDER—A PROBLEM-ORIENTED COURSEBOOK, Second Edition, 1335 pages, 1990. Teacher's Manual available. (Casebook) 1990 Documents Supplement.

Interviewing and Counseling

BINDER AND PRICE'S LEGAL INTERVIEWING AND COUNSELING, 232 pages, 1977. Softcover. Teacher's Manual available. (Coursebook)

BINDER, BERGMAN AND PRICE'S LAWYERS AS COUNSELORS: A CLIENT-CENTERED APPROACH, 427 pages, 1991. Softcover. (Coursebook)

SHAFFER AND ELKINS' LEGAL INTERVIEWING AND COUNSELING IN A NUTSHELL, Second Edition, 487 pages, 1987. Softcover. (Text)

Introduction to Law—see Legal Method and Legal System

Introduction to Law Study

HEGLAND'S INTRODUCTION TO THE STUDY AND PRACTICE OF LAW IN A NUTSHELL, 418 pages, 1983. Softcover. (Text)

KINYON'S INTRODUCTION TO LAW STUDY AND LAW EXAMINATIONS IN A NUTSHELL, 389 pages, 1971. Softcover. (Text)

Judicial Process—see Legal Method and Legal System

Jurisprudence

CHRISTIE'S JURISPRUDENCE—TEXT AND READINGS ON THE PHILOSOPHY OF LAW, 1056 pages, 1973. (Casebook)

SINHA'S JURISPRUDENCE (LEGAL PHILOSOPHY) IN A NUTSHELL. 379 pages, 1993. Softcover. (Text)

Juvenile Justice

FOX'S JUVENILE COURTS IN A NUTSHELL, Third Edition, 291 pages, 1984. Softcover. (Text)

Labor and Employment Law—see also Employment Discrimination, Workers' Compensation

CONISON'S EMPLOYEE BENEFIT PLANS IN A NUTSHELL, Approximately 465 pages, 1993. Softcover. (Text)

FINKIN, GOLDMAN AND SUMMERS' LEGAL PROTECTION OF INDIVIDUAL EMPLOYEES, (The Labor Law Group). 1164 pages, 1989. (Case-

Labor and Employment Law—Cont'd

book)

GORMAN'S BASIC TEXT ON LABOR LAW—UNIONIZATION AND COLLECTIVE BARGAINING, 914 pages, 1976. (Text)

LESLIE'S LABOR LAW IN A NUTSHELL, Third Edition, 388 pages, 1992. Softcover. (Text)

NOLAN'S LABOR ARBITRATION LAW AND PRACTICE IN A NUTSHELL, 358 pages, 1979. Softcover. (Text)

OBERER, HANSLOWE, ANDERSEN AND HEINSZ' CASES AND MATERIALS ON LABOR LAW—COLLECTIVE BARGAINING IN A FREE SOCIETY, Third Edition, 1163 pages, 1986. Teacher's Manual available. (Casebook) 1986 Statutory Supplement. 1991 Case Supplement.

RABIN, SILVERSTEIN AND SCHATZKI'S LABOR AND EMPLOYMENT LAW: PROBLEMS, CASES AND MATERIALS IN THE LAW OF WORK, (The Labor Law Group). 1014 pages, 1988. Teacher's Manual available. (Casebook) 1988 Statutory Supplement.

WOLLETT, GRODIN AND WEISBERGER'S COLLECTIVE BARGAINING IN PUBLIC EMPLOYMENT, (The Labor Law Group). Fourth Edition, approximately 425 pages, 1993. (Casebook)

Land Finance—Property Security—see Real Estate Transactions

Land Use

CALLIES AND FREILICH'S CASES AND MATERIALS ON LAND USE, 1233 pages, 1986. (Casebook) 1991 Supplement.

HAGMAN AND JUERGENSMEYER'S HORNBOOK ON URBAN PLANNING AND LAND DEVELOPMENT CONTROL LAW, Second Edition, Student Edition, 680 pages, 1986. (Text)

WRIGHT AND GITELMAN'S CASES AND MATERIALS ON LAND USE, Fourth Edition, 1255 pages, 1991. Teacher's Manual available. (Casebook)

WRIGHT AND WRIGHT'S LAND USE IN A NUTSHELL, Second Edition, 356 pages, 1985. Softcover. (Text)

Legal History—see also Legal Method and Legal System

PRESSER AND ZAINALDIN'S CASES AND MATERIALS ON LAW AND JURISPRUDENCE IN AMERICAN HISTORY, Second Edition, 1092 pages, 1989. Teacher's Manual available. (Casebook)

Legal Method and Legal System—see also Legal Research, Legal Writing

BERCH, BERCH AND SPRITZER'S INTRODUCTION TO LEGAL METHOD AND PROCESS, Second Edition, 585 pages, 1992. Teacher's Manual available. (Casebook)

BODENHEIMER, OAKLEY AND LOVE'S READINGS AND CASES ON AN INTRODUCTION TO THE ANGLO-AMERICAN LEGAL SYSTEM, Second Edition, 166 pages, 1988. Softcover. (Casebook)

KEETON'S JUDGING, 842 pages, 1990. Softcover. (Coursebook)

KELSO AND KELSO'S STUDYING LAW: AN INTRODUCTION, 587 pages, 1984. (Coursebook)

KEMPIN'S HISTORICAL INTRODUCTION TO ANGLO-AMERICAN LAW IN A NUTSHELL, Third Edition, 323 pages, 1990. Softcover. (Text)

MEADOR'S AMERICAN COURTS, 113 pages, 1991. Softcover. (Text)

REYNOLDS' JUDICIAL PROCESS IN A NUTSHELL, Second Edition, 308 pages, 1991. Softcover. (Text)

Legal Research

COHEN AND OLSON'S LEGAL RESEARCH IN A NUTSHELL, Fifth Edition, 370 pages, 1992. Softcover. (Text)

COHEN, BERRING AND OLSON'S HORNBOOK ON HOW TO FIND THE LAW, Ninth Edition, 716 pages, 1989. (Text)

COHEN, BERRING AND OLSON'S FINDING THE LAW, 570 pages, 1989. Softcover reprint from Cohen, Berring and Olson's How to Find the Law, Ninth Edition. (Coursebook)

Legal Research Exercises, 4th Ed., for use with Cohen, Berring and Olson, 253 pages, 1992. Teacher's Manual available.

HAZELTON'S COMPUTER-ASSISTED LEGAL RESEARCH: THE BASICS, Approximately 70 pages, 1993. Softcover. (Coursebook)

ROMBAUER'S LEGAL PROBLEM SOLVING—ANALYSIS, RESEARCH AND WRITING, Fifth

Legal Research—Cont'd

Edition, 524 pages, 1991. Softcover. Teacher's Manual with problems available. (Coursebook)

TEPLY'S LEGAL RESEARCH AND CITATION, Fourth Edition, 436 pages, 1992. Softcover. (Coursebook)

Student Library Exercises, Fourth Edition, 276 pages, 1992. Answer Key available.

Legal Writing and Drafting

CHILD'S DRAFTING LEGAL DOCUMENTS: PRINCIPLES AND PRACTICES, Second Edition, 425 pages, 1992. Softcover. Teacher's Manual available. (Coursebook)

FELSENFELD AND SIEGEL'S WRITING CONTRACTS IN PLAIN ENGLISH, 290 pages, 1981. Softcover. (Text)

MARTINEAU'S DRAFTING LEGISLATION AND RULES IN PLAIN ENGLISH, 155 pages, 1991. Softcover. Teacher's Manual available. (Text)

MELLINKOFF'S DICTIONARY OF AMERICAN LEGAL USAGE, 703 pages, 1992. Softcover. (Text)

MELLINKOFF'S LEGAL WRITING—SENSE AND NONSENSE, 242 pages, 1982. Softcover. Teacher's Manual available. (Text)

PRATT'S LEGAL WRITING: A SYSTEMATIC APPROACH, Second Edition, 426 pages, 1993. Teacher's Manual available. (Coursebook)

RAY AND COX'S BEYOND THE BASICS: A TEXT FOR ADVANCED LEGAL WRITING, 427 pages, 1991. Softcover. Teacher's Manual available. (Text)

RAY AND RAMSFIELD'S LEGAL WRITING: GETTING IT RIGHT AND GETTING IT WRITTEN, Second Edition, approximately 350 pages, 1993. Softcover. (Text)

SQUIRES AND ROMBAUER'S LEGAL WRITING IN A NUTSHELL, 294 pages, 1982. Softcover. (Text)

STATSKY AND WERNET'S CASE ANALYSIS AND FUNDAMENTALS OF LEGAL WRITING, Third Edition, 424 pages, 1989. Teacher's Manual available. (Text)

TEPLY'S LEGAL WRITING, ANALYSIS AND ORAL ARGUMENT, 576 pages, 1990. Softcover. Teacher's Manual available. (Coursebook)

WEIHOFEN'S LEGAL WRITING STYLE, Second Edition, 332 pages, 1980. (Text)

Legislation—see also Legal Writing and Drafting

DAVIES' LEGISLATIVE LAW AND PROCESS IN A NUTSHELL, Second Edition, 346 pages, 1986. Softcover. (Text)

ESKRIDGE AND FRICKEY'S CASES AND MATERIALS ON LEGISLATION: STATUTES AND THE CREATION OF PUBLIC POLICY, 937 pages, 1988. Teacher's Manual available. (Casebook) 1992 Supplement.

STATSKY'S LEGISLATIVE ANALYSIS AND DRAFTING, Second Edition, 217 pages, 1984. Teacher's Manual available. (Text)

Local Government

FRUG'S CASES AND MATERIALS ON LOCAL GOVERNMENT LAW, 1005 pages, 1988. (Casebook) 1991 Supplement.

MCCARTHY'S LOCAL GOVERNMENT LAW IN A NUTSHELL, Third Edition, 435 pages, 1990. Softcover. (Text)

REYNOLDS' HORNBOOK ON LOCAL GOVERNMENT LAW, 860 pages, 1982 with 1993 pocket part. (Text)

VALENTE AND MCCARTHY'S CASES AND MATERIALS ON LOCAL GOVERNMENT LAW, Fourth Edition, 1158 pages, 1992. Teacher's Manual available. (Casebook)

Mass Communication Law

GILLMOR, BARRON, SIMON AND TERRY'S CASES AND COMMENT ON MASS COMMUNICATION LAW, Fifth Edition, 947 pages, 1990. (Casebook)

GINSBURG, BOTEIN AND DIRECTOR'S REGULATION OF THE ELECTRONIC MASS MEDIA: LAW AND POLICY FOR RADIO, TELEVISION, CABLE AND THE NEW VIDEO TECHNOLOGIES, Second Edition, 657 pages, 1991. (Casebook) 1991 Statutory Supplement.

ZUCKMAN, GAYNES, CARTER AND DEE'S MASS COMMUNICATIONS LAW IN A NUTSHELL, Third Edition, 538 pages, 1988. Softcover. (Text)

Medicine, Law and

FISCINA, BOUMIL, SHARPE AND HEAD'S MEDICAL LIABILITY, 487 pages, 1991. Teacher's

Medicine, Law and—Cont'd

Manual available. (Casebook)

FURROW, JOHNSON, JOST AND SCHWARTZ' HEALTH LAW: CASES, MATERIALS AND PROBLEMS, Second Edition, 1236 pages, 1991. Teacher's Manual available. (Casebook)

FURROW, JOHNSON, JOST AND SCHWARTZ' BIOETHICS: HEALTH CARE LAW AND ETHICS, Reprint from Furrow et al., Health Law, Second Edition. Softcover. Teacher's Manual available. (Casebook)

FURROW, JOHNSON, JOST AND SCHWARTZ' THE LAW OF HEALTH CARE ORGANIZATION AND FINANCE, Reprint from Furrow et al., Health Law, Second Edition. Softcover. Teacher's Manual available.

FURROW, JOHNSON, JOST AND SCHWARTZ' LIABILITY AND QUALITY ISSUES IN HEALTH CARE, Reprint from Furrow et al., Health Law, Second Edition. Softcover. Teacher's Manual available. (Casebook)

HALL AND ELLMAN'S HEALTH CARE LAW AND ETHICS IN A NUTSHELL, 401 pages, 1990. Softcover (Text)

JARVIS, CLOSEN, HERMANN AND LEONARD'S AIDS LAW IN A NUTSHELL, 349 pages, 1991. Softcover. (Text)

KING'S THE LAW OF MEDICAL MALPRACTICE IN A NUTSHELL, Second Edition, 342 pages, 1986. Softcover. (Text)

SHAPIRO AND SPECE'S CASES, MATERIALS AND PROBLEMS ON BIOETHICS AND LAW, 892 pages, 1981. (Casebook) 1991 Supplement.

Mining Law—see Energy and Natural Resources Law

Mortgages—see Real Estate Transactions

Natural Resources Law—see Energy and Natural Resources Law, Environmental Law

Negotiation

GIFFORD'S LEGAL NEGOTIATION: THEORY AND APPLICATIONS, 225 pages, 1989. Softcover. (Text)

TEPLY'S LEGAL NEGOTIATION IN A NUTSHELL, 282 pages, 1992. Softcover. (Text)

WILLIAMS' LEGAL NEGOTIATION AND SETTLEMENT, 207 pages, 1983. Softcover. Teacher's Manual available. (Coursebook)

Office Practice—see also Computers and Law, Interviewing and Counseling, Negotiation

MUNNEKE'S LAW PRACTICE MANAGEMENT: MATERIALS AND CASES, 634 pages, 1991. Teacher's Manual available. (Casebook)

Oil and Gas—see also Energy and Natural Resources Law

HEMINGWAY'S HORNBOOK ON THE LAW OF OIL AND GAS, Third Edition, Student Edition, 711 pages, 1992. (Text)

KUNTZ, LOWE, ANDERSON AND SMITH'S CASES AND MATERIALS ON OIL AND GAS LAW, Second Edition, approximately 1000 pages, 1993. (Casebook) 1993 Forms Manual.

LOWE'S OIL AND GAS LAW IN A NUTSHELL, Second Edition, 465 pages, 1988. Softcover. (Text)

Patents—see Intellectual Property

Partnership—see Agency—Partnership

Products Liability

FISCHER AND POWERS' CASES AND MATERIALS ON PRODUCTS LIABILITY, 685 pages, 1988. Teacher's Manual available. (Casebook)

PHILLIPS' PRODUCTS LIABILITY IN A NUTSHELL, Fourth Edition, approximately 325 pages, 1993. Softcover. (Text)

Professional Responsibility

ARONSON, DEVINE AND FISCH'S PROBLEMS, CASES AND MATERIALS IN PROFESSIONAL RESPONSIBILITY, 745 pages, 1985. Teacher's Manual available. (Casebook)

ARONSON AND WECKSTEIN'S PROFESSIONAL RESPONSIBILITY IN A NUTSHELL, Second Edition, 514 pages, 1991. Softcover. (Text)

DVORKIN, HIMMELSTEIN AND LESNICK'S BECOMING A LAWYER: A HUMANISTIC PERSPECTIVE ON LEGAL EDUCATION AND PROFESSIONALISM, 211 pages, 1981. Softcover. (Text)

LESNICK'S BEING A LAWYER: INDIVIDUAL CHOICE AND RESPONSIBILITY IN THE PRACTICE OF LAW, 422 pages, 1992. Softcover. Teacher's Manual available. (Coursebook)

MELLINKOFF'S THE CONSCIENCE OF A LAWYER, 304 pages, 1973. (Text)

MOLITERNO AND LEVY'S ETHICS OF THE LAWYER'S WORK, 305 pages, 1993. Softcover.

Professional Responsibility—Cont'd

Teacher's Manual available. (Coursebook)

PIRSIG AND KIRWIN'S CASES AND MATERIALS ON PROFESSIONAL RESPONSIBILITY, Fourth Edition, 603 pages, 1984. Teacher's Manual available. (Casebook)

ROTUNDA'S BLACK LETTER ON PROFESSIONAL RESPONSIBILITY, Third Edition, 492 pages, 1992. Softcover. (Review)

SCHWARTZ, WYDICK AND PERSCHBACHER'S PROBLEMS IN LEGAL ETHICS, Third Edition, 402 pages, 1993. (Coursebook)

SELECTED STATUTES, RULES AND STANDARDS ON THE LEGAL PROFESSION. Softcover. Approximately 950 pages, 1993.

SMITH AND MALLEN'S PREVENTING LEGAL MALPRACTICE, 264 pages, 1989. Reprint from Mallen and Smith's Legal Malpractice, Third Edition. (Text)

SUTTON AND DZIENKOWSKI'S CASES AND MATERIALS ON PROFESSIONAL RESPONSIBILITY FOR LAWYERS, 839 pages, 1989. Teacher's Manual available. (Casebook)

WOLFRAM'S HORNBOOK ON MODERN LEGAL ETHICS, Student Edition, 1120 pages, 1986. (Text)

WYDICK AND PERSCHBACHER'S CALIFORNIA LEGAL ETHICS, 439 pages, 1992. Softcover. (Coursebook)

Property—see also Real Estate Transactions, Land Use, Trusts and Estates

BARNES AND STOUT'S THE ECONOMICS OF PROPERTY RIGHTS AND NUISANCE LAW, 87 pages, 1992. Softcover. Teacher's Manual available. (Casebook)

BERNHARDT'S BLACK LETTER ON PROPERTY, Second Edition, 388 pages, 1991. Softcover. (Review)

BERNHARDT'S REAL PROPERTY IN A NUTSHELL, Third Edition, 475 pages, 1993. Softcover. (Text)

BOYER, HOVENKAMP AND KURTZ' THE LAW OF PROPERTY, AN INTRODUCTORY SURVEY, Fourth Edition, 696 pages, 1991. (Text)

BROWDER, CUNNINGHAM, NELSON, STOEBUCK AND WHITMAN'S CASES ON BASIC PROPERTY LAW, Fifth Edition, 1386 pages, 1989. Teacher's Manual available. (Casebook)

BRUCE, ELY AND BOSTICK'S CASES AND MATERIALS ON MODERN PROPERTY LAW, Second Edition, 953 pages, 1989. Teacher's Manual available. (Casebook)

BURKE'S PERSONAL PROPERTY IN A NUTSHELL, Second Edition, 399 pages, 1993. Softcover. (Text)

CUNNINGHAM, STOEBUCK AND WHITMAN'S HORNBOOK ON THE LAW OF PROPERTY, Second Edition, approximately 900 pages, 1993. (Text)

DONAHUE, KAUPER AND MARTIN'S CASES AND MATERIALS ON PROPERTY, AN INTRODUCTION TO THE CONCEPT AND THE INSTITUTION, Third Edition, 1189 pages, 1993. Teacher's Manual available. (Casebook)

HILL'S LANDLORD AND TENANT LAW IN A NUTSHELL, Second Edition, 311 pages, 1986. Softcover. (Text)

JOHNSON, JOST, SALSICH AND SHAFFER'S PROPERTY LAW, CASES, MATERIALS AND PROBLEMS, 908 pages, 1992. Teacher's Manual available. (Casebook)

KURTZ AND HOVENKAMP'S CASES AND MATERIALS ON AMERICAN PROPERTY LAW, Second Edition, 1232 pages, 1993. Teacher's Manual available. (Casebook)

MOYNIHAN'S INTRODUCTION TO REAL PROPERTY, Second Edition, 239 pages, 1988. (Text)

Psychiatry, Law and

REISNER AND SLOBOGIN'S LAW AND THE MENTAL HEALTH SYSTEM, CIVIL AND CRIMINAL ASPECTS, Second Edition, 1117 pages, 1990. Teacher's Manual available. (Casebook) 1992 Supplement.

Real Estate Transactions

BRUCE'S REAL ESTATE FINANCE IN A NUTSHELL, Third Edition, 287 pages, 1991. Softcover. (Text)

MAXWELL, RIESENFELD, HETLAND AND WARREN'S CASES ON CALIFORNIA SECURITY TRANSACTIONS IN LAND, Fourth Edition, 778 pages, 1992. Teacher's Manual available. (Casebook)

NELSON AND WHITMAN'S BLACK LETTER ON LAND TRANSACTIONS AND FINANCE, Second Edition, 466 pages, 1988. Softcover. (Review)

NELSON AND WHITMAN'S CASES AND MATERI-

Real Estate Transactions—Cont'd

ALS ON REAL ESTATE TRANSFER, FINANCE AND DEVELOPMENT, Fourth Edition, 1346 pages, 1992. (Casebook)

NELSON AND WHITMAN'S HORNBOOK ON REAL ESTATE FINANCE LAW, Second Edition, 941 pages, 1985 with 1989 pocket part. (Text)

Regulated Industries—see also Mass Communication Law, Banking Law

GELLHORN AND PIERCE'S REGULATED INDUSTRIES IN A NUTSHELL, Second Edition, 389 pages, 1987. Softcover. (Text)

MORGAN, HARRISON AND VERKUIL'S CASES AND MATERIALS ON ECONOMIC REGULATION OF BUSINESS, Second Edition, 666 pages, 1985. (Casebook)

Remedies

DOBBS' HORNBOOK ON REMEDIES, Second Edition, approximately 900 pages, 1993. (Text)

DOBBS AND KAVANAGH'S PROBLEMS IN REMEDIES, Second Edition, 218 pages, 1993. Softcover. Teacher's Manual available. (Coursebook)

DOBBYN'S INJUNCTIONS IN A NUTSHELL, 264 pages, 1974. Softcover. (Text)

FRIEDMAN'S CONTRACT REMEDIES IN A NUTSHELL, 323 pages, 1981. Softcover. (Text)

LEAVELL, LOVE AND NELSON'S CASES AND MATERIALS ON EQUITABLE REMEDIES, RESTITUTION AND DAMAGES, Fourth Edition, 1111 pages, 1986. Teacher's Manual available. (Casebook)

O'CONNELL'S REMEDIES IN A NUTSHELL, Second Edition, 320 pages, 1985. Softcover. (Text)

SCHOENBROD, MACBETH, LEVINE AND JUNG'S CASES AND MATERIALS ON REMEDIES: PUBLIC AND PRIVATE, 848 pages, 1990. Teacher's Manual available. (Casebook) 1992 Supplement.

YORK, BAUMAN AND RENDLEMAN'S CASES AND MATERIALS ON REMEDIES, Fifth Edition, 1270 pages, 1992. Teacher's Manual available. (Casebook)

Sea, Law of

SOHN AND GUSTAFSON'S THE LAW OF THE SEA IN A NUTSHELL, 264 pages, 1984. Softcover. (Text)

Securities Regulation

HAZEN'S HORNBOOK ON THE LAW OF SECURITIES REGULATION, Second Edition, Student Edition, 1082 pages, 1990. (Text)

RATNER'S SECURITIES REGULATION IN A NUTSHELL, Fourth Edition, 320 pages, 1992. Softcover. (Text)

RATNER AND HAZEN'S SECURITIES REGULATION: CASES AND MATERIALS, Fourth Edition, 1062 pages, 1991. Teacher's Manual available. (Casebook) 1991 Problems and Sample Documents Supplement.

Statutory Supplement. *See Securities Regulation, Selected Statutes*

SECURITIES REGULATION, SELECTED STATUTES, RULES, AND FORMS. Softcover. Approximately 1375 pages, 1993.

Sports Law

CHAMPION'S SPORTS LAW IN A NUTSHELL. 325 pages, 1993. Softcover. (Text)

SCHUBERT, SMITH AND TRENTADUE'S SPORTS LAW, 395 pages, 1986. (Text)

WEILER AND ROBERTS' CASES, MATERIALS, AND PROBLEMS ON THE LAW OF SPORTS, Approximately 765 pages, 1993. (Casebook) 1993 Statutory and Document Supplement.

Tax Policy

DODGE'S THE LOGIC OF TAX, 343 pages, 1989. Softcover. (Text)

UTZ' TAX POLICY: AN INTRODUCTION AND SURVEY OF THE PRINCIPAL DEBATES, 260 pages, 1993. Softcover. Teacher's Manual available. (Coursebook)

Tax Practice and Procedure

GARBIS, RUBIN AND MORGAN'S CASES AND MATERIALS ON TAX PROCEDURE AND TAX FRAUD, Third Edition, 921 pages, 1992. (Casebook)

MORGAN'S TAX PROCEDURE AND TAX FRAUD IN A NUTSHELL, 400 pages, 1990. Softcover. (Text)

Taxation—Corporate

KAHN AND GANN'S CORPORATE TAXATION, Third Edition, 980 pages, 1989. Teacher's Manual available. (Casebook) 1991 Supplement.

SCHWARZ AND LATHROPE'S BLACK LETTER ON

Taxation—Corporate—Cont'd

CORPORATE AND PARTNERSHIP TAXATION, 537 pages, 1991. Softcover. (Review)

WEIDENBRUCH AND BURKE'S FEDERAL INCOME TAXATION OF CORPORATIONS AND STOCKHOLDERS IN A NUTSHELL, Third Edition, 309 pages, 1989. Softcover. (Text)

Taxation—Estate & Gift—see also Estate Planning, Trusts and Estates

MCNULTY'S FEDERAL ESTATE AND GIFT TAXATION IN A NUTSHELL, Fourth Edition, 496 pages, 1989. Softcover. (Text)

PEAT AND WILLBANKS' FEDERAL ESTATE AND GIFT TAXATION: AN ANALYSIS AND CRITIQUE, 265 pages, 1991. Softcover. (Text)

PENNELL'S CASES AND MATERIALS ON INCOME TAXATION OF TRUSTS, ESTATES, GRANTORS AND BENEFICIARIES, 460 pages, 1987. Teacher's Manual available. (Casebook)

Taxation—Individual

GUNN AND WARD'S CASES, TEXT AND PROBLEMS ON FEDERAL INCOME TAXATION, Third Edition, 817 pages, 1992. Teacher's Manual available. (Casebook)

HUDSON AND LIND'S BLACK LETTER ON FEDERAL INCOME TAXATION, Fourth Edition, 410 pages, 1992. Softcover. (Review)

MCNULTY'S FEDERAL INCOME TAXATION OF INDIVIDUALS IN A NUTSHELL, Fourth Edition, 503 pages, 1988. Softcover. (Text)

POSIN'S FEDERAL INCOME TAXATION, Second Edition, approximately 550 pages, 1993. Softcover. (Text)

ROSE AND CHOMMIE'S HORNBOOK ON FEDERAL INCOME TAXATION, Third Edition, 923 pages, 1988, with 1991 pocket part. (Text)

SELECTED FEDERAL TAXATION STATUTES AND REGULATIONS. Softcover. Approximately 1700 pages, 1994.

Taxation—International

DOERNBERG'S INTERNATIONAL TAXATION IN A NUTSHELL, Second Edition, approximately 375 pages, 1993. Softcover. (Text)

KAPLAN'S FEDERAL TAXATION OF INTERNATIONAL TRANSACTIONS: PRINCIPLES, PLANNING AND POLICY, 635 pages, 1988. (Casebook)

Taxation—Partnership

BERGER AND WIEDENBECK'S CASES AND MATERIALS ON PARTNERSHIP TAXATION, 788 pages, 1989. Teacher's Manual available. (Casebook) 1991 Supplement.

BISHOP AND BROOKS' FEDERAL PARTNERSHIP TAXATION: A GUIDE TO THE LEADING CASES, STATUTES, AND REGULATIONS, 545 pages, 1990. Softcover. (Text)

BURKE'S FEDERAL INCOME TAXATION OF PARTNERSHIPS IN A NUTSHELL, 356 pages, 1992. Softcover. (Text)

SCHWARZ AND LATHROPE'S BLACK LETTER ON CORPORATE AND PARTNERSHIP TAXATION, 537 pages, 1991. Softcover. (Review)

Taxation—State & Local

GELFAND AND SALSICH'S STATE AND LOCAL TAXATION AND FINANCE IN A NUTSHELL, 309 pages, 1986. Softcover. (Text)

HELLERSTEIN AND HELLERSTEIN'S CASES AND MATERIALS ON STATE AND LOCAL TAXATION, Fifth Edition, 1071 pages, 1988. (Casebook)

Torts—see also Products Liability

BARNES AND STOUT'S THE ECONOMIC ANALYSIS OF TORT LAW, 161 pages, 1992. Softcover. Teacher's Manual available. (Casebook)

CHRISTIE AND MEEKS' CASES AND MATERIALS ON THE LAW OF TORTS, Second Edition, 1264 pages, 1990. (Casebook)

DOBBS' TORTS AND COMPENSATION—PERSONAL ACCOUNTABILITY AND SOCIAL RESPONSIBILITY FOR INJURY, Second Edition, approximately 1050 pages, 1993. Teacher's Manual available. (Casebook)

KEETON, KEETON, SARGENTICH AND STEINER'S CASES AND MATERIALS ON TORT AND ACCIDENT LAW, Second Edition, 1318 pages, 1989. (Casebook)

KIONKA'S BLACK LETTER ON TORTS, Second Edition, approximately 350 pages, 1993. Softcover. (Review)

KIONKA'S TORTS IN A NUTSHELL, Second Edition, 449 pages, 1992. Softcover. (Text)

PROSSER AND KEETON'S HORNBOOK ON TORTS, Fifth Edition, Student Edition, 1286 pages, 1984 with 1988 pocket part. (Text)

ROBERTSON, POWERS AND ANDERSON'S CASES

Torts—Cont'd

AND MATERIALS ON TORTS, 932 pages, 1989. Teacher's Manual available. (Casebook)

Trade Regulation—see also Antitrust, Regulated Industries

McMANIS' UNFAIR TRADE PRACTICES IN A NUTSHELL, Third Edition, 471 pages, 1993. Softcover. (Text)

SCHECHTER'S BLACK LETTER ON UNFAIR TRADE PRACTICES AND INTELLECTUAL PROPERTY, Second Edition, approximately 300 pages, 1993. Softcover. (Review)

WESTON, MAGGS AND SCHECHTER'S UNFAIR TRADE PRACTICES AND CONSUMER PROTECTION, CASES AND COMMENTS, Fifth Edition, 957 pages, 1992. Teacher's Manual available. (Casebook)

Trial and Appellate Advocacy—see also Civil Procedure

APPELLATE ADVOCACY, HANDBOOK OF, Third Edition, 101 pages, 1993. Softcover. (Text)

BERGMAN'S TRIAL ADVOCACY IN A NUTSHELL, Second Edition, 354 pages, 1989. Softcover. (Text)

BINDER AND BERGMAN'S FACT INVESTIGATION: FROM HYPOTHESIS TO PROOF, 354 pages, 1984. Teacher's Manual available. (Coursebook)

CARLSON'S ADJUDICATION OF CRIMINAL JUSTICE: PROBLEMS AND REFERENCES, 130 pages, 1986. Softcover. (Casebook)

CARLSON AND IMWINKELRIED'S DYNAMICS OF TRIAL PRACTICE: PROBLEMS AND MATERIALS, 414 pages, 1989. Teacher's Manual available. (Coursebook) 1990 Supplement.

CLARY'S PRIMER ON THE ANALYSIS AND PRESENTATION OF LEGAL ARGUMENT, 106 pages, 1992. Softcover. (Text)

DESSEM'S PRETRIAL LITIGATION IN A NUTSHELL, 382 pages, 1992. Softcover. (Text)

DESSEM'S PRETRIAL LITIGATION: LAW, POLICY AND PRACTICE, 608 pages, 1991. Softcover. Teacher's Manual available. (Coursebook)

DEVINE'S NON-JURY CASE FILES FOR TRIAL ADVOCACY, 258 pages, 1991. (Coursebook)

GOLDBERG'S THE FIRST TRIAL (WHERE DO I SIT? WHAT DO I SAY?) IN A NUTSHELL, 396 pages, 1982. Softcover. (Text)

HAYDOCK, HERR, AND STEMPEL'S FUNDAMENTALS OF PRE-TRIAL LITIGATION, Second Edition, 786 pages, 1992. Softcover. Teacher's Manual available. (Coursebook)

HAYDOCK AND SONSTENG'S TRIAL: THEORIES, TACTICS, TECHNIQUES, 711 pages, 1991. Softcover. (Text)

HEGLAND'S TRIAL AND PRACTICE SKILLS IN A NUTSHELL, 346 pages, 1978. Softcover. (Text)

HORNSTEIN'S APPELLATE ADVOCACY IN A NUTSHELL, 325 pages, 1984. Softcover. (Text)

JEANS' TRIAL ADVOCACY, Second Edition, approximately 575 pages, 1993. Softcover. (Text)

LISNEK AND KAUFMAN'S DEPOSITIONS: PROCEDURE, STRATEGY AND TECHNIQUE, Law School and CLE Edition. 250 pages, 1990. Softcover. (Text)

MARTINEAU'S CASES AND MATERIALS ON APPELLATE PRACTICE AND PROCEDURE, 565 pages, 1987. (Casebook)

SONSTENG, HAYDOCK AND BOYD'S THE TRIALBOOK: A TOTAL SYSTEM FOR PREPARATION AND PRESENTATION OF A CASE, 404 pages, 1984. Softcover. (Coursebook)

WHARTON, HAYDOCK AND SONSTENG'S CALIFORNIA CIVIL TRIALBOOK, Law School and CLE Edition. 148 pages, 1990. Softcover. (Text)

Trusts and Estates

ATKINSON'S HORNBOOK ON WILLS, Second Edition, 975 pages, 1953. (Text)

AVERILL'S UNIFORM PROBATE CODE IN A NUTSHELL, Third Edition, approximately 450 pages, 1993. Softcover. (Text)

BOGERT'S HORNBOOK ON TRUSTS, Sixth Edition, Student Edition, 794 pages, 1987. (Text)

CLARK, LUSKY AND MURPHY'S CASES AND MATERIALS ON GRATUITOUS TRANSFERS, Third Edition, 970 pages, 1985. (Casebook)

DODGE'S WILLS, TRUSTS AND ESTATE PLANNING–LAW AND TAXATION, CASES AND MATERIALS, 665 pages, 1988. (Casebook)

McGOVERN, KURTZ AND REIN'S HORNBOOK ON WILLS, TRUSTS AND ESTATES–INCLUDING

Trusts and Estates—Cont'd

TAXATION AND FUTURE INTERESTS, 996 pages, 1988. (Text)

MENNELL'S WILLS AND TRUSTS IN A NUTSHELL, 392 pages, 1979. Softcover. (Text)

SIMES' HORNBOOK ON FUTURE INTERESTS, Second Edition, 355 pages, 1966. (Text)

TURANO AND RADIGAN'S HORNBOOK ON NEW YORK ESTATE ADMINISTRATION, 676 pages, 1986 with 1991 pocket part. (Text)

UNIFORM PROBATE CODE, OFFICIAL TEXT WITH COMMENTS. 863 pages, 1991. Softcover.

WAGGONER'S FUTURE INTERESTS IN A NUTSHELL, 361 pages, 1981. Softcover. (Text)

Water Law—see also Energy and Natural Resources Law, Environmental Law

GETCHES' WATER LAW IN A NUTSHELL, Second Edition, 459 pages, 1990. Softcover. (Text)

SAX, ABRAMS AND THOMPSON'S LEGAL CONTROL OF WATER RESOURCES: CASES AND MATERIALS, Second Edition, 987 pages, 1991. Teacher's Manual available. (Casebook)

TRELEASE AND GOULD'S CASES AND MATERIALS ON WATER LAW, Fourth Edition, 816 pages, 1986. (Casebook) 1993 Supplement.

Wills—see Trusts and Estates

Workers' Compensation

HOOD, HARDY AND LEWIS' WORKERS' COMPENSATION AND EMPLOYEE PROTECTION LAWS IN A NUTSHELL, Second Edition, 361 pages, 1990. Softcover. (Text)

LITTLE, EATON AND SMITH'S CASES AND MATERIALS ON WORKERS' COMPENSATION, 537 pages, 1992. Teacher's Manual available. (Casebook)

WEST'S LAW SCHOOL ADVISORY BOARD

---

*

CASES AND MATERIALS ON
EVIDENCE
Seventh Edition

By

Charles T. McCormick
Late Dean and Professor of Law
University of Texas

John F. Sutton, Jr.
A.W. Walker Centennial Chair in Law Emeritus
and Professor of Law, University of Texas

Olin Guy Wellborn III
William C. Liedtke, Sr. Professor of Law
University of Texas

AMERICAN CASEBOOK SERIES®

WEST PUBLISHING CO.
ST. PAUL, MINN., 1992

American Casebook Series, the key symbol appearing on the front cover and the WP symbol are registered trademarks of West Publishing Co. Registered in the U.S. Patent and Trademark Office.

610 Opperman Drive
P.O. Box 64526
St. Paul, MN 55164–0526

Printed in the United States of America

Library of Congress Cataloging-in-Publication Data

McCormick, Charles Tilford, 1889–1963.
Cases and materials on evidence / by Charles T. McCormick, John F. Sutton, Jr., Olin Guy Wellborn III. — 7th ed.
p. cm. — (American casebook series)
Includes index.
ISBN 0–314–00426–2
1. Evidence (Law)—United States—Cases. I. Sutton, John Floyd, 1918– . II. Wellborn, Olin Guy, 1947– . III. Title.
IV. Series.
KF8934.M27 1992
347.73'6—dc20
[347.3076] 92–5652
CIP

ISBN 0–314–00426–2

(M.,S.&W.) Evidence, 7th Ed. ACB
1st Reprint—1993

PRINTED ON 10% POST CONSUMER RECYCLED PAPER

Preface to the Seventh Edition

This edition is a complete revision rather than merely an updating of its predecessor. We have added much new material and eliminated an even larger amount of old material. Where we have retained items from the Sixth Edition, we have reedited and rearranged them. In other words, this is a new book which includes some cases from the Sixth Edition.

In its present form, this is basically a book about the Federal Rules of Evidence and state codifications based on them. Therefore, few cases decided before 1975 are presented. Materials are organized entirely according to the Federal Rules. Each of the ten chapters corresponds to one of the first ten articles of the Rules. Within chapters and sections we have followed the sequence of the Rules except where logic or pedagogy required reordering. The order of chapters represents our notions of the best presentation, but any teacher familiar with the Rules can easily map a different path.

The latest edition of Federal Rules of Evidence, including the Advisory Committee's Notes and legislative history, is an essential companion to this book. Like many teachers, we assign a state codification as well.

Since the Sixth Edition, which appeared at the beginning of 1987, the Supreme Court of the United States has issued a number of important evidence decisions. We include as principal cases Huddleston v. United States (1988), United States v. Owens (1988), Bourjailly v. United States (1987), Beech Aircraft Corp. v. Rainey (1988), Idaho v. Wright (1990), Rock v. Arkansas (1987), Kentucky v. Stincer (1987), Tanner v. United States (1987), Maryland v. Craig (1990), Doe v. United States (1988), and Braswell v. United States (1988), and we present excerpts from Dowling v. United States (1990) and United States v. Zolin (1989).

One of our late colleagues, paraphrasing a well-known television commercial, admonished his students to "learn the law the old-fashioned way: read it." Perhaps that sentiment underlies our continued preference for the traditional casebook format in a field where many others have adopted some version of "text and problems." A judicial opinion is a text and a (real) problem, and it is more—it is a part of the law.

JOHN F. SUTTON, JR.
OLIN GUY WELLBORN III

February, 1992

*

Summary of Contents

Table of Contents

Table of Cases

The principal cases are in bold type. Cases cited or discussed in the text are roman type. References are to pages. Cases cited in principal cases and within other quoted materials are not included.

CASES AND MATERIALS ON

EVIDENCE

Seventh Edition

*

Chapter 1

RELEVANCY
[FED.R.EVID. ART. IV]

SECTION 1. GENERAL PRINCIPLES *
[FED.R.EVID. 401–403]**

STATE v. KOTSIMPULOS

Supreme Judicial Court of Maine, 1980.
411 A.2d 79.

ROBERTS, JUSTICE.

After trial by jury, Peter Kotsimpulos was convicted of the crime of theft (17–A M.R.S.A. § 353) of five pork tenderloins from the Hannaford Brothers meat plant in South Portland. The sole issue raised by Kotsimpulos on appeal is the exclusion of evidence of the expressed desire of a Hannaford Brothers supervisor to see that the defendant was relieved of his duties as a federal meat inspector. Finding no error, we affirm the judgment of the Superior Court.

The evidence at trial revealed that police officers had established surveillance at the plant because of unexplained disappearances of

* See 1 Wigmore, Evidence §§ 2, 9–12 (Tillers rev. 1983); 1A id. ch. 3 (Tillers rev. 1983); McCormick, Evidence ch. 16 (4th ed. 1992); Dolan, Rule 403: The Prejudice Rule in Evidence, 49 S.Cal.L.Rev. 220 (1976); Gold, Federal Rule of Evidence 403: Observations on the Nature of Unfairly Prejudicial Evidence, 58 Wash.L.Rev. 497 (1983); Lempert, Modeling Relevance, 75 Mich.L.Rev. 1021 (1977); Travers, An Essay on the Determination of Relevancy Under the Federal Rules of Evidence, 1977 Ariz.St.L.J. 327; Wellborn, The Federal Rules of Evidence and the Application of State Law in the Federal Courts, 55 Tex. L.Rev. 371 (1977).

** Each section heading is accompanied by an asterisk footnote citing pertinent provisions of Wigmore's and McCormick's treatises and selected law review articles. The footnotes do not refer to treatises on the Federal Rules of Evidence because they are organized in accordance with the Rules and students can easily locate their pertinent provisions without help. The leading treatises on the Federal Rules of Evidence are Graham, Handbook of Federal Evidence (3d ed. 1991); Louisell & Mueller, Federal Evidence (1977–81); Saltzburg & Martin, Federal Rules of Evidence Manual (5th ed. 1990); Weinstein & Berger, Weinstein's Evidence; Weinstein & Berger, Weinstein's Evidence Manual (1991); Weissenberger, Federal Evidence (1987); and Wright, Graham, & Gold, Federal Practice and Procedure: Evidence (1977–90).

meat. Early on the morning of August 10, 1978, the defendant was observed entering the plant, returning to his car, reentering the plant, and finally returning to his car once again some time later. A spot check of meat within the plant revealed five pork tenderloins missing. Upon arrest, the defendant was found to have five pork tenderloins in his coat pocket.

The defendant testified that he did not take the pork loins, that he did not know how they got in his car, but that they got in his pocket because he picked them up off the floor of the car thinking they were a package of meat he had purchased elsewhere. Defense counsel then attempted to introduce testimony by the defendant that he had been threatened by one Carver. Upon offer of proof, counsel suggested that Carver had expressly warned Kotsimpulos that he was going to see that he, Kotsimpulos, lost his job. The express purpose for offering this evidence was to suggest the possibility that the pork loins had been planted in the defendant's car, thus warranting a reasonable doubt as to his guilt. The presiding justice excluded the testimony on the alternative grounds that (a) it was not relevant (M.R.Evid. 402) and (b) the danger of confusing the jury outweighed the probative value of the evidence. (M.R.Evid. 403).[1]

M.R.Evid. 401 defines relevance as follows:

> "Relevant evidence" means evidence having any tendency to make the existence of any fact that is of consequence to the determination of the action more probable or less probable than it would be without the evidence.

The concept of relevance "rests upon rules of logic or common sense, not of law." Field and Murray, *Maine Evidence* § 401.1 at 53 (1976). Common sense suggests that one measures relevance in a continuum, and that at some stage evidence becomes so remote that its probative impact upon "the existence of any fact that is of consequence" is reduced to zero. When the probative impact reaches zero, the evidence is simply not admissible under Rule 402; but prior to that point, the admission of the evidence may be weighed against other factors under Rule 403.[2]

As we said in *Eaton v. Sontag,* Me., 387 A.2d 33, 38 (1978):

1. The initial ruling was that the evidence was not relevant. After further offer of proof, the presiding justice ruled that "the probative value of this evidence is at best very slight" and that "the evidence rather than assisting the jury is going to confuse the jury and that it will divert their attention from the issue which is before them."

2. M.R.Evid. 402 provides:

> All relevant evidence is admissible, except as limited by constitutional requirements or as otherwise provided by statute or by these rules or by other rules applicable in the courts of this state. Evidence which is not relevant is not admissible.

M.R.Evid. 403 provides:

> Although relevant, evidence may be excluded if its probative value is substantially outweighed by the danger of unfair prejudice, confusion of the issues, or misleading the jury, or by considerations of undue delay, waste of time, or needless presentation of cumulative evidence.

> [T]he determination whether evidence is relevant * * * must necessarily rest largely in the sound discretion of the presiding justice as of the time it is offered.

The presiding justice must exercise his discretion under Rule 403 in determining whether logically relevant evidence is so lacking in probative value that it should be excluded under the circumstances of the case. See Field and Murray, *supra,* § 401.1 at 53–56. The ruling will be reviewed only for abuse of discretion. *State v. Saucier,* Me., 385 A.2d 44, 47 (1978); *see also State v. Doughty,* Me., 399 A.2d 1319, 1323 (1979).

Evidence of animosity toward a party may be relevant on questions of motive or credibility when the alleged animosity was felt by another party or a witness. *See, e.g., State v. Brown,* Me., 321 A.2d 478 (1974). In this case, Carver was neither a party nor a witness, so the evidence of his threat could be relevant only if there is sufficient logical connection to any other fact of consequence. As this Court held in *State v. Berube,* 139 Me. 11, 15, 26 A.2d 654, 656 (1942), evidence of another person's threats toward the defendant, standing alone, is not admissible to show that that other person had anything to do with the crime charged or the prosecution of the defendant. There must be additional evidence connecting the other person with the crime or with the proceedings, before his feelings toward the defendant become admissible. *See* M.R.Evid. 104(b).

In the instant case, the suggested fact of consequence was the possible planting of false evidence in the defendant's car. Carver's threat was not specifically suggestive of any such intent. Upon inquiry by the presiding justice, defense counsel conceded that there was no evidence that Carver had participated in the surveillance or apprehension of the defendant; nor was there any evidence that Carver had an opportunity to plant the pork tenderloins in defendant's car. Under the circumstances of this case, we find no abuse of discretion in the conclusion of the presiding justice that the probative value of the threat was too slight to warrant the risk of confusing the jury.

The entry is:

Appeal denied.

Judgment of conviction affirmed.

STATE v. NICHOLAS

Court of Appeals of Washington, 1983.

34 Wash.App. 775, 663 P.2d 1356, review denied, 100 Wash.2d 1006 (1983).

RINGOLD, JUDGE.

Edward Peter Nicholas, Jr. appeals the judgment and sentence entered on his conviction by a jury of one count of burglary in the first degree (RCW 9A.52.020) and one count of rape in the first degree (RCW 9A.44.040). We affirm.

On January 5, 1981, the victim, Ms. S., was awakened by an intruder in her house. He was wearing a sweatshirt with the hood over his head and it was dark, so she could not see his face. He proceeded to have forcible intercourse with her. At one point during the rape Ms. S. said "Is it Peter?" referring to the defendant, who lived nearby and had done yard work for her the previous summer. The rapist did not respond to her question, and fled from the house. Ms. S. reported the rape to the police, who investigated but did not develop any suspects.

On June 25, 1981, Ms. S. was again raped in her bed by an intruder. She tried to push him away with her hands on his face and chest. After he fled, she notified the police and described the rapist as slender and muscular, with short curly hair and an odor of sweat mixed with cologne. He was wearing two layers of clothing, "like a T-shirt with a shirt over it or a jacket over it." Ms. S. felt that the January and June rapes had been perpetrated by the same person.

K.C., a police dog, picked up a scent on the bushes near the victim's house, but lost it at a nearby street intersection. K.C. picked up a scent again on the other side of the intersection after hunting for a while. The dog and Officer Kummerfeldt, his handler, ran down the street into a schoolyard, where they found Nicholas. K.C. indicated that it was Nicholas's scent he was following. Kummerfeldt described Nicholas as extremely sweaty and red-faced, and as apparently having an erection.

Officer Hambly, who took Nicholas into custody after K.C. found him, testified that Nicholas was sweating profusely and had an erection. Nicholas also had two small fresh scratches on his face, characterized by Officer Hambly as "fingernail scratches." Nicholas was wearing "dirty tennis shoes, a blue, very baggy T-shirt type of affair, and blue jeans." He was not wearing socks or underwear.

After being advised of his rights, Nicholas related his version of events to the police. He had received the scratches earlier that day, when he had fallen into some bushes off a ladder while housepainting; he had been drinking at a local tavern earlier in the evening, had walked home and then to a friend's house; the friend was not home, so he had been returning to his house when he stepped into the school yard to urinate, and K.C. came up to him; he was sweaty because he had been running. After arresting Nicholas, the police searched his residence. Nicholas's mother gave them a sweatshirt of his which was similar to that worn by the January rapist.

Laboratory tests were performed on fingernail scrapings and a vaginal smear taken from Ms. S., for comparison with Nicholas's blood type. The fingernail scrapings proved to contain human blood, but in insufficient quantities to type. The vaginal smear contained sperm, though Ms. S. stated she did not know whether her assailant ejaculated. An acid phosphatase test showed positive for a type O secretor which meant, since Ms. S. is a type O secretor, that the rapist was either a type O secretor or a non-secretor, categories covering about 60 percent of the population. Blood tests showed that Nicholas was a type A non-secretor, so he was not ruled out by the acid phosphatase test. No legible fingerprints were obtained from a pair of sunglasses which had been left by the assailant at the scene of the June rape.

Nicholas was charged with one count of first degree rape and one count of first degree burglary arising from the June 25 rape. Another count of first degree rape and another count of first degree burglary with respect to the January 5th rape were subsequently added by amendment. The charges were tried to a jury, which found Nicholas guilty of the charges dealing with the June 25 incident and not guilty of the charges relating to the January 5th incident.

* * *

Admissibility of Medical Test Results

Nicholas next contends that the results of the secretor type tests had no relevance to the issue of identity, and established only that the sperm could have come from 60 percent of the population. He argues that the test results merely tended to include him in a class of people who might have committed the rape, "thereby increas[ing] the probability of defendant's guilt without connecting him, in any way, to the charged offense." *People v. Sturdivant,* 91 Mich.App. 128, 283 N.W.2d 669, 670 (1979). He urges this court to follow the *Sturdivant* case and hold that the testimony was prejudicial and irrelevant and should have been excluded.

People v. Sturdivant, supra, holds irrelevant secretor test results which merely place the defendant in a category of people who might have committed the crime. *Sturdivant* has subsequently been disapproved by other panels of the Michigan court, *see, e.g., People v. Camon,* 110 Mich.App. 474, 313 N.W.2d 322 (1981); *People v. Horton,* 99 Mich. App. 40, 297 N.W.2d 857 (1980), and even the author of the *Sturdivant* opinion has subsequently qualified his holding in that case by saying that the test is one of balancing probative value with prejudicial effect, not a rule of irrelevance per se. *See People v. White,* 102 Mich.App. 156, 301 N.W.2d 837, 839 (1981) (Kelly, J., concurring); *see also* Annot., 46 A.L.R.2d 1000.

In *State v. Luoma,* 88 Wash.2d 28, 558 P.2d 756 (1977), the court held that the evidence the victim's blood type matched bloodstains found in the defendant's car had probative value, and was admissible; that an objection goes to the weight and not the admissibility of the evidence. Similarly, evidence which tends to limit the field of possible perpetrators is relevant on the issue of identity. The results of the acid phosphatase and secretor type tests tended to some degree to make it more probable that Nicholas was guilty of the rape and burglary. ER 401. Nicholas nowhere alleges prejudice which would merit exclusion of this evidence pursuant to ER 403. The probative value of the evidence or the lack thereof could be argued to the jury. The evidence was properly admitted.

* * *

The judgment and sentence is affirmed.

UNITED STATES v. JOHNSON

United States Court of Appeals, Fifth Circuit, 1977.
558 F.2d 744, cert. denied, 434 U.S. 1065, 98 S.Ct. 1241, 55 L.Ed.2d 766 (1978).

SIMPSON, CIRCUIT JUDGE:

Lewis E. Johnson was convicted on three counts of making and subscribing false and fraudulent corporate income tax returns for two corporations which he controlled. Title 26 U.S.C. § 7206(1) (1970). In appealing his conviction he has raised 14 arguments in favor of reversal. We find none of them meritorious and affirm. Two of the points raised on appeal warrant comment.

Both the original indictment and a superseding indictment to which Johnson pleaded not guilty and went to trial contained seven counts charging violations of law as to income taxes. Counts I and III charged him with income tax evasion on his Individual Income Tax Returns, Forms 1040, for calendar years 1971 and 1972, in violation of Title 26, U.S.C. § 7201. Counts II and IV charged him with making false and fraudulent statements on his Individual Income Tax Returns for the same years, in violation of Title 26, U.S.C. § 7206(1). Counts V, VI and VII, on which Johnson was convicted, charged him with making and subscribing false and fraudulent corporate income tax returns, of corporations controlled by him, in violation of Title 26, U.S.C. § 7206(1). Prior to trial, on motion of the United States, the district court dismissed Counts I, II and III, thus removing the issue of tax evasion from the trial. The jury acquitted appellant as to Count IV.

Many of Johnson's objections to the fairness of his trial stem from the dismissal of the tax evasion charges because, he contends, he was thereby prevented from introducing evidence to establish that, during the period in question, he actually overpaid his taxes by neglecting to make permissible deductions. Because he was tried only for wilfully making false statements on his and his corporations' tax returns, his tax liability or overpayment was irrelevant. Johnson maintains that he was prejudiced because evidence submitted by the government led the jury to believe that he had underpaid his taxes and the trial judge would not allow him to counter this suggestion.

The irrelevancy of Johnson's alleged overpayment of tax to any issue at his trial is firmly established by cases in this and other Circuits. We held the following in *Schepps v. United States,* 395 F.2d 749 (5th Cir.1968), cert. denied, 393 U.S. 925, 89 S.Ct. 256, 21 L.Ed.2d 261:

> The appellant has been found guilty, in two counts, of violating 26 U.S.C., § 7206(1), wilfully making and subscribing a federal income tax return which he did not believe to be true and correct as to every material matter. That the return was false in certain particulars is not disputed. Although not charged with nor being tried for income tax evasion, appellant says that he should have been allowed to

> introduce proof showing that the falsity resulted in no tax deficiency. This proof was not relevant to the issue raised by the indictment and it was not error to reject it, *Siravo v. United States,* 1 Cir., 1967, 377 F.2d 469; *Silverstein v. United States,* 1 Cir., 1967, 377 F.2d 269; *Hoover v. United States,* 5 Cir., 1966, 358 F.2d 87, 89, cert. denied, 385 U.S. 822, 87 S.Ct. 50, 17 L.Ed.2d 59.

See also *United States v. Fritz,* 481 F.2d 644 (9th Cir.1973); *United States v. Jernigan,* 411 F.2d 471 (5th Cir.1969), cert. denied, 396 U.S. 927, 90 S.Ct. 262, 24 L.Ed.2d 225.

These precedents notwithstanding, Johnson raises two objections to the district court's refusal to allow evidence of income tax overpayment. First, Johnson contends that such evidence was relevant in his case to the issue of whether he in good faith relied on his accountants properly to compute and classify reportable items of income and expense. He argues that:

> Had the appellant not left the accounting procedures to his accountants and trusted their computations, surely some of the deductible items which would have reduced Appellant's tax liability would have been picked up by him when he examined his returns.

Brief for Appellant at 39.

We agree that the failure to make permissible deductions, resulting in a tax overpayment, logically tends to prove reliance on the integrity and expertise of one's accountants. Although this evidence might thus have aided the reliance aspect of Johnson's defense, it could have had no appreciable impact on the case as a whole because much of the prosecution's evidence demonstrated that Johnson withheld relevant information from his accountants. Under these circumstances, Johnson's alleged reliance on his accountants is irrelevant. Cf. *United States v. Signer,* 482 F.2d 394, 398 (6th Cir.1973).

Even if we assume that reliance evidence is logically relevant to any issue in the case, our inquiry cannot end there. Under Federal Rule of Evidence 403, admissibility is predicated on more than mere logical relevance:

> Although relevant, evidence may be excluded if its probative value is substantially outweighed by the danger of unfair prejudice, confusion of the issues, or misleading the jury, or by considerations of undue delay, waste of time, or needless presentation of cumulative evidence.

In determining legal relevance, the trial judge has broad discretion. *United States v. Moore,* 522 F.2d 1068, 1079 (9th Cir.1975), cert. denied, 423 U.S. 1049, 96 S.Ct. 775, 46 L.Ed.2d 637 (1976). We may not disturb his ruling unless he has clearly abused his discretion. *United States v. Dwyer,* 539 F.2d 924, 927 (2d Cir.1976).

No showing of abuse of discretion has been made here. Where reliance on the accoutants was relevant, the district court allowed direct evidence on that point. Because it depends on a series of inferences, however, evidence of neglected deductions is only indirectly probative of reliance. Moreover, it carries several risks against which Rule 403 was designed to protect. It could have resulted in unfair prejudice to the government's case by appealing to the emotions of the jury. Indeed, the conduct of Johnson's counsel during the trial made this no small concern of the district court.[1] Also, the danger of confusing the issues was great because tax liability was irrelevant to the offenses for which Johnson was tried. Finally, presenting evidence of overpayment could have resulted in a waste of time on collateral issues. See 1st Supp.Record, Vol. III, at 308. We conclude that the district court properly excluded evidence of neglected tax deductions.

Johnson's second contention in this regard is that the district court erred in overruling his motion for a mistrial when the prosecutor, in his closing argument, implied a tax liability on Johnson's part. Specifically, Johnson objected to the prosecutor's statements that improper business deductions were made "at the expense of the taxpayers of this country". See Tr.Pros.Arg. at 22. We do not agree that this expression implies a tax liability. But, however it is interpreted, any prejudicial effect that it might have had was cured by the district court's instruction to the jury: whether "a tax is due or owing by the defendant is immaterial to the charges before you in this case". The instruction continued:

> Accordingly, whether the Government has or has not suffered a pecuniary or monetary loss as a result of the alleged false return is not relevant and need not be considered by you in your deliberation.[2]

We have carefully examined Johnson's 12 other allegations of error and find them to be without merit.

* * *

The judgment of conviction appealed from is

AFFIRMED.

---

1. The district court repeatedly admonished Johnson's counsel for appealing to the sympathy of the jury in a manner unrelated to the merits of the case. The Court at one point sustained an objection to an attempt to elicit from Mr. Johnson information about his contributions to a religious school: "Counsel, I think you well know that attempts to evoke sympathy on the basis of religious activities is wholly improper to the merits of this case. You have repeatedly gone into this, notwithstanding the Court's rulings". 1st Supp. Record Vol. IV, at 251. In his closing argument, Johnson's counsel noted that his client had gone to war for his government, "subjected himself to the enemy's bullets", and that now the same government had turned his life "into a nightmare". *Id.*, Vol. V, at 46. The district court was moved to comment to Johnson's counsel: "you were able to turn tears on and off like a faucet during your closing argument * * * if there can be such a thing as erudition in tears, you certainly displayed it". *Id.* at 163, 165. This comment occurred during the argument of post-trial motions, and thus *not* in the jury's presence.

2. 1st Supp.Record, Vol. V, at 103. We note also that in his closing argument Johnson's counsel stated: "But bear in mind, this case is not about any taxes that are alleged to be due by Mr. Johnson. No claim, you read these indictments, there is no claim for any amount of taxes". *Id.* at 41.

GEORGE F. JAMES, RELEVANCY, PROBABILITY AND THE LAW, 29 Calif.L.Rev. 689, 690 (1941). "Relevancy, as the word itself indicates, is not an inherent characteristic of any item of evidence but exists as a relation between an item of evidence and a proposition sought to be proved. If an item of evidence tends to prove or to disprove any proposition, it is relevant to that proposition. If the proposition itself is one provable in the case at bar, or if it in turn forms a further link in a chain of proof the final proposition of which is provable in the case at bar, then the offered item of evidence has probative value in the case. Whether the immediate or ultimate proposition sought to be proved is provable in the case at bar is determined by the pleadings, by the procedural rules applicable thereto, and by the substantive law governing the case. Whether the offered item of evidence tends to prove the proposition at which it is ultimately aimed depends upon other factors, shortly to be considered. But because relevancy * * * means tendency to prove a proposition properly provable in the case, an offered item of evidence may be excluded as 'irrelevant' for either of these two quite distinct reasons: because it is not probative of the proposition at which it is directed, or because that proposition is not provable in the case."

UNITED STATES v. HALL, 653 F.2d 1002, 1005 (5th Cir.1981). "The essential prerequisite of admissibility is relevance. Fed.R.Ev. 402. To be relevant, evidence must have some 'tendency to make the existence of any fact that is of consequence to the determination of the action more probable or less probable than it would be without the evidence.' Id. 401. Implicit in that definition are two distinct requirements: (1) The evidence must be probative of the proposition it is offered to prove, and (2) the proposition to be proved must be one that is of consequence to the determination of the action. McCormick on Evidence § 185, at 435 (2d ed. 1972); 1 Weinstein's Evidence ¶ 401[03], at 401–13 (1980); 22 Wright & Graham, Federal Practice and Procedure: Evidence § 5162, at 18 (1978). Whether a proposition is of consequence to the determination of the action is a question that is governed by the substantive law. Simply stated, the proposition to be proved must be part of the hypothesis governing the case—a matter that is in issue, or probative of a matter that is in issue, in the litigation. McCormick on Evidence, supra, § 185, at 434; 1 Weinstein's Evidence, supra, ¶ 401[03]."

PEOPLE v. CARLSON, 712 P.2d 1018, 1021–22 (Colo.1986). "In resolving an issue of relevancy, a court must first ask whether the proffered evidence relates to a fact 'that is of consequence to the determination of the action,' CRE 401—in other words, whether the proferred evidence is legally material to some factual issue in the case.

If this question is answered in the negative, the evidence is simply inadmissible as having no bearing whatever on any issue in the case. If this initial question is answered in the affirmative, the next question centers on the matter of logical relevancy. The appropriate inquiry here is whether, as provided in CRE 401, the evidence makes the existence of a consequential fact 'more probable or less probable than it would be without the evidence.' If the proffered evidence is not logically relevant, the inquiry is at an end and the evidence should not be admitted. If, on the other hand, the evidence is logically relevant to a consequential fact, a third question must then be addressed—that is, whether under CRE 403 the probative value of the evidence is substantially outweighed by the danger of unfair prejudice. People v. Lowe, 660 P.2d 1261, 1265 (Colo.1983); 1 J. Weinstein and M. Berger, Weinstein's Evidence ¶ 403[01], at 403–13 (1982)."

UNITED STATES v. MYERS, 550 F.2d 1036, 1049–51 (5th Cir. 1977). "Analytically, flight is an admission by conduct. E. Cleary McCormick on Evidence § 271, p. 655 (rev. ed. 1972). Its probative value as circumstantial evidence of guilt depends upon the degree of confidence with which four inferences can be drawn: (1) from the defendant's behavior to flight; (2) from flight to consciousness of guilt; (3) from consciousness of guilt to consciousness of guilt concerning the crime charged; and (4) from consciousness of guilt concerning the crime charged to actual guilt of the crime charged. See generally Miller v. United States, 116 U.S.App.D.C. 45, 48, 320 F.2d 767, 770 (1963); 1 J. Wigmore, Evidence § 173, p. 632 (3d ed. 1940). The use of evidence of flight has been criticized on the grounds that the second and fourth inferences are not supported by common experience and it is widely acknowledged that evidence of flight or related conduct is 'only marginally probative as to the ultimate issue of guilt or innocence.' United States v. Robinson, 154 U.S.App.D.C. 265, 273, 475 F.2d 376, 384 (1973). * * *

"Nevertheless, in United States v. Ballard, 423 F.2d 127 (5th Cir.1970), we stated:

> It is today universally conceded that the fact of an accused's flight, escape from custody, resistance to arrest, concealment, assumption of a false name, and related conduct, are admissible as evidence of consciousness of guilt, and thus of guilt itself. Id. at 133.

Quoting 2 J. Wigmore, Evidence § 276, p. 111 (3d ed. 1940). * * *

"Applying these principles to the California incident initially, it is apparent that the events do not support the first of the four inferences. The only evidence that Myers or Coffie attempted to flee from the arresting officers was furnished by Agent Hanlon. But Hanlon's testimony was inconclusive. He first stated that Myers and Coffie were three feet from the motorcycle; then that they were fifty feet from it.

In addition, Hanlon's testimony below conflicted with statements he made at Myers' trial on the Pennsylvania charges. There he testified that neither Myers nor Coffie had attempted to flee. Indeed, it seems unlikely that they would get off of the motorcycle if their purpose was to avoid capture. For a jury to find that Myers fled from federal agents prior to his arrest in California would require conjecture and speculation. It was error to instruct the jury that they could infer consciousness of guilt from an alleged flight which was without support in the record. Cf. United States v. Torrence, 480 F.2d 564 (5th Cir.1973).

"The evidentiary basis for the instruction regarding the California incident is also deficient in another respect. Even assuming that Myers did attempt to flee, giving a flight instruction would still be improper because the third inference upon which the probative value of flight as circumstantial evidence of guilt depends, from consciousness of guilt to consciousness of guilt concerning the crime charged, cannot be drawn. Since it is known that Myers committed an armed bank robbery in Pennsylvania between the date on which the Florida robbery occurred and the date of his arrest in California, the hypothesis that he fled solely because he felt guilty about the Pennsylvania robbery cannot be ruled out. The theory under which evidence of flight is admitted presumes that consciousness of guilt concerning the Pennsylvania robbery could be a sufficient cause of flight. Without knowing whether Myers committed the Florida robbery it is impossible to say whether the California flight resulted from feelings of guilt attributable to the Florida and Pennsylvania robberies or from consciousness of guilt about the Pennsylvania robbery alone. Therefore, even if Myers did flee from the federal agents in California, no inference that he is guilty of the Florida robbery is possible, and it was error for this reason also to instruct the jury that they could draw such an inference. Cf. State v. Whitney, 43 Idaho 745, 254 P. 525 (1927) (attempted escape by prisoner awaiting trial for two district offenses not relevant to show that he is guilty of either); 2 P. Herrick, Underhill's Criminal Evidence § 373, p. 923 (5th ed. 1956).

* * *

"Turning next to the Florida incident, the evidence, though somewhat stronger, was likewise insufficient to support the flight instruction given. The version of Myers' conduct in Florida most favorable to the prosecution's case is that federal agents were unable to contact him at his usual place of residence for three weeks after the robbery, that he had his girlfriend bring his clothing from her house to a rendezvous point in a shopping center, that he fled when an unidentified man ran toward him at the shopping center, and that he left the state between three and six weeks after the date of the robbery. This evidence does not demonstrate intentional flight '*immediately* after the commission of a crime or after [accusation] of a crime' (emphasis added) as the instruction, by its own terms, requires. Compare United States v. Rowan, 518 F.2d 685, 691 (6th Cir.1975) (flight instruction not improper where defendant left the community within 36 hours of the time at which the charged crime was committed) with United States v. White, 488 F.2d 660, 662 (8th Cir.1973) (instruction improper where five months had elapsed between the date of the charged offense and the attempted arrest). See generally United States v. Register, supra; United States v. Deas, 413 F.2d 1371 (5th Cir.1969); Monnette v. United States, 299 F.2d 847 (5th Cir.1962). The immediacy requirement is important. It is the instinctive or impulsive character of the defendant's behavior, like flinching, that indicates fear of apprehension and gives evidence of flight such trustworthiness as it possesses. See generally Hutchins & Slesinger, Some Observations on the Law of Evidence—Consciousness of Guilt, 77 U.Pa.L.Rev. 725, 734–35 (1929). The more remote in time the alleged flight is from the commission or accusation of an offense, the greater the likelihood that it resulted from something other than feelings of guilt concerning that offense. Under the evidence adduced it was error to instruct the jury that they could infer from the Florida incident that Myers committed the crime with which he is charged."

UNITED STATES v. HANKINS, 931 F.2d 1256, 1261–62 (8th Cir.1991), cert. denied, ___ U.S. ___, 112 S.Ct. 243, 116 L.Ed.2d 198 (1991). "Most of the cases on this subject * * * involve evidence of *flight,* usually from the scene of a crime or from an arresting officer. The present case involves evidence of *escape,* but we see no distinction that would warrant an analytical approach different from that which is used in flight cases. Flight and escape are similar evasive acts. See, e.g., United States v. Guerrero, 756 F.2d 1342, 1347 (9th Cir.), cert. denied, 469 U.S. 934, 105 S.Ct. 334, 83 L.Ed.2d 270 (1984) (evidence of escape met the *Myers* inference test); United States v. Clark, 506 F.2d 416, 418 (5th Cir.), cert. denied, 421 U.S. 967, 95 S.Ct. 1957, 44 L.Ed.2d 454 (1975) (evidence of escape from custody analyzed as evidence of flight).

"The second and fourth inferences, it has been said, are often the most difficult to support, and that is true in this case as well. See *Myers,* 550 F.2d at 1049. But given the evidentiary manifestations in this case, the district court did not abuse its discretion in admitting evidence of Hankins's escape. One can confidently infer from Hankins's behavior that he was fleeing from custody. One can also confidently infer that Hankins's behavior was related to the armed bank robbery charges. Hankins gave a number of reasons for why he escaped (e.g., he thought he was being framed and he wanted to see his children) and these are all explanations for the jury to consider in weighing the significance of the escape evidence. But there is nothing in the record to suggest that Hankins escaped because he felt guilty about some other offense (i.e., the third inference above). Before his escape, Hankins had been made fully aware of the charges against him. Thus, 'there is a sufficient basis in the evidence to warrant the inference that the flight "was prompted by considerations related to the issue in question." ' United States v. Roy, 843 F.2d 305, 310 (8th Cir.) (quoting *Peltier,* 585 F.2d at 323), cert. denied, 487 U.S. 1222, 108 S.Ct. 2881, 101 L.Ed.2d 916 (1988). See also *Crosby,* 917 F.2d at 368 (evidence of flight admissible when appellant knew of the charges against him and his scheduled trial date, yet disappeared on day of trial).

"Hankins also argues that an unnecessarily extensive and prejudicial amount of evidence regarding his escape was received by the district court. Given the often marginally probative value of evidence of flight or escape and the risk of its prejudicial effect, district courts should be wary of the amount of evidence permitted on this subject and the way in which it is presented. See, e.g., *Peltier,* 585 F.2d at 324 (court determined that evidence was not presented in an 'inflammatory manner' and, 'in relation to the length of the trial, the time necessary for its presentation was brief'). The evidence of escape in Hankins's trial was not presented in an inflammatory manner, but it is our impression that more testimony than necessary was received by the district court. We do not believe, however, that this constitutes an abuse of the district court's discretion."

UNITED STATES v. MONAHAN, 633 F.2d 984, 985 (1st Cir.1980). "Evidence of threats to witnesses can be relevant to show consciousness of guilt. * * * Although some conduct regarded as obstruction of justice may not be probative because it demonstrates only a preference to avoid legal involvement, the act here was not so innocuous. The offensiveness of threatening personal harm to a witness shows that Monahan was willing to take extreme measures to exclude pertinent evidence from the trial. This surpasses in nature and degree any innocent desire to avoid entanglement. The specificity of this conduct implies a knowledge and fear of particular and damaging testimony intimately related to the prosecution at hand—not a generalized distaste for the courtroom. Because the evidence implicated no irrelevant or collateral matters, any 'prejudice' that arose did so only because of the evidence's probative character. Rule 403 is not contravened by evidence that might show only that the defendant is guilty of the crime charged. * * *

"We have no occasion in this case to consider whether a threat that is inflammatory or macabre in content should be excluded under Rule 403. Cf. United States v. McManaman, 606 F.2d 919, 926 (10th Cir. 1979) ('hearing and reading the taped conversation lead us to the conviction that the inflammatory talk of the plan of murders clearly must have predominated in impact over the discussion of drug dealing'); United States v. Check, 582 F.2d 668, 685–86 (2d Cir.1978) (recognizing the 'severe prejudice' that can result from testimony of death threats); United States v. Weir, 575 F.2d 668, 669–71 (8th Cir.1978) (threats of three assassinations, plus account of attempted killing resulting in bullet wound, held to be reversible error)."

Note

See also United States v. Jackson, 886 F.2d 838, 845–48 (7th Cir.1989) (refusal to provide handwriting exemplars); Brown & Williamson Tobacco Corp. v. Jacobson, 827 F.2d 1119, 1134 (7th Cir.1987) (bad faith destruction of documentary evidence), cert. denied, 485 U.S. 993, 108 S.Ct. 1302, 99 L.Ed.2d 512 (1988); United States v. Mendez—Ortiz, 810 F.2d 76, 79 (6th Cir.1986) (attempts to bribe and threats to witness), cert. denied, 480 U.S. 922, 107 S.Ct. 1384, 94 L.Ed.2d 697 (1987); United States v. Boyle, 675 F.2d 430, 432 (1st Cir.1982) (use of false name after crime); United States v. Morales, 577 F.2d 769, 772–73 (2d Cir.1978) (use of false name during crime); State v. Edwards, 136 Ariz. 177, 665 P.2d 59, 66 (1983) (resisting arrest); State v. Campbell, 146 Mont. 251, 405 P.2d 978, 984–85 (1965) (suicide attempt).

UNITED STATES v. McRAE

United States Court of Appeals, Fifth Circuit, 1979.

593 F.2d 700, cert. denied, 444 U.S. 862, 100 S.Ct. 128, 62 L.Ed.2d 83 (1979).

GEE, CIRCUIT JUDGE:

About two years ago, appellant McRae killed his wife Nancy by shooting her through the head with his deer rifle at point-blank range. That he did so is admitted; his sole defense at trial was that the shooting was not malicious but accidental. The offense having occurred on the Fort Bliss military reservation, McRae was indicted for second-degree murder under 18 U.S.C. § 1111. A jury trial resulted in his conviction and sentence to life imprisonment. * * *

* * *

The remaining two claimed errors involve evidentiary rulings by the district court. As to rulings of this sort, it is a commonplace that the trial court enjoys a wide discretion, one which we do not disturb except for abuse.

The first of these complaints is of the admission of various photographs of the deceased and of the death scene. It is said that these should have been excluded under Rule 403, Federal Rules of Evidence, as relevant matter the probative value of which is substantially outweighed by the danger of unfair prejudice. Two of these color prints are indeed—as the trial court characterized them—gross, distasteful and disturbing. Exhibit 29 is a view of Mrs. McRae's corpse, clothed in her bloody garments, bent forward so as to display an exit wound in the back of her skull produced by part of McRae's dum-dum bullet, which exploded in her brain. Exhibit 22 shows a front view of her body, seated in the chair where she died, her left eye disfigured by the bullet's entry and her head broken by its force. By comparison with these, the other photographs are mild; but these are not pretty even to the hardened eye. Neither, however, was the crime, and these exhibits are not flagrantly or deliberately gruesome depictions of it. *See United States v. Kaiser,* 545 F.2d 467, 496 (5th Cir.1977). The trial court carefully reviewed the government's photographic exhibits, excluding some of little probative value.[7] It found those admitted important to establishing elements of the offense—such as Mrs. McRae's position and that of the rifle when it was fired, as bearing on McRae's defense of accident.

Relevant evidence is inherently prejudicial; but it is only *unfair* prejudice, *substantially* outweighing probative value, which permits exclusion of relevant matter under Rule 403. Unless trials are to be conducted on scenarios, on unreal facts tailored and sanitized for the occasion, the application of Rule 403 must be cautious and sparing. Its major function is limited to excluding matter of scant or cumulative probative force, dragged in by the heels for the sake of its prejudicial effect. As to such, Rule 403 is meant to relax the iron rule of relevance, to permit the trial judge to preserve the fairness of the proceedings by exclusion despite its relevance. It is not designed to permit the court to "even out" the weight of the evidence, to mitigate a crime, or to make a contest where there is little or none. Here was no parade of horrors. We refuse to interfere with the trial court's exercise of its discretion.

Finally, McRae complains of the admission, on rebuttal, of evidence about his intimate relations with certain women. The first of these commenced two months after his wife's death. We have carefully reviewed McRae's own testimony, which dwelt on his grief and his intense devotion to his wife and family, all in an attempt to cast Mrs. McRae's death as accidental. We note that he introduced medical testimony of his hospitalization during a two-week period following the murder for "grief syndrome." We note also that the trial court excluded some of the more prejudicial portions of the proffered rebuttal testimony, such as that recounting a particularly gross expression of contempt by him for his dead wife. In view of his emphasis on his desolation at her death and on his undying devotion, we cannot say that an abuse of discretion occurred in the admission of this rebuttal evidence.

McRae's conviction is therefore

AFFIRMED.

Notes

(1) See also Dollar v. Long Mfg., N.C., Inc., 561 F.2d 613, 618 (5th Cir.1977), cert. denied, 435 U.S. 996, 98 S.Ct. 1648, 56 L.Ed.2d 85 (1978) ("Of course, 'unfair prejudice' as used in Rule 403 is not to be equated with testimony simply adverse to the opposing party. Virtually all evidence is prejudicial or it isn't material. The prejudice must be 'unfair.' "); Carter v. Hewitt, 617 F.2d 961, 972 (3d Cir.1980) (Rule 403 "does not offer protection against evidence that is merely prejudicial, in the sense of being detrimen-

7. Such as the children's handprints in blood on the wall of their home.

tal to a party's case. Rather, the rule only protects against evidence that is *unfairly* prejudicial. Evidence is unfairly prejudicial only if it has 'an undue tendency to suggest decision on an improper basis, commonly, though not necessarily, an emotional one.' Advisory Committee's Note, F.R.Evid. 403. It is unfairly prejudicial if it 'appeals to the jury's sympathies, arouses its sense of horror, provokes its instinct to punish,' or otherwise 'may cause a jury to base its decision on something other than the established propositions in the case.' 1 J. Weinstein & M. Berger, Weinstein's Evidence ¶ 403[03], at 403–15 to 403–17 (1978).").

(2) "An important consideration relating to probative value is the prosecutorial need for such evidence." United States v. Spletzer, 535 F.2d 950, 956 (5th Cir.1976). See also Bolt v. Halifax Hosp. Medical Center, 891 F.2d 810, 822 (11th Cir.1990) (when the tendered evidence is the only evidence on an issue, its probative value is very high), cert. denied, ___ U.S. ___, 110 S.Ct. 1960, 109 L.Ed.2d 322 (1990); United States v. Layton, 767 F.2d 549, 555 (9th Cir.1985) (exclusion of a tape approved in part because the availability of other evidence to prove the same facts "is a factor to be evaluated in the balance"); United States v. Beechum, 582 F.2d 898, 914 (5th Cir.1978) ("Probity in this context is not an absolute; its value must be determined with regard to the extent to which the defendant's unlawful intent is established by other evidence, stipulation, or inference. It is the incremental probity of the evidence that is to be balanced against its potential for undue prejudice."), cert. denied, 440 U.S. 920, 99 S.Ct. 1244, 59 L.Ed.2d 472 (1979).

(3) "Although sec. 904.03 does not list 'surprise' as a specific ground for excluding evidence, testimony which results in surprise may be excluded if the surprise would require a continuance causing undue delay or if surprise is coupled with the danger of prejudice and confusion of issues." Lease America Corp. v. Insurance Co. of North America, 88 Wis.2d 395, 276 N.W.2d 767, 769 (1979). See also United States v. Cole, 857 F.2d 971, 976 (4th Cir.1988) ("[W]hen a prosecutor enters into an informal discovery agreement he must abide by its spirit as well as its letter. * * * Thus, we cannot condone the admission of this statement when the prosecution allowed the defendants to mistakenly believe no such statement existed. Consequently, the testimony should have been excluded under Fed.R.Evid. 403 on the grounds of unfair prejudice and surprise.").

(4) On the concept of "cumulative evidence," see Towner v. State, p. 561 infra.

PEOPLE v. LONG, 38 Cal.App.3d 680, 113 Cal.Rptr. 530, 536–37 (1974). "Preliminarily, two observations might be made: (1) murder is seldom pretty,[2] and pictures, testimony and physical evidence in such a case are always unpleasant; and (2) many attorneys tend to underestimate the stability of the jury. A juror is not some kind of a dithering nincompoop, brought in from never-never land and exposed to the

2. As the defendant said of the decedent, 'He was a pretty ugly sight.'

harsh realities of life for the first time in the jury box. There is nothing magic about being a member of the bench or bar which makes these individuals capable of dispassionately evaluating gruesome testimony which, it is often contended, will throw jurors into a paroxysm of hysteria. Jurors are our peers, often as well educated, as well balanced, as stable, as experienced in the realities of life as the holders of law degrees. The average juror is well able to stomach the unpleasantness of exposure to the facts of a murder without being unduly influenced. The supposed influence on jurors of allegedly gruesome or inflammatory pictures exists more in the imagination of judges and lawyers than in reality.

"In this case, we have reviewed the pictures, both still and motion. They are neither 'better' nor 'worse' than those in the average murder case. Gruesome, yes, but factually gruesome. However, they are not unnecessarily hideous, ghastly, horrible or dreadful. Inflammatory? Definitely not. They are fair, if unpleasant, representations of an unpleasant situation which happened to be brought on by this defendant's actions. Their probative value in showing the jury exactly what happened clearly outweighs any speculative prejudicial effect. The photographs used in this case are not so gruesome or overdone as to 'unnecessarily inflame the passion of the jurors,' to quote the defendant."

NAPIER v. COMMONWEALTH, 426 S.W.2d 121, 122–23 (Ky.1968). "The gun that killed Cox was never found. His billfold was discovered in a toilet bowl in the men's room of the cabaret. The fatal bullet entered his face just to the left of the nose, took a downward course and came out below the right ear.

"Appellant's first contention is that he was entitled to a directed verdict of acquittal and that the verdict was flagrantly against the evidence. Our reaction is that only the Constitution saved him from a directed verdict for the Commonwealth.

"Over appellant's objection the Commonwealth was permitted to introduce a post mortem photograph of the victim's face showing the bullet hole and other marks of the fray. It is described as 'grisly and gruesome.' Since a pathologist had quite clearly demonstrated to the jury the points of entry and exit, we concede that the photograph may not have been strictly necessary. Nevertheless, an accurate photograph is more believable than any chart or second-hand description and in this case, as it developed, appellant's theory that Cox somehow managed to shoot himself made the precise location of the wound vitally important.

"It has been said that if the evidentiary value or necessity of a gruesome photograph outweighs its possible prejudicial effect it may be admitted. 29 Am.Jur.2d 861 (Evidence, § 787). 'The rule prohibiting the exhibition of inflammatory evidence to a jury does not preclude the revelation of the true facts surrounding the commission of a crime when these facts are relevant and necessary.' Salisbury v. Commonwealth, Ky., 417 S.W.2d 244, 246 (1967). But we need not depend on that principle as a basis for holding this particular photograph admissible. The fact is that it was not so gruesome as to be likely to prejudice or inflame the men and women, inured as they are to the horrors of both war and television, who sit on a modern jury. The time has come when it should be presumed that a person capable of serving as a juror in a murder case can, without losing his head, bear the sight of a photograph showing the body of the decedent in the condition or place in which found. 'Where the photographs revealed nothing more than the scene of the crime and the persons of the victims, they were not incompetent.' Salisbury v. Commonwealth, id."

HOLLAND v. COMMONWEALTH, 703 S.W.2d 876, 879–80 (Ky. 1985). "It is the general rule that a photograph, otherwise admissible, does not become inadmissible simply because it is gruesome and the crime is heinous. Brown v. Commonwealth, Ky., 558 S.W.2d 599 (1977). However, we find this case distinguishable in that the presentation of photographs depicting the animal mutilation of the corpse goes far beyond demonstrating proof of a contested relevant fact. Poe v. Commonwealth, Ky., 301 S.W.2d 900 (1957). Proof of identity, condition and lividity was amply established by the testimony of witnesses who found the body and the pathologist. The photographs do not elaborate on the nature of the victim's injuries but serve to arouse passion at the sight of extensive animal mutilation."

BERRY v. STATE, 290 Ark. 223, 718 S.W.2d 447, 450 (1986). "Because of the trial court's carte blanche acceptance of these graphic and repetitive pictures into evidence, it is necessary that we reexamine our position on the admissibility of inflammatory photographs. The analysis should firmly emphasize the need for the trial court to carefully weigh the probative value of the photographs against their prejudicial nature, rather than promoting a general rule of admissibility which essentially allows automatic acceptance of all the photographs of the victim and crime scene the prosecution can offer.

"Other states have been equally liberal in the admission of similar photographs where they were relevant to proof of the state's case. Like we do now, many have found it necessary, however, to stem the resulting influx of inflammatory pictures where the claims of relevance were increasingly tenuous in light of the prejudicial nature of the photographs."

Notes

(1) Although the admissibility of a gruesome, prejudicial photograph in a state court is an evidentiary question not reviewable in federal court, a federal court in a habeas corpus case will consider the constitutional issue whether the admission of the photograph was an error of such magnitude as to be fundamentally unfair and a denial of due process of law. See Osborne v. Wainwright, 720 F.2d 1237 (11th Cir.1983).

(2) "Unlike still photographs, which can generally be viewed by the court while the jury is in the box before they are admitted into evidence, moving pictures and slides should be viewed by the court out of the presence of the jury before their admissibility is determined." Cotlar v. State, 558 S.W.2d 16, 18 n. 1 (Tex.Crim.App.1977).

(3) Not all questionable photographs involve gruesome death scenes. In Douglass v. Hustler Magazine, Inc., 769 F.2d 1128 (7th Cir.1985), cert. denied, 475 U.S. 1094, 106 S.Ct. 1489, 89 L.Ed.2d 892 (1986), plaintiff, an actress and model, sued the magazine for invasion of privacy for unauthorized publication of nude photographs of her. Judgment for plaintiff was reversed and the case remanded. "An expert witness on the issue of *Hustler*'s offensiveness accompanied his testimony with a projection of 128 slides showing some of the vilest photographs and cartoons to have been published in *Hustler* over the years. * * * [T]he prejudicial effect of the parade of filth in the slide show so clearly outweighed its probative value as to require exclusion under Rule 403 of the Federal Rules of Evidence. * * * [B]ad as it is, *Hustler* is not so concentratedly outrageous as the slide show would make a viewer think." 769 F.2d at 1141–42.

SMITH v. STATE

Court of Criminal Appeals of Oklahoma, 1982.
650 P.2d 904.

BUSSEY, JUDGE:

The extraordinary circumstances of this case require that it be reversed and remanded for a new trial. The pertinent facts are as follows:

On Sunday, October 8, 1978, the appellant, Lena Smith, drove her automobile into a Sav–Go gasoline station in Yukon and commenced honking her horn until someone came out of the building to her car. The appellant instructed that person to call an ambulance. It was subsequently discovered that the passengers in the appellant's car, her two young granddaughters, had been gravely wounded by gunshots. One of the children was killed by a .44 caliber slug which passed completely through her body and embedded in the front car seat. The bullet was fired less than thirty (30) inches from the victim. The other child was severely wounded by a .38 caliber slug which likewise passed through her body and embedded itself in the front car seat. That bullet was fired from a distance of twelve (12) inches. The appellant was also severely wounded. A third slug was not found in the automobile.

The appellant was arrested and charged with Murder in the First Degree and Shooting with Intent to Kill. * * *

* * *

Having concluded that the appellant was effectively denied her insanity defense by the action and inaction of counsel for both sides, we address one final issue pertinent to re-trial.

State's Exhibit Number 34, a three-inch by five-inch posed photograph of the victims, which was taken sometime prior to the shootings, was improperly admitted into evidence. We have disapproved of the use of "before" photographs of victims in previous cases. Citing *Hudman v. State,* 89 Okl.Cr. 160, 205 P.2d 1175 (1949)[8] in *Ritchie v. State,* 632 P.2d 1244 (Okl.Cr.1981),[9] we indicated that such pictures lack relevancy in criminal cases;

> The jury should not have been concerned with what the child looked like prior to the offense committed against her, but instead it should have been concerned only with what had been done to the child, how it was done, when it was done, and who did it. 632 P.2d at 1246.

Although the trial court admonished the jury to consider the photograph only insofar as it proved the identity of the victims, we cannot say the error was cured. The prejudicial nature of the photograph was great, especially in light of the fact that it had no relevance. A photograph of this nature may arouse as many passions in a juror's mind as one depicting a gruesome scene. The photograph of the cherubic little girls served only to highlight the unfortunate fact that untimely death and injury had been visited upon them.

The photograph resulted in unfair prejudice which must be avoided on retrial.[10]

* * *

8. In *Hudman,* the trial court permitted the prosecution to introduce photographs of the victim of a homicide which had been taken prior to the homicide. The photographs, which depicted the victim in a sailor's uniform, were held to be of little or no relevance in this case, and of undue prejudice to the jury. The erroneous admission of the photograph was only one of many errors committed at that trial which prompted the reduction of the defendant's sentence for manslaughter in the first degree from thirty years' imprisonment to twenty years' imprisonment.

9. The photograph of the child was only a contributing factor in the *Ritchie* decision. That case was reversed and remanded for a new trial primarily because of the introduction of gruesome photographs of the autopsy performed on the child.

The photograph in the instant case is distinguishable from that in *Ritchie* because it was much smaller and not posted on a bulletin board for the jury to view throughout the trial. The photograph was, however, flashed before the jury at different points in the trial, and was taken into the jury room during deliberations. The principle espoused in *Ritchie* applies to the present case.

10. We note that the introduction of photographs of victims taken prior to criminal acts against them is not reversible error standing alone. However, in the words of *Ritchie,* supra, "In a close case, on appeal, such a photograph may well tip the scales in the appellant's favor." 632 P.2d at 1246. We do not encourage the use of "before" pictures in trials. Should the need to identify the victim(s) in a criminal case arise, there are many alternative forms of identification readily available to the State without resort to items which carry such prejudicial impact.

For the reasons herein stated, the appellant's convictions for Murder in the First Degree and Shooting with Intent to Kill are REVERSED and REMANDED for a new trial.

ROBERTS v. STEVENS CLINIC HOSPITAL, INC.

Supreme Court of Appeals of West Virginia, 1986.
176 W.Va. 492, 345 S.E.2d 791.

NEELY, JUSTICE:

In this appeal we decide whether we should sustain a McDowell County Circuit Court $10,000,000 jury award in favor of the parents and two siblings of Michael Joseph Roberts, a 2½–year–old child who died as the result of medical malpractice. We find no reversible error in the conduct of the trial, but we find it appropriate to enter a remittitur of $7,000,000.

* * *

II

At trial the plaintiff introduced into evidence a professionally prepared, twenty minute, videotape that combined "home movie" video recordings of Michael taken by a neighbor with a series of still, colored, photographs of Michael and the family. The audio background for this video presentation consisted of tape recordings of the child's voice as well as Joyce's voice singing and talking to the child. It is the defendant's contention that this film was a "theatrical" presentation that artistically highlighted certain aspects of Michael's life and Joyce's relationship to Michael in an inaccurate way.

We have reviewed the tape in its entirety and we find nothing inflammatory or prejudicial about it. *W.Va.Code,* 55–7–6 [1982], our wrongful death statute, provides in section (c)(1):

> "The verdict of the jury shall include, but may not be limited to, damages for the following: (A) Sorrow, mental anguish, and solace which may include society, companionship, comfort, guidance, kindly offices and advice of the decedent; * * *".

The purpose of the videotape was to demonstrate that Michael was a healthy, intelligent, enthusiastic, and well loved child. So as a preliminary matter, the videotape was relevant. *W.Va.R.Evid.* 401, 402. In our review of the tape, we find no artistic highlighting that emphasizes some scenes or photographs more than others, and we find no merit in the defendant's assertion that because the mother's voice went on several seconds after the screen turned black, an unduly sentimental atmosphere was evoked that would have prejudiced the jury.

This Court has not previously addressed the admissibility of videotape "Day-in-the-Life" films. The same evidentiary rules that govern the admissibility of recordings and photographs govern the admissibility of videotape evidence. *W.Va.R.Evid.* 1001(2). The general rule is that pictures or photographs that are relevant to any issue in a case are admissible. Furthermore, the trial judge is afforded wide discretion in determining the admissibility of videotapes and motion pictures. *Szeliga v. General Motors Corp.,* 728 F.2d 566, 567 (1st Cir.1984); *Ilosky v. Michelin Tire Corp.,* ___ W.Va. ___, 307 S.E.2d 603, 618 (1983).

We are not unmindful of the potential dangers inherent in such presentations. As one court has explained:

> Almost always an edited tape necessarily raises issues as to every sequence portrayed of whether the event shown is fairly representative of fact, after the editing process, and whether it is unduly prejudicial because of the manner of presentation.

Bolstridge v. Central Maine Power Co., 621 F.Supp. 1202 (D.C.Me.1985) (Plaintiff's "Day-in-the-Life" videotape excluded when open court testimony could demonstrate similar evidence, and admission of videotape would create risk of distracting jury and unfairly prejudicing defendant). A videotape's tone and editing, as well as the availability of similar evidence through in-court testimony, are all factors a trial court should consider in deciding whether to admit a videotape. But, we shall not reverse a trial court's decision in these matters unless the record shows a clear abuse of discretion. *See Gough v. Lopez,* ___ W.Va. ___, 304 S.E.2d 875 (1983) (Evaluation of remoteness of evidence left to trial court's discretion).

* * *

Accordingly, for the reasons set forth above the judgment of the Circuit Court of McDowell County is reversed and the case is remanded to the circuit court with directions to enter a remittitur of $7,000,000 and enter judgment on the verdict for $3,000,000 or, in the alternative, at the option of the plaintiff, to award a new trial.

Reversed and remanded with directions.

GRIMES v. EMPLOYERS MUT. LIABILITY INS. CO., 73 F.R.D. 607 (D.Alaska 1977). "This cause of action in diversity is a suit for personal injuries arising out of an industrial accident. On August 18, 1976, the plaintiff Thomas I. Grimes filed a motion in limine seeking a pretrial ruling on the admissibility of certain motion pictures. Specifically, the plaintiff seeks a ruling on the admissibility of: 1) a film depicting the plaintiff performing various daily activities and conducting clinical tests (hereinafter referred to collectively as 'plaintiff's film') * * *.

* * *

"The plaintiff's film is a 25 minute, 16 mm soundless motion picture consisting of three segments: 1) a section depicting the plaintiff performing daily activities in and near his home, 2) a section depicting the plaintiff performing the Jebsen–Taylor Hand Function Test, and 3) a section depicting the plaintiff performing a range-of-motion, prosthetic device test.

* * *

"The defendant's relevancy objection is in fact an objection to the prejudicial nature of the plaintiff's film. Under Rule 403 of the Federal Rules of Evidence, relevant evidence may be excluded in the court's discretion:

> '* * * if its probative value is substantially outweighed by the danger of unfair prejudice, confusion of the issues, or misleading the jury, or by considerations of undue delay, waste of time, or needless presentation of cumulative evidence.'

See generally 1 Weinstein ¶ 403, at 403–1 (1975). The defendant contends that the film of the plaintiff at home is prejudicial and misleading because the activities filmed were not activities normally performed by the plaintiff and because the filming was selective and non-continuous. The defendant in particular objects to the scenes of the plaintiff hugging his daughter, placing a cigarette in the mouth of his quadriplegic brother, driving a car, loading a gun while not actually hunting, and operating a fishing reel while not actually fishing. The defendant similarly objects to the film of the plaintiff performing clinical tests because the filming was prejudicial.

"The defendant's objections are in part well taken. The scenes of the plaintiff with his daughter and with his quadriplegic brother serve little purpose other than to create sympathy for the plaintiff. The prejudicial effect of these scenes outweighs the probative value of the evidence. In contrast, the other scenes of the plaintiff performing daily functions and the film of the plaintiff performing clinical tests have a probative value greater than any prejudice which might result. The films illustrate, better than words, the impact the injury has had on the plaintiff's life in terms of pain and suffering and loss of enjoyment of life. While the scenes are unpleasant, so is plaintiff's injury. Given that liability will have to be established before the jury will be allowed to view the film, the admission of the film will not be unduly prejudicial if the plaintiff shows that the daily activities were or are typical activities for the plaintiff."

Notes

(1) Compare Thomas v. C.G. Tate Const. Co., 465 F.Supp. 566 (D.S.C. 1979) (excluding videotape of physical therapy sessions of plaintiff burn victim displaying obvious "extreme pain and mental anguish").

(2) "A film depicting the victim in unlikely circumstances or performing improbable tasks cannot be said to fairly portray a typical 'Day in the Life' of the victim. The probative value of a film is greatest, and the possibility of prejudice lowest, when the conduct portrayed is limited to ordinary, day-to-day situations. * * * The film shows Bannister getting around school, getting into his car, pumping gasoline for his car, and performing several different tasks in his home. Although there are a

couple of scenes that show Bannister conducting activities that he would be unlikely to do frequently, the film as a whole demonstrates Bannister's adaptation to his injury. We hold that the district court did not abuse its discretion in admitting the film * * *." Bannister v. Town of Noble, Okl., 812 F.2d 1265, 1269–70 (10th Cir.1987).

SIMON v. KENNEBUNKPORT

Supreme Judicial Court of Maine, 1980.
417 A.2d 982.

GLASSMAN, JUSTICE.

On the morning of July 22, 1977, the appellant, Irene Simon, sustained a broken hip when she stumbled and fell while walking on a sidewalk along Ocean Avenue in Kennebunkport. The elderly woman filed a complaint under 23 M.R.S.A. § 3655 against the appellee, Town of Kennebunkport (Town), alleging that her injury was proximately caused by a defect in the design or construction of the sidewalk. Following a trial in the Superior Court, York County, the jury determined by special verdict that no defect in the sidewalk had proximately caused the appellant to fall, and judgment was entered for the appellee. The appellant contends that the presiding Justice erred in excluding evidence, offered to establish the defective condition of the sidewalk, that during the two years prior to the accident many other persons stumbled or fell at the location. We vacate the judgment.

Greg Quevillon and Anthony Cooper both operated businesses in the building in front of which the appellant fell. At trial Quevillon testified that the condition of the uneven, inclined sidewalk had not changed from the time it was constructed in 1974 or 1975 until the time of the accident in 1977. The appellant then attempted to elicit from this witness whether he had observed other persons fall at the location. The presiding Justice sustained the Town's objection, ruling that although the appellant could establish that the condition of the sidewalk had remained unchanged since its construction she could not offer evidence that other persons had fallen during this period. The appellant then represented that "if permitted to testify both Mr. Quevillon and Mr. Cooper would state that they saw nearly one person a day fall on that particular sidewalk, and * * * evidence of prior fall[s] is admissible where it goes to show a defect." Later, referring to the proposed testimony of Cooper, the appellant stated:

> My offer of proof is that if permitted to testify this witness would indicate that on similar conditions of weather, and under conditions where the road was identical to that, the condition of July 22, 1979 [sic], he saw approximately 100 people stumble or fall on that particular portion of the roadway.
>
> * * *

In a negligence action, evidence of other similar accidents or occurrences may be relevant circumstantially to show a defective or dangerous condition, notice thereof or causation on the occasion in question. The absence of other accidents or occurrences may also be probative on these issues. See generally, C. McCormick, *Handbook of the Law of Evidence* § 200 (2d ed. E. Cleary 1972). Nevertheless, Maine courts, with only rare exceptions, traditionally excluded such evidence on the ground that it " 'tends to draw away the minds of the jury from the point in issue [(negligence of the defendant at the time and place of the accident)], and to excite prejudice, and mislead them; and, moreover, the adverse party, having no notice of such a course of evidence, is not prepared to rebut it.' " [citations omitted.]

The genesis of an inflexible rule excluding other-accident evidence is commonly believed to be the early Massachusetts case of Collins v. Inhabitants of Dorchester, 60 Mass. (6 Cush.) 396 (1850), which reasoned that such evidence was largely irrelevant, involved proof of collateral facts and engendered unfair surprise. Id. at 398. The overwhelming majority of jurisdictions, including Massachusetts, see Robitaille v. Netoco Community Theatres of North Attleboro, Inc., 305 Mass. 265, 267–68, 25 N.E.2d 749, 750 (1940), have since either rejected or abandoned a positive rule of exclusion in favor of a standard of discretion. These courts hold that where the proponent can show that other accidents occurred under circumstances substantially similar to those prevailing at the time of the injury in question such evidence is admissible subject to exclusion by the trial court when the probative value of the evidence on the issues of defect, notice or causation is substantially outweighed by the danger of unfair prejudice or confusion of the issues or by consideration of undue delay. [citations omitted.]

A blanket rule of irrelevance is manifestly incompatible with modern principles of evidence. Although the introduction of other-accident evidence may carry with it the problems associated with inquiry into collateral matters, such evidence may also be highly probative on material issues of a negligence action, as illustrated by the instant case. Early cases failed to discern that admitting this evidence for its circumstantial force is not inconsistent with the fundamental principle that negligence liability is to be predicated on absence of due care under the circumstances at the time and place of injury. See, e.g., Damren v. Trask, 102 Me. 39, 46, 65 A. 513, 516 (1906). Although not rejecting prior case law, several later decisions of this Court appeared to eschew a *per se* rule as unnecessarily broad and to recognize that the similarity requirement, together with the trial court's discretion, adequately safeguards the proper use of this evidence. See Torrey v. Congress Square Hotel Co., supra, 145 Me. at 242, 75 A.2d at 457; Stodder v. Coca–Cola Bottling Plants, Inc., supra, 142 Me. at 144, 48 A.2d at 625; Spence v. Bath Iron Works Corp., supra, 140 Me. at 292–93, 37 A.2d at 176 (evidence of similar accidents permitted to show causation) (dictum); Nadeau v. Perkins, supra, 135 Me. at 217–18, 193 A. at 878 (allowing other-accident evidence on issue of breach of statutory duty where relevant circumstances similar). See generally Field & Murray, Maine Evidence § 403.4 (1976).

Whatever the continued vitality following these cases of an absolute prohibition against other-accident evidence, it is clear that such a rule did not survive the adoption of our new Rules of Evidence in 1976. Because the comprehensive reformulation does not specifically bar the use of this evidence, its admissibility must be determined by reference to the general provisions governing the admission of relevant evidence. M.R.Evid. 401 defines relevancy in terms of probative value and materiality. With exceptions not here pertinent, M.R.Evid. 402 provides that all relevant evidence is admissible. Although relevant, evidence may nevertheless be excluded under M.R.Evid. 403 when the danger of unfair prejudice, confusion or undue delay is disproportionate to the value of the evidence. Under this formulation, therefore, when a party seeks to introduce evidence of other accidents over objection on the ground of irrelevance, M.R.Evid. 401 requires the presiding Justice to determine the relevancy of the evidence on the basis of whether there is a substantial similarity in the operative circumstances between the proffer and the case at bar and whether the evidence is probative on a material issue in the case.[4] He must then consider whether the probative value of such evidence is substantially outweighed by the countervailing considerations of M.R.Evid. 403. As with other determinations of admissibility involving the balancing of probative value against prejudicial effect, the admission of other-accident evidence is committed to the sound discretion of the presiding Justice.[5] See, e.g., Towle v. Aube, Me., 310 A.2d 259, 265 (1973).

In the case at bar, it is readily apparent that the ruling of the presiding Justice constituted an abuse of discretion which rose to the level of prejudicial error. Evidence that in the two years prior to the accident as many as one hundred persons stumbled or fell under similar circumstances at the same location, unchanged in condition, clearly satisfies the substantial-similarity foundational requirement and is highly probative on the material issue whether the sidewalk was in a defective condition at the time of the appellant's fall. See, e.g., District of Columbia v. Armes, 107 U.S. 519, 524–25, 2 S.Ct. 840, 844–46, 27 L.Ed. 618 (1882); City of Lebanon v. Graves, 178 Ky. 749, 758, 199 S.W. 1064, 1068 (1918). See also Louisville & N.R. Co. v. Loesch, 215 Ky. 452, 457, 284 S.W. 1097, 1100 (1926). As demonstrated by its

4. As part of this determination, the presiding Justice must examine the temporal relationship between the proffered evidence and the injury in the case at bar. For example, evidence that other accidents occurred after the injury in question may be relevant to show causation but is without probative force on the issue of notice. Spence v. Bath Iron Works Corp., supra, 140 Me. at 292–93, 37 A.2d at 176; see McCormick, supra, at § 200.

5. At a later stage of the trial, the Town offered evidence that the appellant's husband, who was walking directly in front of the appellant at the time of the accident, did not fall as tending to show the absence of a defect in the sidewalk. Over the appellant's objection, the presiding Justice admitted this evidence, ruling that, unlike the excluded evidence of prior falls, the "non-fall" evidence related to the immediate time frame of the accident. In view of our disposition of this appeal, we need not decide whether this ruling, assigned as an additional ground of error by the appellant, constituted an abuse of discretion and, if so, whether the error was harmless. See M.R.Evid. 103(a).

prepared objection to the introduction of this evidence, the Town was well aware of the evidence before trial and therefore would not have been unfairly surprised by its admission. Because the evidence was to be offered through the personal observations of two witnesses, its introduction would not have consumed an inordinate amount of time or tended to confuse or excite the jury. The excluded evidence was crucial to the case of the appellant. The judgment of the Superior Court cannot stand.

The entry is:

Appeal sustained.

Judgment vacated.

Remanded to the Superior Court for further proceedings consistent with the opinion herein.

Costs allowed to appellant.

All concurring.

GARDNER v. SOUTHERN RY. SYSTEMS, 675 F.2d 949, 952–53 (7th Cir.1982). "We agree with appellant's interpretation of the law applicable to prior accident evidence in railroad collision cases. A railroad can be found negligent not only in the manner in which it operates its trains, but also because it failed to take adequate precautions at a grade crossing which it knew or should have known to be extra-hazardous. Stevens v. Norfolk & W. Ry. Co., 171 Ind.App. 334, 357 N.E.2d 1, 4 (1977); see also Menke v. Southern Railway Company, 603 F.2d 1281 (7th Cir.1979). Evidence of prior accidents which occurred at that crossing under similar conditions may be admitted to show that the railroad had prior knowledge that a dangerous and hazardous condition existed. New York Central Railroad Co. v. Sarich, 133 Ind.App. 516, 180 N.E.2d 388, 398 (Ind.App.Ct.1965); 5A Personal Injury § 1.05[1][j], pp. 124–27. Moreover, as the Third Circuit and other circuits suggest, it is appropriate to relax the requirement of similar conditions when the offer of proof is to show notice of the dangerous character of the crossing rather than defendant's negligence. Evans v. Pennsylvania Railroad Co., 255 F.2d 205, 210 (3rd Cir.1958); McCormick, Evidence (Horn Book Series), p. 352; compare McCormick v. Great Western Power Co., 214 Cal. 658, 8 P.2d 145, 81 ALR 678 (1932); City of Taylorville v. Stafford, 196 Ill. 288, 63 N.E. 624 (1902).

"The controlling principle in cases of this type, however, appears in Rule 403 of the Federal Rules of Evidence, reading:

> Although relevant, evidence may be excluded if its probative value is substantially outweighed by the danger of unfair prejudice, confusion of the issues, or misleading the jury, or by considerations of undue delay, waste of time, or needless presentation of cumulative evidence.

Unless we find, therefore, that the district court abused its discretion in excluding the evidence, we must affirm. United States v. Catalano, 491 F.2d 268, 274 (2nd Cir.), cert. denied, 419 U.S. 825, 95 S.Ct. 42, 42 L.Ed.2d 48 (1974); Shepard v. General Motors Corp., 423 F.2d 406, 408 (1st Cir.1970).

"Judge Brooks undoubtedly considered many factors including photographs in rendering his decision. First, conditions and surrounding circumstances at the crossing at the time of the prior accident on November 30, 1976, were different, at least in some respects, from those which existed on February 24, 1978. Second, because no action was ever brought nor any claim filed on behalf of the previous decedent, it is not known whether conditions at the crossing or decedent's own negligence were responsible for the 1976 accident. That no action was ever brought may suggest the latter. Third, notwithstanding the ambiguity surrounding the prior accident, the jury might infer from evidence of the prior accident alone that ultra-hazardous conditions existed at the site and were the cause of the later accident without those issues ever having been proved. In any case, the district court permitted appellant to present testimony that the conditions which existed at the crossing at the time of the February 24, 1978 collision had been evident some time before. Thus the dangerous conditions were presented in a non-prejudicial manner. These facts could certainly lead a reasonable person to conclude that the danger of prejudice and delay from admitting such evidence would substantially outweigh its probative value. Under these circumstances, we find no abuse of discretion in excluding this evidence."

JONES v. PAK–MOR MANUFACTURING CO.

Supreme Court of Arizona, En Banc, 1985.
145 Ariz. 121, 700 P.2d 819, cert. denied, 474 U.S. 948, 106 S.Ct. 314, 88 L.Ed.2d 295 (1985).

FELDMAN, JUSTICE.

Jerry Jones (plaintiff) was injured on January 27, 1979, while working on a machine manufactured by Pak–Mor Manufacturing Company (defendant). In the product liability action which followed, plaintiff alleged improper design and sought recovery on theories of negligence and strict liability. Before trial, plaintiff moved to exclude all evidence of the absence of prior, similar accidents. The trial court granted plaintiff's motion, ruling that such evidence was inadmissible under Arizona law. After verdict and judgment for plaintiff, defendant appealed, claiming, *inter alia,* that the exclusion ruling was in error. The court of appeals affirmed. *Jones v. Pak–Mor Manufacturing Co.,* 145 Ariz. 132, 700 P.2d 830 (1984). * * *

* * *

While recognizing that there is authority from other jurisdictions supporting the admission of evidence relating to the absence of prior accidents in both negligence and strict liability actions, both the trial judge and the court of appeals correctly noted the existence of Arizona decisions "admit[ting] evidence of prior accidents, but exclud[ing] evidence of the absence of prior accidents." (*Jones v. Pak–Mor,* at 123, 700 P.2d at 821.) As the court of appeals further noted, in Arizona the rule is "applied mechanically." (*Id.*) Although the trial court has discretion to admit evidence of prior accidents, the rule relating to inadmissibility of evidence of the absence of prior accidents is a *per se* rule. *Hlavaty v. Song,* 107 Ariz. 606, 491 P.2d 460 (1971). Evidence of the absence of prior accidents under similar conditions is inadmissible to prove lack of defect, lack of danger, or similar issues. *Id.* * * *

The rule of *per se* inadmissibility was first adopted by this court in *Fox Tucson Theaters Corp. v. Lindsay,* 47 Ariz. 388, 56 P.2d 183 (1936). Defendant argues that *Lindsay* was not meant as a *per se* rule, that it is now a minority rule, that it is unsupported by logic, and that this court should reconsider it. Finding these arguments persuasive, we accepted review. * * *

* * *

We note also that the rule of *per se* inadmissibility, adopted in *Fox Tucson Theaters Corp. v. Lindsay* and followed in other cases, has been criticized by most, if not all, evidence scholars. *See McCormick on Evidence* § 200 at 590–92 (E. Cleary ed. 1984); M. Udall & J. Livermore, *Arizona Law of Evidence* § 85 at 190 (2d ed. 1982); 2 Wigmore, *Evidence* §§ 443–44 at 528–32 (Chadbourn rev. 1979). Observing that few recent decisions have applied a general rule of exclusion, McCormick has criticized the lack of symmetry in the rule allowing a judge discretion to admit proof of other accidents but not proof of the absence of other accidents:

> One might think that if proof of similar accidents is admissible in the judge's discretion to show that a particular condition or defect exists, or that the injury sued for was caused in a certain way, or that a situation is dangerous, or that defendant knew or should have known of the danger, then evidence of the absence of accidents during a period of similar exposure and experience likewise would be receivable to show that these facts do not exist in the case at bar. Indeed, it would seem perverse to tell a jury that one or two persons besides the plaintiff tripped on defendant's stairwell while withholding from them the further information that another thousand persons descended the same stairs without incident.

McCormick, *supra,* § 200 at 590. Similarly, Wigmore has rejected as unsound a fixed rule of admissibility or inadmissibility, favoring instead a general rule of judicial discretion:

> It is much wiser and more practical to leave the possible inconvenience to be determined by the tribunal best fitted to determine it, the trial court, and to sanction the reception of all such relevant evidence subject to this exclusionary discretion based on inconvenience.

2 Wigmore, *supra,* § 444 at 532.

* * *

We hold, therefore, that in product liability cases involving a claim of defective design, whether based on negligence, strict liability, or both, the trial court has discretion under Rule 403 to admit evidence of safety-history concerning both the existence and the nonexistence of prior accidents, provided that the proponent establishes the necessary predicate for the evidence. The evidence of safety-history is admissible on issues pertaining to whether the design caused the product to be defective, whether the defect was unreasonably dangerous, whether it was a cause of the accident, or—in negligence cases—whether the defendant should have foreseen that the design of the product was not reasonably safe for its contemplated uses.

In the case at bench, the trial court held that evidence of the lack of prior accidents was *per se* inadmissible. The court of appeals affirmed that holding. We turn, then, to determine whether that ruling constituted reversible error.

* * *

* * * The probative portion of the offer in the case at bench was simply that during the period of time the product had been in use the defendant had "had no reports to the manufacturer of any injuries" similar to that sustained by plaintiff. As indicated above, the absence of claims and reports is not the relevant fact, nor even one which justifies an inference of the relevant fact (that there have been no accidents), absent a showing that if there had been accidents the witness would have known of them either from the system utilized to track safety-history or from the investigation made at the sources of such information. There may have been no lawsuits filed against defendant, but we have no way of knowing what workers' compensation claims were filed with appropriate administrative bodies nor any way of knowing what injuries were sustained but not pursued. In other words, we have no way to tell whether the testimony contained in the avowal, even if given by the president, would have carried convincing persuasive force, would have been admissible at all, or would have tipped the scales an iota.

* * *

* * * Defendant's offer of proof did not indicate that there existed any evidence to warrant the inference that the absence of claims tended to prove a lack of accidents. On this point the record is silent. Trial counsel offered no evidence of customer surveys, user surveys, safety record search, or any other fact to indicate that the absence of claims was some evidence of the absence of accidents under similar conditions of use. Nor does anything in the depositions, answers to interrogatories, or other discovery data in the file (including the portions not offered in evidence) even hint that defendant could have gone beyond the "I know of no claims and therefore believe there were no accidents" format of testimony from the president of the company.

* * *

We therefore affirm the judgment of the trial court. The portion of the opinion of the court of appeals which deals with admissibility of safety-history is vacated, the remainder of the opinion is approved.

HALE v. FIRESTONE TIRE & RUBBER CO.

United States Court of Appeals, Eighth Circuit, 1987.
820 F.2d 928.

HEANEY, CIRCUIT JUDGE.

The Budd Company (Budd) appeals from a final judgment entered in the United States District Court for the Western District of Missouri upon a jury verdict in an exploding rim case brought by Larry Hale and his wife, Linda Hale. The Hales were awarded $1,733,800 in actual and punitive damages from Budd. For reversal, Budd argues that the district court abused its discretion in 1) admitting into evidence a videotape prepared by the Hales' counsel depicting a mannequin being "killed" by a rim separation; * * *. We affirm in part and reverse in part.

I. BACKGROUND

Larry Hale was injured on October 4, 1977, when a RH5° multi-piece tire rim separated under pressure and struck him. The accident occurred while Hale was inflating a tubed tire mounted on the outer dual RH5° rim of his 1968 Ford F–600 ten-wheel truck. The RH5° rim consists of three parts: a rim base, a side ring, and a disc. Firestone manufactured the rim base and side ring. Budd manufactured the disc, attached the disc to the Firestone rim, and sold the rim/disc combination.

In 1978, the Hales brought an action against Firestone on a strict liability theory. Budd was added as a defendant in 1982. After approximately a two-week jury trial, the Hales were awarded $4,290,000 in actual and punitive damages from Firestone and Budd. Firestone and Budd appealed, and this Court reversed the judgment. *See Hale v. Firestone Tire & Rubber Co.,* 756 F.2d 1322 (8th Cir.1985) (*Hale I*).

In 1985, the parties tried the case a second time before the same district court judge, the Honorable Scott O. Wright. After another approximately two-week trial, Judge Wright declared a mistrial when the jury could not decide whether Plaintiff's Exhibit 1 was the rim involved in the accident.

Just prior to the third trial, Firestone and the Hales reached a settlement for $625,000. The third two-week trial before Judge Wright began against Budd alone on March 3, 1986. The jury awarded Larry Hale $679,000 and Linda Hale $225,000 in actual damages and assessed $1.5 million in punitive damages. The jury also found that Larry Hale was five percent at fault for his injuries. After deducting five percent and crediting Budd $625,000 for the Firestone settlement, the court entered judgment in favor of the Hales in the amount of $1,733,800. 636 F.Supp. 585. Budd appeals.

II. Analysis

A. The Videotape

Budd first argues that the district court abused its discretion in permitting the Hales to show the jury a four-minute videotape depicting a tire rim separation. The videotape was prepared by the Hales' counsel with the assistance of a cameraman and the Hales' expert witness, consulting engineer Donald Gibson. Using a lifesize mannequin, the tape depicts a man, crouched next to a truck, filling a tire with air. The tire then explodes, striking the mannequin and hurling it approximately ten feet in a cloud of smoke. The explosion is repeated two more times and concludes with a closeup shot of the mannequin's face.

Budd argues that 1) the videotape exaggerated the force of explosion because the experimental tire was inflated to approximately seventy-five pounds per square inch (psi) while the accident tire was inflated to no more than fifty-five psi, and 2) the four-minute trial tape is an edited summary of two days of filming, and Budd was not afforded an opportunity to view the "master" tape. In countering Budd's assertions, the Hales argue that: 1) the twenty psi difference between the experimental explosion and the real explosion is only slight, and 2) there is no complete tape of the filming because the cameraman simply taped over the approximately six attempts required to achieve the explosion depicted in the trial tape.

This Court considered the law regarding evidence of experiments in *Hale I:*

> Evidence of experimental tests is not admissible unless a foundational showing is made that the tests were conducted under conditions substantially similar to actual conditions. The admissibility of such evidence rests largely in the discretion of the trial judge and his decision will not be overturned absent a clear showing of an abuse of discretion.

Hale I, 756 F.2d at 1333 (quoting *Collins v. B.F. Goodrich Co.,* 558 F.2d 908, 910 (8th Cir.1977)). *See Petty v. Ideco, Division of Dresser Industries, Inc.,* 761 F.2d 1146 (5th Cir.1985).

In our view, the district court did not abuse its discretion in permitting the videotape to be introduced in evidence. According to the Hales' expert, the mannequin in the film was approximately the same size and weight as Larry Hale. The mannequin was crouched next to an RH5° rim and tire on the axel of a truck, just as Larry Hale was at the time of the accident. Although the tire in the experiment was inflated to twenty more pounds per square inch than the tire in the accident, this difference does not render an otherwise substantially similar demonstration inadmissible, but rather goes to the weight of the evidence. The tire in the experiment was one size smaller than the tire on Larry Hale's truck, 900 × 20 rather than 1000 × 20, and, according to the Hales' expert Dr. Donald Gibson, the explosion force of the smaller tire is somewhat less than the force of the larger tire. Tr. 724. We are satisfied that the trial court balanced the tire size differential against the psi differential and did not abuse its discretion in determining that "the videotape demonstration was relevant because it was made under conditions *very similar* to the conditions involved in the actual accident." District court order denying new trial at 1 (April 25, 1986). Additionally, Budd had ample opportunity to cross-examine Dr. Gibson as to the consequences of the difference in inflation pressure and tire size but chose not to explore those differences.

Finally, the trial court's finding that "the master tape was not intentionally withheld from defendant, but instead was unavailable because it had been erased during the editing process" was not clearly erroneous. While it would have been better had the Hales' counsel instructed the cameraman to save all the film footage, Budd was not prejudiced by this omission. Budd had every opportunity to cross-examine Dr. Gibson as to the number of attempts required before the tire exploded.

* * *

This matter is remanded to the district court for action consistent with section E of this opinion. * * *

CHAMPEAU v. FRUEHAUF CORP., 814 F.2d 1271, 1278 (8th Cir.1987). "Champeau challenges the admission of a videotaped experiment into evidence at the second trial. The experiment showed that if the driver of a tractor-trailer rig traveling thirty-five miles per hour took his foot off of the accelerator one-quarter mile from the curve that was the scene of the accident and never accelerated again, the rig would coast to a stop short of the curve. The purpose of the experiment was not to recreate the accident, but to take Champeau's distance and speed estimates and show that under the applicable laws of physics the accident could not have occurred as Champeau had described.

"Some similarities in conditions existed between the experiment and the accident, but the conditions were far from identical. In order to remedy this situation the district court submitted to the jury lists of differences and similarities written by the attorneys. In light of the similarities in conditions and the lists of similarities and differences submitted to the jury, we cannot find error in the admission of the videotaped experiment into evidence.

"Moreover, the experiment did not need to be performed in similar circumstances in order to be admissible because it did not purport to be a recreation of the accident and it was merely used to demonstrate general principles of physics as applied to Champeau's testimony. See

Nanda v. Ford Motor Co., 509 F.2d 213, 223 (7th Cir.1974); Harkins v. Ford Motor Co., 437 F.2d 276, 278 & n. 5 (3d Cir.1970). We therefore conclude that the court did not abuse its discretion in admitting this evidence."

GLADHILL v. GENERAL MOTORS CORP., 743 F.2d 1049, 1051–52 (4th Cir.1984). "Plaintiffs contend that the district court committed reversible error when it permitted defendants to display a videotaped demonstration of a braking test of the Chevrolet Citation when the circumstances under which the demonstration was conducted were not similar to those involved in the accident. The test, conducted by a General Motors test driver, involved causing one of the rear brakes to lock while the car was in motion. The record indicates that the accident in which Mr. Gladhill was injured occurred at night, on a hill sloping downwards, at a 'sharp curve', 'between the two elbows of the curve.' By contrast, the videotaped demonstration was conducted at a General Motors test facility on a flat, straight, asphalt surface in daylight by an experienced test driver. * * *

* * *

"Defendants are correct that demonstrations of experiments used to illustrate the principles used in forming an expert opinion are not always required to adhere strictly to the circumstances of the events at issue in the trial. Brandt v. French, 638 F.2d 209, 212 (10 Cir.1981). Nevertheless, we are persuaded that this entire test goes well beyond a mere demonstration of a physical principle. The jury was given a view of a Chevrolet Citation on a wide-open asphalt road traveling in a straight line with one of its rear wheels locked and a test driver in control. It is easy to understand why the jury might be unable to visualize plaintiffs' version of the events after this film. Indeed, the circumstances of the accident, as alleged, are so different from this test as to make the results largely irrelevant if not misleading. It is elementary physics that automobiles traveling downhill with their front wheels turned do not behave the same way with their brakes locked as those traveling on a flat surface with their front wheels straight. Thus, we are persuaded that evidence of this test should be excluded entirely on retrial. It is possible to call almost any evidence of this type 'a demonstration to illustrate a principle' but when the demonstration is a physical representation of how an automobile behaves under given conditions, those conditions must be sufficiently close to those involved in the accident at issue to make the probative value of the demonstration outweigh its prejudicial effect. In this instance, the conditions were dissimilar in such fundamental and important respects that the risk of prejudice to plaintiffs outweighed the probative value of the evidence."

GENERAL MOTORS CORP. v. TURNER, 567 S.W.2d 812 (Tex.Civ. App.1978), rev'd on other grounds, 584 S.W.2d 844 (Tex.1979). "For the purposes of this opinion it is sufficient to state that plaintiff, while seeking to avoid a collision with a truck, overturned his car when it left the road. The car rolled over and the roof was deformed when it came in contact with the ground. Plaintiff received a crushed vertebra in the accident which resulted in his paralysis. * * *

* * *

"* * * Plaintiff produced two witnesses, both with an automotive design background, who concluded that the design of the roof of plaintiff's automobile was unreasonably dangerous. They suggested an alternative design consisting of three roll bars extending from the frame of the car over the roof area. * * *

* * *

"We turn now to a third complaint of the defendants, that relating to the exclusion of evidence of a test conducted by a witness for the defendants. After plaintiff's witnesses had testified about the safety of the roll bars, as noted in our discussion of the second complaint, the defendants hired a racing car mechanic to install a NASCAR roll cage system on a car that was the same make and model as plaintiff's vehicle. A NASCAR roll cage is one that is used on racing cars. Then the car was mounted on its side on a dolly, roof in front, and crashed into a stationary barrier at 30 m.p.h. (A film of this was shown this court at oral argument.) The trial court correctly excluded evidence of this experiment.

"The admissibility of out-of-court experiments depends on the particular facts and circumstances of each case. The experiment must be objective and not mislead or confuse the jury. Fort Worth & Denver Railway Co. v. Williams, 375 S.W.2d 279, 282 (Tex.1964); Van Ornum v. Otter Tail Power Co., 210 N.W.2d 188, 197 (N.D.1973). The evidence shows here that the forces involved in a rollover and a barrier crash test are not the same; they are much greater in the barrier crash, and much more likely to damage the roof. It would not be fair to admit this experiment, because it was totally different from our rollover situation."

UNITED STATES v. WANOSKIA, 800 F.2d 235, 237–39 (10th Cir.1986). "Defendant's version was presented primarily through his own testimony. He testified that an argument began between his wife and Menarco shortly after their return home. When he tried to stop the argument, his wife struck him and then Menarco with a frying pan. Defendant testified that his wife then took his .357 revolver from the bedroom and threatened to shoot him. A scuffle ensued between Wanoskia, his wife, and Menarco. Eventually, his wife got control of the gun and after saying, 'Watch this,' shot herself in the head.

"At trial the government sought to show by expert testimony and a demonstration that defendant's wife did not shoot herself. The expert testimony related to the powder burns on the wife's face and how far away the pistol must have been when it discharged. The demonstration was to show that defendant's wife could not have held the weapon that far away from her face.

* * *

"The government next presented Dr. John Smialek, chief medical investigator for the State of New Mexico in Albuquerque. Smialek, who performed the autopsy on Mrs. Wanoskia, testified that he found gun powder on the victim's face in a pattern with a nine inch diameter. Based on the earlier witness' test firings, Smialek estimated that the gun was eighteen inches from Mrs. Wanoskia when fired.

"Smialek also stated that Mrs. Wanoskia weighed 171 pounds and was five feet two inches tall. He estimated the length of her arms to be between nineteen and twenty inches. * * *

"* * * Eventually, a woman with twenty-four-inch arms was used as a model in the demonstration. In the first demonstration, the model held the revolver with her thumb on the trigger and pointed at her head. The distance from the muzzle to her face was twelve inches. Next, the model held the gun with her forefinger on the trigger. In this position, the distance from the muzzle of the gun to her face was roughly four inches. Finally, the model held the gun with both thumbs on the trigger. In this position, the distance from the muzzle of the gun to her face was eleven and three-quarter inches. Defendant objected to this demonstration and a similar one during the prosecution's rebuttal presentation.

"Demonstrative evidence, and in particular, reenactments of events, can be highly persuasive. The opportunity for the jury to see what supposedly happened can accomplish in seconds what might otherwise take days of testimony. By conveying a visual image of what allegedly occurred, one side can imprint on the jury's mind its version of the facts. See generally Carson v. Polley, 689 F.2d 562, 579 (5th Cir.1982); McCormick on Evidence § 215 (3d ed. 1984). Thus the court must take special care to ensure that the demonstration fairly depicts the events at issue. Nevertheless, a trial court's decision to admit or exclude such evidence will be reversed only if the court abused its discretion. United States v. Hart, 729 F.2d 662, 669 (10th Cir.1984).

* * *

"We also note that the trial court took great care in ensuring that the demonstrations did not unduly prejudice defendant. Before permitting the demonstrations during the case-in-chief, the court viewed the demonstrations outside the presence of the jury. Only after being satisfied that these demonstrations were probative did the court permit them. In addition, the court intentionally had the demonstration performed by a woman with arms longer than the estimate of the expert witness. We find no abuse of discretion in the court's allowing the demonstrations. See Hart, 729 F.2d at 669."

MAGNET COVE BARIUM CORP. v. BROWN

Court of Civil Appeals of Texas, Waco, 1967.
419 S.W.2d 697.

WILSON, JUSTICE.

Appellee's action against appellants sought reformation of deeds to Magnet Cove Barium Corporation (Magcobar), alleging that by mutual mistake the conveyances omitted a reservation to appellees of a royalty interest, future bonuses and delay rentals. Alternatively appellees asserted a trespass to try title count. Judgment was rendered on a jury verdict reforming the deeds as prayed for, and decreeing recovery in trespass to try title with merger of estates.

The jury found that it had been agreed that the deeds would reserve 1/2 of the usual 1/8 royalty and 1/2 of future bonuses and delay rentals on oil and gas that may be produced from the land described in appellees' deeds to Magcobar, and that the reservation was omitted by mutual mistake.

Magcobar's first group of points complains of admission in evidence of two mining leases, two deeds and an option to purchase executed by third persons to Magcobar, as contravening the evidence rules concerning res inter alios acta.

In 1961, and again in 1962, appellees granted Magcobar options to purchase 320 acres. These options recited there was excepted and reserved to appellees' predecessor, Killam, "1/2 of the usual 1/8 royalty" on oil and gas, that "acreage is to be determined by survey," and payment "is to be based on actual acreage," at $145 an acre. Magcobar exercised the option, sending appellees a warranty deed describing the 320 acres, and a special warranty deed describing 378.60 acres (which included a 58.60 excess developed by survey). Both deeds excepted "a 1/16th undivided interest in and to the oil and gas located in, on and under the tract or parcel of land herein described." These deeds were executed and delivered by appellees.

The parties agree that after the results of the survey became known they conferred to determine the course of the closing. Appellees contend that "at this time the agreement was made" that in exchange for the excess 58.6 acres appellees "would retain 1/2 of the usual 1/8 royalty and 1/2 of the bonuses and delay rentals on oil and gas in and under the total 378.6 acres." Appellant also says there was an oral modification of the option agreement, but denies there was any further agreement concerning royalty, bonuses or delay rentals. Its position on trial was that the consideration for the conveyance of the excess of 58.6 acres was its agreement to pay a $1200 vendor's lien indebtedness owing to appellees' grantor, Killam. Appellees urged it was improbable and not reasonable to believe that they accepted a $1200 obligation in lieu of a promised cash payment of over $8,000 for the 58.6 acres.

Appellant relies upon the maxim of irrelevancy of res inter alios acta under which evidence of contracts, acts and transactions between one of the parties and others are excluded. The decisions in Texas are the subject of a comment and a case note: Starling Thomas Morris, 24 Tex.L.Rev. 351 (1945)[1]; Frank B. Sheppard, id., 95. No arbitrary or categorical rule governing admissibility has emerged from the Texas decisions.

McCormick & Ray, Texas Law of Evidence, Sec. 1523, p. 370, lists some decisions in which contracts between a party and third persons have been excluded, and states: "It is believed, however, that there is no sound basis for excluding such evidence as a class." In II Wigmore, Evidence (3d ed. 1940) Sec. 377, p. 307, it is said that "no technical rule or general policy obstructs such evidence", noting: "the only question can be whether the instances produced do have any real probative value to show a system or plan or habit". See I Jones, Evidence, (4th ed. 1938), Sec. 141, p. 250; Texas Digest, Evidence, Key Nos. 138, 139.

Appellees seek to sustain admission of five instruments between Magcobar and third persons as establishing a plan, design or pattern by Magcobar by which oil and gas rights were consistently reserved to their grantors in transactions similar to that with appellees.

Magcobar was to "build a plant to process kaolin, sand and rock minerals." It was "not in the oil and gas business." The site it acquired comprised four tracts, including appellees'; and the instruments complained of all related to lands constituting the site. They consisted of (1) and (2) two 1962 mining leases authorizing removal by Magcobar of sand, silica, kaolin and other minerals "except oil and gas", (3) a 1963 purchase option which reserved oil and gas with (4) the conveyance thereunder, and (5) a special warranty deed dated October, 1963 excepting and reserving oil and gas.

In our opinion the trial court was authorized to conclude that these instruments were of some probative value on the issue of mutual mistake in the inadvertent omission of the reservation alleged.

* * *

* * * The judgment is affirmed.

CIBRO PETROLEUM PRODUCTS, INC. v. SOHIO ALASKA PETROLEUM CO., 602 F.Supp. 1520, 1551 (N.D.N.Y.1985), aff'd, 798 F.2d 1421 (Em.App.1986), cert. dism'd, 479 U.S. 979, 107 S.Ct. 562, 93

1. "No one doubts that the existence of a design or plan to do an act is of some probative value on the question whether or not that act was done, or that a pattern, system or course of conduct is of some probative value in tending to establish that the controverted act was done in accordance with that system." P. 357, and see p. 359.

L.Ed.2d 568 (1986). "This court's interpretation of paragraph 7 of the Cibro–Sohio contract is further supported by a review of Sohio's other contracts for the sale of crude oil. * * *

"Notwithstanding defendant's protestations to the contrary, these contracts are admissible to aid the court in interpreting the term clause at issue in this litigation. Judge Weinstein has noted that a party's business transactions with third parties is relevant to prove the meaning of a contract in appropriate cases:

> [t]here are strong arguments in favor of the rejection of proof concerning third party contracts where similarities are weak and comparisons strained, but there is no excuse for absolute exclusion of evidence that outlines a clear course of dealing or habit of doing business. Subsidiary evidence of parallelism must be strong and convincing when dealing with third party situations, and there is every reason to believe that standards of admissibility should be higher than when dealing with transactions between the same parties.

2 J. Weinstein & M. Berger, Weinstein's Evidence, ¶ 406[03] at 406–18 (1982) (quoting Slough, 'Relevancy Unraveled,' 6 Kan.L.Rev. 38–41 (1957).) See also McCormick on Evidence § 198 (2d ed. 1972) (contracts of a party with third persons may show customary practice and course of dealing and be highly probative on the terms of the present agreement). Numerous federal courts are in agreement."

STATE EX REL. CITY OF WICHITA FALLS v. RUST, 468 S.W.2d 581, 586 (Tex.Civ.App.1971). "The degree of similarity of land is largely within the trial court's discretion in determining the admissibility of evidence concerning other sales in a condemnation suit. State v. Reece, 374 S.W.2d 686 (Houston Tex.Civ.App., 1964, no writ hist.); State v. Helvey, 375 S.W.2d 744 (Tyler Tex.Civ.App., 1964, no writ hist.); and State v. Powell, 376 S.W.2d 929 (Dallas Tex.Civ.App., 1964, no writ hist.). The following is from the Powell opinion at page 930 (referring to City of Austin v. Cannizzo, 153 Tex. 324, 267 S.W.2d 808): 'We do not construe that opinion as requiring absolute similarity before properties can be compared for the purpose of forming an opinion as to values. So far as we know, no court has ever made such a requirement. Reason and experience tell us that no two pieces of real property could ever be found which were exactly similar. All the law requires in this respect is that the properties be reasonably similar, and our courts have frequently held that it is within the sound discretion of the trial court to determine whether or not the properties offered for comparison meet the test of similarity.' "

UNITED STATES v. PETROV, 747 F.2d 824, 831–32 (2d Cir.1984), cert. denied, 471 U.S. 1025, 105 S.Ct. 2037, 85 L.Ed.2d 318 (1985). "A key issue in any obscenity case is the degree of community acceptance or toleration of materials similar to those at issue. See United States v. Pinkus, 579 F.2d 1174, 1175 (9th Cir.), cert. dismissed, 439 U.S. 999, 99 S.Ct. 605, 58 L.Ed.2d 674 (1978); United States v. Womack, 509 F.2d 368, 376–78 (D.C.Cir.1974), cert. denied, 422 U.S. 1022, 95 S.Ct. 2644, 45 L.Ed.2d 681 (1975). To establish that some or all of the photographs did not offend community standards, Petrov called a private investigator who testified that he had visited a number of bookstores and newsstands in Syracuse and other cities in the Northern District of New York, where he purchased various magazines and books. In opposing the admission of defendant's comparable materials, the government contended that even assuming their comparability, their availability in the community 'does not automatically make them admissible as tending to prove the nonobscenity of the materials which the defendant is charged with circulating.' Hamling v. United States, 418 U.S. 87, 125, 94 S.Ct. 2887, 2911, 41 L.Ed.2d 590 (1974); see also United States v. Manarite, 448 F.2d 583, 593 (2d Cir.), cert. denied, 404 U.S. 947, 92 S.Ct. 298, 30 L.Ed.2d 264 (1971) ('[m]ere availability of similar materials by itself means nothing more than other persons are engaged in similar activities'). Thus, in addition to availability, the government argued, it must be shown that the proffered materials enjoy 'a reasonable degree of community acceptance', before they will be admitted. Id. The court sustained the government's objection to most of the material, although it admitted as 'comparable' items a series of bondage and genital mutilation photographs from two magazines, 'Penthouse' and 'Bounty'. The court also admitted photographs of the bookstores and outlets where the investigator had purchased these materials.

"We recognize the difficulties inherent in attempting to prove a fact as elusive as a community standard; on the other hand, we are uncomfortable with the circularity of the approach suggested by the government, that, in order for the defendant to place comparable photographs in evidence for the purpose of establishing community acceptance, he must first establish the community acceptance. We are also aware of the practical difficulties that would be created by a rule that admitted all comparable materials on the theory that if they were found in the community they were some evidence of community acceptability and community standards.

"We think a solution is adequately provided for in the Federal Rules of Evidence, which were not in effect when both *Hamling* and *Manarite* were decided. Comparable material that is available in the community can be viewed as relevant under Rule 401; but whether it should be admitted in a particular trial is a delicate question to be determined by the balancing process of Rule 403, which requires the trial judge to determine whether the probative value of the particular offer is substantially outweighed by one or more of a variety of considerations, including confusion of the issues, misleading the jury, waste of time, or needless presentation of cumulative evidence. By judicious application of Rule 403, a trial judge can afford the defendant in an obscenity case a fair opportunity to prove that the community displays a reasonable degree of acceptance of comparable material, without needlessly prolonging the trial with cumulative evidence of minimal probative value.

"When the district court ruled in this case that some of Petrov's proffered comparable evidence was admissible and some was not, it gave no explanation for its ruling. Effective appellate review of such an issue requires the trial court to explain its decision. This is particularly so when the trial court decides an evidentiary question under Rule 403, which requires it to strike a balance between probative value and the competing considerations. If there is a retrial, and if 'comparable' evidence is again offered by Petrov, we expect the trial court to analyze the problem in light of all the circumstances presented at the new trial, and after applying Rule 403, to make clear on the record the reasons for its rulings."

BUNION v. ALLSTATE INSURANCE CO.

United States District Court, Eastern District of Pennsylvania, 1980.
502 F.Supp. 340.

Memorandum and Order

Giles, District Judge.

This is a diversity action arising from an accident in 1976 in which plaintiff's car was allegedly rear-ended by another car, causing injuries to his chest, back, and internal organs. Defendant has now filed two motions, one for reconsideration of a denial of a prior motion for partial summary judgment and the other *in limine* as to the admission as evidence at trial the fact that plaintiff was involved in prior accidents.

* * *

The Motion to Admit Evidence

Defendant also moves to admit as evidence at time of trial facts relating to other accidents involving plaintiff. Such evidence would be proferred in an effort to show that plaintiff is "claim-minded." Defendant alleges that plaintiff has made claims in seven other accidents in the last nine years. Three accidents were falls in plaintiff's house occurring in 1971. One was a rear-end collision in 1974. The remaining incidents occurred in 1972, 1977, and 1979. The details of these three incidents are unclear, but apparently one of these was yet another vehicular accident.

Defendant asserts that, as in the present case, plaintiff was the only eyewitness to four of the incidents—the home falls and the 1974 rear-end collision—and also that, as here, there is no police report for the 1974 accident.

Plaintiff counters that this proferred evidence does not show a pattern of similar claims. In particular, he states that there were several other eyewitnesses to the prior rear-end collision which involved circumstances significantly different from those in this action. Finally, plaintiff argues that such evidence would be irrelevant and prejudicial.

In order to rule that evidence is admissible, this court must find that its probative value is not substantially outweighed by the danger of unfair prejudice. Fed.R.Evid. 403. The admissibility of evidence of claim-mindedness has been the subject of considerable cogent discussion. See *McCormick's Handbook of the Law of Evidence* § 196 (E. Cleary ed. 1972) [hereinafter cited as *McCormick*]; also see 3A J. Wigmore, *Evidence* § 963 (Chadbourn ed. 1970); Annot., 69 A.L.R.2d 593 (1960).

Where it has been proved that a party brought previous claims which were similar in nature *and* fraudulent, most courts have admitted the evidence of the former claims on the ground that it is strongly relevant to falsity of the current claim. *McCormick,* supra, § 196 at 466. Here, inasmuch as there is no proof by defendants that the plaintiff's other claims were fraudulent, defendant's evidence does not fall within an accepted exception for proven false claims.

At the other end of the spectrum, evidence tending to show that a party is a chronic personal-injury claimant generally has been excluded because its slight probative value has been deemed outweighed by the danger of prejudice. Id. In this case, the probative value of any evidence cannot be ascertained presently because defendant has described some of the claims in no greater detail than "automobile or home related accidents." Here, defendant has not shown sufficient similarity between plaintiff's prior claims and the current one to warrant any inference of fraud.

There are the middle ground situations where there has been a showing of repeated similar claims. Id. 466–67. Such evidence may be relevant due to improbability of chance repetitions of similar accidents to the same person. Simultaneously, however, such evidence may be prejudicial to litigants who may be accident prone or otherwise innocent of fraud. McCormick suggests that "the judge, balancing in his discretion probative value against prejudice, should admit the evidence only when the proponent has produced or will produce other evidence of fraud." Id. 467. In this case, defendant offers no such corroborative evidence. Furthermore, the balancing of relevancy against prejudice is impeded, and indeed precluded, by the lack of detail and clarity as to exactly what evidence defendant intends to introduce and the purpose for which it is offered. Defendant has neither identified which depositions or other testimony he wishes to introduce, nor identified any similarity among the accidents or injuries, nor made an offer of proof of fraud, nor stated whether the evidence will be introduced as part of his case-in-chief, on rebuttal, or on cross-examination.

In the case upon which defendant places primary reliance, the evidence of similar accidents or fraud was admitted on cross-examination for the purpose of impeaching the witness. Mintz v. Premier Cab

Association, 127 F.2d 744, 744 (D.C.Cir.1942). Other cases cited by defendant show that the evidence of similar accidents or fraud was either introduced on cross-examination, was introduced by plaintiff, or was admitted for impeachment purposes or as tending to show that injury had been caused by prior accidents as opposed to direct proof of fraud. See Atkinson v. Atchinson, Topeka & Santa Fe Railway, 197 F.2d 244, 245–46 (10th Cir.1952) (evidence was elicited on cross-examination, was admitted as tending to impeach plaintiff's testimony of particular careful driving habits); Manes v. Dowling, 375 A.2d 221, 223–24 (D.C.1977) (evidence introduced by plaintiff, admitted as relevant to the nature and extent of injuries); Evans v. Greyhound Corp., 200 A.2d 194, 196 (D.C.1964) (evidence admitted on cross-examination).

Here, in the absence of a clear showing of the existence of probative and admissible evidence, the motion *in limine* is denied.

Note

On evidence that a complainant in a rape or sexual assault prosecution has made similar, false claims against others, see Smith v. State, p. 477 infra.

SECTION 2. CHARACTER *

[FED.R.EVID. 404, 405, 412]

UNITED STATES v. GILLILAND

United States Court of Appeals, Tenth Circuit, 1978.
586 F.2d 1384.

LOGAN, CIRCUIT JUDGE.

This is an appeal from a jury conviction of Roy Valentine Gilliland for transportation of a stolen automobile across state lines in violation of the Dyer Act, 18 U.S.C. § 2312.

The issues upon appeal relate to the propriety of certain questions asked of Gilliland's stepson, Billy Tull, who appeared as a defense witness, concerning criminal convictions of Gilliland 14 to 34 years prior to the offense involved in this trial.

The federal prosecutors presented their case based principally upon stopping defendant near Guymon, Oklahoma while he was driving a vehicle stolen a few hours earlier in Dumas, Texas. The totality of the

* See 1A Wigmore, Evidence §§ 52–82.1 (Tillers Rev.1983); McCormick, Evidence §§ 186–193 (4th ed. 1992); Imwinkelried, Uncharged Misconduct Evidence (1984); Galvin, Shielding Rape Victims in the State and Federal Courts: A Proposal for the Second Decade, 70 Minn.L.Rev. 763 (1986); Kuhns, The Propensity to Misunderstand the Character of Specific Acts Evidence, 66 Iowa L.Rev. 777 (1981); Tanford & Bocchino, Rape Victim Shield Laws and the Sixth Amendment, 128 U.Pa.L.Rev. 544 (1980); Uviller, Evidence of Character to Prove Conduct: Illusion, Illogic and Injustice in the Courtroom, 130 U.Pa.L.Rev. 845 (1982); Weissenberger, Character Evidence Under the Federal Rules: A Puzzle with Missing Pieces, 48 U.Cin.L.Rev. 1 (1979); Weissenberger, Making Sense of Extrinsic Act Evidence: Federal Rule of Evidence 404(b), 70 Iowa L.Rev. 579 (1985).

government's evidence was ample to support the jury conviction, in the absence of the error discussed herein. The defense was that Gilliland did not steal the car, but bought it on approval from a purported car salesman in a bar in Oklahoma, with a portion of the consideration being repayment of a gambling debt owed by the salesman to Gilliland. Defendant's stepson Billy Tull was a defense witness presented as one who had been present at the transfer and who had personally observed much of the paper work in the exchange of title. After Tull had so testified the government attorney initiated his cross-examination as follows:

Q How long have you known this Defendant, your step father?

A Approximately 11 years.

Q As I understand it, you are telling the ladies and gentlemen of the Jury, he is just the kind of man that would not do this thing; is that right?

A Yes, sir.

Q He is the kind of man who would not steal a car and take it across the state line; it is that correct?

A Yes, sir.

Q And he is certainly the kind of man who would not forge items like you have in front of you there; is that correct?

A Yes, sir.

Q He just wouldn't do that?

A No, sir.

MR. MILLER: May I approach the bench if the Court please?

FOLLOWING PROCEEDINGS HELD AT BENCH OUT OF THE HEARING OF THE JURY:

MR. MILLER: I have got two things to advise the Court. I am going to ask this man about his step father's criminal record because he has been convicted twice of the Dyer Act. He has been convicted twice of Forgery. He has been convicted more times of that. I want to ask him about those particular convictions. Some of these convictions are more than ten years old. Some of them are not more than ten years old, but I knew there is a Rule of Court.

THE COURT: Credibility rule doesn't apply here.

MR. MILLER: I wanted to clear it with the Court.

THE COURT: You may do so over the objection of the Defendant.

(Following proceedings held in Open Court)

THE COURT: Go ahead, Mr. Miller.

Q (By Mr. Miller) Mr. Tull, did you know that your step father in 1942 in Del Rio, Texas, in the Federal Court there was convicted of the Dyer Act, which is transporting motor vehicles across the state line, and was sentenced to two years in the Federal Reformatory?

A I knew he had been in prison, but I did not know why.

Q Mr. Tull, did you know that your step father in October of 1961 was convicted of Dyer Act, which is transporting a motor vehicle across the state line in Los Angeles, California, and was sentenced to five years in the Federal Penitentiary?

A No, sir, I did not know about that.

Q Mr. Tull, did you know that your step father was convicted in November of 1950 in Sacramento, California, of two separate counts of Forgery and was convicted and sentenced to a term of 1 to 14 years on each one of those counts?

A No, sir.

Q Mr. Tull, did you know that your step father was convicted in February of 1962 of Interstate Transportation of Forged Securities in Federal Court in Fort Worth, Texas—that is wrong. It would have been in California that he was convicted, but he was sentenced at that time to another five years in the Federal Reformatory and he was in a Reformatory in Fort Worth, Texas. Did you know that?

A No, sir.

Q Now let me ask you this: Do you think your step father is capable of stealing cars and taking them across the state line?

A Sir, for the 11 years that I have known him, I would say no.

Q Do you think your step father is capable of forging documents like you have got right there in front of you?

A I would say no.

* * *

I

The government attempts to justify its inquiry into the criminal convictions on grounds that Tull was testifying as to the character of the defendant. The general rule is, "Evidence of other crimes, wrongs, or acts is not admissible to prove the character of a person in order to show that he acted in conformity therewith." Fed.R.Evid. 404(b). The rationale for this exclusionary rule is well-stated by Mr. Justice Jackson in Michelson v. United States, 335 U.S. 469, 475–476, 69 S.Ct. 213, 218–219, 93 L.Ed. 168 (1948):

> Courts that follow the common-law tradition almost unanimously have come to disallow resort by the prosecution to any kind of evidence of a defendant's evil character to establish a probability of his guilt. Not that the law invests the defendant with a presumption of good character, Greer v. United States, 245 U.S. 559, 38 S.Ct. 209, 62 L.Ed. 469 but it simply closes the whole matter of character, disposition and reputation on the prosecution's case-in-chief. The state may not show defendant's prior trouble with the law, specific criminal acts, or ill name among his neighbors, even though such facts might logically be persuasive that he is by propensity a probable perpetrator of the crime. The inquiry is not rejected because character is irrelevant; on the

> contrary, it is said to weigh too much with the jury and to so overpersuade them as to prejudge one with a bad general record and deny him a fair opportunity to defend against a particular charge. The overriding policy in excluding such evidence, despite its admitted probative value, is the practical experience that its disallowance tends to prevent confusion of issues, unfair surprise and undue prejudice. (Footnotes omitted.)

The accused defendant may make character an issue, however, for the reasons also outlined in the *Michelson* case:

> But this line of inquiry firmly denied to the State is opened to the defendant because character is relevant in resolving probabilities of guilt. He may introduce affirmative testimony that the general estimate of his character is so favorable that the jury may infer that he would not be likely to commit the offense charged. This privilege is sometimes valuable to a defendant for this Court has held that such testimony alone, in some circumstances, may be enough to raise a reasonable doubt of guilt and that in the federal courts a jury in a proper case should be so instructed. Edgington v. United States, 164 U.S. 361, 17 S.Ct. 72, 41 L.Ed. 467. (Footnotes omitted.)
>
> 335 U.S. at 476, 69 S.Ct. at 219.

If the defendant utilizes a character witness then the government may cross-examine or introduce evidence of prior convictions to rebut the defense evidence of good character. Fed.R.Evid. 404(a)(1), 405(a). The judge, of course, has a duty of continuing surveillance as to whether the evidence's prejudicial effect outweighs its probative value. Id. 403. We do not need to discuss application of Rule 403 here, however, because Billy Tull was not a character witness. His entire testimony on direct examination was as purported eyewitness to the purchase of the automobile. The government may not turn him into a character witness by asking him what kind of a man defendant was, and then use those questions to bootstrap into the case evidence of defendant's prior convictions which it was prohibited from using in its case-in-chief.

II

It is argued the inquiry into the criminal record of defendant may be justified as showing intent, plan, scheme or design, under Fed. R.Evid. 404(b). The jury instructions expressly stated that this was one basis for admitting the evidence.

This Court has rejected such an argument in a case squarely in point and controlling here. United States v. Burkhart, 458 F.2d 201 (10th Cir.1972), was a Dyer Act case, where the government introduced evidence of Dyer Act convictions of defendant 4 and 15 years before as relevant to the elements of criminal intent, knowledge, plan or scheme. This Court, sitting en banc, rejected the evidence and ordered a new trial. Judge Doyle's opinion for the Court contains an exhaustive review of the cases. It makes the following commentary on the reluctance of the courts to admit such evidence:

> Several factors have contributed to formulation of a cautious judicial attitude.
>
> First, the accused is required to defend charges which are not described in the information or indictment. As a result he is required to defend past actions which he may have in the past answered and with respect to which he may have even served his sentence. Thus, he is in effect tried as a recidivist though such a charge is not a part of the federal criminal code.
>
> Secondly, although such evidence may have at least some relevance to the offense being tried, its predominant quality is to show up the defendant's character as a car thief or a bad check artist, for example. Proof of defendant's sociopathic disposition is not a valid object. Showing that a man is generally bad has never been under our system allowable. The defendant has a right to be tried on the truth of the specific charge contained in the indictment.
>
> Third, an obvious truth is that once prior convictions are introduced the trial is, for all practical purposes, completed and the guilty outcome follows as a mere formality. This is true regardless of the care and caution employed by the court in instructing the jury.
>
> Thus, it is clear that the problem is not a simple evidentiary one, but rather goes to the fundamental fairness and justice of the trial itself.
>
> 458 F.2d at 204–205.

In the present case the convictions were from 14 to 34 years prior to the offense charged, which makes them significantly less relevant than were the ones involved in *Burkhart.*

* * *

In oral argument counsel urged that even if error had been committed in this case it was harmless. Certainly we agree there was sufficient evidence of defendant's guilt to support the verdict. But there is also no doubt that when the prior convictions were permitted to be shown during the cross-examination of witness Tull it had a profound effect upon the defense of the case.

* * *

The concept of harmless error is different in a criminal case from what is required in civil litigation, because of the requirement to prove guilt beyond a reasonable doubt. Thus the error must be harmless beyond a reasonable doubt. Chapman v. California, 386 U.S. 18, 24, 87 S.Ct. 824, 17 L.Ed.2d 705 (1967). We have consistently held that error such as that involved here requires reversal, even in the face of other evidence ample to support the verdict. See United States v. Burkhart, 458 F.2d 201 (10th Cir.1972); United States v. Arnold, 425 F.2d 204 (10th Cir.1970).

The judgment of the district court is reversed, and the cause is remanded for a new trial.

Note

"Clearly, the action by the State, in referring to appellant's failure to call character witnesses was, under the circumstances of this case, the functional equivalent of the State injecting appellant's character into the case. It is reversible error for the State to place a defendant's character in issue before a jury when the defendant has not first raised the issue." Brokenberry v. State, 788 S.W.2d 103, 105 (Tex.App.1990).

GOVERNMENT OF VIRGIN ISLANDS v. GRANT, 775 F.2d 508, 513 (3d Cir.1985). "During the course of a trial, it is customary for the defendant to introduce evidence concerning his background, such as information about his education and employment. Such evidence is routinely admitted without objection, and testimony that an accused has never been arrested is commonly admitted as part of this background evidence.

"The jurisprudence of 'background evidence' is essentially undeveloped. 'Background' or 'preliminary' evidence is not mentioned in the evidence codes, nor has it received attention in the treatises. One justification for its admission, at least in terms of the background of a witness *qua* witness, is that it may establish absence of bias or motive by showing the witness' relationship (or non-relationship) to the parties or to the case. It may also be said to bear on the credibility of the witness by showing the witness to be a stable person. The routine admission of evidence that an accused has never been arrested would thus seem to be a function of years of practice and of the common sense notion that it is helpful for the trier of fact to know something about a defendant's background when evaluating his culpability.

"We do not gainsay that the practice of admitting evidence as to a lack of prior arrest, as background evidence (though not as evidence of good character that would require good character charge and open the door to evidence of bad character) makes some sense.[7] In determining whether to admit background evidence, however, wide discretion should remain with the trial court. We hold that the Territorial Court did not abuse its discretion in refusing to permit Grant to testify that he had no prior arrests."

UNITED STATES v. GILLESPIE, 852 F.2d 475, 479–80 (9th Cir. 1988). "The appellant contends the district court erred in admitting the testimony of clinical psychologist Dr. Maloney on characteristics common to child molesters. The appellant contends he did not put his

7. We note that the line between background evidence and character evidence is blurred, and that at some point a defendant who goes too far with evidence indicating good character, despite attempts to characterize it as background evidence, might find that the door to rebuttal evidence has been opened.

general character at issue and did not assert his character was such that he could not sexually abuse a child. * * *

* * *

"A defendant puts his character at issue when he offers testimony as to honesty or his good reputation. * * * Testimony limited to the defendant's background, however, is not sufficient to put the defendant's general character at issue. See United States v. McLister, 608 F.2d 785, 790 (9th Cir.1979). In *McLister,* the court held that the defendant did not put his general character at issue in his drug trial when his counsel told the jury the defendant was well-off, from a privileged background, had no need to enter into an illegal business, and intended to go into a legitimate business. Id.

* * *

"The trial court's admission of the testimony was an abuse of discretion. Neither the appellant, his witnesses, nor his lawyer put his general character at issue or testified he had any specific character traits that rendered him incapable of molesting a female child. The appellant's testimony as to his childhood was general background information, which did not put his character at issue. See *McLister,* 608 F.2d at 789.

"We have stated in dictum that testimony of criminal profiles is highly undesirable as substantive evidence because it is of low probativity and inherently prejudicial. See *Hernandez,* 717 F.2d at 554–55 (testimony of the profile of a drug courier ordinarily inadmissible as substantive evidence of guilt). The jury's perception of the appellant's character and credibility are crucial to the outcome of this case; therefore, admission of Dr. Maloney's testimony was not harmless error."

UNITED STATES v. ANGELINI

United States Court of Appeals, First Circuit, 1982.
678 F.2d 380.

LEVIN H. CAMPBELL, CIRCUIT JUDGE.

Victor Angelini was convicted after a jury trial of possessing with intent to distribute and distributing methaqualone, a controlled substance, in violation of 21 U.S.C. § 841(a)(2), 18 U.S.C. § 2. The evidence presented against him at trial consisted primarily of the testimony of Drug Enforcement Administration Special Agent Keefe. Agent Keefe testified that, while working undercover, he met with one Samuel Jacobs on October 7, 1980, at which time Jacobs informed him of a new drug source from Florida. Jacobs arranged for Keefe to meet the source on October 14. Angelini was introduced as the drug source at this meeting. According to Keefe, Angelini stated that he could obtain various drugs. Angelini also asked Keefe about a small sample of drugs he, Angelini, had given Jacobs. Angelini went on to quote a price for shipments of the drugs.

The defense consisted chiefly of Angelini's denials of what Keefe said transpired at the October 14 meeting. He said that he was not involved in drugs and that while the general subject of drugs may have come up at the meeting, he did not engage in any criminal activity. Angelini's wife also testified on his behalf that he was not involved in drug trafficking.

Angelini sought to introduce evidence through three character witnesses that he was law-abiding and truthful. The district court refused to allow the witnesses to take the stand on the basis that law-abidingness was not relevant to the case; no explicit distinct explanation was given as to the basis of the ruling with respect to truthfulness. On appeal, Angelini asserts that these rulings were in error. While we do not believe it was error for the district court to have excluded the evidence concerning truthfulness, see note 1, infra, we hold that the court erred in excluding evidence concerning Angelini's character as a law-abiding person.

Federal Rule of Evidence 404(a) states that an accused may introduce "[e]vidence of a pertinent trait of his character." The word "pertinent" is read as synonymous with "relevant." United States v. Staggs, 553 F.2d 1073, 1075 (7th Cir.1977); 22 Wright & Graham, *Federal Practice and Procedure: Evidence* § 5236, at 383 (1978). Thus, the basic issue is whether the character trait in question would make any fact "of consequence to the determination" of the case more or less probable than it would be without evidence of the trait. See Fed. R.Evid. 401; United States v. Staggs, 553 F.2d 1073.

Under this analysis, evidence of law-abidingness should have been admitted. Evidence that Angelini was a law-abiding person would tend to make it less likely that he would knowingly break the law. Such evidence has long been recognized as relevant. See 1 Wigmore, *Evidence* § 55 (Chadbourne rev. 1972). In Michelson v. United States, 335 U.S. 469, 69 S.Ct. 213, 93 L.Ed. 168 (1948), the Supreme Court stated that "[p]ossession of * * * characteristics [including law-abidingness] would seem * * * incompatible with offering a bribe to a revenue agent," which was the crime charged. Id., at 483, 69 S.Ct. at 222. Similarly, in State v. Padgett, 93 W.Va. 623, 117 S.E. 493, 495 (1923), the court stated

> A law-abiding trait of character would tend to negative indulgence in the propensity of making moonshine liquor, and that was the nature of the inquiry attempted to be made.

The observations made in these cases apply with equal force to the drug offenses charged here.

In a case directly on point, United States v. Hewitt, 634 F.2d 277 (5th Cir.1981), the Fifth Circuit held that evidence of a defendant's law-abiding character was erroneously excluded in a trial for unlawful possession or receipt of firearms. In the course of its analysis, the court stressed the relevancy of such evidence. Id., at 279. As it noted, however, this inquiry does not end the matter. While the *Hewitt* court went on to ask whether law-abidingness is a "specific" or a "general" trait of character, we think the issue may be better framed as whether it qualifies as a trait at all, or is so diffuse as to be merely synonymous with good character generally, which is not admissible. Rule 404 permits evidence of traits only; an earlier draft was modified, deleting language that would have allowed the introduction of evidence of a defendant's character generally. See Advisory Committee's Note to Rule 404; Proposed Federal Rules of Evidence 4–04(a)(1), 46 F.R.D. 161, 227 (1969). Under the common law, there was a similar distinction made between general good character and particular traits of character. See McCormick, *Evidence* § 191, at 455 (2d ed. 1972); 1 Wigmore, *Evidence* § 59, at 458; 22 Wright & Graham, *Federal Practice and Procedure: Evidence* § 5236, at 382. Since Rule 404 was intended to restate the common law rule, 2 Weinstein & Berger, *Evidence* ¶ 404[05] (1981), it is useful to examine the cases to determine whether evidence of law-abidingness was normally held to be admissible.

With very few exceptions, the cases hold that evidence of a defendant's character as a law-abiding person is admissible. See, e.g., State v. Padgett, 93 W.Va. 623, 117 S.E. 493; State v. Quinn, 344 Mo. 1072, 130 S.W.2d 511 (1939); Bishop v. State, 72 Tex.Crim. 1, 160 S.W. 705 (1913); Livingston v. State, 589 S.W.2d 395 (Tex.Crim.1979); State v. Ervin, 22 Utah 2d 216, 451 P.2d 372 (1969); Finnie v. State, 264 Ark. 638, 593 S.W.2d 32 (1980). See also, e.g., United States v. Jalbert, 504 F.2d 892, 895 (1st Cir.1974) ("character evidence is admissible * * * to show a party's general renown for honesty and lawfulness"); Commonwealth v. Nagle, 157 Mass. 554, 32 N.E. 861, 862 (1893) ("unwillingness to commit crimes generally" apparently assumed a proper subject for character evidence). The only case we have found squarely stating that evidence of law-abidingness is generally inadmissible is Chung Sing v. United States, 4 Ariz. 217, 36 P. 205 (1894), but there is very little discussion of the issue. There is no indication of a general common law rule against the admissibility of evidence of law-abidingness (as distinguished from good character generally which, as noted, was usually held inadmissible).

We hold, therefore, that the trait of law-abidingness was relevant and admissible under Rule 404(a). We cannot say that the exclusion of this evidence was harmless error. Cf. Michelson v. United States, 335 U.S. at 476, 69 S.Ct. at 218 (evidence of good character may in itself raise a reasonable doubt as to defendant's guilt). We therefore remand for a new trial.[1]

Vacated and remanded.

1. As guidance for the district court on retrial, we note our rejection of Angelini's argument that he should have been permitted to introduce evidence of his character for truthfulness. If not pertinent to the crime charged—and Angelini does not argue that it is—such evidence is admissible "only after the character of the witness for truthfulness has been attacked by opinion or reputation evidence or otherwise." Fed.R.Evid. 608(a). The mere fact that an accused takes the stand does not give him the right to present character evidence supporting his veracity. United States v. Jackson, 588 F.2d 1046, 1055 (5th Cir.), *cert. denied,* 442 U.S. 941, 99 S.Ct. 2882, 61 L.Ed.2d 310 (1979). Nor does contradiction of a witness, even the accused, necessarily

---

STATE v. HOOD, 346 N.W.2d 481, 484–85 (Iowa 1984). "*Relevancy of Snodgrass' personality evidence.* Defendant contends the trial court erred in overruling his relevancy objection to the introduction by [codefendant] Sherryl [Snodgrass] of expert testimony concerning an evaluation of her as possessing a 'passive-dependent' personality. The expert testified that a 'passive-dependent' individual will allow others to assume responsibility and will act in a manner to maintain such a dependent relationship. Sherryl offered this testimony to negate evidence that she had the requisite intent to kill her husband. Iowa Code section 707.21(1) requires the State to prove on a first-degree murder charge that a defendant 'willfully, deliberately, and with premeditation kills another person.' In substance she sought to show it was unlikely she would commit such an act. In addition, she sought to show that her actions, especially those subsequent to the killing, did not warrant an inference that she intended to kill her husband but had only been following the direction of someone else.

"Hood claims Snodgrass' personality was not relevant to any issue and should have been excluded under the relevancy rule barring proof of a person's character as evidence of conduct on a particular occasion. E. Cleary, McCormick on Evidence, § 188 (2d ed. 1972). A significant exception to this general rule, however, has been recognized by this court.

> A defendant may introduce evidence of his good character for the traits involved in an offense as bearing on the probability he [or she] did or did not commit the crime charged. This may be done by proof of his real character for such traits or his general reputation for them.

State v. Buckner, 214 N.W.2d 164, 166–67 (Iowa 1974). See also State v. Hamann, 285 N.W.2d 180, 184 (Iowa 1979); State v. Hobbs, 172 N.W.2d 268, 271 (Iowa 1969); E. Cleary, McCormick on Evidence, § 191 (2d ed. 1972). Compare Iowa R.Evid. 404(a)(1), 405(a). The expert's opinion testimony on Snodgrass' unique character trait comes within this exception because it bears on the probability of her committing the crime charged."

Notes

(1) "The prevailing view limits pertinent traits to those involved in the offense charged—proof of honesty in a theft charge or peacefulness in a murder charge. * * * However, it is necessary to allow evidence of defendant's character, as testimony that the general estimate of his charac-

require the admission of proffered evidence for truthfulness. Id. The cross-examination of Angelini conducted here could hardly be characterized as so "slashing," McCormick, *Evidence* § 49, at 104, as to constitute an attack on credibility under Rule 608. While the retrial may take a different course, necessitating a different approach by the presiding judge, we see no error in the exclusion of the evidence under the circumstances which obtained at the trial now under consideration.

ter may be so favorable the jury could infer he would not be likely to commit the offense charged. * * * [T]he defense proffered opinion evidence that Shelton was not a discipline problem and had an aversion to violence. Both of these traits—probative of a law abiding and non-violent nature—have been traditionally admissible in a murder case and should have been admitted. * * * The defense also sought to introduce evidence of Shelton's immaturity and limited intelligence. Both traits were relevant to a lack of intent—a crucial issue here * * *." Shelton v. State, 287 Ark. 322, 699 S.W.2d 728, 734–35 (1985).

(2) "[T]his Court concludes that evidence of poor judgment in commodity trading and handling debts does not constitute a character trait within the meaning of Rule 404(a)(1)." United States v. Buchbinder, 614 F.Supp. 1561, 1568 (N.D.Ill.1985).

UNITED STATES v. BRIGHT

United States Court of Appeals, Fifth Circuit, 1979.

588 F.2d 504, cert. denied, 440 U.S. 972, 99 S.Ct. 1537, 59 L.Ed.2d 789 (1979).

AINSWORTH, CIRCUIT JUDGE:

Edgar Lee Whitten and Louin Ray Bright appeal their convictions for mail fraud under 18 U.S.C. §§ 2 and 1341. * * *

IV. THE CROSS-EXAMINATION OF THE CHARACTER WITNESS

Finally, appellant Whitten asserts that the trial court abused its discretion in allowing the Government to cross-examine one of his character witnesses regarding Whitten's alleged reprimand by a judge and bar association for unprofessional conduct. The witness, an attorney, testified under direct examination that Whitten had a good general reputation in his community for veracity and integrity and declared that he would believe Whitten under oath. On cross-examination, the Government asked this witness whether he had "heard that Mr. Whitten was reprimanded by Judge Dick Thomas in November of last year for unprofessional conduct?", and the witness replied, "No, sir, I had not." During recross-examination, the Government queried, "But you had not heard that Mr. Whitten had been reprimanded by the Bar Association through Judge Thomas in DeSoto County?" Whitten's character witness responded, "I was not aware of either one of them." The Government then asked, "Well, the State Bar then, the Mississippi State Bar?", and the witness answered, "I was not aware of that, no sir." Whitten's counsel objected to each of these questions and, at the close of trial, moved for a mistrial; the lower court overruled the objections and denied the motion.

Arguing that he was "substantially prejudiced by this type of cross-examination," Whitten contends that the district judge should have invoked his discretionary power under Fed.R.Evid. 403 to stop this line of questioning, since "its probative value [was] substantially outweighed by the danger of unfair prejudice." Fed.R.Evid. 403. We disagree. When a witness has testified in support of the defendant's good character, the trial court may in its discretion allow the Government to attempt to undermine the credibility of that witness on cross-examination "by asking him whether he has heard of prior misconduct of the defendant which is inconsistent with the witness' direct testimony." *United States v. Wells,* 5 Cir., 1976, 525 F.2d 974, 976. However, there are "two important limitations upon judicial discretion in admitting inquiries concerning such prior misconduct: first, a requirement that the prosecution have some good-faith factual basis for the incidents inquired about, and second, a requirement that the incidents inquired about are relevant to the character traits involved at trial." *Id.* at 977. Those requirements are both satisfied here. During a conference in chambers after the defendants rested their case, Whitten's lawyer moved for a mistrial, arguing that "the government offered no evidence whatsoever of this highly prejudicial statement" "about a censure from the DeSoto County Bar, the Mississippi State Bar Association for unethical conduct." The Government replied that it was "prepared to show the basis on which we asked the question, that it is a fact, and that our questions were based on that fact." It said that if Whitten's attorney "will stipulate to the letter of reprimand we will introduce that in the record" and volunteered to "move to reopen and call Mr. Whitten for further cross-examination on the matter" if his counsel "thinks it necessary that we prove it." In our view, the Government's proffer of a letter of reprimand for stipulation and its willingness to reopen the case and attempt to prove the fact of Whitten's reprimand demonstrated the necessary "good-faith factual basis for the incidents inquired about." Those incidents were also "relevant to the character traits involved at trial." The character witness, an attorney, testified to Whitten's good reputation for honesty and integrity and the alleged reprimand for unprofessional conduct was relevant to Whitten's community reputation regarding those traits.

AFFIRMED.

UNITED STATES v. CANDELARIA–GONZALEZ, 547 F.2d 291, 293–95 (5th Cir.1977). "We consider first Ledesma's contention that the district judge erroneously permitted grossly improper cross-examination of Ledesma's character witnesses. Several witnesses testified as to his general reputation for truth and veracity. The first such witness testified that such reputation was good. Government counsel on cross-examination asked if Ledesma's indictment would affect the witness's opinion of him and his reputation in general. Defense counsel objected, and the district judge ultimately sustained the objection, at the same time advising government counsel that it would be permissible to ask the witness if Ledesma's reputation *would* be affected *if* he were *convicted* of trafficking in narcotics. Government counsel posed this question to Ledesma's second character witness. The question was permitted over defense counsel's objection. Two other character witnesses for Ledesma were asked the same question, and counsel objected in each instance. Once the objection to the question was overruled, on the other occasion the objection was sustained.

"Control of the cross-examination of character witnesses as well as others is largely within a trial court's discretion. See Michelson v. United States, 1948, 335 U.S. 469, 480, 69 S.Ct. 213, 220–21, 93 L.Ed. 168, 176. 'Wide discretion is accompanied by heavy responsibility on trial courts to protect the practice from any misuse.' Id.

"The district judge below abused this discretion when he permitted the prosecution to ask these hypothetical questions on cross-examination. Once the defendant places his reputation in issue, the prosecution has wide latitude to pursue the reputation of the accused on cross-examination. Id. at 479, 69 S.Ct. at 220, 93 L.Ed. at 175–76; Moore v. United States, 5 Cir.1941, 123 F.2d 207. Nevertheless reputation denotes the formation of definite opinions by the community. See United States v. Lewis, 1973, 157 U.S.App.D.C. 43, 482 F.2d 632; 5 Wigmore, Evidence § 1611 (Chadbourn Ed.1974).

"The nature of the questions put to Ledesma's witnesses by government counsel, however, was a far cry from any concept of formulated community opinion. Rather, the questions posed sought speculative responses resting upon an assumption of guilt. Government counsel asked if Ledesma's reputation *would* be affected *if* he *were* convicted of the alleged crime. These hypothetical questions struck at the very heart of the presumption of innocence which is fundamental to Anglo–Saxon concepts of fair trial. See Gomila v. United States, 5 Cir.1944, 146 F.2d 372; Little v. United States, 8 Cir.1937, 93 F.2d 401, 408. We think that the risk of prejudice to defendant's basic rights from such questions requires reversal. The questions put have no place in a criminal trial.

"Testimony as to reputation should be, as the name indicates, based on repute, which is synonymous with hearsay. It is 'established not by what one knows to be fact concerning another, but by what one has heard in the community about the person in question.' (Citations omitted). United States v. Fink, 5 Cir.1974, 502 F.2d 1, 5. *See* Michelson v. United States, supra, 335 U.S. at 477, 69 S.Ct. at 219, 93 L.Ed. at 174–75. Obviously the character witnesses offered by the appellant Ledesma had heard nothing in the community about his post conviction reputation when he had been convicted of nothing whatsoever. No one yet knew what people would say about him if he were convicted.

"Government counsel also asked, on cross-examination, whether it would be inconsistent with the witness's knowledge of Ledesma *if* a DEA agent testified that Ledesma was known as a major narcotics trafficker. After instructing counsel to rephrase his question, the district judge allowed it. This type of questioning was beyond the scope of permissible interrogation under Michelson v. United States, supra, and the Federal Rules of Evidence. The agent's testimony was raised to the status of accepted fact, and the presumption of innocence was destroyed in the process. See further, Kotteakos v. United States, 1946, 328 U.S. 750, 66 S.Ct. 1239, 90 L.Ed. 1557. The convictions here are due to be reversed for the court's repeated allowance of inherently prejudicial cross-examination by the prosecutor."

UNITED STATES v. HEWITT, 663 F.2d 1381, 1390–91 (11th Cir. 1981). "Finally, Hewitt alleges that the trial judge committed reversible error in allowing the prosecutor to cross-examine one of Hewitt's reputation witnesses improperly. At trial, Hewitt called four reputation witnesses, each of whom testified to Hewitt's good reputation in the community. The prosecution cross-examined each of the four witnesses by asking them whether they had heard that Hewitt had been indicted, arrested, and was to go to trial in Muscogee County Superior Court on two counts of theft of air conditioning units. The first three reputation witnesses testified that they had heard of the impending trial, but that their assessment of Hewitt's reputation in the community was unaltered. The fourth reputation witness, Diane Gibbons, stated that she had not heard of the impending trial. The prosecuting attorney then asked, 'If you heard that would your testimony that his reputation is good, would that still be your testimony?' Gibbons answered that her assessment of Hewitt's reputation would remain unchanged.

"Hewitt does not deny that it was proper to ask the reputation witnesses whether they had heard about his impending trial in Muscogee County. The Supreme Court established long ago in Michelson v. United States, 335 U.S. 469, 478–79, 69 S.Ct. 213, 219–220, 93 L.Ed. 168 (1948), that a reputation witness for the defense may be cross-examined as to whether he has heard of certain facts that tend to reflect negatively on defendant's reputation. This line of cross-examination is allowed for the very specific purpose of impeaching the witness' credibility. If the reputation witness has not heard of a fact that is likely to have caused a negative community impression of the defendant, the government has shown that the witness' knowledge of defendant's reputation is shallow and unreliable. If the reputation witness has heard of this fact but nevertheless testifies that the defendant's reputation is good, then the government has shown that the witness is either lying or is applying a lowered standard by which he assesses the defendant's good reputation. See Michelson v. United States, 335 U.S. at 479, 483, 69 S.Ct. at 220–222; United States v. Curry, 512 F.2d 1299, 1305 (4th Cir.), cert. denied, 423 U.S. 832, 96 S.Ct. 55, 46 L.Ed.2d 50 (1975); C. McCormick, Evidence 457 n. 74 (2d ed. 1972).

"In light of the limited purpose for which Michelson-type cross-examination is appropriate, it is clear that the hypothetical question posed by the prosecuting attorney to Hewitt's reputation witness was highly improper. The government had already shown that Gibbons knew little of Hewitt's reputation in the community by exposing her ignorance of his pending trial. After thus impeaching her credibility as a reputation witness, the government attempted to conscript her as an expert on Hewitt's reputation by asking her what the community would think if it had heard of the theft charges. This question serves no legitimate purpose and, at the very least, was irrelevant.[18]

"It remains to be determined, however, whether this improper cross-examination resulted in prejudice to Hewitt's case so as to warrant reversal. Fed.R.Crim.P. 52(a); Michelson v. United States, 335 U.S. at 480, 69 S.Ct. at 220; United States v. Candelaria–Gonzalez, 547 F.2d 291, 294 (5th Cir.1977); United States v. Curtis, 644 F.2d 263, 269–70 (3d Cir.1981). For several reasons, we conclude that it did not. First, the hypothetical question did not ask the witness to assume the existence of facts that the government could not substantiate. To the contrary, the prosecuting attorney had made a timely proffer of evidence to the judge which established that Hewitt was awaiting trial on charges of theft. See Michelson v. United States, 335 U.S. at 480–81 & n. 17, 69 S.Ct. at 220–221. Cf. Gross v. United States, 394 F.2d 216, 220 (8th Cir.1968), cert. denied, 397 U.S. 1013, 90 S.Ct. 1245, 25 L.Ed.2d 427 (1970) (conviction reversed because no basis for cross-examination established). Also, the question did not ask the witness to assume the guilt of Hewitt in the matter for which he was standing trial, and therefore did not violate the presumption of innocence to which Hewitt was entitled. See United States v. Candelaria–Gonzalez, 547 F.2d at 294. Finally, the hypothetical question did not cause Hewitt's reputation witness to alter her evaluation of Hewitt's reputation in the community. See United States v. Dovalina, 525 F.2d 952, 957 (5th Cir.), cert. denied, 425 U.S. 953, 96 S.Ct. 1729, 48 L.Ed.2d 197 (1976); United States v. Curtis, 644 F.2d at 270.[19]"

Notes

(1) "In cross-examining a reputation witness, the State is permitted to ask the witness if he has heard of a specific act of misconduct by the

18. See, e.g., Gross v. United States, 394 F.2d 216, 221 (8th Cir.1968), cert. denied, 397 U.S. 1013, 90 S.Ct. 1245, 25 L.Ed.2d 427 (1970). This conclusion is not altered by the adoption of Fed.R.Evid. 405. That rule changes preexisting practice by allowing the defendant to prove his good character by means of reputation or opinion evidence. Advis.Comm. Notes, Fed.R.Evid. 405. The fact that the defendant is free to prove his good character by means of opinion evidence does not mean that the government is free to impeach the defendant's reputation witnesses by use of hypotheticals, a means normally appropriate for impeachment of expert opinion testimony. United States v. Curtis, 644 F.2d 263, 268 (3d Cir.1981).

19. The government reads our decision in United States v. Dovalina, 525 F.2d 952 (5th Cir.), cert. denied, 425 U.S. 953, 96 S.Ct. 1729, 48 L.Ed.2d 197 (1976), to hold that whenever a reputation witness responds to an improper hypothetical question with an answer that reaffirms his favorable testimony, the defendant necessarily suffers no prejudice. We reject that reading of *Dovalina*. In several cases, a defendant's conviction has been reversed because of improperly posed hypotheticals despite the fact that the reputation witness refused to change his testimony. See, e.g., United States v. Candelaria–Gonzalez, 547 F.2d 291, 293–94 & n. 3 (5th Cir.1977); Gross v. United States, 394 F.2d at 220–21. Our decision in *Dovalina* establishes only that the response of the reputation witness to the improper hypothetical is one factor to be considered by the court in assessing prejudice. United States v. Curtis, 644 F.2d at 270.

defendant, * * * but the question is not to be framed so as to imply that the act has actually been committed, i.e., an assertion of the truth of the matter. * * * Where improper questions in the cross-examination of a character witness have been asked, the Texas Court of Criminal Appeals has not hesitated to reverse solely on the basis of the improper prejudicial question." Rogers v. State, 725 S.W.2d 350, 358–59 (Tex.App.1987).

(2) "The district court permitted and itself pursued questions to several defense character witnesses that required the witnesses to assume the guilt of the appellants. In light of our recent decision in United States v. Oshatz, 912 F.2d 534 (2nd Cir.1990), this questioning was error. * * * On cross-examination, the government asked Wallace if his opinion of Long would change were he to become 'aware that John Long had accepted cash kickbacks in exchange for investing union members' dues in a particular investment company.' When the witness repeatedly protested that he 'wouldn't believe it,' the court ordered him to assume the fact as posed by the government and respond to the question. When Wallace answered that his opinion of Long was so high that even the government's suggested proof would not change his view, the court intervened again, accused Wallace of answering evasively, and expressed disbelief of Wallace's responses. Wallace then finally answered 'yes' to a series of questions premised on purported conduct for which Long was on trial. * * * We reverse as to all counts." United States v. Long, 917 F.2d 691, 703–04 (2d Cir.1990).

(3) "[T]he power of the state to rebut the character of defendant is limited to the trait or traits introduced by the defendant. * * * A defendant does not open the door to any and all evidence concerning his character merely by basing an argument on some aspects of his character. He opens the door only for evidence that his character is not what he claims it to be." People v. Johnson, 409 Mich. 552, 297 N.W.2d 115, 119 (1980).

HUDDLESTON v. UNITED STATES

Supreme Court of the United States, 1988.
485 U.S. 681, 108 S.Ct. 1496, 99 L.Ed.2d 771.

CHIEF JUSTICE REHNQUIST delivered the opinion of the Court.

Federal Rule of Evidence 404(b) provides:

> "Other crimes, wrongs, or acts.—Evidence of other crimes, wrongs, or acts is not admissible to prove the character of a person in order to show that he acted in conformity therewith. It may, however, be admissible for other purposes, such as proof of motive, opportunity, intent, preparation, plan, knowledge, identity, or absence of mistake or accident."

This case presents the question whether the district court must itself make a preliminary finding that the Government has proved the "other act" by a preponderance of the evidence before it submits the evidence to the jury. We hold that it need not do so.

Petitioner, Guy Rufus Huddleston, was charged with one count of selling stolen goods in interstate commerce, 18 U.S.C. § 2315, and one count of possessing stolen property in interstate commerce, 18 U.S.C. § 659. The two counts related to two portions of a shipment of stolen Memorex video cassette tapes that petitioner was alleged to have possessed and sold, knowing that they were stolen.

The evidence at trial showed that a trailer containing over 32,000 blank Memorex video cassette tapes with a manufacturing cost of $4.53 per tape was stolen from the Overnight Express yard in South Holland, Illinois, sometime between April 11 and 15, 1985. On April 17, 1985, petitioner contacted Karen Curry, the manager of the Magic Rent-to-Own in Ypsilanti, Michigan, seeking her assistance in selling a large number of blank Memorex video cassette tapes. After assuring Curry that the tapes were not stolen, he told her he wished to sell them in lots of at least 500 at $2.75 to $3.00 per tape. Curry subsequently arranged for the sale of a total of 5,000 tapes, which petitioner delivered to the various purchasers—who apparently believed the sales were legitimate.

There was no dispute that the tapes which petitioner sold were stolen; the only material issue at trial was whether petitioner knew they were stolen. The District Court allowed the Government to introduce evidence of "similar acts" under Rule 404(b), concluding that such evidence had "clear relevance as to [petitioner's knowledge]." App. 11. The first piece of similar act evidence offered by the Government was the testimony of Paul Toney, a record store owner. He testified that in February 1985, petitioner offered to sell new 12″ black and white televisions for $28 a piece. According to Toney, petitioner indicated that he could obtain several thousand of these televisions. Petitioner and Toney eventually traveled to the Magic Rent-to-Own, where Toney purchased 20 of the televisions. Several days later, Toney purchased 18 more televisions.

The second piece of similar act evidence was the testimony of Robert Nelson, an undercover FBI agent posing as a buyer for an appliance store. Nelson testified that in May 1985, petitioner offered to sell him a large quantity of Amana appliances—28 refrigerators, 2 ranges, and 40 icemakers. Nelson agreed to pay $8,000 for the appliances. Petitioner was arrested shortly after he arrived at the parking lot where he and Nelson had agreed to transfer the appliances. A truck containing the appliances was stopped a short distance from the parking lot, and Leroy Wesby, who was driving the truck, was also arrested. It was determined that the appliances had a value of approximately $20,000 and were part of a shipment that had been stolen.

Petitioner testified that the Memorex tapes, the televisions, and the appliances had all been provided by Leroy Wesby, who had represented that all of the merchandise was obtained legitimately. Petitioner stated that he had sold 6,500 Memorex tapes for Wesby on a commission basis. Petitioner maintained that all of the sales for Wesby had been on a commission basis and that he had no knowledge that any of the goods were stolen.

In closing, the prosecution explained that petitioner was not on trial for his dealings with the appliances or the televisions. The District Court instructed the jury that the similar acts evidence was to be used only to establish petitioner's knowledge, and not to prove his character. The jury convicted petitioner on the possession count only.

A divided panel of the United States Court of Appeals for the Sixth Circuit initially reversed the conviction, concluding that because the Government had failed to prove by clear and convincing evidence that the televisions were stolen, the District Court erred in admitting the testimony concerning the televisions. 802 F.2d 874 (1986).[1] The panel subsequently granted rehearing to address the decision in *United States v. Ebens,* 800 F.2d 1422 (CA6 1986), in which a different panel had held: "Courts may admit evidence of prior bad acts if the proof shows by a preponderance of the evidence that the defendant did in fact commit the act." *Id.,* at 1432. On rehearing, the court affirmed the conviction. "Applying the preponderance of the evidence standard adopted in *Ebens,* we cannot say that the district court abused its discretion in admitting evidence of the similar acts in question here." 811 F.2d 974, 975 (1987) (*per curiam*). The court noted that the evidence concerning the televisions was admitted for a proper purpose and that the probative value of this evidence was not outweighed by its potential prejudicial effect.

We granted certiorari, 484 U.S. ___, 108 S.Ct. 226, 98 L.Ed.2d 185 (1987), to resolve a conflict among the Courts of Appeals as to whether the trial court must make a preliminary finding before "similar act" and other Rule 404(b) evidence is submitted to the jury.[2] We conclude that such evidence should be admitted if there is sufficient evidence to support a finding by the jury that the defendant committed the similar act.

Federal Rule of Evidence 404(b)—which applies in both civil and criminal cases—generally prohibits the introduction of evidence of

1. "[T]he government's only support for the assertion that the televisions were stolen was [petitioner's] failure to produce a bill of sale at trial and the fact that the televisions were sold at a low price." 802 F.2d, at 876, n. 5.

2. The First, Fourth, Fifth, and Eleventh Circuits allow the admission of similar act evidence if the evidence is sufficient to allow the jury to find that the defendant committed the act. *United States v. Ingraham,* 832 F.2d 229, 235 (CA1 1987); *United States v. Martin,* 773 F.2d 579, 582 (CA4 1985); *United States v. Beechum,* 582 F.2d 898, 914 (CA5 1978) (en banc), cert. denied, 440 U.S. 920, 99 S.Ct. 1244, 59 L.Ed.2d 472 (1979); *United States v. Dothard,* 666 F.2d 498, 502 (CA11 1982). Consistent with the Sixth Circuit, the Second Circuit prohibits the introduction of similar act evidence unless the trial court finds by a preponderance of the evidence that the defendant committed the act. *United States v. Leonard,* 524 F.2d 1076, 1090–1091 (CA2 1975). The Seventh, Eighth, Ninth, and District of Columbia Circuits require the Government to prove to the court by clear and convincing evidence that the defendant committed the similar act. *United States v. Leight,* 818 F.2d 1297, 1302 (CA7), cert. denied, 484 U.S. ___, 108 S.Ct. 356, 98 L.Ed.2d 381 (1987); *United States v. Weber,* 818 F.2d 14 (CA8 1987); *United States v. Vaccaro,* 816 F.2d 443, 452 (CA9), cert. denied, *sub nom. Alvis v. United States,* 484 U.S. ___, 108 S.Ct. 262, 98 L.Ed.2d 220 (1987); *United States v. Lavelle,* 243 U.S.App.D.C. 47, 57, 751 F.2d 1266, 1276, cert. denied, 474 U.S. 817, 106 S.Ct. 62, 88 L.Ed.2d 51 (1985).

extrinsic acts that might adversely reflect on the actor's character, unless that evidence bears upon a relevant issue in the case such as motive, opportunity, or knowledge. Extrinsic acts evidence may be critical to the establishment of the truth as to a disputed issue, especially when that issue involves the actor's state of mind and the only means of ascertaining that mental state is by drawing inferences from conduct. The actor in the instant case was a criminal defendant, and the act in question was "similar" to the one with which he was charged. Our use of these terms is not meant to suggest that our analysis is limited to such circumstances.

Before this Court, petitioner argues that the District Court erred in admitting Toney's testimony as to petitioner's sale of the televisions.[3] The threshold inquiry a court must make before admitting similar acts evidence under Rule 404(b) is whether that evidence is probative of a material issue other than character. The Government's theory of relevance was that the televisions were stolen, and proof that petitioner had engaged in a series of sales of stolen merchandise from the same suspicious source would be strong evidence that he was aware that each of these items, including the Memorex tapes, was stolen.[4] As such, the sale of the televisions was a "similar act" only if the televisions were stolen. Petitioner acknowledges that this evidence was admitted for the proper purpose of showing his knowledge that the Memorex tapes were stolen. He asserts, however, that the evidence should not have been admitted because the Government failed to prove to the District Court that the televisions were in fact stolen.

Petitioner argues from the premise that evidence of similar acts has a grave potential for causing improper prejudice. For instance, the jury may choose to punish the defendant for the similar rather than the charged act, or the jury may infer that the defendant is an evil person inclined to violate the law. Because of this danger, petitioner maintains, the jury ought not to be exposed to similar act evidence until the trial court has heard the evidence and made a determination under Federal Rule of Evidence 104(a) that the defendant committed the similar act. Rule 104(a) provides that "[p]reliminary questions concerning the qualification of a person to be a witness, the existence of a privilege, or the admissibility of evidence shall be determined by the court, subject to the provisions of subdivision (b)." According to petitioner, the trial court must make this preliminary finding by at least a preponderance of the evidence.[5]

3. Petitioner does not dispute that Nelson's testimony concerning the Amana appliances was properly admitted under Rule 404(b).

4. The Government also argues before this Court that the evidence concerning the televisions is relevant even if the jury could not conclude that the sets were stolen. We have found nothing in the record indicating that this theory was suggested to or relied upon by the courts below, and in light of our ruling, we need not address this alternate theory.

5. In his brief, petitioner argued that the Government was required to prove to the trial court the commission of the similar act by clear and convincing proof. At oral argument, his counsel conceded that such a position is untenable in light of our decision last term in *Bourjaily v. United*

We reject petitioner's position, for it is inconsistent with the structure of the Rules of Evidence and with the plain language of Rule 404(b). Article IV of the Rules of Evidence deals with the relevancy of evidence. Rules 401 and 402 establish the broad principle that relevant evidence—evidence that makes the existence of any fact at issue more or less probable—is admissible unless the Rules provide otherwise. Rule 403 allows the trial judge to exclude relevant evidence if, among other things, "its probative value is substantially outweighed by the danger of unfair prejudice." Rules 404 through 412 address specific types of evidence that have generated problems. Generally, these latter Rules do not flatly prohibit the introduction of such evidence but instead limit the purpose for which it may be introduced. Rule 404(b), for example, protects against the introduction of extrinsic act evidence when that evidence is offered solely to prove character. The text contains no intimation, however, that any preliminary showing is necessary before such evidence may be introduced for a proper purpose. If offered for such a proper purpose, the evidence is subject only to general strictures limiting admissibility such as Rules 402 and 403.

Petitioner's reading of Rule 404(b) as mandating a preliminary finding by the trial court that the act in question occurred not only superimposes a level of judicial oversight that is nowhere apparent from the language of that provision, but it is simply inconsistent with the legislative history behind Rule 404(b). The Advisory Committee specifically declined to offer any "mechanical solution" to the admission of evidence under 404(b). Advisory Committee's Notes on Fed.Rule Evid. 404(b), 28 U.S.C.App., p. 691. Rather, the Committee indicated that the trial court should assess such evidence under the usual rules for admissibility: "The determination must be made whether the danger of undue prejudice outweighs the probative value of the evidence in view of the availability of other means of proof and other factors appropriate for making decisions of this kind under Rule 403." *Ibid;* see also S.Rep. No. 93–1277, p. 25 (1974) ("[I]t is anticipated that with respect to permissible uses for such evidence, the trial judge may exclude it only on the basis of those considerations set forth in Rule 403, *i.e.* prejudice, confusion or waste of time").

Petitioner's suggestion that a preliminary finding is necessary to protect the defendant from the potential for unfair prejudice is also belied by the Reports of the House of Representatives and the Senate. The House made clear that the version of Rule 404(b) which became law was intended to "plac[e] greater emphasis on admissibility than did the final Court version." H.R.Rep. No. 93–650, p. 7 (1973). The Senate echoed this theme: "[T]he use of the discretionary word 'may' with

States, 483 U.S. ___, 107 S.Ct. 268, 93 L.Ed.2d 246 (1987), in which we concluded that preliminary factual findings under Rule 104(a) are subject to the preponderance of the evidence standard. Tr. of Oral Arg. 12. Petitioner now asserts that although the Sixth Circuit correctly held that the Government must prove the similar act by preponderant evidence before it is admitted, the court erred in applying that test to these facts. We consider first what preliminary finding, if any, the trial court must make before letting similar acts evidence go to the jury.

respect to the admissibility of evidence of crimes, wrongs, or other acts is not intended to confer any arbitrary discretion on the trial judge." S.Rep. No. 93–1277, at 24. Thus, Congress was not nearly so concerned with the potential prejudicial effect of Rule 404(b) evidence as it was with ensuring that restrictions would not be placed on the admission of such evidence.

We conclude that a preliminary finding by the court that the Government has proved the act by a preponderance of the evidence is not called for under Rule 104(a).[6] This is not to say, however, that the Government may parade past the jury a litany of potentially prejudicial similar acts that have been established or connected to the defendant only by unsubstantiated innuendo. Evidence is admissible under Rule 404(b) only if it is relevant. "Relevancy is not an inherent characteristic of any item of evidence but exists only as a relation between an item of evidence and a matter properly provable in the case." Advisory Committee's Notes on Fed.Rule Evid. 401, 28 U.S.C.App., p. 688. In the Rule 404(b) context, similar act evidence is relevant only if the jury can reasonably conclude that the act occurred and that the defendant was the actor. See *United States v. Beechum,* 582 F.2d 898, 912–913 (CA5 1978) (en banc). In the instant case, the evidence that petitioner was selling the televisions was relevant under the Government's theory only if the jury could reasonably find that the televisions were stolen.

Such questions of relevance conditioned on a fact are dealt with under Federal Rule of Evidence 104(b). *Beechum, supra,* at 912–913; see also E. Imwinkelried, Uncharged Misconduct Evidence § 2.06 (1984). Rule 104(b) provides:

> "When the relevancy of evidence depends upon the fulfillment of a condition of fact, the court shall admit it upon, or subject to, the introduction of evidence sufficient to support a finding of the fulfillment of the condition."

In determining whether the Government has introduced sufficient evidence to meet Rule 104(b), the trial court neither weighs credibility nor makes a finding that the Government has proved the conditional fact by a preponderance of the evidence. The court simply examines all the evidence in the case and decides whether the jury could reasonably find the conditional fact—here, that the televisions were stolen—by a preponderance of the evidence. See 21 C. Wright & K. Graham, Federal Practice and Procedure § 5054, p. 269 (1977). The trial court has traditionally exercised the broadest sort of discretion in

6. Petitioner also suggests that in performing the balancing prescribed by Federal Rule of Evidence 403, the trial court must find that the prejudicial potential of similar acts evidence substantially outweighs its probative value unless the court concludes by a preponderance of the evidence that the defendant committed the similar act. We reject this suggestion because Rule 403 admits of no such gloss and because such a holding would be erroneous for the same reasons that a preliminary finding under Rule 104(a) is inappropriate. We do, however, agree with the Government's concession at oral argument that the strength of the evidence establishing the similar act is one of the factors the court may consider when conducting the Rule 403 balancing. Tr. of Oral Arg. 26.

controlling the order of proof at trial, and we see nothing in the Rules of Evidence that would change this practice. Often the trial court may decide to allow the proponent to introduce evidence concerning a similar act, and at a later point in the trial assess whether sufficient evidence has been offered to permit the jury to make the requisite finding.[7] If the proponent has failed to meet this minimal standard of proof, the trial court must instruct the jury to disregard the evidence.

We emphasize that in assessing the sufficiency of the evidence under Rule 104(b), the trial court must consider all evidence presented to the jury. "[I]ndividual pieces of evidence, insufficient in themselves to prove a point, may in cumulation prove it. The sum of an evidentiary presentation may well be greater than its constituent parts." *Bourjaily v. United States,* 483 U.S. ___, 107 S.Ct. 268, 93 L.Ed.2d 246 (1987). In assessing whether the evidence was sufficient to support a finding that the televisions were stolen, the court here was required to consider not only the direct evidence on that point—the low price of the televisions, the large quantity offered for sale, and petitioner's inability to produce a bill of sale—but also the evidence concerning petitioner's involvement in the sales of other stolen merchandise obtained from Wesby, such as the Memorex tapes and the Amana appliances. Given this evidence, the jury reasonably could have concluded that the televisions were stolen, and the trial court therefore properly allowed the evidence to go to the jury.

We share petitioner's concern that unduly prejudicial evidence might be introduced under Rule 404(b). See *Michelson v. United States,* 335 U.S. 469, 475–476, 69 S.Ct. 213, 218–219, 93 L.Ed. 168 (1948). We think, however, that the protection against such unfair prejudice emanates not from a requirement of a preliminary finding by the trial court, but rather from four other sources: first, from the requirement of Rule 404(b) that the evidence be offered for a proper purpose; second, from the relevancy requirement of Rule 402—as enforced through Rule 104(b); third, from the assessment the trial court must make under Rule 403 to determine whether the probative value of the similar acts evidence is substantially outweighed by its potential for unfair prejudice,[8] see Advisory Committee's Notes on Fed.Rule Evid. 404(b), 28 U.S.C.App., p. 691; S.Rep. No. 93–1277, at 25; and fourth, from Federal Rule of Evidence 105, which provides that the trial court shall, upon request, instruct the jury that the similar acts evidence is to be

7. "When an item of evidence is conditionally relevant, it is often not possible for the offeror to prove the fact upon which relevance is conditioned at the time the evidence is offered. In such cases it is customary to permit him to introduce the evidence and 'connect it up' later. Rule 104(b) continues this practice, specifically authorizing the judge to admit the evidence 'subject to' proof of the preliminary fact. It is, of course, not the responsibility of the judge sua sponte to insure that the foundation evidence is offered; the objector must move to strike the evidence if at the close of the trial the offeror has failed to satisfy the condition." 21 C. Wright & K. Graham, Federal Practice and Procedure § 5054 pp. 269–270 (1977) (footnotes omitted).

8. As petitioner's counsel conceded at oral argument, petitioner did not seek review of the Rule 403 balancing performed by the courts below. Tr. of Oral Arg. 14. We therefore do not address that issue.

considered only for the proper purpose for which it was admitted. See *United States v. Ingraham,* 832 F.2d 229, 235 (CA1 1987).

Affirmed.

DOWLING v. UNITED STATES, 493 U.S. 342, 110 S.Ct. 668, 107 L.Ed.2d 708 (1990). "At petitioner's trial for various offenses arising out of a bank robbery, testimony was admitted under Rule 404(b) of the Federal Rules of Evidence, relating to an alleged crime that the defendant had previously been acquitted of committing. We conclude that neither the Double Jeopardy nor the Due Process Clause barred the use of this testimony.

* * *

"During petitioner's third trial, the Government over petitioner's objection called a woman named Vena Henry to the stand. Ms. Henry testified that a man wearing a knitted mask with cutout eyes and carrying a small handgun had, together with a man named Delroy Christian, entered her home in Frederiksted approximately two weeks after the First Pennsylvania Bank robbery. Ms. Henry testified that a struggle ensued and that she unmasked the intruder, whom she identified as Dowling. Based on this incident, Dowling had been charged under Virgin Islands law with burglary, attempted robbery, assault, and weapons offenses, but had been acquitted after a trial held before his third trial in the bank robbery case.

"The Government assertedly elicited Henry's testimony for two purposes. First, it believed that Henry's description of Dowling as wearing a mask and carrying a gun similar to the mask worn and the gun carried by the robber of the First Pennsylvania Bank strengthened the Government's identification of Dowling as the bank robber. Second, the Government sought to link Dowling with Delroy Christian, the other man who entered Henry's home. The day before the bank robbery, Dowling had borrowed a white Volkswagen from a friend. At Dowling's trial for the First Pennsylvania Bank robbery, a police officer testified that, shortly before the bank robbery, she and her partner had come upon Christian and another man parked in a white Volkswagen in front of the bank with the car door open into the street; Christian was in the backseat. The officers told the two men to close the door, and the men drove away to the north. The police followed the Volkswagen for about a mile and, shortly thereafter, received a radio message that the bank had been robbed. The Government's theory was that Christian and his friend were to drive the getaway car after Dowling robbed the bank.

* * *

"For present purposes, we assume for the sake of argument that Dowling's acquittal established that there was a reasonable doubt as to whether Dowling was the masked man who entered Vena Henry's home with Delroy Christian two weeks after the First Pennsylvania Bank robbery. But to introduce evidence on this point at the bank robbery trial, the Government did not have to demonstrate that Dowling was the man who entered the home beyond a reasonable doubt: the Government sought to introduce Henry's testimony under Rule 404(b), and, as mentioned earlier, in Huddleston v. United States, 485 U.S., at 689, 108 S.Ct., at 1501, we held that '[i]n the Rule 404(b) context, similar act evidence is relevant only if the jury can reasonably conclude that the act occurred and that the defendant was the actor.' Because a jury might reasonably conclude that Dowling was the masked man who entered Henry's home, even if it did not believe beyond a reasonable doubt that Dowling committed the crimes charged at the first trial, the collateral estoppel component of the Double Jeopardy Clause is inapposite.

* * *

"Besides arguing that the introduction of Henry's testimony violated the Double Jeopardy Clause, petitioner also contends that the introduction of this evidence was unconstitutional because it failed the due process test of 'fundamental fairness.' We recognize that the introduction of evidence in circumstances like those involved here has the potential to prejudice the jury or unfairly force the defendant to spend time and money relitigating matters considered at the first trial. The question, however, is whether it is acceptable to deal with the potential for abuse through non-constitutional sources like the Federal Rules of Evidence,[4] or whether the introduction of this type of evidence is so extremely unfair that its admission violates 'fundamental conceptions of justice.' United States v. Lovasco, 431 U.S. 783, 790, 97 S.Ct. 2044, 2048, 52 L.Ed.2d 752 (1977).

"Beyond the specific guarantees enumerated in the Bill of Rights, the Due Process Clause has limited operation. We, therefore, have defined the category of infractions that violate 'fundamental fairness' very narrowly. * * * Especially in light of the limiting instructions provided by the trial judge, we cannot hold that the introduction of Henry's testimony merits this kind of condemnation."

UNITED STATES v. LEWIS

United States Court of Appeals, Ninth Circuit, 1988.
837 F.2d 415.

GOODWIN, CIRCUIT JUDGE:

Lawrence Lewis, Jr., was tried and convicted under 18 U.S.C. § 1111 (1982)[1] for the second-degree murder of his two-year-old stepson, Jordan Francis.

4. The Third Circuit, as noted above, found Henry's testimony inadmissible under both Rule 404(b) and Rule 403. 855 F.2d 114, 122 (1988). The United States urges that this was error, but in affirming we need not pass on the validity of the Court of Appeals' judgment in this respect.

1. Section 1111(b) makes a federal offense of any murder committed "[w]ithin

On appeal, the defendant challenges: * * * 3) the trial court's admission of evidence concerning a prior battery of the same child by the defendant.

On the evening of June 17, 1986, the defendant brought his unconscious stepson to the hospital emergency room at the Fort Huachuca Army base in Arizona. Attempts to revive the child were unsuccessful. Examinations by an Army doctor and an Army criminal investigator revealed recent bruises to the child's thigh, arm, back and forehead. An autopsy indicated that the child died from severe brain swelling as a result of blunt force injuries to his head and body.

At trial, the defendant testified that in disciplining the child for defecating on the floor he had hit him with a belt and slapped him on his head before giving him a bath, which the defendant viewed as punishment. He testified that as a child he had been subjected to severe corporal punishment and that he believed such techniques were necessary to discipline children. Because the defendant conceded that he had killed the child, the only issue at trial was whether he possessed the "malice aforethought" that is an element of second-degree murder under 18 U.S.C. § 1111(a) (1982).

* * *

III. Prior Bad Acts

The defendant challenges the district court's decision to admit the testimony of two maintenance workers that they saw the defendant severely punish his stepson six weeks before the child's death. The two workers testified that the defendant had repeatedly hit his stepson on the head and face because the child was unable to put his shoes on. They also testified that they saw the defendant carrying the child to the bedroom while holding a belt in his hand.

The district court ruled pretrial that this prior incident was admissible, stating:

> Well, to show—both the intent and the absence of mistake and surprise. I think that it negates any inference that this is an isolated incident of overreaction.
>
> * * *
>
> Or reaction in blind anger. And it may be that. But it also shows that the defendant had noticed that he was capable of that kind of action, and—capable of the potential infliction of serious harm on the child.

We review the district court's decision to admit evidence of a prior bad act under Fed.R.Evid. 404(b) for an abuse of discretion. *See United States v. Feldman,* 788 F.2d 544, 557 (9th Cir.1986), *cert. denied,* ——

the special * * * territorial jurisdiction of the United States." 18 U.S.C. § 1111(b) (1982).

U.S. ___, 107 S.Ct. 955, 93 L.Ed.2d 1003 (1987). "Relevant evidence of crimes not charged in the indictment is admissible under Fed.R.Evid. 404(b) unless its only relevance is to show criminal disposition." *United States v. Unruh,* 827 F.2d 501, 516 (9th Cir.1987). However, evidence admissible under Fed.R.Evid. 404(b) must be excluded unless its probative value outweighs its prejudicial effect, as required by Fed.R.Evid. 403. *United States v. Bradshaw,* 690 F.2d 704, 709 (9th Cir.1982), *cert. denied,* 463 U.S. 1210, 103 S.Ct. 3543, 77 L.Ed.2d 1392 (1983).

Under Fed.R.Evid. 404(b), evidence of prior acts is admissible to prove intent when "the prior act is similar and close enough in time to be relevant" and "the evidence of the prior act is clear and convincing." *United States v. Hooton,* 662 F.2d 628, 635 (9th Cir.1981), *cert. denied,* 455 U.S. 1004, 102 S.Ct. 1640, 71 L.Ed.2d 873 (1982). The testimony concerning the prior act was relevant because the prior act occurred only six weeks before the child's death and because it involved the defendant's abuse of the child; as the trial court observed, the prior act tended to demonstrate his intent. Evidence of the prior act was clear and convincing, given that two witnesses testified in court—and the defendant admitted—that he had beaten his stepson on that date.

The defendant argues that the testimony should have been excluded under Fed.R.Evid. 403, which allows exclusion where the evidence's "probative value is substantially outweighed by the danger of unfair prejudice." [8]

Evidence of the prior incident had probative value in disproving claims that the defendant lacked intent or that the child died by accident. *See Hooton,* 662 F.2d at 634–35 (admitting evidence of a prior act where lack of intent will be raised as a defense); *see also United States v. Woods,* 484 F.2d 127, 133–34 (4th Cir.) (finding that prior injuries to a child were relevant in proving the defendant's intent and the absence of accident), *cert. denied,* 415 U.S. 979, 94 S.Ct. 1566, 39 L.Ed.2d 875 (1974); *United States v. Harris,* 661 F.2d 138 (10th Cir.1981) (same). Additionally, the testimony was probative because 18 U.S.C. § 1111(a) (1982) requires the government to prove that the defendant acted with "malice aforethought." *See United States v. Celestine,* 510 F.2d 457, 459 (9th Cir.1975) (holding that malice aforethought "may be inferred from circumstances which show 'a wanton and depraved spirit, a mind bent on evil mischief without regard to its consequences' ") (quoting *Government of Virgin Islands v. Lake,* 362 F.2d 770, 774 (3rd Cir.1966)).

8. The defendant also argues that the government could not introduce evidence of prior bad acts in its case in chief because "[i]t is an accepted principle that only after the defense has presented its case can the trial judge know if intent or knowledge or any other element constituting an exception to the exclusion rule is truly a disputed issue in the case." *Hooton* holds that "even in general intent crimes, the government can offer evidence of other acts as part of its case-in-chief when it is obvious that the defense will raise lack of intent as a defense." *Hooton,* 662 F.2d at 635. Because the defendant had admitted that he committed the act, it was obvious that lack of intent would be raised as a defense.

The evidence was not overly prejudicial because the defendant already had admitted beating the child at the time of his death and on other occasions. Given his admission, we must reject the defendant's claim that the evidence was highly prejudicial because "a jury is likely to infer that, having once committed a crime, the defendant is likely to do it again." *See United States v. Bejar–Matrecios,* 618 F.2d 81, 84 (9th Cir.1980).

The trial court did not abuse its discretion in admitting evidence of the defendant's prior act. The court properly instructed the jury that the prior bad act did not imply that the defendant had a criminal propensity. We therefore find no reversible error.

* * *

[Affirmed.]

Notes

(1) "[T]he distinction between specific intent and general intent is of little help in deciding when intent is really an issue. All crimes other than those imposing strict liability require a degree of culpability, either knowledge, intent, recklessness or willfulness. Whether there is a material issue as to this element of intent depends not on the statutory definition of the offense but on the circumstances of the case and on the nature of the defense. * * * A defendant who admits committing an act but relies on innocence, mistake, or lack of knowledge to exculpate him has made an issue of intent. A defendant who denies participation in an act raises no discrete issue of intent and if the act be proven the intent will usually be inferred. * * * It is only after the defense is presented that the trial judge can know if intent or knowledge or any exception to the exclusion rule is truly a disputed issue in the trial." United States v. Adderly, 529 F.2d 1178, 1181–82 (5th Cir.1976).

(2) "We have instructed that normally evidence of a defendant's prior conviction introduced to show knowledge or intent should not be admitted until the conclusion of the defendant's case, since by that time the court is in a better position to determine whether knowledge or intent is truly a disputed issue and whether the probative value of the evidence outweighs the risk of unfair prejudice." United States v. Alessi, 638 F.2d 466, 477 (2d Cir.1980).

(3) "When the defendant makes intent an important trial issue by taking the stand and 'professing the innocence of his intent,' the defendant waives any right to contest the government's prior presentation of evidence to the contrary." United States v. Smith, 726 F.2d 183, 186 n. 3 (5th Cir.1984).

(4) "[O]ne theory of relevance depends on the doctrine of chances—the more frequently an unusual event occurs, the less likely that it is accidental. Wigmore offers a simple illustration. If A and B go hunting, and B shoots once in A's direction, we may easily conclude B stumbled and fired unintentionally. But if the same event occurs several times, each successive event reduces the chances that B acted unintentionally. The doctrine of chances employs commonsense reasoning based on everyday experience,

and it does not require an inference to the actor's character and thence to the actor's conduct." Wydick, Character Evidence: A Guided Tour of the Grotesque Structure, 21 U.C.Davis L.Rev. 123, 166–67 (1987).

UNITED STATES v. WILLIFORD, 764 F.2d 1493, 1498 (11th Cir. 1985). "The effect of the Willifords' offer to stipulate to intent is not clear in this circuit. Cases dealing specifically with intent state uniformly that if the defendant unequivocally removes intent, as through a stipulation, the extrinsic act evidence cannot be admitted for the purpose of proving intent. E.g., United States v. Russo, 717 F.2d 545, 552 (11th Cir.1983); United States v. Holman, 680 F.2d 1340, 1349 (11th Cir.1982); United States v. Bulman, 667 F.2d 1374, 1382 (11th Cir.), cert. denied, 456 U.S. 1010, 102 S.Ct. 2305, 73 L.Ed.2d 1307 (1982); United States v. Roberts, 619 F.2d 379, 383 n. 2 (5th Cir.1980).

"None of the cases specifically addresses the issue of whether a defendant may force the government to accede or the court to accept such a stipulation. Other circuits have held that whether to accept a stipulation is a matter in the discretion of the trial court. See, e.g., United States v. Pedroza, 750 F.2d 187, 201 (2d Cir.1984); but see United States v. Mohel, 604 F.2d 748, 753 (2d Cir.1979) (unequivocal offer of stipulation removes intent as issue).

* * *

"We have held that a trial court did not abuse its discretion in refusing to require the government to accept a proffered stipulation that defendant was a convicted felon when the charges included a felony conviction as an element of the offense. United States v. O'Shea, 724 F.2d 1514, 1516 (11th Cir.1984) ('a party may not preclude his adversary's offer of proof by admission or stipulation,' citing Parr v. United States, 255 F.2d 86, 88 (5th Cir.), cert. denied, 358 U.S. 824, 79 S.Ct. 40, 3 L.Ed.2d 64 (1958)). This circuit has refused to adopt a per se rule either for or against admission of evidence when that evidence is relevant to an issue to which the defendant offers to stipulate. Rather, we analyze the offer to stipulate as one factor in making the Rule 403 determination. *O'Shea,* 724 F.2d at 1516, 1517.

"We need not reconcile the tension between these two lines of cases. The evidence of the cocaine negotiation was properly admitted to explain the story of the crime.

"Evidence of an uncharged offense arising from the same series of transactions as that charged is not an extrinsic offense within Rule 404(b)."

UNITED STATES v. BENTON, 637 F.2d 1052, 1056–57 (5th Cir. 1981). "Motive has been defined as 'the reason that nudges the will and prods the mind to indulge the criminal intent.' United States v. Beechum, 582 F.2d at 915 n. 15 quoting Slough & Knightly, Other Vices, Other Crimes, 41 Iowa L.Rev. 325, 328 (1956). See also United States v. Day, 591 F.2d 861, 874 (D.C.Cir.1978). While motive is not an element of any offenses charged against appellant, it may be evidence of identity or of deliberateness, malice or specific intent which are elements of the crimes. See McCormick on Evidence, § 190 at 450–51 (2d ed. 1972). We believe that appellant's knowledge that Zambito might implicate him in the Florida homicides constituted a motive for appellant wanting to kill Zambito to obtain his silence.[2] This evidence of motivation was relevant as tending to show the participation of appellant in the crime and to show malice or intent which are elements of the crimes charged."

STATE v. LEFEVER, 102 Wash.2d 777, 690 P.2d 574, 578 (1984). "We concur in the views expressed by the California and Alaska courts in their refusal to admit evidence of heroin addiction to show a link between the robberies and the addictions where the issue was identification. * * * Even if the heroin habit could be used to show motive, where identification is the key element to be proved, the fact that defendant was a heroin user had limited probative value to show that he committed the robberies. When, as here, identification is crucial and eyewitness testimony as to identity is confused at best, it is error for the prosecution to introduce evidence of defendant's addiction to heroin. The resultant prejudice to one accused of a crime completely overwhelms any possible relevance or probativeness."

UNITED STATES v. GREEN, 648 F.2d 587, 591–92 (9th Cir.1981). "Appellants contend that the testimony in the Government's case in chief with respect to appellants' involvement in the tableting and marketing of LSD between 1972 and 1975 was erroneously admitted and does not come within any of the exceptions of Fed.Rule of Evid. 404(b) * * *.

* * *

"The Government argues that the contested evidence was properly admitted to show appellants' knowledge, and their plan and motive to 'frame' Allard and Messenger. Neither party has discussed 'opportunity' as a basis for admissibility, which we consider more pertinent under the facts of this case.

"The appellants were convicted of conspiracy to obstruct justice, conspiracy to violate citizens' rights, and conspiracy to make false

2. The desire to silence a potential adverse witness is a frequently encountered motive for murder. See, e.g., United States v. Harvey, 526 F.2d 529 (2d Cir. 1975), cert. denied 424 U.S. 956, 96 S.Ct. 1432, 47 L.Ed.2d 362 (1976) and case collected in 2 Wigmore on Evidence, § 390 at 423–25 n. 2 (Chadbourn rev'd. ed. 1979).

statements to a government agency. In sum, they were convicted of conspiring to 'frame' the members of Technichem. This required a combination of talents and associations—a working knowledge of illicit drug operations, an awareness of the components of and procedures for making LSD, knowledge of persons in a position and of a character which subjected them to suspicion of drug violations, and connections with a 'reliable' person educated in the illegal drug business who was personally inclined and capable of carrying out the actual 'planting' of the drugs in a convincing manner. Without this specialized background neither of the appellants would have had the capacity, i.e., an opportunity, to commit the crimes charged.

" 'Opportunity' is an express exception of Rule 404(b). Though the word has been little used by the courts it evidently is intended to cover all or a part of a category called 'capacity' (see 22 Wright & Graham, Federal Practice and Procedure: Evidence § 5241 at p. 485 (1978); Wigmore, Code of Evidence §§ 386, 400 (3d ed. 1942)),[5] and has been applied in similar circumstances. For example, in United States v. McPartlin, 595 F.2d 1321, 1343 (7 Cir.), cert. denied, 444 U.S. 833, 100 S.Ct. 65, 62 L.Ed.2d 43 (1979), the court found that evidence that a defendant charged with bribery of public officials was acquainted with a notoriously corrupt state official was relevant to show that he had the kind of political connections to accomplish the charged acts of bribery. See also United States v. Jones, 438 F.2d 461, 466 (7 Cir.1971), where the court found that evidence that a defendant possessed cocaine was admissible to establish that he had the ability to make the sale charged in the indictment.

"Evidence is deemed admissible under Rule 404(b) on appeal if it is admissible on any ground. United States v. Gocke, 507 F.2d 820, 824 n. 4 (8 Cir.1974), cert. denied, 420 U.S. 979, 95 S.Ct. 1407, 43 L.Ed.2d 660 (1975); see SEC v. Chenerey Corp., 318 U.S. 80, 88, 63 S.Ct. 454, 459, 87 L.Ed. 626 (1943). The exceptions of knowledge, plan, motive and opportunity are all closely related. It is unnecessary to specify the exception within which a particular line of inquiry or piece of evidence is admissible. It is enough that the evidence is relevant to an issue in the case other than a defendant's criminal propensity. It is, of course, for the trial court to make the initial determination of relevancy,[6] and

5. Though the draftsman of the Uniform Rules subsequently wrote a manual for practitioners which did not list 'opportunity' among the permissible uses of character evidence it did include the actor's 'ability or capacity to do the wrong.' See 1 Morgan, Basic Problems of Evidence, p. 214 (1961). 22 Wright & Graham § 5241 at p. 485.

6. We recognize the problems confronting a trial judge in determining when evidence is inadmissible under Rule 404 as demonstrative of a criminal propensity or admissible under one of the specified exceptions. The question is more easily resolved, however, where the crimes charged are not of a type necessarily connected in any way to the defendant's past conduct. If the crimes charged here had to do with the sale or distribution of drugs, then the challenged evidence would go more directly to the issue of propensity. Here, however, the crimes charged involve a conspiracy to 'frame' private citizens; the challenged evidence does nothing to establish a propensity for this type of activity, but only establishes the capability of carrying out the elaborate conspiracy charged.

the evidence must be carefully scrutinized to determine probative value. United States v. Aims Back, 588 F.2d 1283, 1287 (9 Cir.1979)."

UNITED STATES v. WOODS, 613 F.2d 629, 634–35 (6th Cir.1980), cert. denied, 446 U.S. 920, 100 S.Ct. 1856, 64 L.Ed.2d 275 (1980). "Prior crimes evidence is admissible if there was a 'plan' (an agreement to commit a series of crimes) or a 'signature' (as device so unusual or distinctive as to be like a signature). F.R.Evid. 404(b). We find the circumstances of this case reveal a 'signature' on the crimes insofar as each was an armed robbery by robbers wearing ski masks, goggles, and jumpsuits and using a stolen vehicle for a getaway car. These factors constitute an unusual and distinctive pattern and since the defendants had been connected to the prior robbery by fingerprints and Woods' confession to it, it would have been permissible to admit that evidence under Rule 404(b)."

UNITED STATES v. POWELL, 587 F.2d 443, 448 (9th Cir.1978). "The probative value of evidence of other crimes where the issue is identity depends upon the extent to which it raises an inference that the perpetrator of the prior offenses was the perpetrator of the offense in issue. Both the existence and the strength of an inference proceeds through an evaluation of the similarities between the prior offense and the charged crime. Thus, if the characteristics of both the prior offense and the charged offense are not in any way distinctive, but are similar to numerous other crimes committed by persons other than the defendant, no inference of identity can arise. An inference of identity from prior crimes can only arise when the elements of the prior offenses and the charged offense, singly or together, are sufficiently distinctive to warrant an inference that the person who committed the prior offense also committed the offense on trial. (United States v. Webb (9th Cir.1972) 466 F.2d 1352.) The probative value of evidence of other crimes on the issue of identity always depends upon the strength of the inference; when the inference of identity is weak, evidence of prior crimes should be excluded because under such circumstances the prejudicial effect of the evidence inevitably outweighs the probative value of that evidence. (United States v. Myers (5th Cir.1977) 550 F.2d 1036; United States v. Foutz (4th Cir.1976) 540 F.2d 733, 2 Weinstein's Evidence ¶ 404[09] at 404–61 et seq.)

"The 1969 marihuana offense bore no resemblance to the offense charged, except that marihuana trafficking was involved. The 1973 marihuana offense resembled the offense charged only in that large quantities of marihuana were stored in a house, but nothing sets that prior offense apart from any other marihuana trafficking that involves large quantities of marihuana."

UNITED STATES v. STEVENS, 935 F.2d 1380, 1401–02, 1404–05 (3d Cir.1991). "To shore up his theory that Smith and McCormack misidentified him as the perpetrator, Stevens sought to introduce under Fed.R.Evid. 404(b) the testimony of Tyrone Mitchell, the victim of a similar crime at Fort Dix. Three days after Smith and McCormack were assaulted, Mitchell, a black man, was robbed at gunpoint by another black man who, according to Mitchell's description, resembled Smith's and McCormack's attacker. Unlike Smith and McCormack, however, Mitchell stated that Stevens was not his assailant. Stevens reasons that Mitchell's failure to identify him tends to establish that he did not assault Smith and McCormack. The syllogism goes as follows. In view of the many parallels between the two crimes, one person very likely committed both; and because Stevens was exonerated by Mitchell, a black man whose identification (or lack thereof) is arguably more reliable than that of the two white victims, Stevens was not that person. The critical question is, of course, one of degree of similarity.

"The similarities between the Mitchell robbery and the Smith and McCormack robbery/sexual assault are significant. Both crimes: (1) took place within a few hundred yards of one another; (2) were armed robberies; (3) involved a handgun; (4) occurred between 9:30 p.m. and 10:30 p.m.; (5) were perpetrated on military personnel; and (6) involved a black assailant who was described similarly by his victims. Indeed, based on these similarities, the United States Army Criminal Investigation Division came to believe, initially, that the same person had committed both crimes. * * *

"An additional, and even more striking, parallel subsequently developed which made the similarities between the two crimes more difficult to dismiss as mere coincidence. Mitchell was robbed of various items, including his military identification card. This card later was used to cash two stolen checks at the Fort Meade exchange in Maryland. Significantly, McCormack's stolen money order, like Mitchell's identification, also ended up near Fort Meade: it was cashed by someone other than Stevens at the Odenton Pharmacy located across the street from Fort Meade. That the fruits of the Mitchell and McCormack robberies, which occurred within days of one another at Fort Dix, New Jersey, both surfaced near Fort Meade, Maryland, is undoubtedly probative that the same individual committed both offenses.

"The analytical basis for Stevens's proffer of Mitchell's testimony was a rarely-used variant of Rule 404(b), known as 'reverse 404(b).' In contrast to ordinary 'other crimes' evidence, which is used to incriminate criminal defendants, 'reverse 404(b)' evidence is utilized to exonerate defendants. * * *

* * *

"* * * In our view, the most persuasive treatment of 'reverse 404(b)' evidence is found in [State v.] Garfole, [76 N.J. 445, 388 A.2d 587 (1978)] wherein the New Jersey Supreme Court observed that a lower standard of similarity should govern 'reverse 404(b)' evidence because prejudice to the defendant is not a factor. We agree with the reasoning of *Garfole* and with its holding that the admissibility of 'reverse 404(b)' evidence depends on a straightforward balancing of the evidence's probative value against considerations such as undue waste of time and confusion of the issues. Recasting this standard in terms of the Federal Rules of Evidence, we therefore conclude that a defendant may introduce 'reverse 404(b)' evidence so long as its probative value under Rule 401 is not substantially outweighed by Rule 403 considerations."

UNITED STATES v. KREZDORN, 639 F.2d 1327, 1331–32 (5th Cir.1981), cert. denied, 465 U.S. 1066, 104 S.Ct. 1416, 79 L.Ed.2d 742 (1984). "Since a 'plan' is not an element of the offense with which Krezdorn was charged,[7] evidence showing a plan must be relevant to some ultimate issue in the case. The contested issues in this case are (1) whether the signatures of Immigration Inspector Francisco Valdez on the applications were forged and, if so, (2) whether Krezdorn forged them. Evidence of extrinsic offenses can be used, inter alia, to establish the identity of a wrongdoer or the doing of a criminal act by raising a preliminary inference of a plan. For instance, evidence of an extrinsic offense may be admissible when it logically raises an inference that the defendant was engaged in a larger, more comprehensive plan. The existence of a plan then tends to prove that the defendant committed the charged crime, since commission of that crime would lead to the completion of the overall plan. This use of extrinsic evidence to establish the existence of a plan is allowed by Rule 404(b) because,

> [it] involves no inference as to the defendant's character; instead his conduct is said to be caused by his conscious commitment to a course of conduct of which the charged crime is only a part. The other crime is admitted to show this larger goal rather than to show defendant's propensity to commit crimes.

22 C. Wright & K. Graham, Federal Practice & Procedure: Evidence § 5244, at 500 (1978) (footnotes omitted).

"The thirty-two additional forgeries do not tend to establish the existence of a larger goal of which the four charged forgeries were only a part. The four forgeries for which Krezdorn was indicted show that Krezdorn was engaged in forgery. That there were thirty-six instead of only four forged I–190's does not establish anything different. It would, at best, merely demonstrate the repetition of similar criminal acts, thus

7. The existence of a plan would be directly at issue in, for instance, a conspiracy charge.

indicating Krezdorn's propensity to commit this crime. Evidence of other crimes is not admissible for this purpose.

"The Court in *Beechum* discussed in some detail another circumstance in which extrinsic evidence would be considered part of a common plan or scheme: 'If the uncharged offense is "so linked together in point of time and circumstances with the crime charged that one cannot be fully shown without proving the other, the general rule of exclusion does not apply."' 582 F.2d at 912 n. 15 (quoting Slough & Knightly, Other Vices, Other Crimes, 41 Iowa L.Rev. 325, 331 (1956)). In the instant case, the district court specifically relied upon this exception to allow the introduction of the contested evidence.

"This exception applies when evidence of uncharged offenses is necessary to explain the circumstances or setting of the charged crime; in such a situation, the extrinsic evidence 'complete[s] the story of the crime on trial by proving its immediate context of happenings near in time and place.'[8] McCormick, Law of Evidence § 190, at 448 (2d ed. E. Cleary 1972) (footnote omitted), quoted in 2 J. Weinstein & M. Berger, Weinstein's Evidence ¶ 404[16], at 404–85 (1980). The justification for this exception is that the evidence is being admitted for a purpose other than to prove propensity:

> It may be quite impossible to prove the case without revealing other crimes. The court cannot 'fragmentize the event under inquiry.' If an understanding of the event in question, or if a description of the immediate circumstances reveals other crimes than those charged, exclusion will lead to a highly artificial situation at the trial making understandable testimony unlikely.

2 J. Weinstein & M. Berger ¶ 404[10], at 404–60 (footnotes omitted). Some courts have labeled this exception *res gestae*, an appellation that tends merely to obscure the analysis underlying the admissibility of the evidence.

"The district court admitted the contested evidence at trial pursuant to this exception, stating that the extrinsic offense evidence was 'so closely blended and inextricably wound up with the crimes charged as to constitute part of the plan or system of criminal action involved.' The trial court misapplied the exception in this instance. The thirty-two extrinsic forgeries are not necessary to explain the circumstances surrounding the forgery of the four applications for which Krezdorn was charged. Evidence that the defendant allegedly committed the charged crime more times than he was charged with does not constitute

8. A closely related concept is that of admitting evidence of an inseparably interrelated uncharged crime because it is viewed as part of the same crime as the charged crime. Since it is part of the charged crime and not a separate crime, Rule 404(b) does not apply to exclude it. See United States v. Aleman, 592 F.2d 881, 885–86 (5th Cir.1979). 'It matters little whether the evidence is viewed as lying beyond the scope of Rule 404, or as satisfying the test of Rule 404(b) since it is being used to enhance the trier's understanding of the event, and not to prove propensity.' 2 J. Weinstein & M. Berger, Weinstein's Evidence ¶ 404[10], at 404–61 (1980).

part of the 'system of criminal action.' The admission of this evidence was an abuse of discretion."

UNITED STATES v. LEVY, 731 F.2d 997, 1002–03 (2d Cir.1984). "Courts and commentators have struggled with the question of when an act or crime is an 'other' act or crime as defined by Rule 404(b). See 22 C. Wright & K. Graham, Federal Practice and Procedure, § 5239, at 445–49 (1978). When the acts or crimes sought to be introduced occurred contemporaneously with the indicted crime, some commentators argue that such contemporaneous crimes or acts are outside of the scope of Rule 404(b) because such crimes or acts are so interwoven with the indicted crime that it would be impossible to prove one without revealing the other. Commentators have suggested that the admission of evidence of contemporaneous crimes appears not to substantially prejudice the defendant. They argue that the other crime or act arises from the same transaction as the indicted crime and the evidence of the 'interwoven' crime is obviously not offered solely to prove the defendant's criminal propensity. See 22 C. Wright & K. Graham, Federal Practice and Procedure, § 5239, at 448 (1978).

"Some courts have extended this inextricably interwoven concept to allow admission of the evidence of crimes or acts occurring prior to or subsequent to the indicted crime. The district court cites several of the cases to support its analysis. In United States v. Aleman, 592 F.2d 881 (5th Cir.1979), the defendant had been indicted for possession and distribution of heroin. The defendant admitted his involvement in heroin trafficking during negotiations for the sale of an ounce of cocaine. The court held that the evidence of the cocaine transaction was admissible because it would have been confusing to have testimony on the admissions without a description of the circumstances surrounding the conversation. In United States v. Torres, 685 F.2d 921 (5th Cir.1982), the Fifth Circuit also allowed the admission of evidence of a sample transaction between DEA agents and defendants that had preceded the larger purchase for which defendants were indicted. Because the plans for the larger transaction had been laid at the time of the sample transaction, the Fifth Circuit ruled that the sample transaction did not constitute ' "other acts" of the type contemplated by Rule 404(b).' 685 F.2d at 924. The Eleventh Circuit adopted the Fifth Circuit's approach in United States v. Costa, 691 F.2d 1358 (11th Cir.1982), where an informant sought to testify about a chain of drug dealings with the defendant that had preceded and led to the sale for which the defendant was indicted. The court upheld the admission of the testimony because 'it formed an integral and natural part of the witness's accounts of the circumstances surrounding the offenses for which the defendant was indicted.' 691 F.2d at 1361.

"Other circuits have included evidence of inextricably interwoven crimes or acts within the scope of Rule 404(b) and have determined the admissibility of the evidence as an exception to Rule 404(b) and under the balancing provisions of Rule 403. The First Circuit in United States v. D'Alora, 585 F.2d 16 (1st Cir.1978), applied Rules 404(b) and 403 to evaluate the admissibility of marked money, paid to a codefendant in a previous drug transaction found on the defendant's person during an arrest for a later drug transaction. The court determined that the evidence was necessary 'to complete the story of the crime,' id. at 20 (quoting 2 J. Weinstein & M. Berger, Weinstein's Evidence, § 404[09] at 404–57 (1975)), found its probative value outweighed its prejudicial impact and ruled in favor of its admission. In United States v. Masters, 622 F.2d 83 (4th Cir.1980), the evidence sought to be admitted was the defendant's descriptions of his other crimes taped during negotiations for illegal gun sales. The Fourth Circuit found the evidence admissible under Rules 404(b) and 403 because the ' "unchanged offense [was] 'so linked together in point of time and circumstances with the crime charged that one cannot be fully shown without proving the other. * * * ' " ' Id. at 86 (quoting United States v. Beechum, 582 F.2d 898, 912 n. 15 (5th Cir.1978), cert. denied, 440 U.S. 920, 99 S.Ct. 1244, 59 L.Ed.2d 472 (1979)).

"The fact that evidence of the sample transaction with Simon Assraf was closely connected with the Elimalich/Dilson transaction did not obviate the need to assess evidence of the sample transaction under Rules 404(b) and 403. The sample and the one ounce transactions occurred at different locations, at different times and with different people. The argument that an act with these distinctions from the charged offense is not 'other' for the purposes of Rule 404(b) is not persuasive."

STATE v. GOODSON, 690 S.W.2d 155, 159 (Mo.App.1985). "State v. Tillman, 454 S.W.2d 923 (Mo.1970) involves facts similar to the present case. Defendant was convicted of carrying a concealed weapon. The arresting officer testified that he found two weapons concealed in a folded jacket on the rear seat of an automobile where defendant and others had been. Over objection the court permitted the officer to testify on direct examination that the occupants of the automobile were arrested for murder and robbery. The state attempted to justify the testimony on the grounds that the jury was entitled to know the circumstances of the arrest. The court rejected that position and refused to recognize 'circumstance of arrest' as an exception to the general rule. *Tillman,* 454 S.W.2d at 926.

"We find that the circumstances of arrest justification is not an exception to the general rule and the court erred in permitting the testimony of defendant's present possession of marijuana. The facts of the crime of carrying a concealed weapon had been fully presented prior to the testimony concerning the officer's search of the car. There was no evidence that the defendant was under the influence of or that his actions in carrying the weapon were in any way related to marijuana. At trial the state justified the inquiry as part of the circumstances of the arrest, a doctrine rejected by the supreme court in *Tillman.* On appeal the state relies upon the complete and coherent picture exception discussed in State v. King, 588 S.W.2d at 150. We find that exception not applicable to the present facts where the charge was carrying a concealed weapon and all the necessary evidence for conviction of that crime was before the jury without the mention of marijuana found in an automobile. The proof of the crime required no further explanation so as to permit the jury to have a complete or coherent picture."

UNITED STATES v. MILLER, 895 F.2d 1431, 1436 (D.C.Cir.1990), cert. denied, ___ U.S. ___, 111 S.Ct. 79, 112 L.Ed.2d 52 (1990). "[Rule 404(b)] was intended not to define the set of permissible purposes for which bad-acts evidence may be admitted but rather to define the *one impermissible* purpose for such evidence. 'Only one series of evidential hypotheses is forbidden in criminal cases by Rule 404: a man who commits a crime probably has a defect of character; a man with such a defect of character is more likely than men generally to have committed the act in question.' 2 J. Weinstein & M. Berger, supra note 9, ¶ 404[8] at 404–52. In other words, under Rule 404(b), *any* purpose for which bad-acts evidence is introduced is a proper purpose so long as the evidence is not offered *solely* to prove character. The Government's right to introduce bad-acts evidence for purposes other than showing a defendant's criminal propensity is by no means unlimited. But the limits derive from the 'general strictures limiting admissibility such as Rules 402 and 403,' not from Rule 404(b). *Huddleston,* 108 S.Ct. at 1500."

Notes

(1) In Jones v. State, 376 S.W.2d 842 (Tex.Crim.App.1964), Jones was charged with stealing money from Hause. Hause testified that Jones entered his place of business, acted drunk, grabbed one man and "propositioned" him, fell, and grabbed Hause when he helped her up. After Jones left, Hause discovered that money was missing from his billfold. The state was permitted to show that Jones had behaved similarly in two other business premises and that on each occasion money disappeared from men's persons. Jones' conviction was affirmed. "The evidence was offered and was admitted only for the purpose of showing identity, intent, motive, malice or common plan or scheme. * * * The intent of the appellant in making physical contact with Mr. Hause was material and was uncertain. Proof that the money was taken as well as the intent of the appellant rested upon the circumstances. The two collateral offenses show more than a similarity in results. They show a common plan and systematic course of action." Id. at 843.

(2) In United States v. Woods, 484 F.2d 127 (4th Cir.1973), cert. denied, 415 U.S. 979, 94 S.Ct. 1566, 39 L.Ed.2d 875 (1974), Woods was convicted of murder of her infant foster son Paul, who died after admission to a hospital for the fifth time with breathing difficulties. The government was permitted to show that over a period of twenty-five years at least twenty episodes of cyanosis (lack of oxygen) occurred among nine children who were in defendant's custody or to whom she had access. Seven of the children died. This evidence was held admissible "to prove that (a) Paul's death was the result of culpable homicide and not of natural causes, and (b) defendant was the perpetrator of the crime. * * * While we conclude that the evidence was admissible generally under the accident and signature exceptions, we prefer to place our decision upon a broader ground. * * * [W]e think that the evidence would prove that a crime had been committed because of the remoteness of the possibility that so many infants in the care and custody of defendant would suffer cyanotic episodes and respiratory difficulties if they were not induced by the defendant's wrongdoing, and at the same time, would prove the identity of defendant as the wrongdoer. * * * [W]e think that its relevance clearly outweighs its prejudicial effect on the jury." 484 F.2d at 133–35.

(3) In United States v. Micke, 859 F.2d 473 (7th Cir.1988), defendant was convicted of aiding preparation of a fraudulent income tax return. "The parties agreed that documents * * * had been executed in January, but backdated to December by defendant. The sole issue at trial was whether the deal had been agreed on in December, or subsequently in January. If * * * the latter, the backdating and the returns were fraudulent." Evidence of an offer by defendant to another person to backdate instruments to a prior year was held admissible "to show defendant's intent to commit the crimes charged in the indictment." Id. at 478–79. A dissenting judge disagreed, saying, "In this case the only issue was whether the taxpayers made their agreements in January, when the documents were executed, or in December, when the documents were dated. Testimony that defendant offered to backdate documents for a different taxpayer was wholly irrelevant in establishing the correct date of the agreements at issue." Id. at 481.

(4) "The laundry list [of Rule 404(b)] is unfortunate because it tempts litigants, and sometimes judges, simply to recite a few items from the list, using incantation rather than analysis to justify admission of specific act evidence. When specific acts evidence is offered, the judge should *require* the proponent to define its relevance. What fact, other than character, is the proponent trying to prove? Is that fact 'of consequence' in the case? Does the evidence really 'help to prove' that fact?" Wydick, Character Evidence: A Guided Tour of the Grotesque Structure, 21 U.C.Davis L.Rev. 123, 166–67 (1987).

ELLIOTT v. STATE

Supreme Court of Wyoming, 1979.
600 P.2d 1044.

THOMAS, JUSTICE.

The major question presented in this case is the admissibility in a trial for second degree sexual assault of testimony of an older sister of the victim concerning prior attempts of a similar nature involving her as a victim. * * *

* * *

We deal with the issue of the testimony of the older sister as to prior sexual assaults in the context of Rule 404(b) and Rule 403, Wyoming Rules of Evidence. Rule 404(b), W.R.E., provides as follows:

> "(b) *Other crimes, wrongs, or acts.*—Evidence of other crimes, wrongs, or acts is not admissible to prove the character of a person in order to show that he acted in conformity therewith. It may, however, be admissible for other purposes, such as proof of motive, opportunity, intent, preparation, plan, knowledge, identity, or absence of mistake or accident."

Rule 403, W.R.E., provides as follows:

> "Although relevant, evidence may be excluded if its probative value is substantially outweighed by the danger of unfair prejudice, confusion of the issues, or misleading the jury, or by considerations of undue delay, waste of time, or needless presentation of cumulative evidence."

Wyoming unquestionably is committed to the general rule that evidence of other crimes or wrongdoing normally is not admissible in the trial of a criminal case. *Newell v. State,* Wyo., 548 P.2d 8 (1976); *Dorador v. State,* Wyo., 520 P.2d 230 (1974); *Gabrielson v. State,* Wyo., 510 P.2d 534 (1973); *Rosencrance v. State,* 33 Wyo. 360, 239 P. 952 (1933). In prior cases, however, the court has recognized that in the context of sexual offenses other similar acts may be admitted if they involved the victim in the charged offense. *State v. Koch,* 64 Wyo. 175, 189 P.2d 162 (1948); *State v. Quirk,* 38 Wyo. 462, 268 P. 189 (1928); *Strand v. State,* 36 Wyo. 78, 252 P. 1030 (1927).

Our analysis of cases from other jurisdictions leads to the conclusion that in recent years a preponderance of the courts have sustained the admissibility of the testimony of third persons as to prior or subsequent similar crimes, wrongs or acts in cases involving sexual offenses. Among the grounds relied upon for the admissibility of such evidence is that it is admissible to show motive or to show plan, with various phrases being used by the courts to describe those concepts. *State v. Thomas,* 110 Ariz. 106, 515 P.2d 851 (1973); *Fields v. State,* 255 Ark. 540, 502 S.W.2d 480 (1973); *People v. Fritts,* 72 Cal.App.3d 319, 140 Cal.Rptr. 94 (1977); *People v. Covert,* 249 Cal.App.2d 81, 57 Cal.Rptr. 220 (1967); *State v. Hauck,* 172 Conn. 140, 374 A.2d 150 (1976); *Hunt v. State,* 233 Ga. 329, 211 S.E.2d 288 (1974); *Staggers v. State,* 120 Ga.App. 875, 172 S.E.2d 462 (1969); *Thornton v. State,* Ind., 376 N.E.2d 492 (1978); *Merry v. State,* Ind.App., 335 N.E.2d 249 (1975); *Thompson v. State,* 162 Ind.App. 381, 319 N.E.2d 670 (1974); *People v. Gonzales,* 60 Ill.App.3d 980, 17 Ill.Dec. 901, 377 N.E.2d 91 (1978); *People v. Middleton,* 38 Ill.App.3d 984, 350 N.E.2d 223 (1976); *State v. Drake,* Iowa, 219 N.W.2d 492 (1974); *State v. Hampton,* 215 Kan. 907, 529 P.2d 127 (1974); *People v. Burton,* 28 Mich.App. 253, 184 N.W.2d 336 (1970); *State v. Jensen,* 153 Mont. 233, 455 P.2d 631 (1969); *State v. Hoffmeyer,*

187 Neb. 701, 193 N.W.2d 760 (1972); *Simpson v. State,* Nev., 587 P.2d 1319 (1978); *Jett v. State,* Okl.Cr., 525 P.2d 1247 (1974); *State v. Jackson,* 82 Ohio App. 318, 81 N.E.2d 546 (1948); *McKinney v. State,* Tex.Cr.App., 505 S.W.2d 536 (1974); *Hendrickson v. State,* 61 Wis.2d 275, 212 N.W.2d 481 (1973); *State v. Tarrell,* 74 Wis.2d 647, 247 N.W.2d 696 (1976).

We note that in cases involving sexual assaults, such as incest, and statutory rape with family members as the victims, the courts in recent years have almost uniformly admitted such testimony. See for example, *People v. Fritts,* supra; *People v. Covert,* supra; *Staggers v. State,* supra; *Merry v. State,* supra; *Simpson v. State,* supra; *Jett v. State,* supra; *State v. Jackson,* supra; *Hendrickson v. State,* supra. The description of the events by the victim's sister here, together with the testimony of the victim, persuades us that the conduct described was sufficiently similar to pass the test of relevancy under Rule 404(b), W.R.E., and was admissible for the purpose of proving the motive of the appellant.

According to these other courts, the remoteness of the other conduct is a factor to be considered in determining the question of relevancy. In this instance the testimony of the older sister described a time frame of not more than three years prior to this instance, which would not inhibit admissibility of her testimony as involving acts that are too remote.

As we have indicated, some courts in comparable circumstances have relied upon the common design or plan manifested by the similarity of the prior crimes, wrongs, or acts to justify their admissibility. That reasoning well might fit these circumstances. The conduct described by the witnesses was sufficiently similar to meet that requirement as set forth in the decisions of other courts. In this particular instance, however, we conclude that admissibility of the evidence is justified as proof of motive. In *Valerio v. State,* Wyo., 429 P.2d 317 (1967), we cited several cases as having held that "testimony about one's previous criminal activity can be introduced in the current trial if the purpose of such introduction is to establish identity, guilty knowledge, intent or motive." In *Thompson v. United States,* 144 F. 14, 18 (1st Cir.1906), the court said:

> "In the sense of the criminal law, motive has been well enough described as 'that which leads or tempts the mind to indulge in a criminal act,' and it is something that may be resorted to as a legitimate help in arriving at the ultimate act in question. * * *"

In Webster's New International Dictionary, Unabridged, page 1475 (G. & C. Merriam Co., Publishers, 1961), there appear, among others, the following definitions of motive and its synonyms:

> "* * * something within a person (as a need, idea, organic state, or emotion) that incites him to action * * * the consideration or object influencing a choice or prompting an action * * * syn motive, spring,

impulse, incentive, inducement, spur, and goad, can mean in common, a stimulus prompting a person to act in a particular way. * * *"

In *State v. Bond,* 12 Idaho 424, 86 P. 43 (1906), the court pointed out that motive is an inferential fact which may be inferred from any previous occurrences having reference to and connected with the commission of the offense.

Turning to the application of these concepts here, we have a case in which a victim whose testimony is corroborated by fresh complaint and some apparent injury, testifying that criminal conduct occurred. The defendant testified that no such conduct occurred, and ascribed a motive to the victim for testifying falsely. Given this evidentiary conflict a finder of fact would be extremely interested in other information that might be available to help resolve the ultimate issue. Evidence of motive would be such information. One who is a paraphiliac, whose preference or addiction for unusual sexual practices occurs in the form of pedophilia, could well be recognized as having a motive to commit the acts complained of by the victim. The fact finder could infer from the acts complained of by the older sister that Elliott was so motivated. Such information would be helpful to any professional in determining whether Elliott was so afflicted. We conclude that on this basis the conduct described by the older sister in her testimony passes the test of relevancy under Rule 404(b), W.R.E., and was admissible for the purpose of proving the motive of the appellant. See e.g., *People v. Fritts,* supra; *Hendrickson v. State,* supra; *State v. Jackson,* supra; and *Staggers v. State,* supra.

The determination of admissibility of the testimony of the victim's older sister under Rule 404(b), W.R.E., is only the first step in connection with the ultimate ruling admitting the evidence. Under Rule 403, W.R.E., in each such instance the trial court is called upon to weigh the probative value against the danger of unfair prejudice, confusion of the issues or misleading the jury, among other factors. The record does not disclose a specific consideration by the trial court of this requirement in this instance.[1] In every such instance it is desirable for the trial court to require a proffer of the evidence urged as admissible under Rule 404(b), W.R.E. See Rule 103(c), W.R.E. In that way the trial court can know before ruling on the admissibility under Rule 404(b), W.R.E., exactly what testimony will be forthcoming, and can then perform its function of comparing probative value to the danger set forth in Rule 403, W.R.E., without the possibility that the jury could be influenced by evidence the court ultimately holds to be inadmissible.

The function of performing the comparisons required by Rule 403, W.R.E., generally is held to be discretionary with the trial court. The fact that the evidence is detrimental to the defendant is neutral. For the prejudice factor to come into play the court must conclude that it is unfair. *United States v. Dolliole,* 597 F.2d 102 (7th Cir.1979). Evaluat-

1. A record of the court's finding under Rule 403, W.R.E., is helpful in reviewing the exercise of discretion. *United States v. Dolliole,* 597 F.2d 102 (7th Cir.1979).

ing this evidence in the light of the decisions of other courts, we cannot hold that the district court in this instance committed an abuse of discretion within the context of Rule 403, W.R.E. *United States v. McPartlin,* 595 F.2d 1321 (6th Cir.1979). Applying the separate tests required by Rules 404(b) and 403, W.R.E., we conclude that the evidence properly was admitted. See *State v. Tarrell,* supra.

Some courts would question the propriety of the older sister's testimony as rebuttal evidence. While such evidence properly could have been brought as part of the State's case in chief, the motive of the defendant only assumed more than ordinary significance when the defendant denied the occurrence of the charged offense and ascribed a motive to the victim for testifying untruthfully. Under these circumstances it was perhaps appropriate for the prosecutor to await an additional necessity for such testimony. Permitting the testimony of the older sister to be presented at a time which in most trials would involve rebuttal evidence was proper.

* * *

The judgment of the trial court is affirmed.

McClintock, Justice, specially concurring.

While I agree with the majority that the testimony of the victim's sister was properly admitted, I cannot agree that the testimony establishes a motive for the crime, as suggested by the majority. Such testimony is admissible to establish a continuing plan to sexually assault family members and to establish a method characteristically employed. Secondly, the testimony was relevant in that it corroborated the credibility of the victim. *People v. Covert,* 249 Cal.App.2d 81, 57 Cal.Rptr. 220, hrg. denied (1967); *People v. Fritts,* 72 Cal.App.3d 319, 140 Cal.Rptr. 94, hrg. denied (1977); *State v. Thomas,* 110 Ariz. 106, 515 P.2d 851, reh. denied (1973).

Rule 404(b), W.R.E., provides that evidence of other crimes may be admitted to prove "motive, opportunity, intent, preparation, plan, knowledge, identity, or absence of mistake or accident." In the instant case the following evidence was introduced:

(1) Both girls were the defendant's stepdaughters.

(2) Both girls were minors when the defendant assaulted them: the victim was nine years old and her sister was 11 and 12 years old.

(3) Both girls were assaulted in a bedroom.

(4) Both girls were told to remove their clothing and after they refused the defendant took off their clothes.

(5) Defendant first fondled the victims' genitalia with his finger and then attempted to force his penis into them. He succeeded in penetrating the nine-year-old.

I find that the testimony of both victims shows a common plan and method of operation and therefore is admissible as an exception under Rule 404(b), supra.

Furthermore, when the defendant took the stand he accused the victim of fabricating the story because he and the victim's mother were having marital difficulties. The defendant's plea of innocence and his testimony concerning the alleged frame-up challenged the credibility of the complaining witness. The testimony of the victim's sister during rebuttal was therefore relevant. *People v. Covert,* supra, 249 Cal. App.2d 81, 57 Cal.Rptr. at 224–225.

STATE v. RAYE, 73 N.C.App. 273, 326 S.E.2d 333 (1985), review denied, 313 N.C. 609, 332 S.E.2d 183 (1985). "Defendant's first and second assignments of error relate to testimony by State's witnesses as to sexual misconduct by the defendant other than the charged offenses. The first challenged testimony was admitted when the older sister of the prosecutrix testified in corroboration of her sister, the alleged victim. After she gave testimony concerning the incidents for which defendant was charged, the State asked the older sister, '* * * what, if anything, did your father do to you sexually.' The older sister testified about several times when her stepfather had made sexual advances to her.

"Although evidence of other wrongdoing by defendant is not admissible to show character or disposition to commit the charged offense, such evidence is admissible if it tends to prove any fact relevant to the charged offense. State v. McClain, 240 N.C. 171, 81 S.E.2d 364 (1954). Our courts have been liberal in allowing evidence of similar sex offenses, especially when the sex impulse manifested is of an unusual or unnatural character. 1 H. Brandis, Brandis on North Carolina Evidence Sec. 92 (2d rev. ed. 1982). In trials for incest it is competent for the State to offer evidence of a defendant's advances to a daughter not involved in the charged offenses for the purpose of showing intent as well as the unnatural lust of the defendant. State v. Edwards, 224 N.C. 527, 31 S.E.2d 516 (1944). In the instant case, testimony of the older sister was offered in corroboration of the prosecutrix. Although some of the older sister's testimony related to her stepfather's sexual advances to her rather than the prosecutrix, in a trial for incest such as this that testimony is allowed."

PENDLETON v. COMMONWEALTH, 685 S.W.2d 549, 554–55 (Ky. 1985) (Leibson, J., dissenting): "The majority opinion holds that this testimony from daughter Janet charging prior instances of sexual misconduct was *not* admissible to prove 'lustful inclination' in the accused, overruling Russell v. Commonwealth, Ky., 482 S.W.2d 584

(1972) to the extent that *Russell* approved use of such evidence to prove 'lustful inclination.' But the majority opinion in the present case then holds that such evidence could be admitted 'to prove intent, motive or a common plan or pattern of activity.' There is no distinction between these two phrases as they apply in the present situation. The *only* issue in this case was did the appellant commit the criminal acts against daughter April charged in the indictment? The *only* reason the past sexual misconduct daughter Janet testified to would have any relevance to the issue in the case would be if it served to show the accused's 'lustful inclination' to commit such acts. Lustful inclination, propensity to commit the crime charged, and 'intent, motive or a common plan or pattern of activity' (which is the current phraseology of the majority opinion), are all of one meaning here. We should not create a formula to do what we say cannot be done."

MONTGOMERY v. STATE, 810 S.W.2d 372, 393–97 (Tex.Crim.App. 1990). "Appellant was tried simultaneously under two indictments for indecency with a child committed against two of his three young daughters. One of appellant's former wives, not the mother of his daughters, testified that in her experience, appellant would 'quite frequently' 'walk around in the nude' in front of his children '[w]ith erections.' * * *

* * *

"* * * It is at least subject to reasonable debate whether the testimony that appellant frequently walked around in front of his daughters naked and with an erection, in combination with other evidence of inappropriate behavior toward them, did have a tendency to show a generalized 'intent to arouse and gratify' his own sexual desire *vis-a-vis* his children. This in turn would support an inference that, if he did in fact touch his daughters' genitals with his hand on the occasions alleged, it was a specific manifestation of that same intent to arouse and gratify his sexual desire, an elemental fact in these prosecutions. * * * [W]e hold it was not an abuse of discretion for the trial court to have found the evidence had relevance apart from character conformity.

"* * * We proceed, then, to review the court of appeals' conclusion 'that the probative value of the extraneous evidence outweighed any possibility of prejudice.' * * *

* * *

"We conclude the State had no compelling need to show that appellant frequently walked around naked, with an erection, in the presence of his children, either to prove specific intent or to shore up testimony of the complainants.

"Inherent probativeness and inherent prejudice also weigh in favor of exclusion. Though relevant, such evidence has only marginal probative value. By contrast, the danger of unfair prejudice from such testimony is substantial. Both sexually related misconduct and misconduct involving children are inherently inflammatory. Many in our society would condemn appellant for his conduct whether they believed it showed sexual arousal directed at his children, an undifferentiated sexual arousal imprudently displayed, or simply an incidental erection coupled with a damnable nonchalance. In any event there was a grave potential for decision on an improper basis, as jurors may have lost sight of specific issues they were called upon to decide and convicted appellant out of a revulsion against his parental demeanor. A substantial portion of the State's case was devoted to showing such extraneous misconduct, and most of appellant's evidence was responsive to it. Under these circumstances a jury instruction would not likely have neutralized the danger. We conclude that probativeness was minimal while the potential for prejudice was great."

STATE v. DEBAERE, 356 N.W.2d 301, 305 (Minn.1984). "In this case the defendant allegedly entered the house of a female acquaintance without consent, forced himself on her, and then, when complaint was made, claimed consent. The other-crime evidence showed a pattern of similar aggressive sexual behavior by defendant against other women in the community. Given our prior cases—e.g., State v. Morrison, 310 N.W.2d 135 (Minn.1981)—we believe that the trial court did not abuse its discretion in admitting the evidence, which was highly relevant to the issue of consent."

DOE v. UNITED STATES

United States Court of Appeals, Fourth Circuit, 1981.
666 F.2d 43.

BUTZNER, CIRCUIT JUDGE:

These appeals concern the district court's evidentiary ruling in a pre-trial proceeding held pursuant to rule 412 of the Federal Rules of Evidence. The court held that evidence concerning the past sexual behavior and habits of the prosecutrix was admissible in the rape trial of Donald Robert Black. We conclude that we have jurisdiction to hear her appeal, and we affirm in part and reverse in part the order of the district court.

I

The appellant is the alleged victim and chief government witness in the impending rape trial of Black. Pursuant to rule 412 of the Federal Rules of Evidence, Black made a pre-trial motion to admit evidence and permit cross-examination concerning the victim's past sexual behavior. After a hearing, the district court ruled that Black could introduce the evidence which he proffered.

Several days later, the district court granted Black's motion for the issuance of subpoenas for individuals who were to testify about the victim's sexual history. These included the victim's former landlord, a social worker who had previously investigated the victim, a sexual partner of the victim, and two people who claimed to be aware of the victim's reputation for promiscuity.

Thereafter, the victim instituted a civil action seeking the permanent sealing of the record of the rule 412 proceedings and other relief. During the course of this civil action, the court learned that the rape victim had not received notice of the earlier proceeding as mandated by subsection (c)(1) of rule 412. Consequently, it reopened the rule 412 hearing. The court then reaffirmed its prior ruling in the criminal case and entered summary judgment in favor of the defendants in the civil action. The victim appeals from the orders in both the civil and criminal actions.[5]

II

Black asserts that this court lacks jurisdiction to entertain the victim's appeal from the district court's order in the rule 412 proceeding. Resolution of this issue requires an examination of the procedural provisions of the rule.

Rule 412 places significant limitations on the admissibility of evidence concerning the past sexual behavior of a rape victim. The rule provides the additional safeguard of a hearing in chambers to determine the admissibility of such evidence. These provisions were adopted "to protect rape victims from the degrading and embarrassing disclosure of intimate details about their private lives." 124 Cong.Rec. at H 11945 (1978). To effectuate this purpose, subsections (c)(1) and (2) of the rule require that rape victims receive notice of the evidentiary hearing and a copy of the defendant's motion and offer of proof. Additionally, subsection (c)(2) makes provision for the victim's testimony at the evidentiary hearing.

The text, purpose, and legislative history of rule 412 clearly indicate that Congress enacted the rule for the special benefit of the victims of rape. The rule makes no reference to the right of a victim to appeal an adverse ruling. Nevertheless, this remedy is implicit as a necessary corollary of the rule's explicit protection of the privacy interests Congress sought to safeguard. Cf. Cort v. Ash, 422 U.S. 66, 95 S.Ct. 2080, 45 L.Ed.2d 26 (1975).[6] No other party in the evidentiary proceeding

5. Counsel for the victim, the United States, and Black filed briefs and argued before this court in these consolidated appeals.

6. In Cort v. Ash, 422 U.S. at 78, 95 S.Ct. at 2087–88, the Supreme Court identified several factors to be considered when "determining whether a private remedy is implicit in a statute not expressly providing one * * *." They are as follows: 1) whether the plaintiff was " 'one of the class for whose *especial* benefit the statute was enacted' " [citation omitted]; 2) whether there is "any indication of legislative intent, explicit or implicit, either to create such a remedy or to deny one;" 3) whether it is "consistent with the underlying purposes of the legislative scheme to imply such a remedy for the plaintiff;" 4) whether "the cause of action [is] one traditionally

shares these interests to the extent that they might be viewed as a champion of the victim's rights.[7] Therefore, the congressional intent embodied in rule 412 will be frustrated if rape victims are not allowed to appeal an erroneous evidentiary ruling made at a pretrial hearing conducted pursuant to the rule.

Section 1291 of title 28 U.S.C. confers on courts of appeals jurisdiction to review final decisions of the district courts. The Supreme Court has held that this finality requirement should be "given a 'practical rather than a technical construction.'" Gillespie v. U.S. Steel Corp., 379 U.S. 148, 152, 85 S.Ct. 308, 310–11, 13 L.Ed.2d 199 (1964). * * *

* * *

* * * [T]he injustice to rape victims in delaying an appeal until after the conclusion of the criminal trial is manifest. Without the right to immediate appeal, victims aggrieved by the court's order will have no opportunity to protect their privacy from invasions forbidden by the rule. Appeal following the defendant's acquittal or conviction is no remedy, for the harm that the rule seeks to prevent already will have occurred. Consequently, we conclude that with respect to the victim the district court's order meets *Gillespie's* test of practical finality, and we have jurisdiction to hear this appeal.

III

At the pre-trial rule 412 evidentiary hearing, Black presented several witnesses who told about the victim's past sexual behavior and reputation. Black testified that although he had talked on the phone with the victim several times, he did not meet her until the night of the alleged crime. Several men previously had told him the victim was promiscuous, and he had read a love letter she had written to another man.

At the conclusion of the hearing, the district court ruled that the following evidence was admissible:

(1) evidence of the victim's "general reputation in and around the Army post * * * where Mr. Black resided;"

(2) evidence of the victim's "habit of calling out to the barracks to speak to various and sundry soldiers;"

(3) evidence of the victim's "habit of coming to the post to meet people and of her habit of being at the barracks at the snack bar;"

(4) evidence from the victim's former landlord regarding "his experience with her" alleged promiscuous behavior;

(5) evidence of what a social worker learned of the victim;

(6) telephone conversations that Black had with the victim;

relegated to state law, in an area basically the concern of States, so that it would be inappropriate to infer a cause of action based solely on federal law."

7. The government does not assert that it has a right of appeal. It, nevertheless, agrees with the victim that the district court erred, and it presented this position by brief and oral argument.

(7) evidence of the defendant's "state of mind as a result of what he knew of her reputation * * * and what she had said to him."

Black argues that all of the evidence delineated in items 1–7 is admissible to support his claim that the victim consented, to show the reasonableness of his belief that she consented, and to corroborate his testimony. He relies on the rule's provision for the admission of constitutionally required evidence. Exclusion of the evidence, he maintains, will deprive him of the rights secured by the due process clause of the fifth amendment and the right of confrontation and compulsory process guaranteed by the sixth amendment.

Rule 412 restricts the admission of evidence in several respects. Subsection (a) excludes reputation or opinion evidence of the past sexual behavior of the victim. Subsection (b) provides that evidence of past sexual behavior, other than reputation and opinion, is only admissible in three circumstances: first, the defendant may introduce this evidence when it is constitutionally required, 412(b)(1); second, when the defendant claims that he was not the source of semen or injury, he may introduce evidence of the victim's relations with other men, 412(b)(2)(A); and third, when the defendant claims the victim consented, he may testify about his prior relations with the victim, 412(b)(2)(B).

The evidence delineated in items 1–5 of the district court's order clearly falls within the proscription of subsection (a) of the rule. Though sometimes couched in terms of habit, this evidence is essentially opinion or reputation evidence. Consequently, the exceptions set forth in subsection (b) do not render it admissible.

The constitutional justification for excluding reputation and opinion evidence rests on a dual premise. First, an accused is not constitutionally entitled to present irrelevant evidence. Second, reputation and opinion concerning a victim's past sexual behavior are not relevant indicators of the likelihood of her consent to a specific sexual act or of her veracity. *Privacy of Rape Victims: Hearings on H.R. 14666 and Other Bills Before the Subcomm. on Criminal Justice of the Committee on the Judiciary,* 94th Cong., 2d Sess. 14–15 (1976). Indeed, even before Congress enacted rule 412, the leading federal case on the subject, United States v. Kasto, 584 F.2d 268, 271–72 (8th Cir.1978), stated that in the absence of extraordinary circumstances:

> evidence of a rape victim's unchastity, whether in the form of testimony concerning her general reputation or direct or cross-examination testimony concerning specific acts with persons other than the defendant, is ordinarily insufficiently probative either of her general credibility as a witness or of her consent to intercourse with the defendant on the particular occasion * * * to outweigh its highly prejudicial effect.

State legislatures and courts have generally reached the same conclusion.[9] We are not prepared to state that extraordinary circumstances

9. Forty-five states have enacted rape shield laws in various forms. For a comprehensive analysis and comparison of these laws, see Tanford and Bocchino,

will never justify admission of such evidence to preserve a defendant's constitutional rights. The record of the rule 412 hearing in this case, however, discloses no circumstances for deeming that the rule's exclusion of the evidence classified in items 1–5 is unconstitutional.

The evidence described in items 6 and 7 of the district court's ruling is admissible. Certainly, the victim's conversations with Black are relevant, and they are not the type of evidence that the rule excludes. Black's knowledge, acquired before the alleged crime, of the victim's past sexual behavior is relevant on the issue of Black's intent. See 2 Weinstein and Berger, *Evidence* ¶ 412(01). Moreover, the rule does not exclude the production of the victim's letter or testimony of the men with whom Black talked if this evidence is introduced to corroborate the existence of the conversations and the letter.

The legislative history discloses that reputation and opinion evidence of the past sexual behavior of an alleged victim was excluded because Congress considered that this evidence was not relevant to the issues of the victims consent or her veracity. *Privacy of Rape Victims: Hearings on H.R. 14666 and Other Bills Before the Subcomm. on Criminal Justice of the Committee on the Judiciary,* 94th Cong., 2d Sess. 14–15, 45 (1976). There is no indication, however, that this evidence was intended to be excluded when offered solely to show the accused's state of mind. Therefore, its admission is governed by the Rules of Evidence dealing with relevancy in general. Knowledge that Black acquired after the incident is irrelevant to this issue.

IV

The prosecutrix also appeals from the district court's adverse grant of summary judgment in the civil suit. At the time of the first rule 412 hearing, counsel initially appointed for Black coincidentally represented the rape victim in a child custody proceeding. To prepare for the custody proceeding, the rape victim had furnished this attorney with confidential information. On the basis of this conflict and the provisions of the rule, she requested that the record of the first rule 412 proceeding be permanently sealed. Also, she requested that the clerk be prohibited from issuing subpoenas duces tecum for the record and files of her earlier child custody proceeding. Presumably, these items would disclose information concerning her past sexual behavior.

Rape Victim Shield Laws and the Sixth Amendment, 128 U.Penn.L.Rev. 544 (1980).

In the following cases, state courts upheld the constitutionality of rape shield laws: State v. Howard, 426 A.2d 457 (N.H. 1981); State v. Fortney, 301 N.C. 31, 269 S.E.2d 110 (1980); State v. Blue, 225 Kan. 576, 592 P.2d 897 (1979); State v. Green, 260 S.E.2d 257 (W.Va.1979); Marion v. State, 590 S.W.2d 288 (Ark.1979); Roberts v. State, 268 Ind. 127, 373 N.E.2d 1103 (Ct.App.1978); People v. Khan, 80 Mich. App. 605, 264 N.W.2d 360 (1978); State v. Ryan, 157 N.J.Super. 121, 384 A.2d 570 (Super.Ct.App.Div.1978); State v. Herrera, 92 N.M. 7, 582 P.2d 384 (Ct.App.1978); People v. Mandel, 61 A.D.2d 563, 403 N.Y.S.2d 63 (App.Div.1978), rev'd on other grounds, 48 N.Y.2d 185, 425 N.Y.S.2d 63, 401 N.E.2d 185 (1979); Smith v. Commonwealth, 566 S.W.2d 181 (Ky.App.1978); People v. McKenna, 196 Colo. 367, 585 P.2d 275 (1978); People v. Blackburn, 56 Cal. App.3d 685, 128 Cal.Rptr. 864 (Ct.App. 1976).

Rule 412 does not mandate the sealing of the record of the pre-trial evidentiary hearing. This is within the sound discretion of the trial court. We are not presented with any facts which suggest that the district court's refusal to seal the record constituted an abuse of discretion. The issuance of subpoenas is also within the discretion of the trial court, and its refusal to grant the victim's request cannot be deemed an abuse of discretion, particularly since Black has not even sought a subpoena for these items. The court also acted properly in dealing with the attorney's conflict of interest. It appointed new counsel to represent Black and instructed them to avoid communicating with the former counsel regarding Black's defense.

In No. 81–5209, the order of the district court is affirmed in part and reversed in part, and this case is remanded.

In No. 81–1995, the judgment of the district court is affirmed.

UNITED STATES v. SHAW, 824 F.2d 601 (8th Cir.1987), cert. denied, 484 U.S. 1068, 108 S.Ct. 1033, 98 L.Ed.2d 997 (1988). "After hearing testimony that James Shaw had engaged in numerous acts of sexual intercourse with S.A., his eleven year old foster daughter, a jury found Shaw guilty of seven counts of carnal knowledge, 18 U.S.C. §§ 1153, 2032 (1982). * * *

* * *

"The government undoubtedly introduced evidence concerning S.A.'s hymen to establish that its condition was consistent with her having engaged in sexual intercourse. This evidence, coupled with S.A.'s testimony, allowed the inference that Shaw caused this condition when they had sexual intercourse. Shaw contends that he should have been allowed to rebut this evidence by showing that someone else was responsible for the condition of S.A.'s hymen. In compliance with Federal Rule of Evidence 412(c)(1), Shaw filed a pretrial written motion, proffering evidence to rebut the government's evidence of the condition of S.A.'s hymen. The motion asserted that seven young boys would testify that they had sexual intercourse with S.A., one that he had sexual intercourse with S.A. fifty times. The district court rejected Shaw's motion, which was raised several times during the trial, ruling as a matter of law that the rupturing of a hymen does not constitute a Rule 412(b)(2)(A) 'injury.'

* * *

"* * * The testimony, in sum, indicated that S.A.'s hymen was not intact; it had been stretched; her vaginal orifice was widened. Even if this physical condition was the result of sexual intercourse, it is not an injury. Unlike a situation where the evidence indicates, for example, that sexual intercourse caused a tearing or bruising of the hymen or unusual bleeding, the evidence concerning S.A.'s hymen, while it may describe a physiological accommodation, falls short of establishing an injury so as to trigger the applicability of Rule 412's injury exception.

"Shaw argues we should read Rule 412's injury exception broadly to authorize the introduction of past sexual behavior evidence when it is offered to establish the source of any physical consequence. Several commentators support this contention. For example, Professors Wright and Graham contend that a defendant should be allowed to introduce past sexual behavior evidence whenever the prosecution introduces evidence of 'any "physical consequences" offered to prove that the act took place.' 23 C. Wright & K. Graham, Federal Practice & Procedure § 5388, at 598 (1980) * * *. * * * We recognize that a compelling argument supporting this contention is that it defies principles of relevancy to allow past sexual behavior evidence to rebut evidence of a physical consequence that constitutes an injury (for example, evidence that the defendant broke the complainant's nose), while prohibiting it for evidence of a physical consequence that does not constitute an injury (for example, evidence that the defendant caused a stretching of the complainant's hymen). The defendant's need to introduce source evidence is equally strong regardless of what type of physical consequence the prosecution contends the defendant caused when he allegedly raped the complainant. Moreover, it can be argued that the type of physical consequence in issue has no bearing on the probative value of the past sexual behavior evidence.

* * *

"In construing the meaning of Rule 412(b)(2)(A), a court 'must begin with the language employed by Congress and the assumption that the ordinary meaning of that language accurately expresses the legislative purpose.' Park 'N Fly, Inc. v. Dollar Park & Fly, Inc., 469 U.S. 189, 194, 105 S.Ct. 658, 662, 83 L.Ed.2d 582 (1985). Our review of the legislative history to Rule 412's injury exception convinces us that Congress had no intention to expand the commonly understood meaning of the word 'injury' to include all physical consequences. We thus hold that the district court did not err in excluding evidence of S.A.'s past sexual behavior."

SUMMITT v. STATE

Supreme Court of Nevada, 1985.
101 Nev. 159, 697 P.2d 1374.

MOWBRAY, JUSTICE:

A jury found appellant Vernon Summitt guilty of two counts of sexual assault. He seeks reversal of his judgment of conviction asserting several assignments of error, only one of which we find to have merit: that the district judge erred in excluding testimony centered about a prior similar sexual experience of the victim. Accordingly, we reverse and remand the case for a new trial.

A grand jury indicted Summitt for three counts of sexual assault committed on a six year old child. A count charging sexual intercourse was dismissed before the trial because of the state's failure to preserve evidence. Summitt was tried and convicted of the remaining counts of cunnilingus and fellatio.

At the jury trial Summitt sought to introduce evidence of a prior sexual experience of the victim which included intercourse, fellatio and the fondling of the victim's genitalia. The prior assault had occurred two years before the crime in issue, in the same trailer park, and involved the same victim and her nine year old girl friend, who was also a witness in the instant case. Summitt offered the testimony to show that the young victim had had prior independent knowledge of similar acts which constituted the basis for the present charge.

The district judge denied Summitt's offer on the ground that the "rape victim shield law," Nevada Revised Statute section 50.090 [1], barred the admission of such evidence. We turn to the construction of the statute.

In 1977 Nevada joined forty-five states and the federal government in passing a "rape shield" statute, limiting inquiry into the sexual history of a complaining witness in a rape or sexual assault case. *See* J.A. Tanford and A.J. Bocchino, *Rape Victim Shield Laws and the Sixth Amendment,* 128 U.Pa.L.Rev. 544, 544 (1980).

Such laws have generally been designed to reverse the common law rule applicable in rape cases, that use of evidence of a female complainant's general reputation for morality and chastity was admissible to infer consent and also to attack credibility generally. Thus, for example, it had been held: "It is a matter of common knowledge that the bad character of a man for chastity does not even in the remotest degree affect his character for truth, when based upon that alone, while it does that of a woman." *State v. Sibley,* 131 Mo. 519, 132 Mo. 102, 33 S.W. 167, 171 (1895), quoted in *State v. Brown,* 636 S.W.2d 929, 933 n. 3 (Mo.1982), *cert. denied sub nom., Brown v. Missouri,* 459 U.S. 1212, 103 S.Ct. 1207, 75 L.Ed.2d 448 (1983). Such statutes as Nevada's have been described as "directed at the misuse of prior sexual conduct evidence based on this antiquated and obviously illogical premise." *State v. Hudlow,* 99 Wash.2d 1, 659 P.2d 514, 519 (1983). *See also People v. McKenna,* 196 Colo. 367, 585 P.2d 275, 278 (1978). An additional purpose of such statutes is " 'to protect rape victims from degrading and embarrassing disclosure of intimate details about their private lives.' " 124 Cong.Rec. at H 11945 (1978), quoted in *Doe v. United States,* 666 F.2d 43, 45 (4th Cir.1981). Finally, "[t]he restrictions placed on the admissibility of certain evidence by the rape-shield laws will, it was hoped, encourage rape victims to come forward and report the crimes

1. NRS 50.090 states in pertinent part: In any prosecution for sexual assault ... the accused may not present evidence of any previous sexual conduct of the victim of the crime to challenge the victim's credibility as a witness unless the prosecutor has presented evidence or the victim has testified concerning such conduct, or the absence of such conduct, in which case the scope of the accused's cross-examination of the victim or rebuttal shall be limited to the evidence presented by the prosecutor or victim.

and testify in court protected from unnecessary indignities and needless probing into their respective sexual histories." *State v. Lemon,* 456 A.2d 261, 264 (R.I.1983).

In construing Nevada's "shield law," we must be mindful of these legislative purposes. Equally important is the rule that "[a] statute should, if it reasonably can, be so construed as to avoid any conflict with the constitution." *State v. Woodbury,* 17 Nev. 337, 356, 30 P. 1006, 1012 (1883). *See also Anaya v. State,* 96 Nev. 119, 606 P.2d 156 (1980); *Milchem, Inc. v. District Court,* 84 Nev. 541, 445 P.2d 148 (1968).

A defendant's rights to present witnesses in his own behalf, to confront and to cross-examine the witnesses against him are fundamental rights, secured by the Sixth Amendment, and applicable to the states through the Fourteenth Amendment. *Chambers v. Mississippi,* 410 U.S. 284, 93 S.Ct. 1038, 35 L.Ed.2d 297 (1973); *Washington v. Texas,* 388 U.S. 14, 87 S.Ct. 1920, 18 L.Ed.2d 1019 (1967); *Pointer v. Texas,* 380 U.S. 400, 85 S.Ct. 1065, 13 L.Ed.2d 923 (1965). The United States Supreme Court has held that the right to confront and cross-examine witnesses may, in appropriate cases, bow to "accommodate other legitimate interests in the criminal trial process." *Chambers v. Mississippi,* 410 U.S. at 295, 93 S.Ct. at 1046. But, the Court has cautioned, "its denial or significant diminution calls into question the ultimate 'integrity of the fact-finding process' and requires that the competing interest be closely examined." *Id.*

Thus in *Davis v. Alaska,* 415 U.S. 308, 320, 94 S.Ct. 1105, 1112, 39 L.Ed.2d 347 (1974), the court held that the legitimate interest of the state in protecting from public scrutiny the juvenile record of a prosecution witness could not "require yielding of so vital a constitutional right as the effective cross-examination for bias of an adverse witness." The court examined the particular interests of the state and the defendant, noting that defense counsel made it clear that he would not introduce the juvenile record as a "general impeachment of [the witness's] character as a truthful person," but rather to show specifically that the witness was on probation for a similar crime, which may have provided a motive for shifting blame to the defendant. *Id.* at 311, 94 S.Ct. at 1107. Similarly in this case, we have a defendant who seeks to introduce evidence which it is the general policy of the state to protect, but which the defendant seeks to use for the sole and limited purpose of challenging the witness's credibility by dispelling an inference which the jury may well draw otherwise from the circumstances, that a six year old child would be unable to describe the occurrences in her testimony unless they had in fact taken place.

Other courts confronted with the necessity of accommodating the competing interests of complaining witnesses and defendants in such cases have concluded that rape shield statutes should be construed and applied so as to uphold the constitutional rights of defendants, while creating the least possible interference with the legislative purpose reflected in the statutes. *See, esp., Bell v. Harrison,* 670 F.2d 656 (6th

Cir.1982) (Tennessee statute); *State v. Blue,* 225 Kan. 576, 592 P.2d 897 (1979); *Commonwealth v. Joyce,* 382 Mass. 222, 415 N.E.2d 181 (1981); *State v. Howard,* 121 N.H. 53, 426 A.2d 457 (1981); *State v. Jalo,* 27 Or.App. 845, 557 P.2d 1359 (1976); *Shockley v. State,* 585 S.W.2d 645 (Tenn.Crim.App.1978); *Winfield v. Commonwealth,* 225 Va. 211, 301 S.E.2d 15 (1983); *State v. Hudlow, supra,* 99 Wash.2d 1, 659 P.2d 514 (1983).

The holdings of two of these state court decisions apply to the case at bar. In *State v. Howard, supra,* the Supreme Court of New Hampshire considered a statute which purported to preclude any evidence of a victim's consensual sexual activity with persons other than a defendant. In that case, as in this one, the defendant sought to introduce such evidence in order to challenge the young complaining witness's credibility, by showing that she had had other experiences which could explain the source of her knowledge of the sexual activity she described in her testimony. The court determined that in order to uphold the constitutionality of the statute, it would require that a defendant in a prosecution to which the shield law was applicable "must, upon motion, be given an opportunity to demonstrate that due process requires the admission of such evidence because the probative value in the context of that particular case outweighs its prejudicial effect on the prosecutrix. Such motion should, of course, be made out of the presence of the jury." 426 A.2d at 461. We are persuaded that this procedure would provide a proper means of deciding, on a case by case basis, whether such evidence should be admitted. *See Anaya v. State, supra,* 96 Nev. 119, 606 P.2d 156 (1980).

We agree with the reasoning of the Supreme Court of Washington that in following this procedure, the trial court must undertake to balance the probative value of the evidence against its prejudicial effect, *see* NRS 48.035(1)[3], and that the inquiry should particularly focus upon "potential prejudice to the truthfinding process itself," *i.e.,* "whether the introduction of the victim's past sexual conduct may confuse the issues, mislead the jury, or cause the jury to decide the case on an improper or emotional basis." *State v. Hudlow, supra,* 659 P.2d at 521.

In the instant case the defendant does not seek to impeach the credibility of the complaining witness by a general allegation of unchastity. Rather, the specific evidence was offered to show knowledge of such acts rather than lack of chastity.[4] We agree with the ruling of the

3. NRS 48.035(1) reads:

> Although relevant, evidence is not admissible if its probative value is substantially outweighed by the danger of unfair prejudice, of confusion of the issues or of misleading the jury.

4. In the affidavit supporting appellant-defendant's motion for a new trial in the proceedings below, it was asserted that Juror No. 1, Richard L. Linton, after the verdict was rendered, stated to both counsel for the state and the appellant that during the jury's deliberations "the question was posed among the jurors why a girl of such a young age would know of such sexual acts unless they had, in fact, occurred as alleged."

Supreme Court of New Hampshire in *State v. Howard, supra,* 426 A.2d at 462:

> We believe that the average juror would perceive the average twelve-year-old girl as a sexual innocent. Therefore, it is probable that jurors would believe that the sexual experience she describes must have occurred in connection with the incident being prosecuted; otherwise, she could not have described it. However, if statutory rape victims have had other sexual experiences, it would be possible for them to provide detailed, realistic testimony concerning an incident that may never have happened. To preclude a defendant from presenting such evidence to the jury, if it is otherwise admissible, would be obvious error. Accordingly, a defendant must be afforded the opportunity to show, by specific incidents of sexual conduct, that the prosecutrix has the experience and ability to contrive a statutory rape charge against him.

We also agree, however, that "[i]n the exercise of its sound discretion, the trial court should be mindful of the important policy considerations underlying the rape-shield statute," and accordingly "should limit the admission of evidence of specific instances of the complainant's sexual conduct to the extent that it is possible without unduly infringing upon the defendant's constitutional right to confrontation." *Id.*

Since the remaining evidence of guilt was not strong, and since "[t]he accuracy and truthfulness of [the complaining witness's] testimony were key elements in * * * the case against [defendant]," *Davis v. Alaska, supra,* 415 U.S. at 317, 94 S.Ct. at 1111, we reverse and remand for further proceedings consistent with this opinion.

SPRINGER, C.J., and GUNDERSON, J., concur.

STEFFEN, JUSTICE, concurring in part and dissenting in part.

I concur in result with my brethren on the fellatio count but dissent as to the count involving cunnilingus.

I agree that the district court committed reversible error in excluding reference to a prior incident involving the same child-victim. The purposes of the "rape victim shield law" (NRS 50.090) would not have been frustrated by the terse admission of facts concerning the earlier experience since the child, then age four, was clearly a victim whose reputation would have been unaffected by such a disclosure. The admission of the prior occurrence would permit the defendant to disabuse jurors who might conclude that the child's familiarity with fellatio could not have existed absent the actuality of the ordeal described at trial by the child. Evidence of the prior incident would not relate to the sexual *conduct* of the child, but rather her experience as a tender-aged victim of a sexual assault.

The error upon which we must reverse the fellatio conviction does not, in my opinion, similarly affect the cunnilingus count. The majority emphasizes that the trial court should allow inquiry into the prior incident only to the extent of "*specific instances* of the complainant's sexual conduct." (Emphasis added.) It is especially significant that there is *no evidence* in the record that the prior violation of the child included an act of cunnilingus. Moreover, there is an equal absence of evidence that the child was even questioned about cunnilingus in connection with the prior incident. We are thus faced with a reversal by this Court of the felony count of cunnilingus based upon a non-event, *i.e.,* the introduction of the then four-year-old victim to cunnilingus as a result of the prior incident.

The majority relies on *State v. Howard,* 426 A.2d 457 (N.H.1981), as authority for reversal of defendant's conviction on both counts. Unfortunately, *State v. Howard* does not support the reversal of the cunnilingus conviction. The Supreme Court of New Hampshire, as quoted by the majority, states that "a defendant must be afforded the opportunity to show, by specific incidents of sexual conduct, that the prosecutrix has the *experience and ability* to contrive a statutory rape charge against him." (Emphasis added.) Aside from the fact that *State v. Howard* involved a twelve-year-old complainant with an allegedly extensive prior history of consensual sexual conduct as opposed to the six-year-old prosecutrix in the instant case whose only "history" was as a four-year-old victim of sexual assault, it must be emphasized that there is no showing that the child-victim in this case had "the experience and ability" to contrive a charge of cunnilingus against the defendant stemming from the prior incident.

Another consequence of the majority ruling is that it actually violates the spirit of the rape shield law by accommodating a general attack on the credibility of the child-victim. In effect, the majority holds that the child's prior experience as a four-year-old victim of sexual assault in the form of fellatio may be admitted as a basis for inferring that she contrived a charge of cunnilingus against Summitt. We are thus propelled into the concept that sexual history in general, as opposed to *specific instances* of sexual experience in particular, may be introduced to attack the credibility of a prosecutrix. It is clear that such a proposition substantially expands both the holding and the *ratio decidendi* of *State v. Howard, supra.* It also appears, given the tender age of the prosecutrix in the instant case, that the proposition created by this decision would apply in virtually all instances involving a child-victim whose sexual "history" is limited to an experience of sexual assault occurring at age four or above. I am simply unable to reconcile the majority ruling "with the necessity of accommodating the competing interests of complaining witnesses and defendants" by construing and applying the rape shield law "so as to uphold the constitutional rights of defendants, while creating the least possible interference with the legislative purpose reflected in the statutes." I therefore conclude that the majority position is in conflict with the basic purpose and spirit of Nevada's rape shield statute.

There is an additional reason why I believe this Court should be particularly sensitive to the peculiar circumstances of the instant case in relation to the rape shield law. Specifically, Nevada's rape shield statute, NRS 50.090, applies to victims who have a prior history of sexual *conduct.* The word "conduct" imports active behavior, and does not comprehend mere experience forced on a tender-aged child by means of a felonious sexual assault. I would therefore conclude that the beneficial concerns and purposes of the rape shield legislation would have even stronger application to a child-victim of sexual assault who has no history of personal sexual conduct. It is one thing to permit the introduction of specific instances of actual sexual experiences forced upon a child as a victim in order to disabuse jurors of the inference that a child's knowledge of such experiences must have necessarily resulted from the alleged acts of the defendant. It is quite another proposition to permit the introduction of evidence of one type of sexual assault previously suffered by the child-victim as a basis for inferring an ability on the part of the child-victim to contrive a different sexual crime against the defendant. The former proposition achieves fairness to the defendant and respect for the youthful victim; the latter provides an advantage to the defendant which is unfair to the state and which diminishes or eliminates the intended statutory protection and respect for the prosecutrix.

My position in dissent is reinforced by the failure of defense counsel to preserve as an issue on appeal the refusal of the district court to admit evidence of the prior incident as it relates to the cunnilingus conviction. Such "failure" was both understandable and justifiable since there was no evidence upon which to create such an issue.[1] Furthermore, in defendant's motion for a new trial the instant issue was directed to the fellatio count. I therefore conclude that this Court should defer to the time-honored rule that an issue not raised in the trial court will not be entertained on appeal. *Merica v. State,* 87 Nev. 457, 488 P.2d 1161 (1971); *Kelley v. State,* 76 Nev. 65, 348 P.2d 966 (1960). Actually, in reversing the cunnilingus conviction, this Court not only disregards the rule precluding the consideration of issues raised initially on appeal—it extends itself to create, *sua sponte,* a non-constitutional issue upon which relief is granted without benefit of legal precedent or authority.

These types of cases are extremely difficult. I am keenly aware of the concern of my brethren in the majority for both the rights of the defendant and the ordeal of the young prosecutrix upon retrial. Moreover, I respect the sense of the majority that I am drawing too thin a line in my dissenting position. I must nevertheless conclude, for

1. Defense counsel did, however, properly object to the trial court's refusal to allow evidence of the prior incident as it related to the fellatio count. In that regard, counsel unsuccessfully proffered the following instruction to the jury:

> "It is improper for you to infer that * * * [the child-victim] would have known of the act of fellatio: that being the insertion of the penis into the mouth, only if the actions she testified to had in fact occurred."

Additionally, in arguing to the court below, defense counsel said:

> "But the fact is that there are normal people in this community, normal people that get called as jurors that sit up there and in their growing up experiences at six years old, did not know of these type [sic] of sexual acts, and maybe cunnilingus was not mentioned in that prior act, but fellatio definitely was, and fellatio is an issue in this case."

reasons noted above, that defendant's conviction on the cunnilingus count should be affirmed. Accordingly, I respectfully dissent.

COMMONWEALTH v. BLACK, 337 Pa.Super. 548, 487 A.2d 396 (1985). "Appellant, 48-year-old Darrell L. Black, was charged with statutory rape, corruption of minors, incest, and attempted involuntary deviate sexual intercourse with respect to his thirteen-year-old daughter, Cynthia. * * *

* * *

"Appellant's version of the events that evening was that although his daughter was present in his room, no sexual contact occurred. As is common in sexual offense cases, the prosecutrix and appellant provided the only direct evidence for their respective versions and the case thus turned on their comparative credibility.

"While the sexual incident was found to have occurred during Christmas, 1979, testimony indicated that Cynthia's complaints began to surface almost three months later, near the end of March, 1980. These complaints coincided with violent arguments between appellant and prosecutrix' fifteen-year-old brother, which culminated in the brother leaving home and separating from the family, including prosecutrix. Cynthia admitted wanting her brother back in the home, and other testimony indicated that as soon as appellant was arrested and removed, the fifteen-year-old brother contacted the family and sought to return home. In his defense, appellant offered to show through cross-examination that Cynthia had maintained an ongoing, consensual sexual relationship with this brother, which ended when the brother left home. Appellant contends that the true extent of prosecutrix' bias against him could only be revealed by showing the abnormal, sexual relationship which she had with her brother and which had been terminated by appellant's dispute with her brother. Specifically, appellant urges that Cynthia's testimony can only be weighed fairly when measured against her desire, first, to punish appellant for his interference with her sexual relationship with her brother, and, second, to remove appellant from the home so that her brother might return and resume the relationship. As noted above, the lower court excluded this evidence of prosecutrix' prior sexual conduct with her brother, relying on the Rape Shield Law.

"We begin by noting the modern rule that prior sexual conduct with third persons is ordinarily inadmissible to attack the character of the prosecutrix in sex offense cases. 1A Wigmore, Evidence § 62 (Tillers rev. 1983). However, in this case the evidence of prior sexual conduct was not offered merely to show any general moral turpitude or defect of the prosecutrix, but rather to reveal a specific bias against and hostility toward appellant and a motive to seek retribution by, perhaps, false accusation. * * *

"In contrast to the broad, common law rule permitting cross-examination to show bias, we are confronted with Pennsylvania's Rape Shield Law, which provides, in pertinent part, that '[e]vidence of specific instances of the alleged victim's past sexual conduct, * * * shall not be admissible in prosecutions under [Chapter 31] * * * ', relating to sexual offenses. 18 Pa.C.S. § 3104(a). The lower court relied on this plain statutory language, as well as our recent opinion in Commonwealth v. Duncan, 279 Pa.Super. 395, 421 A.2d 257 (1980), in holding the evidence inadmissible.

"Appellant, however, contends that the Rape Shield Law, as applied below, improperly infringed upon his right of confrontation guaranteed by the Sixth Amendment to the United States Constitution. Although the United States Supreme Court has not ruled directly on any of the numerous, recently enacted rape shield laws, in Davis v. Alaska, 415 U.S. 308, 94 S.Ct. 1105, 39 L.Ed.2d 347 (1974), it considered a criminal defendant's Sixth Amendment right of confrontation with respect to a juvenile law which shielded a prosecution witness from cross-examination based on his juvenile record.

* * *

"We find the juvenile statutes in Davis and the Rape Shield Law in this case strikingly similar. Both laws are designed to protect designated classes of persons by shielding them from the public humiliation and opprobrium which would naturally flow from the disclosure of the suppressed evidence; both laws seek to afford the designated classes an opportunity to start anew. Compare In re Gault, 387 U.S. 1, 87 S.Ct. 1428, 18 L.Ed.2d 527 (1967) with Commonwealth v. Strube, 274 Pa.Super. 199, 418 A.2d 365 (1979), cert. denied, 449 U.S. 992, 101 S.Ct. 527, 66 L.Ed.2d 288 (1980). We can not distinguish the present case from Davis v. Alaska, supra, and therefore are constrained to reverse and remand for a new trial. In so holding, we note that other jurisdictions which have considered like challenges to their rape shield laws are in accord. See State v. LaClair, 121 N.H. 743, 433 A.2d 1326 (1981); Marion v. State, 267 Ark. 345, 590 S.W.2d 288 (1979); State v. Jalo, 27 Or.App. 845, 557 P.2d 1359 (1976); Maryland v. Delawder, 28 Md.App. 212, 344 A.2d 446 (1975); Annot., 1 A.L.R.4th 283 (1980). See also Tanford and Bocchino, Rape Victim Shield Laws and the Sixth Amendment, 128 U.Pa.L.Rev. 544 (1980).

* * *

"We emphasize that our holding today is not meant to limit the importance of the general principles embodied in the Rape Shield Law, particularly, that evidence of sexual conduct with third persons is irrelevant to prove either general moral defect or consent of the victim. We also reaffirm the trial court's responsibility to limit repetitive and unnecessarily harrassing cross-examination in all cases, but especially these most sensitive situations. But, in spite of the trial court's appropriately broad discretion in controlling the examination of witnesses, we cannot approve the complete elimination of a relevant and

crucial line of cross-examination. We therefore hold that insofar as the Rape Shield Law purports to prohibit the admission of evidence which may logically demonstrate a witness' bias, interest or prejudice or which properly attacks the witness' credibility, it unconstitutionally infringes upon an accused's right of confrontation under the Sixth Amendment to the United States Constitution and Article I, Section 9 of the Pennsylvania Constitution."

Note

On evidence that a complainant in a rape or sexual assault prosecution has made similar, false claims against others, see Smith v. State, p. 477 infra.

GOVERNMENT OF THE VIRGIN ISLANDS v. CARINO, 631 F.2d 226, 229 (3d Cir.1980). Carino was convicted of assault with intent to commit mayhem. He claimed that he acted in self-defense. "Carino may have believed that he could use proof of the prior conviction to show Richardson's character, because the Rules of Evidence treat character of the victim as an exception to the general rule rejecting the circumstantial use of character evidence. However, the nature of evidence permitted for proof of character is limited by Rule 405(a) to opinion and reputation testimony, Government of the Virgin Islands v. Roldan, V.I., 612 F.2d 775, 778 (3d Cir.1979), cert. denied, 100 S.Ct. 1857 (1980); Government of the Virgin Islands v. Petersen, 14 V.I. 24, 32, 553 F.2d 324, 329 (3d Cir.1977). See 2 Louisell & Mueller, Federal Evidence § 139 at 105 (1978) (hereinafter Louisell & Mueller). As we read the record, there was no effort to introduce reputation evidence of Richardson, as distinguished from her *conviction* and prior acts. Therefore, when the court excluded evidence of the conviction to show Richardson's character, it did not err.

"However, the Rules provide an additional basis for the introduction of specific evidence of other crimes. Rule 404(b) provides: * * *

"Carino sought to introduce Richardson's conviction for manslaughter of her prior boyfriend to 'demonstrate the fear' and 'the state of mind' of defendant at the time of the incident. Although there is no specific reference in the Federal Rules of Evidence to admissibility for that purpose, we do not read the Rules as changing the prior precedent under which certain acts of violence by the victim are admissible to corroborate defendant's position that he 'reasonably feared he was in danger of imminent great bodily injury.' United States v. Burks, 470 F.2d 432, 435 (D.C.Cir.1972). Commentators on the Federal Rules of Evidence have reached a similar conclusion. Professors Louisell and Mueller state, 'If it can be established that the accused knew at the time of the alleged crime of prior violent acts by the victim, such evidence is relevant as tending to show a reasonable apprehension on the part of the accused. Since this is not the circumstantial use of character evidence to prove conduct, such use is not barred either by Rule 404 or Rule 405.' Louisell & Mueller, supra § 139, at 108 (emphasis in original). While such use of a victim's prior acts may not fall precisely into any of the enumerated purposes, it is close to some of them, such as 'intent' and 'knowledge.' In any event, the enumerated purposes are not exclusive, as demonstrated by the language of the Rule authorizing use of other crimes evidence 'for other purposes, such as * * *.' (emphasis added)."

PERRIN v. ANDERSON

United States Court of Appeals, Tenth Circuit, 1986.
784 F.2d 1040.

LOGAN, CIRCUIT JUDGE.

* * *

This is a 42 U.S.C. § 1983 civil rights action for compensatory and punitive damages arising from the death of Terry Kim Perrin. Plaintiff, administratrix of Perrin's estate and guardian of his son, alleged that defendants, Donnie Anderson and Roland Von Schriltz, members of the Oklahoma Highway Patrol, deprived Perrin of his civil rights when they shot and killed him while attempting to obtain information concerning a traffic accident in which he had been involved. The jury found in favor of defendants.

In this appeal plaintiff contends that the district court erred in admitting: (1) testimony by four police officers recounting previous violent encounters they had had with Perrin; * * * and (4) evidence that Perrin's home contained many pornographic drawings, sketches, books, and materials.

A simple highway accident set off the bizarre chain of events that culminated in Perrin's death. The incident began when Perrin drove his car into the back of another car on an Oklahoma highway. After determining that the occupants of the car he had hit were uninjured, Perrin walked to his home, which was close to the highway.

Trooper Von Schriltz went to Perrin's home to obtain information concerning the accident. He was joined there by Trooper Anderson. They knocked on and off for ten to twenty minutes before persuading Perrin to open the door. Once Perrin opened the door, the defendant officers noticed Perrin's erratic behavior. The troopers testified that his moods would change quickly and that he was yelling that the accident was not his fault. Von Schriltz testified that he sensed a possibly dangerous situation and slowly moved his hand to his gun in order to secure its hammer with a leather thong. This action apparently provoked Perrin who then slammed the door. The door bounced open and Perrin then attacked Anderson. A fierce battle ensued between Perrin and the two officers, who unsuccessfully applied several chokeholds to Perrin in an attempt to subdue him. Eventually Anderson, who testified that he feared he was about to lose consciousness as a result of having been kicked repeatedly in the face and chest by Perrin, took out his gun, and, without issuing a warning, shot and killed Perrin. Anderson stated that he was convinced Perrin would have killed both officers had he not fired.

I

At trial the court permitted four police officers to testify that they had been involved previously in violent encounters with Perrin. These officers testified to Perrin's apparent hatred or fear of uniformed officers and his consistently violent response to any contact with them. For example, defendants presented evidence that on earlier occasions Perrin was completely uncontrollable and violent in the presence of uniformed officers. On one occasion he rammed his head into the bars and walls of his cell, requiring administration of a tranquilizer. Another time while barefoot, Perrin kicked loose a porcelain toilet bowl that was bolted to the floor. One officer testified that he encountered Perrin while responding to a public drunk call. Perrin attacked him, and during the following struggle Perrin tried to reach for the officer's weapon. The officer and his back-up had to carry Perrin handcuffed, kicking and screaming, to the squad car, where Perrin then kicked the windshield out of the car. Another officer testified that Perrin attacked him after Perrin was stopped at a vehicle checkpoint. During the ensuing struggle three policemen were needed to subdue Perrin, including one 6′2″ officer weighing 250 pounds and one 6′6″ officer weighing 350 pounds.

Defendants introduced this evidence to prove that Perrin was the first aggressor in the fight—a key element in defendants' self-defense claim. The court admitted the evidence over objection, under Federal Rules of Evidence provisions treating both character and habit evidence. Plaintiff contends this was error.

A

Section 404(a) of the Federal Rules of Evidence carefully limits the circumstances under which character evidence may be admitted to prove that an individual, at the time in question, acted in conformity with his character. This rule is necessary because of the high degree of prejudice that inheres in character evidence. *See* Fed.R.Evid. 404 advisory committee note. In most instances we are unwilling to permit a jury to infer that an individual performed the alleged acts based on a particular character trait. The exceptions to Rule 404(a)'s general ban on the use of character evidence permit criminal defendants to offer evidence of their own character or of their victim's character. Fed. R.Evid. 404(a)(1)–(2). Not until such a defendant takes this initial step may the prosecution rebut by offering contrary character evidence. *Id.* advisory committee note. Although the Advisory Committee on the Rules of Evidence has observed that this rule "lies more in history and experience than in logic," *id.*, it does seem desirable to afford a criminal defendant every opportunity to exonerate himself.[2] In offering such potentially prejudicial testimony, the defendant of course proceeds at his own risk. Once he offers evidence of his or his victim's character, the prosecution may offer contrary evidence. Fed.R.Evid. 404(a)(1)–(2).

Although the literal language of the exceptions to Rule 404(a) applies only to criminal cases, we agree with the district court here that, when the central issue involved in a civil case is in nature criminal, the defendant may invoke the exceptions to Rule 404(a). *Accord Carson v. Polley,* 689 F.2d 562, 575–76 (5th Cir.1982) (exceptions to Rule 404(a) apply in 42 U.S.C. § 1983 action alleging assault and battery); *Crumpton v. Confederation Life Insurance Co.,* 672 F.2d 1248, 1253 (5th Cir.1982) (exceptions to Rule 404(a) apply in civil action focusing on whether a rape had occurred); *see also Hackbart v. Cincinnati Bengals, Inc.,* 601 F.2d 516, 525–26 (10th Cir.) (considering Rule 404(a) exceptions in civil action examining whether plaintiff was a "dirty football player"), *cert. denied,* 444 U.S. 931, 100 S.Ct. 275, 62 L.Ed.2d 188 (1979).

In a case of this kind, the civil defendant, like the criminal defendant, stands in a position of great peril. *See* E. Cleary, *McCormick on Evidence* § 192, at 570–71 (3d ed. 1984) (hereinafter *McCormick*). A verdict against the defendants in this case would be tantamount to finding that they killed Perrin without cause. The resulting stigma warrants giving them the same opportunity to present a defense that a criminal defendant could present. Accordingly we hold that defendants were entitled to present evidence of Perrin's character from which the jury could infer that Perrin was the aggressor. The self-defense claim raised in this case is not functionally different from a self-defense claim raised in a criminal case.[3]

Although we agree with the district court that character evidence was admissible in this case, we hold that the district court should not have permitted testimony about prior specific incidents.

Federal Rule of Evidence 405 establishes the permissible methods of proving character:

"(a) **Reputation or opinion.** In all cases in which evidence of character or a trait of character of a person is admissible, proof may be made

2. We agree with Professor Uviller's explanation of why a criminal defendant is entitled to use character evidence to a greater extent than a civil defendant:

> "About the best one can do with this puzzle is to guess that somewhere, somehow the rule was relaxed to allow the criminal defendant with so much at stake and so little available in the way of conventional proof to have special dispensation to tell the factfinder just what sort of person he really is."

Uviller, *Evidence of Character to Prove Conduct: Illusion, Illogic, and Injustice in the Courtroom,* 130 U.Pa.L.Rev. 845, 855 (1982).

3. Plaintiff also argues that, because defendants had no personal knowledge of Perrin's character, evidence of his character was irrelevant. Although plaintiff is correct that this evidence has no bearing on whether defendants had a reasonable fear of Perrin, it is directly relevant to the issue of who was the aggressor in the fight. *See, e.g., United States v. Burks,* 470 F.2d 432, 434–35 & n. 4 (D.C.Cir.1972).

by testimony as to reputation or by testimony in the form of an opinion. On cross-examination, inquiry is allowable into relevant specific instances of conduct.

(b) **Specific instances of conduct.** In cases in which character or a trait of character of a person is an essential element of a charge, claim, or defense, proof may also be made of specific instances of his conduct."

Testimony concerning specific instances of conduct is the most convincing, of course, but it also "possesses the greatest capacity to arouse prejudice, to confuse, to surprise and to consume time." Fed.R.Evid. 405 advisory committee note. Rule 405 therefore concludes that such evidence may be used only when character is in issue "in the strict sense." *Id.*

Character is directly in issue in the strict sense when it is "a material fact that under the substantive law determines rights and liabilities of the parties." *McCormick* § 187, at 551. In such a case the evidence is not being offered to prove that the defendant acted in conformity with the character trait; instead, the existence or nonexistence of the character trait itself "determines the rights and liabilities of the parties." *Id.* at 552 n. 5. In a defamation action, for example, the plaintiff's reputation for honesty is directly at issue when the defendant has called the plaintiff dishonest. *See* Uviller, *Evidence of Character to Prove Conduct: Illusion, Illogic, and Injustice in the Courtroom,* 130 U.Pa.L.Rev. 845, 852 (1982).

Defendants here offered character evidence for the purpose of proving that Perrin was the aggressor. "[E]vidence of a violent disposition to prove that the person was the aggressor in an affray" is given as an example of the circumstantial use of character evidence in the advisory committee notes for Fed.R.Evid. 404(a). When character is used circumstantially, only reputation and opinion are acceptable forms of proof. Fed.R.Evid. 405 advisory committee note.[4] We therefore find that the district court erroneously relied upon the character evidence rules in permitting testimony about specific violent incidents involving Perrin.

B

Character and habit are closely akin. The district court found, alternatively, that the testimony recounting Perrin's previous violent encounters with police officers was admissible as evidence of a habit under Fed.R.Evid. 406. Here, we concur.

Rule 406 provides:

"Evidence of the habit of a person * * *, whether corroborated or not and regardless of the presence of eyewitnesses, is relevant to prove that

4. In *Hackbart v. Cincinnati Bengals, Inc.,* we intimated that character would be at issue in determining who was the aggressor in a fight. 601 F.2d at 526. We now think this statement was inaccurate. Character is "in issue" only when the existence of the character trait itself will affect the rights of the parties. For examples of when character is in issue, see *McCormick* § 187, at 551–52 & nn. 1–4.

the conduct of the person * * * on a particular occasion was in conformity with the habit * * *."

The limitations on the methods of proving character set out in Rule 405 do not apply to proof of habit. Testimony concerning prior specific incidents is allowed. *See McCormick* § 195, at 577.

This court has defined "habit" as "a regular practice of meeting a particular kind of situation with a certain type of conduct, or a reflex behavior in a specific set of circumstances." *Frase v. Henry,* 444 F.2d 1228, 1232 (10th Cir.1971) (defining "habit" under Kansas law). The advisory committee notes to Rule 406 state that, "[w]hile adequacy of sampling and uniformity of response are key factors, precise standards for measuring their sufficiency for evidence purposes cannot be formulated." Fed.R.Evid. 406 advisory committee note. That Perrin might be proved to have a "habit" of reacting violently to uniformed police officers seems rather extraordinary. We believe, however, that defendants did in fact demonstrate that Perrin repeatedly reacted with extreme aggression when dealing with uniformed police officers.

Four police officers testified to at least five separate violent incidents, and plaintiff offered no evidence of any peaceful encounter between Perrin and the police. Five incidents ordinarily would be insufficient to establish the existence of a habit. *See Reyes v. Missouri Pacific Railway Co.,* 589 F.2d 791, 794–95 (5th Cir.1979) (four convictions for public intoxication in three and one-half years insufficient to prove habit). But defendants here had made an offer of proof of testimony from eight police officers concerning numerous different incidents. To prevent undue prejudice to plaintiff, the district court permitted only four of these witnesses to testify, and it explicitly stated that it thought the testimony of the four officers had been sufficient to establish a habit. *Id.* We hold that the district court properly admitted this evidence pursuant to Rule 406. There was adequate testimony to establish that Perrin invariably reacted with extreme violence to any contact with a uniformed police officer.

* * *

IV

Plaintiff's final assertion is that the trial court erred in admitting testimony about numerous sexually explicit pornographic items that were strewn about Perrin's home and were readily accessible to his six-year-old son. Defendants offered evidence that approximately fifty magazines containing pictures of "kinky-type sex" were in the bathroom, a bedroom, and the living room. There also was evidence that hand-drawn pictures signed by Perrin depicting oral sodomy and nude women with straps on them were in every room but the kitchen and one bedroom. Plaintiff contends that this testimony was irrelevant, and, even if relevant, unduly prejudicial. Defendants counter that this testimony was permissible rebuttal to plaintiff's contention that Perrin was a good father and that his son's loss of his companionship should be valued by the jury at $1,000,000.

We agree with defendants that this testimony was relevant on the damages issue. In determining the amount to which Perrin's son was entitled, the jury properly could have considered the nature of the influence Perrin was having on his son. *See, e.g., Smith v. United States,* 587 F.2d 1013, 1017 (3d Cir.1978) (admitting evidence that defendant's mental condition precluded award of damages for loss of services and nurture); *Solomon v. Warren,* 540 F.2d 777, 788 (5th Cir.1976) (evidence must be admitted that deceased parent furnished physical, intellectual, and moral training to child); *In re Paris Air Crash of March 3, 1974,* 423 F.Supp. 367, 373 (C.D.Cal.1976) (instructing jury to consider factors such as the disposition of the decedent in assessing loss to child).

We do not hold, however, that because Perrin exposed his child to pornography, the value of his relationship to the child diminished. We only state that it was within the discretion of the trial judge to admit such evidence. *See Blim v. Western Electric Company, Inc.,* 731 F.2d 1473, 1477 (10th Cir.1984) (trial court has broad discretion to balance probity versus prejudice). Regarding the possible prejudice to plaintiff's case, we would be more convinced that this evidence might have prejudiced plaintiff if the jury had found in plaintiff's favor but rendered only a small award.

AFFIRMED.

DAHLEN v. LANDIS, 314 N.W.2d 63, 71 (N.D.1981). "[Rule 405(b)] permits specific instances of conduct to be used to prove character where character or a character trait is an 'essential element of a charge, claim, or defense.' Traditionally referred to as 'character in issue,' Rule 405(b) applies only when character or a character trait is an operative fact which, under the substantive law, determines the legal rights of the parties. 22 Wright and Graham, Federal Practice and Procedure § 5267 at 602. Scholars agree that true instances of character in issue are 'rather rare.' Wright and Graham, supra, § 5235 at 368, n. 3. Representative instances include chastity under a statute making chastity an element of the crime of seduction, and the competency of a driver in an action for negligent entrustment of a car to a careless driver. See Advisory Committee Notes to Federal Rule 404.

"The question thus raised is whether or not the victim's character is an essential element of self-defense [in a civil suit for assault and battery]. Under the circumstances of this case, Dahlen's character was not 'in issue' in the strict sense of Rule 405(b)."

UNITED STATES v. MURZYN, 631 F.2d 525, 528–29 n. 2 (7th Cir.1980), cert. denied, 450 U.S. 923, 101 S.Ct. 1373, 67 L.Ed.2d 351 (1981). "As we read these rules, assertion of an entrapment defense falls within the ambit of Rule 404(a)(1) because it puts the accused's predisposition to commit the crime in issue. Accordingly, the government is entitled to rebut an entrapment defense by evidence of the accused's character introduced to prove that he 'acted in conformity therewith' and was, at the relevant time, predisposed to commit the crime charged. Under Rule 405(b), the government may do this by resort to evidence of the accused's prior specific acts. This is the case because predisposition is, in effect, an 'essential element' of the government's case once the issue of entrapment has been raised; thereafter, the government is required to prove beyond a reasonable doubt that the accused was predisposed to commit the crime and was not entrapped. E.g., United States v. Townsend, 555 F.2d 152, 158 (7th Cir.), cert. denied, 434 U.S. 897, 98 S.Ct. 277, 54 L.Ed.2d 184 (1977).

"We recognize that the use of prior crimes, wrongs, or specific acts to prove predisposition to commit the crime charged can be viewed as a proof of the accused's character 'in order to show that he acted in conformity therewith,' and thus can be thought in conflict with Rule 404(b). We read Rules 404(a)(1) and 405(b) as being consistent with Rule 404(b), however, and reconcile them by finding that one of the 'other purposes' mentioned in Rule 404(b) is proof of predisposition. Predisposition is similar to other objects of proof mentioned in Rule 404(b) both in that it involves the mental state of the accused at a given time and in that it is often, in effect, an essential element of the government's case. To otherwise interpret Rule 404(b) would, we think, disturb the holding in Sorrells v. United States, [287 U.S. 435, 53 S.Ct. 210, 77 L.Ed. 413 (1932),] that a 'searching' inquiry into predisposition is allowed."

UNITED STATES v. RICHARDSON, 764 F.2d 1514, 1522 n. 2 (11th Cir.1985), cert. denied, 474 U.S. 952, 106 S.Ct. 320, 88 L.Ed.2d 303 (1985). "There is a possibility that evidence of predisposition constitutes evidence of a pertinent trait of a defendant's character that the accused places into issue by making an entrapment defense, and therefore admissible under Rule 404(a)(1). See United States v. Sonntag, 684 F.2d 781, 787–88 (11th Cir.1982) (government's failure to produce evidence related to defendant's predisposition not a violation of discovery order covering all prior acts probative of knowledge or intent, a Rule 404(b) category, because predisposition evidence is admissible under Rule 404(a)(1)). Most courts, however, have analyzed the admissibility of predisposition evidence under Rule 404(b). United States v. Moore, 732 F.2d 983 (D.C.Cir.1984); United States v. Jimenez, 613 F.2d 1373 (5th Cir.1980); United States v. Biggins, 551 F.2d 64, 68 (5th Cir.1977). See also United States v. Daniels, 572 F.2d 535 (5th Cir.1978) (excluding predisposition evidence under Rule 403, no mention of Rule 404(b)). Because predisposition deals with a state of mind at a particular time and Rule 404(a)(1) deals with 'character' in a more general sense, we resolve the question under Rule 404(b). See United States v. Webster, 649 F.2d 346, 350 (5th Cir.1981) (en banc) ('predisposition is a state of mind, not a character trait.')."

Note

"Predisposition, 'the principal element in the defense of entrapment,' * * * focuses upon whether the defendant was an 'unwary innocent' or instead, an 'unwary criminal' who readily availed himself of the opportunity to perpetrate the crime." Mathews v. United States, 485 U.S. 58, 63, 108 S.Ct. 883, 886, 99 L.Ed.2d 54 (1988).

SECTION 3. HABIT AND ROUTINE PRACTICE *

[FED.R.EVID. 406]

PERRIN v. ANDERSON

[p. 103 supra]

WEIL v. SELTZER

United States Court of Appeals, District of Columbia Circuit, 1989.
873 F.2d 1453.

FLOYD R. GIBSON, SENIOR CIRCUIT JUDGE:

* * *

On March 27, 1984, Martin Weil died unexpectedly at the age of 54 years. Weil's treating physicians could not explain the cause of his death nor could they account for a series of recent medical problems which he suffered from prior to his death.[1] An autopsy was performed in order to determine the cause of Weil's death. The autopsy and a subsequent investigation into the treatment that Weil received from his allergist, Dr. Seltzer, were very revealing.

Dr. Seltzer had treated Weil for more than twenty years and over the course of this treatment Dr. Seltzer regularly prescribed medication which Weil was led to believe were antihistamines. After Weil's death, however, it was determined that Dr. Seltzer had been prescribing a drug called prednisone, which is a steroid. Suddenly, Weil's treating physicians were able to explain his bizarre medical problems that predominated the last ten years of his life. It became apparent that Weil's illnesses were attributable to his long-term ingestion of steroids prescribed by Dr. Seltzer.

* See 2 Wigmore, Evidence § 461 (Chadbourn rev. 1979); McCormick, Evidence § 195 (4th ed. 1992); Lewan, Rationale of Habit Evidence, 16 Syracuse L.Rev. 39 (1964).

1. During the ten years leading up to his death, Weil suffered from: severe flu-like symptoms; cysts on his face, neck, and eye lids; a broken hip; a fractured knee; general osteoporosis; a life-threatening drop in blood pressure; an abscess in his groin; pain associated with the collapse of his vertebrae; and a severe infection in his left hand. Many of these illnesses were unusual for a man of Weil's age. Medical experts called to testify on behalf of Weil's estate linked many of these problems to long-term use of steroids.

The autopsy, which was consistent with long-term steroid use, determined that Weil's cause of death was a saddle block embolus (a type of blood clot), which contained several bone marrow fragments. The autopsy also revealed significant atrophy in Weil's adrenal glands and severe osteoporosis.

Medical experts testified that Weil's osteoporosis, which was linked to his steroid use, may have caused his bones to crumble thus explaining the presence of bone marrow fragments in the fatal blood clot. Long-term steroid use also may have been the cause of the atrophy in Weil's adrenal glands. This condition reduces the body's ability to ward off infection.

Weil's estate filed suit against Dr. Seltzer and began discovery. Through its discovery efforts, Weil's estate learned that Dr. Seltzer prescribed steroids to Weil on his first visit in 1963 and continued to prescribe steroids over a period of more than twenty years. Indeed, Dr. Seltzer had prescribed steroids just eight days before Weil's death and on at least three other occasions during the three months immediately preceding Weil's death.

The most startling fact revealed in the discovery was the frequency with which Dr. Seltzer prescribed steroids to his patients. Dr. Seltzer's purchase orders for medication during the years 1980 thru 1984, which were produced during discovery, revealed that he purchased 10,000 tablets of the steroidal drugs. Weil's estate then contacted three of the drug companies named in the purchase orders and learned that Dr. Seltzer had purchased more than 1.7 million tablets containing steroids during the 1980–1984 period alone. Weil's estate then contacted eight of Dr. Seltzer's former patients and learned that each had been treated by Dr. Seltzer for many years and they were prescribed pills which Dr. Seltzer represented to be antihistamines and decongestants. All of the patients later learned that the pills prescribed by Dr. Seltzer were in fact steroids. Finally, a number of boxes and bottles labeled with the names of antihistamines and other non-steroidal medications were found in the possession of Dr. Seltzer, Weil, and several of Dr. Seltzer's former patients. These boxes and bottles were mislabeled because they actually contained cortisone, another type of steroid.

* * *

B. "Former Patient" Evidence

The next issue concerns the testimony of five of Dr. Seltzer's former patients which was admitted in the second trial, over appellant's objection. The substance of this testimony indicated that Dr. Seltzer had prescribed steroids to other allergy patients while representing the drugs to be antihistamines or decongestants.

The district court admitted the evidence under Federal Rule of Evidence 406 which provides:

> Evidence of the habit of a person or of the routine practice of an organization, whether corroborated or not and regardless of the pres-

> ence of eyewitnesses, is relevant to prove that the conduct of the person or organization on a particular occasion was in conformity with the habit or routine practice.

Fed.R.Evid. 406.

Appellant argues that the district court erred in admitting the "former patient" evidence because its admission is forbidden by Federal Rule of Evidence 404(b) which provides:

> Evidence of other crimes, wrongs, or acts is not admissible to prove the character of a person in order to show action in conformity therewith. It may, however, be admissible for other purposes, such as proof of motive, opportunity, intent, preparation, plan, knowledge, identity, or absence of mistake or accident.

Fed.R.Evid. 404(b).

Again, we review the district court's action for an abuse of discretion. *See Carter v. District of Columbia,* 795 F.2d 116, 126 (D.C.Cir. 1986). For the reasons discussed below we believe that the district court abused its discretion in allowing the former patient evidence under Rule 406.

Rule 406 allows certain evidence which would otherwise be inadmissible if it rises to the level of habit. In this context, habit refers to the type of nonvolitional activity that occurs with invariable regularity. It is the nonvolitional character of habit evidence that makes it probative. *See, e.g., Levin v. United States,* 338 F.2d 265, 272 (D.C.Cir.1964) (testimony concerning religious practices not admissible because "the very volitional basis of the activity raises serious questions as to its invariable nature, and hence its probative value"), *cert. denied,* 379 U.S. 999, 85 S.Ct. 713, 13 L.Ed.2d 701 (1965). *But see Perrin v. Anderson,* 784 F.2d 1040, 1046 (10th Cir.1986) (five instances of violent encounters with police sufficient to establish "habit" of reacting violently to uniformed police officers). Thus, habit is a *consistent* method or manner of responding to a particular stimulus. Habits have a reflexive, almost instinctive quality. The advisory committee notes on Rule 406 illustrate this point:

> A habit * * * is the person's regular practice of meeting a particular kind of situation with a specific type of conduct, such as the habit of going down a particular stairway two stairs at a time, or of giving the hand-signal for a left turn, or of alighting from railway cars while they are moving. The doing of the habitual acts may become semi-automatic.

Fed.R.Evid. 406 advisory committee's note (quoting C. McCormick, *Handbook of the Law of Evidence* 340 (1954)). *See also United States v. Troutman,* 814 F.2d 1428, 1455 (10th Cir.1987) (evidence of past official conduct not admissible because "[e]xtortion or refraining from extortion is not a semi-automatic act and does not constitute habit"). The former patient evidence in this case certainly does not meet this criteria.

We do not believe the evidence of Dr. Seltzer's treatment of five former patients constitutes habit as envisioned by Rule 406. *Cf. Cannell v. Rhodes,* 31 Ohio App.3d 183, 509 N.E.2d 963, 966 (1986) (court properly excluded proffered testimony of attorney's other clients regarding discussions they had with attorney concerning fees; evidence was not proper habit evidence under Rule 406). In deciding whether conduct amounts to "habit" significant factors include the "adequacy of sampling and uniformity of responses." Fed.R.Evid. 406 advisory committee's note. Thus, one of the concerns over the reliability of habit testimony is that the conduct at issue may not have occurred with sufficient regularity making it more probable than not that it would be carried out in every instance or in most instances. *Levin,* 338 F.2d at 272. This concern is not allayed by the former patient testimony because none of the former patients had ever observed Dr. Seltzer with another patient. Before the former patient evidence could be properly admitted as habit evidence the witnesses "must have some knowledge of the practice and must demonstrate this knowledge prior to giving testimony concerning the routine practice. Where a witness cannot demonstrate such knowledge, he cannot testify as to the routine nature of the practice." *Laszko v. Cooper Laboratories, Inc.,* 114 Mich.App. 253, 318 N.W.2d 639, 641 (1982). Each witness who testified against Dr. Seltzer only knew of the way Dr. Seltzer treated his own allergies. Although they each saw Dr. Seltzer on more than one occasion, he was treating the same patient (the testifying witness) on each occasion. None of the patients were able to testify concerning Dr. Seltzer's method of treating others. Dr. Seltzer's actions might constitute habit only if he reacted the same way each time he was presented with a new patient with allergies. For the former patient testimony to be at all probative it must show that Dr. Seltzer responded the same way with each patient as he did with the testifying patient. *See generally* Annotation, *Admissibility of Evidence of Habit or Routine Practice Under Rule 406, Federal Rules of Evidence,* 53 A.L.R.Fed. 703, 705 (1981) (when considering evidence under Rule 406 as habit "it has been held that it is necessary to critically examine the ratio of reactions to the situations and to show regularity of conduct by comparison of the number of instances in which any such conduct occurs with the number in which no such conduct takes place") (footnote omitted); *see also Wilson v. Volkswagen of America, Inc.,* 561 F.2d 494, 512 (4th Cir.1977), *cert. denied,* 434 U.S. 1020, 98 S.Ct. 744, 54 L.Ed.2d 768 (1978).

Weil's estate emphasizes the appellant's failure to contradict the testimony of Dr. Seltzer's former patients, noting that evidence concerning Dr. Seltzer's treatment of his other patients was within appellant's control. We note, however, that the admissibility of habit evidence under Rule 406 does not hinge on the ability of the party seeking exclusion of the evidence to disprove the habitual character of the evidence. *But see Perrin v. Anderson,* 784 F.2d at 1046. Rather, the burden of establishing the habitual nature of the evidence rests on the proponent of the evidence.

Evidence concerning Dr. Seltzer's treatment of five former patients is not of the nonvolitional, habitual type that ensures its probative value. Rather the former patient evidence is the type of character evidence contemplated under Rule 404(b). This evidence of Dr. Seltzer's treatment of the former patients was clearly an attempt to show that Dr. Seltzer treated Weil in conformity with his treatment of the five testifying patients. *See, e.g., Outley v. City of New York,* 837 F.2d 587, 592–93 (2d Cir.1988) (evidence of six prior lawsuits filed by litigant improper under Rule 404(b) because it is improper evidence of the character trait of litigiousness); *cf. Carter v. District of Columbia,* 795 F.2d at 131 (admission of police officer's personnel files containing evidence of other bad acts was error because it subjected officers to risk of unfair prejudice). Thus, the evidence was admitted for an improper purpose and was undoubtedly prejudicial to appellant's defense.

We note that under Rule 404(b) the former patient evidence may have been admissible for other purposes, *i.e.,* to show plan, knowledge, identity, or absence of mistake or accident. Indeed, Judge Oberdorfer ruled in the first trial that the evidence could be introduced for that purpose. We, of course, express no view on the correctness of that ruling since that issue is not before us in this case.

Accordingly, the admission of this prejudicial evidence under the standard of "habit" requires us to vacate the district court's judgment.

* * *

SIMPLEX, INC. v. DIVERSIFIED ENERGY SYSTEMS, INC., 847 F.2d 1290, 1293–94 (7th Cir.1988). "Diversified also finds error in Judge Mills's exclusion of evidence regarding other contracts involving Simplex. Diversified argues that it should have been allowed to introduce evidence of Simplex's conduct with respect to other contracts to establish Simplex's routine practice of late deliveries and defective performance pursuant to Rule 406 of the Federal Rules of Evidence.

"We are cautious in permitting the admission of habit or pattern-of-conduct evidence under Rule 406 because it necessarily engenders the very real possibility that such evidence will be used to establish a party's propensity to act in conformity with its general character, thereby thwarting Rule 404's prohibition against the use of character evidence except for narrowly prescribed purposes. See Wilson v. Volkswagen of America, Inc., 561 F.2d 494 (4th Cir.1977). Moreover, such collateral inquiries threaten the orderly conduct of trial while potentially coloring the central inquiry and unfairly prejudicing the party against whom they are directed. Id. at 511. Thus, before a court may admit evidence of habit, the offering party must establish the degree of specificity and frequency of uniform response that ensures more than a mere 'tendency' to act in a given manner, but rather, conduct that is 'semi-automatic' in nature. See Fed.R.Evid. 406 (Notes of Advisory

Committee); 23 Wright and Graham, Federal Practice and Procedure, § 5273 (1980) p. 33 (evidence of habit must be highly particularized); *Wilson,* 561 F.2d at 511 (pattern-of-conduct or habit evidence must be ' "numerous enough to base an inference of systematic conduct" and to establish "one's regular response to a repeated specific situation" ').

"We are extremely dubious of Diversified's contention that late and inadequate performance of other contracts approaches the level of specificity necessary to be considered semi-automatic conduct. Our reluctance is sustained by the numerous but clearly distinguishable cases cited by Diversified. See, e.g., Meyer v. United States, 464 F.Supp. 317 (D.Colo.1979), aff'd. 638 F.2d 155 (10th Cir.1980) (habit established by dentist 'routinely and regularly' informing patients of risks involved in molar extractions); United States v. Callahan, 551 F.2d 733 (6th Cir.1977) (routine pay-offs to local union officials established habit of paying unions 'for the sake of expediency and not fear'); Spartan Grain and Mills Co. v. Ayers, 517 F.2d 214 (5th Cir.1975) (physical manner in which seller routinely collected eggs thereby affecting adversely the hatching rate established habit). Each case involves specific, particularized conduct capable of almost identical repetition. Conversely, the production of defective products could take an endless variety of forms. Beyond the conclusory assertion that 'numerous examples of other instances of lateness and defective performance on similar contracts' exist, Diversified fails to allege any specific, repetitive conduct that might approach evidence of habit. Mere similarity of contracts does not present the kind of 'sufficiently similar circumstances to outweigh the danger * * * of prejudice and of confusion.' See McCormick on Evidence § 162 (1964).

"Nor has Diversified indicated the actual number of other contracts upon which it relies, making it impossible to determine if the examples are ' "numerous enough to infer systematic conduct" * * *.' Wilson, 561 F.2d at 511 (quoting Strauss v. Douglas Aircraft Co., 404 F.2d 1152, 1158 (2nd Cir.1968)). As noted in Wilson, the Rule 406 inquiry also necessitates 'some comparison of the number of instances in which any such conduct occurs with the number in which no such conduct took place.' Id. at 512. Simplex has been in business since 1934; it obviously has been a party to hundreds of different contracts. Diversified fails even to acknowledge, much less make a comparison of the number of late and defectively performed contracts relative to those without such inadequacies. Consequently, Diversified's proffered evidence of other similar contract disputes failed to allege adequately a frequency of specific conduct sufficient to be considered semiautomatic and therefore could not properly be admitted as evidence of habit. See G.M. Brod and Co., Inc. v. U.S. Home Corp., 759 F.2d 1526, 1533 (11th Cir.1985) (['The defendant's former employee's] testimony of specific instances of [defendant's] operation within his personal experience, when considered in the light of [defendant's] contractual dealings with thousands of small subcontractors and the significant differences between the types of contracts involved and the course of dealing required of them, falls short of the adequacy of sampling and uniformity of response which are the controlling considerations governing admissibility. It was, therefore, error for the district court to admit this collateral evidence as evidence of routine practice * * *.')."

MAYNARD v. SAYLES, 817 F.2d 50, 52–53 (8th Cir.1987). "* * * Maynard attempted to introduce the testimony of Cynthia Stein, a former Kansas City police officer, that there exists an unwritten rule of corroboration or 'code of silence' among Kansas City police officers. During an offer of proof, Stein testified that where a fellow officer has used excessive force in arresting a criminal suspect, the witnessing officers will not discuss the incident except to corroborate the fellow officer's version of the arrest. In her testimony, Stein stated that such a rule exists, and gave an account of a specific instance in which she claimed to have violated the rule and to have suffered formal and informal discipline for the transgression.

"The trial court excluded Stein's proposed testimony in its entirety.

"* * * The foundation for Rule 406 evidence can be established by a lay opinion. 23 C. Wright & K. Graham, Federal Practice and Procedure § 5276 (1980). Such an opinion need only comply with Rule 701 of the Federal Rules of Evidence which requires that the witness's testimony be rationally based on perception and helpful to a determination of a fact at issue. Burlington Northern Ry. Co. v. Neb., 802 F.2d 994, 1004 (8th Cir.1986); Greenwood Ranches, Inc. v. Skie Constr. Co., 629 F.2d 518, 522 (8th Cir.1980). Personal knowledge based on industry experience is a sufficient foundation for lay opinion testimony. See, e.g., Farner v. Paccar, Inc., 562 F.2d 518, 520 (8th Cir.1977).

"By her employment experience with the Kansas City Police Department, Stein established that she possessed the personal knowledge necessary to testify to a routine practice at the Kansas City Police Department. Stein worked as a police officer in the Kansas City Police Department for three years; from March 1979 to December 1982. During this time, she worked side by side with three of the defendants—Officers Calegari, Bartlett, and Sayles. Thus Stein possessed firsthand knowledge of departmental practices and the degree to which they had been followed by police officers, including the defendants in this case.

"We believe Stein's theory exhibited a sufficient foundation to be admitted as Rule 406 evidence of a routine practice, despite Maynard's failure to produce more than one witness to testify to what Stein referred to as a 'code of silence.' Realistically, the nature of the routine practice at issue is one to which few police officers would testify. Thus, it is unlikely that additional evidence of this sort of routine practice would be available.

"We do not believe failure to produce more than one witness to testify to the alleged 'code of silence' prohibits admitting Stein's testimony under Rule 406. First, Rule 406 explicitly states that evidence of a routine practice need not be corroborated to be admissible. Second, courts frequently determine that the testimony of one or two witnesses is sufficient to establish a foundation for Rule 406 evidence. See, e.g., United States v. Oddo, 314 F.2d 115 (2d Cir.), cert. denied, 375 U.S. 833, 84 S.Ct. 50, 11 L.Ed.2d 63 (1963) (one official's testimony sufficient to establish foundation for his evidence of a routine recordkeeping practice at INS); Swine Flu Immunization Products Liability Litigation, 533 F.Supp. 567 (D.Colo.1980) (two health department employees' testimony sufficient to establish foundation for their evidence that department routinely obtained consent forms before administering flu shots); Envirex, Inc. v. Ecological Recovery Assoc., Inc., 454 F.Supp. 1329 (M.D.Penn.1978), aff'd, 601 F.2d 574 (1979) (one employee's testimony sufficient to establish foundation for his evidence that company routinely sends complete proposal to all general contractors). See also Wetherill v. University of Chicago, 570 F.Supp. 1124, 1129 (N.D.Ill.1983); 23 C. Wright & K. Graham, Federal Practice and Procedure § 5276 (1980)."

MAYNARD v. SAYLES, 831 F.2d 173 (8th Cir.1987). "The panel opinion filed April 23, 1987 is vacated. The judgment of the district court is affirmed by an evenly divided court, five judges voting to affirm and five judges voting to reverse."

Note

See also Reyes v. Missouri Pacific R. Co., 589 F.2d 791, 794–95 (5th Cir.1979) (four convictions for public intoxication in three and one-half years insufficient to prove habit to prove intoxication on particular occasion); Ritchey v. Murray, 274 Ark. 388, 625 S.W.2d 476 (1981) (evidence that Murray often crossed the center line of the road while driving did not make out habit); Hoffman v. Rengo Oil Co., 20 Mich.App. 575, 174 N.W.2d 155 (1969) (testimony that deceased habitually followed a set pattern in crossing the highway to obtain daily newspaper properly admitted); Reaves v. Mandell, 209 N.J.Super. 465, 507 A.2d 807 (1986) ("Based on a routine developed over a period of 15 years, [the defendant, an obstetrician/gynecologist,] was prepared to testify about the information which he invariably gave to patients who presented a fibroid uterus"; "considering the uniformity of response and the adequacy of the prior instances, [the testimony rises] to the level of habit"); Lapierre v. Sawyer, 131 N.H. 609, 557 A.2d 640 (1989) (plaintiff alleged that during a racquetball match the defendant, losing his temper, negligently struck a ball that was no longer in play, injuring plaintiff's eye; plaintiff offered to show that "the defendant had lost his temper in two or three previous games"; "plaintiff's evidence failed to satisfy the criteria which distinguish habit evidence from character evidence * * * plaintiff needed to show that the defendant's specific response to the repeated situation of falling behind or losing important racquetball points was to strike balls no longer in play, or otherwise to play outside the rules so as to endanger his opponents"); Charmley v. Lewis, 302 Or. 324, 729 P.2d 567 (1986) (plaintiff went to the grocery store nearly every day and invariably took the same route; the evidence "that plaintiff always crossed this particular street within this particular crosswalk demonstrated an ingrained habit that meets the requirements of OEC 406").

SECTION 4. SUBSEQUENT REMEDIAL MEASURES *

[FED.R.EVID. 407]

ANDERSON v. MALLOY

United States Court of Appeals, Eighth Circuit, 1983.
700 F.2d 1208.

LAY, CHIEF JUDGE.

Linda and Derriel Anderson appeal from a judgment on a jury verdict rendered against them in the United States District Court for the Eastern District of Missouri. The Andersons claim the trial court abused its discretion in excluding portions of the plaintiffs' evidence. We agree, and accordingly vacate the district court's judgment and remand the case for a new trial.

In January and February of 1979, the Andersons were guests in a motel in the St. Louis area owned and operated by the defendants, Malloy, Zes, and Gibson. On the evening of February 7, 1979, while Linda Anderson was alone in the motel room, an unknown assailant forcibly entered the room and assaulted and raped her.

The Andersons thereupon filed suit alleging diversity jurisdiction in federal district court in St. Louis, alleging that the defendants negligently failed to provide them with reasonably safe lodging, that the defendants breached an express warranty to provide reasonably safe lodging, and that the defendants fraudulently misrepresented the level of security provided to the motel's guests.

During the trial, the district court made four evidentiary rulings excluding portions of the plaintiffs' evidence. The court refused to admit * * * (4) evidence that, after Linda Anderson was raped, the defendants installed safety chains and "peep holes" in the entrance doors of the motel rooms.

The motel owners argued in defense that they had done everything reasonably necessary to make their motel secure. The defendants also affirmatively claimed that Linda Anderson's injuries were proximately

* See 2 Wigmore, Evidence § 283 (Chadbourn rev.1979); McCormick, Evidence § 267 (4th ed. 1992); Henderson, Products Liability and Admissibility of Subsequent Remedial Measures: Resolving the Conflict by Recognizing the Difference Between Negligence and Strict Tort Liability, 64 Neb.L.Rev. 1 (1985).

caused by her own negligence in opening her door in a strange city to a person she did not know.

The jury returned a verdict for the defendants, and the district court entered judgment on the verdict.

* * *

IV. EVIDENCE OF SUBSEQUENT REMEDIAL MEASURES

The plaintiffs attempted to introduce evidence to show that, after Linda Anderson was assaulted and raped, the defendants installed safety chains and "peep holes" on the doors of all units in the motel. The trial court refused to admit the evidence on the ground that Federal Rule of Evidence 407 "generally prohibits" the admission of such evidence.

Rule 407 prohibits the admission of evidence of subsequent remedial measures when the evidence is offered to prove negligence or culpable conduct. However, the rule expressly does not require the exclusion of such evidence when offered for another purpose. Of course, to be admissible any evidence not excluded by rule 407 must still be relevant (Fed.R.Evid. 402) and its probative value must outweigh any dangers associated with its admission (Fed.R.Evid. 403).

The plaintiffs assert on appeal that the defendants controverted the feasibility of the use of peep holes and safety chains. Thus, the plaintiffs argue that the evidence comes within the exception of rule 407. Although the trial court held to the contrary, we find that the defendants did affirmatively controvert the feasibility of the chain locks and peep holes. We conclude that the trial court committed a prejudicial abuse of discretion when it excluded the evidence.

The first witness called by the plaintiffs was the defendant, Malloy, one of the owners of the motel. Malloy was asked by the plaintiffs' counsel about the security measures taken by the defendants since they purchased the motel in 1974, but he was not asked about the absence of peep holes or chain locks on the doors. On cross-examination defense counsel opened up the issue in the following exchange:

> Q. We've already talked about the additional lighting that was installed. Did [the village police chief] indicate to you anything about putting these peepholes, as they are called, in the solid core doors?
>
> A. He felt like we had six-foot picture windows right next to the door. If we'd put peepholes in, it would be false security.
>
> Q. Did you follow the officer's recommendation in that regard?
>
> A. Yes. We did not put the peepholes in at that time.
>
> Q. Did he indicate to you anything about these chains you see on doors on occasion?
>
> A. He felt like they were unnecessary, also. False security.

On redirect, in rebuttal, the plaintiffs' counsel then asked:

> Do I understand, [the police chief] indicated to you that it wouldn't be feasible to put in peepholes and chain guards on the front doors?

Mr. Malloy replied:

> A. At that time he felt like the picture windows were adequate for—that the peephole would be sort of a false security, because they could look out these picture windows and see the door, the step there.

Whether something is feasible relates not only to actual possibility of operation, and its cost and convenience, but also to its ultimate utility and success in its intended performance. That is to say, "feasible" means not only "possible," but also means "capable of being * * * utilized, or dealt with successfully." *Webster's Third New International Dictionary* 831 (unabridged ed. 1967); see *Black's Law Dictionary* 549 (5th ed. 1979) ("reasonable assurance of success."). See also American Airlines, Inc. v. United States, 418 F.2d 180, 196 (5th Cir.1969) (defendant's witness had testified that an airplane altimeter in issue was "feasible and safe and that there was no reason to change it"; plaintiff allowed to show that defendant changed altimeter design after crash).

For the defendant to suggest that installation of peep holes and chain locks would provide only a false sense of security not only infers that the devices would not successfully provide security, it also infers that the devices would in fact create a lesser level of security if they were installed. With this testimony the defendants controverted the feasibility of the installation of these devices, because the defendant Malloy in effect testified that these devices were not "capable of being utilized or dealt with successfully."

The defendants' counsel took advantage of the situation and in closing argument to the jury said that the evidence showed that the defendants in providing security "did everything anybody recommended that they do. What more can they do? * * * Is there any evidence from any reliable source that [the defendants] could or should have done anything more?" With such a suggestion implanted in the minds of the jurors by Malloy's testimony, the plaintiffs' counsel had every right to rebut that suggestion by showing that the defendants had in fact installed these devices after Linda Anderson was raped.

The plaintiffs were entitled to show affirmatively that these devices were feasible, and furthermore to impeach the credibility of the defendants by showing that, although the defendants testified that they had done everything necessary for a secure motel, and that chain locks and peep holes would not be successful, they in fact took further security measures after Linda Anderson was raped, and in fact installed the same devices that they testified could not be used successfully. Under rule 407 the evidence could not be used by the plaintiffs to prove the defendants' negligence, and a limiting instruction would warn the jury of this restriction in its admission. But we think it was an abuse of discretion for the trial court to refuse to admit the only evidence that would effectively rebut the inferences created by the defendants. See Patrick v. South Central Bell Telephone Co., 641 F.2d 1192, 1196–97

(6th Cir.1980) (trial court allowed evidence of subsequent repairs to telephone line after the defendant inferred that line was not placed below statutory minimum height requirements); Kenny v. Southeastern Pennsylvania Transportation Authority, 581 F.2d 351, 356 (3d Cir.1978), cert. denied, 439 U.S. 1073, 99 S.Ct. 845, 59 L.Ed.2d 39 (1979) (defendant inferred that lighting was adequate on railroad platform at time plaintiff was raped; plaintiff allowed to show that, after the rape, defendant installed new lighting fixtures); American Airlines, Inc. v. United States, supra, 418 F.2d at 196. See also J. Weinstein & M. Berger, *Weinstein's Evidence* ¶ 407[05], at 407–23 to 24 (1981).

We find the trial court committed prejudicial error in the ruling discussed above; accordingly, we vacate the judgment of the district court, and remand the case for a new trial.[8]

JOHN R. GIBSON, CIRCUIT JUDGE, concurring in part and dissenting in part.

I concur with Parts I, II and III of the majority opinion. I respectfully dissent from Part IV of the majority opinion dealing with evidence of subsequent remedial measures and, therefore, would affirm the judgment for defendants.

I disagree that the testimony in this case involves a question of feasibility. This line of Malloy's testimony commences:

> Q Did you also, sir, before you went into operation, meet with a representative of the Village of Edmundson Police Department?
>
> A Yes, I did.
>
> Q And did he also make recommendations to you as to what could or should be done insofar as security is concerned?
>
> A Yes, he did. Uh-huh.

Solid core doors, Triple A door locks, and bar pins in sliding doors were all recommended. The witness was asked:

> Q You did follow his recommendations and you did do that?
>
> A We did, yes.

The testimony set out on page 1213 of the majority opinion followed. There was then testimony of a recommendation of an additional guard from 11:00 p.m. to 7:00 a.m.

When plaintiffs' offer of proof was made, the district court stated:

> There is no question of feasibility in this situation. He said he went on the recommendation, whether it's good, bad, right or wrong. He hasn't said anything which says it wasn't feasible or would cost too much.

8. Since the issues are to be retried and to avoid error on further retrial, we add the following comment. When the security experts advised defendants that security locks and peep holes would be "false security" and the defendants allegedly followed such advice, the defendants as an historical fact controverted the feasibility of such devices. Thus, once the plaintiffs demonstrate this evidence contained in Malloy's prior testimony, plaintiff should be allowed to affirmatively prove defendants' subsequent use of the devices.

In considering evidence questions, we reverse only for abuse of discretion. Haynes v. American Motors Corp., 691 F.2d 1268, 1272 (8th Cir.1982); Auto–Owners Insurance Co. v. Jensen, 667 F.2d 714, 722 (8th Cir.1981). I cannot find that the district court abused its discretion in ruling that the testimony on this issue involved recommendations and not feasibility. The testimony on the sense of false security deals only with the reasons for the recommendations. All of the testimony set out above as well as that in the majority opinion abundantly supports the district court ruling.

The term "feasible" has been defined by the Supreme Court in American Textile Mfrs. Inst. v. Donovan, 452 U.S. 490, 101 S.Ct. 2478, 69 L.Ed.2d 185 (1981). Justice Brennan in his opinion states:

> The plain meaning of the word "feasible" supports respondents' interpretation of the statute. According to Webster's Third New International Dictionary of the English Language 831 (1976), "feasible" means "capable of being done, executed, or effected." Accord, The Oxford English Dictionary 116 (1933) ("Capable of being done, accomplished or carried out"); Funk & Wagnalls New "Standard" Dictionary of the English Language 903 (1957) ("That may be done, performed or effected"). Thus, § 6(b)(5) directs the Secretary to issue the standard that "most adequately assures * * * that no employee will suffer material impairment of health," limited only by the extent to which this is "capable of being done." 452 U.S. 508–9, 101 S.Ct. at 2490, 69 L.Ed.2d 201–202.

The ruling of the district court was consistent with this definition of feasible. While Mr. Justice Brennan's opinion deals with use of the word in 29 U.S.C. § 655(b)(5), his broad treatment of the word "feasible" cannot be limited simply to that statute as opposed to its use in Rule 407, which was presented to Congress and subject to Congressional action.

In *American Textile Mfrs. Inst. v. Donovan,* the dissenting opinion of Justice Rehnquist observed "the remarkable range of interpretation" of the term "to the extent feasible." 452 U.S. at 544, 101 S.Ct. at 2508. The majority opinion here reaches to the second dictionary definition of feasible in order to conclude that feasibility was controverted.[1] Where the district court has made a ruling consistent with the Supreme Court definition of the word "feasible," I think we should not find error in its failing to consider the second meaning of this word that has a "remarkable range of interpretation."

The majority finds feasibility an issue not from direct testimony that feasibility was involved, but rather by inferring that it is an issue from the testimony concerning false sense of security which was given

1. Not only the dictionaries cited by the majority but also The American Heritage Dictionary of the English Language, Funk & Wagnall's, Standard Encyclopedic Dictionary, Webster's New World Dictionary, and The Oxford English Dictionary all give as the first definition that recognized by the Supreme Court in American Textile Mfrs. Inst. v. Donovan, 452 U.S. 490, 101 S.Ct. 2478, 69 L.Ed.2d 185 (1981) and as the second definition that recognized by the majority in its opinion.

as the reason for the recommendation of the police chief. My view is that this testimony relates to the question of necessity or desirability and that the majority stretches the chain of inferences too far.

The view expressed here is supported by decisions from other circuits. The Fourth Circuit in Werner v. Upjohn Co., Inc., 628 F.2d 848 (4th Cir.1980), cert. denied, 449 U.S. 1080, 101 S.Ct. 862, 66 L.Ed.2d 804 (1981), held that defendant did not controvert the feasibility of an additional drug product warning; it merely questioned the necessity of such a warning. Id. at 855. The Seventh Circuit in Oberst v. International Harvester Co., Inc., 640 F.2d 863 (7th Cir.1980) held that evidence of a design change excluded at trial would have been cumulative since it was clear that design alternatives were commercially available. So here the issue was the necessity or reasons for not using peepholes and chain locks which undoubtedly were commercially available. The evidence simply was that they were not recommended and therefore not used.

Plaintiffs make no contention with respect to the impeachment exception to Rule 407, neither did they make such contention at trial. I find no testimony in the record that defendants stated that they had done everything necessary for a secure motel, but simply that they had received recommendations from the chief of police and followed these recommendations. I find no testimony of defendants that chain locks and peepholes could not be used successfully, but only that the majority has inferred such statements from the testimony of false sense of security. I think we should not find impeachment of defendants on the basis of inferences the majority draws from the testimony.

Defendants' closing argument stressed the recommendations given by the chief of police. The closing argument certainly cannot be used to justify introduction of evidence during the course of the trial. While defendants posed the question of "what more can they do" the statement, read in context, simply argues that defendants had followed expert recommendations. The following is the omission from the quotation on page 1214 of the majority opinion:

> You go to the chief of the police or of the area where you're working and you ask him, "What should I do," and he tells you and you do it. You call in Union Electric and they say put in 10 more lights, you put in 10 more lights.

The argument continued:

> These gentlemen were concerned about the safety of their guests, concerned enough to seek professional help from Union Electric and from the chief of police, and not only to seek it, but to follow the advice that was given them. What more could they do?

Defendants' argument viewed in its entirety related to the police chief's recommendation and was fully supported by the evidence.

Plaintiffs' attempted introduction of defendants' subsequent remedial measures was an attempt "solely to raise the spectre of negligence under the guise of feasibility." J. Cotchett & A. Elkind, *Federal Courtroom Evidence,* at 58–59. The trial court is entitled to guard against the improper admission of such evidence. See 10 J. Moore, *Moore's Federal Practice* § 407.04 at p. IV–159 (2d ed. 1982); 2 J. Weinstein & M. Berger, *Weinstein's Evidence* ¶ 407[05] at p. 407–26 (1982).

I cannot conclude that the district court abused its discretion in ruling that the testimony involved matters of recommendation rather than feasibility, and in making a ruling that is consistent with the plain meaning of feasible as recognized in the recent decision of the United States Supreme Court. Accordingly, I would affirm.

MELLER v. HEIL CO., 745 F.2d 1297, 1299–300 (10th Cir.1984), cert. denied, 467 U.S. 1206, 104 S.Ct. 2390, 81 L.Ed.2d 347 (1984). "The Advisory Committee note indicates that the rule has two justifications. First, subsequent remedial measures are of limited probative value as an admission of fault. Second, and more importantly, exclusion of remedial measures favors 'a social policy of encouraging people to take, or at least not discouraging them from taking, steps in furtherance of added safety.' Fed.R.Evid. 407 advisory committee note.

"While Rule 407 recognizes the importance of encouraging safety improvements, it also recognizes that this salutory social policy must be balanced against competing interests. Chief among these other interests is the admission of relevant, probative evidence. Rule 407 strikes a balance by excluding subsequent remedial measures only when used as evidence of the defendant's 'negligence or culpable conduct.' It permits introduction of such measures to prove other controverted issues, provided that introduction of this evidence meets the remaining admissibility requirements of the Federal Rules of Evidence."

WERNER v. UPJOHN CO., 628 F.2d 848 (4th Cir.1980), cert. denied, 449 U.S. 1080, 101 S.Ct. 862, 66 L.Ed.2d 804 (1981). "Plaintiff argues, and we agree, that the exceptions listed in Rule 407—ownership, control or feasibility of precautionary measures (if controverted), and impeachment, are illustrative and not exhaustive. See Advisory Committee Notes to Rule 407. However, we note once again that Rule 407 promotes an important policy of encouraging subsequent remedial measures. If this policy is to be effectuated we should not be too quick to read new exceptions into the rule because by so doing there is a danger of subverting the policy underlying the rule.

"* * * It is clear that in enacting the Federal Rules of Evidence Congress did not intend to wipe out the years of common law development in the field of evidence, indeed the contrary is true. The new rules contain many gaps and omissions and in order to answer these unresolved questions courts certainly should rely on common law precedent. See Redden & Saltzburg, *Federal Rules of Evidence Manual* 411–413 (1975). This is true with respect to Rule 407 which merely enacts the common law rule. * * *

"Of course, exceptions must arise where the defendant attempts to make offensive use of the exclusion of this evidence. Thus, if the defendant denies ownership or control, contends that no such repair or improvement was possible, or makes statements conflicting with the fact of repair, then the plaintiff should be allowed to make use of subsequent remedial measures. As previously noted, the list of exceptions in Rule 407 is illustrative, not exhaustive, but each of the listed exceptions deals with situations where the defendant might gain a direct benefit over and above the fact of exclusion and it seems to us that new exceptions to the rule should follow this rationale if the policy behind the rule is to be protected."

HARDY v. CHEMETRON CORP., 870 F.2d 1007, 1010–11, 1015 (5th Cir.1989). "Evidence of Chemetron's rewiring should have been admitted, Hardy claims, 'to impeach Defendant's trial position that the cause of this accident was not the way the machine was wired, and also * * * Defendant's claim that, after all, this machine had operated properly after the accident.' Thus Hardy first maintains that she should have been allowed to impeach Chemetron's 'trial position' that negligent wiring had not caused her injury, which, minus a double negative, amounts to saying that she should have been allowed to adduce evidence of the rewiring to prove Chemetron's negligence. This is precisely what Rule 407 was designed to prevent. As the Seventh Circuit has explained:

> This exception must be applied with care, since 'any evidence of subsequent remedial measures might be thought to contradict and so in a sense impeach [a party's] testimony that he was using due care at the time of the accident * * * [I]f this counted as "impeachment" the exception would swallow the rule.'

This circuit has recognized that risk and held that the trial judge should guard against the improper admission of evidence to prove prior negligence under the guise of impeachment.

"Evidence of subsequent measures is no more admissible to rebut a claim of non-negligence than it is to prove negligence directly. Hardy's argument is but a semantic manipulation, and must therefore be rejected. * * *

* * *

"GARZA, Circuit Judge, dissenting:

* * *

"* * * I do not believe that Rule 407 permits a defendant who has effected subsequent design changes to make statements which repeatedly imply that no subsequent remedial measures were taken, or that no practical manufacturer would consider taking such measures, or that such changes would, in any event, simply not work. In three different ways, and on at least three different occasions during trial, Chemetron's expert laid these inferences before the jury and then hid within the shelter of Rule 407, notwithstanding the existence of credible impeachment evidence that the trial judge prevented the plaintiff from presenting."

GRENADA STEEL INDUSTRIES v. ALABAMA OXYGEN CO.

United States Court of Appeals, Fifth Circuit, 1983.
695 F.2d 883.

ALVIN B. RUBIN, CIRCUIT JUDGE:

This appeal raises two issues: whether, in this products liability suit, the exclusion of evidence of post-accident design changes was prejudicial error and, if not, whether the evidence as a whole was sufficient to support both the jury verdict for defendants and the trial judge's denial of post-judgment relief. Finding that the district judge erred neither in excluding the proffered testimony nor in finding the evidence sufficient, we affirm.

I.

On June 2, 1977, a fire, followed by an explosion, occurred in a plant owned by Grenada Steel Industries, Inc. (Grenada Steel). In this diversity-based suit, Grenada contends that the fire was caused by a leak of acetylene gas through a valve on the cylinder that contained the gas. Alabama Oxygen Company, Inc., (Alabama Oxygen) sold acetylene gas to Grenada Steel. The gas was delivered in a metal cylinder, which was to be returned when the gas was consumed. The cylinder was equipped with a valve manufactured by Sherwood–Selpac Corporation (SSC) in December, 1972, utilizing a rubber o-ring seal around the valve plug to prevent leakage of acetylene gas. The valve's design was based on a patent issued in 1965. The cylinder, with its SSC valve, was supplied to Alabama Oxygen in 1973. One year later, in 1974, SSC halted production of this type of valve. It was no longer being marketed when the fire occurred in 1977.

Liberty Mutual Insurance Company insured Grenada Steel. It paid $608,990.38 to Grenada Steel for losses resulting from the fire. It then filed this suit, as subrogee, to recover from Alabama Oxygen and SSC the amount paid to Grenada Steel. Grenada Steel later joined in the suit to assert its own claim for damages not covered by its insurance. Since their interests are in most respects identical, we refer to both claimants jointly as Grenada Steel.

In the six-day jury trial, Grenada Steel proffered evidence that, following the fire, Rego, a competitive valve manufacturer, manufactured and designed an acetylene valve based on an alternative design and that SSC had itself manufactured a differently designed model. The district court excluded this evidence. Grenada Steel also introduced the testimony of an expert witness that the valve was defective. SSC countered with testimony that the valve's design had a good reputation in the industry, its valves had been approved by Underwriters Laboratories, and the same design had been used in the industry for a number of years. Each side also presented contradictory factual and expert evidence concerning where the fire originated.

The district court, with counsel's assistance, formulated both special interrogatories and a general verdict. In response to the special interrogatories, the jury found that the valve was not defective or unreasonably dangerous, had undergone substantial changes in condition after it was sold by the manufacturer and before the fire, and was not unfit for ordinary use for the purpose intended. It rendered a general verdict for the defendants. Grenada Steel does not assert that the answers to the special interrogatories were either inconsistent with each other or with the general verdict but only that they are "*incorrect* and do not square with the *facts.*" (Emphasis in Grenada Steel's brief.)

II.

We start with an elementary proposition: in diversity cases, state substantive law applies. Erie Railroad v. Tompkins, 304 U.S. 64, 58 S.Ct. 817, 82 L.Ed. 1188 (1938). Therefore, in determining the sufficiency of the evidence we follow Mississippi courts, which have adopted the American Law Institute's Restatement (Second) of Torts § 402A as the appropriate standard of strict liability for product manufacturers. Page v. Barko Hydraulics, 673 F.2d 134, 136 n. 1 (5th Cir.1982); State Stove Mfg. Co. v. Hodges, 189 So.2d 113, 118 (Miss.1966), cert. denied, 386 U.S. 912, 87 S.Ct. 860, 17 L.Ed.2d 784 (1967). In matters of procedure, however, such as the admissibility of evidence, federal rules apply. Fed.R.Evid. 1101(b); Rabon v. Automatic Fasteners, Inc., 672 F.2d 1231, 1238 n. 14 (5th Cir.1982); Johnson v. C. Ellis & Sons Iron Works, Inc., 604 F.2d 950, 957 (5th Cir.1979).

The district court relied on Rule 407 of the Federal Rules of Evidence to exclude evidence that, after the accident, SSC and Rego marketed valves that were designed differently from the one patented in 1965. That rule provides:

> When, after an event, measures are taken which, if taken previously, would have made the event less likely to occur, evidence of the subsequent measures is not admissible to prove negligence or culpable conduct in connection with the event. This rule does not require the exclusion of evidence of subsequent measures when offered for another purpose, such as proving * * * feasibility of precautionary measures, if controverted * * *.

In excluding the testimony, the district judge held that the rule applies not only to claims of negligence but also to those based on strict liability. He also found that the feasibility of a different design had not been challenged by SSC, and, therefore, ruled that evidence of the new design was inadmissible on that issue.

The initial question is whether Rule 407 applies to product liability cases. This is a question on which we have not yet passed. See Foster v. Ford Motor Co., 616 F.2d 1304, 1309 n. 11 (5th Cir.1980).[1] We examine first its applicability to the evidence concerning changes by SSC because the rule on its face, as discussed more fully below, does not deal with alternative designs or products introduced by third parties.

The Eighth Circuit has held repeatedly that Rule 407 is simply inapplicable to products liability cases. Unterburger v. Snow Co., 630 F.2d 599, 603 (8th Cir.1980); Farner v. Paccar, Inc., 562 F.2d 518, 528 n. 20 (8th Cir.1977); Robbins v. Farmer's Union Grain Terminal Ass'n, 552 F.2d 788, 793 (8th Cir.1977); Abel v. J.C. Penney Co., 488 F.Supp. 891 (D.Minn.1980), aff'd, 660 F.2d 720 (8th Cir.1981). This view rests on two arguments. First, the rule is limited by its terms to efforts to prove negligence or culpable conduct. Yet in strict liability cases, the Eighth Circuit reasons, the focus is not on negligence or culpable conduct. Instead, liability stems from the unreasonably dangerous nature of the product. Second, its decisions rely heavily upon the policy considerations set forth in Ault v. International Harvester Co., 13 Cal.3d 113, 117 Cal.Rptr. 812, 528 P.2d 1148 (1974).

In *Ault,* decided before the adoption of the Federal Rules of Evidence, the court concluded that the blanket exclusionary rule was inapplicable to strict liability cases for economic reasons. The court asserted that it is "manifestly unrealistic to suggest that * * * a producer will forego making improvements in its product, and risk innumerable additional lawsuits and the attendant adverse effect upon its public image, simply because evidence of the adoption may be admitted in an action founded on strict liability." Id. at 121, 117 Cal.Rptr. at 815, 528 P.2d at 1151.[2]

1. The problem has given rise to much commentary. See 23 C. Wright & K. Graham, Federal Practice and Procedure § 5285 (1980); Costello & Weinberger, *The Subsequent Repair Doctrine and Products Liability,* 51 N.Y.S.B.J. 463 (1979); Davis, Evidence of Post-Accident Failures, Modifications and Design Changes in Products Liability Litigation, 6 St. Mary's L.J. 792 (1975); Note, The Case For the Renovated Repair Rule: Admission of Evidence of Subsequent Repairs Against the Mass Producer in Strict Products Liability, 29 Am. U.L.Rev. 135 (1979); Note, Products Liability and Evidence of Subsequent Repairs, 1972 Duke L.J. 837; Note, Evidence of Subsequent Repairs: Yesterday, Today and Tomorrow, 9 U.Cal.D.L.Rev. 421 (1976); Note, Federal Rule of Evidence 407 and its State Variations: The Courts Perform Some "Subsequent Remedial Measures" Of Their Own in Products Liability Cases, 49 U.Mo.K.C.L.Rev. 338 (1981); Comment, Subsequently Remedying Strict Products Liability: Cann v. Ford, 14 Conn.L.Rev. 759 (1982). See also Department of Commerce, Model Uniform Product Liability Act § 107, 44 Fed.Reg. 62,714, 62,728 (October 31, 1979); Annot., 50 A.L.R.Fed. 935 (1980); Annot., 47 A.L.R.3d 1001 (1974).

2. The *Ault* decision has been followed in other states both by decision and by legislative action or court rule. See Caterpillar Tractor Co. v. Beck, 624 P.2d 790, 793–94 (Alaska 1981); Good v. A.B. Chance Co., 39 Colo.App. 70, 78–80, 565 P.2d 217,

Other circuits have taken a different path and held that Rule 407 applies with equal force in strict liability cases. Hall v. American Steamship Co., 688 F.2d 1062 (6th Cir.1982); Josephs v. Harris Corp., 677 F.2d 985, 990–91 (3d Cir.1982); Cann v. Ford Motor Co., 658 F.2d 54 (2d Cir.1981), cert. denied, 456 U.S. 960, 102 S.Ct. 2036, 72 L.Ed.2d 484 (1982); Werner v. Upjohn Co., 628 F.2d 848 (4th Cir.1980); cert. denied, 449 U.S. 1080, 101 S.Ct. 862, 66 L.Ed.2d 804 (1981). In Bauman v. Volkswagenwerk Aktiengesellschaft, 621 F.2d 230 (6th Cir.1980), and Roy v. Star Chopper Co., 584 F.2d 1124, 1134 (1st Cir.1978), the courts applied Rule 407 in product liability cases without discussing the issue. In Oberst v. International Harvester Co., 640 F.2d 863 (7th Cir.1980), the court held evidence of subsequent repairs inadmissible. It is not clear, however, whether this decision was based on Rule 407 or on Illinois law.[3]

In *Werner* the Fourth Circuit noted that one of the basic concerns underlying Rule 407 was the encouragement of voluntary repairs by manufacturers. The court questioned "why this policy should apply any differently where the complaint is based on strict liability as well as negligence." 628 F.2d at 848. The *Werner* opinion further notes that the *Ault* approach would admit subsequent repairs as evidence that the product was defective even in cases where the manufacturer was simply making further improvements to an already safe product. Id. See also Hall v. American Steamship Co., 688 F.2d at 1067 (following *Werner*).

224 (1977); Caprara v. Chrysler Corp., 52 N.Y.2d 114, 124–25, 436 N.Y.S.2d 251, 256, 417 N.E.2d 545, 550 (1981); Ginnis v. Mapes Hotel Corp., 86 Nev. 408, 416–17, 470 P.2d 135, 140 (1970); Shaffer v. Honeywell, Inc., 249 N.W.2d 251 (S.D.1976); Chart v. General Motors Corp., 80 Wis.2d 91, 258 N.W.2d 680 (1977).

Maine admits evidence of subsequent repairs even if they are offered to show negligence. Me.R.Evid. 407(a). There is thus no need for a strict liability exception in that state. The text of Committee Comments to Wyo.R.Evid. 407 and Colo.R.Evid. 407 indicate that, while those states adopted the language of the federal rule, they also incorporated the *Ault* decision. Hawaii R.Evid. 407 is also identical in wording to the federal rule, except that it adds to the list of exceptions: "proving dangerous defect in products liability cases." Alaska R.Evid. 407 contains a similar proviso.

3. Several states have also continued to follow the traditional rule excluding evidence of subsequent repair even in strict liability cases. See Hallmark v. Allied Prods. Corp., 132 Ariz. 434, 440–41, 646 P.2d 319, 325–26 (1982); Moldovan v. Allis Chalmers Mfg. Co., 83 Mich.App. 373, 268 N.W.2d 656 (Mich.Ct.App.1978); Price v. Buckingham Mfg. Co., 110 N.J.Super. 462, 266 A.2d 140, 141 (1970) (per curiam); Lamonica v. Outboard Marine Corp., 48 Ohio App.2d 43, 355 N.E.2d 533, 535 (Ohio Ct. App.1976); Haysom v. Coleman Lantern Co., 89 Wash.2d 474, 573 P.2d 785 (1978) (en banc).

Ariz.Rev.Stat.Ann. § 12–686(a) expressly excludes evidence of subsequent repair to prove evidence of a defect in products liability actions. Neb.Rev.Stat. § 27–407 is identical to the federal rule, but adds at the end: "Negligence or culpable conduct, as used in this rule, shall include, but not be limited to, the manufacture and sale of a defective product."

Other cases continue to apply the traditional rule in products liability actions based upon a failure to warn. In those cases, however, the basis for liability more closely resembles negligence than strict liability. See Ortho Pharmaceutical Corp. v. Chapman, 388 N.E.2d 541, 561–63 (Ind. App.1979); Smith v. E.R. Squibb & Sons, Inc., 405 Mich. 79, 273 N.W.2d 476 (Mich. 1979).

Voluntary change to improve a product and reduce the possible hazard to a user should be encouraged. While there is no evidence concerning whether admission of evidence of change would deter such action by manufacturers, the assumption in the rule that it might have a deterrent effect is not demonstrably inapplicable to manufacturers upon whom strict liability is imposed. But our decision does not rest only on theses about the influence of possible tort liability on human conduct. It rests more firmly on the proposition that evidence of subsequent repair or change has little relevance to whether the product in question was defective at some previous time.

It has been suggested that evidence of a change in the manufacturing process or the design of a product has probative value because "a business is not likely to change a product unless the change promotes safety and is feasible." R. Lempert & S. Saltzburg, A Modern Approach to Evidence 189 (1977). But this argument is based on little direct evidence of why manufacturers make product changes. Similarly, most of the arguments made against admissibility rely on undocumented assumptions about how evidence of such changes might affect litigation. A priori judgments concerning why manufacturers do or do not alter their products, made by such dubious experts as judges, lawyers, and law professors, suffer from excessive reliance on logical deduction and surmise without the benefit of evidence of industry practice or economic factors. It seems to us, with no greater expertise than like-trained lawyers and judges, that changes in design or in manufacturing process might be made after an accident for a number of different reasons: simply to avoid another injury, as a sort of admission of error, because a better way has been discovered, or to implement an idea or plan conceived before the accident. The cost of making the change, the acceptance of the altered product in the market place, and whether the change is one of several that can be made contemporaneously might also be considerations.

We cannot really know why changes are made by industry generally or why a change was made in a particular product in the absence of evidence on the question. Instead, we ought to consider the probative value of such evidence on the point at issue. The real question is whether the product or its design was defective at the time the product was sold. See S. Saltzburg & K. Redden, Federal Rules of Evidence Manual 181 (3d ed. 1982). The jury's attention should be directed to whether the product was reasonably safe at the time it was manufactured. In this case, for example, there was ample expert testimony concerning that very point. The introduction of evidence about subsequent changes in the product or its design threatens to confuse the jury by diverting its attention from whether the product was defective at the relevant time to what was done later. Id. at 182 (addressing only product design). Interpreted to require the evidence to focus on the time when the product was sold, Rule 407 would conform to the policy expressed in Rule 403, the exclusion of relevant information if its probative value is substantially outweighed by the danger of confusion. See 23 C. Wright & K. Graham, supra, § 5288, at 144.

For these reasons, we follow the path taken by the First, Second, Third, Fourth and Sixth Circuits and hold Rule 407 applicable to strict liability cases.

Grenada Steel argues that, even if Rule 407 applies, the evidence was admissible under the exception to that rule for evidence offered to show feasibility of precautionary measures. But this exception pertains if the issue of feasibility is contested. Grenada Steel argues that, in design defect cases, feasibility is "inherently" an issue and an integral element of its proof. This, however, assumes that their claim that another design was feasible makes a contest. It takes two to tango, in court as well as on the ballroom floor, and the mere assertion that the manufacturer did not make a change does not controvert the feasibility of change. The manufacturer raised no issue that the alternative design suggested by Grenada Steel's experts was not feasible. Its defense was only that the design it used was not defective.

Feasibility may "almost always" be in question in design defect cases, as suggested by Professors S. Saltzburg and K. Redden, in their excellent Federal Rules of Evidence Manual 180 (3d ed. 1982). But "almost always" like "hardly ever" admits of the unusual case that prompts the qualifying adverb. Sometimes, as here, the manufacturer does not suggest that another design was impractical but only that it adopted an acceptable one. It is not obliged to prove perfection but only that the product "meets the reasonable expectations of the ordinary consumer as to its safety." Page v. Barko Hydraulics, 673 F.2d at 138.

The Fourth Circuit has ruled that "it is clear from the face of * * * rule [407] that an affirmative concession is not required. Rather, feasibility is not in issue unless controverted by the defendant." Werner v. Upjohn Co., 628 F.2d at 855. Two commentators suggest a uniform rule:

> The administration of Rule 407 would be greatly simplified if the appellate courts were to hold that in all of these [negligence and product liability] situations, feasibility of precautionary measures will be deemed "controverted" unless the defendant is prepared to make an unequivocal admission of feasibility.

23 C. Wright & K. Graham, Federal Practice & Procedure § 5288, at 144 (1980). The defendant manufacturer was not put to that alternative. We need not, therefore, determine whether denial of a request for an admission of feasibility would *per se* create a contest. In this case, however, the defendant clearly stated that feasibility was not controverted. No request for an admission to that effect was made. Therefore, the evidence was properly excluded under rule 407.

The district court also excluded evidence that Rego, another manufacturer, later offered an alternatively designed valve. Grenada Steel argues that the admission of evidence showing that someone other than the defendant made a design change cannot discourage voluntary repairs. The party making the repair is not penalized by the admission of the evidence. Therefore, neither the text of rule 407 nor the policy underlying it excludes evidence of subsequent repairs made by someone other than the defendant. See Louisville & Nashville Railroad Co. v. Williams, 370 F.2d 839, 843–44 (5th Cir.1966); Farner v. Paccar, Inc., 562 F.2d 518, 520 n. 20 (8th Cir.1977); Lolie v. Ohio Brass Co., 502 F.2d 741 (7th Cir.1974) (per curiam); Wallner v. Kitchens of Sara Lee, Inc., 419 F.2d 1028, 1032 (7th Cir.1970); Steele v. Wiedemann Co., 280 F.2d 380 (3d Cir.1960); 10 J. Moore & H. Bendix, Moore's Federal Practice § 407.05 (1982); 23 C. Wright & K. Graham, Federal Practice & Procedure § 5284, at 113 (1980); McCormick on Evidence § 275, at 667 (E. Cleary 2d ed. 1972).

Nevertheless, we think the district court's exclusion of this evidence was proper because it lacked sufficient probative value and injected the dangers of confusion and misleading the jury. In Ward v. Hobart Manufacturing Co., 450 F.2d 1176 (5th Cir.1971), a Mississippi diversity-based negligent design case, we held that it was error for a district court to consider design changes developed after the manufacture of the product in question. Such repairs were simply irrelevant to the reasonableness of the design at the time of manufacture. Alternative designs may indicate that the product was unreasonably dangerous, see Wade, On the Nature of Strict Tort Liability For Products, 44 Miss.L.J. 825, 837 (1973), but only if they were available at the time of manufacture. We fail to see how an alternative design, developed by another person years after the product in question was manufactured, is relevant to whether the product was reasonably safe at the time it was made. Therefore, the district court properly excluded evidence of Rego's alternative design in the absence of an issue on which that evidence would have had sufficient probative value to outweigh its unfair prejudicial effect.

* * *

For these reasons, the judgment is AFFIRMED.

Notes

(1) See also Roberts v. Harnischfeger Corp., 901 F.2d 42, 44 (5th Cir.1989) (reaffirming the *Granada Steel* holding that design changes made after the manufacture of a product are not relevant to the reasonableness of the design at the time of manufacture).

(2) "[I]t is clear from the wording and history of Rule 407 that the term 'event' refers to the time of the accident or injury to the plaintiff, not to the time of manufacture of the product or creation of the hazard"; therefore, evidence of a design change effected after manufacture but before the accident is not barred by Rule 407. Huffman v. Caterpillar Tractor Co., 908 F.2d 1470, 1482 (10th Cir.1990).

(3) The policy underlying Rule 407 "is not served by admitting evidence of subsequent repairs, even if the decision to make such repairs was

made prior to the incident being litigated. Once an accident occurs, there is even more reason to encourage defendants to take remedial measures. Defendants should not fear that if litigation ensues after a particular incident, any remedial measures taken will be admitted to prove their negligence." Rollins v. Board of Governors for Higher Educ., 761 F.Supp. 939, 940 (D.R.I.1991).

(4) Pau v. Yosemite Park & Curry Co., 928 F.2d 880 (9th Cir.1991), was a wrongful death action arising from a bicycle accident on a trail in Yosemite National Park. After the accident, the United States Park Service, rather than the defendant, posted a sign on the trail forbidding bicycles on the "steep hill ahead." Exclusion of evidence of the erection of the sign was held an abuse of discretion because the sign was not a subsequent safety measure undertaken by the defendant. Id. at 888. Accord, D.L. by Friederichs v. Huebner, 110 Wis.2d 581, 329 N.W.2d 890, 907 (1983) (Rule 407 "does not apply to evidence of post-event remedial measures undertaken by entities not charged with liability in the litigation before the court").

(5) "This Court is of the view that the policy considerations underlying Rule 407 are to some extent implicated in the context of post-event tests, but that it would extend the Rule beyond its intended boundaries to include such tests within its ambit. Post-event tests will not, in themselves, result in added safety. Rather it is only if the defects revealed in those tests are remedied and changes implemented that the goal of added safety will be furthered. By its terms Rule 407 includes only the actual remedial measures themselves and not the initial steps toward ascertaining whether any remedial measures are called for." Fasanaro v. Mooney Aircraft Corp., 687 F.Supp. 482, 487 (N.D.Cal.1988).

SECTION 5. COMPROMISE AND OFFERS TO COMPROMISE *

[FED.R.EVID. 408–410]

ROCHESTER MACHINE CORP. v. MULACH STEEL CORP.

Supreme Court of Pennsylvania, 1982.
498 Pa. 545, 449 A.2d 1366.

HUTCHINSON, JUSTICE.

On January 24, 1978, Appellant Rochester Machine Corporation (Rochester) filed a complaint for confession of judgment against Appellee Mulach Steel Corporation (Mulach) pursuant to a warrant of attorney contained in a real estate and equipment lease. The basis for the confession of judgment was Mulach's alleged failure to make repairs to the leased premises and equipment as required in the lease agreement. Judgment was subsequently entered in the amount of $41,738.94,

* See 4 Wigmore, Evidence §§ 1061–1062 (Chadbourn rev. 1972); McCormick, Evidence § 266 (4th ed. 1992).

however, that judgment was opened. On January 23, 1979 a jury returned a verdict in favor of Rochester in the amount of $47,300.00. The trial court denied Mulach's motion for a new trial. A panel of the Superior Court reversed and granted Mulach a new trial on the ground that the trial court erred in admitting certain correspondence between the parties' attorneys. 287 Pa.Super.Ct. 270, 430 A.2d 280 (1981) (Opinion by BROSKY, J.; MONTGOMERY, J. dissenting). We disagree and accordingly reverse the order of the Superior Court.

The background of the case is as follows: On November 14, 1975, Mulach leased certain premises from Rochester for a period of one year. The lease was subsequently extended to November 14, 1977. On August 31, 1977 Rochester, through its attorney, sent a letter to Mulach which presented an itemized list of damages said to be caused during Mulach's occupancy. The letter demanded immediate payment of the estimated cost of repairs. On October 31, 1977, Mulach replied by way of a letter from its attorney. The letter consisted of an item by item response to each claim for damages asserted in Rochester's letter of August 31. With respect to some of the items, Mulach stated "Mulach accepts responsibility." With respect to several others, Mulach declined to accept responsibility, generally offering instead a brief explanation as to why it was not liable for the claimed item.[1]

I

The general rule is that an offer to compromise is not admissible in evidence at trial as an admission that what is offered is rightfully due or that liability exists. Woldow v. Dever, 374 Pa. 370, 376, 97 A.2d 777,

1. Rochester's letter to Mulach, dated August 31, 1977 states, *inter alia:*

> The extensive repairs made necessary by damage during your occupancy are as follows:
>
> * * *
>
> In view of the nature and extent of the damage and the cost of the required repairs (over $30,000), we must insist upon a prompt and definite commitment from you respecting the restoration of the premises to their former good condition.
>
> In conclusion, we wish to inform you that under Pennsylvania law, in a situation of this kind the landlord is entitled not only to the cost of repairs, but also to the rental value of the premises lost during the period while repairs are being made. Thus, you will see that it is in your best interest as well as our client's to resolve this matter as soon as possible.
>
> Please let us have you reply by September 15. Unless we receive a constructive response from you by then, we must assume that you are rejecting our client's claim.

Mulach's reply of October 31 states that "Mulach accepts responsibility" for items 2, 3, 4, 5, 7, 10 & 12. With respect to the remaining items of damage listed by Rochester Mulach's reply states, *inter alia:*

> Client insists that the lay-in ceiling in the toilet room had fallen when they took possession, and they will not do anything about this.
>
> * * *
>
> Mulach does not accept responsibility. Our employees tell us that Mr. Jeffry Bruce cut all the holes in that door, and we will do nothing about it. He denies this, but this is a factual issue.
>
> * * *
>
> We question whether or not the owners' insurance would cover this item. It occurred when the building was broken into by third parties.
>
> * * *
>
> Mulach will accept no responsibility for the cranes except to replace the penants. The cranes are in better shape today than they were when Mulach began its Lease.

781 (1953). Our threshold inquiry, then, is whether the correspondence between Mulach and Rochester can be fairly characterized as relating to an offer of compromise. Although this Court has not, heretofore, defined an offer to compromise, it is generally defined as the settlement of differences by mutual concessions; an adjustment of conflicting claims. Kelly v. Steinberg, 148 Cal.App.2d 211, 219, 306 P.2d 955, 960 (1957) (citing Webster's International Dictionary, (2d ed.)). Under such a definition the demand by Rochester stating items of damages caused by Mulach and demanding the estimated amount for their repair cannot be construed as an offer to compromise a disputed claim. See Gallagher v. Viking Supply Corp., 3 Ariz.App. 55, 411 P.2d 814 (1966). Likewise, Mulach's response cannot be construed as a settlement offer or as a counter-settlement offer. Mulach's response, accepting "responsibility" for some items of damage while refusing "responsibility" for others, does not in any way suggest that it is an offer to compromise a disputed claim. Rather it is nothing more, or less, than what it purports to be, an admission of liability with respect to some items of damages and a disclaimer of liability with respect to others.[2] There is no suggestion in the letter of efforts to negotiate a compromise. In fact, Mulach's letter suggests an exactly opposite intent. That is to say, Mulach's letter suggests that it is unwilling to compromise or to negotiate the disputed items.

We believe that the trial court correctly relied on the opinion of the Montgomery County Court of Common Pleas in Rockledge Municipal Authority v. E. Leva & Son's, Inc., 89 Montg.L.R. 342 (1968), *aff'd per curiam,* 434 Pa. 554, 252 A.2d 195 (1969) in determining the correspondence in the present case was not related to an offer to compromise. * * *

II

Even if the letter of October 31, 1977 is viewed as an offer of compromise, those portions of the letter constituting distinct admissions are, in fact, admissible. It is well settled that this Commonwealth adheres to the Common Law Rule that:

> While an offer to pay a sum of money to compromise a dispute is not admissible in evidence to prove that the sum offered was admitted to be due, the *distinct admission of a fact* is not to be excluded because it was accompanied by an offer to compromise the suit.

Mannella v. City of Pittsburgh, 334 Pa. 396, 403, 6 A.2d 70, 73 (1939) (emphasis added) (citing Rabinowitz v. Silverman, 223 Pa. 139, 72 A. 378 (1909); Bascom v. Danville Stove & Manufacturing Co., 182 Pa. 427,

2. Item 8 of Rochester's letter indicates a new roll-up steel door was required as a result of damage by Mulach. Mulach's reply to item 8 demonstrates its unequivocal intention *not* to settle the disputed questions of liability. Mulach's reply to item 8 states:

> 8. Mulach does not accept responsibility. Our employees tell us that Mr. Jeffrey Bruce cut all the holes in the door, and *we will do nothing about it. He denies this but this is a factual issue.* (emphasis added).

38 A. 510 (1897); Arthur v. James, 28 Pa. 236 (1857); Sailor v. Hertzogg, 2 Pa. 182 (1845)).

The specific acceptance of responsibility for specific items of damages is fairly construed as a distinct admission.[4]

Our rule permitting the introduction of distinct admissions made in the course of settlement negotiations has been subject to some criticism. Moreover, under the Federal Rules of Evidence such admissions, made in the course of settlement negotiations, are inadmissible. Hence, we take this opportunity to reexamine the validity of our rule.

According to *Wigmore on Evidence* § 1061 (Chadbourn rev. ed. 1972), there are three alternative theories which account for the exclusion of evidence related to settlement negotiations. The theory which a particular court adopts will determine the scope of the exclusion. The first theory is grounded in a privilege protecting as confidential all overtures of settlement made to the opposing party. The privilege is based on the belief that expeditious and extrajudicial settlements are to be encouraged and that privacy of communication is necessary in order to encourage them. Under this view, all statements made in the course of settlement negotiations must be excluded. Indeed such a position is ratified by Rule 408 of the Federal Rules of Evidence. See *Weinstein's Evidence* ¶ 408(03).[6]

On the other hand, Professor Wigmore, the leading academic proponent of the relevancy theory states:

> The true reason for excluding an offer of compromise is that it *does not* ordinarily proceed from and *imply a specific belief that the adversary's claim is well founded,* but rather a belief that the further prosecution of that claim, whether well founded or not, would in any event cause such annoyance as is preferably avoided by the payment of the sum offered. In short, the offer implies merely a desire for peace, not a concession of wrong done:
>
> * * *

4. Black's Law Dictionary, p. 1476 (rev. 4th ed. 1968) defines the word responsibility as "the obligation to answer for an act done, and to repair any injury it may have caused." The term responsibility is synonymous with liability. Bostick v. Usry, 221 Ga. 647, 146 S.E.2d 882, 883 (1966) (citing Webster's 3rd Int. Dictionary, p. 1935). The Mary F. Barrett, 279 F. 329, 334 (3d Cir.1922).

6. The criticism of the common law rule made by adherents of the privilege view is that the common law rule discourages freedom of communication in settlement negotiations.

> The practical value of the common law rule has been greatly diminished by its inapplicability to admissions of fact, even though made in the course of compromise negotiations, unless hypothetical, stated to be "without prejudice", or so connected with the offer as to be inseparable from it. McCormick § 251, pp. 540–541. An inevitable effect is to inhibit freedom of communication with respect to compromise, even among lawyers. Another effect is the generation of controversy over whether a given statement falls within or without the protected area.
>
> These considerations account for the expansion of the rule herewith to include evidence of conduct or statements made in compromise negotiations, as well as the offer or completed compromise itself.

Advisory Committee's Note, Fed.R.Evid. 408.

> By this theory, the offer is excluded because, as matter of interpretation or inference, it does not signify an admission at all. There is no concession of claim to be found in it, expressly or by implication. Conversely, if an express admission is in terms made, it is receivable, even though it forms part of an offer to compromise:

Wigmore on Evidence, supra at § 1061, pp. 36–37 (emphasis in original) (footnotes omitted).

The third view, adopted by the courts of England and almost universally rejected by scholars and by courts in the United States is described by Professor Wigmore as follows:

> Another theory, resting apparently on some notion of *contract,* is that an *express reservation* of secrecy (e.g., by the words "*without prejudice* ") assimilates the offer to a contractual offer, so that if the terms are not accepted the offer is null and can have no evidential effect.

Wigmore on Evidence, supra at § 1061, p. 35 (emphasis in original).

Our Court, while recognizing the public policy behind expeditious extrajudicial settlements, has adopted the relevancy view.

> It is never the intendment of the law to shut out the truth, but to repel any *inference* which may arise from a proposition made, not with the design to admit the existence of a fact, but merely to buy one's peace. If, however, an admission is made *because* it is a fact, the evidence to prove it is competent, whatever motive may have prompted the declaration. If A. offers to B. ten pounds in satisfaction of his claim of a hundred pounds, merely to prevent a suit, or purchase tranquillity, this *implies* no admission that any sum is due and therefore the testimony to prove the fact must be rejected, because it evinces nothing concerning the merits of the controversy. But if A. admits a particular item in the account, or any other fact, meaning to make the admission as being true, this is good evidence, although the object of the conversation was to compromise an existing controversy.

Sailor v. Hertzog, 2 Pa. at 186 (quoting Hartford B. Co. v. Granger, 4 Conn. 142, 148) (emphasis in original). See also Heyman v. Hanauer, 302 Pa. 56, 152 A. 910 (1930); Rabinowitz v. Silverman, 223 Pa. 139, 72 A. 378 (1909); Arthur v. James, 28 Pa. 236 (1857).

It should be clear, however, that our refusal to exclude distinct admissions made in the course of settlement negotiations does not act as a significant deterrent to extrajudicial settlements. A party seeking to invoke our exclusionary rule in accordance with the common law needs only to characterize his admissions in hypothetical terms. See Weinstein's Evidence, supra at § 408(03) (citing Factor v. Commissioner, 281 F.2d 100, 125–127 (9th Cir.1960); cert. denied, 364 U.S. 933, 81 S.Ct. 380, 5 L.Ed.2d 367 (1961) Re Evansville Television, Inc., 286 F.2d 65, 70 (7th Cir.1961)). cert denied sub nom., Schepp v. Producers, Inc., 366 U.S. 903, 81 S.Ct. 1048, 6 L.Ed.2d 204 (1961).[7]

7. According to *McCormick on Evidence* § 274 (1972):

The generally accepted doctrine has been that an admission of fact in the course of

A logical concomitant of the Federal Rule is the exclusion of almost all otherwise relevant and competent admissions made between parties to a contractual dispute on the ground that such evidence was made during the course of compromise negotiations.[8] In each instance, the court must first determine whether discussions regarding a dispute between parties constitute "compromise negotiations," an ethereal inquiry at best. In fact, broadly defined, virtually any communication between parties to a dispute involving some "give and take" may be characterized as "compromise negotiations." We, therefore, retain the common law rule permitting introduction into evidence of distinct admissions, even if made in connection with an offer to compromise or in the course of settlement negotiations.

We recognize the public interest is furthered by encouraging parties to settle disputes without invoking the judicial process. However, if in the course of such negotiations a party makes a clear, unequivocal admission, without qualifying it as a hypothetical admission for purposes of compromise, and, in the context and circumstances surrounding the offer it cannot be inferred that the admission is inextricably connected to an offer to compromise, it is admissible. Implicit in our rule is the conclusion that the public policy which protects litigants in the compromise of their disputes must bow before the stronger public policy which requires that issues of fact be determined on the basis of the greatest amount of relevant nonprejudicial testimony. See Annot., 15 A.L.R.3d 13, 30 (1967).

Accordingly, the order of the Superior Court is reversed and the judgment entered in the Court of Common Pleas of Beaver County is affirmed.

ROBERTS, J., files a concurring opinion in which FLAHERTY and McDERMOTT, JJ., join.

NIX, J., concurs in the result.

LARSEN, J., dissents.

ROBERTS, JUSTICE, concurring.

> negotiations is not privileged unless it is hypothetical—"we admit for the sake of the discussion only"—or unless it is expressly stated to be "without prejudice" or unless it is separably connected with the offer, so that it cannot be correctly understood without reading the two together.

While Professor McCormick, a proponent of the privilege theory, is critical of such distinctions, we remain unpersuaded by his view. In the present case, Mulach made distinct admissions of fact, in clear and absolute terms, through its attorney. It cannot be said that Mulach was punished for failing to use highly technical terms of art beyond the comprehension of a layman or that the failure to condition the admissions as hypothetical for purposes of settlement negotiations resulted from counsel's inadvertence. Rather it is apparent that Mulach said exactly what it meant to say, to wit, that it was responsible for some items of damages but that it intended to contest liability with respect to those damages which it believed that it had not caused.

8. The Federal Rule does not merely exclude admissions contained in offers to compromise; the scope of its exclusion includes all "conduct or statements made in compromise negotiations".

I join in Part I of the Opinion of Mr. Justice Hutchinson but not in Part II, which discusses the continuing vitality of our common law rule relating to the admissibility of compromise evidence. Part I properly holds that Mulach's response to the letter of Rochester was an admission of liability, and not an offer to compromise. This holding makes it unnecessary to discuss whether the response would have been admissible had it been an offer to compromise.

FLAHERTY AND MCDERMOTT, JJ., join in this concurring opinion.

Notes

(1) "While it is true that a statement is excludible if the party making it is seeking to reach a compromise, we do not find that any compromise negotiations were actually taking place in the instant situation. The statement by Georgen [an associate at the defendant's law firm] merely refers to the possible institution of suit by both plaintiff and defendant as co-parties against Schacterle. Upon inquiry into the subjective purposes of the parties, we cannot say that this statement, which is figuratively a solicitation to stay on defendant's 'side of the fence' in case of possible litigation, is the legal equivalent of a statement made in the course of compromise negotiations. Accordingly, we deny defendant's motion and admit this letter into evidence.

"We find further support for our determination in the fact that the letter was sent to Harmonay prior to the existence of an actual dispute between the instant parties, and is therefore not privileged as an offer of compromise. * * * It is admissible as an admission by a party." S. Leo Harmonay, Inc. v. Binks Mfg. Co., 597 F.Supp. 1014, 1023 (S.D.N.Y.1984), aff'd, 762 F.2d 990 (2d Cir.1985).

(2) See also Miller v. Component Homes, Inc., 356 N.W.2d 213, 216 (Iowa 1984) (letter from employee demanding $13,000 in commissions admitted because it was not a letter "by an adversary attempting to 'buy his peace' "); Bellino v. Bellino Const. Co., 75 A.D.2d 630, 427 N.Y.S.2d 303, 304 (1980) (letter from plaintiff's counsel admitted as an authorized admission even though written during settlement negotiations, "for while an offer of settlement would be inadmissible, admissions made in the course of such negotiations are not"); Delaney v. Georgia–Pacific Corp., 42 Or.App. 439, 601 P.2d 475 (1979) (in a dispute between joint venturers, G–P offered to buy the interest of the other joint venturer for $1,950,000 the month before suit was filed; evidence of the offer was held admissible because it was an attempt to get control of the company free of the obligation to consult with the other joint venturer rather than an attempt to compromise); Heritage Bank v. Packerland Packing Co., 82 Wis.2d 225, 262 N.W.2d 109 (1978) (demand letter, unconditional and written without prior negotiation, admitted).

CENTRAL SOYA CO. v. EPSTEIN FISHERIES, INC., 676 F.2d 939, 944 (7th Cir.1982). "Second, Epstein Fisheries argues that it was error for the district court to exclude, under Rule 408 of the Federal Rules of

Evidence, the testimony of Larry Haack—an accountant present at the negotiations leading to the first settlement between Central Soya and Aquarium Farms (at which Central Soya paid Aquarium Farms $50,000 and Aquarium Farms agreed to continue buying the catfish feed)—that the parties to the settlement intended to forgive the $13,000 indebtedness of Aquarium Farms to Central Soya for catfish feed already delivered but not paid for. Rule 408 excludes evidence of compromises and offers to compromise, and of 'statements made in compromise negotiations.' Although this language is broad enough to cover Haack's testimony, the purpose of the rule must be considered. It is to encourage settlements. The fear is that settlement negotiations will be inhibited if the parties know that their statements may later be used as admissions of liability. But Haack's testimony was not offered for the purpose of demonstrating that Central Soya was or was not liable to Aquarium Farms for breach of its contract to supply a complete catfish feed. The purpose was to demonstrate what the terms of the settlement of Aquarium Farms' claim were. 'Where the settlement negotiations and terms explain and are a part of another dispute they must often be admitted if the trier is to understand the case.' 2 Weinstein & Berger, Weinstein's Evidence ¶ 408[5], at 27 (1981). That is this case.

"Haack's testimony was not only proper under Rule 408; it was highly germane to the question of Epstein Fisheries' liability to Central Soya on the guaranty. If Haack's testimony was believed, it would follow that although Central Soya sued Aquarium Farms for $24,000 it could not have collected more than $11,000, because that was Aquarium 'Farms' total unpaid indebtedness. If so, then even if the counterclaim was totally worthless, the most Central Soya would be entitled to collect in this suit on the guaranty would be $11,000—not $20,000, as the court below thought. In addition, if the debt was only $11,000, it would be completely offset by a counterclaim having an expected value of $11,000, making it more likely that the dropping of the counterclaim operated to discharge the debt—and Epstein Fisheries, the guarantor—in full."

JOICE v. MISSOURI—KANSAS—TEXAS RY. CO., 354 Mo. 439, 189 S.W.2d 568, 574–75 (1945). "Wilson, the Coweta section foreman, was a witness and testified for the railroad. In some matters his evidence was corroborative of Joice's claims but in many important particulars his evidence was contrary to that of Joice and in denial of his claims. On cross-examination it was first developed that he had been injured in the collision. He was then asked if he had not made a claim against the railroad and whether the railroad had settled with him. The court permitted the question and admitted the answer that the railroad had settled with him though the amount of the settlement was not disclosed. It was objected then, as it is now, that it was error to permit Wilson to say, on cross-examination, that he had been injured in the same accident and that the railroad had settled with him. It is urged that the evidence was prejudicial in that it could only be considered by the jury as an admission of liability, especially so because it was admitted without limitation or restriction by the court.

"It is true that proof of a compromise or settlement with a third person is not admissible for the purpose of establishing either the validity or the invalidity of a claim. Sec. 309, American Law Institute's Model Code of Evidence; 31 C.J.S., Evidence, § 292, pp. 1055, 1056; Hawthorne v. Eckerson Co., 2 Cir., 77 F.2d 844. It may not be used as an admission against interest or as probative of whether an agent was acting within the scope of his employment. National Battery Co. v. Levy, 8 Cir., 126 F.2d 33; Domarek v. Bates Motor Transport Lines, 7 Cir., 93 F.2d 522. And certainly a plaintiff may not prove by his own favorable witness that the witness was injured in the same accident and that the defendant had settled with the witness. Pfiffner v. Kroger Grocer & Baking Co., Mo.App., 140 S.W.2d 79. * * *

"Here Joice's counsel, in the presence of the jury, disavowed any intention of asking the question for the mere purpose of prejudicing the jury and argued that he had a right to show the compromise as affecting Wilson's credibility as a witness for the railroad. The court explained that it thought the evidence admissible to show interest and bias on the part of the witness. Mo.R.S.A. § 1887. Under the circumstances and so limited, in this jurisdiction, it is permissible to show by cross-examination that an adversary witness, injured in the same accident, has compromised and settled his claim with the defendant for the purpose of reflecting his credibility and the weight to be given his evidence, as an inference of interest or bias may be drawn from such fact. Sommer v. Continental Portland Cement Co., 295 Mo. 519, 527, 246 S.W. 212, 214; Breitschaft v. Wyatt, Mo.App., 167 S.W.2d 931, 934; Gurley v. St. Louis Transit Co., Mo.App., 259 S.W. 895. Conversely, defendants may show interest and bias on the part of plaintiffs' witness by developing the fact that the witness was injured in the same accident and had filed a suit or made claim against the defendant. Riner v. Riek, Mo.App., 57 S.W.2d 724; Golden v. Onerem, Mo.App., 123 S.W.2d 617."

JOHNSON v. MOBERG, 334 N.W.2d 411, 414–15 (Minn.1983). "Minutes before closing arguments were to begin, counsel for plaintiff and defendant Moberg agreed orally as follows: (1) defendant Moberg guaranteed plaintiff a minimum recovery of $25,000; (2) plaintiff promised defendant Moberg that his maximum exposure to plaintiff was $25,000; and also (3) that if the verdict required defendant Moberg to pay less than $25,000, Moberg would pay only the lesser amount.

"Settlement agreements such as this are becoming increasingly prevalent. Termed 'Mary Carter' agreements from their first appearance in Booth v. Mary Carter Paint Co., 202 So.2d 8 (Fla.1967), they have been described by the Florida court in Ward v. Ochoa, 284 So.2d 385, 387 (Fla.1973), as 'basically a contract by which one co-defendant secretly agrees with the plaintiff that, if such defendant will proceed to defend himself in court, his own maximum liability will be diminished proportionately by increasing the liability of the other co-defendants.'

"We hold that 'Mary Carter' settlement agreements must be disclosed, and disclosed promptly, to the trial court and to the other litigants. This kind of settlement can affect the motivation of the parties and, indeed, the credibility of witnesses, and only by bringing these settlements into the open can a trial proceed in a fair and proper adversarial setting. The overwhelming majority of courts that have considered the issue have required that the trier of fact be apprised promptly of any such agreements. See, e.g., Sequoia Manufacturing Co. v. Halec Construction Co., 117 Ariz. 11, 24, 570 P.2d 782, 794 (Ariz.Ct. App.1977); Pellet v. Sonotone Corp., 26 Cal.2d 705, 713, 160 P.2d 783, 788 (1945); Ward v. Ochoa, 284 So.2d 385, 388 (Fla.1973); Gatto v. Walgreen, 61 Ill.2d 513, 523, 337 N.E.2d 23, 29 (1975), cert. denied, 425 U.S. 936, 96 S.Ct. 1669, 48 L.Ed.2d 178 (1976); Burkett v. Crulo Trucking Co., 171 Ind.App. 166, 355 N.E.2d 253 (1976); General Motors Corp. v. Lahocki, 286 Md. 714, 410 A.2d 1039 (1980); Grillo v. Burke's Paint Co., 275 Or. 421, 427, 551 P.2d 449, 453 (1976); General Motors Corp. v. Simmons, 558 S.W.2d 855 (Tex.1977)."

NAACP LEGAL DEFENSE & EDUCATIONAL FUND, INC. v. UNITED STATES DEPT OF JUSTICE, 612 F.Supp. 1143, 1146 (D.D.C. 1985). "DOJ further argues that a settlement negotiation privilege exists under FRE 408. The Court does not agree. Indeed, the Court finds that the holding in Center for Auto Safety v. Dept. of Justice, 576 F.Supp. 739 (D.D.C.1983), while not controlling on this Court, is definitive on this issue. In *Center for Auto Safety,* DOJ refused to release certain documents requested by the plaintiffs pursuant to a FOIA request. These documents concerned DOJ's consent to the modification of certain restrictions in a 1969 consent decree by the automotive industry. DOJ argued in that case, as it does in the instant actions, that there existed an implicit exemption to FOIA disclosure under FRE 408 involving settlement negotiations. The Court in *Center for Auto Safety* stated that 'DOJ's argument for this settlement negotiations privilege is misplaced. FRE 408 limits a document's relevance at trial, not its disclosure for other purposes.' Although the intent of FRE 408 is to foster settlement negotiations, the sole means used to effectuate that end is a limitation on the admission of evidence produced during settlement negotiations for the purpose of proving liability at trial. It was never intended to be a broad discovery privilege."

UNITED STATES v. BAKER, 926 F.2d 179, 180 (2d Cir.1991). "We believe it fairly evident that the Rule [408] applies only to civil litigation. The reference to 'a claim which was disputed as to either validity or amount' does not easily embrace an attempt to bargain over criminal charges. Negotiations over immunity from criminal charges or a plea bargain do not in ordinary parlance constitute discussions of a 'claim' over which there is a dispute as to 'validity' or 'amount.' Moreover, Fed.R.Crim.P. 11(e)(6) [identical to Fed.R.Evid. 410] explicitly addresses the exclusion of plea bargain negotiations and limits the statements excluded to those made to an 'attorney' for the government. The very existence of Rule 11(e)(6) strongly supports the conclusion that Rule 408 applies only to civil matters. We therefore hold that Rule 408 did not preclude testimony as to Mazzilli's statements to Nichols."

UNITED STATES v. LAWSON

United States Court of Appeals, Second Circuit, 1982.
683 F.2d 688.

Ralph K. Winter, Circuit Judge:

David R. Lawson appeals his conviction for bank robbery in the United States District Court for the Western District of New York, John T. Curtin, *Chief Judge,* after a jury trial. Appellant was sentenced on three counts to concurrent prison terms of 12 years, 10 years and 12 years, respectively. Lawson raises numerous issues on this appeal, including (1) the admission of statements he made in connection with an offer to plead guilty * * *.

For the reasons set out below, we reverse.

The Facts Summarized

* * *

Throughout the case, Lawson maintained his innocence. He testified that he did not participate in the robbery and spent most of that day with an Ann Robinson. Lawson also stated that Bell had admitted that he falsely implicated him in the Niagara robbery solely because of Bell's belief that Lawson had alerted the police to Bell's role in the earlier robbery. On cross-examination, the government sought to impeach Lawson through statements he had made to F.B.I. Agent Corcoran while in custody. Lawson had suggested a "deal" to Corcoran in which he would plead guilty and testify against his three accomplices in exchange for a four-year sentence to run concurrently with a state sentence he was about to begin.

* * *

The prosecution called Agent Corcoran in rebuttal. He testified that Lawson had told him while in custody that "he would make a deal if the Government could guarantee him a maximum of four years and thereby he would plead guilty and testify."

* * *

Discussion

A. Lawson's Statements to Agent Corcoran

At the time Lawson made the statements described above to Agent Corcoran, Fed.R.Evid. 410 and Fed.R.Crim.P. 11(e)(6) made inadmissible any statement made "in connection with" any offer to plead guilty or *nolo contendere* to a crime.[5] Both rules have been amended in the interim so as to apply only to statements made to prosecuting attorneys. The government expressly waived at oral argument any claim that the new version is applicable either to Lawson's original trial or to a new trial.

Lawson claims that all testimony as to his statements to Agent Corcoran should have been excluded under Rules 410 and 11(e)(6). At a pre-trial hearing, the District Court expressed reservations about the admissibility of Lawson's statements. On November 18, 1980, the government wrote the District Court:

> Please be advised that after further consideration, the Government does not intend to attempt to introduce at trial any statements made by Mr. Lawson to F.B.I. Agent James Corcoran. This is in view of the fact that it is our opinion that the introduction of the statements would be precluded under Rule 410 of the Federal Rules of Evidence.

Nevertheless, the government used these statements to impeach Lawson's testimony. Two grounds are asserted in support of this use of the statements. First, it is argued that the statements were not made in the course of plea negotiations. The letter of November 18 clearly waives any such claim, however. If the statements were not made in plea negotiations, then Rules 410 and 11(e)(6) would be wholly inapplicable and the statements could have been used in the government's main case. The government was familiar with all the circumstances surrounding Lawson's conversations with Corcoran and the letter of November 18 plainly treats them as within Rule 410. That letter thus waives any position to the contrary. We need not, therefore, determine the impact of our decisions in United States v. Levy, 578 F.2d 896 (2d Cir.1978), United States v. Stirling, 571 F.2d 708 (2d Cir.1978), and United States v. Arroyo–Angulo, 580 F.2d 1137 (2d Cir.1978), which in any event involve very different facts.

---

5. The relevant version of both Fed. R.Evid. 410 and Fed.R.Crim.P. 11(e)(6) read:

> *Inadmissibility of Pleas, Offers of Pleas, and Related Statements.* Except as otherwise provided in this rule [paragraph], evidence of a plea of guilty, later withdrawn, or a plea of nolo contendere, or of an offer to plead guilty or nolo contendere to the crime charged or any other crime, or of statements made in connection with, and relevant to, any of the foregoing pleas or offers, is not admissible in any civil or criminal proceeding against the person who made the plea or offer. However, evidence of a statement made in connection with, and relevant to, a plea of guilty, later withdrawn, a plea of nolo contendere, or an offer to plead guilty or nolo contendere to the crime charged or any other crime, is admissible in a criminal proceeding for perjury or false statement if the statement was made by the defendant under oath, on the record and in the presence of counsel.

The second ground offered to support use of Lawson's statements relies on the language of Rules 410 and 11(e)(6) that such statements are not admissible "against the person who made the plea or offer. * * *" It is argued that "against the person" means use in the government's case-in-chief and not use for impeachment or rebuttal purposes. Whether the November 18, 1980 letter also waives this claim is a closer question. The letter does not qualify the denial of any intention to use the statements, and we hardly think that a pre-trial hearing was held solely to determine admissibility in the main case. Nevertheless, there is no indication that use for impeachment purposes was ever focused upon by the parties. Therefore, we reach the issue of admissibility.

In admitting the statements, the District Court relied upon United States v. Havens, 446 U.S. 620, 100 S.Ct. 1912, 64 L.Ed.2d 559 (1979). *Havens* held that pre-trial statements by a criminal defendant which would have been inadmissible as part of the prosecution's main case under Miranda v. Arizona, 384 U.S. 436, 86 S.Ct. 1602, 16 L.Ed.2d 694 (1966), might be used to impeach the defendant if he or she took the stand. We believe *Havens* is inapposite, however. A principal purpose of the exclusionary rule under *Miranda* is to deter police officers while Rules 410 and 11(e)(6) are designed to encourage plea bargaining. So far as deterrence in the former case is concerned, exclusion from the case-in-chief provides the needed deterrence. It is somewhat far-fetched to believe that police conduct of an interrogation of a suspect will involve fine calculations as to whether the particular suspect will take the stand in a trial months or years in the future. Plea bargaining involves a wholly different context. Not only does it usually occur closer to trial but it will in all but a few cases involve attorneys. Calculations as to use for impeachment purposes will clearly affect the discussions and impair the frank and open atmosphere Rules 410 and 11(e)(6) were designed to foster.

We are aided in resolving this question by an unusually clear legislative history. In considering these rules, Congress debated and rejected proposals that statements made in connection with an offer to plead guilty be available for impeachment purposes. Fed.R.Evid. 410, as originally promulgated by the Supreme Court, provided that "an offer to plead guilty * * * or statements made in connection with [an offer to plead guilty], is not admissible in any civil or criminal proceeding against the person who made the * * * offer." In 1974, the Senate proposed the addition of the following specific language to Rule 410:

> This rule should not apply to the introduction of voluntary and reliable statements made in court on the record in connection with [an offer to plead guilty] where offered for impeachment purposes or in a subsequent prosecution of the declarant for perjury or false statement.

See S.Rep. No. 93–1277, 93d Cong., 2d Sess. 2 (October 18, 1974); see also id. at 10–11, reprinted in 1974 U.S.Code Cong. & Ad.News 7051, 7057–58. The Senate amendment was adopted by the Conference

Committee but with a provision that Rule 410 would be superseded by any amendment to the Federal Rules of Criminal Procedure, which was inconsistent with it and was effective after the date of the Act establishing the Federal Rules of Evidence. See H.Conf.Rep. No. 93–1597, 93d Cong., 2d Sess. 1 (December 14, 1974). The Conference Report explained that the issue was about to arise again in Congress' deliberations over Fed.R.Crim.P. 11(e)(6), which, as proposed by the Supreme Court, was "inconsistent" with the Conference Committee's Rule 410. H.Conf.Rep. No. 93–1597 at 6–7, reprinted in 1974 U.S.Code Cong. & Ad.News 7098, 7100. On January 2, 1975, the latter rule was enacted with the proviso described above. Pub.L. No. 93–595; 88 Stat. 1926, 1933 (1975).

Congress thereupon turned to the proposed Fed.R.Crim.P. 11(e)(6). Consistent with its prior position that offers to plead should be admissible for impeachment purposes, the Senate voted to eliminate Fed. R.Crim.P. 11(e)(6) so that the newly-enacted Rule 410 would prevail, thereby permitting use of plea bargaining statements for impeachment purposes. See 121 Cong.Rec. 23318–30 (July 17, 1975). The House, on the other hand, opposed the use of such statements for impeachment. See H.Rep. No. 94–247, 94th Cong., 1st Sess. 7 (May 29, 1975), reprinted in 1975 U.S.Code Cong. & Ad.News 674, 679. The Conference Committee resolved the dispute in favor of the House view. The Conference Report states:

> Rule 11(e)(6) deals with the use of statements made in connection with plea agreements. The House version permits a limited use of pleas of guilty, later withdrawn, or nolo contendere, offers of such pleas, and statements made in connection with such pleas or offers. Such evidence can be used in a perjury or false statement prosecution if the plea, offer, or related statement was made under oath, on the record, and in the presence of counsel. The Senate version permits evidence of voluntary and reliable statements made in court on the record to be used for the purpose of impeaching the credibility of the declarant or in a perjury or false statement prosecution.
>
> The Conference adopts the House version * * *

See H.Conf.Rep. No. 94–414, 94th Cong., 1st Sess. 10 (July 28, 1975), reprinted in 1975 U.S.Code Cong. & Ad.News 713, 714. As finally adopted, Fed.R.Crim.P. 11(e)(6) was enacted on July 31, 1975, Pub.L. No. 94–64, § 3(10), 89 Stat. 370, 372 (1975), and became effective on August 1, 1975. Fed.R.Evid. 410 as enacted on January 2, 1975, thus never became effective because Fed.R.Crim.P. 11(e)(6) was inconsistent with it. On December 12, 1975, a version of Rule 410 identical to Fed.R.Crim.P. 11(e)(6), was adopted by the Congress. Pub.L. No. 94–149, § 1(9), 89 Stat. 805 (1975).

We regard this legislative history as demonstrating Congress' explicit intention to preclude use of statements made in plea negotiations for impeachment purposes. Indeed, even the Senate version would not have permitted use of the statements at issue here since they were not made in court and on the record. Their inadmissibility under Rules 410 and 11(e)(6) is thus beyond serious dispute.

The admission of Lawson's statements to Corcoran was not harmless error. The government's evidence was composed largely of uncertain eyewitness testimony and witnesses impeached for bias. Use of these statements to attack Lawson's credibility was thus no insignificant event and may well have altered the balance of the credible evidence in the eyes of the jury.

* * *

Reversed and remanded.

TIMBERS, CIRCUIT JUDGE, concurring in part and dissenting in part:

* * *

The majority holds that the government was precluded from using the plea negotiation evidence for impeachment purposes. It says that the government waived its right to introduce the evidence by its pretrial letter stating that such evidence would not be introduced at trial. The majority further holds that in any event the use of such evidence for impeachment purposes is barred by Fed.R.Crim.P. 11(e)(6) and Fed.R.Evid. 410.

I disagree, under the circumstances of this case where there was no prejudice to appellant, that the letter should be regarded as having waived any right the government may have had to use the evidence. The government did not introduce the evidence in its case in chief; rather, it used the evidence only for impeachment. It strikes me as an overly restrictive view of prosecutorial discretion to hold that the government was forever precluded from using the evidence, despite the possibility of a change of circumstances after making the declaration.

To me, the only arguable reason for the majority's holding—curiously, not relied on by the majority—is the possible prejudice to a defendant in stating that the evidence will not be used and then using it. Here, however, there was no prejudice or surprise whatsoever. The government notified appellant before the defense began its case that it would use the evidence. This is a significantly different situation from one in which the government might use the evidence with no advance warning at all. The most that appellant can complain of here is that the evidence was damaging. He cannot claim any bona fide prejudice or surprise.

I do not dispute the proposition that, if the evidence was inadmissible under the Federal Rules in the government's case in chief, it likewise would be inadmissible for impeachment purposes. The wording of the Rules and the legislative history make this clear. First, the Rules provide that the evidence cannot be used "against the defendant"; the use of the evidence for impeachment clearly is against the defendant. Second, the failure of Congress to include an exception allowing for use of the evidence for impeachment, despite the Senate's interest in having such a provision, suggests that the use of such evidence for impeachment is foreclosed.

Nevertheless, in my view the Rules do not apply here. Undoubtedly the evidence would be admissible under the current versions of Fed.R.Evid. 410 and Fed.R.Crim.P. 11(e)(6). I would reach the same result here under the previous versions of the Rules in view of the circumstances of this case.

First, appellant contacted an FBI agent—not a prosecutor or an attorney—to try to arrange a deal. Although the Rules in effect at that time did not limit the contacts explicitly to those between a defendant and government attorneys, both the Advisory Committee on Criminal Rules and certain cases concluded that Congress had intended the earlier Rules to be so limited. See 77 F.R.D. 507, 534–35 (1978) (Advisory Committee Note to Fed.R.Crim.P. 11(e)(6)); e.g., United States v. Grant, 622 F.2d 308, 313 & n. 3 (8 Cir.1980).

Second, if we are to be faithful to prior decisions of our Court, there simply were no "plea discussions" within the meaning of the Rules. In United States v. Arroyo–Angulo, 580 F.2d 1137, 1148 (2 Cir.), cert. denied, 439 U.S. 913 (1978), we held that there was no violation of Fed.R.Crim.P. 11(e)(6) when the government used evidence of plea discussions. We stated that factors in deciding whether the Rule forbids such use were that no criminal charges had been filed when the contact was made and that the purpose of the contact by defendant was to stave off his prosecution. In the instant case, no charges had been filed and appellant later admitted that he was negotiating to gain time on the streets. In addition, the agent was not a prosecutor, as appellant knew. Finally, in *Arroyo–Angulo* the evidence was introduced in the government's case in chief, not merely for impeachment as here. Thus there is even stronger reason for holding that the use of the evidence in the instant case was proper.

Furthermore, in United States v. Levy, 578 F.2d 896, 901 (2 Cir.1978), we held that, notwithstanding Rules 410 and 11(e)(6), the admissions could be received in evidence where the offers of cooperation were made to agents who did not initiate the conversation. Here, by appellant's own admission, he initiated the contact at which what the majority characterizes as "plea discussions" were held.

* * *

I would affirm appellant's conviction and 12 year sentence for armed bank robbery. From the majority's refusal to do so, I respectfully dissent.

Notes

(1) It is "reasonable to read the phrase 'plea discussions' * * * to include offers of immunity, dismissal of all charges, or no prosecution, as well as offers to allow pleas to lesser or related offenses * * *." United States v. Boltz, 663 F.Supp. 956, 961 (D.Alaska 1987).

(2) The Federal Rules of Evidence do not apply during sentencing; therefore, incriminating statements made by defendant during plea negotiations may be admissible in the sentencing phase of the trial. United States v. Paden, 908 F.2d 1229, 1234–35 (5th Cir.1990), cert. denied, ___ U.S. ___, 111 S.Ct. 710, 112 L.Ed.2d 699 (1991).

(3) In Lichon v. American Universal Ins. Co., 435 Mich. 408, 459 N.W.2d 288, 293–95 (1990), the insured's nolo contendere plea to a charge of attempted burning of real property was held inadmissible against him in his subsequent civil suit for fire insurance proceeds, based upon Mich. R.Evid. 410. Contra, Walker v. Schaeffer, 854 F.2d 138, 143 (6th Cir.1988) (while Fed.R.Evid. 410 would bar introduction of nolo contendere plea against a defendant in a subsequent civil action, it does not bar evidence of the plea against a plaintiff); Levin v. State Farm Fire & Cas. Co., 735 F.Supp. 236 (E.D.Mich.1990) (rejecting reasoning but "constrained to follow" *Walker v. Schaeffer* on facts similar to *Lichon*).

SECTION 6. LIABILITY INSURANCE *

[FED.R.EVID. 411]

CHARTER v. CHLEBORAD

United States Court of Appeals, Eighth Circuit, 1977.
551 F.2d 246, cert. denied, 434 U.S. 856, 98 S.Ct. 176, 54 L.Ed.2d 128 (1977).

PER CURIAM.

This is a diversity action to recover damages for alleged medical malpractice. In June of 1973, plaintiff was struck by a truck while working as a highway flagman. The accident caused extensive injuries to both of plaintiff's legs. Plaintiff was hospitalized and placed under the care of a general practitioner and defendant, a surgeon. Surgery was performed on both legs. As a result of severe complications plaintiff was transferred to another hospital where both legs were amputated above the knee.

The trial of the matter resulted in a jury verdict for defendant and the district court denied plaintiff's motion for a new trial. Plaintiff presents two issues on appeal. First, plaintiff argues that the district court erred in limiting the cross-examination of a rebuttal witness for the defense. Second, plaintiff objects to an instruction given to the jury relating to causation. We deal first with the evidentiary issue.

Plaintiff offered the testimony of Dr. Joseph Lichtor, M.D., a Kansas City, Missouri orthopedic surgeon. Dr. Lichtor testified as to his opinion of the requisite standard of care defendant should have used when treating plaintiff. He compared the treatment given and concluded that defendant had been negligent. Finally, Dr. Lichtor testified that the cause of the complications and subsequent amputations was defendant's negligence.

* See 2 Wigmore, Evidence § 282a (Chadbourn rev. 1979); McCormick, Evidence § 201 (4th ed. 1992).

As a part of his rebuttal case, defendant offered the testimony of John J. Alder, an attorney from the Kansas City area. Mr. Alder testified that Dr. Lichtor's reputation for truth and veracity in the Kansas City area was bad. On cross-examination Mr. Alder testified that he did some defense work in medical malpractice cases. He also stated that some of his clients in those cases were insurance companies.

Plaintiff's counsel then asked him to name some of those companies and defendant objected to the relevancy of the matter. After a conference at the Bench[1] the district court refused to allow further questioning on the subject of insurance. As plaintiff stated in his motion for a new trial, Mr. Alder was employed in part by the same liability carrier who represents defendant in this action.

It is well established that the existence of a liability insurance policy is not admissible to show one's negligence or other wrongful conduct. Fed.R.Evid. 411 (1975); C. McCormick, Evidence § 201, at 479 (2d ed. 1972). This rule has its basis in the belief that such evidence is of questionable probative value or relevance and is often prejudicial. Advisory Committee's note Fed.R.Evid. 411 (1975); 2 J. Wigmore, Evidence § 282a, at 133–34 (3d ed. 1940). Evidence of the existence of insurance may be offered for other purposes, however. See, e.g., Corbett v. Borandi, 375 F.2d 265 (3d Cir.1967); Newell v. Harold Shaffer Leasing Co., 489 F.2d 103 (5th Cir.1974). Rule 411 of the Federal Rules of Evidence provides several examples:

> This Rule does not require the exclusion of evidence of insurance against liability when offered for another purpose, such as proof of agency, ownership, or control, *or bias or prejudice of a witness.*

(Emphasis added.)

In this case the fact that defendant's insurer employed Mr. Alder was clearly admissible to show possible bias of that witness. Defendant does not dispute this obvious import of Rule 411 but urges that for several reasons the district court's exclusion of the evidence was not reversible error.

First, defendant argues that plaintiff was required to make a formal offer of proof. Rule 103(a)(2) of the Federal Rules of Evidence provides that error may not be predicated upon a ruling excluding evidence unless:

1. Defense counsel moved for a mistrial which was denied by the district court. The following discussion then occurred:

PLAINTIFF'S COUNSEL: We are certainly entitled to go into this for the purpose of showing his interest when he comes in and goes into his reputation.

THE COURT: But now I don't want insurance to enter this case at all. We've been at this over a week.

PLAINTIFF'S COUNSEL: Alright. I am not going into that. I just want to show—

DEFENDANT'S COUNSEL: He has already.

THE COURT: Stay away from that or I will declare a mistrial and we can start all over. Don't go into it any further or I sure will. Do you understand?

PLAINTIFF'S COUNSEL: I understand, Your Honor.

> The substance of the evidence was made known to the court by offer or was apparent from the context within which questions were asked.

However, it is clear from the transcript, particularly the conversation between counsel out of the hearing of the jury, that the court was aware of the general nature of the evidence to be offered.

Based upon Rule 403 of the Federal Rules of Evidence defendant also argues that the trial court acted within its discretion in excluding evidence of insurance. This argument is without merit. In our opinion the probative value of the evidence far outweighs any danger of unfair prejudice. Also, there is no indication in the record or briefs of the parties that any particular prejudice was threatened in this case. Rule 403 was not designed to allow the blanket exclusion of evidence of insurance absent some indicia of prejudice. Such a result would defeat the obvious purpose of Rule 411.

Defendant's final argument against reversal is that any error was harmless and did not affect a substantial right of the plaintiff. To pass on this argument we must view the total circumstances of the case. Plaintiff's claim rested for the most part on the credibility of his expert witness. When defendant undertook to impeach that witness plaintiff was entitled to attempt to show possible bias of Mr. Alder as surrebuttal. Considering the importance of expert testimony in this case we cannot conclude that the trial court's exclusionary ruling was mere harmless error.

Because we find that the exclusion of the above mentioned evidence requires reversal, we do not consider the validity of the causation instruction given to the jury. Accordingly, the judgment of the district court is reversed and the action is remanded with directions to grant the plaintiff a new trial.

Notes

(1) "Since the main point of contention in this lawsuit was the matter of ownership of the vehicle, evidence of insurance was admissible under rule 411." Jacobini v. Hall, 719 S.W.2d 396, 401 (Tex.App.1986).

(2) "The converse, a showing that the defendant had no insurance is equally immaterial and erroneous for it amounts to nothing more than a plea of poverty." Modern Elec. Co. v. Dennis, 259 N.C. 354, 130 S.E.2d 547, 550 (1963).

(3) Rule 411 addresses only liability insurance. As an aspect of the collateral source rule, evidence that the plaintiff was covered by health, disability, or accident insurance is also normally inadmissible. See, e.g., Evans v. Wilson, 279 Ark. 224, 650 S.W.2d 569 (1983). As with liability insurance, the normal exclusion may be overridden where the collateral insurance has special relevancy. See, e.g., Mac Tyres, Inc. v. Vigil, 92 N.M. 446, 589 P.2d 1037 (1979) (trial court should have permitted defendant to impeach plaintiff by showing that he lied about the accident to obtain workers' compensation benefits); McDonald v. Alamo Motor Lines, 222

S.W.2d 1013 (Tex.Civ.App.1949) (plaintiff claimed his injuries caused an inability to write; his handwritten proof of loss on health and accident policy admitted).

Chapter 2

HEARSAY

[FED.R.EVID. ART. VIII]

SECTION 1. DEFINITION *

[FED.R.EVID. 801(a)–(c)]

COMMONWEALTH v. FARRIS

Superior Court of Pennsylvania, 1977.
251 Pa.Super. 277, 380 A.2d 486.

SPAETH, JUDGE:

Appellant was held for trial on five bills of indictment. Two of the bills were for robbery, two for weapons offenses, and one for conspiracy. The Commonwealth did not move for trial on the two weapons bills, and eventually these were not prossed. A jury found appellant not guilty on the two robbery bills, and guilty on the conspiracy bill. Appellant's post-trial motions were denied, and he was sentenced to 18 months to 3 years in prison. On this appeal he raises several issues, but we find it necessary to consider only one.

At the trial the only issue of substance was identification. On October 14, 1975, at about 8:00 p.m., a man burst through the door of Dave's Tavern in Philadelphia, brandished a gun, and ordered everyone to "hit the floor." The proprietor of the bar identified this man as appellant. He saw the man's face for "a matter of seconds." The man with the gun and another man took money from the cash register and from the occupants of the tavern, and left. An off-duty police officer happened to be outside the tavern. He saw two men with guns run out and get into a car. The officer identified appellant as one of the two men. He saw the man he identified as appellant for no more than

* See 5 Wigmore, Evidence §§ 1361–1365 (Chadbourn rev. 1974); 6 id. §§ 1766–1792 (Chadbourn rev. 1976); McCormick, Evidence ch. 24 (4th ed. 1992); Morgan, Hearsay Dangers and the Application of the Hearsay Concept, 62 Harv.L.Rev. 177 (1948); Park, McCormick on Evidence and the Concept of Hearsay: A Critical Analysis Followed by Suggestions for Law Teachers, 65 Minn.L.Rev. 423 (1981); Tribe, Triangulating Hearsay, 87 Harv.L.Rev. 957 (1974); Wellborn, The Definition of Hearsay in the Federal Rules of Evidence, 61 Tex.L.Rev. 49 (1982).

fifteen seconds, during most of which time he saw only the man's back; he saw the man's face for "I would say three seconds." The officer was able to get the license number of the car the two men got into, and before the car drove away, he got a full-face view of the driver, whom he later identified as one Gary Moore. The officer was not able to see well enough to be sure how many men were in the car, but there may have been a fourth man.

The bartender testified, but he could not identify the robbers. There was also testimony regarding recovery of guns from a car identified as belonging to Gary Moore.

In addition, a detective, Robert Aiken, testified; it is his testimony that concerns us. The testimony was as follows:

By [LEONARD ROSS] the Assistant District Attorney:

Q. What, if anything was the first thing you did once you received the assignment in [the robbery of Dave's Tavern] case?

A. Well, one of the first things I did was interrogate Gary Moore.

Q. Was he already in police custody at that time?

A. Yes, he was.

Q. Did Gary Moore say something to you?

A. He made a statement to me, yes.

MISS MAGUIGAN [Appellant's counsel]: Objected to, Your Honor.

MR. ROSS: Your Honor, it is a statement of fact, not hearsay.

THE COURT: All right. Objection overruled. Go ahead.

Q. As a result of what Gary Moore told you, what if anything did you do?

A. I arrested Emanuel Farris.

We hold that the objection by appellant's counsel should have been sustained. We hold further that on the facts of this case the failure to sustain the objection requires a new trial.

The Commonwealth argues that since "the statement itself was never read to the jury * * * Detective Aiken's testimony * * * does not constitute hearsay." Commonwealth's Brief at 19. According to the Commonwealth, "Moore's statement * * * was merely referred to as part of the investigation * * *." Id. The lower court accepted this argument, saying that "Detective Aiken merely described the steps in his investigation leading to the arrest of Emanuel Farris." Slip Opinion of Lower Court at 2.

To regard the testimony in this manner is disingenuous. By no means did the detective "merely describe [ ]" his investigation; what he did—that is, what the testimony elicited from him by the assistant district attorney did—was to tell the jury: "I interrogated Gary Moore, and he told me that one of the men involved in the robbery was Emanuel Farris, and so I arrested Farris."

There can be little doubt—we have none—that this is just what the jury understood the detective to say. Common sense tells us so: a jury is not likely to make nice legal distinctions between a flat-out narrative ("Moore told me that * * *). and an oblique narrative ("as a result of what Moore told me, I did * * *). Furthermore, it is plain that the jury did not have much confidence in either the proprietor's or the police officer's identification of appellant, or else it would not have acquitted appellant on both of the robbery bills; the conviction of appellant on the conspiracy bill must have derived from, or depended upon, some juror saying to the other jurors, "But the detective said Moore told him Farris was involved." (In this regard it should be noted that the identifications of appellant, both based as mentioned above on very brief observation, were the only evidence against appellant. No physical evidence was recovered from appellant; no statement was attributed to him; and he did not testify.)

There can also be little doubt—and again, we have none—that the assistant district attorney intended to get across to the jury that Moore had identified appellant as involved in the robbery. That was the only reason to question the detective as he was questioned. Sometimes, to be sure, it will be relevant to ask a law enforcement officer to "describe the steps in your investigation," for example, when the issue is whether the officer had reasonable cause to get a search warrant or to make an arrest. Here, however, the facts that the detective had taken "a statement" from Moore, and had then "[a]s a result of" that statement arrested appellant, were of no possible relevance—*except* to show that Moore had told the detective that appellant was involved in the robbery.

Had the detective testified flat-out, "Moore told me that one of the men involved was Farris," it would be clear beyond reasonable argument that the testimony would have been hearsay: it would have been an assertion by someone not in court (Moore), offered for its truth (that one of the men was Farris), and thus depending for its value upon the credibility of the out-of-court asserter. See generally McCormick on Evidence § 246 (Cleary ed. 1972). The Commonwealth should not be permitted to evade this principle by having the detective testify obliquely rather than flat-out. As McCormick observes:

> *Indirect versions of hearsay statements; negative results of inquiries.* If the apparent purpose of offered testimony is to use an out-of-court statement to evidence the truth of facts stated therein, the hearsay objection cannot be obviated by eliciting the purport of the statements in indirect form. Thus evidence as to the purport of "information received" by the witness, or a statement of the result of investigation made by other persons, offered as evidence of the facts asserted out of court, have been held to be hearsay.

McCormick, supra, § 249, at 593–94 (footnotes omitted).[2]

2. In one of these omitted footnotes McCormick cites Falknor, "Indirect Hearsay," 31 Tul.L.Rev. 3 (1956). There, characterizing this sort of hearsay as "ob-

Here, Moore, the out-of-court asserter, did not testify. He was therefore not subject to cross-examination, either to test the basis of his statement to the detective that appellant had been one of the men involved in the robbery, or to uncover any motive he might have had to lie about appellant's involvement. As in all hearsay situations, cross-examination of the detective could not test either Moore's accuracy or his bias.

* * *

Accordingly the judgment of sentence is vacated and a new trial is granted.

SCHAFFER v. STATE, 777 S.W.2d 111, 112–13 (Tex.Crim.App. 1989). "A McAllen police officer arrested appellant in a stolen van which contained approximately 1,700 grams of bagged and loose peyote buttons. Appellant testified at trial. He admitted to being inside the stolen van and to knowing that the van contained the controlled substance. Appellant's defense, however, was that he was acting as a police informer. He named 'Jimmy Seals' as the Abilene police officer with whom he had worked for two years previous to his arrest. He further testified that during those two years he had provided authorities information leading to the arrests and convictions of several drug dealers.

"Apparently surprised, the prosecutor asked Manuel A. Segovia, a narcotics investigator for the Hidalgo County Sheriff's Office who had testified earlier on behalf of the State, to phone officer Seals. Thereafter, in rebuttal to appellant's testimony, Officer Segovia testified as follows:

'Q. Officer Segovia, when was the first time you heard the name of—a person by the name of Jimmy Seals?

'A. This morning.

'Q. And who, if anybody, informed you of that name?

'A. You did, sir.

'Q. And were you able to contact Officer Seals?

'A. Yes, sir.

'Q. And when was this?

'A. This morning.

'Q. And did you have occasion to talk to him?

'A. Yes, sir, I did.

scured" hearsay, id., Professor Falknor collects many cases where the statement of the witness was in its effect a statement of what someone not in court had told the witness.

'Q. Without telling us what he told you, Officer Segovia, would you, at this time, ask the State to drop charges against Mr. Schaffer?

'A. No, sir.

"* * * Seals did not testify at trial.

"At trial and upon appeal, appellant asserted that the State had elicited hearsay testimony before the jury when it received a negative answer from Officer Segovia in response to its question of whether the Officer would request that the State drop charges against appellant after talking with Officer Seals. The trial court overruled appellant's hearsay objection but the Corpus Christi Court of Appeals reversed the conviction * * *. We agree with the Court of Appeals and hold that the trial court should have sustained appellant's hearsay objection."

HANSON v. JOHNSON

Supreme Court of Minnesota, 1924.
161 Minn. 229, 201 N.W. 322.

WILSON, C.J.

Action in conversion. Appeal from judgment by defendants. Case was tried to the court without a jury.

It is claimed that the court erred in the reception of evidence. Plaintiff owned and leased a farm to one Schrik under a written lease, the terms of which gave plaintiff two-fifths of the corn grown. The tenant gave a mortgage to defendant bank on his share of the crops. The tenant's mortgaged property was sold at auction by the bank with his permission. At this sale a crib of corn containing 393 bushels was sold by the bank to defendant Johnson. If plaintiff owned the corn it was converted by defendants.

1. In an effort to prove that the corn was owned by plaintiff, and that it was a part of his share, he testified over the objection of hearsay and self-serving, that when the tenant was about through husking corn he was on the farm and the tenant pointed out the corn in question (and a double crib of corn) and said:

> "Mr. Hanson, here is your corn for this year, this double crib here and this single crib here is your share for this year's corn; this belongs to you, Mr. Hanson."

A bystander was called, and against the same objection testified to having heard the talk in substantially the same language.

There is no question but that plaintiff owned some corn. It was necessary to identify it. The division made his share definite. This division and identity was made by acts of tenant in husking the corn and putting it in separate cribs and then his telling Hanson which was his share, and the latter's acquiescence therein. The language of the tenant was the very fact necessary to be proved. The verbal part of the transaction between plaintiff and the tenant was necessary to prove the fact. The words were the verbal acts. They aid in giving legal significance to the conduct of the parties. They accompanied the conduct. There could be no division without words or gestures identifying the respective shares. This was a fact to be shown in the chain of proof of title. It was competent evidence. It was not hearsay nor self-serving. 3 Wigmore on Ev. (2d Ed.) §§ 1770, 1772–1777. As between plaintiff and the tenant, this evidence would be admissible. It was original evidence. The issues here being between different persons does not change the rule. Fredin v. Richards, 66 Minn. 46, 68 N.W. 402; State Bank of Winsted v. Strandberg, 148 Minn. 108, 180 N.W. 1006; Hughes on Ev. (1907 Ed.) p. 139, § 12.

2. The court refused to permit defendant to prove what the tenant told the bank officials at the time of the sale as to who owned this corn. The cashier of the bank testified that plaintiff had told him over the phone that Schrik would show him where the corn was. Defendant claimed this was sufficient to justify the court in receiving the excluded evidence. We think not. It was insufficient to make the tenant plaintiff's agent to determine ownership. In the absence of such, it was not admissible upon any theory.

There is evidence to sustain the findings of the court, and the record is free from error.

Affirmed.

Notes

(1) See 6 Wigmore, Evidence §§ 1770–1777 (Chadbourn rev. 1976); McCormick, Evidence § 249 (4th ed. 1992).

(2) "West Coast argues on appeal that evidence regarding an oral agreement to charge the reduced rates was inadmissible hearsay. This argument is without merit. Evidence of an oral agreement is not offered to prove the truth of the matter stated. Rather, such evidence is offered simply to show that the statement was made. It is well established that statements which may themselves affect the legal rights of the parties are not considered hearsay under the Federal Rules of Evidence. Fed.R.Evid. 801(c) advisory committee's note." West Coast Truck Lines v. Arcata Community Recycling, 846 F.2d 1239, 1246 n. 5 (9th Cir.1988), cert. denied, 488 U.S. 856, 109 S.Ct. 147, 102 L.Ed.2d 119 (1988).

(3) "The statement at issue is paradigmatic nonhearsay; it was offered because it contains threats made against officers of the federal courts, i.e., it contains the operative words of this criminal action. It was not 'offered in evidence to prove the truth of the matter asserted,' [Fed.R.Evid.] 801(c)." United States v. Jones, 663 F.2d 567, 571 (5th Cir.1981).

what is not hearsay

(4) "Felbro objects that the individual votes are hearsay and may not be admitted through the testimony of the tellers, Machuca and Zayas. See Fed.R.Evid. 801(c). The ballots were apparently destroyed after the meeting and could not be admitted into evidence.

"This testimony was not hearsay as it was *not* 'offered in evidence to prove the truth of the matter asserted.' Rule 801(c). The testimony as to the individual ballots was offered solely to prove that such a vote was cast. We are not concerned with the 'truth' of any matter expressed by the individual casting the ballot. The casting of a vote is a verbal act, in which the statement itself has legal effect.

"As stated in the advisory committee notes on proposed Rule 801:

> If the significance of an offered statement lies solely in the fact that it was made, no issue is raised as to the truth of anything asserted, and the statement is not hearsay. Emich Motors Corp. v. General Motors Corp., 181 F.2d 70 (7th Cir.1950), rev'd on other grounds 340 U.S. 558, 71 S.Ct. 408, 95 L.Ed. 534 [1951], letters of complaint from customers offered as a reason for cancellation of dealer's franchise, to rebut contention that franchise was revoked for refusal to finance sales through affiliated finance company. The effect is to exclude from hearsay the entire category of 'verbal acts' and 'verbal parts of an act,' in which the statement itself affects the legal rights of the parties or is a circumstance bearing on conduct affecting their rights."

Local 512, Warehouse & Office Workers' Union v. N.L.R.B., 795 F.2d 705, 713 n. 4 (9th Cir.1986).

McCLURE v. STATE

Court of Criminal Appeals of Texas, 1979.
575 S.W.2d 564.

ONION, PRESIDING JUDGE.

This is an appeal from a conviction for the offense of murder; punishment is imprisonment for ninety-nine (99) years.

* * *

Appellant's testimony raised the issue of voluntary manslaughter, and the court instructed the jury thereon. See V.T.C.A., Penal Code, § 19.04. * * *

* * *

V.T.C.A., Penal Code, § 19.06, provides, as did Article 1257a, V.A.P.C., that the jury be allowed to consider *all* relevant facts and circumstances going to show the condition of the mind of the accused at the time of the homicide. It long has been the rule in this state that evidence such as that offered by appellant to prove his wife's infidelity is admissible as bearing on the accused's state of mind.

> "We think the court erred in rejecting the evidence offered by defendant to prove the adulterous intercourse between his wife and the man Stephenson, and that recently before the homicide he had been informed of this fact. This and any other evidence which tended to show that he had reasonable cause to be excited, troubled, distracted and frenzied, that he had knowledge of facts well calculated to destroy his mental equilibrium, to dethrone his reason, to render it improbable that he could and did act with a cool, sedate and deliberate mind in committing the homicide, was in our opinion admissible."

Burkhard v. State, 18 Tex.App. 599 (1885).

In order for the evidence of the deceased's infidelity to be admissible, appellant was required to show that he had knowledge thereof. See *Jamar v. State,* 142 Tex.Cr.R. 91, 150 S.W.2d 1031 (1941); *Newchurch v. State,* 135 Tex.Cr.R. 619, 121 S.W.2d 998 (1938); *Black v. State,* 82 Tex.Cr.R. 358, 198 S.W. 959 (1917); *Ashley v. State,* 362 S.W.2d 847 (Tex.Cr.App.1962).

To prove that he had knowledge of the deceased having had sexual relations with Crowder and Davis, appellant offered to testify that Cindy Haynes had so informed him. The court erred in refusing to allow appellant to testify as to what Haynes had told him on the ground that such testimony would have been hearsay.

> "When it is proved that D made a statement to X, with the purpose of showing the probable state of mind thereby induced in X, such as being put on notice or having knowledge, or motive, or to show the information which X had as bearing on the reasonableness or good faith of the subsequent conduct of X, or anxiety, the evidence is not subject to attack as hearsay."

McCormick, Evidence, § 249, pp. 589–90 (2nd ed. 1972).

> "Whenever an utterance is offered to evidence the *state of mind* which ensued *in another person* in consequence of the utterance, it is obvious that no assertive or testimonial use is to be made of it, and the utterance is therefore admissible, so far as the hearsay rule is concerned."

6 Wigmore, Evidence, § 1789, p. 314 (Chadbourn rev. 1976). The court should have allowed appellant to testify as to what Cindy Haynes had told him, since that testimony would have shown he had knowledge of the deceased's indiscretions with Crowder and Davis. See *Thompson v. State,* 115 Tex.Cr.R. 337, 29 S.W.2d 343 (1929).

* * *

The judgment is reversed and the cause remanded.

SMEDRA v. STANEK

United States Court of Appeals, Tenth Circuit, 1951.
187 F.2d 892.

HUXMAN, CIRCUIT JUDGE.

Appellant, Zig Smedra, brought this action against Doctors Stanek and Matchett, for damages and expenses alleged to have resulted from negligent acts of the defendants in leaving "one or more sponges or pieces of surgical gauze in the person of the plaintiff" during an operation. The jury returned a verdict for defendants. From the judgment on the verdict Smedra has appealed.

A number of assignments are urged for reversal. The decision, however, turns on one question—did the trial court err in excluding relevant and material evidence as hearsay.

* * *

There was a great deal of evidence introduced with regard to the manner in which the operation was conducted, the kind and nature of surgical dressings in use at the hospital, as well as other evidence bearing upon the manner in which the operation was performed and the treatment received by Smedra from the appellee doctors. So also there was a great deal of evidence as to the suffering of Smedra and evidence which would tend to support a conclusion that the incision refused to heal because of some foreign substance in the wound. But since the question is not whether the evidence is sufficient to support a verdict for appellant or falls short of making a case in his behalf, no useful purpose would be served by recounting it in detail.

As stated, the sole question is whether the court erred in excluding certain evidence offered by appellant. Dr. Matchett, the other appellee, had testified by deposition that his recollection "was that Dr. Stanek had been told by someone in the operating room that the sponge count did not come out right." Appellant was not allowed to bring out this answer on trial. Dr. Stanek was asked and permitted to answer that there was a conversation in the operating room, the inference being that the conversation related to a sponge count. He was not permitted to state the substance of the conversation. Appellant then made an offer of proof, offering to prove that Dr. Stanek had been warned that the sponge count was off. This offer was refused on the ground that there had been no evidence that the sponge count had been taken and that in the absence of such proof the proffered testimony would be hearsay.

Dr. Freed, who was one of the prominent physicians and surgeons practicing in this hospital, testified that it was a common practice in this type of a case to have a sponge count taken; that the actual count was taken by the nurses in attendance and that its purpose was to prevent the loss of a sponge during the operation. He testified that a sponge count was taken at the close of his part of the operation. While he did not specifically mention this hospital in his testimony that it was common practice to take such a count, we think the inference that such was the practice in this hospital is properly deducible from what he said.

To establish liability, it was necessary to prove, first, that a sponge or gauze, or part thereof, was left in the incision, and, second, that it was left there as the result of failure on the part of the doctors to exercise that degree of skill and care required of practitioners in that environment.

The relevancy of the excluded evidence was not to establish that a sponge count had been taken and that it failed to check out, nor, yet, was its purpose to establish that the doctor had knowledge that such a count had been taken. For that purpose, it would be hearsay and inadmissible. Its purpose was to warn the doctor that a sponge might have been left in the incision. The effect of the proffered testimony was the same as though the nurse had said, "Doctor, there must be a sponge in the wound because one is missing," or, if she had said, "Doctor, I think a sponge has been left in the incision."

For the purpose of establishing that this warning, with regard to the condition or possible condition of the incision was brought home to the doctor, the testimony was not hearsay and was admissible. This evidence of a warning that a foreign substance might have been left in the incision is important on the question whether, in the light of this warning, the doctors thereafter exercised due care to ascertain that no foreign substance was left in the incision.

* * *

The judgment is reversed and the cause is remanded to proceed in conformity with the views expressed herein.

UNITED STATES v. RUBIN, 591 F.2d 278, 283 (5th Cir.1979), cert. denied, 444 U.S. 864, 100 S.Ct. 133, 62 L.Ed.2d 87 (1979). "Rubin also argues that the trial court improperly excluded as hearsay certain proffered testimony. To decide whether the testimony was inadmissible hearsay, some background information is necessary. One of Rubin's defenses in this case was lack of criminal intent. He claimed that because he interpreted the unions' constitutions as allowing the salary increases, he was unaware that the increases were actually unauthorized. The constitutions, however, appear clearly to mandate a different procedure for obtaining salary increases from the procedure followed by Rubin. To explain why he nonetheless believed the salary increases were authorized, Rubin testified that his understanding was that the constitutions were not to be interpreted literally. Rubin wanted to explain further that both present and past presidents of the unions, those individuals given the duty of interpreting the constitutions, had told him that the constitutions were flexible, living documents that could be interpreted to fit the needs of a particular local. The trial judge excluded this testimony as hearsay.

"The Federal Rules of Evidence define hearsay as 'a statement, other than one made by the declarant while testifying at the trial or hearing, offered in evidence *to prove the truth of the matter asserted.*' Fed.R.Evid. 801 (emphasis added). As Rubin explained at trial, he did not offer the statements to prove the truth of the matter asserted, but instead to prove that he had heard them and to establish their effect on his state of mind. See Dutton v. Evans, 400 U.S. 74, 88, 91 S.Ct. 210, 27 L.Ed.2d 213 (1970). Thus, Rubin's proffered testimony was not hearsay, and because it was relevant to his state of mind, it should have been admitted. See Fed.R.Evid. 401 & 402.

"Since the trial court allowed Rubin to testify to his understanding of what the constitutions meant, the government argues that the excluded testimony would have been cumulative only. Thus, the government claims that the trial court's exclusion of the testimony constitutes harmless error. We disagree. Rubin's testimony about what he considered to be the proper interpretation of the unions' constitutions would have been much more believable had he also testified to the conversations on which he based his conclusions—especially since those conversations were with the officials charged with interpreting the constitutions. Since the testimony was admissible and would have significantly helped establish Rubin's defense, we hold that its exclusion was reversible error."

UNITED STATES v. ZENNI

United States District Court, Eastern District of Kentucky, 1980.
492 F.Supp. 464.

BERTELSMAN, DISTRICT JUDGE.

This prosecution for illegal bookmaking activities presents a classic problem in the law of evidence, namely, whether implied assertions are hearsay. The problem was a controversial one at common law, the discussion of which has filled many pages in the treatises and learned journals.[2] Although the answer to the problem is clear under the Federal Rules of Evidence, there has been little judicial treatment of the matter, and many members of the bar are unfamiliar with the marked departure from the common law the Federal Rules have effected on this issue.

FACTS

The relevant facts are simply stated. While conducting a search of the premises of the defendant, Ruby Humphrey, pursuant to a lawful search warrant which authorized a search for evidence of bookmaking activity, government agents answered the telephone several times. The unknown callers stated directions for the placing of bets on various sporting events. The government proposes to introduce this evidence to show that the callers believed that the premises were used in betting operations. The existence of such belief tends to prove that they were so used. The defendants object on the ground of hearsay.

COMMON LAW BACKGROUND

At common law,[3] the hearsay rule applied "only to evidence of out-of-court statements [4] offered for the purpose of proving that the facts are as asserted in the statement."

2. *See e.g., McCormick on Evidence* § 250 (2d Ed.1972) [*hereinafter McCormick*]; Morgan, *Basic Problems of Evidence* (1976); *Weinstein's Evidence* ¶ 801 [hereinafter *Weinstein*]. Falknor, *The "Hear-Say" Rule as a "See-Do" Rule: Evidence of Conduct,* 33 Rocky Mt.L.Rev. 133 (1961) [hereinafter Falknor] contains a particularly penetrating and succinct analysis. (*See also* authorities in note 15, *infra.*)

3. As used in this opinion the term "common law" refers primarily to case law, as distinguished from the Federal Rules of Evidence, or other evidence codes.

4. It should be noted at the outset that the word *statement* as used in the Federal Rules of Evidence has a more restricted meaning than as used at common law. F.R.Ev. 801(a). See further discussion below.

On the other hand, not all out-of-court expression is common law hearsay. For instance, an utterance offered to show the publication of a slander, or that a person was given notice of a fact, or orally entered into a contract, is not hearsay.

In the instant case, the utterances of the absent declarants are not offered for the truth of the words,[7] and the mere fact that the words were uttered has no relevance of itself.[8] Rather they are offered to show the declarants' belief in a fact sought to be proved. At common law this situation occupied a controversial no-man's land. It was argued on the one hand that the out-of-court utterance was not hearsay, because the evidence was not offered for any truth stated in it, but for the truth of some other proposition inferred from it. On the other hand, it was also argued that the reasons for excluding hearsay applied, in that the evidence was being offered to show declarant's belief in the implied proposition, and he was not available to be cross-examined. Thus, the latter argument was that there existed strong policy reasons for ruling that such utterances were hearsay.

The classic case, which is discussed in virtually every textbook on evidence, is *Wright v. Tatham,* 7 Adolph. & E. 313, 386, 112 Eng.Rep. 488 (Exch. Ch. 1837), and 5 Cl. & F. 670, 739, 47 Rev.Rep. 136 (H.L.1838). Described as a "celebrated and hard-fought cause," *Wright v. Tatham* was a will contest, in which the will was sought to be set aside on the grounds of the incompetency of the testator at the time of its execution. The proponents of the will offered to introduce into evidence letters to the testator from certain absent individuals on various business and social matters. The purpose of the offer was to show that the writers of the letters believed the testator was able to make intelligent decisions concerning such matters, and thus was competent.

One of the illustrations advanced in the judicial opinions in *Wright v. Tatham* is perhaps even more famous than the case itself. This is Baron Parke's famous sea captain example. Is it hearsay to offer as proof of the seaworthiness of a vessel that its captain, after thoroughly inspecting it, embarked on an ocean voyage upon it with his family?

The court in *Wright v. Tatham* held that implied assertions[11] of this kind were hearsay. The rationale, as stated by Baron Parke, was as follows:

7. That is, the utterance, "Put $2 to win on Paul Revere in the third at Pimlico," is a direction and not an assertion of any kind, and therefore can be neither true nor false.

8. *Cf. United States v. McLennan,* 563 F.2d 943 (9th Cir.1977), in a criminal case, the defense was advice of counsel. Statements made by counsel to the defendant were not hearsay, because it was relevant what the advice was. Of a similar nature would be a policeman's statement, "Go through the stop sign," if it were illegal to go through it unless directed by an officer. Other examples of expression admissible as non-hearsay, because they are verbal acts, relevant merely because they occurred, are "I agree" offered to show a contract was made; or "He took a bribe," offered to show a slander was published.

11. The problem is the same whether the relevant assertion is implied from verbal expression, such as that of the betters in the instant case or the letter writers in

"The conclusion at which I have arrived is, that proof of a particular fact which is not of itself a matter in issue, but which is relevant only as implying a statement or opinion of a third person on the matter in issue, is inadmissible in all cases where such a statement or opinion not on oath would be of itself inadmissible; and, therefore, in this case the letters which are offered only to prove the competence of the testator, that is the truth of the implied statements therein contained, were properly rejected, as the mere statement or opinion of the writer would certainly have been inadmissible."

This was the prevailing common law view,[12] where the hearsay issue was recognized. But frequently, it was not recognized.[13] Thus, two federal appellate cases involving facts virtually identical to those in the case at bar did not even discuss the hearsay issue, although the evidence admitted in them would have been objectionable hearsay under the common law view.[14]

The Federal Rules of Evidence

The common law rule that implied assertions were subject to hearsay treatment was criticized by respected commentators for several reasons. A leading work on the Federal Rules of Evidence, referring to the hotly debated question whether an implied assertion stands on better ground with respect to the hearsay rule than an express assertion, states:

"By the time the federal rules were drafted, a number of eminent scholars and revisers had concluded that it does. Two principal arguments were usually expressed for removing implied assertions from the scope of the hearsay rule. First, when a person acts in a way consistent with a belief but without intending by his act to communicate that belief, one of the principal reasons for the hearsay rule—to exclude declarations whose veracity cannot be tested by cross-examination—does not apply, because the declarant's sincerity is not then involved. In the second place, the underlying belief is in some cases self-verifying:

'There is frequently a guarantee of the trustworthiness of the inference to be drawn * * * because the actor has based his actions on the correctness of his belief, i.e. his actions speak louder than words.' "[15]

In a frequently cited article the following analysis appears:

"But ought the hearsay rule be deemed applicable to evidence of conduct? As McCormick has observed, the problem 'has only once received any adequate discussion in any decided case,' *i.e.*, in *Wright v.*

Wright, or from conduct, as in the sea captain example. *See* F.R.Ev. 801(a); Falknor, *supra* note 2, at 134.

12. Falknor, *supra* note 2, at 133.

13. *McCormick, supra* note 2, § 250 at 598; *Weinstein, supra* note 2, ¶ 801(a)[02] at 801–57.

14. *Reynolds v. United States,* 225 F.2d 123 (5th Cir.1955); *Billeci v. United States,* 184 F.2d 394 (D.C.Cir.1950). *See Weinstein* ¶ 801(a)[02] at 801–57—801–58.

15. *Weinstein* ¶ 801(a)[01], at 801–55. *See also* Morgan, Hearsay, 25 Miss.L.J. 1, 8 (1953); Maguire, *The Hearsay System: Around and Through the Thicket,* 14 Vand. L.Rev. 741 (1961); McCormick, *The Borderland of Hearsay,* 39 Yale L.J. 489 (1930); Falknor, *supra* note 2 at 133.

Tatham, already referred to. And even in that case the court did not pursue its inquiry beyond the point of concluding that evidence of an 'implied' assertion must necessarily be excluded wherever evidence of an 'express' assertion would be inadmissible. But as has been pointed out more than once (although I find no *judicial* recognition of the difference), the 'implied' assertion is, from the hearsay standpoint, not nearly as vulnerable as an express assertion of the fact which the evidence is offered to establish.

"This is on the assumption that the conduct was 'nonassertive;' that the passers-by had their umbrellas up for the sake of keeping dry, not for the purpose of telling anyone it was raining; that the truck driver started up for the sake of resuming his journey, not for the purpose of telling anyone that the light had changed; that the vicar wrote the letter to the testator for the purpose of settling the dispute with the latter, rather than with any idea of expressing his opinion of the testator's sanity. And in the typical 'conduct as hearsay' case this assumption will be quite justifiable.

"On this assumption, it is clear that evidence of conduct must be taken as freed from at least one of the hearsay dangers, *i.e.*, mendacity. A man does not lie to himself. Put otherwise, if in doing what he does a man has no intention of asserting the existence or non-existence of a fact, it would appear that the trustworthiness of evidence of this conduct is the same whether he is an egregious liar or a paragon of veracity. Accordingly, the lack of opportunity for cross-examination in relation to his veracity or lack of it, would seem to be of no substantial importance. Accordingly, the usual judicial disposition to equate the 'implied' to the 'express' assertion is very questionable." [16]

The drafters of the Federal Rules agreed with the criticisms of the common law rule that implied assertions should be treated as hearsay and expressly abolished it. They did this by providing that no oral or written expression was to be considered as hearsay, unless it was an "assertion" concerning the matter sought to be proved and that no nonverbal conduct should be considered as hearsay, unless it was intended to be an "assertion" concerning said matter.[18] * * *

"Assertion" is not defined in the rules, but has the connotation of a

16. Falknor, *supra* note 2, at 136. The context makes clear that the author would apply the same analysis "where the conduct, although 'verbal,' is relevant, not as tending to prove the truth of what was said, but circumstantially, that is, as manifesting a belief in the existence of the fact the evidence is offered to prove." *Id.* at 134.

18. See the sea captain illustration discussed, *supra.* In an unpublished ruling this court recently held admissible as non-hearsay the fact that a U.S. mining inspector ate his lunch in an area in a coal mine now alleged to have been unsafe, and that other inspectors who observed operations prior to a disastrous explosion issued no citations, when it would have been their duty to do so, if there had been safety violations. These non-assertive acts would have been hearsay under the rule of *Wright v. Tatham* but are not hearsay under Rule 801 of the Federal Rules of Evidence, because the inspectors did not intend to make assertions under the circumstances. *Boggs v. Blue Diamond Coal Company* (E.D.Ky. No. 77–69, Pikeville Division).

forceful or positive declaration.[19]

The Advisory Committee note concerning this problem states:

"The definition of 'statement' assumes importance because the term is used in the definition of hearsay in subdivision (c). *The effect of the definition of 'statement' is to exclude from the operation of the hearsay rule all evidence of conduct, verbal or nonverbal, not intended as an assertion. The key to the definition is that nothing is an assertion unless intended to be one.*

"* * * The situations giving rise to the nonverbal conduct are such as virtually to eliminate questions of sincerity. Motivation, the nature of the conduct, and the presence or absence of reliance will bear heavily upon the weight to be given .the evidence. Falknor, "The 'Hear-Say' Rule as a 'See-Do' Rule: Evidence of Conduct," 33 Rocky Mt.L.Rev. 133 (1961). *Similar considerations govern nonassertive verbal conduct and verbal conduct which is assertive but offered as a basis for inferring something other than the matter asserted,* also excluded from the definition of hearsay by the language of subdivision (c)." (Emphasis added).

This court, therefore, holds that, "Subdivision (a)(2) of Rule 801 removes implied assertions from the definition of statement and consequently from the operation of the hearsay rule." [20]

Applying the principles discussed above to the case at bar, this court holds that the utterances of the betters telephoning in their bets were nonassertive verbal conduct, offered as relevant for an implied assertion to be inferred from them, namely that bets could be placed at the premises being telephoned. The language is not an assertion on its face, and it is obvious these persons did not intend to make an assertion about the fact sought to be proved or anything else.[21]

As an implied assertion, the proffered evidence is expressly excluded from the operation of the hearsay rule by Rule 801 of the Federal Rules of Evidence, and the objection thereto must be overruled. An order to that effect has previously been entered.

---

19. Random House *Dictionary of the English Language* (1969 Ed.)

20. *Weinstein,* ¶ 801(a)[01] at 801-56; *McCormick* § 250 at 599.

21. A somewhat different type of analysis would be required by words non-assertive in form, but which under the circumstances might be intended as an assertion. For example, an inspector at an airport security station might run a metal detector over a passenger and say "go on through." In the absence of the inspector, would testimony of this event be objectionable hearsay, if offered for the proposition that the passenger did not have a gun on him at that time? Although Rule 801(a) does not seem to require a preliminary determination by the trial court whether verbal conduct is intended as an assertion, it is submitted that such a determination would be required in the example given. If an assertion were intended the evidence would be excluded. If not, it would be admissible. This result is implicit in the policy of the drafters of the Federal Rules of Evidence that the touchstone for hearsay is the intention to make an assertion. *See* S. Saltzburg and K. Redden, Federal Rules of Evidence Manual 456 (2d ed. 1977).

UNITED STATES v. LEWIS, 902 F.2d 1176, 1179 (5th Cir.1990). "At the time of their arrest, each appellant had in his possession an electronic pager or 'beeper'. These pagers were seized by the Ridgeland Police. Later that day, at the police station, the pager associated with Lewis began beeping. Officer Jerry Price called the number displayed on the pager and identified himself as Lewis. The person on the other end asked Price 'Did you get the stuff?' Price answered affirmatively. The unidentified person then asked 'Where is Dog?' Price responded that 'Dog' was not available. He then tried to arrange a meeting with the unknown caller, but no one showed up at the appointed rendezvous. The evidence at trial revealed that 'Dog' is Wade's nickname.

"Lewis and Wade contend that the district court erred by allowing Officer Price to testify to the questions asked by the unidentified caller. They argue that the questions are hearsay that should have been excluded pursuant to Fed.R.Evid. 802. We disagree. Officer Price's testimony was not hearsay because the questions asked by the unknown caller were not 'statements' within the definition of hearsay.

"The Federal Rules of Evidence define hearsay as 'a statement, other than one made by the declarant while testifying at the trial or hearing, offered in evidence to prove the truth of the matter asserted.' Fed.R.Evid. 801(c). A 'statement' is then defined as an *oral or written assertion* or nonverbal conduct intended as an assertion. Fed.R.Evid. 801(a). The effect of this definition is to remove from the operation of the hearsay rule 'all evidence of conduct, verbal or nonverbal, not intended as an assertion.' Fed.R.Evid. 801(a) advisory committee's note; United States v. Jackson, 588 F.2d 1046, 1049 n. 4 (5th Cir.), cert. denied, 442 U.S. 941, 99 S.Ct. 2882, 61 L.Ed.2d 310 (1979). While 'assertion' is not defined in the rule, the term has the connotation of a positive declaration. See Webster's Ninth New Collegiate Dictionary 109 (1985 ed.). The questions asked by the unknown caller, like most questions and inquiries, are not hearsay because they do not, and were not intended to, assert anything. D. Binder, Hearsay Handbook § 2.03 (2d. ed. & 1989 supp.); Inc. Publishing Corp. v. Manhattan Magazine, Inc., 616 F.Supp. 370, 388 (S.D.N.Y.1985).

"Appellants argue that while the questions in this case are not direct assertions, there are certain assertions implicit in the questions. For example, they argue that implicit in the question 'Did you get the stuff?' is an assertion that Lewis and/or Wade were expecting to receive some 'stuff'. However, Rule 801, through its definition of statement, forecloses appellants' argument by removing implied assertions from the coverage of the hearsay rule. United States v. Groce, 682 F.2d 1359, 1364 (11th Cir.1982); United States v. Zenni, 492 F.Supp. 464, 469 (E.D.Ky.1980); 4 J. Weinstein & M. Berger, Weinstein's Evidence ¶ 801(a)[01] (1988). Accordingly, we conclude that because the questions asked by the unknown caller were not assertions, the questions were not hearsay, and the district court properly allowed Officer Price to repeat them in his testimony."

Notes

(1) Compare United States v. Reynolds, 715 F.2d 99 (3d Cir.1983) (D2's statement to D1, in presence of arresting officers, "I didn't tell them anything about you," inadmissible hearsay against D1 to prove D1's complicity by the "implied assertion").

(2) The defendant in State v. McGann, 132 Ariz. 296, 645 P.2d 811 (1982), was convicted of forging the signature of the holder of a Chevron credit card. "The station manager's testimony about Chevron back-billing him was also hearsay. The back-billing act by Chevron was nonverbal conduct intended as an assertion of unauthorized signatures, not made during the trial, and offered to prove the truth of the matter asserted therein. See Ariz.R.Evid. 801. It too does not fall within any of the exceptions to Ariz.R.Evid. 803 or 804, so it also was inadmissible under Ariz..R.Evid. 802." 645 P.2d at 813.

(3) In addition to the authorities cited in *Zenni,* see 2 Wigmore, Evidence §§ 267–273 (Chadbourn rev. 1979); Bacigal, Implied Hearsay: Defusing the Battle Line Between Pragmatism and Theory, 11 So.Ill.U.L.J. 1127 (1987); Milich, Re–Examining Hearsay Under the Federal Rules: Some Method for the Madness, 39 Kan.L.Rev. 893 (1991); Park, "I Didn't Tell Them Anything About You": Implied Assertions as Hearsay Under the Federal Rules of Evidence, 74 Minn.L.Rev. 783 (1990); Seidelson, Implied Assertions and Federal Rule of Evidence 801: A Quandary for Federal Courts, 24 Duquesne L.Rev. 741 (1986); Wellborn, The Definition of Hearsay in the Federal Rules of Evidence, 61 Tex.L.Rev. 49 (1982).

(4) To prove that a product design or lot was not defective, or that premises were not dangerous, a defendant offers evidence that other purchasers or patrons did not complain. Hearsay? See St. Louis Southwestern Ry. Co. v. Arkansas & Texas Grain Co., 42 Tex.Civ.App. 125, 95 S.W. 656, 660 (1906) (no); Cain v. George, 411 F.2d 572, 573 (5th Cir.1969) (no); Falknor, Silence as Hearsay, 89 U.Pa.L.Rev. 192 (1940).

SECTION 2. PRIOR STATEMENT BY WITNESS *

[FED.R.EVID. 801(d)(1)]

UNITED STATES v. CASTRO–AYON

United States Court of Appeals, Ninth Circuit, 1976.

537 F.2d 1055, cert. denied, 429 U.S. 983, 97 S.Ct. 501, 50 L.Ed.2d 594 (1976).

GOODWIN, CIRCUIT JUDGE:

Rafael Castro–Ayon appeals his conviction for violating 8 U.S.C. § 1324 and 18 U.S.C. § 371 (inducing illegal immigration, transporting

* See 3A Wigmore, Evidence § 1018 (Chadbourn rev. 1970); 4 id. §§ 1122–1132 (Chadbourn rev. 1972); McCormick, Evidence § 251 (4th ed. 1992); Bein, Prior Inconsistent Statements: The Hearsay Rule, 801(d)(1)(A) and 803(24), 26 U.C.L.A.L.Rev. 967 (1979); Blakey, Substantive Use of Prior Inconsistent Statements Under the Federal Rules of Evidence, 64 Ky.L.J. 3 (1976); Graham, Examination of a Party's Own Witness Under the Federal Rules of Evidence: A Promise Unfulfilled, 54 Tex.L.Rev. 917 (1976); Graham, The Relationship Among Federal Rules of Evidence 607, 801(d)(1)(A), and 403: A Reply to Weinstein's Evidence, 55 Tex.L.Rev. 573 (1977); Graham, Employing Inconsistent Statements for Impeachment

illegal immigrants, and conspiracy). He challenges the admission of "prior inconsistent statements" of witnesses and an instruction allowing the jury to use this testimony as substantive evidence of guilt. We affirm.

On August 29, 1975, a border patrol agent stopped a van carrying eleven illegal aliens, including the driver. The van was registered to Castro–Ayon, a United States citizen residing in Richmond, California. The aliens were taken to the Chula Vista Border Patrol Station where Agent Pearce advised them of their "Miranda" rights, placed them under oath and interrogated them. The interrogation was tape-recorded.

At the trial, three of the aliens were called by the government and were asked questions about Castro–Ayon. These witnesses all tended to exculpate him. The prosecutor thereupon asked foundation questions for impeachment. Each witness admitted that she had made a statement to Agent Pearce shortly after she was arrested. The prosecutor next called Agent Pearce. Pearce testified to the substance of the prior statements all of which were inconsistent with the testimony that the witnesses had given in court. Castro–Ayon objected to the admission of this evidence.

At the close of the trial, the court instructed the jury to weigh the prior inconsistent statements of the witnesses, not only in testing the credibility of the witnesses, but also in considering the defendant's guilt.

Historically, courts have limited the use of "prior inconsistent statements" of witnesses to impeachment of the witnesses' credibility. Most circuits have excluded prior inconsistent statements when offered as substantive evidence. United States v. Lester, 491 F.2d 680 (6th Cir.1974); United States v. Eaton, 485 F.2d 102 (10th Cir.1973); Subecz v. Curtis, 483 F.2d 263 (1st Cir.1973); United States v. Small, 443 F.2d 497 (3d Cir.1971); Byrd v. United States, 119 U.S.App.D.C. 360, 342 F.2d 939 (1965); Century Indemnity Co. v. Serafine, 311 F.2d 676 (7th Cir.1963). Our own court has long held this view. Kuhn v. United States, 24 F.2d 910 (9th Cir.1928); Isaac v. United States, 431 F.2d 11 (9th Cir.1970).

We recently underscored our adherence to the "orthodox rule" that prior inconsistent statements were admissible only for purposes of

and as Substantive Evidence: A Critical Review and Proposed Amendment of Federal Rules of Evidence 801(d)(1)(A), 613, and 607, 75 Mich.L.Rev. 1565 (1977); Graham, Prior Consistent Statements: Rule 801(d)(1)(B) of the Federal Rules of Evidence, Critique and Proposal, 30 Hast.L.J. 575 (1979); Mauet, Prior Identification in Criminal Cases: Hearsay and Confrontation Issues, 24 Ariz.L.Rev. 29 (1982); Ohlbaum, The Hobgoblin of the Federal Rules of Evidence: An Analysis of Rule 801(d)(1)(B), Prior Consistent Statements and a New Proposal, 1987 B.Y.U.L.Rev. 231; Ordover, Surprise! That Damaging Turncoat Witness Is Still With Us: An Analysis of Federal Rules of Evidence 607, 801(d)(1)(A) and 403, 5 Hofstra L.Rev. 65 (1976).

impeachment. United States v. Tavares, 512 F.2d 872 (9th Cir.1975). Except where independent grounds exist for their admission, such statements have been excluded, for all but their impeachment value, by the hearsay rule. See, e.g., Wheeler v. United States, 382 F.2d 998 (10th Cir.1967).

The new Federal Rules of Evidence have changed the hearsay rule. Some prior statements are now admissible for their substantive value as well as for impeachment. Fed.R.Evid. 801(d)(1), 88 Stat. 1938 (1975).

The new rule defines a statement as "not hearsay if the declarant testifies at the trial or hearing and is subject to cross-examination concerning the statement and the statement is (A) inconsistent with his testimony, and was given under oath subject to the penalty of perjury at a trial, hearing, or other proceeding * * *"[1]

The statements Agent Pearce recorded satisfy the conditions of rule 801(d)(1) if the interrogation of the smuggled aliens constituted a "trial, hearing, or other proceeding". Certainly, interrogation by Agent Pearce was not a trial or hearing. But was it an "other proceeding"?

The term "other proceeding" does not, in itself, reveal its own dimension. But reference to the legislative history[2] helps define the term. The original version of rule 801(d)(1), drafted by the Advisory Committee and passed by the Senate, would have allowed substantive use of *any* prior inconsistent statement. The House of Representatives, however, passed a much more restrictive version of the rule: The House version allowed substantive admissibility only if the prior inconsistent statement was (1) given under oath; (2) subject to prosecution for perjury; (3) subject to cross-examination; and (4) given in a trial or hearing, or in a deposition.

The conference committee reported out a compromise version which purported to adopt the Senate version; but an "amendment" added the requirements that the prior statement be (1) given under oath; (2) subject to prosecution for perjury; and (3) given in a "trial, hearing, or other proceeding". The compromise version passed both houses of Congress. 88 Stat. 1938 (1975).

By not requiring the prior statement to be subject to cross-examination and by adding the term "other proceeding" to the limitation of "trial or hearing", the conference committee allowed admission of prior

1. The term "prior inconsistent statement" as used in the remainder of this opinion shall mean a prior inconsistent statement made by a declarant who later testifies at the trial or hearing and is subject to cross-examination concerning the statement. The issues in this case involve the circumstances of the prior statement, not the circumstances of introducing the statement into evidence at trial.

2. The legislative history is found in the committee reports to Congress. S.Rep. No. 93–1277, 93rd Cong., 2d Sess. (Note to Rule 801(d)(1)(A)) (1974); H.Rep. No. 93–650, 93rd Cong., 2d Sess. (Note to Rule 801(d)(1)) (1974); H.Rep. No. 93–1597, 93rd Cong., 2d Sess. (Note to Rule 801(d)(1)(A)) (1974) (Conference Committee). The pertinent parts of these reports are reprinted in U.S.C.A. The Federal Rules of Evidence and in 4 U.S.Code Cong. and Adm.News pp. 7062, 7086, 7104 (1974).

inconsistent statements given before a grand jury.[3] The committee consciously intended to include grand-jury proceedings within the ambit of "other proceedings." [4]

Our reading of the legislative history leads us to the conclusion that Congress intended the term "other proceeding" to include the immigration interrogation held by Agent Pearce.

First, we note that Congress intended the term "other proceeding" to extend beyond grand jury proceedings. If the conference committee had intended to limit the reach of this rule to grand-jury proceedings, words were at hand to do so; the choice of the open-ended term "other proceedings" was intentional.

The conference committee adopted the Senate version with some limiting amendments. It could have chosen the House version and deleted some of its restrictions. We are impressed by the spirit of the unamended version, especially where the limitation deliberately uses an open-ended term like "other proceeding".

Second, we note that the immigration proceeding before Agent Pearce bears many similarities to a grand-jury proceeding: both are investigatory, ex parte, inquisitive, sworn, basically prosecutorial, held before an officer other than the arresting officer, recorded, and held in circumstances of some legal formality. Indeed, this immigration proceeding provides more legal rights for the witnesses than does a grand jury: the right to remain totally silent, the right to counsel, and the right to have the interrogator inform the witness of these rights.[5]

We do not hold, as the question is not before us, that every sworn statement given during a police-station interrogation would be admissible. While this immigration proceeding bears many similarities to the station-house interrogation, we believe that it qualifies as an "other proceeding" within the meaning of the statute.

Castro–Ayon relies heavily on United States v. Tavares, 512 F.2d 872 (9th Cir.1975). There, before the new rules of evidence had become effective, we underscored our adherence to the "orthodox rule" that prior inconsistent statements were not admissible except for impeachment purposes. In discussing the prior law, we characterized rule 801(d)(1) as reflecting the orthodox rule with an exception for statements given during a prior judicial proceeding. While the new rule clearly does allow statements made in prior judicial proceedings to be received as exceptions to the hearsay rule, there was nothing before the court in the *Tavares* case which required a definition of "other proceed-

3. "The rule as adopted covers statements before a grand jury." H.Rep. No. 93–1597, 93rd Cong., 2d Sess. (Note to Rule 801(d)(1)(A)) (1974), *reprinted in* U.S.C.A. The Federal Rules of Evidence and in 4 U.S.Code Cong. and Adm.News 7104 (1974).

4. See note 3. We also note that the rule in the Second Circuit, which excepted from the exclusions of the orthodox rule statements made before a grand jury, was known to the conferees. See H.Rep. No. 93–650, supra, note 2.

5. See United States v. Mandujano, — U.S. —, 96 S.Ct. 1768, 48 L.Ed.2d 212 (1976).

ings". Accordingly, we are not precluded from examining the matter afresh now that the question is before us.[6] Congress has changed the law.

The trial court committed no error in receiving the challenged evidence, and correctly instructed the jury that it could consider the evidence upon the substantive issues in the case.

Other assignments of error were briefed and argued, but none requires a comment. One bit of inadmissible hearsay came into the record with reference to one count, but in view of the concurrent sentences, it is not necessary to notice the error.

Affirmed.

Note

Compare United States v. Dietrich, 854 F.2d 1056, 1060–62 (7th Cir. 1988), holding that a prior sworn written statement given by a witness to Secret Service agents was not admissible as substantive evidence under Rule 801(d)(1)(A) because the interview was not an "other proceeding" within the meaning of the rule. "Thomas' statement was given to the same agents who had the authority to arrest her, the interview was not prosecutorial, it was not recorded, and there were no indicia of legal formality. The circumstances surrounding Thomas' statement did not differ significantly from a typical police station interrogation." Id. at 1062.

CAMPBELL v. STATE

Court of Criminal Appeals of Texas, 1986.
718 S.W.2d 712.

MILLER, JUDGE.

Appellant was indicted and convicted by a jury for the offense of murder. See V.T.C.A. Penal Code, § 19.02. The jury assessed punishment at life imprisonment in the Texas Department of Corrections. Appellant urged seven grounds of error in his appeal to the First District Court of Appeals in Houston, but the Court of Appeals affirmed his conviction in an unpublished opinion. *Campbell v. State,* No. 01–83–0755–CR (August 23, 1984). By petition for discretionary review to this Court, appellant raised five grounds of review. We granted appellant's petition on grounds of review four and five, which claim that the trial court erroneously allowed the prosecution to bolster the testimony of its witness, Ms. Oakreter Jackson, by evidence of prior consistent statements. We will reverse the judgment of the Court of Appeals.

Appellant killed the deceased in appellant's front yard on Saturday night, July 2, 1983, by striking him in the head with a heavy object. The people at the scene and appellant's neighbors did not volunteer any

6. A grand-jury proceeding is not technically a "judicial proceeding". Neither are administrative hearings, which would arguably be covered by the term "trial, hearing, or other proceeding".

information to the officers investigating the homicide. One month later, however, the police were informed by the Crime Stoppers Program that Jackson was a witness, and Jackson subsequently gave statements to the police.

Jackson was the State's eyewitness at trial. She testified that she was on the porch of the house across the street when an argument began between appellant and the deceased, evidently over some lawnmowers belonging to the deceased that appellant had sold. Jackson stated that appellant was handling an iron bumper jack during the argument, and that when the deceased turned to walk away, appellant struck him from behind with the jack. The deceased started to turn and face appellant, when appellant struck him again in the forehead, fatally wounding him. Jackson testified that appellant then removed an envelope from the deceased's shirt pocket (the envelope purportedly contained money that the deceased had shown to appellant during the argument), went into his house to change his clothes, and left the scene.

Appellant and two eyewitnesses for the defense testified to a different version of the incident. They said that there was no argument about lawnmowers, that the deceased brandished a knife, that the blow was delivered by a piece of lumber that appellant picked up in the yard in response to this provocation from the deceased, that the deceased was threatening to get a gun when appellant struck him (only once), and that they did not see Jackson around the scene at all. Appellant's entire case turned on self-defense, which his witnesses supported and Jackson refuted. The jury apparently believed Jackson.

After Jackson testified for the State on direct examination, the defense attorney opened a number of avenues of impeachment on cross and recross examination. Jackson testified that she had never been intimately involved with appellant, which was refuted by defense witnesses, that she had not been convicted of any crimes involving moral turpitude, which was refuted by a conviction for theft, and that she had never used the name "Broadway," which was also refuted by the documents showing her conviction. The defense attorney also asked her if she had been paid for the reporting of the crime, and if so, when and how much. She stated that she had been paid one month after giving the information.

Jackson was later returned to the stand to rehabilitate herself by describing why she did not realize she had actually been convicted, and by stating that she did not think that the defense attorney had used the exact name "Broadway" when questioning her on that issue. The State also elicited her testimony that she received the $400.00 from the Crime Stoppers Program in September, a month and a half after her initial statements to the police were made, and that she was not receiving any additional money for testifying at the trial.

Detective Osterberg, the last witness called, testified for the State on rebuttal. Over objection, he was asked about his three prior conversations with Jackson that began with her approaching him through Crime Stoppers. He testified that she said the "same things" in each conversation or statement, and that "[s]he has never changed her story. It has always been the same."

During closing argument, the defense attorney referred to Jackson as "the four hundred dollar witness," and said, "here they want you to believe a woman who a month later turns in a man for four hundred dollars * * *." The prosecutor responded in closing argument by stating that Jackson was a believable witness because "she told Detective Osterberg the same thing each time she talked to him." Defense counsel's objection to this statement was sustained over the prosecutor's argument that what the prosecutor alluded to was in evidence.

Appellant's grounds of review numbers four and five complain that the Court of Appeals erred: (a) in holding that the prosecutor's bolstering of Jackson was not improper and did not constitute reversible error; and (b) in holding that the trial court's admission of evidence over objection of Jackson's prior consistent statements, when no predicate had been laid for the admission of such evidence, was proper. In response to the latter, we must answer two questions regarding the admissibility of prior consistent statements:

> 1) whether the predicate for such statements was laid in this case; and
>
> 2) whether such statements were admissible although they were made at a time when the motive to fabricate was present.

The prevailing rule for criminal cases in Texas is set out in *Rains v. State,* 146 S.W.2d 176, 178 (Tex.Cr.App.1940):

> "In *Browney v. State,* 128 Tex.Cr.R. 81, 79 S.W.2d 311, 315, the rule is stated as follows: 'It is well settled that where a witness has been impeached by showing that he made other and different statements in regard to the matter than those testified to by him on trial, he can be supported by showing that he made similar statements to those testified to by him recently after the occurrence. However, if the supporting statement was made after a motive or inducement existed to fabricate, the supporting statement is inadmissible.' "

On Motion for Rehearing, this Court in *Rains,* supra, thoroughly reviewed Texas precedent, found that the above-stated rule has been consistent from the beginning, and reaffirmed it. *Id.* at 179–180.

Under this rule, appellant makes a strong case on both counts: that there was no predicate laid that Jackson made prior inconsistent statements, which would open the door to evidence of prior consistent statements; and that the prior consistent statements about which evidence was admitted were made at a time when the motive to fabricate—the reward money—existed.

The Court of Appeals found against appellant on both issues. It held that the defense challenged Jackson's credibility by "implying that she had fabricated her story to collect the Crime Stoppers' reward and to get even with the appellant." *Campbell,* supra at 5. It continued, "[a]lthough the statements by Ms. Jackson to the police investigator were given after she had received the Crime Stoppers' reward money [which is not strictly true, but close enough because the motivation was present when all the statements were made], that merely affected the *weight,* not the admissibility of the rehabilitation testimony." *Id.* (Emphasis and comment added.) The latter comment is a misstatement of the controlling rule, and we reverse the Court of Appeals for the reasons developed below.

With regard to the second question, admissibility of the statement after the predicate is laid, our holding on this issue follows the precedent set out in *Rains,* supra at 178.

> "'* * * [I]f the supporting statement was made after a motive or inducement existed to fabricate, the supporting statement is inadmissible.'"

Prior consistent statements then are not admissible if they were made after the motive for fabrication came into existence.

It is appropriate at this juncture to examine the continued viability of *Rains,* supra, in light of the recent promulgation of new rules of evidence in Texas. On December 18, 1985, this Court promulgated the new Texas Rules of Criminal Evidence [cited as Tex.R.Cr.Evid.], which were effective on September 1, 1986. Germane to this case is the rule regarding a witness' prior consistent statement, set forth in Tex.R.Cr. Evid. 801(e)(1), which states that a statement is not hearsay if:

> * * * The declarant testifies at the trial or hearing and is subject to cross-examination concerning the statement, and the statement is * * * (B) consistent with his testimony and is offered to rebut an express or implied charge against him of recent fabrication or improper influence or motive, * * *.

This rule is simply a codification of well established Texas caselaw. Under the new rule of criminal evidence or under Texas caselaw, a proper predicate for admission is laid when the witness testifies at trial and is subject to cross-examination about the statement and there has been an express or implied charge against him of recent fabrication or improper influence or motive. In the instant case, the witness Jackson did testify, was subject to cross-examination and was expressly charged with improper motive and fabrication concerning the statement. Thus, a proper predicate for admission of the prior consistent statement was established.

With regard to the second question, the admissibility of the statement vis-a-vis the motive to lie, we note at the outset that Tex.R.Cr. Evid. 801(e)(1), supra, contains no requirement of admissibility that prior consistent statements be made before the time when the motive to fabricate arose. No Texas civil cases have been decided on this point since the adoption of the new Civil Rules of Evidence, but the requirement is strongly entrenched in prior case law. See *McInnes v. Yamaha Motor Corp., U.S.A.,* 673 S.W.2d 185 (Tex.1984); *Skillern & Sons, Inc. v. Rosen,* 359 S.W.2d 298, 301–303 (Tex.1962).

Federal courts interpreting the identical language have tended to incorporate the requirement of absence of motive to fabricate, the leading case being *United States v. Quinto,* 582 F.2d 224 (2nd Cir.1978). The court's discussion in *Quinto* supra, of the rationale for this rule is helpful to our analysis:

> "The rationale for excluding most, but not all, prior consistent statements being offered to establish the witness's credibility is one of relevance. 'The witness is not helped by [the prior consistent statement] even if it is an improbable or untrustworthy story, it is not made more probable or more trustworthy by any number of repetitions of it.' * * * 'Prior consistent statements traditionally have been admissible to rebut charges of recent fabrication or improper influence or motive.' * * * But the prior consistent statements have been so admissible only when the statements were made prior to the time the supposed motive to falsify arose * * *. *Only then was the prior consistent statement 'relevant' on the issue of credibility;* that is, it tended to make the trustworthiness of the witness's in-court testimony more probable, after that testimony had been assailed, inasmuch as the consistency of the prior statement with the witness's testimony at trial made it 'appear that the statement in the form now uttered was independent of the [alleged] discrediting influence.' "

Id. at 232–233 (Emphasis added; citations omitted; bracketed words in the original.)

The court in *Quinto,* supra, went on to note that Fed.R.Evid. 801(d)(1)(B) [hereinafter Fed.Rule(s)] altered the preexisting evidentiary law on the use of prior consistent statements, by allowing those statements that meet its standards to be used as non-hearsay "substantive evidence," to prove the truth of the matter asserted, rather than merely for rehabilitation. Notwithstanding the language of the rule, however, it held that the *standards* for admissibility are precisely the same as the traditional standards, which include the requirement that the prior consistent statement be made prior to the time that the supposed motive to falsify arose. *Id.* at 233–234.

Other federal courts have noted that *Quinto,* supra, and its progeny read this requirement into the Rule, while the Rule itself includes no such limitation upon admissibility for the purpose of corroborating an allegedly impeached witness' testimony. *United States v. Parodi,* 703 F.2d 768, 784 (4th Cir.1983); and *United States v. Harris,* 761 F.2d 394 (7th Cir.1985). See also, *United States v. Pierre,* 781 F.2d 329 (2nd Cir.1986); *United States v. Obayagbona,* 627 F.Supp. 329 (1985). These cases hold that *Quinto,* supra, was concerned only with the application of Fed.Rule 801(d)(1)(B), supra, to prior statements as substantive evidence, and did not deal with their use for the more limited purpose of rehabilitation.

> "Since the only mention of prior consistent statements in the Federal Rules of Evidence is in Rule 801(d)(1)(B) and this limits admissibility to cases where the statement 'is offered to rebut an express or implied charge against him of recent fabrication of improper influence,' law-

yers and judges can be forgiven for being misled into concluding, as was done by dictum in *United States v. Quinto,* * * * that the limitation applies to the use of prior consistent statements for rehabilitation as well as for direct evidence. However, analysis makes it clear that *Rule 801(d)(1)(B) simply does not deal with the extent to which prior consistent statements may be used for rehabilitation.*" (Emphasis added.)

United States v. Rubin, 609 F.2d 51, 68–69 (2d Cir.1979, Friendly, J., concurring), *aff'd.,* 449 U.S. 424, 101 S.Ct. 698, 66 L.Ed.2d 633 (1981), quoted in *Parodi,* supra at 785, n. 13.

This split in federal authority is confusing, and the cases (*Rubin, Parodi,* and *Harris,* supra, among others) that support the rule that motive to fabricate goes only to the weight and not to the admissibility of a prior consistent statement are of only limited assistance. Judge Friendly's underscored comment is difficult to accept in view of the plain language of the Rule, which certainly appears to contemplate rehabilitation. We are also confronted with the additional reference to prior consistent statements in Tex.R.Cr.Evid. 612(c), which limits admissibility of such statements to situations allowed by Tex.R.Cr.Evid. 801(e)(1)(B). The Federal Rules lack this provision, and the express absence of other references to prior consistent statements is relied upon in Judge Friendly's analysis.

When the new Rules of Criminal Evidence were promulgated, a decision was made to adopt the wording of Fed.Rule 801(d)(1)(B), supra, for Tex.R.Cr.Evid. 801(e)(1)(B), supra. The intent was to adopt not only the wording of the Federal Rule but its interpretation as well. The Federal Rule has been interpreted in *Quinto,* supra, to require that a prior consistent statement be made prior to the time there was a motive to testify falsely in order to be admissible, even though the statute does not explicitly set out this requirement. Therefore, the Texas rule will also include this requirement. This decision is more in keeping with the precedent laid down by this Court in *Rains,* supra, which shall remain intact.

In the instant case, Officer Osterberg testified about three prior statements made by Jackson that were all consistent with the testimony she gave at trial. There is no dispute that all three statements were made after Jackson was promised money in return for information. All the statements were made after Jackson had a motive to testify falsely. Therefore, none of them were admissible to rebut a claim of recent fabrication.

We therefore reverse the judgment of the Court of Appeals because of the error in the admission, over proper objection, of evidence of Jackson's prior consistent statements. Such error must of course be assayed for harm to the appellant, a task the Court of Appeals necessarily never reached in their disposition of these grounds of error.

The case is therefore remanded to the Court of Appeals for proper disposition not inconsistent with this opinion.

MISSOURI PACIFIC R. CO. v. VLACH, 687 S.W.2d 414, 417–18 (Tex.App.1985). "Appellant contends in its eighth point of error that the trial court erred in refusing to admit into evidence the prior consistent statements of certain witnesses. A railroad signal crew was working at the scene of the accident. Their testimony was favorable to appellant's defense. Appellant alleged that appellees' attorney charged the signal crew with discussing their evidence together in a meeting before trial and argued that their testimony was orchestrated by appellant. Appellant offered the prior consistent statements of these witnesses to rebut the charges of recent fabrication. The exception to the hearsay rule relied upon by appellant is Rule 801(e)(1)(B) of the Texas Rules of Evidence which states:

> A statement is not hearsay if * * * The declarant testifies at the trial or hearing *and is subject to cross-examination concerning the statement,* and the statement is * * * consistent with his testimony and is offered to rebut an express or implied charge against him of recent fabrication or improper influence or motive * * * (Emphasis added.)

The trial court denied admission of the statements. This action was correct because the statements were not offered until after the witnesses had been excused from the courtroom. If the statements were admitted, appellee would not have had an opportunity to cross-examine the witnesses concerning the statements as required by Rule 801(e)(1). The trial court acted within its discretion in excluding these prior statements under the circumstances. Point of error eight is overruled."

UNITED STATES v. LEWIS

United States Court of Appeals, Second Circuit, 1977.
565 F.2d 1248, cert. denied, 435 U.S. 973, 98 S.Ct. 1618, 56 L.Ed.2d 66 (1978).

FEINBERG, CIRCUIT JUDGE:

After a jury trial in the United States District Court for the Eastern District of New York before Thomas C. Platt, J., appellant Frank Tillman Lewis was convicted of armed bank robbery and conspiracy to commit that crime, 18 U.S.C. §§ 2113(a) and (d), and 371. * * *

* * *

The photographic identification

In his thorough brief and argument, appellant's counsel maintains that the district judge committed a number of errors of law. The most substantial arguments on appeal stem from Norma Sharpe's pre-trial identification of appellant from a display of photographs. At trial, Mrs. Sharpe was unable to identify appellant in the courtroom and mistakenly picked out a Deputy United States Marshal instead. When Mrs. Sharpe was then shown the photographic display, she testified that she had previously identified one of the bank robbers from the group of pictures, and she then picked out the photograph she had earlier selected. This picture, which was of appellant, was then admitted into evidence. After Mrs. Sharpe's testimony, FBI Agent Leo Farrell testified as to the way in which he had prepared the photographic spread. He also confirmed that Mrs. Sharpe had selected appellant's picture shortly after the bank robbery.

* * *

Appellant next argues that the identification testimony should have been excluded as hearsay, and is not permitted by the new Federal Rules of Evidence. Appellant directs our attention to Rule 801(d), which contains various definitions, and provides in relevant part that:

> (d) Statements which are not hearsay. A statement is not hearsay if—
>
> (1) Prior statement by witness. The declarant testifies at the trial or hearing and is subject to cross-examination concerning the statement, and the statement is (A) inconsistent with his testimony, and was given under oath subject to the penalty of perjury at a trial, hearing, or other proceeding, or in a deposition, or (B) consistent with his testimony and is offered to rebut an express or implied charge against him of recent fabrication or improper influence or motive, or (C) *one of identification of a person made after perceiving him;* * * * (Emphasis supplied).

Appellant argues that Agent Farrell's testimony should have been excluded because "identification of a person made after perceiving him" contemplates only corporeal, not photographic, identification; and because it was improper to allow Farrell to testify in the absence of an in-court identification by Mrs. Sharpe. Appellant also claims that Mrs. Sharpe's testimony about her prior identification after she erroneously identified someone else in court amounted to testimony about a prior inconsistent statement not made under oath, rendering it improper under subsection (A), which overrides subsection (C).

Subsection (C) of Rule 801(d)(1), the focal point of appellant's arguments, appeared in its present form in the Rules as promulgated by the Supreme Court in November 1972. However, the Senate deleted the subsection before the Rules were approved by Congress in December 1974. Not long thereafter, the subsection was resurrected in an amendment to Rule 801, effective October 31, 1975.[5] The Senate Report on the 1975 amendment attributed the initial opposition to the subsection to concern over convicting a defendant solely on "unsworn, out-of-court testimony." [6] The Report noted, however, that the Rule required the identifier to be available for cross-examination at the trial, and in support of the view that such evidence should be admissible, cited, among other recent decisions, the Supreme Court's discussion in

5. Pub.L. No. 94–113, 89 Stat. 576.

6. S.Rep. No. 199, 94th Cong., 1st Sess. 2 (1975), hereafter "Senate Report." See also S.Rep. No. 1277, 93rd Cong., 2d Sess. (1974).

Gilbert v. California, 388 U.S. 263, 272 n. 3, 87 S.Ct. 1951, 18 L.Ed.2d 1178 (1967), the opinion of Judge Friendly in *United States v. Miller,* 381 F.2d 529, 538 (2d Cir.1967), cert. denied, 392 U.S. 929, 88 S.Ct. 2273, 20 L.Ed.2d 1387 (1968), and the en banc decision of the Court of Appeals for the District of Columbia, *Clemons v. United States,* 408 F.2d 1230 (1968), cert. denied, 394 U.S. 964, 89 S.Ct. 1318, 22 L.Ed.2d 567 (1969). The controversy over, and the rationale of, subsection (C) are both admirably summarized in 4 Weinstein's Evidence, 801–3ff., ¶ 801(d)(1)(C)[01]. We agree with the observation there made that

> Congress has recognized, as do most trial judges, that identification in the courtroom is a formality that offers little in the way of reliability and much in the way of suggestibility. The experienced trial judge gives much greater credence to the out-of-court identification.

Id. at 801–103. This court recently pointed out that "[t]he purpose of the rule was to permit the introduction of identifications made by a witness when memory was fresher and there had been less opportunity for influence to be exerted upon him." *United States v. Marchand,* 564 F.2d 983, 996 (2d Cir.1977).

With these considerations in mind, we turn to appellant's specific contentions. The legislative history makes clear that Congress intended "nonsuggestive * * * photographic," as well as lineup, identifications to be covered by subsection (C). Senate Report, at 2.[7] This conclusion is confirmed by our recent holding in *United States v. Marchand,* supra, 564 F.2d at 996. We can see no sound principle for construing "identification of a person" to exclude identification by a photograph. True, there are dangers peculiar to photographic identification and these, like the dangers of a lineup or even those of an on-the-spot identification, must be taken into account in assessing reliability. But they do not justify a limiting construction of subsection (C).

Appellant's second argument on this point is that the failure of Mrs. Sharpe to identify appellant in court made inadmissible Agent Farrell's evidence that she had identified appellant a month or two earlier. Appellant may be confusing this situation with that posed by the failure or refusal of the identifying witness to recall in court the earlier identification, which is discussed in Judge Weinstein's treatise from which appellant's brief extensively quotes. In that situation, testimony like Agent Farrell's might well raise questions concerning the adequacy of cross-examination and the right to confront the original identifying witness. In this case, however, Mrs. Sharpe did recall her prior identification and so testified. Even before the new Rule, we approved of admitting evidence of prior identification, albeit corporeal, by the declarant's "own testimony and also by that of others corroborating his version of the details," see *United States v. Miller,* supra, 381 F.2d at 538, cited by the Senate Report in support of subsection (C). Cf.

7. See also the House Report on subsection (C), H.Rep. No. 355, 94th Cong., 1st Sess. 2–3 (1975), hereafter "House Report."

United States v. Jenkins, 496 F.2d 57, 68–70 (2d Cir.), cert. denied, 420 U.S. 925, 95 S.Ct. 1119, 43 L.Ed.2d 394 (1975) (declarant could not recall prior photographic nonidentification of Jenkins and identification of another; evidence of same through third party excluded). If appellant is suggesting that under the new Rule testimony like Agent Farrell's may only be used to bolster an accurate in-court identification, we disagree. It seems clear both from the text and the legislative history of the amended Rule that testimony concerning extra-judicial identifications is admissible regardless of whether there has been an accurate in-court identification. The Senate Report recognizes the possibility that there may be a "discrepancy * * * between the witness's in-court and out-of-court testimony,"[8] and the House Report praises the amended Rule as a means of ensuring that "delays in the criminal justice system do not lead to cases falling through because the witness can no longer recall the identity of the person he saw commit the crime."[9] The occurrence of the very contingency foreseen by the Congress will obviously not serve, of itself, to bar the Farrell testimony.

Appellant's final point seems to be that subsection (C) does not apply at all when the identifier has made an erroneous in-court identification because the prior identification is inconsistent with it and was not given under oath, as required by subsection (A). The Government responds that since appellant's appearance had changed significantly by the time of trial, there was no inconsistency. More significantly, even though Rule 801(d)(1) embraces subsection (C), the latter is not limited by the earlier subsections. Subsection (C) represents a legislative decision to admit statements of identification provided the declarant "testifies at * * * trial * * * and is subject to cross-examination concerning the statement." These conditions were met here, and we do not think that subsection (C) is rendered inoperative by Mrs. Sharpe's misidentification in court.

* * *

Judgment affirmed.

Notes

(1) "In this case, Fishman testified at trial that he had identified Salerno before trial as one of the persons who extorted the money from him, but at trial recanted this statement and denied that Salerno had extorted money from him. Further, he was subject to cross-examination concerning his earlier statement made before trial identifying Salerno as one of the extortionists. Thus, Elder's testimony was properly admitted since the elements of Rule 801(d)(1)(C) were satisfied. * * * Salerno's reliance on United States v. Hogan, 763 F.2d 697 (5th Cir.1985) and United States v. Webster, 734 F.2d 1191 (7th Cir.1984) is inapposite. Both cases condemned the practice of the government calling a witness, knowing in advance that he would give unfavorable testimony, in order to impeach his testimony by introducing hearsay evidence against the defendant under

8. Senate Report, supra note 6, at 2.

9. House Report, supra note 7, at 3.

Fed.R.Evid. 607 since the 'purpose [of introducing the hearsay evidence] would not be to impeach the witness but to put in hearsay as substantive evidence against the defendant' that would be otherwise inadmissible. *Webster,* 234 F.2d at 1192. We initially note that the record does not reflect, nor have the defendants presented, any evidence whatsoever establishing that the government had any knowledge that Fishman would recant his prior testimony and not identify Salerno at trial. Further in our case, the trial court admitted Elder's testimony regarding Fishman's identification of Salerno not as impeachment evidence under Rule 607 but as independently admissible substantive evidence under Rule 801(d)(1)(C). * * * Since Agent Elder's testimony was independently admissible under Fed.R.Evid. 801(d)(1)(C) (and Salerno does not contend otherwise) and was not introduced as hearsay impeachment under Rule 607, his testimony was properly admitted at trial." United States v. O'Malley, 796 F.2d 891, 899 (7th Cir.1986).

(2) "This Circuit has held that this rule permits 'a witness to testify regarding identifications made by another witness.' * * * Where, as here, both the agent and the witness testify and are available for cross-examination, the statement of identification is not hearsay. * * * [T]he rule was intended to solve the problem of a witness who identifies a defendant before trial, but then at trial refused to acknowledge the identification because of fear of reprisal." United States v. Jarrad, 754 F.2d 1451, 1456 (9th Cir.1985), cert. denied, 474 U.S. 830, 106 S.Ct. 96, 88 L.Ed.2d 78 (1985).

UNITED STATES v. OWENS

Supreme Court of the United States, 1988.
484 U.S. 554, 108 S.Ct. 838, 98 L.Ed.2d 951.

JUSTICE SCALIA delivered the opinion of the Court.

This case requires us to determine whether either the Confrontation Clause of the Sixth Amendment or Rule 802 of the Federal Rules of Evidence bars testimony concerning a prior, out-of-court identification when the identifying witness is unable, because of memory loss, to explain the basis for the identification.

I

On April 12, 1982, John Foster, a correctional counselor at the federal prison in Lompoc, California, was attacked and brutally beaten with a metal pipe. His skull was fractured, and he remained hospitalized for almost a month. As a result of his injuries, Foster's memory was severely impaired. When Thomas Mansfield, an FBI agent investigating the assault, first attempted to interview Foster, on April 19, he found Foster lethargic and unable to remember his attacker's name. On May 5, Mansfield again spoke to Foster, who was much improved and able to describe the attack. Foster named respondent as his attacker and identified respondent from an array of photographs.

Respondent was tried in Federal District Court for assault with intent to commit murder under 18 U.S.C. § 113(a). At trial, Foster recounted his activities just before the attack, and described feeling the blows to his head and seeing blood on the floor. He testified that he clearly remembered identifying respondent as his assailant during his May 5th interview with Mansfield. On cross-examination, he admitted that he could not remember seeing his assailant. He also admitted that, although there was evidence that he had received numerous visitors in the hospital, he was unable to remember any of them except Mansfield, and could not remember whether any of these visitors had suggested that respondent was the assailant. Defense counsel unsuccessfully sought to refresh his recollection with hospital records, including one indicating that Foster had attributed the assault to someone other than respondent. Respondent was convicted and sentenced to 20 years' imprisonment to be served consecutively to a previous sentence.

On appeal, the United States Court of Appeals for the Ninth Circuit considered challenges based on the Confrontation Clause and Rule 802 of the Federal Rules of Evidence.[1] By divided vote it upheld both challenges (though finding the Rule 802 violation harmless error), and reversed the judgment of the District Court. 789 F.2d 750 (1986). We granted certiorari, 479 U.S. ___, 107 S.Ct. 1284, 94 L.Ed.2d 143 (1987), to resolve the conflict with other Circuits on the significance of a hearsay declarant's memory loss both with respect to the Confrontation Clause, see, *e.g., United States ex rel. Thomas v. Cuyler,* 548 F.2d 460, 462–463 (CA3 1977), and with respect to Rule 802, see, *e.g., United States v. Lewis,* 565 F.2d 1248, 1252 (CA2 1977), cert. denied, 435 U.S. 973, 98 S.Ct. 1618, 56 L.Ed.2d 66 (1978).

II

The Confrontation Clause of the Sixth Amendment gives the accused the right "to be confronted with the witnesses against him." This has long been read as securing an adequate opportunity to cross-examine adverse witnesses. See, *e.g., Mattox v. United States,* 156 U.S. 237, 242–243, 15 S.Ct. 337, 339, 39 L.Ed. 409 (1895); *Douglas v. Alabama,* 380 U.S. 415, 418, 85 S.Ct. 1074, 1076, 13 L.Ed.2d 934 (1965). This Court has never held that a Confrontation Clause violation can be founded upon a witness's loss of memory, but in two cases has expressly left that possibility open.

In *California v. Green,* 399 U.S. 149, 157–164, 90 S.Ct. 1930, 1934–38, 26 L.Ed.2d 489 (1970), we found no constitutional violation in the admission of testimony that had been given at a preliminary hearing, relying on (as one of two independent grounds) the proposition that the opportunity to cross-examine the witness at trial satisfied the Sixth Amendment's requirements. We declined, however, to decide the admissibility of the same witness's out-of-court statement to a police officer concerning events that at trial he was unable to recall. In remanding on this point, we noted that the state court had not con-

1. This case has been argued, both here and below, as though Fed.Rule Evid. 801(d)(1)(C) were the basis of the challenge. That is substantially but not technically correct. If respondent's arguments are accepted, it is Rule 802 that would render the out-of-court statement inadmissible as hearsay; but as explained in Part III, it is ultimately Rule 801(d)(1)(C) that determines whether Rule 802 is applicable.

sidered, and the parties had not briefed, the possibility that the witness's memory loss so affected the petitioner's right to cross-examine as to violate the Confrontation Clause.[2] *Id.,* at 168–169, 90 S.Ct., at 1940–41. Justice Harlan, in a scholarly concurrence, stated that he would have reached the issue of the out-of-court statement, and would have held that a witness's inability to "recall either the underlying events that are the subject of an extra-judicial statement or previous testimony or recollect the circumstances under which the statement was given, does not have Sixth Amendment consequence." *Id.,* at 188, 90 S.Ct., at 1951.

In *Delaware v. Fensterer,* 474 U.S. 15, 106 S.Ct. 292, 88 L.Ed.2d 15 (1985) (*per curiam*), we determined that there was no Confrontation Clause violation when an expert witness testified as to what opinion he had formed, but could not recollect the basis on which he had formed it. We said:

> "The Confrontation Clause includes no guarantee that every witness called by the prosecution will refrain from giving testimony that is marred by forgetfulness, confusion, or evasion. To the contrary, the Confrontation Clause is generally satisfied when the defense is given a full and fair opportunity to probe and expose these infirmities through cross-examination, thereby calling to the attention of the factfinder the reasons for giving scant weight to the witness' testimony." *Id.,* at 21–22, 106 S.Ct., at 296.

Our opinion noted that a defendant seeking to discredit a forgetful expert witness is not without ammunition, since the jury may be persuaded "that his opinion is as unreliable as his memory." *Id.,* at 19, 106 S.Ct., at 294. We distinguished, however, the unresolved issue in *Green* on the basis that that involved the introduction of an out-of-court statement. 474 U.S., at 18, 106 S.Ct., at 294. Justice Stevens, concurring in the judgment, suggested that the question at hand was in fact quite close to the question left open in *Green.* 474 U.S., at 23–24, 106 S.Ct., at 297.

Here that question is squarely presented, and we agree with the answer suggested 18 years ago by Justice Harlan. "[T]he Confrontation Clause guarantees only 'an *opportunity* for effective cross-examination, not cross-examination that is effective in whatever way, and to whatever extent, the defense might wish.'" *Kentucky v. Stincer,* ___ U.S. ___, ___, 107 S.Ct. 2658, 2664, 96 L.Ed.2d 631 (1987), quoting from *Fensterer, supra,* 474 U.S. at 22, 106 S.Ct. at 296 (emphasis added); *Delaware v. Van Arsdall,* 475 U.S. 673, 679, 106 S.Ct. 1431, 1435, 89 L.Ed.2d 674 (1986); *Ohio v. Roberts,* 448 U.S. 56, 73, n. 12, 100 S.Ct. 2531, 2543, n. 12, 65 L.Ed.2d 597 (1980). As *Fensterer* demonstrates, that opportunity is not denied when a witness testifies as to his current belief but is unable to recollect the reason for that belief. It is sufficient that the

2. On remand, the California Supreme Court concluded that the Confrontation Clause was not violated by the out-of-court statement, because the declarant testified under oath, subject to cross-examination, and the jury was able to observe his demeanor. *People v. Green,* 3 Cal.3d 981, 92 Cal.Rptr. 494, 479 P.2d 998, cert. dism'd, 404 U.S. 801, 92 S.Ct. 20, 30 L.Ed.2d 34 (1971).

defendant has the opportunity to bring out such matters as the witness's bias, his lack of care and attentiveness, his poor eyesight, and even (what is often a prime objective of cross-examination, see 3A J. Wigmore, Evidence § 995, pp. 931–932 (J. Chadbourn rev. 1970)) the very fact that he has a bad memory. If the ability to inquire into these matters suffices to establish the constitutionally requisite opportunity for cross-examination when a witness testifies as to his current belief, the basis for which he cannot recall, we see no reason why it should not suffice when the witness's past belief is introduced and he is unable to recollect the reason for that past belief. In both cases the foundation for the belief (current or past) cannot effectively be elicited, but other means of impugning the belief are available. Indeed, if there is any difference in persuasive impact between the statement "I believe this to be the man who assaulted me, but can't remember why" and the statement "I don't know whether this is the man who assaulted me, but I told the police I believed so earlier," the former would seem, if anything, more damaging and hence give rise to a greater need for memory-testing, if that is to be considered essential to an opportunity for effective cross-examination. We conclude with respect to this latter example, as we did in *Fensterer* with respect to the former, that it is not. The weapons available to impugn the witness's statement when memory loss is asserted will of course not always achieve success, but successful cross-examination is not the constitutional guarantee. They are, however, realistic weapons, as is demonstrated by defense counsel's summation in this very case, which emphasized Foster's memory loss and argued that his identification of respondent was the result of the suggestions of people who visited him in the hospital.

Our constitutional analysis is not altered by the fact that the testimony here involved an out-of-court identification that would traditionally be categorized as hearsay. See Advisory Committee's Notes on Fed.Rule Evid. 801(d)(1)(C), 28 U.S.C.App., p. 717. This Court has recognized a partial (and somewhat indeterminate) overlap between the requirements of the traditional hearsay rule and the Confrontation Clause. See *Green,* 399 U.S., at 155–156, 90 S.Ct., at 1933–34; *id.,* at 173, 90 S.Ct., at 1943 (Harlan, J., concurring). The dangers associated with hearsay inspired the Court of Appeals in the present case to believe that the Constitution required the testimony to be examined for "indicia of reliability," *Dutton v. Evans,* 400 U.S. 74, 89, 91 S.Ct. 210, 220, 27 L.Ed.2d 213 (1970), or "particularized guarantees of trustworthiness," *Roberts, supra,* at 66, 100 S.Ct. at 2539. We do not think such an inquiry is called for when a hearsay declarant is present at trial and subject to unrestricted cross-examination. In that situation, as the Court recognized in *Green,* the traditional protections of the oath, cross-examination, and opportunity for the jury to observe the witness's demeanor satisfy the constitutional requirements. 399 U.S., at 158–161, 90 S.Ct., at 1935–36. We do not think that a constitutional line drawn by the Confrontation Clause falls between a forgetful witness's live testimony that he once believed this defendant to be the perpetrator of the crime, and the introduction of the witness's earlier statement to that effect.

Respondent has argued that this Court's jurisprudence concerning suggestive identification procedures shows the special dangers of identification testimony, and the special importance of cross-examination when such hearsay is proffered. See, *e.g., Manson v. Brathwaite,* 432 U.S. 98, 97 S.Ct. 2243, 53 L.Ed.2d 140 (1977); *Neil v. Biggers,* 409 U.S. 188, 93 S.Ct. 375, 34 L.Ed.2d 401 (1972). Respondent has not, however, argued that the identification procedure used here was in any way suggestive. There does not appear in our opinions, and we decline to adopt today, the principle that, because of the mere possibility of suggestive procedures, out-of-court statements of identification are inherently less reliable than other out-of-court statements.

III

Respondent urges as an alternative basis for affirmance a violation of Fed.Rule Evid. 802, which generally excludes hearsay. Rule 801(d)(1)(C) defines as not hearsay a prior statement "of identification of a person made after perceiving the person," if the declarant "testifies at the trial or hearing and is subject to cross-examination concerning the statement." The Court of Appeals found that Foster's identification statement did not come within this exclusion because his memory loss prevented his being "subject to cross-examination concerning the statement." Although the Court of Appeals concluded that the violation of the Rules of Evidence was harmless (applying for purposes of that determination a "more-probable-than-not" standard, rather than the "beyond-a-reasonable-doubt" standard applicable to the Confrontation Clause violation, see *Delaware v. Van Arsdall,* 475 U.S., at 684, 106 S.Ct., at 1438), respondent argues to the contrary.

It seems to us that the more natural reading of "subject to cross-examination concerning the statement" includes what was available here. Ordinarily a witness is regarded as "subject to cross-examination" when he is placed on the stand, under oath, and responds willingly to questions. Just as with the constitutional prohibition, limitations on the scope of examination by the trial court or assertions of privilege by the witness may undermine the process to such a degree that meaningful cross-examination within the intent of the rule no longer exists. But that effect is not produced by the witness's assertion of memory loss—which, as discussed earlier, is often the very result sought to be produced by cross-examination, and can be effective in destroying the force of the prior statement. Rule 801(d)(1)(C), which specifies that the cross-examination need only "concer[n] the statement," does not on its face require more.

This reading seems even more compelling when the rule is compared with Rule 804(a)(3), which defines "Unavailability as a witness" to include situations in which a declarant "testifies to a lack of memory of the subject matter of the declarant's statement." Congress plainly was aware of the recurrent evidentiary problem at issue here—witness forgetfulness of an underlying event—but chose not to make it an exception to Rule 801(d)(1)(C).

The reasons for that choice are apparent from the Advisory Committee's Notes on Rule 801 and its legislative history. The premise for Rule 801(d)(1)(C) was that, given adequate safeguards against suggestiveness, out-of-court identifications were generally preferable to courtroom identifications. Advisory Committee's Notes on Rule 801, 28 U.S.C.App., p. 717. Thus, despite the traditional view that such statements were hearsay, the Advisory Committee believed that their use was to be fostered rather than discouraged. Similarly, the House Report on the Rule noted that since, "[a]s time goes by, a witness' memory will fade and his identification will become less reliable," minimizing the barriers to admission of more contemporaneous identification is fairer to defendants and prevents "cases falling through because the witness can no longer recall the identity of the person he saw commit the crime." H.R.Rep. No. 94–355, p. 3 (1975). See also S.Rep. No. 94–199, p. 2 (1975), U.S.Code Cong. & Admin.News, 1975, pp. 1092, 1094. To judge from the House and Senate Reports, Rule 801(d)(1)(C) was in part directed to the very problem here at issue: a memory loss that makes it impossible for the witness to provide an in-court identification or testify about details of the events underlying an earlier identification.

Respondent argues that this reading is impermissible because it creates an internal inconsistency in the Rules, since the forgetful witness who is deemed "subject to cross-examination" under 801(d)(1)(C) is simultaneously deemed "unavailable" under 804(a)(3). This is the position espoused by a prominent commentary on the Rules, see 4 J. Weinstein & M. Berger, Weinstein's Evidence 801–120 to 801–121, 801–178 (1987). It seems to use, however, that this is not a substantive inconsistency, but only a semantic oddity resulting from the fact that Rule 804(a) has for convenience of reference in Rule 804(b) chosen to describe the circumstances necessary in order to admit certain categories of hearsay testimony under the rubric "Unavailability as a witness." These circumstances include not only absence from the hearing, but also claims of privilege, refusals to obey a court's order to testify, and inability to testify based on physical or mental illness or memory loss. Had the rubric instead been "Unavailability as a witness, memory loss, and other special circumstances" there would be no apparent inconsistency with Rule 801, which is a definition section excluding certain statements entirely from the category of "hearsay." The semantic inconsistency exists not only with respect to Rule 801(d)(1)(C), but also with respect to the other subparagraphs of Rule 801(d)(1). It would seem strange, for example, to assert that a witness can avoid introduction of testimony from a prior proceeding that is inconsistent with his trial testimony, see Rule 801(d)(1)(A), by simply asserting lack of memory of the facts to which the prior testimony related. See *United States v. Murphy,* 696 F.2d 282, 283–284 (CA4 1982), cert. denied, 461 U.S. 945, 103 S.Ct. 2123, 77 L.Ed.2d 1303 (1983). But that situation, like this one, presents the verbal curiosity that the witness is "subject to cross-examination" under Rule 801 while at the same time "unavailable" under Rule 804(a)(3). Quite obviously, the two characterizations are made for two entirely different purposes and there is no requirement or expectation that they should coincide.

For the reasons stated, we hold that neither the Confrontation Clause nor Fed.Rule Evid. 802 is violated by admission of an identification statement of a witness who is unable, because of a memory loss, to testify concerning the basis for the identification. The decision of the Court of Appeals is reversed and remanded for proceedings consistent with this opinion.

So ordered.

JUSTICE KENNEDY took no part in the consideration or decision of this case.

JUSTICE BRENNAN, with whom JUSTICE MARSHALL joins, dissenting.

* * *

Although the Court suggests that the result it reaches today follows naturally from our earlier cases, we have never before held that the Confrontation Clause protects nothing more than a defendant's right to question live witnesses, no matter how futile that questioning might be. On the contrary, as the Court's own recitation of our prior case law reveals, we have repeatedly affirmed that the right of confrontation ensures "an opportunity for *effective* cross-examination." *Delaware v. Fensterer,* 474 U.S. 15, 20, 106 S.Ct. 292, 295, 88 L.Ed.2d 15 (1985) (*per curiam*) (emphasis added); see also *Nelson v. O'Neil,* 402 U.S. 622, 629, 91 S.Ct. 1723, 1727, 29 L.Ed.2d 222 (1971) (Confrontation Clause does not bar admission of out-of-court statement where defendant has "the benefit of full and *effective* cross-examination of [declarant]") (emphasis added); *California v. Green,* 399 U.S., at 159, 90 S.Ct., at 1935 (introduction of out-of-court statement does not violate Confrontation Clause "as long as the defendant is assured of full and *effective* cross-examination at the time of trial") (emphasis added). While we have rejected the notion that effectiveness should be measured in terms of a defendant's ultimate success, we have never, until today, equated effectiveness with the mere opportunity to pose questions. Rather, consistent with the Confrontation Clause's mission of "advanc[ing] a practical concern for the accuracy of the truth-determining process in criminal trials," *Dutton v. Evans,* 400 U.S. 74, 89, 91 S.Ct. 210, 220, 27 L.Ed.2d 213 (1970), we have suggested that the touchstone of effectiveness is whether the cross-examination affords " 'the trier of fact * * * a satisfactory basis for evaluating the truth of the prior statement.' " *Ibid.* (quoting *California v. Green, supra,* at 161, 90 S.Ct., at 1936). See also *Ohio v. Roberts,* 448 U.S. 56, 73, 100 S.Ct. 2531, 2542, 65 L.Ed.2d 597 (1980) (introduction of prior testimony where the declarant was unavailable at trial did not violate Confrontation Clause where previous cross-examination of declarant "afforded the trier of fact a satisfactory basis for evaluating the truth of the prior statement" (citation omitted; internal quotation marks omitted)), *Mancusi v. Stubbs,* 408 U.S. 204, 216, 92 S.Ct. 2308, 2315, 33 L.Ed.2d 293 (1972) (same). Where no opportunity for such cross-examination exists, we have recognized that the Sixth Amendment permits the introduction of out-of-court statements only when they bear sufficient independent "indicia of reliability." *Dutton v. Evans, supra,* 400 U.S. at 89, 91 S.Ct. at 220.

* * *

I agree with the Court that the Confrontation Clause does not guarantee defendants the right to confront only those witnesses whose testimony is not marred by forgetfulness, confusion, or evasion, and that the right of confrontation " 'is generally satisfied when the defense is given a full and fair opportunity to probe and expose these infirmities through cross-examination.' " *Ante* (quoting *Fensterer,* 474 U.S., at 22, 106 S.Ct., at 296). But as we stressed just last Term, this right to cross-examination "is essentially a 'functional' right designed to promote reliability in the truth-finding functions of a criminal trial." *Kentucky v. Stincer,* 482 U.S. ___, ___, 107 S.Ct. at 2658, 2662, 96 L.Ed.2d 631 (1987). In the present case, respondent Owens was afforded no opportunity to probe and expose the infirmities of Foster's May 5, 1982 recollections, for here cross-examination, the "greatest legal engine ever invented for the discovery of truth," *California v. Green,* 399 U.S., at 158, 90 S.Ct. at 1935, stood as helpless as current medical technology before Foster's profound memory loss. In concluding that respondent's Sixth Amendment rights were satisfied by Foster's mere presence in the courtroom, the Court reduces the right of confrontation to a hollow formalism. Because I believe the Confrontation Clause guarantees more than the right to ask questions of a live witness, no matter how dead that witness's memory proves to be, I dissent.

Note

See Haddad, The Future of Confrontation Clause Developments: What Will Emerge When the Supreme Court Synthesizes the Diverse Lines of Confrontation Decisions? 81 J.Crim.L. & Criminology 77 (1990); Shaviro, The Supreme Court's Bifurcated Interpretation of the Confrontation Clause, 17 Hastings Const.L.Q. 383 (1990).

SECTION 3. FORMER TESTIMONY *

[FED.R.EVID. 804(b)(1)]

STATE v. AYERS

Supreme Judicial Court of Maine, 1983.

468 A.2d 606, cert. denied, 466 U.S. 941, 104 S.Ct. 1919, 80 L.Ed.2d 466 (1984).

McKusick, Chief Justice.

* * *

John Cheponis, former husband of defendant, was shot and beaten to death in his J–P Cash Market in Presque Isle on April 6, 1979.

* See 5 Wigmore, Evidence §§ 1367–1394, 1401–1418 (Chadbourn rev. 1974); McCormick, Evidence ch. 31 (4th ed. 1992); Martin, The Former–Testimony Exception in the Proposed Federal Rules of Evidence, 57 Iowa L.Rev. 547 (1972); Weissenberger, The Former Testimony Hearsay Exception: A Study in Rulemaking, Judicial Revision-

Defendant and Donald Ayers, whom she later married, were jointly indicted for murder and conspiracy. Both defendants testified at their joint trial held June 25 to July 2, 1980, in the Superior Court (Aroostook County). The jury found the defendants guilty on both counts of the indictment. On appeal, this court upheld the judgments of conspiracy, but set aside the convictions of murder, finding that a confession given by Barbara Ayers had been obtained in violation of her Miranda rights and that the murder weapon had been discovered as a result of that illegally obtained confession. State v. Ayers, 433 A.2d 356 (Me. 1981). Donald Ayers was separately retried on the murder charge, and his conviction was recently affirmed by this court. State v. Ayers, 464 A.2d 963 (Me.1983).

At Barbara Ayers' second trial on the murder charge, this time by herself, the defense sought and procured suppression of the confession and the pistol. Following the granting of her motions to suppress, the State, at the pretrial hearing, called Donald Ayers to testify. Mr. Ayers refused to answer any questions, even after the court found that he lacked a valid fifth amendment claim and ordered him to testify. The State then moved the court to admit into evidence, pursuant to M.R.Evid. 804(b)(1), portions of the testimony Donald Ayers had previously given when he was on trial jointly with Barbara Ayers. The court found that all the preconditions were met to the invocation of Rule 804(b)(1) in that Mr. Ayers was an "unavailable" witness and that Barbara Ayers, at the former proceeding, had had "an opportunity and similar motive to develop [his] testimony by direct, cross, or redirect examination." Therefore, portions of Mr. Ayers' former testimony describing the murder plot, the procurement of the murder weapon, and the commission of the crime were read to the jury, over Barbara's continuing objection.

Defendant Barbara Ayers now assigns error to the court's ruling on the admissibility of the former testimony. She asserts that she lacked the requisite "similar motive" to examine Mr. Ayers at the two trials and that therefore the Rule 804(b)(1) exception was not properly applicable. Defendant's claim is that at her first trial, where her illegally obtained confession was improperly admitted, she was forced to employ the tactic of admitting, but then attempting to justify, the killing of John Cheponis. In contrast, she asserts that, at the second trial, with the confession suppressed, she planned to refrain from testifying herself and intended to attack the State's case by introducing circumstantial evidence to suggest that individuals other than herself had committed the crime. In fact, although she did not take the stand at her retrial, she never offered evidence pointing an accusatory finger at others.

ism, and the Separation of Powers, 67 N.C.L.Rev. 295 (1989).

The presiding justice's findings of fact necessary for admissibility under the hearsay exception of Rule 804(b)(1)—namely, the unavailability of the witness and the opportunity and similar motive to examine—must be upheld unless clearly erroneous. See State v. Caouette, 462 A.2d 1171, 1175–76 (Me.1983); State v. Hafford, 410 A.2d 219, 220 (Me.1980). The justice could rationally conclude from the evidence that defendant had the same motive to challenge Mr. Ayers' testimony at the first trial, if it was not truthful, as she had at her second trial. His testimony implicated her in the murder of John Cheponis, and her guilt or innocence of that crime was the identical issue of both trials.

To support her argument that a "similar motive" was lacking, defendant finds her "greatest assistance" in a decision of a single trial judge: United States v. Franklin, 235 F.Supp. 338 (D.D.C.1964). Even if we were inclined to give much weight to one opinion of a single judge from another jurisdiction, we find *Franklin* readily distinguishable on its facts. In *Franklin,* a federal district judge found no similar motive to examine where the government sought to introduce against a defendant testimony given by his former co-defendants at their previous joint trial. The judge on the facts of that particular case found that at the first trial the co-defendants' testimony "did not accuse the defendant" and that "a vigorous cross-examination of an associate might have reflected badly on the defendant." Accordingly, the judge concluded on the fact circumstances of Franklin's first trial that he had had "no real need or incentive to thoroughly cross-examine his then co-defendant[s]." 235 F.Supp. at 341. Such is not the case with Barbara Ayers. At both of her trials the all-encompassing question being tried was whether she was guilty of murder, and Donald Ayers' testimony pointed toward her guilt. It clearly did "accuse the defendant." The presiding justice at Barbara Ayers' second trial was fully entitled to discredit her assertion that her newly devised plan to pursue different tactics at her second trial precluded her from having a similar motive to cross-examine Mr. Ayers at both trials. Particularly is this true when as it turned out she never fully pursued her alleged change of tactics.

The "opportunity and similar motive" test of Rule 804(b)(1) has been usefully analyzed in terms of whether "an attorney making every effort within reason [at the prior trial] to bring out facts on behalf of his client *might* have developed the testimony fully." Martin, The Former–Testimony Exception in the Proposed Federal Rules of Evidence, 57 Iowa L.Rev. 547, 559 (1972) (emphasis in original). The author noted:

> It is unfair to hold a party to the former examination if no reasonable attorney would be expected to have elicited the now-relevant facts; *but if the circumstances were such that those facts could have been brought out if they were available, the present opponent can fairly be held.*

Id. (emphasis added). The author further states that any inquiry into matters of tactical choice is precluded; that "it is * * * indisputable that no authority considers them sufficient factors for excluding former testimony; the question is always phrased in terms of 'opportunity' and 'motive and interest,' rather than 'actual examination' and 'ability' to develop the testimony fully." Id. As so analyzed, the trial justice's preliminary determination on the admissibility of prior testimony is a fact-finding, subject to review only for clear error. We can find no such error in the admission against Barbara Ayers of the prior testimony of Donald Ayers directly incriminating her in the murder for which she was standing trial in both cases.

* * *

Judgment affirmed.

NICHOLS, JUSTICE, dissenting.

I cannot agree with today's majority when in such cavalier fashion it permits the former testimony of a witness, Donald Ayers, to be admitted into evidence against the Defendant, Barbara Thibodeau Ayers, in this, her second trial for murder.

The witness's testimony at the earlier trial was nothing but hearsay at this trial. Its admission into evidence by the Superior Court was a violation of the Defendant's right of confrontation guaranteed to her by Amendment VI (through Amendment XIV) of the United States Constitution.

In a very limited way our Maine Rules of Evidence (tracking the Federal Rules of Evidence in this particular) permit the testimony of a witness given at a former trial to come in when the declarant is unavailable as a witness. Our rules provide that such hearsay is not excluded by the hearsay rule only if the party against whom the testimony is offered at the second trial

> had an opportunity and similar motive to develop the testimony by direct, cross, or redirect examination. M.R.Evid. 804(b)(1).

The central issue here is whether the Defendant had a "similar motive" to cross-examine this witness at an earlier time when he and she were being jointly tried for murder. The answer is that the Defendant did not.

The counsel who represented her at the first trial defended on the grounds of justification. He had no reason in that trial vigorously to cross-examine this witness as to the Defendant's role in the slaying. Nor did he do so. Months later in a second trial the Defendant was represented by new counsel. It is clear from the record that at the second trial new counsel grounded their defense on a different issue entirely—whether there was insufficient evidence that it was the Defendant who killed the victim. On this issue cross-examination of Donald Ayers became of critical importance to the Defendant.

The "motive" had become dramatically dissimilar, yet today's majority gloss over that difference.

First, it is simplistic indeed to suggest, as the majority does, that guilt or innocence was "all-encompassing" and "the identical issue of both trials." They close their eyes to the fact that if a *new* trial is to be just that, client and counsel must have the opportunity to decide anew the trial strategy to be pursued.

Second, after the defense has settled upon their strategy for a jury trial, it is unrealistic to imply, as today's majority does, that instead of presenting their case in the manner and with a selectivity counsel deem most persuasive to the jury, they must digress by cross-examining witnesses at length on matters not relevant to the issues of the day, all at the peril that at some possible second trial the witnesses' former testimony would be admitted on the "all-encompassing" issue of "guilt or innocence." Jury persuasion becomes subordinated to making a record for an appellate court.

Even before the rulemakers inserted this requirement of "similar motive" to develop the testimony by cross-examination, it had been recognized that where a defendant has had no opportunity to cross-examine that is "full, substantial and meaningful in view of the realities of the situation," the former testimony is not excludable from the hearsay rule. United States v. Franklin, 235 F.Supp. 338, 341 (D.D.C.1964).

Since this requirement was codified in Fed.R.Evid. 804(b)(1) rare has been the case decided under that rule on "similar motive" grounds. For two cases decided under that rule at least in part on "similar motive" grounds, see Black Hills Jewelry Manufacturing Co. v. Gold Rush, Inc., 633 F.2d 746, 752–3 (8th Cir.1980); Hewitt v. Hutter, 432 F.Supp. 795, 799 (W.D.Va.1977); *aff'd.* 568 F.2d 773 (4th Cir.1978).[1]

To admit into evidence at this second trial of the Defendant the former testimony here challenged certainly offends the rule and violates as well her constitutional right to be confronted by the witnesses against her.[2] In view of the realities of the situation, with a different defense being pressed in the first trial, the Defendant had no meaningful opportunity at that time to cross-examine on the issue being urged in the second trial. The former testimony remains pure hearsay, and its admission at this second trial offends the Defendant's right of confrontation.[3]

Years ago, when a somewhat different issue was joined in a second case, our Court had occasion to observe that "[c]ross-examination upon

1. See generally 4 *Weinstein's Evidence* ¶ 804(b)(1)[04] (1981).

2. See Ohio v. Roberts, 448 U.S. 56, 66, 100 S.Ct. 2531, 2539, 65 L.Ed.2d 597 (1980); Pointer v. Texas, 380 U.S. 400, 407, 85 S.Ct. 1065, 1069, 13 L.Ed.2d 923 (1965); Mattox v. United States, 156 U.S. 237, 244, 15 S.Ct. 337, 340, 39 L.Ed. 409 (1895).

3. Just as the issue is novel in this jurisdiction, so few, indeed, have been the cases which have tested the federal equivalent, Fed.R.Evid. 804(b)(1), in a second trial situation; most involved challenges to the admission of testimony first given at some preliminary hearing. The case before us is unique in that it is conceded that at the first trial certain constitutional safeguards to which this Defendant was entitled had been infringed. If her in-court confession was a "fruit of the poisonous tree" as our Court indicated in State v. Ayers, 433 A.2d 356 (Me.1981), why was not Donald Ayers' prior testimony, which followed that confession and suffers from the same constitutional infirmity, every bit as much a fruit of that tree?

the one issue might differ from cross-examination on the other." Ellsworth v. Waltham, 125 Me. 214, 216, 132 A. 423 (1926). That observation is pertinent here today.

When this Defendant's defense was justification, as it was in her first trial, no reasonable attorney, striving to focus the jury's attention on the validity of this defense, could be expected to have diverted the fact finders' attention by a lengthy cross-examination of Donald Ayers on matters irrelevant to this defense.

I advert to the same sentence from Professor Martin's law review article as does the majority:

> It is unfair to hold a party to the former examination if no reasonable attorney would be expected to have elicited the now-relevant facts; but if the circumstances could have been brought out if they were available, the present opponent can fairly be held.

Martin, The Former–Testimony Exception in the Proposed Federal Rules of Evidence, 57 Iowa L.Rev. 547, 559 (1972). However, I submit that it is the first clause of that sentence which is pertinent here, and not the second clause, which the majority underscores.

As an eminent authority declares, "When the issue to which the former testimony is directed in the subsequent proceeding was not an issue in the earlier proceeding, then the similar motive requirement will not be satisfied." 11 *Moore's Federal Practice* 270 (1982). See Peterson v. United States, 344 F.2d 419 (5th Cir.1965) (former testimony not admissible when a new issue of conspiracy was joined at the second trial).[4]

In sum, the majority's interpretation of Evid.R. 804(b)(1) drains all meaning from the words "similar motive." Surely, the federal rulemakers introduced this phrase for a purpose. I would interpret "similar motive" in a way that makes those words a vital safeguard of defendants' right of confrontation. I would conclude that the "similar motive" requirement was not satisfied in the case before us. I would vacate the judgment of conviction.

CLAY v. JOHNS–MANVILLE SALES CORP.

United States Court of Appeals, Sixth Circuit, 1983.

722 F.2d 1289, cert. denied sub nom. Raymark Indus., Inc. v. Clay, 467 U.S. 1253, 104 S.Ct. 3537, 82 L.Ed.2d 842 (1984).

George Clifton Edwards, Jr., Circuit Judge.

In these two cases plaintiffs John Ed Clay and Curtis Bailey, each joined by his wife, brought actions for damages against defendants Johns–Manville Sales Corporation and Raybestos–Manhattan, Inc., on

4. See also United States v. Wingate, 520 F.2d 309 (2d Cir.1975), *cert. denied,* 423 U.S. 1074, 96 S.Ct. 858, 47 L.Ed.2d 84 (1976) (issue at a suppression hearing held to be so different from issue at subsequent trial as not to exclude former testimony from the hearsay rule).

the basis of products liability claims resulting from plaintiffs' exposure to asbestos containing products manufactured by the defendants. The cases were tried in the United States District Court for the Eastern District of Tennessee and ended in jury verdicts for the defendants.

* * *

We turn now to the second issue which requires our consideration, namely whether the District Judge erred in excluding a deposition taken from a witness, Dr. Kenneth Wallace Smith, in DeRocco v. Forty-eight Installation, Inc., No. 7880 (W.D.Pa.1974). At the time of the *DeRocco* proceeding, Dr. Smith was 63 years of age and had acquired his knowledge about asbestos disease in the employment of the Johns–Manville Corporation, the largest asbestos manufacturer in the field. Serving Johns–Manville during a good portion of his 22 years of employment as the only full-time physician in the organization, Dr. Smith's deposition is peculiarly relevant to the extent of the knowledge possessed by manufacturers of the hazards of asbestos containing products during the years when appellants Clay and Bailey allege they were exposed to asbestos.

Dr. Smith had died before the trial of this case. The key question in relation to the admissibility of this evidence is posed by the language of Rule 804(b)(1) of the Federal Rules of Evidence, which reads:

Rule 804. Hearsay Exceptions; Declarant Unavailable

(a) Definition of unavailability. "Unavailability as a witness" includes situations in which the declarant—

* * *

(b) Hearsay exceptions. The following are not excluded by the hearsay rule if the declarant is unavailable as a witness:

(1) Former testimony. Testimony given as a witness at another hearing of the same or a different proceeding, or in a deposition taken in compliance with law in the course of the same or another proceeding, if the party against whom the testimony is now offered, or, in a civil action or proceeding, a predecessor in interest, had an opportunity and similar motive to develop the testimony by direct, cross, or redirect examination.

To ascertain the meaning of "predecessor in interest," an examination of legislative history is necessary. As originally proposed by the Supreme Court, Rule 804(b)(1) would have admitted prior testimony of an unavailable witness if the party against whom it is offered or a person "with a motive and interest" similar to him had an opportunity to examine that witness. H.R.Rep. No. 650, 93d Cong., 1st Sess. 15 (1973), *reprinted in* 1974 U.S.Code Cong. & Ad.News 7051, 7088. The House of Representatives substituted the current "predecessor in interest" language. The House Committee on the Judiciary offered the following explanation for the alteration:

The Committee considered that it is generally unfair to impose upon the party against whom the hearsay evidence is being offered

> responsibility for the manner in which the witness was previously handled by another party. The sole exception to this, in the Committee's view, is when a party's predecessor in interest in a civil action or proceeding had an opportunity and similar motive to examine the witness. The Committee amended the Rule to reflect these policy determinations.

H.R.Rep. No. 650, U.S.Code Cong. & Admin.News 1974, p. 7088, supra.

Although the Senate accepted the change proposed by the House, the Senate Committee on the Judiciary made the following observation about the import of the House actions:

> Former testimony.—Rule 804(b)(1) as submitted by the Court allowed prior testimony of an unavailable witness to be admissible if the party against whom it is offered or a person "with motive and interest similar" to his had an opportunity to examine the witness.
>
> The House amended the rule to apply only to a party's predecessor in interest. Although the committee recognizes considerable merit to the rule submitted by the Supreme Court, a position which has been advocated by many scholars and judges, we have concluded that the difference between the two versions is not great and we accept the House amendment.

S.Rep. No. 1277, 93d Cong., 2d Sess. 28 (1974), *reprinted in* 1974 U.S.Code Cong. & Ad.News 7051, 7074.

We join the Third Circuit in agreeing with the Senate Committee that the difference between the ultimate revision and the Rule, as originally proposed, is "not great." Lloyd v. American Export Lines, Inc., 580 F.2d 1179, 1185 (3d Cir.), *cert. denied,* 439 U.S. 969, 99 S.Ct. 461, 58 L.Ed.2d 428 (1978). Accordingly, we adopt the position taken by the *Lloyd* court which it expressed in the following language:

> While we do not endorse an extravagant interpretation of who or what constitutes a "predecessor in interest," we prefer one that is realistically generous over one that is formalistically grudging. We believe that what has been described as "the practical and expedient view" expresses the congressional intention: "if it appears that in the former suit a party having a like motive to cross-examine about the same matters as the present party would have, was accorded an adequate opportunity for such examination, the testimony may be received against the present party." Under these circumstances, the previous party having like motive to develop the testimony about the same material facts is, in the final analysis, a predecessor in interest to the present party.

Id. at 1187. See also Rule v. International Association of Bridge, Structural Ornamental Iron Workers, Local 396, 568 F.2d 558, 569 (8th Cir.1977); *Weinstein & Berger, Evidence* § 804(b)(1)[04] at 804–67 (1969) ("[C]ases decided since the enactment of Rule 804(b)(1) for the most part indicate a reluctance to interpret 'predecessor in interest' in its old, narrow, and substantive law sense, of privity"). Contra In re IBM

Peripheral EDP Devices Antitrust Litigation, 444 F.Supp. 110 (N.D.Cal. 1978).

Our examination of the record submitted in this case satisfies us that defendants in the *DeRocco* case had a similar motive in confronting Dr. Smith's testimony, both in terms of appropriate objections and searching cross-examination, to that which Raybestos has in the current litigation. We therefore hold that the purposes of Rule 804(b)(1) will be fulfilled by the admission of Dr. Smith's deposition on retrial.

* * *

The judgments entered below against plaintiffs are vacated and the cases are remanded for retrial against defendant Raybestos in accordance with this opinion.

Notes

(1) United States v. McDonald, 837 F.2d 1287 (5th Cir.1988), was a prosecution of McDonald and Minteer for fraud against ANICO. The trial court rejected McDonald's offer of testimony given by Minteer in a deposition in a civil case in which ANICO sought to recover for the fraud. McDonald contended that ANICO was a predecessor in interest to the government because both wanted to prove that Minteer defrauded ANICO. The government contended that the "predecessor in interest" provision of Rule 804(b)(1) applies only when a deposition taken in a civil action is sought to be introduced in a subsequent civil action. The court observed that neither "the language nor the legislative history of Rule 804 is dispositive," that the Tenth and Seventh Circuits have reached different results on the issue, and that scholars "are divided on the issue, although there is some common ground that the predecessor in interest clause is inapplicable when testimony is sought to be introduced against a criminal defendant. * * * The idea travels on the right of a criminal defendant to present evidence in his own defense. * * * [W]e are not persuaded that we are limited to the two extremes. * * *

"Of course, the phrase 'predecessor in interest' contemplates a situation where a litigant had not itself examined a witness. If a party in a civil case and the government in a later criminal case have sufficiently similar incentives to develop the testimony, we see no reason to conclude that the rule is necessarily and always unavailable to a criminal defendant.

"Here, although ANICO and the government had similar status in their respective claims, we find that the trial strategies were not sufficiently similar to admit the Minteer deposition." Id. at 1291–1293.

(2) See also United States v. Miller, 904 F.2d 65 (D.C.Cir.1990) (defendants were entitled to introduce at trial the testimony of a witness who testified favorably to the defendants before the grand jury and who asserted his fifth amendment privilege at trial); United States v. Powell, 894 F.2d 895, 901 (7th Cir.1990) (not error to exclude Heet's testimony at guilty plea hearing; "[e]ven if the government's presence at Heet's plea hearing gave it the 'opportunity' to cross-examine Heet required by the rule, the government does not * * * have the same motive at a plea hearing as it does at

other proceedings"), cert. denied, ___ U.S. ___, 110 S.Ct. 2189, 109 L.Ed.2d 517 (1990).

SECTION 4. ADMISSIONS BY PARTY-OPPONENT *

[FED.R.EVID. 801(d)(2)]

UNITED STATES v. UNITED SHOE MACHINERY CORP.

United States District Court, District of Massachusetts, 1950.
89 F.Supp. 349.

WYZANSKI, DISTRICT JUDGE.

* * *

It has sometimes been erroneously said that extrajudicial admissions are receivable against a party as an exception to the hearsay rule and that the reason for the exception is either because in that party's eyes the statement must at one time have seemed trustworthy or because it is only fair to put upon that party the burden of explaining his own declaration. But the masters of the law of evidence now agree that this is not the correct rationale. Morgan, The Rationale of Vicarious Admissions, 42 Harv.L.Rev. 461; Wigmore, Evidence, 3d Ed., § 1048. See Napier v. Bossard, 2 Cir., 102 F.2d 467, 468; Milton v. United States, 71 App.D.C. 394, 110 F.2d 556, 560. Unlike statements of fact against interest (sometimes loosely called admissions), an extrajudicial admission of a party is receivable against him not as an exception to the hearsay rule but as not being within the purpose of the hearsay rule. The hearsay rule is a feature of the adversary system of the common law. It allows a party to object to the introduction of a statement not made under oath and not subject to cross-examination. Its purpose is to afford a party the privilege if he desires it of requiring the declarant to be sworn and subjected to questions. That purpose does not apply, and so the hearsay rule does not apply, where the evidence offered against a party are *his* statements.

The question remains as to what are "his" statements. * * *

* * *

MAHLANDT v. WILD CANID SURVIVAL & RESEARCH CENTER, INC.

United States Court of Appeals, Eighth Circuit, 1978.
588 F.2d 626.

VAN SICKLE, DISTRICT JUDGE.

This is a civil action for damages arising out of an alleged attack by a wolf on a child. The sole issues on appeal are as to the correctness of

* See 4 Wigmore, Evidence §§ 1048–1087 (Chadbourn rev. 1972); McCormick, Evidence ch. 25 (4th ed. 1992); Bein, Parties' Admissions, Agents' Admissions: Hearsay Wolves in Sheep's Clothing, 12 Hofstra L.Rev. 393 (1984); Maguire & Vincent, Admissions Implied from Spoilation or Related Conduct, 45 Yale L.J. 226 (1935); Morgan, Admissions as an Exception to the Hearsay Rule, 30 Yale L.J. 355 (1921); Morgan, Admissions, 12 Wash.L.Rev. 181 (1937); Morgan, Admissions, 1 U.C.L.A.L.Rev. 18 (1953); Strahorn, A Reconsideration of the Hearsay Rule and Admissions, 85 U.Pa.L.Rev. 484, 564 (1937).

three rulings which excluded conclusionary statements against interest. Two of them were made by a defendant, who was also an employee of the corporate defendant; and the third was in the form of a statement appearing in the records of a board meeting of the corporate defendant.

On March 23, 1973, Daniel Mahlandt, then 3 years, 10 months, and 8 days old, was sent by his mother to a neighbor's home on an adjoining street to get his older brother, Donald. Daniel's mother watched him cross the street, and then turned into the house to get her car keys. Daniel's path took him along a walkway adjacent to the Poos' residence. Next to the walkway was a five foot chain link fence to which Sophie had been chained with a six foot chain. In other words, Sophie was free to move in a half circle having a six foot radius on the side of the fence opposite from Daniel.

Sophie was a bitch wolf, 11 months and 28 days old, who had been born at the St. Louis Zoo, and kept there until she reached 6 months of age, at which time she was given to the Wild Canid Survival and Research Center, Inc. It was the policy of the Zoo to remove wolves from the Children's Zoo after they reached the age of 5 or 6 months. Sophie was supposed to be kept at the Tyson Research Center, but Kenneth Poos, as Director of Education for the Wild Canid Survival and Research Center, Inc., had been keeping her at his home because he was taking Sophie to schools and institutions where he showed films and gave programs with respect to the nature of wolves. Sophie was known as a very gentle wolf who had proved herself to be good natured and stable during her contacts with thousands of children, while she was in the St. Louis Children's Zoo.

Sophie was chained because the evening before she had jumped the fence and attacked a beagle who was running along the fence and yapping at her.

A neighbor who was ill in bed in the second floor of his home heard a child's screams and went to his window, where he saw a boy lying on his back within the enclosure, with a wolf straddling him. The wolf's face was near Daniel's face, but the distance was so great that he could not see what the wolf was doing, and did not see any biting. Within about 15 seconds the neighbor saw Clarke Poos, about seventeen, run around the house, get the wolf off of the boy, and disappear with the child in his arms to the back of the house. Clarke took the boy in and laid him on the kitchen floor.

Clarke had been returning from his friend's home immediately west when he heard a child's cries and ran around to the enclosure. He found Daniel lying within the enclosure, about three feet from the fence, and Sophie standing back from the boy the length of her chain, and wailing. An expert in the behavior of wolves stated that when a wolf licks a child's face that it is a sign of care, and not a sign of attack; that a wolf's wail is a sign of compassion, and an effort to get attention, not a sign of attack. No witness saw or knew how Daniel was injured. Clarke and his sister ran over to get Daniel's mother. She says that Clarke told her, "a wolf got Danny and he is dying." Clarke denies that statement. The defendant, Mr. Poos, arrived home while Daniel and his mother were in the kitchen. After Daniel was taken in an ambulance, Mr. Poos talked to everyone present, including a neighbor who came in. Within an hour after he arrived home, Mr. Poos went to Washington University to inform Owen Sexton, President of Wild Canid Survival and Research Center, Inc., of the incident. Mr. Sexton was not in his office so Mr. Poos left the following note on his door:

> Owen, would call me at home, 727–5080? Sophie bit a child that came in our back yard. All has been taken care of. I need to convey what happened to you. (Exhibit 11)

Denial of admission of this note is one of the issues on appeal.

Later that day, Mr. Poos found Mr. Sexton at the Tyson Research Center and told him what had happened. Denial of plaintiff's offer to prove that Mr. Poos told Mr. Sexton that, "Sophie had bit a child that day," is the second issue on appeal.

A meeting of the Directors of the Wild Canid Survival and Research Center, Inc., was held on April 4, 1973. Mr. Poos was not present at that meeting. The minutes of that meeting reflect that there was a "great deal of discussion * * * about the legal aspects of the incident of Sophie biting the child." Plaintiff offered an abstract of the minutes containing that reference. Denial of the offer of that abstract is the third issue on appeal.

Daniel had lacerations of the face, left thigh, left calf, and right thigh, and abrasions and bruises of the abdomen and chest. Mr. Mahlandt was permitted to state that Daniel had indicated that he had gone under the fence. Mr. Mahlandt and Mr. Poos, about a month after the incident, examined the fence to determine what caused Daniel's lacerations. Mr. Mahlandt felt that they did not look like animal bites. The parallel scars on Daniel's thigh appeared to match the configuration of the barbs or tines on the fence. The expert as to the behavior of wolves opined that the lacerations were not wolf bites or wounds caused by wolf claws. Wolves have powerful jaws and a wolf bite will result in massive crushing or severing of a limb. He stated that if Sophie had bitten Daniel there would have been clear apposition of teeth and massive crushing of Daniel's hands and arms which were not injured. Also, if Sophie had pulled Daniel under the fence, tooth marks on the foot or leg would have been present, although Sophie possessed enough strength to pull the boy under the fence.

The jury brought in a verdict for the defense.

The trial judge's rationale for excluding the note, the statement, and the corporate minutes, was the same in each case. He reasoned that Mr. Poos did not have any personal knowledge of the facts, and accordingly, the first two admissions were based on hearsay; and the third admission contained in the minutes of the board meeting was subject to the same objection of hearsay, and unreliability because of lack of personal knowledge.

The Federal Rules of Evidence became effective in July 1975 (180 days after passage of the Act). Thus, at this time, there is very little case law to rely upon for resolution of the problems of interpretation.

The relevant rule here is:

Rule 801. Definitions.

* * * (d) Statements which are not hearsay. A statement is not hearsay if—

* * * (2) Admission by party-opponent. The statement is offered against a party and is

* * * (A) his own statement, in either his individual or representative capacity or

(B) a statement of which he has manifested his adoption or belief in its truth, or

(C) a statement by a person authorized by him to make a statement concerning the subject, or

(D) a statement by his agent or servant concerning a matter within the scope of his agency or employment, made during the existence of the relationship, * * *.

So the statement in the note pinned on the door is not hearsay, and is admissible against Mr. Poos. It was his own statement, and as such was clearly different from the reported statement of another. Example, "I was told that * * *." See Cedeck v. Hamiltonian Fed. Sav. & L. Ass'n., 551 F.2d 1136 (8th Cir.1977). It was also a statement of which he had manifested his adoption or belief in its truth. And the same observations may be made of the statement made later in the day to Mr. Sexton that, "Sophie had bit a child * * *."

Are these statements admissible against Wild Canid Survival and Research Center, Inc.? They were made by Mr. Poos when he was an agent or servant of the Wild Canid Survival and Research Center, Inc., and they concerned a matter within the scope of his agency, or employment, i.e., his custody of Sophie, and were made during the existence of that relationship.

Defendant argues that Rule 801(d)(2) does not provide for the admission of "in house" statements; that is, it allows only admissions made to third parties.

The notes of the Advisory Committee on the Proposed Rules (28 U.S.C.A., Volume on Federal Rules of Evidence, Rule 801, p. 527 at p. 530), discuss the problem of "in house" admissions with reference to Rule 801(d)(2)(C) situations. This is not a (C) situation because Mr. Poos was not authorized or directed to make a statement on the matter by anyone. But the rationale developed in that comment does apply to this (D) situation. Mr. Poos had actual physical custody of Sophie. His conclusions, his opinions, were obviously accepted as a basis for action by his principal. See minutes of corporate meeting. As the Advisory Committee points out in its note on (C) situations:

> * * * communication to an outsider has not generally been thought to be an essential characteristic of an admission. Thus a party's books or records are usable against him, without regard to any intent to disclose to third persons. V. Wigmore on Evidence § 1557.

Weinstein's discussion of Rule 801(d)(2)(D) (Weinstein's Evidence § 801(d)(2)(D)(01), p. 801–137), states that:

> Rule 801(d)(2)(D) adopts the approach * * * which, as a general proposition, makes statement made by agents within the scope of their employment admissible * * *. Once agency, and the making of the statement while the relationship continues, are established, the statement is exempt from the hearsay rule so long as it relates to a matter within the scope of the agency.

After reciting a lengthy quotation which justifies the rule as necessary, and suggests that such admissions are trustworthy and reliable, Weinstein states categorically that although an express requirement of personal knowledge on the part of the declarant of the facts underlying his statement is not written into the rule, it should be. He feels that is mandated by Rules 805 and 403.

Rule 805 recites, in effect, that a statement containing hearsay within hearsay is admissible if each part of the statement falls within an exception to the hearsay rule. Rule 805, however, deals only with hearsay exceptions. A statement based on the personal knowledge of the declarant of facts underlying his statement is not the repetition of the statement of another, thus not hearsay. It is merely opinion testimony. Rule 805 cannot mandate the implied condition desired by Judge Weinstein.

Rule 403 provides for the exclusion of relevant evidence if its probative value is substantially outweighed by the danger of unfair prejudice, confusion of the issues, or misleading the jury, or by consideration of undue delay, waste of time, or needless presentation of cumulative evidence. Nor does Rule 403 mandate the implied condition desired by Judge Weinstein.

Thus, while both Rule 805 and Rule 403 provide additional bases for excluding otherwise acceptable evidence, neither rule mandates the introduction into Rule 801(d)(2)(D) of an implied requirement that the declarant have personal knowledge of the facts underlying his statement. So we conclude that the two statements made by Mr. Poos were admissible against Wild Canid Survival and Research Center, Inc.

As to the entry in the records of a corporate meeting, the directors as primary officers of the corporation had the authority to include their conclusions in the record of the meeting. So the evidence would fall within 801(d)(2)(C) as to Wild Canid Survival and Research Center, Inc., and be admissible. The "in house" aspect of this admission has already been discussed, Rule 801(d)(2)(D), supra.

But there was no servant, or agency, relationship which justified admitting the evidence of the board minutes as against Mr. Poos.

None of the conditions of 801(d)(2) cover the claim that minutes of a corporate board meeting can be used against a non-attending, non-participating employee of that corporation. The evidence was not admissible as against Mr. Poos.

There is left only the question of whether the trial court's rulings which excluded all three items of evidence are justified under Rule 403. He clearly found that the evidence was not reliable, pointing out that none of the statements were based on the personal knowledge of the declarant.

Again, that problem was faced by the Advisory Committee on Proposed Rules. In its discussion of 801(d)(2) exceptions to the hearsay rule, the Committee said:

> The freedom which admissions have enjoyed from technical demands of searching for an assurance of trustworthiness in some against-interest circumstances, and from the restrictive influences of the opinion rule and the rule requiring first hand knowledge, when taken with the apparently prevalent satisfaction with the results, calls for generous treatment of this avenue to admissibility. 28 U.S.C.A., Volume of Federal Rules of Evidence, Rule 801, p. 527, at p. 530.

So here, remembering that relevant evidence is usually prejudicial to the cause of the side against which it is presented, and that the prejudice which concerns us is unreasonable prejudice; and applying the spirit of Rule 801(d)(2), we hold that Rule 403 does not warrant the exclusion of the evidence of Mr. Poos' statements as against himself or Wild Canid Survival and Research Center, Inc.

But the limited admissibility of the corporate minutes, coupled with the repetitive nature of the evidence and the low probative value of the minute record, all justify supporting the judgment of the trial court under Rule 403.

The judgment of the District Court is reversed and the matter remanded to the District Court for a new trial consistent with this opinion.

Notes

(1) Relaxation of the personal knowledge requirement and the opinion rule with regard to party admissions is traditional. See McCormick, Evidence §§ 255, 256 (4th ed. 1992).

(2) Prior to the Federal Rules of Evidence, statements by a party's employee or agent were commonly held to be admissible against him as admissions only to the extent of the authority of the declarant to make

statements to others on the principal's behalf. See, e.g., Big Mack Trucking Co. v. Dickerson, 497 S.W.2d 283 (Tex.1973).

UNITED STATES v. MORGAN

United States Court of Appeals, District of Columbia Circuit, 1978.
581 F.2d 933.

BAZELON, CIRCUIT JUDGE:

Appellant, William Morgan, was found guilty by a jury of possessing phenmetrazine with intent to distribute in violation of 21 U.S.C.A. § 841(a)(1970). We agree with his contention that the trial judge erred in excluding certain evidence from the jury.

I

On January 6, 1977, officers of the Metropolitan Police Department obtained a warrant to search for illegal drugs in a single-family dwelling in Northwest Washington, D.C. The warrant was issued upon the affidavit of Detective Mathis, stating that a reliable informant had advised him that a black male, age 22 to 24 and known as "Timmy," was selling drugs from inside the house; that "within the past 48 hours" Mathis had gone to the house with the informant and waited outside while the informant made a "controlled" buy; that upon rejoining Mathis, the informant handed him some pink pills, later identified as phenmetrazine; and that the informant said he had purchased these pills from Timmy.

When the officers arrived at the house at 10 p.m. to execute the warrant, they did not find Timmy but instead came across appellant and four other persons in the front hallway. [Citations to transcript omitted.] Appellant was holding the leash on a snarling German shepherd. According to the officers, appellant immediately reached in his pocket with his free hand, grabbed some pink pills, threw them on the floor, and started to mash them with his foot. Detective Mathis managed to recover intact twelve of the pills, which subsequently were determined to be phenmetrazine. A search of the basement resulted in seizure of seventy-seven additional such pills and $30 cash, found in a shaving kit secreted in a hole in the ceiling; $4,280 cash, found in a fuse box; $410 cash, found in a dresser drawer; the birth certificate of a Kelsey Etheridge, found in an unidentified article of clothing on a chair; and Etheridge's school identification, found on top of a television. No fingerprints were taken from any of these particular items, and no fingerprints were introduced at trial. Besides appellant, at least six other persons were in the house when the police arrived, including the four who were in the hallway.

At trial, the government sought to connect appellant not merely with the twelve pills seized from the floor in the hallway but also with the seventy-seven pills and $4,280 cash found in the basement. The owner of the house, Mrs. McKnight, testified that she had known appellant for about two years and that he came to her home daily to feed and exercise her dogs, which were chained in the basement. Appellant, she said, was the only person regularly in the house who was not afraid of the dogs. She also stated, however, that with the exception of Etheridge, who used the basement bathroom, no one had lived in the basement since October 1976.

Appellant testified that he resided in Southeast Washington with his sister and brother. On the evening of the search, he had gone to Mrs. McKnight's house to invite one of the occupants, a William Taylor, to go with him to a party. He denied dropping any phenmetrazine, and claimed to have no knowledge of the drugs or money found in the basement. He admitted that he did take care of the dogs, however, and thus came to the house and entered the basement every other day.

Three times during the trial defense counsel sought to establish that Timmy, Mrs. McKnight's son, lived in the house and was selling drugs. Counsel proffered as evidence of this fact the statements made by the informant to Detective Mathis that are contained in the affidavit supporting the search warrant. The trial judge excluded this evidence on grounds that it was irrelevant and was hearsay.

* * *

The Federal Rules of Evidence specifically provide that certain categories of out-of-court statements offered to show the truth of the matter asserted shall not be regarded as "hearsay." Under Rule 801(d)(2)(B) such a statement is not barred as hearsay if a party-opponent "has manifested his adoption or belief in its truth * * *." This Rule plainly applies to the informant's statements to Detective Mathis. The government manifested its belief in the truth of the informant's statements about Timmy by characterizing them as "reliable" in a sworn affidavit to a United States Magistrate.[10]

Notwithstanding the plain language of the Rule, the government urges us to hold it inapplicable to the prosecution in criminal cases. The government's position is based on public policy grounds, and has been accepted, it says, by the Courts of Appeals for the Second, Sixth, and Seventh Circuits.[11] All of the cases on which it relies, however,

10. We note that the Federal Rules clearly contemplate that the federal government is a party-opponent of the defendant in criminal cases, and specifically provide that in certain circumstances statements made by government agents are admissible against the government as substantive evidence. See Rule 803(8). We note also that, at least in this jurisdiction, Assistant United States Attorneys, who represent the government in criminal cases, approve applications for warrants before they are presented to the Magistrates. See United States v. Strother, 188 U.S.App.D.C. 155, at 159, 578 F.2d 397, at 401 (D.C.Cir.1978); Dorman v. United States, 140 U.S.App.D.C. 313, 323, 435 F.2d 385, 395 (1970). Though the proposition seems self-evident, it bears mention that when the government authorizes its agent to present his sworn assurances to a judicial officer that certain matters are true and justify issuance of a warrant, the statements of fact or belief in the officer's affidavit represent the position of the government itself, not merely the views of its agent. Cf. United States v. Powers, 467 F.2d 1089, 1097 n. 1 (7th Cir.1972), cert. denied, 410 U.S. 983, 93 S.Ct. 1499, 36 L.Ed.2d 178 (1973) (dissenting opinion of then Circuit Judge Stevens).

11. The government relies on United States v. Pandilidis, 524 F.2d 644, 650 (6th Cir.1975), cert. denied, 424 U.S. 933, 96

save one, were decided before the Federal Rules of Evidence were made effective by Congress. And that one, United States v. Pandilidis, 524 F.2d 644 (6th Cir.1975), cert. denied, 424 U.S. 933, 96 S.Ct. 1146, 47 L.Ed.2d 340 (1976), decided several months after the effective date of the Rules, does not discuss their possible applicability. Moreover, there is nothing in the history of the Rules generally or in Rule 801(d)(2)(B) particularly to suggest that it does not apply to the prosecution in criminal cases.

Most basically, we think the government reads too much into the position taken by our sister Circuits. None of the cases on which it relies deals with the problem of out-of-court statements in which the government itself has manifested its "adoption or belief." Rather, to the extent these cases survive publication of the Federal Rules, a question we need not decide here, they establish only that the prosecution is excepted from the general rule that admissions made by an agent during the course of the agency and concerning matters within the scope of the agency are binding on his principal.[15] Clearly, state-

S.Ct. 1146, 47 L.Ed.2d 340 (1976); United States v. Powers, 467 F.2d 1089, 1095 (7th Cir.1972), cert. denied, 410 U.S. 983, 93 S.Ct. 1499, 36 L.Ed.2d 178 (1973); and United States v. Santos, 372 F.2d 177, 180 (2d Cir.1967).

The public policy argument is explained only in the *Santos* opinion and, we think is somewhat difficult to grasp. The court in that case seemed to be distinguishing government agents from nongovernment agents (whose statements regarding matters within the scope of the agency may be attributed to their principals, see note 15 infra and accompanying text) on the rationale that government agents are "supposedly uninterested *personally* in the outcome of the trial." 372 F.2d at 180 (emphasis supplied). The court did not explain the significance of this premise. We are not told whether it follows that (a) it would be unfair to impute to the government responsibility for the statements of its agents, or (b) such statements lack the special assurances of trustworthiness that attend the out-of-court statements of nongovernment agents.

Whether or not this view of public policy survives publication of the Federal Rules of Evidence, see note 15 infra, we fail to see what possible bearing it could have on this case. It may be true that the informant was not interested personally in the outcome of a particular criminal proceeding when he spoke to Detective Mathis, that it would be unfair to find that he was speaking for the government at the time, and that, at that time, his statements lacked special assurances of trustworthiness. But the question we must consider is whether, once the government indicates its belief that an informant's assertions are trustworthy, it may *then* turn around and object to their admission on hearsay grounds. On that question the *Santos* policy argument has nothing to say.

15. In United States v. Pandilidis, supra, the court held that it was not error to exclude evidence that an agent of the Internal Revenue Service (IRS) believed defendant guilty of nothing more than a civil offense. 524 F.2d at 650. In United States v. Powers, supra, the court approved exclusion of an IRS agent's opinions about whether the proceeds from certain checks were taxable income. 467 F.2d at 1095. And in United States v. Santos, supra, the court held that the trial judge properly excluded a sworn statement by a narcotics agent indicating that he had witnessed the assault and that persons other than defendant were responsible for it. 372 F.2d at 179. It should be noted that in two of these cases, *Pandilidis* and *Santos,* the court did not address the question whether the government itself had taken the position that its agent's statements were true. In *Powers,* however, the court implied that if the government had in fact taken such a position, a different result might have been required. 467 F.2d at 1095.

It is not clear whether these cases survive the Federal Rules. Rule 801(d)(2)(D) provides that statements made by an "agent or servant concerning a matter within the scope of his agency or employment, made during the existence of the relationship" shall be treated as admissions by his principal. As in the case of

ments in which the government has manifested its "adoption or belief" stand on more solid ground than mere out-of-court assertions by a government agent. We do not decide that just *any* statement the informant might have made is admissible against the government. We decide only that where, as here, the government has indicated in a sworn affidavit to a judicial officer that it believes particular statements are trustworthy, it may not sustain an objection to the subsequent introduction of those statements on grounds that they are hearsay.

* * *

Reversed and remanded for a new trial.

PEOPLE v. GREEN

Colorado Court of Appeals, 1981.
629 P.2d 1098.

KIRSHBAUM, JUDGE.

Defendant, Winifred Mitchell Green, appeals his conviction of conspiracy to commit first degree murder, attempt to commit first degree murder, and criminal solicitation. We reverse.

The record reveals that one Frank Moore was seriously injured when he was shot several times outside a pool hall in Colorado Springs. Moore had robbed defendant's home prior to the shooting, and had fathered a child with defendant's wife, Eunice Green, before she and defendant were married. At the time of the shooting, Eunice Green and the child resided with defendant.

At trial, one Clifford Muse gave testimony to the effect that defendant had hired James Mitchell to hurt or kill Moore. Over defendant's objection, defendant's sister-in-law, Lela Mae Clark, testified respecting an incident which occurred several weeks after the shooting.

During an *in camera* hearing, Clark testified that several weeks after the shooting defendant's wife ran into Clark's home barefoot and distraught, said she had just been arguing with defendant about defendant's relationship with another woman, and lay down in Clark's bedroom; that defendant arrived moments later and went into the bedroom; that she, Clark, entered the bedroom while defendant's wife was yelling at defendant; that defendant's wife told defendant "she wasn't scared of him just * * * because he had Frank [Moore] shot"; and that defendant did not respond to that statement. Clark also stated during a subsequent *in camera* hearing that as she entered the bedroom defendant told her that his wife had a gun, and that defen-

Rule 801(d)(2)(B), there is no indication in the history of the Rules that the draftsmen meant to except the government from operation of Rule 801(d)(2)(D) in criminal cases. But consider in this connection the possible significance of Rule 803(8).

dant's wife raised a pillow and revealed a pistol to Clark before making the accusatory statement.[1]

Defendant contends that the trial court erroneously concluded that Clark's testimony was admissible under the adoptive admission exemption to the prohibition against hearsay. We agree.

An incriminating statement uttered by a third party in the presence of a defendant is deemed not to be hearsay, and therefore admissible against the defendant, when the evidence establishes that the defendant demonstrated his or her adoption of the statement or belief in its truth. Cook v. People, 56 Colo. 477, 138 P. 756 (1914); Colorado Rules of Evidence 801(d)(2)(B). Underlying this "adoptive admission" exemption from normal hearsay concepts is the general assumption that it would be reasonable to expect any person who hears a statement accusing him or her of misconduct to deny such statement. See *McCormick on Evidence* § 270 (E. Cleary 2d ed. 1972). The assumption is a weak one, and evidence of such statements must be scrutinized with special concern in criminal cases, where there are constitutional limits to the permissible inferences from a defendant's silence. See Doyle v. Ohio, 426 U.S. 610, 96 S.Ct. 2240, 49 L.Ed.2d 91 (1976), United States v. Hale, 422 U.S. 71, 95 S.Ct. 2133, 45 L.Ed.2d 99 (1975); See also United States v. Coppola, 526 F.2d 764 (10th Cir.1975); People v. Cole, 195 Colo. 483, 584 P.2d 71 (1978).

Indeed, there is authority in other jurisdictions for the principle that, because of Fifth Amendment considerations, a defendant's total silence when confronted with accusations of criminal conduct may never be deemed an adoptive admission in subsequent criminal proceedings. People v. Parks, 57 Mich.App. 738, 226 N.W.2d 710 (1975); see Commonwealth v. Dravecz, 424 Pa. 582, 227 A.2d 904 (1967).

The ultimate fact question is whether the defendant adopted or acquiesced in the statement, or in some manner indicated his or her belief in its truth. United States v. Moore, 522 F.2d 1068 (9th Cir. 1975), *cert. denied,* 423 U.S. 1049, 96 S.Ct. 775, 46 L.Ed.2d 637 (1976); see Cook v. People, supra; see Russell v. People, 125 Colo. 290, 242 P.2d 610 (1952). Before admitting any such statement into evidence a trial court must determine preliminarily, normally by means of an *in camera* hearing, that the party offering the statement can produce evidence to support the factual conclusions that the defendant heard and understood the statement, had knowledge of the contents thereof, and was free from any emotional or physical impediment which would inhibit an immediate response. See *McCormick on Evidence,* supra, § 270; *Notes of the Advisory Committee on Federal Rule of Evidence* 104(b); see also J. Quinn, Hearsay in Criminal Cases under the Colora-

1. The record reveals two *in camera* hearings. The trial court's conclusion that the statement was admissible was based on the evidence presented at those hearings. Clark's testimony before the jury differed to some extent from her *in camera* testimony; she told the jury that when defendant arrived at her house he told her that his wife had a gun and had threatened "to blow his so and so off" a few minutes earlier.

do Rules of Evidence: An Overview, 50 U.Colo.L.Rev. 277 (1979). The issue should then be submitted to the jury under appropriate instructions.

Here, the *only* circumstance suggesting that defendant adopted the incriminating statement of his wife was his failure to respond. His silence, at best a neutral factor, must be weighed against the uncontroverted facts that he knew Eunice had a gun, that a heated domestic dispute over another woman was in progress, and that Eunice had threatened him with violence minutes before. In these circumstances, we conclude that defendant was not free from emotional impediments to an immediate response; hence, Clark's testimony was not admissible. Because the attributed admission could well have affected the outcome beyond a reasonable doubt, the error was prejudicial. See People v. Taylor, 197 Colo. 161, 591 P.2d 1017 (1979).

Because the conviction must be reversed, it is unnecessary to treat the other issues raised on appeal.

The judgment is reversed and the cause is remanded for a new trial in conformity with the procedures and conclusions contained herein.

FLETCHER v. WEIR

Supreme Court of the United States, 1982.
455 U.S. 603, 102 S.Ct. 1309, 71 L.Ed.2d 490.

PER CURIAM.

In the course of a fight in a nightclub parking lot, Ronnie Buchanan pinned respondent Weir to the ground. Buchanan then jumped to his feet and shouted that he had been stabbed; he ultimately died from his stab wounds. Respondent immediately left the scene, and did not report the incident to the police.

At his trial for intentional murder, respondent took the stand in his own defense. He admitted stabbing Buchanan, but claimed that he acted in self-defense and that the stabbing was accidental. This in-court statement was the first occasion on which respondent offered an exculpatory version of the stabbing. The prosecutor cross-examined him as to why he had, when arrested, failed either to advance his exculpatory explanation to the arresting officers or to disclose the location of the knife he had used to stab Buchanan. Respondent was ultimately found guilty by a jury of first-degree manslaughter. The conviction was affirmed on appeal to the Supreme Court of Kentucky.

The United States District Court for the Western District of Kentucky then granted respondent a writ of habeas corpus, and the Court of Appeals, for the Sixth Circuit affirmed. 658 F.2d 1126 (1981). The Court of Appeals concluded that respondent was denied due process of law guaranteed by the Fourteenth Amendment when the prosecutor used his postarrest silence for impeachment purposes.[1] Although it did

1. During cross-examination, the prosecutor also questioned respondent concerning his failure *prior to his arrest* to report the incident to the police and offer his

not appear from the record that the arresting officers had immediately read respondent his *Miranda* warnings,[2] the court concluded that a defendant cannot be impeached by use of his postarrest silence even if no *Miranda* warnings had been given. The court held that "it is inherently unfair to allow cross-examination concerning post-arrest silence," 658 F.2d, at 1130, and rejected the contention that our decision in Doyle v. Ohio, 426 U.S. 610, 96 S.Ct. 2240, 49 L.Ed.2d 91 (1976), applied only where the police had read *Miranda* warnings to a defendant. Because we think that the Court of Appeals gave an overly broad reading to our decision in Doyle v. Ohio, supra, we reverse its judgment.

One year prior to our decision in *Doyle,* we held in the exercise of our supervisory power over the federal courts that silence following the giving of *Miranda* warnings was ordinarily so ambiguous as to have little probative value. United States v. Hale, 422 U.S. 171, 95 S.Ct. 2133, 45 L.Ed.2d 99 (1975). There we said:

> "In light of the many alternative explanations for his pretrial silence, we do not think it sufficiently probative of an inconsistency with his in-court testimony to warrant admission of evidence thereof." Id., at 180, 95 S.Ct., at 2138.

The principles which evolved on the basis of decisional law dealing with appeals within the federal court system are not, of course, necessarily based on any constitutional principle. Where they are not, the States are free to follow or to disregard them so long as the state procedure as a whole remains consistent with due process of law. See Cupp v. Naughten, 414 U.S. 141, 146, 94 S.Ct. 396, 400, 38 L.Ed.2d 368 (1973). The year after our decision in *Hale,* we were called upon to decide an issue similar to that presented in *Hale* in the context of a state criminal proceeding. While recognizing the importance of cross-examination and of exposing fabricated defenses, we held in Doyle v. Ohio, supra, that because of the nature of *Miranda* warnings it would be a violation of due process to allow comment on the silence which the warnings may well have encouraged:

> "[W]hile it is true that the *Miranda* warnings contain no express assurance that silence will carry no penalty, such assurance is implicit to any person who receives the warnings. In such circumstances, it would be fundamentally unfair and a deprivation of due process to allow the arrested person's silence to be used to impeach an explanation subsequently offered at trial." Id., at 618, 96 S.Ct., at 2245 (footnote omitted).

The significant difference between the present case and *Doyle* is that the record does not indicate that respondent Weir received any *Miranda* warnings during the period in which he remained silent

exculpatory story. Relying on our decision in Jenkins v. Anderson, 447 U.S. 231, 100 S.Ct. 2124, 65 L.Ed.2d 86 (1980), the Court of Appeals correctly held that there was no constitutional impropriety in the prosecutor's use of respondent's pre-arrest silence for impeachment purposes.

2. Miranda v. Arizona, 384 U.S. 436, 86 S.Ct. 1602, 16 L.Ed.2d 694 (1966).

immediately after his arrest. The majority of the Court of Appeals recognized the difference, but sought to extend *Doyle* to cover Weir's situation by stating that "[w]e think an arrest, by itself, is governmental action which implicitly induces a defendant to remain silent." 658 F.2d, at 1131. We think that this broadening of *Doyle* is unsupported by the reasoning of that case and contrary to our post-*Doyle* decisions.

In Jenkins v. Anderson, 447 U.S. 231, 239, 100 S.Ct. 2124, 2129, 65 L.Ed.2d 86 (1980), a case dealing with pre-arrest silence, we said:

> "Common law traditionally has allowed witnesses to be impeached by their previous failure to state a fact in circumstances in which that fact naturally would have been asserted. 3A J. Wigmore, Evidence § 1042, p. 1056 (Chadbourn rev. 1970). Each jurisdiction may formulate its own rules of evidence to determine when prior silence is so inconsistent with present statements that impeachment by reference to such silence is probative."

In *Jenkins,* as in other post-*Doyle* cases, we have consistently explained *Doyle* as a case where the government had induced silence by implicitly assuring the defendant that his silence would not be used against him. In Roberts v. United States, 445 U.S. 552, 561, 100 S.Ct. 1358, 1365, 63 L.Ed.2d 622 (1980), we observed that the post-conviction, presentencing silence of the defendant did not resemble "postarrest silence that may be induced by the assurances contained in *Miranda* warnings." In *Jenkins,* we noted that the failure to speak involved in that case occurred before the defendant was taken into custody and was given his *Miranda* warnings, commenting that no governmental action induced the defendant to remain silent before his arrest. 447 U.S., at 239–240, 100 S.Ct., at 2130. Finally, in Anderson v. Charles, 447 U.S. 404, 407–408, 100 S.Ct. 2180, 2182, 65 L.Ed.2d 222 (1980), we explained that use of silence for impeachment was fundamentally unfair in *Doyle* because "*Miranda* warnings inform a person of his right to remain silent and assure him, at least implicitly, that his silence will not be used against him. * * * *Doyle* bars the use against a criminal defendant of silence maintained after receipt of governmental assurances."

In the absence of the sort of affirmative assurances embodied in the *Miranda* warnings, we do not believe that it violates due process of law for a State to permit cross-examination as to postarrest silence when a defendant chooses to take the stand. A State is entitled, in such situations, to leave to the judge and jury under its own rules of evidence the resolution of the extent to which postarrest silence may be deemed to impeach a criminal defendant's own testimony.

The motion of respondent for leave to proceed *in forma pauperis* is granted.

The petition for certiorari is granted, the judgment of the Court of Appeals is reversed, and the case is remanded for proceedings consistent with this opinion.

It is so ordered.

JUSTICE BRENNAN would set the case for oral argument.

JUSTICE MARSHALL dissents from the summary reversal of this case.

UNITED STATES v. INADI

Supreme Court of the United States, 1986.
475 U.S. 387, 106 S.Ct. 1121, 89 L.Ed.2d 390.

JUSTICE POWELL delivered the opinion of the Court.

This case presents the question whether the Confrontation Clause requires the Government to show that a nontestifying co-conspirator is unavailable to testify, as a condition for admission of that co-conspirator's out-of-court statements.

I

Following a jury trial in the Eastern District of Pennsylvania, respondent Joseph Inadi was convicted of conspiring to manufacture and distribute methamphetamine, and related offenses. * * *

From May 23 to May 27, 1980, the Cape May County Prosecutor's Office lawfully intercepted and recorded five telephone conversations between various participants in the conspiracy. These taped conversations were played for the jury at trial.

The Court of Appeals for the Third Circuit reversed. The court agreed that the Government had satisfied Rule 801(d)(2)(E), but decided that the Confrontation Clause established an independent requirement that the Government, as a condition to admission of any out-of-court statements, must show the unavailability of the declarant. * * *

II

A

The Court of Appeals derived its rule that the Government must demonstrate unavailability from our decision in Ohio v. Roberts [448 U.S. 56 (1980)]. It quoted *Roberts* as holding that "in conformance with the Framers' preference for face-to-face accusation, the Sixth Amendment establishes a rule of necessity. In the usual case * * * the prosecution must either produce, or demonstrate the unavailability of, the declarant whose statement it wishes to use against the defendant." 448 U.S., at 65, 100 S.Ct., at 2538. The Court of Appeals viewed this language as setting forth a "clear constitutional rule" applicable before any hearsay can be admitted. 748 F.2d, at 818. Under this interpretation of *Roberts,* no out-of-court statement would be admissible without a showing of unavailability.

Roberts, however, does not stand for such a wholesale revision of the law of evidence, nor does it support such a broad interpretation of the Confrontation Clause. *Roberts* itself disclaimed any intention of proposing a general answer to the many difficult questions arising out of the relationship between the Confrontation Clause and hearsay. "The Court has not sought to 'map out a theory of the Confrontation

Clause that would determine the validity of all * * * hearsay "exceptions."' '" 448 U.S., at 64–65, 100 S.Ct., at 2538–39, quoting California v. Green, 399 U.S. 149, 162, 90 S.Ct. 1930, 1937, 26 L.Ed.2d 489 (1970). The Court in *Roberts* remained "[c]onvinced that 'no rule will perfectly resolve all possible problems'" and rejected the "invitation to overrule a near-century of jurisprudence" in order to create such a rule. 448 U.S., at 68, n. 9, 100 S.Ct., at 2540, n. 9, quoting Natali, Green, Dutton, and Chambers: Three Cases in Search of a Theory, 7 Rutgers–Camden L.J. 43, 73 (1975). In addition, the Court specifically noted that a "demonstration of unavailability * * * is not always required." 448 U.S., at 65, n. 7, 100 S.Ct., at 2539, n. 7. In light of these limiting statements, *Roberts* should not be read as an abstract answer to questions not presented in that case, but rather as a resolution of the issue the Court said it was examining: "the constitutional propriety of the introduction in evidence of the preliminary hearing testimony of a witness not produced at the defendant's subsequent state criminal trial." Id., at 58.

The Confrontation Clause analysis in *Roberts* focuses on those factors that come into play when the prosecution seeks to admit testimony from a prior judicial proceeding in place of live testimony at trial. See Fed.Rule Evid. 804(b)(1). In particular, the *Roberts* Court examined the requirement, found in a long line of Confrontation Clause cases involving prior testimony, that before such statements can be admitted the government must demonstrate that the declarant is unavailable. See Mancusi v. Stubbs, 408 U.S. 204, 92 S.Ct. 2308, 33 L.Ed.2d 293 (1972); California v. Green, supra; Barber v. Page, 390 U.S. 719, 88 S.Ct. 1318, 20 L.Ed.2d 258 (1968); Berger v. California, 393 U.S. 314, 89 S.Ct. 540, 21 L.Ed.2d 508 (1969). All of the cases cited in *Roberts* for this "unavailability rule" concern prior testimony. In particular, the Court focused on two cases, *Barber* and *Mancusi,* that directly "explored the issue of constitutional unavailability." 448 U.S., at 76, 100 S.Ct., at 2544. Both cases specifically limited the unavailability exception to prior testimony. *Barber,* supra, 390 U.S., at 722, 88 S.Ct., at 1320; *Mancusi,* supra, 408 U.S., at 211, 92 S.Ct., at 2312.

Roberts must be read consistently with the question it answered, the authority it cited, and its own facts. All of these indicate that *Roberts* simply reaffirmed a longstanding rule, foreshadowed in Pointer v. Texas, 380 U.S. 400, 89 S.Ct. 540, 21 L.Ed.2d 508 (1965), established in *Barber,* and refined in a line of cases up through *Roberts,* that applies unavailability analysis to prior testimony. *Roberts* cannot fairly be read to stand for the radical proposition that no out-of-court statement can be introduced by the government without a showing that the declarant is unavailable.

B

There are good reasons why the unavailability rule, developed in cases involving former testimony, is not applicable to coconspirators' out-of-court statements. Unlike some other exceptions to the hearsay rules, or the exemption from the hearsay definition involved in this case, former testimony often is only a weaker substitute for live testimony. It seldom has independent evidentiary significance of its own, but is intended to replace live testimony. If the declarant is available and the same information can be presented to the trier of fact in the form of live testimony, with full cross-examination and the opportunity to view the demeanor of the declarant, there is little justification for relying on the weaker version. When two versions of the same evidence are available, longstanding principles of the law of hearsay, applicable as well to Confrontation Clause analysis, favor the better evidence. See Graham, The Right of Confrontation and the Hearsay Rule: Sir Walter Raleigh Loses Another One, 8 Crim.L.Bull. 99, 143 (1972). But if the declarant is unavailable, no "better" version of the evidence exists, and the former testimony may be admitted as a substitute for live testimony on the same point.

Those same principles do not apply to co-conspirator statements. Because they are made while the conspiracy is in progress, such statements provide evidence of the conspiracy's context that cannot be replicated, even if the declarant testifies to the same matters in court. When the Government—as here—offers the statement of one drug dealer to another in furtherance of an illegal conspiracy, the statement often will derive its significance from the circumstances in which it was made. Conspirators are likely to speak differently when talking to each other in furtherance of their illegal aims than when testifying on the witness stand. Even when the declarant takes the stand, his in-court testimony seldom will reproduce a significant portion of the evidentiary value of his statements during the course of the conspiracy.

In addition, the relative positions of the parties will have changed substantially between the time of the statements and the trial. The declarant and the defendant will have changed from partners in an illegal conspiracy to suspects or defendants in a criminal trial, each with information potentially damaging to the other. The declarant himself may be facing indictment or trial, in which case he has little incentive to aid the prosecution, and yet will be equally wary of coming to the aid of his former partners in crime. In that situation, it is extremely unlikely that in-court testimony will recapture the evidentiary significance of statements made when the conspiracy was operating in full force.

These points distinguish co-conspirators' statements from the statements involved in *Roberts* and our other prior testimony cases. Those cases rested in part on the strong similarities between the prior judicial proceedings and the trial. No such strong similarities exist between co-conspirator statements and live testimony at trial. To the contrary, co-conspirator statements derive much of their value from the fact that they are made in a context very different from trial, and therefore are usually irreplaceable as substantive evidence. Under these circumstances, "only clear folly would dictate an across the board policy of doing without" such statements. Advisory Committee's Introductory

Note on the Hearsay Problem, quoted in Westen, The Future of Confrontation, 77 Mich.L.Rev. 1185, 1193 (1979). The admission of co-conspirators' declarations into evidence thus actually furthers the "Confrontation Clause's very mission" which is to "advance 'the accuracy of the truth-determining process in criminal trials.'" Tennessee v. Street, 471 U.S. —, —, 105 S.Ct. 2078, 85 L.Ed.2d 425 (1985), quoting Dutton v. Evans, 400 U.S. 74, 89, 91 S.Ct. 210, 220, 27 L.Ed.2d 213 (1970).

* * *

We accordingly reverse the judgment of the Court of Appeals for the Third Circuit.

It is so ordered.

JUSTICE MARSHALL, with whom JUSTICE BRENNAN joins, dissenting. * * *

BOURJAILY v. UNITED STATES

Supreme Court of the United States, 1987.
483 U.S. 171, 107 S.Ct. 2775, 97 L.Ed.2d 144.

CHIEF JUSTICE REHNQUIST delivered the opinion of the Court.

Federal Rule of Evidence 801(d)(2)(E) provides: "A statement is not hearsay if * * * [t]he statement is offered against a party and is * * * a statement by a coconspirator of a party during the course and in furtherance of the conspiracy." We granted certiorari to answer three questions regarding the admission of statements under Rule 801(d)(2)(E): (1) whether the court must determine by independent evidence that the conspiracy existed and that the defendant and the declarant were members of this conspiracy; (2) the quantum of proof on which such determinations must be based; and (3) whether a court must in each case examine the circumstances of such a statement to determine its reliability. 479 U.S. 881, 107 S.Ct. 268, 93 L.Ed.2d 246 (1986).

In May 1984, Clarence Greathouse, an informant working for the Federal Bureau of Investigation (FBI), arranged to sell a kilogram of cocaine to Angelo Lonardo. Lonardo agreed that he would find individuals to distribute the drug. When the sale became imminent, Lonardo stated in a tape-recorded telephone conversation that he had a "gentleman friend" who had some questions to ask about the cocaine. In a subsequent telephone call, Greathouse spoke to the "friend" about the quality of the drug and the price. Greathouse then spoke again with Lonardo, and the two arranged the details of the purchase. They agreed that the sale would take place in a designated hotel parking lot, and Lonardo would transfer the drug from Greathouse's car to the "friend," who would be waiting in the parking lot in his own car. Greathouse proceeded with the transaction as planned, and FBI agents arrested Lonardo and petitioner immediately after Lonardo placed a kilogram of cocaine into petitioner's car in the hotel parking lot. In petitioner's car, the agents found over $20,000 in cash.

Petitioner was charged with conspiring to distribute cocaine, in violation of 21 U.S.C. § 846, and possession of cocaine with intent to distribute, a violation of 21 U.S.C. § 841(a)(1). The Government introduced, over petitioner's objection, Angelo Lonardo's telephone statements regarding the participation of the "friend" in the transaction. The District Court found that, considering the events in the parking lot and Lonardo's statements over the telephone, the Government had established by a preponderance of the evidence that a conspiracy involving Lonardo and petitioner existed, and that Lonardo's statements over the telephone had been made in the course of and in furtherance of the conspiracy. App. 66–75. Accordingly, the trial court held that Lonardo's out-of-court statements satisfied Rule 801(d)(2)(E) and were not hearsay. Petitioner was convicted on both counts and sentenced to 15 years. The United States Court of Appeals for the Sixth Circuit affirmed. 781 F.2d 539 (1986). The Court of Appeals agreed with the District Court's analysis and conclusion that Lonardo's out-of-court statements were admissible under the Federal Rules of Evidence. The court also rejected petitioner's contention that because he could not cross-examine Lonardo, the admission of these statements violated his constitutional right to confront the witnesses against him. We affirm.

Before admitting a co-conspirator's statement over an objection that it does not qualify under Rule 801(d)(2)(E), a court must be satisfied that the statement actually falls within the definition of the Rule. There must be evidence that there was a conspiracy involving the declarant and the nonoffering party, and that the statement was made "during the course and in furtherance of the conspiracy." Federal Rule of Evidence 104(a) provides: "Preliminary questions concerning * * * the admissibility of evidence shall be determined by the court." Petitioner and the Government agree that the existence of a conspiracy and petitioner's involvement in it are preliminary questions of fact that, under Rule 104, must be resolved by the court. The Federal Rules, however, nowhere define the standard of proof the court must observe in resolving these questions.

We are therefore guided by our prior decisions regarding admissibility determinations that hinge on preliminary factual questions. We have traditionally required that these matters be established by a preponderance of proof. Evidence is placed before the jury when it satisfies the technical requirements of the evidentiary Rules, which embody certain legal and policy determinations. The inquiry made by a court concerned with these matters is not whether the proponent of the evidence wins or loses his case on the merits, but whether the evidentiary Rules have been satisfied. Thus, the evidentiary standard is unrelated to the burden of proof on the substantive issues, be it a criminal case, see *In re Winship,* 397 U.S. 358, 90 S.Ct. 1068, 25 L.Ed.2d 368 (1970), or a civil case. See generally *Colorado v. Connelly,* 479 U.S.

157, 167–169, 107 S.Ct. 515, 522–523, 93 L.Ed.2d 473 (1986). The preponderance standard ensures that before admitting evidence, the court will have found it more likely than not that the technical issues and policy concerns addressed by the Federal Rules of Evidence have been afforded due consideration. As in *Lego v. Twomey,* 404 U.S. 477, 488, 92 S.Ct. 619, 626, 30 L.Ed.2d 618 (1972), we find "nothing to suggest that admissibility rulings have been unreliable or otherwise wanting in quality because not based on some higher standard." We think that our previous decisions in this area resolve the matter. See, *e.g., Colorado v. Connelly, supra* (preliminary fact that custodial confessant waived rights must be proved by preponderance of the evidence); *Nix v. Williams,* 467 U.S. 431, 444, n. 5, 104 S.Ct. 2501, 2509, n. 5, 81 L.Ed.2d 377 (1984) (inevitable discovery of illegally seized evidence must be shown to have been more likely than not); *United States v. Matlock,* 415 U.S. 164, 94 S.Ct. 988, 39 L.Ed.2d 242 (1974) (voluntariness of consent to search must be shown by preponderance of the evidence); *Lego v. Twomey, supra* (voluntariness of confession must be demonstrated by a preponderance of the evidence). Therefore, we hold that when the preliminary facts relevant to Rule 801(d)(2)(E) are disputed, the offering party must prove them by a preponderance of the evidence.[1]

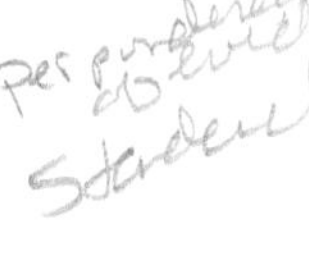

Even though petitioner agrees that the courts below applied the proper standard of proof with regard to the preliminary facts relevant to Rule 801(d)(2)(E), he nevertheless challenges the admission of Lonardo's statements. Petitioner argues that in determining whether a conspiracy exists and whether the defendant was a member of it, the court must look only to independent evidence—that is, evidence other than the statements sought to be admitted. Petitioner relies on *Glasser v. United States,* 315 U.S. 60, 62 S.Ct. 457, 86 L.Ed. 680 (1942), in which this Court first mentioned the so-called "bootstrapping rule." The relevant issue in *Glasser* was whether Glasser's counsel, who also represented another defendant, faced such a conflict of interest that Glasser received ineffective assistance. Glasser contended that conflicting loyalties led his lawyer not to object to statements made by one of Glasser's co-conspirators. The Government argued that any objection would have been fruitless because the statements were admissible. The Court rejected this proposition:

> "[S]uch declarations are admissible over the objection of an alleged co-conspirator, who was not present when they were made, only if there is proof *aliunde* that he is connected with the conspiracy * * *. Otherwise, hearsay would lift itself by its own bootstraps to the level of competent evidence." *Id.,* at 74–75, 62 S.Ct., at 467.

1. We intimate no view on the proper standard of proof for questions falling under Federal Rule of Evidence 104(b) (conditional relevancy). We also decline to address the circumstances in which the burden of coming forward to show that the proffered evidence is inadmissible is appropriately placed on the nonoffering party. See E. Cleary, McCormick on Evidence § 53, p. 136, n. 8 (3d ed. 1984). Finally, we do not express an opinion on the proper order of proof that trial courts should follow in concluding that the preponderance standard has been satisfied in an ongoing trial.

The Court revisited the bootstrapping rule in *United States v. Nixon,* 418 U.S. 683, 94 S.Ct. 3090, 41 L.Ed.2d 1039 (1974), where again, in passing, the Court stated: "Declarations by one defendant may also be admissible against other defendants upon a sufficient showing, *by independent evidence,* of a conspiracy among one or more other defendants and the declarant and if the declarations at issue were in furtherance of that conspiracy." *Id.,* at 701, and n. 14, 94 S.Ct., at 3104, and n. 14 (emphasis added) (footnote omitted). Read in the light most favorable to petitioner, *Glasser* could mean that a court should not consider hearsay statements at all in determining preliminary facts under Rule 801(d)(2)(E). Petitioner, of course, adopts this view of the bootstrapping rule. *Glasser,* however, could also mean that a court must have *some* proof *aliunde,* but may look at the hearsay statements themselves in light of this independent evidence to determine whether a conspiracy has been shown by a preponderance of the evidence. The Courts of Appeals have widely adopted the former view and held that in determining the preliminary facts relevant to co-conspirators' out-of-court statements, a court may not look at the hearsay statements themselves for their evidentiary value.

Both *Glasser* and *Nixon,* however, were decided before Congress enacted the Federal Rules of Evidence in 1975. These Rules now govern the treatment of evidentiary questions in federal courts. Rule 104(a) provides: "Preliminary questions concerning * * * the admissibility of evidence shall be determined by the court * * *. In making its determination it is not bound by the rules of evidence except those with respect to privileges." Similarly, Rule 1101(d)(1) states that the Rules of Evidence (other than with respect to privileges) shall not apply to "[t]he determination of questions of fact preliminary to admissibility of evidence when the issue is to be determined by the court under rule 104." The question thus presented is whether any aspect of *Glasser*'s bootstrapping rule remains viable after the enactment of the Federal Rules of Evidence.

Petitioner concedes that Rule 104, on its face, appears to allow the court to make the preliminary factual determinations relevant to Rule 801(d)(2)(E) by considering any evidence it wishes, unhindered by considerations of admissibility. Brief for Petitioner 27. That would seem to many to be the end of the matter. Congress has decided that courts may consider hearsay in making these factual determinations. Out-of-court statements made by anyone, including putative co-conspirators, are often hearsay. Even if they are, they may be considered, *Glasser* and the bootstrapping rule notwithstanding. But petitioner nevertheless argues that the bootstrapping rule, as most Courts of Appeals have construed it, survived this apparently unequivocal change in the law unscathed and that Rule 104, as applied to the admission of co-conspirator's statements, does not mean what it says. We disagree.

Petitioner claims that Congress evidenced no intent to disturb the bootstrapping rule, which was embedded in the previous approach, and we should not find that Congress altered the rule without affirmative evidence so indicating. It would be extraordinary to require legislative history to *confirm* the plain meaning of Rule 104. The Rule on its face allows the trial judge to consider any evidence whatsoever, bound only by the rules of privilege. We think that the Rule is sufficiently clear that to the extent that it is inconsistent with petitioner's interpretation of *Glasser* and *Nixon,* the Rule prevails.[2]

Nor do we agree with petitioner that this construction of Rule 104(a) will allow courts to admit hearsay statements without any credible proof of the conspiracy, thus fundamentally changing the nature of the co-conspirator exception. Petitioner starts with the proposition that co-conspirators' out-of-court statements are deemed unreliable and are inadmissible, at least until a conspiracy is shown. Since these statements are unreliable, petitioner contends that they should not form any part of the basis for establishing a conspiracy, the very antecedent that renders them admissible.

Petitioner's theory ignores two simple facts of evidentiary life. First, out-of-court statements are only *presumed* unreliable. The presumption may be rebutted by appropriate proof. See Fed.Rule Evid. 803(24) (otherwise inadmissible hearsay may be admitted if circumstantial guarantees of trustworthiness demonstrated). Second, individual pieces of evidence, insufficient in themselves to prove a point, may in cumulation prove it. The sum of an evidentiary presentation may well be greater than its constituent parts. Taken together, these two propositions demonstrate that a piece of evidence, unreliable in isolation, may become quite probative when corroborated by other evidence. A *per se* rule barring consideration of these hearsay statements during preliminary factfinding is not therefore required. Even if out-of-court declarations by co-conspirators are presumptively unreliable, trial courts must be permitted to evaluate these statements for their evidentiary worth as revealed by the particular circumstances of the case. Courts often act as factfinders, and there is no reason to believe that courts are any less able to properly recognize the probative value of evidence in this particular area. The party opposing admission has

2. The Advisory Committee Notes show that the Rule was not adopted in a fit of absentmindedness. The Note to Rule 104 specifically addresses the process by which a federal court should make the factual determinations requisite to a finding of admissibility:

> "If the question is factual in nature, the judge will of necessity receive evidence pro and con on the issue. The rule provides that the rules of evidence in general do not apply to this process. McCormick § 53, p. 123, n. 8, points out that the authorities are 'scattered and inconclusive,' and observes:
>
> " 'Should the exclusionary law of evidence, "the child of the jury system" in Thayer's phrase, be applied to this hearing before the judge? Sound sense backs the view that it should not, and that the judge should be empowered to hear *any relevant evidence,* such as affidavits *or other reliable hearsay.*' " 28 U.S.C.App., p. 681 (emphasis added).

The Advisory Committee further noted: "An item, offered and objected to, *may itself be considered in ruling on admissibility,* though not yet admitted in evidence." *Ibid.* (emphasis added). We think this language makes plain the drafters' intent to abolish any kind of bootstrapping rule. Silence is at best ambiguous, and we decline the invitation to rely on speculation to import ambiguity into what is otherwise a clear rule.

an adequate incentive to point out the shortcomings in such evidence before the trial court finds the preliminary facts. If the opposing party is unsuccessful in keeping the evidence from the factfinder, he still has the opportunity to attack the probative value of the evidence as it relates to the substantive issue in the case. See, *e.g.,* Fed.Rule Evid. 806 (allowing attack on credibility of out-of-court declarant).

We think that there is little doubt that a co-conspirator's statements could themselves be probative of the existence of a conspiracy and the participation of both the defendant and the declarant in the conspiracy. Petitioner's case presents a paradigm. The out-of-court statements of Lonardo indicated that Lonardo was involved in a conspiracy with a "friend." The statements indicated that the friend had agreed with Lonardo to buy a kilogram of cocaine and to distribute it. The statements also revealed that the friend would be at the hotel parking lot, in his car, and would accept the cocaine from Greathouse's car after Greathouse gave Lonardo the keys. Each one of Lonardo's statements may itself be unreliable, but taken as a whole, the entire conversation between Lonardo and Greathouse was corroborated by independent evidence. The friend, who turned out to be petitioner, showed up at the prearranged spot at the prearranged time. He picked up the cocaine, and a significant sum of money was found in his car. On these facts, the trial court concluded, in our view correctly, that the Government had established the existence of a conspiracy and petitioner's participation in it.

We need not decide in this case whether the courts below could have relied solely upon Lonardo's hearsay statements to determine that a conspiracy had been established by a preponderance of the evidence. To the extent that *Glasser* meant that courts could not look to the hearsay statements themselves for any purpose, it has clearly been superseded by Rule 104(a). It is sufficient for today to hold that a court, in making a preliminary factual determination under Rule 801(d)(2)(E), may examine the hearsay statements sought to be admitted. As we have held in other cases concerning admissibility determinations, "the judge should receive the evidence and give it such weight as his judgment and experience counsel." *United States v. Matlock,* 415 U.S., at 175, 94 S.Ct., at 995. The courts below properly considered the statements of Lonardo and the subsequent events in finding that the Government had established by a preponderance of the evidence that Lonardo was involved in a conspiracy with petitioner. We have no reason to believe that the District Court's factfinding of this point was clearly erroneous. We hold that Lonardo's out-of-court statements were properly admitted against petitioner.

We also reject any suggestion that admission of these statements against petitioner violated his rights under the Confrontation Clause of the Sixth Amendment. That Clause provides: "In all criminal prosecutions, the accused shall enjoy the right * * * to be confronted with the witnesses against him." At petitioner's trial, Lonardo exercised his right not to testify. Petitioner argued that Lonardo's unavailability rendered the admission of his out-of-court statements unconstitutional since petitioner had no opportunity to confront Lonardo as to these statements. The Court of Appeals held that the requirements for admission under Rule 801(d)(2)(E) are identical to the requirements of the Confrontation Clause, and since the statements were admissible under the Rule, there was no constitutional problem. We agree.

While a literal interpretation of the Confrontation Clause could bar the use of any out-of-court statements when the declarant is unavailable, this Court has rejected that view as "unintended and too extreme." *Ohio v. Roberts,* 448 U.S. 56, 63, 100 S.Ct. 2531, 2537, 65 L.Ed.2d 597 (1980). Rather, we have attempted to harmonize the goal of the Clause—placing limits on the kind of evidence that may be received against a defendant—with a societal interest in accurate factfinding, which may require consideration of out-of-court statements. To accommodate these competing interests, the Court has, as a general matter only, required the prosecution to demonstrate both the unavailability of the declarant and the "indicia of reliability" surrounding the out-of-court declaration. *Id.,* at 65–66, 100 S.Ct., at 2538–2539. Last Term in *United States v. Inadi,* 475 U.S. 387, 106 S.Ct. 1121, 89 L.Ed.2d 390 (1986), we held that the first of these two generalized inquiries, unavailability, was not required when the hearsay statement is the out-of-court declaration of a co-conspirator. Today, we conclude that the second inquiry, independent indicia of reliability, is also not mandated by the Constitution.

The Court's decision in *Ohio v. Roberts* laid down only "a general approach to the problem" of reconciling hearsay exceptions with the Confrontation Clause. See 448 U.S., at 65, 100 S.Ct., at 2538. In fact, *Roberts* itself limits the requirement that a court make a separate inquiry into the reliability of an out-of-court statement. Because " 'hearsay rules and the Confrontation Clause are generally designed to protect similar values,' *California v. Green,* 399 U.S. [149, 155, 90 S.Ct. 1930, 1933, 26 L.Ed.2d 489 (1970)], and 'stem from the same roots,' *Dutton v. Evans,* 400 U.S. 74, 86, 91 S.Ct. 210, 218, 27 L.Ed.2d 213 (1970)," *id.,* at 66, 100 S.Ct., at 2539, we concluded in *Roberts* that no independent inquiry into reliability is required when the evidence "falls within a firmly rooted hearsay exception." *Ibid.* We think that the co-conspirator exception to the hearsay rule is firmly enough rooted in our jurisprudence that, under this Court's holding in *Roberts,* a court need not independently inquire into the reliability of such statements. Cf. *Dutton v. Evans,* 400 U.S. 74, 91 S.Ct. 210, 27 L.Ed.2d 213 (1970) (reliability inquiry required where evidentiary rule deviates from common-law approach, admitting co-conspirators' hearsay statements made after termination of conspiracy). The admissibility of co-conspirators' statements was first established in this Court over a century and a half ago in *United States v. Gooding,* 12 Wheat. 460, 6 L.Ed. 693 (1827) (interpreting statements of co-conspirator as *res gestae* and thus admissible against defendant), and the Court has repeatedly reaffirmed the exception as accepted practice. In fact, two of the most prominent approvals of the rule came in cases that petitioner maintains are still vital today, *Glasser v. United States,* 315 U.S. 60, 62 S.Ct. 457, 86 L.Ed. 680 (1942), and *United States v. Nixon,* 418 U.S. 683, 94 S.Ct. 3090, 41 L.Ed.2d 1039 (1974). To the extent that these cases have not been superseded by the Federal Rules of Evidence, they demonstrate that the co-conspirator exception to the hearsay rule is steeped in our jurisprudence. In *Delaney v. United States,* 263 U.S. 586, 590, 44 S.Ct. 206, 207, 68 L.Ed. 462 (1924), the Court rejected the very challenge petitioner brings today, holding that there can be no separate Confrontation Clause challenge to the admission of a co-conspirator's out-of-court statement. In so ruling, the Court relied on established precedent holding such statements competent evidence. We think that these cases demonstrate that co-conspirators' statements, when made in the course and in furtherance of the conspiracy, have a long tradition of being outside the compass of the general hearsay exclusion. Accordingly, we hold that the Confrontation Clause does not require a court to embark on an independent inquiry into the reliability of statements that satisfy the requirements of Rule 801(d)(2)(E).[4]

The judgment of the Court of Appeals is

Affirmed.

JUSTICE STEVENS, concurring.

The rule against "bootstrapping" announced in *Glasser v. United States,* 315 U.S. 60, 74–75, 62 S.Ct. 457, 467, 86 L.Ed. 680 (1942), has two possible interpretations. The more prevalent interpretation adopted by the Courts of Appeals is that the admissibility of the declaration under the co-conspirator rule must be determined *entirely* by independent evidence. The Court correctly holds that this reading of the *Glasser* rule is foreclosed by the plain language of Rule 104(a) of the Federal Rules of Evidence. That Rule unambiguously authorizes the trial judge to consider the contents of a proffered declaration in determining its admissibility.

I have never been persuaded, however, that this interpretation of the *Glasser* rule is correct. In my view, *Glasser* holds that a declarant's out-of-court statement is inadmissible against his alleged co-conspirators unless there is some corroborating evidence to support the triple conclusion that there was a conspiracy among those defendants, that the declarant was a member of the conspiracy, and that the statement furthered the objectives of the conspiracy. An otherwise inadmissible hearsay statement cannot provide the sole evidentiary support for its own admissibility—it cannot lift itself into admissibility entirely by tugging on its own bootstraps. It may, however, use its own bootstraps, together with other support, to overcome the objection. In the words of the *Glasser* opinion, there must be proof "*aliunde,*" that is, evidence

4. We reject any suggestion that by abolishing the bootstrapping rule, the Federal Rules of Evidence have changed the co-conspirator hearsay exception such that it is no longer "firmly rooted" in our legal tradition. The bootstrapping rule relates only to the *method of proof* that the exception has been satisfied. It does not change any element of the co-conspirator exception, which has remained substantively unchanged since its adoption in this country.

from another source, that together with the contents of the statement satisfies the preliminary conditions for admission of the statement. *Id.,* at 74, 62 S.Ct., at 467.[1] This interpretation of *Glasser* as requiring some but not complete proof "*aliunde,*" is fully consistent with the plain language of Rule 104(a). If, as I assume they did, the drafters of Rule 104(a) understood the *Glasser* rule as I do, they had no reason to indicate that it would be affected by the new Rule.

Thus, the absence of any legislative history indicating an intent to change the *Glasser* rule is entirely consistent with the reasoning of the Court's opinion, which I join.

JUSTICE BLACKMUN, with whom JUSTICE BRENNAN and JUSTICE MARSHALL join, dissenting.

I disagree with the Court in three respects: [1] First, I do not believe that the Federal Rules of Evidence changed the long- and well-settled law to the effect that the preliminary questions of fact, relating to admissibility of a nontestifying co-conspirator's statement, must be established by evidence independent of that statement itself. Second, I disagree with the Court's conclusion that allowing the co-conspirator's statement to be considered in the resolution of these factual questions will remedy problems of the statement's unreliability. In my view, the abandonment of the independent-evidence requirement will lead, instead, to the opposite result. This is because the abandonment will eliminate one of the few safeguards of reliability that this exemption from the hearsay definition possesses. Third, because the Court alters the traditional hearsay exemption—especially an aspect of it that contributes to the reliability of an admitted statement—I do not believe that the Court can rely on the "firmly rooted hearsay exception" rationale, see *Ohio v. Roberts,* 448 U.S. 56, 66, 100 S.Ct. 2531, 2539, 65 L.Ed.2d 597 (1980), to avoid a determination whether any "indicia of reliability" support the co-conspirator's statement, as the Confrontation Clause surely demands.

* * *

MENDOZA v. FIDELITY & GUARANTY INSURANCE UNDERWRITERS, INC.

Supreme Court of Texas, 1980.
606 S.W.2d 692.

DENTON, JUSTICE.

Celedonio R. Mendoza brought this suit against Fidelity & Guaranty Insurance Underwriters, Inc., seeking an increase in his worker's compensation benefits under Art. 8306 § 12d, Tex.Rev.Civ.Stat.Ann.

1. Glasser had argued that "independently of the statements complained of, there is *no proof* connecting him with the conspiracy." 315 U.S., at 75, 62 S.Ct., at 467 (emphasis added).

1. I do agree with the Court that the standard of proof by which an offering party establishes the preliminary facts of Rule 801(d)(2)(E) is the preponderance of the evidence.

relative to an alleged change of condition to the worker. The trial court entered judgment for Mendoza upon a jury verdict. The court of civil appeals reversed and rendered. 588 S.W.2d 612. We reverse the judgment of the court of civil appeals and affirm the judgment of the trial court.

In January 1976, Celedonio Mendoza received an upper back injury while employed as a laborer. At that time his condition was diagnosed as a mild thoracic spine injury. In July of that year he was diagnosed as having a dorsal spine strain, however he continued to work on "electrical projects." In November 1976, Mendoza filed a claim for worker's compensation benefits pursuant to Art. 8306, Tex.Rev.Civ.Stat. Ann. On November 30, 1976 the Industrial Accident Board (the Board) ordered a compensation award which included four weeks for temporary total disability at $70.00 per week and $6.67 per week for permanent partial disability for three hundred weeks. This award was not appealed and became final under Art. 8307 § 5. In December 1976, Mendoza again sought medical treatment for new physical complications. He was hospitalized for further diagnosis of additional complaints, and he received numerous medical treatments.

In January 1977, Mendoza filed an application with the Board to modify the prior award on the basis of a subsequent change in his physical condition as authorized by Art. 8306 § 12d. On April 1, 1977, the Board refused to modify the previous award. Mendoza then filed suit in district court to obtain a de novo review of the Board's action. At the time this suit was filed, Mendoza's condition had been diagnosed as myositis.[2] The position of the insurer, Fidelity & Guaranty Insurance Underwriters, Inc., at trial was that Mendoza's physical condition had not changed since the Board's first order so that there was no further loss of wage earning capacity after that time.

At trial, the evidence of Mendoza's changed physical condition included medical records prior to and after the original award, testimony from lay witnesses, and testimony from Mendoza. Mendoza testified on cross-examination that he had been totally unable to do any kind of work since his injury.

The jury verdict in favor of Mendoza found that his physical condition had substantially deteriorated after his back injury, and that this change had been the producing cause of total, permanent incapacity beginning December 16, 1976.

The court of civil appeals reversed and rendered a take nothing judgment, holding that Mendoza's testimony that he was totally unable to work prior to the award of November 30th, 1976 was a judicial admission that he was totally disabled at that time so that there could not have been a further change in his work capacity.[3]

2. Mendoza testified at trial that he could only lift his arms for short periods of time, that he had weakness in his legs, and pain in his intestines, neck, and back.

3. 588 S.W.2d 612, 615. A dissenting opinion concluded that the November 30, 1976 award and determination of perma-

The testimony which the court of civil appeals held to be a judicial admission was elicited from Mendoza on cross-examination. That testimony is as follows:

> Q. But on September—in September of 1976, you were totally unable to do any work?
>
> A. Yes, sir.
>
> Q. In October of 1976, you were totally unable to do any kind of work?
>
> A. In October 1976?
>
> Q. That is still before you were put in the hospital.
>
> A. Yes, sir.
>
> Q. Up to November 30, 1976, you were totally unable to do any kind of work.
>
> A. Yes, sir.
>
> Q. In December of 1976, you were totally unable to do any kind of work?
>
> A. Yes, sir.
>
> Q. Right up to the present time?
>
> A. Yes, sir.

In order to set aside the prior Board award under Art. 8306 § 12d, Mendoza must prove that his physical condition became substantially worse after the November 30, 1976 award. In addition, Mendoza must prove an increasing incapacity to work due to his changed physical condition. Employers Reinsurance Corp. v. Holland, 162 Tex. 394, 347 S.W.2d 605 (1961). The issue on this appeal is whether the court of civil appeals erred in holding that Mendoza's testimony was a judicial admission which conclusively established his total incapacity prior to the Board's order of November 30, 1976.

A party's testimonial declarations which are contrary to his position are quasi-admissions. They are merely some evidence, and they are not conclusive upon the admitter. Harris County v. Hall, 141 Tex. 388, 172 S.W.2d 691 (1943); Texas Distiller's, Inc. v. Howell, 409 S.W.2d 888 (Tex.Civ.App.—San Antonio 1966, writ ref'd n.r.e.). The weight to be given such admissions is decided by the trier of fact. These are to be distinguished from the true judicial admission which is a formal waiver of proof usually found in pleadings or the stipulations of the parties. A judicial admission is conclusive upon the party making it, and it relieves the opposing party's burden of proving the admitted fact, and bars the admitting party from disputing it. Gevinson v. Manhattan Construction Co. of Oklahoma, 449 S.W.2d 458, 467 (Tex.1969); McCormick and Ray, Texas Law of Evidence § 1127 (2d ed. 1956).

nent partial incapacity was res judicata on the issue of Mendoza's prior physical capabilities and would bar the use of Mendoza's testimony as a judicial admission.

However, as a matter of public policy, a party's testimonial quasi-admission will preclude recovery if it meets the requirements set out in Griffin v. Superior Insurance Co., 338 S.W.2d 415, 419 (Tex.1960) and United States Fidelity & Guaranty Co. v. Carr, 242 S.W.2d 224, 229 (Tex.Civ.App.—San Antonio 1951, writ refused). The public policy underlying this rule is that it would be unjust to permit a party to recover after he has sworn himself out of court by clear, unequivocal testimony. *Carr,* supra. A quasi-admission will be treated as a judicial admission if it appears:

> (1) That the declaration relied upon was made during the course of a judicial proceeding. * * *
>
> (2) That the statement is contrary to an essential fact embraced in the theory of recovery or defense asserted by the person giving the testimony. * * *
>
> (3) *That the statement is deliberate, clear, and unequivocal. The hypothesis of mere mistake or slip of the tongue must be eliminated.* * * *
>
> (4) That the giving of conclusive effect to the declaration will be consistent with the public policy upon which the rule is based.
>
> (5) That the statement is not also destructive of the opposing party's theory of recovery.

Id. at 229. (Emphasis added).

Petitioner Mendoza contends that his testimony consisted only of personal opinion, and therefore is excluded from the application of the rule set out in *Griffin* and *Carr,* supra. However, the fact that an admission is an opinion or conclusion, does not prevent its use for impeachment or as substantive evidence on a material issue. Commercial Standard Insurance Co. v. Barron, 495 S.W.2d 276 (Tex.Civ.App.—Tyler 1973, writ ref'd n.r.e.); Snyder v. Schill, 388 S.W.2d 208 (Tex.Civ.App.—Houston 1964, writ ref'd n.r.e.); Taylor v. Owen, 290 S.W.2d 771 (Tex.Civ.App.—San Antonio 1956, writ ref'd n.r.e.); 2 C. McCormick & Ray, Texas Evidence § 1126 (2d ed. 1956). This is especially true if, unlike this case, the statement relates to facts peculiarly within the declarant's own knowledge. Gevinson v. Manhattan Construction Co. of Oklahoma, 449 S.W.2d 458, 466 (Tex.1969).

Here the court of civil appeals has correctly stated the requirements for a quasi-admission to be treated as a conclusive judicial admission. 588 S.W.2d at 615. However, we disagree with their conclusion that Mendoza's testimony met those requirements. We are of the opinion that Mendoza's opinion testimony was not so clear and unequivocal as to come under the rule announced in *Carr,* and that the possibility of a mistake has not been eliminated.

The issue of whether a claimant's physical condition is such that he is totally incapacitated due to an injury is a fact question. It calls for the expression of an opinion concerning the claimant's physical condition and does not involve a conclusion as to the legal effect of the physical condition. Usually medical experts are called to offer opinion testimony concerning the nature of the injury, whether it is temporary or permanent, and the extent of disability or incapacity resulting from the injury. Federal Underwriters Exchange v. Cost, 132 Tex. 299, 123 S.W.2d 332, 335 (1938). The opinions of medical experts on such matters are based upon training and experience, and involve a prognosis of the claimant's physical condition. By contrast, the testimony of a lay witness on such matters can only be based on his observation of physical facts such as the presence of pain or limitation of movement. There are certain medical areas in which the average lay person would not possess sufficient knowledge to form an opinion which would be of any aid to the jury. Scott v. Liberty Mutual Insurance Co., 204 S.W.2d 16 (Tex.Civ.App.—Austin 1947, writ ref'd n.r.e.). An opinion that would conclusively admit that a back injury has resulted in a total temporary, total permanent, or merely partial inability to work requires medical knowledge beyond that of the average lay person. Also, the testimony of Mendoza does not exclude the possibility that his opinion was mistaken in that it may have comprehended factors other than his physical condition such as his ability to obtain employment as a manual laborer or the availability of jobs in his community. Therefore Mendoza's testimony that his physical condition was such that he was totally unable to work prior to November 30, 1976 was not deliberate, clear and unequivocal, so as to preclude his recovery by a judicial admission.

The judgment of the court of civil appeals is reversed and the judgment of the trial court is affirmed.

DEICHMILLER v. INDUSTRIAL COMMISSION OF ILLINOIS, 147 Ill.App.3d 66, 497 N.E.2d 452, 456–57 (1986). "Claimant also points out that Mr. Zonca testified that based upon his experience as a plumber, his knowledge of the claimant's skills and the difficulty of the examination, he believed that claimant would have passed the examination. Claimant contends that Mr. Zonca's testimonial admissions against interest are binding against Zonca and that the Commission afforded insufficient weight to such admissions.

"We recognize that judicial admissions are conclusive and may not be contradicted. A testimonial judicial admission is one within the particular knowledge of the witness. If testimony is deliberate, clear and unequivocal as to facts within the party's peculiar knowledge, he will be held to such testimony as a judicial admission. (Bishop v. Crowther (1st Dist.1980), 92 Ill.App.3d 1, 12–13, 47 Ill.Dec. 594, 603, 415 N.E.2d 599, 608.) However, Mr. Zonca's testimony amounts to no more than his opinion that claimant would have passed the union journeymen plumber examination. His subjective, individual opinion is not a 'concrete fact' and thus could not be a judicial admission. Accordingly, the Commission properly could have discounted his opinion."

Note

Statements admitted as evidential but not judicial admissions: answers to interrogatories under Fed.R.Civ.P. 33, Freed v. Erie Lackawanna Ry. Co., 445 F.2d 619 (6th Cir.1971), cert. denied, 404 U.S. 1017, 92 S.Ct. 678, 30 L.Ed.2d 665 (1972); superseded pleadings in the same case, Haynes v. Manning, 717 F.Supp. 730, 733 (D.Kan.1989), aff'd in part, rev'd in part on other grounds, 917 F.2d 450 (10th Cir.1990); pleadings in another, related civil case, Frank R. Jelleff, Inc. v. Braden, 233 F.2d 671, 675–77 (D.C.Cir. 1956); plea of guilty in a related criminal case, State Farm Mut. Auto. Ins. Co. v. Worthington, 405 F.2d 683 (8th Cir.1968); Hinslaw v. Keith, p. 342 infra. As for withdrawn pleas of guilty and pleas of nolo contendre, see Fed.R.Evid. 410.

SECTION 5. STATEMENT AGAINST INTEREST *

[FED.R.EVID. 804(b)(3)]

ROBINSON v. HARKINS & CO.

Supreme Court of Texas, 1986.
711 S.W.2d 619.

PER CURIAM.

This is a personal injury action brought under the doctrine of *respondeat superior,* arising from a motor vehicle-train collision. The questions before us are whether the trial court erred in (1) sustaining a hearsay objection to certain evidence offered as declarations against interest * * *. The court of appeals held there was no error and affirmed the trial court's judgment denying recovery. 704 S.W.2d 554. We hold that the trial court did so err and accordingly grant petitioner's writ of error and, without hearing oral argument, reverse the judgment of the court of appeals.

Jerry Robinson worked for Harkins & Company as a mechanic. He was on 24–hour call and was provided with a company truck to move between work sites. On November 4, 1980, Jerry was working at a job site near Runge, Texas. Margaret Robinson accompanied her husband to the site. The Robinsons left the job site at approximately 3:30 p.m. and, on the way home to Alice, stopped to visit Jerry's stepfather and mother at their bar near Kenedy. The Robinsons left the bar at approximately 12:00 a.m. Their truck collided with the fifth car of a Southern Pacific Railroad train four or five miles from the bar at approximately 12:05 a.m. Margaret was rendered a paraplegic as a result of the accident. Jerry was not seriously injured. The Robinsons have since divorced and Jerry moved away. His whereabouts were unknown to all parties at the time of trial.

* See 5 Wigmore, Evidence §§ 1455–1477 (Chadbourn rev. 1974); McCormick, Evidence ch. 33 (4th ed. 1992); Jefferson, Declarations Against Interest: An Exception to the Hearsay Rule, 58 Harv.L.Rev. 1 (1944); Morgan, Declarations Against Interest, 5 Vand.L.Rev. 451 (1952).

In order to recover under the doctrine of *respondeat superior,* Margaret had to prove that Jerry was driving the truck. This was the major dispute at trial. The evidence on this point was conflicting, and the jury failed to find that Jerry was the driver. No issue was submitted as to Margaret. In her appeal, Margaret contends that the trial court excluded evidence tending to show that Jerry was driving that was vital to her case. This evidence consisted of (1) a notice of injury report filed by Jerry with the Industrial Accident Board and (2) inculpating statements made by Jerry to Margaret. The trial court sustained Harkins' hearsay objection to this evidence. * * *

We first address the admissibility of the excluded evidence. Margaret argues that both the IAB report and the inculpating statements are admissible under the declarations against interest exceptions to the hearsay rule. TEX.R.EVID. 803(24) (Vernon Supp.1986). This rule provides:

> *Statement against interest.* A statement which was at the time of its making so far contrary to the declarant's pecuniary or proprietary interest, or so far tended to subject him to civil or criminal liability, or to render invalid a claim by him against another, or to make him an object of hatred, ridicule, or disgrace, that a reasonable man in his position would not have made the statement unless he believed it to be true.

All hearsay exceptions require a showing of trustworthiness. TEX. R.EVID. 803(24) is founded on the principle that the ramifications of making a statement is so contrary to the declarant's interest that he would not make the statement unless it was true. There are three general interests considered under the rule: pecuniary, penal, and social. Thus, while a particular statement may be self-serving in one respect, it may simultaneously be contrary to another interest. Admissibility, then, necessarily requires a weighing and balancing of competing interests.

In the present case, the evidence offered by Margaret serves as a declaration against all three of the "interests" embodied in TEX. R.EVID. 803(24). By admitting to be the driver, Jerry subjected himself to potential liability for negligence, which is against his pecuniary interest. Further, he has opened himself up to possible criminal charges for the accident itself and if he lied in order to recover worker's compensation benefits. Finally, he has announced to the world that he was partly responsible for making his wife a paraplegic, which goes against his social interest. On the other hand, the IAB report is self-serving in that it might allow Jerry to recover worker's compensation benefits. While there is some degree of competing interest, the disserving nature of the proffered evidence outweighs the self-serving aspect relied on by the court of appeals. We hold that both the IAB report and the extrinsic statements fall within the parameters of a declaration against interest and thus qualify as exceptions to the hearsay rule. TEX.R.EVID. 803(24).

* * *

TIMBER ACCESS INDUSTRIES, INC. v. UNITED STATES PLYWOOD—CHAMPION PAPERS, INC., 263 Or. 509, 503 P.2d 482, 487–88 (1972). "Timber Access also contends that the testimony comes within the exception to the hearsay rule which admits declarations against the interest of the declarer. * * * The exception presently under discussion requires the statement to be made against the *declarer's pecuniary* interest. Hagberg v. Haas, 237 Or. 34, 38, 390 P.2d 361 (1964). Plaintiff argues that the statement made by Girard was against his pecuniary interest since it made him subject to the loss of his job. There is no basis for this argument because there is no evidence indicating that at the time he made the statement Girard had any knowledge that it might cause him to lose his position.

"In the present situation, Girard's purported statement concerning the conditions under which the logs were purchased does not fit nicely under any of the generally recognized exceptions to the hearsay rule. However, if the words were spoken, there is an aura of trustworthiness about them which makes evidence of them admissible. A manager of a plywood plant gets to be manager because of his employer's confidence in his business acumen. His ability to buy logs advantageously in a widely fluctuating market is one of the reasons he holds his position. If he admits that he obligated his employer to buy unconditionally a volume of logs at a set price without a definite deadline, he is admitting that he made a disadvantageous deal and this would necessarily reflect adversely upon his ability. It is not natural, normal, or usual for a person to admit that he made what has turned out to be a poor deal unless, in fact, he did make it. Testimony concerning his statement should be an exception to the hearsay rule * * * because he was in a position to have knowledge of the facts, and a person in his position normally would not have made the statement unless it was the truth. The declarant's interest, although not pecuniary, was sufficient to assure that he was not lying and that the statement was not the result of any mistake of fact.

"The limitation of admission of declarations against interest to those which fit neatly within the classifications of pecuniary or proprietary has long been questioned. Wigmore states that the exception is subject to arbitrary limitations resting on no reason at all. 5 Wigmore on Evidence § 1455, at 259 (3d ed.).

"McCormick, in discussing this exception, argues:

> 'Moreover, the restriction to material interests, ignoring as it does other motives just as influential upon the minds and hearts of men, should be more widely relaxed. Declarations against social interests, such as acknowledgments of facts which would subject the declarant to ridicule or disgrace, or facts calculated to arouse in the declarant a sense of shame or remorse, seem adequately buttressed in trustworthi-

ness and should be received under the present principle.' McCormick on Evidence § 278, at 674–75 (2d ed. 1972). (Footnotes omitted.)"

STATE v. ARNOLD

Supreme Court of Texas, 1989.
778 S.W.2d 68.

PER CURIAM.

This case concerns the forfeiture of a 1988 Ford Bronco to the State of Texas under the Controlled Substances Act, Tex.Rev.Civ.Stat.Ann. art. 4476–15, § 5.03(a)(5) (Vernon Supp.1989). Under that Act, the State must prove knowledge or consent to an offense by the owner of a vehicle before forfeiture is permitted.

The Bronco was registered to Albert Arnold but was being driven by Jody Curry, Arnold's brother-in-law, at the time it was stopped. At trial, the state sought to prove Curry was the true owner rather than Arnold.

Hearsay testimony was admitted at trial, without objection, that Curry had stated that the vehicle was really his and only registered in Arnold's name to avoid forfeiture to the State. The trial court relied on this testimony, together with other circumstantial evidence, in finding that Curry was the true owner of the Bronco. Consequently, the vehicle was ordered to be forfeited to the State.

In an unpublished opinion, the court of appeals reversed the trial court on the ground that the evidence was legally insufficient to rebut the presumption of title in Arnold, the registered owner. In the opinion, Curry's statements that he owned the vehicle were characterized as a self-serving claim that constituted no evidence on the question of actual ownership.

The evidence reveals no dispute between Curry and Arnold over ownership at the time Curry stated he owned the vehicle. His statements then are not merely self-serving declarations made with the intent to support a position in a property ownership dispute. The cases to that effect relied on by the court of appeals are thus inapposite. See *Segal v. Saunders,* 220 S.W.2d 339, 341 (Tex.Civ.App.—Fort Worth 1949, writ ref'd n.r.e.); *Chenoworth v. Flannery,* 202 S.W.2d 480, 483 (Tex.Civ. App.—Amarillo 1947, no writ).

Curry's statements should instead be analyzed as statements against interest under Texas Rule of Civil Evidence 803(24). That rule deems trustworthy a hearsay statement that is so contrary to the declarant's interest that he would not make the statement unless true. A statement may be self-serving in one respect but contrary to another interest. The court must balance these competing interests to determine their predominant nature and ultimately the level of trustworthiness to be accorded. *Robinson v. Harkins & Co.,* 711 S.W.2d 619, 621 (Tex.1986).

Balance test

If Curry was the true owner, his assertions to that effect w contrary to his pecuniary and proprietary interest. They tended expose him to the possibility of losing a new, expensive vehicle. ' same statements subjected him to civil liability under the forfeiture provisions of the Controlled Substances Act, Tex.Rev.Stat.Ann. art. 4476–15 (Vernon Supp.1989). Curry would not make statements so contrary to his interest unless they were true.

There is little self-serving content in the statements to outweigh the negative exposure of his pecuniary interests. Nothing in the record suggests Curry might need to employ such statements in a self-serving manner in anticipation of an ownership dispute between Curry and Arnold. Balancing these internally competing interests, Curry's statements are more accurately categorized as statements against interest when viewed under the relevant circumstances. For the same reason that statements against interest are admissible under the hearsay exception of Texas Rule of Civil Evidence 803(24), whereas predominantly self-serving statements are not, we find Curry's statements sufficiently trustworthy to be probative on the issue of ownership.

The court of appeals, in reviewing a no evidence challenge in a non-jury setting, must disregard all evidence contrary to the trial court's finding. "[I]f there is any remaining evidence which would support the verdict or judgment, the trial court's judgment must be upheld." *McGalliard v. Kuhlmann,* 722 S.W.2d 694, 696–97 (Tex.1986). Curry's statements against interest, being trustworthy, constitute more than a scintilla of evidence to support the conclusion that Curry and not Arnold owned the vehicle.

Because the court of appeals failed to analyze Curry's statements in their proper context, we grant the application for writ of error and, without hearing oral argument, a majority of the court reverses the judgment of the court of appeals as in conflict with our decision in *McGalliard.* See Tex.R.App.P. 133(b). We remand to the court of appeals for consideration of the factual insufficiency points of error left unaddressed in its original opinion.

UNITED STATES v. BARRETT

United States Court of Appeals, First Circuit, 1976.
539 F.2d 244.

LEVIN H. CAMPBELL, CIRCUIT JUDGE.

Arthur Barrett appeals from his conviction after a jury trial for crimes arising from the theft and sale of a collection of postage stamps from the Cardinal Spellman Philatelic Museum in Weston, Massachusetts. * * *

II

Barrett next argues that the court below erred by refusing to admit the testimony of three defense witnesses. The first was James Melvin.

Melvin testified that in February, 1974, he was at a card game on Bowdoin Street, in Dorchester, Massachusetts, with Ben Tilley. When Melvin was asked to recount a conversation which he had there with Tilley, the Government objected. Barrett made an offer of proof that Melvin would testify that Tilley had told Melvin "that he, Tilley, and Buzzy [Adams] were going to have some trouble from the people from California" with respect to the "stamp theft or matter" and that "[Melvin] asked him did he mean Bucky or Buzzy, and then he said, 'No, Bucky [Barrett] wasn't involved. It was Buzzy.'" Barrett argued at the bench that this testimony was admissible under Chambers v. Mississippi, 410 U.S. 284, 93 S.Ct. 1038, 35 L.Ed.2d 297 (1973), and Fed.R.Evid. 804(b)(3) as a declaration against self-interest, apparently on the theory that Tilley's display of inside knowledge of "the people from California" (presumably Bass and his associates), the stamp theft, and the identity of persons "involved", all tended against Tilley's penal interest at the time by advertising his likely complicity. The court excluded the proffered testimony as hearsay on the ground that the relevant part, that Buzzy, not Bucky, was involved, was not against Tilley's interest. The court said, "You are offering it not to prove anything prejudicial to the alleged maker of the statement but to prove that [Buzzy] rather than [Bucky] did it * * *." Barrett argues on appeal that the entire statement, including the portion exculpating Barrett, should have been admitted.

Rule 804(b)(3) of the new Federal Rules of Evidence provides, with an important qualification, for the admission of a statement by an unavailable declarant that at the time of making tended to subject him to criminal liability. The rule provides in pertinent part,

> "(b) *Hearsay exceptions.* The following are not excluded by the hearsay rule if the declarant is unavailable as a witness:
>
> "* * *
>
> "(3) *Statement against interest.* A statement which was at the time of its making so far contrary to the declarant's pecuniary or proprietary interest, or so far tended to subject him to civil or criminal liability * * * that a reasonable man in his position would not have made the statement unless he believed it to be true. A statement tending to expose the declarant to criminal liability and offered to exculpate the accused is not admissable [sic] unless corroborating circumstances clearly indicate the trustworthiness of the statement."

Rule 804(b)(3) is a departure from the principle laid down in Donnelly v. United States, 228 U.S. 243, 33 S.Ct. 449, 57 L.Ed. 820 (1913), in which the Supreme Court endorsed the exclusion from evidence of a third party's extra-judicial confession to the murder for which the defendant was on trial. In conformity with English precedent, the *Donnelly* court limited the hearsay exception for declarations against interest to declarations against interest to declarations against interest of a pecuniary character. Id. at 272–77, 33 S.Ct. 449. Statements subjecting the declarant to criminal liability were held to be outside the exception.

Half a century later, when the present Federal Rules of Evidence were being formulated, *Donnelly* was in disfavor, and provision was made in the various drafts of the new code for the admission of declarations against penal interest. See M.S. Walker, Inc. v. Travelers Indemnity Co., 470 F.2d 951 (1st Cir.1973). The text underwent several revisions prior to enactment. A provision forbidding prosecutorial use of third party statements or confessions which implicated an accused as well as the declarant was deleted, with the result that subject to sixth amendment and other constraints, a third party's out of court statements against penal interest may now be used against, as well as in favor of, an accused. And, more relevant here, the second sentence of clause (3) was rewritten to require that statements offered to exculpate the accused be corroborated so as to "clearly indicate the trustworthiness of the statement".

As submitted to Congress by the Supreme Court, the Rule required simply that a statement offered to exculpate the accused be corroborated. 56 F.R.D. 183, 321 (Rule 804(b)(4)). The Advisory Committee explained this requirement as a way of accommodating the common law's distrust of confessions offered to exculpate an accused:

> "The refusal of the common law to concede the adequacy of a penal interest was no doubt indefensible in logic [citing Holmes' *Donnelly* dissent], but one senses in the decisions a distrust of evidence of confessions by third persons offered to exculpate the accused arising from suspicions of fabrication either of the fact of the making of the confession or in its contents, enhanced in either instance by the required unavailability of the declarant. Nevertheless, an increasing amount of decisional law recognizes exposure to punishment for crime as a sufficient stake. The requirement of corroboration is included in the rule in order to effect an accommodation between these competing considerations. When the statement is offered by the accused by way of exculpation, the resulting situation is not adapted to control by rulings as to the weight of the evidence, and hence the provision is cast in terms of a requirement preliminary to admissibility. The requirement of corroboration should be construed in such a manner as to effectuate its purpose of circumventing fabrication." [Citations omitted.]

Notes of Advisory Committee on Proposed Rules, at 28 U.S.C.A.Fed. R.Evid. 804.

The House Judiciary Committee strengthened this corroboration requirement by adding the present language. The Committee noted,

> "[The Committee] believed * * * as did the [Supreme] Court [in its earlier version] that statements of this type tending to exculpate the accused are more suspect and so should have their admissibility conditioned upon some further provision insuring trustworthiness. The proposal in the Court Rule to add a requirement of simple corroboration was, however, deemed ineffective to accomplish this purpose since

> the accused's own testimony might suffice while not necessarily increasing the reliability of the hearsay statement. The Committee settled upon the language 'unless corroborating circumstances clearly indicate the trustworthiness of the statement' as affording a proper standard and degree of discretion. It was contemplated that the result in such cases as Donnelly v. United States, 228 U.S. 243 [33 S.Ct. 449, 57 L.Ed. 820] (1912), where the circumstances plainly indicated reliability, would be changed."

Notes of Committee on the Judiciary, H.R.Rep. No. 93–650, Note to Subdivision (b)(3), at 28 U.S.C.A.Fed.R.Evid. 804, U.S.Code Cong. & Admin.News 1974, pp. 7051, 7089.

As finally enacted, Rule 804(b)(3) requires a two-stage analysis: first, do the offered remarks come within the hearsay exception as a "statement against interest"? and second, if they do, is there sufficient corroboration to clearly indicate trustworthiness? Here we believe that the remarks offered were statements against interest within the Rule, and that the district court should have gone on to determine whether there was sufficient corroboration so as to warrant their admission.

Turning to the first stage of analysis, we think that Tilley's alleged remarks sufficiently tended to subject him to criminal liability "that a reasonable man in his position would not have made the statement unless he believed it to be true." Although the remarks did not amount to a clear confession to a crime as did the declarations in cases like *Donnelly* and Chambers v. Mississippi, supra, we do not understand the hearsay exception to be limited to direct confessions. See Note, Declarations Against Penal Interest: Standards of Admissibility Under an Emerging Majority Rule, 57 Bost.U.L.Rev. 148, 158 (1976). A reasonable person would have realized that remarks of the sort attributed to Tilley strongly implied his personal participation in the stamp crimes and hence would tend to subject him to criminal liability. Though by no means conclusive, the statement would be important evidence against Tilley were he himself on trial for the stamp crimes. We cannot say, therefore, that it did not pose the sort of threat to Tilley's interest that the hearsay exception contemplates. See id. at 156–58.

We do not overlook the fact that the proffered remarks came in the course of conversation with acquaintances over cards. In such circumstances, Tilley might not so readily have perceived the disserving character of what was said nor have expected his words to be repeated to the police. See id. at 159–65 and cases cited therein. But we are unable to say that the contextual circumstances so far impugn the reliability presumed from the remarks' disserving character as to take them outside the first part of the Rule. See *Chambers,* supra, 410 U.S. at 300, 93 S.Ct. 1038 (confession made "spontaneously to a close acquaintance"); cf. McClain v. Anderson Free Press, 232 S.C. 448, 467, 102 S.E.2d 750, 760 (1958) (Oxner, J., concurring), *cited in* Note, *Declarations Against Penal Interest,* supra, at 159. The factors in question seem better considered under the second part of the Rule in determining whether, overall, there is enough corroboration to "clearly indicate * * * trustworthiness".

Nor do we overlook the fact that exculpating Barrett was not in itself against Tilley's interest, since both could have participated in the crime. Tilley's remarks differ in this respect from the third-party confessions in *Chambers* and *Donnelly.* In Barrett's trial, the relevance of Tilley's participation is limited to the credence it gives to his views on who else took part. The district court seemed to suggest that in order for exculpatory remarks such as Tilley's to be admissible as against interest, the innocence of the accused must itself be prejudicial to the declarant. On the present facts, we read the first part of Rule 804(b)(3) more broadly, and conclude that so much of Tilley's remarks as exculpated "Bucky" and inculpated "Buzzy" should here be considered as part of the statement against Tilley's interest.

Under the common law exception for declarations against interest, the treatment to be given portions of a declaration collateral to the declarant's interest has been the subject of much debate. A leading commentator, after acknowledging the traditional liberality with which courts have admitted collateral statements, has expressed the opinion that,

> "As long as the courts adhere to the exceptions to the hearsay rule it would be more reasonable to confine the use of statements against interest in all cases to the proof of the fact which is against interest, since the reliability of other parts of the statement is conjectural."

B. Jefferson, Declarations Against Interest: An Exception to the Hearsay Rule, 58 Harv.L.Rev. 1, 62–63 (1944). And more pointedly, in an article criticizing certain conventional exceptions to the hearsay rule, another author has said,

> "Nonetheless, the naming of another as a compatriot will almost never be against the declarant's own interest and thus will contain little assurance of reliability on this ground. * * * The invocation of a name may be gratuitous, may be deliberately false in order to gain advantages for the declarant greater than those that would flow from naming a real participant or no one at all, may be a cover for concealment purposes (another kind of 'advantage'), or may represent an effort to gain some kind of personal revenge." [Footnote omitted.]

D. Davenport, The Confrontation Clause and the Coconspirator Exception in Criminal Prosecutions: A Functional Analysis, 85 Harv.L.Rev. 1378, 1396 (1972).

There are two reasons, however, which make it difficult for us to agree with the district court's view of the statement in issue. First, the Buzzy–Bucky statement, especially in context, is itself arguably disserving to Tilley, since it strengthened the impression that he had an insider's knowledge of the crimes. And second, the case law, while far from settled, has tended to grant at least "[a] certain latitude as to contextual statements, neutral as to interest giving meaning to the declaration against interest * * * ", McCormick on Evidence § 279(a), at 676 (2d ed. 1972); see United States v. Goodlow, 500 F.2d 954 (8th Cir.1974); cf. United States v. Seyfried, 435 F.2d 696 (7th Cir.1970), *cert. denied,* 402 U.S. 912, 91 S.Ct. 1393, 28 L.Ed.2d 654 (1971). See also cases cited in Wigmore, supra, § 1465. But see United States v. Marquez, 462 F.2d 893, 895 (2d Cir.1972). While we do not read the federal rule as incorporating the rather broad formulation put forward by Wigmore, who saw the against-interest exception as permitting reception not only of the "specific fact against interest, but also * * * *every fact contained in the same statement* ", Wigmore, supra, § 1465, at 339 (emphasis in original), neither does it appear that Congress intended to constrict the scope of a declaration against interest to the point of excluding "collateral" material that, as here, actually tended to fortify the statement's disserving aspects. See Notes of Advisory Committee, supra; Notes of Committee on the Judiciary, supra. We hold that the Buzzy–Bucky remark was sufficiently integral to the entire statement, and the latter sufficiently against interest, as to come within the first part of Rule 804(b)(3).

It follows that the district court was under an obligation to determine, under the second sentence of the Rule, whether "corroborating circumstances clearly indicate[d] the trustworthiness of the statement", including, we would add, the trustworthiness of that part exculpating Barrett. We emphasize that admissibility is conditional upon separate compliance with that standard, which, it is clear from both the statutory language and the legislative history, is not an insignificant hurdle. However, because the court below believed that the Buzzy–Bucky remark was inadmissible because outside Tilley's statement against interest, it never expressly analyzed the proposed testimony in light of that standard. And because for other reasons, see infra, there must be a new trial, we ourselves take no position at this time on the admissibility of the testimony under this standard. Unlike the first part of the Rule, which must be read in light of the case law that has evolved under the common law hearsay exception, the second part breaks new ground. We read the Rule as investing the district court with a substantial degree of discretion in making this important finding on trustworthiness, and therefore prefer to let the district court rule first in the course of the new proceeding. We would, nonetheless, make two observations to guide the district court's judgment, should the question arise upon retrial.

First we would not read the standard of trustworthiness as imposing a standard so strict as to be utterly unrealistic. Even in *Donnelly* and *Chambers* the evidence, while strongly corroborated, could have been disbelieved by the jury. On the other hand, there is no question but that Congress meant to preclude reception of exculpatory hearsay statements against penal interest unless accompanied by circumstances solidly indicating trustworthiness. This requirement goes beyond minimal corroboration. Trial judges will have to make an assessment case by case and in attempting to understand the standard may be aided by the legislative comments quoted above. In cases that are open to reasonable differences, this court is unlikely to substitute its judgment for that of the district court.

Second, in ruling on trustworthiness courts should be mindful of the possible relationship between constitutional cases such as *Chambers* and the new federal rule. *Chambers* holds, on facts far more compelling than anything here, that it is a violation of due process to exclude such exculpatory evidence as a well established confession of another to the crime for which the accused is on trial. Rule 804(b)(3) reflects Congress' attempt to strike a fair balance between exclusion of trustworthy evidence, as in *Chambers* and *Donnelly,* and indiscriminate admission of less trustworthy evidence which, because of the lack of opportunity for cross-examination and the absence of the declarant, is open to easy fabrication. Clearly the federal rule is no more restrictive than the Constitution permits, and may in some situations be more inclusive. We do not suggest that there is any issue of constitutional dimension in the present case.

UNITED STATES v. KATSOUGRAKIS

United States Court of Appeals, Second Circuit, 1983.
715 F.2d 769, cert. denied, 464 U.S. 1040, 104 S.Ct. 704, 79 L.Ed.2d 169 (1984).

[Katsougrakis and Hiotis were convicted on several charges arising from their procurement of the arson of an unprofitable business they had owned, the Kings Villa Diner. Chrisanthou and Kynegos, the arsonists hired by the appellants, were accidentally trapped in the fire, and both died several days later of burns.]

MESKILL, CIRCUIT JUDGE:

* * *

II. EVIDENTIARY RULINGS

A. *Chrisanthou's "Nodding of Head"*

On the day following the Kings Villa fire, Fitos Vasiliou visited his friend Charlie Chrisanthou at the Nassau County Medical Center. Although Chrisanthou was badly burned and wrapped virtually from head to toe in bandages, Vasiliou was permitted to converse briefly with his friend. As recounted by Vasiliou at trial, the following colloquy took place during their visit:

> [Prosecutor]: What did he [Chrisanthou] say? What did you say to him and what did you do?
>
> [Vasiliou]: I said to him, you think they [Katsougrakis and Hiotis] set you up?
>
> The Court: Say it again. The jurors don't hear you. Say it slowly and louder.
>
> The Witness: I asked him if they set him up and they burned him in the diner. So he said, no.
>
> The Court: Did he say, no, or did he just shake his head?

The Witness: No, he didn't say, no. He go like this.

The Court: Indicating the negative. All right.

The Witness: Go like this. I asked him—I said to him, you got paid to burn this place up. He go like this.

The Court: He indicated by shaking his head up and down [indicating the affirmative].

* * *

The district court, over the objection of defense counsel, permitted Vasiliou to recount his October 5, 1981 conversation with Chrisanthou in the Nassau County Hospital, including the various "nods" made by the decedent in response to Vasiliou's inquiries. On appeal, Katsougrakis and Hiotis charge that their constitutional rights under the Confrontation Clause were abridged by the admission of this hearsay testimony and further that the "nods" constitute inadmissible hearsay not falling within one of the recognized exceptions to that rule.[4]

A troublesome evidentiary question is presented when the government seeks to introduce a hearsay statement which is against the declarant's penal interest and which also inculpates the accused. Ordinarily, a statement against penal interest has clear guarantees of trustworthiness because, human nature being what it is, a person is unlikely to implicate himself criminally unless he was in fact involved in the criminal undertaking. The veracity of the hearsay statement may be questioned, however, when the declarant also inculpates a third party. For example, if during custodial interrogation the declarant perceived an opportunity to curry favor with the government by implicating both himself and a third party, he may choose this course in the hope of gaining immunity or a reduced sentence. See United States v. Oliver, 626 F.2d 254, 261 (2d Cir.1980). Since the declarant may in that circumstance have less than honorable motives for volunteering his "statement," that portion of the hearsay which inculpates the accused must be scrutinized carefully. The importance of this issue has prompted much scholarly debate, see, e.g., Tague, Perils of the Rulemaking Process: The Development, Application, and Unconstitutionality of Rule 804(b)(3)'s Penal Interest Exception, 69 Geo.L.J. 851 (1981); Westen, The Future of Confrontation, 77 Mich.L.Rev. 1185 (1979); Younger, Confrontation and Hearsay: A Look Backward, A Peek Forward, 1 Hofstra L.Rev. 32 (1973), and although divergent views have been expressed, the courts generally agree on the relevant legal standard. See, e.g., Ohio v. Roberts, 448 U.S. 56, 65–66, 100 S.Ct. 2531, 2538–39, 65 L.Ed.2d 597 (1980); United States v. Oliver, 626 F.2d at

4. The parties correctly concede that a "nod" is a statement for purposes of the hearsay rule and will be held to constitute hearsay if introduced to prove the truth of the matter asserted (i.e., a positive or negative answer in response to a particular question). See United States v. Ross, 321 F.2d 61, 69 (2d Cir.), *cert. denied,* 375 U.S. 894, 84 S.Ct. 170, 11 L.Ed.2d 123 (1963) (pointing of finger held to be a statement for purposes of hearsay rule). Here, the government unquestionably offered this testimony to prove the truth of the matter asserted, i.e., that appellants participated in the arson scheme.

260–63; United States v. Garris, 616 F.2d 626, 629–31 (2d Cir.), *cert. denied,* 447 U.S. 926, 100 S.Ct. 3021, 65 L.Ed.2d 1119 (1980). The moving party must show by a preponderance of the evidence that the "dual inculpatory" statement falls within a recognized exception to the hearsay rule and that attending circumstances confirm its trustworthiness. United States v. Oliver, 626 F.2d at 262; United States v. Garris, 616 F.2d at 630. Introduction of the hearsay statement under these circumstances does not offend the Confrontation Clause because there is strong indicia of reliability.

In this case, the government relied on Rule 804(b)(3) of the Federal Rules of Evidence, the penal interest exception to the hearsay rule, to meet its threshold burden. To satisfy this exception, the proponent must show "(1) that the declarant is 'unavailable' as a witness, (2) that the statement is sufficiently reliable to warrant an inference that 'a reasonable man in [the declarant's] position would not have made the statement unless he believed it to be true,' and (3) that 'corroborating circumstances clearly indicate the trustworthiness of the statement.' " United States v. Oliver, 626 F.2d at 260 (quoting Fed.R.Evid. 804(b)(3)); see United States v. Lieberman, 637 F.2d 95, 103–04 (2d Cir.1980).

Chrisanthou was unavailable to testify since he had died prior to trial. The "nods" clearly tended to subject Chrisanthou to criminal liability—by affirmative nod he admitted complicity in the criminal undertaking. Moreover, circumstances surrounding the conversation confirmed the reliability of the hearsay declaration and Chrisanthou's belief in its truth. The declarant was approaching death and was talking privately with his friend when the challenged admission was made. He was not conversing with police or other government agents whose favor he might be expected to curry. See, e.g., United States v. Lieberman, 637 F.2d at 103; United States v. Garris, 616 F.2d at 631–32. Indeed, if his intent was to implicate appellants falsely, he could have responded in the affirmative when asked whether Katsougrakis and Hiotis "set him up." Finally, corroborating circumstances confirm the trustworthiness of the statement. The evidence at trial showed that the Great Neck Kings Villa was experiencing recurring financial problems and that appellants twice tried to sell the diner. Expert testimony proved that the fire was intentionally set and the jury was free to infer that Katsougrakis and Hiotis were the only persons with a strong motive to have the diner destroyed by fire. In fact, Karagiannis testified that appellants asked him several months before the fire whether he knew anyone who could "do the job." Finally, the testimony of Rose Marie Chrisanthou and the non-hearsay testimony of Vasiliou concerning his meeting with Hiotis and the $6,000 payment provide further corroboration. The hearsay "nods" fall safely within the penal interest exception to the hearsay rule.

Appellants argue that even if the Chrisanthou "nods" satisfy Rule 804(b)(3), they do not survive constitutional scrutiny under the Confrontation Clause. Katsougrakis and Hiotis correctly point out that even though a hearsay statement may fall within a hearsay exception, the statement of an unavailable declarant will nonetheless be excluded under the Confrontation Clause unless the court is satisfied that "it bears adequate 'indicia of reliability.'" See Ohio v. Roberts, 448 U.S. 56, 66, 100 S.Ct. 2531, 2539, 65 L.Ed.2d 597 (1980) (quoting Dutton v. Evans, 400 U.S. 74, 89, 91 S.Ct. 210, 220, 27 L.Ed.2d 213 (1970)); Mancusi v. Stubbs, 408 U.S. 204, 213, 92 S.Ct. 2308, 2313, 33 L.Ed.2d 293 (1972). As a practical matter, however, a hearsay statement that satisfies the penal interest exception usually will survive Confrontation Clause scrutiny because the "trustworthiness" issue has already been decided in favor of admissibility. The Supreme Court has reaffirmed this view, holding that "[r]eliability can be inferred without more in a case where the evidence falls within a firmly rooted hearsay exception." Ohio v. Roberts, 448 U.S. at 66, 100 S.Ct. at 2539.

Chrisanthou's nods fall within a "firmly rooted hearsay exception" and the corroborating circumstances detailed previously fully confirm their trustworthiness. As noted earlier, the principal danger of hearsay statements that implicate both the declarant and the accused is that the declarant may have some ulterior motive for volunteering evidence against both parties—the declarant may confess hoping to gain immunity or a reduced sentence in return for his cooperation in convicting the accused. See United States v. Garris, 616 F.2d at 631; United States v. Lang, 589 F.2d 92, 97 (2d Cir.1978) (this Court intimates in dictum that a hearsay statement which satisfies the penal interest exception may have been inadmissible if the declarant knew he was volunteering this information to a government informant); see generally 4 J. Weinstein & M. Berger, Weinstein's Evidence ¶ 804(b)(3)[03], at 804–94–96 (1976). Here, there is no persuasive showing that Chrisanthou had an ulterior motive when conversing with his friend Vasiliou. His nods were entirely consistent with the evidence presented at trial; no confrontation problems are shown here.

* * *

UNITED STATES v. GARCIA, 897 F.2d 1413, 1420–21 (7th Cir. 1990). "Rule 804(b)(3) requires that corroborating circumstances clearly indicate the trustworthiness of a statement against interest. * * * This applies to both inculpatory and exculpatory statements. * * *

"Jose argues that the hearsay statements lack reliability because they were made during the custodial interrogation of Carlos without an attorney and as such may have been made merely to curry favor with the authorities. * * * There is nothing in the record that indicates Carlos was motivated by a desire to curry favor with his interrogators. He voluntarily made his statement after being advised of his *Miranda* rights and did not enter into any plea agreements with the government. Under this analysis, we find there was sufficient evidence for the district court to conclude that Carlos' statements were corroborated by *some* other evidence in the case. In sum, the trial court's decision to admit the statements was not clearly erroneous."

UNITED STATES v. HARTY, 930 F.2d 1257, 1263 (7th Cir.1991), cert. denied, ___ U.S. ___, 112 S.Ct. 262, 116 L.Ed.2d 215 (1991). "In United States v. Alvarez, 584 F.2d 694 (5th Cir.1978), the Fifth Circuit chose to adopt the third requirement of Rule 804(b)(3), the existence of 'corroborating circumstances [that] clearly indicate the trustworthiness of the statement,' as a prerequisite to the admission of Rule 804(b)(3) evidence inculpating a defendant in order to pass constitutional muster under the Sixth Amendment Confrontation Clause. Id. at 700–01. As the *Alvarez* court noted, Congress intentionally avoided codifying constitutional evidentiary principles such as those required under the Sixth Amendment Confrontation Clause when it adopted the Federal Rules of Evidence:

> '[T]he basic approach of the rules is to avoid codifying, or attempting to codify, constitutional evidentiary principles, such as the * * * sixth amendment's right of confrontation. Codification of a constitutional principle is unnecessary and, where the principle is under development, often unwise.'

Id. at 700 (quoting S.Rep. No. 93–1277, 93d Cong., 2d Sess., reprinted in 1974 U.S.Code Cong. & Admin.News 7051, 7068). Congress properly left the question of the constitutional parameters for determining the admissibility of hearsay evidence to the courts. In *Alvarez,* the Fifth Circuit consolidated the requirements of Rule 804(b)(3) and the Confrontation Clause in dealing with the admission of incriminating, out-of-court statements by an unavailable declarant when offered to inculpate a defendant.

"We recently adopted the Fifth Circuit's approach to Rule 804(b)(3) in United States v. Garcia, 897 F.2d 1413 (7th Cir.1990), while retaining a separate Confrontation Clause analysis. Under the three-prong 804(b)(3) test we established in *Garcia,* 'a court must find that, (1) the declarant's statement was against the penal interest of the declarant, (2) corroborating circumstances exist indicating the trustworthiness of the statement, and (3) the declarant must be unavailable.' 897 F.2d at 1420. Our Confrontation Clause test has long required 'that the declarant actually made the statement * * * [and (2) that] there must be circumstantial evidence supporting the truth of the statement.' United States v. Blakey, 607 F.2d 779, 786 (7th Cir.1979). Under the Supreme Court's recent holding in Idaho v. Wright, ___ U.S. ___, 110 S.Ct. 3139, 3150, 111 L.Ed.2d 638 (1990), however, the second prong of *Blakey* is invalid and the test must now conform to the requirement that the hearsay must be reliable 'by virtue of its inherent trustworthiness.' "

Note

See also Lee v. Illinois, 476 U.S. 530, 106 S.Ct. 2056, 90 L.Ed.2d 514 (1986); United States v. Winley, 638 F.2d 560 (2d Cir.1981) (statement by coconspirator inadmissible under Rule 801(d)(2)(E) because made after termination of conspiracy may be admissible as statement against penal interest).

SECTION 6. STATEMENT UNDER BELIEF OF IMPENDING DEATH *

[FED.R.EVID. 804(b)(2)]

STATE v. QUINTANA

Supreme Court of New Mexico, 1982.
98 N.M. 17, 644 P.2d 531.

RIORDAN, JUSTICE.

Rosinaldo Quintana (Quintana) was convicted of voluntary manslaughter. Quintana alleged on appeal that the deathbed statement of Telesfor Lopez (Lopez), the decedent, was erroneously admitted into evidence. The Court of Appeals held that the admission of the statement was reversible error. We granted certiorari; and we reverse the Court of Appeals.

The issue on appeal is:

> Whether Lopez' deathbed statement was a dying declaration that was properly admitted into evidence.

* * *

Lopez died May 26, 1980 from infection caused by a single gunshot wound. The bullet removed during the autopsy on Lopez was tested and found to have come from Quintana's rifle. Quintana was then charged with Lopez' death.

At trial, the State sought admission of a hearsay statement made by Lopez just before his death. The statement had been elicited at the hospital by the attorney retained by Lopez' family to investigate the civil liability aspect of the shooting. The statement was admitted over Quintana's objection.

The family attorney testified that he went to the hospital on May 26th for the express purpose of obtaining a dying declaration from Lopez. He spoke to Lopez for two to six minutes. The attorney testified that when he went to the intensive care unit, he saw Lopez:

> wired to any number of machines. They were monitoring his heartbeat. They were monitoring his blood pressure. He had oxygen—he was breathing oxygen. They had his feet elevated. It was my understanding—and I saw that myself—it was my understanding that the

* See 5 Wigmore, Evidence §§ 1430–1452 (Chadbourn rev. 1974); McCormick, Evidence ch. 32 (4th ed. 1992); Quick, Some Reflections on Dying Declarations, 6 How. L.J. 109 (1960).

> reason they had his feet slightly elevated was because the kid was choking on his own blood. When I saw him and during the time that I spoke to him, his breathing was labored; his speech was somewhat difficult. During the entire time that I talked to him, the blood continued to ooze out of his nose and mouth and he was in great pain.

The attorney testified that during the conversation Lopez was conversant, conscious and lucid. Lopez was *never* told by his doctors that he was going to die; however, Lopez told the attorney that he knew he was very seriously injured; he knew that his back was broken, and he was paralyzed; and he knew that there was a strong possibility of dying. During the interview, the attorney elicited answers from Lopez as to circumstances surrounding the shooting; however, Lopez was not able to identify the person who shot him.

The State asserts that Lopez' statements made to the attorney are admissible under New Mexico's Evidence Rule 804(b)(3), N.M.S.A.1978. Rule 804(b)(3) states:

> (b) *Hearsay exceptions.* The following are not excluded by the hearsay rule if the declarant is unavailable as a witness:
>
> * * *
>
> (3) *Statement under belief of impending death.* A statement made by a declarant while believing that his death was imminent, concerning the cause or circumstances of what he believed to be his impending death.

The admissibility of evidence is within the sound discretion of the trial court, and its ruling will be upheld unless there is a showing of an abuse of that discretion. State v. Smith, 92 N.M. 533, 591 P.2d 664 (1979). We find there was no abuse of the trial judge's discretion.

A dying declaration is admissible when there is a showing that the statement was made under a sense of "impending death". When such a declaration is made, the declarant must be conscious and the realization of approaching death must exist. State v. Stewart, 30 N.M. 227, 231 P. 692 (1924). The determination as to whether the particular testimony is admissible must depend upon the particular circumstances of each case. State v. Sanford, 44 N.M. 66, 97 P.2d 915 (1939).

In determining "impending death", one is to look to the state of mind of the victim. *Stewart,* supra. Fear or even the belief that the illness will end in death is not enough for a dying declaration. There must be a settled hopeless expectation that death is near, and what is said must have been spoken in the hush of impending death. Shepard v. United States, 290 U.S. 96, 100, 54 S.Ct. 22, 24, 78 L.Ed. 196 (1933); *Stewart,* supra. The state of mind must be exhibited in the evidence and not left to conjecture. *Shepard,* supra. Therefore, a dying person can declare that he believes he is dying; however, there are no specific words that have to be spoken by the declarant. *Stewart,* supra. Alternatively, if it can reasonably be inferred from the state of the wound or the state of the illness that the dying person was aware of his danger, then the requirement of impending death is met. Id.; Territory v. Dick Eagle, 15 N.M. 609, 110 P. 862 (1910). *Stewart,* supra, stated:

> "In the trial of a murder case, if at the time of making declarations the condition of the wounded party making them, the nature of his wounds, the length of time after making the declarations before he expired, and all the circumstances make a prima facie case that he was in the article of death and conscious of his condition when he made the declarations, and [sic] such declarations should be admitted in evidence by the court. * * * "

Id., 30 N.M. at 234, 231 P. at 695 (quoting Jones v. State, 130 Ga. 274, 60 S.E. 840, 840 (1908)). Therefore, a decedent does not have to be told he is dying; it can be obvious from the circumstances that death is impending. Territory v. Dick Eagle, supra; Shuman v. State, 94 Nev. 265, 578 P.2d 1183 (1978).

In Johnson v. State, 579 P.2d 20 (Alaska 1978), the court stated that under the Federal Rules of Evidence there is no longer the requirement that there be an abandonment of all hope of recovery. The only requirement is that the statement be made by a declarant while believing that his death was imminent. The Alaska Supreme Court stated that:

> We believe that to require that the declarant have abandoned all hope of recovery is overly demanding. In light of modern medical science it is rare indeed that all hope of recovery is abandoned, yet a victim may be aware of the probability that his death is impending to the extent necessary to create sufficient solemnity to give adequate assurance of the trustworthiness of his testimony. What is required for a dying declaration to be admissible is that the declarant have such a belief that he is facing death as to remove ordinary worldly motives for misstatement. In that regard, the court may consider the totality of the circumstances including the presence or absence of motive to falsify and the manner in which the statement was volunteered or elicited.

Id. at 25 (footnote omitted). Also, the Nevada Supreme Court in *Shuman,* supra, stated that:

> "[I]t is not necessary for the declarant to state to anyone, expressly, that he knows or believes he is going to die, or that death is certain or near, or to indulge in any like expression; nor is it deemed essential that his physician, or anyone else, state to the injured person that he will probably die as a result of his wounds, or that they employ any similar expression. It is sufficient if the wounds are of such a nature that the usual or probable effect upon the average person so injured would be mortal; and that such probable mortal effect is not hidden, but, from experience in like cases, it may be *reasonably concluded* that such probable effect has revealed itself upon the human consciousness of the wounded person. * * *" [Emphasis in *Shuman.*]

Id. 94 Nev. at 269, 578 P.2d at 1185 (quoting State v. Teeter, 65 Nev. 584, 628, 200 P.2d 657, 679 (1948)). We agree with the Alaska and Nevada opinions.

Lopez' statements and circumstances surrounding his statements are sufficient to show that he believed his death was imminent. He stated that he knew that he was seriously injured; he knew his back was broken, and he was paralyzed; he also stated that there was a strong possibility of dying. The attorney also testified as to what he witnessed about Lopez' condition. He stated that he was hooked up to several machines and was oozing blood from his nose and mouth. Lopez died about three hours after giving the statement. Therefore, we hold that the dying declaration was properly admitted into evidence.

However, a dying declaration by no means implies absolute verity. It can be impeached. Carver v. United States, 164 U.S. 694, 17 S.Ct. 228, 41 L.Ed. 602 (1897). After the declaration has been found to be admissible, the defendant can impeach the statement in the same manner as the defendant could impeach a witness. He can discredit the statement by showing that the deceased bore a bad reputation or that he did not believe in a future state of rewards or punishment. Id.; State v. Gallegos, 28 N.M. 403, 213 P. 1030 (1923).

Therefore, we find that the trial court did not abuse its discretion in admitting the dying declaration. The Court of Appeals is reversed and the trial court's verdict is affirmed.

PEOPLE v. SILER, 171 Mich.App. 246, 429 N.W.2d 865, 867–68 (1988). "The evidence at trial showed that on March 15, 1987, at 8:00 p.m., the Grand Rapids Police Emergency Communications Operator received a call from a person, later identified as Gordon Darwin. All incoming calls are taped directly from the telephone. A copy of the tape was admitted into evidence over defendant's objection and played for the jury. It reads as follows:

'OPERATOR: At the tone the time will be 8:02 and forty seconds. At the tone the time will be 8:02 and.

'DISPATCHER: Grand Rapids Police.

'CALLER: I need an ambulance right away.

'DISPATCHER: Where?

'CALLER: 21 Weston, apartment 514.

'DISPATCHER: What's going on there?

'CALLER: My heart's stabbed.

'DISPATCHER: Your heart is what?

'CALLER: I've been stabbed in the heart.

'DISPATCHER: And who did it?

'CALLER: Just come with the ambulance.* * *

'DISPATCHER: Who did it?

'CALLER: A friend of mine.

'DISPATCHER: Is he there?

'CALLER: William Siler, yeah.

'DISPATCHER: William Tyler.

'CALLER: Siler, he's looking out for me in the meantime.

'DISPATCHER: That would be apartment 514?

'CALLER: 21 Weston, hurry please.

'DISPATCHER: What is the phone number there, sir?

'CALLER: 456–6725. Hurry with the ambulance.

'DISPATCHER: Okay. William Siler did it, huh?

'CALLER: Yeah.

'DISPATCHER: Okay. What's he wearing? They're on the way.

'CALLER: Hurry with the ambulance.

'DISPATCHER: Right, they're on the way. Just tell me what he's wearing. Operator.'

"Police Officer Robert Winters was dispatched to Darwin's apartment and found him lying unconscious on the floor in a fetal position. Winters located a bleeding stab wound in Darwin's left chest. Darwin was transported to St. Mary's Hospital where he died at around 9:30 p.m.

* * *

"The condition in dispute in this case is whether Darwin was conscious of impending death. 'Consciousness of death' requires, first, that it be established that the declarant was in fact in extremis at the time the statement was made and, secondly, that the decedent believed his death was impending. But, it is not necessary for the declarant to have actually stated that he knew he was dying in order for the statement to be admissible as a dying declaration. * * *

"Darwin called the emergency number, stating that he had been stabbed in the heart and that he needed an ambulance right away. Three times he repeated his request for an ambulance and told the police to hurry. A forensic pathologist testified that Darwin remained conscious for four to five minutes after the wound was inflicted. Approximately one and a half hours later, he was pronounced dead without having regained consciousness. Taking these circumstances into account, we find that Darwin was conscious of impending death when he telephoned the emergency number. The tape recording reflects a dying declaration. The magistrate did not abuse his discretion."

SECTION 7. EXCITED UTTERANCE *

[FED.R.EVID. 803(2)]

CITY OF DALLAS v. DONOVAN

Court of Appeals of Texas, 1989.
768 S.W.2d 905.

BAKER, JUSTICE.

The city appeals from an adverse judgment in a negligence lawsuit. In three points of error, the city contends that the trial court erred by admitting hearsay testimony, and that there was no evidence or insufficient evidence to support the judgment. We overrule these points of error and affirm the trial court's judgment.

Michael and Victoria Donovan, individually and on behalf of Erin, Timothy, and Mary Donovan, sued the city because of injuries that they suffered in a collision on January 14, 1984. The accident happened at an intersection in the Dallas city limits. A stop sign, which would have controlled traffic moving in the direction of the Donovan's travel, was down at the time of the accident. A governmental unit is immune from liability for damages based on a claim arising from the removal or destruction of a traffic or road sign by a third party unless the governmental unit fails to correct the situation within a reasonable time after actual notice. *See* TEX.CIV.PRAC. & REM.CODE ANN. § 101.060(a)(3) (Vernon 1986) (formerly TEX.REV.CIV.STAT.ANN. art. 6252–19, § 14(12) (Vernon 1970)). The jury found that a third party had removed the stop sign, that the city did have actual notice that the sign was down, that the city failed to replace the sign within a reasonable time after receiving notice, and that this failure was a proximate cause of the collision.

In its first point of error, the city argues that the trial court erred in admitting certain testimony of Ladd William Backhaus. He testified that a middle-aged woman drove up to the scene of the accident minutes after the collision. She observed the injured children, and Backhaus could tell that she was affected by what she saw, based on her facial expression and tone of voice. He said that she was very excited or upset, she was emotional, her hands were shaking, and her voice was "crackling." He said that she volunteered the statement that days prior to the accident she had reported to the city that the stop sign was down.

The city objected to the woman's statement, contending that it was inadmissible hearsay, and the city makes the same argument on appeal. The Donovans contend that the statement was admissible as an excited utterance under rule 803(2) of the Texas Rules of Civil Evidence. The pertinent part of the rule states:

* See 6 Wigmore, Evidence §§ 1745–1764 (Chadbourn rev. 1976); McCormick, Evidence §§ 268, 270, 272, 272.1 (4th ed. 1992); Hutchins & Slesinger, Some Observations on the Law of Evidence: Spontaneous Exclamations, 28 Colum.L.Rev. 432 (1928); Slough, Spontaneous Statements and State of Mind, 46 Iowa L.Rev. 224 (1961).

> The following are not excluded by the hearsay rule, even though the declarant is available as a witness:
>
> * * *.
>
> (2) Excited utterance. A statement relating to a startling event or condition made while the declarant was under the stress of excitement caused by the event or condition.

TEX.R.CIV.EVID. 803(2).

The city argues that the woman's statement lacks the necessary relationship to the startling event. The city asserts that the statement bears no relationship to the events immediately preceding the accident, the accident itself, or the resulting injuries. In support of this argument, the city cites *American General Insurance Co. v. Coleman,* 157 Tex. 377, 303 S.W.2d 370 (1957). In that case, the Texas Supreme Court held that an injured worker's statement made to a treating doctor was not admissible under the res gestae exception to the hearsay rule. The Court said that the statement was lacking in the requirement that it tend to illuminate or explain the exciting event, and it did not relate to happenings which were causative or descriptive of the accident. *Coleman,* 303 S.W.2d at 373.

We note that the Supreme Court has since suggested that use of the term "res gestae" in this context should be abandoned because it is vague and imprecise and has been used indiscriminately. *See Sanders v. Worthington,* 382 S.W.2d 910, 915 (Tex.1964). In any case, we conclude that *Coleman* does not support the city's position. In our view, the woman's statement about her report to the city concerning the stop sign does tend to explain or illuminate the accident, and it does relate to happenings causative of the accident. The Donovans argued at trial that the city's failure to restore the stop sign after actual notice was a proximate cause of the collision, and the jury so found. Since the woman's statement is probative of actual notice to the city that the stop sign was down, it does tend to explain the accident, and it relates to happenings causative of the accident. Therefore, we view *Coleman* as supportive of the Donovan's argument that the statement was admissible as an excited utterance.

The city also relies upon *Gulf, Colorado, & Santa Fe Railway Co. v. Southwick,* 30 S.W. 592 (Tex.Civ.App.1895, no writ). This case provides an excellent example of one of the reasons for avoidance of the term "res gestae." *Southwick* involved testimony by two witnesses who said that they heard a train conductor state, "I told those people that those stools would yet be the death of some one." The court held that it was error to allow this testimony because it was not admissible as an opinion of the conductor, as part of the res gestae, or for impeachment purposes. *Southwick,* 30 S.W. at 593. Since the court never explained what it meant by "res gestae," we can only speculate about its meaning as used by the court. The term "res gestae" has been used in determining the admissibility of declarations of mental state, declarations of bodily condition, admissions by parties, various classes of spontaneous exclamations, and other kinds of evidence. *See* 1A R. RAY, TEXAS LAW OF EVIDENCE § 911, at 146–49 (Texas Practice 3d ed. 1980). We will not speculate about which of the above meanings, if any, the *Southwick* court intended. Therefore, we do not view *Southwick* as authoritative on the issue before us, which concerns the admissibility of an alleged excited utterance.

We also observe that the Texas and federal rules on excited utterances are identical, and that Texas adopted the federal rule. *See* FED.R.EVID. 803(2); H. WENDORF & D. SCHLUETER, TEXAS RULES OF EVIDENCE MANUAL 326 (2d ed. 1988). A number of Texas commentators have considered the advisory committee's notes on the federal rules as persuasive. *See, e.g.,* WENDORF & SCHLUETER, *supra,* at 328–29; 33 S. GOODE, O. WELLBORN, & M. SHARLOT, GUIDE TO THE TEXAS RULES OF EVIDENCE § 803.3, at 579 (Texas Practice 1988). As to the content of statements excepted from the hearsay rule, the advisory committee note states:

> Permissible *subject matter* of the statement is limited under Exception (1) [rule 803(1) on present sense impressions] to description or explanation of the event or condition * * *. In Exception (2) [rule 803(2) on excited utterances], however, the statement need only "relate" to the startling event or condition, thus affording a broader scope of subject matter coverage.

FED.R.EVID. 803 advisory committee's note (emphasis in original).

In a case applying the federal rule, there was testimony by the plaintiff's father that after the plaintiff fell in the defendant's store, another shopper stated that she had informed "them" about a substance on the floor about an hour and a half ago. The trial court admitted the statement as an excited utterance. The federal appellate court held that the three required conditions for admission had been satisfied: a startling occasion, a statement made before time to fabricate, and a statement relating to the circumstances of the occurrence. The statement was probative of notice of the premises defect, and the court stated that "it is undisputed that [the declarant's] statement directly concerned the 'circumstance' surrounding the occurrence." *See David v. Pueblo Supermarket,* 740 F.2d 230, 234–35 (3d Cir.1984).

In the present case, the necessary relationship between the statement and the event is disputed, but we resolve that dispute in favor of the Donovans. We conclude that the statement was clearly related to the event, since it was probative of actual notice and therefore relates to happenings causative of the accident and tends to at least partially explain the accident. We agree with the advisory committee's note that excited utterances are not confined to statements describing or explaining the startling event itself. *See* FED.R.EVID. 803 advisory committee's note; TEX.R.CIV.EVID. 803(2).

The city also argues that the statement was inadmissible because it referred to an incident remote from the startling event in terms of time. We disagree with the premise of this argument. The advisory committee suggests that the time element is important only with respect to the duration of the declarant's state of excitement. *See* FED.R.EVID. 803 advisory committee's note. A statement made while in a condition of excitement theoretically stills the capacity for reflection and prevents fabrication. *See id.; David,* 740 F.2d at 235. One commentator suggests that it is well-settled that declarations concerning incidents occurring before the accident regarding the cause of the accident are admissible. *See* RAY, *supra,* § 918, at 170–72 & n. 51. We conclude that the only requirement concerning time with respect to admission of excited utterances is the necessity that the statement be made while in a state of excitement caused by the startling event. *See* TEX.R.CIV.EVID. 803(2).

The city further contends that there must be independent evidence of the incident sought to be proved by the excited utterance. The city notes that the woman's statement was introduced to prove that she had reported the downed stop sign to the city. The city relies on *Richardson v. Green,* 677 S.W.2d 497 (Tex.1984), and *Truck Insurance Exchange v. Michling,* 364 S.W.2d 172 (Tex.1963). This reliance is misplaced. These cases require that there be independent evidence of the *startling event itself. Richardson,* 677 S.W.2d at 500; *Michling,* 364 S.W.2d at 174–75. In this case, the woman's statement was offered to prove an incident distinct from, but related to, the startling occurrence. Therefore, *Richardson* and *Michling* are inapplicable.

We hold that it was not error to admit Backhaus' testimony about the woman's statement. The statement was admissible as an excited utterance. *See* TEX.R.CIV.EVID. 803(2). We overrule the city's first point of error.

* * *

We affirm the trial court's judgment.

Note

Regarding excited utterances by unidentified bystanders, see also Miller v. Keating, 754 F.2d 507, 510 (3d Cir.1985) (statements by unidentified declarants are not "ipso facto inadmissible" but "are admissible if they otherwise meet the criteria of 803(2)"); State v. Smith, 285 So.2d 240, 244–45 (La.1973) (unidentified bystander who "apparently viewed the armed robbery in progress at scene of robbery" handed the victim a slip of paper bearing automobile license number within thirty seconds after the conclusion of the robbery; the writing was properly admitted as an excited utterance or a present sense impression).

UNITED STATES v. NAPIER, 518 F.2d 316, 317–18 (9th Cir.1975), cert. denied, 423 U.S. 895, 96 S.Ct. 196, 46 L.Ed.2d 128 (1975). "Caruso was hospitalized for seven weeks following the assault, during which time she underwent two brain operations. There was testimony that she suffered brain damage which rendered her unable to comprehend the significance of an oath and therefore incapable of testifying at trial. It was also testified, although her memory was intact, that her communication with others was restricted to isolated words and simple phrases, often precipitated by situations of stress and strain. Approximately one week after Caruso returned home from the hospital, her sister, Eileen Moore, showed her a newspaper article containing a photograph of the defendant. Moore testified that Caruso looked at the photograph (but did not read the accompanying article), and her 'immediate reaction was one of great distress and horror and upset,' and that Caruso 'pointed to it and she said very clearly, "He killed me, he killed me." ' Moore also testified that no member of the family had attempted to discuss the incident with Caruso prior to the display of the photograph. The court admitted the statement, over defendant's objection that it was inadmissible hearsay, as a 'spontaneous exclamation.' We hold that the statement was properly admitted.

"Although the government insists that the statement is a 'verbal act' and thus not hearsay at all, we do not pass on this contention because it is our view that even if the statement is hearsay it falls within the exception for 'spontaneous exclamation' or 'excited utterances.' Fed.R.Evid. 803(2) provides: 'A statement relating to a startling event or condition made while the declarant was under the stress of excitement caused by the event or condition [is not excluded by the hearsay rule].' Appellant disputes the applicability of the 'spontaneous exclamation' exception. He argues that, since the statement 'he killed me' refers to the assault, that event constitutes the 'startling' event. Because the statement was not made under the stress of excitement caused by the assault, appellant insists that the statement is not within the exception. We reject appellant's analysis. The display of the photograph, on the facts of this case, qualifies as a sufficiently 'startling' event to render the statement made in response thereto admissible.

"Although in most cases the 'startling' events which prompt 'spontaneous exclamations' are accidents, assaults, and the like, cf. McCormick, Evidence § 297 at 705 (2d ed. 1972), there is no reason to restrict the exception to those situations. Wigmore, in the classic statement of the admissibility of spontaneous exclamations, writes:

> This general principle is based on the experience that, under certain external circumstances of physical shock, a stress of nervous excitement may be produced which stills the reflective faculties and removes their control, so that the utterance which then occurs is a spontaneous and sincere response to the actual sensations and perceptions already produced by the external shock. Since this utterance is made under the immediate and uncontrolled domination of the senses, and during the brief period when considerations of self-interest could not have been brought fully to bear by reasoned reflection, the utterance may be taken as particularly trustworthy (or, at least, as lacking the usual grounds of untrustworthiness), and thus as expressing the real tenor of the speaker's belief as to the facts just observed by him; and may

therefore be received as testimony to those facts. The ordinary situation presenting these conditions is an affray or a railroad accident. But the principle itself is a broad one.

6 Wigmore, Evidence § 1747, at 135 (3d ed. 1940) (footnote omitted). And McCormick writes of the nature of the event which underlies the exception: 'The courts seem to look primarily to the effect upon the declarant and, if satisfied that the event was such as to cause adequate excitement, the inquiry is ended.' McCormick, Evidence § 297, at 705 (2d ed. 1972). In the instant case where Caruso, having never discussed the assault with her family, was suddenly and unexpectedly confronted with a photograph of her alleged assailant, there can be no doubt that the event was sufficiently 'startling' to provide adequate safeguards against reflection and fabrication."

HAWKINS v. STATE, 792 S.W.2d 491, 494–95 (Tex.App.1990). "In his third point of error, Hawkins argues that the trial court erred in overruling his objection to the testimony of the husband about the complainant's identification of her assailants. The husband testified that when he arrived at the scene, about an hour and a half after the assault, his wife 'was very nervous and she was crying.' She immediately identified, through sign language, 'our friend with the bulgy eyes, Charles,' as one of her assailants. The trial court overruled Hawkins' objection that this testimony was hearsay.

* * *

"The trial court admitted the complainant's identification of her attacker as an excited utterance. An excited utterance is defined as a 'statement relating to a startling event or condition made while the declarant was under the stress of excitement caused by the event or condition.' TEX.R.CRIM.EVID. 803(2). Hawkins argues that too much time elapsed between the assault and the identification for the latter to have qualified as an excited utterance.

"In determining the admissibility of statements under the excited utterance exception to the hearsay rule, the element of time is an important, but not controlling, factor. Fisk v. State, 432 S.W.2d 912, 914–15 (Tex.Crim.App.1968); Short v. State, 658 S.W.2d 250, 255 (Tex. App.—Houston [1st Dist.] 1983), aff'd, 671 S.W.2d 888 (Tex.Crim.App. 1984). The critical factor is whether the person who made the statement was still dominated by the emotions arising from the exciting event. *Fisk,* 432 S.W.2d at 915; *Short,* 658 S.W.2d at 255. In *Short,* for example, we held that the exception applied to a statement made at least four and one-half hours after the exciting event. 658 S.W.2d at 255.

"By overruling the objection, the trial court ruled that the complainant was still under the stress of her assault when she identified Hawkins as her attacker. That ruling is supported by the husband's testimony that his wife was nervous and crying when she told him Hawkins attacked her. Hawkins, who had the right to conduct a voir dire examination of the witness, did not elicit any controverting testimony when the court admitted the statement. Instead, Hawkins argued that one and one-half hours was too long a period, as a matter of law, between the event and the statement. Because we have held that four and one-half hours was not too long a period, we find no error. See Short, 658 S.W.2d at 255."

Note

Many cases consider whether a hearsay statement of a young child qualifies for admission as an excited utterance. Some representative cases are State v. Bauer, 146 Ariz. 134, 704 P.2d 264, 267 (App.1985) (upholding admission of statement of two-and-one-half-year-old girl; "In Arizona excited utterances of children who are incompetent to testify because of their age are admissible in evidence."); State v. Roy, 214 Neb. 204, 333 N.W.2d 398, 401 (1983) (in response to emergency room nurse's question, "Who hurt you?," two-year-old stepdaughter of defendant answered, "Daddy"; admission approved; "[T]he tender age of the victim, her battered physical condition, the startling nature of the event and attendant hospital trip and examination, and the fact that the response was elicited in connection with the child's fear of further injury resulted in the response having been made under the stress of the excitement caused by the event, and created sufficient indicia of reliability to qualify the response as an excited utterance such as to overcome both the hearsay and right of confrontation objections."); State v. Smith, 315 N.C. 76, 337 S.E.2d 833 (1985) (descriptive statements volunteered by four- and five-year-old children to grandmother two or three days after sexual assault, one girl saying she was "scared," admitted as excited utterances); State v. Wallace, 37 Ohio St.3d 87, 524 N.E.2d 466 (1988) (in felonious assault prosecution, statements of five-year-old, drifting in and out of consciousness, in response to questions by a social worker fifteen hours after assault, properly admitted as excited utterances, even though the child was not competent to testify at trial); Beavers v. State, 709 P.2d 702, 704 (Okl.Crim.1985) (statements by ten- and eleven-year-old girls to their mothers "when the girls were dropped off at their apartments by appellant" held admissible); Richardson v. Green, 677 S.W.2d 497, 500 (Tex.1984) (statement by three-year-old boy; "A hearsay statement by a small child may be admitted as res gestae if the usual requirements are shown, that is, the statement was a spontaneous utterance made under the immediate influence of an exciting event. * * * Spontaneity was not established. The alleged abuse preceded the statements by several days and the claimed spontaneous statement resulted from questions long after the event."); King v. State, 631 S.W.2d 486, 493 (Tex.Crim.App.) ("the authorities make it clear that the fact that a statement is a response to a question is but one factor to consider in determining its spontaneity"), cert. denied, 459 U.S. 928, 103 S.Ct. 238, 74 L.Ed.2d 188 (1982); State v. Bouchard, 31 Wash.App. 381, 639 P.2d 761, 763 (1982) (statements by three-old-child, in response "to the mother's inquiries as to how the blood got in the little girl's pants," admissible as excited utterances); and State v. Padilla, 110 Wis.2d 414, 329 N.W.2d 263 (App.1982) (upholding admission of statement of ten-year-old girl to mother three days after the last of three sexual assaults).

STATE v. HAFFORD, 410 A.2d 219, 220–21 (Me.1980) "We interpret the presiding justice's admission of evidence of Cook's statement under the *res gestae* doctrine as an invocation of the 'excited utterance' exception to the hearsay rule. See M.R.Evid. 802, 803(2). * * *

* * *

"Although no error was committed in admitting the statement, we take this occasion to express our disapproval of the use of the term *res gestae.* As stated in 6 Wigmore, Evidence § 1767, at 255 (Chadbourne rev.1976):

> The phrase res gestae has long been not only entirely useless, but even positively harmful. It is useless, because every rule of evidence to which it has ever been applied exists as a part of some other well-established principle and can be explained in the terms of that principle. It is harmful, because by its ambiguity it invites the confusion of one rule with another and thus creates uncertainty as to the limitations of both. It ought therefore wholly to be repudiated as a vicious element in our legal phraseology.

See also Morgan, 'A Suggested Classification of Utterances Admissible as Res Gestae,' 31 Yale L.J. 229, 229 (1922). Since the promulgation of the Rules of Evidence in 1976, we look there to determine when hearsay may be received in evidence. Rule 802 specifically declares that '[h]earsay is not admissible except as provided by law or by these rules.'

"Although many of our pre-Rules cases have in terms discussed the '*res gestae* exception,' * * * and although Rule 803(2) was intended to codify the decisional law as developed in that line of cases, see Advisors' Note to Rule 803, Field & Murray, infra at 202–03, the drafters of our Rules of Evidences specifically avoided using the term *res gestae* in order to expunge that phrase from our Maine law of evidence. See Field & Murray, Maine Evidence § 803.2 (1976). Continued use of that label by the bench and bar would serve only to confuse and mislead."

STATE v. LENARCHICK, 74 Wis.2d 425, 247 N.W.2d 80, 93 (1976). "Nolte was also allowed to testify that, shortly after the stabbing, a person known as Popeye stated, 'Joe really fucked Williams up bad.' This evidence was objected to on the single ground that there was no evidence to show that the witness Popeye actually witnessed the event to which his declaration related.

"The declaration was admitted as a *res gestae* statement. Under the Code of Evidence, the *res gestae* exception to the hearsay rule is denominated an excited utterance. The rule is codified in sec. 908.-03(2), Stats. The rule permits such utterance as an exception to the hearsay rule:

> 'A statement relating to a startling event or condition made while the declarant was under the stress of excitement caused by the event or condition.'

"There is no independent evidence to show that Popeye in fact observed the stabbing. However, the rule quoted above does not require such independent evidence. McCormick's observations are in accord with the conclusion that personal observation of a startling event is not required if the declarant is under the influence of the startling event. He states:

> 'Under generally prevailing practice, the declaration itself is taken as sufficient proof of the exciting event and therefore the declaration is admissible despite absence of other proof that an exciting event occurred. * * * Nor is it necessary that he have actually observed the event. * * *.' McCormick, Evidence (2d ed.), sec. 297, p. 705.

"It is reasoned that the inference that the declarant saw the event should be permitted from the utterance itself and from the circumstances in which it was given. The rationale of the excited-utterance exception is that the utterance stems from the nonrational, and thus objectively truthful, process of the person at the event. Accordingly, it belies the rationale of the exception to conclude that the declarant made the excited utterance on the basis of an event of which he had no knowledge."

SECTION 8. PRESENT SENSE IMPRESSION *

[FED.R.EVID. 803(1)]

HOUSTON OXYGEN CO. v. DAVIS

Commission of Appeals of Texas, 1942.
139 Tex. 1, 161 S.W.2d 474.

TAYLOR, COMMISSIONER.

Pearl Davis, joined by her present husband, Johnie Davis, filed this suit against Houston Oxygen Company, Inc., and Oliver O. Stanbury, for damages for injuries sustained by Charles Applebhy, Pearl's minor son * * *.

* * *

Defendants contend that the courts below erred in holding inadmissible a statement offered by them, made (according to their testimony) by Mrs. Sally Cooper shortly before the accident occurred. Mrs. Cooper testified that on the date of the accident a Plymouth car headed north

* See McCormick, Evidence § 271 (4th ed. 1992); Waltz, The Present Sense Impression Exception to the Rule Against Hearsay: Origins and Attributes, 66 Iowa L.Rev. 869 (1981).

on state highway No. 35 (in which the minor and several other colored passengers were riding) passed her about four or five miles from the scene of the accident; that she at the time was driving a car in the same direction on the highway and that Jack Sanders and M.C. Cooper, her brother-in-law, were passengers with her. Sanders testified the Plymouth passed them on a curve of the highway, rough and uneven at that point, travelling "sixty or sixty-five miles" an hour, about four miles from the scene of the accident and that as it went out of sight it was "bouncing up and down in the back and zig zagging." When Sanders was asked if anyone in the car made any statement as the Plymouth went by, plaintiffs objected. Defendants' bill of exception discloses that the excluded statement of Mrs. Cooper, made just after the Plymouth passed by, was, as testified to by Sanders for inclusion in the bill, "they must have been drunk, that we would find them somewhere on the road wrecked if they kept that rate of speed up." * * *

* * *

We have concluded, though the question is not free from difficulty, that the statement of Mrs. Cooper was admissible; that the trial court erred in not admitting the proffered testimony of Cooper and Sanders that Mrs. Cooper made it, and in not permitting Mrs. Cooper herself to testify she made the statement; and that the Court of Civil Appeals erred in sustaining the trial court's ruling holding the statement was hearsay. Missouri Pac. R. Co. et al. v. Collier, 62 Tex. 318; Gulf, C. & S.F. Ry. Co. v. Compton, 75 Tex. 667, 13 S.W. 667; Beaumont, S.L. & W.R. Co. v. Schmidt, 123 Tex. 580, 72 S.W.2d 899; St. Louis, B. & M.R. Co. v. Watkins, Tex.Civ.App., 245 S.W. 794, writ dismissed; Missouri, K. & T. Ry. Co. v. Vance, Tex.Civ.App., 41 S.W. 167; McCormick & Ray's Texas Law of Evidence, p. 548, sec. 430. It is sufficiently spontaneous to save it from the suspicion of being manufactured evidence. There was no time for a calculated statement. McCormick & Ray in the section cited say: "In one class of cases the requirement of spontaneity is somewhat attenuated. If a person observes some situation or happening which is not at all startling or shocking in its nature, nor actually producing excitement in the observer, the observer may yet have occasion to comment on what he sees (or learns from other senses) at the very time that he is receiving the impression. Such a comment, as to a situation then before the declarant, does not have the safeguard of impulse, emotion, or excitement, but there are other safeguards. In the first place, the report at the moment of the thing then seen, heard, etc., is safe from any error from defect of memory of the declarant. Secondly, there is little or no time for calculated misstatement, and thirdly, the statement will usually be made to another (the witness who reports it) who would have equal opportunities to observe and hence to check a misstatement. Consequently, it is believed that such comments, strictly limited, to reports of present sense-impressions, have such exceptional reliability as to warrant their inclusion within the hearsay exception for Spontaneous Declarations."

* * *

The statement of Mrs. Cooper is not one the evidential value of which is purely cumulative, nor is it such as to relegate the determination of its admissibility to the trial court's discretion. Rather it was one in which the witness was alluding to an occurrence within her own knowledge in language calculated to make her "meaning clearer to the jury" than would a mere expression of opinion as to the speed at which the passing car was moving. The Collier, Compton and Vance cases, supra. We find neither in the statement nor in the circumstances under which it was made (if it was) any basis upon which to invoke the discretion of the trial court as to its admissibility. It is competent evidence the consideration of which, since it is relevant and not merely cumulative, is determinable as a matter of law under an established rule of evidence. Authorities cited supra. The inference to be drawn as to whether the statement was made, and the inferences flowing from it (if made) are solely for the jury, and the trial court erred in excluding the testimony from its consideration.

Defendants contend the making of the statement was too remote in point of time. Had it been made under the stress of emotion, or if the party seeking the benefit of its admission were the one who made it, a different question would be presented. See illustrations referred to in cases noted under the text in McCormick & Ray, sec. 431, pp. 550, 551. It is stated in Vol. 17, Tex.Jur. pp. 623, 624, sec. 262, in discussing the element of time as affecting the admissibility of res gestae statements, that "if they sprang out of the principal transaction (wreck, in the present case), tend to explain it and were voluntary and spontaneous, and made at a time so near it as to preclude the idea of deliberate design, they may be regarded as contemporaneous in point of time and are admissible"; and, further, that "the declarations * * * may either precede the * * * transaction in question, or follow it," citing Gulf, C. & S.F. Ry. Co. v. Compton, 75 Tex. 667, 13 S.W. 667, and other cases in which the point of time preceded the accident. Certainly the statement in the present case (made, if it was, about four miles before the witness reached the scene of the collision) was not so remote in point of time as to be without relevance to its cause. The Court of Civil Appeals erred in affirming the action of the trial court in excluding the testimony. Authorities cited above and McGowen v. McGowen, 52 Tex. 657.

* * *

The judgment of the Court of Civil Appeals affirming that of the trial court is reversed and the case is remanded for another trial.

Opinion adopted by the Supreme Court.

Note

In United States v. Phelps, 572 F.Supp. 262 (E.D.Ky.1983), the court excluded Phelps' offer of his own statement to officers, "That is my gym bag, but Taylor put it in the trunk." The subject matter of the statement "was not what the declarant was presently perceiving when the statement was made, but rather something which had occurred at a remote previous time, namely whenever the gym bag was placed in the trunk." Id. at 265.

SECTION 9. STATEMENTS FOR PURPOSES OF MEDICAL DIAGNOSIS OR TREATMENT *

[FED.R.EVID. 803(4)]

STATE v. MOEN

Supreme Court of Oregon, 1990.
309 Or. 45, 786 P.2d 111.

JONES, JUSTICE.

This is a criminal case in which the defendant seeks reversal of his conviction of the offense of aggravated murder. In the alternative, he requests that his death sentence be vacated.

SUMMARY OF FACTS

Guilt Phase

The bodies of Hazel Chatfield and Judith Moen were found in Hazel Chatfield's residence on Friday, March 14, 1986, by a neighbor and two friends.

Dr. Karen Gunson, the medical examiner, testified that both victims died of gunshot wounds to the head. In addition to the fatal wound to the head, Judith Moen had been shot in the chest after death had occurred. Dr. Gunson also found some bruises and other minor injuries on Judith Moen. The time of death was estimated to be Thursday night or some time before then.

The police officers and crime laboratory technicians found that some areas of the house had been ransacked, but discounted theories of burglary because a portable television and stereo were not taken. Further, no footprints were found in soft soil outside what the officers otherwise might have treated as a suspected entry point. The spent bullets from what appeared to be the fatal gunshots were recovered and all three had eight lands and grooves with a right-hand twist and appeared to have been fired from a .38 caliber revolver.

The state's theory was that defendant had killed Judith Moen during a domestic quarrel and that he had killed Hazel Chatfield when she became involved in the dispute. Blood splatter evidence indicated that some injury had occurred to Judith Moen on her bed, that she had been upright and mobile at some time while bleeding, then was shot through the head, moved, and shot again through the chest. The second gunshot wound probably occurred one-half hour or longer after the first gunshot wound to Judith Moen. Other physical evidence indicated that Hazel Chatfield may have been holding a towel to one of

* See 6 Wigmore, Evidence §§ 1718–1723 (Chadbourn rev. 1976); McCormick, Evidence ch. 27 (4th ed. 1992); Mosteller, Child Sexual Abuse and Statements for the Purpose of Medical Diagnosis or Treatment, 67 N.C.L.Rev. 257 (1989).

Judity Moen's wounds when she was shot. All of the blood samples taken from the residence were matched to Judith Moen.

The police investigation focused on defendant because he had been seen with Judith Moen on Wednesday evening, March 12, 1986, at approximately 9:30 to 10:00 at a local restaurant.

When questioned by police after the crime, defendant had a mark on his left hand and made a statement to the officers that a dog had bitten him. A dentist made casts of the victims' teeth and a veterinarian took tooth impressions of several dogs known to have been in contact with defendant during the relevant times. Those casts were submitted to Dr. Gary Bell, who was presented to the court as a specialist in forensic dentistry. Dr. Bell concluded that the tooth mark or teeth marks on defendant's hand were consistent with Hazel Chatfield's teeth and that neither Judith Moen nor any of the three dogs examined could have caused the mark.

Through a series of transactions, defendant had been in possession of a .38 caliber revolver known as an RG38s, and the state presented evidence that the bullets that killed the victims came from that weapon.

The remainder of the state's case focused on actions by defendant that the state characterized as suspicious, such as taking a raincoat to be cleaned and washing his hands with gasoline, and on statements made by defendant or by the victims.

Dr. Daniel Mulkey testified that he treated Hazel Chatfield from August 1985 up to and including visits on February 11 and March 11, 1986. During the latter two visits, Mrs. Chatfield complained of depression and despondency since her daughter and son-in-law (defendant) had moved into her home. Mrs. Chatfield appeared agitated, anxious, nervous, very tearful, and crying. Dr. Mulkey attempted to treat her for a potentially fatal lesion but, because of her situation at home, was unable to convince her that she needed treatment. Dr. Mulkey further testified that Mrs. Chatfield told him that she was upset about her daughter and son-in-law, that her son-in-law had been physically abusive to her daughter, and that "she felt he might kill them both." Dr. Mulkey diagnosed her condition as situational depression and recommended that defendant be removed from the home.

* * *

Defendant argues that Dr. Mulkey's testimony concerning Hazel Chatfield's statements should not have been admitted under OEC 803(4) because: (1) "the declarant's motivation for giving the information is highly suspect," and (2) the doctor "did not specifically rely upon the statement[s] as reasonably pertinent to his diagnosis of depression."

OEC 803(4) recognizes a hearsay exception for statements made for the purposes of medical diagnosis or treatment. The rule provides:

> "The following are not excluded by [OEC 802, the general rule against the admission of hearsay], even though the declarant is available as a witness:
>
> "* * *
>
> "(4) Statements made for purposes of medical diagnosis or treatment and describing medical history, or past or present symptoms, pain or sensations, or the inception or general character of the cause [or] external source thereof insofar as reasonably pertinent to diagnosis or treatment."

The Legislative Commentary to the rule states, in pertinent part:

> "In this subsection, an exception to the hearsay rule is created for statements made for the purposes of medical diagnosis or treatment. Several changes to Oregon law result.
>
> "Even those few jurisdictions which have shied away from admitting statements of present condition generally, see [OEC] 803(3), supra, have allowed them if made to a person for the purpose of diagnosis or treatment in view of the declarant's strong motivation to be truthful. McCormick[, Evidence,] section 292 at 690. The guaranty of trustworthiness extends to statements of past condition made for the purpose of diagnosis or treatment, i.e., medical history, although until now Oregon courts have not accepted this. See *Reid v. Yellow Cab Co.,* 131 Or 27, 279 P 635 (1929). The guaranty also extends to statements regarding causation of a condition, if reasonably pertinent, in accord with the current trend. *Shell Oil Co. v. Industrial Commission,* 2 Ill.2d 590, 119 NE2d 224 (1954); McCormick[, Evidence,] section 292 at 691, 692; New Jersey Evidence Rule 63(12)(c).
>
> "Statements as to fault ordinarily would not qualify under the language of this subsection. Thus, a statement that the declarant was struck by an automobile would not be excluded, as touching causation; a statement that the car was driven through a red light would [be excluded], as touching fault."

Professor Laird Kirkpatrick explains that "[t]he rationale underlying this exception is that the patient's desire for proper treatment or diagnosis outweighs any motive to falsify." Kirkpatrick, Oregon Evidence 361 (1982).

Judge Weinstein, referring to the identical hearsay exception under the Federal Rules of Evidence, FRE 803(4), suggests a second policy ground for the admissibility of these statements, *i.e.,* "a fact reliable enough to serve as the basis for a diagnosis is also reliable enough to escape hearsay proscription." 4 Weinstein & Berger, Weinstein's Evidence 803–146 (1988).

To be admissible under OEC 803(4), a statement must meet three requirements:

(a) The statement must be "made for purposes of medical diagnosis or treatment";

(b) The statement must describe or relate "medical history, or past or present symptoms, pain or sensations, or the inception or general character of the cause [or] external source thereof";

(c) The statement must be "reasonably pertinent to diagnosis or treatment."

The challenged testimony in this case satisfies these criteria:

a. *Were Hazel Chatfield's statements "made for purposes of medical diagnosis [and] treatment"?*

Mrs. Chatfield's motive in making the statements at issue must necessarily be determined by reference to the circumstances in which they were made. As explained in 4 Louisell & Mueller, Federal Evidence 593–94, § 444 (1980) (concerning the identical federal provision):

> "The principal reason for admitting statements made for purposes of obtaining medical treatment is that they are considered trustworthy. *Usually such statements are made by the patient to his physician, and usually they describe the patient's own past and present physical sensations, and things which happened to him personally.* Thus, risks of misperception and of faulty memory are minimal. Moreover, the patient will understand that his description is important in determining the treatment he will receive, so he has every reason to speak not only truthfully, but carefully, so that the risks of insincerity and ambiguity are likewise minimal." (Emphasis added; footnote omitted.)

On February 11, 1986, Mrs. Chatfield came to her physician's as a patient as "part of a routine follow up for high blood pressure and some other medical problems." She was so "anxious" and "extremely nervous" that Dr. Mulkey could not conduct the planned interview and she "indicated" to him for the first time "that she was suffering from depression or anxiety." When she first referred to her son-in-law's presence in her home, she did so only in response to Dr. Mulkey's question why she was depressed. When he saw her as a patient one month later, she exhibited symptoms "absolutely" associated with extreme depression and was so emotionally distressed that, as before, Dr. Mulkey was unable to talk with her about other medical problems, one of which was "potentially life-threatening." Through his professional training and practice, he knew the symptoms of depression and anxiety and previously had diagnosed her as suffering from situational depression. In this context, Mrs. Chatfield again talked with Dr. Mulkey about defendant's presence in her home, his abusive conduct, and her resulting fears. He determined that she still suffered from the illness of depression and prescribed anti-depressant medication and defendant's removal from the home.

Mrs. Chatfield made these statements as a patient to her treating physician during regularly scheduled visits to his office. The statements related directly to the severe emotional distress that she was suffering at the time of those visits. The depression that she experienced is a medically recognized illness that her physician had the training and experience to diagnose *and* to treat. Her complaints focused on her feelings of depression. Dr. Mulkey responded to her statements with clinical inquiries, a medical diagnosis, and a prescribed course of treatment.

The trial court was entitled to conclude that the statements in question were "made for purposes of medical diagnosis [and] treatment."

b. *Was the subject matter of the statements proper?*

Mrs. Chatfield's statements to her physician quite clearly described "the inception or general character of the cause [or] external source" of her continuing depression. Defendant does not contend otherwise.

c. *Were Mrs. Chatfield's statements "reasonably pertinent" to diagnosis and treatment?*

OEC 803(4) authorizes the admission of a patient's out-of-court statements (made for purposes of diagnosis or treatment) to her physician concerning "the inception or general character of the *cause* [or] external *source* " of her condition, to the extent that such information is "*reasonably* pertinent to [the physician's] diagnosis or treatment." (Emphasis added.) The commentary to the rule confirms the reliability of statements satisfying that condition, *i.e.:*

> "The guaranty [of trustworthiness] also extends to statements regarding *causation of a condition,* if reasonably pertinent, in accord with the current trend." (Emphasis added.)

In this case, Mrs. Chatfield gave Dr. Mulkey information concerning the *cause* of her depression and, in doing so, identified defendant. Defendant argues that such statements are "accusations of personal fault" and not reasonably pertinent to diagnosis or treatment. Defendant's argument ignores the wording of OEC 803(4). OEC 803(4) expressly authorizes the admission of statements concerning the "cause [or] external source" of an illness, provided the statements are "made for purposes of medical diagnosis or treatment" and are "reasonably pertinent" to either endeavor. Mrs. Chatfield's statements concerning defendant communicated to Dr. Mulkey the ongoing *cause* of her situational depression. He used that information first, to diagnose, and, then, to treat her illness. The information and his professional skills permitted him to distinguish her depression from other forms of that illness and to prescribe specific treatment for it. The requirements of the rule are satisfied. The fact that the continuing cause of her illness was the presence and conduct of a named individual is not a basis for excluding the statements.

In interpreting an identical evidentiary rule, FRE 803(4), the leading federal decision is consistent with our analysis and conclusion. In *United States v. Renville,* 779 F.2d 430 (8th Cir.1985), an 11–year–old child was sexually abused by her stepfather. The defendant claimed that a doctor should not have been permitted to testify to statements of the victim, made during an examination, that identified the defendant as her abuser. He argued that FRE 803(4) did "not encompass statements of fault or identity made to medical personnel." 779 F.2d at 435–36. While acknowledging that such statements relating to identity ordinarily are not admissible, the court determined that where such statements were relevant to the physician's diagnosis or treatment, FRE 803(4) authorized their admission. Because the victim's statements were relevant for those purposes, the court held that their admission was proper. That court's analysis is applicable to this case:

> "The crucial question under the rule is whether the out-of-court statement of the declarant was 'reasonably pertinent' to diagnosis or treatment. In *United States v. Iron Shell,* 633 F.2d 77 (8th Cir.1980), *cert. denied* 450 U.S. 1001, 101 S.Ct. 1709, 68 L.Ed.2d 203 (1981), this court set forth a two-part test for the admissibility of hearsay statements under rule 803(4): first, the declarant's motive in making the statement must be consistent with the purposes of promoting treatment; and second, the content of the statement must be such as is reasonably relied on by a physician in treatment or diagnosis. *Id.* at 84. *See also Roberts v. Hollocher,* 664 F.2d 200, 204 (8th Cir.1981). The test reflects the twin policy justifications advanced to support the rule. First, it is assumed that a patient has a strong motive to speak truthfully and accurately because the treatment or diagnosis will depend in part upon the information conveyed. The declarant's motive thus provides a sufficient guarantee of trustworthiness to permit an exception to the hearsay rule. *Iron Shell,* 633 F.2d at 84. Second, we have recognized that 'a fact reliable enough to serve as the basis for a diagnosis is also reliable enough to escape hearsay proscription.' *Id.* * * *
>
> "* * *

"* * * We believe that a statement by a child abuse victim that the abuser is a member of the victim's immediate household presents a sufficiently different case from that envisaged by the drafters of rule 803(4) that it should not fall under the general rule. Statements by a child abuse victim to a physician during an examination that the abuser is a member of the victim's immediate household *are* reasonably pertinent to treatment.

> "* * *
>
> "* * * *Information that the abuser is a member of the household is therefore 'reasonably pertinent' to a course of treatment which includes removing the child from the home.*" 779 F.2d at 436–38 (first emphasis in original; second emphasis added).[4]

4. Many state courts have reached the same conclusion as the *Renville* court: *State v. Robinson,* 153 Ariz. 191, 735 P.2d 801 (1987) (while the official commentary to FRE 803(4) excludes attributions of fault from the category of admissible statements made to a treating physician, this concerns only somatic injuries, such as result from automobile accidents. In child sexual abuse cases statements concerning the assailant's identity are crucial to effective treatment of the psychological trauma of the abuse and to the prevention of future abuse); *Stallnacker v. State,* 19 Ark.App. 9, 715 S.W.2d 883 (1986) (because there was a need to prevent recurring abuse and to treat the child emotionally, the child's statements identifying her father as the abuser were admissible); *Oldsen v. People,* 732 P.2d 1132 (Colo.1986) (because the child victim was found to be incompetent

Admissibility of statements of the type challenged here is not limited to cases involving child abuse.

The testimony of Dr. Mulkey relating statements made to him by his patient, Mrs. Chatfield, concerning defendant's presence and conduct in her home was admissible under OEC 803(4) against defendant's hearsay objection.

* * *

The judgment is affirmed as to the guilt phase and reversed as to the penalty phase, and the case is remanded to the circuit court for further proceedings consistent with this opinion.

FADELEY, J., filed a dissenting opinion in which LINDE, J., joined.

FADELEY, JUSTICE, dissenting.

* * *

None of the authorities cited by the majority are about a statement used to prove the intent or identity of a future, but predicted, homicide. No authority can be found to support admission under the diagnosis and treatment exception, to prove a future event. Rather, the authorities cited, or which can be found, require that the declaration of the patient be about past causation of a currently existing condition. At most, the declaration, under those authorities, would be admissible to prove that the mother-in-law's existing condition of depression was caused by fear of her son-in-law. These cases do not support admission of a prediction of who will commit a future crime as to which there can be no present motive to be truthful to obtain proper treatment. These cases are not at all about an accusation that "He will kill me" in the future. Nor do they involve declarants who told the doctor-witness "No, he has never abused me."

* * *

The *Renville* court justified a special exception from the restrictions of FRE 803(4) upon which the majority seizes and expands. A treatment statement normally may not be used for attributing past fault. The special exception is for "a statement of a child abuse victim that the abuser is a member of the victim's immediate household." 779 F.2d at 436. The majority quotes this special exception but, then, without any analysis whatever or citation of any authority, states as a holding that:

> "Admissibility of statements of the type challenged here is not limited to cases involving child abuse." At 59, 786 P.2d at 120.

The cases relied upon by the majority in footnote 4 do not support the misapplication of the rule by the majority. Rather, they are about

to testify and because the proponent of the hearsay testimony could produce no other evidence that the child was capable of recognizing the need to prove accurate information for purposes of diagnosis or treatment, the child's statements to the treating physician were admissible under Rule 803(4)); *but see People v. Lalone,* 432 Mich. 103, 437 N.W.2d 611 (1989).

identifying the perpetrator of child sex abuse which has occurred within a family. * * *

JOHNSON v. STATE, 579 P.2d 20, 21–22 (Alaska 1978). "On December 30, 1975, Mrs. Johnson was taken by ambulance to the emergency room at Mt. Edgecumbe Hospital. She was attended by Vera Marvin who found Mrs. Johnson having trouble breathing and in considerable pain. Initially, due to the extent of her injuries, Ms. Marvin thought that Mrs. Johnson might have been run over by an automobile. In answer to inquiries, however, Mrs. Johnson indicated that she had been at a house party and was beaten by another man. Ms. Marvin testified:

> I think that both the doctor and myself, you know it was hard to believe that it was done by a person, by beating because it looked like a car ran over her and we kept asking—I kept asking Elizabeth so finally I told Elizabeth the doctor has to know what happened to you. And like I said, it looked like a car ran over her, so finally she took my wrist and pulled me over by her and she said I promised that, I promised my husband that I wouldn't tell who did it, that the story that they told was the story that they were going to stick to. She told me then that her husband beat her. Then I turned around and told the doctor and Mrs. Vinsant he had beat her.

Subsequently, Mrs. Johnson gave Dr. Silver essentially the same information.

"The trial judge denied the motion to suppress this testimony based on an exception to the hearsay rule for statements made for the purpose of medical diagnosis or treatment. * * *

"Statements of a patient as to presently existing body conditions are generally admitted as evidence of the facts stated because there is a high likelihood of truthfulness resulting from the patient's belief that the doctor will rely on such statements in his diagnosis and treatment. Where statements going to the cause of a patient's condition relate information desirable for diagnosis and treatment, they are also admissible based on the same indicia of reliability. Thus, the trial court was correct in admitting Mrs. Johnson's statements as to the general cause of her condition. The statements, however, also revealed the identity of her alleged assailant. This information did not relate to diagnosis or treatment, and as to that portion of the statements, the court's denial of the motion to suppress was erroneous. The situation presents the same distinction identified by McCormick and the commentary on the Federal Rules of Evidence, between general statements made going to the cause of injury which are important to diagnosis and treatment, and statements entering the realm of fixing fault. Since statements fixing fault and indicating the identity of an assailant are not relevant to medical diagnosis or treatment, they lack assurances of reliability and should be excluded."

O'GEE v. DOBBS HOUSES, INC., 570 F.2d 1084 2d Cir.1978). "Prior to the adoption of the Federal Rules of Evidence, a non-treating doctor such as Dr. Koven would have been permitted to recite his patient's statements to him, not as proof of the facts stated, but only to show the basis of his opinion. W. McCormick, Evidence § 267 (1954). The Federal Rules, however, rejected this distinction as being too esoteric for a jury to recognize. 4 Weinstein & Berger, Evidence ¶ 803(4)[01]. Rule 803(4) clearly permits the admission into evidence of what O'Gee told Dr. Koven about her condition, so long as it was relied on by Dr. Koven in formulating his opinion—a foundation that was properly laid."

SECTION 10. THEN EXISTING MENTAL, EMOTIONAL OR PHYSICAL CONDITION *

[FED.R.EVID. 803(3)]

CASUALTY INSURANCE CO. v. SALINAS

Supreme Court of Texas, 1960.
160 Tex. 445, 333 S.W.2d 109.

NORVELL, JUSTICE.

This is a workmen's compensation case in which the Court of Civil Appeals sustained the sole point contained in appellant's brief and reversed the judgment of the trial court because of the exclusion of evidence proffered by the plaintiff, Martin A. Salinas. See, Salinas v. Casualty Insurance Company of California, Tex.Civ.App., 323 S.W.2d 600.

* * * Salinas, while employed by Howel Refining Company was injured when a fellow workman dropped a large bolt upon his right shoulder. He claimed a temporary total incapacity, and a permanent partial incapacity of thirty per cent. The jury found, however, that the partial incapacity was limited to 52 weeks.

Upon the trial, Salinas testified as to his injury, the extent and duration of a disabling pain in his shoulder and back, and maintained that such pain persisted to the date of trial. Two doctors testifying for the insurance carrier stated that Salinas was not seriously injured, had suffered little or no pain except for a short period after the injury, and in effect was malingering. To offset this medical testimony, Salinas called three lay witnesses and tendered proof that Salinas had complained of present existing pain at various times subsequent to his injury. The trial court excluded this testimony.

* See 6 Wigmore, Evidence §§ 1714–1719, 1725–1740 (Chadbourn rev. 1976); McCormick, Evidence §§ 269, 273–276 (4th ed. 1992); Hinton, States of Mind and the Hearsay Rule, 1 U.Chi.L.Rev. 394 (1934).

* * *

Upon consideration of the merits of the case, our investigation has led us to the conclusion that the overwhelming weight of American authority supports the position of the Court of Civil Appeals in holding that Salinas' proffered witnesses should have been permitted to testify as to his complaints of presently existing pain. In Roth v. Travelers' Protective Ass'n of America, 1909, 102 Tex. 241, 115 S.W. 31, 35, cited by the Court of Civil Appeals, Mr. Justice Brown, writing for this Court, carefully considered numerous items of evidence in connection with various objections made thereto. It was held that the following statement of a witness was admissible, viz.:

> "He was not so talkative as he had been. Mr. Roth (the injured person) complained each day while he was with me, and said that he was feeling badly, and told me that his head hurt him."

In Northern Pacific Railroad Company v. Urlin, 1894, 158 U.S. 271, 15 S.Ct. 840, 842, 39 L.Ed. 977, the Supreme Court of the United States quoted the following with approval from Fleming v. City of Springfield, 154 Mass. 520, 28 N.E. 910:

> "The declarations of a party himself, to whomsoever made, are competent evidence, when confined strictly to such complaints, expressions, and exclamations as furnish evidence of a present, existing pain or malady, to prove his condition, ills, pains, and symptoms, whether arising from sickness, or from an injury by accident or violence."

This matter is fully covered by Dean Wigmore and it appears that statements of existing bodily pain have been recognized as an exception to the hearsay rule since the early part of the 19th century. The basis for the exception is stated by Wigmore with a wealth of supporting authorities as follows:

> "Applied specifically to the present Exception, the judicial doctrine has been that there is a fair necessity for lack of other better evidence, for resorting to a person's own contemporary statements of his mental or physical condition. It is indeed possible to obtain by circumstantial evidence (chiefly of conduct) some knowledge of a human being's internal state of pain, emotion, motive, design, and the like; but in directness, amount, and value, this source of evidence must usually be decidedly inferior to the person's own contemporary assertions of those conditions. It might be argued, however, that the person's own statements on the stand would amply satisfy the need for his testimonial evidence. The answer is that statements of this sort on the stand, where there is ample opportunity for deliberate misrepresentation and small means for checking it by other evidence or testing it by cross-examination, are comparatively inferior to statements made at times when circumstances lessened the possible inducement to misrepresentation." Wigmore on Evidence (3rd Ed.) § 1714.

* * *

Statements of existing bodily pain need not be made to a physician in order to be admissible, Wigmore (3rd Ed.) § 1719, although this circumstance may have some bearing upon the weight given the declaration by a jury. Northern Pacific Railroad Co. v. Urlin, supra, nor is it essential that the expression of pain concerning which testimony is offered be of an involuntary nature such as a scream or a groan or the like. A verbal and articulate statement of complaint comes within the exception to the hearsay rule. Wigmore (3rd Ed.) § 1719.

* * *

The judgment of the Court of Civil Appeals is affirmed.

ADKINS v. BRETT

Supreme Court of California, 1920.
184 Cal. 252, 193 P. 251.

OLNEY, J.

The action involved in the present appeal is one for damages for the alienation by the defendant of the plaintiff's wife. The cause was tried before a jury, a verdict was returned for the plaintiff, and from the judgment entered upon the verdict the defendant appeals.

* * *

The serious questions in the case arise in connection with the admission of evidence of conversations between the plaintiff and his wife, wherein the latter admitted or stated that she had gone automobile riding with the defendant, had dined with him, had received flowers from him, that he was able to give her a good time, and the plaintiff was not, that she intended to continue to accept the defendant's attentions and the plaintiff could do what he pleased about it, and that he was distasteful to her.

* * *

The real objection to such evidence as that under consideration is that it is hearsay. The evidence was plainly relevant; that is, it tended to prove matters in issue, and was therefore admissible unless there is some rule of exclusion applicable to it. The only rule of exclusion to which it can be subject is the rule against hearsay. The evidence was, in fact, hearsay, both as to the past matters stated in the conversations and as to the wife's statements of her then feelings toward the plaintiff and the defendant. But the rule is thoroughly well settled that, when the intention, feelings or other mental state of a certain person at a particular time, including his bodily feelings, is material to the issues under trial, evidence of such person's declarations at the time indicative of his then mental state, even though hearsay, is competent as within an exception to the hearsay rule. In the present case the state of the wife's feelings at the time of these conversations, both toward her husband and toward the defendant, was material, and the conversations were indicative of her feelings, and, this being so, evidence of them was admissible to show her then state of feelings. This much can hardly be questioned, in view of the settled character of the general rule just stated, its plain applicability to just such cases as the present, and the fact that it has very generally been so applied. See Cripe v. Cripe, 170 Cal. 91, 148 P. 520, and authorities there cited; 13 R.C.L. 1477; 21 Cyc. 1624.

The difficulty in regard to such declarations as those involved here lies in the fact that, while they may be competent upon the point of the wife's feelings, they go very much further. They contain statements as to matters such as automobile rides, dinners, flowers, and attentions generally by the defendant to the wife, as proof of which the statements are not within any exception to the hearsay rule and are wholly incompetent. The situation is intensified by the fact that those matters are themselves material to the issues, and, if true, very detrimental to the defendant, so that the admission of the evidence involves the placing before the jury of evidence tending to prove matters in issue, for proving which such evidence is not competent, and the proof of which is very prejudicial to the party against whom it is introduced.

Nevertheless it is clear enough that the evidence, competent for the purpose of showing the state of the wife's feelings, is not rendered incompetent by the fact that it also tends to prove other material matters, to prove which it is not competent. The rule upon this point, which is one of well-nigh every-day application in actual trial, is thus stated by Wigmore (volume 1, p. 42):

> "In other words, when an evidentiary fact is offered for one purpose, and becomes admissible by satisfying all the rules applicable to it in that capacity, it is not inadmissible because it does not satisfy the rules applicable to it in some other capacity, and because the jury might improperly consider it in the latter capacity. This doctrine, although involving certain risks, is indispensable as a practical rule."

Cripe v. Cripe, supra, is an illustration of this. A father was sued by the wife of his son for the alienation from her of the son, and at the trial the following question was asked of the father as a witness:

> "After the marriage of your son and daughter, and before Dolly [the son's wife] left the ranch at Huasua in August, 1911, did your son ever tell you that Dolly drank to such an extent that he could not control her, or did he ever tell you during that time that she abused him so bad that he could not live with her?"

It is plain that as to the facts that the wife drank to excess and abused her husband, so that he could not live with her, the evidence was hearsay, was not within any exception to the hearsay rule, and was wholly incompetent, and at the same time those facts were material to the case, and, if true, very detrimental to the cause of the wife, so that the introduction of the evidence would be very prejudicial to her as to facts which the evidence was wholly incompetent to prove. Nevertheless the question was held to be proper, and the refusal of the trial court to permit it to be answered reversible error, on the ground that the testimony which it called for was competent to show the state of the son's feelings.

The rule, then, is that the admissibility of such evidence as that under discussion, admissible because competent as to one point, is not destroyed by its incompetency as to other points which it yet logically tends to prove. The danger, however, of the jury misusing such evidence and giving it weight in determining the points as to which it is incompetent is manifest. In such a situation, as Prof. Wigmore puts it immediately following the quotation already made, "the only question can be what the proper means are for avoiding the risk of misusing the evidence." Answering this question, Prof. Wigmore says:

> "It is uniformly conceded that the instruction [to the jury] of the court [that the evidence is competent only as proof of one point and must not be considered as proof of others] suffices for that purpose; and the better opinion is that the opponent of the evidence must ask for that instruction; otherwise he may be supposed to have waived it as unnecessary for his protection."

The general correctness of this statement cannot be doubted. But we doubt if the learned author intended to say more than that the opponent of such evidence is always entitled to such an instruction for his protection, if he asks for it, and that generally it will suffice. But it is not difficult to imagine cases where it would not suffice, and the opponent could justly ask for more. The matter is largely one of discretion on the part of the trial judge. If the point to prove which the evidence is competent can just as well be proven by other evidence, or if it is of but slight weight or importance upon that point, the trial judge might well be justified in excluding it entirely, because of its prejudicial and dangerous character as to other points. A number of the authorities cited by defendant's counsel are distinguishable from the present case upon this ground. This would emphatically be true where there is good reason for believing that the real object for which the evidence is offered is not to prove the point for which it is ostensibly offered and is competent, but is to get before the jury declarations as to other points, to prove which the evidence is incompetent. The same thing would be true as to the introduction of repeated declarations, when once the point for which they are competent has been amply shown. It may also be that the portions of the declaration which there is danger may be misused by the jury are not so interwoven with the balance of the declaration but that they can be disassociated from it without impairing the meaning or effect of the declaration for the purpose for which it is admissible. In such a case evidence of such portions of the declaration may be excluded on proper objection, when offered, if there is opportunity for such objection, or, if there is not, may be stricken out on motion subsequently. The point of the matter is that the opponent of such evidence, so likely to be misused against him, is entitled to such protection against its misuse as can reasonably be given him without impairing the ability of the other party to prove his case, or depriving him of the use of competent evidence reasonably necessary for that purpose.

The question, then, in the present case in connection with the evidence of declarations of the wife reduces itself to a question as to whether the defendant was properly protected from the danger of this evidence being misused by the jury, and considered by them as proof of matters other than that for proving which it was admitted. We think that there can be no doubt but that the defendant was not properly protected in this respect.

[The court reviewed the instructions given below and found them inadequate.]

Judgment reversed.

ELMER v. FESSENDEN

Supreme Judicial Court of Massachusetts, 1889.
151 Mass. 359, 24 N.E. 208.

This is an action of tort by Samuel Elmer against George R. Fessenden. The declaration, as amended, and answer are made part of these exceptions. At the trial, which was before a jury, the plaintiff introduced evidence tending to show that he was, during 1887, a manufacturer of whip-snaps from silk thread, in Ashfield, which thread his employes there resident were compelled to manipulate, and that in the month of June, 1887, the defendant, who was a physician in that town, had circulated the report that he had sent some of the silk thread used in the manufacture to the state board of health for analysis, and received from that board a report that it contained arsenic in sufficient quantities to be dangerous to the employes using it in the way they did. The witness who testified to these facts had also testified that he was, and had been from March, 1887, the agent of the plaintiff who superintended this business, and he was permitted, on the assurance of the plaintiff's counsel that he expected to prove later that certain of the employes, for the loss of whose services damages were specified in the declaration, had stopped work by reason of the statement of the defendant to them, above referred to, relative to the report of the board of health, to testify that these employes stopped work on the 11th day of June, 1887, for some time. The plaintiff then, to prove the reason why they stopped work, asked the witness "whether they gave any reason for stopping work." This question was excluded by the court. The plaintiff afterwards asked: "What, if anything, did they say as reason for stopping?" This question the court also excluded. * * * The plaintiff having duly excepted to the several exclusions of evidence above set forth, and the jury having returned a verdict for the defendant, the plaintiff brings exceptions.

HOLMES, J.

1. It was a part of the plaintiff's case that the cause of his workmen's leaving his employment was the defendant's false story. If, as may be assumed, the excluded testimony would have shown that the workmen, when they left, gave as their reason to the superintendent

that the defendant had told them that the board of health reported arsenic in the silk, the evidence was admissible to show that their belief in the presence of poison was their reason in fact. Lund v. Tyngsborough, 9 Cush. 36, 41, 43; Aveson v. Kinnaird, 6 East, 188, 193; Hadley v. Carter, 8 N.H. 40, 43; U.S. v. Penn, 13 N.B.R. 464, 467. We cannot follow the ruling at *nisi prius* in Tilk v. Parsons, 2 Car. & P. 201, that the testimony of the persons concerned is the only evidence to prove their motives. We rather agree with Mr. Starkie, that such declarations, made with no apparent motive for misstatement, may be better evidence of the maker's state of mind at the time than the subsequent testimony of the same persons. Starkie, Ev., 10th Amer.Ed., *89. As a rule, such declarations are not evidence of the past facts which they may recite. The cases in which they have been admitted to prove the cause of a wound or injury, when the declarations were made at the time, or immediately after the event, if not exceptions to the general rule, at least mark the limit of admissibility. Com. v. Hackett, 2 Allen, 136, 140; Com. v. McPike, 3 Cush. 184; Travelers' Insurance Co. v. Mosley, 8 Wall. 397, 19 L.Ed. 437. The excluded testimony was not competent to prove that the defendant did tell the workmen the story. As to that it was mere hearsay, and was not within the scope of the special reasons which led to the decisions last cited. Roosa v. Loan Co., 132 Mass. 439; Chapin v. Marlborough, 9 Gray, 244; Bacon v. Charlton, 7 Cush. 581, 586; Aveson v. Kinnaird, ubi supra; People v. Thornton, 74 Cal. 482, 486, 16 P. 244. It is admitted, however, that there was independent testimony that the defendant spoke to the workmen, and therefore the exceptions must be sustained.

* * *

ZIPPO MANUFACTURING CO. v. ROGERS IMPORTS, INC.

United States District Court, Southern District of New York, 1963.
216 F.Supp. 670.

FEINBERG, DISTRICT JUDGE.

This case involves the attempt of a manufacturer of a popular cigarette lighter to keep others from imitating the lighter's shape and appearance. Plaintiff Zippo Manufacturing Company ("Zippo"), a Pennsylvania corporation, alleges both trademark infringement and unfair competition on the part of defendant Rogers, Inc. ("Rogers"), a New York corporation, by reason of Rogers' sale of pocket lighters closely resembling Zippo's. * * *

* * *

Plaintiff has relied heavily on a consumer study to prove the elements of its case. This study was prepared and conducted by the sampling and market research firm of W.R. Simmons & Associates Research, Inc. Mr. Simmons, the head of this firm, and Donald F. Bowdren, the project supervisor, appeared as witnesses; both are qualified experts in the field of consumer surveys. Mr. Bowdren testified that the purpose of the study was to determine whether the physical attributes of the Zippo standard and slim-lighters serve as indicators of the source of the lighters to potential customers and whether the similar physical attributes of the Rogers lighters cause public confusion. The study or project consisted of three separate surveys. In Survey A, the respondents, or interviewees, were shown a Zippo standard lighter which had all the Zippo identification markings removed and were asked, among other things, what brand of lighter they thought it was and why. In Survey B, the same procedure was followed for the Zippo slim-lighter. In Survey C, respondents were shown a Rogers standard lighter that was being sold at the time of the survey, with all of its identifying markings and they were asked, among other things, what brand of lighter they thought it was and why.

* * *

Defendant objects to the admission of the surveys into evidence. It first contends that the surveys are hearsay. The weight of case authority, the consensus of legal writers, and reasoned policy considerations all indicate that the hearsay rule should not bar the admission of properly conducted public surveys. Although courts were at first reluctant to accept survey evidence or to give it weight, the more recent trend is clearly contrary. Surveys are not admitted over the hearsay objection on two technically distinct bases. Some cases hold that surveys are not hearsay at all; other cases hold that surveys are hearsay but are admissible because they are within the recognized exception to the hearsay rule for statements of present state of mind, attitude, or belief. Still other cases admit surveys without stating the ground on which they are admitted.

The cases holding that surveys are not hearsay do so on the basis that the surveys are not offered to prove the truth of what respondents said and, therefore, do not fall within the classic definition of hearsay. This approach has been criticized because, it is said, the answers to questions in a survey designed to prove the existence of a specific idea in the public mind are offered to prove the truth of the matter contained in these answers. Under this argument, when a respondent is asked to identify the brand of an unmarked lighter, the answer of each respondent who thinks the lighter is a Zippo is regarded as if he said, "I believe that this unmarked lighter is a Zippo." Since the matter to be proved in a secondary meaning case is respondent's belief that the lighter shown him is a Zippo lighter, a respondent's answer is hearsay in the classic sense. Others have criticized the non-hearsay characterization, regardless of whether surveys are offered to prove the truth of what respondents said, because the answers in a survey depend for their probative value on the sincerity of respondents. One of the purposes of the hearsay rule is to subject to cross-examination statements which depend on the declarant's narrative sincerity. See Morgan, Hearsay Dangers and the Application of the Hearsay Concept, 62 Harv.L.Rev. 177 (1948). The answer of a respondent that he thinks an unmarked lighter is a Zippo is relevant to the issue of secondary meaning only if, in fact, the respondent really does believe that the unmarked lighter is a Zippo. Under this view, therefore, answers in a survey should be regarded as hearsay.

Regardless of whether the surveys in this case could be admitted under the non-hearsay approach, they are admissible because the answers of respondents are expressions of presently existing state of mind, attitude, or belief. There is a recognized exception to the hearsay rule for such statements, and under it the statements are admissible to prove the truth of the matter contained therein.

Even if the surveys did not fit within this exception, well reasoned authority justifies their admission under the following approach: the determination that a statement is hearsay does not end the inquiry into admissibility; there must still be a further examination of the need for the statement at trial and the circumstantial guaranty of trustworthiness surrounding the making of the statement. This approach has been used to justify the admissibility of a survey. Necessity in this context requires a comparison of the probative value of the survey with the evidence, if any, which as a practical matter could be used if the survey were excluded. If the survey is more valuable, then necessity exists for the survey, i.e., it is the inability to get "evidence of the same value" which makes the hearsay statement necessary. When, as here, the state of mind of the smoking population (115,000,000 people) is the issue, a scientifically conducted survey is necessary because the practical alternatives do not produce equally probative evidence. With such a survey, the results are probably approximately the same as would be obtained if each of the 115,000,000 people were interviewed. The alternative of having 115,000,000 people testify in court is obviously impractical. The alternatives of having a much smaller section of the public testify (such as eighty witnesses) or using expert witnesses to testify to the state of the public mind are clearly not as valuable because the inferences which can be drawn from such testimony to the public state of mind are not as strong or as direct as the justifiable inferences from a scientific survey.

The second element involved in this approach is the guaranty of trustworthiness supplied by the circumstances under which the out-of-court statements were made. A logical step in this inquiry is to see which of the hearsay dangers are present. With regard to these surveys: there is no danger of faulty memory; the danger of faulty perception is negligible because respondents need only examine two or three cigarette lighters at most; the danger of faulty narration is equally negligible since the answers called for are simple. The only appreciable danger is that the respondent is insincere. But this danger is minimized by the circumstances of this or any public opinion poll in which scientific sampling is employed, because members of the public who are asked questions about things in which they have no interest have no reason to falsify their feelings. While the sampling procedure substantially guarantees trustworthiness insofar as the respondent's sincerity is concerned, other survey techniques substantially insure trustworthiness in other respects. If questions are unfairly worded to suggest answers favorable to the party sponsoring the survey, the element of trustworthiness in the poll would be lacking. The same result would follow if the interviewers asked fair questions in a leading manner. Thus, the methodology of the survey bears directly on trustworthiness, as it does on necessity. Since the two elements of necessity and trustworthiness are satisfied, I would admit these surveys under this approach to the hearsay rule, even apart from the state of mind exception.

* * *

LOETSCH v. NEW YORK CITY OMNIBUS CORP.

Court of Appeals of New York, 1943.
291 N.Y. 308, 52 N.E.2d 448.

THACHER, JUDGE.

Appeal by defendant from the nonunanimous judgment of the Appellate Division affirming a judgment of the Supreme Court, New York County, in favor of plaintiff in a wrongful death action.

Upon the trial of this action counsel for defendants-appellants offered in evidence the will of the decedent dated December 2, 1940, for the purpose of proving the statement of the decedent with respect to her relations with her husband. The statement was as follows: "Whereas I have been a faithful, dutiful, and loving wife to my husband, Dean Yankovich, and whereas he reciprocated my tender affections for him with acts of cruelty and indifference, and whereas he has failed to support and maintain me in that station of life which would have been possible and proper for him, I hereby limit my bequest to him to one dollar."

On plaintiff's objection the will was excluded from evidence, and the exception taken presents the only question for our consideration. The will, executed within four months prior to decedent's death, was relevant to an understanding of the relations which existed between the decedent and her husband. It is always proper to make proof of the relations of the decedent to the person for whose benefit the action is maintained, because such proof has a bearing upon the pecuniary loss suffered by the person entitled to the recovery, and this is true whether the beneficiary is the surviving husband or wife or one or more of the next of kin. Murphy v. Erie R. Co., 202 N.Y. 242, 245, 95 N.E. 699; Houghkirk v. President, etc., of Delaware & H. Canal Co., 92 N.Y. 219, 44 Am.Rep. 370; Sternfels v. Metropolitan St. R. Co., 73 App.Div. 494, 77 N.Y.S. 309, affirmed 174 N.Y. 512, 66 N.E. 1117; Farley v. New York, N.H. & H.R. Co., 87 Conn. 328, 87 A. 990.

The measure of loss is to be determined solely from the standpoint of the surviving spouse and is strictly limited to compensation for pecuniary loss. Decedent Estate Law, § 132, Consol.Laws, c. 13. Accordingly, the amount recoverable in any particular case must be very largely influenced by the nature of the relationship between the beneficiary and the deceased. When the deceased is one who was under no legal obligation to provide support for the beneficiary during life, his or her disposition voluntarily to do so is of essential importance to the jury in determining pecuniary loss. Evidence showing such a disposition or the lack of it should not be excluded.

Question remains as to the character of the proof offered, which was a declaration in writing of the decedent made within four months of her death. Such declarations are evidence of the decedent's state of mind and are probative of a disposition on the part of the declarant which has a very vital bearing upon the reasonable expectancy, or lack of it, of future assistance or support if life continues. This expectancy, disappointed by death, is the basis of recovery (Michigan Cent. R. Co. v. Vreeland, 227 U.S. 59, 70, 33 S.Ct. 192, 57 L.Ed. 417, Ann.Cas.1914C, 176) and is the measure of pecuniary loss for which the jury must award fair and just compensation. No testimonial effect need be given to the declaration, but the fact that such a declaration was made by the decedent, whether true or false, is compelling evidence of her feelings toward, and relations to, her husband. As such it is not excluded under the hearsay rule but is admissible as a verbal act.

* * *

The judgments should be reversed and a new trial granted, with costs to the appellant to abide the event.

POSNER v. DALLAS COUNTY CHILD WELFARE, 784 S.W.2d 585, 586, 587 (Tex.App.1990). "The Texas Department of Human Services sued to terminate the parental rights of Penelope and Robert Posner to their two daughters. Both parents appeal the judgment terminating their parental rights. We affirm.

* * *

"Appellants first complain about the testimony of Pamela Lynn Mings. Mings testified that, while observing her four-year-old son and J., appellants' older daughter, playing with dolls, she overheard J. say, '[G]ive me your doll, and I'll show you with mine how daddies sex their little girls.'

"This testimony was not offered to prove the truth of the declarant's statement as to how daddies 'sex their little girls.' Rather, it was offered to show that J. made the statement which was relevant to the issue of her emotional well-being and state of mind. Hence, the statement clearly falls within the hearsay exception, TEX.R.CIV.EVID. 803(3), as it was a statement of J.'s then existing emotional condition and state of mind."

MUTUAL LIFE INSURANCE CO. v. HILLMON

Supreme Court of the United States, 1892.
145 U.S. 285, 12 S.Ct. 909, 36 L.Ed. 706.

In error to the circuit court of the United States for the district of Kansas. Reversed.

STATEMENT BY MR. JUSTICE GRAY

On July 13, 1880, Sallie E. Hillmon, a citizen of Kansas, brought an action against the Mutual Life Insurance Company, a corporation of New York, on a policy of insurance, dated December 10, 1878, on the life of her husband, John W. Hillmon, in the sum of $10,000, payable to her within 60 days after notice and proof of his death. On the same day the plaintiff brought two other actions,—the one against the New York Life Insurance Company, a corporation of New York, on two similar policies of life insurance, dated, respectively, November 30, 1878, and December 10, 1878, for the sum of $5,000 each; and the other against the Connecticut Mutual Life Insurance Company, a corporation of Connecticut, on a similar policy, dated March 4, 1879, for the sum of $5,000.

In each case the declaration alleged that Hillmon died on March 17, 1879, during the continuance of the policy, but that the defendant, though duly notified of the fact, had refused to pay the amount of the policy, or any part thereof; and the answer denied the death of Hillmon, and alleged that he, together with John H. Brown and divers other persons, on or before November 30, 1878, conspiring to defraud the defendant, procured the issue of all the policies, and afterwards, in March and April, 1879, falsely pretended and represented that Hillmon was dead, and that a dead body which they had procured was his, whereas in reality he was alive and in hiding.

* * *

At the trial plaintiff introduced evidence tending to show that on or about March 5, 1879, Hillmon and Brown left Wichita, in the state of Kansas, and traveled together through southern Kansas in search of a site for a cattle ranch; that on the night of March 18th, while they were in camp at a place called "Crooked Creek," Hillmon was killed by the accidental discharge of a gun; that Brown at once notified persons living in the neighborhood, and that the body was thereupon taken to a neighboring town, where, after an inquest, it was buried. The defendants introduced evidence tending to show that the body found in the camp at Crooked creek on the night of March 18th was not the body of Hillmon, but was the body of one Frederick Adolph Walters. Upon the question whose body this was there was much conflicting evidence, including photographs and descriptions of the corpse, and of the marks and scars upon it, and testimony to its likeness to Hillmon and to Walters.

The defendants introduced testimony that Walters left his home at Ft. Madison, in the state of Iowa, in March, 1878, and was afterwards in Kansas in 1878, and in January and February, 1879; that during that time his family frequently received letters from him, the last of which was written from Wichita; and that he had not been heard from since March, 1879. The defendants also offered the following evidence:

Elizabeth Rieffenach testified that she was a sister of Frederick Adolph Walters, and lived at Ft. Madison; and thereupon, as shown by the bill of exceptions, the following proceedings took place:

"Witness further testified that she had received a letter written from Wichita, Kansas, about the 4th or 5th day of March, 1879, by her brother Frederick Adolph; that the letter was dated at Wichita, and was in the handwriting of her brother; that she had searched for the letter, but could not find the same, it being lost; that she remembered and could state the contents of the letter.

"Thereupon the defendants' counsel asked the question, 'State the contents of that letter;'" to which the plaintiff objected, on the ground that the same is incompetent, irrelevant, and hearsay. The objection was sustained, and the defendants duly excepted. The following is the letter as stated by witness:

> "Wichita, Kansas, March 4th or 5th or 3d or 4th,—I don't know,—1879. Dear Sister and All: I now in my usual style drop you a few lines to let you know that I expect to leave Wichita on or about March the 5th with a certain Mr. Hillmon, a sheep trader, for Colorado, or parts unknown to me. I expect to see the country now. News are of no interest to you, as you are not acquainted here. I will close with compliments to all inquiring friends. Love to all. I am truly your brother, FRED. ADOLPH WALTERS."

Alvina D. Kasten testified that she was 21 years of age, and resided in Ft. Madison; that she was engaged to be married to Frederick Adolph Walters; that she last saw him on March 24, 1878, at Ft. Madison; that he left there at that time, and had not returned; that she corresponded regularly with him, and received a letter about every two weeks until March 3, 1879, which was the last time she received a letter from him; that this letter was dated at Wichita, March 1, 1879, and was addressed to her at Ft. Madison, and the envelope was postmarked "Wichita, Kansas, March 2, 1879;" and that she had never heard from or seen him since that time.

The defendants put in evidence the envelope with the postmark and address, and thereupon offered to read the letter in evidence. The plaintiff objected to the reading of the letter. The court sustained the objection, and the defendants excepted.

This letter was dated "Wichita, March 1, 1879," was signed by Walters, and began as follows:

> "Dearest Alvina: Your kind and ever welcome letter was received yesterday afternoon about an hour before I left Emporia. I will stay

here until the fore part of next week, and then will leave here to see a part of the country that I never expected to see when I left home, as I am going with a man by the name of Hillmon, who intends to start a sheep ranch, and, as he promised me more wages than I could make at anything else, I concluded to take it, for a while at least, until I strike something better. There is so many folks in this country that have got the Leadville fever, and if I could not of got the situation that I have now I would have went there myself; but as it is at present I get to see the best portion of Kansas, Indian Territory, Colorado, and Mexico. The route that we intend to take would cost a man to travel from $150 to $200, but it will not cost me a cent; besides, I get good wages. I will drop you a letter occasionally until I get settled down. Then I want you to answer it."

* * *

The jury * * * returned verdicts for the plaintiff against the three defendants respectively for the amounts of their policies and interest, upon which separate judgments were rendered. * * *

MR. JUSTICE GRAY, after stating the case as above, delivered the opinion of the court.

* * *

The evidence that Walters was at Wichita on or before March 5th, and had not been heard from since, together with the evidence to identify as his the body found at Crooked Creek on March 18th, tended to show that he went from Wichita to Crooked Creek between those dates. Evidence that just before March 5th he had the intention of leaving Wichita with Hillmon would tend to corroborate the evidence already admitted, and to show that he went from Wichita to Crooked Creek with Hillmon. Letters from him to his family and his betrothed were the natural, if not the only attainable, evidence of his intention.

The position taken at the bar that the letters were competent evidence, within the rule stated in Nicholls v. Webb, 8 Wheat. 326, 337, as memoranda made in the ordinary course of business, cannot be maintained, for they were clearly not such.

But upon another ground suggested they should have been admitted. A man's state of mind or feeling can only be manifested to others by countenance, attitude, or gesture, or by sounds or words, spoken or written. The nature of the fact to be proved is the same, and evidence of its proper tokens is equally competent to prove it, whether expressed by aspect or conduct, by voice or pen. When the intention to be proved is important only as qualifying an act, its connection with that act must be shown, in order to warrant the admission of declarations of the intention. But whenever the intention is of itself a distinct and material fact in a chain of circumstances, it may be proved by contemporaneous oral or written declarations of the party.

The existence of a particular intention in a certain person at a certain time being a material fact to be proved, evidence that he expressed that intention at that time is as direct evidence of the fact as his own testimony that he then had that intention would be. After his death there can hardly be any other way of proving it, and while he is still alive his own memory of his state of mind at a former time is no more likely to be clear and true than a bystander's recollection of what he then said, and is less trustworthy than letters written by him at the very time and under circumstances precluding a suspicion of misrepresentation.

The letters in question were competent, not as narratives of facts communicated to the writer by others, nor yet as proof that he actually went away from Wichita, but as evidence that, shortly before the time when other evidence tended to show that he went away, he had the intention of going, and of going with Hillmon, which made it more probable both that he did go and that he went with Hillmon than if there had been no proof of such intention. In view of the mass of conflicting testimony introduced upon the question whether it was the body of Walters that was found in Hillmon's camp, this evidence might properly influence the jury in determining that question.

The rule applicable to this case has been thus stated by this court: "Wherever the bodily or mental feelings of an individual are material to be proved, the usual expressions of such feelings are original and competent evidence. Those expressions are the natural reflexes of what it might be impossible to show by other testimony. If there be such other testimony, this may be necessary to set the facts thus developed in their true light, and to give them their proper effect. As independent, explanatory, or corroborative evidence it is often indispensable to the due administration of justice. Such declarations are regarded as verbal acts, and are as competent as any other testimony, when relevant to the issue. Their truth or falsity is an inquiry for the jury." Insurance Co. v. Mosley, 8 Wall. 397, 404, 405, 19 L.Ed. 437.

In accordance with this rule, a bankrupt's declarations, oral or by letter, at or before the time of leaving or staying away from home, as to his reason for going abroad, have always been held by the English courts to be competent, in an action by his assignees against a creditor, as evidence that his departure was with intent to defraud his creditors, and therefore an act of bankruptcy. Bateman v. Bailey, 5 Term.R. 512; Rawson v. Haigh, 9 J.B. Moore, 217, 2 Bing. 99; Smith v. Cramer, 1 Scott, 541, 1 Bing.N.C. 585.

The highest courts of New Hampshire and Massachusetts have held declarations of a servant, at the time of leaving his master's service, to be competent evidence, in actions between third persons, of his reasons for doing so. Hadley v. Carter, 8 N.H. 40; Elmer v. Fessenden, 151 Mass. 359, 24 N.E. 208. And the supreme court of Ohio has held that, for the purpose of proving that a person was at a railroad station intending to take passage on a train, previous declarations made by him at the time of leaving his hotel were admissible. Railroad Co. v. Herrick, 29 N.E. 1052. See, also, Jackson v. Boneham, 15 Johns, 226;

Gorham v. Canton, 5 Greenl. 266; Kilburn v. Bennett, 3 Metc., Mass., 199; Lund v. Tyngsborough, 9 Cush. 36.

In actions for criminal conversation, letters by the wife to her husband or to third persons are competent to show her affection towards her husband, and her reasons for living apart from him, if written before any misconduct on her part, and if there is no ground to suspect collusion. Trelawney v. Colman, 2 Stark, 191, and 1 Barn. & Ald. 90; Willis v. Bernard, 5 Car. & P. 342, and 1 Moore & S. 584, 8 Bing. 376; 1 Greenl.Ev. § 102. So letters from a husband to a third person, showing his state of feeling affection, and sympathy for his wife, have been held by this court to be competent evidence, bearing on the validity of the marriage, when the legitimacy of their children is in issue. Gaines v. Relf, 12 How. 472, 520, 534, 13 L.Ed. 1071.

Even in the probate of wills, which are required by law to be in writing, executed and attested in prescribed forms, yet, where the validity of a will is questioned for want of mental capacity, or by reason of fraud and undue influence, or where the will is lost, and it becomes necessary to prove its contents, written or oral evidence of declarations of the testator before the date of the will has been admitted, in Massachusetts and in England, to show his real intention as to the disposition of his property, although there has been a difference of opinion as to the admissibility, for such purposes, of his subsequent declarations. Shailer v. Bumstead, 99 Mass. 112; Sugden v. St. Leonards, 1 Prob.Div. 154; Woodward v. Goulstone, 11 App.Cas. 469, 478, 484, 486.

* * *

In Sugden v. St. Leonards, which arose upon the probate of the lost will of Lord Chancellor St. Leonards, the English court of appeal was unanimous in holding oral as well as written declarations made by the testator before the date of the will to be admissible in evidence. Lord Chief Justice Cockburn said: "I entertain no doubt that prior instructions, or a draft authenticated by the testator, or verbal declarations of what he was about to do, though of course not conclusive evidence, are yet legally admissible as secondary evidence, of the contents of a lost will." 1 Prob.Div. 226. Sir George Jessel, M.R., said: "It is not strictly evidence of the contents of the instrument, it is simply evidence of the intention of the person who afterwards executes the instrument. It is simply evidence of probability,—no doubt of a high degree of probability in some cases, and of a low degree of probability in others. The cogency of the evidence depends very much on the nearness in point of time of the declaration of intention to the period of the execution of the instrument." Id. 242. * * *

Upon an indictment of one Hunter for the murder of one Armstrong at Camden, the court of errors and appeals of New Jersey unanimously held that Armstrong's oral declarations to his son at Philadelphia, on the afternoon before the night of the murder, as well as a letter written by him at the same time and place to his wife, each stating that he was going with Hunter to Camden on business, were rightly admitted in evidence. Chief Justice Beasley said: "In the ordinary course of things, it was the usual information that a man about leaving home would communicate, for the convenience of his family, the information of his friends, or the regulation of his business. At the time it was given, such declarations could, in the nature of things, mean harm to no one. He who uttered them was bent on no expedition of mischief or wrong, and the attitude of affairs at the time entirely explodes the idea that such utterances were intended to serve any purpose but that for which they were obviously designed. If it be said that such notice of an intention of leaving home could have been given without introducing in it the name of Mr. Hunter, the obvious answer to the suggestion, I think, is that a reference to the companion who is to accompany the person leaving is as natural a part of the transaction as is any other incident or quality of it. If it is legitimate to show by a man's own declarations that he left his home to be gone a week, or for a certain destination, which seems incontestable, why may it not be proved in the same way that a designated person was to bear him company? At the time the words were uttered or written they imported no wrongdoing to any one, and the reference to the companion who was to go with him was nothing more, as matters then stood, than an indication of an additional circumstance of his going. If it was in the ordinary train of events for this man to leave word or to state where he was going, it seems to me it was equally so for him to say with whom he was going." Hunter v. State, 40 N.J.L. 495, 534, 536–538.

Upon principle and authority, therefore, we are of opinion that the two letters were competent evidence of the intention of Walters at the time of writing them, which was a material fact bearing upon the question in controversy; and that for the exclusion of these letters, as well as for the undue restriction of the defendants' challenges, the verdicts must be set aside, and a new trial had.

* * *

Note

See Hinton, States of Mind and the Hearsay Rule, 1 U.Chi.L.Rev. 394 (1934); Hutchins & Slesinger, Some Observations on the Law of Evidence: State of Mind to Prove an Act, 38 Yale L.J. 283 (1929); MacCracken, The Case of the Anonymous Corpse, 19 American Heritage No. 4, at 51 (June 1968); Maguire, The Hillmon Case—Thirty-Three Years After, 38 Harv. L.Rev. 709 (1925); McFarland, Dead Men Tell Tales: Thirty Times Three Years of the Judicial Process After Hillmon, 30 Vill.L.Rev. 1 (1985); Payne, The Hillmon Case—An Old Problem Revisited, 41 Va.L.Rev. 1011 (1955); Rice, The State of Mind Exception to the Hearsay Rule: A Response to "'Secondary' Relevance," 14 Duquesne L.Rev. 219 (1976); Seidelson, The State of Mind Exception to the Hearsay Rule, 13 Duquesne L.Rev. 251 (1974); Seligman, An Exception to the Hearsay Rule, 26 Harv.L.Rev. 146 (1912); Weissenberger, Hearsay Puzzles: An Essay on Federal Evidence Rule 803(3), 64 Temp.L.Rev. 145 (1991).

UNITED STATES v. PHEASTER

United States Court of Appeals, Ninth Circuit, 1976.
544 F.2d 353, cert. denied, 429 U.S. 1099, 97 S.Ct. 1118, 51 L.Ed.2d 546 (1977).

RENFREW, DISTRICT JUDGE:

* * *

I. FACTS

This case arises from the disappearance of Larry Adell, the 16–year–old son of Palm Springs multi-millionaire Robert Adell. At approximately 9:30 P.M. on June 1, 1974, Larry Adell left a group of his high school friends in a Palm Springs restaurant known as Sambo's North. He walked into the parking lot of the restaurant with the expressed intention of meeting a man named Angelo who was supposed to deliver a pound of free marijuana. Larry never returned to his friends in the restaurant that evening, and his family never saw him thereafter.

The long, agonizing, and ultimately unsuccessful effort to find Larry began shortly after his disappearance. At about 2:30 A.M. on June 2, 1974, Larry's father was telephoned by a male caller who told him that his son was being held and that further instructions would be left in Larry's car in the parking lot of Sambo's North. Those instructions included a demand for a ransom of $400,000 for the release of Larry. Further instructions regarding the delivery of the ransom were promised within a week. Although the caller had warned Mr. Adell that he would never see Larry again if the police or the F.B.I. were notified, Mr. Adell immediately called the F.B.I., and that agency was actively involved in the investigation of the case from the beginning.

Numerous difficulties were encountered in attempting to deliver the ransom, necessitating a number of communications between the kidnappers and Mr. Adell. The communications from the kidnappers included a mixture of instructions and threats, as well as messages from Larry. Before the kidnappers finally broke off communications on June 30, 1974, Mr. Adell had received a total of ten letters from the kidnappers, nine of which were typed in a "script" style and one of which was handwritten. In addition, Mr. Adell had received two telephone calls from the kidnappers, one of which was tape-recorded by the F.B.I. In these communications, the kidnappers gave instructions for a total of four attempts to deliver the ransom, but it was never delivered for a number of reasons, and Larry was never released.

The instructions for the first delivery, set for June 8th, were nullified by the late delivery of the letter containing them on June 9th. The second delivery failed when, on June 12th, Mr. Adell balked at turning over the money without more adequate assurances that his son would be released. The third delivery on June 23d was aborted, apparently because of the kidnappers' awareness that the pick-up site was being monitored. A duffel bag containing the ransom money was thrown into the designated spot, but it was never retrieved by the kidnappers. The fourth and final attempt never really began. On June 30th, pursuant to instructions, Mr. Adell went to a designated hotel pay telephone to await further instructions but was never contacted. No further communications were received from the kidnappers, despite Mr. Adell's attempt to renew contact by messages published in the Los Angeles Times.

When it appeared that further efforts to communicate with the kidnappers would be futile, the F.B.I. arrested appellants, who had been under surveillance for some time, in a coordinated operation on July 14, 1974.

* * *

III. Errors Asserted by Inciso

A. Admissibility of Hearsay Testimony Concerning Statements of Larry Adell

Appellant Inciso argues that the district court erred in admitting hearsay testimony by two teenaged friends of Larry Adell concerning statements made by Larry on June 1, 1974, the day that he disappeared. Timely objections were made to the questions which elicited the testimony on the ground that the questions called for hearsay. In response, the Government attorney stated that the testimony was offered for the limited purpose of showing the "state of mind of Larry". After instructing the jury that it could only consider the testimony for that limited purpose and not for "the truth or falsity of what [Larry] said", the district court allowed the witnesses to answer the questions. Francine Gomes, Larry's date on the evening that he disappeared, testified that when Larry picked her up that evening, he told her that he was going to meet Angelo at Sambo's North at 9:30 P.M. to "pick up a pound of marijuana which Angelo had promised him for free". She also testified that she had been with Larry on another occasion when he met a man named Angelo, and she identified the defendant as that man. Miss Gomes stated that it was approximately 9:15 P.M. when Larry went into the parking lot. Doug Sendejas, one of Larry's friends who was with him at Sambo's North just prior to his disappearance, testified that Larry had made similar statements to him in the afternoon and early evening of June 1st regarding a meeting that evening with Angelo. Mr. Sendejas also testified that when Larry left the table at Sambo's North to go into the parking lot, Larry stated that "he was going to meet Angelo and he'd be right back."

Inciso's contention that the district court erred in admitting the hearsay testimony of Larry's friends is premised on the view that the statements could not properly be used by the jury to conclude that Larry did in fact meet Inciso in the parking lot of Sambo's North at approximately 9:30 P.M. on June 1, 1974. The correctness of that assumption is, in our view, the key to the analysis of this contention of error. The Government argues that Larry's statements were relevant to two issues in the case. First the statements are said to be relevant to an issue created by the defense when Inciso's attorney attempted to show that Larry had not been kidnapped but had disappeared voluntarily as part of a simulated kidnapping designed to extort money from his wealthy father from whom he was allegedly estranged. In his brief on appeal, Inciso concedes the relevance and, presumably, the admissibility of the statements to "show that Larry did not voluntarily disappear". However, Inciso argues that for this limited purpose, there was no need to name the person with whom Larry intended to meet, and that the district court's limiting instruction was insufficient to overcome the prejudice to which he was exposed by the testimony. Second, the Government argues that the statements are relevant and admissible to show that, as intended, Larry did meet Inciso in the parking lot at Sambo's North on the evening of June 1, 1974. If the Government's second theory of admissibility is successful, Inciso's arguments regarding the excision of his name from the statements admitted under the first theory is obviously mooted.

In determining the admissibility of the disputed evidence, we apply the standard of Rule 26 of the Federal Rules of Criminal Procedure which governed at the time of the trial below. Under that standard, the District Court was required to decide issues concerning the "admissibility of evidence" according to "the principles of the common law as they may be interpreted by the courts of the United States in the light of reason and experience."

The Government's position that Larry Adell's statements can be used to prove that the meeting with Inciso did occur raises a difficult and important question concerning the scope of the so-called "*Hillmon* doctrine", a particular species of the "state of mind" exception to the general rule that hearsay evidence is inadmissible. The doctrine takes its name from the famous Supreme Court decision in Mutual Life Insurance Co. v. Hillmon, 145 U.S. 285, 12 S.Ct. 909, 36 L.Ed. 706 (1892). That the *Hillmon* doctrine should create controversy and confusion is not surprising, for it is an extraordinary doctrine. Under the state of mind exception, hearsay evidence is admissible if it bears on the state of mind of the declarant and if that state of mind is an issue in the case. For example, statements by a testator which demonstrate that he had the necessary testamentary intent are admissible to show that intent when it is in issue. The exception embodied in the *Hillmon* doctrine is fundamentally different, because it does not require that the state of mind of the declarant be an actual issue in the case. Instead, under the *Hillmon* doctrine the state of mind of the declarant is used inferentially to prove other matters which are in issue. Stated simply, the doctrine provides that when the performance of a particular act by an individual is an issue in a case, his intention (state of mind) to perform that act may be shown. From that intention, the trier of fact may draw the inference that the person carried out his intention and performed the act. Within this conceptual framework, hearsay evidence of statements by the person which tend to show his intention is deemed admissible under the state of mind exception. Inciso's objection to the doctrine concerns its application in situations in which the declarant has stated his intention to do something *with another person,* and the issue is whether he did so. There can be no doubt that the theory of the *Hillmon* doctrine is different when the declarant's statement of intention necessarily requires the action of one or more others if it is to be fulfilled.

When hearsay evidence concerns the declarant's statement of his intention to do something with another person, the *Hillmon* doctrine requires that the trier of fact infer from the state of mind of the declarant the probability of a particular act not only by the declarant but also by the other person. Several objections can be raised against a doctrine that would allow such an inference to be made. One such objection is based on the unreliability of the inference [13] but is not, in our view, compelling.[14] A much more significant and troubling objection is based on the inconsistency of such an inference with the state of mind exception. This problem is more easily perceived when one divides what is really a compound statement into its component parts. In the instant case, the statement by Larry Adell, "I am going to meet Angelo in the parking lot to get a pound of grass", is really two statements. The first is the obvious statement of Larry's intention. The second is an implicit statement of Angelo's intention. Surely, if the meeting is to take place in a location which Angelo does not habitually frequent, one must assume that Angelo intended to meet Larry there if one is to make the inference that Angelo was in the parking lot and the meeting occurred. The important point is that the second, implicit statement has nothing to do with Larry's state of mind. For example, if Larry's friends had testified that Larry had said, "Angelo is going to be in the parking lot of Sambo's North tonight with a pound of grass", no state of mind exception or any other exception to the hearsay rule would be available. Yet, this is in effect at least half of what the testimony did attribute to Larry.

Despite the theoretical awkwardness associated with the application of the *Hillmon* doctrine to facts such as those now before us, the authority in favor of such an application is impressive, beginning with the seminal *Hillmon* decision itself. *Hillmon,* supra, 145 U.S. 285, 12

13. Because of this concern, one treatise states that, "Use of declarations of state of mind to prove subsequent conduct might, then, be limited to proof of conduct that would not have required the substantial cooperation of persons other than the declarant." McCormick's Handbook of the Law of Evidence 698 (E. Cleary ed.1972). However, that same authority also recognizes that "courts have not imposed the limitation". Id. at 698–699.

14. The inference from a statement of present intention that the act intended was in fact performed is nothing more than an inference. Even where no actions by other parties are necessary in order for the intended act to be performed, a myriad of contingencies could intervene to frustrate the fulfillment of the intention. The fact that the cooperation of another party is necessary if the intended act is to be performed adds another important contingency, but the difference is one of degree rather than kind. The possible unreliability of the inference to be drawn from the present intention is a matter going to the weight of the evidence which might be argued to the trier of fact, but it should not be a ground for completely excluding the admittedly relevant evidence.

S.Ct. 909, was a civil case involving a colorful dispute over certain life insurance claims. The factual issue in the case was whether *Hillmon,* who had purchased a number of life insurance policies naming his wife as beneficiary, had been killed by the accidental discharge of a gun in a campsite near Crooked Creek, Kansas. If he had been so killed, his wife was entitled to the benefits under the insurance policies. The defendant insurance companies contended, however, that Hillmon was not dead but was in hiding, and that the claims were part of a conspiracy to defraud the companies. While it was undisputed that someone had been killed in the campsite at Crooked Creek, there was complete disagreement as to who the victim was. The defendants in *Hillmon* introduced evidence which tended to show that the body at Crooked Creek was not that of Hillmon, but was that of another man, Frederick Adolph Walters. As part of this attempt to show that it was Walters who was killed at Crooked Creek, the defendants attempted to introduce two letters written by Walters from Wichita, Kansas, shortly before he disappeared, never to be heard from again. In the letters, one written to his sister and the other to his fiancee, Walters stated that he intended to leave Wichita in the near future and to travel with a man named Hillmon. In the letter to his fiancee, Walters explained that Hillmon was making the expedition to search for a suitable site for a sheep ranch, and that Hillmon had promised him employment at the ranch on very favorable terms. Plaintiff's objection to the introduction of the letters on the ground that they were incompetent, irrelevant, and hearsay was sustained by the trial court.

The Supreme Court summarily rejected the argument that the letters were admissible "as memoranda made in the ordinary course of business," 145 U.S. at 295, 12 S.Ct. at 912, but then held that they were admissible as evidence of Walters' intention:

> " 'The letters in question were competent, not as narratives of facts communicated to the writer by others, nor yet as proof that he actually went away from Wichita, but *as evidence that,* shortly before the time when other evidence tended to show that he went away, *he had the intention of going, and of going with Hillmon, which made it more probable both that he did go and that he went with Hillmon, than if there had been no proof of such intention.* In view of the mass of conflicting testimony introduced upon the question of whether it was the body of Walters that was found in Hillmon's camp, this evidence might properly influence the jury in determining that question.' 145 U.S. at 295–296, 12 S.Ct. at 912–913 (emphasis added)."

Although *Hillmon* was a civil case, the Supreme Court cited with approval a number of criminal cases in support of its decision. One of them, Hunter v. State, 11 Vroom (40 N.J.L.) 495, involved facts remarkably similar to those before us here. The Court summarized the facts and the holding of that case as follows:

> " 'Upon an indictment of one Hunter for the murder of one Armstrong at Camden, the Court of Errors and Appeals of New Jersey unanimously held that Armstrong's oral declarations to his son at

Philadelphia, on the afternoon before the night of the murder, as well as a letter written by him at the same time and place to his wife, each stating that he was going with Hunter to Camden on business, were rightly admitted in evidence.' 145 U.S. at 299, 12 S.Ct. at 914."

The Court then quoted a long passage from the opinion of Chief Justice Beasley in *Hunter.* The primary concern expressed in that passage was whether there was anything unnatural about the victim's statements that might suggest an ulterior purpose and, hence, unreliability. Having found no indicia of unreliability, Chief Justice Beasley brushed aside the suggestion that the specific reference to the defendant should have been omitted. Speaking rhetorically, Chief Justice Beasley asked:

> "If it is legitimate to show by a man's own declarations that he left his home to be gone a week, or for a certain destination, which seems incontestable, why may it not be proved in the same way that a designated person was to bear him company?"

The Chief Justice then concluded:

> " ' "If it was in the ordinary train of events for this man to leave word or to state where he was going, it seems to me it was equally so for him to say with whom he was going." Hunter v. State [11 Vroom], 40 N.J. Law. 495, 534, 536, 538.' 145 U.S. at 299, 12 S.Ct. at 914."

The *Hillmon* doctrine has been applied by the California Supreme Court in People v. Alcalde, 24 Cal.2d 177, 148 P.2d 627 (1944), a criminal case with facts which closely parallel those in *Hunter.* In *Alcalde* the defendant was tried and convicted of first degree murder for the brutal slaying of a woman whom he had been seeing socially. One of the issues before the California Supreme Court was the asserted error by the trial court in allowing the introduction of certain hearsay testimony concerning statements made by the victim on the day of her murder. As in the instant case, the testimony was highly incriminating, because the victim reportedly said that she was going out with Frank, the defendant, on the evening she was murdered. On appeal, a majority of the California Supreme Court affirmed the defendant's conviction, holding that *Hillmon* was "the leading case on the admissibility of declarations of intent to do an act as proof that the act thereafter was accomplished." 148 P.2d at 631. Without purporting to "define or summarize all the limitations or restrictions upon the admissibility of" such evidence, id. at 632, the court did mention several prudential considerations not unlike those mentioned by Chief Justice Beasley in *Hunter.* Thus, the declarant should be dead or otherwise unavailable, and the testimony concerning his statements should be relevant and possess a high degree of trustworthiness. Id. at 631. The court also noted that there was other evidence from which the defendant's guilt could be inferred. Applying these standards, the court found no error in the trial court's admission of the disputed hearsay testimony. "Unquestionably the deceased's statement of her intent and the logical inference to be drawn therefrom, namely, that she was with the defendant that night, were relevant to the issue of the guilt of the defendant." Id. at 632.

In addition to the decisions in *Hillmon* and *Alcalde,* support for the Government's position can be found in the California Evidence Code and the new Federal Rules of Evidence, although in each instance resort must be made to the comments to the relevant provisions.

Section 1250 of the California Evidence Code carves out an exception to the general hearsay rule for statements of a declarant's "then existing mental or physical state". The *Hillmon* doctrine is codified in Section 1250(2) which allows the use of such hearsay evidence when it "is offered to prove or explain acts or conduct of the declarant." The comment to Section 1250(2) states that, "Thus, a statement of the declarant's intent to do certain acts is admissible to prove that he did those acts." Although neither the language of the statute nor that of the comment specifically addresses the particular issue now before us, the comment does cite the *Alcalde* decision and, therefore, indirectly rejects the limitation urged by Inciso.

Although the new Federal Rules of Evidence were not in force at the time of the trial below, we refer to them for any light that they might shed on the status of the common law at the time of the trial. The codification of the state of mind exception in Rule 803(3) does not provide a direct statement of the *Hillmon* doctrine. Rule 803(3) provides an exemption from the hearsay rule for the following evidence:

> "*Then existing mental, emotional, or physical condition.* A statement of the declarant's then existing state of mind, emotion, sensation, or physical condition (such as intent, plan, motive, design, mental feeling, pain, and bodily health), but not including a statement of memory or belief to prove the fact remembered or believed unless it relates to the execution, revocation, identification, or terms of declarant's will."

Although Rule 803(3) is silent regarding the *Hillmon* doctrine, both the Advisory Committee on the Proposed Rules and the House Committee on the Judiciary specifically addressed the doctrine. After noting that Rule 803(3) would not allow the admission of statements of memory, the Advisory Committee stated broadly that

> " 'The rule of Mutual Life Ins. Co. v. Hillmon [citation omitted] allowing evidence of intention as tending to prove the doing of the act intended, is, of course, left undisturbed.' Note to Paragraph (3), 28 U.S.C.A. at 585."

Significantly, the Notes of the House Committee on the Judiciary regarding Rule 803(3) are far more specific and revealing:

> " 'However, the Committee intends that the Rule be construed to limit the doctrine of Mutual Life Insurance Co. v. Hillmon [citation omitted] so as to render statements of intent by a declarant admissible *only to prove his future conduct, not the future conduct of another person.*' House Report No. 93–650, Note to Paragraph (3), 28 U.S.C.A. at 579 (emphasis added)."

Although the matter is certainly not free from doubt, we read the note of the Advisory Committee as presuming that the *Hillmon* doctrine would be incorporated in full force, including necessarily the application in *Hillmon* itself. The language suggests that the Advisory Committee presumed that such a broad interpretation was the prevailing common law position. The notes of the House Committee on the Judiciary are significantly different. The language used there suggests a legislative intention to cut back on what that body also perceived to be the prevailing common law view, namely, that the *Hillmon* doctrine could be applied to facts such as those now before us.

Although we recognize the force of the objection to the application of the *Hillmon* doctrine in the instant case,[18] we cannot conclude that

18. Criticism of the *Hillmon* doctrine has come from very distinguished quarters, both judicial and academic. However, the position of the judicial critics is definitely the minority position, stated primarily in dicta and dissent.

In his opinion for the Court in Shepard v. United States, 290 U.S. 96, 54 S.Ct. 22, 78 L.Ed.2d 196 (1933), Justice Cardozo indicated in dicta an apparent hostility to the *Hillmon* doctrine. *Shepard* involved hearsay testimony of a dramatically different character from that in the instant case. The Court reviewed the conviction of an army medical officer for the murder of his wife by poison. The asserted error by the trial court was its admission, over defense objection, of certain hearsay testimony by Mrs. Shepard's nurse concerning statements that Mrs. Shepard had made during her final illness. The nurse's testimony was that, after asking whether there was enough whiskey left in the bottle from which she had drunk just prior to her collapse to make a test for poison, Mrs. Shepard stated, "Dr. Shepard has poisoned me." One theory advanced by the Government on appeal was that the testimony was admissible to show that Mrs. Shepard did not have suicidal tendencies and, thus, to refute the defense argument that she took her own life. The Court rejected that theory, holding that the testimony had not been admitted for the limited purpose suggested by the Government and that, even if it had been admitted for that purpose, its relevance was far outweighed by the extreme prejudice it would create for the defendant. In rejecting the Government's theory, the Court refused to extend the state of mind exception to statements of memory. In his survey of the state of mind exception, Justice Cardozo appeared to suggest that the *Hillmon* doctrine is limited to "suits upon insurance policies", id. at 105, 54 S.Ct. 22, although the cases cited by the Court in *Hillmon* refute that suggestion.

The decision in *Shepard* was relied upon by Justice Traynor of the California Supreme Court in his vigorous dissent from the decision reached by the majority in People v. Alcalde, supra, 148 P.2d 627. Justice Traynor argued that the victim's declarations regarding her meeting with Frank could not be used to "induce the belief that the defendant went out with the deceased, took her to the scene of the crime and there murdered her * * * without setting aside the rule against hearsay." Id. at 633. Any other legitimate use of the declaration, in his opinion, was so insignificant that it was outweighed by the enormous prejudice to the defendant in allowing the jury to hear it.

Finally, the exhaustive analysis of a different, but related, hearsay issue by the Court of Appeals for the District of Columbia in United States v. Brown, 160 U.S.App.D.C. 190, 490 F.2d 758 (1974), provides inferential support for the position urged by Inciso. The issue in that case was the admissibility of hearsay testimony concerning a victim's extrajudicial declarations that he was "[f]rightened that he may be killed" by the defendant. Id. at 762. After surveying the relevant cases, the court stated a "synthesis" of the governing principles. One of the cases which was criticized by the court was the decision of the California Supreme Court in People v. Merkouris, 52 Cal.2d 672, 344 P.2d 1 (1959), a case relied upon by the Government in the instant case. The court in *Merkouris* held that hearsay testimony showing the victim's fear of the defendant could properly be admitted to show the probable identity of the killer. The court in *Brown* expressed the following criticism of that holding, a criticism which might also apply to the application of the *Hillmon* doctrine in the instant case:

the district court erred in allowing the testimony concerning Larry Adell's statements to be introduced.

* * *

For the reasons set out above, we affirm the convictions.

ELY, CIRCUIT JUDGE (concurring and dissenting):

My Brother Renfrew, in his customary way, has written a scholarly and thoughtful opinion in this sad and difficult case. I concur in the affirmance of Pheaster's conviction on the substantive charges, none of which involved kidnapping *per se,* but I must respectfully dissent from the majority's affirmance of Inciso's conviction on the charge of conspiracy. * * *

In respect to Inciso's participation in the kidnapping conspiracy, there is no doubt that Adell's hearsay statement that the latter was going to meet "Angelo" was the strongest evidence linking Inciso to the conspiracy. The statement was obviously relevant to Adell's state of mind and his future intent. But it was also highly prejudicial to Inciso. Adell's statement could not be admitted without the attendant and substantial risk that, despite the judge's limiting instruction, the jury would rely on the statement to prove not only the act of Adell, but also those of Inciso.

I am obligated by the almost century-old precedent of Mutual Life Insurance Co. v. Hillmon, 145 U.S. 285, 12 S.Ct. 909 (1892) to concur in the majority's decision that the trial court did not commit reversible error in admitting Adell's alleged statement. Nevertheless, while my Brother Renfrew is doubtless correct that a majority of courts have adhered to the so-called *Hillmon* doctrine, it is also true that the holding has been subjected to severe criticism by some of our Nation's most distinguished and judicial scholars. I am impelled, therefore, strongly to emphasize my own agreement with the views of Mr. Justice Cardozo in Shepard v. United States, 290 U.S. 96, 54 S.Ct. 22, 78 L.Ed. 196 (1933) and Chief Justice Traynor in his dissenting opinion in People v. Alcalde, 24 Cal.2d 177, 148 P.2d 627 (1944). As Justice Traynor wrote, "A declaration as to what one person intended to do * * * cannot safely be accepted as evidence of what another probably did." Id. at 189, 148 P.2d at 633. The fact that the members of the House Judiciary Committee specifically noted their intent to limit the *Hillmon* doctrine in Rule 803(3) of the new Federal Rules of Evidence indicates that the sound criticisms voiced by those two eminent members of the judiciary, as well as other legal scholars, are now widely believed to be valid.

"Such an approach violates the fundamental safeguards necessary to the use of such testimony [citation omitted]. Through a circuitous series of inferences, the court reverses the effect of the statement so as to reflect on *defendant's* intent and actions rather than the state of mind of the declarant (victim). This is the very result that it is hoped the limiting instruction will prevent." 490 F.2d at 771 (emphasis in original).

For a frequently cited academic critique of the *Hillmon* doctrine, see Maguire, The Hillmon Case—Thirty-Three Years After, 38 Harv.L.Rev. 709 (1925).

NORTON v. STATE, 771 S.W.2d 160, 165–66 (Tex.App.1989). "Norton contends that the trial court erred by admitting specific testimony by Bailey's widow over his objection of hearsay and that the improperly admitted testimony was harmful. * * * The testimony in question by Paula Bailey was as follows:

Q Now late that night did your husband receive a telephone call?

A Yes, sir, he did.

Q And did you awaken?

A Yes, sir.

Q And as it—when you awakened, what did you observe?

A My husband was—he just had talked to Ray on the phone, and he told him to pick up Preston and go—come help him work at the shop.

MR. GOLDSTEIN: Your Honor, we're going to object to the witness's hearsay response as to what her husband told her was told to him.

Q Once again, Your Honor, that would be pro—offered for the limited purpose to show that as a result of a telephone call, that the defendant—the state of mine—I mean, the state of mind of the deceased, and that based upon that, he did in fact perform an act thereafter.

"On cross-examination, the witness stated that she had no personal knowledge of the telephone call because she was asleep and did not hear the telephone ring.

"There are two distinct elements in this testimony: (1) Bailey was informing his wife of his intention to go to Norton's shop, and (2) Bailey was telling his wife that he was going there because Norton had called and asked him to come. The testimony was offered for the limited purpose of showing Bailey's state of mind under the exception to the hearsay rule codified at Tex.R.Crim.Evid. 803(3). This exception includes a statement 'of the declarant's then existing state of mind, emotion, sensation, of physical condition (such as intent, plan, motive, design, mental feeling, pain, or bodily health), *but not including a statement of memory or belief to prove the fact remembered or believed* * * * (emphasis added).'

* * *

"To admit memory declarations under the state-of-mind exception would defeat the entire hearsay rule. Maguire, The Hillmon Case—Thirty Three Years After, 38 Harv.L.Rev. 709 (1925), quoted in H. Wendorf & D. Schlueter, Texas Rules of Evidence Manual 329 (2d ed. 1988). That is the reason that memory declarations are expressly excluded by the rule.

"Thus, Bailey's statement to his wife that he intended to go to Norton's shop was admissible for the limited purpose to show that he intended to go to the shop to help Norton. But the second factor communicated that Bailey was going there because Norton had called and asked him to come clearly states a fact remembered which is specifically excluded from the exception."

STATE v. CHARO, 156 Ariz. 561, 754 P.2d 288, 291–92 (1988). "The rule that a murder victim's fear could be used to prove the perpetrator's identity was recognized in California. People v. Merkouris, 52 Cal.2d 672, 344 P.2d 1 (1959). It found some support in a few other jurisdictions despite an apparently contrary position implicit in Shepard v. United States, 290 U.S. 96, 54 S.Ct. 22, 78 L.Ed. 196 (1933). Subsequently the California rules of evidence were revised so that a hearsay statement of fear by a murder victim was admissible and relevant to prove or explain subsequent acts of the *decedent,* but not as a basis to infer a defendant's conduct. Thus, a victim's state of mind was held to be relevant in cases where the issue was suicide, State v. Duke, 110 Ariz. 320, 518 P.2d 570 (1974), or self-defense, People v. Atchley, 53 Cal.2d 160, 346 P.2d 764 (1959), cert. dismissed, 366 U.S. 207, 81 S.Ct. 1051, 6 L.Ed.2d 233 (1961). However, the idea of proving that a victim was afraid of the defendant as admissible to prove identity has been thoroughly rejected. People v. Armendariz, 37 Cal.3d 573, 581, 209 Cal.Rptr. 664, 672, 693 P.2d 243, 251 (1984) ('A victim's out-of-court statements of fear of an accused are admissible * * * only when the victim's conduct in conformity with that fear is in dispute. Absent such dispute, the statements are irrelevant.'); See also, United States v. Brown, 490 F.2d 758 (D.C.Cir.1973) (victim's fear of the defendant is irrelevant to prove identity).

"The Arizona Rules of Evidence are consonant with the above view on the state of mind exception * * *."

JOHNSON v. CHRANS, 844 F.2d 482, 483, 485–86 (7th Cir.1988), cert. denied, 488 U.S. 835, 109 S.Ct. 95, 102 L.Ed.2d 71 (1988). "At trial Johnson's counsel sought to establish that Mitchell had been threatened by a supplier, 'Larry T.,' whom Mitchell said he owed $10,000. The trial court rebuffed defense counsel's attempt to call witnesses to testify as to Mitchell's statements about Larry T., ruling that the proffered testimony was inadmissible hearsay. Defense counsel contended that this testimony was admissible under the state-of-mind exception to Illinois' hearsay rule. * * *

* * *

"* * * Illinois courts admit out-of-court statements under the state-of-mind exception if the declarant's state of mind is directly in issue, e.g., People v. Adams, 102 Ill.App.3d 1129, 1135, 58 Ill.Dec. 325, 331, 430 N.E.2d 267, 273 (2d Dist.1981) (victim's state of mind relevant to defendant's claim of self defense), or if the declarant's state of mind gives rise to reliable inferences about the declarant's later conduct, e.g., People v. Lang, 106 Ill.App.3d 808, 815, 62 Ill.Dec. 510, 516, 436 N.E.2d 260, 266 (3d Dist.1982) (victim's state of mind casts doubt on defendant's claim that marriage was happy and shooting of wife was accidental). See also People v. Coleman, 116 Ill.App.3d 28, 33, 71 Ill.Dec. 819, 822, 451 N.E.2d 973, 976 (3d Dist.1983) (explaining relevance requirement for state-of-mind exception). Illinois courts do not, however, admit out-of-court statements regarding the defendant's state of mind as proof of subsequent conduct by a person other than the declarant. See People v. Goodman, 77 Ill.App.3d 569, 574, 33 Ill.Dec. 49, 53, 396 N.E.2d 274, 278 (4th Dist.1979) (distinguishing between permissible use of state-of-mind declarations to prove declarant's subsequent actions and impermissible use to prove someone else's subsequent actions); People v. Reddock, 13 Ill.App.3d 296, 305, 300 N.E.2d 31, 38 (2d Dist.1973) (statements of deceased that he was going with defendant to look at real estate inadmissible to show any intent on part of defendant to set out on such a mission). * * *

"Johnson claims that the Illinois rule expresses an unsupported preference for state-of-mind evidence that goes to the declarant's conduct and mental state. This contention, however, ignores a clear distinction between the reliability of out-of-court statements as proof of a declarant's state of mind and the reliability of such statements as proof of subsequent conduct by someone other than the declarant. If Johnson were offering hearsay evidence concerning Mitchell's statements to prove Mitchell's state of mind, there would be something of a reliability problem due to the prosecution's inability to cross-examine Mitchell to determine whether he had honestly described his state of mind to the witness. Illinois' state-of-mind exception reflects a judgment that this measure of unreliability is acceptable where the declarant's state of mind is directly relevant.

"Johnson, however, proposes to use Mitchell's out-of-court statements to suggest that Larry T. actually threatened Mitchell and that Larry T. should therefore be considered an alternative suspect. This proposed use introduces additional sources of unreliability. In addition to the danger that Mitchell misrepresented his state of mind to the witness, there is the possibility that Larry T. misrepresented his intentions or that Mitchell misunderstood him."

BRIDGES v. STATE

Supreme Court of Wisconsin, 1945.
247 Wis. 350, 19 N.W.2d 529.

[Bridges was convicted of taking indecent liberties with Sharon Schunk, a child of seven. The identification of Bridges depended significantly upon the identification of his residence at 125 East Johnson Street as the place where Sharon was taken and assaulted.]

FRITZ, JUSTICE.

* * *

* * * There is testimony by police officers and also Mrs. Schunk as to statements which were made to them by Sharon on February 26 and 27, 1945, and also during the course of their subsequent investigations to ascertain the identity of the man who committed the offense and of the house and room in which it was committed. In those statements she spoke, as hereinbefore stated, of various matters and features which she remembered and which were descriptive of the exterior and surroundings of the house; and of the room and various articles and the location thereof therein. It is true that testimony as to such statements was hearsay and, as such, inadmissible if the purpose for which it was received had been to establish thereby that there were in fact the stated articles in the room, or that they were located as stated, or that the exterior features or surroundings of the house were as Sharon stated. That, however, was not in this case the purpose for which the evidence as to those statements was admitted. It was admissible in so far as the fact that she had made the statements can be deemed to tend to show that at the time those statements were made—which was a month prior to the subsequent discovery of the room and house at 125 East Johnson Street—she had knowledge as to articles and descriptive features which, as was proven by other evidence, were in fact in or about that room and house. If in relation thereto Sharon made the statements as to which the officers and her mother testified, then those statements, although they were extra judicial utterances, constituted at least circumstantial evidence that she then had such knowledge; and that such state of mind on her part was acquired by reason of her having been in that room and house prior to making the statements. Under these circumstances there are applicable to the hearsay testimony in question the following propositions stated in Wigmore on Evidence, 3rd Ed., to-wit:

> "The condition of a speaker's mind, as to knowledge, belief, rationality, emotion, or the like may be evidenced by his utterances, either used testimonially as assertions to be believed, or used circumstantially as affording indirect inferences. * * * The usual resort is to utterances which circumstantially indicate a specific state of mind causing them. To such a use, then the hearsay rule makes no opposition, because the utterance is not used for the sake of inducing belief in any assertion it may contain. The assertion, if in form there is one, is to be disregarded and the direct inference alone regarded. This discrimination, though well accepted in law, is easy to be ignored, and it needs perhaps to be emphasized." Vol. 6, p. 237, sec. 1790. See also p. 234, sec. 1788; p. 240, sec. 1791.

* * *

So in this case the proof that Sharon made the statements in question before there was any possibility of having what she stated she remembered about the house, and room, and articles therein, from her first contact therewith, affected or changed by what she learned after the discovery and location thereof, at 125 East Johnson Street, is material and significant in so far as it tended to show that she had knowledge of certain things in and about the house and room. The existence of those things in fact could not, however, be established by her hearsay statements, but had to be proven by other evidence which was competent. In other words, although proof of her extra judicial assertions was competent to show such knowledge on her part, it could not be deemed to prove the facts asserted thereby. When for instance, it was proven that Sharon stated during the evening after the alleged assault that there was a picture of the lady in the room, her statement did not constitute competent evidence to prove that there was such a picture in the room. But her statement was competent as evidence to prove that she had knowledge of such an object in the room and for this purpose the utterance is not inadmissible hearsay, but is a circumstantial fact indicating knowledge on the part of Sharon Schunk at a particular time.

* * *

Judgment affirmed.

ATHERTON v. GASLIN

Court of Appeals of Kentucky, 1922.
194 Ky. 460, 239 S.W. 771.

CLAY, J.

The principal question on this appeal is whether, in a contest of a will, on the sole ground of forgery, the declarations of the testator are admissible in corroboration of other and more direct evidence tending to show the genuineness of the will.

The question arises in the following way: J.F. Atherton, a bachelor, died March 6, 1919. * * * Upon the death of J.F. Atherton, there was probated in the Nelson county court a paper purporting to be his holographic will, by which he devised all of his property to his nephew, Roscoe Gaslin. Thereupon William B. Atherton and others prosecuted an appeal to the Nelson circuit court, where the will was contested on the ground of forgery. A trial before a jury resulted in a verdict sustaining the will, and the contestants appeal.

After showing by several witnesses, who were qualified to testify on the subject, that the will was wholly in the handwriting of the testator, the contestees were permitted to show that the testator stated before making his will that he intended to leave his property to Roscoe Gaslin, and that he stated after the date of the will that he had made a will making Roscoe Gaslin his sole devisee.

There is little, if any, dissent from the rule that the declarations of the testator are admissible on the issue of mental incapacity, for they are outward manifestations of a state of mind and tend more or less directly to show what that state of mind was. Alexander's Commentaries on Wills, § 362. Though it was held in Throckmorton v. Holt, 180 U.S. 552, 21 S.Ct. 474, 45 L.Ed. 663, that the declarations of the testator were not admissible to prove or disprove the making of a will, and that there was no distinction between ante-testamentary and post-testamentary statements, Mr. Wigmore says that the admissibility of the former is entirely settled, and our investigation of the question has led to the same conclusion. Wigmore on Evidence, vol. 3, § 1735; State v. Ready, 78 N.J.L. 599, 75 A. 564, 28 L.R.A., N.S., 240.

Admissibility of such statements proceeds on the principle that a design or plan to do or not do a specific act has probative value to show that the act was in fact done or not done. Wigmore on Evidence, vol. 1, § 102. Hence if the issue is whether a will, or a will of a particular tenor, was executed, the pre-existing testamentary design of the testator is relevant, and such design may be evidenced by his statements. Wigmore on Evidence, vol. 3, § 1735.

When we come to post-testamentary statements of the testator as to the execution, contents, or revocation of a will, we find that there is a great diversity of opinion. Many of the courts take the unqualified position that such statements are mere assertions of an external fact offered as evidence of the truth of the assertion, and do not fall within any of the exceptions to the hearsay rule. Illustrative cases taking this view of the question are: Meeker v. Boylan, 28 N.J.L. 276; In re Gordon's Case, 50 N.J.Eq. 397, 26 A. 268, affirmed in Gordon v. Old, 52 N.J.Eq. 317, 30 A. 19; Leslie v. McMurtry, 60 Ark. 301, 30 S.W. 33; Dan v. Brown, 4 Cow., N.Y., 490, 15 Am.Dec. 395; Grant v. Grant, 1 Sandf.Ch., N.Y., 235; Kennedy's Will, 167 N.Y. 163, 60 N.E. 442; Earp v. Edgington, 107 Tenn. 23, 64 S.W. 40; Walton v. Kendrick, 122 Mo. 504, 27 S.W.2d 872, 25 L.R.A. 701. Among the cases holding that such evidence is admissible are the following: Sugden v. St. Leonards, L.R.I.P.D. 154; Conoly v. Gayle, 61 Ala. 116; Patterson v. Hickey, 32 Ga. 159; Lane v. Hill, 68 N.H. 275, 44 A. 393, 73 Am.St.Rep. 591; Tynan v. Paschal, 27 Tex. 300, 84 Am.Dec. 619; Hoppe v. Byers, 60 Md. 381; Glockner v. Glockner, 263 Pa. 393, 106 A. 731; In re Johnson's Estate, 170 Wis. 436, 175 N.W. 917. In Hoppe v. Byers, supra, it was held that post-testamentary declarations of a testator, that he had made a will of a particular tenor, though not admissible to establish the paper, were admissible in corroboration of direct evidence of execution. In the case of In re Johnson's Estate, supra, it was held that post-testamentary declarations of a testator, to the effect that he had made a will, and for the benefit of proponent, were admissible in proceedings to probate a will contested for lack of genuineness of signature. The courts, in taking this view of the question, either make a special exception to the hearsay rule, or admit the testimony as indicating the testator's belief or state of mind, from which we may infer the doing of the act which produced that belief or state of mind.

Taking up the opinions of this court, we find that in the case of Beauchamp's Will, 4 T.B.Mon. 361, the question involved was one of revocation. The same witness, who wrote and proved the execution of the will, testified that some days after its publication he informed the testator that the will was burned. Whereupon testator replied that it was done by his orders, and that the law would make a will for him. In holding that the will had been revoked, the court said:

> "Revocation is an act of the mind; it consists in the will and purpose to destroy, or annul the operation of the instrument. This will or purpose of mind must be made known by some one or other of those outward signs or symbols of revocation, pointed out by the statute. Any one of these signs or symbols performed in the slightest manner, joined with the declared intent, or settled purpose of revoking, will be a good revocation. It is the intention that must govern. The question is, Has he revoked or not—revocavit vel non? It is a question of fact and intention. In pursuing the enquiry, the existence of one fact may be inferred from the proof of other facts.
>
> "From the facts proved, of the destruction of the instrument, the knowledge thereof by the decedent, his declarations that he had ordered it, that the law would make a will for him, and his abstaining from any attempt to supply the loss or destruction of the paper, the intention to revoke must be inferred. It cannot be necessary to prove positively and in terms, the total destruction of the paper in the presence of the testator, by a witness who saw it. It is enough that the inward intent to revoke, and the outward symbol of revocation are so knit together and bound by the evidence that they cannot be separated."

We also held in Steele v. Price, 5 B.Mon. 58, that the failure of one, who is informed of the destruction of his will, to publish another, furnished a prima facie presumption of intention to revoke the will destroyed, but that this presumption could be rebutted by evidence of the same grade, such as the declarations of the testator respecting his testamentary intentions. In the case of Chisholm's Heirs v. Ben, etc., 7 B.Mon. 408, it was held that the declarations of a decedent in his lifetime, tending to show that he had a will at the time in existence, are admissible to repel the presumption of a revocation, but only as corroborative and as the lowest species of evidence. It was further held that the declarations of a decedent as to the execution and contents of his will are only admissible in corroboration of other evidence, and, when there is no other evidence, his declarations should be rejected. In Wall v. Dimmitt, 114 Ky. 923, 72 S.W. 300, 24 Ky.Law Rep. 1749, we held that declarations of the testator, whether made before or after the execution of the will, were not competent as direct and substantive evidence of undue influence or to show that the will was procured thereby, but are admissible to show the mental condition of the testator at the time of making the will and his susceptibility to influences by which he was surrounded. While the opinion in the case of Mercer's Adm'r v. Mackin, 14 Bush. 434, employs certain language from which it might be inferred that the court was of the opinion that the declarations of a testator as to the execution and contents of his will are not admissible for any purpose, a careful examination of the opinion will show that all the court intended to hold was that the declarations of the testator are not alone sufficient to prove the due execution or contents of his will, and are admissible only in corroboration of other evidence. * * *

We perceive no reason for making any distinction between the testator's declaration as to the contents of his will and his declaration as to the making of a will. Each shows the testator's belief or state of mind, from which we may naturally infer the existence of the fact or the doing of the act which produced that belief or state of mind. Not only so, but we have affirmed cases involving the genuineness of a will and based our conclusion on the testator's post-testamentary declaration as to its execution. Furthermore, there is a plain intimation in the case of Mercer's Adm'r v. Mackin, supra, that the testator's declarations as to the execution of his will are admissible in corroboration of other evidence. That such declarations are of a persuasive character, and may often throw light on a doubtful issue, cannot be doubted. The fact that they may be manufactured goes to their weight and not to their admissibility. In view of these considerations and of the manifest tendency of the courts of to-day to enlarge rather than restrict the character of evidence that may be received, we conclude that both the ante-testamentary and post-testamentary declarations of the testator were admissible in corroboration of the other evidence tending to show the genuineness of the will.

We have examined with care the other errors assigned, but find none of them of sufficient importance to authorize a reversal.

Judgment affirmed.

Note

See 6 Wigmore, Evidence §§ 1734–1740 (Chadbourn rev. 1976); McCormick, Evidence § 276 (4th ed. 1992).

SECTION 11. RECORDED RECOLLECTION *

[FED.R.EVID. 803(5)]

UNITED STATES v. PATTERSON

United States Court of Appeals, Ninth Circuit, 1982.
678 F.2d 774, cert. denied, 459 U.S. 911, 103 S.Ct. 219, 74 L.Ed.2d 174 (1982).

JAMES M. BURNS, DISTRICT JUDGE.

Defendant James Patterson appeals his conviction on two counts of receiving stolen property, 18 U.S.C. § 2313, and on one count of conspiracy to transport stolen motor vehicles in interstate commerce, 18 U.S.C. §§ 371 and 2312. He assigns several errors: 1) the grand jury testimony of a witness was erroneously admitted into evidence; * * *.

* See 3 Wigmore, Evidence §§ 734–757 (Chadbourn rev. 1970); McCormick, Evidence ch. 28 (4th ed. 1992); Blakely, Past Recollection Recorded: Restrictions on Use as Exhibit and Proposals for Change, 17 Hous.L.Rev. 411 (1980)

* * *

I. Grand Jury Testimony

Testifying under a grant of immunity, James McKay (defendant's nephew) told the grand jury on March 10, 1980, the defendant had told him the forklifts were obtained from a man in California and they had been stolen. At trial McKay testified he could not remember the defendant telling him about the source or legality of the forklifts.[1] After the prosecutor tried without success to refresh McKay's memory with a transcript of his grand jury testimony, the trial judge allowed the pertinent portion of the grand jury testimony to be read into the record as a past recorded recollection exception to the hearsay rule.[2]

A document is admissible as past recorded recollection if 1) the witness once had knowledge about the matters in the document, 2) the witness now has insufficient recollection to testify fully and accurately, and 3) the record was made at a time when the matter was fresh in the witness' memory and reflected the witness' knowledge correctly. *United States v. Edwards,* 539 F.2d 689, 691–692 (9th Cir.), *cert. denied,* 429 U.S. 984, 97 S.Ct. 501, 50 L.Ed.2d 594 (1976). *Accord, Clark v. City of Los Angeles,* 650 F.2d 1033, 1037–1038 (9th Cir.1981) (stating the rule but not reaching the issue of admissibility).

Defendant claims the third foundation requirement of Fed.R.Evid. 803(5) was not met and thus admission of the grand jury transcript was error. The defendant specifically contends the government failed to show 1) the matter was fresh in McKay's mind when he testified before

1. Knowledge that the property in question has been stolen is one of the essential elements of the crime of receiving stolen property. 18 U.S.C. § 2313 (1970).

2. The government first attempted to refresh McKay's memory by showing him a transcript of his testimony before the grand jury:

> McKay: I get a recollection in my memory saying that I must have said that. But as I sit here right now I cannot say that I can remember Mr. Patterson or him saying this to me at that time. It's been a long time, you know. This is almost two years ago, and I've got to swear under oath right now, and I can't say that I can actually remember him saying that. If I can say that, I can go off with that and say—

The testimony continued:

> Q. As you sit here today, you can't remember what Mr. Patterson said to you about where he got the forklifts?
>
> A. Right.
>
> Q. But at the time you appeared before the Grand Jury back in March and testified to what he said, at that time apparently you were able to recall; is that correct?
>
> A. Yeah, I was a lot madder at him then.
>
> Q. Well, were you able to recall a little bit better?
>
> A. I must have been.
>
> Q. You say you were mad at them (sic) then. Were you lying before the Grand Jury?
>
> A. No, I don't think so.

The government then offered a portion of the grand jury transcript into evidence. After defense counsel objected, the following exchange occurred:

> THE COURT: I think this is admissible. You can't remember this at this time; is that true?
>
> THE WITNESS: Yes.
>
> THE COURT: But is the Grand Jury transcript which you read, is it accurate?
>
> THE WITNESS: I believe so.
>
> THE COURT: I'm going to allow this to be read under Rule 803(5), past recollection recorded.

the grand jury, and 2) McKay's statements to the grand jury were an accurate reflection of his knowledge at that time. We disagree.

* * *

A traditional rule, commonly applied before adoption of Rule 803(5), was that freshness is defined by contemporaneousness, i.e., the witness' recollection must have been recorded at or near the time of the event. 3 J. Wigmore, *Wigmore on Evidence,* § 745 (Chadbourne rev. 1970). In this case McKay's grand jury testimony occurred at least ten months after the conversation in which the defendant told him the forklifts were stolen. Even before the adoption of Rule 803(5), though, some courts used a more flexible rule giving the trial judge discretion to determine freshness on a "case-by-case basis giving consideration to all pertinent aspects including the lapse of time which reasonably and properly bear upon the likelihood of the statement being an accurate recordation of the event to which the memory related." *United States v. Senak,* 527 F.2d 129, 141 (7th Cir.1975), *cert. denied,* 425 U.S. 907, 96 S.Ct. 1500, 47 L.Ed.2d 758 (1976) (pre-Rules case).[4] Broad discretion for the trial judge is clearly intended under Fed.R.Evid. 803(5), as the advisory committee notes indicate: "No attempt is made in the exception to spell out the method of establishing the initial knowledge or the contemporaneity and accuracy of the record, leaving them to be dealt with as the circumstances of the particular case might indicate." 28 U.S.C.App. p. 581 (1976). *See United States v. Williams,* 571 F.2d 344, 348–50 (6th Cir.), *cert. denied,* 439 U.S. 841, 99 S.Ct. 131, 58 L.Ed.2d 139 (1978) (finding no abuse of discretion in admitting under Rule 803(5) statement of witness to agent relating conversation that took place six months earlier).

We cannot say the trial judge abused his discretion in finding that McKay's memory was fresh at the time he testified before the grand jury, although the question admittedly is a close one. At least ten months elapsed between McKay's conversation with the defendant and his grand jury testimony. McKay admitted he was angry with the defendant when he appeared before the grand jury. In attempting to lay the foundation, the prosecutor and trial judge asked ambiguous questions, and McKay equivocated wherever possible. Still, the trial judge elicited responses showing that at trial McKay could not remember his conversation with the defendant and that before the grand jury

4. In *Senak* the court rejected contemporaneousness as the sole test of whether an event was fresh in a witness' mind at the time the record was made. There, the trial court admitted a witness' statement made three years after the event in question; here, the period is only ten months. In *Senak,* however, the court noted the existence of unusual circumstances indicating the witness' fresh memory and reliability of her knowledge at the time she made the statement. The recorded statement displayed no lapses in the witness' memory. The statement was specific and detailed. The witness had read her statement and had edited it before signing it as a true account of her knowledge at that time. The court observed that the witness had been trying to remember not a routine transaction but arrangements with a lawyer who was defending her boyfriend against criminal charges. Finally, the witness testified explicitly at trial that her statement had been true at the time she made it.

he had remembered the crucial conversation. Thus, it was well within the discretion of the trial judge to determine, under all of the circumstances, that the conversation had been fresh in McKay's mind when he appeared before the grand jury.

The past recorded recollection exception also requires a showing that the record accurately reflected the witness' knowledge at the time the record was made. The defendant characterizes the trial court's inquiry of McKay on that subject as asking McKay whether the grand jury *transcript* was accurate rather than whether his grand jury *testimony* was accurate. We reject the defendant's characterization as frivolous. We deem the trial court's question to have required from McKay a response regarding the accuracy of his statements to the grand jury (as embodied in the transcript). McKay told the trial court he did not think he had lied to the grand jury. He also said he had recalled the events in question better when he testified before the grand jury. Moreover, the indications of reliability are stronger in this case than in *United States v. Edwards,* 539 F.2d at 691–692.[5] Therefore, we find no abuse of discretion in the trial court's determination that McKay's grand jury testimony was an accurate reflection of his knowledge at that time.

In summary, the grand jury testimony was admissible as past recorded recollection. * * *

* * *

Affirmed in part and reversed in part.

STATE v. SUTTON, 253 Or. 24, 450 P.2d 748 (1969). "The writing in question met all but one of the qualifications of past recollection recorded. The witness identified the written memorandum, recalled the making of it at the time of the event when his recollection was fresh, and testified as to its accuracy. He did not say 'it was accurate' but he testified to the actual performance of each step reflected in the memorandum. This testimony would qualify the writing to be received in evidence except for a rule, adopted in Oregon and many other states that, before a memorandum of past recollection recorded may be received in evidence, the witness must have no present recollection of the subject matter of which the memorandum is a record. * * *

5. In *Edwards* this court upheld admission of a statement made by a companion of the defendant, describing events leading to the crime, even though the companion admittedly was drunk when he gave the statement to police. The statement was made the day after the events in question, was signed by the witness and contained an inscription in his handwriting acknowledging he had read the statement and it was correct to the best of his knowledge. At trial the companion testified he recalled making the statement, and, although he had no memory of the underlying facts, "he believed the statement accurately reflected his recollection at the time it was made." 539 F.2d at 692.

The indications of reliability are stronger, we believe, in the instant case. McKay recalled testifying before the grand jury, he remembered being under oath at that time and, although he admitted exaggerating his testimony to the grand jury, he also said he thought he had told the truth.

"We have come to the conclusion that the above and similar cases are in error which held that the absence of a present recollection by the writer is a prerequisite to the receiving in evidence of a past recollection recorded. Professor Wigmore has put his finger upon the fallacy in our present rule. In disapproving such a rule he states:

'* * * Is the use of past recollection necessary (1) because in the case in hand there is not available a present actual recollection in the specific witness, or (2) because in the usual case a faithful record of past recollection, if it exists, is more trustworthy and desirable than a present recollection of greater or less vividness?

'The latter view, it would seem is more in harmony with general experience, as well as with the attitude of the judges who early vindicated the use of past recollection. A faithful memorandum is acceptable, not conditionally on the total or partial absence of a present remnant of actual recollection in the particular witness, but *unconditionally;* because, for every moment of time which elapses between the act of recording and the occasion of testifying, the actual recollection must be inferior in vividness to the recollection perpetuated in the record.' (Emphasis theirs.) Wigmore Evidence (3d ed.) 76 § 738."

ELAM v. SOARES, 282 Or. 93, 577 P.2d 1336, 1338–39 (1978). "Defendant contends, in the alternative, that the 'recorded statement' falls within the exception to the hearsay rule as a 'record of past recollection' and says that in State v. Sutton, 253 Or. 24, 26–27, 450 P.2d 748 (1969), this court removed the previous requirement of that exception to the effect that there must be an absence of a present recollection by a writer-witness as a 'necessary pre-requisite.'

"The abandonment of that requirement has been criticized because of possible abuses by use of statements prepared for purposes of litigation under the supervision of claim adjusters or attorneys. (See McCormick, supra, 715, § 302, and 603, § 251.) See also Federal Rules of Evidence § 803(5) (1975), Advisory Committee's Note 111.

"Indeed, since our decision in 1969 in *Sutton,* and apparently for these reasons, the following rule has been adopted as Rule 803(5) of the Federal Rules of Evidence, effective July 1, 1975: * * *

"We agree with this rule and, accordingly, hold that a writing is admissible as a 'recorded recollection' only when the witness 'has insufficient recollection to enable him to testify fully and accurately.' Because this requirement was not satisfied in this case, it follows that this recorded statement was not admissible as a statement of past recorded recollection. To the extent that what was said in State v. Sutton, supra, is inconsistent with our holding in this case, that case is overruled."

UNITED STATES v. BOOZ, 451 F.2d 719, 725 (3d Cir.1971). "It is not entirely clear on this record whether Kulp's memory had, in fact, been refreshed. If not, resort must be had by the prosecution to the hearsay exception for past recollection recorded. If Mr. Kulp's memory is not revived by the FBI Report, he may nevertheless testify from its contents if certain conditions are met. A prerequisite of such testimony is ascertaining the identity and accuracy of the record used. 3 Wigmore, Evidence § 747, supra. If Kulp had testified that he read the report over after the FBI Agent made it and was, at that time, satisfied that it was correct, sufficient proof of the report's accuracy would have been made out. Since Kulp did not so testify, the more difficult question is whether there is any other basis for admitting the license plate number.

"Some courts and textwriters have taken the view that where as here, a record is the joint product of two individuals, one who makes an oral statement and one who embodies it in a writing, if both parties are available to testify at trial as to the accuracy with which each performed his role, the recollection may be admitted. See e.g., Swart v. United States, 394 F.2d 5 (9th Cir.1968); 3 Wigmore, Evidence § 751, supra; Morgan, The Relation Between Hearsay and Preserved Memory, 40 Harv.L.Rev. 712, 720 (1927). We think such an exception to the hearsay rule is sound and adopt it here. If Agent Bass can verify the accuracy of his transcription and if Kulp can testify he related an accurate recollection of the number to Agent Bass, we believe that, even though Kulp may not have read the report, sufficient indicia of its accuracy exist to let the evidence go to the jury. If the appropriate evidentiary basis is established at the retrial we think that the appellant would be entitled to an instruction on this point to the effect that in view of the elapsed time since Kulp reported to the FBI, the jurors should cautiously consider the degree of reliability the offered recollection deserves and that no more weight should be accorded it than such degree dictates."

SECTION 12. RECORDS OF REGULARLY CONDUCTED ACTIVITY *

[FED.R.EVID. 803(6), (7)]

KEOGH v. COMMISSIONER OF INTERNAL REVENUE

United States Court of Appeals, Ninth Circuit, 1983.
713 F.2d 496.

DUNIWAY, CIRCUIT JUDGE:

In this case we review the tax court's finding of income tax deficiencies against a Las Vegas casino employee. The wife of the

* See 5 Wigmore, Evidence §§ 1517–1561 (Chadbourn rev. 1974); McCormick, Evidence ch. 29 (4th ed. 1992).

employee is a party solely because the two filed a joint return. We affirm.

I. Facts

Appellant husband here, petitioner in the tax court, was employed at the Dunes Hotel & Country Club, in Las Vegas. He worked in the casino, where he dealt blackjack or ran "big wheel" or roulette games and was known as a 21 dealer. The 21 dealers earned regular wages paid semimonthly. In addition, 21 players sometimes gave them tips or "tokes" in the form of coins or casino chips. Players often gave tokes to the dealers directly; at other times, they placed bets for the dealers, with a player determining after a winning bet how much of the winnings was the dealer's to keep.

The tax court found that during the years in question, 1969–1971, all 21 dealers at the Dunes pooled their tokes, and that the pool was divided equally once a day among all the dealers who had worked during that day's three shifts. Dealers who were off work sick for more than three days in a row were paid $20 off the top of the pool, but dealers who worked as temporary supervisors, or "floormen," did not share in the tokes. During the years in question, the dealers earned annual wages ranging from $5,946.52 to $9,113.79. They reported to their employer total annual toke incomes ranging from $632.50 to $1,022.60, and the reported amounts were shown on the employer's W–2 forms and on the dealers' tax returns.

The Commissioner asserted that the Keoghs had underreported tip income in 1969, 1970, and 1971. He calculated Keogh's toke income through a statistical analysis based on entries in a diary kept by one John Whitlock, Jr., not a party to this action, who worked at the Dunes from March 4, 1967 to May 7, 1970. In the diary, the date of the month and the day of the week were listed on the left side of each page, and separate vertical columns were designated "gross," "net," "tax," and "tips." Beginning in January, 1968, there was an additional column designated "F.I.C.A.," and beginning in April, 1969, a further column designated "insurance." Wage entries were made in the notebook approximately every two weeks in amounts that were the same as those in the Dunes' payroll records for Whitlock. An entry of "off," "sick," "vac," or a dollar amount was made in the diary in the "tips" column for each day.

The Commissioner's statistical analysis of the tip entries resulted in an average daily toke income per dealer of between $42.04 and $74.24, depending on the year and the day of the week. For days on which Whitlock and Keogh both worked, the Commissioner's estimate for him reflected the diary figure. The appropriate average daily toke entry was used for days worked by Keogh but not by Whitlock. Finally, the Commissioner reduced his total estimated toke income for Keogh by 10 percent to account for variability in statistical projections.

There were some problems in the Commissioner's analysis. First, Whitlock's diary did not cover the entire period for which the Commissioner alleged income deficiencies in Keogh's reported tokes; the Commissioner's calculations for part of 1970 and for all of 1971 were extrapolations of the amounts Whitlock entered in previous years. Second, Whitlock did not work as a 21 dealer for the entire period covered by his diary; he first was a craps dealer before he switched to 21. It is undisputed that craps dealers generally made more in tokes than 21 dealers, and that craps dealers did not share their tokes with 21 dealers. It is unclear, however, when Whitlock switched from craps to 21. Third, as the tax court found, the Commissioner's analysis did not reflect consultations with any gaming industry experts outside the I.R.S. and did not consider factors such as the economy, type of game, limits on amounts that could be bet for dealers, amount of money bet, percentage won by the Dunes, season of the year, or holiday periods. Fourth, it is undisputed that Whitlock had, as the tax court found, "a poor reputation for honesty and truthfulness," was dismissed by the Dunes for unsatisfactory work, and had been convicted, with his wife, of receiving stolen property. Despite the larger amounts entered in his diary, he reported total toke income of $419 in 1968, $382 in 1969, and $58 from January through April of 1970.

At trial before the tax court, the principal evidence was a photocopy of the Whitlock diary and testimony by Barbara Mikle, by then Whitlock's former wife. Whitlock, though subpoenaed by the Commissioner, failed to appear. Keogh claimed that he had recorded his daily toke income, but had thrown the records out monthly after reporting toke income to the Dunes each month.

The tax court issued a memorandum findings of fact and opinion on August 17, 1981. Essentially, it accepted the Commissioner's analysis, but reduced the tax deficiency the Commissioner had asserted against Keogh by approximately 20 percent. The tax court found that the Keoghs owed in additional taxes $2,050.52 for 1969, $1,757.46 for 1970, and $1,672.10 for 1971.

II. Evidential Issues

A. Hearsay

The Whitlock diary, offered in evidence to prove the truth of its contents as they related to tokes received by Dunes 21 dealers, was hearsay and thus inadmissible unless excepted by one or more rules of evidence. F.R.Evid. 801, 802. In admitting the diary, the tax court cited the exceptions contained in Rules 803(6) and 804(b)(3). Because we find the diary admissible under Rule 803(6), we do not address the 804(b)(3) exception.

Rule 803(6), the "business records" exception to the hearsay rule, permits the admission of

> A * * * record, * * * in any form, of acts [or] events, * * * made at or near the time by, * * * a person with knowledge, if kept in the course

> of a regularly conducted business activity, and if it was the regular practice of that business activity to make the * * * record, * * * all as shown by the testimony of the custodian or other qualified witness, unless the source of information or the method or circumstances of preparation indicate lack of trustworthiness. The term "business" as used in this paragraph includes business, * * * occupation, and calling of every kind, whether or not conducted for profit.

We hold that the tax court did not abuse its discretion in admitting the diary in evidence. United States v. Perlmuter, 9 Cir., 1982, 693 F.2d 1290, 1293.

The Keoghs' first argument is that Rule 803(6) does not apply to the diary because it was not a business record. They argue that the diary was Whitlock's personal record, not a record of the business enterprise involved, the Dunes. But Whitlock's diary, even though personal to him, shows every indication of being kept "in the course of" his own "business activity," "occupation, and calling." See 4 Weinstein's Evidence ¶ 803(6)[03] (1981 ed.) at 803–155: "[P]ersonal records kept for business reasons may be able to qualify. A housekeeper's records kept neatly and accurately for purposes of balancing bank statements, keeping strict budgets and preparing income tax returns could qualify under the statute."

The reliability usually found in records kept by business concerns may be established in personal business records if they are systematically checked and regularly and continually maintained. See United States v. Hedman, 7 Cir., 1980, 630 F.2d 1184, 1197–1198 (diary of payoffs by extortion victim); United States v. McPartlin, 7 Cir., 1979, 595 F.2d 1321, 1347–1350 (desk calendar-appointment diary, and cases there cited); Weinstein, supra, (reliability determined from "testimony indicating that they were kept meticulously"); Advisory Committee Note to Rule 803(6). But see Buckley v. Altheimer, 7 Cir., 1946, 152 F.2d 502, 507–508 (private financial diary inadmissible, distinguished from "account books or individual memoranda of particular transactions"), a case decided before the adoption of the Federal Rules of Evidence.

Here, Mikle testified that she saw Whitlock and only Whitlock make entries in the diary; that he usually made them after night shifts of work; that when he made no entries for three to four days, he would copy entries for those days from a record kept in his wallet; that he usually made no entries in the diary on his days off; and that she understood the diary to contain a record of tokes he received from his work as a dealer.

The cases that the Keoghs cite for the proposition that Rule 803(6) applies only to commercial business records that are kept by those under a business duty to do so arose in the commercial context, but in fact stress just the sort of timeliness and regularity of entries that are present here. See, e.g., United States v. Kim, D.C.Cir.,1979, 595 F.2d 755, 759–764 (telex prepared in response to subpoena and summarizing two-year-old bank deposits not admissible); Seattle–First National Bank v. Randall, 9 Cir.,1976, 532 F.2d 1291, 1296 (bank's loan procedure manual not admissible).

More to the point is Sabatino v. Curtiss National Bank of Miami Springs, 5 Cir.,1969, 415 F.2d 632, reversing a trial court's refusal to admit in evidence a personal check record. That case construed the Federal Business Records Act, 28 U.S.C. § 1732, but its reasoning is instructive here. United States v. Smith, 9 Cir.,1979, 609 F.2d 1294, 1301. The *Sabatino* court said, "A man has a direct financial interest in keeping accurate accounts in his personal business. * * * The cases indicate that private records, if kept regularly and if incidental to some personal business pursuit, are competent evidence under § 1732." 415 F.2d at 636. It made no difference whether the check account was used for any specific business. Id. at n. 5. "Moreover, it is settled that the business 'need not be commercial.'" Id., citing C. McCormick, Evidence § 283 (1954).

The Keoghs dispute the general trustworthiness of the diary entries. They cite Palmer v. Hoffman, 1943, 318 U.S. 109, 113–114, 63 S.Ct. 477, 480–481, 87 L.Ed. 645, alleging that Whitlock's motives in preparing the diary were never explained. *Palmer v. Hoffman* is not in point because there is no evidence that Whitlock's motives in making the entries were suspect. The diary contained his own personal financial records; there is no reason put forward for him to have lied to himself. The reliability of the tip entries is corroborated by the fact that other entries corresponded with Dunes' payroll records, and that reliability is not tarnished by the fact that Whitlock, as the Keoghs are alleged to have done, reported to the government smaller amounts of tip income than he in fact received and recorded in the diary. Neither is Rule 803(6) made inapplicable by the fact that Mikle, not Whitlock, testified to lay the foundation for the diary. She testified adequately as to the regularity of the entries. See United States v. Smith, supra, 609 F.2d at 1301–1302.

The Keoghs contend that the testimony of Whitlock as custodian of the diary was required because only he could speak to his reliance on the records kept there. But the record gives us no reason to believe that Whitlock did not rely on his personal financial diary; therefore, we do not find that the tax court abused its discretion in admitting it without Whitlock's personal testimony.

* * *

Affirmed.

Notes

(1) In United States v. Evans, 572 F.2d 455 (5th Cir.1978), cert. denied, 439 U.S. 870, 99 S.Ct. 200, 58 L.Ed.2d 182 (1978), one defendant, Gent, objected to the introduction against him of a series of pocket-size calendars, or "daytimers," which he had maintained. "At the outset, it is interesting to note that here, for all intents and purposes, the 'declarants' are objecting

to the introduction of the so-called 'hearsay.' This is an ironic twist in that the rule against hearsay has as its primary purpose the protection of the right of litigants to confront witnesses against them and to test their credibility through cross-examination. * * * This unique situation certainly colors our consideration of these claims. See Fed.R.Evid. 102. There is some support in the record for the government's proposition, accepted by the district court, that the daytimers were made and maintained as business records of CRCAP and, as such, were admissible under Rule 803(6). * * * Even aside from this testimony, there is a compelling reason why the daytimers were admissible. The entries were, in fact, statements made by Gent himself and offered against him. Thus, they were not hearsay at all under Rule 801(d)(2)(A), Federal Rules of Evidence. Any and all statements of an accused person, so far as are not excluded by the doctrine of confessions or by the privilege against self-incrimination, are usable against the accused as admissions and are not hearsay." 572 F.2d at 487–88.

(2) "FBI agent Snider testified that he had checked various records, which included police records, sheriff's office records, credit records, and city directories, and contacted other sources in Lewiston and that there was no trace of a person named Dale Olson who might have borrowed appellant's automobile. * * * Case law predating the Federal Rules of Evidence differed on the question whether evidence of the lack of entries in records constitutes hearsay, and if so, whether any exception permitted its admittance. * * * The Federal Rules of Evidence, however, have resolved the issue. Rule 803(7) treats evidence of the absence of entries in records of a regularly conducted activity as an exception to the hearsay rule * * *. The authors of the Advisory Committee Note explained that such evidence was 'probably not hearsay as defined in Rule 801,' but the drafters of the Rules opted for a specific treatment of the subject in order to resolve the question definitively in favor of admissibility." United States v. Rich, 580 F.2d 929, 937–38 (9th Cir.1978), cert. denied, 439 U.S. 935, 99 S.Ct. 330, 58 L.Ed.2d 331 (1978).

UNITED STATES v. VELA

United States Court of Appeals, Fifth Circuit, 1982.
673 F.2d 86.

CLARK, CHIEF JUDGE:

Ricardo "Ricky" Vela assigns a plethora of errors in this appeal from conviction of conspiracy to commit a drug-related offense. After considering each of his arguments, we affirm his conviction.

* * *

III. ADMISSION OF TELEPHONE RECORDS

Vela argues that the district court erred in admitting copies of the telephone bills of Vela, Caballero, and Gutierrez under the business records exception to the hearsay rule because a proper foundation was not laid to support the reliability of Southwestern Bell Company's computer-billing process. We hold that the foundation was adequate to support admissibility under Rule 803(6).

At trial, an employee of Southwestern Bell described as custodian of the records sponsored copies of the telephone bills. He testified that the copies were made from microfiche records prepared by the comptroller's department of the company, that the records were prepared in the usual course of the company's regularly-conducted business activity, and that it was part of that activity to prepare such records. When questioned by Vela's counsel outside of the jury's presence, the employee explained the process by which automatic call identification equipment registers the dialing of long-distance telephone calls on electronic tapes. The tapes are then transmitted to the comptroller's office where the information is transferred onto billing tapes. Computers are used at two stages: first, in the recording of the initial dialing, and second, in the computation and preparation of bills in the comptroller's office. The testifying employee vouched only for the general reliability of the process. He was unable to identify the brand, type, and model of each computer, or to vouch for the working condition of the specific equipment during the billing periods covered.

The district court admitted the bills under Rule 803(6) declaring that they "would be even more reliable than * * * average business record[s] because they are not even touched by the hand of man." * * *

Vela's central attack on admissibility of the bills under Rule 803(6) is that the prosecution did not lay a satisfactory foundation. Vela does not dispute that insofar as the custodian of the records testified that the records were kept in the regular course of business the dictates of Rule 803(6) were satisfied. What Vela does argue is that by failing to establish that the computers involved in the billing process were in proper working order a satisfactory foundation was not made and Vela was denied confrontation rights.

Our review of a trial court's decision to admit business records is a limited one. We test it only for abuse of discretion. See Rosenberg v. Collins, 624 F.2d 659, 665 (5th Cir.1980). While the suggestion has been made that there are unique foundation requirements for the admission of computerized business records under Rule 803(6), see generally United States v. Scholle, 553 F.2d 1109, 1125 (8th Cir.), *cert. denied,* 434 U.S. 940, 98 S.Ct. 432, 54 L.Ed.2d 300 (1977); *McCormick's Handbook of the Law of Evidence* 733–34 (2d ed. 1972), this court has previously held that "computer data compilations * * * should be treated as any other record of regularly conducted activity." Rosenberg v. Collins, 624 F.2d at 665. Like the computer records in the *Rosenberg* case, the telephone company's long distance billing records are "sufficiently trustworthy in the eyes of this disinterested company to be relied on by the company in conducting its day to day business affairs." Id.

The prosecution laid a proper predicate for the admission of the bills. A telephone company employee explained the precise manner in which the billing data are compiled. The failure to certify the brand or proper operating condition of the machinery involved does not betray a circumstance of preparation indicating any lack of trustworthiness. Fed.R.Evid. 803(6). This court has previously stated that computer evidence is not intrinsically unreliable. United States v. Fendley, 522 F.2d 181, 187 (5th Cir.1975); Olympic Insurance Co. v. H.D. Harrison, Inc., 418 F.2d 669, 670 (5th Cir.1969). Vela's arguments for a level of authentication greater than that regularly practiced by the company in its own business activities go beyond the rule and its reasonable purpose to admit truthful evidence. The court did not abuse its discretion in admitting the bills or deny Vela his confrontation rights. At best, the arguments made go to the weight that should be accorded the evidence, not its admissibility. See United States v. Scholle, 553 F.2d at 1125.

* * *

Affirmed.

Notes

(1) The subject of computer-generated evidence has engendered a voluminous literature. See, e.g., Bender, Computer Law: Evidence and Procedure (1978); Fromholtz, Discovery, Evidence, Confidentiality, and Security Problems Associated with the Use of Computer–Based Litigation Support Systems, 1977 Wash.U.L.Q. 445; Horning, Electronically Stored Evidence: Answers to Some Recurring Questions Concerning Pretrial Discovery and Trial Usage, 41 Wash. & Lee L.Rev. 1335 (1984); Peritz, Computer Data and Reliability: A Call for Authentication of Business Records Under the Federal Rules of Evidence, 80 Nw.U.L.Rev. 956 (1986); Roberts, A Practitioner's Primer on Computer–Generated Evidence, 41 U.Chi.L.Rev. 254 (1974).

(2) "[A]ppellant objects to admission into evidence of a computer printout which recorded the 6:29 p.m. telephone call from Adler's room to appellant's hotel. * * * Appellant argues that, since the Sheraton's Director of Communications, Ms. Fry, 'did not understand the distinctions between "menus," "data bases," and computer "code," she was "confused and inadequately trained," ' and thus without personal knowledge of the way in which the computer printout was generated. This argument is frivolous. The record was generated automatically, as the trial transcript demonstrated, and was retained in the ordinary course of business, as records of outgoing telephone calls regularly are. Fry was a 'qualified witness,' even though she was not a computer programmer. * * * In any event, telephone records are business records for the purposes of Fed. R.Evid. 803(6)." United States v. Linn, 880 F.2d 209, 216 (9th Cir.1989).

(3) "The determination of whether a foundation has been properly laid for application of Federal Rule of Evidence 803(6) and whether the circumstances indicate lack of trustworthiness is within the discretion of the district court. * * * As for the requirement that the record-keeping process be attested to by a qualified witness, it is well established that the witness need not be the person who actually prepared the record. * * * A qualified witness is simply one who can explain and be cross-examined concerning the manner in which the records are made and kept." Wallace

Motor Sales, Inc. v. American Motor Sales Corp., 780 F.2d 1049, 1060–61 (1st Cir.1985).

(4) "Contrary to Staudinger's assertion, there is no requirement that the party offering a business record produce the author of the item. ¶ 803(6)[02] Weinstein's Evidence at 803–179 to –181 (1985). Furthermore, '[a] foundation for admissibility may at times be predicated on judicial notice of the nature of the business and the nature of the records as observed by the court, particularly in the case of bank and similar statements.' Id. at p. 803–178. In this case, the records admitted were the type of records maintained by banks in the ordinary course of business. In addition, the PSB custodian testified that the records were of a type normally maintained in the ordinary course of the bank's business and that the records would be made in close proximity to the time of their origin." Federal Deposit Ins. Corp. v. Staudinger, 797 F.2d 908, 910 (10th Cir.1986).

UNITED STATES v. BAKER

United States Court of Appeals, District of Columbia Circuit, 1982.
693 F.2d 183.

TAMM, CIRCUIT JUDGE:

* * *

On June 1, 1981, a United States Secret Service special agent assigned to undercover duty purchased two treasury checks in the amounts of $1,008 and $807 from defendant for $350. The next day the agent purchased treasury checks in the amounts of $10,000 and $1,008 from defendant for $1,000. The following day the agent purchased a treasury check in the amount of $10,000 from defendant for $500. By having each of the intended payees fill out and return Form 1133, the Secret Service confirmed that the payees did not receive the checks nor authorize anyone else to negotiate them. Defendant was indicted on September 3, 1981, on three counts of selling government property in violation of 18 U.S.C. § 641. After a jury trial on December 14 and 15, 1981, he was found guilty on all three counts and was sentenced to imprisonment for not less than two and not more than six years.

* * *

Fourth, defendant argues that it was error to receive Form 1133 into evidence and that the forms are the only evidence of his lack of authority to sell the checks, an essential element of the charge against him. A.T.F.S. Form 1133 is routinely sent to intended payees of government checks who the Treasury Department believes have not received their checks. The form inquires whether the payee received the check and whether he authorized anyone else to receive or negotiate it. The filing of the form facilitates the prompt issuance of a replacement check. Each of the intended payees of the checks sold by defendant completed Form 1133 and answered that he had not received his check and that he had not authorized anyone else to receive it. These completed forms were admitted into evidence over the defense counsel's objection, for the alleged purpose of proving that the payees submitted claim forms.

The forms, which were filled out by the intended payees and mailed back to the Treasury Department, are out-of-court statements offered to prove the truth of the matter asserted and, therefore, are hearsay under Federal Rule of Evidence 801(c). The forms are relevant only to prove that the payees did not receive the checks and did not authorize defendant to possess them, which is the matter asserted in the forms. Hearsay, of course, is inadmissible unless it falls within one of the exceptions to the rule. Fed.R.Evid. 802.

Contrary to the government's argument, the forms do not fall within the hearsay exception for records of regularly conducted activity. Federal Rule of Evidence 803(6) provides:

* * *

The justification for this exception is that business records have a high degree of accuracy because the nation's business demands it, because the records are customarily checked for correctness, and because recordkeepers are trained in habits of precision. McCormick, *Evidence* § 306, at 720 (2d ed. 1972). Double hearsay exists when a business record is prepared by one employee from information supplied by another employee. If both the source and the recorder of the information, as well as every other participant in the chain producing the record, are acting in the regular course of business, the multiple hearsay is excused by Rule 803(6). However, if the source of the information is an outsider, Rule 803(6) does not, by itself, permit the admission of the business record. The outsider's statement must fall within another hearsay exception to be admissible because it does not have the presumption of accuracy that statements made during the regular course of business have. See United States v. Davis, 571 F.2d 1354 (5th Cir.1978); 4 D. Louisell & C. Mueller, *Federal Evidence* § 448 (1980); McCormick, *Evidence* § 310, at 725–26 (2d ed. 1972); 4 J. Weinstein & M. Berger, *Weinstein's Evidence* ¶ 803(6)[04] (1981). In the present case, the intended payees were not acting in the regular course of business, and their statements do not fall within any other hearsay exception. Therefore, the forms are inadmissible hearsay. If the issue were relevant, the forms would be admissible to show that they were in fact filed, which is in the firsthand knowledge of Treasury Department officials. But even if the filing of the forms were relevant, the forms would not be admissible to prove that the payees did not receive their checks. See United States v. Tompkins, 487 F.2d 146, 151 (8th Cir. 1973).

Although admission of the claim forms was error, it was merely harmless error. * * *

* * *

Affirmed.

LEWIS v. BAKER

United States Court of Appeals, Second Circuit, 1975.
526 F.2d 470.

WATERMAN, CIRCUIT JUDGE:

Plaintiff, Clifford J. Lewis, Jr., brought this action in the United States District Court for the Southern District of New York pursuant to the Federal Employers' Liability Act, 45 U.S.C. § 51 et seq. and the Federal Safety Appliance Act, 45 U.S.C. § 1 et seq. alleging he suffered a disabling injury while employed by the Penn Central Railroad. Judgment was entered in favor of defendants after a jury trial. Plaintiff appeals and seeks a new trial on the following grounds: (1) accident reports were improperly admitted into evidence; * * *. Finding no merit to the above contentions, we affirm.

On the date of his injury, October 26, 1969, plaintiff was employed as a freight brakeman or car dropper in the Penn Central railroad freight yard in Morrisville, Pennsylvania. His work called for him to move freight cars in a railroad yard by riding them down a slope while applying the brake manually. Plaintiff testified that immediately before the incident in question, he climbed onto the lead car of two box-cars, stationed himself on the rear brake platform of that car, applied the brake to test it, and found that the brake held. Upon his signal, another employee of the railroad released the two box-cars from the rest of the train at the top of a hill, at which time they started to roll down the slope. Plaintiff then started to turn the vertical brake wheel so that the car would slow down as it descended the slope and would ease into the train with which it was to couple on a track beyond the bottom of the slope. He claims that the brake did not hold, that the car continued to gather momentum, and that he then decided to leap off the car to avoid injury. As a result of the fall, he claims to have sustained substantial knee injury and the aggravation of a preexisting psychiatric condition which has precluded his returning to his job. There were no witnesses to the accident other than the plaintiff.

At the trial, defendants sought to rebut plaintiff's allegations of a faulty brake with evidence that the brake had functioned properly immediately prior to the accident when the plaintiff tested it, and immediately after the accident when it was checked in connection with the preparation of an accident report. It was the defendants' contention that plaintiff improperly set, or forgot to set, a necessary brake handle, panicked, and then leapt from the car.

In support of their interpretation of the events, defendants offered into evidence a "personal injury report" and an "inspection report." Frank Talbott, a trainmaster, testified that the personal injury report was signed by him and prepared under his supervision. The information had been provided to him by William F. Campbell, the night trainmaster. Talbott confirmed the authenticity of the record and testified that he was required to make out such reports of injuries as part of the regular course of business. At the trial David W. Halderman, an assistant general foreman for the defendants, identified the inspection report which had been prepared by Campbell and by Alfred Zuchero, a gang foreman. This report was based upon an inspection of the car Campbell and Zuchero had conducted less than four hours after the accident. Halderman testified that Zuchero was dead and that Campbell was employed by a railroad in Virginia. The latter was thus beyond the reach of subpoena. Halderman also confirmed that following every accident involving injury to an employee his office was required to complete inspection reports, and that such reports were regularly kept in the course of business. Over objection, the court admitted both reports into evidence.

Determination of the admissibility of these reports under the Federal Business Records Act involves two problems: whether the reports are business records within that statute, and whether the fact that the accident report was prepared by an employee who had neither firsthand knowledge of the accident nor had inspected the purportedly defective car and brake affects admissibility into evidence.

As a preliminary matter, there is little doubt that these reports are each a "writing or record, whether in the form of an entry in a book or otherwise, made as a memorandum or record of any act, transaction, occurrence, or event. * * *" 28 U.S.C. § 1732 (1966). Furthermore, it is beyond dispute that these reports were made pursuant to a regular procedure at the railroad yard, and that Talbott, Campbell and Zuchero made the reports within a reasonable time after the accident. Appellant argues, however, that notwithstanding the presence of those factors which would indicate a full compliance with 28 U.S.C. § 1732, the Supreme Court's decision in Palmer v. Hoffman, 318 U.S. 109, 63 S.Ct. 477, 87 L.Ed. 645 (1943), precludes their admission into evidence. There the Court upheld the inadmissibility of an accident report offered by the defendant railroad that had been prepared by one of its locomotive engineers. The Court stated that since the report was not prepared "for the systematic conduct of the business as a business," it was not "made 'in the regular course' of the business" of the railroad. 318 U.S. at 113, 63 S.Ct. at 481. We find significant differences between the report and the circumstances of its making in that case and the facts here, and we uphold the district court's admission of the records below.

In *Palmer v. Hoffman,* the engineer preparing the report had been personally involved in the accident, and, as Circuit Judge Frank stated in his opinion for the Court of Appeals, the engineer knew "at the time of making it that he [was] very likely, in a probable law suit relating to that accident, to be charged with wrongdoing as a participant in the accident, so that he [was] almost certain, when making the memorandum or report, to be sharply affected by a desire to exculpate himself and to relieve himself or his employer of liability." 129 F.2d 976, 991 (2d Cir.1942) (italics omitted). Here there could have been no similar motivation on the part of Talbott, Campbell or Zuchero, for not one of them was involved in the accident, or could have possibly been the target of a lawsuit by Lewis. In United States v. New York Foreign Trade Zone Operators, 304 F.2d 792 (2d Cir.1962), we sustained the admissibility of a similar report by the co-employee of the injured party which had been prepared as part of the regular business of the defendant pier-owner and operator. As we explained there, the mere fact that a record might ultimately be of some value in the event of litigation does not *per se* mandate its exclusion. In *Palmer v. Hoffman,* "[o]bviously the Supreme Court was concerned about a likely untrustworthiness of materials prepared specifically by a prospective litigant for courtroom use." 304 F.2d at 797. The fact that a report embodies an employee's version of the accident, Taylor v. Baltimore & Ohio R.R. Co., 344 F.2d 281 (2d Cir.1965), or happens to work in favor of the entrant's employer, Naylor v. Isthmian S.S. Co., 187 F.2d 538 (2d Cir.1951) does not, without more, indicate untrustworthiness. See Pekelis v. Transcontinental & W. Air, Inc., 187 F.2d 122 (2d Cir.), *cert. denied,* 341 U.S. 951, 71 S.Ct. 1020, 95 L.Ed. 1374 (1951). In the absence of a motive to fabricate, a motive so clearly spelled out in *Palmer v. Hoffman,* the holding in that case is not controlling to emasculate the Business Records Act. Therefore the trial court must look to those earmarks of reliability which otherwise establish the trustworthiness of the record. See Gaussen v. United Fruit Co., 412 F.2d 72, 74 (2d Cir.1969).

Here the ICC requires the employer to prepare and file monthly reports of all accidents involving railroad employees. Assistant general foreman Halderman testified that following every injury he was required to inspect the equipment involved and to report the results of the inspection on a regular printed form. As we stated in Taylor v. Baltimore & Ohio R.R. Co., supra, "[i]t would ill become a court to say that the regular making of reports required by law is not in the regular course of business." 344 F.2d at 285. In addition to their use by the railroad in making reports to the ICC, the reports here were undoubtedly of utility to the employer in ascertaining whether the equipment involved was defective so that future accidents might be prevented. These factors, we think, are sufficient indicia of trustworthiness to establish the admissibility of the reports into evidence under the Federal Business Records Act.

The fact that the trainmaster Talbott completed the personal injury report based on information supplied to him by a third person, Campbell, does not render the report inadmissible. 28 U.S.C. § 1732 explicitly states that "lack of personal knowledge by the entrant or maker" shall not affect the admissibility of the record, and may only affect its weight. See also United States v. Re, 336 F.2d 306, 313–14 (2d Cir.), *cert. denied,* 379 U.S. 904, 85 S.Ct. 188, 13 L.Ed.2d 177 (1964). Nor does the fact that the entrant does not testify preclude the admission of the record. All that is required is that someone who is sufficiently familiar with business practices be able to testify that the record was made regularly as part of those business practices and that the record is a truly authentic one. United States v. Dawson, 400 F.2d 194, 198–99 (2d Cir.1968), *cert. denied,* 393 U.S. 1023, 89 S.Ct. 632, 21 L.Ed.2d 567 (1969); United States v. Teague, 445 F.2d 114, 119 (7th Cir.1971). Witnesses Talbott and Halderman met those requirements.

* * *

Affirmed.

LOPER v. ANDREWS

Supreme Court of Texas, 1966.
404 S.W.2d 300.

STEAKLEY, JUSTICE.

We granted writ of error in this case to review the problem of the admissibility under Article 3737e of medical opinion entries in hospital records.

* * *

Article 3737e says that a record of an act, event or condition shall be competent evidence of the occurrence of the act or event *or the existence of the condition* when the statutory conditions to admissibility are otherwise present. The problem here is whether the recorded entry of a medical diagnosis can qualify as a memorandum or record of a condition and as competent evidence of the existence of the condition described therein. Medical diagnoses analyze the cause and nature of a patient's condition and may be classified into three broad types. The medical facts may be such that the medical condition is apparent and observable by all. Or, the facts and findings may be such that an expert interpretation is required but the medical condition is nevertheless well recognized and reasonably certain. Or, the facts and findings may be such that their meaning and the resulting medical opinion as to the patient's condition rests primarily in expert medical opinion, conjecture and speculation. A severed limb or an open wound illustrates the first and states the obvious. The diagnosis of leukemia in *Rodriguez* illustrates the second. Leukemia was considered to be an affliction subject to reliable diagnosis and as not partaking of opinion or conjecture in any consequential sense. We were of the view that such a recorded diagnosis could properly be said to be within the statutory contemplation of a record of a condition and as competent evidence of the existence of the condition. A third situation is represented by the opinion entry here and was also illustrated by references in the *Rodriguez* opinion to consideration of the problem in other cases. In approving the *Rodriguez* construction of the statute we did not hold that diagnostic entries in hospital records may be considered as competent evidence of the condition they describe where they are genuinely disputed and necessarily rest largely in expert opinion, speculation or conjecture.

A witness is generally permitted to testify only to facts within his personal knowledge. He does not have to possess special qualifications to do so. He is not permitted to express an opinion since this invades the province of the trier of the facts. An exception to the personal knowledge prerequisite is represented by the testimony of a qualified expert in the expression of an opinion in the field of his qualifications. This is permitted because experts are considered to have a special knowledge not generally possessed by jurors and are better able to draw conclusions from the facts than the jurors. The diagnosis or medical opinion of a doctor is an example. Such testimony is in the nature of an expert opinion based on the application of the expertise of the doctor to the facts within his knowledge. The opportunity of cross-examination is unusually important to adversely affected parties. We do not read Article 3737e as purporting to render entries of such character admissible without exception; we construe the statute as doing so only in those instances where it can be said that the diagnosis records a condition resting in reasonable medical certainty.

The opinion and conjectural nature of the important sentence in the entry in question here is self-evident. The finding is that the boy suffered a "papilledema of the left optic disc of about two diopters." The medical opinion attributed to Dr. Hutchings is that "he believes" that such condition resulted from "a fracture of the base of the skull, and some left optic nerve pressure." The entry does not purport to rest upon demonstrable medical facts and was the subject of genuine dispute between the doctors. It is an expert conjecture of Dr. Hutchings on the question of whether or not the boy suffered a skull fracture and in our view is lacking the requisite medical certainty to qualify under Article 3737e.

We are of the further opinion, however, that the admission in evidence of the hospital record with the inadmissible opinion entry of Dr. Hutchings was not reversibly harmful to Petitioner * * *.

* * *

POPE, JUSTICE (concurring).

* * *

The majority, in holding that opinion testimony should be excluded, has announced a new exclusionary rule with respect to medical opinions. The Court treats expert medical opinion as speculation or conjecture in spite of medical evidence to the contrary. The majority says that because there was a dispute between the doctors who examined the injured boy, the diagnostic entries "necessarily rest largely in expert opinion, speculation or conjecture."

When a doctor gives his expert opinion about medical causes lawyers and judges, who are not medical experts, are bold indeed to say that the evidence is mere conjecture or speculation. Dr. Swetland's entry in the hospital records was that Dr. Hutchings "* * * believes * * * definitely * * *" that the condition resulted from a fracture of the base of the skull. The evidence did not relate to the future, in which case the doctor would be limited to probabilities in the expression of his opinion. We exclude this evidence though the doctor said, "I definitely believe." The predicate for admission of this opinion evidence was laid.

The real basis for the exclusion is that the non-expert Court believes that the evidence was speculative. If it be such, Dr. Swetland and Dr. Hutchings did not so state. The Court in this case, and apparently for the future, has committed itself as an overseeing expert to pass upon medical conditions, diseases, treatments, prognoses, and to announce to both the medical and legal professions, which medical opinions are sound and which are conjectural. I would leave this to the doctors. 2 McCormick & Ray, Texas Law of Evidence, § 1427.

I concur in the result.

Note

The Texas Supreme Court's official comment to Tex.R.Civ.Evid. 803(6) reads: "This provision rejects the doctrine of Loper v. Andrews, 404 S.W.2d 300, 305 (Tex.1966), which required that an entry of a medical opinion or diagnosis meet a test of 'reasonable medical certainty.' "

SECTION 13. PUBLIC RECORDS AND REPORTS *

[FED.R.EVID. 803(8)–(10)]

UNITED STATES v. QUEZADA

United States Court of Appeals, Fifth Circuit, 1985.
754 F.2d 1190.

JOHN R. BROWN, CIRCUIT JUDGE:

In this appeal from a conviction under 8 U.S.C. § 1326 for illegal reentry after deportation, appellant challenges the admission of certain evidence at his bench trial. We review the proceedings below, find that properly admitted evidence sufficiently supports the conviction, and affirm.

BACKGROUND

Appellant Oscar Ramos Quezada, an illegal alien, was deported from this country on April 25, 1982, pursuant to a warrant of deportation (Form I–205) issued by the United States Immigration and Naturalization Service (INS). Seven months later, on November 17, 1983, a Border Patrol officer arrested Quezada at the El Paso County Jail, where he was incarcerated on a public intoxication charge. Quezada

* See 5 Wigmore, Evidence §§ 1630–1684 (Chadbourn rev. 1974); McCormick, Evidence ch. 30 (4th ed. 1992); Alexander, Hearsay Exception for Public Records in Federal Criminal Trials, 47 Albany L.Rev. 699 (1983); Imwinkelried, The Constitutionality of Introducing Evaluative Laboratory Reports Against Criminal Defendants, 30 Hast.L.J. 621 (1979).

was subsequently indicted by a federal grand jury for illegally reentering the country after having been previously arrested and deported, in violation of 8 U.S.C. § 1326. After a bench trial, he was convicted and sentenced to a prison term of two years, all but six months of which were suspended in lieu of supervised probation.

At trial, the principal part of the government's case was devoted to proving that Quezada had been "deported and arrested" as required for conviction under the statute. In order to establish these statutory requisites, the government called as a witness Border Patrol Agent David Meshirer. Agent Meshirer first testified that he had been designated the custodian of appellant's immigration file. The government then used the witness to introduce its exhibits.

Two exhibits are of particular importance in this appeal. The first is INS Form I–205, the warrant of deportation which authorized the deportation of appellant. The second, INS Form I–294, is a letter to appellant in his native language, warning him of the penalties for illegal reentry after deportation. Both exhibits were admitted into evidence over appellant's objections.

The testimony of Agent Meshirer also figures prominently in this appeal. His testimony described the use and function of the INS forms put in evidence. First, he explained that on the back of Form I–205 are spaces to be filled out by the deporting officer, as well as a space for the thumbprint of the deportee. Agent Meshirer also observed that the back of Form I–205 reflected that appellant had been deported on April 25, 1982, and that this deportation had been witnessed by an immigration officer whose signature appeared on the exhibit. Finally, he pointed out a thumbprint on the back of the exhibit, which subsequent testimony established to be that of appellant.

Agent Meshirer next testified as to the normal procedure followed in executing warrants of deportation. He stated that when a person has been ordered deported, an immigration officer will pick up the deportee, fill in the blanks on the back of the warrant, and sign the warrant as having witnessed the departure. He also testified that in the course of a normal deportation, the deportee's right thumbprint is taken. As to Form I–294, the letter informing the deportee of the penalties for illegal reentry, Agent Meshirer observed that it is given to the deportee along with a copy of the warrant of deportation. Thus, according to this testimony, the deported individual is fully apprised of the fact of his deportation, and that he is subject to criminal penalties for illegal reentry.

On cross-examination, appellant's counsel first focused on an apparent irregularity in the manner in which the warrant of deportation had been filled out in this case. Along with the other information on the back of the warrant, there is a space for the signature of the officer executing the warrant. Appellant's cross-examination established that, while the other information on the back of the warrant had been supplied, there was no signature from an executing officer.[6]

Next, appellant's counsel examined Agent Meshirer on the process of deportation. As the witness was questioned on the procedure followed in executing warrants of deportation, the following colloquy occurred:

Q. Okay. So then have you ever executed a warrant?

A. No, sir; not a Warrant of Deportation.

Q. So you have no personal knowledge of actually how it's done, do you?

A. The knowledge I have is what I have been told by detention officers.

Q. All right. So that any testimony that you have given us as to the procedure is based simply upon what other people have told you outside of Court, is that correct?

A. Based on the normal rule of things and the normal processes of deportation.

Q. You have never seen it done, have you?

A. But I haven't been there personally and personally deported a person and executed this warrant.

Q. All right.

Trial Transcript at p. 24. Thus it was revealed that Agent Meshirer had never actually executed a warrant of deportation. Appellant's hearsay objections to the testimony were overruled, and this appeal followed.

DISCUSSION

Appellant urges that the evidence below was insufficient to prove the "arrest" necessary for prosecution under 8 U.S.C. § 1326, as that term has been interpreted by this court. In *United States v. Wong Kim Bo,* 466 F.2d 1298 (5th Cir.1972) *rehearing denied,* 472 F.2d 720 (5th Cir.1972), we discussed that term as it fits into the scheme of the statute in question. First, we observed that there are five elements which the government must prove in order to obtain a conviction for illegal reentry after deportation: [i] that defendant was an alien; [ii] that he was "arrested" and [iii] "deported" as those terms are contemplated by the statute; [iv] that he was subsequently found within this country and [v] that he did not have consent from the Attorney General to reapply for admission. *Id.* at 1303.[7]

6. As stated previously, the warrant did contain the signature of the immigration officer witnessing appellant's departure. The separate line for signature of the officer executing the warrant, presumably the same officer, was not signed.

7. Of these five elements, appellant challenges only the second, whether or not he was properly "arrested."

We next turned to an analysis of the "arrest" requirement. After examining the legislative and Congressional purpose underlying the Act, we concluded that an "arrest" under the statute is accomplished by service on the alien of the warrant of deportation, thus providing the requisite notice to trigger criminal sanctions for illegal reentry thereafter. *Id.* at 1304–05. This notice is critical, we observed, for it insures that criminal sanctions are not imposed for reentry where the alien does not know that he has previously been officially deported. *Id.* at 1304.

The argument presented on appeal is that the government failed to prove that appellant was actually served with a warrant of deportation issued by INS. This argument implicates important questions respecting the use of public documents in criminal proceedings, and the means of proving the customary practice of a governmental agency.

Documentary Evidence

Initially, our attention is drawn to the question of the admissibility of INS Form I–205, the warrant of deportation. This document is crucial to the government's case, as it contains virtually all of the information proving appellant's prior arrest and deportation. Thus is implicated F.R.Evid. 803(8)(B), the public records exception to the hearsay rule, which provides as follows:

> Rule 803. Hearsay Exceptions: Availability of Declarant Immaterial
>
> The following are not excluded by the hearsay rule, even though the declarant is available as a witness:
>
> * * *
>
> (8) Public records and reports. Records, reports, statements, or data compilations, in any form, of public offices or agencies setting forth * * * (B) matters observed pursuant to duty imposed by law as to which matters there was a duty to report, excluding, however, in criminal cases matters observed by police officers and other law enforcement personnel.

Two principal reasons underlie this exception to the general rule excluding hearsay: the presumed trustworthiness of public documents prepared in the discharge of official functions, and the necessity of using such documents, due to the likelihood that a public official would have no independent memory of a particular action or entry where his duties require the constant repetition of routine tasks. *See generally,* 4 D. Louisell and C. Mueller, Federal Evidence, Public Records § 454.

Despite this policy favoring the admissibility of public records, Congress was also obviously concerned about the use of such documents in criminal cases. In an apparent attempt to avoid a collision between the hearsay rule and the confrontation clause of the Sixth Amendment, Congress excluded from the public records exception "in criminal cases matters observed by police officers and other law enforcement personnel * * *." Rule 803(8)(B). In so doing, however, Congress did not make clear whether the Rule was designed to exclude all reports made by a government employee which are offered against a criminal defendant, or whether only certain types of reports were intended to be excluded.

While some courts have inflexibly applied the Rule 803(8)(B) proscription to all law enforcement records in criminal cases, *see, e.g., United States v. Oates,* 560 F.2d 45, 83–84 (2d Cir.1977), we are not persuaded that such a narrow application of the rule is warranted here.[9] The law enforcement exception in Rule 803(8)(B) is based in part on the presumed unreliability of observations made by law enforcement officials at the scene of a crime, or in the course of investigating a crime:

> [o]stensibly, the reason for this exclusion is that observations by police officers at the scene of the crime or the apprehension of the defendant were not as reliable as observations by public officials in other cases because of the adversarial nature of the confrontation between the police and the defendant in criminal cases.

Senate Report No. 1277, 93d Cong.2d Sess., *reprinted in* [1974] U.S.Code Cong. & Ad.News 7051, 7064. Thus, a number of courts have drawn a distinction for purposes of Rule 803(8)(B) between law enforcement reports prepared in a routine, non-adversarial setting, and those resulting from the arguably more subjective endeavor of investigating a crime and evaluating the results of that investigation. *See, e.g., United States v. Orozco,* 590 F.2d 789, 793–94 (9th Cir.1979) (admitting computer records of license plates on cars crossing the border due to non-adversarial setting in which information was gathered) *cert. denied,* 439 U.S. 1049, 99 S.Ct. 728, 58 L.Ed.2d 709 (1978); *United States v. Union Nacional De Trabajadores,* 576 F.2d 388, 390–91 (1st Cir.1978) (admitting Marshal's return of service); *United States v. Grady,* 544 F.2d 598 (2d Cir.1976) (admitting reports on firearms serial numbers for Northern Ireland law enforcement agency on basis that they were records of a routine function).

Under this analysis, a warrant of deportation was deemed properly admissible in a § 1326 action in *United States v. Hernandez–Rojas,* 617 F.2d 533 (9th Cir.1980), *cert. denied,* 449 U.S. 864, 101 S.Ct. 170, 66 L.Ed.2d 81 (1980). The Ninth Circuit there concluded that the notations on the warrant indicating the defendant's deportation were the result of a ministerial, objective observation, and thus had none of the subjective features of reports made in a more adversarial setting, such as an investigation of a crime scene. *Id.* at 535.

9. While we cited *Oates* with approval in *United States v. Cain,* 615 F.2d 380 (5th Cir.1980), that case is not contrary to our decision today. First, we cited *Oates* only for the proposition that a document inadmissible under Rule 803(8)(B) may not be received in evidence merely because it satisfies Rule 803(6), the exception for business records. *Id.* at 382. Further, unlike the case here, the public record at issue in *Cain* reported actual criminal activity on the part of the defendant. Finally, the *Cain* court apparently was not faced with a situation in which the very number of cases handled by the government agency made reliance on such records an administrative and evidentiary necessity. * * *

We find the reasoning of these cases persuasive. This circuit has recognized that Rule 803(8) is designed to permit the admission into evidence of public records prepared for purposes independent of specific litigation. *United States v. Stone,* 604 F.2d 922 (5th Cir.1979) (Rule 803(8)(A)). In the case of documents recording routine, objective observations, made as part of the everyday function of the preparing official or agency, the factors likely to cloud the perception of an official engaged in the more traditional law enforcement functions of observation and investigation of crime are simply not present. Due to the lack of any motivation on the part of the recording official to do other than mechanically register an unambiguous factual matter (here, appellant's departure from the country), such records are, like other public documents, inherently reliable. *See Smith v. Ithaca,* 612 F.2d 215, 222 (5th Cir.1980) (records trustworthy where recording official has no reason to be other than objective).

We further believe that the warrant of deportation in this case establishes the service required by *Wong Kim Bo.* Appellant's thumbprint on the warrant indicates that the warrant was presented to him prior to departure. Additionally, testimony of Border Patrol Agent Meshirer conclusively established the authenticity and reliability of this record of deportation. *See* F.R.Evid. 901(b)(7). He testified that the warrants of deportation are kept in the normal course of business of the INS. Trial Transcript at 11. He further testified that the warrants of deportation are kept as a matter of course with the individual file maintained for each alien being processed. *Id.* at 9–10. This testimony clearly indicated the extent to which such records are relied on by the INS in its day-to-day operations.

Moreover, in a case like the one at bar, the absolute necessity of proving the government's case through the use of public records is unquestionable. In the years 1977–1981, the INS processed for departure from the country, on average, more than 1,000,000 aliens annually. In 1981, more than 260,000 aliens were processed in the State of Texas alone, with over 6,000 of those having been officially deported. Given these numbers, it is unlikely that testimony by an INS officer as to the deportation of a particular individual could be based on anything other than recorded observations, with such testimony being merely cumulative to the more reliable written record of deportation.

We thus conclude that the warrant of deportation, containing appellant's thumbprint and indicating the date and location of his deportation, sufficiently established the arrest requirement contemplated by the statute. Given the overwhelming number of immigration cases processed each year, the INS must be permitted to rely on such records to establish certain elements of a violation of § 1326.

Testimonial Evidence

The proof of service of the warrant contained on the document itself was further corroborated by the testimony of Agent Meshirer. His testimony was designed to demonstrate the normal procedure followed in executing a warrant of deportation: that the deporting officer obtains the thumbprint of the deportee on the back of the warrant, as well as providing the deportee with copies of the warrant and INS Form I–294.

On cross-examination, counsel for appellant elicited Agent Meshirer's testimony that he had never personally observed the execution of a warrant, and that his knowledge of the procedures was based "on what he had been told by detention officers," as well as "the normal rule of things and the normal processes of deportation." Transcript at p. 24. Appellant's counsel thereafter objected to the testimony as hearsay, an objection which he reasserts here.

We believe that appellant's argument, phrased and briefed in terms of the hearsay rule, is more appropriately understood as implicating the personal knowledge requirement of F.R.Evid. 602. Of course, the hearsay rule and the personal knowledge requirement are cut at least in part from the same cloth, as the Advisory Committee Notes to Rule 602 acknowledge: "This rule would, however, prevent [a witness] from testifying to the subject matter of [a] hearsay statement, as he has no personal knowledge of it." In the present case, however, the most important question is not whether the trial court improperly admitted hearsay testimony, but rather whether the witness had adequate knowledge to testify to the normal practice followed by INS agents in executing warrants of deportation.

The government's strategy was clearly to use Agent Meshirer's testimony to establish the normal practice of the INS in order to prove conduct in conformity therewith, in accordance with F.R.Evid. 406. This court has recognized the admissibility of such evidence. *See, e.g., Spartan Grain and Mill Company v. Ayers,* 517 F.2d 214, 219 (5th Cir.1975); *Stevens v. U.S.,* 306 F.2d 834 (5th Cir.1962).

It is true, as appellant urges, that Agent Meshirer cannot be allowed to testify as to the subject matter of a hearsay statement, in this case, the out-of-court statements of detention officers as to the procedures followed at deportations. Nor in this case may the witness satisfy the personal knowledge requirement of Rule 602 by reliance on inadmissible hearsay. However, our inquiry does not end there—for even if testimony is based in part on inadmissible hearsay, Rule 602 will be satisfied if "evidence is introduced sufficient to support a finding that [the witness] has personal knowledge of the matter." Rule 602. We believe the government's witness met this standard. He testified that he had performed various functions for the Border Patrol, including traffic check, line watch, and service as a warrant officer. He gave extensive testimony relating to the procedures followed in keeping the records of all persons deported. Moreover, his testimony revealed that his knowledge of the procedure followed in executing warrants of deportation was based not only on what he had been told by detention officers, but also on "the normal rule of things and the normal processes of deportation." Transcript at p. 24.

Thus, while Agent Meshirer's testimony does not reveal that he had physically observed the execution of a warrant of deportation, we believe it is sufficient to permit the conclusion that he was familiar with the procedure.[14] The properly admitted testimony corroborated the proof of deportation contained on the warrant itself. Additionally, the testimony permits the conclusion that, through the use of Form I-294, appellant was informed in his native language of the penalties for illegal reentry. In this matter, the requirements of *Wong Kim Bo* were clearly satisfied.

CONCLUSION

We conclude that the government has adduced sufficient, competent evidence to prove an arrest under 8 U.S.C. § 1326. Given the sheer volume of cases handled by the INS, it is crucial that the government be able to rely on properly maintained and authenticated records to establish violations. As we have already observed, a requirement of direct testimony by the deporting officer would add little to the weight of evidence, considering the improbability that he would recall the facts surrounding any one particular deportation.

Here, the documentary evidence of deportation with appellant's thumbprint thereon, corroborated by the testimony as to the regular practice of deporting officers, adequately supports the trial court's conclusion.

Affirmed.

BEECH AIRCRAFT CORP. v. RAINEY

Supreme Court of the United States, 1988.
488 U.S. 153, 109 S.Ct. 439, 102 L.Ed.2d 445.

JUSTICE BRENNAN delivered the opinion of the Court.

In this case we address a longstanding conflict among the federal courts of appeal over whether Federal Rule of Evidence 803(8)(C), which provides an exception to the hearsay rule for public investigatory reports containing "factual findings," extends to conclusions and opinions contained in such reports. * * *

I

This litigation stems from the crash of a Navy training aircraft at Middleton Field, Alabama, on July 13, 1982, which took the lives of both pilots on board, Lieutenant Commander Barbara Ann Rainey and

14. The situation is similar to that presented where testimony is given concerning the mailing of a letter in the normal course of business. This circuit has long accepted proof of the normal practice of the use of the mails by means of circumstantial evidence, without requiring the testimony of a business' mail clerk, ostensibly the only person who could testify directly to the business practice of mailing and receiving letters. *See, e.g., Stevens v. United States,* 306 F.2d 834 (5th Cir.1962); *see generally* 2 D. Luisell and C. Mueller, § 159 at p. 225. In such cases, as here, all that is necessary is some competent evidence as to the routine practice followed by the organization, given by someone familiar with these procedures.

Ensign Donald Bruce Knowlton. The accident took place while Rainey, a Navy flight instructor, and Knowlton, her student, were flying "touch-and-go" exercises in a T–34C Turbo–Mentor aircraft, number 3E955. Their aircraft and several others flew in an oval pattern, each plane making successive landing/takeoff maneuvers on the runway. Following its fourth pass at the runway, 3E955 appeared to make a left turn prematurely, cutting out the aircraft ahead of it in the pattern and threatening a collision. After radio warnings from two other pilots, the plane banked sharply to the right in order to avoid the other aircraft. At that point it lost altitude rapidly, crashed, and burned.

Because of the damage to the plane and the lack of any survivors, the cause of the accident could not be determined with certainty. The two pilots' surviving spouses brought a product liability suit against petitioners Beech Aircraft Corporation, the plane's manufacturer, and Beech Aerospace Services, which serviced the plane under contract with the Navy.[1] The plaintiffs alleged that the crash had been caused by a loss of engine power, known as "rollback," due to some defect in the aircraft's fuel control system. The defendants, on the other hand, advanced the theory of pilot error, suggesting that the plane had stalled during the abrupt avoidance maneuver.

At trial, the only seriously disputed question was whether pilot error or equipment malfunction had caused the crash. Both sides relied primarily on expert testimony. One piece of evidence presented by the defense was an investigative report prepared by Lieutenant Commander William Morgan on order of the training squadron's commanding officer and pursuant to authority granted in the Manual of the Judge Advocate General. This "JAG Report," completed during the six weeks following the accident, was organized into sections labeled "finding of fact," "opinions," and "recommendations," and was supported by some 60 attachments. The "finding of fact" included statements like the following:

> "13. At approximately 1020, while turning crosswind without proper interval, 3E955 crashed, immediately caught fire and burned.
>
> * * *
>
> "27. At the time of impact, the engine of 3E955 was operating but was operating at reduced power." App. 10–12.

Among his "opinions" Lieutenant Commander Morgan stated, in paragraph five, that due to the deaths of the two pilots and the destruction of the aircraft "it is almost impossible to determine exactly what happened to Navy 3E955 from the time it left the runway on its last touch and go until it impacted the ground." He nonetheless continued with a detailed reconstruction of a possible set of events, based on pilot

1. The manufacturer of the plane's engine, Pratt & Whitney Canada, Ltd., was also a defendant, but it subsequently settled with respondents and is no longer a party to this action.

error, that could have caused the accident.[2] The next two paragraphs stated a caveat and a conclusion:

"6. Although the above sequence of events is the most likely to have occurred, it does not change the possibility that a 'rollback' did occur.

"7. The most probable cause of the accident was the pilots [*sic*] failure to maintain proper interval." *Id.,* at 15.

The trial judge initially determined, at a pretrial conference, that the JAG Report was sufficiently trustworthy to be admissible, but that it "would be admissible only on its factual findings and would not be admissible insofar as any opinions or conclusions are concerned." *Id.,* at 35. The day before trial, however, the court reversed itself and ruled, over the plaintiffs' objection, that certain of the conclusions would be admitted. *Id.,* at 40–41. Accordingly, the court admitted most of the report's "opinions," including the first sentence of paragraph five about the impossibility of determining exactly what happened, and paragraph seven, which opined about failure to maintain proper interval as "[t]he most probable cause of the accident." *Id.,* at 97. On the other hand, the remainder of paragraph five was barred as "nothing but a possible scenario," *id.,* at 40, and paragraph six, in which investigator Morgan refused to rule out rollback, was deleted as

2. Paragraph five reads in its entirety as follows: "Because both pilots were killed in the crash and because of the nearly total destruction of the aircraft by fire, it is almost impossible to determine exactly what happened to Navy 3E955 from the time it left the runway on its last touch and go until it impacted the ground. However, from evidence available and the information gained from eyewitnesses, a possible scenario can be constructed as follows:

"a. 3E955 entered the Middleton pattern with ENS Knowlton at the controls attempting to make normal landings.

"b. After two unsuccessful attempts, LCDR Rainey took the aircraft and demonstrated two landings 'on the numbers.' After getting the aircraft safely airborne from the touch and go, LCDR Rainey transferred control to ENS Knowlton.

"c. Due to his physical strength, ENS Knowlton did not trim down elevator as the aircraft accelerated toward 100 knots; in fact, due to his inexperience, he may have trimmed incorrectly, putting in more up elevator.

"d. As ENS Knowlton was climbing to pattern altitude, he did not see the aircraft established on downwind so he began his crosswind turn. Due to ENS Knowlton's large size, LCDR Rainey was unable to see the conflicting traffic.

"e. Hearing the first call, LCDR Rainey probably cautioned ENS Knowlton to check for traffic. Hearing the second call, she took immediate action and told ENS Knowlton she had the aircraft as she initiated a turn toward an upwind heading.

"f. As the aircraft was rolling from a climbing left turn to a climbing right turn, ENS Knowlton released the stick letting the up elevator trim take effect causing the nose of the aircraft to pitch abruptly up.

"g. The large angle of bank used trying to maneuver for aircraft separation coupled with the abrupt pitch up caused the aircraft to stall. As the aircraft stalled and went into a nose low attitude, LCDR Rainey reduced the PCL (power control lever) toward idle. As she was rolling toward wings level, she advanced the PCL to maximum to stop the loss of altitude but due to the 2 to 4 second lag in engine response, the aircraft impacted the ground before power was available." App. 14–15.

well.[3]

* * *

Following a two-week trial, the jury returned a verdict for the petitioners. A panel of the Eleventh Circuit reversed and remanded for a new trial. 784 F.2d 1523 (CA11 1986). Considering itself bound by the Fifth Circuit precedent of *Smith v. Ithaca Corp.*, 612 F.2d 215 (CA5 1980),[4] the panel agreed with Rainey's argument that Federal Rule of Evidence 803(8)(C), which excepts investigatory reports from the hearsay rule, did not encompass evaluative conclusions or opinions. Therefore, it held, the "conclusions" contained in the JAG Report should have been excluded. One member of the panel, concurring specially, urged however that the Circuit reconsider its interpretation of Rule 803(8)(C), suggesting that "*Smith* is an anomaly among the circuits." 784 F.2d at 1530 (opinion of Johnson, J.). * * *

On rehearing en banc, the Court of Appeals divided evenly on the question of Rule 803(8)(C). 827 F.2d 1498 (CA11 1987). It therefore held that *Smith* was controlling and consequently reinstated the panel judgment. * * *

II

Federal Rule of Evidence 803 provides that certain types of hearsay statements are not made excludable by the hearsay rule, whether or not the declarant is available to testify. Rule 803(8) defines the "public records and reports" which are not excludable, as follows:

> "Records, reports, statements, or data compilations, in any form, of public offices or agencies, setting forth (A) the activities of the office or agency, or (B) matters observed pursuant to duty imposed by law as to which matters there was a duty to report, * * * or (C) in civil actions and proceedings and against the Government in criminal cases, factual findings resulting from an investigation made pursuant to authority granted by law, unless the sources of information or other circumstances indicate lack of trustworthiness."

Controversy over what "public records and reports" are made not excludable by Rule 803(8)(C) has divided the federal courts from the beginning. In the present case, the Court of Appeals followed the "narrow" interpretation of *Smith v. Ithaca Corp.*, 612 F.2d 215, 220–223 (CA5 1980), which held that the term "factual findings" did not encompass "opinions" or "conclusions." Courts of appeal other than those of the Fifth and Eleventh Circuits, however, have generally adopted a broader interpretation. For example, the Court of Appeals for the Sixth Circuit, in *Baker v. Elcona Homes Corp.*, 588 F.2d 551, 557–558 (1978), cert. denied, 441 U.S. 933, 99 S.Ct. 2054, 60 L.Ed.2d 661 (1979),

3. The record gives no indication why paragraph six was deleted. See, *e.g., id.*, at 40 (striking most of ¶ 5, as well as ¶¶ 8 and 9, but silent on ¶ 6). Neither at trial nor on appeal have respondents raised any objection to the deletion of paragraph six.

4. In *Bonner v. Prichard, Ala.*, 661 F.2d 1206 (CA11 1981), the newly created Eleventh Circuit adopted as binding precedent Fifth Circuit decisions rendered prior to October 1981.

held that "factual findings admissible under Rule 803(8)(C) may be those which are made by the preparer of the report from disputed evidence * * *."[6] The other courts of appeal that have squarely confronted the issue have also adopted the broader interpretation.[7] We agree and hold that factually based conclusions or opinions are not on that account excluded from the scope of Rule 803(8)(C).

Because the Federal Rules of Evidence are a legislative enactment, we turn to the "traditional tools of statutory construction," *INS v. Cardoza–Fonseca,* 480 U.S. 421, 446, 107 S.Ct. 1207, 1221, 94 L.Ed.2d 434 (1987), in order to construe their provisions. We begin with the language of the Rule itself. Proponents of the narrow view have generally relied heavily on a perceived dichotomy between "fact" and "opinion" in arguing for the limited scope of the phrase "factual findings." *Smith v. Ithaca Corp., supra,* contrasted the term "factual findings" in Rule 803(8)(C) with the language of Rule 803(6) (records of regularly conducted activity), which expressly refers to "opinions" and "diagnoses." "Factual findings," the court opined, must be something other than opinions. *Smith, supra,* at 221–222.[8]

6. *Baker* involved a police officer's report on an automobile accident. While there was no direct witness as to the color of the traffic lights at the moment of the accident, the court held admissible the officer's conclusion on the basis of his investigations at the accident scene and an interview with one of the drivers that "apparently unit # 2 * * * entered the intersection against a red light." 588 F.2d, at 555.

7. See *Melville v. American Home Assurance Co.,* 584 F.2d 1306, 1315–1316 (CA3 1978); *Ellis v. International Playtex, Inc.,* 745 F.2d 292, 300–301 (CA4 1984); *Kehm v. Proctor & Gamble Mfg. Co.,* 724 F.2d 613, 618 (CA8 1983); *Jenkins v. Whittaker Corp.,* 785 F.2d 720, 726 (CA9), cert. denied, 479 U.S. 918, 107 S.Ct. 324, 93 L.Ed.2d 296 (1986); *Perrin v. Anderson,* 784 F.2d 1040, 1046–1047 (CA10 1986).

Nor is the scope of Rule 803(8)(C) unexplored terrain among legal scholars. The leading evidence treatises are virtually unanimous in recommending the broad approach. See E. Cleary, McCormick on Evidence 890, n. 7 (3d ed. 1984); M. Graham, Handbook of Federal Evidence 886 (2d ed. 1986); R. Lempert & S. Saltzburg, A Modern Approach to Evidence 449–450 (2d ed. 1982); G. Lilly, An Introduction to the Law of Evidence 275–276 (2d ed. 1987); 4 D. Louisell & C. Mueller, Federal Evidence § 455, pp. 740–741 (1980); 4 J. Weinstein & M. Berger, Weinstein's Evidence ¶ 803(8)[03], pp. 803–250 to 803–252 (1987). See generally Grant, The Trustworthiness Standard for the Public Records and Reports Hearsay Exception, 12 Western St. U.L.Rev. 53, 81–85 (1984) (favoring broad admissibility); Note, The Scope of Federal Rule of Evidence 803(8)(C), 59 Texas L.Rev. 155 (1980) (advocating narrow interpretation); Comment, The Public Documents Hearsay Exception for Evaluative Reports: Fact or Fiction?, 63 Tulane L.Rev. 121 (1988) (same).

8. The court in *Smith* found it significant that different language was used in Rules 803(6) and 803(8)(C): "Since these terms are used in similar context within the same Rule, it is logical to assume that Congress intended that the terms have different and distinct meanings." 612 F.2d, at 222. The Advisory Committee notes to Rule 803(6) make clear, however, that the Committee was motivated by a particular concern in drafting the language of that Rule. While opinions were rarely found in traditional "business records," the expansion of that category to encompass documents such as medical diagnoses and test results brought with it some uncertainty in earlier versions of the Rule as to whether diagnoses and the like were admissible. "In order to make clear its adherence to the [position favoring admissibility]," the Committee stated, "the rule specifically includes both diagnoses and opinions, in addition to acts, events, and conditions, as proper subjects of admissible entries." Advisory Committee's Notes on Fed.Rule Evid. 803(6), 28 U.S.C.App., p. 723. Since that specific concern was not present in the context of Rule 803(8)(C), the absence of identical language should not be accorded much significance. See *Rainey v. Beech Aircraft Corp.,* 827 F.2d 1498, 1511–1512

For several reasons, we do not agree. In the first place, it is not apparent that the term "factual findings" should be read to mean simply "facts" (as opposed to "opinions" or "conclusions"). A common definition of "finding of fact" is, for example, "[a] conclusion by way of reasonable inference from the evidence." Black's Law Dictionary 569 (5th ed. 1979). To say the least, the language of the Rule does not compel us to reject the interpretation that "factual findings" includes conclusions or opinions that flow from a factual investigation. Second, we note that, contrary to what is often assumed, the language of the Rule does not state that "factual findings" are admissible, but that "*reports* * * * setting forth * * * factual findings" (emphasis added) are admissible. On this reading, the language of the Rule does not create a distinction between "fact" and "opinion" contained in such reports.

Turning next to the legislative history of Rule 803(8)(C), we find no clear answer to the question of how the Rule's language should be interpreted. Indeed, in this case the legislative history may well be at the origin of the dispute. Rather than the more usual situation where a court must attempt to glean meaning from ambiguous comments of legislators who did not focus directly on the problem at hand, here the Committees in both Houses of Congress clearly recognized and expressed their opinions on the precise question at issue. Unfortunately, however, they took diametrically opposite positions. Moreover, the two Houses made no effort to reconcile their views, either through changes in the Rule's language or through a statement in the Report of the Conference Committee.

The House Judiciary Committee, which dealt first with the proposed rules after they had been transmitted to Congress by this Court, included in its Report but one brief paragraph on Rule 803(8):

> "The Committee approved Rule 803(8) without substantive change from the form in which it was submitted by the Court. The Committee intends that the phrase 'factual findings' be strictly construed and that evaluations or opinions contained in public reports shall not be admissible under this Rule." H.R.Rep. No. 93–650, p. 14 (1973), U.S.Code Cong. & Admin.News 1974, pp. 7051, 7088.

The Senate Committee responded at somewhat greater length, but equally emphatically:

> "The House Judiciary Committee report contained a statement of intent that 'the phrase "factual findings" in subdivision (c) be strictly construed and that evaluations or opinions contained in public reports shall not be admissible under this rule.' The committee takes strong exception to this limiting understanding of the application of the rule. We do not think it reflects an understanding of the intended operation

(CA11 1987) (en banc) (Tjoflat, J., concurring). What is more, the Committee's report on Rule 803(8)(C) strongly suggests that that Rule has the same scope of admissibility as does Rule 803(6): "Hence the rule, *as in Exception [paragraph] (6)*, assumes admissibility in the first instance but with ample provision for escape if sufficient negative factors are present." Advisory Committee's Notes on Fed.Rule Evid. 803(8), 28 U.S.C.App., p. 725 (emphasis added).

of the rule as explained in the Advisory Committee notes to this subsection * * *. We think the restrictive interpretation of the House overlooks the fact that while the Advisory Committee assumes admissibility in the first instance of evaluative reports, they are not admissible if, as the rule states, 'the sources of information or other circumstances indicate lack of trustworthiness.'

* * *

"The committee concludes that the language of the rule together with the explanation provided by the Advisory Committee furnish sufficient guidance on the admissibility of evaluative reports." S.Rep. No. 93–1277, p. 18 (1974), U.S.Code Cong. & Admin.News 1974, p. 7064.

Clearly this legislative history reveals a difference of view between the Senate and the House that affords no definitive guide to the congressional understanding. It seems clear however that the Senate understanding is more in accord with the wording of the Rule and with the comments of the Advisory Committee.[9]

The Advisory Committee's comments are notable, first, in that they contain no mention of any dichotomy between statements of "fact" and "opinions" or "conclusions." What was on the Committee's mind was simply whether what it called "evaluative reports" should be admissible. Illustrating the previous division among the courts on this subject, the Committee cited numerous cases in which the admissibility of such reports had been both sustained and denied. It also took note of various federal statutes that made certain kinds of evaluative reports admissible in evidence. What is striking about all of these examples is that these were *reports that stated conclusions. E.g., Moran v. Pittsburgh–Des Moines Steel Co.,* 183 F.2d 467, 472–473 (CA3 1950) (report of Bureau of Mines concerning the cause of a gas tank explosion admissible); *Franklin v. Skelly Oil Co.,* 141 F.2d 568, 571–572 (CA10 1944) (report of state fire marshal on the cause of a gas explosion inadmissible); 42 U.S.C. § 269(b) (bill of health by appropriate official admissible as prima facie evidence of vessel's sanitary history and condition). The Committee's concern was clearly whether reports of this kind should be admissible. Nowhere in its comments is there the slightest indication that it even considered the solution of admitting only "factual" statements from such reports.[10] Rather, the Committee referred throughout

9. See Advisory Committee's Notes on Fed.Rule Evid. 803(8), 28 U.S.C.App., pp. 724–725. As Congress did not amend the Advisory Committee's draft in any way that touches on the question before us, the Committee's commentary is particularly relevant in determining the meaning of the document Congress enacted.

10. Our conclusion that the Committee was concerned only about the question of the admissibility *vel non* of "evaluative reports," without any distinction between statements of "fact" and "conclusions," draws support from the fact that this was the focus of scholarly debate on the official reports question prior to adoption of the Federal Rules. Indeed, the problem was often phrased as one of whether official reports could be admitted *in view of the fact that they contained the investigator's conclusions.* Thus Professor McCormick, in an influential article relied upon by the Committee, stated his position as follows: "that evaluative reports of official investigators, though partly based upon statements of others, *and though embracing conclusions,* are admissible as evidence of the facts reported." McCormick, Can the

to "reports," without any such differentiation regarding the statements they contained. What the Committee referred to in the Rule's language as "reports * * * setting forth * * * factual findings" is surely nothing more or less than what in its commentary it called "evaluative reports." Its solution as to their admissibility is clearly stated in the final paragraph of its report on this Rule. That solution consists of two principles: First, "the rule * * * assumes admissibility in the first instance * * *." Second, it provides "ample provision for escape if sufficient negative factors are present."

That "provision for escape" is contained in the final clause of the Rule: evaluative reports are admissible "unless the sources of information or other circumstances indicate lack of trustworthiness." This trustworthiness inquiry—and not an arbitrary distinction between "fact" and "opinion"—was the Committee's primary safeguard against the admission of unreliable evidence, and it is important to note that it applies to all elements of the report. Thus, a trial judge has the discretion, and indeed the obligation, to exclude an entire report or portions thereof—whether narrow "factual" statements or broader "conclusions"—that she determines to be untrustworthy.[11] Moreover, safeguards built in to other portions of the Federal Rules, such as those dealing with relevance and prejudice, provide the court with additional means of scrutinizing and, where appropriate, excluding evaluative reports or portions of them. And of course it goes without saying that the admission of a report containing "conclusions" is subject to the ultimate safeguard—the opponent's right to present evidence tending to contradict or diminish the weight of those conclusions.

Our conclusion that neither the language of the Rule nor the intent of its framers calls for a distinction between "fact" and "opinion" is strengthened by the analytical difficulty of drawing such a line. It has frequently been remarked that the distinction between statements of fact and opinion is, at best, one of degree:

> "All statements in language are statements of opinion, i.e., statements of mental processes or perceptions. So-called 'statements of fact' are

Courts Make Wider Use of Reports of Official Investigations?, 42 Iowa L.Rev. 363, 365 (1957) (emphasis added).

11. The Advisory Committee proposed a nonexclusive list of four factors it thought would be helpful in passing on this question: (1) the timeliness of the investigation; (2) the investigator's skill or experience; (3) whether a hearing was held; and (4) possible bias when reports are prepared with a view to possible litigation (citing *Palmer v. Hoffman,* 318 U.S. 109, 63 S.Ct. 477, 87 L.Ed. 645 (1943)). Advisory Committee's Notes on Fed.Rule Evid. 803(8), 28 U.S.C.App., p. 725; see Note, The Trustworthiness of Government Evaluative Reports under Federal Rule of Evidence 803(8)(C), 96 Harv.L.Rev. 492 (1982).

In a case similar in many respects to this one, the trial court applied the trustworthiness requirement to hold inadmissible a JAG Report on the causes of a Navy airplane accident; it found the report untrustworthy because it "was prepared by an inexperienced investigator in a highly complex field of investigation." *Fraley v. Rockwell Int'l Corp.,* 470 F.Supp. 1264, 1267 (SD Ohio 1979). In the present case, the District Court found the JAG Report to be trustworthy. App. 35. As no party has challenged that finding, we have no occasion to express an opinion on it.

only more specific statements of opinion. What the judge means to say, when he asks the witness to state the facts, is: 'The nature of this case requires that you be more specific, if you can, in your description of what you saw.' " W. King & D. Pillinger, Opinion Evidence in Illinois 4 (1942) (footnote omitted), quoted in 3 J. Weinstein & M. Berger, Weinstein's Evidence ¶ 701[01], p. 701–6 (1988).

See also E. Cleary, McCormick on Evidence 27 (3d ed. 1984) ("There is no conceivable statement however specific, detailed and 'factual,' that is not in some measure the product of inference and reflection as well as observation and memory"); R. Lempert & S. Saltzburg, A Modern Approach to Evidence 449 (2d ed. 1982) ("A factual finding, unless it is a simple report of something observed, is an opinion as to what more basic facts imply"). Thus, the traditional requirement that lay witnesses give statements of fact rather than opinion may be considered, "[l]ike the hearsay and original documents rules * * * a 'best evidence' rule." McCormick, Opinion Evidence in Iowa, 19 Drake L.Rev. 245, 246 (1970).

In the present case, the trial court had no difficulty in admitting as a factual finding the statement in the JAG Report that "[a]t the time of impact, the engine of 3E955 was operating but was operating at reduced power." Surely this "factual finding" could also be characterized as an opinion, which the investigator presumably arrived at on the basis of clues contained in the airplane wreckage. Rather than requiring that we draw some inevitably arbitrary line between the various shades of fact/opinion that invariably will be present in investigatory reports, we believe the Rule instructs us—as its plain language states—to admit "reports * * * setting forth * * * factual findings." The Rule's limitations and safeguards lie elsewhere: First, the requirement that reports contain factual findings bars the admission of statements not based on factual investigation. Second, the trustworthiness provision requires the court to make a determination as to whether the report, or any portion thereof, is sufficiently trustworthy to be admitted.

A broad approach to admissibility under Rule 803(8)(C), as we have outlined it, is also consistent with the Federal Rules' general approach of relaxing the traditional barriers to "opinion" testimony. Rules 702–705 permit experts to testify in the form of an opinion, and without any exclusion of opinions on "ultimate issues." And Rule 701 permits even a lay witness to testify in the form of opinions or inferences drawn from her observations when testimony in that form will be helpful to the trier of fact. We see no reason to strain to reach an interpretation of Rule 803(8)(C) that is contrary to the liberal thrust of the Federal Rules.[12]

12. The cited Rules refer, of course, to situations—unlike that at issue—where the opinion testimony is subject to cross-examination. But the determination that cross-examination was not indispensable in regard to official investigatory reports has already been made, and our point is merely that imposing a rigid distinction between fact and opinion would run against the Rules' tendency to de-emphasize that dichotomy.

We hold, therefore, that portions of investigatory reports otherwise admissible under Rule 803(8)(C) are not inadmissible merely because they state a conclusion or opinion. As long as the conclusion is based on a factual investigation and satisfies the Rule's trustworthiness requirement, it should be admissible along with other portions of the report.[13] As the trial judge in this case determined that certain of the JAG Report's conclusions were trustworthy, he rightly allowed them to be admitted into evidence. We therefore reverse the judgment of the Court of Appeals in respect of the Rule 803(8)(C) issue.

* * *

HINES v. BRANDON STEEL DECKS, INC., 886 F.2d 299, 302–03 (11th Cir.1989). "In footnote thirteen of the Supreme Court *Rainey* opinion, the Court cautioned that it expressed no view as to whether a legal conclusion as opposed to a factual conclusion was admissible under Rule 803(8)(C) * * *. In his concurring opinion in the Eleventh Circuit *Rainey* case, Judge Tjoflat suggested that, indeed, legal conclusions contained in reports would not fall within Rule 803(8)(C) as a 'finding.' 'The common meaning of finding * * * comports with investigative conclusions (i.e., the results derived from the examination of facts), but not with idle speculation or legal conclusions: "a finding does not include legal conclusions that may have been reached by an investigator and is necessarily something more than a mere recitation of evidence * * *." ' *Rainey,* 827 F.2d at 1510 (citation omitted). We agree that Rule 803(8)(C) does not provide for the admissibility of the legal conclusions contained within an otherwise admissible public report. Thus, one approach that the district court might take is to determine whether any of the excluded portions of the OSHA report contain legal conclusions that fall outside the purview of Rule 803(8)(C). Legal conclusions are inadmissible because the jury would have no way of knowing whether the preparer of the report was cognizant of the requirements underlying the legal conclusion and, if not, whether the preparer might have a higher or lower standard than the law requires.

"We caution, however, that the amorphous line between 'factual' and 'legal' conclusions may obscure a practical analysis under this rubric. While a legal conclusion encompasses 'the idea that the State will habitually sanction and enforce a legal relation of a specific content,' a factual conclusion is one of a number of 'contingencies on which the State predicates this relation.' Isaacs, Law and the Facts, 22 Colum.L.Rev. 1 (1922). Another way of looking at this inquiry is: Would the conclusion, if made by the district court, be subject to the

13. We emphasize that the issue in this case is whether Rule 803(8)(C) recognizes any difference between statements of "fact" and "opinion." There is no question in this case of any distinction between "fact" and "law." We thus express no opinion on whether legal conclusions contained in an official report are admissible as "findings of fact" under Rule 803(8)(C).

clearly erroneous standard of review on appeal? If so, then the conclusion is factual; if not, then the conclusion is legal. In addition, for those conclusions which are a mixed question of law and fact, a potential framework for analysis would be to ask whether the investigator made a finding of the 'ultimate facts' underlying the legal conclusion.

"We further note that most cases analyzing the admissibility of reports under 803(8)(C) do not frame the issue in terms of factual versus legal conclusions. Instead, almost all of the courts frame the inquiry in terms of trustworthiness. Comment, The Trustworthiness of Government Evaluation Reports under Federal Rule of Evidence 803(8)(C), 96 Harv.L.Rev. 492, 497–98 (1982)."

GENTILE v. COUNTY OF SUFFOLK, 129 F.R.D. 435, 448 (E.D.N.Y.1990), aff'd, 926 F.2d 142 (2d Cir.1991). "There are practical reasons for allowing public reports to be admitted. It would be almost impossible to require individual investigators to appear in court to testify any time the results of an investigation were probative of issues in individual litigation. Few individual litigants—particularly in civil rights cases—have the resources to duplicate the type of exhaustive reports produced by public agencies and funded by the taxpayers. See Note, The Trustworthiness of Government Evaluative Reports Under Federal Rule of Evidence 803(8)(C), 96 Harv.L.Rev. 492, 509 (1982) (suggesting that Rule 803(8)(C) operates as an important link between administrative and judicial systems by allowing private litigants to take advantage of a valuable and generally reliable public resource). Litigants should not be denied use of critical evidence because they lack the financial ability to duplicate it. See id. at 505–06 (placing restrictions on admissibility of government reports favors institutional parties and suggests class bias)."

Notes

(1) A public record or report that meets the requirements of Rule 803(8) may nevertheless be rendered inadmissible by statute or regulation. See, e.g., Huber v. United States, 838 F.2d 398, 401–03 ([illegible]th Cir.1988) (Coast Guard investigative report on maritime accident inadmissible in civil action by Coast Guard regulation); Budden v. United States, 748 F.Supp. 1374, 1376–78 (D.Neb.1990) (National Transportation Safety Board investigative report on helicopter accident inadmissible in civil action by 49 U.S.C.A. § 1441(e)).

(2) With regard to multiple hearsay problems, public records and reports are typically treated similarly to private business records. See, e.g., Budden v. United States, 748 F.Supp. 1374, 1377 (D.Neb.1990); In re Air Crash Disaster at Stapleton International Airport, 720 F.Supp. 1493, 1497 (D.Colo.1989).

SECTION 14. LEARNED TREATISES *

[FED.R.EVID. 803(18)]

ZWACK v. STATE

Court of Appeals of Texas, 1988.
757 S.W.2d 66.

ROBERTSON, JUSTICE.

The jury rejected appellant's not guilty plea to attempted capital murder of a peace officer and assessed his punishment at confinement for 45 years. Issues on appeal concern the refusal to permit appellant to read portions of a learned treatise into evidence, the constitutionality of the provision which prohibits informing the jury of the effect of a verdict of not guilty by reason of insanity, denial of a requested instruction on self-defense and whether error was committed in charging on the parole laws. We affirm.

Appellant does not challenge the sufficiency of the evidence. It will be briefly summarized only as necessary to a discussion of the issues.

In his first point of error appellant contends the trial court erred in refusing to permit his counsel to read portions of the book, H. Capland & B. Saddock, Modern Synopsis, a Comprehensive Textbook of Psychiatry (4th ed.). Appellant's defense was insanity. A psychiatrist and a clinical psychologist, called by appellant, testified that from their examinations they concluded appellant was suffering from paranoia and the psychologist additionally concluded appellant was "borderline schizophrenic." A psychiatrist and a psychologist called by the state testified that they found no evidence of a major mental illness from which appellant was suffering and that he was legally sane. On direct examination of his two experts and on cross-examination of the state's two experts, appellant established that each was familiar with the book in question and that it was recognized as authoritative in the field of psychiatry; however, none of the witnesses were then questioned as to the contents of the work. After the state rested, appellant sought to read portions of the book to the jury, stating that "it's my opinion that I do it now after I have had each witness identify it as authoritative." The trial court denied appellant's request. While during appellant's argument to the trial court he stated that he "would ask leave to recall the witness and do it with the witness sitting there," this request was not pursued and is thus not before us. Thus the issue is simply whether either side may read as substantive evidence, under the facts as presented here, excerpts from a learned treatise. We hold they may not.

* See 6 Wigmore, Evidence §§ 1690–1700 (Chadbourn rev. 1976); McCormick, Evidence § 321 (4th ed. 1992).

Prior to the adoption of the new rules of evidence, it was well-established that standard medical texts could not be introduced as direct evidence but could only be used to discredit or test the weight of the testimony of the expert if he stated he recognized the text as standard authority. *Aliff v. State,* 627 S.W.2d 166, 170 (Tex.Crim.App. 1982); *Long v. State,* 649 S.W.2d 363, 364–65 (Tex.App.—Fort Worth 1983, pet. ref'd); *Seeley v. Eaton,* 506 S.W.2d 719, 723 (Tex.Civ.App.—Houston [14th Dist.] 1974, writ ref'd n.r.e.). Tex.R.Crim.Evid. 803(18) changed this rule. It excludes from the rule against hearsay learned treatises

> To the extent called to the attention of an expert witness upon cross-examination or relied upon by him in direct examination, statements contained in published treatises, periodicals, or pamphlets on a subject of history, medicine, or other science or art, established as a reliable authority by the testimony or admission of the witness or by other expert testimony or by judicial notice. If admitted, the statements may be read into evidence but may not be received as exhibits.

In commenting on this new rule Professor Wellborn stated:

> An important feature of rule 803(18) is that, unlike the earlier Model Code and Uniform Rules, the federal and Texas provisions permit learned publications to be used only in conjunction with testimony by an expert witness, either on direct or cross-examination—even when the authority of the publication is otherwise established. The reason for this limitation is to ensure that a jury will not receive arcane information without some guidance from a live witness. Consequently, it would not be proper under the new rule for an attorney to read into evidence from a publication, however fully authenticated and established as authoritative, except while examining an expert witness.

Wellborn, *Article VIII: Hearsay,* 20 Hous.L.Rev. 477, 526–27 (1983). (citations omitted).

While Rule 803(18) has not yet been interpreted by a Texas court, it has been in issue in several federal courts. In *Tart v. McGann,* 697 F.2d 75 (2d Cir.1982), the change in the rule was discussed:

> Prior to the enactment of Rule 803(18), learned treatises were generally usable only on cross-examination, and then only for impeachment purposes. See Weinstein, supra, 803(18)[01]. Most commentators found the hearsay objections to learned treatise evidence unconvincing, and recommended that treatises be admitted as substantive evidence. Some commentators went so far as to suggest that treatises be admitted independently of an expert's testimony. Id. 803(18)[02]. The Advisory Committee rejected this position, noting that a treatise might be "misunderstood and misapplied without expert assistance and supervision." FED.R.EVID. 803(18) advisory committee notes. Accordingly, the Rule permits the admission of learned treatises as substantive evidence, but only when "an expert is on the stand and available to explain and assist in the application of the treatise * * *." Id.

Tart, 697 F.2d at 78. The first circuit rejected the argument "that the contents of all issues of a periodical may be qualified wholesale under

Rule 803(18) by testimony that the magazine was highly regarded" in *Meschino v. North Am. Drager, Inc.,* 841 F.2d 429, 434 (1st Cir.1988). And our own circuit used the following language in *Dartez v. Fibreboard Corp.,* 765 F.2d 456 (5th Cir.1985):

> The reason for the Rule's restrictions on the use of learned treatises is to avoid the possibility that the jury will misunderstand and misapply the technical language within such an article if they are allowed to consider the publication itself instead of receiving the information through the testimony of an expert in the field. Fed.R.Evid. 803(18) advisory committee note.

Dartez, 765 F.2d at 465. We agree with the above interpretations and hold that learned treatises are to be used only in conjunction with testimony by an expert witness, either on direct or cross-examination, even though the authority of the publication is otherwise established. Appellant's first point of error is overruled.

* * *

The judgment is affirmed.

MENDOZA v. STATE, 787 S.W.2d 502 (Tex.App.1990). "Appellant first complains of error in permitting the State's expert witness to read a portion of an FBI manual into evidence. Donna Stanley, a serologist with the Department of Public Safety, testified regarding tests she ran on items of evidence submitted to her by the Austin police. The results of her tests revealed no presence of sperm fluid in the victim's mouth or vagina, but Stanley testified that such negative findings were not unusual in sexual assault cases. One of the manuals Stanley relied upon as an authoritative source for this proposition is a scientific publication of the Federal Bureau of Investigation. The manual contains a study and analysis of sexual assault evidence compiled from various police labs across the country. After a voir dire examination of the witness, the trial court allowed Stanley to read into evidence a portion of an article written by a Larry Brown from a Virginia FBI laboratory.

"A witness may read into evidence, either on direct or cross-examination, parts of a treatise, periodical, or pamphlet, assuming that the witness is an expert in the relevant area and establishes by her testimony that the publication is a reliable source in her field. Tex. R.Cr.Evid.Ann. 803(18) (Pamph.1990). See Zwack v. State, 757 S.W.2d 66, 68–9 (Tex.App.1988, pet. ref'd).

"Appellant objected to this evidence because Stanley admitted she knew nothing about Larry Brown, one of the authors who contributed to the manual, and because the State had not established that Larry Brown was a recognized authority. However, Rule 803(18) does not require that the State show the publication was written by an authority but requires instead that the expert witness relies on it and considers it a reliable authority in the field. The State established Stanley as an expert, and Stanley testified she considered the FBI publication to be an authoritative source in her field. The fact that Stanley did not know the author or credentials of a particular article of the publication does not vitiate compliance with the rule. Appellant's first point of error is overruled."

MESCHINO v. NORTH AMERICAN DRAGER, INC., 841 F.2d 429, 433–34 (1st Cir.1988). "Plaintiff further objects to the court's exclusion of two articles published in *Health Devices Magazine.* She sought to introduce a December 1985 article entitled 'PEEP Valves' against Boehringer, and a July 1981 article entitled 'Ventilation Alarms' against NAD. The basic question was qualification under Fed.R.Evid. 803(18), whether the article had been 'established as a reliable authority.' * * *

" * * * [W]e would not accept plaintiff's argument that the contents of all issues of a periodical may be qualified wholesale under Rule 803(18) by testimony that the magazine was highly regarded. In these days of quantified research, and pressure to publish, an article does not reach the dignity of a 'reliable authority' merely because some editor, even a most reputable one, sees fit to circulate it. Physicians engaged in research may write dozens of papers during a lifetime. Mere publication cannot make them automatically reliable authority. The price of escape from cross-examination is a higher standard than 'qualified,' set for live witnesses who do not. The words have a serious meaning, such as recognition of the authoritive stature of the writer, or affirmative acceptance of the article itself in the profession."

SECTION 15. JUDGMENT OF PREVIOUS CONVICTION *

[FED.R.EVID. 803(22)]

HINSHAW v. KEITH

United States District Court, Maine, 1986.
645 F.Supp. 180.

MEMORANDUM AND ORDER DENYING DEFENDANT'S MOTION IN LIMINE

CYR, CHIEF JUDGE.

On September 5, 1984, plaintiff filed a complaint alleging that on or about September 6, 1982, defendant Keith, an employee of Dysart's, negligently operated a motor vehicle on the Maine Turnpike, resulting in a collision with the plaintiff's vehicle and in personal injuries to the plaintiff. Subsequent to the filing of the complaint, it was stipulated by

* See 4 Wigmore, Evidence § 1346a (Chadbourn rev. 1972); 5 id. § 1671a (Chadbourn rev. 1974); McCormick, Evidence § 298 (4th ed. 1992).

all parties that on November 5, 1982, defendant Keith was convicted of leaving the scene of the subject accident, in violation of Me.Rev.Stat. Ann. tit. 29, § 894. It is further stipulated that the conviction followed upon a plea of guilty entered on defendant's behalf through his attorney, that the attorney had been authorized to enter the plea, and that in doing so the attorney had not acted improperly.

On December 29, 1985, defendant Keith filed a motion *in limine*, asking that the plaintiff be prohibited from introducing the conviction in evidence, on the ground that such evidence is barred by Rule 803(22) of the Federal Rules of Evidence. The motion was granted on May 22, 1986, by order of the United States Magistrate. As plaintiff filed a timely objection to the Magistrate's decision, the court undertakes *de novo* review of the order granting defendant's motion *in limine*. 28 U.S.C. § 636(b).

I.

Rule 803 of the Federal Rules of Evidence lists exceptions to the hearsay rule, including in pertinent part:

> The following are not excluded by the hearsay rule, even though the declarant is available as a witness:
>
> * * *
>
> (22) *Judgment of previous conviction.* Evidence of a final judgment, entered after a trial or upon a plea of guilty * * * adjudging a person guilty of a crime punishable by death or imprisonment in excess of one year, to prove any fact essential to sustain the judgment.

The Notes of the Advisory Committee state that "the direction of the decisions * * * manifest an increasing reluctance to reject *in toto* the validity of the law's factfinding process outside the confines of res judicata and collateral estoppel." In explaining the limitation of the exclusion to felony convictions, the Notes add that "[p]ractical considerations require exclusion of convictions of minor offenses, not because the administration of justice in its lower echelons must be inferior, but because motivation to defend at this level is often minimal or non-existent."

It is clear that, if determinative, Rule 803(22) would preclude admission of the judgment of conviction in the present case, since the crime of which defendant Keith was convicted was not a felony. However, Rule 803(22) is not a rule of exclusion, but rather an exception to the broad exclusionary rule known as the hearsay rule.

Although a judgment of conviction comes under the hearsay rule, Fed.R.Evid. 802, a plea of guilty is admissible on a different basis. Unwithdrawn guilty pleas in criminal cases have been held admissible in a subsequent civil suit arising out of the same factual situation, generally as an admission by a party-opponent under Rule 801(d)(2), and sometimes as a declaration against interest under Rule 804(b)(3).

In *Rain v. Pavkov,* 357 F.2d 506, 510 (3d Cir.1966), the court held such a plea admissible despite a state statute declaring a guilty plea in traffic offenses inadmissible. And in *McCormick v. United States,* 539 F.Supp. 1179, 1183 (D.Colo.1982), a case involving a truck driver's guilty plea to a charge of running a red light, the court held that "a guilty plea may be * * * introduced in a subsequent civil proceeding as an admission," although "this admission does not conclusively establish liability." *See also Hillyer v. David Phillips Trucking Co.,* 606 F.2d 619 (5th Cir.1979).

II.

In granting the defendant's motion *in limine,* the Magistrate declared that there is a conflict between Rule 803(22) and Rules 801(d)(2) and 804(b)(3). This conflict is said to arise from the fact that Rule 803(22), although merely an exception to the hearsay rule, is based on a policy that has a wider application: namely, that evidence of a conviction for a minor offense should not be admissible in subsequent civil actions, because of the lack of motivation to contest on the part of the defendant. (*See* Magistrate's Order, at 3–4). To hold that a guilty plea is admissible under Rule 801(d)(2) or Rule 804(b)(3), while a conviction is not, would undercut this policy and "would serve to negate the full import of Rule 803(22)." *Id.* at 4. Accordingly, the Magistrate recommended that " 'evidence of guilty pleas in nonfelony cases should not be allowed,' " either as admissions or as statements against interest. *Id.* at 3, *quoting* J. Weinstein & M. Berger, *Weinstein's Evidence* § 803(22)(01) at 803–354 to 803–355 (1985). Rather, the conflict between the rules should be resolved under Fed.R.Evid. 403 by "the application by the court of a *per se* rule that the result of the introduction of a guilty plea in this type of situation would be more prejudicial than probative." *Id.* at 5.

III.

The only authority cited for creating a *per se* rule of the kind recommended is *Weinstein's Evidence, supra. Weinstein,* in turn, cites only four case notes to support its position.[1] *See id.* at nn. 26 & 27. *Weinstein* acknowledges two cases which hold that guilty pleas in nonfelony cases are admissible in subsequent civil actions, *Rain v. Pavkov,* 357 F.2d 506 (3d Cir.1966), and *M.F.A. Mutual Insurance Co. v. Dixon,* 243 F.Supp. 806 (W.D.Ark.1965), but merely concludes, without explication, that "[t]hese decisions should not be followed," *id.* at n. 28. *Weinstein* notwithstanding, the fact is that these two cases represent current law on this issue. Indeed, *all* case law interpreting the Federal Rules of Evidence on the issue of the admissibility of guilty pleas in nonfelony traffic cases holds that such pleas may be admitted either as admissions under Rule 801(d)(2) or as statements against interest under Rule 804(b)(3). *See Rain v. Pavkov,* 357 F.2d 506 (3d Cir.1966); *Dun-*

1. Note, *Admissibility and Weight of a Criminal Conviction in a Subsequent Civil Action,* 39 Va.L.Rev. 995 (1953); Note, *Evidence: Judgments: Admissibility in Evidence in a Civil Action of Party's Conviction of Traffic Infraction,* 35 Cornell L.Q. 872 (1950); Note, *Evidence—Traffic Infraction—Admissibility as Proof of Underlying Fact,* 16 Brooklyn L.Rev. 286 (1950); Note, *Admissibility of Traffic Conviction as Proof of Facts in Subsequent Civil Action,* 50 Colum.L.Rev. 529 (1950).

ham v. Pannell, 263 F.2d 725 (5th Cir.1959); *Levelle v. Powers,* 248 F.2d 774 (10th Cir.1957); *McCormick v. United States,* 539 F.Supp. 1179 (D.Colo.1982); *M.F.A. Mutual Insurance Co. v. Dixon,* 243 F.Supp. 806 (W.D.Ark.1965); *see also Hillyer v. David Phillips Trucking Co.,* 606 F.2d 619 (5th Cir.1979); *Sharp v. Frazier,* 519 F.Supp. 74 (E.D.Tenn. 1981).

Weinstein also states, however, that "[c]are should be taken not to confuse the issue of the admissibility of a prior criminal conviction and of an unwithdrawn plea of guilty," *Weinstein's Evidence, supra,* § 401(06) at 410–38, thus tacitly recognizing the importance of the distinction between the two. In explaining the reason for the distinction, the commentary quotes Judge Wisdom in *Dunham v. Pannell,* 263 F.2d at 730: "A plea of guilty * * * is not offered to prove the facts recited in the charge, but to prove that the offender * * * *admitted* the facts." *Id.* at 410–39. And the commentary finds "persuasive" the following statement by Judge Fuld, in *Ando v. Woodberry,* 8 N.Y.2d 165, 203 N.Y.S.2d 74, 78, 168 N.E.2d 520, 524 (1960), upholding the admissibility of such a plea: "If voluntarily and deliberately made, the plea was a statement of guilt, an admission by the defendant that he committed the acts charged, and it should be accorded no less force or effect than if made outside of court to a stranger." *Id.*

Another purpose served by refraining from the imposition of a *per se* rule is that the admission of such evidence gives the jury the opportunity to decide questions of fact on a more fully adequate evidentiary basis. As Judge Fuld stated: "To the claim that the jury will be unduly prejudiced by the introduction of a plea of guilt despite the opportunity to explain it away, we content ourselves with the statement that this underestimates the intelligence of jurors." 168 N.E.2d at 524.

The court possesses discretionary power, *see* Fed.R.Evid. 403, to determine whether the probative value of a guilty plea to a traffic-related nonfelony charge is outweighed, *inter alia,* by the risk of unfair prejudice. *See Hillyer v. David Phillips Trucking Co.,* 606 F.2d 619 (5th Cir.1979). Therefore, it seems to the court altogether inadvisable to create a hard-and-fast rule that such pleas should not be allowed as admissions or as statements against interest.

It is to be expected that the competing policy considerations underlying particular rules of evidence will result in tensions in the application of these rules. Although judicial establishment of a *per se* rule would resolve the rules conflict once and for all, by giving complete sway to one rule over another, the resultant eclipse of certain policy considerations in favor of others seems too high a price to pay. it seems preferable as a jurisprudential matter that the court balance the competing policy considerations reflected in these rules of evidence on a case-by-case basis, rather than by recourse to a *per se* rule.

* * *

V.

The court holds that an unwithdrawn guilty plea made to a nonfelony charge may be admissible as evidence in a subsequent civil suit arising out of the same factual situation, as a nonhearsay admission pursuant to Fed.R.Evid. 801(d)(2). In the present case, it is stipulated that defendant Keith entered a plea of guilty to the charge of leaving the scene of an accident, in violation of Me.Rev.Stat.Ann. tit. 29, § 894. This plea constitutes an admission by a party-opponent under Fed.R.Evid. 801(d)(2) and therefore is not inadmissible hearsay. Whether the guilty plea should be admitted in the circumstances of this case may depend upon a balancing of the considerations contemplated by Fed.R.Evid. 403, which task is better left to trial.

Accordingly, the order of the U.S. Magistrate granting defendant's motion *in limine* is vacated, and defendant's motion *in limine* is hereby *DENIED.*

SECTION 16. OTHER EXCEPTIONS *

[FED.R.EVID. 803(11)–(17), (19)–(21), (23)–(24); 804(b)(4), (5)]

IDAHO v. WRIGHT

Supreme Court of the United States, 1990.
___ U.S. ___, 110 S.Ct. 3139, 111 L.Ed.2d 638.

JUSTICE O'CONNOR delivered the opinion of the Court.

This case requires us to decide whether the admission at trial of certain hearsay statements made by a child declarant to an examining pediatrician violates a defendant's rights under the Confrontation Clause of the Sixth Amendment.

I

Respondent Laura Lee Wright was jointly charged with Robert L. Giles of two counts of lewd conduct with a minor under 16, in violation of Idaho Code § 18–1508 (1987). The alleged victims were respondent's two daughters, one of whom was 5½ and the other 2½ years old at the time the crimes were charged.

Respondent and her ex-husband, Louis Wright, the father of the older daughter, had reached an informal agreement whereby each parent would have custody of the older daughter for six consecutive months. The allegations surfaced in November 1986 when the older daughter told Cynthia Goodman, Louis Wright's female companion, that Giles had had sexual intercourse with her while respondent held her down and covered her mouth, App. 47–55; 3 Tr. 456–460, and that she had seen respondent and Giles do the same thing to respondent's younger daughter, App. 48–49, 61; 3 Tr. 460. The younger daughter was living with her parents—respondent and Giles—at the time of the alleged offenses.

* See McCormick, Evidence ch. 33 (4th ed. 1992).

Goodman reported the older daughter's disclosures to the police the next day and took the older daughter to the hospital. A medical examination of the older daughter revealed evidence of sexual abuse. One of the examining physicians was Dr. John Jambura, a pediatrician with extensive experience in child abuse cases. App. 91–94. Police and welfare officials took the younger daughter into custody that day for protection and investigation. Dr. Jambura examined her the following day and found conditions "strongly suggestive of sexual abuse with vaginal contact," occurring approximately two to three days prior to the examination. *Id.*, at 105, 106.

At the joint trial of respondent and Giles, the trial court conducted a *voir dire* examination of the younger daughter, who was three years old at the time of trial, to determine whether she was capable of testifying. *Id.*, at 32–38. The court concluded, and the parties agreed, that the younger daughter was "not capable of communicating to the jury." *Id.*, at 39.

At issue in this case is the admission at trial of certain statements made by the younger daughter to Dr. Jambura in response to questions he asked regarding the alleged abuse. Over objection by respondent and Giles, the trial court permitted Dr. Jambura to testify before the jury as follows:

> "Q. [By the prosecutor] Now, calling your attention then to your examination of Kathy Wright on November 10th. What—would you describe any interview dialogue that you had with Kathy at that time? Excuse me, before you get into that, would you lay a setting of where this took place and who else might have been present?
>
> "A. This took place in my office, in my examining room, and, as I recall, I believe previous testimony I said that I recall a female attendant being present, I don't recall her identity.
>
> "I started out with basically, 'Hi, how are you,' you know, 'What did you have for breakfast this morning?' Essentially a few minutes of just sort of chitchat.
>
> "Q. Was there response from Kathy to that first—those first questions?
>
> "A. There was. She started to carry on a very relaxed animated conversation. I then proceeded to just gently start asking questions about, 'Well, how are things at home,' you know, those sorts. Gently moving into the domestic situation and then moved into four questions in particular, as I reflected in my records, 'Do you play with daddy? Does daddy play with you? Does daddy touch you with his pee-pee? Do you touch his pee-pee?' And again we then established what was meant by pee-pee, it was a generic term for genital area.
>
> "Q. Before you get into that, what was, as best you recollect, what was her response to the question 'Do you play with daddy?'
>
> "A. Yes, we play—I remember her making a comment about yes we play a lot and expanding on that and talking about spending time with daddy.

"Q. And 'Does daddy play with you?' Was there any response?

"A. She responded to that as well, that they played together in a variety of circumstances and, you know, seemed very unaffected by the question.

"Q. And then what did you say and her response?

"A. When I asked her 'Does daddy touch you with his pee-pee,' she did admit to that. When I asked, 'Do you touch his pee-pee,' she did not have any response.

"Q. Excuse me. Did you notice any change in her affect or attitude in that line of questioning?

"A. Yes.

"Q. What did you observe?

"A. She would not—oh, she did not talk any further about that. She would not elucidate what exactly—what kind of touching was taking place, or how it was happening. She did, however, say that daddy does do this with me, but he does it a lot more with my sister than with me.

"Q. And how did she offer that last statement? Was that in response to a question or was that just a volunteered statement?

"A. That was a volunteered statement as I sat and waited for her to respond, again after she sort of clammed-up, and that was the next statement that she made after just allowing some silence to occur." *Id.,* at 121–123.

On cross-examination, Dr. Jambura acknowledged that a picture that he drew during his questioning of the younger daughter had been discarded. *Id.,* at 124. Dr. Jambura also stated that although he had dictated notes to summarize the conversation, his notes were not detailed and did not record any changes in the child's affect or attitude. *Id.,* at 123–124.

The trial court admitted these statements under Idaho's residual hearsay exception, which provides in relevant part:

"Rule 803. Hearsay exceptions; availability of declarant immaterial.—The following are not excluded by the hearsay rule, even though the declarant is available as a witness.

* * *

"(24) Other exceptions. A statement not specifically covered by any of the foregoing exceptions but having equivalent circumstantial guarantees of trustworthiness, if the court determines that (A) the statement is offered as evidence of a material fact; (B) the statement is more probative on the point for which it is offered than any other evidence which the proponent can procure through reasonable efforts; and (C) the general purposes of these rules and the interests of justice will best be served by admission of the statement into evidence." Idaho Rule Evid. 803(24).

Respondent and Giles were each convicted of two counts of lewd conduct with a minor under 16 and sentenced to 20 years imprisonment. Each appealed only from the conviction involving the younger daughter. Giles contended that the trial court erred in admitting Dr. Jambura's testimony under Idaho's residual hearsay exception. The Idaho Supreme Court disagreed and affirmed his conviction. *State v. Giles,* 115 Idaho 984, 772 P.2d 191 (1989). Respondent asserted that the admission of Dr. Jambura's testimony under the residual hearsay exception nevertheless violated her rights under the Confrontation Clause. The Idaho Supreme Court agreed and reversed respondent's conviction. 116 Idaho 382, 775 P.2d 1224 (1989).

The Supreme Court of Idaho held that the admission of the inculpatory hearsay testimony violated respondent's federal constitutional right to confrontation because the testimony did not fall within a traditional hearsay exception and was based on an interview that lacked procedural safeguards. *Id.,* at 385, 775 P.2d, at 1227. The court found Dr. Jambura's interview technique inadequate because "the questions and answers were not recorded on videotape for preservation and perusal by the defense at or before trial; and, blatantly leading questions were used in the interrogation." *Ibid.* The statements also lacked trustworthiness, according to the court, because "this interrogation was performed by someone with a preconceived idea of what the child should be disclosing." *Ibid.* Noting that expert testimony and child psychology texts indicated that children are susceptible to suggestion and are therefore likely to be misled by leading questions, the court found that "[t]he circumstances surrounding this interview demonstrate dangers of unreliability which, because the interview was not [audio or video] recorded, can never be fully assessed." *Id.,* at 388, 775 P.2d, at 1230. The court concluded that the younger daughter's statements lacked the particularized guarantees of trustworthiness necessary to satisfy the requirements of the Confrontation Clause and that therefore the trial court erred in admitting them. *Id.,* at 389, 775 P.2d, at 1231. Because the court was not convinced, beyond a reasonable doubt, that the jury would have reached the same result had the error not occurred, the court reversed respondent's conviction on the count involving the younger daughter and remanded for a new trial. *Ibid.*

We granted certiorari, 493 U.S. ___, 110 S.Ct. 833, 107 L.Ed.2d 829 (1990), and now affirm.

II

The Confrontation Clause of the Sixth Amendment, made applicable to the States through the Fourteenth Amendment, provides: "In all criminal prosecutions, the accused shall enjoy the right * * * to be confronted with the witnesses against him."

From the earliest days of our Confrontation Clause jurisprudence, we have consistently held that the Clause does not necessarily prohibit the admission of hearsay statements against a criminal defendant, even though the admission of such statements might be thought to violate the literal terms of the Clause. See, *e.g., Mattox v. United States,* 156 U.S. 237, 243, 15 S.Ct. 337, 339, 39 L.Ed. 409 (1895); *Pointer v. Texas,* 380 U.S. 400, 407, 85 S.Ct. 1065, 1069, 13 L.Ed.2d 923 (1965). We reaffirmed only recently that "[w]hile a literal interpretation of the Confrontation Clause could bar the use of any out-of-court statements when the declarant is unavailable, this Court has rejected that view as 'unintended and too extreme.'" *Bourjaily v. United States,* 483 U.S. 171, 182, 107 S.Ct. 2775, 2782, 97 L.Ed.2d 144 (1987) (quoting *Ohio v. Roberts,* 448 U.S. 56, 63, 100 S.Ct. 2531, 2537, 65 L.Ed.2d 597 (1980)); see also *Maryland v. Craig,* ___ U.S. ___, 110 S.Ct. 3157, ___ L.Ed.2d ___ ("[T]he [Confrontation] Clause permits, where necessary, the admission of certain hearsay statements against a defendant despite the defendant's inability to confront the declarant at trial").

Although we have recognized that hearsay rules and the Confrontation Clause are generally designed to protect similar values, we have also been careful not to equate the Confrontation Clause's prohibitions with the general rule prohibiting the admission of hearsay statements. See *California v. Green,* 399 U.S. 149, 155–156, 90 S.Ct. 1930, 1933–1934, 26 L.Ed.2d 489 (1970); *Dutton v. Evans,* 400 U.S. 74, 86, 91 S.Ct. 210, 218, 27 L.Ed.2d 213 (1970) (plurality opinion); *United States v. Inadi,* 475 U.S. 387, 393, n. 5, 106 S.Ct. 1121, 1125, n. 5, 89 L.Ed.2d 390 (1986). The Confrontation Clause, in other words, bars the admission of some evidence that would otherwise be admissible under an exception to the hearsay rule. See, *e.g., Green, supra,* 399 U.S., at 155–156, 90 S.Ct., at 1933–1934; *Bruton v. United States,* 391 U.S. 123, 88 S.Ct. 1620, 20 L.Ed.2d 476 (1968); *Barber v. Page,* 390 U.S. 719, 88 S.Ct. 1318, 20 L.Ed.2d 255 (1968); *Pointer, supra.*

In *Ohio v. Roberts,* we set forth "a general approach" for determining when incriminating statements admissible under an exception to the hearsay rule also meet the requirements of the Confrontation Clause. 448 U.S., at 65, 100 S.Ct., at 2538. We noted that the Confrontation Clause "operates in two separate ways to restrict the range of admissible hearsay." *Ibid.* "First, in conformance with the Framers' preference for face-to-face accusation, the Sixth Amendment establishes a rule of necessity. In the usual case * * * the prosecution must either produce or demonstrate the unavailability of, the declarant whose statement it wishes to use against the defendant." *Ibid.* (citations omitted). Second, once a witness is shown to be unavailable, "his statement is admissible only if it bears adequate 'indicia of reliability.' Reliability can be inferred without more in a case where the evidence falls within a firmly rooted hearsay exception. In other cases, the evidence must be excluded, at least absent a showing of particularized guarantees of trustworthiness." *Id.,* at 66, 100 S.Ct., at 2539 (footnote omitted); see also *Mancusi v. Stubbs,* 408 U.S. 204, 213, 92 S.Ct. 2308, 2313, 33 L.Ed.2d 293 (1972).

Applying this general analytical framework to the facts of *Roberts, supra,* we held that the admission of testimony given at a preliminary hearing, where the declarant failed to appear at trial despite the State's having issued five separate subpoenas to her, did not violate the Confrontation Clause. *Id.*, 448 U.S., at 67–77, 100 S.Ct., at 2540–2545. Specifically, we found that the State had carried its burden of showing that the declarant was unavailable to testify at trial, see *Barber, supra*, 390 U.S., at 724–725, 88 S.Ct., at 1321–1322; *Mancusi, supra*, 408 U.S., at 212, 92 S.Ct., at 2312, and that the testimony at the preliminary hearing bore sufficient indicia of reliability, particularly because defense counsel had had an adequate opportunity to cross-examine the declarant at the preliminary hearing, see *Mancusi, supra*, at 216, 92 S.Ct., at 2314.

We have applied the general approach articulated in *Roberts* to subsequent cases raising Confrontation Clause and hearsay issues. In *United States v. Inadi, supra*, we held that the general requirement of unavailability did not apply to incriminating out-of-court statements made by a non-testifying co-conspirator and that therefore the Confrontation Clause did not prohibit the admission of such statements, even though the government had not shown that the declarant was unavailable to testify at trial. 475 U.S., at 394–400, 106 S.Ct., at 1125–1129. In *Bourjaily v. United States, supra*, we held that such statements also carried with them sufficient "indicia of reliability" because the hearsay exception for co-conspirator statements was a firmly rooted one. 483 U.S., at 182–184, 107 S.Ct., at 2782–2783.

Applying the *Roberts* approach to this case, we first note that this case does not raise the question whether, before a child's out-of-court statements are admitted, the Confrontation Clause requires the prosecution to show that a child witness is unavailable at trial—and, if so, what that showing requires. The trial court in this case found that respondent's younger daughter was incapable of communicating with the jury, and defense counsel agreed. App. 39. The court below neither questioned this finding nor discussed the general requirement of unavailability. For purposes of deciding this case, we assume without deciding that, to the extent the unavailability requirement applies in this case, the younger daughter was an unavailable witness within the meaning of the Confrontation Clause.

The crux of the question presented is therefore whether the State, as the proponent of evidence presumptively barred by the hearsay rule and the Confrontation Clause, has carried its burden of proving that the younger daughter's incriminating statements to Dr. Jambura bore sufficient indicia of reliability to withstand scrutiny under the Clause. The court below held that, although the trial court had properly admitted the statements under the State's residual hearsay exception, the statements were "fraught with the dangers of unreliability which the Confrontation Clause is designed to highlight and obviate." 116 Idaho, at 389, 775 P.2d, at 1231. The State asserts that the court below erected too stringent a standard for admitting the statements and that the statements were, under the totality of the circumstances, sufficiently reliable for Confrontation Clause purposes.

In *Roberts,* we suggested that the "indicia of reliability" requirement could be met in either of two circumstances: where the hearsay statement "falls within a firmly rooted hearsay exception," or where it is supported by "a showing of particularized guarantees of trustworthiness." 448 U.S., at 66, 100 S.Ct., at 2539; see also *Bourjaily,* 483 U.S., at 183, 107 S.Ct., at 2782 ("[T]he co-conspirator exception to the hearsay rule is firmly enough rooted in our jurisprudence that, under this Court's holding in *Roberts,* a court need not independently inquire into the reliability of such statements"); *Lee v. Illinois,* 476 U.S. 530, 543, 106 S.Ct. 2056, 2063, 90 L.Ed.2d 514 (1986) ("[E]ven if certain hearsay evidence does not fall within 'a firmly rooted hearsay exception' and is thus presumptively unreliable and inadmissible for Confrontation Clause purposes, it may nonetheless meet Confrontation Clause reliability standards if it is supported by a 'showing of particularized guarantees of trustworthiness' ") (footnote and citation omitted).

We note at the outset that Idaho's residual hearsay exception, Idaho Rule Evid. 803(24), under which the challenged statements were admitted, App. 113–115, is not a firmly rooted hearsay exception for Confrontation Clause purposes. Admission under a firmly rooted hearsay exception satisfies the constitutional requirement of reliability because of the weight accorded longstanding judicial and legislative experience in assessing the trustworthiness of certain types of out-of-court statements. See *Mattox,* 156 U.S., at 243, 15 S.Ct., at 339; *Roberts,* 448 U.S., at 66, 100 S.Ct., at 2539; *Bourjaily,* 483 U.S., at 183, 107 S.Ct., at 2782; see also *Lee,* 476 U.S., at 551–552, 106 S.Ct., at 2067–2068 (Blackmun, J., dissenting) ("[S]tatements squarely within established hearsay exceptions possess 'the imprimatur of judicial and legislative experience' * * * and that fact must weigh heavily in our assessment of their reliability for constitutional purposes") (citation omitted). The residual hearsay exception, by contrast, accommodates ad hoc instances in which statements not otherwise falling within a recognized hearsay exception might nevertheless be sufficiently reliable to be admissible at trial. See, *e.g.,* Senate Judiciary Committee's Note on Fed.Rule Evid. 803(24), 28 U.S.C.App., pp. 786–787; E. Cleary, McCormick on Evidence § 324.1, pp. 907–909 (3d ed. 1984). Hearsay statements admitted under the residual exception, almost by definition, therefore do not share the same tradition of reliability that supports the admissibility of statements under a firmly rooted hearsay exception. Moreover, were we to agree that the admission of hearsay statements under the residual exception automatically passed Confrontation Clause scrutiny, virtually every codified hearsay exception would assume constitutional stature, a step this Court has repeatedly declined to take. See *Green,* 399 U.S., at 155–156, 90 S.Ct., at 1933–1934; *Evans,* 400 U.S., at 86–87, 91 S.Ct., at 218–219 (plurality opinion); *Inadi,* 475 U.S., at 393, n. 5, 106 S.Ct., at 1125, n. 5; see also *Evans, supra,* 400 U.S., at 94–95, 91 S.Ct., at 222–223 (Harlan, J., concurring in result).

The State in any event does not press the matter strongly and recognizes that, because the younger daughter's hearsay statements do not fall within a firmly rooted hearsay exception, they are "presumptively unreliable and inadmissible for Confrontation Clause purposes," *Lee,* 476 U.S., at 543, 106 S.Ct., at 2063, and "must be excluded, at least absent a showing of particularized guarantees of trustworthiness," *Roberts,* 448 U.S., at 66, 100 S.Ct., at 2539. The court below concluded that the State had not made such a showing, in large measure because the statements resulted from an interview lacking certain procedural safeguards. The court below specifically noted that Dr. Jambura failed to record the interview on videotape, asked leading questions, and questioned the child with a preconceived idea of what she should be disclosing. See 116 Idaho, at 388, 775 P.2d, at 1230.

Although we agree with the court below that the Confrontation Clause bars the admission of the younger daughter's hearsay statements, we reject the apparently dispositive weight placed by that court on the lack of procedural safeguards at the interview. Out-of-court statements made by children regarding sexual abuse arise in a wide variety of circumstances, and we do not believe the Constitution imposes a fixed set of procedural prerequisites to the admission of such statements at trial. The procedural requirements identified by the court below, to the extent regarded as conditions precedent to the admission of child hearsay statements in child sexual abuse cases, may in many instances be inappropriate or unnecessary to a determination whether a given statement is sufficiently trustworthy for Confrontation Clause purposes. See, *e.g., Nelson v. Farrey,* 874 F.2d 1222, 1229 (CA7 1989) (videotape requirement not feasible, especially where defendant had not yet been criminally charged), cert. denied, 493 U.S. ___, 110 S.Ct. 835, 107 L.Ed.2d 831 (1990); J. Myers, Child Witness Law and Practice § 4.6, pp. 129–134 (1987) (use of leading questions with children, when appropriate, does not necessarily render responses untrustworthy). Although the procedural guidelines propounded by the court below may well enhance the reliability of out-of-court statements of children regarding sexual abuse, we decline to read into the Confrontation Clause a preconceived and artificial litmus test for the procedural propriety of professional interviews in which children make hearsay statements against a defendant.

The State responds that a finding of "particularized guarantees of trustworthiness" should instead be based on a consideration of the totality of the circumstances, including not only the circumstances surrounding the making of the statement, but also other evidence at trial that corroborates the truth of the statement. We agree that "particularized guarantees of trustworthiness" must be shown from the totality of the circumstances, but we think the relevant circumstances include only those that surround the making of the statement and that render the declarant particularly worthy of belief. This conclusion derives from the rationale for permitting exceptions to the general rule against hearsay:

> "The theory of the hearsay rule * * * is that the many possible sources of inaccuracy and untrustworthiness which may lie underneath

> the bare untested assertion of a witness can best be brought to light and exposed, if they exist, by the test of cross-examination. But this test or security may in a given instance be superfluous; it may be sufficiently clear, in that instance, that the statement offered is free enough from the risk of inaccuracy and untrustworthiness, so that the test of cross-examination would be a work of supererogation." 5 J. Wigmore, Evidence § 1420, p. 251 (J. Chadbourne rev. 1974).

In other words, if the declarant's truthfulness is so clear from the surrounding circumstances that the test of cross-examination would be of marginal utility, then the hearsay rule does not bar admission of the statement at trial. The basis for the "excited utterance" exception, for example, is that such statements are given under circumstances that eliminate the possibility of fabrication, coaching, or confabulation, and that therefore the circumstances surrounding the making of the statement provide sufficient assurance that the statement is trustworthy and that cross-examination would be superfluous. See, *e.g.,* 6 Wigmore, *supra,* §§ 1745–1764; 4 J. Weinstein & M. Berger, Weinstein's Evidence ¶ 803(2)[01] (1988); Advisory Committee's Note on Fed.Rule Evid. 803(2), 28 U.S.C.App., p. 778. Likewise, the "dying declaration" and "medical treatment" exceptions to the hearsay rule are based on the belief that persons making such statements are highly unlikely to lie. See, *e.g., Mattox,* 156 U.S., at 244, 15 S.Ct., at 340 ("[T]he sense of impending death is presumed to remove all temptation to falsehood, and to enforce as strict an adherence to the truth as would the obligation of oath"); *Queen v. Osman,* 15 Cox Crim.Cas. 1, 3 (Eng. N.Wales Cir.1881) (Lush, L.J.) ("[N]o person, who is immediately going into the presence of his Maker, will do so with a lie upon his lips"); Mosteller, Child Sexual Abuse and Statements for the Purpose of Medical Diagnosis or Treatment, 67 N.C.L.Rev. 257 (1989). "The circumstantial guarantees of trustworthiness on which the various specific exceptions to the hearsay rule are based are those that existed at the time the statement was made and do not include those that may be added by using hindsight." *Huff v. White Motor Corp.,* 609 F.2d 286, 292 (CA7 1979).

We think the "particularized guarantees of trustworthiness" required for admission under the Confrontation Clause must likewise be drawn from the totality of circumstances that surround the making of the statement and that render the declarant particularly worthy of belief. Our precedents have recognized that statements admitted under a "firmly rooted" hearsay exception are so trustworthy that adversarial testing would add little to their reliability. See *Green,* 399 U.S., at 161, 90 S.Ct., at 1936 (examining "whether subsequent cross-examination at the defendant's trial will still afford the trier of fact a satisfactory basis for evaluating the truth of the prior statement"); see also *Mattox,* 156 U.S., at 244, 15 S.Ct., at 340; *Evans,* 400 U.S., at 88–89, 91 S.Ct., at 219–220 (plurality opinion); *Roberts,* 448 U.S., at 65, 73, 100 S.Ct., at 2538, 2542. Because evidence possessing "particularized guarantees of trustworthiness" must be at least as reliable as evidence admitted under a firmly rooted hearsay exception, see *Roberts, supra,* at 66, 100 S.Ct., at 2539, we think that evidence admitted under the former requirement must similarly be so trustworthy that adversarial testing would add little to its reliability. See *Lee v. Illinois,* 476 U.S., at 544, 106 S.Ct., at 2063 (determining indicia of reliability from the circumstances surrounding the making of the statement); see also *State v. Ryan,* 103 Wash.2d 165, 174, 691 P.2d 197, 204 (1984) ("Adequate indicia of reliability [under *Roberts*] must be found in reference to circumstances surrounding the making of the out-of-court statement, and not from subsequent corroboration of the criminal act"). Thus, unless an affirmative reason, arising from the circumstances in which the statement was made, provides a basis for rebutting the presumption that a hearsay statement is not worthy of reliance at trial, the Confrontation Clause requires exclusion of the out-of-court statement.

The state and federal courts have identified a number of factors that we think properly relate to whether hearsay statements made by a child witness in child sexual abuse cases are reliable. See, *e.g., State v. Robinson,* 153 Ariz. 191, 201, 735 P.2d 801, 811 (1987) (spontaneity and consistent repetition); *Morgan v. Foretich,* 846 F.2d 941, 948 (CA4 1988) (mental state of the declarant); *State v. Sorenson,* 143 Wis.2d 226, 246, 421 N.W.2d 77, 85 (1988) (use of terminology unexpected of a child of similar age); *State v. Kuone,* 243 Kan. 218, 221–222, 757 P.2d 289, 292–293 (1988) (lack of motive to fabricate). Although these cases (which we cite for the factors they discuss and not necessarily to approve the results that they reach) involve the application of various hearsay exceptions to statements of child declarants, we think the factors identified also apply to whether such statements bear "particularized guarantees of trustworthiness" under the Confrontation Clause. These factors are, of course, not exclusive, and courts have considerable leeway in their consideration of appropriate factors. We therefore decline to endorse a mechanical test for determining "particularized guarantees of trustworthiness" under the Clause. Rather, the unifying principle is that these factors relate to whether the child declarant was particularly likely to be telling the truth when the statement was made.

As our discussion above suggests, we are unpersuaded by the State's contention that evidence corroborating the truth of a hearsay statement may properly support a finding that the statement bears "particularlized guarantees of trustworthiness." To be admissible under the Confrontation Clause, hearsay evidence used to convict a defendant must possess indicia of reliability by virtue of its inherent trustworthiness, not by reference to other evidence at trial. Cf. *Delaware v. Van Arsdall,* 475 U.S. 673, 680, 106 S.Ct. 1431, 1435, 89 L.Ed.2d 674 (1986). "[T]he Clause countenances only hearsay marked with such trustworthiness that 'there is no material departure from the reason of the general rule.'" *Roberts,* 448 U.S., at 65, 100 S.Ct., at 2538 (quoting *Snyder v. Massachusetts,* 291 U.S. 97, 107, 54 S.Ct. 330, 332, 78 L.Ed. 674 (1934)). A statement made under duress, for example, may happen to be a true statement, but the circumstances under which it is made may provide no basis for supposing that the declarant is particularly likely to be telling the truth—indeed, the circumstances may even be such that the declarant is particularly *un*likely to be telling the truth. In such a case, cross-examination at trial would be highly useful to probe the declarant's state-of-mind when he made the statements; the presence of evidence tending to corroborate the truth of the statement would be no substitute for cross-examination of the declarant at trial.

In short, the use of corroborating evidence to support a hearsay statement's "particularized guarantees of trustworthiness" would permit admission of a presumptively unreliable statement by bootstrapping on the trustworthiness of other evidence at trial, a result we think at odds with the requirement that hearsay evidence admitted under the Confrontation Clause be so trustworthy that cross-examination of the declarant would be of marginal utility. Indeed, although a plurality of the Court in *Dutton v. Evans* looked to corroborating evidence as one of four factors in determining whether a particular hearsay statement possessed sufficient indicia of reliability, see 400 U.S., at 88, 91 S.Ct., at 219, we think the presence of corroborating evidence more appropriately indicates that any error in admitting the statement might be harmless,* rather than that any basis exists for presuming the declarant to be trustworthy. See *id.*, at 90, 91 S.Ct., at 220 (Blackmun, J., joined by Burger, C.J., concurring) (finding admission of the statement at issue to be harmless error, if error at all); see also 4 D. Louisell & C. Mueller, Federal Evidence § 418, p. 143 (1980) (discussing *Evans*).

Moreover, although we considered in *Lee v. Illinois* the "interlocking" nature of a codefendant's and a defendant's confessions to determine whether the codefendant's confession was sufficiently trustworthy for confrontation purposes, we declined to rely on corroborative physical evidence and indeed rejected the "interlock" theory in that case. 476 U.S., at 545–546, 106 S.Ct., at 2064–2065. We cautioned that "[t]he true danger inherent in this type of hearsay is, in fact, its selective reliability." *Id.*, at 545, 106 S.Ct., at 2064. This concern applies in the child hearsay context as well: Corroboration of a child's allegations of sexual abuse by medical evidence of abuse, for example, sheds no light on the reliability of the child's allegations regarding the identity of the

* The dissent suggests that the Court unequivocally rejected this view in *Cruz v. New York,* 481 U.S. 186, 192, 107 S.Ct. 1714, 1718, 95 L.Ed.2d 162 (1987), but the quoted language on which the dissent relies is taken out of context. *Cruz* involved the admission at a joint trial of a nontestifying codefendant's confession that incriminated the defendant, where the jury was instructed to consider that confession only against the codefendant, and where the defendant's own confession, corroborating that of his codefendant, was introduced against him. The Court in *Cruz,* relying squarely on *Bruton v. United States,* 391 U.S. 123, 88 S.Ct. 1620, 20 L.Ed.2d 476 (1968), held that the admission of the codefendant's confession violated the Confrontation Clause. 481 U.S., at 193, 107 S.Ct., at 1788. The language on which the dissent relies appears in a paragraph discussing whether the "interlocking" nature of the confessions was relevant to the applicability of *Bruton* (the Court concluded that it was not). The Court in that case said nothing about whether the codefendant's confession would be admissible against the defendant simply because it may have "interlocked" with the defendant's confession.

abuser. There is a very real danger that a jury will rely on partial corroboration to mistakenly infer the trustworthiness of the entire statement. Furthermore, we recognized the similarity between harmless-error analysis and the corroboration inquiry when we noted in *Lee* that the harm of "admission of the [hearsay] statement [was that it] poses too serious a threat to the accuracy of the verdict to be countenanced by the Sixth Amendment." *Ibid.* (emphasis added).

Finally, we reject respondent's contention that the younger daughter's out-of-court statements in this case are *per se* unreliable, or at least presumptively unreliable, on the ground that the trial court found the younger daughter incompetent to testify at trial. First, respondent's contention rests upon a questionable reading of the record in this case. The trial court found only that the younger daughter was "not capable of communicating to the jury." App. 39. Although Idaho law provides that a child witness may not testify if he "appear[s] incapable of receiving just impressions of the facts respecting which they are examined, or of relating them truly," Idaho Code § 9–202 (Supp.1989); Idaho Rule Evid. 601(a), the trial court in this case made no such findings. Indeed, the more reasonable inference is that, by ruling that the statements were admissible under Idaho's residual hearsay exception, the trial court implicitly found that the younger daughter, at the time she made the statements, was capable of receiving just impressions of the facts and of relating them truly. See App. 115. In addition, we have in any event held that the Confrontation Clause does not erect a *per se* rule barring the admission of prior statements of a declarant who is unable to communicate to the jury at the time of trial. See, *e.g., Mattox,* 156 U.S., at 243–244, 15 S.Ct., at 339–340; see also 4 Louisell & Mueller, *supra,* § 486, pp. 1041–1045. Although such inability might be relevant to whether the earlier hearsay statement possessed particularized guarantees of trustworthiness, a *per se* rule of exclusion would not only frustrate the truth-seeking purpose of the Confrontation Clause, but would also hinder States in their own "enlightened development in the law of evidence," *Evans,* 400 U.S., at 95, 91 S.Ct., at 222 (Harlan, J., concurring in result).

III

The trial court in this case, in ruling that the Confrontation Clause did not prohibit admission of the younger daughter's hearsay statements, relied on the following factors:

> "In this case, of course, there is physical evidence to corroborate that sexual abuse occurred. It would also seem to be the case that there is no motive to make up a story of this nature in a child of these years. We're not talking about a pubescent youth who may fantasize. The nature of the statements themselves as to sexual abuse are such that they fall outside the general believability that a child could make them up or would make them up. This is simply not the type of statement, I believe, that one would expect a child to fabricate.

> We come then to the identification itself. Are there any indicia of reliability as to identification? From the doctor's testimony it appears that the injuries testified to occurred at the time that the victim was in the custody of the Defendants. The [older daughter] has testified as to identification of [the] perpetrators. Those—the identification of the perpetrators in this case are persons well known to the [younger daughter]. This is not a case in which a child is called upon to identify a stranger or a person with whom they would have no knowledge of their identity or ability to recollect and recall. Those factors are sufficient indicia of reliability to permit the admission of the statements." App. 115.

Of the factors the trial court found relevant, only two relate to circumstances surrounding the making of the statements: whether the child had a motive to "make up a story of this nature," and whether, given the child's age, the statements are of the type "that one would expect a child to fabricate." *Ibid.* The other factors on which the trial court relied, however, such as the presence of physical evidence of abuse, the opportunity of respondent to commit the offense, and the older daughter's corroborating identification, relate instead to whether other evidence existed to corroborate the truth of the statement. These factors, as we have discussed, are irrelevant to a showing of the "particularized guarantees of trustworthiness" necessary for admission of hearsay statements under the Confrontation Clause.

We think the Supreme Court of Idaho properly focused on the presumptive unreliability of the out-of-court statements and on the suggestive manner in which Dr. Jambura conducted the interview. Viewing the totality of the circumstances surrounding the younger daughter's responses to Dr. Jambura's questions, we find no special reason for supposing that the incriminating statements were particularly trustworthy. The younger daughter's last statement regarding the abuse of the older daughter, however, presents a closer question. According to Dr. Jambura, the younger daughter "volunteered" that statement "after she sort of clammed-up." *Id.*, at 123. Although the spontaneity of the statement and the change in demeanor suggest that the younger daughter was telling the truth when she made the statement, we note that it is possible that "[i]f there is evidence of prior interrogation, prompting, or manipulation by adults, spontaneity may be an inaccurate indicator of trustworthiness." *Robinson*, 153 Ariz., at 201, 735 P.2d, at 811. Moreover, the statement was not made under circumstances of reliability comparable to those required, for example, for the admission of excited utterances or statements made for purposes of medical diagnosis or treatment. Given the presumption of inadmissibility accorded accusatory hearsay statements not admitted pursuant to a firmly rooted hearsay exception, *Lee*, 476 U.S., at 543, 106 S.Ct., at 2058, we agree with the court below that the State has failed to show that the younger daughter's incriminating statements to the pediatrician possessed sufficient "particularized guarantees of trustworthiness" under the Confrontation Clause to overcome that presumption.

The State does not challenge the Idaho Supreme Court's conclusion that the Confrontation Clause error in this case was not harmless beyond a reasonable doubt, and we see no reason to revisit the issue. We therefore agree with that court that respondent's conviction involving the younger daughter must be reversed and the case remanded for further proceedings. Accordingly, the judgment of the Supreme Court of Idaho is affirmed.

It is so ordered.

JUSTICE KENNEDY, with whom THE CHIEF JUSTICE, JUSTICE WHITE and JUSTICE BLACKMUN join, dissenting.

The issue is whether the Sixth Amendment right of confrontation is violated when statements from a child who is unavailable to testify at trial are admitted under a hearsay exception against a defendant who stands accused of abusing her. The Court today holds that it is not, provided that the child's statements bear "particularized guarantees of trustworthiness." *Ohio v. Roberts,* 448 U.S. 56, 66, 100 S.Ct. 2531, 2539, 65 L.Ed.2d 597 (1980). I agree. My disagreement is with the rule the Court invents to control this inquiry, and with the Court's ultimate determination that the statements in question here must be inadmissible as violative of the Confrontation Clause.

Given the principle, for cases involving hearsay statements that do not come within one of the traditional hearsay exceptions, that admissibility depends upon finding particular guarantees of trustworthiness in each case, it is difficult to state rules of general application. I believe the Court recognizes this. The majority errs, in my view, by adopting a rule that corroboration of the statement by other evidence is an impermissible part of the trustworthiness inquiry. The Court's apparent ruling is that corroborating evidence may not be considered in whole or in part for this purpose.[1] This limitation, at least on a facial interpretation of the Court's analytic categories, is a new creation by the Court; it likely will prove unworkable and does not even square with the examples of reliability indicators the Court itself invokes; and it is contrary to our own precedents.

I see no constitutional justification for this decision to prescind corroborating evidence from consideration of the question whether a child's statements are reliable. It is a matter of common sense for most people that one of the best ways to determine whether what someone says is trustworthy is to see if it is corroborated by other evidence. In

1. The Court also states that the child's hearsay statements are "presumptively unreliable." I take this to mean only that the government bears the burden of coming forward with indicia of reliability sufficient for the purposes of the Confrontation Clause, and that if it fails to do so the statements are inadmissible. A presumption of unreliability exists as a counterweight to the indicia of reliability offered by the government only where there is an affirmative reason to believe that a particular category of hearsay may be unreliable. See, *e.g., Lee v. Illinois,* 476 U.S. 530, 545, 106 S.Ct. 2056, 2064, 90 L.Ed.2d 514 (1986) ("[A] codefendant's confession is presumptively unreliable as to the passages detailing the defendant's conduct or culpability because those passages may well be the product of the codefendant's desire to shift or spread blame, curry favor, avenge himself, or divert attention to another").

the context of child abuse, for example, if part of the child's hearsay statement is that the assailant tied her wrists or had a scar on his lower abdomen, and there is physical evidence or testimony to corroborate the child's statement, evidence which the child could not have fabricated, we are more likely to believe that what the child says is true. Conversely, one can imagine a situation in which a child makes a statement which is spontaneous or is otherwise made under circumstances indicating that it is reliable, but which also contains undisputed factual inaccuracies so great that the credibility of the child's statements is substantially undermined. Under the Court's analysis, the statement would satisfy the requirements of the Confrontation Clause despite substantial doubt about its reliability. Nothing in the law of evidence or the law of the Confrontation Clause countenances such a result; on the contrary, most federal courts have looked to the existence of corroborating evidence or the lack thereof to determine the reliability of hearsay statements not coming within one of the traditional hearsay exceptions. See 4 D. Louisell & C. Mueller, Federal Evidence § 472, p. 929 (1980) (collecting cases); 4 J. Weinstein & M. Berger, Weinstein's Evidence ¶ 804(b)(5)[01] (1988) (same). Specifically with reference to hearsay statements by children, a review of the cases has led a leading commentator on child witness law to conclude flatly: "If the content of an out-of-court statement is supported or corroborated by other evidence, the reliability of the hearsay is strengthened." J. Myers, Child Witness Law and Practice § 5.37, p. 364 (1987).[2] The

2. A sampling of cases using corroborating evidence as to support a finding that a child's statements were reliable includes: *United States v. Dorian,* 803 F.2d 1439, 1445 (CA8 1986); *United States v. Cree,* 778 F.2d 474, 477 (CA8 1985); *United States v. Nick,* 604 F.2d 1199, 1204 (CA9 1979); *State v. Allen,* 157 Ariz. 165, 176–178, 755 P.2d 1153, 1164–1166 (1988); *State v. Robinson,* 153 Ariz. 191, 204, 735 P.2d 801, 814 (1987); *State v. Bellotti,* 383 N.W.2d 308, 315 (Minn.App.1986); *State v. Soukup,* 376 N.W.2d 498, 501 (Minn.App.1985); *State v. Doe,* 94 N.M. 637, 639, 614 P.2d 1086, 1088 (App.1980); *State v. McCafferty,* 356 N.W.2d 159, 164 (S.D.1984); *United States v. Quick,* 22 M.J. 722, 724 (A.C.M.R.1986). Numerous other cases rely upon corroboration pursuant to state statutory rules regarding hearsay statements by children. See J. Myers § 5.38.

Aside from *Lee v. Illinois, supra,* discussed *infra,* the only case cited by the Court for the proposition that corroborative evidence is irrelevant to reliability is *State v. Ryan,* 103 Wash.2d 165, 174, 691 P.2d 197, 204 (1984). The Court quotes the opinion out of context. In holding that corroborating evidence could not be used to demonstrate reliability, the Washington Supreme Court was not interpreting the Confrontation Clause; rather, its opinion clearly reveals that the court's holding was an interpretation of a Washington statute, Wash.Rev.Code Ann. § 9A.44.120 (1988), which provided that hearsay statements from an unavailable child declarant could be admitted into evidence at trial only if they were reliable *and* corroborated by other evidence. The portion of the opinion following the sentence quoted by the majority reveals the true nature of its holding:

> "The trial court was apparently persuaded that the statements of the children must be reliable, if, in hindsight they prove to be true. *RCW 9A.44.120 demands more.*
>
> "*The statute* requires separate determinations of reliability *and* corroboration when the child is unavailable. The word "and" is conjunctive * * *. The Legislature would have used the word "or" had they intended the disjunctive * * *. Although defendant's confession was offered as corroboration, wholly absent are the requisite circumstantial guarantees of reliability." *State v. Ryan, supra,* at 174, 691 P.2d, at 204. (citations omitted; emphasis added).

Other States also have expressly recognized the need for and legitimacy of consid-

Court's apparent misgivings about the weight to be given corroborating evidence may or may not be correct, but those misgivings do not justify wholesale elimination of this evidence from consideration, in derogation of an overwhelming judicial and legislative consensus to the contrary. States are of course free, as a matter of state law, to demand corroboration of an unavailable child declarant's statements as well as other indicia of reliability before allowing the statements to be admitted into evidence. Until today, however, no similar distinction could be found in our precedents interpreting the Confrontation Clause. If anything, the many state statutes requiring corroboration of a child declarant's statements emphasize the relevance, not the irrelevance, of corroborating evidence to the determination whether an unavailable child witness's statements bear particularized guarantees of trustworthiness, which is the ultimate inquiry under the Confrontation Clause. In sum, whatever doubt the Court has with the weight to be given the corroborating evidence found in this case is no justification for rejecting the considered wisdom of virtually the entire legal community that corroborating evidence is relevant to reliability and trustworthiness.

Far from rejecting this commonsense proposition, the very cases relied upon by the Court today embrace it. In *Lee v. Illinois,* 476 U.S. 530, 106 S.Ct. 2056, 90 L.Ed.2d 514 (1986), we considered whether the confession of a codefendant that "interlocked" with a defendant's own confession bore particularized guarantees of trustworthiness so that its admission into evidence against the defendant did not violate the Confrontation Clause. Although the Court's ultimate conclusion was that the confession did not bear sufficient indicia of reliability, its analysis was far different from that utilized by the Court in the present case. The Court today notes that, in *Lee,* we determined the trustworthiness of the confession by looking to the circumstances surrounding its making; what the Court omits from its discussion of *Lee* is the fact that we also considered the extent of the "interlock," that is, the extent to which the two confessions corroborated each other. The Court in *Lee* was unanimous in its recognition of corroboration as a legitimate indicator of reliability; the only disagreement was whether the corroborative nature of the confessions and the circumstances of their making were sufficient to satisfy the Confrontation Clause. See 476 U.S., at 546, 106 S.Ct., at 2064 (finding insufficient indicia of reliability, "*flowing from either the circumstances surrounding the confession or the 'interlocking' character of the confessions,*" to support admission of the codefendant's confession) (emphasis added); *id.,* at 557, 106 S.Ct., at

ering corroborating evidence in determining whether a child declarant's statements are trustworthy and should be admitted into evidence. See Ariz.Rev.Stat.Ann. § 13–1416 (1989); Ark.Rule Evid. 803(25)(A); Cal.Evid.Code Ann. § 1228 (West 1990); Colo.Rev.Stat. § 13–25–129 (1987); Fla.Stat. § 90.803(23) (1989); Idaho Code § 19–3024 (1987); Ill.Rev.Stat., ch. 38, ¶ 115–10 (1989); Ind.Code § 35–37–4–6 (1988); Md.Cts. & Jud.Proc.Code Ann. § 9–103.1 (1989); Minn.Stat. § 595.02(3) (1988); Miss.Code.Ann. § 13–1–403 (Supp.1989); N.J.R.Evid. 63 (1989); N.D.Rule Evid. 803(24); Okla.Stat.Tit. 12, § 2803.1 (1989); Oregon Rev.Stat. § 40.460 (1989); 42 Pa. Cons.Stat. § 5985.1 (1989); S.D.Codified Laws § 19–16–38 (1987); Utah Code Ann. § 76–5–411 (1990).

2070 (Blackmun, J., dissenting) (finding the codefendant's confession supported by sufficient indicia of reliability including, *inter alia,* "extensive and convincing corroboration by petitioner's own confession" and "further corroboration provided by the physical evidence"). See also *New Mexico v. Earnest,* 477 U.S. 648, 649, n. *, 106 S.Ct. 2734, 2735, n. *, 91 L.Ed.2d 539 (1986) (Rehnquist, J., concurring); *Dutton v. Evans,* 400 U.S. 74, 88–89, 91 S.Ct. 210, 219–220, 27 L.Ed.2d 213 (1970) (plurality opinion).

The Court today suggests that the presence of corroborating evidence goes more to the issue of whether the admission of the hearsay statements was harmless error than whether the statements themselves were reliable and therefore admissible. Once again, in the context of interlocking confessions, our previous cases have been unequivocal in rejecting this suggestion:

> "Quite obviously, what the 'interlocking' nature of the codefendant's confession pertains to is not its *harmfulness* but rather its *reliability:* If it confirms essentially the same facts as the defendant's own confession it is more likely to be true." *Cruz v. New York,* 481 U.S. 186, 192, 107 S.Ct. 1714, 1718, 95 L.Ed.2d 162 (1987) (emphasis in original).

It was precisely because the "interlocking" nature of the confessions heightened their reliability as hearsay that we noted in *Cruz* that "[o]f course, the defendant's confession may be considered at trial in assessing whether his codefendant's statements are supported by sufficient 'indicia of reliability' to be directly admissible against him." *Id.,* at 193–194, 107 S.Ct., at 1718–1719 (citing *Lee, supra,* 476 U.S., at 543–544, 106 S.Ct., at 2063–2064). In short, corroboration has been an essential element in our past hearsay cases, and there is no justification for a categorical refusal to consider it here.

Our Fourth Amendment cases are also premised upon the idea that corroboration is a legitimate indicator of reliability. We have long held that corroboration is an essential element in determining whether police may act on the basis of an informant's tip, for the simple reason that "because an informant is shown to be right about some things, he is probably right about other facts that he has alleged." *Alabama v. White,* 496 U.S. ___, ___, 110 S.Ct. 2412, ___, ___ L.Ed.2d ___ (1990). See also *Illinois v. Gates,* 462 U.S. 213, 244, 245, 103 S.Ct. 2317, 2335, 2336, 76 L.Ed.2d 527 (1983); *Spinelli v. United States,* 393 U.S. 410, 415, 89 S.Ct. 584, 588, 21 L.Ed.2d 637 (1969); *Jones v. United States,* 362 U.S. 257, 271, 80 S.Ct. 725, 736, 4 L.Ed.2d 697 (1960).

The Court does not offer any justification for barring the consideration of corroborating evidence, other than the suggestion that corroborating evidence does not bolster the "inherent trustworthiness" of the statements. But for purposes of determining the reliability of the statements, I can discern no difference between the factors that the Court believes indicate "inherent trustworthiness" and those, like corroborating evidence, that apparently do not. Even the factors endorsed by the Court will involve consideration of the very evidence the Court purports to exclude from the reliability analysis. The Court notes that one test of reliability is whether the child "use[d] * * * terminology unexpected of a child of similar age." But making this determination requires consideration of the child's vocabulary skills and past opportunity, or lack thereof, to learn the terminology at issue. And, when all of the extrinsic circumstances of a case are considered, it may be shown that use of a particular word or vocabulary in fact supports the inference of prolonged contact with the defendant, who was known to use the vocabulary in question. As a further example, the Court notes that motive to fabricate is an index of reliability. But if the suspect charges that a third person concocted a false case against him and coached the child, surely it is relevant to show that the third person had no contact with the child or no opportunity to suggest false testimony. Given the contradictions inherent in the Court's test when measured against its own examples, I expect its holding will soon prove to be as unworkable as it is illogical.

The short of the matter is that both the circumstances existing at the time the child makes the statements and the existence of corroborating evidence indicate, to a greater or lesser degree, whether the statements are reliable. If the Court means to suggest that the circumstances surrounding the making of a statement are the best indicators of reliability, I doubt this is so in every instance. And, if it were true in a particular case, that does not warrant ignoring other indicators of reliability such as corroborating evidence, absent some other reason for excluding it. If anything, I should think that corroborating evidence in the form of testimony or physical evidence, apart from the narrow circumstances in which the statement was made, would be a preferred means of determining a statement's reliability for purposes of the Confrontation Clause, for the simple reason that, unlike other indicators of trustworthiness, corroborating evidence can be addressed by the defendant and assessed by the trial court in an objective and critical way.

In this case, the younger daughter's statements are corroborated in at least four respects: (1) physical evidence that she was the victim of sexual abuse; (2) evidence that she had been in the custody of the suspect at the time the injuries occurred; (3) testimony of the older daughter that their father abused the younger daughter, thus corroborating the younger daughter's statement; and (4) the testimony of the older daughter that she herself was abused by their father, thus corroborating the younger daughter's statement that her sister had also been abused. These facts, coupled with the circumstances surrounding the making of the statements acknowledged by the Court as suggesting that the statements are reliable, give rise to a legitimate argument that admission of the statements did not violate the Confrontation Clause. Because the Idaho Supreme Court did not consider these factors, I would vacate its judgment reversing respondent's conviction and remand for it to consider in the first instance whether the child's statements bore "particularized guarantees of trustworthiness" under the analysis set forth in this separate opinion.

For these reasons, I respectfully dissent.

Notes

(1) On the residual exceptions in general, see Black, Federal Rules of Evidence 803(24) & 804(b)(5)—The Residual Exceptions—An Overview, 25 Hous.L.Rev. 13 (1988); Imwinkelried, The Scope of the Residual Hearsay Exceptions in the Federal Rules of Evidence, 15 San Diego L.Rev. 239 (1978); Sonenshein, The Residual Exception to the Federal Hearsay Rule: Two Exceptions in Search of a Rule, 57 N.Y.U.L.Rev. 867 (1982).

(2) Several of the states that have adopted versions of the Federal Rules of Evidence have omitted any residual exceptions. In Maine, the drafters explained this decision as follows:

> "The Court decided not to adopt any catch-all provision. It was impressed by the theoretical undesirability of foreclosing further development of the law of evidence on a case-by-case basis. It concluded, however, that despite the purported safeguards, there was a serious risk that trial judges would differ greatly in applying the elastic standard of equivalent trustworthiness. The result would be a lack of uniformity which would make preparation for trial difficult. Nor would it be likely that the Law Court on appeal could effectively apply corrective measures. There would indeed be doubt whether an affirmance of an admission of evidence under the catch-all provision amounted to the creation of a new exception with the force of precedent or merely a refusal to rule that the trial judge had abused his discretion.
>
> "Flexibility in construction of the rules so as to promote growth and development of the law of evidence is called for by Rule 102. Under this mandate there will be room to construe an existing hearsay exception broadly in the interest of ascertaining truth, as distinguished from creating an entirely new exception based upon the trial judge's determination of equivalent trustworthiness, a guideline which the most conscientious of judges would find extremely difficult to follow."

Me.R.Evid. 803 advisory committee note.

(3) Montana, on the other hand, not only adopted the exceptions, but deleted the restrictive amendments that Congress added to the Federal versions. The Montana drafters explained:

> "The Commission believed this exception should allow 'room for growth and development of the law of evidence in the area of hearsay' * * * and that the amendments by Congress are too restrictive and contrary to the purpose of the provision. These amendments can be criticized as follows: the requirement that the statement be offered as evidence of a "material" fact is redundant in requiring relevance as defined in Rule 401 and uses outmoded language. * * * The requirement that the evidence be more probative on the point for which it is offered restricts the use of these types of exceptions by imposing a requirement similar to that of unavailability under Rule 804; this restriction would have the effect of severely limiting the instances in

> which the exception would be used and be impractical in the sense that a party would generally offer the strongest evidence available regardless of the existence of this requirement. The requirement that the general purposes of these rules and interests of justice will be served is unnecessarily repetitive in view of Rule 102. Finally, the notice requirement is unnecessary because of discovery procedures and the discretion of the court in allowing advance rulings on the admissibility of evidence."

Mont.R.Evid. 803(24) commission comments.

Chapter 3

PROCEDURES FOR ADMITTING AND EXCLUDING EVIDENCE *

[FED.R.EVID. ART. I]

McEWEN v. TEXAS & P. RY. CO.

Court of Civil Appeals of Texas, 1936.
92 S.W.2d 308.

FUNDERBURK, JUSTICE.

By this suit J.D. McEwen sought recovery of damages from the Texas & Pacific Railway Company for personal injuries to his wife, alleged to have been sustained by reason of the negligence of the defendant, through its employee, in assisting her to alight from a passenger train at Abilene, Tex. Special issues were submitted to a jury upon which was returned a verdict finding that Mrs. McEwen was a passenger; that she fell when she started to get off the train; that she received personal injuries when she fell; that defendant's employee was negligent in the way and manner he undertook to help her get off the train; that such negligence was the proximate cause of the injuries and resulted in damages in the sum of $2,500. By said verdict it was also found that when Mrs. McEwen started to get off the train she failed to exercise ordinary care for her own safety which was a proximate cause of her injuries. Based upon the issues and findings relating to contributory negligence, the trial court gave judgment for the defendant, from which the plaintiff has appealed.

Appellant's first assignment of error is that: "The court erred in permitting the defendant to prove over the plaintiff's objection that

* See 1 Wigmore, Evidence §§ 13–21 (Tillers rev. 1983); 8 id. ch. 73 (McNaughten rev. 1961); McCormick, Evidence ch. 6 (4th ed. 1992); Ball, The Myth of Conditional Relevancy, 14 Ga.L.Rev. 435 (1980); Kaplan, Of Mabrus and Zorgs—An Essay in Honor of David Louisell, 66 Calif.L.Rev. 987 (1978); Saltzburg, The Harm of Harmless Error, 59 Va.L.Rev. 988 (1973); Saltzburg, Another Ground for Decision—Harmless Trial Court Errors, 47 Temple L.Q. 193 (1974); Saltzburg, Standards of Proof and Preliminary Questions of Fact, 27 Stan.L.Rev. 271 (1975); Seidelson, Conditional Relevancy and Federal Rule of Evidence 104(b), 47 Geo.Wash.L.Rev. 1048 (1979).

plaintiff's wife was fond of playing bridge." The proposition submitted under said assignment is that: "The court erred in permitting the defendant, over the objection of the plaintiff, to prove by plaintiff's wife that she was fond of playing cards. Such testimony was immaterial, not pertinent to any issue in the case, and was prejudicial and inflammatory." Counsel for defendant asked the witness the question: "Mrs. McEwen, is it not a fact that you are rather fond of playing bridge?" Counsel for plaintiff said: "We object to that. I do not think that is material." The court overruled the objection. Then counsel for plaintiff said: "Note our exception. May it please the court as to whether or not she was fond of playing bridge—." The court replied: "The court has already ruled." Then counsel replied: "I want to get my exception; on the ground that whatever may be her mode of amusement could not have any bearing on the extent of her injury." There is no bill of exception and the nature of the objection and the action of the court is to be determined only from the proceedings just detailed.

It is our view that the objection was in substance and effect only that the testimony was immaterial, or at most irrelevant and immaterial, and therefore came within the classification of a general objection. The authorities, we think, support a proposition of law which may be stated as follows: A general objection to evidence—meaning one which does not definitely and specifically state the grounds on which it is based so that the court may intelligently rule on it—is, as a general rule, insufficient. 64 C.J. 180, § 203. For examples of such general objections with the objection in some of the cases parenthetically noted, see Early–Foster Co. v. Mid–Tex Oil Mills (Tex.Civ.App.) 208 S.W. 224 (immaterial); Morgan v. Gordon (Tex.Civ.App.) 13 S.W.(2d) 905 (irrelevant and immaterial); Padgitt Bros. Co. v. Dorsey (Tex.Civ.App.) 206 S.W. 851 (irrelevant and immaterial); Moorman v. Small (Tex.Civ.App.) 220 S.W. 127 (irrelevant and immaterial and might prejudice the jury); Moore v. Miller (Tex.Civ.App.) 155 S.W. 573 (irrelevant and immaterial); Matthews v. Monzingo (Tex.Civ.App.) 46 S.W.(2d) 424 (immaterial, irrelevant and prejudicial); Capitol Hotel Co. v. Rittenberry (Tex.Civ. App.) 41 S.W.(2d) 697; Glens Falls Ins. Co. v. Bendy (Tex.Civ.App.) 39 S.W.(2d) 628 (prejudicial); Kansas City, M. & O. R. Co. v. Foster (Tex.Civ.App.) 38 S.W.(2d) 391 (immaterial and irrelevant); * * *.

To said general rule certain exceptions have been declared as follows: "where the ground therefor is so manifest that the trial court could not fail to understand it" [Cheatham v. Riddle, 8 Tex. 162; St. Louis, B. & M. Ry. Co. v. Fielder, supra; Missouri, K. & T. Ry. Co. v. Johnson (Tex.Civ.App.) 126 S.W. 672; Texas Brewing Co. v. Dickey (Tex.Civ.App.) 43 S.W. 577], or "when the evidence offered is clearly irrelevant and incompetent" [J.I. Case Threshing Mach. Co. v. O'Keefe (Tex.Civ.App.) 259 S.W. 222; Farmers' Mill & Elevator Co. v. Hodges (Tex.Civ.App.) 248 S.W. 72; McDannell v. Horrell, 1 Posey, Unrep.Cas. 521], or, "inadmissible for any purpose." Stiles v. Giddens, 21 Tex. 783; Cheatham v. Riddle, supra; Missouri, K. & T. Ry. Co. v. Johnson, supra.

Or, "the objection is of such nature that it could not have been obviated." 64 C.J. 185, § 205.

The gist of the complaint against the introduction of the evidence as set forth in the brief is that it was prejudicial. We think it is correct to say that the objection, aside from the matter of its being general and not one coming within any of the exceptions to the general rule, did not include the element that it was prejudicial. C.W. Hahl Co. v. Cunningham & Hardy (Tex.Civ.App.) 246 S.W. 108; Moore v. Miller (Tex.Civ. App.) 155 S.W. 573. In De Garca v. Galvan, 55 Tex. 53, the court said: "An objection which does not state the reasons for the rejection of the testimony, if, under any contingency, the evidence offered would be properly admitted, will not be considered on appeal." We think if it should be conceded that the testimony in question under any contingency was of a nature calculated to be prejudicial, it was not so clearly and certainly so as to relieve the appellant of the necessity of pointing out in his objection why it was so, in order to have the court's action reversed.

* * *

Being of the opinion that no error in the judgment is shown, and that it should be affirmed, it is accordingly so ordered.

BUCKLEY v. STATE, 630 S.W.2d 740, 743 (Tex.App.1982). "Appellant's fourth and fifth grounds of error complain of the trial court's admission into evidence of a State's exhibit consisting of a Houston Police Department supplemental offense report, an evidence submission slip and a rape kit workup sheet. This exhibit was submitted by the State under the Texas Business Record Act, Article 3737e, V.A.C.S. (1973). Before the trial court, the appellant contended that the exhibit was hearsay as to one Peter Christian, Jr. of the Houston Police Department, through whom the State sought to introduce it, and hence was inadmissible. Appellant tendered the further argument that no proper predicate had been made for admission of the exhibit under art. 3737e and that although the State later called J.R. Daniels, who actually conducted the evidence analysis contained in the exhibit, the error in admitting the exhibit was not cured. Kistler v. State, 591 S.W.2d 836 (Tex.Cr.App.1980); United States v. Brown, 451 F.2d 1231 (5th Cir.1971). So far as the record shows, appellant's objection was to the effect that Christian's testimony was based on hearsay and the objection was directed at the entire exhibit. While the State admits that certain portions of the exhibit were probably not admissible under the holdings of the *Coulter* and *Kistler* cases, there can be no doubt that other portions of the exhibit consisting of the supplemental offense report and rape workup sheet were admissible, for which the proper predicate had been laid as required by art. 3737e. Garcia v. State, 581 S.W.2d 168 (Tex.Cr.App.1979). If the contents of an exhibit are such that some portions, but not all, are inadmissible, it is incumbent upon the objecting party to identify and specify the exact portions of the exhibit sought to be excluded and state the grounds for such objection, if he wishes to preserve error. Hernandez v. State, 599 S.W.2d 614 (Tex.Cr.App.1980). Appellant's fourth and fifth grounds of error are overruled."

POWELL v. POWELL, 554 S.W.2d 850, 855 (Tex.Civ.App.1977). "Since the statements attributed to the deceased were hearsay, it could have no relevance except for a limited purpose for which it was never offered. Skillern & Sons, Inc. v. Rosen, 359 S.W.2d 298, 301 (Tex.1962); Singleton v. Carmichael, 305 S.W.2d 379, 384 (Tex.Civ.App.—Houston 1957, writ ref'd n.r.e.). A general objection to the offer having been sustained, counsel's failure to re-offer the statement for limited purpose was a waiver. Gottschald v. Reaves, 457 S.W.2d 307, 309–310 (Tex.Civ. App.—Houston [1st Dist.] 1970, n.w.h.). Where evidence, only a part of which is admissible, is offered as a whole, the court does not commit error in sustaining an objection to such testimony, and it is not the duty of the court nor the party objecting to separate the admissible from the inadmissible. Texas General Indemnity Company v. Ellis, 421 S.W.2d 467, 473 (Tex.Civ.App.—Tyler 1967, n.w.h.).

"Even if the statement had been offered for a limited purpose, the court was correct in excluding the proffered evidence, because the statement itself was coupled with a superfluous, inadmissible statement by Pearl Hartsfield that: '* * * I told him he wasn't thinking straight. He said he was, and so I told him I didn't think he was.' Appellant's failure to segregate that inadmissible evidence from the statement attributed to N.P. Powell was likewise a sufficient ground for refusing the tender. In Texas General Indemnity Co. v. Ellis, supra, this court stated the rule that: 'It seems to be the settled law of this state that where evidence is offered as a whole, only a part of which is admissible, the court does not commit error in sustaining an objection to such testimony and in such case it is not the duty of the court nor the party objecting to the same to separate the admissible from the inadmissible.' "

HACKENSON v. CITY OF WATERBURY

Supreme Court of Errors of Connecticut, 1938.
124 Conn. 679, 2 A.2d 215.

BROWN, JUDGE.

It is undisputed that upon the evidence the jury could properly have found that the plaintiff, while walking southerly across North Main Street in Waterbury from the northwesterly corner of its intersection with Bishop Street to the southerly side of North Main Street, in the exercise of due care, stepped into a hole or depression in the pavement located somewhere between the double trolley tracks near the center of the street, which caused her to fall, resulting in the injuries complained of. The question determinative of this appeal is whether the evidence warranted the finding of the further fact essential to a verdict against the defendant, that this hole or depression was not located within eight inches of a trolley rail, the defendant not being liable for a defect within this area by virtue of §§ 3752 and 3755 of the General Statutes.

* * * [Plaintiff's] testimony on cross-examination was:

"Q. You say you fell on a raised part of the pavement; is that it? A. No, I stepped into a hole.

"Q. In a hole? A. I certainly did.

"Q. And is that near the track? A. It certainly was.

"Q. Was it right on the track? A. No.

"Q. How close to the track was it? * * * A. Well, I should say two and one-half inches.

"Q. From the rail? A. Yes.

"Q. * * * Your foot went into that hole, two and one-half inches from the rail, and you fell? A. Yes."

This testimony, aside from that offered through the plaintiff after the defendant had rested its case, which is hereinafter referred to, was the only direct evidence as to where the hole in question was located.

The plaintiff's final contention is predicated upon what she claims to be evidence in the record disclosed by the transcript of what occurred when she was recalled to the stand after the defendant had rested its case. In the absence of a finding, the plaintiff's claim can only be tested by what is revealed by this transcript, made a part of the record by order of this court in response to the plaintiff's motion. This shows that the plaintiff's counsel, after the defendant had closed its case, recalled the plaintiff and the following transpired:

"Q. And where your foot went into the hole, measuring from the toe of your foot to the center of the north rail of the north bound traffic (the third rail), can you tell how far that was? A. Twenty eight inches.

"Mr. Sullivan: I object to that if Your Honor pleases."

The court sustained the objection to the question, ruling that it was not proper rebuttal, and denying the plaintiff's request to reopen the plaintiff's case to permit the inquiry. An exception to this ruling was duly granted to the plaintiff. Her claim now is that in the absence of a motion to strike it out, her answer having been given before the defendant's objection was made to the question, it remains in the record and constituted evidence that the hole was more than eight inches from the rail, which is sufficient to warrant the verdict.

The generally accepted rule as to when objection to a question must be interposed has been stated to be: "For evidence contained in a specific question, the objection must ordinarily be made as soon as the question is stated, and before the answer is given; unless the inadmissibility was due, not to the subject of the question, but to some feature of the answer." 1 Wigmore, Evidence (2d Ed.) 175, § 18, a, (1). This rule, however, is to be reasonably applied. Thus in an opinion quoted by Wigmore in this connection, the court, in referring to a rule of court of similar import, said: "It must have a reasonable interpretation. Its object is to prevent a party from knowingly withholding his objection, until he discovers the effect of the testimony, and then if it turns out to be unfavorable to interpose his objection." Marsh v. Hand, 35 Md. 123, 127. The record here discloses no violation of the rule as so interpreted. The obvious purpose of the plaintiff's counsel in recalling her and in asking this question was to save her case by getting before the jury some evidence to afford a basis for finding that the defect was more than eight inches away from the rail. Under such circumstances the only reasonable inference from the transcript is, that the plaintiff must have been fully aware of the significance to her case of this answer, and that in her anxiety to get the benefit thereof, gave it before counsel for the defendant had the opportunity to object. As the evidence stood, it is clear that the defendant's counsel was not, as in D'Andrea v. Rende, 123 Conn. 377, 383, 195 A. 741, 744, "gambling on the answer" by his delay, if any, in interposing his objection.

There is authority that where the court in sustaining an objection to the question has not directed the jury not to consider the reply given, a motion to strike it out is essential to its proper elimination. 26 R.C.L. 1047, § 55; Sorenson v. Smith, 65 Or. 78, 129 P. 757, 131 P. 1022, 51 L.R.A.,N.S., 612, Ann.Cas. 1915A, 1127; Wightman v. Campbell, 217 N.Y. 479, 112 N.E. 184, Ann.Cas. 1917E, 673; Dawley v. Congdon, 42 R.I. 64, 105 A. 393, 395. We adopt, however, a rule upon the situation before us which is less technical, yet sufficient for the ample protection of the parties' right. "If the question is put and the answer given in such rapid succession that the party objecting has not fair opportunity to state his objection, it is the duty of the court to entertain the objection when thereafter promptly made." Adler & Co. v. Pruitt, 169 Ala. 213, 229, 53 So. 315, 320, 32 L.R.A.,N.S., 889. This the court did here, and so far as appears it was within its discretion to sustain the objection to the question as not proper rebuttal. We are not here concerned with a situation presenting the question whether the jury might have failed to understand the effect of the ruling and so something more than the mere sustaining of the objection would be necessary in order to protect the rights of the parties. The only basis upon which the plaintiff can claim error in the ruling of the trial court in setting aside the verdict is that the jury could, in the absence of a motion to strike out, properly consider the testimony. That is not the law in this jurisdiction. The plaintiff has failed to protect any rights she had by an appeal from the ruling made. Under these circumstances, even in the absence of a motion to strike out the answer, no testimony indicating the hole was not within eight inches from the rail is available in support of the jury's verdict.

There is no error.

Notes

(1) "Counsel's failure to object at the time such evidence was admitted is precisely the type of 'inexcusable procedural default' discussed in Estelle v. Williams [425 U.S. 501, 96 S.Ct. 1691, 48 L.Ed.2d 126 (1976)].

> '[T]here are two situations in which a conviction should be left standing despite the claimed infringement of a constitutional right. The first situation arises when it can be shown that the substantive right in question was consensually relinquished. The other situation arises *when a defendant has made an "inexcusable procedural default" in failing to object at a time when a substantive right could have been protected.*'

425 U.S. at 513, 96 S.Ct. at 1697 (Powell, J., concurring) (emphasis added). A timely objection could have prevented the introduction of this evidence; a motion to strike or to give a limiting instruction could have cured some of the prejudicial effect. In light of Estelle v. Williams, counsel's failure to object to the infringement of a trial-type right bars the client from later raising this substantive right in a collateral proceeding." St. John v. Estelle, 544 F.2d 894, 895 (5th Cir.1977), cert. denied, 436 U.S. 914, 98 S.Ct. 2255, 56 L.Ed.2d 415 (1978).

(2) "Under ordinary circumstances, an objection not made until after an answer is given is not timely. * * * A recognized exception to this rule occurs in a situation where the record shows that no opportunity was afforded the complaining party to voice an objection between the question and a responsive answer because the witness answered so quickly as to preclude the interjection of the objection or for some other reason apparent on the record. * * * When such a trial situation develops, the proper procedure is to voice the objection at the earliest possible opportunity and move to strike the answer. In the absence of such a motion to strike, the ruling of the trial court is not preserved for review." State v. Peterson, 546 S.W.2d 175, 179–80 (Mo.App.1976).

(3) "It is well-settled that a motion to strike is the correct means of removing from consideration evidence properly admitted when such evidence later becomes inadmissible." State ex rel. Utility Consumers Council v. Public Serv. Com'n of Missouri, 562 S.W.2d 688, 695 (Mo.App.1978), cert. denied, 439 U.S. 866, 99 S.Ct. 192, 58 L.Ed.2d 177 (1978).

STEVEN GOODE, OLIN GUY WELLBORN III & M. MICHAEL SHARLOT, GUIDE TO THE TEXAS RULES OF EVIDENCE: CIVIL AND CRIMINAL (1988)

§ 103.2 Rule 103(a)(1): Objection

* * * The basic principle that runs through all doctrines about preserving error is party responsibility.[1] It is not the role of the judge to present evidence, or to render the proponent's evidence into a form required by the rules of evidence; nor is it his responsibility to exclude

1. See McCormick, Evidence §§ 51, 52 (3d ed. 1984).

or to limit evidence as provided by evidence law, except insofar as the party opposing the evidence precisely and timely requests that he do so.

To the question, *which* party has the responsibility regarding any particular matter, it is infallibly accurate to answer with another question: which party is complaining now on appeal? This is because in a real sense both parties are always responsible for the application of any evidence rule to any evidence. Whichever party complains on appeal about the trial judge's action must, at the earliest opportunity, have done everything necessary to bring to the judge's attention the evidence rule in question. If he has failed in any respect to do those things, his complaint will in all likelihood be ignored. These rules concerning preservation of error are quite neutral between the parties, proponent and opponent; they place total responsibility, simultaneously, on both. The "party" who is favored or protected by the doctrines is the trial judge.

The idea that responsibility rests upon both parties may be illustrated by the following example. Suppose proponent offers a group of documents, some of which are competent evidence and some of which are inadmissible hearsay. Opponent objects to the entire offer on the ground of hearsay. In this state of the record, the trial judge can do no wrong, in the sense that he may either sustain or overrule the objection and either ruling will be invulnerable on appeal. If he sustains the objection, excluding the competent documents along with the incompetent, the proponent may not successfully complain on appeal that his competent evidence was excluded, even though it was. He will be told by the appellate court that it was his responsibility to separate the admissible from the inadmissible parts of the offer, and an objection that was good as to part of the unsegregated mass may be sustained as to all.[2] On the other hand, if the trial judge overrules the overbroad objection, admitting the incompetent portions of the offer along with the competent, the ruling will be equally impervious to review on appeal by the objector. He will be told that his objection to the whole offer, which did not point out precisely which parts were inadmissible, was properly overruled if any part of the offer was admissible.[3]

This example shows how the responsibilities of both parties in the invocation and application of evidence rules are independent of one another. A party who wishes to complain on appeal must have fully acquitted his responsibilities to alert the trial judge to the proper rule and its proper application. If he failed to do so he is barred from complaint, and it is immaterial that the other party below also failed in his coordinate responsibilities.

2. See Interest of T.L.H., 630 S.W.2d 441, 445 (Tex.App.—Corpus Christi 1982, no writ); Lister v. Employers Reinsurance Corp., 590 S.W.2d 803, 805 (Tex.Civ.App.—Houston [14th Dist.] 1979, writ ref'd n.r.e.).

3. See Speier v. Webster College, 616 S.W.2d 617, 619 (Tex.1981); Brown & Root, Inc. v. Haddad, 142 Tex. 624, 628, 180 S.W.2d 339, 341 (1944); Ramos v. State, 419 S.W.2d 359, 364 (Tex.Crim.App.1967); Eubanks v. Winn, 469 S.W.2d 292, 296 (Tex.Civ.App.—Houston [1st Dist.] 1971, writ ref'd n.r.e.).

To preserve error in the admission of evidence, Rule 103(a)(1) requires a timely and specific objection or motion to strike. The Rule is a restatement of the common law, and does not change the law in any way.[4] The reasons why all courts have insisted upon timely and specific objections to invoke evidence rules are not difficult to discern. The Texas Court of Criminal Appeals explained the bases of the requirements as follows:

> The generally acknowledged policies of requiring specific objections are two-fold. First, a specific objection is required to inform the trial judge of the basis of the objection and afford him the opportunity to rule on it. Second, a specific objection is required to afford opposing counsel an opportunity to remove the objection or supply other testimony.[5]

There are four aspects as to which an objection may be wanting in specificity and may therefore be inadequate to protect the rights of the objector: grounds, parts, parties, and purposes. A failure of specificity in any of the four respects may have the result that the objector cannot successfully complain on appeal if the objection is overruled, even though the evidence was in fact not properly admissible or not admissible as offered. The problems of specificity of objections as to parties and purposes are addressed in Rule 105, and are examined in the discussion of that provision.[6] Rule 103(a)(1) refers to "stating the specific ground of objection." This language is interpreted to refer to specificity as to parts as well as to legal grounds.[7]

An objection only preserves the specific ground or grounds named. A so-called "general" objection, such as the notorious "irrelevant, incompetent, and immaterial," preserves no ground for appeal, except perhaps the ground of total irrelevancy to any issue in the case.[8] Rule 103(a)(1) contemplates that an objection general by itself may acquire specific meaning in the context, which will be recognized on appeal. This is in accord with prior Texas practice.[9]

4. See Advisory Committee's Note to Federal Rule 103(a) ("Subdivision (a) states the law as generally accepted today.").

5. Zillender v. State, 557 S.W.2d 515, 517 (Tex.Crim.App.1977). Accord, Texas Mun. Power Agency v. Berger, 600 S.W.2d 850, 854 (Tex.Civ.App.—Houston [1st Dist.] 1980, no writ).

6. See § 105.1 infra.

7. See Graham, Handbook of Federal Evidence § 103.2, at 13 (2d ed. 1986); 1 Louisell & Mueller, Federal Evidence § 9, at 43 (1977).

8. See Bridges v. City of Richardson, 163 Tex. 292, 293, 354 S.W.2d 366, 368 (1962); Xanthull v. State, 172 Tex.Crim.R. 481, 482, 358 S.W.2d 631, 632 (1962); Capitol Hotel Co. v. Rittenberry, 41 S.W.2d 697, 705 (Tex.Civ.App.—Amarillo 1931, writ dism'd) ("[I]t is uniformly held that a general objection to the introduction of testimony because it is irrelevant, incompetent, and immaterial is tantamount to no objection and unless the objection specifically states why the proffered testimony is irrelevant, immaterial or incompetent the objection will not support an assignment in the appellate court."); Graham, Handbook of Federal Evidence § 103.2, at 14 (2d ed. 1986).

9. See Zillender v. State, 557 S.W.2d 515, 517 (Tex.Crim.App.1977); Coca Cola Bottling Co. v. Tannahill, 235 S.W.2d 224, 225 (Tex.Civ.App.—Fort Worth 1950, writ dism'd); Turner v. Hodges' Estate, 219 S.W.2d 522, 524 (Tex.Civ.App.—Fort Worth 1949, writ ref'd n.r.e.).

Since an objection only preserves the specific grounds named, if an objection naming an untenable ground is overruled, the ruling will be affirmed on appeal even though a good but unnamed ground existed for exclusion of the evidence.[10] If an objection naming an untenable ground is sustained, the ruling will not be upheld on appeal on the basis of an unnamed valid ground if the valid ground might have been obviated by the proponent had it been raised at the trial.[11]

An objection must be specific as to parts as well as grounds. If part of an offer is admissible and part inadmissible, an objection to the whole, even if it names a valid specific ground, may be properly overruled, and the entire offer admitted, if the objector fails to specify properly which part or parts of the offer are inadmissible.[12] If the objector does point out parts of the offer that are inadmissible on specified grounds, the court may not thereafter admit the whole, but must at least exclude the parts designated as inadmissible by the objection.[13]

In addition to the requirement of specificity as to grounds and parts, Rule 103(a)(1) codifies the common-law requirement that objections and motions to strike be "timely." To be timely, a party must invoke an evidence point as soon as the ground for it becomes manifest. In the case of an offer of real or documentary evidence, the proper time for objection is when the item is formally offered; after it has been admitted is too late.[14] In the case of oral testimony, normally the objection must precede the witness' answer.[15] In some circumstances an objection after the answer, accompanied by a motion to strike and a request for an instruction to the jury to disregard the answer, will be timely; for example, where a witness gives an objectionable answer to a question that is unobjectionable.[16] Subsequent objection is also timely where the witness answers an objectionable question too quickly for the

10. See Williams v. State, 549 S.W.2d 183, 187 (Tex.Crim.App.1977); Harrington v. State, 547 S.W.2d 616, 620 (Tex.Crim. App.1977); Douglas v. Winkle, 623 S.W.2d 764, 768 (Tex.App.—Texarkana 1981, no writ); Eubanks v. Winn, 469 S.W.2d 292, 296 (Tex.Civ.App.—Houston [1st Dist.] 1971, writ ref'd n.r.e.).

11. See Graham, Handbook of Federal Evidence § 103.2, at 13–14 (2d ed. 1986); McCormick, Evidence § 52, at 131 (3d ed. 1984); 1 Ray, Texas Law of Evidence § 26, at 35 (3d ed. 1980).

12. See Speier v. Webster College, 616 S.W.2d 617, 619 (Tex.1981); Brown & Root, Inc. v. Haddad, 142 Tex. 624, 628, 180 S.W.2d 339, 341 (1944); Ramos v. State, 419 S.W.2d 359, 364 (Tex.Crim.App.1967); Eubanks v. Winn, 469 S.W.2d 292, 296 (Tex.Civ.App.—Houston [1st Dist.] 1971, writ ref'd n.r.e.); Graham, Handbook of Federal Evidence § 103.2, at 13 (2d ed. 1986); 1 Louisell & Mueller, Federal Evidence § 9, at 43 (1977).

13. See Hurtado v. Texas Employers' Ins. Ass'n, 574 S.W.2d 536, 538 (Tex.1978).

14. See J.A. Robinson Sons, Inc. v. Wigart, 420 S.W.2d 474, 486 (Tex.Civ.App.—Amarillo 1967), rev'd on other grounds, 431 S.W.2d 327 (Tex.1968); 1 Louisell & Mueller, Federal Evidence § 8, at 37 (1977); 21 Wright & Graham, Federal Practice and Procedure § 5037, at 188 (1977).

15. See Guzman v. State, 521 S.W.2d 267, 269 (Tex.Crim.App.1975); Meza v. State, 172 Tex.Crim.R. 544, 550, 360 S.W.2d 403, 406 (1962); Zamora v. Romero, 581 S.W.2d 742, 747 (Tex.Civ.App.—Corpus Christi 1979, writ ref'd n.r.e.); Fox v. Amarillo Nat. Bank, 552 S.W.2d 547, 551 (Tex.Civ.App.—Amarillo 1977, writ ref'd n.r.e.).

16. See Johnson v. Hodges, 121 S.W.2d 371, 373 (Tex.Civ.App.—Fort Worth 1938, writ dism'd).

objection to be interposed; where the witness volunteers an objectionable statement; or where the defect does not appear on the face of the testimony but is revealed later, such as where a witness testifies on direct examination as if from first-hand knowledge but cross-examination or voir dire reveals that in fact his testimony is based upon hearsay.[17] Of course, the motion to strike is itself subject to a requirement of timeliness.[18] In addition, a motion to strike, like an objection, must be specific. If it is overbroad, asking for the deletion of admissible as well as inadmissible evidence, it will not be error to overrule it.[19]

Texas courts have recognized the "running objection" as sufficient to preserve error with regard to a series of similar offers of evidence.[20] Indeed, they have gone further and held that "[w]here a party makes a proper objection to the introduction of testimony and is overruled, he is entitled to assume that the judge will make the same ruling as to the other offers of similar testimony, and he is not required to repeat the objection." [21] All authorities have interpreted Rule 103(a)(1) to be consistent with these practices.[22]

* * *

It has been repeatedly held in Texas that a ruling denying a motion in limine does not suffice to preserve error in the admission of evidence; the party must object when the evidence is offered at trial.[24] If a

17. See generally Graham, Handbook of Federal Evidence § 103.3, at 16–17 (2d ed. 1986); 1 Louisell & Mueller, Federal Evidence § 8, at 36–37 (1977); McCormick, Evidence § 52, at 127 (3d ed. 1984); 1 Ray, Texas Law of Evidence § 23, at 28–29 (3d ed. 1980).

18. See 1 Louisell & Mueller, Federal Evidence § 8, at 37–38 (1977); 21 Wright & Graham, Federal Practice and Procedure § 5037, at 190 (1977).

19. See City of Kennedale v. City of Arlington, 532 S.W.2d 668, 678 (Tex.Civ. App.—Fort Worth 1976, writ dism'd).

20. See Baldwin v. State, 697 S.W.2d 725, 732 (Tex.App.—Corpus Christi 1985, no pet.); City of Baytown v. Bayshore Constructors, Inc., 615 S.W.2d 792, 794 (Tex. Civ.App.—Houston [1st Dist.] 1980, no writ).

21. Bunnett/Smallwood & Co. v. Helton Oil Co., 577 S.W.2d 291, 295 (Tex.Civ. App.—Amarillo 1978, no writ). Accord, Welch v. Texas Employers' Ins. Ass'n, 636 S.W.2d 450, 453 (Tex.App.—Eastland 1982, no writ), writ refused 643 S.W.2d 919 (1982); D.L.N. v. State, 590 S.W.2d 820, 823 (Tex.Civ.App.—Dallas 1979, no writ) ("failure to repeat objections to similar evidence may not be a waiver when previous objections have been overruled.").

22. See Graham, Handbook of Federal Evidence § 103.2, at 15 (2d ed. 1986) ("A party who has objected and obtained a ruling clearly indicating the attitude of the court to the admissibility of the evidence is not required to repeat the objection each time such evidence is offered whether during the examination of the same witness or another witness. Where the court has clearly ruled, repetition of the objection serves only to waste time and prejudice the objecting party in the eyes of the jury. A request for a continuing objection * * * offers counsel additional protection * * *."). Accord, 1 Louisell & Mueller, Federal Evidence § 10, at 44–45 (1977); 21 Wright & Graham, Federal Practice and Procedure § 5037, at 191–92 (1977).

24. See Hartford Accident & Indemnity Co. v. McCardell, 369 S.W.2d 331, 335 (Tex. 1963); Harrington v. State, 547 S.W.2d 616 (Tex.Crim.App.1977); Simpson v. State, 507 S.W.2d 530 (Tex.Crim.App.1974); Crider v. Appelt, 696 S.W.2d 55 (Tex.App.—Austin 1985, no writ) (applying Rule 103(a)(1)). For an extensive discussion of motion in limine practice in Texas, see Hazel, The Motion in Limine: A Texas Proposal, 21 Hous.L.Rev. 919 (1984).

motion in limine is granted, a proper objection at trial is required to preserve error with regard to questions that are claimed to violate it.[25]

* * *

§ 105.1 Rule 105: Limited Admissibility

* * *

* * * If evidence is offered that is admissible against party-opponent A but not against party-opponent B—for example, A's admission—Rule 105 codifies the common-law practice of admission with a limiting instruction.[3] If party B fails to request the instruction, however, he may not complain on appeal if the judge admits the evidence without limitation. The same doctrine obtained in Texas prior to the Rules.[4] Similarly, if evidence is admissible only for a limited purpose, such as impeachment, Rule 105 authorizes admitting it with a limiting instruction; but as held many times prior to the Rules,[5] if the opponent fails to request the instruction, he may not complain on appeal if the evidence is admitted without limitation.

* * * If evidence is admissible against one party-opponent but not against another, and proponent fails to limit his offer accordingly, he may not complain on appeal if the evidence is excluded altogether.[6] Similarly, if evidence is admissible only for a particular purpose, and the offering party fails to specify the purpose or specifies a purpose for which it is not admissible, he cannot complain if the trial judge excludes the evidence entirely.[7]

* * *

25. See Pool v. Ford Motor Co., 715 S.W.2d 629, 637 (Tex.1986).

3. The effectiveness (or ineffectiveness) of the limiting instruction in the particular circumstances must be considered in the decision whether to admit the partly admissible offer or to exclude it for unfair prejudice under Rule 403. See Advisory Committee's Note to Federal Rule 105; Advisory Committee's Note to Federal Rule 403.

4. See Wolfe v. East Texas Seed Co., 583 S.W.2d 481, 482 (Tex.Civ.App.—Houston [1st Dist.] 1979, writ dism'd); Fort Worth Hotel Co. v. Waggoman, 126 S.W.2d 578, 586 (Tex.Civ.App.—Fort Worth 1939, writ dism'd judgmt cor.).

5. See Scotchcraft Bldg. Materials, Inc. v. Parker, 618 S.W.2d 835, 837 (Tex.Civ. App.—Houston [1st Dist.] 1981, writ ref'd n.r.e.); Bristol-Myers Co. v. Gonzales, 548 S.W.2d 416, 430–31 (Tex.Civ.App.—Corpus Christi 1976), rev'd on other grounds, 561 S.W.2d 801 (1978); Miller v. Hardy, 564 S.W.2d 102, 105 (Tex.Civ.App.—El Paso 1978, writ ref'd n.r.e.).

6. See Luvual v. Henke & Pillot, Div. of Kroger Co., 366 S.W.2d 831, 839 (Tex.Civ. App.—Houston 1963, writ ref'd n.r.e.) ("Where evidence is inadmissible against one of the parties and admissible against the other, the party offering it must offer it against the party against whom it is admissible. If he does not do so, but offers it generally and the court sustains an objection, there is no error in exclusion.").

7. See Texas Employers' Ins. Ass'n v. Garza, 557 S.W.2d 843, 847 (Tex.Civ.App.—Corpus Christi 1977, writ ref'd n.r.e.); Powell v. Powell, 554 S.W.2d 850, 855 (Tex.Civ. App.—Tyler 1977, writ ref'd n.r.e.); Kaplan v. Goodfried, 497 S.W.2d 101, 104 (Tex. Civ.App.—Dallas 1973, no writ); Gottschald v. Reaves, 457 S.W.2d 307, 309–10 (Tex. Civ.App.—Houston [1st Dist.] 1970, no writ).

PALMERIN v. CITY OF RIVERSIDE

United States Court of Appeals, Ninth Circuit, 1986.
794 F.2d 1409.

PREGERSON, CIRCUIT JUDGE.

While investigating a narcotics violation, two City of Riverside police officers scuffled with two suspects and members of the suspects' family. Four people subsequently pled guilty to various misdemeanor charges. Family members sued the officers and the City of Riverside under 42 U.S.C. § 1983 alleging the use of excessive force during the arrests. A jury found no constitutional violations and acquitted the officers. The district court then dismissed all claims against the City. One of the suspects and his brother appeal, contending that the introduction of guilty pleas and of seized marijuana into evidence was reversible error. They also assert that the dismissal of the City was premature. We affirm.

* * *

I. *THE GUILTY PLEAS*

Before trial, counsel for Cruz and Richard Palmerin unsuccessfully sought to exclude admission of the guilty pleas from evidence by a motion *in limine*. The district court held that the pleas were relevant to the issue of excessive force because the pleas constituted admissions of resistance to the officers. The Palmerins argue that the guilty pleas are not relevant to their claims of excessive force by the officers, that they constitute impermissible character evidence, and that, even if relevant, the prejudice to the Palmerins substantially outweighed the probative value.

A. Timeliness of Objections

The City argues that the Palmerins' failure to object contemporaneously during trial to the admissibility of the pleas into evidence bars them from raising the issue on appeal. *See* Fed.R.Evid. 103(a)(1). The law in this circuit is unclear regarding whether an unsuccessful pretrial motion *in limine* will preserve for appeal an objection to the introduction of disputed evidence at trial. *See Burgess v. Premier Corp.,* 727 F.2d 826, 836 (9th Cir.1984). In *Burgess,* however, we were able to resolve the appeal without reaching the issue. *Id.* Two apparently conflicting decisions, decided in different contexts, generated this confusion.

In *United States v. Helina,* 549 F.2d 713 (9th Cir.1977), a criminal prosecution for tax evasion, defense counsel made a pretrial motion *in limine* to exclude any evidence that Helina had exercised his fifth amendment rights and had refused to provide records to the IRS. *Id.* at 715. The trial court sustained the motion with respect to direct testimony, but refused to prevent cross-examination and rebuttal on these issues. *Id.* This court denied Helina's contention that the prosecutor's questions to Helina on cross-examination relating to Helina's failure to provide records to the IRS amounted to improper prosecutorial conduct in violation of his fifth amendment rights. *Id.* at

717–18. The court reviewed the prosecutor's behavior for plain error because defense counsel had failed to object contemporaneously during trial when the comments were made. *Id.* at 718. The court stated: "His *in limine* motion having been denied * * *, defense counsel once more bore the burden of making a proper objection at the appropriate time." *Id.*

Three years later, in *Sheehy v. Southern Pacific Transportation Co.,* 631 F.2d 649 (9th Cir.1980), we reached an apparently contrary conclusion. Sheehy sued his employer for workplace injuries under the FELA. In a pretrial motion *in limine,* plaintiff's counsel sought to exclude references to collateral benefits received by Sheehy. The trial court ruled that evidence of the amount of benefits was admissible on the issue of Sheehy's motivation to resume working and malingering, but that the source of the benefits and the term "pension" could not be mentioned. *Id.* at 651. On cross-examination, defense counsel questioned Sheehy about his benefits income during his extended time off work. *Id.* No contemporaneous objection was made. *Id.* This court found that the admission of evidence of collateral benefits was reversible error under *Eichel v. New York Central Railroad Co.,* 375 U.S. 253, 255, 84 S.Ct. 316, 317, 11 L.Ed.2d 307 (1963). *Sheehy,* 631 F.2d at 651–52. In so holding, this court without citing *Helina,* rejected the contention that Sheehy waived his right to raise the matter on appeal by failing to object contemporaneously to the evidence: "Sheehy's attorney objected during the pretrial arguments to the court's ruling that the evidence was admissible. The objection at that time was on record and at least under these circumstances was adequate to preserve the right on appeal." *Id.* at 652–53.

Helina and *Sheehy* are distinguishable from each other. The disputed matter in *Helina* related to whether the prosecutor's behavior in asking questions permitted by the *in limine* motion violated Helina's constitutional rights by improperly commenting on his invocation of the privilege against self-incrimination. The issue is not precisely the one that was the subject of the motion *in limine,* and it is one that is highly dependent upon the trial context. We therefore required contemporaneous objection to review for more than plain error. By contrast, the evidence in *Sheehy* was elicited in direct response to questions sanctioned through the rejection of the *in limine* motion by the court. The objection was adequately covered by the motion *in limine* and we held that the point was preserved for appeal. We therefore do not interpret either *Helina* or *Sheehy* as requiring us to adopt an all-or-nothing rule.

The uncertainty in this circuit concerning whether a contemporaneous objection is required following an unsuccessful pretrial motion *in limine* is mirrored by a sharp division of views among the circuits.

Some circuits require that "[o]bjection must be made in the trial court unless a good reason exists not to do so," notwithstanding an unsuccessful pretrial motion *in limine.* *Rojas v. Richardson,* 703 F.2d

186, 189–90 & n. 3, *opinion set aside for other reasons on rehearing,* 713 F.2d 116 (5th Cir.1983); *see also Northwestern Flyers, Inc. v. Olson Bros. Manufacturing Co.,* 679 F.2d 1264, 1275 n. 27 (8th Cir.1982).

In contrast, the Third Circuit recently held that no formal objection at trial is necessary where the pretrial motion adequately resolves the admissibility of the disputed evidence "with no suggestion that [the trial court] would reconsider the matter at trial." *American Home Assurance Co. v. Sunshine Supermarket, Inc.,* 753 F.2d 321, 324–25 (3d Cir.1985). The Third Circuit panel concluded that "if an issue is fully briefed and the trial court is able to make a definitive ruling, then the motion *in limine* provides a useful tool for eliminating unnecessary trial interruptions." *Id.* at 324. Similarly, the District of Columbia Circuit has stated that where the court has already indicated its views in no uncertain terms, it would "exalt form over substance" to require further objection. *United States v. Williams,* 561 F.2d 859, 863 (D.C.Cir.1977).[3]

The rule followed by the Fifth and Eighth Circuits requires a contemporaneous objection to the admissibility of the evidence during trial to preserve the matter for appeal. This rule ensures that the evidentiary appeal is based on the actual form and timing of the attempt to introduce the evidence, rather than on an essentially hypothetical situation suggested by the pretrial motion *in limine.* However, despite its "bright line" advantages, we reject this approach because it raises the danger that an unsuccessful motion *in limine* will serve as a trap for unwary counsel and bar an appeal of a meritorious issue on essentially technical grounds. We prefer the more flexible approach of *Sheehy* and the Third Circuit.

Pretrial motions are useful tools to resolve issues which would otherwise "clutter up" the trial. Such motions reduce the need for sidebar conferences and argument outside the hearing of the jury, thereby saving jurors' time and eliminating distractions. *See Judge's Manual for the Management of Complex Criminal Jury Cases* § 2.2 (1982) (District judges should "[e]ncourage counsel to bring motions *in limine* on evidentiary questions. This will prevent disruptions at trial which could render the proceedings incoherent to the jurors.") *Manual*

3. *See also* 21 C. Wright & K. Graham, *Federal Practice and Procedure,* § 5037 at 195 (1977) ("If a ruling is made at the pretrial stage, it is 'timely' and there is no need to renew the objection at trial."); 1 J. Weinstein and M. Berger, *Weinstein's Evidence* ¶ 103[02] at 103–17 (1982) ("Ultimately, whether or not the pretrial objection is deemed sufficient to preserve error may well depend upon whether the appellate court feels that justice was done at the trial level.").

State courts are split on whether a contemporaneous objection during trial is required to preserve a right to appeal on an evidentiary matter admitted over a denied motion *in limine.* *Compare Reeve v. McBrearety,* 8 Kan.App.2d 419, 422, 660 P.2d 75, 77 (1983); *State v. Harper,* 215 Neb. 686, 687–88, 340 N.W.2d 391, 393 (1983); *Kaiser v. State,* 673 P.2d 160, 161–62 (Okla.Crim.1983); *State v. Lesley,* 672 P.2d 79, 82 (Utah 1983); Gamble, *The Motion in Limine: A Pretrial Procedure That Has Come of Age,* 33 Ala.L.Rev. 1, 16 (1981) (objection during trial required); *with State v. Sisneros,* 137 Ariz. 323, 325, 670 P.2d 721, 723 (1983); *Harley–Davidson Motor Co. v. Daniel,* 244 Ga. 284, 285–86, 260 S.E.2d 20, 22 (1979) (*in limine* motion preserves objection for appeal).

for Complex Litigation Second § 32.23 at 271–72 (1985) ("By addressing these [evidentiary issues] before trial [through motions *in limine*], judge and the attorneys may be able to give them more deliberate and careful consideration than if the issues were raised for the first time during trial, and pretrial rulings on critical evidentiary questions permit the trial to be conducted more efficiently and effectively.").

The Federal Rules of Civil Procedure state that formal exceptions to court rulings are unnecessary. Fed.R.Civ.P. 46. To require invariably a contemporaneous objection after a rejected *in limine* motion would be tantamount to requiring formal exceptions. This would exalt the form of timely objection over the substance of whether a proper objection has been made and considered by the trial court.

We, therefore, reject an invariable requirement that an objection that is the subject of an unsuccessful motion *in limine* be renewed at trial. We adopt the approach of *Sheehy* and *American Home*. Accordingly, we hold that where the substance of the objection has been thoroughly explored during the hearing on the motion *in limine,* and the trial court's ruling permitting introduction of evidence was explicit and definitive, no further action is required to preserve for appeal the issue of admissibility of that evidence. In applying this approach, we find that the Palmerins have preserved their objection for appeal. The substance of the objection to the admission of the guilty pleas was thoroughly explored during the hearing on the motion *in limine,* and the trial judge's ruling was explicit and definitive. There was no hint that the ruling might be subject to reconsideration. Perhaps most important, there was nothing in the manner or context in which the guilty pleas were introduced at trial that was unforeseen or that cast any doubt on the applicability of the trial court's *in limine* ruling. Accordingly, we permit the Palmerins to raise on appeal their objections to introduction of the guilty pleas.[4]

* * *

AFFIRMED.

4. It is important to distinguish the situation here, where the *in limine* motion fails and the evidence is introduced at trial, from the situation where the result of the *in limine* motion is that the evidence is not used at trial. In *Luce v. United States,* 469 U.S. 38, 105 S.Ct. 460, 464, 83 L.Ed.2d 443 (1984), the Supreme Court concluded that a defendant could not appeal an unsuccessful *in limine* motion to exclude certain impeaching evidence when he did not take the stand to testify because the disputed evidence was never before the jury. Two concurring justices stated that *Luce* was limited to the prior felony impeachment rule of Fed.R.Evid. 609(a), 105 S.Ct. at 464 (Brennan J., concurring). The Court's principal rationale was that the subtleties of timing and manner of introduction of the disputed evidence were critical to appellate determinations of prejudicial effect and harmless error. *Id.* at 463–64; *cf. Coursen v. A.H. Robins Co.,* 764 F.2d 1329, 1342 (9th Cir.1985) (no interlocutory appeal available for *in limine* motion excluding evidence of prior sexual history because reviewing court cannot determine prejudice absent a trial). However, where the evidence is in the record over an *in limine* objection, even though an additional contemporaneous objection was not made when the evidence was admitted at trial, an appellate court's ability to review the impact of the disputed evidence on the jury is unimpaired.

PADILLA v. STATE

Supreme Court of Wyoming, 1979.
601 P.2d 189.

ROONEY, JUSTICE.

Appellant-defendant appeals from the judgment and sentence of the trial court rendered on a jury verdict of guilty of first degree sexual assault * * *.

* * *

IMPEACHMENT RULING

The following occurred during recross examination of victim by appellant's attorney, Terry Tharp:

"Q. [Victim's first name], do you recall your appearance at the preliminary hearing, I asked you about it on my examination the last time, that was the hearing we had before in Lovell.

"A. Yes.

"Q. And you testified at that hearing that you hadn't known Mike [appellant]?

"MR. GARRETT: I am going to object. I think she should be furnished with a copy of the transcript rather than counsel saying what she testified.

"THE COURT: He should use the transcript and refer to questions and answers.

"MR. THARP: I have a tape recording.

"THE COURT: Well, really the proper way to do that is to refer, as you know, to page and line number and say, on such and such a day you were asked this question and didn't you answer such and such.

"MR. THARP: I know, Your Honor, but the transcript of the preliminary hearing, one was never made. As a matter of fact, the copy of the preliminary hearing is, the Justice of the Peace recorded over some of it. I have portions of it, however.

"THE COURT: Well, based on that, the objection is sustained."

Appellant contends that Rule 613(a), W.R.E. authorizes the approach used by appellant in this respect, and that the trial court erred in sustaining appellee's objection. Appellee–State contends that not only was the ruling of the trial court proper, but the error, if any, was not properly preserved for consideration on appeal pursuant to Rule 103(a)(2), W.R.E.

We agree that the error, if one, was not properly preserved for consideration on appeal. The requirements of Rule 103(a)(2), W.R.E., were not met. Meredith v. Hardy, 5th Cir., 554 F.2d 764 (1977); Yost v. A.O. Smith Corporation, 8th Cir., 562 F.2d 592 (1977).

Not only did appellant fail to make an offer of the substance of the evidence proposed to be presented if the objection were not sustained, but he advised the court that the transcript reflecting the same did not exist in a suitable or admissible form.

After the court sustained the objection, appellant made no further reference to the issue—in the form of an offer of proof or otherwise. In addition to insuring "that the record will be sufficiently detailed to permit appraisal by an appellate court of the scope and effect of the ruling," 1 Weinstein's Evidence ¶ 103[03], p. 103–27, the offer of proof serves the function of calling the nature of the error "to the attention of the judge, so as to alert him to the proper course of action and enable opposing counsel to take proper corrective measures," Advisory Committee's Note to Rule 103 of Federal Rules of Evidence.[9] Appellant's failure to make an offer of proof prevented the attainment of these purposes.

Appellant argues that the question itself was sufficient foundation as to time and place of the alleged inconsistent statement. He argues that he could have impeached the witness if she denied making the statement by allowing the prosecution to hear the tape of the testimony at the preliminary hearing or by calling as a witness someone present at the hearing. But, as of the time of the objection and ruling thereon, this presupposes the fact that such inconsistent statement was made at the hearing. These arguments are the precise items which should have been presented as an offer of proof so that this court would know whether or not from the record there was a potential for establishment of inconsistent statements, so that the trial court could appraise its ruling in context with the proposed proof, and so that opposing counsel could make the request authorized by Rule 103(a)(2). In this latter respect, appellant advised the court that a transcript of the preliminary hearing was not made. He inferred that it was recorded on tape but that only portions remained and that some of the tape was recorded over. He apparently had nothing certified or verified as to accuracy. Possibly, he had enough to satisfy the opposing counsel on the precise issue; but, here again, an offer of proof as to exactly what he had was necessary to preclude speculation by us or by the trial court.

Rule 103(a)(2) does make unnecessary an offer of proof if the substance of the evidence was apparent from the context within which questions were asked. Such exception was recognized before the adoption of the rules. Taylor v. MacDonald, Wyo., 409 P.2d 762 (1966) (exclusion of conversation had with defendant concerning matters otherwise presented to the jury where "nature of the expected testimony clearly appears"); State v. Ditzel, 77 Wyo. 233, 311 P.2d 961, reh. den. 77 Wyo. 233, 314 P.2d 832 (1957) (exclusion of defendant's testimony in embezzlement trial as to whether diversion of funds was done with approval of representative of victim where nature of testimony *otherwise* clearly appears); Gregg v. Gregg, Wyo., 469 P.2d 406 (1970)

9. Source of Rule 103, W.R.E., and identical to Rule 103, W.R.E.

(exclusion of testimony of 11–year old when counsel advised testimony to corroborate mother's testimony and the nature of testimony clearly appears). In each case the nature of the testimony appeared otherwise than in the question itself. In this case the only indication of the expected testimony is in the question "[a]nd you testified at that hearing that you hadn't known Mike?" This does not meet the exception of Rule 103(a)(2) which requires the substance of the evidence to be apparent "from the *context within which* questions were asked." To allow the question itself, coupled with advice to the court that a transcript containing the impeachment statement did not exist and that the tape containing such was recorded over to a great extent, to set the stage for the exception would be to invite the damage which is one of the concerns of the rules of evidence and of fair trial generally and which is expressed in the Advisory Committee's Note to Rule 613(a), Federal Rules of Evidence: [12]

> "The provision for disclosure to counsel is designed to protect against unwarranted insinuations that a statement has been made when the fact is to the contrary."

Affirmed.

STEVEN GOODE, OLIN GUY WELLBORN III & M. MICHAEL SHARLOT, GUIDE TO THE TEXAS RULES OF EVIDENCE: CIVIL AND CRIMINAL (1988)

§ 103.3 Rule 103(a)(2): Offer of Proof

To preserve error in the exclusion of evidence, Rule 103(a)(2), like the common law, requires that the substance of the evidence be shown by offer of proof. The primary purpose of the offer of proof is to enable an appellate court to determine whether the exclusion was erroneous and harmful.[1] A secondary purpose is to permit the trial judge to reconsider his ruling in light of the actual evidence.[2]

Texas courts have consistently held that error in the exclusion of evidence may not be urged unless the proponent perfected an offer of proof or bill of exception.[3] There has been some doubt whether the requirement of an offer of proof to preserve error applies to questions posed on cross-examination. It has been suggested that since counsel may not know the answer that an adverse witness would give to his question, the requirement does not ordinarily apply.[4] Yet this circum-

12. Source of Rule 613(a), W.R.E., and identical to Rule 613(a), W.R.E.

1. See McCormick, Evidence § 51, at 123–24 (3d ed. 1984).

2. See id.

3. See Moore v. State, 462 S.W.2d 574, 576 (Tex.Crim.App.1970); Davidson v. State, 162 Tex.Crim.R. 640, 646–47, 288 S.W.2d 93, 97 (1956); Texas Employers' Ins. Ass'n v. Garza, 557 S.W.2d 843, 847 (Tex.Civ.App.—Corpus Christi 1977, writ ref'd n.r.e.); Morris v. City of Houston, 466 S.W.2d 851, 856 (Tex.Civ.App.—Houston [14th Dist.] 1971, no writ); Bell v. Hoskins, 357 S.W.2d 585, 588 (Tex.Civ.App.—Dallas 1962, no writ); City of Houston v. Huber, 311 S.W.2d 488, 495 (Tex.Civ.App.—Houston 1958, no writ).

4. See McCormick, Evidence § 51, at 124 n. 9 (3d ed. 1984).

stance would not preclude an offer in question-and-answer form, and on the issues of admissibility and harm a complete record would be of equal value on cross-examination as on direct examination. Texas authority is divided.[5] Criminal Rule 103(a)(2), like the federal version, permits an exception to the requirement of offer of proof, where "the substance of the evidence * * * was apparent from the context within which questions were asked." This exception may frequently apply during cross-examination.[6]

* * *

As noted in a previous section, Texas courts have consistently held that a motion in limine does not by itself preserve error in the admission of evidence; the complainant must make a timely and specific objection at trial as well.[9] Texas courts have also consistently held that if a motion in limine is granted, the party against whom the exclusion operates must make an offer of proof in order to preserve error.[10] Rule 103(a)(2) continues this requirement.

BOURJAILY v. UNITED STATES

[p. 216 supra]

HUDDLESTON v. UNITED STATES

[p. 58 supra]

THOMPSON v. STATE

Court of Appeals of Texas, 1988.

752 S.W.2d 12, pet. for discretionary review dismissed,
795 S.W.2d 177 (Tex.Crim.App.1990).

DEVANY, JUSTICE.

Fred Lee Thompson, appellant, was convicted of murder and sentenced to 55 years in prison. He presents five points of error which

5. Compare Texas Employers' Ins. Ass'n v. Garza, 557 S.W.2d 843, 847 (Tex. Civ.App.—Corpus Christi 1977, writ ref'd n.r.e.) ("[W]hen tendered evidence is excluded, whether testimony of one's own witness on direct examination or testimony of the opponent's witness on cross-examination, in order to later complain it is necessary for the complainant to make an offer of proof on a bill of exception to show what the witness' testimony would have been. Otherwise there is nothing before the appellate court to show reversible error in the trial court's ruling.") with Foster v. Bailey, 691 S.W.2d 801, 803 (Tex.App.—Houston [1st Dist.] 1985, no writ) (offer of proof not required to show error in sustaining objection to relevant inquiry on cross-examination of opposing party; "The right to cross-examine the sole adverse party on an ultimate disputed issue should not depend upon a showing that the cross-examination will be successful.") and Ledisco Financial Services, Inc. v. Viracola, 533 S.W.2d 951, 958 (Tex.Civ.App.—Texarkana 1976, no writ) (requirement of offer of proof or bill of exception to preserve error does not apply to cross-examination of adverse party).

6. See Graham, Handbook of Federal Evidence § 103.7, at 25–26 (2d ed. 1986); 1 Louisell & Mueller, Federal Evidence § 12, at 69–71 (1977); 21 Wright & Graham, Federal Practice and Procedure § 5040, at 219–21.

9. See § 103.2 supra.

10. See Tempo Tamers, Inc. v. Crow-Houston Four, Ltd., 715 S.W.2d 658, 662–63 (Tex.App.—Dallas 1986, writ ref'd n.r.e.); Roberts v. Tatum, 575 S.W.2d 138, 144 (Tex.Civ.App.—Corpus Christi 1978, writ ref'd n.r.e.).

may be summarized as follows: his first three points of error complain that the trial court failed to instruct the jury of the limited purpose of admissibility of certain evidence *at the time* the evidence was offered by the State at the guilt/innocence phase of the trial; * * *. For the reasons stated below, we overrule appellant's points of error and affirm the judgment of the trial court.

The pertinent facts necessary to review this case on appeal show that the victim of the crime was killed with a shotgun blast. An investigation of the crime by the police allegedly revealed that there were three witnesses who implicated appellant in the crime. However, as State's witnesses at trial, each denied that he gave any such statements to the police. The State impeached each of those witnesses by offering as evidence the three signed statements given to the police. Appellant requested that the jury be instructed to consider the statements only for the limited purposes of attacking the credibility of the witnesses rather than to prove the contents of the statements. The trial court refused this request at the time, but included in the jury charge at the conclusion of testimony and arguments that such evidence could not be considered by the jury to establish the guilt of the appellant. Appellant complains that such instructions should have been given to the jury at the time of the request in order that the jury would understand *then* that such evidence did not constitute proof that appellant committed the crime. Appellant argues that the jury would have already used the evidence in its observations of the testimony and evidence and that it was too late to instruct the jury at the end of the trial that the evidence only attacks the credibility of the State's own witnesses.

The pertinent governing evidence rule provides:

> When evidence which is admissible * * * for one purpose but not admissible * * * for another purpose is admitted, the court, upon request, shall restrict the evidence to its proper scope and instruct the jury accordingly; * * *.

TEX.R.CRIM.EVID. 105 (which became effective September 1, 1986). This rule is new and there are no cases giving us guidance in its use. However, we find almost identical provisions in the comparable rule 105 for civil cases as well as in the federal rule 105. Therefore, we have referred to Federal Practice and Procedure by Wright and Graham, which contains the following commentary on the federal rule: "It appears that the language originated in the proposed Missouri Evidence Code of 1948, with this comment: 'This section but codifies in a simple, condensed form the procedure recognized in many decisions.'" 21 C. Wright & K. Graham, *Federal Practice and Procedure* § 5067 (1977). At section 5066 of that authority, we find the following: "Limiting instructions may be given when the evidence is being introduced or during the judge's charge at the end of the case. It is preferable that the jury be instructed on the limited use of the evidence at the point of admission." 21 C. Wright & K. Graham, *Federal Practice and Procedure* § 5066 (1977).

The criminal evidence rule 105, applicable in this case, clearly entitles the appellant to a binding instruction not to use the evidence for any purpose other than the purpose for which the evidence was admitted. While the better practice appears to be to give the instruction at the time the evidence is admitted, our concern is satisfied by the fact that the limiting instruction was given to the jury in the jury charge. The trial judge has broad powers in the conduct of a trial. When he charges the jury at the conclusion of the trial on what it should consider and what it should not consider, we must assume that the jury will follow those instructions. Furthermore, the closing arguments of counsel give another opportunity for an appellant to explain why the evidence is limited. We are mindful of the degree of harm that may be suffered by an accused when evidence of this nature is admitted *even with limiting instructions given at the time of its admission.* However, we leave to the sound discretion of the trial court the conduct of the trial in a just and impartial manner following the pertinent rules. In the instant case, limiting instructions were given to the jury in compliance with rule 105. Limiting instructions in the jury charge on the effect of impeaching evidence is proper and should be sufficient protection for appellant. *Goodman v. State,* 665 S.W.2d 788, 792 (Tex.Crim.App.1984); *Castillo v. State,* 421 S.W.2d 112, 114 (Tex. Crim.App.1967). Appellant's first three points of error are overruled.

* * *

The judgment of conviction is affirmed.

McNIEL v. STATE, 757 S.W.2d 129, 136 (Tex.App.1988). "Appellant asserts in her tenth point of error that the trial court erred by failing to instruct the jury on the limited admissibility of the prior misdemeanor conviction. We note that appellant made no request for any limiting instruction until after both sides had closed and argued the case. However, prior to the Court's charge, the appellant objected to the omission of a limiting instruction on the purpose of the prior conviction.

"Tex.R.Crim.Evid. 105(a), upon which appellant relies, provides:

> (a) When evidence which is admissible as to one party or for one purpose but not admissible as to another party or for another purpose is admitted, the court, upon request, shall restrict the evidence to its proper scope and instruct the jury accordingly.

"This rule provides a basis for the trial court to instruct the jury on the limited admissibility of certain evidence *at the time it is admitted.* The rule provides no support for the contention that error is preserved by a request for a limiting instruction made, not during the presentation of evidence, but as an objection to the court's charge."

UNITED STATES v. SWEISS

United States Court of Appeals, Seventh Circuit, 1987.
814 F.2d 1208.

FLAUM, CIRCUIT JUDGE.

Musa "Moses" Sweiss was the manager and part owner of a Super Low grocery store in Chicago, Illinois. Sweiss was convicted of conspiring to destroy a competing grocery store and of attempting to obstruct the government's investigation of that crime. Sweiss appeals the district court's refusal to allow the jury to hear the first of two tape-recorded conversations between the defendant and one of the main prosecution witnesses. After examining the transcript of the conversation, we conclude that because of a decision made by defendant's counsel as to trial strategy, the district court did not abuse its discretion in refusing to admit the conversation at the time it was offered. We therefore affirm the district court's holding.

I.

Moses Sweiss was indicted in September, 1984, on charges that he conspired with Bassam Faraj to commit arson and aided and abetted an attempted arson. Moses Sweiss was also indicted for assisting Bassam Faraj in his plans to flee the jurisdiction of the United States and for attempting to persuade a grand jury witness to retract or change his testimony against Sweiss. Moses Sweiss' defense at trial was that he was "framed" in order to "take the fall" for the true instigator of the conspiracy, his "millionaire uncle," Michael Sweiss, who was the controlling partner of the Super Low grocery store that Moses Sweiss operated.

Faraj, who was working as a butcher at the Super Low, asked a frequent customer by the name of William Franklin to "torch the One Stop" supermarket. That same day Franklin contacted the Chicago Police Department Bomb and Arson Hotline and told them that Faraj had offered him $1,500 to burn down the One Stop. Agents of the Department of Alcohol, Tobacco and Firearms ("ATF") outfitted Franklin with a hidden recording device that was then used to tape nine conversations that detailed Faraj's plans to destroy the One Stop. During Faraj's conversations with Franklin, Faraj never revealed the name of the person who had hired him, but referred to that person as "the man," "my uncle," and "one of my uncles." On one occasion, when Franklin walked into the Super Low, he saw Faraj speaking to Moses Sweiss. Faraj later said to Franklin that, "Man, I was inside, you know, talking to the man."

Faraj was arrested on May 3, 1984, and after hearing the tape-recorded conversations between himself and Franklin, Faraj named Moses Sweiss as the person for whom he was working. Faraj remained in custody until several members of the Sweiss family, including Moses Sweiss, posted a $15,000 cash bond. Three months later, Faraj called an ATF agent and told him that he wanted to talk to the government about Moses Sweiss. Faraj then agreed to wear a hidden recording device, and secretly recorded two conversations that Moses Sweiss was involved in, one on August 14, 1984, and the other on September 10, 1984. Faraj became a trial witness for the government.

The government introduced a transcript of the September conversation into evidence at Moses Sweiss' trial; however, the district court refused to admit a transcript of the August conversation which was offered by the defense after the prosecution rested its case. Both conversations were in Arabic. Both parties stipulated to the use of an English translation of the September conversation. During the September conversation, Faraj and Moses discussed how Faraj could flee to Mexico and how Faraj had been solicited to bomb the One Stop grocery store. Although Sweiss did not say anything in the conversation that directly incriminated himself, the government argued to the jury that his statements implicated him in the crime.

* * *

B.

1.

The defendant argues that the tape recording of the August 14, 1984 conversation should have been admitted to explain his later statements recorded in September. He argues that the complete truth could only have been ascertained if both tapes had been played to the jury. This is particularly crucial, the defendant argues, because of the importance the prosecution placed on specific statements made in the September conversation.

Federal Rule of Evidence 106 codifies the common law rule of completeness:

> When a writing or recorded statement or part thereof is introduced by a party, an adverse party may require him at that time to introduce any other part or any other writing or recorded statement which ought in fairness to be considered contemporaneously with it.

"This rule is circumscribed by two qualifications. The portions sought to be admitted (1) must be relevant to the issues and (2) only those parts which qualify or explain the subject matter of the portion offered by the opponent need be admitted." *United States v. Walker,* 652 F.2d 708, 710 (7th Cir.1981) (en banc) (*citing United States v. McCorkle,* 511 F.2d 482, 486–87 (7th Cir.), *cert. denied,* 423 U.S. 826, 96 S.Ct. 43, 46 L.Ed.2d 43 (1975)). The Second Circuit in *United States v. Marin,* 669 F.2d 73, 82–83 (2d Cir.1982), and the Third Circuit in *United States v. Soures,* 736 F.2d 87, 91 (3d Cir.1984), *cert. denied,* 469 U.S. 1161, 105 S.Ct. 914, 83 L.Ed.2d 927 (1985), have both adopted and amplified the test we articulated in *Walker.* Under the doctrine of completeness, another writing or tape recording is "required to be read [or heard] if it is necessary to (1) explain the admitted portion, (2) place the admitted portion in context, (3) avoid misleading the trier of fact, or (4) insure a fair and impartial understanding." *Soures,* 736 F.2d at 91 (*citing Marin,* 669 F.2d at 84).

In *Walker* the defendant was found guilty of extortion after a second trial (the first ended in a deadlocked jury). The defendant elected not to testify at his second trial, but portions of his testimony from the first trial were admitted into evidence during his second trial. The defendant argued on appeal that the trial judge violated Rule 106 by allowing the prosecution to introduce selected portions of the defendant's prior testimony while refusing to admit other relevant parts. We found that "substantial portions" of the excluded testimony were "relevant to specific elements of the Government's proof and explanatory of the excerpts already admitted." *Walker,* 652 F.2d at 711. In contrast to *Walker,* in this case, because the excluded conversation, although perhaps useful to the jury, was not *necessary to explain* evidence already admitted, Rule 106 was not implicated. Therefore, the trial court did not abuse its discretion in denying its admission.

2.

To lay a sufficient foundation at trial for a rule of completeness claim, the offeror need only specify the portion of the testimony that is relevant to the issue at trial and that qualifies or explains portions already admitted. *Walker,* 652 F.2d at 710. This is a minimal burden that can be met without unreasonable specificity. For example, in *United States v. Littwin,* 338 F.2d 141, 146 (6th Cir.1964), the defendant's counsel did not point out "what word, remark or phrase in that part of the tape which was played he would like to have explained or rebutted, or what part of the unplayed tape would be relevant or would throw light upon any word, phrase or remark which the jury had heard." The court concluded that the district court did not abuse its discretion in excluding the statements.

In this case, Sweiss' trial counsel did not argue that the August tape was admissible under the rule of completeness, nor did he even hint at this. After extensive questioning by the district court the defense counsel did not state what portions of the August tape explained the September tape. Furthermore, the defendant's counsel did not mention Federal Rule of Evidence 106, nor did he state any of the substance of the rule. In fact, even when directly asked, he was unable to give the court any case law on the point. Moreover, the nature of the August conversation was vague and rambling. Unless the conversation was heavily edited, its admission may well have confused the jury. Consequently, the trial counsel should have precisely delineated the relevant portions of the tape that he wished the jury to hear.

At the time that the defense offered the August tape for admission, the prosecution had not yet stated what it believed was the "key" evidence against Sweiss. However, after Sweiss' cross-examination it became clear that the prosecution was focusing on the portion of the September tape that demonstrated that Sweiss knew that Eddie Al–Abbasi was a corroborating witness. At that point, the defense could have offered portions of the August tape recording again because the defense counsel clearly knew what inference the government was arguing should be drawn from the September tape recording. Alternatively, the defense could have recalled Faraj, asked him what he said in the August conversation, and used the August tape recording to impeach him. But Sweiss' trial counsel chose not to follow either of these paths.

Furthermore, the prejudicial impact of the exclusion, if any, was diminished because, unlike *Walker,* the defendant in this case did take the stand and thus did have a chance to explain his statements. While on the stand, Sweiss did not refer to the August conversation. In addition, the defense did not examine the government's witnesses as to the August conversation. Thus, the defense failed to use its ample opportunity to refer to the relevant portions of the August conversation that allegedly corroborated Sweiss' story. The trial judge's refusal to admit the August tape, moreover, was without prejudice, so that the defendant could have offered the portions of the tape recording again when and if they became relevant and explanatory.[2] The defendant, however, did not offer the tape again.

The August tape, if edited, may have aided the jury in understanding the September conversation. However, the defendant failed to lay a sufficient foundation for its admission under Federal Rule of Evidence 106. Moreover, because of the defense counsel's failure to make a focused and specific request outlining the relevant portions of the August conversation, the district court had discretion in refusing its admission. Therefore, the district court's refusal to admit the tape recording was not an abuse of discretion *when it was offered. See Walker,* 652 F.2d at 713.

* * *

Affirmed.

REECE v. STATE, 772 S.W.2d 198, 202–04 (Tex.App.1989). "In his third point of error, appellant contends the trial court erred by allowing the State to introduce 'only portions' of his confession. Appellant bases his complaint on the State's changing a sentence from his confession which originally read 'I want to say that I do believe that I did not kill Mr. Smith cause [sic] I did not do nothing [sic] but hit him three times with my hand' by deleting words so that it ultimately read: '*I did kill Mr. Smith* (emphasis added).' The State's deletions represent a flagrant abuse of a long accepted trial tactic. But while we condemn the

2. The record indicates that the judge held the prosecutor's objections up to particular scrutiny. The court's action was correct, because it ensured that the government did not select for trial strategy purposes half of the recordings that helped the prosecution, but then object on evidentiary grounds to the defendant's offer of the other half.

abuse, we cannot conclude beyond a reasonable doubt that reversible error occurred in this case.

* * *

"We further find no violation of Rule 106. In light of the prosecutor's deletions, the original sentence from appellant's confession 'I want to say that I do believe I did not kill Mr. Smith' was clearly one 'which ought in fairness to be considered contemporaneously' with the edited statement. Tex.R.Crim.Evid. 106. But although appellant complains on appeal that he was 'forced to introduce portions' of the confession while at the same time disputing its accuracy, appellant did not invoke the very rule which would have entitled him to timely correct the prosecutor by introducing only the remainder of the edited sentence 'then and there' during the prosecutor's reading. Tex.R.Crim.Evid. 106. Nothing required appellant to read all but one paragraph of his entire original statement in order to correct the error he claims here. By deferring his corrections to his case-in-chief, * * * appellant waived his right, under Rule 106, to timely remedy the prosecutor's abusive tactic. In our opinion, the general objection 'Well, I still object' would not suffice to preserve error under Rule 106 in this case because, at the time appellant's counsel made the objection, the prosecutor had not yet read the statement of which appellant complains."

BEECH AIRCRAFT CORP. v. RAINEY, 488 U.S. 153, 171–72, 109 S.Ct. 439, 450–51, 102 L.Ed.2d 445 (1988). "Respondents also contended on appeal that reversal was required because the District Court improperly restricted the cross-examination of plaintiff Rainey by his own counsel in regard to the letter Rainey had addressed to Lieutenant Commander Morgan. We agree with the unanimous holding of the Court of Appeals en banc that the District Court erred in refusing to permit Rainey to present a more complete picture of what he had written to Morgan.

* * *

"The common-law 'rule of completeness,' which underlies Federal Rule of Evidence 106, was designed to prevent exactly the type of prejudice of which Rainey complains. In its aspect relevant to this case, the rule of completeness was stated succinctly by Wigmore: 'the opponent, against whom a part of an utterance has been put in, may in his turn complement it by putting in the remainder, in order to secure for the tribunal a complete understanding of the total tenor and effect of the utterance.' 7 J. Wigmore, Evidence in Trials at Common Law § 2113, p. 653 (J. Chadbourn rev. 1978). The Federal Rules of Evidence have partially codified the doctrine of completeness in Rule 106:

* * *

"In proposing Rule 106, the Advisory Committee stressed that it 'does not in any way circumscribe the right of the adversary to develop the matter on cross-examination or as part of his own case.' Advisory Committee's Notes on Fed.Rule Evid. 106, 28 U.S.C.App., p. 682. We take this to be a reaffirmation of the obvious: that when one party has made use of a portion of a document, such that misunderstanding or distortion can be averted only through presentation of another portion, the material required for completeness is *ipso facto* relevant and therefore admissible under Rules 401 and 402. See 1 J. Weinstein & M. Berger, Weinstein's Evidence ¶ 106[02], p. 106–20 (1986). The District Court's refusal to admit the proffered completion evidence was a clear abuse of discretion.

"While much of the controversy in this case has centered on whether Rule 106 applies, we find it unnecessary to address that issue. Clearly the concerns underlying Rule 106 are relevant here, but, as the general rules of relevancy permit a ready resolution to this case, we need go no further in exploring the scope and meaning of Rule 106."

UNITED STATES v. BARRENTINE, 591 F.2d 1069 (5th Cir.1979), cert. denied, 444 U.S. 990, 100 S.Ct. 521, 62 L.Ed.2d 419 (1979). A number of defendants were convicted of conspiring to transport gambling paraphernalia in interstate commerce and to conduct an illegal gambling business. Barbara and Bobby Smith were among those convicted. Charles Michael Bland was a member of the conspiracy but he had become a government informant and was not indicted.

"The Smiths raise two evidentiary issues that require treatment. Bland testified on redirect examination that he made a trip to Texas to pick up 100 pounds of marijuana at the direction of Bobby Smith. A few moments later Bland also testified that Smith was 'seeing' Bland's wife. The Smiths first contend that this evidence placed Bobby Smith's character in evidence in violation of Rule 404 of the Federal Rules of Evidence and was not offered to show motive, plan, scheme, intent or identity.

"The questioned evidence was allowed only after the defense had cross-examined Bland concerning his prior arrests in Texas and Georgia and the reason for his decision to talk to the FBI. On redirect the prosecution probed into these matters to develop Bland's testimony that he had been directed to purchase the marijuana by Bobby Smith and had elected to talk to the FBI because of Smith's involvement with his wife.

"We find no fault with defense counsel's cross-examination of Bland concerning his arrests. * * * When the witness is the star witness, or was an accomplice or participant in the crime for which the defendant is being prosecuted, the importance of full cross-examination to disclose possible bias is necessarily increased. See Beaudine v. United States, 368 F.2d 417, 424 (5th Cir.1966).

"Bland's cross-examination, however, opened the door to a new line of questioning on redirect. Cross-examination on a part of a transaction enables the opposing party to elicit evidence on redirect examination of the whole transaction at least to the extent that it relates to the same subject. Harrison v. United States, 387 F.2d 614 (5th Cir.1968). We are assisted in our resolution of the present problem by Beck v. United States, 317 F.2d 865 (5th Cir.1963):

> When the defense opened up the question * * * the prosecution was properly allowed to counteract that evidence or rehabilitate the witness, even if in doing so the evidence offered made the defendant appear as an unsavory character."

DANIELSON v. HANFORD

Court of Appeals of Minnesota, 1984.
352 N.W.2d 758.

LESLIE, JUDGE.

Plaintiffs brought wrongful death and personal injury actions against the estate of Debra Hanford, alleging that her negligent driving caused a head-on collision. Plaintiffs' actions were consolidated for trial on the issue of liability alone, and a jury found that Hanford had not been driving at the time of the accident. Judgment was entered in favor of Hanford's estate, and plaintiffs' motions for judgment notwithstanding the verdict or for a new trial were denied. Plaintiffs appeal, alleging errors of law occurring at trial. We affirm.

FACTS

These actions arose out of a two-car, head-on collision, which occurred on August 17, 1980. Ray Willard was driving one vehicle with Maxine Willard, Ronald Danielson, and Emma Danielson riding as passengers. The other vehicle—a Camaro—was occupied by Duane Voges, Sandra Voges, Debra Hanford and Gary Ottum. Gary Ottum was the only occupant of the Camaro who survived the accident.

Following the accident numerous lawsuits were commenced for personal injury and wrongful death. Because it was uncertain whether Duane Voges or Debra Hanford had been driving the Camaro at the time of the accident, this trial was commenced to determine who was the driver of the Camaro.

Prior to trial the court ruled that neither experts nor lay persons would be allowed to render any opinion concerning who had been driving the vehicle. The court reasoned that the severity of the accident and the almost total destruction of the Camaro left no basis for any person to render a meaningful or helpful opinion concerning the driver of the vehicle. The court concluded, in accordance with Rule 701 and Rule 702, Minn.R.Evid., that any opinion on this issue would be prejudicial and would not assist the jury's understanding of the evidence.

Therefore, the parties agreed that a portion of the investigating trooper's accident report would not be allowed into evidence. That report contained a statement by Gary Ottum that he was "95 percent sure" *Debra Hanford* had been driving the Camaro, with a notation by the trooper immediately following which indicated in parentheses: "Positions of the victims trapped in the vehicle showed *Duane Voges* as the driver." (Emphasis supplied.)

During the course of the trial, however, counsel for appellant Willard began to cross-examine the trooper as follows:

> Q. Did you record anything in your notes or in your official report that would indicate that you disbelieved or doubted what Mr. Ottum told you? Did you write anything critical of what he said to you?
>
> A. I guess I did, in my official report.
>
> Q. I want you to tell me, looking at the official report, if you said anything that Mr. Ottum—recorded anything that Mr. Ottum said to you was incorrect or not the truth specific reference to Mr. Ottum?
>
> A. In reference to Mr. Ottum's statements to me, I did in parenthesis put my observation, which was contrary to what Mr. Ottum had told me in a portion of his statement. I put in parenthesis—
>
> Q. Listen to me one more second, Officer. Did you write anything in that statement, did you write anything or make any notation or did you tell anyone else in your department or your supervisor that Mr. Ottum told you something that was not the truth, and I am talking about specific reference to Mr. Ottum, not your own surmise?
>
> A. I believe I am referring to Mr. Ottum when I am in the portion where I am conversing with Mr. Ottum—excuse me—and logging his statements, I did write something that was contrary to a portion of what Ottum said.
>
> * * *

Following this questioning and outside the hearing of the jury, counsel for respondent Debra Hanford requested that the court allow redirect examination of the trooper to indicate what he had noted in his report, since counsel for appellant Willard had allegedly "opened the door" to this evidence. Counsel for appellant Willard objected, asserting that his questioning had been designed simply to demonstrate that Gary Ottum had appeared credible to the trooper, whereas the notation by the trooper consisted of the trooper's opinion on who had been driving the Camaro. Counsel for all other appellants joined in the objection.

After considering the arguments by counsel, the court concluded that the door was opened for receipt of the trooper's accident report notation, although the purpose of admission would be limited by an appropriate instruction. The court allowed the trooper to testify concerning his notation in the accident report. In its final instructions the trial court cautioned:

> You also heard testimony from [the trooper] by way of his reading from his report that he had indicated in the report that the position of the bodies indicated to him Duane Voges was the driver. This statement of [the trooper] does not go to the ultimate issue of who was driving the car, but is only to show that [the trooper] did in fact question the accuracy of Gary Ottum's statement that he was 95 percent sure Debra Hanford was driving the car.

The jury returned a verdict determining that Duane Voges had been the driver of the Camaro. Appellants Willard, Ottum, Voges and Danielsons moved for a judgment notwithstanding the verdict or a new trial. This appeal is from the trial court's denial of those motions.

* * *

ANALYSIS

I.

The trial court properly applied the doctrine of curative admissibility in this instance.

The appellants claim that the trial court erred by allowing the trooper's notation concerning the positions of the bodies to be offered into evidence, since that notation constituted an opinion by the trooper which had been previously disallowed by the court. The appellants argue that counsel for appellant Willard was only questioning the trooper about Gary Ottum's credibility, and not about the trooper's personal opinions concerning who had been driving the Camaro.

The respondent replies that the questioning by counsel for appellant Willard created the inference that the trooper believed Gary Ottum; thus, the door was opened to rebuttal testimony consisting of the trooper's notation to the contrary. The respondent argues that the doctrine of curative admissibility was properly applied by the court in this instance to allow the introduction of the trooper's notations.

The doctrine of curative admissibility, expressed in Busch v. Busch Construction, Inc., 262 N.W.2d 377, 386 (Minn.1977), "allows a party to present otherwise inadmissible evidence on an evidentiary point where an opponent has 'opened the door' by introducing similarly inadmissible evidence on the same point." *Busch* explains:

> In order to be entitled as a matter of right to present rebutting evidence on an evidentiary fact: (a) the original evidence must be inadmissible and prejudicial, (b) the rebuttal evidence must be similarly inadmissible, and (c) the rebuttal evidence must be limited to the same evidentiary fact as the original inadmissible evidence.

Id., 262 N.W.2d at 387. (Footnote omitted.)

When the above doctrine is applied to the contested portion of the cross-examination in this instance it is apparent that the trooper's original replies to appellant Willard's questions were not prejudicial to respondent Hanford—rather, the trooper's replies to the questions consistently indicated that he did not agree with Gary Ottum's statement that respondent Hanford had been driving the Camaro. Although the actual replies by the trooper were not prejudicial, however, appellant Willard's questions to the trooper themselves created an inadmissible and prejudicial impression that the trooper did not disbelieve Gary Ottum. The Minnesota Supreme Court has not addressed the question whether inquiry alone may trigger the doctrine of curative admissibility, but Professor McCormick has stated:

> [I]f the incompetent evidence, *or even the inquiry eliciting it,* is so prejudice-arousing that an objection or motion to strike can not have erased the harm, then it seems that the adversary should be entitled to answer it as of right.

McCormick, *Handbook of the Law of Evidence,* § 57 (2d ed., 1972). (Footnote omitted; emphasis supplied.) In this instance the prejudice by appellant Willard's questions could not have been eliminated by a motion to strike; thus, the doctrine of curative admissibility was properly applied in this instance, and the trooper's responses concerning the accident report were properly admitted.

II.

A new trial was properly denied appellants Ottum, Danielsons and Voges, since the questioning by counsel for appellant Willard did not constitute prejudicial error.

The appellants claim that the questioning by counsel for appellant Willard constituted an irregularity in the trial proceedings which deprived them of a fair trial. See Rule 59.01(1), Minn.R.Civ.P.

In view of the determination that evidence of the trooper's notation was properly admitted, any conclusion that the appellants were deprived of a fair trial must rest upon a decision that the limiting instruction of the court was not sufficient to avoid prejudice to the appellants.

After considering appellants' motions for judgment notwithstanding the verdict or a new trial, the court determined that its limiting instruction was sufficient to avoid any potential prejudice to appellants. This determination by the trial court was an exercise of its sound discretion should not be reversed, absent abuse. Cambern v. Sioux Tools, Inc., 323 N.W.2d 795 (Minn.1982).

We find that the trial court's determination was reasonable.

* * *

III.

The trial court properly excluded rebuttal opinion testimony on the issue of the driver's identity.

Once the notation of the trooper concerning the driver of the Camaro was introduced, the appellants argue they should have been allowed to offer rebuttal opinion testimony. Specifically, the appellants claim they should have been allowed to introduce evidence that the trooper demanded blood samples from the bodies of both Debra Hanford and Duane Voges, indicating that the trooper did not actually know who had been driving the Camaro. In addition, the appellants claim they were erroneously denied the opportunity to present testimony by a medical doctor concerning the location of bruises on Debra Hanford and Duane Voges, and the doctor's opinion concerning where Hanford and Voges had been seated when they received those bruises. The appellants offer two reasons why this evidence should have been allowed: (a) the doctrine of curative admissibility, and (b) independent admissibility of the evidence.

(a) *Doctrine of curative admissibility.* As indicated above, the doctrine of curative admissibility requires that the original evidence be inadmissible and prejudicial. Busch v. Busch Construction, Inc., 262 N.W.2d 377 (Minn.1977). Since the trooper's testimony concerning his notation has been determined admissible, the doctrine is not applicable here to allow rebuttal opinion testimony.

(b) *Independent admissibility of the evidence.* Since the original evidence concerning Trooper Garvey's notation was admissible, it was within the trial court's discretion to determine whether rebuttal opinion testimony should be allowed. Busch v. Busch Construction, Inc., 262 N.W.2d at 387; Thurman v. Pepsi–Cola Bottling Co., 289 N.W.2d 141, 145 (Minn.1980). The trial court clearly indicated to the parties prior to trial that expert opinion testimony would be prejudicial and would not assist the jury. This decision is justified by the almost total destruction of the vehicle. The allowance of testimony concerning the trooper's notation with an appropriate limiting instruction does not alter the conclusion that any additional opinion testimony would still be prejudicial and of little assistance to the jury. It is therefore our determination that the trial court's decision to disallow this evidence, and its reaffirmance of that decision upon the motion for a new trial, did not constitute an abuse of discretion. See Renne v. Gustafson, 292 Minn. 218, 194 N.W.2d 267 (1972).

* * *

Decision

The trial court's rulings upon the various evidentiary issues raised at trial were correct, and the court therefore properly denied appellants' post-trial motions contesting the propriety of those rulings.

Affirmed.

Note

When the evidence to be answered has been admitted over objection, Wigmore argued that the objector should be precluded from responding with counter-evidence, as his exception on appeal should suffice. See 1 Wigmore, Evidence § 15 (Tillers rev. 1983). Compare Lake Roland Elevated Ry. Co. v. Weir, 86 Md. 273, 37 A. 714, 715 (1897) ("If, after objection is made to testimony, the trial court admits it, the plainest principles of justice, to say nothing of consistency in the court's rulings, would require that the other party be permitted to meet it.").

CANTRELL v. SUPERIOR LOAN CORPORATION, 603 S.W.2d 627, 643–44 (Mo.App.1980). "In addition the curative admissibility doctrine can be invoked only if the cross-examination of appellant about his purported attempt to get Mrs. Clark to testify falsely was improper cross-examination. Watson v. Landvatter, 517 S.W.2d 117, 122[8–9] (Mo. banc 1974). If it were proper cross-examination, this rule cannot be utilized by appellants, as it is used only to refute adverse inferences created by irrelevant evidence.

"A witness may properly be interrogated as to attempts to tamper with, or influence, other witnesses for purposes of impeachment for interest and bias. Strahl v. Turner, 310 S.W.2d 833, 844[15] (Mo.1958); State v. Preslar, 318 Mo. 679, 300 S.W. 687 (1927); 98 C.J.S. Witnesses § 560(p), pages 515–516. Thus the cross-examination of appellant as to this issue was proper and the curative admissibility doctrine could not be invoked."

BARSON v. E.R. SQUIBB & SONS, INC., 682 P.2d 832, 840 (Utah 1984). "Squibb introduced the issue of efficacy, beginning with the first witness at trial. During cross-examination of Mrs. Barson, plaintiffs' first witness, counsel for defendant solicited testimony relating to whether the injection of Delalutin did what it was supposed to do, that is, stop spotting. Squibb next solicited cross-examination testimony from plaintiffs' second witness, Dr. Parkinson, as to his opinion concerning the effectiveness of Delalutin. Plaintiffs did not raise the issue of efficacy with either witness.

"We do not need to reach the issue of whether or not efficacy evidence was in and of itself admissible, since, even if the evidence was inadmissible, 'if a party interjects into a case incompetent evidence tending to establish immaterial or unrelated facts, he cannot complain on appeal that his adversary subsequently offered and was permitted to introduce the same kind of evidence.'"

MAYNARD v. STATE, 685 S.W.2d 60, 65–66 (Tex.Crim.App.1985). "It is the general rule that when the defendant offers the same evidence to which he earlier objected, he is not in a position to complain on appeal. Womble v. State, 618 S.W.2d 59 (Tex.Cr.App.1981); Cameron v. State, 530 S.W.2d 841 (Tex.Cr.App.1975); Palmer v. State, 475 S.W.2d 797 (Tex.Cr.App.1972). This principle is better known as the doctrine of curative admissibility. The court of appeals relied on this doctrine in holding that appellant waived his objection to the admission of the extraneous offense. There exists, however, a corollary to this rule, unmentioned by the court of appeals, that the harmful effect of improperly admitted evidence is not cured by the fact that the defendant sought to meet, destroy, or explain it by the introduction of rebutting evidence. Such testimony does not act as a waiver of the right to challenge the admissibility of the evidence originally admitted. Evers v. State, 576 S.W.2d 46 (Tex.Cr.App.1978); Alvarez v. State, 511 S.W.2d 493 (Tex.Cr.App.1973); Nicholas v. State, 502 S.W.2d 169 (Tex. Cr.App.1973). Under these authorities, the appellant did not waive his objection to the legal admissibility of the inventory if he testified to meet, destroy, or explain the existence of the marihuana and the switchblade knife in his car. In Thomas v. State, 572 S.W.2d 507 (Tex.Cr.App.1978), Presiding Judge Onion explained the operation of the rule and its exception thusly:

> '[I]f a defendant takes the witness stand to refute, deny, contradict, or impeach evidence or testimony properly objected to, no waiver of the objection occurs. But if a defendant in testifying admits or confirms the truth of the facts or evidence objected to, even if attempting to create a defense based on or beyond those facts, a waiver of the objection does occur. The one possible exception to this principle is that no waiver will be found where a defendant objects to evidence or testimony not tied directly or indirectly to the elements of the case and then in testifying himself admits those facts to be true. This exception is illustrated by Alvarez v. State, supra, in which a portion of a confession saying "I always carry a pistol with me because I shot and killed a man in Lubbock not too long ago and am afraid of his people," was properly objected to as showing an extraneous offense. This Court found that the objection was not waived when the defendant took the stand and admitted on direct examination that the statement was true in attempting to explain the incident. This was an extraneous offense, not tied to the elements of the case but useful only to show the character of the defendant. However, this case appears to contradict Robbins v. State, 481 S.W.2d 419 (Tex.Cr.App.1972); Cook v. State, 409 S.W.2d 857 (Tex.Cr.App.1966); and Meadowes v. State, 368 S.W.2d 203 (Tex.Cr.App.1963), all of which held that objection to improper evidence of an extraneous offense was waived when the defendant on direct examination confirmed such facts. We express no opinion now as to this point.'

"We are now squarely confronted with the issue and we hold that no waiver occurs when, after the admission over objection of *evidence of an extraneous offense,* the defendant subsequently testifies to essentially the same facts to which he had earlier objected. This is sound policy because it is fair policy. An extraneous offense is collateral to the facts in issue at trial and is inherently prejudicial. That it actually took place does not affect its lack of relevance. To require the defendant to sit mute in the face of such harmful evidence to preserve the issue for appellate review is to unfairly hamstring the defendant at trial. Once the evidence is admitted, correctly or incorrectly, the defendant is compelled by the exigencies of trial to mitigate such inherently prejudicial evidence as best as he or she can. To the extent that *Robbins,* supra, *Cook,* supra, and *Meadowes,* supra, are inconsistent with this holding, they are overruled."

STEVEN GOODE, OLIN GUY WELLBORN III & M. MICHAEL SHARLOT, GUIDE TO THE TEXAS RULES OF EVIDENCE: CIVIL AND CRIMINAL (1988)

§ 103.1 Rule 103: Rulings on Evidence; Rule 103(a): Effect of Erroneous Ruling

* * *

Two doctrines concerning harmless error merit special mention. One is stated by the Texas Supreme Court as follows:

> The general rule is that error in the admission of testimony is deemed harmless if the objecting party subsequently permits the same or similar evidence to be introduced without objection.[9]

The Court of Criminal Appeals has announced the same principle:

> It has long been held that the admission of improper evidence will not require reversal if the same facts are proved by "other and proper" testimony.[10]

In recent years the Court of Criminal Appeals has referred to this principle as "the doctrine of curative admissibility." [11] This is an incorrect use of the term. The correct meaning of the term "curative admissibility" is exemplified by the following statement by the Supreme Court of Minnesota:

> The doctrine of curative admissibility allows a party to present otherwise inadmissible evidence on an evidentiary point where an opponent has "opened the door" by introducing similarly inadmissible evidence on the same point.[12]

Thus, the doctrine of curative admissibility, correctly identified, is closely related to the doctrine of optional completeness codified in Texas Criminal Rule 107.[13] Curative admissibility, as the term itself suggests, is a doctrine of admissibility, not of harmless error. In the cases where the Court of Criminal Appeals misuses the term, admissibility of the defendant's responsive evidence is not challenged. If it

9. Richardson v. Green, 677 S.W.2d 497, 501 (Tex.1984) (Pope, J.). But see Bunnett/Smallwood & Co. v. Helton Oil Co., 577 S.W.2d 291, 295 (Tex.Civ.App.—Amarillo 1978, no writ) ("Where a party makes a proper objection to the introduction of testimony and is overruled, he is entitled to assume that the judge will make the same ruling as to the other offers of similar testimony, and he is not required to repeat the objection.").

10. Alvarez v. State, 511 S.W.2d 493, 498 (Tex.Crim.App.1973). Accord, Nicholas v. State, 502 S.W.2d 169, 175 (Tex. Crim.App.1973) ("[I]f a fact is proven without objection, its erroneous proof over objection, although still error, is harmless error since the same facts have been proven without objection.").

11. Maynard v. State, 685 S.W.2d 60, 65 (Tex.Crim.App.1985); Thomas v. State, 572 S.W.2d 507, 512 (Tex.Crim.App.1976).

12. Busch v. Busch Constr., Inc., 262 N.W.2d 377, 386 (Minn.1977). See generally 1 Wigmore, Evidence § 15 (Tillers rev. 1983) (collecting numerous cases from many jurisdictions).

13. See §§ 106.1 & 107.1 infra.

were, the true doctrine of curative admissibility would apply and provide admissibility. The issue in these cases is whether the evidence presented by the defendant in response to inadmissible evidence improperly admitted over his objection has the effect of rendering the original error harmless, or of "waiving" it. This is a matter quite distinct from curative admissibility.

Even though misnamed by the Court of Criminal Appeals, the general rule is well established in both civil and criminal cases that an error in admitting evidence may be rendered harmless or waived if the aggrieved party himself introduces evidence to the same effect, or permits the opponent to do so at another point in the trial without objection. The general rule is subject to an important qualification, however. In criminal cases,

> While an accused may waive the error of improper admission of evidence if such evidence comes in elsewhere without objection, he does not waive the error if he offers "testimony to rebut, destroy, or explain" the improperly admitted evidence.[14]

The same qualification is recognized in civil cases:

> If incompetent evidence is admitted over proper objection, the objecting party is not left to suffer injury in the instant trial and take his chances on appeal and retrial. He may defend himself without waiving his objection. He may explain or rebut or demonstrate the untruthfulness of the incompetent evidence.[15]

The second special doctrine about harmless error concerns nonjury cases. In a case tried to the court, an appellate court will presume that the trial judge disregarded any incompetent evidence.[16] Therefore, reception of inadmissible evidence in a nonjury case will not require reversal unless the record shows an absence of competent evidence to support the judgment.[17]

14. Alvarez v. State, 511 S.W.2d 493, 499 (Tex.Crim.App.1973). Accord, Maynard v. State, 685 S.W.2d 60, 65 (Tex.Crim. App.1985); Thomas v. State, 572 S.W.2d 507, 512 (Tex.Crim.App.1976); Nicholas v. State, 502 S.W.2d 169, 175 (Tex.Crim.App. 1973).

15. State v. Chavers, 454 S.W.2d 395, 398 (Tex.1970). Accord, 1 Wigmore, Evidence § 18, at 836–38 (Tillers rev. 1983) ("[A]n opponent ordinarily waives his own objection if he makes subsequent use of evidence similar to that which he had previously objected, except where such subsequent use was done merely in self-defense, to explain or rebut the original evidence.").

16. See Gillespie v. Gillespie, 644 S.W.2d 449, 450 (Tex.1982).

17. See id.

Chapter 4

WITNESSES
[FED.R.EVID. ART. VI]

SECTION 1. COMPETENCY *
[FED.R.EVID. 601–606]

ROCK v. ARKANSAS

Supreme Court of the United States, 1987.
483 U.S. 44, 107 S.Ct. 2704, 97 L.Ed.2d 37 (1987).

JUSTICE BLACKMUN delivered the opinion of the Court.

The issue presented in this case is whether Arkansas' evidentiary rule prohibiting the admission of hypnotically refreshed testimony violated petitioner's constitutional right to testify on her own behalf as a defendant in a criminal case.

I

Petitioner Vickie Lorene Rock was charged with manslaughter in the death of her husband, Frank Rock, on July 2, 1983. A dispute had been simmering about Frank's wish to move from the couple's small apartment adjacent to Vickie's beauty parlor to a trailer she owned outside town. That night a fight erupted when Frank refused to let petitioner eat some pizza and prevented her from leaving the apartment to get something else to eat. App. 98, 103–104. When police arrived on the scene they found Frank on the floor with a bullet wound in his chest. Petitioner urged the officers to help her husband, Tr. 230, and cried to a sergeant who took her in charge, "please save him" and "don't let him die." *Id.*, at 268. The police removed her from the

* See 2 Wigmore, Evidence chs. 19–22, 24, 26 (Chadbourn rev. 1979); 6 id. §§ 1815–1829 (Chadbourn rev. 1976); 8 id. §§ 2345–2356 (McNaughton rev. 1961); McCormick, Evidence ch. 7 (4th ed. 1992); Crump, Jury Misconduct, Jury Interviews, and the Federal Rules of Evidence: Is the Broad Exclusionary Principle of Rule 606(b) Justified?, 66 N.C.L.Rev. 509 (1988); Melton, Children's Competency to Testify, 5 Law & Human Behavior 73 (1981); Thompson, Challenge to the Decisionmaking Process—Federal Rule of Evidence 606(b) and the Constitutional Right to a Fair Trial, 38 Sw.L.J. 1187 (1985).

building because she was upset and because she interfered with their investigation by her repeated attempts to use the telephone to call her husband's parents. *Id.,* at 263–264, 267–268. According to the testimony of one of the investigating officers, petitioner told him that "she stood up to leave the room and [her husband] grabbed her by the throat and choked her and threw her against the wall and * * * at that time she walked over and picked up the weapon and pointed it toward the floor and he hit her again and she shot him." *Id.,* at 281.

Because petitioner could not remember the precise details of the shooting, her attorney suggested that she submit to hypnosis in order to refresh her memory. Petitioner was hypnotized twice by Doctor Bettye Back, a licensed neuropsychologist with training in the field of hypnosis. *Id.,* at 901–903. Doctor Back interviewed petitioner for an hour prior to the first hypnosis session, taking notes on petitioner's general history and her recollections of the shooting. App. 46–47. Both hypnosis sessions were recorded on tape. *Id.,* at 53. Petitioner did not relate any new information during either of the sessions, *id.,* at 78, 83, but, after the hypnosis, she was able to remember that at the time of the incident she had her thumb on the hammer of the gun, but had not held her finger on the trigger. She also recalled that the gun had discharged when her husband grabbed her arm during the scuffle. *Id.,* at 29, 38. As a result of the details that petitioner was able to remember about the shooting, her counsel arranged for a gun expert to examine the handgun, a single-action Hawes .22 Deputy Marshal. That inspection revealed that the gun was defective and prone to fire, when hit or dropped, without the trigger's being pulled. Tr. 662–663, 711.

When the prosecutor learned of the hypnosis sessions, he filed a motion to exclude petitioner's testimony. The trial judge held a pretrial hearing on the motion and concluded that no hypnotically refreshed testimony would be admitted. The court issued an order limiting petitioner's testimony to "matters remembered and stated to the examiner prior to being placed under hypnosis." App. to Pet. for Cert. xvii. At trial, petitioner introduced testimony by the gun expert, Tr. 647–712, but the court limited petitioner's own description of the events on the day of the shooting to a reiteration of the sketchy information in Doctor Back's notes. See App. 96–104. The jury convicted petitioner on the manslaughter charge and she was sentenced to 10 years' imprisonment and a $10,000 fine.

On appeal, the Supreme Court of Arkansas rejected petitioner's claim that the limitations on her testimony violated her right to present her defense. The court concluded that "the dangers of admitting this kind of testimony outweigh whatever probative value it may have," and decided to follow the approach of States that have held hypnotically refreshed testimony of witnesses inadmissible *per se.* 288 Ark. 566, 573, 708 S.W.2d 78, 81 (1986). Although the court acknowledged that "a defendant's right to testify is fundamental," *id.,* at 578, 708 S.W.2d, at 84, it ruled that the exclusion of petitioner's testimony did not violate her constitutional rights. Any "prejudice or deprivation" she suffered "was minimal and resulted from her own actions and not by any erroneous ruling of the court." *Id.*, at 580, 708 S.W.2d, at 86. We granted certiorari, 479 U.S. 947, 107 S.Ct. 430, 93 L.Ed.2d 381 (1986), to consider the constitutionality of Arkansas' *per se* rule excluding a criminal defendant's hypnotically refreshed testimony.

II

Petitioner's claim that her testimony was impermissibly excluded is bottomed on her constitutional right to testify in her own defense. At this point in the development of our adversary system, it cannot be doubted that a defendant in a criminal case has the right to take the witness stand and to testify in his or her own defense. This, of course, is a change from the historic common-law view, which was that all parties to litigation, including criminal defendants, were disqualified from testifying because of their interest in the outcome of the trial. See generally 2 J. Wigmore, Evidence §§ 576, 579 (J. Chadbourn rev. 1979). The principal rationale for this rule was the possible untrustworthiness of a party's testimony. Under the common law, the practice did develop of permitting criminal defendants to tell their side of the story, but they were limited to making an unsworn statement that could not be elicited through direct examination by counsel and was not subject to cross-examination. *Id.*, at § 579, p. 827.

This Court in *Ferguson v. Georgia*, 365 U.S. 570, 573–582, 81 S.Ct. 756, 758–763, 5 L.Ed.2d 783 (1961), detailed the history of the transition from a rule of a defendant's incompetency to a rule of competency. As the Court there recounted, it came to be recognized that permitting a defendant to testify advances both the " 'detection of guilt' " and " 'the protection of innocence,' " *id.*, at 581, 81 S.Ct., at 762, quoting 1 Am.L.Rev. 396 (1867), and by the end of the second half of the 19th century,[5] all States except Georgia had enacted statutes that declared criminal defendants competent to testify. See 365 U.S., at 577 and n. 6, 596–598, 81 S.Ct., at 760 and n. 6, 770–771.[6] Congress enacted a general competency statute in the Act of Mar. 16, 1878, 20 Stat. 30, as amended, 18 U.S.C. § 3481, and similar developments followed in other common-law countries. Thus, more than 25 years ago this Court was able to state:

5. The removal of the disqualifications for accused persons occurred later than the establishment of the competence to testify of civil parties. 2 J. Wigmore, Evidence § 579, p. 826 (J. Chadbourn rev. 1979). This was not due to concern that criminal defendants were more likely to be unreliable than other witnesses, but to a concern for the accused:

> "If, being competent, he failed to testify, that (it was believed) would damage his cause more seriously than if he were able to claim that his silence were enforced by law. Moreover, if he did testify, that (it was believed) would injure more than assist his cause, since by undergoing the ordeal of cross-examination, he would appear at a disadvantage dangerous even to an innocent man." *Id.*, at 828.

6. The Arkansas Constitution guarantees an accused the right "to be heard by himself and his counsel." Art. 2, § 10. Rule 601 of the Arkansas Rules of Evidence provides a general rule of competency: "Every person is competent to be a witness except as otherwise provided in these rules."

"In sum, decades ago the considered consensus of the English-speaking world came to be that there was no rational justification for prohibiting the sworn testimony of the accused, who above all others may be in a position to meet the prosecution's case." *Ferguson v. Georgia,* 365 U.S., at 582, 81 S.Ct., at 763.

The right to testify on one's own behalf at a criminal trial has sources in several provisions of the Constitution. It is one of the rights that "are essential to due process of law in a fair adversary process." *Faretta v. California,* 422 U.S. 806, 819, n. 15, 95 S.Ct. 2525, 2533 n. 15, 45 L.Ed.2d 562 (1975). The necessary ingredients of the Fourteenth Amendment's guarantee that no one shall be deprived of liberty without due process of law include a right to be heard and to offer testimony:

"A person's right to reasonable notice of a charge against him, and *an opportunity to be heard in his defense*—a right to his day in court—are basic in our system of jurisprudence; and these rights include, as a minimum, a right to examine the witnesses against him, to offer testimony, and to be represented by counsel." (Emphasis added.) *In re Oliver,* 333 U.S. 257, 273, 68 S.Ct. 499, 507, 92 L.Ed. 682 (1948).

See also *Ferguson v. Georgia,* 365 U.S., at 602, 81 S.Ct., at 773. (Clark, J., concurring) (Fourteenth Amendment secures "right of a criminal defendant to choose between silence and testifying in his own behalf").

The right to testify is also found in the Compulsory Process Clause of the Sixth Amendment, which grants a defendant the right to call "witnesses in his favor," a right that is guaranteed in the criminal courts of the States by the Fourteenth Amendment. *Washington v. Texas,* 388 U.S. 14, 17–19, 87 S.Ct. 1920, 1922–1923, 18 L.Ed.2d 1019 (1967). Logically included in the accused's right to call witnesses whose testimony is "material and favorable to his defense," *United States v. Valenzuela-Bernal,* 458 U.S. 858, 867, 102 S.Ct. 3440, 3446, 73 L.Ed.2d 1193 (1982), is a right to testify himself, should he decide it is in his favor to do so. In fact, the most important witness for the defense in many criminal cases is the defendant himself. There is no justification today for a rule that denies an accused the opportunity to offer his own testimony. Like the truthfulness of other witnesses, the defendant's veracity, which was the concern behind the original common-law rule, can be tested adequately by cross-examination. See generally Westen, The Compulsory Process Clause, 73 Mich.L.Rev. 71, 119–120 (1974).

Moreover, in *Faretta v. California,* 422 U.S., at 819, 95 S.Ct., at 2533, the Court recognized that the Sixth Amendment

"grants to the accused *personally* the right to make his defense. It is the accused, not counsel, who must be 'informed of the nature and cause of the accusation,' who must be 'confronted with the witnesses against him,' and who must be accorded 'compulsory process for obtaining witnesses in his favor.'" (Emphasis added.)

Even more fundamental to a personal defense than the right of self-representation, which was found to be "necessarily implied by the structure of the Amendment," *ibid.,* is an accused's right to present his own version of events in his own words. A defendant's opportunity to conduct his own defense by calling witnesses is incomplete if he may not present himself as a witness.

The opportunity to testify is also a necessary corollary to the Fifth Amendment's guarantee against compelled testimony. In *Harris v. New York,* 401 U.S. 222, 230, 91 S.Ct. 643, 648, 28 L.Ed.2d 1 (1971), the Court stated: "Every criminal defendant is privileged to testify in his own defense, or to refuse to do so." *Id.,* at 225, 91 S.Ct., at 645. Three of the dissenting Justices in that case agreed that the Fifth Amendment encompasses this right: "[The Fifth Amendment's privilege against self-incrimination] is fulfilled only when an accused is guaranteed the right 'to remain silent unless he chooses to speak in the unfettered exercise of his own will.' * * * The choice of whether to testify in one's own defense * * * is an exercise of the constitutional privilege." *Id.,* at 230, 91 S.Ct., at 648, quoting *Malloy v. Hogan,* 378 U.S. 1, 8, 84 S.Ct. 1489, 1493, 9 L.Ed.2d 653 (1964). (Emphasis removed.)

III

The question now before the Court is whether a criminal defendant's right to testify may be restricted by a state rule that excludes her posthypnosis testimony. This is not the first time this Court has faced a constitutional challenge to a state rule, designed to ensure trustworthy evidence, that interfered with the ability of a defendant to offer testimony. In *Washington v. Texas,* 388 U.S. 14, 87 S.Ct. 1920, 18 L.Ed.2d 1019 (1967), the Court was confronted with a state statute that prevented persons charged as principals, accomplices, or accessories in the same crime from being introduced as witnesses for one another. The statute, like the original common-law prohibition on testimony by the accused, was grounded in a concern for the reliability of evidence presented by an interested party:

> "It was thought that if two persons charged with the same crime were allowed to testify on behalf of each other, 'each would try to swear the other out of the charge.' This rule, as well as the other disqualifications for interest, rested on the unstated premises that the right to present witnesses was subordinate to the court's interest in preventing perjury, and that erroneous decisions were best avoided by preventing the jury from hearing any testimony that might be perjured, even if it were the only testimony available on a crucial issue." (Footnote omitted.) *Id.,* at 21, 87 S.Ct., at 1924, quoting *Benson v. United States,* 146 U.S. 325, 335, 13 S.Ct. 60, 63, 36 L.Ed. 991 (1892).

As the Court recognized, the incompetency of a codefendant to testify had been rejected on nonconstitutional grounds in 1918, when the Court, refusing to be bound by "the dead hand of the common-law rule of 1789," stated:

> " '[T]he conviction of our time [is] that the truth is more likely to be arrived at by hearing the testimony of all persons of competent understanding who may seem to have knowledge of the facts involved

> in a case, leaving the credit and weight of such testimony to be determined by the jury or by the court. * * * '" 388 U.S., at 22, 87 S.Ct., at 1924, quoting *Rosen v. United States,* 245 U.S. 467, 471, 38 S.Ct. 148, 150, 62 L.Ed. 406 (1918).

The Court concluded that this reasoning was compelled by the Sixth Amendment's protections for the accused. In particular, the Court reasoned that the Sixth Amendment was designed in part "to make the testimony of a defendant's witnesses admissible on his behalf in court." 388 U.S., at 22, 87 S.Ct., at 1925.

With the rationale for the common-law incompetency rule thus rejected on constitutional grounds, the Court found that the mere presence of the witness in the courtroom was not enough to satisfy the Constitution's Compulsory Process Clause. By preventing the defendant from having the benefit of his accomplice's testimony, "the State *arbitrarily* denied him the right to put on the stand a witness who was physically and mentally capable of testifying to events that he had personally observed, and whose testimony would have been relevant and material to the defense." (Emphasis added.) *Id.,* at 23, 87 S.Ct., at 1925.

Just as a State may not apply an arbitrary rule of competence to exclude a material defense witness from taking the stand, it also may not apply a rule of evidence that permits a witness to take the stand, but arbitrarily excludes material portions of his testimony. In *Chambers v. Mississippi,* 410 U.S. 284, 93 S.Ct. 1038, 35 L.Ed.2d 297 (1973), the Court invalidated a State's hearsay rule on the ground that it abridged the defendant's right to "present witnesses in his own defense." *Id.,* at 302, 93 S.Ct., at 1049. Chambers was tried for a murder to which another person repeatedly had confessed in the presence of acquaintances. The State's hearsay rule, coupled with a "voucher" rule that did not allow the defendant to cross-examine the confessed murderer directly, prevented Chambers from introducing testimony concerning these confessions, which were critical to his defense. This Court reversed the judgment of conviction, holding that when a state rule of evidence conflicts with the right to present witnesses, the rule may "not be applied mechanistically to defeat the ends of justice," but must meet the fundamental standards of due process. *Ibid.* In the Court's view, the State in *Chambers* did not demonstrate that the hearsay testimony in that case, which bore "assurances of trustworthiness" including corroboration by other evidence, would be unreliable, and thus the defendant should have been able to introduce the exculpatory testimony. *Ibid.*

Of course, the right to present relevant testimony is not without limitation. The right "may, in appropriate cases, bow to accommodate other legitimate interests in the criminal trial process." *Id.,* at 295, 93 S.Ct., at 1046.[11] But restrictions of a defendant's right to testify may

11. Numerous state procedural and evidentiary rules control the presentation of evidence and do not offend the defendant's right to testify. See, *e.g., Chambers v. Mis-*

not be arbitrary or disproportionate to the purposes they are designed to serve. In applying its evidentiary rules a State must evaluate whether the interests served by a rule justify the limitation imposed on the defendant's constitutional right to testify.

IV

The Arkansas rule enunciated by the state courts does not allow a trial court to consider whether posthypnosis testimony may be admissible in a particular case; it is a *per se* rule prohibiting the admission at trial of any defendant's hypnotically refreshed testimony on the ground that such testimony is always unreliable. Thus, in Arkansas, an accused's testimony is limited to matters that he or she can prove were remembered *before* hypnosis. This rule operates to the detriment of any defendant who undergoes hypnosis, without regard to the reasons for it, the circumstances under which it took place, or any independent verification of the information it produced.[13]

In this case, the application of that rule had a significant adverse effect on petitioner's ability to testify. It virtually prevented her from describing any of the events that occurred on the day of the shooting, despite corroboration of many of those events by other witnesses. Even more importantly, under the court's rule petitioner was not permitted to describe the actual shooting except in the words contained in Doctor Back's notes. The expert's description of the gun's tendency to misfire would have taken on greater significance if the jury had heard petitioner testify that she did not have her finger on the trigger and that the gun went off when her husband hit her arm.

In establishing its *per se* rule, the Arkansas Supreme Court simply followed the approach taken by a number of States that have decided that hypnotically enhanced testimony should be excluded at trial on the ground that it tends to be unreliable.[14] Other States that have

sissippi, 410 U.S., at 284, 302, 93 S.Ct., at 1049 ("In the exercise of this right, the accused, as is required of the State, must comply with established rules of procedure and evidence designed to assure both fairness and reliability in the ascertainment of guilt and innocence"); *Washington v. Texas,* 388 U.S. 14, 23, n. 21, 87 S.Ct. 1920, 1925, n. 21, 18 L.Ed.2d 1019 (1967) (opinion should not be construed as disapproving testimonial privileges or nonarbitrary rules that disqualify those incapable of observing events due to mental infirmity or infancy from being witnesses).

13. The Arkansas Supreme Court took the position that petitioner was fully responsible for any prejudice that resulted from the restriction on her testimony because it was she who chose to resort to the technique of hypnosis. 288 Ark. 566, 580, 708 S.W.2d 78, 86 (1986). The prosecution and the trial court each expressed a similar view and the theme was renewed repeatedly at trial as a justification for limiting petitioner's testimony. See App. 15, 20, 21–22, 24, 36. It should be noted, however, that Arkansas had given no previous indication that it looked with disfavor on the use of hypnosis to assist in the preparation for trial and there were no previous state-court rulings on the issue.

14. See, *e.g., Contreras v. State,* 718 P.2d 129 (Alaska 1986); *State ex rel. Collins v. Superior Court, County of Maricopa,* 132 Ariz. 180, 207–208, 644 P.2d 1266, 1293–1294 (1982); *People v. Quintanar,* 659 P.2d 710, 711 (Colo.App.1982); *State v. Davis,* 490 A.2d 601 (Del.Super.1985); *Bundy v. State,* 471 So.2d 9, 18–19 (Fla.1985), cert. denied, 479 U.S. 894, 107 S.Ct. 295, 93 L.Ed.2d 269 (1986); *State v. Moreno,* 68 Haw. 233, 709 P.2d 103 (1985); *State v. Haislip,* 237 Kan. 461, 482, 701 P.2d 909, 925–926, cert. denied, 474 U.S. 1022, 106 S.Ct. 575, 88 L.Ed.2d 558 (1985); *State v.*

adopted an exclusionary rule, however, have done so for the testimony of *witnesses,* not for the testimony of a *defendant.* The Arkansas Supreme Court failed to perform the constitutional analysis that is necessary when a defendant's right to testify is at stake.[15]

Although the Arkansas court concluded that any testimony that cannot be proved to be the product of prehypnosis memory is unreliable, many courts have eschewed a *per se* rule and permit the admission of hypnotically refreshed testimony.[16] Hypnosis by trained physicians or psychologists has been recognized as a valid therapeutic technique since 1958, although there is no generally accepted theory to explain the phenomenon, or even a consensus on a single definition of hypnosis. See Council on Scientific Affairs, Scientific Status of Refreshing Recollection by the Use of Hypnosis, 253 J.A.M.A. 1918, 1918–1919 (1985)

Collins, 296 Md. 670, 464 A.2d 1028 (1983); *Commonwealth v. Kater,* 388 Mass. 519, 447 N.E.2d 1190 (1983); *People v. Gonzales,* 415 Mich. 615, 329 N.W.2d 743 (1982), opinion added to, 417 Mich. 1129, 336 N.W.2d 751 (1983); *Alsbach v. Bader,* 700 S.W.2d 823 (Mo.1985); *State v. Palmer,* 210 Neb. 206, 218, 313 N.W.2d 648, 655 (1981); *People v. Hughes,* 59 N.Y.2d 523, 466 N.Y.S.2d 255, 453 N.E.2d 484 (1983); *Robison v. State,* 677 P.2d 1080, 1085 (Okla.Crim. App.), cert. denied, 467 U.S. 1246, 104 S.Ct. 3524, 82 L.Ed.2d 831 (1984); *Commonwealth v. Nazarovitch,* 496 Pa. 97, 110, 436 A.2d 170, 177 (1981); *State v. Martin,* 101 Wash.2d 713, 684 P.2d 651 (1984). See *State v. Ture,* 353 N.W.2d 502, 513–514 (Minn.1984).

15. The Arkansas court relied on a California case, *People v. Shirley,* 31 Cal.3d 18, 181 Cal.Rptr. 243, 723 P.2d 1354, cert. denied, 459 U.S. 860, 103 S.Ct. 133, 74 L.Ed.2d 114 (1982), for much of its reasoning as to the unreliability of hypnosis. 288 Ark., at 575–578, 708 S.W.2d, at 83–84. But while the California court adopted a far stricter general rule—barring entirely testimony by any witness who has been hypnotized—it explicitly excepted testimony by an accused:

> "[W]hen it is the defendant himself—not merely a defense witness—who submits to pretrial hypnosis, the experience will not render his testimony inadmissible if he elects to take the stand. In that case, the rule we adopt herein is subject to a necessary exception to avoid impairing the fundamental right of an accused to testify in his own behalf." 31 Cal.3d, at 67, 723 P.2d, at 1384.

This case does not involve the admissibility of testimony of previously hypnotized witnesses other than criminal defendants and we express no opinion on that issue.

16. Some jurisdictions have adopted a rule that hypnosis affects the credibility, but not the admissibility, of testimony. See, *e.g., Beck v. Norris,* 801 F.2d 242, 244–245 (CA6 1986); *United States v. Awkard,* 597 F.2d 667, 669 (CA9), cert. denied, 444 U.S. 885, 100 S.Ct. 179, 62 L.Ed.2d 116 (1979); *State v. Wren,* 425 So.2d 756 (La. 1983); *State v. Brown,* 337 N.W.2d 138, 151 (N.D.1983); *State v. Glebock,* 616 S.W.2d 897, 903–904 (Tenn.Crim.App.1981); *Chapman v. State,* 638 P.2d 1280, 1282 (Wyo. 1982).

Other courts conduct an individualized inquiry in each case. See, *e.g., McQueen v. Garrison,* 814 F.2d 951, 958 (CA4 1987) (reliability evaluation); *Wicker v. McCotter,* 783 F.2d 487, 492–493 (CA5) (probative value of the testimony weighed against its prejudicial effect), cert. denied, 478 U.S. 1010, 106 S.Ct. 3310, 92 L.Ed.2d 723 (1986); *State v. Iwakiri,* 106 Idaho 618, 625, 682 P.2d 571, 578 (1984) (weigh "totality of circumstances").

In some jurisdictions, courts have established procedural prerequisites for admissibility in order to reduce the risks associated with hypnosis. Perhaps the leading case in this line is *State v. Hurd,* 86 N.J. 525, 432 A.2d 86 (1981). See also *Sprynczynatyk v. General Motors Corp.,* 771 F.2d 1112, 1122–1123 (CA8 1985), cert. denied, 475 U.S. 1046, 106 S.Ct. 1263, 89 L.Ed.2d 572 (1986); *United States v. Harrington,* 18 M.J. 797, 803 (A.C.M.R.1984); *House v. State,* 445 So.2d 815, 826–827 (Miss.1984); *State v. Beachum,* 97 N.M. 682, 689–690, 643 P.2d 246, 253–254 (App.1981), writ quashed, 98 N.M. 51, 644 P.2d 1040 (1982); *State v. Weston,* 16 Ohio App.3d 279, 287, 475 N.E.2d 805, 813 (1984); *State v. Armstrong,* 110 Wis.2d 555, 329 N.W.2d 386, cert. denied, 461 U.S. 946, 103 S.Ct. 2125, 77 L.Ed.2d 1304 (1983).

(Council Report).[17] The use of hypnosis in criminal investigations, however, is controversial, and the current medical and legal view of its appropriate role is unsettled.

Responses of individuals to hypnosis vary greatly. The popular belief that hypnosis guarantees the accuracy of recall is as yet without established foundation and, in fact, hypnosis often has no effect at all on memory. The most common response to hypnosis, however, appears to be an increase in both correct and incorrect recollections.[18] Three general characteristics of hypnosis may lead to the introduction of inaccurate memories: the subject becomes "suggestible" and may try to please the hypnotist with answers the subject thinks will be met with approval; the subject is likely to "confabulate," that is, to fill in details from the imagination in order to make an answer more coherent and complete; and, the subject experiences "memory hardening," which gives him great confidence in both true and false memories, making effective cross-examination more difficult. See generally M. Orne et al., Hypnotically Induced Testimony, in Eyewitness Testimony: Psychological Perspectives 171 (G. Wells & E. Loftus, eds., 1984); Diamond, Inherent Problems in the Use of Pretrial Hypnosis on a Prospective Witness, 68 Calif.L.Rev. 313, 333–342 (1980). Despite the unreliability that hypnosis concededly may introduce, however, the procedure has been credited as instrumental in obtaining investigative leads or identifications that were later confirmed by independent evidence. See, *e.g., People v. Hughes,* 59 N.Y.2d 523, 533, 466 N.Y.S.2d 255, 453 N.E.2d 484, 488 (1983); see generally R. Udolf, Forensic Hypnosis 11–16 (1983).

The inaccuracies the process introduces can be reduced, although perhaps not eliminated, by the use of procedural safeguards. One set of suggested guidelines calls for hypnosis to be performed only by a psychologist or psychiatrist with special training in its use and who is independent of the investigation. See Orne, The Use and Misuse of Hypnosis in Court, 27 Int'l J. Clinical and Experimental Hypnosis 311, 335–336 (1979). These procedures reduce the possibility that biases will be communicated to the hypersuggestive subject by the hypnotist. Suggestion will be less likely also if the hypnosis is conducted in a neutral setting with no one present but the hypnotist and the subject. Tape or video recording of all interrogations, before, during, and after

17. Hypnosis has been described as "involv[ing] the focusing of attention; increased responsiveness to suggestions; suspension of disbelief with a lowering of critical judgment; potential for altering perception, motor control, or memory in response to suggestions; and the subjective experience of responding involuntarily." Council Report, 253 J.A.M.A., at 1919.

18. "[W]hen hypnosis is used to refresh recollection, one of the following outcomes occurs: (1) hypnosis produces recollections that are not substantially different from nonhypnotic recollections; (2) it yields recollections that are more inaccurate than nonhypnotic memory; or, most frequently, (3) it results in more information being reported, but these recollections contain both accurate and inaccurate details * * * There are no data to support a fourth alternative, namely, that hypnosis increas-

hypnosis, can help reveal if leading questions were asked. *Id.*, at 336.[19] Such guidelines do not guarantee the accuracy of the testimony, because they cannot control the subject's own motivations or any tendency to confabulate, but they do provide a means of controlling overt suggestions.

The more traditional means of assessing accuracy of testimony also remain applicable in the case of a previously hypnotized defendant. Certain information recalled as a result of hypnosis may be verified as highly accurate by corroborating evidence. Cross-examination, even in the face of a confident defendant, is an effective tool for revealing inconsistencies. Moreover, a jury can be educated to the risks of hypnosis through expert testimony and cautionary instructions. Indeed, it is probably to a defendant's advantage to establish carefully the extent of his memory prior to hypnosis, in order to minimize the decrease in credibility the procedure might introduce.

We are not now prepared to endorse without qualifications the use of hypnosis as an investigative tool; scientific understanding of the phenomenon and of the means to control the effects of hypnosis is still in its infancy. Arkansas, however, has not justified the exclusion of *all* of a defendant's testimony that the defendant is unable to prove to be the product of prehypnosis memory. A State's legitimate interest in barring unreliable evidence does not extend to *per se* exclusions that may be reliable in an individual case. Wholesale inadmissibility of a defendant's testimony is an arbitrary restriction on the right to testify in the absence of clear evidence by the State repudiating the validity of all posthypnosis recollections. The State would be well within its powers if it established guidelines to aid trial courts in the evaluation of posthypnosis testimony and it may be able to show that testimony in a particular case is so unreliable that exclusion is justified. But it has not shown that hypnotically enhanced testimony is always so untrustworthy and so immune to the traditional means of evaluating credibility that it should disable a defendant from presenting her version of the events for which she is on trial.

In this case, the defective condition of the gun corroborated the details petitioner remembered about the shooting. The tape recordings provided some means to evaluate the hypnosis and the trial judge concluded that Doctor Back did not suggest responses with leading questions. * * * Those circumstances present an argument for admissibility of petitioner's testimony in this particular case, an argument that must be considered by the trial court. Arkansas' *per se* rule excluding all posthypnosis testimony infringes impermissibly on the right of a defendant to testify on his own behalf.

es remembering of only accurate information." *Id.*, at 1921.

19. Courts have adopted varying versions of these safeguards. See n. 16, *supra*. Oregon by statute has a requirement for procedural safeguards for hypnosis. Ore. Rev.Stat. § 136.675 (1985).

The judgment of the Supreme Court of Arkansas is vacated, and the case is remanded to that court for further proceedings not inconsistent with this opinion.

It is so ordered.

CHIEF JUSTICE REHNQUIST, with whom JUSTICE WHITE, JUSTICE O'CONNOR, and JUSTICE SCALIA join, dissenting.

In deciding that petitioner Rock's testimony was properly limited at her trial, the Arkansas Supreme Court cited several factors that undermine the reliability of hypnotically induced testimony. Like the Court today, the Arkansas Supreme Court observed that a hypnotized individual becomes subject to suggestion, is likely to confabulate, and experiences artificially increased confidence in both true and false memories following hypnosis. No known set of procedures, both courts agree, can insure against the inherently unreliable nature of such testimony. Having acceded to the factual premises of the Arkansas Supreme Court, the Court nevertheless concludes that a state trial court must attempt to make its own scientific assessment of reliability in each case it is confronted with a request for the admission of hypnotically induced testimony. I find no justification in the Constitution for such a ruling.

In the Court's words, the decision today is "bottomed" on recognition of Rock's "constitutional right to testify in her own defense." While it is true that this Court, in dictum, has recognized the existence of such a right, see, *e.g., Faretta v. California,* 422 U.S. 806, 819, n. 15, 95 S.Ct. 2525, 2533 n. 15, 45 L.Ed.2d 562 (1975), the principles identified by the Court as underlying this right provide little support for invalidating the evidentiary rule applied by the Arkansas Supreme Court.

As a general matter, the Court first recites, a defendant's right to testify facilitates the truth-seeking function of a criminal trial by advancing both the " 'detection of guilt' " and " 'the protection of innocence.' " Such reasoning is hardly controlling here, where advancement of the truth-seeking function of Rock's trial was the sole motivation behind limiting her testimony. The Court also posits, however, that "a rule that denies an accused the opportunity to offer his own testimony" cannot be upheld because, "[l]ike the truthfulness of other witnesses, the defendant's veracity * * * can be tested adequately by cross-examination." But the Court candidly admits that the increased confidence inspired by hypnotism makes "cross-examination more difficult," thereby diminishing an adverse party's ability to test the truthfulness of defendants such as Rock. Nevertheless, we are told, the exclusion of a defendant's testimony cannot be sanctioned because the defendant " 'above all others may be in a position to meet the prosecution's case.' " In relying on such reasoning, the Court apparently forgets that the issue before us arises only by virtue of Rock's memory loss, which rendered her less able "to meet the prosecution's case."

In conjunction with its reliance on broad principles that have little relevance here, the Court barely concerns itself with the recognition, present throughout our decisions, that an individual's right to present evidence is subject always to reasonable restrictions. Indeed, the due process decisions relied on by the Court all envision that an individual's right to present evidence on his behalf is not absolute and must oftentimes give way to countervailing considerations. See, *e.g., In re Oliver,* 333 U.S. 257, 273, 275, 68 S.Ct. 499, 508, 92 L.Ed. 682 (1948); *Morrissey v. Brewer,* 408 U.S. 471, 481–482, 92 S.Ct. 2593, 2600–2601, 33 L.Ed.2d 484 (1972); *Goldberg v. Kelly,* 397 U.S. 254, 263, 90 S.Ct. 1011, 1018, 25 L.Ed.2d 287 (1970). Similarly, our Compulsory Process Clause decisions make clear that the right to present relevant testimony "may, in appropriate cases, bow to accommodate other legitimate interests in the criminal trial process." *Chambers v. Mississippi,* 410 U.S. 284, 295, 93 S.Ct. 1038, 1046, 35 L.Ed.2d 297 (1973); see *Washington v. Texas,* 388 U.S. 14, 22, 87 S.Ct. 1920, 1925, 18 L.Ed.2d 1019 (1967). The Constitution does not in any way relieve a defendant from compliance with "rules of procedure and evidence designed to assure both fairness and reliability in the ascertainment of guilt and innocence." *Chambers v. Mississippi, supra,* 410 U.S., at 302, 93 S.Ct., at 1049. Surely a rule designed to exclude testimony whose trustworthiness is inherently suspect cannot be said to fall outside this description.*

This Court has traditionally accorded the States "respect * * * in the establishment and implementation of their own criminal trial rules and procedures." 410 U.S., at 302–303, 93 S.Ct., at 1049–1050; see, *e.g., Marshall v. Lonberger,* 459 U.S. 422, 438, n. 6, 103 S.Ct. 843, 853, n. 6, 74 L.Ed.2d 646 (1983) ("[T]he Due Process Clause does not permit the federal courts to engage in a finely tuned review of the wisdom of state evidentiary rules"); *Patterson v. New York,* 432 U.S. 197, 201, 97 S.Ct. 2319, 2322, 53 L.Ed.2d 281 (1977) ("[W]e should not lightly construe the Constitution so as to intrude upon the administration of justice by the individual States"). One would think that this deference would be at its highest in an area such as this, where, as the Court concedes, "scientific understanding * * * is still in its infancy." Turning a blind eye to this concession, the Court chooses instead to restrict the ability of both state and federal courts to respond to changes in the understanding of hypnosis.

The Supreme Court of Arkansas' decision was an entirely permissible response to a novel and difficult question. See National Institute of Justice, Issues and Practices, M. Orne et al., Hypnotically Refreshed Testimony: Enhanced Memory or Tampering with Evidence? 51 (1985). As an original proposition, the solution this Court imposes upon Arkansas may be equally sensible, though requiring the matter to be

* The Court recognizes, as it must, that rules governing "testimonial privileges [and] nonarbitrary rules that disqualify those incapable of observing events due to mental infirmity or infancy from being witnesses" do not "offend the defendant's right to testify." I fail to discern any meaningful constitutional difference between such rules and the one at issue here.

considered *res nova* by every single trial judge in every single case might seem to some to pose serious administrative difficulties. But until there is much more of a consensus on the use of hypnosis than there is now, the Constitution does not warrant this Court's mandating its own view of how to deal with the issue.

KENTUCKY v. STINCER

Supreme Court of the United States, 1987.
482 U.S. 730, 107 S.Ct. 2658, 96 L.Ed.2d 631.

JUSTICE BLACKMUN delivered the opinion of the Court.

The question presented in this case is whether the exclusion of a defendant from a hearing held to determine the competency of two child witnesses to testify violates the defendant's rights under the Confrontation Clause of the Sixth Amendment or the Due Process Clause of the Fourteenth Amendment.

* * *

* * * Under Kentucky law, when a child's competency to testify is raised, the judge is required to resolve three basic issues: whether the child is capable of observing and recollecting facts, whether the child is capable of narrating those facts to a court or jury, and whether the child has a moral sense of the obligation to tell the truth. See *Moore v. Commonwealth,* 384 S.W.2d 498, 500 (Ky.1964) ("When the competency of an infant to testify is properly raised it is then the duty of the trial court to carefully examine the witness to ascertain whether she (or he) is sufficiently intelligent to observe, recollect and narrate the facts and has a moral sense of obligation to speak the truth"); *Capps v. Commonwealth,* 560 S.W.2d 559, 560 (Ky.1977); *Hendricks v. Commonwealth,* 550 S.W.2d 551, 554 (Ky.1977); see also *Thomas v. Commonwealth,* 300 Ky. 480, 481–482, 189 S.W.2d 686, 686–687 (1945); Comment, An Overview of the Competency of Child Testimony, 13 No.Ky.L.Rev. 181, 184 (1986).[11] Thus, questions at a competency hearing usually are limited to matters that are unrelated to the basic issues of the trial. Children often are asked their names, where they go to school, how old they are, whether they know who the judge is, whether they know what a lie is, and whether they know what happens when one tells a lie. See Comment, The Competency Requirement for the Child Victim of Sexual Abuse: Must We Abandon It?, 40 U.Miami L.Rev. 245, 263, and n. 78 (1985); Comment, Defendants' Rights in Child Witness Competency Hearings: Establishing Constitutional Procedures for Sexual Abuse Cases, 69 Minn.L.Rev. 1377, 1381–1383, and nn. 9–11 (1985).[12]

11. Similar requirements for establishing competency to testify were set forth in *Wheeler v. United States,* 159 U.S. 523, 16 S.Ct. 93, 40 L.Ed. 244 (1895): "[T]here is no precise age which determines the question of competency. This depends on the capacity and intelligence of the child, his appreciation of the difference between truth and falsehood, as well as of his duty to tell the former." *Id.,* at 524, 16 S.Ct., at 93. See generally 2 Wigmore §§ 505–507.

12. Some States explicitly allow children to testify without requiring a prior competency qualification, while others sim-

In Kentucky, as in certain other States, it is the responsibility of the judge, not the jury, to decide whether a witness is competent to testify based on the witness' answers to such questions. *Whitehead v. Stith,* 268 Ky. 703, 709, 105 S.W.2d 834, 837 (1937) (question of competency is one for court, not jury, and if court finds witness lacks qualification, "it commits a palpable abuse of its discretion" should it then permit witness to testify); *Payne v. Commonwealth,* 623 S.W.2d 867, 878 (Ky.1981); *Capps v. Commonwealth,* 560 S.W.2d, at 560. See 2 Wigmore § 507, p. 714 (citing cases). In those States where the judge has the responsibility for determining competency, that responsibility usually continues throughout the trial.[13] A motion by defense counsel that the court reconsider its earlier decision that a child is competent may be raised after the child testifies on direct examination, see, *e.g., In re R.R.,* 79 N.J. 97, 106, 398 A.2d 76, 80 (1979) (at close of State's case, defense attorney moved that 4–year–old boy be declared incompetent on basis of actual testimony given by boy),[14] or after direct and cross-examination of the witness. See, *e.g.,* Reply Brief for Petitioner 12 ("If, during trial, there arises some basis for challenging the judge's competency determination, the judge may be asked to reconsider," referring to respondent's motion to that effect, Tr. 126–127). Moreover, appellate

ply provide that all persons, including children, are deemed competent unless otherwise limited by statute. See B. Battman & J. Bulkley, National Legal Resource Center for Child Advocacy and Protection, Protecting Child Victim/Witnesses: Sample Laws and Materials 43–44 (1986) (listing statutes) (Protecting Child Victim/Witnesses); Bulkley, Evidentiary and Procedural Trends in State Legislation and Other Emerging Legal Issues in Child Sexual Abuse Cases, 89 Dick.L.Rev. 645, 645 (1985). Some commentators have urged that children be allowed to testify without undergoing a prior competency qualification. See Protecting Child Victim/Witnesses, at 38 (proposing sample competency statute according children same rebuttable presumption of competency granted other witnesses); 2 Wigmore § 509, p. 719 ("it must be concluded that the sensible way is to put the child upon the stand to give testimony for what it may seem to be worth").

A number of States, however, mandate by statute that a trial judge assess a child's competency to testify on the basis of specified requirements. These usually include a determination that the child is capable of expression, is capable of understanding the duty to tell the truth, and is capable of receiving just impressions of the facts about which he or she is called to testify. See, *e.g.,* Ariz.Rev.Stat.Ann. § 12–2202 (1982); Ga.Code Ann. § 24–9–5 (1982); Idaho Code § 9–202 (Supp.1987); Ind.Code § 34–1–14–5 (1986); Mich.Comp.Laws § 600.2163 (1986); Minn.Stat. § 595.02, subd. 1(f) (Supp.1987); N.Y.Crim.Proc.Law § 60.20 (McKinney 1981); Ohio Rev.Code Ann. § 2317.01 (1981); see Protecting Child Victim/Witnesses, at 45 (listing statutes). The recent reforms in some States of presuming the competency of young children and allowing juries to assess credibility at trial is not called into question by this opinion. We are concerned solely with those States that retain competency qualification requirements.

13. See, *e.g., Litzkuhn v. Clark,* 85 Ariz. 355, 360, 339 P.2d 389, 392 (1959) ("[I]t is the duty of the trial judge who has permitted a child to be sworn as a witness, at any time to change his mind upon due occasion therefor, to remove the child from the stand and to instruct the jury to disregard his testimony"); *Davis v. Weber,* 93 Ariz. 312, 317, 380 P.2d 608, 611 (1963) ("The right of a trial judge to change his mind [regarding a child's competency] can hardly be denied").

14. California recently amended its statute governing the disqualification of incompetent witnesses to provide explicitly: "In any proceeding held outside the presence of a jury, a court may reserve challenges to the competency of a witness until the conclusion of the direct examination of that witness." Cal.Evid.Code Ann. § 701(b) (West Supp.1987).

courts reviewing a trial judge's determination of competency also often will look at the full testimony at trial.[15]

In this case both T.G. and N.G. were asked several background questions during the competency hearing, as well as several questions directed at what it meant to tell the truth. Some of the questions regarding the witnesses' backgrounds were repeated by the prosecutor on direct examination, while others—particularly those regarding the witnesses' ability to tell the difference between truth and falsehood—were repeated by respondent's counsel on cross-examination. At the close of the children's testimony, respondent's counsel, had he thought it appropriate, was in a position to move that the court reconsider its competency rulings on the ground that the direct and cross-examination had elicited evidence that the young girls lacked the basic requisites for serving as competent witnesses. Thus, the critical tool of cross-examination was available to counsel as a means of establishing that the witnesses were not competent to testify, as well as a means of undermining the credibility of their testimony.

Because respondent had the opportunity for full and effective cross-examination of the two witnesses during trial, and because of the nature of the competency hearing at issue in this case, we conclude that respondent's rights under the Confrontation Clause were not violated by his exclusion from the competency hearing of the two girls.

* * *

We conclude that respondent's due process rights were not violated by his exclusion from the competency hearing in this case. * * *

* * *

JUSTICE MARSHALL, with whom JUSTICE BRENNAN and JUSTICE STEVENS join, dissenting.

The Court today defines respondent's Sixth Amendment right to be confronted with the witnesses against him as guaranteeing nothing more than an opportunity to cross-examine these witnesses *at some point* during his trial. The Confrontation Clause protects much more. In this case, it secures at a minimum respondent's right of presence to assist his lawyer at the in-chambers hearing to determine the competency of the key prosecution witnesses. Respondent's claim under the Due Process Clause of the Fourteenth Amendment, though similar in this testimonial context to his claim under the Confrontation Clause,

15. See, *e.g., Payne v. Commonwealth,* 623 S.W.2d 867, 878 (Ky.1981) (review of children's testimony at trial reveals that trial court's ruling of competency was appropriate); *Hendricks v. Commonwealth,* 550 S.W.2d 551, 554 (Ky.1977) ("Not only did the trial judge determine that the children were competent to testify, but the transcript of the testimony of these children clearly demonstrates their intellectual ability to observe, recollect and narrate the facts and to recognize their moral obligation to tell the truth"); see also *In re R.R.,* 79 N.J. 97, 113, 398 A.2d 76, 84 (1979) ("[I]n determining the propriety of the trial judge's determination, an appellate court need not limit its view to the responses given by the witness during the *voir dire* examination; instead, it can consider the entire record—including the testimony in fact given by the witness under oath—in order to arrive at its decision").

was not addressed by the court below and should not be decided here. Were this issue properly before the Court, however, I would again dissent. Due process requires that respondent be allowed to attend every critical stage of his trial.

* * *

UNITED STATES v. ODOM

United States Court of Appeals, Fourth Circuit, 1984.
736 F.2d 104.

DONALD RUSSELL, CIRCUIT JUDGE:

The defendants appeal their convictions arising out of absentee voting in a federal and state election conducted in Alexander County, North Carolina in November 1982. In the first twenty-eight counts of the mail fraud indictment the defendants Odom, Beach, Dyson and Lackey were charged with participation in a scheme to cast false and fraudulent absentee ballots and in counts twenty-nine and thirty, the defendants were charged with conspiracy to vote more than once and with the substantive offense of so voting in the election.[1] The defendants were convicted on all counts and received concurrent sentences. Three of the defendants (Odom, Beach and Dyson) have appealed their convictions on a number of grounds. The defendant Lackey chose not to appeal. We find no basis for reversal in any of the grounds and accordingly affirm the judgments of convictions.

I

In the general election held on November 2, 1982, the sheriff and clerk of court of Alexander County were candidates for reelection. In that same election there were federal candidates for the United States House of Representatives. The defendant Odom was a deputy sheriff under the incumbent Alexander County sheriff who was a candidate for reelection; the defendant Lackey was also employed part time by the County sheriff; the defendant Beach was an employee in the office of the County Clerk of Court, who was similarly a candidate for reelection; and the defendant Dyson was a friend of Odom.

The alleged scheme involved casting absentee votes in the name of residents of The Belle's View Rest Home in Alexander County. The residents were generally persons of advanced years, feeble both physically and mentally. * * *

* * *

IV

The defendants complain next that the district court "erred in permitting unsworn and otherwise incompetent witnesses to testify for the prosecution." By this claim they challenge the mental competency of the residents of the Rest Home, either to appear or to testify at trial.

1. 18 U.S.C. §§ 2, 1341; 42 U.S.C. § 1973i(e) and 18 U.S.C. 371.

In connection with that issue, the defendants fault the manner in which the district judge chose to resolve the issue of the competency of such witnesses. It was their position on the procedural question that the district judge should have ruled on the witnesses' competency in an *in camera* hearing. They made a motion for such a hearing, but only at trial during the Government's case in chief.[5] It was denied. The defendants question this denial. On the substantive issue of the witnesses' competency, they assert that the district judge should not have permitted these residents of the Rest Home to testify at all or to appear before the jury but should have found them incompetent.

We address, first, the contention that the district court erred in not granting an *in camera* hearing on the competency of the residents of the Home to appear as witnesses. The defendants' motion for such hearing was not made until near the conclusion of the Government's case-in-chief. They would excuse their delay in submitting such motion with the claim that they had not anticipated that the Government would present these residents of the Home as witnesses. We find this excuse difficult to accept. The heart of the Government's case was whether these residents had knowingly or intelligently voted absentee in the election. On this issue, it would seem inconceivable that the Government would not have subpoenaed the residents at trial. Leaving to the side this matter of delay in submitting the motion, though, the conclusion is inescapable that to grant the motion when made would have required the district judge to interrupt the trial and to excuse the jury while he examined separately *in camera* approximately thirty witnesses, and, to the extent that he found them competent under federal practice, to recall the jury and to go over again much of the testimony that would have been taken *in camera.* Such an interruption in the trial and interference with the orderly process of the case was certainly not required or even prudent.

Rule 104(c), Fed.R.Evid., prescribes the procedure to be followed in connection with motions for *in camera* or out-of-the-presence-of-the-jury hearings, such as the one sought by the defendants. That Rule specifies only one motion on which a defendant is entitled to of right an *in camera* hearing and that is a motion challenging the validity of a confession. In all situations other than an assault on the voluntariness of a confession, the granting of the motion is a matter committed to the discretion of the trial judge. While the Rule itself is silent as to any preference with respect to whether an *in camera* hearing should be granted in this discretionary area, the Advisory Committee's Notes on

5. The motion and the ruling of the district judge appear thus in the record:

"May it please the Court, may we put the motion in the record before we bring the jury in? Your Honor, we would move that, prior to any of these people that Mr. Cogburn has told us about in Chambers being allowed to testify before the jury in this matter, that we be allowed to voir dire them outside the presence of the jury to determine whether or not they are competent witnesses.

"COURT: I think you can do it in the presence of the jury as well as outside the presence of the jury, Mr. Gray. We'll just have to take them one at a time."

the Rule leave little doubt as to what its opinion was on the question. It said critically that an *in camera* hearing is "time consuming" and "[n]ot infrequently the same evidence which is relevant to the issue of establishment of fulfillment of a condition precedent to admissibility is also relevant to weight or credibility." It suggested that "time is saved by taking foundation proof in the presence of the jury" and opined that "[m]uch evidence on preliminary questions, though not relevant to jury issues, may be heard by the jury with no adverse effect." It concluded that "[a] great deal must be left to the discretion of the judge who will act as the interests of justice require."

The considerations which the Advisory Committee found militated against an *in camera* hearing are present in this case. The motion, if granted, would have been "time consuming," would have interrupted the trial and its orderly proceedings, and would have required the taking of testimony *in camera* which would have been largely repeated in later testimony before the jury.

Beyond these considerations found by the Advisory Committee to militate against an *in camera* hearing there is the additional consideration arising out of the provisions of Rule 601, Fed.R.Evid. Most writers are of the opinion that "[t]he trial court's responsibility under Rule 104(a) to determine preliminary questions concerning the qualification of witnesses is largely vitiated by Rule 601 which makes all witnesses competent except where state law applied the rule of decision and declares a witness incompetent." 1 Weinstein's *Evidence,* § 104[03], pp. 104–26. With particular reference to any necessity for a preliminary or *in camera* hearing on the issue of witness competency, 3 Weinstein's *Evidence,* § 601[04], pp. 601–28 states:

> "Since Rule 601 abolishes all grounds for disqualifying a witness [except when state law furnishes the rule of decision], a preliminary hearing pursuant to Rule 104(a) for the purpose of determining competency is usually no longer required. This does not mean that the trial judge no longer has any power to keep a witness from testifying. It merely means that the judge must shift his attention from the proposed witness to the proffered testimony; instead of ruling on the basis of competency he must recast the problem in terms of relevancy."

Moreover, the authorities decided before the adoption of the Federal Rules of Evidence, generally have recognized that there is no requirement for an *in camera* preliminary hearing on the competency of witnesses. * * *

* * *

We turn now to the substantive objection to the competency of the Rest Home residents as witnesses. Other than for the motion for an *in camera* hearing, the defendants made no objection to these residents when they were called as witnesses. Neither did they move to strike the testimony of such witnesses when the latter had concluded their testimony. The general rule is that any objection to the competency of a witness should be raised at the time the party is presented as a witness and, absent objection at that time, any claim of incompetency of the witness is waived; and this is particularly so, if there is no motion to strike at the conclusion of the witness' testimony * * *. * * *

It is unnecessary, however, for us to rest our decision on the competency of the residents who were sworn on principles of waiver, since federal procedure as well as common law supports their qualifications. Rule 601, Fed.R.Evid., which is the controlling guide in federal criminal courts on qualifications of witnesses, represents, in the words of the leading commentator on the Rules, "the culmination of the modern trend which has converted questions of competency into questions of credibility while 'steadily moving towards a realization that judicial determination of the question of whether a witness should be heard at all should be abrogated in favor of hearing the testimony for what it is worth.' " 3 Weinstein's *Evidence,* Witnesses, § 601[05], p. 601–37, citing Comment, "Witnesses under Article VI of the Proposed Federal Rules of Evidence," 15 Wayne L.Rev. 1236, 1250 (1969). *See also, McCormick on Evidence,* § 62, pp. 140–41 (Cleary ed. 1972). As a consequence of this purpose of the Rule, Weinstein suggests that it is "probably more accurate to say that [in determining questions under Rule 601], the Court will decide not competency but minimum credibility." *See* 3 Weinstein § 601[01], p. 601–10. Under this rule every witness is presumed to be competent. Neither feeble-mindedness nor insanity renders a witness incompetent or disqualified. The defendants so concede and we specifically so held recently in *United States v. Lightly, supra,* 677 F.2d at 1028. The only grounds for disqualifying a party as a witness under Rule 601, according to *Lightly,* are that the witness "does not have knowledge of the matters about which he is to testify, that he does not have the capacity to recall, or that he does not understand the duty to testify truthfully." *Id.* at 1028. Most of the state decisions are to the same effect. *See for instance, Commonwealth v. Pronkoskie,* 477 Pa. 132, 383 A.2d 858, 860–61 (1978); *People v. Coca,* 39 Colo.App. 264, 564 P.2d 431, 433 (1977). Whether the witness has such competency is a matter for determination by the trial judge after such examination as he deems appropriate and his exercise of discretion in this regard is to be reversed only for clear error. *United States v. Martino,* 648 F.2d 367, 389 (5th Cir.1981), *cert. denied,* 456 U.S. 943, 102 S.Ct. 2006, 72 L.Ed.2d 465. Judged by this standard we find no error in the ruling of the district judge on the competency of the witnesses who were sworn.

The defendants do not seem, however, to center their argument in this connection on incompetency of the residents as witnesses *per se,* or on the irrelevance of their testimony; their objection is rather one to the very right of the residents to appear at trial. Their contention is basically that the "mentally debilitated" condition of these residents, "evident both in their appearance and testimony," is such as to create inescapably in the minds of the jury "[t]he manifest implication" that "the [defendants] *must* have been guilty of vote fraud because the patients were incapable of formulating a voluntary or informed choice"[7] when their ballots were voted in the November election. Under those circumstances, the defendants argue that they were prejudiced by the appearance at trial of the residents, and for that reason the district court should not have permitted such parties to be presented as witnesses at trial. The flaw in this argument is that it fails to state a ground for disqualification under Rule 601 and, more than that it is contrary to a rule applied from time immemorial in determining insanity or incompetence. From the earliest days, the rule at common law has been that when mental competency or capacity is in issue, it is approved practice that the chancellor or the jury (dependent on which is to resolve the issue) should observe the person whose competency is in issue, to note his demeanor and his responses to questions, in reaching a decision. This rule was stated with precision in *Mettetal v. Hall,* 288 Mich. 200, 284 N.W. 698, 700 (1939):

> "It seems to have been the established rule of the common law that it was proper that the person alleged to be mentally incompetent should appear before the chancellor for inspection. Abbot of Strata Marcella's Case, 9 Coke's Rep. 31 a; 3 Blackstone's Commentaries, p. 332. In case mental incompetency became involved in such a way that the mental condition of a person was to be determined by the jury, inspection by the jury was an allowable mode of acquiring knowledge on an issue of insanity. 1 Hale's Pleas of the Crown, pp. 29, 33. See, also, 2 Wigmore on Evidence, § 1160."

Wigmore is to the same effect (2 Wigmore on *Evidence,* § 1160, p. 360):

> "On an issue of *idiocy* or *insanity,* it was from an early period regarded proper that the person should appear before the Chancellor for inspection. Since the Chancellor is upon the subject of insanity no less a layman than is a juryman, it seems equally proper, and has been perhaps equally long established, that inspection by the jury should be an allowable mode of acquiring knowledge on an issue of insanity." (Emphasis in text)

The most important factual issue in this case was the competency of these residents to exercise what the defendants characterize as "a voluntary or informed choice." For the jury to resolve this issue, it was not merely relevant, it was actually compelling that the jury be permitted to see the residents and to hear their responses, and to judge for themselves first-hand the conduct and comprehensiveness of the persons whose competency was the dispositive issue. If the very appearance, demeanor and conduct of these witnesses marked them as being "incapable of formulating a voluntary and informed choice," as the defendants suggest, that appearance and demeanor were properly relevant for the consideration of the jury. If the defendants were prejudiced in their defense by these "manifest" demonstrations of inability on the part of the residents to make such a choice and to give such an authorization, it is a prejudice for which the defendants must

7. Emphasis in brief.

accept the responsibility. It follows that however the question may be considered—whether under Rule 601 or at common law—the district judge did not commit clear error or abuse his discretion in permitting the residents to be presented as witnesses and in allowing those he ordered sworn to testify.

There were, however, nine witnesses called, whom the district judge refused to allow the clerk to swear. There was no objection to the competency of these witnesses when they were presented. The Government was permitted to examine these parties and the defendants were given the opportunity to cross-examine them. In some instances, the defendants exercised the right to cross-examine the parties in question. Of the residents of the Home who did not testify, five did not even respond to their names or show any ability to comprehend the questions directed to them or to give any testimony whatsoever. Because of this obvious incapacity, the Government made no effort to continue the examination of these witnesses and the defendants forewent the opportunity to cross-examine them. The other four gave such contradictory answers in direct and cross-examination that the district judge concluded that such persons were not competent and should not be sworn. At no time during the presentation or examination of these witnesses and the failure of the clerk to administer the oath to them did the defendants offer any objection. It was not until the day after these witnesses had been called that any question was raised about the propriety of the parties' being presented as witnesses or to their testifying to such extent as it could be said they had testified. And the objection made at this late time was only in response to an inquiry made of counsel by the district judge. The circumstances under which the district judge raised the point deserve to be examined.

The morning after the residents of the Rest Home had been presented as witnesses and nine of them had not been sworn, the district judge, out of the presence of the jury, brought up the fact that some of the persons called had not been sworn by the clerk pursuant to his instruction.[8] The defendants then moved to strike the testimony of the witnesses. In making the motion, the defendants stated no grounds. The district judge responded that he would recall the witnesses who had not been sworn and permit re-cross-examination. The defendants, after a conference, advised the court that they would withdraw their objections to the appearance and testimony (such as it

8. The Court's statement was as follows:

"Before we start this morning, yesterday afternoon we had these people from the nursing home here, as you know. I directed the Clerk, in my discretion, not to bother to try to swear some of them, because obviously they couldn't even talk when you got them up here. They didn't know the answers, didn't know their names, how old they were or anything else. Of course, the Court is conversant with the fact that witnesses ought to be sworn. I want to know now on the record if any of you gentlemen have any questions, that is, the defense counsel, with the Court's procedure in that way. If you do, I want to know it now."

was) of the witnesses and would not request the recalling of the witnesses. On this appeal, however, the defendants now complain of the absence of an oath by these nine persons. We find the complaint without merit.

It is well settled that the swearing of a witness is waived by failure to raise the point during the witness' testimony, thus denying the trial court an opportunity to correct what has been characterized as an "irregularity." [9] The rationale of this principle was declared a century and a half ago in the oft-cited case of *Cady v. Norton,* 14 Pick. 236, 237 (Mass.1833). The Court in that case stated two justifications for the rule: First, the defect or failure could have been corrected if a timely objection had been made; second, in the absence of a waiver rule counsel might deliberately avoid objecting to a witness being unsworn in order to have a ground of appeal.

* * *

CONCLUSION

Having considered all the defendants' claims of error and finding none requiring a reversal, we affirm the judgments of convictions.

Affirmed.

FARLEY v. COLLINS

Supreme Court of Florida, 1962.
146 So.2d 366.

THORNAL, JUSTICE.

By a petition for a writ of certiorari we are requested to review a decision of the District Court of Appeal, Third District, which has been certified by that court as passing upon a question of great public interest. Collins v. Farley, Fla.App., 137 So.2d 31; Art. V, Section 4(2), Florida Constitution, F.S.A.

We must determine whether an automobile collision constitutes a "transaction" within the contemplation of Section 90.05, Florida Statutes, F.S.A., otherwise known as "The Dead Man's Statute."

The factual situation is delineated in detail in the cited decision of the Court of Appeal which has been submitted for review. Farley, while driving a motorcycle, collided with an automobile then being

9. In the Note, *A Reconsideration of the Sworn Testimony Requirement: Securing Truth in the Twentieth Century,* 75 *Mich. L.Rev.* 1681 (1977), the author concludes after an exhaustive discussion of the background and rationale of the oath requirement, at p. 1707:

"Yet the oath is largely an historical artifact: to borrow Justice Holmes' oft-quoted phrase, to a significant extent 'the grounds upon which [the traditional rule] was laid down have vanished long since, and the rule simply persists from blind imitation of the past.'* This being the case, the deep and uncritical confidence placed in the sworn nature of testimony cannot longer be justified." [*O.W. Holmes, Collected Legal Papers 187 (1920) (footnote in original)].

See, also, United States v. Looper, 419 F.2d 1405, 1406–07 (4th Cir.1969).

driven by one Dann, who was deceased at the time of the trial. Farley instituted an action for damages allegedly resulting from the collision. The action was brought against Collins as administrator of the estate of Dann. The trial judge permitted Farley to testify as to the movements of his motorcycle immediately prior to the collision. He also testified as to the movements of his motorcycle and the Dann automobile during the occurrence of the collision. The detailed testimony was set out in the opinion of the Court of Appeal in Collins v. Farley, supra. The administrator objected to the testimony on the ground that it related to a "transaction" between the plaintiff and a party deceased at the time of the trial. The trial judge overruled the objection and allowed the testimony. The Court of Appeal, Collins v. Farley, supra, reversed this ruling with a holding that the collision between Farley's motorcycle and the automobile of the decedent constituted a "transaction" between the two so that the testimony was inadmissible under Section 90.05, Florida Statutes, F.S.A. It is this decision which has been submitted for review.

The petitioner Farley contends that the fortuitous occurrence of a collision does not constitute a "transaction" within the meaning of the cited statute.

The respondent insists that the language of the statute is sufficiently broad to comprehend every type of occurrence between a testifying party and a deceased adversary.

* * *

The pertinent part of Section 90.05, Florida Statutes, F.S.A., is as follows:

> "* * * no party * * * shall be examined as a witness in regard to any transaction or communication between such witness and a person at the time of such examination deceased * * *."

At common law, no party or person interested in the results of litigation was permitted to testify. The interest of the witness was an absolute disqualification which precluded him from giving testimony. 58 Am.Jur., Witnesses, Section 169, page 120. In 1843 the disqualification of interested persons was removed in England by statute. 6 and 7 Vict. c. 85. In 1851 the disqualification of parties was removed by statute in England. 14 and 15, Vict. c. 99. Since then these disqualifying elements have been removed by statute in practically all of the states. The Florida statute, Section 90.05, supra, was enacted as chapter 1983, Laws of Florida, 1874. Its statutory predecessor in this country was enacted originally by the State of New York, and is now cited as Section 347, New York Civil Practice Act. To the extent, therefore, that the Florida statute and the New York statute are in harmony we would look to the New York decisions as a guide to our own conclusion. Adams v. Board of Trustees of the Internal Improvement Fund, 37 Fla. 266, 20 So. 266.

Although, admittedly, Section 90.05, supra, is in derogation of the common law, nevertheless to the extent that it removes the disqualification of a witness because of interest, it should be construed liberally for the reason that it is remedial in nature. 58 Am.Jur. Witnesses, Section 169, page 120; Texas v. Chiles, 21 Wall. (U.S.) 488, 22 Law Ed. 650; Nolan v. Moore, 81 Fla. 600, 88 So. 601. The objective of statutes which eliminate disqualifications is to expand the opportunities for making available previously excluded evidence. It has generally been concluded that the exclusion of the testimony of a party merely because of interest will more likely result in wide-spread injustices than would a rule permitting the testimony subject to traditional tests of credibility. On the other hand, the exception to the rule of admissibility which is comprehended by exclusions under the Dead Man's Statute is to be strictly construed. The restriction against admitting the testimony of an interested party in a cause against the representatives of a deceased adversary is a limitation on the remedial aspects of the statute which permits interested parties to testify. Hence, the language of the Dead Man proviso should be strictly construed and limited to its narrowest application. By applying this rule we reduce to a minimum the restrictions on the broader remedial statute. Day v. Stickle, Fla.App., 113 So.2d 559, 80 A.L.R.2d 1291, cert. den. 115 So.2d 414; Harper v. Johnson, Tex.1961, 345 S.W.2d 277; Jones on Evidence (5th Ed.) Vol. 3, Section 774, page 1440; Wigmore on Evidence (3rd Ed.1940), Section 578.

With a view to the rules of statutory construction and the historical background of the subject statute, we return to our consideration of the prime question which is whether the word "transaction" as used in the exception contained in the Florida Statutes, should be construed broadly to include an automobile collision.

This Court has recognized that the so-called Dead Man's Statute may in proper cases be applied to tort actions. In some of those cases a broad definition of the word "transaction" has been cited. Embrey v. Southern Gas and Electric Corp., Fla., 63 So.2d 258; Herring v. Eiland, Fla., 81 So.2d 645. However, as emphasized by the certificate of the Court of Appeal certifying the instant case to us, this Court has never been confronted squarely with the problem which challenges our present considerations.

Herring v. Eiland, supra, involved a suit by the guardian of an incompetent passenger against the driver of a vehicle in which the passenger was injured as a result of a collision. The trial court considered upon motion for a summary judgment the deposition of the defendant driver regarding the activities of the parties shortly preceding the accident, as well as his own actions and the speed and movement of his automobile immediately before the accident. On appeal this Court held that the occurrence of the accident allegedly resulting from the negligence of the driver was not such a "transaction" between the driver and his incompetent guest that would bar the testimony of the driver in defense of the claim asserted against him.

In Day v. Stickle, supra, a passenger in one automobile brought suit against a personal representative of the driver of another automobile involved in a collision resulting in injury to the passenger. The Court of Appeal which has certified the instant problem to us held that the injured passenger could testify regarding the circumstances of the collision. The Court correctly recognized the rule of strict construction applicable to the Dead Man's Statute. It held in summary that the collision between the automobile in which the injured plaintiff was a passenger and the automobile driven by the deceased whose estate was being sued did not constitute a "transaction" between the two.

Admittedly, there is a difference of view among the courts as to whether an automobile collision constitutes a "transaction" between the drivers of the two vehicles involved. Some courts adhere to the position that such a collision is a "transaction" and that the testimony of a surviving driver is inadmissible in an action against the estate of his adversary. In re Mueller's Estate, 166 Neb. 376, 89 N.W.2d 137; Countrymen v. Sullivan, 344 Ill.App. 371, 100 N.E.2d 799; Zeigler v. Moore, 75 Nev. 91, 335 P.2d 425. On the other hand, a number of courts have adopted the contrary view by limiting the Dead Man's Statute to its most restrictive interpretation. These courts construe the word "transaction" as requiring something in the nature of a negotiation or a course of conduct or a mutuality of responsibility resulting from the voluntary conduct of opposing parties. In this view a "transaction" results when one enters upon a course of conduct after a knowing exchange of reciprocal acts or conversations. We have the opinion that the latter view is the better view and should govern the instant case. In addition to the decisions which we shall cite, we are supported by the leading authorities on the rules of evidence. Jones on Evidence, Vol. 3, Section 774; Wigmore on Evidence (3rd Ed.1940) Section 578. Recently, in Harper v. Johnson, Tex.1961, 345 S.W.2d 277, the Supreme Court of Texas, when confronted by a statute very similar to ours, held that a "transaction" involves a mutuality or concert of action. It does not include the circumstances "surrounding an involuntary and fortuitous collision between two motor vehicles driven by two complete strangers." To apply the statute to such a situation, said the Texas court, would be to extend the language of the Dead Man's Statute beyond the bounds of the rule of strict construction applicable to it. The court then directly held, as do we here, that the survivor of an automobile collision may testify as to his observations and may describe the physical situation and the movements of the vehicles prior to and at the time of the accident.

While the foregoing conclusion has not been reached without some difficulty, it appears to us to provide a rule more nearly consistent with the legislative intent as announced by the subject statute. It is also consistent with the policy of the law to make available all relevant evidence in its quest for the truth in any particular factual situation. The credibility of the testifying survivor who is under oath may certainly be evaluated by the jury and tested by cross-examination. In the ultimate, we agree with those courts which have taken the position that the exclusion of such testimony will work greater injustices by preventing recovery on legitimate claims as against the view that admissibility might result in the establishment of fraudulent claims against decedents' estates. The view which we have above announced is also supported by Knoepfle v. Suko, N.D., 108 N.W.2d 456; Rankin v. Morgan, 193 Ark. 751, 102 S.W.2d 552; Krause v. Emmons, 6 Boyce 104, 29 Del. 104, 97 A. 238. In other decisions, although there was a slight difference in the language of the statute, we are of the opinion that the difference is not of controlling materiality and the result was the same as that reached by us here. Shaneybrook v. Blizzard, 209 Md. 304, 121 A.2d 218; Seligman v. Orth, 205 Wis. 199, 236 N.W. 115; McCarthy v. Woolston, 210 App.Div. 152, 205 N.Y.S. 507; Turbot v. Repp, 247 Iowa 69, 72 N.W.2d 565.

We, therefore, hold that the collision in the instant case did not constitute a "transaction or communication between" the surviving driver of the motorcycle and the deceased driver of the automobile. The testimony of the surviving driver of the motorcycle which was permitted in evidence by the trial judge, was not inadmissible under Section 90.05, Florida Statutes, F.S.A. The trial judge, therefore, ruled correctly in allowing the testimony. By the decision certified to us for review the District Court of Appeal committed error in reversing the trial court on this ruling.

The writ of certiorari having been issued, judgment of the Court of Appeal is quashed to the extent considered by the foregoing opinion and the cause is remanded to the Court of Appeal for further proceedings consistent herewith.

It is so ordered.

FLORIDA EVIDENCE CODE (1976)

§ 90.602 Testimony of interested persons

(1) No person interested in an action or proceeding against the personal representative, heir-at-law, assignee, legatee, devisee, or survivor of a deceased person, or against the assignee, committee, or guardian of an insane person, shall be examined as a witness regarding any oral communication between the interested person and the person who is deceased or insane at the time of the examination.

(2) This section does not apply when:

(a) A personal representative, heir-at-law, assignee, legatee, devisee, or survivor of a deceased person, or the assignee, committee, or guardian of an insane person, is examined on his own behalf regarding the oral communication.

(b) Evidence of the subject matter of the oral communication is offered by the personal representative, heir-at-law, assignee, legatee, devisee, or survivor of a deceased person, or the assignee, committee, or guardian of an insane person.

LAW REVISION COUNCIL NOTE—1976

This section, commonly known as the "Deadman's Statute," provides protection for the estates of the deceased and the insane by making certain interested persons incompetent to testify in an action against the estate regarding oral communications with the deceased or insane person. Existing Fla.Stat. § 90.05 is substantially restated and the same class of persons are protected. However, the section is applicable only to "oral communications" and not to "transactions" because of problems that have arisen therewith. Although the section is applicable only to persons "interested" in certain actions and proceedings, the language encompasses those covered by the existing statute.

The preliminary drafts of this section eliminated the "Deadman's Statute" because "The practical consequence of these statutes is that if a survivor has rendered services, furnished goods or lent money to a person whom he trusted, without an outside witness or admissible written evidence, he is helpless if the other dies and the representative of his estate declines to pay." McCormick, Evidence § 65 (2nd ed. 1972). See Jackson v. Parker, 153 Fla. 622, 15 So.2d 451 (1943); 3 Wigmore, Evidence § 578 (1940). However, this provision was adopted since there is generally no opposing testimony to meet the allegation of the interested claimant and fraud and hardship could result if the surviving party was permitted to testify concerning the oral communication.

Note

Ray, Dead Man's Statutes, 24 Ohio St.L.J. 89 (1963), counted thirty-four states with some form of the statute. Since then, many of the statutes have been repealed (see, e.g., Davis v. Hare, 262 Ark. 818, 561 S.W.2d 321 (1978); Kirk v. Marquis, 391 A.2d 335 (Me.1978)), or, as in Florida, relaxed, usually in connection with the adoption of a codification based upon the Federal Rules of Evidence.

ELIZARRARAS v. BANK OF EL PASO

United States Court of Appeals, Fifth Circuit, 1980.
631 F.2d 366.

KRAVITCH, CIRCUIT JUDGE.

In a jury trial, appellee Elizarraras was awarded damages of $89,800 due to appellant bank's failure to honor appellee's check. * * * We * * * affirm on the issue of liability. Because, however, we find insufficient evidence to support the award of damages, we reverse the judgment and remand for a new trial solely on the issue of damages.

* * *

* * * The jury awarded damages in the amount of $89,800: $75,000 for loss of credit and damage to reputation, $12,800 for the penalty the Mexican bank charged appellee, and $2,000 for interest on the $64,000 still owed to the Mexican bank.

* * *

Appellant contends that essential evidence to support the award of $12,800 penalty and $2,000 interest to the Mexican bank was wrongfully admitted and that evidence to sustain the $75,000 award for loss of credit and damage to reputation was insufficient.

At trial appellant objected to the following statement made by appellee: "I paid the $64,000; then $12,800 and twenty-three and something else." Under Fed.R.Evid. 602, a "witness may not testify to a matter unless evidence is introduced sufficient to support a finding that he has personal knowledge of the matter." The Advisory Committee on the Federal Rules, in its notes on Rule 602, points out that "[t]his rule would prevent [a witness] from testifying to the subject matter of [a] hearsay statement, as he has no personal knowledge of it." The problem in the instant case is that the appellee did not carry the burden Rule 602 puts on him of showing personal knowledge of the matter testified to (although appellant objected on hearsay grounds, not personal knowledge, we will not draw such a fine line). In context, it is clear that as to the penalty and interest appellee was not testifying to any act of payment he committed, but rather to the fact his account was charged $12,800 and $2,000; thus, this is not an instance where one can infer personal knowledge from the testimony itself.[21] The only basis appellee appeared to have for his testimony concerning the payment of the penalty and interest was the Mexican bank officers' oral assertions [22] and the Mexican bank notice appellant received; yet this evidence had been excluded as inadmissible hearsay.[23] Neither the conversation nor notice is in the record on appeal. Therefore, we do not rule on the admissibility of this evidence.

Nor can we agree that admission of the appellee's testimony was harmless error. * * * We therefore reverse the judgment insofar as it awards the appellee $12,800 and $2,000 and remand for a new trial on those issues.

* * *

For the above reasons, we also reverse the award of $75,000 for loss of credit and or reputation and remand for a new trial on this issue.

AFFIRMED IN PART, REVERSED IN PART. REMANDED FOR A NEW TRIAL ON DAMAGES.

21. An example would be "I saw X in the room."

22. On voir dire, appellee began to testify that the Mexican bank officials told him about the $12,800 penalty and the $2,000 interest (in context this seemed to be what he was about to say), but an objection to this as hearsay was sustained.

23. If his testimony had been based on admissible hearsay, this would presumably satisfy Rule 602, though we do not decide the question.

TANNER v. UNITED STATES

Supreme Court of the United States, 1987.
483 U.S. 107, 107 S.Ct. 2739, 97 L.Ed.2d 90.

JUSTICE O'CONNOR delivered the opinion of the Court.

Petitioners William Conover and Anthony Tanner were convicted of conspiring to defraud the United States in violation of 18 U.S.C. § 371, and of committing mail fraud in violation of 18 U.S.C. § 1341. The United States Court of Appeals for the Eleventh Circuit affirmed the convictions. 772 F.2d 765 (1985). Petitioners argue that the District Court erred in refusing to admit juror testimony at a post-verdict hearing on juror intoxication during the trial; and that the conspiracy count of the indictment failed to charge a crime against the United States. We affirm in part and remand.

* * *

The day before petitioners were scheduled to be sentenced, Tanner filed a motion, in which Conover subsequently joined, seeking continuance of the sentencing date, permission to interview jurors, an evidentiary hearing, and a new trial. According to an affidavit accompanying the motion, Tanner's attorney had received an unsolicited telephone call from one of the trial jurors, Vera Asbul. App. 246. Juror Asbul informed Tanner's attorney that several of the jurors consumed alcohol during the lunch breaks at various times throughout the trial, causing them to sleep through the afternoons. *Id.,* at 247. The District Court continued the sentencing date, ordered the parties to file memoranda, and heard argument on the motion to interview jurors. The District Court concluded that juror testimony on intoxication was inadmissible under Federal Rule of Evidence 606(b) to impeach the jury's verdict. The District Court invited petitioners to call any nonjuror witnesses, such as courtroom personnel, in support of the motion for new trial. Tanner's counsel took the stand and testified that he had observed one of the jurors "in a sort of giggly mood" at one point during the trial but did not bring this to anyone's attention at the time. *Id.,* at 170.

* * *

Following the hearing the District Court filed an order stating that "[o]n the basis of the admissible evidence offered I specifically find that the motions for leave to interview jurors or for an evidentiary hearing at which jurors would be witnesses is not required or appropriate." The District Court also denied the motion for new trial. *Id.,* at 181–182.

While the appeal of this case was pending before the Eleventh Circuit, petitioners filed another new trial motion based on additional evidence of jury misconduct. In another affidavit, Tanner's attorney stated that he received an unsolicited visit at his residence from a second juror, Daniel Hardy. *Id.,* at 241. Despite the fact that the District Court had denied petitioners' motion for leave to interview jurors, two days after Hardy's visit Tanner's attorney arranged for Hardy to be interviewed by two private investigators. *Id.,* at 242. The interview was transcribed, sworn to by the juror, and attached to the new trial motion. In the interview Hardy stated that he "felt like * * * the jury was on one big party." *Id.,* at 209. Hardy indicated that seven of the jurors drank alcohol during the noon recess. Four jurors, including Hardy, consumed between them "a pitcher to three pitchers" of beer during various recesses. *Id.,* at 212. Of the three other jurors who were alleged to have consumed alcohol, Hardy stated that on several occasions he observed two jurors having one or two mixed drinks during the lunch recess, and one other juror, who was also the foreperson, having a liter of wine on each of three occasions. *Id.,* at 213–215. Juror Hardy also stated that he and three other jurors smoked marijuana quite regularly during the trial. *Id.,* at 216–223. Moreover, Hardy stated that during the trial he observed one juror ingest cocaine five times and another juror ingest cocaine two or three times. *Id.,* at 227. One juror sold a quarter pound of marijuana to another juror during the trial, and took marijuana, cocaine, and drug paraphernalia into the courthouse. *Id.,* at 234–235. Hardy noted that some of the jurors were falling asleep during the trial, and that one of the jurors described himself to Hardy as "flying." *Id.,* at 229. Hardy stated that before he visited Tanner's attorney at his residence, no one had contacted him concerning the jury's conduct, and Hardy had not been offered anything in return for his statement. *Id.,* at 232. Hardy said that he came forward "to clear my conscience" and "[b]ecause I felt * * * that the people on the jury didn't have no business being on the jury. I felt * * * that Mr. Tanner should have a better opportunity to get somebody that would review the facts right." *Id.,* at 231–232.

The District Court, stating that the motions "contain supplemental allegations which differ quantitatively but not qualitatively from those in the April motions," *id.,* at 256, denied petitioners' motion for a new trial.

The Court of Appeals for the Eleventh Circuit affirmed. 772 F.2d 765 (1985). We granted certiorari, 479 U.S. 929, 107 S.Ct. 397, 93 L.Ed.2d 351 (1986), to consider whether the District Court was required to hold an evidentiary hearing, including juror testimony, on juror alcohol and drug use during the trial, and to consider whether petitioners' actions constituted a conspiracy to defraud the United States within the meaning of 18 U.S.C. § 371.

II

Petitioners argue that the District Court erred in not ordering an additional evidentiary hearing at which jurors would testify concerning drug and alcohol use during the trial. Petitioners assert that, contrary to the holdings of the District Court and the Court of Appeals, juror testimony on ingestion of drugs or alcohol during the trial is not barred by Federal Rule of Evidence 606(b). Moreover, petitioners argue that whether or not authorized by Rule 606(b), an evidentiary hearing including juror testimony on drug and alcohol use is compelled by their Sixth Amendment right to trial by a competent jury.

By the beginning of this century, if not earlier, the near-universal and firmly established common-law rule in the United States flatly prohibited the admission of juror testimony to impeach a jury verdict. See 8 J. Wigmore, Evidence § 2352, pp. 696–697 (J. McNaughton rev. ed. 1961) (common-law rule, originating from 1785 opinion of Lord Mansfield, "came to receive in the United States an adherence almost unquestioned").

Exceptions to the common-law rule were recognized only in situations in which an "extraneous influence," *Mattox v. United States,* 146 U.S. 140, 149, 13 S.Ct. 50, 53, 36 L.Ed. 917 (1892), was alleged to have affected the jury. In *Mattox,* this Court held admissible the testimony of jurors describing how they heard and read prejudicial information not admitted into evidence. The Court allowed juror testimony on influence by outsiders in *Parker v. Gladden,* 385 U.S. 363, 365, 87 S.Ct. 468, 470, 17 L.Ed.2d 420 (1966) (bailiff's comments on defendant), and *Remmer v. United States,* 347 U.S. 227, 228–230, 74 S.Ct. 450, 450–452, 98 L.Ed. 654 (1954) (bribe offered to juror). See also *Smith v. Phillips,* 455 U.S. 209, 102 S.Ct. 940, 71 L.Ed.2d 78 (1982) (juror in criminal trial had submitted an application for employment at the District Attorney's office). In situations that did not fall into this exception for external influence, however, the Court adhered to the common-law rule against admitting juror testimony to impeach a verdict. *McDonald v. Pless,* 238 U.S. 264, 35 S.Ct. 783, 59 L.Ed. 1300 (1915); *Hyde v. United States,* 225 U.S. 347, 384, 32 S.Ct. 793, 808, 56 L.Ed. 1114 (1912).

Lower courts used this external/internal distinction to identify those instances in which juror testimony impeaching a verdict would be admissible. The distinction was not based on whether the juror was literally inside or outside the jury room when the alleged irregularity took place; rather, the distinction was based on the nature of the allegation. Clearly a rigid distinction based only on whether the event took place inside or outside the jury room would have been quite unhelpful. For example, under a distinction based on location a juror could not testify concerning a newspaper read inside the jury room. Instead, of course, this has been considered an external influence about which juror testimony is admissible. See *United States v. Thomas,* 463 F.2d 1061 (CA7 1972). Similarly, under a rigid locational distinction jurors could be regularly required to testify after the verdict as to whether they heard and comprehended the judge's instructions, since the charge to the jury takes place outside the jury room. Courts wisely have treated allegations of a juror's inability to hear or comprehend at trial as an internal matter. See *Government of the Virgin Islands v. Nicholas,* 759 F.2d 1073 (CA3 1985); *Davis v. United States,* 47 F.2d 1071 (CA5 1931) (rejecting juror testimony impeaching verdict, including testimony that jurors had not heard a particular instruction of the court).

Most significant for the present case, however, is the fact that lower federal courts treated allegations of the physical or mental incompetence of a juror as "internal" rather than "external" matters. In *United States v. Dioguardi,* 492 F.2d 70 (CA2 1974), the defendant Dioguardi received a letter from one of the jurors soon after the trial in which the juror explained that she had "eyes and ears that * * * see things before [they] happen," but that her eyes "are only partly open" because "a curse was put upon them some years ago." *Id.,* at 75. Armed with this letter and the opinions of seven psychiatrists that the letter suggested that the juror was suffering from a psychological disorder, Dioguardi sought a new trial or in the alternative an evidentiary hearing on the juror's competence. The District Court denied the motion and the Court of Appeals affirmed. The Court of Appeals noted "[t]he strong policy against any post-verdict inquiry into a juror's state of mind," *id.,* at 79, and observed:

> "The quickness with which jury findings will be set aside when there is proof of tampering or *external* influence, * * * parallel the reluctance of courts to inquire into jury deliberations when a verdict is valid on its face * * *. Such exceptions support rather than undermine the rationale of the rule that possible *internal* abnormalities in a jury will not be inquired into except 'in the gravest and most important cases.'" *Id.,* at 79, n. 12, quoting *McDonald v. Pless, supra,* 238 U.S., at 269, 35 S.Ct., at 785 (emphasis in original).

The Court of Appeals concluded that when faced with allegations that a juror was mentally incompetent, "courts have refused to set aside a verdict, or even to make further inquiry, unless there be proof of an adjudication of insanity or mental incompetence closely in advance * * * of jury service," or proof of "a closely contemporaneous and independent post-trial adjudication of incompetency." 492 F.2d, at 80. See also *Sullivan v. Fogg,* 613 F.2d 465, 467 (CA2 1980) (allegation of juror insanity is internal consideration); *United States v. Allen,* 588 F.2d 1100, 1106, n. 12 (CA5 1979) (noting "specific reluctance to probe the minds of jurors once they have deliberated their verdict"); *United States v. Pellegrini,* 441 F.Supp. 1367 (ED Pa.1977), aff'd, 586 F.2d 836 (CA3), cert. denied, 439 U.S. 1050, 99 S.Ct. 731, 58 L.Ed.2d 711 (1978) (whether juror sufficiently understood English language was not a question of "extraneous influence"). This line of federal decisions was reviewed in *Government of the Virgin Islands v. Nicholas, supra,* in which the Court of Appeals concluded that a juror's allegation that a hearing impairment interfered with his understanding of the evidence at trial was not a matter of "external influence." *Id.,* at 1079.

Substantial policy considerations support the common-law rule against the admission of jury testimony to impeach a verdict. As early as 1915 this Court explained the necessity of shielding jury deliberations from public scrutiny:

> "[L]et it once be established that verdicts solemnly made and publicly returned into court can be attacked and set aside on the testimony of those who took part in their publication and all verdicts could be, and

> many would be, followed by an inquiry in the hope of discovering something which might invalidate the finding. Jurors would be harassed and beset by the defeated party in an effort to secure from them evidence of facts which might establish misconduct sufficient to set aside a verdict. If evidence thus secured could be thus used, the result would be to make what was intended to be a private deliberation, the constant subject of public investigation—to the destruction of all frankness and freedom of discussion and conference." *McDonald v. Pless,* 238 U.S., at 267–268, 35 S.Ct., at 784.

See also *Mattox v. United States,* 146 U.S. 140, 13 S.Ct. 50, 36 L.Ed. 917 (1892).

The Court's holdings requiring an evidentiary hearing where extrinsic influence or relationships have tainted the deliberations do not detract from, but rather harmonize with, the weighty government interest in insulating the jury's deliberative process. See *Smith v. Phillips,* 455 U.S. 209, 102 S.Ct. 940, 71 L.Ed.2d 78 (1982) (juror in criminal trial had submitted an application for employment at the District Attorney's office); *Remmer v. United States,* 347 U.S. 227, 74 S.Ct. 450, 98 L.Ed. 654 (1954) (juror reported attempted bribe during trial and was subjected to investigation). The Court's statement in *Remmer* that "[t]he integrity of jury proceedings must not be jeopardized by unauthorized invasions," *id.,* at 229, 74 S.Ct., at 451, could also be applied to the inquiry petitioners seek to make into the internal processes of the jury.

There is little doubt that postverdict investigation into juror misconduct would in some instances lead to the invalidation of verdicts reached after irresponsible or improper juror behavior. It is not at all clear, however, that the jury system could survive such efforts to perfect it. Allegations of juror misconduct, incompetency, or inattentiveness, raised for the first time days, weeks, or months after the verdict, seriously disrupt the finality of the process. See, *e.g., Government of Virgin Islands v. Nicholas, supra,* at 1081 (one year and eight months after verdict rendered, juror alleged that hearing difficulties affected his understanding of the evidence). Moreover, full and frank discussion in the jury room, jurors' willingness to return an unpopular verdict, and the community's trust in a system that relies on the decisions of laypeople would all be undermined by a barrage of postverdict scrutiny of juror conduct. See Note, Public Disclosures of Jury Deliberations, 96 Harv.L.Rev. 886, 888–892 (1983).

Federal Rule of Evidence 606(b) is grounded in the common-law rule against admission of jury testimony to impeach a verdict and the exception for juror testimony relating to extraneous influences. See *Government of Virgin Islands v. Gereau,* 523 F.2d 140, 149, n. 22 (CA3 1975); S.Rep. No. 93–1277, p. 13 (1974), U.S.Code Cong. & Admin.News 1974, p. 7051 (observing that Rule 606(b) "embodied long-accepted Federal law").

Rule 606(b) states:

"Upon an inquiry into the validity of a verdict or indictment, a juror may not testify as to any matter or statement occurring during the course of the jury's deliberations or to the effect of anything upon his or any other juror's mind or emotions as influencing him to assent to or dissent from the verdict or indictment or concerning his mental processes in connection therewith, except that a juror may testify on the question whether extraneous prejudicial information was improperly brought to the jury's attention or whether any outside influence was improperly brought to bear upon any juror. Nor may his affidavit or evidence of any statement by him concerning a matter about which he would be precluded from testifying be received for these purposes."

Petitioners have presented no argument that Rule 606(b) is inapplicable to the juror affidavits and the further inquiry they sought in this case, and, in fact, there appears to be virtually no support for such a proposition. See 3 D. Louisell & C. Mueller, Federal Evidence § 287, pp. 121–125 (1979) (under Rule 606(b), "proof to the following effects is excludable * * *: that one or more jurors was inattentive during trial or deliberations, sleeping or thinking about other matters"); cf. Note, Impeachment of Verdicts by Jurors—Rule of Evidence 606(b), 4 Wm. Mitchell L.Rev. 417, 430–431, and n. 88 (1978) (observing that under Rule 606(b), "juror testimony as to * * * juror intoxication probably will be inadmissible"; note author suggests that "[o]ne possibility is for the courts to determine that certain acts, such as a juror becoming intoxicated outside the jury room, simply are not within the rule," but cites no authority in support of the suggestion). Rather, petitioners argue that substance abuse constitutes an improper "outside influence" about which jurors may testify under Rule 606(b). In our view the language of the Rule cannot easily be stretched to cover this circumstance. However severe their effect and improper their use, drugs or alcohol voluntarily ingested by a juror seems no more an "outside influence" than a virus, poorly prepared food, or a lack of sleep.

In any case, whatever ambiguity might linger in the language of Rule 606(b) as applied to juror intoxication is resolved by the legislative history of the Rule. In 1972, following criticism of a proposed rule that would have allowed considerably broader use of juror testimony to impeach verdicts, the Advisory Committee drafted the present version of Rule 606(b). Compare 51 F.R.D. 315, 387 (1971) with 56 F.R.D. 183, 265 (1972); see 117 Cong.Rec. 33642, 33645 (1971) (letter from Sen. McClellan to Advisory Committee criticizing earlier proposal); *id.,* at 33655 (letter from Department of Justice to Advisory Committee criticizing earlier proposal and arguing that "[s]trong policy considerations continue to support the rule that jurors should not be permitted to testify about what occurred during the course of their deliberations"). This Court adopted the present version of Rule 606(b) and transmitted it to Congress.

The House Judiciary Committee described the effect of the version of Rule 606(b) transmitted by the Court as follows:

"As proposed by the Court, Rule 606(b) limited testimony by a juror in the course of an inquiry into the validity of a verdict or indictment. He could testify as to the influence of extraneous prejudicial information brought to the jury's attention (e.g. a radio newscast or a newspaper account) or an outside influence which improperly had been brought to bear upon a juror (e.g. a threat to the safety of a member of his family), but he could not testify as to other irregularities which occurred in the jury room. Under this formulation a quotient verdict could not be attacked through the testimony of juror, *nor could a juror testify to the drunken condition of a fellow juror which so disabled him that he could not participate in the jury's deliberations.*" H.R.Rep. No. 93–650, pp. 9–10 (1973), U.S.Code Cong. & Admin.News 1974, p. 7083 (emphasis supplied).

The House Judiciary Committee, persuaded that the better practice was to allow juror testimony on any "objective juror misconduct," amended the Rule so as to comport with the more expansive versions proposed by the Advisory Committee in earlier drafts,* and the House passed this amended version.

The Senate Judiciary Committee did not voice any disagreement with the House's interpretation of the Rule proposed by the Court, or the version passed by the House. Indeed, the Senate Report described the House version as "considerably broader" than the version proposed by the Court, and noted that the House version "would permit the impeachment of verdicts by inquiry into, not the mental processes of the jurors, but what happened in terms of conduct in the jury room." S.Rep. No. 93–1277, p. 13 (1974), U.S.Code Cong. & Admin.News 1974, p. 7060. With this understanding of the differences between the two versions of Rule 606(b)—an understanding identical to that of the House—the Senate decided to reject the broader House version and adopt the narrower version approved by the Court. The Senate Report explained:

"[The House version's] extension of the ability to impeach a verdict is felt to be unwarranted and ill-advised.

"The rule passed by the House embodies a suggestion by the Advisory Committee of the Judicial Conference that is considerably broader than the final version adopted by the Supreme Court, which embodied long-accepted Federal law. Although forbidding the impeachment of verdicts by inquiry into the jurors' mental processes, it deletes from the Supreme Court version the proscription against testimony 'as to any matter or statement occurring during the course of the jury's deliberations.' This deletion would have the effect of opening verdicts up to challenge on the basis of what happened during the

* The House version, which adopted the earlier Advisory Committee proposal, read as follows: "Upon an inquiry into the validity of a verdict or indictment, a juror may not testify concerning the effect of anything upon his or any other juror's mind or emotions as influencing him to assent to or dissent from the verdict or indictment or concerning his mental processes in connection therewith. Nor may his affidavit or evidence of any statement by him indicating an effect of this kind be received for these purposes." H.R. 5463, 93d Cong., 2d Sess. (1974).

jury's internal deliberations, for example, where a juror alleged that the jury refused to follow the trial judge's instructions or that some of the jurors did not take part in deliberations.

"Permitting an individual to attack a jury verdict based upon the jury's internal deliberations has long been recognized as unwise by the Supreme Court.

* * *

"As it stands then, the rule would permit the harassment of former jurors by losing parties as well as the possible exploitation of disgruntled or otherwise badly-motivated ex-jurors.

"Public policy requires a finality to litigation. And common fairness requires that absolute privacy be preserved for jurors to engage in the full and free debate necessary to the attainment of just verdicts. Jurors will not be able to function effectively if their deliberations are to be scrutinized in post-trial litigation. In the interest of protecting the jury system and the citizens who make it work, rule 606 should not permit any inquiry into the internal deliberations of the jurors." *Id.*, at 13–14, U.S.Code Cong. & Admin.News 1974, p. 7060.

The Conference Committee Report reaffirms Congress' understanding of the differences between the House and Senate versions of Rule 606(b): "[T]he House bill allows a juror to testify about objective matters occurring during the jury's deliberation, such as the misconduct of another juror or the reaching of a quotient verdict. The Senate bill does not permit juror testimony about any matter or statement occurring during the course of the jury's deliberations." H.R.Conf.Rep. No. 93–1597, p. 8 (1974), U.S.Code Cong. & Admin.News 1974, p. 7102. The Conference Committee adopted, and Congress enacted, the Senate version of Rule 606(b).

Thus, the legislative history demonstrates with uncommon clarity that Congress specifically understood, considered, and rejected a version of Rule 606(b) that would have allowed jurors to testify on juror conduct during deliberations, including juror intoxication. This legislative history provides strong support for the most reasonable reading of the language of Rule 606(b)—that juror intoxication is not an "outside influence" about which jurors may testify to impeach their verdict.

Finally, even if Rule 606(b) is interpreted to retain the common-law exception allowing postverdict inquiry of juror incompetence in cases of "substantial if not wholly conclusive evidence of incompetency," *Dioguardi,* 492 F.2d, at 80, the showing made by petitioners falls far short of this standard. The affidavits and testimony presented in support of the first new trial motion suggested, at worst, that several of the jurors fell asleep at times during the afternoons. The District Court Judge appropriately considered the fact that he had "an unobstructed view" of the jury, and did not see any juror sleeping. App. 147–149, 167–168; See *Government of Virgin Islands v. Nicholas,* 759 F.2d, at 1077 ("[I]t was appropriate for the trial judge to draw upon his personal knowledge and recollection in considering the factual allegations * * * that related to events that occurred in his presence"). The juror affidavit submitted in support of the second new trial motion was obtained in clear violation of the District Court's order and the court's local rule against juror interviews, MD Fla.Rule 2.04(c); on this basis alone the District Court would have been acting within its discretion in disregarding the affidavit. In any case, although the affidavit of juror Hardy describes more dramatic instances of misconduct, Hardy's allegations of *incompetence* are meager. Hardy stated that the alcohol consumption he engaged in with three other jurors did not leave any of them intoxicated. App. to Pet. for Cert. 47 ("I told [the prosecutor] that we would just go out and get us a pitcher of beer and drink it, but as far as us being drunk, no we wasn't"). The only allegations concerning the jurors' ability to properly consider the evidence were Hardy's observations that some jurors were "falling asleep all the time during the trial," and that his own reasoning ability was affected on one day of the trial. App. to Pet. for Cert. 46, 55. These allegations would not suffice to bring this case under the common-law exception allowing post-verdict inquiry when an extremely strong showing of incompetency has been made.

Petitioners also argue that the refusal to hold an additional evidentiary hearing at which jurors would testify as to their conduct "violates the sixth amendment's guarantee to a fair trial before an impartial and *competent* jury." Brief for Petitioners 34 (emphasis in original).

This Court has recognized that a defendant has a right to "a tribunal both impartial and mentally competent to afford a hearing." *Jordan v. Massachusetts,* 225 U.S. 167, 176, 32 S.Ct. 651, 652, 56 L.Ed. 1038 (1912). In this case the District Court held an evidentiary hearing in response to petitioners' first new trial motion at which the judge invited petitioners to introduce any admissible evidence in support of their allegations. At issue in this case is whether the Constitution compelled the District Court to hold an additional evidentiary hearing including one particular kind of evidence inadmissible under the Federal Rules.

As described above, long-recognized and very substantial concerns support the protection of jury deliberations from intrusive inquiry. Petitioners' Sixth Amendment interests in an unimpaired jury, on the other hand, are protected by several aspects of the trial process. The suitability of an individual for the responsibility of jury service, of course, is examined during *voir dire.* Moreover, during the trial the jury is observable by the court, by counsel, and by court personnel. See *United States v. Provenzano,* 620 F.2d 985, 996–997 (CA3 1980) (marshal discovered sequestered juror smoking marijuana during early morning hours). Moreover, jurors are observable by each other, and may report inappropriate juror behavior to the court *before* they render a verdict. See *Lee v. United States,* 454 A.2d 770 (DC App.1982), cert. denied *sub nom. McIlwain v. United States,* 464 U.S. 972, 104 S.Ct. 409, 78 L.Ed.2d 349 (1983) (on second day of deliberations, jurors sent judge a note suggesting that foreperson was incapacitated). Finally, after the trial a party may seek to impeach the verdict by nonjuror evidence of misconduct. See *United States v. Taliaferro,* 558 F.2d 724, 725–726 (CA4 1977) (court considered records of club where jurors dined, and testimony of marshal who accompanied jurors, to determine whether jurors were intoxicated during deliberations). Indeed, in this case the District Court held an evidentiary hearing giving petitioners ample opportunity to produce nonjuror evidence supporting their allegations.

In light of these other sources of protection of petitioners' right to a competent jury, we conclude that the District Court did not err in deciding, based on the inadmissibility of juror testimony and the clear insufficiency of the nonjuror evidence offered by petitioners, that an additional postverdict evidentiary hearing was unnecessary.

* * *

The judgment of the Court of Appeals is affirmed in part and remanded for further proceedings consistent with this opinion.

It is so ordered.

JUSTICE MARSHALL, with whom JUSTICE BRENNAN, JUSTICE BLACKMUN, and JUSTICE STEVENS join, concurring in part and dissenting in part.

Every criminal defendant has a constitutional right to be tried by competent jurors. This Court has long recognized that "[d]ue process implies a tribunal both impartial and mentally competent to afford a hearing," *Jordan v. Massachusetts,* 225 U.S. 167, 176, 32 S.Ct. 651, 652, 56 L.Ed. 1038 (1912), "a jury capable and willing to decide the case solely on the evidence before it." *Smith v. Phillips,* 455 U.S. 209, 217, 102 S.Ct. 940, 946, 71 L.Ed.2d 78 (1982). If, as is charged, members of petitioners' jury were intoxicated as a result of their use of drugs and alcohol to the point of sleeping through material portions of the trial, the verdict in this case must be set aside. In directing district courts to ignore sworn allegations that jurors engaged in gross and debilitating misconduct, this Court denigrates the precious right to a competent jury. Accordingly, I dissent from that part of the Court's opinion.

* * *

Despite the seriousness of the charges, the Court refuses to allow petitioners an opportunity to vindicate their fundamental right to a competent jury. The Court holds that petitioners are absolutely barred from exploring allegations of juror misconduct and incompetency through the only means available to them—examination of the jurors who have already voluntarily come forward. The basis for the Court's ruling is the mistaken belief that juror testimony concerning drug and alcohol abuse at trial is inadmissible under Federal Rule of Evidence 606(b) and is contrary to the policies the Rule was intended to advance.

I readily acknowledge the important policy considerations supporting the common-law rule against admission of jury testimony to impeach a verdict, now embodied in Federal Rule of Evidence 606(b): freedom of deliberation, finality of verdicts, and protection of jurors against harassment by dissatisfied litigants. See, *e.g., McDonald v.*

Pless, 238 U.S. 264, 267–268, 35 S.Ct. 783, 784–785, 59 L.Ed. 1300 (1915); Advisory Committee's Notes on Fed.Rule Evid. 606(b), 28 U.S.C.App., p. 700. It has been simultaneously recognized, however, that "simply putting verdicts beyond effective reach can only promote irregularity and injustice." *Ibid.* If the above-referenced policy considerations seriously threaten the constitutional right to trial by a fair and impartial jury, they must give way. See *Parker v. Gladden,* 385 U.S. 363, 87 S.Ct. 468, 17 L.Ed.2d 420 (1966); *Mattox v. United States,* 146 U.S. 140, 13 S.Ct. 50, 36 L.Ed. 917 (1892).

In this case, however, we are not faced with a conflict between the policy considerations underlying Rule 606(b) and petitioners' Sixth Amendment rights. Rule 606(b) is not applicable to juror testimony on matters *unrelated* to the jury's deliberations. By its terms, Rule 606(b) renders jurors incompetent to testify only as to three subjects: (i) any "matter or statement" occurring during deliberations; (ii) the "effect" of anything upon the "mind or emotions" of any juror as it relates to his or her "assent to or dissent from the verdict"; and (iii) the "mental processes" of the juror in connection with his "assent to or dissent from the verdict." Even as to matters involving deliberations, the bar is not absolute.[6]

It is undisputed that Rule 606(b) does not exclude juror testimony as to matters occurring before or after deliberations. See 3 D. Louisell & C. Mueller, Federal Evidence, § 290, p. 151 (1979); cf. Note, Impeachment of Verdicts by Jurors—Rule of Evidence 606(b), 4 Wm. Mitchell L.Rev. 417, 431, n. 88 (1978). But, more particularly, the Rule only "operates to prohibit testimony as to *certain* conduct by the jurors which has no verifiable manifestations," 3 J. Weinstein & M. Berger, Weinstein's Evidence ¶ 606[04], p. 606–28 (1985) (emphasis added); as to other matters, jurors remain competent to testify. See Fed.Rule Evid. 601. Because petitioners' claim of juror misconduct and incompetency involves objectively verifiable conduct occurring prior to deliberations, juror testimony in support of the claims is admissible under Rule 606(b).

The Court's analysis of legislative history confirms the inapplicability of Rule 606(b) to the type of misconduct alleged in this case. As the Court emphasizes, the debate over two proposed versions of the Rule—the more restrictive Senate version ultimately adopted and the permissive House version, focused on the extent to which jurors would be permitted to testify as to what transpired *during the course of the deliberations themselves.*[7] Similarly, the Conference Committee Re-

6. Rule 606(b) expressly authorizes jurors to testify as to "extraneous prejudicial information" or "outside influence." See *infra.*

7. Proponents of the more restrictive Senate version were reluctant to allow juror testimony as to irregularities in the process by which a verdict was reached, such as the resort to a "quotient verdict." See, *e.g.,* 120 Cong.Rec. 2374–2375 (1974) (statement of Rep. Wiggins); 117 Cong.Rec. 33642, 33645 (1971) (letter from Sen. McClellan); *id.,* at 33649, 33655 (Dept. of Justice Analysis and Recommendations Regarding Revised Draft of Proposed Rules of

port, quoted by the Court, compares the two versions solely in terms of the admissibility of testimony as to matters occurring during, or relating to, the jury's deliberations: "[T]he House bill allows a juror to testify about objective matters occurring during the jury's deliberation, such as the misconduct of another juror or the reaching of a quotient verdict. The Senate bill does not permit juror testimony about any matter or statement occurring *during the course of the jury's deliberations.*" H.R.Conf.Rep. No. 93–1597, p. 8 (1974), U.S.Code Cong. & Admin.News 1974, p. 7102 (emphasis added). The obvious conclusion, and the one compelled by Rule 601, is that *both* versions of Rule 606(b) would have permitted jurors to testify as to matters not involving deliberations. The House Report's passing reference to juror intoxication during deliberations is not to the contrary. Reflecting Congress' consistent focus on the deliberative process, it suggests only that the authors of the House Report believed that the Senate version of Rule 606(b) did not allow testimony as to juror intoxication during deliberations.[8]

In this case, no invasion of the jury deliberations is contemplated. Permitting a limited postverdict inquiry into juror consumption of alcohol and drugs *during trial* would not "make what was intended to be a private deliberation, the constant subject of public investigation—to the destruction of all frankness and freedom of discussion and conference." *McDonald v. Pless,* 238 U.S., at 267–268, 35 S.Ct., at 784. "Allowing [jurors] to testify as to matters other than their own inner reactions involves no particular hazard to the values sought to be protected." Advisory Committee's Notes of Fed.Rule Evid. 606(b), 28 U.S.C.App., p. 701.

Even if I agreed with the Court's expansive construction of Rule 606(b), I would nonetheless find the testimony of juror intoxication admissible under the Rule's "outside influence" exception.[9] As a com-

Evidence for the U.S. Courts and Magistrates).

As the Court explains, the Senate rejected the House version because it "would have the effect of opening verdicts up to challenge on the basis of what happened during the jury's *internal deliberations,* for example, where a juror alleged that the jury refused to follow the trial judge's instructions or that some of the jurors did not take part in deliberations." S.Rep. No. 93–1277, p. 13 (1974), U.S.Code Cong. & Admin.News 1974, p. 7060 (emphasis added). See also *id.,* at 14, U.S.Code Cong. & Admin.News 1974, p. 7060 ("[R]ule 606 should not permit any inquiry into the internal deliberations of the jurors").

8. H.R.Rep. No. 93–650, p. 10 (1973), U.S.Code Cong. & Admin.News 1974, p. 7083 ("Under this formulation a quotient verdict could not be attacked through the testimony of a juror, nor could a juror testify to the drunken condition of a fellow juror which so disabled him that he could not participate in the jury's deliberations").

9. The sole support for the Court's cramped interpretation of this exception is the isolated reference to juror intoxication *at deliberations,* contained in the House Report, quoted *supra,* n. 8. The source for the reference is a letter to the House Subcommittee, to the effect that the version of the Rule adopted by the Senate would not allow inquiry into juror consumption of alcohol during deliberations. The letter was offered in support of reinstatement of the original form of the Rule (the version adopted by the House); the letter focused primarily on the question whether inquiry into quotient verdicts should be permitted. See Rules of Evidence, Hearings before the Special Subcommittee on Reform of Federal Criminal Laws of the House Committee

monsense matter, drugs and alcohol *are* outside influences on jury members. Commentators have suggested that testimony as to drug and alcohol abuse, even during deliberations, falls within this exception. "[T]he present exception paves the way for proof by the affidavit or testimony of a juror that one or more jurors became intoxicated during deliberations * * *. Of course the use of hallucinogenic or narcotic drugs during deliberations should similarly be provable." 3 Louisell & Mueller, Federal Evidence, § 289, pp. 143–145 (footnote omitted). See 3 Weinstein & Berger, Weinstein's Evidence, *supra,* ¶ 606[04], pp. 606–29—606–32 ("Rule 606(b) would not render a witness incompetent to testify to juror irregularities such as intoxication * * * regardless of whether the jury misconduct occurred within or without the jury room"). The Court suggests that, if these are outside influences, "a virus, poorly prepared food, or a lack of sleep" would also qualify. Distinguishing between a virus, for example, and a narcotic drug is a matter of line-drawing. Courts are asked to make these sorts of distinctions in numerous contexts; I have no doubt they would be capable of differentiating between the intoxicants involved in this case and minor indispositions not affecting juror competency.

The Court assures us that petitioners' Sixth Amendment interests are adequately protected by other aspects of the trial process: *voir dire;* observation during trial by the court, counsel, and courtroom personnel; and observation by fellow jurors (so long as they report inappropriate juror behavior to the court before a verdict is rendered). Reliance on these safeguards, to the exclusion of an evidentiary hearing, is misguided. *Voir dire* cannot disclose whether a juror will choose to abuse drugs and alcohol during the trial. Moreover, the type of misconduct alleged here is not readily verifiable through nonjuror testimony. The jurors were not supervised by courtroom personnel during the noon recess, when they consumed alcoholic beverages and used drugs. Hardy reported that he and his three companions purposely avoided observation. They smoked marijuana and used cocaine first in a municipal parking garage and later "[d]own past the Hyatt Regency" because it was "away from everybody." App. 218, 222.

Finally, any reliance on observations of the court is particularly inappropriate on the facts of this case. The District Judge maintained that he had a view of the jury during the trial, and "[y]ou might infer * * * that if I had seen somebody sleeping I would have done something about that." *Id.,* at 167. However, as the portions of the trial transcript quoted indicate, the judge had abdicated any responsibility for monitoring the jury. He stated: "I'm going to—not going to take on

on the Judiciary, 93d Cong., 1st Sess., 389 (1973). In a subsequent letter, the writer dropped any reference to the question of intoxication, focusing exclusively on the issue of quotient verdicts. See Rules of Evidence (Supplement), Hearings before the Subcommittee on Criminal Justice of the House Committee on the Judiciary, 93d Cong., 1st Sess., 27–28 (1973). Moreover, this reference is hardly dispositive. The comparison was provided to show that the House version was "the better practice." H.R.Rep. No. 93–650, *supra,* at 10. None of the subsequent Committee Reports make any allusion to juror intoxication.

that responsibility" and "I'm not going to sit here and watch. I'm—among other things, I'm not going to see—* * *." Tr. 12–100—12–101.

III

The Court acknowledges that "postverdict investigation into juror misconduct would in some instances lead to the invalidation of verdicts reached after irresponsible or improper juror behavior," but maintains that "[i]t is not at all clear * * * that the jury system could survive such efforts to perfect it." Petitioners are not asking for a perfect jury. They are seeking to determine whether the jury that heard their case behaved in a manner consonant with the minimum requirements of the Sixth Amendment. If we deny them this opportunity, the jury system may survive, but the constitutional guarantee on which it is based will become meaningless.

I dissent.

SECTION 2. IMPEACHMENT *

[FED.R.EVID. 607–610, 613]

FOREWORD

There are five main categories of impeachment evidence, representing five types of attack upon the credibility of a witness:

(1) Evidence that the witness has made a *prior inconsistent statement;*

(2) Evidence that the witness has a *bias or interest,* either legitimate or corrupt, relating to one or more of the parties or to the outcome of the case;

(3) Evidence that the witness has a *bad character for truthfulness,* as shown by his previous conviction of a crime, or other misconduct, or by reputation or opinion evidence as to his character;

(4) Evidence of a *defect of capacity* of the witness to observe, remember, or relate;

(5) Evidence that any matter in the witness' testimony is false—sometimes called *specific contradiction* of the witness.

A distinction may be drawn concerning the source of evidence offered for impeachment, between (1) evidence elicited (or attempted to be elicited) from the witness during cross-examination, and (2) evidence from another witness or a document. The second category is called *extrinsic* evidence. In some circumstances resort to extrinsic evidence is prohibited, and it is said that the party "must take the answer" of the witness. This restriction is usually explained by designation of the impeaching matter as *collateral.* Thus the generalization is sometimes made, "A party may not introduce extrinsic evidence to contradict a witness on a collateral matter solely for purposes of impeachment." As

* See 3A Wigmore, Evidence (Chadbourn rev. 1970); 4 id. ch. 38 (Chadbourn rev. 1972); McCormick, Evidence ch. 5 (4th ed. 1992).

the ensuing materials illustrate, determining what matters are "collateral" in this sense is one of the difficult and important problems in the law of impeachment.

The credibility of a witness may not be supported until it has been attacked. The nature of the attack determines the permissible types of rehabilitation evidence.

STATE v. HINES

Supreme Court of Arizona, 1981.
130 Ariz. 68, 633 P.2d 1384.

STRUCKMEYER, CHIEF JUSTICE.

Appellant Donald Ray Hines was convicted by jury of illegal possession of marijuana and appeals. Affirmed.

On the evening of April 6, 1979, Willie Jewel Haynie was allegedly sexually assaulted. The following morning, Haynie accompanied the police to appellant's home where she identified the appellant as one of the persons who had assaulted her. The police then placed the appellant under arrest. Following a search after his arrest, the police found a matchbox containing marijuana in the pocket of his pants. Subsequently, the appellant was tried on charges of kidnapping, sexual assault and possession of marijuana. The jury found appellant guilty of possession of marijuana, but was unable to reach a verdict as to the other asserted offenses.

On appeal, appellant urges that the cross-examination of Susan Robinson, the appellant's chief alibi witness, by the prosecution was improper. Appellant called Susan Robinson, the woman with whom he had been living, to the stand. According to Robinson's testimony, she spent the evening of the alleged assault with the appellant's family. At about 11:15 p.m. that night, the appellant telephoned her at his parents' home, at which time she told him she was ready to leave. He arrived to take her home at about 11:30 p.m., but they did not leave then. First, appellant went to pick up Robinson's brother, Daryl. The appellant returned for Robinson at about 12:00 or 12:30 a.m. As she was leaving the Hines' home, she saw her brothers Daryl and Jimmy sitting in Daryl's car parked alongside of the Hines' house. She also saw a young woman in the car, but failed to recognize her. Robinson and appellant went to where they were living and retired for the evening.

On cross-examination, the prosecutor tried to establish that much of Robinson's testimony was fabricated. He repeatedly called her attention to a prior interview he had had with her on September 13, 1979, and the fact that she had not related to him anything about the telephone call at 11:15 p.m., the appellant's initial visit to his parents' home, or the fact that she had seen her brothers in the company of a woman outside the Hines' residence. He also cross-examined her about what she had told him at the prior interview concerning the vehicle appellant was driving the night of April 6th and about statements she made to an investigating detective the day of appellant's arrest.

Appellant urges that the attempted impeachment was improper. The first impeaching questions of which appellant complains consisted of the prosecutor asking Robinson if she remembered the prior interview of September 13, 1979, and the fact that during that interview she had not said anything to him about the telephone call, the appellant's first visit to his parents' home, or the fact that she had seen her brothers in the company of a woman outside the home of appellant's parents. The question is whether Robinson's September 13, 1979 statements were, in fact, consistent with her testimony at appellant's trial.

At the outset, it should be said that what is being dealt with here is not a direct contradiction between testimony at trial and a previous statement, but, rather, that during a prior interview the witness omitted certain facts to which she later testified at trial. Whether an omission to state a fact constitutes an inconsistency sufficient to discredit a witness depends at least in part upon the circumstances under which the prior statement was made. A prior omission will constitute an inconsistency only where it was made under circumstances rendering it incumbent upon the witness to, or be likely to, state such a fact. See Ball v. State, 43 Ariz. 556, 559, 33 P.2d 601, 602 (1934); Carroll v. Krause, 295 Ill.App. 552, 562, 15 N.E.2d 323, 328 (1938); Asato v. Furtado, 52 Haw. 284, 288, 474 P.2d 288, 292 (1970); Sims v. State, 530 P.2d 1176, 1179–1180 (Wyo.1975). The rationale for allowing impeachment in these circumstances is that "a *failure to assert* a fact, when it would have been natural to assert it, amounts in effect to assertion of the non-existence of the fact." [1] IIIA Wigmore, Evidence § 1042 (Chadbourn rev. 1970). The underlying test as stated in *Wigmore,* supra is: would it have been natural for the person to make the assertion in question?

Here, during the course of the September 13, 1979 interview, the prosecutor questioned Robinson at some length concerning the events of April 6, 1979. She knew that the prosecutor was interested in her

1. It is true that under Rule 19.3, Rules of Criminal Procedure, 17 A.R.S., no prior statement of a witness may be admitted for purposes of impeachment unless it varies materially from his testimony at trial. The comments to Rule 19.3 make it clear that the actual standard embodied in the rule is theoretically no different from the one used prior to adoption of the rule. The standard as stated in IIIA Wigmore, Evidence § 1040 (Chadbourn ed. 1970), is:

> "[T]he purpose [of impeachment by use of a prior inconsistent statement] is to induce the tribunal to discard the one statement because the witness has also made another statement which cannot at the same time be true. * * * Thus, it is not a mere difference of statement that suffices; nor yet is an absolute oppositeness essential; it is an inconsistency that is required."

It would seem apparent, based on the rationale for considering a prior omission a prior inconsistent statement, that an omission which qualifies as a prior inconsistent statement will vary materially from the latter trial testimony as required by Rule 19.3, since on the first occasion the person is in effect saying that the fact does not exist, while on the second occasion he is saying that it does exist. Both statements cannot possibly be true, hence an inconsistency.

because of her relationship with appellant. It could be inferred that she should have realized she was to tell him everything she knew about the appellant's activities that day. The 11:15 p.m. telephone call, the initial appearance of the appellant at his parents' home and the observation of her brothers outside the appellant's parents' home are all facts which it would have been natural to relate when questioned about appellant's activities on April 6, 1979. Her failure to do so constituted proper grounds for impeachment.

Next, appellant contends that even if the omissions were prior inconsistent statements, impeachment should not have been permitted because the prosecutor failed to lay the proper foundation. It is true that in the past a cross-examiner in attempting to impeach a witness by use of prior inconsistent statements was required to ask the witness whether he made the alleged statement, giving it substance and naming the time, the place, and the person to whom made. See McCormick, Evidence, § 37 (1972 ed.). However, these foundational requirements have been explicitly abolished by Rule 613(a), Rules of Evidence, 17A A.R.S., which states: "In examining a witness concerning a prior statement made by him, whether written or not, the statement need not be shown nor its contents disclosed to him at that time * * *." The only requirement is that upon request, the statement must be shown or disclosed to opposing counsel. See 3 Weinstein and Berger, Weinstein's Evidence 631–1 et seq. (1978), and Am.Jur.2d, Federal Rules of Evidence 77 (1975), discussing the provisions of the similar federal rule. Here, the transcript of the relevant interview was made available to defense counsel at her request. Thus, Rule 613(a), Rules of Evidence, 17A A.R.S. was fully complied with.

Appellant contends that even if the prior omissions were inconsistent, and no foundation was necessary, the impeachment was improper because the prosecutor failed to follow up his questions by introducing extrinsic evidence of the omissions. Such impeachment, appellant contends, constitutes impeachment by insinuation and is improper. It has long been the rule that a cross-examiner may not impeach a witness by implying the existence or non-existence of statements or facts which he is not prepared to prove. State v. Hill, 109 Ariz. 93, 95, 505 P.2d 553 (1973). Here, Robinson's testimony was not impeached by insinuation. Impeachment by insinuation occurs when the cross-examiner asks questions for which there is no basis in fact. Robinson admitted that she had previously been asked about the events of April 6, 1979 and at that time had failed to say anything about the telephone call, the fact that appellant had first appeared at his parents' home at about 11:30 p.m. or that she saw her brothers outside the Hines' home. No further proof was necessary. See Udall, Arizona Law of Evidence § 63 (1960); United States v. Hibler, 463 F.2d 455 (9th Cir.1972).[2] As

2. In fact, the real controversy in this area is whether the cross-examiner *may* introduce extrinsic evidence after the witness admits to having made the prior inconsistent statement. See Weinstein and Berger, Weinstein's Evidence 613 (1978). Compare McCormick, Evidence § 37 (1972

such, any impeachment which the jury might infer was not by insinuation.

* * *

Affirmed.

BALTIMORE TRANSIT CO. v. STATE FOR THE USE OF CASTRANDA, 194 Md. 421, 71 A.2d 442, 449–50 (1950). "*Seventh.* Defendant contended that, when it called its investigator to the stand to impeach Elliott, the judge erred in not allowing it to ask him: 'What did Elliott tell you about the accident?' It is an invariable rule that in order to impeach a witness by proof of prior contradictory statements, a foundation for such impeachment must be laid by asking the witness on cross-examination whether he had made contradictory statements to a designated person and informing him of the place where and the time when the statements were supposed to have been made. Baltimore & Ohio R. Co. v. State, to Use of Welch, 114 Md. 536, 544, 80 A. 170; Conrades v. Heller, 119 Md. 448, 451, 87 A. 28; Pindell v. Rubenstein, 139 Md. 567, 574, 115 A. 859. 'This,' Judge Robinson said in Brown v. State, 72 Md. 468, 475, 20 A. 186, 188, 'is but fair and just to the witness, in order that he may be enabled to refresh his recollection in regard to such statements, and afforded the opportunity of making such explanations as he may deem necessary and proper.' If the witness denies that he made the alleged statements, he may then be contradicted by any witness who heard him make them, and the jury will then determine what value to give to his testimony.

* * *

"*Eighth.* Defendant complained because the judge would not permit its investigator to impeach Elliott by telling whether Elliott had said anything to him about being requested by Castranda to go to Snyder's Bar 'to tow an automobile back.' Such a conversation was irrelevant to the issues of the case and hence it was properly excluded. It is an accepted rule that a witness cannot be cross-examined as to any irrelevant fact for the purpose of impeaching him by other evidence. If the witness should answer an irrelevant question without objection, evidence cannot afterwards be admitted to contradict his testimony on the collateral matter. Sloan v. Edwards, 61 Md. 89, 105; Baltimore City Passenger Ry. Co. v. Tanner, 90 Md. 315, 320, 45 A. 188."

GLENN v. GLEASON, 61 Iowa 28, 15 N.W. 659, 661–62 (1883). "In the course of the cross-examination of the witness her attention was called to certain letters said to have been written and signed by her. As to one of these letters she was asked this question: 'Examine that writing and signature, and see if that is your writing or not.'

ed.) with IIIA Wigmore, Evidence § 1043 (Chadbourn rev. 1970).

"Thereupon her counsel requested 'that the witness have the privilege of examining the contents of the letter before being required to answer if it was her signature.' This request was refused, and plaintiff excepted. The witness answered that she would not be positive that the signatures to the letters were her signatures. She stated at one time that she thought that the signature to one of them was her own signature, but was not certain. Thereupon counsel for the defendants proceeded to read certain clauses in the letters, and asked the witness if she had written them. The following are examples of the questions asked the witness as to the contents of these letters: 'Did you in the same letter say to him, "Don't let them draw anything out of you that will conflict with the statement I give you." "No one to love them; none to caress them;" did you write that?' The counsel for the plaintiff protested against this mode of examination of the witness for the reason that the letters were the best evidence of their contents, and the witness should not be compelled to give her recollection of what she had written when the letters in question were in court. The court overruled the objections and permitted counsel to proceed, and the witness answered all the interrogatories, in effect, that she did not remember. In overruling this objection and permitting this course to be pursued in the examination of the witness we think the court erred.

"In volume 1, § 463, of Greenleaf on Evidence, it is said: 'The counsel will not be permitted to represent in the statement of a question the contents of a letter, and to ask the witness whether he wrote a letter to any person with such contents, or contents to the like effect, without having first shown to the witness the letter, and having asked him whether he wrote that letter, and his admitting that he wrote it; for the contents of every written paper, according to the ordinary and well-established rules of evidence, are to be proved by the paper itself, and by that alone, if in existence. But it is not required that the whole paper should be shown to the witness. Two or three lines only of a letter may be exhibited to him, and he may be asked whether he wrote the part exhibited. If he denies or does not admit that he wrote that part, he cannot be examined as to the contents of such letter, for the reason already given; nor is the opposite counsel entitled in that case to look at the paper; and if he admits the letter to be his writing, he cannot be asked whether statements, such as the counsel may suggest, are contained in it, but the whole letter must be read as the only competent evidence of that fact. * * *'

"That the course of examination pursued in this case was in plain violation of these rules must be conceded. It is plain from the mere reading of the record that it tended to embarrass and confuse the witness, and prejudice her in the minds of the jury."

KEEFER v. C.R. BARD, INC., 110 Mich.App. 563, 313 N.W.2d 151, 159–60 (1981). "We also find to be unpersuasive defendant Bard's argument that error requiring reversal was committed where the trial judge permitted Bard's expert witness to be cross-examined and impeached by reference to his prior deposition testimony where he was not first shown a copy of his prior testimony.

"Under MRE 613(a), a written statement must be first shown to a witness before it can be used as a source of impeachment:

> 'In examining a witness concerning a prior statement made by the witness, if written the statement must be shown to the witness and if oral, its substance and the time, place, and person to whom the statement was made must be disclosed to the witness, and on request must be shown or disclosed to opposing counsel.'

"Thus, the question presented is whether the deposition testimony of defendant Bard's expert constituted 'a written statement'.

"The issue before us has not been addressed previously by a Michigan appellate court. However, it appears that the language of this rule of evidence is unambiguous to the extent that it provides that if a prior statement of a witness is written then it must be shown to that witness before impeachment can take place.

"Plaintiff's contention that the rule applies only where the statement is written *by* the witness does not appear to be correct. This follows from the opinion of this Court in People v. Johnson, 100 Mich.App. 594, 598, 300 N.W.2d 332 (1980), where this Court held:

> 'In construing MRE 613, words are to be given their ordinary meanings. See Samuel Reiter Painting Co. v. Bill Miedler Homes, Inc., 87 Mich.App. 75, 273 N.W.2d 592 (1978), *lv. den.* 406 Mich. 911 (1979). We believe that the plain meaning of "written" in the rule belies any claim that tape recordings should be considered as written statements.'

"While this issue addressed by the *Johnson* Court is not the same as that before us here, we believe that that Court was correct in stating that the plain language of this rule of evidence must be construed in accordance with this ordinary meaning.

"To a similar effect, is the opinion of this Court in People v. Donald, 103 Mich.App. 613, 303 N.W.2d 247 (1981). In that case, this Court refuted a defendant's claim that a witness may be impeached only by written statements and that a tape recorded preliminary examination does not qualify unless transcribed into written form. As with *Johnson,* the *Donald* Court distinguished between tape recordings and 'written statements'. Significantly, the Court did not distinguish between all statements written *by* a litigant and all statements given orally by the litigant, some of which may have been reduced to a written form.

"Thus, in these two cases, the Court seems to have implicitly understood that if either of the defendants in these two cases had had his preliminary examination testimony reduced to a transcript form, it would have been a 'written statement' for purposes of MRE 613(a). Therefore, it follows that the trial judge erred in the instant case by permitting defendant Bard's expert witness to be impeached without first giving him an opportunity to examine his deposition testimony. Nonetheless, we find that error requiring reversal has not occurred.

"Even though the trial judge's evidentiary ruling was erroneous, defendant Bard was not prejudiced in such a way as to require a new trial. Mr. Child was told of his prior deposition statement before that statement was used for impeachment. Thus, whatever error occurred arose only from the fact that Bard's expert was orally told of his prior statement rather than being shown it in writing. Further, it is difficult to fathom how the jury's verdict has been affected significantly by the erroneous evidentiary ruling. It is extremely unlikely that the verdict would have been different if plaintiff's counsel would have shown Mr. Child his deposition testimony before using it to impeach him. Mr. Child was given a full and ample opportunity to explain any inconsistency. Therefore, we hold that the complained-of error is harmless beyond a reasonable doubt and does not warrant reversal."

PEOPLE v. RAINFORD, 58 Ill.App.2d 312, 208 N.E.2d 314, 316, 318–19 (1965). "The complaining witness was the 13–year–old stepdaughter of the defendant. Her testimony was that on March 1, 1958, she lived with her mother and stepfather and six brothers and sisters in a four room home in South Holland, Illinois. She testified that on that morning her mother told her to return to the children's bedroom and undress and get into bed with her stepfather. She did this. The defendant was undressed and kneeled over her in a straddled position. At this moment her stepbrother, Bill Rainford, 17, walked through the room into a bathroom which adjoined the bedroom. The defendant then covered himself and she started to cry. After her stepbrother left the bathroom her stepfather told her to get up and get dressed. This testimony was corroborated by Bill Rainford who testified on behalf of the State. Both the defendant and his wife denied the occurrence. * * *

"The defendant next argues that the court erred in sustaining objections to three questions which attempted to elicit from the complaining witness the admission that she continued to live in the Rainford home after the alleged occurrence. The claim is that such conduct was incompatible with the charge she was making against her parents. It is proper to cross-examine as to acts or conduct on the part of a witness which are inconsistent with what would be the natural or probable course of conduct if the witness is testifying truthfully about the occurrence in dispute. People v. Boston, 309 Ill. 77, 139 N.E. 880; 98 C.J.S. Witnesses § 379, pp. 138–139. It has been held that evidence of the inconsistent conduct of the prosecutrix should be especially considered in cases of this kind where the charges are difficult to disprove. People v. Nunes, 30 Ill.2d 143, 195 N.E.2d 706. While these questions were proper we do not believe the fact that a 13–year–old girl remained at home with parents after such an incident would have much probative value. There is nothing in the record to disclose where or to whom she might have turned. It is more natural and probable that a girl of her age would continue to stay with her family. This consideration, however, would go to the weight to be given the evidence rather than its admissibility and the questions should have been allowed.

"The third error alleged concerns the refusal of the court to permit the defendant to cross-examine the complaining witness with respect to her testimony at a prior trial. The defendant and his wife had previously been indicted for the rape of the same girl. They were tried and acquitted of this offense which allegedly occurred on February 15, 1958, approximately two weeks before the attempted rape under consideration here.

"After establishing that the prosecutrix had testified at the earlier trial, defense counsel proceeded to inquire if she remembered certain questions asked her and her specific answers thereto. These questions and answers dealt with the alleged rape of February 15th and referred to her stepfather being undressed in the same bedroom and her stepbrother, Bill Rainford, walking into the bedroom at that time. The State objected to these questions on the grounds that there were two separate offenses and that anything she had testified to regarding the February 15th date could in no way impeach her testimony about the attempted rape of March 1. The defense counsel explained that precisely the same questions were asked of her and that the same answers were given by her in both trials; that her former testimony as to the facts surrounding the rape was identical to her testimony on direct examination pertaining to the attempted rape. The court indicated that it was only concerned with the events of March 1, 1958, and ordered all of the questions and answers stricken.

"The issue drawn is whether a witness may be discredited by her prior testimony concerning one event when that prior testimony is identical with her present testimony about an independent and unrelated second event. No governing decision has been cited to us.

"Generally, a prior statement of a witness, in order to be capable of being proved for purposes of impeachment, must be materially inconsistent with his testimony. The test to be applied in determining inconsistency has been variously stated but basically is that the inconsistent statement must have a reasonable tendency to discredit the direct testimony on a material matter. McCormick on Evidence, chap. 5, sec. 34, p. 64 (1954); 98 C.J.S. Witnesses § 583, p. 559. In the present instance the defense was not attempting to impeach the witness by prior inconsistent statements, but was trying to discredit her by prior identical statements, which by the very reason of their being identical, laid them open to suspicion. We see no reason why this cannot be done—why consistency cannot be shown as well as inconsistency, if the implication from the circumstances of the consistency discredits the testimony of a witness. It would be myopic to rule that inconsistency only can be material and that the inconsistency must be restricted exclusively to prior statements regarding the same event. The complaining witness purportedly testified at the former trial that an exactly same albeit extraordinary chain of events occurred in identical sequence between the same parties, under the same circumstances and before the same witness on a date two weeks before the offense which was then being tried. Such testimony would tend to cast doubt upon her statements concerning the subsequent occurrence. Common sense dictates that human behavior of such a heinous nature and involving three persons would rarely repeat itself in such precise detail. We think it evident that if her prior testimony was as indicated then the witness was either confused, or testified falsely, or was a victim of such highly unlikely circumstances that the court in its pursuit of truth should have required an explanation."

Notes

(1) See 3A Wigmore, Evidence ch. 36 (Chadbourn rev. 1970); McCormick, Evidence §§ 28, 34–37 (4th ed. 1992).

(2) On use of a prior inconsistent statement as substantive evidence, see Fed.R.Evid. 801(d)(1)(A); United States v. Castro–Ayon, p. 169 supra. On impeaching one's own witness by prior inconsistent statement, see United States v. Webster, p. 496 infra.

TRI–STATE TRANSFER CO. v. NOWOTNY

Supreme Court of Minnesota, 1936.
198 Minn. 537, 270 N.W. 684.

HILTON, JUSTICE.

* * *

This is an action to recover for the loss sustained from property damage occasioned by a collision between a tractor-trailer unit owned by the plaintiff corporation, and driven by Leon Thompson, now deceased, and a Ford coach, driven by Charles Reichenbach, defendant's intestate. The accident occurred on a 20–foot paved highway with good shoulders at about 2:15 in the morning of October 3, 1934. There were but two eyewitnesses to the accident who are now available. One was Hollister, an employee of the plaintiff, who was driving another of plaintiff's units and was following the Thompson one at a distance of about 300 feet. The other was Gustav Brockhoff, a passenger in the Reichenbach car. As admitted by counsel for both parties, the stories of these two witnesses are diametrically opposed. Hollister claimed that the Ford, on its wrong side of the highway, was driven into the right side of the Thompson machine, which was on its right side of the highway, and that both the driver, Reichenbach, and Brockhoff appeared intoxicated. Brockhoff testified that the Ford was on its right side of the highway; that the Thompson unit was on its wrong side thereof, and that it had only one headlight, the one on the right side, functioning as the Ford approached it. The jury returned a verdict for the defendant.

* * *

Defendant called one Morrison as a witness. On direct examination he testified that he saw and observed Reichenbach shortly after the accident and that he was sober. On cross-examination it was brought out that Morrison at another time had stated that he could not tell whether or not Reichenbach was sober. On redirect, defendant's counsel, claiming surprise, was permitted to show that Morrison at other times had made statements consistent with his testimony on direct examination. Clearly this was error. "Where the adverse party, for the purpose of discrediting a witness, presents evidence that the witness has previously made statements inconsistent with his testimony, it is well settled that the party producing the witness cannot present other statements previously made by him, consistent with his testimony, to offset or overcome the discrediting effect of such contradictory statements." State v. La Bar, 131 Minn. 432, 155 N.W. 211. See George Gorton Machine Co. v. Grignon, 137 Minn. 378, 163 N.W. 748; Barrett v. Van Duzee, 139 Minn. 351, 166 N.W. 407. To allow such procedure whenever a witness has been discredited by cross-examination would destroy the usefulness of the latter. However, in this case the error was not prejudicial. There was testimony of several other witnesses that Reichenbach was sober and even had Morrison not been called there was ample evidence upon which a finding by the jury that Reichenbach was sober could be sustained.

Brockhoff, who, as stated before, was the principal witness for defendant, testified at length as to the manner of the happening of the accident. On cross-examination he was asked if he knew of an attorney by the name of McDonald, to which he replied in the affirmative. He also admitted that he had retained McDonald. It was then brought out by plaintiff that Brockhoff had commenced an action in the district court of Hennepin county to recover damages for his injuries against both the plaintiff here and Reichenbach. He testified that he told McDonald about his "case." The complaint in that action then was introduced in evidence by plaintiff, without objection and with but a very meager foundation first having been laid, in order to impeach Brockhoff. The version of the accident as related in that complaint was much different than and contradictory to the version testified to in the trial of this case. In rebuttal defendant called McDonald, who was permitted to testify, over objection, as to what Brockhoff had told him at the time he was retained. McDonald's story lent credence to Brockhoff's testimony here. The information was elicited from McDonald that he had prepared the complaint (which was unverified) on his own initiative and that Brockhoff had not read it and did not even know what it contained. The admission of that testimony is claimed to be reversible error.

There is no dispute but that a pleading in one action may be used as an admission against the same party in another action. 2 Wig.Evid. § 1063 et seq.; Carpenter v. Tri–State Tel. & Tel. Co., 169 Minn. 287, 211 N.W. 463; Bakkensen v. Minneapolis Street Railway Co., 184 Minn. 274, 238 N.W. 489. Likewise any statement contradictory to one made by a witness on the stand may be used for the purpose of impeachment. The form or nature of the contradictory assertion is immaterial; i.e., it may be oral or written. 2 Wigmore, Evidence, § 1040. Thus a pleading may be so used, as in the case of admissions. However, the impeached witness may always explain away the inconsistency. See 2 Wigmore, Evidence, § 1044, p. 501. It is possible that the apparent inconsistency may not be the result of dishonesty or poor memory but rather because of a temporary misunderstanding. Plaintiff contends, however, that, even if that be true, the explanation can only be made by the impeached witness himself and not by a third party. See Dufresne v. Weise, 46 Wis. 290, 297, 1 N.W. 59. Therefore it is claimed that defendant had no legal right to call McDonald for that purpose. Assuming, without deciding, that the rule is as contended for by plaintiff, even then it would not necessarily follow that there was prejudicial error in permitting McDonald to testify as he did. Third parties may be called to prove that the purportedly contradictory statement used to impeach the witness was never made. 2 Wigmore, Evidence, § 1045, p. 502. That is all defendant did here. By introducing the complaint in evidence, plaintiff made it appear as if Brockhoff had made the statements therein; but, although it might be presumed that those statements were made by him, evidence could be introduced to rebut it. See Carpenter v. Tri–State Tel. & Tel. Co., 169 Minn. 287, 211 N.W. 463. Plaintiff by introducing the pleading in evidence opened wide the door for testimony to the effect that the pleading actually was not the real utterance of the witness concerned but rather the work of his attorney. McDonald testified as to what Brockhoff actually told him. It should make no difference that he was allowed so to testify rather than to limit his testimony to relating that Brockhoff did not tell him the matters alleged in the complaint. It merely was another way of showing that the statements attributed to Brockhoff were not made by him.

McDonald's testimony was not subject to the objection of the hearsay rule, for the reason that no reliance was to be placed in the truthfulness of the statements made to him by Brockhoff. The only point was to find out whether any statements were made and, if so, just exactly what they were. The circumstances surrounding the preparation of the complaint was the source of the information upon which the allegations therein were based and would seem admissible to explain why the pleading was drawn without regard to the version of the interested party.

* * *

Affirmed.

CAMPBELL v. STATE

[p. 173 supra].

Note

On rehabilitation by prior consistent statement, see also 4 Wigmore, Evidence §§ 1122–1133 (Chadbourn rev. 1972); McCormick, Evidence § 47 (4th ed. 1992); Graham, Prior Consistent Statements: Rule 801(d)(1)(B) of the Federal Rules of Evidence, Critique and Proposal, 30 Hast.L.J. 575 (1979).

CHARTER v. CHLEBORAD

[p. 149 supra].

Notes

(1) See also Fed.R.Evid. 408; Fed.R.Evid. 610 advisory committee note.

(2) See generally 3A Wigmore, Evidence ch. 33 (Chadbourn rev. 1970); McCormick, Evidence § 39 (4th ed. 1992); Hale, Bias as Affecting Credibility, 1 Hastings L.J. 1 (1949).

UNITED STATES v. HARVEY

United States Court of Appeals, Second Circuit, 1976.
547 F.2d 720.

KELLEHER, DISTRICT JUDGE:

Defendant appeals from a judgment of conviction after a jury trial in which a verdict of guilty was found as to each of the two counts of the indictment, the first charging the appellant with bank robbery and the second with bank larceny.

The sole question presented on appeal is whether the trial court committed reversible error in excluding evidence proffered by the defendant as to possible bias on the part of the government's chief identification witness. The question presented is of a type likely to occur with some frequency under the Federal Rules of Evidence, which are still rather new, and which at the time of the trial below had been in effect for approximately five months.

On the afternoon of April 22, 1975, the Main–High branch of the Marine Midland Bank–Western was robbed by a man dressed as a woman. Mrs. Florida Strickland, a teller at the bank, described the robber as a medium complexioned black male in his early twenties, 5′11″ to 6′ in height, 160 lbs., slender build with broad shoulders, five o'clock shadow and a prominent Adam's apple. According to Mrs. Strickland, the robber was wearing a straight-haired wig pulled back into a bun, a blue denim hat, which did not obstruct a full view of the robber's face, gold wire framed dark glasses, lipstick, rouge, a dark coat, and was carrying a 10″ wide red print cloth shoulder bag.

Mrs. Strickland was not able to make a positive identification of the robber, and much of the evidence against appellant at the trial consisted of her description of the robber's personal features and bank surveillance photos which the jury was asked to compare to appellant. The sole identification witness at the trial was a Priscilla Martin who testified that on the afternoon of April 22, while passing by on a bus, she observed a man she identified as appellant walk down the steps of the Salvation Army and touch one of the two doors of the Main–High branch of the Marine Midland Bank. Mrs. Martin described the man as wearing red pants, a black coat, black platform shoes and a black floppy hat whose brim obstructed a view of his face from the nose up. She described his hair style as a frizzled bush, "an afro," but could not say whether it was a wig. Mrs. Martin stated that the man was not wearing glasses and that she could not recall lipstick but did remember seeing rouge.

Mrs. Martin first learned of the robbery of the Main–High branch on the six o'clock news the evening of the 22nd. A week and a half later, she telephoned the bank to find out the time of the bank robbery, but did not leave her name or reveal any information about the robbery. She eventually spoke about the robbery with the Federal Bureau of Investigation, which had learned of her involvement through a friend of Mrs. Martin's husband.

Mrs. Martin had been acquainted with appellant for a number of years. She testified that she knew the appellant for nineteen years and at one time had lived in the same house with him. On cross-examination, defense counsel questioned Mrs. Martin on whether she had ever had any trouble with appellant or ever had any arguments or disagreements with him, and specifically whether she had ever accused appellant of fathering her child and then failing to support this child. Mrs. Martin denied these charges and further denied that appellant visited her in the hospital after birth of the child. Mrs. Martin also denied that she confided in appellant's mother, Mrs. Catherine Harvey, that appellant was the father of the child or that she stated that she would "take revenge" on appellant for not "owning up" to this child.

Following Mrs. Martin's testimony, appellant sought to introduce testimony of Mrs. Harvey which would have shown that Mrs. Harvey was a long-time acquaintance of Mrs. Martin, and that while Mrs. Harvey was on duty as a nurse in a Buffalo hospital, she encountered Mrs. Martin, who was there for treatment of a broken leg. Mrs. Harvey would have testified that during this encounter Mrs. Martin accused appellant of fathering her child and refusing to support it and that Mrs. Martin further explained that when her husband learned of this he beat her and broke her leg, necessitating the hospital treatment. The trial judge refused this proffer of testimony, considering it "collateral" and inadmissible under Federal Rule of Evidence 613(b). It is this ruling which appellant maintains was error and which requires our consideration.

The law is well settled in this Circuit, as in others, that bias of a witness is not a collateral issue and extrinsic evidence is admissible to prove that a witness has a motive to testify falsely. See United States v. Haggett, 438 F.2d 396, 399 (2d Cir.1971); United States v. Lester, 248 F.2d 329, 334 (2d Cir.1957); United States v. Battaglia, 394 F.2d 304, 314 n. 7 (7th Cir.1968). The law of evidence has long recognized that a cross-examiner is not required to "take the answer" of a witness concerning possible bias, but may proffer extrinsic evidence, including the testimony of other witnesses, to prove the facts showing a bias in favor of or against a party. McCormick, Evidence, § 41 (2d Ed. 1972). Special treatment is accorded evidence which is probative of a special motive to lie "for if believed it colors every bit of testimony given by the witness whose motives are bared." United States v. Blackwood, 456 F.2d 526, 530 (2d Cir.1972). This Circuit follows the rule, applicable in a number of other Circuits, that a proper foundation must be laid before extrinsic evidence of bias may be introduced. See United States v. Kahn, 472 F.2d 272, 281–82 (2d Cir.), *cert. denied,* 411 U.S. 982, 93 S.Ct. 2270, 36 L.Ed.2d 958 (1973); United States v. Hayutin, 398 F.2d 944, 953 (2d Cir.), *cert. denied,* 393 U.S. 961, 89 S.Ct. 400, 21 L.Ed.2d 374 (1968). Prior to the proffer of extrinsic evidence, a witness must be provided an opportunity to explain the circumstances suggesting bias. See United States v. Kahn, supra. Federal Rule of Evidence 613(b), which applies to extrinsic evidence of prior inconsistent statements, similarly requires that a witness be "afforded an opportunity to explain or deny" the prior inconsistent statement. Because the testimony of Mrs. Harvey would have impeached Mrs. Martin's credibility by bringing before the jury prior inconsistent statements as well as demonstrate a possible bias on Mrs. Martin's part, Rule 613(b), in effect at the time of trial, required that a proper foundation be laid by appellant's counsel. Rule 613(b), however, relaxes the traditional foundation requirement that a witness's attention on cross-examination be directed specifically to the time and place of the statement and the person to whom made. Cf. Advisory Comm. Notes, Fed.R.Evid. 613(b); McCormick, Evidence, § 37 n. 45. The Rule provides, as has this Court in prior decisions concerning extrinsic bias testimony, that the witness be provided an "opportunity to explain or deny a prior inconsistent statement." Fed.R.Evid. 613(b); see United States v. Kahn, supra at 281–82; United States v. Hayutin, supra at 953. In cross-examining Mrs. Martin, defense counsel clearly asked her whether she had ever accused defendant of fathering her child, whether she had ever stated she would "take revenge" on the defendant and whether she had confided in Mrs. Harvey that defendant was the father of her child. To each of the questions, Mrs. Martin answered no. Thus, on at least three occasions, the witness was afforded an opportunity to explain or deny circumstances suggesting prejudice. Since Mrs. Harvey would have testified that all statements heard by her were made at the same identifiable time and identified place, the reference to Mrs. Harvey as the other party to the conversation should have obviated any surprise to the government as to the when and where of the proffered testimony. Cf. Smith v. United States, 283 F.2d 16, 20–21 (6th Cir.1960). While

defense counsel could have been more expansive in establishing his foundation, we find that it was sufficiently established.

Although the scope of a defendant's right to introduce evidence of bias is not limitless, and may be restricted as the trial court in its sound discretion deems proper, United States v. Blackwood, supra at 530, it is rarely proper to cut off completely a probative inquiry that bears on a feasible defense. Cf. Alford v. United States, 282 U.S. 687, 694, 51 S.Ct. 218, 75 L.Ed. 624 (1931). "(A) defendant should be afforded the opportunity to present facts which, if believed, could lead to the conclusion that a witness who has testified against him either favored the prosecution or was hostile to the defendant. Evidence of all facts and circumstances which 'tend to show that a witness may shade his testimony for the purpose of helping to establish one side of a cause only,' should be received. * * * Although we are mindful that it is within the sound discretion of the trial judge to determine the extent to which he will receive independent evidence for the purpose of proving a witness' hostility, we do not believe that he may, as was done below, exclude all such evidence for that purpose." United States v. Haggett, supra at 399–400 (citations omitted). Since Mrs. Martin was the sole identification witness at the trial, we cannot say that her testimony was not critical to the government's case against appellant. With identity as a principal issue in the trial, appellant was denied an important opportunity to raise a reasonable doubt about his participation in the bank robbery by undermining the credibility of Mrs. Martin. Although Federal Rule of Evidence 403 vests trial courts with discretion to exclude evidence if its probative value is substantially outweighed by the danger of prejudice, confusion, or delay, the trial court apparently did not exclude Mrs. Harvey's testimony on the basis of this consideration. There is no indication in the record that Mrs. Harvey's testimony posed a realistic possibility of confusion or prejudice, see United States v. Aloi, 511 F.2d 585, 602 (2d Cir.1975), or would have caused a significant delay in the proceedings. Indeed, given the importance of the bias testimony to the defense, whatever confusion or delay that may have resulted from its admission would have to have been overwhelming to satisfy Rule 403's balancing test.

We now must consider whether the trial court's error in refusing to admit the testimony of Mrs. Harvey was so prejudicial as to require reversal of appellant's conviction. The right to "place the witness in his proper setting and put the weight of his testimony and his credibility to a test" is an essential safeguard to a fair trial. Alford v. United States, supra at 692, 51 S.Ct. at 219. Exercise of this right is particularly crucial where the witness offers damaging identification testimony, for in the absence of independent contrary evidence, a defendant must rely upon impeachment of the witness's credibility. The record reveals that appellant's conviction rests on the testimony of Mrs. Strickland as to a description of the robber, bank surveillance photos which the jury had an opportunity to review and compare to appellant's appearance, and the identification of Mrs. Martin. We are not convinced that Mrs. Martin's testimony was an insignificant part of the case against appellant and therefore find that denial of the opportunity to raise a reasonable doubt as to identification by showing possible bias was prejudicial to appellant's right to a fair trial.

Accordingly, we reverse appellant's conviction and remand for a new trial.

KIDD v. PEOPLE, 97 Colo. 480, 51 P.2d 1020, 1022 (1935). "In their petition for a rehearing, counsel for the people call attention for the first time to the fact that Stanton was not asked on cross-examination whether or not he had arrested the witness Hobbs and had told Hobbs that unless he would testify to what he knew of and concerning the defendant, he (Stanton) would 'pin something on him' or 'hang something on him.' They urge that in such circumstances it was not error to sustain the objection to defendant's offer to prove by Hobbs that Stanton had placed him under arrest and had made that statement to him.

"In Jaynes v. People, 44 Colo. 535, 99 P. 325, 16 Ann.Cas. 787, we held that one not a party cannot be discredited by proof of contradictory statements unless first himself interrogated as to the alleged contradictory statements. It is contended that the rule should be extended to cover statements that are not contradictory, but that show bias on the part of the witness. On that question the authorities are not harmonious, and we have not heretofore passed upon the question.

"The rule with reference to contradictory statements is so firmly established that it would be inadvisable to change it, though it was adopted upon the assumption that if the witness were not given the opportunity on cross-examination to explain the statement or to deny that he made it, he never would have the opportunity to do so. That assumption is without substantial foundation. The witness who is said to have made the contradictory statement may be recalled to the stand and permitted to explain such alleged statement or to deny that he made it. Wigmore says that 'the rule requiring such an inquiry before proving a prior self-contradiction has been pushed so far, and applied so stiffly and arbitrarily that on the whole it now does quite as much harm as good.' 2 Wigmore, Evidence, 2d Ed., § 953. Discussing the question whether the rule should be extended to cover former statements that are not contradictory, but that show bias, the same author adds: 'To import it in its present shape into any subject where it does not strictly belong by precedent seems unwise.' The authorities are in conflict. It has been stated that in most jurisdictions the rule applied in the case of prior contradictory statements should be extended to cases involving statements that are not contradictory, but that show bias. See note, 16 A.L.R. 984; 20 Ann.Cas. 224; 70 C.J. p. 995. However, we believe that the rule requiring interrogation on cross-examination before admitting evidence of contradictory statements, though firmly established, is of doubtful value at best, and that the rule should not be extended to statements that are not contradictory, but that show bias."

STATE v. ROY

Supreme Judicial Court of Maine, 1978.
385 A.2d 795.

GODFREY, JUSTICE.

In September, 1976, appellant Percy Roy was tried and convicted of the crime of taking indecent liberties in violation of former 17 M.R.S.A. § 1951 (1964). The State's evidence tended to prove that he took indecent liberties with the fifteen-and-a-half-year-old daughter of a woman he had been living with for several years. Appellant took the stand and denied the charge, testifying that there was animosity between himself and the child that grew out of his attempts to discipline her. Appellant did not place his own character in issue by introducing evidence of good character, but merely testified as to his difficulties with the child.

The State cross-examined Roy about a prior conviction. Appellant's counsel objected to that cross-examination and moved for a mistrial. Denying the motion for a mistrial, the trial court admitted the testimony, instructing the jury that the testimony was to be considered only as bearing on Roy's credibility as a witness.

The prior crime involved a charge which was substantially similar to the crime charged in the present case. The text of the cross-examination follows:

> "Q Are you the same Percy Roy who, at Edmundston, New Brunswick, Canada on the 28th day of May, 1970, was convicted of the crime in Canada of having had sexual intercourse with a Nancy Roy, knowing that she was your daughter and was sentenced to a term of three years at the Maritime Penitentiary in Dorchester?
>
> A Yes, I am.
>
> Q How old was Nancy Roy?
>
> A 15."

Appellant objected strongly to cross-examination about the New Brunswick conviction. His objection having been overruled, he did not specifically object to the question concerning the age of Nancy Roy. As one of his points on appeal, appellant argues that the admission of that entire testimony was reversible error.

Admissibility of a prior conviction for impeachment of a witness is governed by Rule 609(a) of the Maine Rules of Evidence.[1] State v.

1. Maine Rules of Evidence, Rule 609:

"(a) *General rule.* For the purpose of attacking the credibility of a witness, evidence that he has been convicted of a crime is admissible but only if the crime (1) was punishable by death or imprison-

Pinkham, 383 A.2d 1355 (Me.1978). Under the Rule, before such evidence is admitted the trial court must determine that its probative value outweighs the prejudicial effect to the defendant. In balancing the two considerations the trial court must exercise its discretion in accordance with the directives of the Rule. State v. Pinkham, supra. The provision of subsection (a)(1) of the Rule, that prior conviction of a relatively serious crime is admissible for impeachment whether or not the crime involved dishonesty, must be taken in the context of the last sentence of subsection (a), that admissibility depends upon the court's determining that the probative value of the evidence outweighs its prejudicial effect. As we pointed out in *Pinkham,* the probative value referred to relates to the veracity of the witness, not to some predisposition on his part to commit a crime similar to the one with which he is charged.

This case is not one in which the testimony in question was offered as evidence of appellant's bad character. Such testimony is not admissible until the defendant puts his character in issue by introducing evidence of good character. Though defendant testified concerning his attempts to discipline the complainant, his testimony was offered to show animosity by her toward him. Thus, the probative value of his prior conviction must be determined solely by reference to its bearing on his general credibility.

The prior conviction for incest had little bearing on the likelihood that the appellant would testify untruthfully. On the other hand, the prejudice to him in the trial of this case was especially great because of the high degree of similarity between the crime of incest and the crime with which he was charged.

Two purposes lie behind the balancing test called for by Rule 609. First, the public has an interest in the fairness of trials which is served by application of evidentiary rules in a way that does not unjustifiably discourage witnesses, particularly defendants, from testifying. See United States v. Jackson, 405 F.Supp. 938, 942 (D.C.N.Y.1975). The public interest in having the benefit of a defendant's testimony is especially strong in a case such as this one where the complainant and the accused were the only witnesses to the acts charged. Without the protection afforded by Rule 609 and the balancing of interests required by it, even a defendant who was innocent of the particular crime charged would decide not to testify rather than run the risk of having evidence of a prior conviction, especially one for a similar offense, used against him.

Second, in a case where the earlier conviction and the present charge are similar, the likelihood is substantially increased that the finder of facts will make improper use of the evidence of prior convic-

ment for one year or more under the law under which he was convicted, or (2) involved dishonesty or false statement, regardless of the punishment. In either case admissibility shall depend upon a determination by the court that the probative value of this evidence outweighs the prejudicial effect to the defendant."

tion, that is, will use it as evidence of defendant's disposition to commit the crime rather than his general lack of credibility. When the earlier crime similar to the present charge did not involve dishonesty, its bearing on defendant's veracity is so tenuous that the fact-finder is likely to have difficulty in focusing on the limited purpose for which the evidence of it is offered. We recognized the problem in several cases before adoption of the Maine Rules of Evidence, e.g., State v. Strollo, Me., 370 A.2d 675 (1977); State v. Gervais, Me., 317 A.2d 796 (1974); State v. Toppi, Me., 275 A.2d 805, 810 n. 5 (1971).[2] The difficulty was compounded in the present case by additional interrogation of the defendant eliciting testimony about the length of his prior sentence and the age of the former victim. See United States v. Harding, 525 F.2d 84, 88 (7th Cir.1975); Martin v. United States, 404 F.2d 640, 642–43 (10th Cir.1968).

The federal courts have addressed the same problem as it arises in the application of Rule 609 of the Federal Rules of Evidence on which the Maine rule is modeled. See, e.g., United States v. Jackson, 405 F.Supp. 938 (D.C.N.Y.1975). Chief Justice Burger had occasion to deal with the problem when he sat in the United States Court of Appeals in a case that arose before the Federal Rules of Evidence were adopted. He said,

> " 'A special and even more difficult problem arises when the prior conviction is for the same or substantially the same conduct for which the accused is on trial. Where multiple convictions of various kinds can be shown, strong reasons arise for excluding those which are for the same crime because of the inevitable pressure on lay jurors to believe that "if he did it before he probably did so this time." As a general guide, those convictions which are for the same crime should be admitted sparingly * * *.' Gordon v. United States, 127 U.S.App. D.C. 343, 347, 383 F.2d 936, 940 (1967), cert. denied, 390 U.S. 1029, 88 S.Ct. 1421, 20 L.Ed.2d 287 (1968)."

In the case before us there was strong similarity between the prior conviction for incest with a fifteen-year-old daughter and the present charge of indecent liberties with the 15½–year–old daughter of the woman with whom he had been living for several years. That similarity created a great likelihood that the evidence could be put to improper use by the jury. Indeed, it would be most difficult for a finder of fact to disregard the similarity. Rule 404 of the Maine Rules of Evidence, relating to admissibility of evidence of character, though not directly applicable in this case, clearly establishes the principle that an accused must be tried for the present crime and that evidence of past crimes will not be used to show he has a predisposition to commit crimes of

2. A party who proposes to offer evidence of prior conviction of a witness to be called by the adverse party is reminded of our admonition in State v. Toppi, Me., 275 A.2d 805, 813 (1971), that the question of its admissibility should be first presented to the presiding justice in the absence of the jury. A party who wishes to exclude evidence of prior convictions of his witness should seek such exclusion by a threshold motion. Among other things, such procedure avoids any question that the issue has been properly raised.

that sort. That principle is necessary and desirable to avoid conviction of individuals because of their reputation or past history. See Commentary to Rule 404, Maine Rules of Evidence, in R. Field & P. Murray, Maine Evidence 67–71 (1976). That principle could be served in this case only by excluding evidence of the prior conviction.

A review of the factors to be considered in determining admissibility leads unavoidably to the conclusion that the trial court exceeded the limits of its discretion in its application of Rule 609. The appellant's prior conviction had little probative value with regard to his honesty as a witness. The public interest in encouraging defendants to testify was ill-served by subjecting this defendant to the admission of highly prejudicial evidence of an earlier conviction of a closely similar offense having little bearing on his veracity. The interrogation of appellant on cross-examination involved not only the fact of prior conviction but also details concerning duration of the sentence imposed and the age of the victim. In the circumstances the probative value of the conviction cannot be reasonably viewed as outweighing the prejudice created by admitting the testimony. The trial court should not have admitted evidence of the conviction in this case.

The entry must be:

Appeal sustained.

Judgment vacated.

Remanded for new trial.

* * *

DELAHANTY, JUSTICE, with whom ARCHIBALD, J., concurs, concurring in result:

I agree with the majority that the appeal herein must be sustained. I do not believe, however, that it is necessary—in fact, in these circumstances it may be presumptuous for want of an articulated Rule 609 evaluation below—to reach the issue upon which the majority rests its reversal. With deference, I would rely on what appears to be prosecutorial "overkill."

True, our Maine Rules of Evidence recognize that within the limits of Rule 609, the prosecution may use evidence of a prior conviction to impeach the credibility of a defendant who testifies in his own behalf. Assuming, for the nonce, that the presiding Justice correctly ruled under M.R.Evid. 609 that the defendant could be impeached by evidence of a prior conviction, an issue that need not be reached, the State exceeded the permissible scope of cross-examination.

In State v. Toppi, Me., 275 A.2d 805 (1971), we suggested a permissible form of questioning on cross-examination when attacking a witness' credibility by evidence of a prior conviction.

> Are you the same * * * who was convicted of the crime of * * * in the Superior Court for * * * County on * * *. Id. at 813.

In the instant case, the prosecution did not so confine the cross-examination but also inquired into the length of the defendant's conviction. More egregiously, the question disclosed details of the crime including the relationship of the defendant to the female victim and her name and age. Given the circumstances of this case, the nature and breadth of such inquiry were highly improper and alone are sufficient to warrant a new trial.

Tangential questioning is considered impermissible for two reasons:

First, it leads to an unnecessary delay in the trial.

Second, it introduces extraneous and possibly prejudicial or inflammatory matters unrelated to the effort of properly discrediting the defendant as a witness. Martin v. United States, 404 F.2d 640 (10th Cir.1968).

Although we have never intimated that the form of question approved in State v. Toppi, supra, is a shibboleth which must be blindly and precisely followed, in the absence of extenuating circumstances any substantial departure from inquiring about the name of the crime and the time and place of conviction is improper for the above-mentioned reasons. Accordingly, the gross departure by the prosecution from acceptable inquiry is quite sufficient to warrant reversal.

Note

See generally 3A Wigmore, Evidence §§ 980–987 (Chadbourn rev. 1970); McCormick, Evidence § 42 (4th ed. 1992).

UNITED STATES v. TONEY

United States Court of Appeals, Fifth Circuit, 1980.

615 F.2d 277, cert. denied, 449 U.S. 985, 101 S.Ct. 403, 66 L.Ed.2d 248 (1980).

JAMES C. HILL, CIRCUIT JUDGE:

This case presents the question whether a district court has the discretion under rule 403 of the Federal Rules of Evidence [1] to prohibit the impeachment of a witness with a conviction for a crime involving dishonesty or false statement (a *crimen falsi*).[2] We hold that the court

1. Fed.R.Evid. 403 provides:

Although relevant, evidence may be excluded if its probative value is substantially outweighed by the danger of unfair prejudice, confusion of the issues, or misleading the jury, or by considerations of undue delay, waste of time, or needless presentation of cumulative evidence.

2. The use of prior convictions for impeachment purposes is authorized by Fed. R.Evid. 609(a), which provides:

For the purpose of attacking the credibility of a witness, evidence that he has been convicted of a crime shall be admitted if elicited from him or established by public record during cross-examination but only if the crime (1) was punishable by death or imprisonment in excess of one year under the law under which he was convicted, and the court determines that the probative value of admitting this evidence outweighs its prejudicial effect to the defendant, or (2) involved dishonesty or false statement, regardless of the punishment.

has no such discretion and that a cross-examiner has an absolute right to introduce a *crimen falsi* conviction for impeachment purposes.[3]

I

On April 4, 1978, James Finis Toney, Jr. was convicted by a jury of mail fraud, 18 U.S.C. §§ 2, 1341 (1976). Prior to trial, Toney filed a motion in limine to preclude the Government from impeaching his credibility with a prior mail fraud conviction [4] if he chose to testify in his own defense. The district court deferred ruling on Toney's motion until trial. During the defense case, the court, in colloquy with counsel, expressed the view that use of the conviction for impeachment would be so prejudicial to Toney that he would probably decide not to testify. Record, vol. 9, at 931–32. No one considered, apparently, whether Fed.R.Evid. 609(a)(2) gave the prosecutor an unqualified right to impeach Toney with the conviction. Before it came time for Toney to testify, however, the Government called rule 609(a)(2) to the court's attention, and the court concluded that the rule required it to permit the impeachment. Record, vol. 10, at 1157. Toney did not take the stand and claims that the court's ruling prevented him from doing so.

Though Toney did not testify or even proffer his proposed testimony, and though the jury could not have been influenced by the allegedly prejudicial mail fraud conviction, Toney may, nevertheless, claim reversible error in the district court's disposition, albeit tentative, of his motion to foreclose the prosecution from attempting a line of impeachment. United States v. Langston, 576 F.2d 1138, 1139 (5th Cir.) (per curiam), *cert. denied,* 439 U.S. 932, 99 S.Ct. 324, 58 L.Ed.2d 327 (1978); see United States v. Hitsman, 604 F.2d 443, 447 (5th Cir.1979). We conclude that the district court read rule 609(a)(2) correctly, however; it had no discretion to prevent the prosecution's use of the *crimen falsi* as impeachment evidence. We, therefore, affirm Toney's conviction.

II

It is established that mail fraud is a crime involving "dishonesty or false statement." United States v. Cohen, 544 F.2d 781, 785 (5th Cir.), *cert. denied,* 431 U.S. 914, 97 S.Ct. 2175, 53 L.Ed.2d 224 (1977); accord, United States v. Brashier, 548 F.2d 1315, 1326–27 (9th Cir.1976), *cert. denied,* 429 U.S. 1111, 97 S.Ct. 1149, 51 L.Ed.2d 565 (1977). Subsection (a)(2) rather than (a)(1) of rule 609 therefore applies in determining the admissibility of a mail fraud conviction for impeachment. Rule 609(a)(2) contains no provision for excluding evidence of a *crimen falsi* on the ground of undue prejudice; that ground can serve as a basis for excluding such evidence only if rule 403, with its prejudice versus probative value weighing provision, is applicable. Rule 609(a)(2) pro-

3. Our holding is, of course, limited by the provisions of Fed.R.Evid. 609(b)–(d) that grant a court discretion, under certain circumstances, to exclude a *crimen falsi* conviction.

4. The prior conviction occurred on October 18, 1977, and arose from the same type of illegal conduct that gave rise to the conviction we now review. This previous conviction was affirmed, United States v. Toney, 598 F.2d 1349 (5th Cir.1979), *cert. den.,* — U.S. —, 100 S.Ct. 706, 62 L.Ed.2d 670 (1979), as was a third mail fraud charge, United States v. Toney, 605 F.2d 200 (5th Cir.1979).

vides that evidence of a prior criminal conviction for a *crimen falsi* offense *shall* be admitted to attack a witness's credibility during cross-examination. When discussing rule 609(a)(2) Congress made this clear:

> The admission of prior convictions involving dishonesty and false statement is not within the discretion of the Court. Such convictions are peculiarly probative of credibility and under this rule, are always to be admitted. Thus, *judicial discretion granted with respect to the admissibility of other prior convictions is not applicable to those involving dishonesty or false statement.*

H.R.Conf.Rep. No. 93–1597, 93d Cong., 2d Sess. 9, *reprinted in* [1974] U.S. Code Cong. & Admin.News, pp. 7098, 7103 (emphasis added). A number of courts have adhered to this congressional intent, observing that a court has no discretion to exclude evidence of a prior *crimen falsi* conviction. See, e.g., United States v. Fearwell, 193 U.S.App.D.C. 386, 392, 595 F.2d 771, 777 (D.C.Cir.1979); United States v. Hawley, 554 F.2d 50, 52 (2d Cir.1977).

Despite the unambiguous language of both rule 609(a)(2) and its legislative history, however, both courts and commentators have posed the question whether the general weighing test of rule 403 determines admissibility where prejudice, which always inheres in the introduction of a conviction for impeachment, is likely. See, e.g., United States v. Papia, 560 F.2d 827, 845 n. 10 (7th Cir.1977); United States v. Hayes, 553 F.2d 824, 827 n. 4 (2d Cir.), *cert. denied,* 434 U.S. 867, 98 S.Ct. 204, 54 L.Ed.2d 143 (1977); United States v. Smith, 179 U.S.App.D.C. 162, 172–79 n. 20, 551 F.2d 348, 358–59 n. 20 (D.C.Cir.1976); United States v. Dixon, 547 F.2d 1079, 1083 n. 4 (9th Cir.1976); P. Rothstein, Rules of Evidence 211 (2d ed. 1978); 3 J. Weinstein & M. Berger, Evidence ¶ 609[03a], at 609–73 (1978). At least one commentator has expressed the view that rule 403 should control. Younger, Three Essays on Character and Credibility Under the Federal Rules of Evidence, 5 Hofstra L.Rev. 7, 12 (1976). We hold, however, that Congress meant what it said in rule 609(a)(2)—that the fact of a prior conviction for an offense such as mail fraud is always admissible for impeachment purposes.

As we have observed, Congress used absolute language when discussing the admissibility of rule 609(a)(2) offenses. Congress carefully and extensively considered the prior crimes impeachment issue, devoting more time to it than any other rule of evidence. *See* J. Weinstein & M. Berger, supra. Rule 403 is a general rule, "designed as a guide for the handling of situations for which no specific rules have been formulated." 28 U.S.C. Rules of Evid. Advisory Comm. Notes at 550 (1976). Rule 609(a)(2) is a well-considered, specific provision enacted to cover a distinct issue in the law of evidence. Congress thoroughly considered the pros and cons of the mandatory admissibility of limited types of prior crimes evidence and determined that in certain cases it was to be the rule. Rule 403 simply has no application where impeachment is sought through a *crimen falsi.* See Note, *Impeachment Under Rule 609(a):* Suggestions for Confining and Guiding Trial Court Discretion,

71 Nw.U.L.Rev. 655, 661 (1976). The district court was correct when it held that, if Toney took the stand, the Government had the right to impeach him with his prior mail fraud conviction. Accordingly, the judgment of that court is

Affirmed.

TUTTLE, CIRCUIT JUDGE, dissenting:

I respectfully dissent from the majority's establishment of an absolute rule requiring admission of a prior *crimen falsi* conviction. I would hold that a district court judge may exclude evidence of a prior conviction involving dishonesty when the prejudicial effect of the evidence is overwhelming.

In formulating the Federal Rules of Evidence, Congress authorized introduction of two types of prior convictions for impeachment purposes—felony convictions and convictions involving dishonesty or false statement. After lengthy debate, Congress chose to treat these two classes of convictions differently, according greater value to convictions involving dishonesty. Under rule 609(a) of the Federal Rules of Evidence, crimes punishable by death or imprisonment for more than one year shall be admitted if "the court determines that the probative value of admitting this evidence outweighs its prejudicial effect to the defendant." Fed.R.Evid. 609(a). This limitation on the admission of felony convictions reflects the traditional concern over admission of prior convictions for impeachment purposes—that the relevance of a conviction to the defendant's credibility will not justify the prejudice that occurs if the jury considers the prior conviction as evidence of present guilt. The judge, in considering felony convictions, is instructed to apply a simple balancing test, measuring probative value against prejudicial effect. This test is not, however, applied to convictions involving dishonesty. Congress determined that these convictions are particularly probative of a defendant's credibility and therefore should not be subjected to the simple balancing between probative value and prejudicial effect.

I do not believe that application of rule 403 of the Federal Rules of Evidence to rule 609(a) will necessarily contravene the intent of Congress to treat these two types of convictions differently. Rule 403 is a general rule which provides the flexibility that is essential in any set of procedural or evidentiary rules. The rule expresses recognition that evidence which is relevant, probative, and admissible under other rules, may nonetheless be so prejudicial that it should be excluded. Rule 403 does not, however, sanction general application of a simple balancing test, such as that in rule 609(a)(1), to evidence admissible under other rules. Instead, it permits only the use of a much more stringent test; evidence may be excluded "if its probative value is *substantially* outweighed by the danger of *unfair* prejudice." Fed.R.Evid. 403 [emphasis added]. To apply the rule 403 test for exclusion to rule 609(a) would not subject convictions involving dishonesty to the same treatment as felony convictions. While felony convictions may be excluded if their prejudicial effect outweighs their value as impeachment evidence, convictions involving dishonesty could be excluded only upon a strong showing of overwhelming prejudice to the defendant.

Because of the Congressional recognition, embodied in rule 609(a)(2), of the great probative value of a *crimen falsi* conviction, it is unlikely that a defendant would often be able to make the necessary showing to require exclusion. Nonetheless, the purpose of rule 403 was to provide judges some flexibility in cases where the possibility of prejudice is extremely great, and I feel that this case comes within that limited group of cases. The defendant's prior conviction for mail fraud was offered to impeach the defendant's credibility as a witness; it was, of course, not relevant as substantive evidence to prove the defendant's guilt in the offense at trial. Despite the undeniable relevance of the prior conviction to the issue of credibility, the prejudice inherent in admission of this conviction is so great that its use should have been limited. It would be hard to imagine evidence more prejudicial, in a trial for mail fraud, then the defendant's prior conviction for mail fraud. I would suggest that the probative value of a conviction involving dishonesty is substantially outweighed by the danger of unfair prejudice to the defendant, when the prior conviction concerns the same kind of offense as that for which the defendant is being tried. A judge should not be prohibited from excluding this evidence by a rigid holding that rule 403 can never be applied to rule 609(a)(2).

UNITED STATES v. SMITH, 551 F.2d 348, 362–63 (D.C.Cir.1976). "Attempted robbery is not a crime involving 'dishonesty or false statement' within the meaning of Rule 609(a)(2). If Gartrell's prior conviction is to be admitted at all, it must be admitted only after the court makes the determination prescribed in Rule 609(a)(1).

"The Conference Committee Report fully supports this position:

> 'By the phrase "dishonesty and false statement" the Conference means crimes such as perjury or subornation of perjury, false statement, criminal fraud, embezzlement, or false pretense, or any other offense in the nature of crimen falsi, the commission of which involves some element of deceit, untruthfulness, or falsification bearing on the accused's propensity to testify truthfully.'

H.R.Conf.Rep. No. 93–1597, 93d Cong., 2d Sess. 9, *reprinted in* [1974] U.S.Code Cong. & Admin.News, pp. 7098, 7103. Numerous remarks made in the course of floor debate, set forth in the Appendix to this opinion, substantiate the interpretation that robbery may not be classified legitimately as an 'offense in the nature of crimen falsi.' Congress clearly intended the phrase to denote a fairly narrow subset of criminal activity. Moreover, research into the derivation of the term 'crimen falsi' indicates that Congress's restrictive construction comports with historical practice. While commentators have uncovered some divergence between civil and common law usage, the expression has never been thought to comprehend robbery or other crimes involving force. Even in its broadest sense, the term 'crimen falsi' has encompassed only those crimes characterized by an element of deceit or deliberate interference with a court's ascertainment of truth. As graphically observed by Senator McClellan, robbery is not such a crime:

> 'There is no deceit in armed robbery. You take a gun, walk out, and put it in a man's face and say, "Give me your money," or walk up to the counter of the cashier and say, "this is a holdup; give me your money." There is no deceit in that. They are not lying. They mean business. They will murder you if you do not do it.'

120 Cong.Rec.S. 19913 (daily ed. Nov. 22, 1974)."

UNITED STATES v. BOYER, 150 F.2d 595 (D.C.Cir.1945). "The fact that a witness has been convicted of a crime may be shown, on the theory that it diminishes the value of his testimony. The question is whether he may then explain the circumstances of his conviction in order to mitigate its apparent effect on his credibility. We agree with the Municipal Court of Appeals that it is unfair to the witness to permit no explanation, particularly when he is at the same time a defendant in a criminal case and 'the prior conviction, though permitted solely for the purpose of affecting the credibility of the defendant, may have some tendency in the minds of the jury to prove his guilt of the crime for which he is then on trial.' It may have such a tendency even when it has no actual bearing on his credibility. Whether the witness is or is not a defendant, if the opposing party introduces his previous convictions we think the witness should be allowed to make such reasonably brief 'protestations on his own behalf as he may feel able to make with a due regard to the penalties of perjury.' Since not all guilty men are equally guilty and some convicted men are innocent, we think the witness should be allowed either to extenuate his guilt or to assert his innocence of the previous charges.

"The government contends that if an explanation or denial is permitted it opens the way to a collateral inquiry which may be long and confusing. Fear of such a result has led some courts to exclude all evidence designed to mitigate or rebut the impeachment which results from proof of a prior conviction. But there is respectable authority to the contrary. It is generally agreed that in order to save time and avoid confusion of issues, inquiry into a previous crime must be stopped before its logical possibilities are exhausted; the witness cannot call other witnesses to corroborate his story and the opposing party cannot call other witnesses to refute it. The disputed question is whether inquiry into a previous crime should stop (1) with proof of the conviction of the witness or (2) with any reasonably brief 'protestations on his own behalf' which he may wish to make. The second alternative will seldom be materially more confusing or time-consuming than the first, if the trial judge duly exercises his 'considerable discretion in admitting or rejecting evidence.' And we think the second alternative is more conducive to the ends of justice. The jury is not likely to give undue weight to an ex-convict's uncorroborated assertion of innocence or of extenuating circumstances."

UNITED STATES v. PENNIX, 313 F.2d 524, 529 (4th Cir.1963). "But it is clearly established that the cross-examiner may not go further and inquire of a defendant concerning only his prior arrest or indictment for crime. This rule is based upon a clear recognition of the fact that the probative value of such evidence is so overwhelmingly outweighed by its inevitable tendency to inflame and prejudice the jury against the defendant that total and complete exclusion is required in order that the right to trial by a fair and impartial jury may not be impaired. In Coyne v. United States, 246 F. 120, 121 (5th Cir.1917), the court made the following observations concerning the introduction of evidence of prior indictment:

> '* * * The fact that an unproven charge has been made against one has no logical tendency to prove that he has been guilty of any offense, or to impair the credibility of his testimony. An indictment is a mere accusation, and raises no presumption of guilt. On the contrary, the indicted person is presumed to be innocent until his guilt is established, by legal evidence beyond a reasonable doubt, in a court of competent jurisdiction.' "

GUSTAFSON v. STATE

Supreme Court of Arkansas, 1979.
267 Ark. 278, 590 S.W.2d 853.

HICKMAN, JUSTICE.

Jack L. Gustafson, Sr. was convicted in the Independence County Circuit Court of burglary, attempted theft and soliciting capital murder. He was sentenced to a total of 50 years imprisonment.

He raises numerous issues on appeal. We find prejudicial error was committed and reverse his conviction and remand the matter for a new trial.

* * *

When Gustafson took the witness stand, as a witness in his own behalf, he was asked by the prosecuting attorney about previous criminal convictions and previous misconduct. The trial judge permitted some of the questions over the objections of Gustafson's lawyer.

There are circumstances where it is possible for the State to introduce into a criminal trial evidence that the defendant has committed crimes unrelated to those with which he is charged. One circumstance is in its case in chief, where, in very limited circumstances, the State may offer evidence of other offenses. Ordinarily, such evidence is not permitted. It is prejudicial by nature and should only be used against a defendant in a criminal action in rare cases. See Alford v. State, 223 Ark. 330, 266 S.W.2d 804 (1954). Another circumstance is when a defendant in a criminal case takes the witness stand in his own behalf. His credibility becomes an issue and the State may, under certain circumstances, test that credibility by asking the defendant if he has been convicted of certain crimes or if he is guilty of certain misconduct. Moore v. State, 256 Ark. 385, 507 S.W.2d 711 (1974). Gustafson was cross-examined both about previous convictions and about acts of misconduct.

First, Gustafson was asked on cross-examination if he had been convicted of burglary and larceny in Sharp County, Arkansas. He admitted that he had been. It does not appear from the record that this question was improper under Uniform Rules of Evidence, Rule 609. Rule 609 permits such a question only if the crime was punishable by death or imprisonment in excess of one year or if the conviction involves dishonesty or a false statement regardless of the punishment. The trial judge must determine if the probative value of the question outweighs its prejudicial effect. There are other restrictions, for example a 10-year time limit and a provision regarding the effect of a pardon. If a defendant denies being convicted of such a crime, the conviction can be proved by extrinsic evidence.

Next, he was asked if he was not, in fact, guilty of possessing several thousand dollars worth of CB radio equipment which had been stolen from Jay's CB Shop at Batesville. The trial judge sustained an objection to this question. He was then asked if he was not guilty of knowingly possessing a 4-wheel drive Chevrolet pickup truck which had been stolen from Richard Thomas at Arkansas College in Batesville. Gustafson refused to answer this question, claiming his privilege under the Fifth Amendment. The judge ordered him to answer and he did. These two questions about Gustafson's previous misconduct, because they were not related to convictions but to misconduct, are governed by Rule 608(b) of the Uniform Rules of Evidence which reads:

> (b) Specific Instances of Conduct. Specific instances of the conduct of a witness, for the purpose of attacking or supporting his credibility, other than conviction of crime as provided in Rule 609, may not be proved by extrinsic evidence. They may, however, in the discretion of the court, if probative of truthfulness or untruthfulness, be inquired into on cross-examination of the witness (1) concerning his character for truthfulness or untruthfulness, or (2) concerning the character for truthfulness or untruthfulness of another witness as to which character the witness being cross-examined has testified.
>
> The giving of testimony, whether by an accused or by any other witness, does not operate as a waiver of his privilege against self-incrimination when examined with respect to matters which relate only to credibility.

Rule 608(b) of the Uniform Rules of Evidence changes Arkansas law. Before the adoption of the Uniform Rules it was proper to ask on cross-examination if a defendant was guilty of most any kind of felony. In Butler v. State, 255 Ark. 1028, 504 S.W.2d 747 (1974), we reviewed some of our prior decisions which had held that it was proper in certain circumstances to ask a defendant if he was guilty of robbery, interstate transportation of stolen property, rape, larceny or assassination. The rationale of permitting such a question was that a person committing such a crime might be prone to lie.

There is no doubt that Rule 608(b) was intended to restrict the use of such evidence, especially in a criminal case. Our rule is based on the federal rule and most commentators take the position that Rule 608(b) should be interpreted restrictively. See McCormick, Evidence, § 42 (2d ed. 1972); Weinstein, Evidence, § 608[05] (1978).

We read Rule 608(b) to provide that the trial court may, if it finds good faith and that the probative value of such information outweighs the prejudicial effect, allow such a question about certain offenses. The most important change is that the question must be concerning misconduct which relates to truthfulness or untruthfulness. That is, one element of the offense alleged must be an act of dishonesty. The question cannot regard misconduct which has no relation at all to honesty. *Weinstein,* supra, indicates that misconduct relating to truthfulness would include forgery, perjury, bribery, false pretense and embezzlement. Obviously, some misconduct would not bear on truthfulness. For example, murder, manslaughter or assault do not *per se* relate to dishonesty. Burglary and breaking and entering would not be such misconduct unless the crime involved the element of theft. Ark. Stat.Ann. §§ 41–2002, 41–2203. We believe that theft, as it is defined in the Arkansas Criminal Code, involves dishonesty. Ark.Stat.Ann. § 41–2201, et seq.

We are aware that the use of such information can be highly prejudicial to a defendant in a criminal case and that the use of such information may well be abused. No doubt Rule 608(b) was designed to curb this possible abuse. We find three conditions on the use of such information. First, the question must be asked in good faith. This has always been our rule. Balentine v. State, 259 Ark. 590, 535 S.W.2d 221 (1976); Moore v. State, supra, and Butler v. State, supra. This means the court may require evidence of good faith before it permits such a question to be asked; that is, that the questioner must have credible knowledge that the offense has been committed, not just information based on rumor or speculation. Next, the court in its discretion should decide if the probative value of the question outweighs the prejudicial effect of such a question. Rule 403, Uniform Rules of Evidence, provides for excluding relevant evidence of its prejudicial effect outweighs its probative value. Finally, of course, the misconduct must relate to truthfulness or untruthfulness and that character trait.

The questions asked of Gustafson relate to misconduct which is defined as theft by receiving in Ark.Stat.Ann. § 41–2206.

The prosecuting attorney asked Gustafson two questions: Both were, had he not, in fact, knowingly possessed certain stolen property, and the prosecuting attorney identified the property, time and place in both questions, as he should have. Those were, on their face, proper questions. The offense of theft by receiving requires that one *receive, retain* or *dispose* of stolen property *knowing* that it was stolen or *having good reason* to believe that it was stolen. Ark.Stat.Ann. § 41-2206. The witness should be able to answer such a question by a simple yes or no. The State may not go beyond that answer, as it may in the case of a conviction, and prove the misconduct by extrinsic evidence.

In the case of State v. Miller, 92 N.M. 520, 590 P.2d 1175 (1979), the New Mexico Court dealt with the identical problem. In the *Miller* case there were some fourteen questions asked of the defendant relating to his guilt of various crimes. The Court said:

> * * * The only purpose of the questions was to test defendant's credibility. State v. Coca, supra [80 N.M. 95, 451 P.2d 999]. The crimes involved in the questions could not be proved by extrinsic evidence. Evidence Rule 608(b). Defendant answered each of the questions in the negative.
>
> What then was the probative value of the questions? There was none. Under the balancing test required by Evidence Rule 403, the trial court abused its discretion in permitting the questioning because the questions were prejudicial and, in light of the answers, there was no probative value.
>
> We do not hold that a question under Evidence Rule 608(b), which asks for an admission concerning a felony, can never be asked. Our holding is that any one of such questions is prejudicial, see State v. Rowell, 77 N.M. 124, 419 P.2d 966 (1966) and, if there is nothing indicating the question has probative value on the question of credibility, it is an abuse of discretion to permit the question. When the question is under Evidence Rule 608(b), a prosecutor, who seeks to have a defendant make an admission concerning a felony when there has been no conviction, hazards a reversal absent a showing of probative value because of the prejudicial nature of the question.

We arrive at the same conclusions.

In Cox v. State, 264 Ark. 608, 573 S.W.2d 906 (1978), two statements were made which are inconsistent with this opinion. It may have been the question asked in *Cox* was improper for other reasons, but our opinion does not show that. We said in *Cox* that it was improper to ask a defendant if he had not, in fact, committed a robbery on the same day of the offense with which he was charged. We said that the question itself was improper and in that regard we were mistaken. Such a question would not be impermissible under Rule 608 if it were asked in good faith and permitted in the discretion of the judge because robbery is an act of dishonesty.

We were also mistaken in *Cox* if we left the impression that a negative answer to an improper question results in no prejudicial error.

There is no doubt that such a question harms a defendant's case. When it is proper, about a type of misconduct that is relevant, it is allowed only because it is relevant to the determination of the credibility of the defendant. But to say that a negative answer always removes the prejudice in every case goes too far. Prejudicial error may result whether the question is properly phrased or not. We cannot predict whether prejudice can be removed in every case.

The trial court sustained an objection to the first question regarding the stolen CB radios. For what reason we cannot say. Then the trial court required Gustafson to answer the question about the 4-wheel drive truck. Gustafson claimed his privilege against self-incrimination regarding this question. The trial court, clearly in error, ordered Gustafson to answer the question. Rule 608(b), specifically the last paragraph, provides that the privilege against self-incrimination is preserved in such circumstances. This was prejudicial error that requires us to reverse the judgment of the court.

The difficult question for us is whether both of these questions may be asked of Gustafson at a retrial if he takes the witness stand. That presumes too much. First of all the judge sustained an objection to the first question for some reason finding it improper. No doubt the trial judge had good reasons for sustaining that objection. We would not presume that those reasons no longer exist, although they might. Obviously that question should not be asked again in this case unless the trial judge in advance makes a decision that it is a proper question, asked in good faith and its probative value outweighs its prejudicial error. The second question, also on its face a proper question, must withstand the same scrutiny by the trial judge whose discretionary judgment we cannot predict. That would no doubt, have some bearing on possible prejudice. If both questions were deemed improper by the trial judge, it would be difficult to say prejudicial error was not committed by the asking alone.

We cannot predict for future cases what questions will or will not be so improper as to require a new trial. We do not intend to be so restrictive in our application of Rule 608(b) as to remove a valuable tool in garnering the truth. However, we do want it made clear that the use of such evidence in a criminal case creates a real hazard of a mistrial or a reversal. Prosecuting attorneys would be well advised to procure a ruling from the trial judge before asking such questions before a jury.

Reversed and remanded.

BYRD, J., concurs.

HOLT, J., dissents.

HARRIS, C.J., not participating.

HOLT, JUSTICE, dissenting in part.

I would adhere to the views expressed in Cox v. State, 264 Ark. 608, 573 S.W.2d 906 (1978), which is overruled today. The majority's view meets the prophecy of *Weinstein* when he wrote: "Such an approach paves the way to an exception which will swallow the rule." Rule 608(b) was not meant to include every act of dishonesty but only those going to the veracity of the witness.

RHODES v. STATE, 276 Ark. 203, 634 S.W.2d 107, 112–14 (1982) (Hickman, J., dissenting). "The majority opinion expresses dissatisfaction with our conclusion in *Gustafson* and are overruling it *sua sponte* prospectively. If I understand it they are holding that theft has no bearing on the character trait of honesty and such misconduct may not be used to impeach a witness or defendant. The opinion states:

> Thus, in the future with the same set of facts before us, we would hold that while an absence of respect for the property rights of others is an undesirable trait, it does not directly indicate an impairment of the trait of truthfulness, and cross-examination would not be allowed on specific acts of shoplifting for which there was no conviction.
>
> * * *

"After careful deliberation we decided in *Gustafson* that there was a relationship between stealing and a lack of veracity. We stated that burglary and robbery would not bear on veracity unless a theft was involved. See People v. Burdine, 99 Cal.App.3d 442, 160 Cal.Rptr. 375 (1979). A jury should know if a witness or a defendant has stolen before. Evidently the majority does not believe thieves tend to lie."

SITZ v. STATE, 23 Ark.App. 126, 743 S.W.2d 18, 19–20 (1988). "After a jury trial, James Sitz was convicted of driving while intoxicated. The State's only witness was James Walker, the Tyronza Chief of Police.

"On cross-examination, appellant's counsel sought to ask Walker about the circumstances surrounding his leaving his position as the Chief of Police for the City of Harrisburg. * * * [H]e was seeking to show that Walker had embezzled funds from the City of Harrisburg. * * *

* * *

" * * * In Gustafson v. State, 267 Ark. 278, 590 S.W.2d 853 (1979), the supreme court held that theft was probative of untruthfulness and therefore could be inquired about on cross under Rule 608(b). *Gustafson* was overruled in Rhodes v. State, 276 Ark. 203, 634 S.W.2d 107 (1982), in which the court held that, although theft is probative of dishonesty, it is not probative of untruthfulness and therefore cannot be inquired about on cross under Rule 608(b). Although *Gustafson* involved theft by receiving and *Rhodes* involved shoplifting, we do not believe that either decision turned on the particular type of theft offense involved. Appellant relies primarily on the dissenting opinion in *Rhodes.* While we might agree with appellant that the dissent is well reasoned we are not at liberty to follow it.

"Embezzlement was not an offense at common law. It has been defined as common-law larceny extended by statute to cover cases where the stolen property comes originally into the possession of the defendant without a trespass. Moody v. People, 65 Colo. 339, 176 P. 476 (1918). It was made a separate offense by statute in this state until the adoption of the Arkansas Criminal Code in 1975, at which time it was consolidated with other theft offenses. Arkansas Statutes Annotated § 41–2202 (Repl.1977). There is dicta in at least two federal cases stating that inquiry into specific acts which would have constituted embezzlement is permissible under Rule 608(b) of the Federal Rules of Evidence. United States v. Amahia, 825 F.2d 177 (8th Cir.1987); United States v. Leake, 642 F.2d 715 (4th Cir.1981). These statements appear to be derived from an article by Dean Ladd, Credibility Tests—Current Trends, 89 U.Pa.L.Rev. 166, 180 (1940). But Dean Ladd also argued that robbery, larceny, and burglary might be probative of untruthfulness.

"Our conclusion is that this case is controlled by the supreme court's holding in *Rhodes.* We do not think a meaningful distinction can be drawn, for purposes of Rule 608(b), between embezzlement and other forms of theft."

Note

See 3A Wigmore, Evidence §§ 979–987 (Chadbourn rev. 1970); McCormick, Evidence § 41 (4th ed. 1992).

SMITH v. STATE

Supreme Court of Georgia, 1989.
259 Ga. 135, 377 S.E.2d 158, cert. denied, 493 U.S. 825, 110 S.Ct. 88, 107 L.Ed.2d 53 (1989).

BELL, JUSTICE.

The appellant, Michael Smith, was convicted of rape, statutory rape, child molestation, and cruelty to children, and was sentenced to terms of imprisonment. Smith appeals and we reverse. The main issue on appeal is whether OCGA § 24–2–3, commonly referred to as the rape-shield law, bars admission of testimony regarding the victim's alleged past false accusations against persons other than the defendant.

Smith and his son lived with the victim, her brother, and her mother. As proof of the alleged offenses, the state offered testimony of an expert witness on "child abuse syndrome," testimony of two social workers, testimony of an investigator from the sheriff's department, and the victim's own testimony.

Outside the presence of the jury, Smith proffered the testimony of ten witnesses, including himself, regarding alleged past false accusations by the victim of sexual misconduct by men other than the defendant. Five testified that they had heard that the victim made similar allegations against them; each witness denied any such wrongdoing. Another witness testified that he had heard about similar allegations against him and that the victim had recanted in his presence; this witness also denied any wrongdoing. Two other witnesses testified that they were present when the victim recanted some of the allegations against persons other than Smith, and a ninth witness testified that she heard similar allegations and that she heard the victim recant these allegations. The defendant stated that the victim had made similar allegations against "ten or twelve" people and had recanted at least some of these accusations.

The court did not admit this evidence because it found that the rape-shield law, as construed in *Taylor v. State,* 183 Ga.App. 314, 316(7), 358 S.E.2d 845 (1987), barred its admission.[2] The court did allow testimony from several defense witnesses regarding the victim's reputation for truthfulness. These witnesses stated that the victim had a poor reputation for truthfulness and that they would not believe her under oath.

1. Initially, Smith contends that the rape-shield law does not prohibit evidence that the victim had lied about sexual misconduct by men other than him, and that if the law is so construed, the law is unconstitutional as violating his right of confrontation. We agree that the rape-shield law does not prohibit such testimony.

OCGA § 24-2-3 prohibits testimony regarding the victim's "past sexual behavior." Numerous other courts have faced the issue presented by this appeal, and have ruled that evidence of prior false allegations by the victim does not fall within the proscription of rape-shield laws. The courts have reasoned that the evidence does not involve the victim's past sexual conduct but rather the victim's propensity to make false statements regarding sexual misconduct. E.g., *Clinebell v. Commonwealth,* 235 Va. 319, 368 S.E.2d 263, 264–265(1) (1988); *Commonwealth v. Bohannon,* 376 Mass. 90, 378 N.E.2d 987, 991–92(10) (1978); *Little v. State,* 413 N.E.2d 639, 643 (Ind.App.1980); *Cox v. State,* 51 Md.App. 271, 443 A.2d 607, 613 (1982). We find the reasoning of these cases persuasive, and hold that § 24-2-3 does not prohibit testimony of previous false allegations by the victim.

We now turn to the state's argument that, even if the rape-shield law does not prohibit such testimony, the testimony relates to the victim's character, which can only be attacked by evidence of the victim's general reputation for veracity. See OCGA §§ 24-2-2; 24-9-84. The state argues that any specific instances of untruthfulness are prohibited. However, regarding evidence that the prosecutrix in a sex-

2. Some of the proffered testimony may be subject to other objections, such as hearsay. However, because the objection to this proffered evidence was based solely on the rape-shield law, and because the trial court excluded the testimony on that ground, we need not rule on this question now.

offense case has made prior false accusations against men other than the defendant, a majority of jurisdictions that have considered the question have held that the evidentiary rule preventing evidence of specific acts of untruthfulness must yield to the defendant's right of confrontation and right to present a full defense. These courts have held that evidence of prior false accusations is admissible to attack the credibility of the prosecutrix and as substantive evidence tending to prove that the instant offense did not occur. E.g., *Clinebell,* supra, 368 S.E.2d at 265–266; *Commonwealth v. Bohannon,* supra, 378 N.E.2d at 990–991; *West v. State,* 290 Ark. 329, 719 S.W.2d 684, 687 (1986); *People v. Adams,* 198 Cal.App.3d 10, 243 Cal.Rptr. 580, 583–584 (1988); *People v. Hurlburt,* 166 Cal.App.2d 334, 333 P.2d 82, 87–88 (1958); *State v. Anderson,* 211 Mont. 272, 686 P.2d 193, 198–201 (1984). See generally Galvin, *Shielding Rape Victims in the State and Federal Courts: A Proposal for the Second Decade,* 70 Minn.L.Rev. 763, 858–863 (1986).

However, the courts that have considered the admissibility of such evidence have ruled that, before such evidence can be admitted, the trial court must make a "threshold determination [outside the presence of the jury] that a reasonable probability of falsity exists. [Cites omitted]." *Clinebell,* supra, 368 S.E.2d at 266. This rule helps protect the prosecutrix from unfounded allegations that she has made similar allegations in the past, and we hereby adopt it for future cases in this state.

Because the trial court erred in excluding the proffered testimony based on the rape-shield statute, and because we cannot conclude that such error was harmless, we must reverse Smith's convictions. * * *

* * *

Judgment reversed.

STATE v. DeSANTIS, 155 Wis.2d 774, 456 N.W.2d 600, 606–07 (1990). "All courts that have considered the issue, according to one commentator, have concluded that the defendant must establish some factual basis before the trial court admits the evidence of untruthful allegations.[6] We conclude that the defendant should produce evidence at the pre-trial hearing sufficient to support a reasonable person's finding that the complainant made prior untruthful allegations. Before the circuit court admits the evidence the circuit court must make a preliminary finding based on the offer of proof that the jury could reasonably find that the complainant made prior untruthful allegations.[7] In other words, in order to admit evidence of untruthful prior

6. Galvin, Rape Shield Victims in the State and Federal Courts: A Proposal for the Second Decade, 70 Minn.L.Rev. 763, 861 (1986).

7. Courts have divided regarding the appropriate standard of proof for determining the admissibility of evidence of prior untruthful allegations of sexual assault. A number of courts have determined that the

allegations of sexual assault, a circuit court must be able to conclude from the proffered evidence that a reasonable person could reasonably infer that the complainant made prior untruthful allegations of sexual assault."

UNITED STATES v. LOLLAR

United States Court of Appeals, Fifth Circuit, 1979.
606 F.2d 587.

JAMES C. HILL, CIRCUIT JUDGE:

Howard Lollar appeals from his conviction for interstate transportation of stolen property valued in excess of $5,000, 18 U.S.C.A. § 2314. The property was alleged to have been stolen by appellant and several of his employees from a warehouse in West Milford, New Jersey. We affirm.

After appellant testified at trial, the government recalled one of its witnesses and asked him whether he would believe appellant under oath. Defense counsel's objection was overruled, and the witness, a former employer, answered the question in the negative. Appellant now argues that it was error to allow the witness to offer his opinion on appellant's veracity.

Although a criminal defendant cannot be compelled to take the stand in his own defense, once he chooses to testify "he places his credibility in issue as does any other witness." United States v. Jackson, 588 F.2d 1046, 1055 (5th Cir.1979); * * *. While the defendant's decision to testify does not open the door to attacks on his general character, it does free the government to offer evidence bearing on the defendant's believability as a witness. Historically, the most widely used method of impeaching a defendant's credibility was to call witnesses to testify that the defendant's reputation for truth and veracity was bad. The propriety of asking a more direct question, such as "would you believe this person under oath," caused a great deal of conflict among the courts and the commentators. Early cases in this Circuit adopted the position that such testimony could be used to impeach a witness' credibility. See Miller v. United States, 288 F. 816, 818 (5th Cir.1923); Held v. United States, 260 F. 932, 933 (5th Cir.1919). While this was the minority view among the courts, many commentators agreed that "the exclusion of opinion evidence was 'historically

offering party must show that a prior allegation of sexual assault is demonstrably false. See State v. Schwartzmiller, 107 Idaho 89, 685 P.2d 830, 833 (1984); Little v. State, 413 N.E.2d 639, 643 (Ind.Ct.App. 1980); State v. Johnson, 102 N.M. 110, 692 P.2d 35, 43 (Ct.App.1984); State v. Sieler, 397 N.W.2d 89, 92 (S.D.1986).

Still other courts hold that the trial court must, before admitting the evidence, determine that a reasonable probability of falsity exists. Clinebell v. Commonwealth, 235 Va. 319, 368 S.E.2d 263, 266 (1988); Smith v. State, 259 Ga. 135, 377 S.E.2d 158, 160 (1989).

See also People v. Alexander, 116 Ill. App.3d 855, 72 Ill.Dec. 338, 452 N.E.2d 591, 594–95 (1983) (evidence of prior false accusation inconclusive and not admissible); State v. Hutchinson, 141 Ariz. 583, 688 P.2d 209 (Ariz.App.1984) (sufficient facts to show prior charge was unsubstantiated).

unsound.'" 3 Weinstein's Evidence ¶ 608[04], at 608–20 (1978); see McCormick, Evidence § 44, at 95 (1954); 7 Wigmore, Evidence §§ 1981–1986 (3d ed. 1940); Ladd, Techniques of Character Testimony, 24 Iowa L.Rev. 498, 509–13 (1939). This conflict was resolved in 1976 with the enactment of Rule 608(a) of the Federal Rules of Evidence. Recognizing that "witnesses who testify to reputation seem in fact often to be giving their opinions, disguised somewhat misleadingly as reputation," Advisory Committee's Notes, Fed.R.Evid. 608(a), Rule 608(a) provides that the credibility of a witness may be attacked "by evidence in the form of *opinion or reputation*", Fed.R.Evid. 608(a) (emphasis added). While it may be more desirable to have counsel first ask the impeaching witness about his knowledge of the defendant's reputation for truth and veracity, and whether based on that knowledge he would believe the defendant under oath, Rule 608(a) imposes no such requirement:

> Witnesses may now be asked directly to state their opinion of the principal witness' character for truthfulness and they may answer for example, "I think X is a liar." The rule imposes no prerequisite conditioned upon long acquaintance or recent information about the witness; cross-examination can be expected to expose defects of lack of familiarity and to reveal reliance on isolated or irrelevant instances of misconduct or the existence of feelings of personal hostility towards the principal witness.

Weinstein's Evidence ¶ 608[04], at 608–20 (1978).

Accordingly, we hold that the district court was acting well within its discretion in overruling defense counsel's objection.

* * *

AFFIRMED.

STATE v. MAULE, 35 Wash.App. 287, 667 P.2d 96, 101 (1983). "The defense called three of Maule's neighbors to testify as to Kimberly's and Denise's reputation for truth and veracity. Each testified that the girls' reputations for truth and veracity were poor. The State's objections to further inquiry as to whether, from the witness' knowledge of the girls' reputation, the witness would believe the girls 'under oath' were sustained. Maule contends the trial judge erred in sustaining the State's objection to these questions. We do not agree.

"ER 608(a) provides:

> The credibility of a witness may be attacked or supported by evidence in the form of reputation, but subject to the limitations: (1) the evidence may refer only to character for truthfulness or untruthfulness, * * *

ER 608 'differs from Federal Rule 608 in that it does not authorize the introduction of evidence of character in the form of an opinion.' Comment, ER 608, 91 Wash.2d 1148 (1978). To ask a witness if he would believe another witness under oath, without further qualification, is to call for the witness' personal opinion and is therefore impermissible. State v. Swenson, 62 Wash.2d 259, 282–83, 382 P.2d 614 (1963). The early case of State v. Hooker, 99 Wash. 661, 666–72, 170 P. 374 (1918), would permit the question and answer objected to. ER 608 is to the contrary. The trial judge did not err in sustaining the State's objections to these questions."

Note

See 3A Wigmore, Evidence §§ 920–930 (Chadbourn rev. 1970); 8 id. §§ 1980–1986 (McNaughton rev. 1961); McCormick, Evidence § 43 (4th ed. 1992); Wilkins, Impeaching by Showing Reputation for Truth, 1 St. Louis U.L.J. 277 (1951).

UNITED STATES v. MEDICAL THERAPY SCIENCES, INC.

United States Court of Appeals, Second Circuit, 1978.
583 F.2d 36, cert. denied, 439 U.S. 1130, 99 S.Ct. 1049, 59 L.Ed.2d 91 (1979).

MOORE, CIRCUIT JUDGE:

After a jury trial, appellants Stanley Berman and his company, Medical Therapy Sciences, Inc. ("Medical Therapy"), were convicted of having filed false claims to obtain Medicare payments during the period of 1971–1976, and of having conspired to do the same along with unindicted co-conspirators, including one Barbara Russell, formerly a trusted employee and personal intimate of Berman. Berman was also convicted of perjury in connection with the grand jury's investigation of Medicare abuses.

* * *

Berman does not challenge the sufficiency of the evidence as to the substantive counts. Rather, his final claim is that his convictions should be reversed because error was committed when, over defense objection, the trial judge permitted the Government to present character witnesses to bolster Russell's credibility. Berman claims that a new trial is required in view of the fact that Russell's credibility was crucial under the defense theory of the case—i.e., that it was Russell alone who had perpetrated the frauds.

Rule 608(a) of the Federal Rules of Evidence provides that character evidence may be used to support a witness, but limits its use so that "evidence of truthful character is admissible only after the character of the witness for truthfulness has been attacked by opinion or reputation evidence or otherwise." Berman's claim is that the foundation for character evidence was not present in this case because Russell's character for truthfulness had not been attacked within the meaning of the Rule. He argues that cross examination elicited only matters of Russell's bias in favor of the Government and against Berman and that, in any event, the Government itself initially brought to the jury's attention, on its direct examination of Russell, the facts that she had had two prior convictions and that she had been accused by Berman of having embezzled money from Medical Therapy. Berman contends that the Government should not thereafter have been allowed to bolster her credibility when the defense cross examined only as to matters brought out on direct.

The Government's argument is that, in questioning Russell on direct as to her prior convictions, the prosecutor was only anticipating defense impeachment, as it had the right to do, so that the jury would not gain the impression that the Government was attempting to hide information from them. United States v. Stassi, 544 F.2d 579, 583 (2d Cir.1976), cert. denied, 430 U.S. 907, 97 S.Ct. 1176, 51 L.Ed.2d 582 (1977); United States v. Rothman, 463 F.2d 488, 490 (2d Cir.), cert. denied, 409 U.S. 956, 93 S.Ct. 291, 34 L.Ed.2d 231 (1972). Because Russell's truthfulness was "attacked" on cross examination, the Government argues that Rule 608(a) by its terms permits it the use of character evidence, notwithstanding its own elicitation of Russell's background. Although the issue is a close one, we believe that the decision to permit the evidence in question was one within the trial judge's discretion.

As to the point that the Government first elicited the impeaching facts, we agree that the Government had the right to proceed as it did. Rule 608 itself contains no limitation that precludes a party from offering character evidence under circumstances where it anticipates impeachment; rather, the event that triggers the applicability of the Rule is an "attack" on the witness' veracity. While under the Federal Rules, a party *may* impeach his own witness, Fed.R.Evid. 607, there is a vast difference between putting that witness' veracity in issue by eliciting the impeaching facts and merely revealing the witness' background. Indeed, even in jurisdictions where a party may not discredit his own witness, it has been held that the fact of prior convictions may be brought out on direct examination for non-impeachment purposes. As stated by the New York Court of Appeals,

> " 'The law does not limit a party to witnesses of good character, nor does it compel a party to conceal the bad record of his witnesses from the jury, to have it afterwards revealed by the opposing party with telling effect. Such a rule would be unfair alike to the party calling the witness and the jury. * * * [W]hen a disreputable witness is called and frankly presented to the jury as such, the party calling him represents him for the occasion and the purposes of the trial as worthy of belief.' People v. Minsky, 227 N.Y. 94, 98, 124 N.E. 126, 127 (1919)."

See also Richardson, Evidence, § 509 (Prince 10th ed.).

While we do not think that Rule 608(a) should make supporting character evidence available to a party who elicits impeachment material on direct examination for impeaching purposes, we do believe that, when the tenor of the direct examination does not suggest an "attack" on veracity, and when cross examination *can* be characterized as such 

an attack, the trial judge should retain the discretion to permit the use of character witnesses. His proximity to the situation allows him to make the determination of when, and by whom, an attack is made. Were the rule to be otherwise, a party would have to choose between revealing, on direct, the background of a witness and its right to use character evidence if the witness' veracity is subsequently impugned.

In the instant case, the Government's direct questioning of Russell was brief and to the point. She was simply asked whether, when she left Medical Therapy to establish a business which was in competition with Berman's, she had taken patients from Berman's operation; she answered in the negative. This questioning covered about one page. (*See,* Tr. 1003). The prosecutor also elicited the fact that, near the end of Russell's employment with Berman, at a time when relations between the two were strained, Berman had accused Russell of taking $70 from him, and that she had denied the charge (claiming, in fact, that Berman had owed her and her husband for past loans), but had repaid the money to avoid any further problem. (Tr. 1015). Finally, she admitted her two prior convictions for obtaining amphetamines by fraudulent practices, but explained that she had committed the acts at a time when she had been addicted to the drug for weight control purposes and that she had sought help after her second conviction. Even this interchange covered only five pages of transcript. (Tr. 1016–1020). At least on the basis of the cold record before us, it appears that, in a very real sense, the Government did not put Russell's veracity in issue. Thus, though we believe that the trial judge should retain discretion to disallow the use of character evidence under circumstances such as this, we think he must also be permitted to allow it when, subsequent to the revelation of a witness' problems on direct, the opponent paints the witness with more accusatory strokes—especially where, as here, wrongdoing which implicates veracity is alleged and denied.

In this case, however, Berman argues that his counsel did not open the door to character evidence because his cross examination of Russell did not constitute an "attack on veracity". We conclude, however, that Judge Carter could have properly characterized the defense's treatment of Russell as an attack within the meaning of Rule 608(a).

In this case, cross examination of Russell included sharp questioning about her prior convictions, which were predicated on activities characterized as fraudulent. When such convictions are used for impeachment purposes, as they were on cross examination here, we think that the door is opened to evidence in support of truthfulness. See 3 Weinstein & Berger, Evidence ¶ 608[08], at 608–41 (1977); Advisory Committee Note to Rule 608(a); McCormick, Evidence ¶ 49; 4 Wigmore, Evidence §§ 1106–1107.

Russell's character was also attacked by "specific act" evidence, to wit, allegations that she had embezzled money and stolen patients from Berman's company. While Berman argues that such evidence, because it involved her efforts to set up a competing business, bore solely on her bias against him, and, as such, did not constitute an attack on character, see Weinstein & Berger, supra, at 608–42; 4 Wigmore, supra, § 1107, we do not think that the implications were so limited. As noted by the commentators, evidence of bias can take many forms. See McCormick, Evidence § 40. Some types of bias, for example bias stemming from a relationship with a party, do not necessarily involve any issue relating to the moral character of the witness, but suggest only that the witness' testimony may perhaps unwittingly be slanted for reasons unrelated to general propensity for untruthfulness. As such, character evidence is not relevant to meet such an attack. On the other hand, alleged partiality based on hostility or self-interest may assume greater significance if it is sought to be proven by conduct rising to the level of corruption. The commentators agree that "[e]vidence of corrupt conduct on the part of a witness should be regarded as an attack on his truthfulness warranting supportive evidence * * *." 3 Weinstein & Berger, supra, at 608–42, citing McCormick, Evidence § 49, at 107 (1954). Certainly, the embezzlement and theft of which Russell was accused can be said to fall within the category of corrupt conduct, within the contemplation of Rule 608(a). See Weinstein & Berger, supra, ¶ 608[05] and authorities therein discussed. Furthermore, Russell consistently denied the larceny that was ascribed to her by the defense attack.[6] Under such a circumstance, the commentators again agree that "rehabilitating evidence should be allowed in the judge's discretion if he finds the witness' denial has not erased the jury's doubts". Weinstein & Berger, supra, at 608–41–42, citing the agreement of Wigmore and McCormick on this point.

We think, in sum, that the decision to permit the character evidence must be affirmed on the facts. We emphasize, however, that discretion in this area must be exercised with circumspection so that

6. * * * [T]he defense attack here went far beyond mere accusation by cross-examination and denial. Other witnesses were called to contradict Russell's denials in order to support the defense's theory that Russell had the motive to commit the frauds, on her own, and for her own purposes—that she could have submitted false claims to cover up for her embezzlement. Though contradiction cannot usually be characterized as an "attack" on character, Weinstein & Berger, supra, ¶ 608[08], at 608–43, citing McCormick, Evidence § 49, here the contradiction specifically implicated Russell's veracity.

As Judge Weinstein and Professor Berger suggest,

> "the mandate in Rule 401 to admit all relevant evidence should be construed to authorize—but not to require—the admission of supportive character evidence if the trial judge finds in the circumstances of the particular case that the contradiction amounted to an attack on veracity." 1 608[08], at 608–43.

This suggestion, in essence, is the conclusion we adopt today. Accord, Advisory Committee Note to Rule 608. We think that trial judges should be permitted, under Rule 608, to exercise sound discretion to permit or deny a party the use of character evidence to support veracity. As is always the case, the balancing test under Rule 403 must be considered before any such evidence is permitted over objection. Furthermore, it is always open to the trial judge to deny a party the opportunity to present only cumulative evidence bearing solely on credibility. See United States v. Augello, 452 F.2d 1135, 1140 (2d Cir.1971) (character evidence should be used with great circumspection, and may be disallowed), cert. denied, 406 U.S. 922, 92 S.Ct. 1787, 32 L.Ed.2d 122; 409 U.S. 859, 93 S.Ct. 145, 34 L.Ed.2d 105 (1972).

the jury's attention is not diverted from the main issues to be tried. It is not every cross examination that should trigger the authority of Rule 608(a)'s provision for supporting character evidence. However, since the attack in this case went even beyond cross examination, and since Berman's guilt was established not only by Russell's testimony, but also by ample supporting evidence, both documentary and in the form of testimony from the Blue Cross specialist and from other employees of Medical Therapy, we affirm.

Judgment affirmed.

Note

See 4 Wigmore, Evidence §§ 1104–1119 (Chadbourn rev. 1970); McCormick, Evidence § 47 (4th ed. 1992).

UNITED STATES v. LINDSTROM

United States Court of Appeals, Eleventh Circuit, 1983.
698 F.2d 1154, cert. denied sub nom. Zuniga v. United States, 464 U.S. 983, 104 S.Ct. 426, 78 L.Ed.2d 361 (1983).

VANCE, CIRCUIT JUDGE:

* * *

Dennis Slater and Joanne Lindstrom appeal convictions and sentences for mail fraud, 18 U.S.C. § 1341 and § 1342, and conspiracy to commit mail fraud, 18 U.S.C. § 371. * * *

* * *

Appellants contend that the district court improperly (1) placed limitations on defense questioning of the government's chief witness relating to her prior psychiatric treatment and confinement, and (2) denied the defense access to medical records suggesting that the government's witness suffered from psychiatric illnesses, including delusions. * * *

* * *

Certain forms of mental disorder have high probative value on the issue of credibility. Although the debate over the proper legal role of mental health professionals continues to rage, even those who would limit the availability of psychiatric evidence acknowledge that many types of "emotional or mental defect may materially affect the accuracy of testimony; a conservative list of such defects would have to include the psychoses, most or all of the neuroses, defects in the structure of the nervous system, mental deficiency, alcoholism, drug addiction and psychopathic personality." Juviler, Psychiatric Opinions as to Credibility of Witnesses: A Suggested Approach, 48 Cal.L.Rev. 648, 648 (1960). Mental illness may tend to produce bias in a witness' testimony. A psychotic's veracity may be impaired by lack of capacity to observe, correlate or recollect actual events. A paranoid person may interpret a reality skewed by suspicions, antipathies or fantasies. A schizophrenic may have difficulty distinguishing fact from fantasy and may have his memory distorted by delusions, hallucinations and paranoid thinking. A paranoid schizophrenic, though he may appear normal and his judgment on matters outside his delusional system may remain intact, may harbor delusions of grandeur or persecution that grossly distort his reactions to events. As one commentator succinctly summarized the interplay between mental disorders and legal issues of credibility:

> [T]he delusions of the litigious paranoiac make him believe he has grievances, which he feels can be corrected only through the courts. His career as a litigant is frequently touched off by a lawsuit or legal controversy whose outcome left him dissatisfied. Often he will insist on conducting his own case, quoting voluminously from cases and statutes. Because he is likely to be of better-than-average intelligence, he may mislead a jury that is uninformed about his paranoiac career and actually convince them that his cause is just.
>
> Trivial incidents and casual remarks may be interpreted in a markedly biased way, as eloquent proof of conspiracy or injustice. In his telling them, these trivial incidents may by retrospective falsification be given a grossly distorted and sinister significance. Even incidents of a decade or more ago may now suddenly be remembered as supporting his suspicions, and narrated in minute detail.
>
> On the other hand, so far as the power of observation is concerned, the paranoid witness may be quite as competent as anyone, and perhaps more than most; his suspiciousness may make him more alert and keen-eyed in watching what goes on.
>
> Delusions of persecution may evoke intense hatred. This may lead to counter-accusations resting on false memory, which may be very real to the accuser and be narrated by him with strong and convincing feeling. And indeed they may have a kernel of truth; because of his personality and his behavior, many people probably do dislike him. As Freud said, a paranoid does not project into a vacuum. Such a person not infrequently feels the need for vengeance.

Weihofen, Testimonial Competence and Credibility, 34 Geo.Wash.L.Rev. 53, 82 (1965) (footnotes omitted).

The government in this case contends that psychiatric evidence merely raises a collateral issue. But such labels cannot substitute for analysis. Whether called "collateral" or not, the issue of a witness' credibility is committed to the providence of the jury. Although the use of psychiatric evidence "does not fall within the traditional pattern of impeachment, the law should be flexible enough to make use of new resources." *Weihofen,* supra at 68. By this late date, use of this kind of evidence can hardly be termed "new."

At trial the defense sought to show that the key witness for the government was not credible, arguing that her motive for initiating and pursuing the investigation of Bay Therapy was based on hatred of the appellants.[4] Lindstrom and Slater argued to the district court that this

4. Appellants also contended that the witness was not competent to testify at all an issue quite different from that of credibility. Credibility is a jury question,

witness was carrying out a vendetta against them because she had not received a promised percentage of Bay Therapy when the business was sold. Appellants further sought to impeach the witness' credibility by demonstrating that her alleged vendetta resulted from a continuing mental illness, for which she had been periodically treated and confined. From public sources and from psychiatric records which the district court permitted defense counsel to review, the defense gathered material suggesting that in 1971 the witness was hospitalized following a serious suicide attempt; that in 1977 the witness, while she was running Bay Therapy, offered a patient of Bay Therapy $3,000 to murder the wife of the witness' alleged lover; that in 1978 she was involuntarily committed under Florida's Baker Act after taking an overdose of drugs; that in 1980 she was arrested and charged with aggravated assault for having allegedly fired a shotgun through the window of her purported lover's house; that following this incident she was briefly placed in a stockade until, at the urging of her psychiatrist, she was transferred to Hillsborough County Hospital where she was involuntarily committed under the Baker Act; that during this confinement she was diagnosed "schizophrenic reaction, chronic undifferentiated type" and described by the Chief of Psychology at Hillsborough as being "immature, egocentric, [and] manipulative," having superficial relationships causing "marital problems and sexual conflicts in general" and seeing authority as something to be manipulated for self gratification and as an obstacle; that an unsigned chart entry noted that the patient had a "history of hallucinations" and was "suicidal—homicidal and delusional." Through effective questioning in these areas, appellants contend that they could have shown the witness' past pattern of aggressive and manipulative conduct toward persons close to her and that they could have demonstrated the witness' motivation and determination in pursuing a vendetta.

The trial court, fearing that the defense would attempt to put the witness herself on trial, stated:

> I think we should discuss, too, the extent of the cross-examination of this witness in regard to these activities. I am trying to think this through. I am not fully convinced it's a 608–B question, although I think it's akin to that. But any questions along this line probably would go further than what seems to be envisioned by 608–B, because you're testing the witness's credibility is what you're attempting to do, I would suppose.[6] *So, within reason, there are two or three properly*

whereas competency is a "threshold question of law to be answered by the judge." United States v. Martino, 648 F.2d 367, 384 (5th Cir.1981), *cert. denied,* 456 U.S. 943, 102 S.Ct. 2006, 2007, 72 L.Ed.2d 465 (1982). We find no reversible error in the district court's resolution of the competency issue.

6. We agree with the trial court that Federal Rule of Evidence 608 is not controlling:

> The credibility of a witness can always be attacked by showing that his capacity to observe, remember or narrate is impaired. Consequently, the witness' capacity at the time of the event, as well as at the time of trial, are significant. Defects of this nature reflect on *mental* capacity for truth-telling rather than on

framed questions I'm going to allow you to at least let this jury know about the fact that this witness has had some mental and emotional problems in the past.

I'm not going to allow the defense to try this witness, so to speak.

Three examples suffice to illustrate the extremely narrow limits within which the district judge permitted cross-examination of the witness. First, the court refused to allow the defense to question the witness about the murder contract that she allegedly offered to a Bay Therapy patient. The defense proffered testimony by the patient to the effect that the witness had approached him and offered him $3,000 to shoot the wife of the witness' purported lover. The court sustained the government's objection to the questions, and also denied a defense request to ask the witness the questions out of the hearing of the jury. Secondly, the district court denied appellants the opportunity to cross-examine the witness about her own alleged attempt to shoot a shotgun through the window of her purported lover's house, after which she was committed under the Baker Act. Thirdly, the judge sustained the government's objection to defense questions focusing on whether, during her commitment, the witness had told hospital personnel that she had attempted suicide for the purpose of manipulating and punishing her boyfriend. Defense counsel proffered hospital records showing that the witness had in fact made such statements. During the ensuing side bar conference, defense counsel stated that the witness' history of manipulation was "the whole point of our defense. It's those people that cross her, Dennis Slater, Joanne Lindstrom, [or her alleged lover], she goes out to get them with a vendetta. She manipulated them. She did it to him on numerous occasions. She's doing the same thing to him. She's told two people that I have a witness for that she's out to get Dennis Slater."

These rulings by the district court constituted an abuse of discretion contradicting Supreme Court and former fifth circuit authority on the right of confrontation in general and the right to examine the psychiatric history of adverse witnesses in particular. * * *

* * *

The government further argued that the excluded evidence would have confused the jury. Such a notion, that juries misconstrue evidence of mental illness because of passion and prejudice, might have been appropriate in the last century. But juries nowadays regularly deal with this sort of evidence.

We "cannot speculate as to whether the jury, as sole judge of the credibility of a witness, would have accepted this line of reasoning had counsel been permitted to fully present it. But we do conclude that the jurors were entitled to have the benefit of the defense theory before them so that they could make an informed judgment * * *." Davis v.

moral inducements for truth-telling, and consequently Rule 608 does not apply. J. Weinstein, Weinstein's Evidence ¶ 607[4] (1981) (footnotes omitted) (emphasis in original).

Alaska, 415 U.S. at 317, 94 S.Ct. at 1111. We hold that the jury was denied evidence necessary for it to make an informed determination of whether the witness' testimony was based on historical facts as she perceived them or whether it was the product of a psychotic hallucination. The jury was denied any evidence on whether this key witness was a schizophrenic, what schizophrenia means and whether it affects one's perceptions of external reality. The jury was denied any evidence of whether the witness was capable of distinguishing reality from hallucinations. Such denial was reversible error.

REVERSED and REMANDED.

STATE v. ARMSTRONG, 232 N.C. 727, 62 S.E.2d 50, 51 (1950). "What could be more effective for the purpose than to impeach the mentality or the intellectual grasp of the witness? If his interest, bias, indelicate way of life, insobriety and general bad reputation in the community may be shown as bearing upon his unworthiness of belief, why not his imbecility, want of understanding, or moronic comprehension, which go more directly to the point?"

Notes

(1) "[The trial judge] did not understand the purpose of a psychiatric examination in the premises is not to determine whether, in the opinion of the psychiatrist, the witness is telling the truth in the case at bench but to determine whether or not the emotional or mental condition of the witness may affect his ability to tell the truth." People v. Francis, 5 Cal.App.3d 414, 85 Cal.Rptr. 61, 64 (1970).

(2) See 3A Wigmore, Evidence §§ 931–935, 989–995 (Chadbourn rev. 1970); McCormick, Evidence § 44 (4th ed. 1992); O'Neale, Court Ordered Psychiatric Examination of a Rape Victim in a Criminal Rape Prosecution—Or How Many Times Must a Woman Be Raped? 18 Santa Clara L.Rev. 119 (1978).

KELLENSWORTH v. STATE

Supreme Court of Arkansas, 1982.
275 Ark. 252, 631 S.W.2d 1.

HICKMAN, JUSTICE.

John Herbert Kellensworth, Jr. was convicted and sentenced to ten years imprisonment for rape and three years for burglary.

* * *

Kellensworth's conviction must be reversed because the trial court erroneously permitted certain testimony by Kellensworth's former wife. The State called her after the defense rested and the sole purpose of her testimony was to impeach testimony by Kellensworth and his parents. Kellensworth's mother had testified that Kellensworth "worshipped" his former wife and child. On cross-examination Kellensworth and his father testified that Kellensworth loved his former wife. The former wife, Vickie Kellensworth, was allowed to rebut this by testifying that Kellensworth, at various times, pulled a gun on her, tried to run her off the road, knocked her up against a brick wall, and on a separate occasion struck her.

The trial judge admitted the testimony because he considered it simple rebuttal evidence. But it was more than mere rebuttal testimony. It was offered to impeach, or discredit, the testimony of Kellensworth and his parents.

A witness cannot be impeached on a collateral matter by calling another witness to contradict the testimony of the first witness. 3A Wigmore on Evidence § 1001; Swaim v. State, 257 Ark. 166, 514 S.W.2d 706 (1974); See Haight v. State, 259 Ark. 478, 533 S.W.2d 510 (1976); Mathis v. State, 267 Ark.App. 904, 591 S.W.2d 679 (1980). The reason for the rule is that to permit such a tactic would only distract the jury from the main issue, waste time and prejudice a defendant. McCormick's Evidence § 47 (1972).

The rule does not mean a witness can never be discredited on a collateral matter. Cross-examination is the usual tool available. Or in some instances, judicial notice can be taken of a fact which will contradict testimony of a witness.

The question of whether the matter was collateral in this case is not easy. One test of whether a fact is collateral is whether the fact is independently provable. If the fact is independently provable it is not collateral. Generally, two kinds of facts meet this test: Those that are relevant to the substantive issue in the case and those facts that show bias, interest, conviction of a crime, or want of capacity, opportunity, or knowledge of the witness. 3A Wigmore on Evidence §§ 1004, 1005. The mother's testimony does not seem to fall into either category and is therefore collateral.

At most, the statement by the mother would be one of "good character," a fact any defendant can choose to place before a jury. Ark.Stat.Ann. § 28–1001, Rule 404 (Repl.1979); Finnie v. State, 267 Ark. 638, 593 S.W.2d 32 (1980). In that narrow sense the evidence might not be deemed collateral. Ark.Stat.Ann. § 28–1001, Rule 405, permits a defendant to offer evidence of his good character but that evidence is limited to testimony as to his reputation and opinion testimony. Such evidence may be directly challenged through cross-examination. Michelson v. U.S., 335 U.S. 469, 69 S.Ct. 213, 93 L.Ed. 168 (1948). Or the State can rebut the evidence in kind with contrary evidence of reputation. But the State cannot produce witnesses to testify to specific acts of misconduct. McCormick's Evidence states: "* * * The witnesses for the prosecution are limited on direct [of their witnesses called in rebuttal] to assertions about the reputation and may not testify to particular acts or rumors thereof." McCormick's Evidence § 192. Also see 29 Ark.L.Rev. 14. Rule 405(b) provides that when character or a character trait is an essential element of a charge, claim or defense, proof may be made of specific instances of misconduct. But obviously the evidence offered is not an essential element of a charge of rape. Rule 404(a)(1) speaks to a "pertinent trait of character." But there is no such character trait at issue in this case. McCormick's Evidence identifies character traits as either moral or nonmoral. The nonmoral traits are ones of care, competence, skill or sanity; the moral character traits being peacefulness, honesty and the like. McCormick's Evidence § 187. Our Rules of Evidence mention only peacefulness as a trait, Rule 404(a)(2), but do not exclude generally accepted character traits. In our judgment it is not a character trait to "worship" one's wife. As we said, if anything, such a statement might qualify as a statement of good character in general, and only that. The State chose to disprove this general statement in a completely unacceptable way; they called Kellensworth's former wife to tell the jury of specific acts of misconduct to contradict the testimony of the mother that Kellensworth "worshipped" his former wife and child. The prejudicial effect of the testimony cannot be denied. Threatening another with a deadly weapon and striking another are both criminal offenses. So, regardless of whether the statement by the mother was collateral, the court was wrong in permitting the prejudicial evidence to go to the jury.

* * *

Reversed and remanded.

HAYS, J., dissents.

HAYS, JUSTICE, dissenting.

I do not agree that the trial court abused its discretion in permitting the rebuttal testimony of appellant's former wife relative to his conduct toward her. The testimony was initiated, not by the prosecution but by the defense in repeated questions to appellant's mother as to appellant's behavior and conduct toward his wife and son. The obvious purpose was to create an impression by the jury that appellant was an adoring and devoted husband and father. No other inference is possible. Where that occurs the State is entitled to some latitude to rebut that kind of evidence with facts from which other inferences could be drawn. Otherwise, the prosecution is rendered helpless where the defense affirmatively elicits testimony which portrays the character of the accused in a false light. The testimony was not collateral and the means by which the State answered it in rebuttal falls within the "wide discretion" of the trial court, which we will not reverse absent manifest abuse. Shipman v. State, 252 Ark. 285, 478 S.W.2d 421 (1972); City of Fayetteville v. Stone, 194 Ark. 218, 106 S.W.2d 158 (1937).

SUPPLEMENTAL OPINION

HICKMAN, JUSTICE.

The State in its petition for rehearing argues that the case of Howell v. State, 141 Ark. 487, 217 S.W.2d 457 (1920), is directly in point and holds that the State can impeach testimony brought out on direct examination with contradictory testimony. In *Howell* the victim in a rape case stated on direct examination that she had never had sexual intercourse with any man except the defendant. The defense was not allowed to impeach this testimony by offering the testimony of another man. We held this was error, pointing out that the State brought up the issue on direct examination, and since it did, the defense ought to be allowed to impeach it with contradictory testimony. If the counterpoint of that situation existed in this case it would have been as follows: Kellensworth would have stated on direct examination that he had never mistreated his wife in any way by striking her or beating her. In *Howell* the testimony was not that the victim was chaste or had a reputation for chastity, an issue permitted to be raised in those days, but was that the victim herself had never had intercourse with anyone except the defendant. The statement was not made by a third party but by the victim herself. In this case the statement was a general statement by Kellensworth's mother and at best could only have been a statement of opinion as to general character, not specific instances of good conduct. Furthermore, the State elicited from Kellensworth and his father on cross-examination testimony about how Kellensworth treated his wife; this subject was never raised by the defense during the direct examination of these witnesses. Due to these differences we deem Howell v. State, supra, distinguishable.

UNITED STATES v. BENEDETTO, 571 F.2d 1246, 1250 (2d Cir. 1978). "What ultimately tips the scale, after reviewing the particular amalgam of facts in this case, is that Benedetto testified on direct examination that he had never taken bribes from anybody. Once a witness (especially a defendant-witness) testifies as to any specific fact on direct testimony, the trial judge has broad discretion to admit extrinsic evidence tending to contradict the specific statement, even if such statement concerns a collateral matter in the case. See Walder v. United States, 347 U.S. 62, 74 S.Ct. 354, 98 L.Ed. 503 (1954); United States v. Beno, supra, 324 F.2d at 588. Moreover, here Benedetto's statement was closely intertwined with the central issue of this case, namely whether he had received money in connection with his official duties at certain plants. The admission of contradictory evidence to impeach Benedetto's credibility was thus warranted."

SIMMONS, INC. v. PINKERTON'S, INC., 762 F.2d 591, 604–05 (7th Cir.1985). "Impeachment by contradiction simply involves presenting evidence that part or all of a witness' testimony is incorrect. Thus if an eyewitness to an auto accident testified that the car that caused the accident was red, impeachment by contradiction relies on evidence that the car actually was yellow. The inference to be drawn is not that the witness was lying, but that the witness made a mistake of fact, and so perhaps her testimony may contain other errors and should be discounted accordingly.

"Of course, a particular misstatement may or may not be probative of the witness' general accuracy, depending on the circumstances, and thus may or may not be worth the time it takes to establish it. For this reason the collateral evidence rule developed. In the above example, assuming the color of the car was not directly relevant to any substantive issue in the case (e.g., if the identity of the car were stipulated), it presumably would not be worth the fact finder's time to entertain a 'mini-trial' on the issue of the car's color, simply to prove that the witness was mistaken as to this fact. Thus, while the accuracy of a witness' perception or memory can always be tested through traditional cross-examination techniques, the collateral evidence rule limits the extent to which the witness' testimony about non-essential matters may be contradicted by extrinsic proof. In short, if a matter is collateral (that is, if it could not be introduced into evidence as substantive proof) then it cannot be proven simply to contradict the witness' testimony for impeachment purposes. 3 J. Weinstein and M. Berger, Weinstein's Evidence ¶ 607[05], 607-61—607-72 (1984)."

LOUISVILLE & N.R. CO. v. McCLISH, 115 Fed. 268, 270–71 (6th Cir.1902). "Did the contradiction of Wright by the witnesses who claim that he was not where he says he was, and consequently could not have seen what he attempted to describe, put in issue the general character of the witness for truth, and thereby justify the introduction of witnesses to sustain it? Greenleaf, who goes farther upon this subject than many of the authorities are willing to follow in admitting this class of testimony, supports the doctrine that the contradiction of a witness by other testimony does not lay the foundation for the introduction of other testimony supporting his general reputation for truth. Greenl. Ev. § 469, and notes. What more is there in this case than the contradiction of Wright by other testimony? It is true that the contradiction is of that character that admits of no reconciliation of the testimony upon any theory of honest mistake or failure of memory. This is often true of witnesses whose general character for truth is unassailable. If, in every case where the witnesses are in direct and irreconcilable conflict, general character proof can be introduced, the disputed issues of fact will be lost sight of in a mass of testimony sustaining or impeaching the various witnesses in the case. The present case affords a striking illustration of the effect of the introduction of this class of testimony, for we find no less than six other witnesses at the trial whom it was deemed necessary to sustain by proof of general reputation. If this practice is to be followed, as is said in Russell v. Coffin, 8 Pick. 142, 'great delay and confusion would rise;

and, as almost all cases are tried upon controverted testimony, each witness must bring his compurgators to support him when he is contradicted, and, indeed, it would be a trial of the witnesses, and not of the action.' An attentive consideration of the cases and of the reasons upon which they are founded leads us to the conclusion that the introduction of this class of testimony should be confined to cases where an attack has been made upon the character of the witness by some method which tends to impeach his general character for truth. It is true that contradicting testimony may have an effect indirectly to impeach in the mind of the trior the character of the witness contradicted, but that is not the purpose of the testimony. It does not matter how much a witness may be contradicted, his general character is presumed good until it is assailed by some recognized method of impeachment. This may be undertaken by showing that the general reputation of the witness for truth is bad, by showing by direct proof or upon cross-examination that he has been convicted of an infamous crime. In these instances the attack is made upon his character, and is not so much upon his testimony in the particular case as upon his unreliability as a witness. When his character is thus assailed, the attack may be repelled by proof of general good reputation for truth. Until it is impeached it is not in issue, and we think the ends of justice will be subserved by confining the testimony to the issues of fact essential to the determination of the controversy before the court. While, as we have said, the cases are by no means uniform upon this subject, the conclusion reached is sustained by many well considered cases; among others; Wertz v. May, 21 Pa. 274; Brann v. Campbell, 86 Ind. 516; State v. Ward, 49 Conn. 429; Webb v. State, 29 Ohio St. 351; State v. Archer, 73 Iowa 320, 35 N.W. 241; Russell v. Coffin, 8 Pick. 142; Brown v. Mooers, 6 Gray, 451; Gertz v. Railroad, 137 Mass. 77, 50 Am.Rep. 285; Stevenson v. Gunning's Estate, 64 Vt. 609, 25 Atl. 697; People v. Gay, 7 N.Y. 378; Tedens v. Schumers, 112 Ill. 263.

"Whether the introduction of proof tending to show that the witness has made statements out of court inconsistent with his testimony is such an attack upon his character as justifies the introduction of sustaining testimony of general reputation is not a question involved in the record now before us. The cases are much in conflict upon the question, as a perusal of them will show. We cannot say that the admission of this sustaining testimony was harmless error. It tended to give undue weight and influence to the testimony of Wright over witnesses who rested upon the presumption of the law as to good character. Brann v. Campbell, 86 Ind. 516."

Note

See 3A Wigmore, Evidence §§ 1000–1008 (Chadbourn rev. 1970); McCormick, Evidence §§ 45, 49 (4th ed. 1992).

UNITED STATES v. WEBSTER

United States Court of Appeals, Seventh Circuit, 1984.
734 F.2d 1191.

POSNER, CIRCUIT JUDGE.

The defendant, Webster, was convicted of aiding and abetting the robbery of a federally insured bank and receiving stolen bank funds, was sentenced to nine years in prison, and appeals. Only one issue need be discussed. The government called the bank robber, King (who had pleaded guilty and been given a long prison term), as a witness against Webster. King gave testimony that if believed would have exculpated the defendant, whereupon the government introduced prior inconsistent statements that King had given the FBI inculpating Webster. Although the court instructed the jury that it could consider the statements only for purposes of impeachment, Webster argues that this was not good enough, that the government should not be allowed to get inadmissible evidence before the jury by calling a hostile witness and then using his out-of-court statements, which would otherwise be inadmissible hearsay, to impeach him.

Rule 607 of the Federal Rules of Evidence provides: "The credibility of a witness may be attacked by any party, including the party calling him." But it would be an abuse of the rule, in a criminal case, for the prosecution to call a witness that it knew would not give it useful evidence, just so it could introduce hearsay evidence against the defendant in the hope that the jury would miss the subtle distinction between impeachment and substantive evidence—or, if it didn't miss it, would ignore it. The purpose would not be to impeach the witness but to put in hearsay as substantive evidence against the defendant, which Rule 607 does not contemplate or authorize. We thus agree that "impeachment by prior inconsistent statement may not be permitted where employed as a mere subterfuge to get before the jury evidence not otherwise admissible." United States v. Morlang, 531 F.2d 183, 190 (4th Cir.1975). Although *Morlang* was decided before the Federal Rules of Evidence became effective, the limitation that we have quoted on the prosecutor's rights under Rule 607 has been accepted in all circuits that have considered the issue. See, e.g., United States v. Miller, 664 F.2d 94, 97 (5th Cir.1981); United States v. DeLillo, 620 F.2d 939, 946 (2d Cir.1980); Whitehurst v. Wright, 592 F.2d 834, 839–40 (5th Cir.1979); United States v. Rogers, 549 F.2d 490, 497 (8th Cir.1976). We agree with these decisions. See also United States v. Gorny, 732 F.2d 597, 603–04 (7th Cir.1984).

But it is quite plain that there was no bad faith here. Before the prosecutor called King to the stand she asked the judge to allow her to examine him outside the presence of the jury, because she didn't know what he would say. The defendant's counsel objected and the voir dire was not held. We do not see how in these circumstances it can be thought that the prosecutor put King on the stand knowing he would give no useful evidence. If she had known that, she would not have offered to voir dire him, as the voir dire would have provided a foundation for defense counsel to object, under *Morlang,* to the admission of King's prior inconsistent statements.

Webster urges us, on the authority of Graham, Handbook of Federal Evidence § 607.3 (1981 and Supp.1983), to go beyond the good-faith standard and hold that the government may not impeach a witness with his prior inconsistent statements unless it is surprised and harmed by the witness's testimony. But we think it would be a mistake to graft such a requirement to Rule 607, even if such a graft would be within the power of judicial interpretation of the rule. Suppose the government called an adverse witness that it thought would give evidence both helpful and harmful to it, but it also thought that the harmful aspect could be nullified by introducing the witness's prior inconsistent statement. As there would be no element of surprise, Professor Graham would forbid the introduction of the prior statements; yet we are at a loss to understand why the government should be put to the choice between the Scylla of forgoing impeachment and the Charybdis of not calling at all a witness from whom it expects to elicit genuinely helpful evidence. The good-faith standard strikes a better balance; and it is always open to the defendant to argue that the probative value of the evidence offered to impeach the witness is clearly outweighed by the prejudicial impact it might have on the jury, because the jury would have difficulty confining use of the evidence to impeachment. See Fed.R.Evid. 403.

The judgment of conviction is

AFFIRMED.

Notes

(1) "Judge Posner misses a very simple point. The government is not put to the choice he presents. It may elicit the helpful testimony without eliciting the known harmful testimony as well. If the defendant chooses to elicit the harmful testimony, the government can impeach with the prior inconsistent statement. If the defendant does not elicit such testimony, the prior inconsistent statement will never be presented to the jury. The only reason the government has to elicit the harmful testimony in the first instance is its belief that the effect of impeachment will more than nullify the harmful effect." Graham, Handbook of Federal Evidence § 607.3, at 429 n. 15 (3d ed. 1991).

(2) See also United States v. Castro–Ayon, p. 169 supra; Graham, Examination of a Party's Own Witness Under the Federal Rules of Evidence: A Promise Unfulfilled, 54 Tex.L.Rev. 917 (1976); Graham, The Relationship Among Federal Rules of Evidence 607, 801(d)(1)(A), and 403: A Reply to Weinstein's Evidence, 55 Tex.L.Rev. 573 (1977); Graham, Employing Inconsistent Statements for Impeachment and as Substantive Evidence: A Critical Review and Proposed Amendments of Federal Rules of Evidence 801(d)(1)(A), 613, and 607, 75 Mich.L.Rev. 1565 (1977); Ordover, surprise! That Damaging Turncoat Witness Is Still With Us: An Analysis

of Federal Rules of Evidence 607, 801(d)(1)(A) and 403, 5 Hofstra L.Rev. 65 (1976).

(3) For background on the traditional prohibition against impeaching one's own witness, see 3A Wigmore, Evidence §§ 896–918 (Chadbourn rev. 1970); McCormick, Evidence § 38 (4th ed. 1992).

SECTION 3. MODE AND ORDER OF INTERROGATION AND PRESENTATION *

[FED.R.EVID. 611]

UNITED STATES v. CAUDLE

United States Court of Appeals, Fourth Circuit, 1979.
606 F.2d 451.

WIDENER, CIRCUIT JUDGE:

The defendants were indicted for several offenses, all arising out of the procuring of a loan from the Economic Development Administration of the United States Department of Commerce, in the amount of $650,000.00, to Brevard Wood Products, Inc. At the time, the defendant, Russell Jack Hawke, Jr. (hereinafter Hawke) was Federal Co–Chairman of the Coastal Plains Regional Commission; the defendant Herbert L. Caudle, Jr. (hereinafter Caudle) was an entrepreneur interested in establishing a plant in the United States to process lumber imported from South America.

Count One charged both defendants with conspiring to defraud the United States in violation of 18 U.S.C. § 371. Count Two charged Hawke with the commission of an act as an employee of the United States affecting a personal financial interest, in violation of 18 U.S.C. § 208(a), in that he had a prospective employment interest and financial interest in Brevard Wood Products. Count Three charged both defendants with concealing a material fact in a matter within the jurisdiction of the United States in violation of 18 U.S.C. § 1001, by concealing the fact that Hawke would be employed with, and receive twenty percent of the stock of, Brevard Wood Products as soon as he terminated his position as Federal Co–Chairman of the Coastal Plains Regional Commission. Both defendants were charged, in the Fourth Count, with making a false statement as to a material fact in a matter within the jurisdiction of the United States, in violation of 18 U.S.C. § 1001, by submitting to the Economic Development Administration *A Feasibility Study for Brevard Wood Products, Inc.*, which included the allegedly false statement that the study was prepared by Albert Levy Associates, Inc. The Fifth Count charged Caudle with making a false

* See 3 Wigmore, Evidence §§ 766–783 (Chadbourn rev. 1970); 6 id. ch. 65 (Chadbourn rev. 1976); McCormick, Evidence §§ 4–7, 19–27, 29–32 (4th ed. 1992); Degnan, Non–Rules Evidence Law: Cross–Examination, 6 Utah L.Rev. 322 (1959); McCormick, The Scope and Art of Cross–Examination, 47 Nw.L.Rev. 177 (1952); Wellborn, Demeanor, 76 Cornell L.Rev. 1075 (1991).

statement as to a material fact in a matter within the jurisdiction of the United States in violation of 18 U.S.C. § 1001, by submitting to the Economic Development Administration a financial statement (in support of the Brevard Wood Products loan application) which falsely stated Caudle's net worth and which omitted liens and judgments that were outstanding against him.

Both defendants were found not guilty on Counts 1 and 3. The jury found Hawke guilty on Counts 2 and 4, and found Caudle guilty on Counts 4 and 5. From the judgments of conviction, both defendants appeal.

In early June 1976, Hawke, in his capacity as Federal Co–Chairman of the Coastal Plains Regional Commission, asked Dr. Albert Levy (of Albert Levy Associates, Inc.) to prepare a feasibility study to determine the possibility of locating a plant to process lumber imported from South America in the United States, possibly at a location within the jurisdiction of the Coastal Plains Regional Commission. Caudle furnished basic information and materials pertaining to the lumber business either to Dr. Levy directly or to Mr. Hawke, who turned the material over to Dr. Levy. On June 14, the Department of Commerce and the Coastal Plains Regional Commission awarded a $3,500.00 contract to Albert Levy Associates to prepare this study. Dr. Levy completed his report (hereinafter referred to as the "first study"), gave it to Hawke on or about July 15, 1976, and was paid from federal funds. Dr. Levy testified that he had then satisfied his legal obligations to the Coastal Plains Regional Commission. There may have been some question as to the length of this study (the report was four pages), and since Dr. Levy expected to obtain additional material relevant to the study, he agreed to turn these additional materials over to Hawke when he received them.

Caudle, the initiator of the idea that brought on the first study by the government, planned to obtain a loan from the Economic Development Administration (EDA) in order to start a proposed lumber processing company (which would eventually be named Brevard Wood Products, Inc.). The EDA requires that a feasibility study be submitted with the loan application, and that the study be made by a source independent of the entrepreneur seeking the loan. The defendants' position, both at trial and on appeal, is that Caudle commissioned Dr. Levy to do a feasibility study of Caudle's proposed wood processing business (hereinafter referred to as the "second study"). Caudle supplied some basic materials for this second study. Dr. Levy verified some of the material submitted to him and wrote some material in rough form, but was unable to get the study put together in time. Dr. Levy, in his line of work, apparently customarily prepared the two studies, the first general, the second specific. On September 24, 1976, with Hawke's permission, Dr. Levy turned the materials for the second study over to Caudle. Over the weekend of September 25 and 26, at Hawke's residence, the defendants and several other people compiled the second study. Dr. Levy knew they were compiling the study. This study, *A Feasibility*

Study for Brevard Wood Products, Inc., consisted of seventy pages, plus exhibits, and a cover letter purporting to be signed by Dr. Levy. The letter was actually a photocopy paste-up of an earlier letter from Dr. Levy. It included the Levy letterhead and signature but the body of the letter was composed by Hawke. The letter stated that "enclosed is the feasibility study prepared by Albert Levy Associates, Inc., for Brevard Wood Products." This case centers around the truth or falsity of the statement that the study was prepared by Dr. Levy.

In October 1976, the defendants gave Dr. Levy a copy of the study they had assembled. Dr. Levy then signed a letter identical to the photocopy paste-up letter prepared earlier, and delivered it to the defendants.

The government's position is that Dr. Levy did not prepare this second feasibility study, and therefore the first cover letter contained a false statement. It construes the testimony at trial to indicate that while some of the study was Dr. Levy's work, much of it was prepared by the defendants. The defendants' position is that Dr. Levy did prepare the second feasibility study, which they merely typed and assembled.

The defendants submitted this study to the EDA on October 4, 1976 as an early part of the loan application. It was apparently on the nineteenth of October that Dr. Levy saw the finished study, approved it, and signed a letter identical to the one prepared earlier by the defendants, which stated that the study was prepared by Albert Levy Associates, Inc. Caudle submitted the loan application on November 4, 1976, and accepted the loan offer on February 25, 1977. On August 14, 1978, one month before the trial, the EDA placed the loan in default.

* * *

One of the principal issues at trial was the truthfulness of the statement in the first cover letter to the second study, that Albert Levy Associates, Inc. prepared the feasibility study on Brevard Wood Products which was submitted with the loan application. On direct examination by the government, Dr. Levy testified that he prepared the first feasibility study and submitted it to Hawke, as Federal Co–Chairman of the Coastal Plains Regional Commission; that he agreed to submit additional materials to Hawke as he received them; that he validated some of the information supplied by Caudle for the second study; that some of the materials he gave to Caudle on September 24 were "created by my [Levy's] handwriting," while some of the information had been originally supplied by Caudle; and that no one who was at the Hawke residence when the second study was compiled was employed by Albert Levy Associates, Inc.

On cross-examination by the defendant Caudle, Dr. Levy testified that he had made the first (general or government) study and implied that having the same consultant prepare the second (specific or entrepreneur) study was usual practice; that when he turned the materials over to Caudle, he knew they would be compiled into a final feasibility study; that he requested a copy of the finished product; that he had no objection to his name being used; that, when he saw the finished product, he adopted it and gave Hawke a letter saying that he, Dr. Levy, had prepared the study; that he considered Caudle's proposed wood products company to be a feasible business project; and that it was normal for the study consultant to get a large amount of materials from the entrepreneur.

On cross-examination by the defendant Hawke, Dr. Levy's testimony chiefly concerned the ownership of the first study and of the materials. He also testified, with regard to the second study, that he was embarrassed because he had not produced a more finished product than he did, and when he saw the finished second study, including the photocopy paste-up letter, he typed and signed a genuine letter. Thus, at the conclusion of the direct and cross-examination, it could not be said that the question of who prepared the study was not in doubt.

On redirect examination, the United States Attorney took Dr. Levy through a page-by-page examination of the second feasibility study. Such detailed testimony had not been asked for on direct examination. With respect to each page, the question was put as to what part of that page represented Dr. Levy's "original work." Although the U.S. Attorney's questions were phrased in terms of the contents of each page, Dr. Levy answered, in many instances, in terms of whether the particular words, names, spelling, or punctuation were his original work.[2] Dr.

2. Defense counsel had adequate justification, at the very least, for taking Dr. Levy through a page by page examination of the second study in order to clarify whether Dr. Levy's testimony on redirect, concerning whether parts of the study were his original work, referred to the words of the study or the sense of the study. The following excerpts from Dr. Levy's redirect examination are not atypical:

Q. Directing your attention to page 11. What portion of the contents of page 11 is your original work?

A. Again, the contents only?

Q. Yes, sir. I am speaking now only to contents. * * *

A. Some of the words could be from my notes, but there is a word that I didn't write and that is why I definitely did not write the entire sentence because I don't spell it that way. * * *

* * *

Q. Directing your attention to page 13. What portion of page 13 is, the contents of page 13, is your original work?

A. I believe that most of that full paragraph on that page. I am not sure whether the words 'six to eight percent' are mine * * *.

* * *

Q. What portion of page 22 is your original work?

A. Like I said before. I believe that most of the headings is—are mine, because that is where I also recognized the table of contents that I was looking at before.

The phrasing here and the whole first line here is mine. I did not type it on this page 22, though.

Q. Well, what portion of the contents of page 22 is your original work?

A. Well, many of the words in the first paragraph, sir, are mine. But not the—I did not deal with the figure of 130 employees.

Q. What about the contents, Dr. Levy?

A. The contents?

Q. The contents of page 22. What portion of that is your original work?

A. Well, most of the wording is what I used in the draft. The figures I did not—specially the number 130, I did not use that.

Levy also testified that he regarded himself as the legal owner of the materials for the second study that he turned over to Caudle.

Counsel for the defendants, on recross examination, sought to take Dr. Levy through a page-by-page examination of the second study as the government had just done. The U.S. Attorney objected "on the basis that he has already been asked that question and answered that question on redirect examination." Defendants' counsel stated that he wanted to ask Dr. Levy "not as to whether the words were the same, but whether the sense of that is the same." Defense counsel requested "the same privilege that the United States Attorney had in going through these individual pages," in order "to show the sense of what this study is and what is his work and what pages in here aren't his or his materials." The court sustained the government's objection on the ground that "this would be essentially the same as going over it on redirect again." The court sustained several objections on these grounds. Based on this, defendants argue that recross examination was denied with respect to crucial points that had been the subject matter of the redirect examination; that this constituted a denial of the right of a criminal accused to cross-examine the witnesses against him; and therefore they are entitled to a new trial. We agree.

The convictions for making a false statement with respect to the feasibility study (Count 4) cannot be allowed to stand for two reasons. Although overlapping, in that both concern the rules of evidence, they are nevertheless not the same. The first is largely procedural and concerns the trial court's power to prohibit cross-examination in a given manner. The second concerns the power of the trial court to prohibit cross-examination at all.

It is properly within the trial judge's discretion to prevent one party from repeating a question already asked by that party. Where there is more than one defendant or defense attorney, it may also be proper to prevent one defense attorney from repeating a question already asked by another defense attorney. See, e.g., *United States v. Miller,* 463 F.2d 600, 601 (1st Cir.1972); see also 3 Wigmore, *Evidence* § 782(4) (Chadbourn rev. 1970). It is quite a different thing, however, to prevent the defense from asking a question on the grounds that it has already been asked by the prosecution. "Repeating the same testimonial matter of the direct examination, by questioning the witness anew on cross-examination, is a process which often becomes desirable * * * in order to test the witness' capacity to recollect what he has just stated and to ascertain whether he falls easily into inconsistencies and thus betrays falsification." 3 Wigmore, *Evidence* § 782(3), p. 182 (Chadbourn rev. 1970). The goals of cross-examination cannot be achieved "except by the direct and personal putting of questions." *Davis v. Alaska,* 415 U.S. 308, 316, 94 S.Ct. 1105, 1110, 39 L.Ed.2d 347 (1974), quoting 5 J. Wigmore, *Evidence* § 1395, p. 123 (3d ed. 1940). "Cross-examination is a right, because of its efficacy in securing more than could have been expected from a direct examination by a friendly examiner." 3A Wigmore, *Evidence* § 944 (Chadbourn rev. 1970). A defendant's right to cross-examine the witnesses on the subject matter of their direct testimony, cannot be denied merely because the prosecutor has already asked the same or similar questions. The questions involved having been asked for the first time on redirect examination, the fact that they had been asked and answered is a reason to permit cross-examination, not a reason to deny it.

"There are few subjects, perhaps, upon which [the Supreme] Court and other courts have been more nearly unanimous than in their expressions of belief that the right of confrontation and cross-examination is an essential and fundamental requirement for the kind of fair trial which is this country's constitutional goal." *Pointer v. Texas,* 380 U.S. 400, 405, 85 S.Ct. 1065, 1068, 13 L.Ed.2d 923 (1965). A full cross-examination of a witness upon the subjects of his examination in chief is the right, not the mere privilege, of the party against whom he is called. *Lindsey v. United States,* 77 U.S.App.D.C. 1, 2, 133 F.2d 368, 369 (D.C.Cir.1942); *Heard v. United States,* 255 F. 829 (8 Cir.1919). See, e.g., *Douglas v. Alabama,* 380 U.S. 415, 418, 85 S.Ct. 1074, 13 L.Ed.2d 934 (1965); *Alford v. United States,* 282 U.S. 687, 691, 51 S.Ct. 218, 75 L.Ed. 624 (1931); 2 Wright, *Federal Practice and Procedure,* Criminal § 416 (1969).

It may not be an exaggeration to claim, as Wigmore does, that cross-examination "is beyond any doubt the greatest legal engine ever invented for the discovery of truth." 5 Wigmore, *Evidence* § 1367 (Chadbourn rev. 1976). And, its efficacy in testing the accuracy and completeness of testimony is so well understood that the right of cross-examination is "one of the safeguards essential to a fair trial." *Alford v. United States,* supra, 282 U.S. at 692, 51 S.Ct. at 219. Evidence supplied through the lips of witnesses is subject not only to the possible infirmities of falsification or bias; it is also subject to the inaccuracies which inevitably flow from the fallibility of human powers of observation, memory, and description. "The annals of the legal profession are filled with instances in which testimony, plausible when supplied on examination in chief, has by cross-examination been shown to be, for one or more of the reasons mentioned, faulty or worthless." *Lindsey v. United States,* 77 U.S.App.D.C. at 2, 133 F.2d at 369; see, e.g., 3 Wigmore, *Evidence* § 782(3), (4) (Chadbourn rev. 1970). Certainly no one experienced in the trial of lawsuits would deny the value of cross-examination in bringing out the truth; indeed, "[c]ross-examination is the principal means by which the believability of a witness and the truth of his testimony are tested." *Davis v. Alaska,* 415 U.S. 308, 316, 94 S.Ct. 1105, 1110, 39 L.Ed.2d 347 (1974).

The theory of cross-examination supports what has been learned from years of practical experience. On direct examination, a witness, even if completely unbiased, only discloses part of the necessary facts, chiefly because his testimony is given only by way of answers to specific questions, and the attorney producing him will usually ask only for the facts favorable to his side of the case. Someone must probe for the remaining facts and qualifying circumstances, and ensure that the testimony is accurate, complete, and clearly understood. The best person to do this is the one most vitally interested, namely the opponent.[3] 5 Wigmore, *Evidence* § 1368 (Chadbourn rev. 1974). For these reasons, cross-examination is "a right long deemed so essential for the due protection of life and liberty that it is guarded against legislative and judicial action by provisions in the Constitution of the United States and in the constitutions of most if not all the States composing the Union." *Pointer v. Texas,* 380 U.S. at 404, 85 S.Ct. at 1068, quoting *Kirby v. United States,* 174 U.S. 47, 55–56, 19 S.Ct. 574, 43 L.Ed. 890 (1899).

In this case, issue is taken with the trial court's limitation of recross examination. However, the reasons we have given in support of the right of cross-examination apply with equal strength to recross examination where new matter is brought out on redirect examination. Examining counsel is normally expected to elicit everything from a witness, so far as possible, at the first opportunity. Where, as here, new matter is brought out on redirect examination, the defendant's first opportunity to test the truthfulness, accuracy, and completeness of that testimony is on recross examination. 6 Wigmore, *Evidence* § 1896 (Chadbourn rev. 1976); McCormick, *Evidence* § 32 (1972). To deny recross examination on matter first drawn out on redirect is to deny the defendant the right of any cross-examination as to that new matter. The prejudice of the denial cannot be doubted.

In *Cossack v. United States,* 63 F.2d 511 (9th Cir.1933), the government called an important witness after it had rested its case. After direct examination by the government and "considerable cross-examination," there was redirect examination and recross examination, after which the witness was excused. At the defendant's request, the witness was recalled for further recross examination for the purpose of laying a foundation for impeachment. The trial court's refusal to allow this line of questioning on recross examination was held to be reversible error, because the defendant was denied the right to cross-examine the witnesses against him. *United States v. Morris,* 485 F.2d 1385 (5th Cir.1973), held that where no new matter is brought out on redirect examination, there is no constitutional right to recross examination, but the court reiterated that the right to recross examination does exist where new matter is brought out in the redirect. See also *United States v. Dana,* 457 F.2d 205 (7th Cir.1972) (no undue limit in confining the recross examination to the scope of the redirect).

Wigmore takes the same view as the cases. "No doubt cases may arise in which redirect examination may make relevant certain new evidence for which there was no prior need or opportunity, and for this

3. The second major function of cross-examination (which is not involved in the instant case) is to show that the witness is biased, prejudiced, or untrustworthy for any reason. "The *facts which diminish the personal trustworthiness or credit of the witness* will also, in every likelihood, have remained undisclosed on the direct examination." 5 Wigmore, *Evidence* § 1368, p. 37 (Chadbourn rev. 1974). (Italics in original.)

purpose a recross examination becomes proper; in such cases it is sometimes said to be a matter of right. But for other matters there is ordinarily no such need, and the allowance of recross examination depends in such cases on the consent of the trial court." VI Wigmore, *Evidence* (Chadbourn rev. 1976) § 1897.

The government argues that the trial court properly exercised its discretion by restricting the defendants' questions on the recross examination of Dr. Levy.[4] Many decisions do recognize that the trial judge has broad discretion to control the scope and extent of cross-examination. E.g. *Davis v. Alaska,* 415 U.S. 308, 316, 94 S.Ct. 1105, 39 L.Ed.2d 347 (1974); *Alford v. United States,* 282 U.S. 687, 694, 51 S.Ct. 218, 75 L.Ed. 624 (1931). However, entirely consistent with that rule, the cases also recognize that it "is only after the right of cross-examination has been substantially and thoroughly exercised that the allowance of further cross-examination becomes discretionary with the trial court." *Hartzell v. United States,* 72 F.2d 569, 585 (8th Cir.1934). See, e.g., *United States v. Pugh,* 141 U.S.App.D.C. 68, 436 F.2d 222 (D.C.Cir.1970); *Arnold v. United States,* 94 F.2d 499, 506 (10th Cir.1938). Other cases state the same rule in somewhat different terms, e.g., *United States v. Mayer,* 556 F.2d 245, 250 (5th Cir.1977) (The trial court's "discretionary authority to limit cross-examination comes into play only after there has been permitted as a matter of right sufficient cross-examination to satisfy the Sixth Amendment"); *United States v. Greenberg,* 423 F.2d 1106, 1108 (5th Cir.1970) ("discretion of the court to limit the scope of cross-examination does not become operative until a party has had an opportunity to exercise the right of cross-examination"); *United States v. Jordan,* 466 F.2d 99, 105 (4th Cir.1972) (Judge Sobeloff dissenting) ("But all issues concerning cross-examination do not melt away upon invocation of the trial judge's discretion * * *. In concrete terms, then, the trial judge's discretion insulates only his decision that an area of cross-examination has been *sufficiently explored* and that further inquiry would be pointless. * * * A considerably stricter standard applies when an appellate court is called upon to review a ruling which *foreclosed altogether* a valid area of cross-examination. * * *") (Emphasis in original.)

The trial court's ruling in this case precluded all cross-examination of Dr. Levy as to what part of each page of the second study was his original work. Since the defendants did not have an opportunity to exercise the right of cross-examination on this issue, the trial court's

4. Federal Rule of Evidence 611(a) and (b):

(a) Control by court. The court shall exercise reasonable control over the mode and order of interrogating witnesses and presenting evidence so as to (1) make the interrogation and presentation effective for the ascertainment of the truth, (2) avoid needless consumption of time, and (3) protect witnesses from harassment or undue embarrassment.

(b) Scope of cross-examination. Cross-examination should be limited to the subject matter of the direct examination and matters affecting the credibility of the witness. The court may, in the exercise of its discretion, permit inquiry into additional matters as if on direct examination.

discretion to limit cross-examination simply did not become operative. Put another way, the trial court does not have discretion to curtail cross-examination until after the questioner has had a reasonable chance to pursue the matters raised on direct. "It is the essence of a fair trial that reasonable latitude be given the cross-examiner, even though he is unable to state to the court what facts a reasonable cross-examination might develop." *Alford v. United States,* 282 U.S. 687, 692, 51 S.Ct. 218, 219, 75 L.Ed. 624 (1931). The trial court here did not give the defendants that reasonable latitude in cross-examination which is essential to a fair trial.

In summary, we are of opinion the defendants had the right to cross-examine Dr. Levy on the matter of the page by page explanation of the report, first brought into the case by the government on redirect examination. The denial by the trial court of this right is prejudicial error. We do not believe the discretion of the trial court to limit the scope or extent of cross-examination came into play in this case because the defendants never had the opportunity to cross-examine Dr. Levy at all on the subject raised by the redirect examination. The discretion of the trial court to limit the extent and scope of cross-examination does not extend so far as to preclude cross-examination at all. We do not construe FRE 611(a) and (b) as contrary to this opinion.

Each of the defendants was convicted on two separate counts. In addition to conviction for submitting the false statement regarding authorship of the second feasibility study (Count 4), Hawke was convicted on the conflict of interest charge (Count 2), and Caudle was convicted for submitting a false financial statement (Count 5). The entire case, however, including these counts, centered around one transaction—procuring a loan from the Economic Development Administration. Although the erroneous restriction of cross-examination may have directly affected Count 4 only, it is highly probable that the defendants were prejudiced on the other counts as well. In these circumstances, our duty to "require such further proceedings to be had as may be just under the circumstances," 28 U.S.C. § 2106, requires a remand for a new trial on all counts. See, e.g., *United States v. Stevenson,* 409 F.2d 354 (7th Cir.), cert. den., 404 U.S. 857, 92 S.Ct. 108, 30 L.Ed.2d 99 (1969); *United States v. Barash,* 365 F.2d 395, 400 (2d Cir.1966), cert. den., 396 U.S. 832, 90 S.Ct. 86, 24 L.Ed.2d 82 (1967); *Edwards v. United States,* 265 F.2d 302 (9th Cir.1959). See also *Benton v. Maryland,* 395 U.S. 784, 798, 89 S.Ct. 2056, 23 L.Ed.2d 707 (1969).

Because we believe that a new trial must be awarded in all events, we do not reach the other errors assigned. The judgments of conviction must be vacated and a new trial awarded.

VACATED AND REMANDED FOR A NEW TRIAL.

GEDERS v. UNITED STATES, 425 U.S. 80, 86–87, 96 S.Ct. 1330, 1334–35, 47 L.Ed.2d 592 (1976). "Our cases have consistently recognized the important role the trial judge plays in the federal system of criminal justice. '[T]he judge is not a mere moderator, but is the governor of the trial for the purpose of assuring its proper conduct and of determining questions of law.' Quercia v. United States, 289 U.S. 466, 469, 53 S.Ct. 698, 77 L.Ed. 1321, 1324 (1933). A criminal trial does not unfold like a play with actors following a script; there is no scenario and can be none. The trial judge must meet situations as they arise and to do this must have broad power to cope with the complexities and contingencies inherent in the adversary process. To this end, he may determine generally the order in which parties will adduce proof; his determination will be reviewed only for abuse of discretion. Goldsby v. United States, 160 U.S. 70, 74, 16 S.Ct. 216, 218, 40 L.Ed. 343, 345 (1895); United States v. Martinez–Villanueva, 463 F.2d 1336 (CA9 1972); Nelson v. United States, 415 F.2d 483, 487 (CA5 1969), cert. denied, 396 U.S. 1060, 90 S.Ct. 751, 24 L.Ed.2d 754 (1970). Within limits, the judge may control the scope of rebuttal testimony, United States v. Chrzanowski, 502 F.2d 573, 575–576 (CA3 1974); United States v. Perez, 491 F.2d 167, 173 (CA9), cert. denied sub nom., Lombera v. United States, 419 U.S. 858, 95 S.Ct. 106, 42 L.Ed.2d 92 (1974); may refuse to allow cumulative, repetitive, or irrelevant testimony, Hamling v. United States, 418 U.S. 87, 127, 94 S.Ct. 2887, 2912, 41 L.Ed.2d 590, 626 (1974); County of Macon v. Shores, 97 U.S. 272, 24 L.Ed. 889 (1877); and may control the scope of examination of witnesses, United States v. Nobles, 422 U.S. 225, 231, 95 S.Ct. 2160, 2166, 45 L.Ed.2d 141, 149 (1975); Glasser v. United States, 315 U.S. 60, 83, 62 S.Ct. 457, 470, 86 L.Ed. 680, 706 (1942). If truth and fairness are not to be sacrificed, the judge must exert substantial control over the proceedings."

BERROYER v. HERTZ, 672 F.2d 334, 339 (3d Cir.1982). "The defendant next argues that the district court abused its discretion in permitting the plaintiff to call a 'rebuttal' witness during her case in chief.

"It is undisputed that 'the mode and order of interrogating witnesses and presenting evidence' is a matter within the discretion of the trial judge. Fed.R.Evid. 611(a). Thus, we have held it to be within the trial court's discretion to permit a defense expert to testify during the plaintiff's case in order to accommodate the schedule of the witness:

> 'Trial courts in this circuit traditionally have accommodated the schedules of expert witnesses. It would exalt form over substance to require a physician to return to a courtroom at a later date, once he has already appeared for one party. Thus, although calling a defense witness out of turn for reception of his testimony during the plaintiff's case in chief may technically disrupt the normal presentation of the case, this decision is committed to the discretion of the trial court. If convinced that practical reasons justify calling a witness out of turn

and that the testimony will not produce undue confusion in the minds of the jurors, experienced trial courts will permit the practice. If it is the product of an informed discretion, the decision will not be disturbed.'

Lis v. Robert Packer Hospital, 579 F.2d 819, 823 (3d Cir.), cert. denied, 439 U.S. 955, 99 S.Ct. 354, 58 L.Ed.2d 346 (1978). This is precisely the accommodation made in this case for the defendant's expert witness, Dr. Shira.

"The defendant argues, however, that there is a difference in kind between direct and rebuttal testimony and that the latter is impermissible per se until the defense has had an opportunity to present its entire case. We disagree. Absent a showing of specific prejudice, we do not believe that an expert witness testifying in rebuttal should be entitled to any less accommodation than one testifying in a party's case-in-chief where, as here, the specific defense testimony to be rebutted is already in evidence. Dr. Shira testified that the plaintiff could not have been in severe pain because the defendant had merely prescribed Wygesic, a mild analgesic. Mr. Thomas testified that the plaintiff never presented a prescription for Wygesic, but rather presented a prescription from the defendant for Percodan, a strong pain-killer. Put simply, one witness asserted a fact and the second contradicted it. The factual question was narrow and relatively uncomplicated. We see no possibility of jury confusion or other prejudice to the defendant and, thus, no clear abuse of discretion."

UNITED STATES v. YOUNG, 745 F.2d 733, 760–61 (2d Cir.1984), cert. denied, 470 U.S. 1084, 105 S.Ct. 1842, 85 L.Ed.2d 142 (1985). "Little more need be said to dispose of the challenge to officer Hight's testimony. Like Magaletti and Wall, Hight was unquestionably qualified as an expert. The only difference in his testimony was that he narrated and offered his opinions as the government played for the jury the videotape upon which he based his opinions. We will not second guess Judge Sand's implicit determinations that this technique was helpful in assisting the jury to understand the evidence, and in enabling the jury to evaluate the basis upon which Hight formed his opinion.

"Generally speaking, a trial judge has broad discretion in deciding whether or not to allow narrative testimony. Fed.R.Evid. 611(a); Hutter Northern Trust v. Door County Chamber of Commerce, 467 F.2d 1075, 1078 (7th Cir.1972); see Goings v. United States, 377 F.2d 753, 762–63 (8th Cir.1967). We see no reason to apply a different rule here, where the narrative testimony accompanied and explained videotaped evidence."

MARYLAND v. CRAIG

Supreme Court of the United States, 1990.
__ U.S. __, 110 S.Ct. 3157, 111 L.Ed.2d 666.

JUSTICE O'CONNOR delivered the opinion of the Court.

This case requires us to decide whether the Confrontation Clause of the Sixth Amendment categorically prohibits a child witness in a child abuse case from testifying against a defendant at trial, outside the defendant's physical presence, by one-way closed circuit television.

I

In October 1986, a Howard County grand jury charged respondent, Sandra Ann Craig, with child abuse, first and second degree sexual offenses, perverted sexual practice, assault, and battery. The named victim in each count was Brooke Etze, a six-year-old child who, from August 1984 to June 1986, had attended a kindergarten and prekindergarten center owned and operated by Craig.

In March 1987, before the case went to trial, the State sought to invoke a Maryland statutory procedure that permits a judge to receive, by one-way closed circuit television, the testimony of a child witness who is alleged to be a victim of child abuse. To invoke the procedure, the trial judge must first "determin[e] that testimony by the child victim in the courtroom will result in the child suffering serious emotional distress such that the child cannot reasonably communicate." Md.Cts. & Jud.Proc.Code Ann. § 9–102(a)(1)(ii) (1989). Once the procedure is invoked, the child witness, prosecutor, and defense counsel withdraw to a separate room; the judge, jury, and defendant remain in the courtroom. The child witness is then examined and cross-examined in the separate room, while a video monitor records and displays the witness' testimony to those in the courtroom. During this time the witness cannot see the defendant. The defendant remains in electronic communication with defense counsel, and objections may be made and ruled on as if the witness were testifying in the courtroom.

In support of its motion invoking the one-way closed circuit television procedure, the State presented expert testimony that Brooke, as well as a number of other children who were alleged to have been sexually abused by Craig, would suffer "serious emotional distress such that [they could not] reasonably communicate," § 9–102(a)(1)(ii), if required to testify in the courtroom. App. 7–59. The Maryland Court of Appeals characterized the evidence as follows:

> "The expert testimony in each case suggested that each child would have some or considerable difficulty in testifying in Craig's presence. For example, as to one child, the expert said that what 'would cause him the most anxiety would be to testify in front of Mrs. Craig * * *.' The child 'wouldn't be able to communicate effectively.' As to another, an expert said she 'would probably stop talking and she would withdraw and curl up.' With respect to two others, the testimony was that

one would 'become highly agitated, that he may refuse to talk or if he did talk, that he would choose his subject regardless of the questions' while the other would 'become extremely timid and unwilling to talk.'" 316 Md. 551, 568–569, 560 A.2d 1120, 1128–1129 (1989).

Craig objected to the use of the procedure on Confrontation Clause grounds, but the trial court rejected that contention, concluding that although the statute "take[s] away the right of the defendant to be face to face with his or her accuser," the defendant retains the "essence of the right of confrontation," including the right to observe, cross-examine, and have the jury view the demeanor of the witness. App. 65–66. The trial court further found that, "based upon the evidence presented * * * the testimony of each of these children in a courtroom will result in each child suffering serious emotional distress * * * such that each of these children cannot reasonably communicate." *Id.*, at 66. The trial court then found Brooke and three other children competent to testify and accordingly permitted them to testify against Craig via the one-way closed circuit television procedure. The jury convicted Craig on all counts, and the Maryland Court of Special Appeals affirmed the convictions, 76 Md.App. 250, 544 A.2d 784 (1988).

The Court of Appeals of Maryland reversed and remanded for a new trial. 316 Md. 551, 560 A.2d 1120 (1989). The Court of Appeals rejected Craig's argument that the Confrontation Clause requires in all cases a face-to-face courtroom encounter between the accused and his accusers, *id.*, at 556–562, 560 A.2d, at 1122–1125, but concluded:

> "[U]nder § 9–102(a)(1)(ii), the operative 'serious emotional distress' which renders a child victim unable to 'reasonably communicate' must be determined to arise, at least primarily, from face-to-face confrontation with the defendant. Thus, we construe the phrase 'in the courtroom' as meaning, for sixth amendment and [state constitution] confrontation purposes, 'in the courtroom in the presence of the defendant.' Unless prevention of 'eyeball-to-eyeball' confrontation is necessary to obtain the trial testimony of the child, the defendant cannot be denied that right." *Id.*, at 566, 560 A.2d, at 1127.

Reviewing the trial court's finding and the evidence presented in support of the § 9–102 procedure, the Court of Appeals held that, "as [it] read *Coy* [*v. Iowa,* 487 U.S. 1012, 108 S.Ct. 2798, 101 L.Ed.2d 857 (1988)], the showing made by the State was insufficient to reach the high threshold required by that case before § 9–102 may be invoked." *Id.* 316 Md., at 554–555, 560 A.2d, at 1121 (footnote omitted).

We granted certiorari to resolve the important Confrontation Clause issues raised by this case. 439 U.S. ___, 110 S.Ct. 834, 107 L.Ed.2d 830 (1990).

II

The Confrontation Clause of the Sixth Amendment, made applicable to the States through the Fourteenth Amendment, provides: "In all criminal prosecutions, the accused shall enjoy the right * * * to be confronted with the witnesses against him."

We observed in *Coy v. Iowa* that "the Confrontation Clause guarantees the defendant a face-to-face meeting with witnesses appearing before the trier of fact." 487 U.S., at 1016, 108 S.Ct., at 2800 (citing *Kentucky v. Stincer,* 482 U.S. 730, 748, 749–750, 107 S.Ct. 2658, 2668–2669, 2669, 96 L.Ed.2d 631 (1987) (MARSHALL, J., dissenting)); see also *Pennsylvania v. Ritchie,* 480 U.S. 39, 51, 107 S.Ct. 989, 998, 94 L.Ed.2d 40 (1987) (plurality opinion); *California v. Green,* 399 U.S. 149, 157, 90 S.Ct. 1930, 1934, 26 L.Ed.2d 489 (1970); *Snyder v. Massachusetts,* 291 U.S. 97, 106, 54 S.Ct. 330, 332, 78 L.Ed. 674 (1934); *Dowdell v. United States,* 221 U.S. 325, 330, 31 S.Ct. 590, 592, 55 L.Ed. 753 (1911); *Kirby v. United States,* 174 U.S. 47, 55, 19 S.Ct. 574, 577, 43 L.Ed. 890 (1899); *Mattox v. United States,* 156 U.S. 237, 244, 15 S.Ct. 337, 340, 39 L.Ed. 409 (1895). This interpretation derives not only from the literal text of the Clause, but also from our understanding of its historical roots. See *Coy, supra,* 487 U.S., at 1015–1016, 108 S.Ct., at 2800; *Mattox, supra,* 156 U.S., at 242, 15 S.Ct., at 339 (Confrontation Clause intended to prevent conviction by affidavit); *Green, supra,* 399 U.S., at 156, 90 S.Ct., at 1934 (same); cf. 3 J. Story, Commentaries § 1785, p. 662 (1833).

We have never held, however, that the Confrontation Clause guarantees criminal defendants the *absolute* right to a face-to-face meeting with witnesses against them at trial. Indeed, in *Coy v. Iowa,* we expressly "le[ft] for another day * * * the question whether any exceptions exist" to the "irreducible literal meaning of the Clause: 'a right to *meet face to face* all those who appear and give evidence *at trial.*' " 487 U.S., at 1021, 108 S.Ct., at 2802–2803 (quoting *Green, supra,* 399 U.S., at 175, 90 S.Ct., at 1943 (Harlan, J., concurring)). The procedure challenged in *Coy* involved the placement of a screen that prevented two child witnesses in a child abuse case from seeing the defendant as they testified against him at trial. See 487 U.S., at 1014–1015, 108 S.Ct., at 2799–2800. In holding that the use of this procedure violated the defendant's right to confront witnesses against him, we suggested that any exception to the right "would surely be allowed only when necessary to further an important public policy"—*i.e.,* only upon a showing of something more than the generalized, "legislatively imposed presumption of trauma" underlying the statute at issue in that case. *Id.,* at 1021, 108 S.Ct., at 2802–2803; see also *id.,* at 1025, 108 S.Ct., at 2804 (concurring opinion). We concluded that "[s]ince there ha[d] been no individualized findings that these particular witnesses needed special protection, the judgment [in the case before us] could not be sustained by any conceivable exception." *Id.,* at 1021, 108 S.Ct., at 2802–2803. Because the trial court in this case made individualized findings that each of the child witnesses needed special protection, this case requires us to decide the question reserved in *Coy.*

The central concern of the Confrontation Clause is to ensure the reliability of the evidence against a criminal defendant by subjecting it to rigorous testing in the context of an adversary proceeding before the trier of fact. The word "confront," after all, also means a clashing of forces or ideas, thus carrying with it the notion of adversariness. As we noted in our earliest case interpreting the Clause:

> "The primary object of the constitutional provision in question was to prevent depositions or *ex parte* affidavits, such as were sometimes admitted in civil cases, being used against the prisoner in lieu of a personal examination and cross-examination of the witness in which the accused has an opportunity, not only of testing the recollection and sifting the conscience of the witness, but of compelling him to stand face to face with the jury in order that they may look at him, and judge by his demeanor upon the stand and the manner in which he gives his testimony whether he is worthy of belief." *Mattox, supra,* 156 U.S., at 242–243, 15 S.Ct., at 339–340.

As this description indicates, the right guaranteed by the Confrontation Clause includes not only a "personal examination," *id.,* at 242, 15 S.Ct., at 339, but also "(1) insures that the witness will give his statements under oath—thus impressing him with the seriousness of the matter and guarding against the lie by the possibility of a penalty for perjury; (2) forces the witness to submit to cross-examination, the 'greatest legal engine ever invented for the discovery of truth'; [and] (3) permits the jury that is to decide the defendant's fate to observe the demeanor of the witness in making his statement, thus aiding the jury in assessing his credibility." *Green,* 399 U.S., at 158, 90 S.Ct., at 1935 (footnote omitted).

The combined effect of these elements of confrontation—physical presence, oath, cross-examination, and observation of demeanor by the trier of fact—serves the purposes of the Confrontation Clause by ensuring that evidence admitted against an accused is reliable and subject to the rigorous adversarial testing that is the norm of Anglo–American criminal proceedings. See *Stincer, supra,* 482 U.S., at 739, 107 S.Ct., at 2664 ("[T]he right to confrontation is a functional one for the purpose of promoting reliability in a criminal trial"); *Dutton v. Evans,* 400 U.S. 74, 89, 91 S.Ct. 210, 219, 27 L.Ed.2d 213 (1970) (plurality opinion) ("[T]he mission of the Confrontation Clause is to advance a practical concern for the accuracy of the truth-determining process in criminal trials by assuring that 'the trier of fact [has] a satisfactory basis for evaluating the truth of the [testimony]' "); *Lee v. Illinois,* 476 U.S. 530, 540, 106 S.Ct. 2056, 2061, 90 L.Ed.2d 514 (1986) (confrontation guarantee serves "symbolic goals" and "promotes reliability"); see also *Faretta v. California,* 422 U.S. 806, 818, 95 S.Ct. 2525, 2532, 45 L.Ed.2d 562 (1975) (Sixth Amendment "constitutionalizes the right in an adversary criminal trial to make a defense as we know it"); *Strickland v. Washington,* 466 U.S. 668, 684–685, 104 S.Ct. 2052, 2062–2063, 80 L.Ed.2d 674 (1984).

We have recognized, for example, that face-to-face confrontation enhances the accuracy of factfinding by reducing the risk that a witness will wrongfully implicate an innocent person. See *Coy,* 487 U.S., at 1019–1020, 108 S.Ct., at 2802 ("It is always more difficult to tell a lie about a person 'to his face' than 'behind his back.' * * * That face-to-face presence may, unfortunately, upset the truthful rape victim or abused child; but by the same token it may confound and undo the false accuser, or reveal the child coached by a malevolent adult"); *Ohio v. Roberts,* 448 U.S. 56, 63, n. 6, 100 S.Ct. 2531, 2537 n. 6, 65 L.Ed.2d 597 (1980); see also 3 W. Blackstone, Commentaries *373–*374. We have also noted the strong symbolic purpose served by requiring adverse witnesses at trial to testify in the accused's presence. See *Coy, supra,* 487 U.S., at 1017, 108 S.Ct., at 2800 ("[T]here is something deep in human nature that regards face-to-face confrontation between accused and accuser as 'essential to a fair trial in a criminal prosecution' ") (quoting *Pointer v. Texas,* 380 U.S. 400, 404, 85 S.Ct. 1065, 1068, 13 L.Ed.2d 923 (1965)).

Although face-to-face confrontation forms "the core of the values furthered by the Confrontation Clause," *Green, supra,* 399 U.S., at 157, 90 S.Ct., at 1934, we have nevertheless recognized that it is not the *sine qua non* of the confrontation right. See *Delaware v. Fensterer,* 474 U.S. 15, 22, 106 S.Ct. 292, 295, 88 L.Ed.2d 15 (1985) (*per curiam*) ("[T]he Confrontation Clause is generally satisfied when the defense is given a full and fair opportunity to probe and expose [testimonial] infirmities [such as forgetfulness, confusion, or evasion] through cross-examination, thereby calling to the attention of the factfinder the reasons for giving scant weight to the witness' testimony"); *Roberts, supra,* 448 U.S., at 69, 100 S.Ct., at 2540 (oath, cross-examination, and demeanor provide "all that the Sixth Amendment demands: 'substantial compliance with the purposes behind the confrontation requirement' ") (quoting *Green, supra,* 399 U.S., at 166, 90 S.Ct., at 1939); see also *Stincer, supra,* 482 U.S., at 739–744, 107 S.Ct., at 2664 (confrontation right not violated by exclusion of defendant from competency hearing of child witnesses, where defendant had opportunity for full and effective cross-examination at trial); *Davis v. Alaska,* 415 U.S. 308, 315–316, 94 S.Ct. 1105, 1109–1110, 39 L.Ed.2d 347 (1974); *Douglas v. Alabama,* 380 U.S. 415, 418, 85 S.Ct. 1074, 1076, 13 L.Ed.2d 934 (1965); *Pointer, supra,* 380 U.S., at 406–407, 85 S.Ct., at 1069; 5 J. Wigmore, Evidence § 1395, p. 150 (J. Chadbourne rev. ed. 1974).

For this reason, we have never insisted on an actual face-to-face encounter at trial in *every* instance in which testimony is admitted against a defendant. Instead, we have repeatedly held that the Clause permits, where necessary, the admission of certain hearsay statements against a defendant despite the defendant's inability to confront the declarant at trial. See, *e.g., Mattox,* 156 U.S., at 243, 15 S.Ct., at 339 ("[T]here could be nothing more directly contrary to the letter of the provision in question than the admission of dying declarations"); *Pointer, supra,* 380 U.S., at 407, 85 S.Ct., at 1069 (noting exceptions to the confrontation right for dying declarations and "other analogous situations"). In *Mattox,* for example, we held that the testimony of a government witness at a former trial against the defendant, where the witness was fully cross-examined but had died after the first trial, was admissible in evidence against the defendant at his second trial. See 156 U.S., at 240–244, 15 S.Ct., at 338–340. * * *

* * *

In sum, our precedents establish that "the Confrontation Clause reflects a *preference* for face-to-face confrontation at trial," *Roberts, supra,* 448 U.S., at 63, 100 S.Ct., at 2537 (emphasis added; footnote omitted), a preference that "must occasionally give way to considerations of public policy and the necessities of the case," *Mattox, supra,* 156 U.S., at 243, 15 S.Ct., at 339–340. * * *

* * *

That the face-to-face confrontation requirement is not absolute does not, of course, mean that it may easily be dispensed with. As we suggested in *Coy,* our precedents confirm that a defendant's right to confront accusatory witnesses may be satisfied absent a physical, face-to-face confrontation at trial only where denial of such confrontation is necessary to further an important public policy and only where the reliability of the testimony is otherwise assured. See *Coy,* 487 U.S., at 1021, 108 S.Ct., at 2802–2803 (citing *Roberts, supra,* 448 U.S., at 64, 100 S.Ct., at 2538; *Chambers, supra,* 410 U.S., at 295, 93 S.Ct., at 1045); *Coy, supra,* 487 U.S., at 1025, 108 S.Ct., at 2804 (concurring opinion).

III

Maryland's statutory procedure, when invoked, prevents a child witness from seeing the defendant as he or she testifies against the defendant at trial. We find it significant, however, that Maryland's procedure preserves all of the other elements of the confrontation right: the child witness must be competent to testify and must testify under oath; the defendant retains full opportunity for contemporaneous cross-examination; and the judge, jury, and defendant are able to view (albeit by video monitor) the demeanor (and body) of the witness as he or she testifies. Although we are mindful of the many subtle effects face-to-face confrontation may have on an adversary criminal proceeding, the presence of these other elements of confrontation—oath, cross-examination, and observation of the witness' demeanor—adequately ensures that the testimony is both reliable and subject to rigorous adversarial testing in a manner functionally equivalent to that accorded live, in-person testimony. These safeguards of reliability and adversariness render the use of such a procedure a far cry from the undisputed prohibition of the Confrontation Clause: trial by *ex parte* affidavit or inquisition, see *Mattox,* 156 U.S., at 242, 15 S.Ct., at 389; see also *Green,* 399 U.S., at 179, 90 S.Ct., at 1946 (HARLAN, J., concurring) ("[T]he Confrontation Clause was meant to constitutionalize a barrier against flagrant abuses, trials by anonymous accusers, and absentee witnesses"). Rather, we think these elements of effective confrontation not only permit a defendant to "confound and undo the false accuser, or reveal the child coached by a malevolent adult," *Coy,* 487 U.S., at 1020, 108 S.Ct., at 2802, but may well aid a defendant in eliciting favorable testimony from the child witness. Indeed, to the extent the child witness' testimony may be said to be technically given out-of-court (though we do not so hold), these assurances of reliability and adversariness are far greater than those required for admission of hearsay testimony under the Confrontation Clause. See *Roberts,* 448 U.S., at 66, 100 S.Ct., at 2539. We are therefore confident that use of the one-way closed-circuit television procedure, where necessary to further an important state interest, does not impinge upon the truth-seeking or symbolic purposes of the Confrontation Clause.

The critical inquiry in this case, therefore, is whether use of the procedure is necessary to further an important state interest. The State contends that it has a substantial interest in protecting children who are allegedly victims of child abuse from the trauma of testifying against the alleged perpetrator and that its statutory procedure for receiving testimony from such witnesses is necessary to further that interest.

We have of course recognized that a State's interest in "the protection of minor victims of sex crimes from further trauma and embarrassment" is a "compelling" one. *Globe Newspaper Co. v. Superior Court,* 457 U.S. 596, 607, 102 S.Ct. 2613, 2620, 73 L.Ed.2d 248 (1982); see also *New York v. Ferber,* 458 U.S. 747, 756–757, 102 S.Ct. 3348, 3354, 73 L.Ed.2d 1113 (1982); *FCC v. Pacifica Foundation,* 438 U.S. 726, 749–750, 98 S.Ct. 3026, 3040–3041, 57 L.Ed.2d 1073 (1978); *Ginsberg v. New York,* 390 U.S. 629, 640, 88 S.Ct. 1274, 1281, 20 L.Ed.2d 195 (1968); *Prince v. Massachusetts,* 321 U.S. 158, 168, 64 S.Ct. 438, 443, 88 L.Ed. 645 (1944). "[W]e have sustained legislation aimed at protecting the physical and emotional well-being of youth even when the laws have operated in the sensitive area of constitutionally protected rights." *Ferber, supra,* 458 U.S., at 757, 102 S.Ct., at 3354. In *Globe Newspaper,* for example, we held that a State's interest in the physical and psychological well-being of a minor victim was sufficiently weighty to justify depriving the press and public of their constitutional right to attend criminal trials, where the trial court makes a case-specific finding that closure of the trial is necessary to protect the welfare of the minor. See 457 U.S., at 608–609, 102 S.Ct., at 2620–21. This Term, in *Osborne v. Ohio,* 495 U.S. ___, 110 S.Ct. 1691, 109 L.Ed.2d 98 (1990), we upheld a state statute that proscribed the possession and viewing of child pornography, reaffirming that " '[i]t is evident beyond the need for elaboration that a State's interest in "safeguarding the physical and psychological well-being of a minor" is "compelling." ' " *Id.,* at ___, 110 S.Ct., at 1696 (quoting *Ferber, supra,* 458 U.S., at 756–757, 102 S.Ct., at 3354–55).

We likewise conclude today that a State's interest in the physical and psychological well-being of child abuse victims may be sufficiently important to outweigh, at least in some cases, a defendant's right to face his or her accusers in court. That a significant majority of States has enacted statutes to protect child witnesses from the trauma of giving testimony in child abuse cases attests to the widespread belief in the importance of such a public policy. See *Coy,* 487 U.S., at 1022–1023, 108 S.Ct., at 2803–04 (concurring opinion) ("Many States have determined that a child victim may suffer trauma from exposure to the harsh atmosphere of the typical courtroom and have undertaken to shield the child through a variety of ameliorative measures"). Thirty-seven States, for example, permit the use of videotaped testimony of sexually abused children; 24 States have authorized the use of one-way closed circuit television testimony in child abuse cases; and 8 States authorize the use of a two-way system in which the child-witness is permitted to see the courtroom and the defendant on a video monitor and in which the jury and judge is permitted to view the child during the testimony.

The statute at issue in this case, for example, was specifically intended "to safeguard the physical and psychological well-being of child victims by avoiding, or at least minimizing, the emotional trauma produced by testifying." *Wildermuth v. State,* 310 Md. 496, 518, 530 A.2d 275, 286 (1987). The *Wildermuth* court noted:

> "In Maryland, the Governor's Task Force on Child Abuse in its *Interim Report* (Nov. 1984) documented the existence of the [child abuse] problem in our State. *Interim Report* at 1. It brought the picture up to date in its *Final Report* (Dec. 1985). In the first six months of 1985, investigations of child abuse were 12 percent more numerous than during the same period of 1984. In 1979, 4,615 cases of child abuse were investigated; in 1984, 8,321. *Final Report* at iii. In its *Interim Report* at 2, the Commission proposed legislation that, with some changes, became § 9–102. The proposal was 'aimed at alleviating the trauma to a child victim in the courtroom atmosphere by allowing the child's testimony to be obtained outside of the courtroom.' *Id.,* at 2. This would both protect the child and enhance the public interest by encouraging effective prosecution of the alleged abuser." *Id.,* at 517, 530 A.2d, at 285.

Given the State's traditional and " 'transcendent interest in protecting the welfare of children,' " *Ginsberg,* 390 U.S., at 640, 88 S.Ct., at 1281 (citation omitted), and buttressed by the growing body of academic literature documenting the psychological trauma suffered by child abuse victims who must testify in court, see Brief for American Psychological Association as *Amicus Curiae* 7–13; G. Goodman et al., Emotional Effects of Criminal Court Testimony on Child Sexual Assault Victims, Final Report to the National Institute of Justice (presented as conference paper at annual convention of American Psychological Assn., Aug. 1989), we will not second-guess the considered judgment of the Maryland Legislature regarding the importance of its interest in protecting child abuse victims from the emotional trauma of testifying. Accordingly, we hold that, if the State makes an adequate showing of necessity, the state interest in protecting child witnesses from the trauma of testifying in a child abuse case is sufficiently important to justify the use of a special procedure that permits a child witness in such cases to testify at trial against a defendant in the absence of face-to-face confrontation with the defendant.

The requisite finding of necessity must of course be a case-specific one: the trial court must hear evidence and determine whether use of the one-way closed circuit television procedure is necessary to protect the welfare of the particular child witness who seeks to testify. See *Globe Newspaper Co.,* 457 U.S., at 608–609, 102 S.Ct., at 2621 (compelling interest in protecting child victims does not justify a *mandatory* trial closure rule); *Coy,* 487 U.S., at 1021, 108 S.Ct., at 2803; *id.,* at 1025, 108 S.Ct., at 2805 (concurring opinion); see also *Hochheiser v. Superior Court,* 161 Cal.App.3d 777, 793, 208 Cal.Rptr. 273, 283 (1984). The trial court must also find that the child witness would be traumatized, not by the courtroom generally, but by the presence of the defendant. See, *e.g., State v. Wilhite,* 160 Ariz. 228, 772 P.2d 582 (1989); *State v. Bonello,* 210 Conn. 51, 554 A.2d 277 (1989); *State v. Davidson,* 764 S.W.2d 731 (Mo.App.1989); *Commonwealth v. Ludwig,* 366 Pa.Super. 361, 531 A.2d 459 (1987). Denial of face-to-face confrontation is not needed to further the state interest in protecting the child witness from trauma unless it is the presence of the defendant that causes the trauma. In other words, if the state interest were merely the interest in protecting child witnesses from courtroom trauma generally, denial of face-to-face confrontation would be unnecessary because the child could be permitted to testify in less intimidating surroundings, albeit with the defendant present. Finally, the trial court must find that the emotional distress suffered by the child witness in the presence of the defendant is more than *de minimis, i.e.,* more than "mere nervousness or excitement or some reluctance to testify," *Wildermuth,* 310 Md., at 524, 530 A.2d, at 289; see also *State v. Mannion,* 19 Utah 505, 511–512, 57 P. 542, 543–544 (1899). We need not decide the minimum showing of emotional trauma required for use of the special procedure, however, because the Maryland statute, which requires a determination that the child witness will suffer "serious emotional distress such that the child cannot reasonably communicate," § 9–102(a)(1)(ii), clearly suffices to meet constitutional standards.

To be sure, face-to-face confrontation may be said to cause trauma for the very purpose of eliciting truth, cf. *Coy, supra,* 487 U.S., at 1019–1020, 108 S.Ct., at 2802–03, but we think that the use of Maryland's special procedure, where necessary to further the important state interest in preventing trauma to child witnesses in child abuse cases, adequately ensures the accuracy of the testimony and preserves the adversary nature of the trial. See *supra,* at 3166. Indeed, where face-to-face confrontation causes significant emotional distress in a child witness, there is evidence that such confrontation would in fact *disserve* the Confrontation Clause's truth-seeking goal. See, *e.g., Coy, supra,* 487 U.S., at 1032, 108 S.Ct., at 2809 (Blackmun, J., dissenting) (face-to-face confrontation "may so overwhelm the child as to prevent the possibility of effective testimony, thereby undermining the truth-finding function of the trial itself"); Brief for American Psychological Association as *Amicus Curiae* 18–24; *State v. Sheppard,* 197 N.J.Super. 411, 416, 484 A.2d 1330, 1332 (1984); Goodman & Helgeson, Child Sexual Assault: Children's Memory and the Law, 40 U.Miami L.Rev. 181, 203–204

(1985); Note, Videotaping Children's Testimony: An Empirical View, 85 Mich.L.Rev. 809, 813–820 (1987).

In sum, we conclude that where necessary to protect a child witness from trauma that would be caused by testifying in the physical presence of the defendant, at least where such trauma would impair the child's ability to communicate, the Confrontation Clause does not prohibit use of a procedure that, despite the absence of face-to-face confrontation, ensures the reliability of the evidence by subjecting it to rigorous adversarial testing and thereby preserves the essence of effective confrontation. Because there is no dispute that the child witnesses in this case testified under oath, were subject to full cross-examination, and were able to be observed by the judge, jury, and defendant as they testified, we conclude that, to the extent that a proper finding of necessity has been made, the admission of such testimony would be consonant with the Confrontation Clause.

IV

The Maryland Court of Appeals held, as we do today, that although face-to-face confrontation is not an absolute constitutional requirement, it may be abridged only where there is a "'case-specific finding of necessity.'" 316 Md., at 564, 560 A.2d, at 1126 (quoting *Coy, supra,* 487 U.S., at 1025, 108 S.Ct., at 2805 (concurring opinion)). Given this latter requirement, the Court of Appeals reasoned that "[t]he question of whether a child is unavailable to testify * * * should not be asked in terms of inability to testify in the ordinary courtroom setting, but in the much narrower terms of the witness's inability to testify in the presence of the accused." 316 Md., at 564, 560 A.2d, at 1126 (footnote omitted). "[T]he determinative inquiry required to preclude face-to-face confrontation is the effect of the presence of the defendant on the witness or the witness's testimony." *Id.,* at 565, 560 A.2d, at 1127. The Court of Appeals accordingly concluded that, as a prerequisite to use of the § 9–102 procedure, the Confrontation Clause requires the trial court to make a specific finding that testimony by the child in the courtroom *in the presence of the defendant* would result in the child suffering serious emotional distress such that the child could not reasonably communicate. *Id.,* at 566, 560 A.2d, at 1127. This conclusion, of course, is consistent with our holding today.

In addition, however, the Court of Appeals interpreted our decision in *Coy* to impose two subsidiary requirements. First, the court held that "§ 9–102 ordinarily cannot be invoked unless the child witness initially is questioned (either in or outside the courtroom) in the defendant's presence." *Id.,* at 566, 560 A.2d, at 1127; see also *Wildermuth,* 310 Md., at 523–524, 530 A.2d, at 289 (personal observation by the judge should be the rule rather than the exception). Second, the court asserted that, before using the one-way television procedure, a trial judge must determine whether a child would suffer "severe emotional distress" if he or she were to testify by *two*-way closed circuit television. 316 Md., at 567, 560 A.2d, at 1128.

Reviewing the evidence presented to the trial court in support of the finding required under § 9–102(a)(1)(ii), the Court of Appeals determined that "the finding of necessity required to limit the defendant's right of confrontation through invocation of § 9–102 * * * was not made here." *Id.*, at 570–571, 560 A.2d, at 1129. The Court of Appeals noted that the trial judge "had the benefit only of expert testimony on the ability of the children to communicate; he did not question any of the children himself, nor did he observe any child's behavior on the witness stand before making his ruling. He did not explore any alternatives to the use of one-way closed-circuit television." *Id.*, at 568, 560 A.2d, at 1128 (footnote omitted). * * *

The Court of Appeals appears to have rested its conclusion at least in part on the trial court's failure to observe the children's behavior in the defendant's presence and its failure to explore less restrictive alternatives to the use of the one-way closed circuit television procedure. See *id.*, at 568–571, 560 A.2d, at 1128–1129. Although we think such evidentiary requirements could strengthen the grounds for use of protective measures, we decline to establish, as a matter of federal constitutional law, any such categorical evidentiary prerequisites for the use of the one-way television procedure. The trial court in this case, for example, could well have found, on the basis of the expert testimony before it, that testimony by the child witnesses in the courtroom in the defendant's presence "will result in [each] child suffering serious emotional distress such that the child cannot reasonably communicate," § 9–102(a)(1)(ii). See *id.*, at 568–569, 560 A.2d, at 1128–1129; see also App. 22–25, 39, 41, 43, 44–45, 54–57. So long as a trial court makes such a case-specific finding of necessity, the Confrontation Clause does not prohibit a State from using a one-way closed circuit television procedure for the receipt of testimony by a child witness in a child abuse case. Because the Court of Appeals held that the trial court had not made the requisite finding of necessity under its interpretation of "the high threshold required by [*Coy*] before § 9–102 may be invoked," 316 Md., at 554–555, 560 A.2d, at 1121 (footnote omitted), we cannot be certain whether the Court of Appeals would reach the same conclusion in light of the legal standard we establish today. We therefore vacate the judgment of the Court of Appeals of Maryland and remand the case for further proceedings not inconsistent with this opinion.

It is so ordered.

JUSTICE SCALIA, with whom JUSTICE BRENNAN, JUSTICE MARSHALL, and JUSTICE STEVENS join, dissenting.

Seldom has this Court failed so conspicuously to sustain a categorical guarantee of the Constitution against the tide of prevailing current opinion. The Sixth Amendment provides, with unmistakable clarity, that "[i]n all criminal prosecutions, the accused shall enjoy the right * * * to be confronted with the witnesses against him." The purpose of enshrining this protection in the Constitution was to assure that none of the many policy interests from time to time pursued by statutory law could overcome a defendant's right to face his or her accusers in court. The Court, however, says:

> "We * * * conclude today that a State's interest in the physical and psychological well-being of child abuse victims may be sufficiently important to outweigh, at least in some cases, a defendant's right to face his or her accusers in court. That a significant majority of States has enacted statutes to protect child witnesses from the trauma of giving testimony in child abuse cases attests to the widespread belief in the importance of such a public policy."

Because of this subordination of explicit constitutional text to currently favored public policy, the following scene can be played out in an American courtroom for the first time in two centuries: A father whose young daughter has been given over to the exclusive custody of his estranged wife, or a mother whose young son has been taken into custody by the State's child welfare department, is sentenced to prison for sexual abuse on the basis of testimony by a child the parent has not seen or spoken to for many months; and the guilty verdict is rendered without giving the parent so much as the opportunity to sit in the presence of the child, and to ask, personally or through counsel, "it is really not true, is it, that I—your father (or mother) whom you see before you—did these terrible things?" Perhaps that is a procedure today's society desires; perhaps (though I doubt it) it is even a fair procedure; but it is assuredly not a procedure permitted by the Constitution.

Because the text of the Sixth Amendment is clear, and because the Constitution is meant to protect against, rather than conform to, current "widespread belief," I respectfully dissent.

I

According to the Court, "we cannot say that [face-to-face] confrontation [with witnesses appearing at trial] is an indispensable element of the Sixth Amendment's guarantee of the right to confront one's accusers." That is rather like saying "we cannot say that being tried before a jury is an indispensable element of the Sixth Amendment's guarantee of the right to jury trial." The Court makes the impossible plausible by recharacterizing the Confrontation Clause, so that confrontation (redesignated "face-to-face confrontation") becomes only one of many "elements of confrontation." The reasoning is as follows: The Confrontation Clause guarantees not only what it explicitly provides for—"face-to-face" confrontation—but also implied and collateral rights such as cross-examination, oath, and observation of demeanor (TRUE); the purpose of this entire cluster of rights is to ensure the reliability of evidence (TRUE); the Maryland procedure preserves the implied and collateral rights (TRUE), which adequately ensure the reliability of evidence (perhaps TRUE); therefore the Confrontation Clause is not violated by denying what it explicitly provides for—"face-to-face" confrontation (unquestionably FALSE). This reasoning abstracts from the right to its purposes, and then eliminates the right. It is wrong because the Confrontation Clause does not guarantee reliable evidence; it guarantees specific trial procedures that were thought to *assure* reliable evidence, undeniably among which was "face-to-face" confrontation. Whatever else it may mean in addition, the defendant's constitutional right "to be confronted with the witnesses against him" means, always and everywhere, at least what it explicitly says: the " 'right to meet face to face all those who appear and give evidence at trial.' " *Coy v. Iowa,* 487 U.S. 1012, 1016, 108 S.Ct. 2798, 2800, 101 L.Ed.2d 857 (1988), quoting *California v. Green,* 399 U.S. 149, 175, 90 S.Ct. 1930, 1943–44, 26 L.Ed.2d 489 (1970) (Harlan, J. concurring).

The Court supports its antitextual conclusion by cobbling together scraps of dicta from various cases that have no bearing here. It will suffice to discuss one of them, since they are all of a kind: Quoting *Ohio v. Roberts,* 448 U.S. 56, 63, 100 S.Ct. 2531, 2537, 65 L.Ed.2d 597 (1980), the Court says that "[i]n sum, our precedents establish that 'the Confrontation Clause reflects a *preference* for face-to-face confrontation at trial' " (emphasis added by the Court). But *Roberts,* and all the other "precedents" the Court enlists to prove the implausible, dealt with the *implications* of the Confrontation Clause, and not its literal, unavoidable text. When *Roberts* said that the Clause merely "reflects a preference for face-to-face confrontation at trial," what it had in mind as the nonpreferred alternative was not (as the Court implies) the appearance of a witness at trial without confronting the defendant. That has been, until today, not merely "nonpreferred" but utterly unheard-of. What *Roberts* had in mind was the receipt of *other-than-first-hand testimony* from witnesses at trial—that is, witnesses' recounting of hearsay statements by absent parties who, *since they did not appear at trial,* did not have to endure face-to-face confrontation. Rejecting that, I agree, was merely giving effect to an evident constitutional preference; there are, after all, many exceptions to the Confrontation Clause's hearsay rule. But that the defendant should be confronted by the witnesses who appear at trial is not a preference "reflected" by the Confrontation Clause; it is a constitutional right unqualifiedly guaranteed.

The Court claims that its interpretation of the Confrontation Clause "is consistent with our cases holding that other Sixth Amendment rights must also be interpreted in the context of the necessities of trial and the adversary process." I disagree. It is true enough that the "necessities of trial and the adversary process" limit the *manner* in which Sixth Amendment rights may be exercised, and limit the *scope* of Sixth Amendment guarantees to the extent that scope is textually indeterminate. Thus (to describe the cases the Court cites): The right to confront is not the right to confront in a manner that disrupts the trial. *Illinois v. Allen,* 397 U.S. 337, 90 S.Ct. 1057, 25 L.Ed.2d 353 (1970). The right "to have compulsory process for obtaining witnesses" is not the right to call witnesses in a manner that violates fair and orderly procedures. *Taylor v. Illinois,* 484 U.S. 400, 108 S.Ct. 646, 98

L.Ed.2d 798 (1988). The scope of the right "to have the assistance of counsel" does not include consultation with counsel at all times during the trial. *Perry v. Leeke,* 488 U.S. 272, 109 S.Ct. 594, 102 L.Ed.2d 624 (1989). The scope of the right to cross-examine does not include access to the State's investigative files. *Pennsylvania v. Ritchie,* 480 U.S. 39, 107 S.Ct. 989, 94 L.Ed.2d 40 (1987). But we are not talking here about denying expansive scope to a Sixth Amendment provision whose scope for the purpose at issue is textually unclear; "to confront" plainly means to encounter face-to-face, whatever else it may mean in addition. And we are not talking about the manner of arranging that face-to-face encounter, but about whether it shall occur at all. The "necessities of trial and the adversary process" are irrelevant here, since they cannot alter the constitutional text.

II

Much of the Court's opinion consists of applying to this case the mode of analysis we have used in the admission of hearsay evidence. The Sixth Amendment does not literally contain a prohibition upon such evidence, since it guarantees the defendant only the right to confront "the witnesses against him." As applied in the Sixth Amendment's context of a prosecution, the noun "witness"—in 1791 as today—could mean either (a) one "who knows or sees any thing; one personally present" or (b) "one who gives testimony" or who "testifies," *i.e.,* "[i]n *judicial proceedings,* [one who] make[s] a solemn declaration under oath, for the purpose of establishing or making proof of some fact to a court." 2 N. Webster, An American Dictionary of the English Language (1828) (emphasis added). See also J. Buchanan, Linguae Britannicae Vera Pronunciatio (1757). The former meaning (one "who knows or sees") would cover hearsay evidence, but is excluded in the Sixth Amendment by the words following the noun: "witnesses *against him.*" The phrase obviously refers to those who give testimony against the defendant at trial. We have nonetheless found implicit in the Confrontation Clause some limitation upon hearsay evidence, since otherwise the Government could subvert the confrontation right by putting on witnesses who know nothing except what an absent declarant said. And in determining the scope of that implicit limitation, we have focused upon whether the reliability of the hearsay statements (which are not *expressly* excluded by the Confrontation Clause) "is otherwise assured." The same test cannot be applied, however, to permit what is explicitly forbidden by the constitutional text; there is simply no room for interpretation with regard to "the irreducible literal meaning of the Clause." *Coy, supra,* 487 U.S., at 1020–1021, 108 S.Ct., at 2803.

Some of the Court's analysis seems to suggest that the children's testimony here was itself hearsay of the sort permissible under our Confrontation Clause cases. That cannot be. Our Confrontation Clause conditions for the admission of hearsay have long included a "general requirement of unavailability" of the declarant. *Idaho v. Wright,* ___ U.S. ___, ___, 110 S.Ct. 3139, ___, ___ L.Ed.2d ___. "In the usual case * * *, the prosecution must either produce or demonstrate the unavailability of, the declarant whose statement it wishes to use against the defendant." *Ohio v. Roberts,* 448 U.S., at 65, 100 S.Ct., at 2538. We have permitted a few exceptions to this general rule—*e.g.,* for co-conspirators' statements, whose effect cannot be replicated by live testimony because they "derive [their] significance from the circumstances in which [they were] made," *United States v. Inadi,* 475 U.S. 387, 395, 106 S.Ct. 1121, 1126, 89 L.Ed.2d 390 (1986). "Live" closed-circuit television testimony, however—if it can be called hearsay at all—is surely an example of hearsay as "a weaker substitute for live testimony," *id.,* at 394, 106 S.Ct., at 1126, which can be employed only when the genuine article is unavailable. "When two versions of the same evidence are available, longstanding principles of the law of hearsay, applicable as well to Confrontation Clause analysis, favor the better evidence." *Ibid.* See also *Roberts, supra* (requiring unavailability as precondition for admission of prior testimony); *Barber v. Page,* 390 U.S. 719, 88 S.Ct. 1318, 20 L.Ed.2d 255 (1968) (same).

The Court's test today requires unavailability only in the sense that the child is unable to testify in the presence of the defendant.[1] That cannot possibly be the relevant sense. If unconfronted testimony is admissible hearsay when the witness is unable to confront the defendant, then presumably there are other categories of admissible hearsay consisting of unsworn testimony when the witness is unable to risk perjury, uncross-examined testimony when the witness is unable to undergo hostile questioning, etc. *California v. Green,* 399 U.S. 149, 90 S.Ct. 1930, 26 L.Ed.2d 489 (1970), is not precedent for such a silly system. That case held that the Confrontation Clause does not bar admission of prior testimony when the declarant is sworn as a witness but refuses to answer. But in *Green,* as in most cases of refusal, we could not know *why* the declarant refused to testify. Here, by contrast, we know that it is precisely because the child is unwilling to testify in the presence of the defendant. That unwillingness cannot be a valid excuse under the Confrontation Clause, whose very object is to place the witness under the sometimes hostile glare of the defendant. "That face-to-face presence may, unfortunately, upset the truthful rape victim or abused child; but by the same token it may confound and undo the false accuser, or reveal the child coached by a malevolent adult." *Coy,* 487 U.S., at 1020, 108 S.Ct., at 2802. To say that a defendant loses his right to confront a witness when that would cause the witness not to testify is rather like saying that the defendant loses his right to counsel when counsel would save him, or his right to subpoena witnesses when they would exculpate him, or his right not to give testimony against himself when that would prove him guilty.

1. I presume that when the Court says "trauma would impair the child's ability to communicate," it means that trauma would make it impossible for the child to communicate. That is the requirement of the Maryland law at issue here: "serious emotional distress such that the child cannot reasonably communicate." Md.Cts. & Jud.Proc.Code Ann. § 9–102(a)(1)(ii) (1989). Any implication beyond that would in any event be dictum.

III

The Court characterizes the State's interest which "outweigh[s]" the explicit text of the Constitution as an "interest in the physical and psychological well-being of child abuse victims," an "interest in protecting" such victims "from the emotional trauma of testifying." That is not so. A child who meets the Maryland statute's requirement of suffering such "serious emotional distress" from confrontation that he "cannot reasonably communicate" would seem entirely safe. Why would a prosecutor want to call a witness who cannot reasonably communicate? And if he did, it would be the State's own fault. Protection of the child's interest—as far as the Confrontation Clause is concerned [2]—is entirely within Maryland's control. The State's interest here is in fact no more and no less than what the State's interest always is when it seeks to get a class of evidence admitted in criminal proceedings: more convictions of guilty defendants. That is not an unworthy interest, but it should not be dressed up as a humanitarian one.

And the interest on the other side is also what it usually is when the State seeks to get a new class of evidence admitted: fewer convictions of innocent defendants—specifically, in the present context, innocent defendants accused of particularly heinous crimes. The "special" reasons that exist for suspending one of the usual guarantees of reliability in the case of children's testimony are perhaps matched by "special" reasons for being particularly insistent upon it in the case of children's testimony. Some studies show that children are substantially more vulnerable to suggestion than adults, and often unable to separate recollected fantasy (or suggestion) from reality. See Lindsay & Johnson, Reality Monitoring and Suggestibility: Children's Ability to Discriminate Among Memories From Different Sources, in Children's Eyewitness Memory 92 (S. Ceci, M. Toglia, & D. Ross eds. 1987); Feher, The Alleged Molestation Victim, The Rules of Evidence, and the Constitution: Should Children Really Be Seen and Not Heard?, 14 Am. J.Crim.L. 227, 230–233 (1987); Christiansen, The Testimony of Child Witnesses: Fact, Fantasy, and the Influence of Pretrial Interviews, 62 Wash.L.Rev. 705, 708–711 (1987). The injustice their erroneous testimony can produce is evidenced by the tragic Scott County investigations of 1983–1984, which disrupted the lives of many (as far as we know) innocent people in the small town of Jordan, Minnesota. At one stage those investigations were pursuing allegations by at least eight children of multiple murders, but the prosecutions actually initiated charged only sexual abuse. Specifically, 24 adults were charged with molesting 37 children. In the course of the investigations, 25 children were placed in foster homes. Of the 24 indicted defendants, one

2. A different situation would be presented if the defendant sought to call the child. In that event, the State's refusal to compel the child to appear, or its insistence upon a procedure such as that set forth in the Maryland statute as a condition of its compelling him to do so, would call into question—initially, at least, and perhaps exclusively—the scope of the defendant's Sixth Amendment right "to have compulsory process for obtaining witnesses in his favor."

pleaded guilty, two were acquitted at trial, and the charges against the remaining 21 were voluntarily dismissed. See Feher, *supra,* at 239–240. There is no doubt that some sexual abuse took place in Jordan; but there is no reason to believe it was as widespread as charged. A report by the Minnesota Attorney General's office, based on inquiries conducted by the Minnesota Bureau of Criminal Apprehension and the Federal Bureau of Investigation, concluded that there was an "absence of credible testimony and [a] lack of significant corroboration" to support reinstitution of sex-abuse charges, and "no credible evidence of murders." H. Humphrey, report on Scott County Investigation 8, 7 (1985). The report describes an investigation full of well-intentioned techniques employed by the prosecution team, police, child protection workers, and foster parents, that distorted and in some cases even coerced the children's recollection. Children were interrogated repeatedly, in some cases as many as 50 times, *id.,* at 9; answers were suggested by telling the children what other witnesses had said, *id.,* at 11; and children (even some who did not at first complain of abuse) were separated from their parents for months, *id.,* at 9. The report describes the consequences as follows:

> "As children continued to be interviewed the list of accused citizens grew. In a number of cases, it was only after weeks or months of questioning that children would 'admit' their parents abused them.
>
> * * *
>
> "In some instances, over a period of time, the allegations of sexual abuse turned to stories of mutilations, and eventually homicide." *Id.,* at 10–11.

The value of the confrontation right in guarding against a child's distorted or coerced recollections is dramatically evident with respect to one of the misguided investigative techniques the report cited: some children were told by their foster parents that reunion with their real parents would be hastened by "admission" of their parents' abuse. *Id.,* at 9. Is it difficult to imagine how unconvincing such a testimonial admission might be to a jury that witnessed the child's delight at seeing his parents in the courtroom? Or how devastating it might be if, pursuant to a psychiatric evaluation that "trauma would impair the child's ability to communicate" in front of his parents, the child were permitted to tell his story to the jury on closed-circuit television?

In the last analysis, however, this debate is not an appropriate one. I have no need to defend the value of confrontation, because the Court has no authority to question it. It is not within our charge to speculate that, "where face-to-face confrontation causes significant emotional distress in a child witness," confrontation might "in fact *disserve* the Confrontation Clause's truth-seeking goal." If so, that is a defect in the Constitution—which should be amended by the procedures provided for such an eventuality, but cannot be corrected by judicial pronouncement that it is archaic, contrary to "widespread belief" and thus null and void. For good or bad, the Sixth Amendment requires confrontation, and we are not at liberty to ignore it. To quote the document one last time (for it plainly says all that need be said): "In *all* criminal prosecutions, the accused shall enjoy the right * * * to be confronted with the witnesses against him" (emphasis added).

The Court today has applied "interest-balancing" analysis where the text of the Constitution simply does not permit it. We are not free to conduct a cost-benefit analysis of clear and explicit constitutional guarantees, and then to adjust their meaning to comport with our findings. The Court has convincingly proved that the Maryland procedure serves a valid interest, and gives the defendant virtually everything the Confrontation Clause guarantees (everything, that is, except confrontation). I am persuaded, therefore, that the Maryland procedure is virtually constitutional. Since it is not, however, actually constitutional I would affirm the judgment of the Maryland Court of Appeals reversing the judgment of conviction.

BOLLER v. COFRANCES

Supreme Court of Wisconsin, 1969.
42 Wis.2d 170, 166 N.W.2d 129.

This is an appeal from a judgment of the circuit court for LaCrosse county, which, after a jury verdict assessing the negligence of each driver at 50 percent, dismissed the complaint of Virginia M. Boller, the administratrix of Henry W. Boller, deceased.

The action arose out of an automobile accident that occurred in the city of LaCrosse on May 23, 1965. Henry W. Boller and his passenger, Catherine Case, were both killed in the accident.

Just prior to the accident, Henry W. Boller, who was proceeding east on Main street, came to a halt at the stop sign protecting arterial traffic on Losey Boulevard, a four-lane arterial highway. The car driven by Cofrances was at that time approaching the intersection from the south at a rate of speed, estimated by the witnesses, in excess of the twenty-five miles an hour that was permitted at that point. The Boller car moved out into Losey Boulevard, where it was struck broadside by the Cofrances car. The evidence adduced at trial indicated that both Boller and Cofrances had been drinking, and each showed a blood alcohol test indicating intoxication. Boller's blood tested .150 percent and Cofrances' tested .180 percent. In view of the undisputed evidence, the trial judge found, as a matter of law, that Cofrances was negligent as to speed.

The jury concluded, additionally, that Cofrances was negligent as to lookout, and Boller was negligent as to lookout and failure to yield the right of way. All items of negligence were found to be causal, and the jury apportioned 50 percent of the negligence to each party.

In motions after verdict, the plaintiff, Virginia M. Boller, asked for a new trial because of errors in the instructions, prejudicial conduct on the part of defendant's counsel, and in the interest of justice. These motions were denied, and judgment on the verdict was entered for the defendant. The plaintiff has appealed to this court.

HEFFERNAN, JUSTICE.

* * *

The plaintiff argues that a new trial should be granted because Virginia Boller was asked the following question on cross-examination by defense counsel:

"Q. Were you aware of the affair that your husband was having with Mrs. Case [the passenger in the car]?

"MR. ARNESON: I object to this, Your Honor, as improper cross examination. There's no foundation for any kind of questioning about that. It's beyond the scope of direct examination in every respect.

"THE COURT: *Beyond the scope,* Mr. Crosby. Objection sustained. [Emphasis supplied.]

"MR. ARNESON: And I ask that the jury be instructed to disregard it.

"THE COURT: Jury will be instructed to disregard it.

"MR. CROSBY: That's all."

* * *

Was it error to exclude the question in regard to Henry Boller's affair with Mrs. Case?

While the trial judge excluded the question, "Were you [Virginia Boller] aware of the affair that your husband was having with Mrs. Case?"—and the plaintiff assumes that such ruling was correct—the defendant on this appeal stoutly contends that the question was proper and Virginia Boller's answer should have been admitted into evidence. Defendant points out in his brief that the plaintiff on direct examination testified, "that she and her husband had a close relationship and were very happily married."

When defendant's counsel asked his question, it was objected to and that objection was sustained on the grounds that it was *beyond the scope of the direct* examination. We do not agree with the ruling of the trial judge. One of the major issues to be resolved by the jury was the evaluation, to the extent possible, of the loss Virginia Boller sustained by losing the society and companionship of Henry Boller. Certainly, the existence of an "affair" with another woman and Virginia Boller's knowledge of it were probative of the value to be placed upon Virginia Boller's loss. Moreover, the question was directly related to, and in impeachment of, her testimony on direct examination. We are satisfied that the question was relevant to the questions posed on direct examination and was within its scope. Of course, despite its probativeness, it is within the discretion of the trial judge to exclude evidence if its probativeness is offset by possible jury prejudice. State v. Hutnik (1968), 39 Wis.2d 754, 763, 764, 159 N.W.2d 733; Price v. State (1967), 37 Wis.2d 117, 133, 154 N.W.2d 222; State v. Smith (1967), 36 Wis.2d

584, 153 N.W.2d 538; Whitty v. State (1967), 34 Wis.2d 278, 149 N.W.2d 557. Here, however, such discretion was not in fact exercised, and in view of the state of the record, such evidence should not have been excluded. While we find the disputed question to be within the scope of the direct examination, we have grave doubts that such rule of exclusion should be followed, particularly when the witness on the stand is a party and subject to be called, in a civil case at least, by the opponent. Abbott v. Truck Insurance Exchange Co. (1967), 33 Wis.2d 671, 681, 148 N.W.2d 116; Musha v. United States Fidelity & Guaranty Co. (1960), 10 Wis.2d 176, 102 N.W.2d 243; Ward v. Thompson (1911), 146 Wis. 376, 131 N.W. 1006; Schultz v. Chicago & N.W.R. Co. (1887), 67 Wis. 616, 31 N.W. 321. The rule against questioning any witness "beyond the scope of direct examination" has no intrinsic merit and does not demonstrably assist in the search for the truth. Rather, by encouraging pettifogging objections that go to form and not substance, the rule is likely to be disruptive of trial procedure and results in appeals that basically have no merit.

The only claimed virtue for the rule is that it ensures the orderly presentation of evidence, i.e., that a plaintiff's witness should not be expected to help make the defendant's case on cross-examination. But why shouldn't he? If the question is relevant and is otherwise admissible and the information solicited is within the knowledge of the witness, it should be within the sound discretion of the trial judge to determine whether or not questions on cross-examination prevent an orderly and cogent presentation of the evidence. They well might, and usually would, contribute to the intelligent search for the truth.

This test, which leaves the admission or exclusion to the discretion of the trial judge, is infinitely preferable to the artificial and meaningless rule that excludes all evidence whether it should then logically come into the record or not, simply because it is "beyond the scope." The Model Code of Evidence recommends the following rule to supplant the present practice:

> "Rule 105. Control of Judge over Presentation of Evidence. The judge controls the conduct of the trial to the end that the evidence shall be presented honestly, expeditiously and in such form as to be readily understood, and in his discretion determines, among other things, * * *
>
> "(h) to what extent and in what circumstances a party cross-examining a witness may be forbidden to examine him concerning material matters not inquired about on a previous examination by the judge or by an adverse party."

Wigmore points out that the present rule, as practiced in Wisconsin, is a recent one, and that the historical or orthodox rule permitted:

> " * * * the opposite party * * * not only [to] cross-examine him in relation to the point which he was called to prove, but he may examine him as to any matter embraced in the issue. He may establish his defence by him without calling any other witnesses. If he is a

competent witness to the jury for any purpose he is so for all purposes." 6 Wigmore, Evidence (3d ed.), sec. 1885, p. 532, quoting Sutherland, J., Fulton Bank v. Stafford, 2 Wend. 483, 485.

Wigmore in that volume, sec. 1885ff., discusses in detail the shortcomings of the present rule. In his Students' Textbook, Wigmore on Evidence, he summarizes the effect of the present rule:

> "Cross examination is the greatest engine for getting at the truth; * * * and a rule which needlessly hampers its exercise as this one does cannot be a sound one."

McCormick, in his treatise on Evidence (hornbook series), sec. 27, p. 51, points out that, when all relevant factors are considered, "the balance [is] overwhelmingly in favor of the wide-open rule." He points out that:

> "The restrictive practice in all its forms * * * is productive * * * of continual bickering over the choice of the numerous variations of the 'scope of the direct' criterion, and of their application to particular cross-questions. These controversies are often reventilated on appeal, and reversals for error in their determination are frequent. Observance of these vague and ambiguous restrictions is a matter of constant and hampering concern to the cross-examiner. If these efforts, delays and misprisions were the necessary incidents to the guarding of substantive rights or the fundamentals of fair trial, they might be worth the cost. As the price of the choice of an obviously debatable regulation of the order of evidence, the sacrifice seems misguided."

McCormick also emphasizes the deleterious effect of the present rule in the prosecution of criminals:

> "* * * the accused may limit his direct examination to some single aspect of the case, such as age, sanity or alibi, and then invoke the court's ruling that the cross-examination be limited to the matter thus opened. Surely the according of a privilege to the accused to select out a favorable fact and testify to that alone, and thus get credit for testifying but escape a searching inquiry on the whole charge, is a travesty on criminal administration * * *"
>
> "In jurisdictions following the wide-open practice there is of course no obstacle to cross-examining the accused upon any matters relevant to any issue in the entire case." Sec. 26, pp. 49, 50.

While the Wisconsin cases appear to allow greater latitude in the cross-examination of a criminal defendant, they appear to permit examination of all facets of an alleged crime only when the defendant has opened the door on direct by testifying on the merits of the case. Sprague v. State (1925), 188 Wis. 432, 206 N.W. 69.

We are satisfied that the wide-open rule should be adopted by this court. The appeal herein is founded upon the exclusion from the record of relevant evidence on the grounds that it elicited information not covered by, or within, the scope of the direct evidence. The evidence, in reason, ought not to have been excluded. Because the plaintiff, by invoking the spurious "beyond the scope" rule, contends that the jury made use of improper and inadmissible evidence, he has brought a patently specious appeal. The exclusion of the evidence on the basis of the restrictive rule is founded in neither reason nor the interest of justice. It is productive of confusion and super-technical appeals similar to the one brought in this instance.

Had the rule been the one permitting wide-open cross-examination, the answer to the question would have been clearly admissible and the subsequent bickering would have been avoided. Of course, as stated above, otherwise admissible evidence can still be excluded in the discretion of the trial judge if its harmful effects on the legal process outweigh its probative value. In such event, e.g., had it been clearly admissible under the wide-open rule, the question would have hinged upon the question of abuse of discretion by the trial judge and not upon a mechanistic rule of evidence.

* * * We * * * conclude that the disputed question properly should have been allowed as eliciting evidence relevant to the issue or in impeachment. On both scores the answer would be admissible even under the restrictive rule heretofore in use. It would without a doubt have been a proper question under the wide-open rule which we herein adopt. Under this rule the trial judge shall exercise discretion to assure an orderly and intelligible presentation of the facts without the requirement of slavish compliance with the "beyond the scope" rule.

We conclude that the plaintiff was not prejudiced by the proceedings and the apportionment of negligence is supported by substantial evidence. The interest of justice would not be secured by a new trial.

Judgment affirmed.

LIS v. ROBERT PACKER HOSPITAL, 579 F.2d 819, 822–25 (3d Cir.1978), cert. denied, 439 U.S. 955, 99 S.Ct. 354, 58 L.Ed.2d 346 (1978). "Appellants allege that the trial judge's statement, 'I have the right to permit inquiry beyond the scope of direct examination and I do it in every case unless it causes confusion', runs a collision course with Federal Rule of Evidence 611(b):

> (b) *Scope of cross-examination.* Cross-examination should be limited to the subject matter of the direct examination and matters affecting the credibility of the witness. The court may, in the exercise of discretion, permit inquiry into additional matters as if on direct examination.

"The rule as adopted by Congress changed the rule submitted to it by the Supreme Court. As submitted, Rule 611(b) provided:

> A witness may be cross-examined on any matter relevant to any issue in the case, including credibility. In the interests of justice, the judge may limit cross-examination with respect to matters not testified to on direct examination.

"The House of Representatives adopted the present language, the Committee on the Judiciary offering this rationale:

> The Committee amended this provision to return to the rule which prevails in the federal courts and thirty-nine State jurisdictions. As amended, the Rule is in the text of the 1969 Advisory Committee draft. It limits cross-examination to credibility and to matters testified to on direct examination, unless the judge permits more, in which event the cross-examiner must proceed as if on direct examination. This traditional rule facilitates orderly presentation by each party at trial. Further, in light of existing discovery procedures, there appears to be no need to abandon the traditional rule.

The Senate Committee stated similar views:

> The House narrowed the Rule to the more traditional practice of limiting cross-examination to the subject matter of direct examination (and credibility), but with discretion in the judge to permit inquiry into additional matters in situations where that would aid in the development of the evidence or otherwise facilitate the conduct of the trial.
>
> The committee agrees with the House amendment. Although there are good arguments in support of broad cross-examination from prospectives of developing all relevant evidence, we believe the factors of insuring an orderly and predictable development of the evidence weigh in favor of the narrower rule, especially when discretion is given to the trial judge to permit inquiry into additional matters. The committee expressly approves this discretion and believes it will permit sufficient flexibility allowing a broader scope of cross-examination whenever appropriate.

"Clearly then, the Rule in its present form establishes a predictable and orderly procedure for the presentation of the various sides to a dispute. The first sentence of the Rule declares that '[c]ross examination should be limited to the subject matter of the direct examination'. The second sentence, affording courts the power to expand the inquiry, clearly contemplates special circumstances.

"We agree with appellants that, notwithstanding the trial court's laudable motives, its ruling effectuated neither the letter nor the spirit of Rule 611(b). Simply stated, the Rule does not confer upon a federal judge 'the right to permit inquiry beyond the scope of the direct * * * in every case'. Rather, the general prescription is precisely the opposite. Any right to counter the stated procedure is granted to the trial court only 'in the exercise of discretion'. To follow the practice announced by the trial judge in this case is not to exercise discretion; it is to use no discretion whatever.

* * *

"Nevertheless, although the trial court apparently failed to exercise discretion in applying Fed.R.Evid. 611(b) * * * we do not reverse in this case because appellants have not persuaded us that they were visited with such prejudice as to entitle them to a new trial. Because of the dearth of case law construing Rule 611(b) in this court, we hesitate to invoke the draconian remedy of a new trial simply because the trial court followed a certain practice in all cases. For the future, however, it may be that a showing of prejudice will not be necessary to obtain relief from this court where, as here, it is demonstrated that the trial court has failed to heed the congressional command. Trial courts in this circuit can reasonably assume that in future cases this court will treat the congressional formulation as a prophylactic rule which, if not followed, requires the most severe sanction—irrespective of demonstrably prejudicial effect."

LAWRENCE v. STATE

Court of Criminal Appeals of Texas, 1970.
457 S.W.2d 561.

BELCHER, JUDGE.

The appellants were jointly indicted and jointly tried for the offense of felony theft, and their punishment assessed at two years.

The appellants contend that the trial court erred in allowing the state to ask its principal witness a leading question that was highly prejudicial to the appellant.

During the examination of the state's witness, Oliver J. Johnson, the following occurred:

"Q (By Mr. Hirtz) Directing your attention back to July, 1966, did you buy some virgin metal, virgin nickel from anyone in July, 1966?

"A (By witness) Yes, sir, I did.

"Q Did you buy approximately eleven hundred ninety-nine pounds of metal back at that time?

"A I did.

"Mr. Cutler: I object to leading. He should know how much he bought.

"The Court: I sustain the objection.

"Mr. Cutler: I ask that the jury be instructed.

"The Court: The jury is instructed they are not to consider the question for any purpose. I sustained the objection.

"Q (By Mr. Hirtz) Do you recall how much of this virgin nickel you bought back in July of 1966?

"A (By witness) I bought eleven hundred ninety-nine pounds.

"Mr. Cutler: I objected after a leading question was asked of him and he turned around and asked how much. As important as that is to this case, I object to that being brought into evidence. He put words in his mouth and then asked him again.

"The Court: That's overruled.

"Mr. Cutler: Note our exception."

The appellants received all the relief that they had requested when the trial court instructed the jury not to consider the leading question for any purpose. The objections were directed to the quantity purchased and not to whether a purchase was made. A case will not be reversed in the absence of a showing of an abuse of the trial court's discretion in allowing a leading question, and where a question has been improperly put, counsel may propound a proper question free from the defects in the former question. McCormick and Ray on Evidence 2d, Secs. 579, 580; 62 Tex.Jur.2d 18, Sec. 147; Bell v. State, 166 Tex.Cr.R. 340, 313 S.W.2d 606. No abuse of discretion is shown.

* * *

The judgment is affirmed.

ALEXANDER v. CHAPMAN, 289 Ark. 238, 711 S.W.2d 765, 769–70 (1986). "Improper leading includes improper suggestion and improper ratification. Wigmore, Treatise on the Law of Evidence § 769: Callahan v. Farm Equipment, Inc., 225 Ark. 547, 283 S.W.2d 692 (1955). Suggestion occurs when a question indicates the answer desired and ratification occurs when a question is suggestive, contains factual detail which could and should originate with the witness and the witness adopts the detail and the form in which it is expressed. Denbeaux and Risinger, Questioning Questions: Objections to Form in Interrogation of Witnesses, 33 Ark.L.Rev. 439 (1979).

* * *

"Some of the sanctions for leading questions recommended by the authors of the cited law review article are: striking the improper question and permitting a proper one, admonishment at the bench or before the jury, striking the improper question and refusing to allow counsel to reask, contempt, and mistrial. Denbeaux and Risinger, supra.

"Here counsel repeatedly ignored the trial court's warnings concerning leading questions. The court conceded it could not or would not take action beyond admonishment. Only once did it instruct the witness not to respond. If counsel will not comply with the trial court's requests, then some sanction, with teeth, must be used against him. We are certain the leading would have stopped had the trial court granted appellants' motion to preclude further inquiry. The appellants were entitled to have the leading stopped.

"Trial courts by necessity are granted great power and discretion to preserve the order of their courtrooms. They have at their command numerous sanctions to see that rules are followed. Because the sanctions exist they are usually not necessary, but sometimes they must be used. Some sanctions should have been used in this case. The appellants were entitled to have the case presented to the jury in the words of witnesses not counsel."

PASCALL v. SMITH, 263 Ark. 428, 569 S.W.2d 89, 91 (1978). "However, we cannot agree that the chancellor erred in permitting the direct examination of appellee to be conducted by leading questions. Ark.Stat.Ann. § 28–1001, Rule 611(c) (Supp.1977) permits leading questions on direct examination 'as may be necessary to develop his testimony.' Here the court, in overruling appellant's objection. stated he was aware the witness was being asked leading questions 'but at the same time this witness is elderly and can't hear too well and I am allowing a little bit more leeway in leading than I ordinarily would.' "

HANEY v. MIZELL MEMORIAL HOSPITAL, 744 F.2d 1467, 1477–78 (11th Cir.1984). "Haney also objects to the district court's refusal to allow him to ask leading questions of a witness he called in his case-in-chief. He reasons that Nurse Williamson, the emergency room technician who first met Haney upon arrival at Mizell Memorial Hospital, was 'a witness identified with an adverse party,' Fed.R.Evid. 611(c), and the use of leading questions therefore was permissible. The hospital argues that since Haney failed to make a threshold showing of actual hostility, the district court acted properly. Although we agree with Haney's reading of Rule 611(c), we nonetheless refuse to reverse the district court on this basis alone.

"Prior to the adoption of Rule 611(c), before a party could lead a witness on direct examination, it had to be shown that the witness was actually hostile or was an adverse party, officer, director, or managing agent of such adverse party. Ellis v. City of Chicago, 667 F.2d 606, 612 (7th Cir.1981). Rule 611(c), however, significantly enlarged the class of witnesses presumed hostile, 'and therefore subject to interrogation by leading questions without further showing of actual hostility.' *Ellis,* 667 F.2d at 613 (citing Fed.R.Evid. 611 advisory committee note); see also Perkins v. Volkswagen of America, Inc., 596 F.2d 681, 682 (5th Cir.1979) (error for trial court to rule that employee of defendant would be plaintiff's witness if plaintiff called him). Since Nurse Williamson, an employee of one of the defendants present when the alleged malpractice may have occurred, certainly was identified with a party adverse to Haney, the district court misread Rule 611(c) when it refused to allow Haney to lead him until actual hostility was established. See 3 J. Weinstein & M. Berger, supra, at 611–60 to –61.

"This mistake does not, however, mandate reversal. Firstly, Haney fails to identify just what information he was unable to elicit from Nurse Williamson because of the district court's ruling. Secondly, the record indicates that this witness was extensively examined and repeatedly impeached by Haney. Under these circumstances, we discern no abuse of the district court's discretion. Moreover, the district court's decision 'will not be reversed absent a clear showing of prejudice to [Haney].' *Ellis,* 667 F.2d at 613. We find no such prejudice in this case."

Notes

(1) See also United States v. Hicks, 748 F.2d 854, 859 (4th Cir.1984) (defendant's girlfriend was "a witness identified with an adverse party" when called by the government); United States v. DeFiore, 720 F.2d 757, 764 (2d Cir.1983) (Rule 611(c)'s provision that leading questions "should not be used on direct examination" constitutes "words of suggestion, not command"), cert. denied, 467 U.S. 1241, 104 S.Ct. 3511, 82 L.Ed.2d 820 (1984); State v. Branom, 689 S.W.2d 778 (Mo.App.1985) (approving testimony of thirteen-year-old statutory rape victim consisting largely of "yes" and "no" responses to leading questions); State v. Lupo, 676 S.W.2d 30, 33 (Mo.App.1984) (evasive witness who contradicted previous statements properly questioned by state as hostile witness); State v. Jenkins, 326 N.W.2d 67, 69–71 (N.D.1982) (leading questions to nine-year-old rape victim proper). Compare Dehring v. Northern Michigan Exploration Co., 104 Mich.App. 300, 304 N.W.2d 560, 568–69 (1981) (trial judge's refusal to permit leading questions to hearing-impaired witness not abuse of discretion).

(2) A question is "argumentative" if it is in the nature of a jury argument rather than an attempt to elicit information from the witness. See, e.g., Smith v. Estelle, 602 F.2d 694, 700 n. 7 (5th Cir 1979) ("Dr. Grigson, you're kind of the hatchet man down here for the District Attorney's Office, aren't you?"; "Did you ever meet a person you didn't think was a sociopath?"), aff'd, 451 U.S. 454, 101 S.Ct. 1866, 68 L.Ed.2d 359 (1981); United States v. Micklus, 581 F.2d 612, 617 n. 3 (7th Cir 1978) ("I'm asking you. It wouldn't bother you any, to come in here and lie from the time you started to the time you stopped, would it?"); United States v. Cash, 499 F.2d 26, 29 (9th Cir.1974) ("As a matter of fact, you drove the car that was parked outside the liquor store when he went in and stole some liquor; is that not a fact?"). "A still more common vice is for the examiner to couch as true matters to which the witness has not testified, and which are in dispute between the parties." McCormick, Evidence § 7 (4th ed. 1992). See, e.g., United States v. Medel, 592 F.2d 1305, 1314 (5th Cir.1979). This is sometimes called a "misleading" question.

SECTION 4. WRITING USED TO REFRESH MEMORY *

[FED.R.EVID. 612]

UNITED STATES v. RICCARDI

United States Court of Appeals, Third Circuit, 1949.

174 F.2d 883, cert. denied, 337 U.S. 941, 69 S.Ct. 1519, 93 L.Ed. 1746 (1949).

KALODNER, CIRCUIT JUDGE.

The defendant was indicted under 18 U.S.C. (1940 ed.) Sections 415 and 417 in four counts charging him with wilfully, unlawfully and

* See 3 Wigmore, Evidence §§ 758–765 (Chadbourn rev. 1970); McCormick, Evidence § 9 (4th ed. 1992).

feloniously having transported or having caused to be transported in interstate commerce certain chattels of the value of $5,000 or more. The first and third counts were dismissed, and the defendant was convicted on the second and fourth counts, from which conviction he appeals.

We are not here primarily concerned with the particular fraudulent representations which the defendant made. Rather we are called upon to decide the propriety of the method utilized at the trial to prove what chattels the defendant obtained and transported, and their value. In short, the principal question is whether the witnesses who testified to these essentials were properly permitted to refresh their memory. In addition, the defendant also asserts error in the acceptance of evidence relating to the transactions between the defendant and the complaining witness, but which was not necessarily a part of the indictment.

The chattels involved are numerous items of bric-a-bric, linens, silverware, and other household articles of quality and distinction. They were the property of Doris Farid es Sultaneh, and were kept in her home at Morristown, New Jersey, from which the defendant is alleged to have transported them to Arizona in a truck and station wagon. The defendant did not deny receiving some of the lady's chattels, but did deny both the quantity and quality alleged. Moreover, it does not appear open to doubt that the truck made but one trip, and the station wagon three, carrying the goods in controversy.

To prove the specific chattels involved, the government relied on the testimony of Doris Farid; to prove their value, it relied on the testimony of an expert, one Leo Berlow.

Farid testified that as the chattels were being moved from the house, she made longhand notes, and that later she copied these notes on her typewriter. Only one of the original notes was produced, and became part of the evidence of the case, a search by Farid having failed to disclose the others. The government sought to have Farid testify with respect to the chattels by using the typewritten notes for the purpose of refreshing her recollection.[2] Although the defendant's objection was overruled, the government, on the next day of the trial, submitted to Farid lists of chattels taken out of a copy of the indict-

2. At pages 114a–115a of Appellant's Appendix, the following appears:

"The Court: That isn't the question. When you look at that typewritten sheet, does that refresh your recollection as to the items therein mentioned?

"The Witness: It does.

"The Court: In what way?

"The Witness: Well, every item here—for instance: '2 Chinese vases octagonal shape Satsuma, light for mantel' I remember.

"The Court: You remember those items individually as packed?

"The Witness: Individually, each one.

"The Court: I will allow her to refresh her recollection, but I will expect you to produce the original notes."

ment, but from which had been deleted such information as dates and values.[3] With the aid of these lists, the witness testified that her recollection was refreshed [4] and that she presently recognized and could identify each item. She was then permitted to read the lists aloud, and testified that she knew that the items were loaded on the truck or station wagon, as the case was. The lists were neither offered nor received in evidence.

The expert, Berlow, testified that he had visited Doris Farid's home on numerous occasions in his professional capacity as dealer in antiques, bric-a-bric, etc.; that he was very familiar with the furnishings therein, having examined the household for the purpose of buying items from Farid or selling them for her on commission. He was shown the same lists which Farid had used to refresh her recollection, and with their aid testified that he could recall the items individually, with some exceptions; that he remembered them to the extent that he could not only describe the items, but in many instances could state where in the house he had seen them; and that he could give an opinion as to their value. This he was permitted to do.

In denying the acceptability of the evidence related, the defendant rests primarily on Putnam v. United States, 1896, 162 U.S. 687, 16 S.Ct. 923, 40 L.Ed. 1118, and refers to this Court's decision in Delaney v. United States, 3 Cir., 1935, 77 F.2d 916. It is his position that the lists should not have been used because they were not made by the witnesses at or shortly after the time of the transaction while the facts were fresh in memory. It is further contended that the witnesses were not hostile to the government, and what Farid did, in fact, was to read off the lists as proof of the actual articles loaded on the vehicles.

The government, on the other hand, asserts that the witnesses gave their independent recollection, which is admissible, albeit refreshed, because it is the recollection and not the writing which is the evidence. It goes further, and urges that where the witness has an independent recollection, anything may be used to stimulate and vitalize that recollection without regard to source or origin.

3. At page 136a of Appellant's Appendix it appears that government counsel began by showing to Farid a list which did not have values. At page 137a, the following appears:

"The Court: Well, I think with these evaluations cut off it is all right. This is the same paper that was shown to the witness yesterday?

"Mr. Pearse (defendant's counsel): No, sir, this is the indictment.

"Mr. Tyne (U.S. Attorney): No, sir, this is the indictment."

Following this, at the suggestion of the trial judge, the dates on the lists, to which defendant had previously objected, were cut off. The lists were then shown to the witness.

4. For example, at page 140a of Appellant's Appendix:

"The Court: Well, Madam, as you look at that list does it refresh your recollection?

"The Witness: I lived with these things, your Honor, I know them.

"The Court: You lived with them yourself?

"The Witness: I did.

"The Court: So when you look at that paper, it does refresh your recollection?

"The Witness: Absolutely."

Refreshing the recollection of a witness is not an uncommon trial practice, but as a theory of evidentiary law its content and application are far from clear. The large collection of cases found in 125 A.L.R. 19–250 illustrates the point. An analysis as good and trustworthy as presently exists appears in Chapter XXVIII, 3 Wigmore on Evidence (3rd ed. 1940). Professor Wigmore separated, broadly, what he called "past recollection recorded" from "present recollection revived", attributing much of the confusion in the cases to a failure to make this distinction and to the use of the phrase "refreshing the recollection" for both classes of testimony. The primary difference between the two classifications is the ability of the witness to testify from present knowledge: where the witness' memory is revived, and he presently recollects the facts and swears to them, he is obviously in a different position from the witness who cannot directly state the facts from present memory and who must ask the court to accept a writing for the truth of its contents because he is willing to swear, for one reason or another, that its contents are true.

Recognition of the basic difference between the two categories of evidence referred to is explicit in the federal cases, although in some the distinction is obscured by the lack of necessity for it. * * *

The difference between present recollection revived and past recollection recorded has a demonstrable effect upon the method of proof. In the instance of past recollection recorded, the witness, by hypothesis, has no present recollection of the matter contained in the writing. Whether the record is directly admitted into evidence, or indirectly by the permissive parroting of the witness, it is nevertheless a substitute for his memory and is offered for the truth of its contents. It assumes a distinct significance as an independent probative force, and is therefore ordinarily required to meet certain standards. These requirements are the more understandable in consideration of the fact that the court is at once desirous of determining whether the writing may be safely received as a substitute for the witness' memory and for the truth of the matter therein asserted, and of affording to the trier of fact information upon which it can form a reliable judgment as to its worth for the purposes offered.

In the case of present recollection revived, the witness, by hypothesis, relates his present recollection, and under oath and subject to cross-examination asserts that it is true; his capacities for memory and perception may be attacked and tested; his determination to tell the truth investigated and revealed; protestations of lack of memory, which escape criticism and indeed constitute a refuge in the situation of past recollection recorded, merely undermine the probative worth of his testimony. It is in recognition of these factors that we find:

> "The law of contemporary writing or entry qualifying it as primary evidence has no application. The primary evidence here is not the writing. It was not introduced in evidence. It was not offered. The primary evidence is the oral statement of the hostile witness. It is

not so important when the statement was made or by whom if it serves the purpose to refresh the mind and unfold the truth." Hoffman v. United States, 9 Cir., 1937, 87 F.2d 410, 411.

"When a party uses an earlier statement of his own witness to refresh the witness' memory, the only evidence recognized as such is the testimony so refreshed. * * * Anything may in fact revive a memory: a song, a scent, a photograph, an allusion, even a past statement known to be false. When a witness declares that any of these has evoked a memory, the opposite party may show, either that it has not evoked what appears to the witness as a memory, or that, although it may so appear to him, the memory is a phantom and not a reliable record of its content. When the evoking stimulus is not itself an account of the relevant occasion, no question of its truth can arise; but when it is an account of that occasion, its falsity, if raised by the opposing party, will become a relevant issue if the witness has declared that the evoked memory accords with it. * * *" United States v. Rappy, 2 Cir., 1947, 157 F.2d 964, 967–968, certiorari denied 329 U.S. 806, 67 S.Ct. 501, 91 L.Ed. 688.

* * *

Since the purpose of the writing is to activate the memory of the witness, there is always the possibility, if not probability, that the writing will exert a strong influence upon the direction of the memory, that is, the nearer the writing to the truth, the lesser the deviation of the witness' memory from the truth. But this is not a binding reason for insistence upon establishing the reliability of the writing previous to permitting the witness to state whether his memory is refreshed. The reception of a witness' testimony does not depend upon whether it is true; truth is a matter for the trier of fact unless, of course, the evidence is so improbable that reasonable men would not differ upon it. When the witness testifies that he has a present recollection, that is the evidence in the case, and not the writing which stimulates it. If his recollection agrees with the writing, it is pointless to require proof of the accuracy of the writing, for such proof can only amount to corroborative evidence. The testimony is received for what it is worth. New York & Colorado Mining Syndicate v. Fraser, 1889, 130 U.S. 611, 620, 9 S.Ct. 665, 32 L.Ed. 1031. And the testimony should be received if it is capable of a reasonably satisfactory evaluation. Undoubtedly, the nature of the writing which the witness says is effective to stimulate his memory plays a part in that evaluation, and the dangers from deficiencies in the witness' testimonial qualifications are not less susceptible of evaluation by the trier of fact than in the case of past perception recorded; indeed, they are more readily subject to test for the witness, as already noted, asserts a present memory and cannot gain protection from a denial of the very memory which he claims to have.

Of course, the categories, present recollection revived and past recollection recorded, are clearest in their extremes, but they are, in practice, converging rather than parallel lines; the difference is frequently one of degree. Moreover, it is in complication thereof that a cooperative witness, yielding to suggestion, deceives himself, that a hostile witness seizes an opportunity, or that a writing is used to convey an improper suggestion. Circumstances, or the nature of the testimony, may belie an assertion of present memory; more often the credibility of the witness generally, and the cross-examiner's attack upon the reliability of his memory, will decide the claim to an independent recollection.

Properly, the burden to ascertain the state of affairs, as near as may be, devolves upon the trial judge, who should in the first instance satisfy himself as to whether the witness testifies upon a record or from his own recollection. It is upon this satisfaction that the reception of the evidence depends, for if it appear to the court that the witness is wholly dependent for the fact upon the memorandum he holds in his hand, the memorandum acquires a significance which, as stated, brings into operation certain guiding rules. Similarly, the trial judge must determine whether the device of refreshing recollection is merely a subterfuge to improperly suggest to the witness the testimony expected of him. It is axiomatic, particularly with respect to the reception of evidence, that much depends upon the discretion of the trial judge. * * *

In the instant case, the learned trial judge determined that both Farid and the expert, Berlow, testified from present recollection. On the record, we cannot say that it was plainly not so. Both witnesses stated that they knew the chattels and could identify them. Farid, who testified that she was present and helped to pack them, said she could remember which were transported; Berlow said he could give an opinion of their value. On a number of occasions the trial judge investigated the foundations of their claim to present recollection and satisfied himself as to its bona fides. The case is, therefore, distinguishable from Jewett v. United States, supra, wherein it was held that the witness had no independent recollection, and from Delaney v. United States, supra, where the Court concluded that the witness did no more than read from a photostatic copy. While the defendant asserts that neither Farid nor Berlow did more, the trial judge immediately recognized that the items of property involved were so numerous that in the ordinary course of events no one would be expected to recite them without having learned a list by rote memory. On the other hand, the items were such that a person familiar with them reasonably could be expected to recognize them and tell what he knows. Under these circumstances, the District Judge might well have permitted the government, in lieu of the procedure followed, to ask Farid leading questions, directing her attention to specific items, and asking her whether she knew what happened to them. This is especially true of Berlow, who did not purport to have any knowledge of the movement of the articles. Clearly, it would have been pointless to ask him to give the value of every article he had ever seen in Farid's home. The same result could have been achieved legitimately without the use of the lists by orally directing his attention to any specific article previously identified by Farid and asking him whether he had seen it, presently remembered it, and could give an opinion as to its value. By the use of lists, nothing more or different was accomplished.

Moreover, we think the procedure followed lay within the discretion of the trial court, and that no prejudicial error ensued. The evidence was capable of a reasonably satisfactory evaluation and was receivable for what it was worth. In the long run, the primary issue of the case was that of credibility, and it is sufficient that the jury had as sound a basis for weighing the testimony as it would in any other instance. The defense had at its disposal the customary opportunities and all the necessary material to test the witness' recollection and other testimonial qualifications, including the single original longhand list which Farid located, the typewritten lists which she said were made at the time of the events involved, and the lists the prosecution used. It might very well have put Farid through severe cross-examination with respect to each chattel she identified on direct examination, but chose instead to attack the reliability of her memory by other means.

Accordingly, it is our conclusion that the learned trial judge did not abuse his discretion, either in determining that the witnesses testified from present recollection, or in permitting the use of the lists described herein.

* * *

For the reasons stated, the judgment of the District Court will be affirmed.

S & A PAINTING CO. v. O.W.B. CORP., 103 F.R.D. 407 (W.D.Pa. 1984). "(3) Defendants deposed Nick S. Frangopoulos on March 6, 1984. During the course of the deposition, Frangopoulos referred to 24 pages of handwritten notes, prepared earlier at the request of counsel, setting forth the events relevant to this litigation. The parties dispute the frequency of the deponent's reference to notes.

"(4) The transcript establishes that Frangopoulos examined the notes three times in order to ascertain dates and read from the notes on one occasion. Defendants seek production of the entire document pursuant to Federal Rule of Evidence 612.

"(5) Plaintiff contends that the attorney-client privilege protects the notes from disclosure. * * * Rule 612(1) applies even though Frangopoulos testified at a deposition, not a trial. Fed.R.Civ.P. 30(c).

"(6) The attorney-client privilege is applicable to the notes in question because they constitute a communication from the client to his lawyer which both expected to be confidential. See Upjohn v. United States, 449 U.S. 383, 101 S.Ct. 677, 66 L.Ed.2d 584 (1981). Moreover, the notes fall within the work-product doctrine as embodied in Fed. R.Civ.P. 26(b)(3) because they were prepared 'in anticipation of litigation' for the attorney for S & A Painting Co., the party's representative under the Rule. * * *

"(7) The issue here is whether Frangopoulos, by referring to his notes during the deposition, waived the attorney-client privilege and work-product protection for all or part of the document. We hold that a waiver occurred as to those portions of the notes to which reference was made, but that the bulk of the notes are protected from disclosure.

"(8) Confronted with the conflict between the command of Rule 612 to disclose materials used to refresh recollection and the protections afforded by the attorney-client privilege and the work-product doctrine, the weight of authority holds that the privilege and protections are waived. James Julian, Inc. v. Raytheon Co., 93 F.R.D. 138 (D.Del.1982) (work-product protection waived); Marshall v. United States Postal Service, 88 F.R.D. 348, 350 (D.D.C.1980) (attorney-client privilege waived); Wheeling–Pittsburgh Steel Corp. v. Underwriters Laboratories, Inc., 81 F.R.D. 8, 9 (N.D.Ill.1978) (attorney-client privilege waived); Bailey v. Meister–Brau, Inc., 57 F.R.D. 11, 13 (N.D.Ill.1972) (attorney-client privilege and work-product protection waived). Given the lack of discretion of Fed.R.Evid. 612(1), applicable here, as compared with Fed.R.Evid. 612(2), we conclude that disclosure is required of those parts of the notes to which reference was made.

"(9) Defendants assert that we must order disclosure of the entire 24–page document. While such broad disclosure has been ordered when deponents reviewed entire files prior to testifying, defendants cite no case in which production was ordered of the entire material separate from those portions actually examined while testifying. * * *

* * *

"(13) The purposes of disclosure under Rule 612 are to test the credibility of a witness's claim that memory has been revived and to expose any discrepancies between the writing and the testimony. McCormick, *Evidence* § 9 at 17 (1972). Both purposes are served by ordering disclosure of only those portions of the document actually used to refresh recollection. A witness cannot be improperly "prompted" by material that he has not examined. Discrepancies may exist between refreshed testimony and portions of documents not referred to during testimony. But Rule 612 is not a mechanism for uncovering all prior inconsistent statements of a witness. Statements of a witness, inconsistent with testimony or not, which have not been used to refresh recollection are simply irrelevant for purposes of Rule 612.

"(14) Rule 612 authorizes a court to excise portions of the writing which are not related to the subject matter of the testimony. Considering the policies and authorities rehearsed, we do not interpret 'testimony' to mean the entire testimony of a witness during a deposition or trial. Instead, we believe that 'testimony' should be interpreted to mean only testimony which was refreshed by the writing. Our interpretation prevents the unfairness which would result from broad disclosure merely because other parts of the writing, not used to refresh recollection, may coincide with other parts of the deponent's or witness's testimony.

"(15) We will order that plaintiff produce a copy of the 24-page set of handwritten notes for *in camera* inspection. We will then order disclosure of all portions of the notes to which Frangopoulos referred during the deposition as established by the transcript. Fed.R.Civ.P. 37(a)."

SECTION 5. CALLING AND INTERROGATION OF WITNESSES BY COURT *

[FED.R.EVID. 614]

UNITED STATES v. KARNES

United States Court of Appeals, Fourth Circuit, 1976.
531 F.2d 214.

WINTER, CIRCUIT JUDGE:

After the jury was unable to agree upon a verdict and was discharged at his first trial, Robert Lee Karnes was tried a second time and convicted by a jury of concealing a motor vehicle moving as, or which is part of, or which constitutes interstate or foreign commerce, knowing the vehicle to have been stolen, in violation of 18 U.S.C. § 2313 (1970). Karnes has appealed, asserting as grounds of reversible error that the district court * * * (b) improperly called as court witnesses two witnesses whose testimony was essential to the government's case * * *.

We conclude that defendant's contention with respect to the court witnesses is of sufficient merit to reverse and grant a new trial. * * *

I.

The somewhat complex facts need not be recited because in oral argument the government conceded that it had no case against Karnes without the testimony of the co-defendant, Fred Cassity, and Cassity's wife. At the bench, the government represented that it would not call them as its witnesses because they previously had made conflicting statements and had withheld information and the government could not therefore vouch for their candor. The district court then called the Cassitys as its own witnesses and in accordance with usual practice permitted both sides to cross-examine them. Fred Cassity was also questioned by the court to permit him to identify a witness who testified about an incident which was a crucial part of the chain of proof. The district court made no statement to the jury in explanation of why these two witnesses were called as its own.

* See 3 Wigmore, Evidence §§ 784, 784a (Chadbourn rev. 1970); 9 id. § 2484 (Chadbourn rev. 1981); McCormick, Evidence § 8 (4th ed. 1992); Saltzburg, The Unnecessarily Expanding Role of the American Trial Judge, 64 Va.L.Rev. 1 (1978).

II.

We agree with the parties that ordinarily the utilization of court witnesses is a matter within the discretion of the trial judge. The leading texts, supported by a plethora of precedents, support the rule. *See* McCormick on Evidence § 8 (1972); 9 Wigmore on Evidence § 2484 (1940). The power to call and to interrogate court witnesses is said to be derived from the judicial system's basic functions of disclosing truth and administering justice.[1] Indeed, the rule is codified in Rule 614 of the new Federal Rules of Evidence, although that rule was not in effect at the time of Karnes' prosecution.

A trial judge is not captive within the case as made by the parties.[2] He has the authority, if not the duty, to call witnesses who possess relevant information affecting the outcome of the issues when the parties decline to call them. But the due process clause requires that a court be impartial.[3] This impartiality is destroyed when the court assumes the role of prosecutor and undertakes to produce evidence, *essential* to overcome the defendant's presumption of innocence, which the government has declined to present. Further, in this case the jury was never told why the witnesses were called as court witnesses and the jury was not instructed that these witnesses were entitled to no greater credibility because they had been called by the court. The jury, thus, may well have afforded them greater credibility than if they had been called as government witnesses. The jury's determination of credibility of witnesses may therefore have been unfairly, albeit unintentionally, influenced and the government's case thereby strengthened.

We have no doubt that, failing to appreciate that the government could not prove its case without them, the district court's motive in calling the witnesses was to get at the truth and to enable the government to cross-examine and perhaps to impeach them with regard to any testimony unfavorable to the government which was inconsist-

1. McCormick, *supra*, p. 12:

Under the Anglo–American adversary trial system, the parties and their counsel have the primary responsibility for finding, selecting, and presenting the evidence. However, our system of party-investigation and party-presentation has some limitations. It is a means to the end of disclosing truth and administering justice; and for reaching this end the judge may exercise various powers.

Prominent among these powers is his power to call and question witnesses.

The judge in his discretion may examine any witness to bring out needed facts which have not been elicited by the parties. Also, it is sometimes said that the judge may have a duty to question witnesses, although the exercise of such a duty does not appear to have been enforced by any appellate court decisions (footnotes omitted).

2. See Advisory Committee's Note to subdivision (a), Rule 614, Fed.R.Ev.

3. With respect to the manner of a court's interrogation of witnesses called by it, the Advisory Committee's note to subdivision (b), Rule 614, Fed.R.Ev., states: "The authority of the judge to question witnesses is * * * well established * * *. The authority is, of course, abused when the judge abandons his proper role and assumes that of advocate * * *." We see no abuse in the form of the district court's questions to Cassity, but we think that when the court called witnesses essential to the government's case whom the government declined to call, there was an analogous abuse.

ent with their prior statements. But the same result could have been achieved by an accepted means. The government must, of course, use its witnesses as it finds them. In many cases the prosecution must depend upon the testimony of persons who are co-defendants, co-conspirators, felons, accomplices, etc., and such witnesses often evidence hostility, are impeachable from their past or current activities, or change or slant their testimony from what, based upon prior statements, the government expects them to say. Under such circumstances, a district judge may afford wide latitude to the government to lead, to cross-examine, and partially to impeach such witnesses. Illustrative of current practice is Rule 607, Fed.R.Ev., which states flatly "[t]he credibility of a witness may be attacked by any party, including the party calling him." *See also St. Clair v. United States,* 154 U.S. 134, 150, 14 S.Ct. 1002 (1894); *United States v. Baldivid,* 465 F.2d 1277, 1279 (4 Cir.), cert. denied, 409 U.S. 1047, 93 S.Ct. 519, 34 L.Ed.2d 499 (1972); *United States v. Stubin,* 446 F.2d 457, 463 (3 Cir.1971); *United States v. Holsey,* 414 F.2d 458, 461 (10 Cir.1969).

Finally, we are not persuaded to a contrary view by *United States v. Wilson,* 361 F.2d 134 (7 Cir.1966), and *Smith v. United States,* 331 F.2d 265 (8 Cir.1964), on which the government relies for affirmance. In both cases, the propriety of the court's calling a witness in a criminal case who gave testimony unfavorable to the defendant was sustained. But in *Wilson,* the witness was not called until the government had closed its case and made a *prima facie* showing of defendant's guilt. Moreover, the testimony was taken out of the presence of the jury and, at the instance of the defendant, it was not revealed to the jury. In *Smith,* although the government had not closed its case before the witness was called, it is clear that the government had proved a case before the witness was called. We disagree with the result in neither case, but we do not think that either is in point here. Our holding is confined to an instance where the government's case would be insufficient as a matter of law without the court witnesses. Neither *Wilson* nor *Smith* arose in that context.

* * *

Reversed; new trial granted.

WIDENER, CIRCUIT JUDGE (concurring):

I

I concur in the result reached by Judge Winter in part II of his opinion and in much of that part of the opinion, but in some respects my reasoning differs.

I decline to base reversal on the already overworked due process clause but rather would base it solely on the too great departure of the trial judge from his historic dispassionate role. After all, the burden of the production of evidence is on the United States, not upon the defendant, and certainly not upon the court. I would classify the error solely as one of federal criminal procedure.

The dissent of Judge Russell accentuates my thoughts on this matter as he recites that it is no more the duty of a trial judge to permit a guilty defendant to escape because of the reluctance of a prosecutor to call a material and available witness than to stand idly by and let an innocent defendant be convicted because of the hesitancy of defendant's counsel to call a witness. If I thought for even one second that, should a defendant's attorney move the court to call an available witness, explaining that he would not call the witness because the witness had made conflicting statements and he could not vouch for the witness' credibility, and should the motion be denied, this court would hold it reversible error, I would vote to affirm on this point. But I cannot imagine such a result and accordingly vote to reverse, because evenhanded justice is equally or more important than the substance of an applicable rule.

* * *

III

I do not share the apparent apprehension of Judge Russell that we have departed from precedent or that our opinion should in any way inhibit the calling of a witness by the court in the ordinary case. My view of this case is predicated in no small part on the fact that, in this criminal trial, the court called the witness at the instance of the United States having previously been advised that the government would not call him.

* * *

DONALD RUSSELL, CIRCUIT JUDGE (dissenting):

I concur fully in all the opinion of Judge Winter herein, except for the finding that the trial court committed error in calling as court's witnesses Fred Cassity and his wife.

While the opinion freely concedes that all the authorities affirm unequivocally the right of the trial judge to call as a court witness any available person or persons possessing relevant testimony, especially if the government or the defendant is unwilling or hesitant to call the person as a witness, it would justify departure from that rule in this case for two reasons, neither of which finds support either in the authorities or, I respectfully suggest, in reason. The first reason for departing from the rule is that the trial judge assumed "the role of prosecutor and [undertook] to produce evidence necessary to overcome the defendant's presumption of innocence." Certainly, the opinion cannot mean that by merely calling a person as a court's witness the trial judge assumes the improper "role of prosecutor." If this were true, the trial judge would be prohibited in all instances from calling a person as a court witness. It is the added qualification that the "evidence of the witnesses" is necessary to the Government's case and makes it impermissible under this reasoning for the court to call the witnesses as court witnesses.

I, however, fail to see why the importance of the witness' testimony is determinative of the right of the trial judge to call him or her as a witness. The very importance of the testimony provides its own justification for the action of the trial judge. There is no real warrant for the trial court to call as a court's witness a person whose testimony lacks special relevancy; the power should not be exercised in order merely to add to the record evidence that at best is peripherally pertinent. But when, as here, there are persons whose testimony, if believed by the jury, could either lead to the defendant's conviction or could go far to absolve the defendant, the trial judge has both a right and a duty, if the Government refused to call the persons, to have them sworn as court witnesses. The trial judge does not abandon his role of required impartiality in the case merely by calling as a court witness one whose testimony is vital but whom the Government or the defendant, for some reason, is reluctant to call. This, I am sure, is a rule that the majority would accept if the witness could supply an essential link in the defense. The same rule should follow when the witness is vital to the Government's case. After all, the trial judge has a responsibility to society and the public. Courts must never forget that the function of the criminal court is as much to shield "the public from criminal behavior" as it is to protect the innocent defendant from undeserved punishment. *Cf., United States Ex Rel. Selikoff v. Com. of Corr.* (2d Cir.1975) 524 F.2d 650, 654. Unfortunately, this double obligation is too often forgotten and too frequently courts conceive of their function simply as the guardians of a defendant's rights and not as the protector of the public itself from crime. I do not conceive it any more the duty of a trial judge to permit a guilty defendant to escape because of the reluctance of a prosecutor to call a material witness available to him than to stand idly by and let an innocent defendant be convicted because of the hesitancy of defendant's counsel to call the witness.

The second reason assigned in the opinion is that the trial judge did not advise the jury "why the witnesses were called as court witnesses" and that they "were entitled to no greater credibility because they had been called by the court." Perhaps in the ordinary case, the rule suggested in the opinion is the proper one. There was no necessity for such advice in this case and the failure to give it, if error, was harmless beyond a reasonable doubt. The prosecutor stated in open court that he was unwilling to call the witnesses because he would not vouch for their credibility. The Government itself thereby cast a heavy shadow over the reliability of their testimony. Anything that the trial judge could have added after that would have been superfluous.

I submit the action of the trial judge was entirely proper. He did no more than his duty.

UNITED STATES v. MAZZILLI

United States Court of Appeals, Second Circuit, 1988.
848 F.2d 384.

ALTIMARI, CIRCUIT JUDGE:

Defendant-appellant Paul Mazzilli appeals from a judgment of conviction entered in the United States District Court for the Eastern District of New York. After a three day jury trial, Mazzilli was convicted of receiving stolen property in violation of 18 U.S.C. § 2315, possession of stolen property in violation of 18 U.S.C. § 659, and conspiracy to possess and distribute stolen property in violation of 18 U.S.C. § 371. Thereafter, he was sentenced to concurrent five-year terms of imprisonment on each count, of which four and one-half years were suspended, concurrent five-year terms of probation and was ordered to pay an aggregate $25,000 fine, a special assessment of $50.00 on each count, and to make restitution. Execution of the sentence was stayed pending appeal.

On appeal, Mazzilli presents several arguments in support of his contention that he was denied a fair trial. In particular, Mazzilli claims that the district court's intensive questioning while he testified caused the jury to conclude that the court disbelieved his account of the facts and swayed the jury's views during its deliberations.[1] In addition, Mazzilli points out that the court inquired into prejudicial, collateral matters during its questioning of him and he argues that, because the government's attorney would have been prohibited from inquiring into these matters, the district court erred in doing so. Because we conclude that the district court's intensive questioning of Mazzilli denied him a fair trial, we reverse.

BACKGROUND

The instant case arose out of the theft of a shipment of various electronic products and electronic children's games. On November 7, 1986, two tractor-trailers containing 500 Soundesign television sets, 3,408 Soundesign telephones and 1,428 Entertech Photon Warrior games were stolen from a truck yard located in New Brunswick, New Jersey. Shortly thereafter, the stolen merchandise surfaced in Brooklyn, New York. On November 19, 1986, FBI agents who were investigating the theft seized 284 of the stolen televisions and 411 of the stolen games from the home of defendant-appellant Paul Mazzilli. On the same day, government agents also seized 3,188 of the stolen telephones from Albert Baker, who owned a Brooklyn, New York wholesale video

1. We observe that defendant did not raise an objection at trial to the questions posed by the district court, and apparently sought no curative instructions. We also note that the government does not argue here that Mazzilli's challenge was not properly preserved for appeal. Because the government has failed to raise this issue on appeal and because we conclude that the district court's conduct was such that it prejudiced Mazzilli's fair trial rights, we conclude that it is appropriate to address the merits of this claim.

equipment outlet. On November 24, 1986, Mazzilli was arrested and charged with possession of the stolen merchandise.

At trial, Baker, who cooperated with the government in Mazzilli's prosecution, testified that on November 12, 1986 he was approached by an acquaintance named Joey who offered to sell him Photon Warrior games. The games normally sell for between $59 and $69 per game, but Joey offered them to Baker for between $35 and $45 each. Joey accounted for the low price by explaining that, although the games had been ordered for a North Carolina store, they were part of an "overage of a shipment" and had been "refused." Baker bought 800 games for a total cost of $30,000. Baker explained, however, that Joey wanted to be paid in cash and would not provide him with an invoice or bill of lading for the goods. Although Baker initially did not suspect that the merchandise he purchased from Joey was stolen, the cash terms and the lack of invoices led him to believe that the games were stolen.

Subsequently, on November 18, having sold the first shipment of games, Baker sought to buy more, but Joey did not have any to sell. Joey then asked Baker to "store" some Soundesign telephones for ten days as a "favor," and stated that "[i]f you can't sell them, I'll take them back from you and I'll give you a dollar to store and to handle each one." The next day two FBI agents visited Baker's store and seized the telephones. The agents then asked Baker whether he had information regarding Soundesign television sets. Baker told the agents that "they [the television sets] were on the streets and * * * [that] there [was] other stuff on the streets." He explained that he believed that this merchandise was stolen. He also told the agents that Mazzilli had offered to sell him some television sets but that he was not interested.

In addition to Baker's testimony, the government's case against Mazzilli included the testimony of the two FBI agents, Andy Conlin and Colleen Nichols, who had seized the Soundesign television sets from Mazzilli's home. Agent Nichols explained that after she and Agent Conlin had identified themselves and had explained to Mazzilli that they were looking for merchandise that had been stolen, Mazzilli directed them to his basement where he had stored the television sets. Agent Nichols testified that Mazzilli then approached her and sought to make a "deal" with the agents.

To rebut the government's case, Mazzilli testified on his own behalf. Mazzilli described himself as an inexperienced businessman who ran a small videocassette rental store in Brooklyn, New York. He stated that he was on a first-name basis with most of his customers, who largely were from the same neighborhood. Mazzilli explained that Joey, with whom he was acquainted, offered to sell him some Soundesign television sets, providing that he could return any unsold televisions in 30 days time and pay for only those sets which he had actually sold. He purchased 325 Soundesign television sets from Joey at $62 each and he resold them for $129, almost invariably for cash and without issuing a receipt. To counter the inference that, when he received the discounted merchandise, he should have known it was stolen, Mazzilli explained that, due to his inexperience, he simply thought he was getting a good deal on "overage" merchandise, which is commonly sold at deep discount throughout New York City. Mazzilli also challenged Agent Nichols' account of the conversation in which he allegedly sought a deal.

During the course of Mazzilli's testimony, the district court interrupted on several occasions to ask questions. At one point during cross-examination, while the government's attorney was attempting to impeach Mazzilli's testimony regarding his lack of knowledge that the goods were stolen, the district court intervened to ask questions regarding his transaction with Joey:

THE COURT: Let me see if I understand, on these terms. They were net 30 or open. So that you either paid him within 30 days or you could return the unsold balance and just pay for what you sold?

[MAZZILLI]: Right.

THE COURT: All of these items?

[MAZZILLI]: Yes.

THE COURT: And there-he didn't require you to put any money down?

[MAZZILLI]: No.

THE COURT: Nothing?

[MAZZILLI]: No.

THE COURT: He just brought them and put them in your cellar?

[MAZZILLI]: Yes.

THE COURT: Is that the way the invoice reads from Global?

[MAZZILLI]: I don't remember. Probably says net on it. Probably net 30.

THE COURT: Didn't say anything open?

[MAZZILLI]: I don't know. I'm pretty sure it said net 30.

THE COURT: It didn't say anything about open and right to return?

[MAZZILLI]: No. That's normal.

THE COURT: That's normal? That's the way all your customers do it?

[MAZZILLI]: All my distributors, sure. If I take a large delivery and I can't sell them, I can return them. Otherwise I won't take—

THE COURT: It doesn't say anything on the Global, though?

[MAZZILLI]: Doesn't say it's net 30?

THE COURT: Doesn't say anything about right to return.

[MAZZILLI]: That's normal. Normal on net 30, as long as I have been in business. I have always been able to return what was unsold.

After this exchange, the government's attorney proceeded with his cross-examination, asking a few more questions, when the district court again intervened:

THE COURT: You have a record of these sales that you made of 41 TVs and 39 toys?

[MAZZILLI]: The fact that they were sold, yes.

THE COURT: No. You have a record of the individual sales that you made?

[MAZZILLI]: Sure.

THE COURT: His question is, did you search for the records of those sales?

[MAZZILLI]: No. Have I searched for them, no.

THE COURT: No.

[AUSA]: So you haven't gone through Precision Video's records to look for records about any sales you made of these TVs or toys, is that right?

[MAZZILLI]: Just the one with the Master Charge.

THE COURT: Is that Global invoice read to—it is addressed to you? Paul Precision?

[MAZZILLI]: I don't remember. I don't have it here.

* * *

THE COURT: Did they call you up and ask you to return this merchandise after the 30 days were up?

[MAZZILLI]: Someone did contact me in reference to the thing after I was arrested.

THE COURT: They did?

[MAZZILLI]: Yes.

THE COURT: You got his name?

[MAZZILLI]: Yes. His name is Joe.

THE COURT: Joe?

[MAZZILLI]: Joe.

THE COURT: The same Joey?

[MAZZILLI]: At this time the same Joey. But I told him I couldn't say anything about it because of my attorney's request.

THE COURT: You didn't say to Joey, listen, those are hot goods?

[MAZZILLI]: Joey never said that.

THE COURT: You didn't say that to Joey?

[MAZZILLI]: No.

THE COURT: You didn't?

[MAZZILLI]: My attorney advised me not to talk about the case.

THE COURT: Wait a minute. This guy had just sold you and got you in all this trouble for some $30,000 worth of hot goods and you never said, hey listen, that stuff you sold—you sold to me was hot?

[MAZZILLI]: I never said that to him.

THE COURT: He called you up?

[MAZZILLI]: Yes.

THE COURT: Did you ask him where he was?

[MAZZILLI]: No.

THE COURT: You didn't ask him for his last name either at that point?

[MAZZILLI]: No.

THE COURT: Or his address?

[MAZZILLI]: No.

On other occasions, the district court questioned Mazzilli on the fact that he had sold all the television sets for cash and about various inadequacies in the invoices he received for the merchandise. In addition, the district court returned to the point made earlier regarding the fact that Mazzilli did not immediately contact Joey after the FBI agents seized the television sets:

THE COURT: When you found out from the agent these were stolen and eight days later I think you told us you found this invoice, did you attempt to locate the location of where Global was?

[MAZZILLI]: No, I didn't. I called my attorney.

THE COURT: You never looked up in a phone book or anything like that?

[MAZZILLI]: No.

THE COURT: No. When Joey called you, you didn't say where is Global located?

[MAZZILLI]: No.

THE COURT: Okay.

The court in its questioning returned to Mazzilli's failure to contact Joey during three other exchanges, each subsequent colloquy essentially repeating the same line of inquiry.

The court did not limit its intervention to cross-examination. While Mazzilli testified on direct examination and after he disputed Agent Nichols' account of the circumstances surrounding his alleged offer to make a deal, the district court interrupted:

THE COURT: Wait a minute. You heard—you saw the demonstration that was put on here when Ms. Nichols described what happened where she was standing right alongside of him. As you recollect it, as I understand it, he was—

[MAZZILLI]: He was not next to her.

THE COURT: She made that up?

[MAZZILLI]: That is correct.

THE COURT: All right.

[MAZZILLI]: Or she was mistaken.

THE COURT: Just mistaken?

[MAZZILLI]: One or the other.

DISCUSSION

Mazzilli contends on this appeal that the district court's conduct denied him a fair trial. He asserts that because the sole issue at trial was whether he knew that the merchandise he possessed was stolen, the jury's evaluation of his credibility was critical to his defense that he lacked such knowledge. He argues that the court's intensive questioning while he testified communicated to the jury its impression that his testimony was unworthy of belief. In addition, Mazzilli argues that the district court's instruction—telling the jury not to be swayed by the court's questions—did not mitigate the adverse impact of its active intervention. We agree.

A district court's role at the trial "is not restricted to that of a mere umpire or referee," *United States v. DiTommaso,* 817 F.2d 201, 221 (2d Cir.1987); "a trial judge need not sit like 'a bump on a log' throughout the trial." *United States v. Pisani,* 773 F.2d 397, 403 (2d Cir.1985). In recognition of the fact that the district court bears the responsibility for insuring that the facts in each case are presented to the jury in a clear and straightforward manner, we have consistently held that " 'the questioning of witnesses by a trial judge, if for a proper purpose such as clarifying ambiguities, correcting misstatements, or obtaining information needed to make rulings, is well within' the court's 'active responsibility to insure that issues clearly are presented to the jury.' " *United States v. Victoria,* 837 F.2d 50, 54 (2d Cir.1988) (quoting *Pisani,* 773 F.2d at 403); *see United States v. Nazzaro,* 472 F.2d 302, 313 (2d Cir.1973).

Fundamental to the right to a fair trial, however, is that the court's responsibility to assist the jury in understanding the evidence should not be so zealously pursued as to give the impression to the jury that the judge believes one version of the evidence and disbelieves or doubts another. *See Victoria,* 837 F.2d at 55, *Nazzaro,* 472 F.2d at 303. While it is unquestionably proper for the government to seek to impeach a defendant's testimony, this is not a proper function of the court for it must at all times maintain the appearance of impartiality and detachment. *See Nazzaro,* 472 F.2d at 313.

In the instant case, Mazzilli relied almost exclusively on his own testimony at trial to rebut the government's case. The jury's evaluation of Mazzilli's credibility therefore was critical to its determination of his guilt or innocence. Indeed, because the government lacked direct evidence to tie Mazzilli to the thefts, and because Mazzilli had an explanation for nearly every piece of circumstantial evidence offered against him, the government necessarily had to discredit Mazzilli's testimony through impeachment. Where, as here, the defendant's credibility is crucial to his defense, a jury's impression that the court disbelieves his testimony surely affects its deliberations. The jury cannot be regarded as having freely come to its own conclusions about the defendant's credibility when the court has already indicated, directly or indirectly, that it disbelieves his testimony.

The record demonstrates that the district court played an overly intrusive role during Mazzilli's testimony. Through its questions, the district court imparted a message of skepticism to the jury and seemingly invited the jury to infer that Mazzilli possessed knowledge that the merchandise was stolen. It was up to the government to establish Mazzilli's knowledge beyond a reasonable doubt and not to be assisted by the court's questioning. The court's questioning left the jury with the indelible impression that the court did not believe Mazzilli's account of the facts. This was error.

As a separate matter, we observe that the district court asked Mazzilli to characterize Agent Nichols' testimony. We have held that it is improper for a court to require a witness to characterize the testimony of a government agent as a lie. *See Victoria,* 837 F.2d at 55; *cf. United States v. Richter,* 826 F.2d 206, 208 (2d Cir.1987). Although this alone would not necessarily merit reversal, because the determination of whether to believe the agent's testimony or Mazzilli's is left to the jury alone, we find that the court's questions in this regard were also improper. *See Victoria,* 837 F.2d at 55.

We note that the district court instructed the jury not to infer anything from its questions posed to Mazzilli. We nevertheless conclude that on this record the court's instruction could not have adequately mitigated the harm caused by its vigorous and extensive questioning.

Conclusion

It is always difficult to evaluate a claim that specific conduct of the district court denied a defendant of a fair trial. In these cases, our review can only be guided by the cold black and white of the printed record. From the record, it is difficult to gleen tone of voice, whether sarcastic or neutral, facial expression, whether reflecting disbelief or sober thoughtfulness, or physical demeanor, whether self-contained or expressing opinion and emotion. Therefore, it is only after an examination of the entire record that we can come to a conclusion about the conduct of the district court.

Having conducted such a review, we conclude that the district court exceeded its proper bounds by assuming the role of advocate to undermine Mazzilli's credibility. We find, therefore, that the court's prejudicial questioning and its compelling Mazzilli to characterize the agent's testimony resulted in denying him a fair trial. Accordingly, we reverse the judgment of conviction entered against Mazzilli and remand for a new trial.

UNITED STATES v. VEGA, 589 F.2d 1147, 1153 (2d Cir.1978). "The argument that trial counsel's failure to object at trial might be due to timidity or fear of antagonizing the judge totally overlooks Fed.R.Evid. 614(c), which provides that objections to the interrogation of witnesses by the court are to 'be made at the time or at the next available opportunity when the jury is not present.' The original draft of rule 614 retained an automatic objection until the conclusion of the trial. 3 Weinstein's Evidence ¶ 614[04] at 614–15. However, this draft was criticized as 'unrealistic and impractical' by The Committee of New York Trial Lawyers which noted: 'Judges are not so sensitive that counsel should be reluctant to make a proper objection merely because the question came from the bench.' Id. Thus the present language of Fed.R.Evid. 614(c), recommended by the American College of Trial Lawyers Committee, id. at n. 1, was adopted in place of the preliminary draft's automatic objection."

DEBENEDETTO v. GOODYEAR TIRE & RUBBER CO.

United States Court of Appeals, Fourth Circuit, 1985.
754 F.2d 512.

MICHAEL, DISTRICT JUDGE:

Deborah Samluck Drier and Melissa E. DeBenedetto (by her guardian ad Litem, Frances DeBenedetto) appeal from the jury verdict in favor of the defendant Goodyear Tire & Rubber Company (Goodyear) in these consolidated product liability cases. Appellants assert that the trial court committed three reversible errors in the conduct of the trial: * * * (2) allowing the jurors to question witnesses during the trial * * *. Despite the reservations stated herein about the practice of allowing questions by jurors, we find no reversible error.

* * *

The second assignment of error is based on the trial court's decision allowing jurors to question witnesses.[1] Appellants maintain that since

1. In his opening comments to the jury, the trial judge expounded his policy of permitting questions by jurors. After counsel completed their examination of a witness, the court allowed jurors to direct questions to the bench. If the trial judge deemed the question proper, he instructed the witness to answer it. Counsel were given the op-

the Federal Rules of Evidence do not explicitly permit this practice, it is error for a trial court to permit it.

First, as an important point in the ultimate decision on this issue, we note that appellants did not object during the trial either to the policy of allowing questions by jurors or to any specific juror question. Appellants indicate that they did not object because they did not want to risk alienating the jury. This argument has some merit with regard to objections to a specific question. However, counsel certainly must have had opportunities during a three-week trial to object and to put on the record—outside the presence of the jury—their objection to an individual question or to the entire practice of juror questioning. Where there is no objection in trial below, this court ordinarily does not consider the issue. Nevertheless, because of the way we view this matter, we address the merits of this issue.

The Federal Rules of Evidence neither explicitly allow nor disallow the practice of permitting jurors to question witnesses. The only guidance to be found is in Fed.R.Evid. 611(a) which instructs the court to "exercise reasonable control over the mode and order of interrogating witnesses * * *." Those courts considering the propriety of juror questions have concluded that it is a matter within the discretion of the trial judge. *See, e.g., United States v. Callahan,* 588 F.2d 1078 (5th Cir.), *cert. denied,* 444 U.S. 826, 100 S.Ct. 49, 62 L.Ed.2d 33 (1979); *United States v. Witt,* 215 F.2d 580 (2d Cir.), *cert. denied,* 348 U.S. 887, 75 S.Ct. 207, 99 L.Ed. 697 (1954). In *Callahan,* the court advised the jury, before opening statements, that it would permit jurors to submit in writing to the court any question a juror might wish to put to a witness, and, if not legally improper, the judge would put the question to the witness. Only one question from a juror was thus submitted; this question was "relatively innocuous and could have had no measurable impact on the outcome". 588 F.2d at 1086. In *Witt,* the opinion recites only that: "During the trial, some of the jurors, with the judge's consent, put questions to witnesses and received answers. We think that a matter within the judge's discretion like witness-questioning by the judge himself, * * *." 215 F.2d at 584. The brevity of the treatment of the point in the *Witt* opinion may well indicate that the appellate court considered the questions to be of the same "relatively innocuous" character as the questions in *Callahan.*

While we agree that allowing juror questions is a matter within the discretion of the trial court, we do not agree that such questions are analogous to or even comparable to questioning of witnesses by the judge. Suffice it to say that the judge is not "an umpire or * * * moderator at a town meeting," but he sits "to see that justice is done in the cases heard before him." *United States v. Rosenberg,* 195 F.2d 583, 594 (2d Cir.), *cert. denied,* 344 U.S. 838, 73 S.Ct. 20, 97 L.Ed. 652 (1952), quoting *Simon v. United States,* 123 F.2d 80, 83 (4th Cir.), *cert. denied,* 314 U.S. 694, 62 S.Ct. 412, 86 L.Ed. 555 (1941). One simply cannot

portunity to re-question each witness after all inquiries from the jury were resolved.

compare the questioning by the trial judge—who is trained in the law and instructed to "see that justice is done"—with the questioning by members of the jury—who are untutored in the law, and instructed to sit as a neutral fact-finding body. Thus, we believe that juror questioning and questioning by the trial judge are clearly and properly distinguishable, although both forms of questioning are matters within the trial court's discretion.

Notwithstanding our belief that juror questioning is a matter within the trial court's discretion, we believe that the practice of juror questioning is fraught with dangers which can undermine the orderly progress of the trial to verdict. Our judicial system is founded upon the presence of a body constituted as a neutral factfinder to discern the truth from the positions presented by the adverse parties. The law of evidence has as its purpose the provision of a set of rules by which only relevant and admissible evidence is put before that neutral factfinder. Individuals not trained in the law cannot be expected to know and understand what is legally relevant, and perhaps more importantly, what is legally admissible.

Since jurors generally are not trained in the law, the potential risk that a juror question will be improper or prejudicial is simply greater than a trial court should take, absent such compelling circumstances as will justify the exercise of that judicial discretion set out above.

While the procedure utilized in the trial below permitted screening of the questions before an answer was given, the statement of the question itself was in the hearing of the other jurors, bringing with it the unknown, and perhaps unknowable, mental reactions of those other jurors. In the case where such a question is rejected, not only the questioning juror but the other jurors are likely to retain whatever mind-set has been generated by the question, leaving the court and counsel to ponder, under the stress of trial, how much influence a *juror* question, answered or unanswered, may have had on the perceptions of the jury as a whole.

Although the court can take remedial steps once such an improper or prejudicial question is asked, it is questionable how effective remedial steps are after the jury has heard the question, as noted *supra.* More importantly, the remedial steps may well make the questioning juror feel abashed and uncomfortable, and perhaps even angry if he feels his pursuit of truth has been thwarted by rules he does not understand. Under the tension and time pressure of a trial, such a reaction is all the more likely. Of course, under the worst case, a juror question may emerge which is so prejudicial as to leave only a declaration of mistrial as an appropriate remedial step, with all the waste that flows from a mistrial.

One further aspect of this practice deserves comment. Human nature being what it is, one or two jurors often will be stronger than the other jurors, and will dominate the jury inquiries. Indeed, this appears to have happened in this case, as discussed *infra.* Moreover, since these questions are from one or more jurors, the possibility that the jury will attach more significance to the answers to these jury questions is great. Every trial judge has noted the development in most lengthy trials of a cohesiveness in the jury as the trial goes on, coming eventually almost to a spirit of camaraderie, in which the actions and reactions of any individual juror are perceived by the jurors as those of the whole jury. In such a setting, the individual juror's question, and the answer elicited, almost certainly will take on a stronger significance to the jury than those questions and answers presented and received in the normal adversarial way.

To the extent that such juror questions reflect consideration of the evidence—and such questions inevitably must do so—then, at the least, the questioning juror has begun the deliberating process with his fellow jurors. Certainly, this is not by design, but stating the question and receiving the answer in the hearing of the remaining jurors begins the reasoning process in the minds of the jurors, stimulates further questions among the jurors, whether asked or not, and generally affects the deliberative process.

With these concerns in mind, we examine the record to determine whether in this instance appellants were prejudiced by the jurors' questions.

There were some 95 questions by jurors during this three-week trial; over half of the questions were asked by the foreman. As noted *supra,* the foreman's number of questions indicates that he was one of the stronger, more vocal members of the jury. Appellants claim that if nothing else, the sheer volume of juror questions indicates a loss of control by the court, thereby prejudicing the appellants' rights.

We have examined carefully each of the questions propounded by jurors and we perceive no bias in any of the questions. The vast majority of the juror questions were technical in nature and reflect a commendable degree of understanding and objectivity by the jury. That such a salutary conclusion is to be reached in this case does not by any means assure that the same or a similar result would come about with other juries.

Because we detect no prejudice to any party, and because appellants did not object to the procedure at the time of trial, we do not find error in the use of juror questions in this case. However, for the reasons set out above, such juror questioning is a course fraught with peril for the trial court. No bright-line rule is adopted here, but the dangers in the practice are very considerable.

* * *

For the reasons stated, we

AFFIRM.

SECTION 6. EXCLUSION OF WITNESSES *

[FED.R.EVID. 615]

SUSANNA AND THE ELDERS

The Bible, Apocrypha, King James Version.

There dwelt a man in Babylon, called Joacim: and he took a wife, whose name was Susanna, the daughter of Chelcias, a very fair woman, and one that feared the Lord. Her parents also were righteous, and taught their daughter according to the law of Moses.

Now Joacim was a great rich man, and had a fair garden joining unto his house: and to him resorted the Jews; because he was more honourable than all others.

The same year were appointed two of the ancients of the people to be judges, such as the Lord spoke of, that wickedness came from Babylon from ancient judges, who seemed to govern the people. These kept much at Joacim's house: and all that had any suits in law came unto them.

Now when the people departed away at noon, Susanna went into her husband's garden to walk. And the two elders saw her going in every day, and walking; so that their lust was inflamed toward her. * * *

And it fell out, as they watched a fit time, she went in as before with two maids only, and she was desirous to wash herself in the garden: for it was hot. And there was nobody there save the two elders, that had hid themselves, and watched her.

Then she said to her maids, "Bring me oil and washing balls, and shut the garden doors, that I may wash me." * * *

Now when the maids were gone forth, the two elders rose up, and ran unto her, saying, "Behold, the garden doors are shut, that no man can see us, and we are in love with thee: therefore consent unto us, and lie with us. If thou wilt not, we will bear witness against thee, that a young man was with thee: and therefore thou didst send away thy maids from thee."

Then Susanna sighed, and said, "I am straitened on every side: for if I do this thing, it is death unto me: and if I do it not, I cannot escape your hands. It is better for me to fall into your hands, and not do it, than to sin in the sight of the Lord."

With that Susanna cried with a loud voice: and the two elders cried out against her. * * *

And it came to pass the next day, when the people were assembled to her husband Joacim, the two elders came also full of mischievous

* See 6 Wigmore, Evidence ch. 63 (Chadbourn rev. 1976); McCormick, Evidence § 50 (4th ed. 1992).

imagination against Susanna to put her to death; and said before the people, "Send for Susanna, the daughter of Chelcias, Joacim's wife." * * *

Then the two elders stood up in the midst of the people, and laid their hands upon her head. And she weeping looked up toward heaven: for her heart trusted in the Lord. And the elders said, "As we walked in the garden alone, this woman came in with two maids, and shut the garden doors, and sent the maids away. Then a young man, who there was hid, came unto her, and lay with her. Then we that stood in a corner of the garden, seeing this wickedness, ran unto them. And when we saw them together, the man we could not hold: for he was stronger than we, and opened the door, and leaped out. But having taken this woman, we asked who the young man was, but she would not tell us: these things do we testify."

Then the assembly believed them, as those that were the elders and judges of the people: so they condemned her to death.

Then Susanna cried out with a loud voice, and said, "O everlasting God, that knowest the secrets, and knowest all things before they be: thou knowest that they have borne false witness against me, and, behold, I must die; whereas I never did such things as these men have maliciously invented against me."

And the Lord heard her voice.

Therefore when she was led to be put to death, the Lord raised up the holy spirit of a young youth, whose name was Daniel: who cried with a loud voice, "I am clear from the blood of this woman."

Then all the people turned them toward him, and said, "What mean these words that thou hast spoken?"

So he standing in the midst of them said, "Are ye such fools, ye sons of Israel, that without examination or knowledge of the truth ye have condemned a daughter of Israel? Return again to the place of judgment: for they have borne false witness against her."

Wherefore all the people turned again in haste, and the elders said unto him, "Come, sit down among us, and show it us, seeing God hath given thee the honour of an elder."

Then said Daniel unto them, "Put these two aside one far from another, and I will examine them."

So when they were put asunder one from another, he called one of them, and said unto him, * * * "Now then, if thou hast seen her, tell me under what tree sawest thou them companying together?"

Who answered, "Under the mastic tree."

And Daniel said, "Very well; thou hast lied against thine own head; for even now the angel of God hath received the sentence of God to cut thee in two."

So he put him aside, and commanded to bring the other, and said unto him, * * * "Now therefore tell me under what tree didst thou take them companying together?"

Who answered, "Under a holm tree."

Then said Daniel unto him, "Well; thou hast also lied against thine own head: for the angel of God waiteth with the sword to cut thee in two, that he may destroy you."

With that all the assembly cried out with a loud voice, and praised God, who saveth them that trust in him. And they arose against the two elders, for Daniel had convicted them of false witness by their own mouth: and according to the law of Moses they did unto them in such sort as they maliciously intended to do to their neighbour: and they put them to death. * * *

From that day forth was Daniel had in great reputation in the sight of the people.

TOWNER v. STATE

Supreme Court of Wyoming, 1984.
685 P.2d 45.

CARDINE, JUSTICE.

Appellant Charles Towner was convicted of four counts of concealing stolen goods in violation of § 6–7–304, W.S.1977.

We will reverse.

Appellant's trial began on February 7, 1983. A motion to sequester the witnesses was granted. The State presented several witnesses who testified to various burglaries, the items which were taken, and the value of those items. Police officers testified concerning the search of the Towner residence and interview of appellant. There is no dispute that the stolen items were found in appellant's living quarters in the basement of his parents' home.

Appellant based his defense on lack of requisite knowledge that the items were stolen. One element necessary for conviction is that the person charged buy, receive or conceal stolen goods "knowing the same to have been stolen." § 6–7–304, supra. Appellant testified that his wife had brought the property into the residence; that he had believed her explanation that she was purchasing and had acquired the property lawfully. Appellant's wife was not available to be called as a witness at the trial. The defense then planned to call Mr. Towner, appellant's father, and Gloria Towner, appellant's sister, to testify that appellant's wife had made similar statements concerning her acquisition of the property to them.

Appellant's attorney was informed by the court and the prosecuting attorney that Mr. Towner and Gloria Towner had been seen in the courtroom during appellant's testimony, thereby violating the sequestration order. The court excluded their testimony because of the violation. The defense, therefore, rested. Subsequently appellant's attorney learned from Mr. Towner and Gloria Towner that an agent of the district attorney's office had attempted to interview them; that they had been asked by the agent to enter the courtroom, and they did so because of this request. Appellant's attorney informed the court of the Towners' explanation of their being in the courtroom, protested the exclusion of their testimony, and asked that they be permitted to testify. The prosecution read a statement from the agent relating to a conversation he had with Mr. Towner shortly before Mr. Towner entered the courtroom. It is unclear from this statement whether or not the agent induced the witnesses to enter the courtroom. He may have; at the very least, that matter was in dispute.

The court asked for an offer of proof as to what the testimony of these witnesses would be if permitted to testify. Appellant's counsel stated that Mr. Towner would testify that appellant's wife had told him that she was buying the property items found in appellant's living quarters, and that she was going to get the bill of sale and show it to him. He was also going to testify that appellant's wife had told him that she was getting the money to pay for the items from her parents. Gloria Towner was essentially going to testify to similar conversations. The court ruled that this testimony

> "is not only of dubious relevance but is also cumulative to what the defendant has already testified to, and which no one has challenged"

and, therefore, affirmed his previous ruling excluding the testimony of the witnesses.

The question presented to us is whether the trial court erred in excluding the defense witnesses' testimony due to their apparent violation of the sequestration order. Rule 615, W.R.E., provides for exclusion of witnesses. Under this rule, sequestration of witnesses is a matter of right for either party. The purpose is to prevent the tailoring of evidence to conform to prior testimony and to assist the parties in detecting falsehoods and testimony which is less than candid. *United States v. Ell,* 718 F.2d 291 (9th Cir.1983); *Geders v. United States,* 425 U.S. 80, 96 S.Ct. 1330, 47 L.Ed.2d 592 (1976); 3 Louisell & Mueller § 370 (1979). Although Rule 615, W.R.E., does not provide for sanctions for violations of the rule, the most often invoked remedies are (1) to hold the witness in contempt; (2) to make the violation a subject for cross-examination and comment; and (3) to disallow the testimony altogether. 3 Louisell & Mueller § 371; 13 Land & Water L.Rev. 909 (1978), "Article VI of the Wyoming Rules of Evidence: Witnesses."

The United States Supreme Court held in *Holder v. United States,* 150 U.S. 91, 14 S.Ct. 10, 37 L.Ed. 1010 (1893):

> "If a witness disobeys the order of withdrawal, while he may be proceeded against for contempt, and his testimony is open to comment to the jury by reason of his conduct, he is not thereby disqualified, and the weight of authority is that he cannot be excluded on that ground, merely, although the right to exclude under particular circumstances

may be supported as within the sound discretion of the trial court." 14 S.Ct. at 10.

We have previously addressed this question in circumstances where the judge allowed witnesses to testify although they had been in the courtroom in violation of a sequestration order. We affirmed the allowance of that testimony, stating that permitting witnesses to testify was a matter addressed to the discretion of the court and that we would reverse only for gross abuse of that discretion. *Whiteley v. State,* Wyo., 418 P.2d 164 (1966); *Pixley v. State,* Wyo., 406 P.2d 662 (1965). We have not, however, addressed the question of the propriety of excluding testimony because of a violation of a sequestration order.

The general rule is that a party who does not know of nor procures the violation should not be deprived of essential testimony. 88 C.J.S. Trial § 70. However, when a party knows that a witness is violating the rule and allows the violation to continue, he may lose the right to present the witness or to object on those grounds. 23 C.J.S. Criminal Law § 1013.

> "A party should not be denied his witness because of misconduct which the party has not caused. 'Refusal to permit a witness to testify in a criminal case on the ground that he had violated the order excluding witnesses is reversible error where neither the state nor the defendant was responsible for the violation of the order and did not know he was present.' Excluding testimony is not an appropriate remedy. Rather, the jury should be instructed on the credibility of the witness. If the order is willfully violated, the court may properly hold the witness in contempt of court." (Citations omitted.) *State v. Wells,* Mont., 658 P.2d 381 (1983).

Exclusion of the witness' testimony is too grave a sanction where the violation was not intentional and was not procured by the connivance of the party or his counsel. A practical and sensitive accommodation between the defendant's right to present a defense and the trial court's need to control the proceedings must be maintained. Exclusion should be allowed only when it is necessary to preserve the integrity of the fact finding process. *State v. Burdge,* 295 Or. 1, 664 P.2d 1076 (1983).

United States v. Schaefer, 299 F.2d 625, 631, 14 A.L.R.3d 1 (7th Cir.1962), held that exclusion of testimony was too harsh in situations where the witness did not willfully violate the sequestration order and there was no indication that the witness was in court with

> "'the consent, connivance, procurement or knowledge of the appellant or his counsel.' * * * [D]isqualification of the offending witness absent particular circumstances is too harsh a penalty on the innocent litigant." See also, *United States v. Johnston,* 578 F.2d 1352 (10th Cir.1978), cert. denied 439 U.S. 931, 99 S.Ct. 321, 58 L.Ed.2d 325.

Braswell v. Wainwright, 463 F.2d 1148 (5th Cir.1972), found error in excluding testimony because of a sequestration violation on grounds of Sixth Amendment rights and due process, stating that the defendant's right to obtain witnesses in his behalf was violated. Since neither the defendant nor his counsel was involved in the violation, there could not have been a waiver of a constitutional right which would render the exclusion proper. Testimony was considered properly excluded when the court found connivance of the government's counsel and prejudice to the defendant, *United States v. Blasco,* 702 F.2d 1315 (11th Cir.1983), and where a defendant violated the sequestration order by comparing testimony with another witness. *United States v. Torbert,* 496 F.2d 154 (9th Cir.1974), cert. denied 419 U.S. 857, 95 S.Ct. 105, 42 L.Ed.2d 91.

United States v. Gibson, 675 F.2d 825 (6th Cir.1982), cert. denied 459 U.S. 972, 103 S.Ct. 305, 74 L.Ed.2d 285, stated that most authorities agree that the "particular circumstances" of *Holder v. United States,* supra, sufficient for exclusion are indications that the witness violated the order with the consent, connivance, procurement or knowledge of the party seeking the testimony. This case held there was no abuse of discretion in excluding testimony because the witness stayed in the courtroom with the knowledge of the defendant *and* another witness gave substantially identical testimony. Excluding two witnesses for a violation was held not to deprive the defendant of his right to obtain witnesses in his behalf where three other witnesses testified to the same facts and the defendant and his counsel knew of their presence in the courtroom. *Calloway v. Blackburn,* 612 F.2d 201 (5th Cir.1980).

There was no evidence presented nor was it claimed that Mr. Towner and Gloria Towner entered the courtroom with the knowledge or consent of appellant or his counsel. The only allegations concerned the possible inducement of their presence by an agent for the county attorney's office. Therefore, we find that exclusion of their testimony as a sanction for violating the sequestration order was an abuse of discretion.

The State contends, however, that even if the exclusion of the witnesses for violation of the sequestration order was improper, the ruling should still be upheld on the grounds that the testimony was cumulative and irrelevant. Rule 403, W.R.E., states:

> "Although relevant, evidence may be excluded if its probative value is substantially outweighed by the danger of unfair prejudice, confusion of the issues, or misleading the jury, or by considerations of undue delay, waste of time, or *needless presentation of cumulative evidence.*" (Emphasis added.)

We have stated that the trial court's discretion in ruling on evidence will not be overturned except for clear abuse. *Buhrle v. State,* Wyo., 627 P.2d 1374 (1981). However, Rule 403 is an extraordinary remedy which should be used sparingly since it allows the court to exclude evidence which is concededly relevant and probative. Its major function is to exclude scant or cumulative evidence which may be unfairly prejudicial, confusing, or needlessly cumulative. *United States v. Thevis,* 665 F.2d 616 (5th Cir.1982). It has been held error to exclude evidence which is corroborative of the defendant's testimony. *People v.*

Linder, 5 Cal.3d 342, 96 Cal.Rptr. 26, 486 P.2d 1226 (1971). If there were no independent corroborative evidence on the points that the defendant testified to other than the excluded testimony, it is improperly excluded. *State v. Conklin,* 79 Wash.2d 805, 489 P.2d 1130 (1971).

United States v. Davis, 639 F.2d 239 (5th Cir.1981), held that it was error to deny the defendant his right to call witnesses in circumstances where the exclusion resulted from noncompliance with a discovery order even though the judge also ruled that the evidence was cumulative. Another court refused to allow defendant to call witnesses who would corroborate his testimony that he lacked the necessary intent, stating that the evidence was hearsay. On appeal there was a reversal, the court holding that even if the testimony were cumulative, it should not be excluded if introduced to corroborate the defendant's own statement because,

> "[t]o deny defendant the right to present any independent corroborative testimony on a material issue must be considered prejudicial error. Such testimony is 'cumulative' to the extent that the defendant testifies to the same facts or events. However, '[w]e know of no rule that prohibits a person on trial for a criminal offense from introducing cumulative testimony upon any fact material to the case, within reasonable limits, and it is manifest that [such testimony should not be prohibited when it] is sought to be introduced to corroborate his own statement, which, by reason of his interest in the result of the trial, may be, and often is, looked upon by the jury with some degree of suspicion.' [Citations.]" (Emphasis omitted.) *People v. Green,* 38 Colo.App. 165, 553 P.2d 839 (1976).

Louisell & Mueller, Federal Evidence § 128 states that:

> "Not all evidence which is entirely duplicative is therefore cumulative and excludable. Evidence may vary in degree of persuasiveness, and when an item of proof which is offered on a point is very different in character or persuasive impact from an item of proof previously received, the former cannot be considered merely 'cumulative' of the latter."

Appellant's case is different from one where many witnesses could testify to the same facts and the trial court limits the witnesses to a few. Appellant testified in his own behalf. With the exclusion of the testimony of his father and his sister, there was no other testimony to the fact that appellant's wife had allegedly brought the items into the house and explained their presence. Appellant's knowledge of the stolen property was necessary for a conviction. The excluded testimony was relevant to a material element and corroborative of appellant's testimony.

The State contends that "the prosecution never challenged the existence or veracity of these statements" made to appellant by his wife. The prosecuting attorney, however, did not admit or stipulate to this fact; and, in closing arguments, he stated that appellant had told several different stories concerning the stolen items when he said:

"* * * However, we think there is a clear showing on actual knowledge that those items were stolen. It is an element of the crime. You cannot find the Defendant guilty unless he knew those items were stolen, and you will just have to determine his credibility and the simple fact that he told two different stories to law enforcement and a different story to you today, which goes a long way towards circumstantial evidence that there was guilty knowledge, he would have told one consistent story. We have a harder question, that he tells two different stories and tells you a different story, and you add that to the fact of all of these suspicious circumstances, how the wheeling and dealing was going on, and he told you obvious that she had this money."

It is possible that the jury believed appellant had fabricated his testimony after he was charged. When appellant's case went to the jury, his testimony denying knowledge that the goods were stolen was uncorroborated. It stood alone against the State's total case and all of its witnesses. It is possible that the jury may have believed Mr. Towner or Gloria Towner irrespective of their close relationship with appellant. This corroborative evidence, when added to appellant's testimony, may or may not have been of sufficient weight to tip the scales in his favor. We do not know what the jury might have decided. We do know that defendant had the right to present this testimony and these witnesses that would tend to corroborate his testimony and would refute a material element of the crime charged. Therefore, we reverse and remand this case for a new trial or such further proceedings as are not inconsistent with this opinion.

ROONEY, CHIEF JUSTICE, dissenting, with whom BROWN, JUSTICE, joins.

The majority opinion concludes that the sanction for violation of the sequestration order in this case (disallowing the testimony of the two witnesses) was too severe. While not saying so, such opinion implies that the trial court should have allowed the testimony with comment to the jury by the court that the witnesses had violated the sequestration order.

I believe the analysis should go beyond this point, and I believe the analysis by the trial court did so. The trial court held the testimony to be

"* * * not only of dubious relevance but is also cumulative to what the Defendant has already testified to, and to which no one has challenged. * * *"

Thus, the court considered allowing the testimony accompanied by the cautionary comment of the court, and then it considered such testimony in light of Rule 403, W.R.E. That rule provides:

"Although relevant, evidence may be excluded if its probative value is substantially outweighed by the danger of unfair prejudice, confusion of the issues, or misleading the jury, or by considerations of undue delay, waste of time, or needless presentation of cumulative evidence."

I believe the court acted in this matter within the discretion afforded to it by Rule 403, W.R.E. Within the scope of this rule we have said that admission of evidence is within the sound discretion of the trial court, which discretion will not be disturbed absent a clear abuse of it. *Sanville v. State,* Wyo., 593 P.2d 1340, 1345 (1979); *Hopkinson v. State,* Wyo., 632 P.2d 79, 101 (1981), cert. denied 455 U.S. 922, 102 S.Ct. 1280, 71 L.Ed.2d 463 (1982). And appellant has the burden of demonstrating an abuse of discretion. *Nimmo v. State,* Wyo., 603 P.2d 386, 392 (1979); *Buhrle v. State,* Wyo., 627 P.2d 1374, 1380 (1981).

Applying the rule to this case, we must ascertain (1) the probative value of the evidence, and (2) the consideration of needless presentation of cumulative evidence. Then, we must weigh the first determination against the second to conclude whether or not there was a clear abuse of the trial court's discretion.

If the trial court had admitted the evidence under the conditions set forth in the majority opinion, the jury would have had to be advised that the credibility of the testimony of appellant's father and of his sister should be considered in view of the fact that they were in the courtroom at the time appellant testified in violation of the direct order of the court that they be then excluded, and that the potential existed for them to have tailored their testimony to conform with the testimony of appellant. The jury would then have heard them testify that appellant's wife told them that she had purchased the property in question, appellant having already told the jury that his wife had told him the same thing. The stolen property consisted of a commercial microwave oven taken from the Casper Hilton Inn; a stereo, television and microwave oven taken from the Lundine residence; a toolbox, calculator, and resin taken from Moltec; drill bits taken from Triangle Sales and Service, Inc.; and an auger taken from Michaels Fence. Appellant testified that these items found in his bedroom were obtained by his wife who said she purchased them from her cousin's friend. The probative value of testimony by appellant's father and sister to the effect that appellant's wife had told them she purchased this random assortment of personal property from her cousin's friend would not only be weakened by the relationship between appellant and the two witnesses but also by the court's comment relative to their violation of the sequestration order.

Against this "probative value" of the testimony of the two witnesses, the trial court had to weigh the desirability for not presenting cumulative evidence.[1] In doing so, the court found the latter to outweigh the former.

The question on appeal is not whether the decision of the trial court was that which we would have made. We are not to weigh the factors ourselves. Our determination is whether or not the trial court's decision was a *clear* abuse of discretion.

1. Cumulative evidence is "additional or corroborative evidence to the same point." Black's Law Dictionary (5th ed. 1979), p. 343.

"A court does not abuse its discretion unless it acts in a manner which exceeds the bounds of reason under the circumstances. In determining whether there has been an abuse of discretion, the ultimate issue is whether or not the court could reasonably conclude as it did. An abuse of discretion has been said to mean an error of law committed by the court under the circumstances. * * *" *Martinez v. State,* Wyo., 611 P.2d 831, 838 (1980).

I do not believe the trial court acted in a manner which *clearly* exceeded the bounds of reason under the circumstances; which *clearly* was other than in a reasonable manner; or which was *clearly* an error of law committed under the circumstances.

Not finding a clear abuse of discretion in excluding the testimony of the two sequestered witnesses, I would affirm.

Chapter 5

OPINIONS AND EXPERT TESTIMONY
[FED. R. EVID. ART. VII]

SECTION 1. OPINION TESTIMONY BY LAY WITNESSES *
[FED.R.EVID. 701]

STATE v. THORP

Supreme Court of North Carolina, 1875.
72 N.C. 186.

READE, J.

The prisoner was charged with drowning her child in a river. A witness saw her going towards the river with a child in her arms. The witness said he knew the prisoner and identified her, he knew the child also, but he was one hundred yards off and was not sure who the child in her arms was. He was then asked if he recognized the child as the deceased? Which question was objected to by the prisoner and ruled out by the Court: for what reason we cannot conceive, as it was clearly competent. Possibly it was ruled out as being a leading question. The Solicitor then asked, "Is it your best impression that the child she had in her arms, was her son Robert Thorp?" The witness said it was. This question was objected to but was admitted. If the former question was leading, this was more so, but there is a more substantial objection to it.

It is true that in very many cases a witness may give "his impressions" or his "opinions" as to facts. Indeed memory is so treacherous, knowledge so imperfect, and even the senses so deceptive, that we can seldom give to positive assertions any other interpretation than that they are the impressions or opinions of the witness. Do you know when a certain act was done? I do. When was it? I think it was

* See 2 Wigmore, Evidence §§ 658–663 (Chadbourn rev. 1979); 7 id. ch. 67 (Chadbourn rev. 1978); McCormick, Evidence §§ 11, 18 (4th ed. 1992).

in January. Where was it? It was in Raleigh. At what place in Raleigh? I think it was at the hotel, it may have been at the capitol. Who did it? Mr. A. Was it not Mr. B? It was one or the other and my best impression is that it was Mr. A. All that would be proper, because the witness is speaking of facts within his knowledge and as he understands them. So if in this case the witness had been asked "Did you know the deceased child? Yes. Did you see it in the person's arms? Yes. Did you recognize it as the deceased? Yes, I think it was, that is my best impression." All that would have been proper. But we think the case presented to us will bear the interpretation that the witness said, "I saw the prisoner have a child in her arms. I was so far off that I could not tell what child it was, but I knew that she had a child of her own, and I suppose she would not have been carrying any other child than her own, therefore I think it was her own child. That is my best impression." And this was clearly improper. This was but his *inference* from what he saw and knew. And we suppose that any bystander in the Court who heard the trial might have been called up and he would have testified that his "best impression" was that it was her child, from the evidence. A witness must speak of facts within his knowledge. He knew that the prisoner had a child of her own, and he knew that she had a child in her arms, and these facts it was proper for him to state, but he could not go further and say, "from these facts which I know I infer that the child was her own, I am not sure but that is my best impression." This may not have been the sense in which he intended to be understood, but we think it will bear that construction. And in favor of life we so construe it. He certainly did not mean to say that he recognized the child as the child of the prisoner, and yet he knew her child very well. Why did he not recognize the child as he did the prisoner? Evidently because at that distance he could not recognize one child from another in the arms of the prisoner. It was probably but little more distinct than a bundle and he just took it to be her child because she had it in her arms. Probably this was all he meant by his "best impression." And it was error to allow it.

DRACKETT PRODUCTS CO. v. BLUE, 152 So.2d 463 (Fla.1963). "The sole question presented here is whether the District Court of Appeal, Third District, was correct in reversing a judgment for the defendant and granting a new trial because the trial court sustained an objection to and instructed the jury to disregard the following question and answer in a suit to recover damages resulting from the explosion of a can of Drano, viz.:

> 'Q. I want to ask if she knew that day what she knew after the accident, that this would explode with water in it, would she have kept it on the shelf.
>
> 'A. I would not.'

* * *

"Conjecture has no place in proceedings of this sort. It would be a manifest impossibility for the defendant to have disproved the statement elicited from the mother because it involved not the proof of a fact but a state of mind concerning which only the mother could establish. Moreover, the answer to such a question would be obvious from the inception. The law seems well established that testimony consisting of guesses, conjecture or speculation—suppositions without a premise of fact—are clearly inadmissible in the trial of causes in the courts of this country. A statement by a witness as to what action he would have taken if something had occurred which did not occur—particularly in those instances where such testimony is offered for the purpose of supporting a claim for relief or damages—or what course of action a person would have pursued under certain circumstances which the witness says did not exist will ordinarily be rejected as inadmissible and as proving nothing."

Note

See also Kloepfer v. Honda Motor Co., 898 F.2d 1452, 1459 (10th Cir.1990) (proper to exclude testimony of child decedent's mother that she would have followed a hypothetical warning on all-terrain vehicle); Evanston Bank v. Brink's, Inc., 853 F.2d 512, 515 (7th Cir.1988) (question to witness asking what bank would have done under hypothetical circumstances properly excluded as speculative).

UNITED STATES v. CARLOCK, 806 F.2d 535, 552 (5th Cir.1986), cert. denied, 480 U.S. 949, 107 S.Ct. 1611, 94 L.Ed.2d 796 (1987). "Della Ardoin, the secretary for Pullman–Torkelson and Carlock, Sr.'s former secretary at Local 406, testified that she knew he owned the heavy equipment rented to Pullman–Torkelson because she saw an invoice and put 'two-and-two' together with other information, the nature of which she can no longer recall. The government argues that Ardoin's testimony was within the ambit of Rule 701.

"We are persuaded that receipt of this testimony as lay opinion was error. There was no showing of a basis for her opinion beyond her work in the office. Thus, we cannot ascertain if the testimony was based upon facts within her personal knowledge sufficient to make her opinion more than an educated guess."

Note

"Testimony about matters outside [a lay witness's] personal knowledge is not admissible, and if not admissible at trial neither is it admissible in an affidavit used to support or resist the grant of summary judgment. * * * It is true that 'personal knowledge' includes inferences—all knowledge is inferential—and therefore opinions. * * * But the inferences and opinions must be grounded in observation or other first-hand personal experience. They must not be flights of fancy, speculations, hunches, intuitions, or rumors about matters remote from that experience." Visser v. Packer Engineering Associates, Inc., 924 F.2d 655, 659 (7th Cir.1991).

CRAGIN v. LOBBEY, 537 S.W.2d 193, 198–99 (Mo.App.1976). "Love had his back to the site of the impact when he 'heard the screeching of brakes' and looked around to see the Lobbey automobile 'within 8 feet of the north edge of the intersection' and the collision occurred thereafter in 'just a fraction of a second.' Over the objections of defendant Lobbey that the policeman had not observed the car for a sufficient time and distance to permit him to make an informed estimate of speed, the officer was permitted to testify that 'I estimated the speed [of the Lobbey car] at 35 miles per hour.' On cross-examination when asked 'Did you guess at the speed, Mr. Love?' the officer replied, 'It would be a guess, yes, sir.' He was then asked 'You didn't have any distance that you saw them travel at which you could form any true estimate of speed, did you?' The officer's answer was, 'You are right. No, sir.' Defendant Lobbey's motion to strike the speed-testimony of Officer Love because it 'was merely a guess [and] has no probative value' was refused. The officer 'estimated' the speed of the Hinkle car at twenty miles per hour and described the impact as 'very slight.'

* * *

"We agree with defendant Lobbey that the trial court erred in permitting the speed-testimony of Officer Love to remain in the record for final consideration in determining the speed of defendant Lobbey's automobile. There is considerable authority that before a witness should be permitted to testify as to the speed of a motor vehicle, he should first demonstrate that he had a reasonable opportunity to judge that speed. 8 Am.Jur.2d, Automobiles and Highway Traffic, § 985, pp. 537–539, and cases there cited. However, and seemingly to the contrary, there are Missouri cases which permit a witness to express an opinion or judgment (as opposed to a guess) as to speed where the opportunity to judge the speed was limited to 'only for about $1/16$ or $1/18$ of a second,' to a ' "fleeting second before the impact," ' or to ' " * * * a split second or so." ' Vaeth v. Gegg, 486 S.W.2d 625, 627[3] (Mo.1972); Johnson v. Cox, 262 S.W.2d 13, 15[3, 4] (Mo.1953); Schneider v. Dannegger, 435 S.W.2d 413, 415 (Mo.App.1968); Lafferty v. Wattle, 349 S.W.2d 519, 527–528 (Mo.App.1961). These authorities opine that the brevity of the observation does not destroy the credibility of the testimony but only goes to its weight and value. On the other hand, a witness who observed a truck moving only six inches in a given direction, should not have been allowed to say that it was moving 10 m.p.h. because such an opinion was bound to have been based on guess, speculation and conjecture and, therefore, was not regarded as substantial evidence. Prince v. Bennett, 322 S.W.2d 886, 890–891 (Mo.1959). Divination is not our forte, and we do not undertake the impossibility of striking a line, either for time or distance, to delineate when an estimate, judgment or opinion as to speed is credible for jury consideration or deteriorates into a mere guess of no probative value. Nevertheless, until it became known that Officer Love's estimate of defendant Lobbey's speed was just a guess, and as long as it appeared the given estimate was an expression of his judgment or opinion, under *Vaeth, Johnson, Schneider,* and *Lafferty,* supra, we cannot say the trial court erred in permitting the testimony albeit the opportunity to judge the speed was limited to 'just a fraction of a second.' But when Officer Love stated that his estimate 'would be a guess, yes, sir,' the trial court erred in not striking that testimony as requested.

"If, upon consideration of a witness's entire testimony, it is apparent his use of the word 'guess' is a colloquial effort to express an opinion or judgment (39 C.J.S. Guess, p. 415), then his employment of that word is not necessarily destructive of his testimony. Hinrichs v. Young, 403 S.W.2d 642, 646[5] (Mo.1966). However, if a witness cedes his prior testimony on a given issue was, in fact, predicated on a mere guess, i.e., upon speculation with no factual basis, or if he admits to facts, conditions or circumstances which make it evident the testimony was a mere guess on his part, then his testimony does not constitute substantial evidence and has no probative value. Zeigenbein v. Thornsberry, 401 S.W.2d 389, 391[3] (Mo.1966); Abernathy v. Coca–Cola Bottling Company of Jackson, 370 S.W.2d 175, 177 (Mo.App.1963); Denney v. Spot Martin, Inc., 328 S.W.2d 399, 405[8] (Mo.App.1959); Christner v. Chicago, R.I. & P. Ry. Co., 228 Mo.App. 220, 228[7], 64 S.W.2d 752, 756[7] (1933); O'Neil Implement Mfg. Co. v. Gordon, 269 S.W. 636, 640[6] (Mo.App.1925). What Officer Love said on direct examination regarding his estimate of the speed of defendant Lobbey's car was admitted on cross-examination to have been a mere guess on his part because, as he agreed, he did not have sufficient opportunity to 'form any true estimate of the speed.' Van Bibber v. Swift & Co., 286 Mo. 317, 337, 228 S.W. 69, 76[9] (banc 1921); Barnhart v. Ripka, 297 S.W.2d 787, 791[7] (Mo.App.1956). With the speed-testimony of Officer Love having thus been dispossessed of probative value, the court should have disposed of that issue as if the witness had not spoken. Oglesby v. Missouri Pac. Ry. Co., 177 Mo. 272, 296, 76 S.W. 623, 627–628 (banc 1903)."

STATE v. HUNT, 3 Wash.App. 754, 477 P.2d 645, 646 (1970). "Defendant's remaining assignment of error involves an evidentiary question. Jimmy Dale Purdy, an uninvolved witness to the accident, testified he had observed defendant's vehicle 10 to 15 feet prior to impact and that it was traveling at 'a very high rate of speed.' When the prosecutor questioned him further on the subject, Purdy stated, in his opinion, the defendant's vehicle was traveling in excess of 65 miles per hour. Defendant assigns error to Purdy's testimony on the basis that he did not have sufficient time to view defendant's vehicle so as to form an opinion concerning its speed. Gray v. Pistoresi, 64 Wash.2d 106, 390 P.2d 697 (1964); Sanders v. Crimmins, 63 Wash.2d 702, 388 P.2d 913 (1964); Charlton v. Baker, 61 Wash.2d 369, 378 P.2d 432 (1963). We disagree.

"A witness may state an opinion concerning the speed of a vehicle provided his testimony does not possess a quality of extravagance which would automatically preclude its believability. McKinney v. City of Seattle, 139 Wash. 148, 245 P. 913 (1926); Day v. Frazer, 59 Wash.2d 659, 369 P.2d 859 (1962). We find no debilitating extravagance in Purdy testifying that defendant's vehicle was traveling "very fast" in a 35-mile-per-hour speed zone. The fact that the state pursued this topic and eventually elicited Purdy's final speed estimate goes merely to the weight of that testimony and not its initial admissibility."

Notes

(1) "Testimony should not be excluded for lack of personal knowledge unless no reasonable juror could believe that the witness had the ability and opportunity to perceive the event that he testifies about." United States v. Hickey, 917 F.2d 901, 904 (6th Cir.1990).

(2) See also United States v. Jackson, 688 F.2d 1121, 1125 (7th Cir. 1982) ("The amount of time that the witness had to observe the defendant goes to the weight to be accorded to the [identification] testimony by the jury rather than to its admissibility."), cert. denied, 460 U.S. 1043, 103 S.Ct. 1441, 75 L.Ed.2d 797 (1983); United States v. Evans, 484 F.2d 1178, 1181 (2d Cir.1973) ("it has long been established that 'the result of the witness' observation need not be positive or absolute certainty * * *; it suffices if he had an opportunity of personal observation and did get some impressions from this observation.' [2 Wigmore, Evidence] § 660 [(3d ed. 1940)].").

UNITED STATES v. SKEET

United States Court of Appeals, Ninth Circuit, 1982.
665 F.2d 983.

KELLAM, SENIOR DISTRICT JUDGE:

Tried to the jury Raymond Carl Skeet (Raymond) was convicted of assault resulting in serious bodily harm in violation of 18 U.S.C. §§ 113(f) and 1153. The victim of Raymond's assault was his brother, Robert Skeet (Robert).

I.

Raymond, Robert, Jasper Walker (Walker) and Robert's common-law wife, Shirley, had spent Saturday morning visiting bars. They returned home to the Navajo Reservation about noon. All were intoxicated except Shirley. There had been some argument between the parties. Upon returning home, Raymond, an ex-Navajo Tribal police officer, went into the hogan and loaded his police revolver. He told Shirley they were laughing about him and he would show what he could do. Robert and Walker were out in front of the hogan working on a pickup truck; Raymond walked out of the hogan and fired three or four shots. Shirley was returning from an outhouse when Raymond pointed the gun at her and told her to "Get over here, damn it." [Tr. of Ev. p. 136]. She called for her husband Robert. He came over and stood next to her, and told Raymond to put the gun away. Raymond had been pointing the gun at Shirley, and when Robert spoke to him, Raymond fired a shot between Robert and Shirley. Robert tried to grab the pistol from Raymond, but Raymond moved back, and Robert struck him in the mouth. Raymond moved back and appeared to trip on some fence posts. As he did he shot striking Robert in the neck. Raymond contended that the facts showed that as he was backing away he stumbled and fell backwards over some metal fence posts that were lying on the ground behind him, and that as he was falling backwards the gun went off. He did not fall to the ground. The prosecution contended that the evidence is clear that while Raymond did stagger backwards he never fell, and was standing on both feet when he fired the gun. Robert was shot in the neck and fell to the ground. When arrested by a police officer, Raymond told the officer he had shot his brother, and that he was lying in front of the hogan. He was read his rights, after which Raymond said he could have easily shot and killed his brother if he had wanted to, but he elected to teach him a lesson, that he only wanted to inflict a small wound on him, that he shot him only with the intention of inflicting a small wound on him. Upon a subsequent questioning he related he and Robert had been fighting and scuffling; that Robert reached out and grabbed his hand, trying to pull the gun away, and that as he was pulling the gun away, it discharged accidentally. Robert testified he never touched the gun. He told quite a different story. There is no question that Robert was seriously injured, as defendant never contested this fact. Defendant did not testify or present evidence.

At trial Raymond unsuccessfully sought to elicit from Robert and Shirley their opinion as to whether the shooting was accidental. The Court declined to admit such opinions and defendant noted his objection.

II.

In his appeal, Raymond raises three issues:

1. Do Rules 701 and 704 of the Federal Rules of Evidence permit a defendant to present evidence of whether a shooting was accidental?

* * *

A.

United States raises the point that Raymond did not offer proof of the substance of the rejected testimony. However, the record shows clearly proof was offered and exception taken and that all parties knew the substance of the rejected testimony.

Turning to the first issue, Rule 701 of the Federal Rules of Evidence provides:

Rule 701. Opinion Testimony by Lay Witnesses

> If the witness is not testifying as an expert, his testimony in the form of opinions or inferences is limited to those opinions or inferences which are (a) rationally based on the perception of the witness and (b) helpful to a clear understanding of his testimony or the determination of a fact in issue.

Rule 704 merely provides that testimony of opinions or inferences otherwise admissible is not objectionable because it embraces an issue to be decided by the jury.

We commence with the proposition that the trial court's rejection of such testimony is not to be overruled absent a showing of clear abuse. *United States v. Butcher,* 557 F.2d 666 at 670 (9th Cir.1977); *United States v. Tsinnijinnie,* 601 F.2d 1035 (9th Cir.1979).

The admissibility of such testimony is governed by whether the opinion is (a) rationally based on the perception of the witness, and (b) is helpful to a clear understanding of his testimony or the determination of a fact in issue.

Opinions of non-experts may be admitted where the facts could not otherwise be adequately presented or described to the jury in such a way as to enable the jury to form an opinion or reach an intelligent conclusion. If it is impossible or difficult to reproduce the data observed by the witnesses, or the facts are difficult of explanation, or complex, or are of a combination of circumstances and appearances which cannot be adequately described and presented with the force and clearness as they appeared to the witness, the witness may state his impressions and opinions based upon what he observed. It is a means of conveying to the jury what the witness has seen or heard. If the jury can be put into a position of equal vantage with the witness for drawing the opinion, then the witness may not give an opinion. Because it is sometimes difficult to describe the mental or physical condition of a person, his character or reputation, the emotions manifest by his acts; speed of a moving object or other things that arise in a day to day observation of lay witnesses; things that are of common occurrence and observation, such as size, heights, odors, flavors, color, heat, and so on; witnesses may relate their opinions or conclusions of what they observed.

The testimony to be admissible must be "predicated upon concrete facts within their own observation and recollection—that is facts perceived from their own senses, as distinguished from their opinions or conclusions drawn from such facts." *Randolph v. Collectramatic, Inc.,* 590 F.2d 844, 847–48 (10th Cir.1979). *See also United States v. Brown,* 540 F.2d 1048, 1053 (10th Cir.1976), *cert. denied,* 429 U.S. 1100, 97 S.Ct. 1122, 51 L.Ed.2d 549 (1977). The question of whether or not a "lay witness is qualified to testify as to any matter of opinion is a preliminary determination within the sound discretion of the trial court whose decision must be upheld unless shown to be clearly erroneous or a clear result of an abuse of judicial discretion." *Id. See also Cardwell v. C & O Ry. Co.,* 504 F.2d 444 (6th Cir.1974). "A certain latitude may rightly be given the Court in permitting a witness on direct examination to testify as to his conclusions, based on common knowledge or experience." *United States v. Trenton Potteries Co.,* 273 U.S. 392, 407, 47 S.Ct. 377, 383, 71 L.Ed. 700 (1927).

There was no error in the trial court's ruling.

* * *

[Reversed on other grounds.]

PARKER v. HOEFER, 118 Vt. 1, 100 A.2d 434, 442–43 (1953). "We next have exceptions to the admission of evidence, and to the refusal of the court to strike out answers to questions, mainly relating to opinion testimony. While waiting with the defendant and another for Parker to attend an ice show the defendant wanted to telephone him and the plaintiff noticed defendant's 'anxiety', 'her impatience' and that she appeared 'very agitated'. * * * That she noticed the defendant's actions in regard to her husband, noticed her interest, her taking him aside and that there was great intimacy between them. That she noticed that the defendant was absorbed in him. That she noticed that her husband's appearance was abnormal, he was exhausted and had lipstick on his collar, he smelled as though he had been drinking and he looked very haggard. * * * The defendant argues that this evidence relative to what the plaintiff noticed about how the defendant appeared and acted and about how Parker appeared were inadmissible as opinions and conclusions, and that no proper foundation had been laid for its admission.

"As a general rule witnesses are to state facts and not give their inferences or opinions; but this rule is subject to the exception that 'where the facts are of such a character as to be incapable of being presented with their proper force to anyone but the observer himself, so as to enable the triers to draw a correct or intelligent conclusion from them without the aid of the judgment or opinion of the witness who had the benefit of personal observation, he is allowed to a certain extent, to add his conclusion, judgment or opinion.' Bates v. Town of Sharon, 45 Vt. 474, 481.

"Under this exception to the rule, it is permissible for a witness to testify that a horse appeared tired, State v. Ward, 61 Vt. 153, 181, 17 A. 483; that a man appeared worried, State v. Bradley, 64 Vt. 466, 470, 24 A. 1053; that two persons were very intimate, State v. Marsh, 70 Vt. 288, 299, 40 A. 836; that a person was domineering, Mathewson v. Mathewson, 81 Vt. 173, 185, 69 A. 646, 18 L.R.A., N.S., 300; that there was nothing peculiar in one's talk or action, In re Esterbrook's Will, 83 Vt. 229, 234, 75 A. 1; the expression of the respondent's face and eyes,

State v. Felch, 92 Vt. 477, 486, 105 A. 23; that the respondent was under the influence of intoxicating liquor, State v. Hedding, 114 Vt. 212, 214, 42 A.2d 438; that cattle were not strong, State v. Persons, 114 Vt. 435, 438, 46 A.2d 854. In this connection we quote State v. Felch, supra [92 Vt. 477, 105 A. 27]: 'So, too, it is held that a witness may testify that one spoke affectionately of another, Appeal of Spencer, 77 Conn. 638, 60 A. 289; that a respondent acted "sneaky," Com. v. Borasky, 214 Mass. 313, 101 N.E. 377; and that one was affectionate toward another, McKee v. Nelson, 4 Cow., N.Y. 355, 15 Am.Dec. 384. And speaking generally, an ordinary observer may be allowed to state that one appeared pleased, angry, excited, friendly, insulting, affectionate, or the like. * * * The raising of an eyebrow, the wave of a handkerchief, or the flash of an eye may give character to an act otherwise too trivial to notice.'

"As to laying a foundation for the admission of this evidence it is not pointed out in what respect the witness could have stated more facts than she did."

BROWN v. STATE, 561 S.W.2d 484, 489 (Tex.Crim.App.1978). "Lastly, appellant contends that the court erred in overruling his objection to the testimony of a police officer that he believed that appellant was 'trying to act like he was unconscious.'

"Officer Cawyer of the Wichita Falls Police Department testified that he saw appellant when he arrived at the scene of the homicide, that appellant was seated, 'slumped backwards and being supported,' and that he was 'kind of groaning, moaning and whimpering-type sounds.' In response to a question as to what he 'observed concerning his condition,' the witness responded, 'He was trying to act like he was unconscious in my opinion.' Cawyer further testified that when he told appellant to open his eyes that 'he [appellant] opened his eyes immediately.' Objection was made to the testimony relative to appellant 'trying to act like he was unconscious' for the reason that the witness was not qualified as a medical expert. The objection was overruled by the court.

"We find the complained of statement to be a shorthand rendition of the facts. See Silva v. State, Tex.Cr.App., 546 S.W.2d 618 (that defendant and his brother had *ambushed* the declarant); Dabbs v. State, 507 S.W.2d 567 (the cigarette *appeared to be fresh*); Ashley v. State, Tex.Cr.App., 527 S.W.2d 302 ('I would say *she was very upset*'); Gardner v. State, Tex.Cr.App., 486 S.W.2d 805 (that mark on door had been caused by object having been 'slid in the door between the door and the trim'); see also McCormick and Ray, Texas Practice, Vol. 2, Evidence, 2d Ed., Sec. 1397. No error is shown."

UNITED STATES v. PETRONE, 185 F.2d 334, 336 (2d Cir.1950), cert. denied, 340 U.S. 931, 71 S.Ct. 493, 95 L.Ed. 672 (1951). "* * * [T]he question is at most one of discretion, turning upon how the judge thinks the truth may best be extracted from the particular witness who chances to be on the stand. Made obligatory, not only may the canon become a substantial obstacle to developing the truth, but it presupposes a logical solecism; for our perceptions—even our most immediate sense perceptions—are always 'conclusions.' The question ought always to be whether it is more convenient to insist that the witness disentangle in his own mind—which, much more often than not, he is quite unable to do—those constituent factors on which his opinion is based; or to let him state his opinion and leave to cross examination a searching inquisition to uncover its foundations. Yet such is the inveterate habit in American courts of treating rules of evidence as though they were sacred tables, that it is apparently impossible to substitute the view that they should be lightly held as wise admonitions for the general conduct of the trial. We do not forget that that attitude is not possible as to all—e.g., as to hearsay—but in this instance it was, not only possible, but required. Nothing is less within the powers of the ordinary witness than to analyze the agglomerate of sensations which combine in his mind to give him an 'impression' of the contents of another's mind. To require him to unravel that nexus will, unless he is much practiced in self scrutiny, generally make him substitute an utterly unreal—though honest—set of constituents, or will altogether paralyze his powers of expression. Nor is it in the least an objection—as apparently the judge here supposed—that the opinion is upon a crucial issue."

STATE v. LERCH

Supreme Court of Oregon, 1984.
296 Or. 377, 677 P.2d 678.

CAMPBELL, JUSTICE.

The defendant was indicted and convicted of the murder of Michael Hanset. He appealed his conviction to the Court of Appeals setting out numerous assignments of error. The Court of Appeals affirmed. *State v. Lerch,* 63 Or.App. 707, 666 P.2d 840 (1983).

* * *

In his brief in the Court of Appeals, the defendant alleged among other assignments that the trial court had erred in allowing: (1) one of the detectives to testify that in his opinion one of the stains on the defendant's kitchen floor was fecal matter; (2) "opinion testimony regarding the smell of decomposing human flesh;" * * *.

* * *

Kerry Taylor was one of the Portland detectives who searched the defendant's apartment in the early morning hours of August 1st. At the trial he testified that on the defendant's kitchen floor he "observed a stain that I believed to be fecal matter." In the defendant's confession he said that he strangled the victim in the kitchen. A pathologist for the State testified that it was common for strangulation victims to defecate. A photograph of the stain taken on August 1st was received in evidence.

Detective Taylor's statement was offered and received as an opinion by a lay witness under OEC 701:

> "If the witness is not testifying as an expert, testimony of the witness in the form of opinions or inferences is limited to those opinions or inferences which are:
>
> "(1) Rationally based on the perception of the witness; and
>
> "(2) Helpful to a clear understanding of testimony of the witness or the determination of a fact in issue."

In the context of this case, Taylor's opinion that he believed the stain to be fecal matter was admissible if it was rationally based upon his perception and was helpful to the determination of a fact in issue.

In the Court of Appeals, the defendant contended that Taylor's opinion was not "rationally based" because his perception of the reddish brown stain on the kitchen linoleum would permit several different inferences to be drawn as to the source of the stain, e.g., "shoe polish, food stains, or mud." The defendant also claims that Taylor's testimony was not necessary because he could have described the stain without giving his opinion and that the "most accurate portrayal of the stain" was the photograph which was received in evidence. The defendant argues that in spite of the lack of Detective Taylor's qualifications as an expert witness, the State set him up "as a sort of mini-expert" in the field which caused his opinion as to a crucial question in the case to have "the aura of an expert witness."

Oregon Rule of Evidence 701 is identical in substance to Rule 701 of the Federal Rules of Evidence. The rule adopts a liberal standard for the admissibility of lay opinions. Kirkpatrick, Oregon Evidence, 292 (1982). The commentary by the legislature approves the proposition from an earlier Oregon case, *State v. Garver,* 190 Or. 291, 315–316, 225 P.2d 771 (1950), that a lay witness may testify as to what he has perceived by using a "shorthand" description which in reality is an opinion. The admission of opinion evidence is within the discretion of the trial court and it will only be reversed for an abuse of discretion. Commentary, OEC 701, 137; *Unitec Corporation v. Beatty Safway Scaffold Co. of Oregon,* 358 F.2d 470, 477–478 (9th Cir.1966); *Fidelity Sec. Corp. v. Brugman et al.,* 137 Or. 38, 1 P.2d 131 (1931).

An essential difference between opinion testimony by a lay witness and an expert witness is that the lay witness is restricted to his personal perceptions while an expert witness may also testify from facts "made known to him at or before the hearing." OEC 703; FRE 703; *Teen-ed, Inc. v. Kimball Intern., Inc.,* 620 F.2d 399, 404 (3rd Cir.1980). 2

Jones on Evidence, § 14:4, 591–592 (6th ed 1972) explains that a lay witness and an expert witness may testify as to the same subject matter:

> "The testimony of the chemist who has analyzed blood, and that of the observer who has merely recognized it by the use of the senses belong to the same legal grade of evidence, and though the one may be entitled to greater weight than the other with the jury, the exclusion of either is not sustainable."

11 Moore's Federal Practice § 701.02 (2d ed. 1983) states that to ensure:

> "* * * the most reliable and useful information is presented for consideration of the trier of fact * * * the rule [FRE 701] relies on the dynamics of the adversary system in which the proponent tries to elicit detailed testimony from a witness supporting his position to increase the weight given the testimony, while the opponent will try to discredit such evidence by bringing out on cross-examination any detail omitted. In any case, the fact finder is not bound to accept an assertion made in the form of opinion testimony."

We hold that the trial court did not abuse its discretion in allowing Detective Taylor to testify as to his opinion of the type of stain found on the defendant's kitchen floor. The opinion was rationally or reasonably based upon what Taylor may have seen on August 1st. The opinion was helpful to the jury to decide an issue—was the victim in fact strangled in the defendant's kitchen? We agree with the Court of Appeals that the photograph of the stain is not a complete and full substitute for Taylor's observation. It was taken at night. It shows a brown and yellow patterned linoleum with the stain in question spotlighted. Even with the added light it is difficult to describe the stain except to say that it is a brownish-yellow smear.

Taylor's opinion was "rationally based" upon the mere fact that he was a human being of the age of reason who could see. He was merely giving a "shorthand description" of what he saw. It is difficult to see how his opinion is different from that of another person describing a spot on a white shirt as "blood," "catsup," or "lipstick." The fact that Taylor was a detective with the homicide division may have added to or detracted from the weight of his testimony—that was for the jury to determine.[5]

The defendant also claims that it was error to admit "opinion testimony regarding the smell of decomposing human flesh." This assignment of error is aimed at the testimony of Joseph George Jaha who testified that on the afternoon of July 29th, he smelled the odor of

5. On cross-examination Taylor testified: (1) when he observed the stain on August 1st (prior to the defendant's confession) he did not form an opinion that it was a fecal stain; (2) at the same time one of the state crime lab people tested the stain for blood with negative results; (3) the stain did not have a characteristic odor; and (4) that he did not mention the stain in

decomposing human flesh coming from the garbage drop box[6] behind his fish market on Southeast Belmont.

Jaha's testimony was offered and received as the opinion of a lay witness under OEC 701, *supra.*

Jaha testified that he had been in the wholesale and retail fish business all his life—"from father to son." He served in an infantry unit with the United States Army for a period of 13 months during the Korean conflict. During that period of time he saw and smelled decomposing human bodies. He could not describe the smell, except that it is worse than fish. Portland Police Detective Emil Bladow, a 24 year member of the force who had been assigned to the homicide division for 9 years, testified that he had personally smelled between 50 and 100 human corpses, and decomposing human flesh has a distinctive odor. Dr. William J. Brady, the State Medical Examiner, testified he had personally conducted 5,000 autopsies and that decomposing human flesh has a distinct and characteristic odor.[7]

The defendant contends that the possible prejudice of Jaha's testimony outweighs its probative value because there are striking and disturbing aspects of the testimony which throw extreme doubt on the credibility of his ultimate opinion. In his brief in the Court of Appeals the defendant states:

> "The disturbing factors included witness Jaha's inconsistent testimony; the fact that he did not even examine the drop box after claiming to have smelled a body; that he did not immediately notify anyone of his perceptions; that his perception was inconsistent with the probable decaying process of Michael Hanset's body according to expert witnesses, this even assuming that said body was in the dumpster in question; that any smell would have been masked by the smell of rotting fish in the box; and the improbability of identifying a smell one hadn't sensed in 30 years." Appellant's brief, pp. 37–38.

It appears the defendant is objecting to the admission of this evidence under OEC 403:

> "Although relevant, evidence may be excluded if its probative value is substantially outweighed by the danger of unfair prejudice, confusion of the issues, or misleading the jury, or by considerations of undue delay or needless presentation of cumulative evidence."

The determination of whether the possible prejudice of Jaha's testimony outweighed its probative value was within the discretion of the trial court. *Wilson v. Piper Aircraft Corporation,* 282 Or. 61, 77, 577 P.2d 1322 (1978). We hold that the trial court did not abuse its discretion.

the report he wrote concerning the search of the defendant's apartment.

6. Jaha also testified that there was a television set and an old mattress on the top of the garbage drop box. This corroborated the defendant's statement to the officer on July 31st and the admissions to his sisters.

7. Dr. William J. Brady's testimony would fit within the assignment of error, but the defendant does not challenge it directly.

The fact that Jaha could not describe the smell does not make his testimony objectionable. In *People v. Reed,* 333 Ill. 397, 164 N.E. 847 (1929), the defendant was convicted of maliciously damaging and defacing a schoolhouse by the use of dynamite. The evidence showed the defendant placed dynamite in the stove and when the school teacher started a fire with paper and corncobs, it exploded. Several witnesses testified they were familiar with the odor and fumes of dynamite and that after the school house explosion they recognized the smell. The testimony was objected to because the witnesses were unable to describe the odor of dynamite. The Illinois Supreme Court affirmed the conviction:

> "Most persons would probably find it difficult to describe the odor of a rose, whiskey, beer, or limburger cheese, but this difficulty could scarcely be regarded as affecting the value of their testimony that they were familiar with and recognized the particular odor." 333 Ill. at 401, 164 N.E. at 850.[8]

We hold that the trial court did not abuse its discretion in admitting the testimony of Joseph George Jaha as an opinion by a lay witness under OEC 701. The defendant's objections go to the weight and not the admissibility of the opinion. Jaha's testimony was rationally based upon his perception in that he had previously experienced and recognized the smell of decomposing human flesh. The testimony was also helpful to the determination of a fact in issue—did the defendant put the victim's body in the garbage drop box?

The defendant also contends that even if Jaha's opinion were rationally based, it is not a proper lay opinion under OEC 701. He states that "this is really expert opinion masquerading as lay opinion." As we have previously pointed out, the same matter may be the subject of both lay and expert testimony. Jones on Evidence, supra. In this case perhaps Dr. William J. Brady, who had performed 5,000 autopsies, could have testified as an expert witness if he had personally smelled the odor.[9] It is doubtful that Brady could have testified on the basis of "facts or data * * * made known" to him "at or before the hearing" because Jaha could not describe the smell.

8. The same rule of law is demonstrated in a different manner in *United States v. Arrasmith,* 557 F.2d 1093 (5th Cir.1977) where the defendant was convicted of possession of 134 pounds of marijuana. A question on appeal was whether the smell of marijuana gave the border patrol agent probable cause to search the defendant's car. The following occurred during the agent's cross-examination:

> "Q. What does marijuana smell like?
>
> "A. Marijuana.
>
> "[Defense Counsel]: Your honor, I don't think that answer is responsive.
>
> "[THE COURT]: It is responsive. It smells like marijuana.
>
> "[Defense Counsel]: Marijuana smells like marijuana?
>
> "THE COURT: Yes, sir."
>
> 557 F.2d at 1094.

The conviction was affirmed.

9. OEC 703 states:

> "The facts or data in the particular case upon which an expert bases an opinion or inference may be those perceived by or made known to the expert at or before the hearing. If of a type reasonably relied upon by experts in the particular field in forming opinions or inferences upon the subject, the facts or data need not be admissible in evidence."

One of the differences between Detective Taylor's opinion and Jaha's opinion is that Taylor was testifying to a common everyday subject matter while Jaha was testifying to a smell that would be a rare experience to the average person. Jaha's prior experience allowed the judge in the first instance to pass upon his qualifications to testify as to the subject matter and secondly gave the jury a basis upon which to weigh his opinion. Perhaps Jaha's "specialized knowledge" would have allowed him to testify as an expert under OEC 702. His opinion was not offered as expert testimony and that question is not before us.

* * *

The conviction of the defendant is affirmed.

MYDLARZ v. PALMER/DUNCAN CONST. CO., 209 Mont. 325, 682 P.2d 695, 704–05 (1984). "Mydlarz next asserts that the lay opinion of one Ron Lins was improperly excluded. Prior to Mydlarz's accident Lins performed the same job that caused Mydlarz's accident. Lins fell under the same circumstances and was injured. Mydlarz argues that Lins's opinion concerning the safety of the device should have been allowed.

"Respondent Palmer/Duncan contends the testimony was properly excluded since it was an opinion on the ultimate issue of the action. Further, Lins was never identified as an expert witness in interrogatories and would not qualify as such.

"Respondent Rice Motors argues that since Lins did not perceive Mydlarz's accident, he could not give an opinion on it.

"We hold that Lins's opinion should have been admitted into evidence. Lay opinion is admissible pursuant to Rule 701, Mont. R.Evid. The opinion must be based on actual perceptions of the witness and helpful to the jury to understand the facts in issue. State v. Fitzpatrick (1980), 186 Mont. 187, 606 P.2d 1343, 37 St.Rep. 194. In this case, Lins's opinion as a *layman* should have been allowed. His opinion of the safety of the workplace was based on his perceptions from working the same job as Mydlarz. Further, his testimony would help the jury understand the conditions under which Mydlarz was working. Finally, the respondents' objections to Lins's testimony were generally based on the failure to meet the expert testimony requirements, and the court rejected the opinion on that basis. The question of lay opinion testimony was not addressed."

WESTERN INDUSTRIES, INC. v. NEWCOR CANADA LTD., 739 F.2d 1198, 1202–03 (7th Cir.1984). "Of course testimony of trade custom is testimony to a conclusion; and though all evidence, even eyewitness testimony, is inferential to a degree (see Hoffman, The

Interpretation of Visual Illusions, Scientific American, Dec. 1983, at p. 154), the chain of inference is longer when the fact testified to is the existence of a trade custom than when it is the color of the defendant's hair. If the members of this court had been called as witnesses in this case and asked whether it was the custom of the specialty welding machine trade not to give disappointed buyers consequential damages, we would not have been competent to answer. But Newcor's witnesses were experienced executives in the trade, and the existence of the alleged custom was a matter they could infer from their own observations and experience, since each had negotiated many sale contracts such as the one in issue in this case. Any doubt about the admissibility of their testimony is dispelled by section 701 of the Federal Rules of Evidence, which makes lay opinion evidence of the kind involved here admissible, see Bohannon v. Pegelow, 652 F.2d 729, 731–32 (7th Cir. 1981), and by the fact that under the liberal definition of 'expert witness' in Rule 702 all of these witnesses could readily have been qualified as expert witnesses on the question of trade custom. The Advisory Committee's Notes on Proposed Rule 702 state that 'within the scope of the rule are * * * the large group sometimes called "skilled" witnesses, such as bankers or landowners testifying to land values.' "

Notes

(1) In Williams Enterprises, Inc. v. Sherman R. Smoot Co., 938 F.2d 230 (D.C.Cir.1991), Smoot's insurance broker was permitted to testify as a lay witness to his opinion concerning the cause of an increase in Smoot's insurance premiums. The broker's opinion was based on facts personally known to him and the trial judge found that the testimony would be helpful. "The fact that the broker based his opinion on specialized knowledge and might have been able to offer his opinion as an expert does not mean he was required to do so. As long as he had personal knowledge of the facts, he was entitled to draw conclusions and inferences from those facts—regardless of whether he applied any special expertise." Id. at 234.

(2) "Burlington Northern also challenges the district court's exclusion of the lay opinion testimony of four executives of railroads that had initiated cabooseless operations prior to the 1982 collective bargaining agreement. * * * These officers testified, or were expected to testify that, in their experience, trains with cabooses were no safer than cabooseless trains. * * * Personal knowledge or perception acquired through review of records prepared in the ordinary course of business, or perceptions based on industry experience, is a sufficient foundation for lay opinion testimony. * * * The railroad executives' testimony, based on knowledge derived from supervising railroad operations, years of experience in the industry, and review of employee accident reports prepared in the ordinary course of business, satisfies the foundation requirements for lay opinion testimony. * * * We conclude that the district court's failure to consider this evidence was an abuse of discretion." Burlington Northern R. Co. v. State of Nebraska, 802 F.2d 994, 1004–05 (8th Cir.1986).

(3) See also Soden v. Freightliner Corp., 714 F.2d 498, 511 (5th Cir. 1983) (a witness with "very considerable practical experience and specialized knowledge" was properly permitted to testify to his opinions as a layman; "a layman can under certain circumstances express an opinion even on matters appropriate for expert testimony"); Teen–Ed, Inc. v. Kimball International, Inc., 620 F.2d 399, 403 (3d Cir.1980) ("The fact that Zeitz might have been able to qualify as an expert witness on the use of accepted accounting principles in the calculation of business losses should not have prevented his testifying on the basis of his knowledge of appellant's records about how lost profits could be calculated from the data contained therein."); McAway v. Holland, 266 Ark. 878, 599 S.W.2d 387, 389 (App.1979) ("Wigmore states there are two questions which need to be resolved before opinion testimony may be given by a lay witness. Is it a subject or topic which requires the witness to have more than ordinary experience, and if so, does this witness have this special experience? Wigmore on Evidence § 1925, Vol. VII, P. 35.").

SECTION 2. TESTIMONY BY EXPERTS *

[FED.R.EVID. 702–706]

WULFF v. SPROUSE–REITZ CO.

Supreme Court of Oregon, 1972.
262 Or. 293, 498 P.2d 766.

BRYSON, JUSTICE.

This is an action at law by the owners of a house and personal property and the insurance company which insured the property, to recover damages against the defendants Northern Electric Co., a corporation, and Sprouse–Reitz Co., Inc., a corporation, the manufacturer and retailer, respectively, of an electric blanket which allegedly caused a fire and destroyed the owners' property.

The complaint sets forth two counts: that defendants were strictly liable for the manufacture and sale to plaintiffs Wulff of said blanket in a defective condition; that defendant Northern Electric was negligent in failing to test the blanket and in failing to warn of the volatile nature of the blanket.

Judgment was entered on the jury's verdict in favor of plaintiffs against both defendants. Defendants appeal, seeking a new trial, setting forth twelve assignments of error.

* See 2 Wigmore, Evidence ch. 23, §§ 672–686 (Chadbourn rev. 1979); 3 id. §§ 687–689 (Chadbourn rev. 1970); 7 id. chs. 67–68 (Chadbourn rev. 1978); McCormick, Evidence §§ 12–17, 203–211 (4th ed. 1992); Gianelli, The Admissibility of Novel Scientific Evidence: Frye v. United States, A Half Century Later, 80 Colum.L.Rev. 1197 (1980); Graham, Expert Witness Testimony and the Federal Rules of Evidence: Insuring Adequate Assurance of Trustworthiness, 1986 U.Ill.L.Rev. 43; Imwinkelried, The "Bases" of Expert Testimony: The Syllogistic Structure of Scientific Testimony, 67 N.C.L.Rev. 1 (1988); McCormick, Scientific Evidence: Defining a New Approach to Admissibility, 67 Iowa L.Rev. 879 (1982); McElhaney, Expert Witnesses and the Federal Rules of Evidence, 28 Mercer L.Rev. 463 (1977); O'Toole, Hearsay Bases of Psychiatric Opinion Testimony: A Critique of Federal Rule of Evidence 703, 51 S.Cal.L.Rev. 129 (1977); Pratt, A Judicial Perspective on Opinion Evidence Under the Federal Rules, 29 Wash. & Lee L.Rev. 313 (1982).

In August or September, 1968, Mrs. Wulff purchased two electric blankets from Sprouse–Reitz. The blankets were alleged to have been manufactured by defendant Northern Electric. Mrs. Wulff stored the blankets in a closet until October or November, 1968. At that time one of the blankets was placed on the bed of her younger daughter, Miss Olga Wulff. Mrs. Wulff reread the instructions before connecting the blanket and was careful not to tuck the blanket under the mattress. The instructions stated that the blanket was not to be left on when not being used; that it should not be allowed to "bunch together"; and objects should not be left on the blanket.

Miss Olga Wulff also read the instructions. She testified that the blanket was not used every night and the electric controls were never set more than one-third of the maximum heat. Miss Olga Wulff occupied a small second-floor bedroom in the Wulff home. There were three electrical outlets in Miss Wulff's carpeted room. On the day of the fire, December 17, 1968, the electric blanket was plugged into one of the outlets and a floor lamp was connected to another. No one was in the house from 7:30 a.m. until approximately 5 p.m., when Mrs. Wulff's older daughter, Maria, returned home.

After sleeping several hours, Maria was awakened by a phone ringing. She noticed a peculiar odor and began searching for its source. After looking downstairs, she went to the second floor and noticed the odor becoming more intense as she approached her sister's bedroom. She opened the door of that bedroom and found the room filled with thick smoke. She opened a window in the hall to let the smoke out. The smoke had risen, allowing Maria to see the blanket "[c]harred and glowing with little red sort of like glowing sparks." The charred area was confined to the middle part of the blanket, which lay perfectly flat on the bed. She then ran downstairs and attempted to phone the fire department but the phone was dead. She secured a garden hose and ran it upstairs; switched off the upstairs electricity; and turned on the water. She soaked the bed thoroughly and sprayed water on the carpet, walls and ceiling. She returned downstairs and, discovering water dripping through the ceiling of the living room, placed a number of pans to protect the carpet. She then fainted.

Sometime later Maria was awakened by a loud noise. She saw flames engulfing the stairwell and a bright orange color from the fire. She ran to a neighbor's house and called the fire department. Testimony and exhibits reveal the house and contents were almost totally destroyed by the fire.

* * *

Defendants assign as error the trial court's (1) "allowing plaintiffs' witness, Mr. J.A. Anderson, to express numerous opinions as an expert," and (2) "in allowing Mr. Anderson to answer a hypothetical question which was not based on substantial evidence in the record." We gather from the questions asked Dr. Anderson by defendants' counsel in aid of objecting to his qualifications that at the time of trial they did not feel he was qualified as an expert because he had no specific experience in the manufacture of electric blankets. Dr. Anderson is a consulting chemical engineer with a BS degree in chemical engineering from Lafayette College, a Master's degree in chemical engineering and heat flow, and a "PHD" [sic] in chemical engineering from Iowa State College, and taught at the university level for four years. This included heat transference, fuels and combustions. He studied some electrical engineering as a requirement for receiving his degree in chemical engineering. He was employed by Dupont and spent a year and a half "in instruments," working with electricity and wires. He worked for American Cyanamid Company for five years and designed and laid out equipment "which involved resistance wiring and involved heat work." This work required him to consider problems in the use of electrical current. He was also employed by Georgia–Pacific Company as an engineer in charge of the research department in developing useful products from waste wood. He was then employed by Pacific Power and Light Company until 1967, and he served as a consultant on a special project which related to safety of electric hot water heaters. Defendants' objection to his qualification was:

> "Well, I would on the basis of the man's testimony now object to his answering the question on what caused this blanket or whatever the problem was with the blanket in glowing and so forth, on the ground I don't think he qualified from the electrical standpoint and I think he so indicated."

Even though the witness was a chemical engineer and not an electrical engineer, he had sufficient training, study, background, and experience to qualify as an expert witness. He does not necessarily have to be an expert in the specific item under question in a products liability case. Whether he is the best expert witness on the specific subject or what credibility will be given to the witness's testimony are matters that go to the weight of his testimony and not to his qualification. The court instructed the jury:

> "* * * In determining the weight to be given to such opinion, you should consider the qualifications and credibility of the expert and the reasons given for his opinion. You are not bound by such opinion. You shall give it such weight, if any, that you feel the opinion is entitled to."

In Highway Com. v. Parker et al., 225 Or. 143, 162, 357 P.2d 548, 556 (1960), this court stated:

> "* * * [T]he competency of a witness who is called as an expert is a preliminary matter which is addressed to the sound discretion of the trial judge. Wigmore on Evidence, 3rd ed. § 561, is a vigorous proponent of the rule that the competency of the would-be expert must be left with the trial judge. He says:
>
> > 'Secondly, and emphatically, the *trial Court must be left to determine,* absolutely and without review, the fact of possession of the required qualification by a particular witness.'

"This court has not gone so far as to assign completely to the trial judge's province a ruling upon the would-be expert's qualifications, but it has gone far in that direction: W.D. Miller Construction Co. v. Donald M. Drake Co., 221 Or. 249, 351 P.2d 41."

The court did not err in allowing the witness to testify as an expert.

Defendants next contend that even if Dr. Anderson was qualified as an expert witness, "[t]he hypothetical question which Mr. Anderson was asked relating to the probable source of the glowing 'embers' included numerous assumptions which were unsubstantiated by competent evidence * * *." The only example, from the record, of unsubstantiated assumptions is:

" * * * it is assumed by the person who is using it [the electric blanket] that they probably turned it off, but they are not sure."

In the trial of a case, one of the most troublesome problems to counsel and trial judges is the putting of a proper hypothetical question to an expert witness based on substantial evidence in the record in order to allow the expert witness to express opinions or inferences.

Much has been written on the use of the hypothetical question. The writers have stated that the use of the hypothetical question in presenting expert opinion has been so grossly abused that it creates a scandal. Judge Learned Hand referred to the practice as "the most horrific and grotesque wen on the fair face of justice." Lectures on Legal Topics, New York Bar Association (1921–1922).

2 Wigmore, Evidence (3d ed.) 812, § 686 poses the question, "*Must the Hypothetical Question go,* as a requirement?" and states:

"Its abuses have become so obstructive and nauseous that no remedy short of extirpation will suffice. It is a logical necessity, but a practical incubus; and logic must here be sacrificed. After all, Law (in Mr. Justice Holmes' phrase) is much more than Logic. It is a strange irony that the hypothetical question, which is one of the few truly scientific features of the rules of Evidence, should have become that feature which does most to disgust men of science with the law of Evidence.

"The hypothetical question, misused by the clumsy and abused by the clever, has in practice led to intolerable obstruction of truth. In the first place, it has artificially clamped the mouth of the expert witness, so that his answer to a complex question may not express his actual opinion on the actual case. This is because the question may be so built up and contrived by counsel as to represent only a partisan conclusion. In the second place, it has tended to mislead the jury as to the purport of actual expert opinion. This is due to the same reason. In the third place, it has tended to confuse the jury, so that its employment becomes a mere waste of time and a futile obstruction.

"No partial limitation of its use seems feasible, by specific rules * * *."

The National Conference of Commissioners on Uniform State Laws, after four years of debate and redrafting, adopted the Uniform Act on Expert Testimony with their comment as follows:

> "Rule 58. *Hypothesis for Expert Opinion Not Necessary.* Questions calling for the opinion of an expert witness need not be hypothetical in form unless the judge in his discretion so requires, but the witness may state his opinion and reasons therefor without first specifying data on which it is based as an hypothesis or otherwise; but upon cross examination he may be required to specify such data.
>
> "COMMENT
>
> "This rule does away with the necessity of following the practice (grossly abused) of using the hypothetical question, but does not forbid its use. It is consistent with the provisions of the Model Expert Testimony Act drafted by this Conference * * *."

An analysis of the problem and the one presented by this assignment leads us to the conclusion that "Rule 58," adopted by the National Conference of Commissioners on Uniform State Laws, is a reasonable rule of law and we adopt its language as the law in Oregon. This rule contemplates that the expert witness is acquainted with the pertinent facts of the case or has heard testimony given, or has read pertinent depositions of witnesses or has examined and considered exhibits before being called to testify. This is expressed by Wigmore, supra at 813, as follows:

> "1. *Where an expert witness has not had personal observation of matters of fact in the case in hand, but has listened to or read any or all of the testimony or depositions to such matter of fact, he may be asked, by the party calling him, to state his conclusion, without specifying in the question the data forming the basis of the conclusion;* * * *.
>
> "2. *Where an expert witness has considered data presented him otherwise than through the testimony or deposition of a witness in the case, he may be asked to state his conclusions thereon, if qualified by personal observation or by general experience, in which case the question need not be in hypothetical form;* * * *.
>
> "3. *In either of the foregoing classes of cases, the opposite party on cross-examination may require the witness to specify the data on the hypothesis of which his conclusion was based.*" (Emphasis theirs.)

The above rule does not do away with the use of the hypothetical question, but it does eliminate the necessity of following the practice.

The record indicates that Dr. Anderson heard a large portion of testimony of other witnesses before he was called to testify and had conducted experiments with material from an electric blanket received in evidence and stipulated to have been similar to the one destroyed in the fire. Great latitude should be given counsel on the cross-examination of an expert witness and this right was accorded counsel for defendant. The facts are that the electric blanket in question was used on the bed of Olga M. Wulff, daughter of plaintiffs. She testified as follows:

> "Q And do you know for sure whether or not you turned off the controls?
>
> "A No, I don't. It was my habit to turn them off and I did it within the limitation of human fallability [sic], but I believe to have turned them off because I always tried to, but I can't be sure."

In the total context of the expert's testimony, the inclusion of the statement in the hypothetical question, "it is assumed by the person who is using it [blanket] that they probably turned it off but they are not sure," was of no consequence. It is an equivocal statement and had no effect on the testimony given by Dr. Anderson. We find no error in this assignment.

* * *

Notwithstanding all of the assignments of error, some involving difficult problems of law, we are of the opinion that no reversible error was committed.

Affirmed.

ALOE COAL CO. v. CLARK EQUIPMENT CO., 816 F.2d 110, 114–15 (3d Cir.1987), cert. denied, 484 U.S. 853, 108 S.Ct. 156, 98 L.Ed.2d 111 (1987). "After a thorough review of the testimony in this case, we conclude that there was not sufficient proof of causation to allow Aloe's negligence claim to go to the jury. Aloe's theory was that 'a fire originated within the * * * 475B Michigan hi-lift tractor as a result of a ruptured hydraulic pressure line.' App. at 8a. Aloe contended that the ruptured line was due to Clark's negligence in manufacturing the tractor shovel. Id. The critical question is whether Aloe supported its allegation regarding the cause of the fire.

"Aloe relied solely on the testimony of one person to establish causation. He was Michael Drewnoski, a sales representative for Mendes & Company, whose position required him to determine the costs of repairing and replacing damaged equipment. Over Clark's objections, the district court allowed Drewnoski to give expert testimony regarding the cause of the tractor shovel fire. Drewnoski's opinion was that the fire was caused by a leak in one of the hydraulic lines. App. at 318a. This testimony presents the threshold question of whether Drewnoski was competent to serve in this expert witness capacity.

"Guiding us are settled legal precepts. An expert witness must have such skill, knowledge, or experience in the field as to make it appear that his opinion will probably aid the trier of fact in his search for the truth. Caisson Corp. v. Ingersoll–Rand Co., 622 F.2d 672, 682 (3d Cir.1980); Universal Athletic Sales Co. v. American Gym, Recreational & Athletic Equipment Corp., 546 F.2d 530, 537 (3d Cir.1976), cert. denied, 430 U.S. 984, 97 S.Ct. 1681, 52 L.Ed.2d 378 (1977); see also Rule 702, F.R.Evid. The determination of competency of an expert witness rests with the discretion of the district court. *Caisson Corp.,* 622 F.2d at 682; Knight v. Otis Elevator Co., 596 F.2d 84, 87 (3d Cir.1979); *Universal Athletic Sales,* 546 F.2d at 537. The Supreme Court has stated that 'the trial judge has broad discretion in the matter of the admission or exclusion of expert evidence, and his action is to be sustained unless manifestly erroneous.' Salem v. United States Lines Co., 370 U.S. 31, 35, 82 S.Ct. 1119, 1122, 8 L.Ed.2d 313 (1962).

"After carefully reviewing Mr. Drewnoski's credentials, we conclude that the district court abused its discretion by allowing the witness to testify regarding the cause of the tractor shovel fire. Drewnoski was not an engineer. He had no experience in designing construction machinery. He had no knowledge or experience in determining the cause of equipment fires. App. at 300a. He had no training as a mechanic. He had never operated construction machinery in the course of business. Id. at 303a–04a. He was a salesman, who at times prepared damage estimates.

"We are well aware of 'the liberal policy of permitting expert testimony which will "probably aid" the trier of fact.' *Knight,* 596 F.2d at 87. But, at a minimum, a proffered expert witness on causation must possess skill or knowledge greater than the average layman in determining causation. Drewnoski did not. We therefore conclude that the district court abused its discretion in allowing him to testify as an expert on the cause of the tractor shovel fire."

WILLIAMS v. CARR, 263 Ark. 326, 565 S.W.2d 400, 404 (1978). "Marvin Thompson, a licensed embalmer and funeral director, who testified that he attended the Dallas Institute of Mortuary Science at Dallas, Texas, and that he obtained his license in late 1950, over the objections of appellants, was qualified by the trial court as an expert witness on the question of grief and mental anguish.

"Mr. Thompson was excused from the rule and, accordingly, he sat in the courtroom during the two days of trial; he heard all of the testimony given by the plaintiffs concerning the grief and mental anguish that they had sustained. Marvin Thompson concluded, from this limited observation of the appellants-plaintiffs, that appellants had sustained nothing more than normal grief as a consequence of the loss of their loved ones.

"The action of the trial court in qualifying a mortician as an expert on the issue of mental anguish and grief is rather shocking and disturbing to this Court. It is well settled that a witness may testify as an expert if he possesses special skill or knowledge with respect to the matter involved so superior to that of men in general as to make his formation of a judgment a fact of probative value. Blanton v. Missouri Pacific Railroad Company, 182 Ark. 543, 31 S.W.2d 947.

"Also, under Rule 702 of the Uniform Rules of Evidence, it is provided as follows:

> 'Testimony by experts.—If scientific, technical, or other specialized knowledge will assist the trier of fact to understand the evidence or to determine a fact in issue, a witness qualified as an expert by knowledge, skill, experience, training, or education, may testify thereto in the form of an opinion or otherwise.'

"We are not persuaded that Mr. Thompson's attendance at an institute of mortuary science and his participation in approximately 200 funerals would qualify him as an expert to offer any constructive and objective testimony relating to the degree and intensity of the mental anguish and grief realized by the appellants-plaintiffs.

"We submit that Mr. Thompson's definition of extraordinary grief illustrates his very limited knowledge of the subject matter and not only does it not represent the law, but was devastating to appellants' claim of damages for mental suffering and grief:

> 'In my opinion, extraordinary grief is that grief that a person cannot overcome and he or she has to be treated by a doctor, psychiatrist or put in a mental hospital.' "

WOLFF v. COMMONWEALTH OF PUERTO RICO, 341 F.2d 945, 948 (1st Cir.1965). "One final matter. It was error not to permit appellants' expert to state his qualifications. The fact that the Commonwealth 'accepted' his qualifications went only to whether the court should permit him to testify. It did not meet the further question of what weight the jury might wish to give his opinion, which might well be governed by its appraisal of his background and experience."

Note

See also United States v. Barletta, 565 F.2d 985, 991–92 (8th Cir.1977) (FBI agent testified as an expert in interpreting "the peculiar argot of bookmakers"); Corbin v. Hittle, 34 Mich.App. 631, 192 N.W.2d 38, 40 (1971) (chiropractor testified that plaintiff's injuries were permanent); Kastner v. Wermerskirschen, 295 Minn. 391, 205 N.W.2d 336, 338–39 (1973) (a chicken hatchery operator could testify as expert on chicken diseases, for "the care of animals is generally in the hands of practical men" and therefore the courts "apply a lower standard of qualification to witnesses giving opinion testimony on such matters than is generally applied to expert witnesses offering testimony as to the diseases and ailments of humans"); State v. Briner, 198 Neb. 766, 255 N.W.2d 422 (1977) ("it would be hard to find a person more qualified as an expert witness on the subject at hand" than the five-times convicted, retired burglar who testified that the tools found in defendant's possession at 3:30 a.m. were suitable for breaking and entering); Dowling v. L.H. Shattuck, Inc., 91 N.H. 234, 17 A.2d 529, 532 (1941) (laborer who had worked in ditches sufficiently expert to give opinion as to proper way to shore ditch in sandy soil against a cave-in); Warren v. Hartnett, 561 S.W.2d 860 (Tex.Civ.App.1977) ("handwriting expert" could not properly testify on basis of handwriting comparison that deceased did not have sufficient mental ability to understand her business or the natural objects of her bounty).

NAT HARRISON ASSOCIATES, INC. v. BYRD, 256 So.2d 50, 52–54 (Fla.App.1971). "During her case in chief, the appellee submitted the following 'hypothetical' questions to the expert in the following order:

> (1) '* * * I will refer Mr. Dollar to two photographs, Plaintiff's Exhibit No. 9 and Exhibit No. 6, which are the plaintiff's vehicle and the defendant's vehicle, and ask you, from the extent of the damage as shown in these two photographs can you give an opinion based upon your knowledge of accidents that have taken place, and so forth, as to the speed differential of these two vehicles at the time of the impact?'
>
> * * *
>
> (3) 'Would you assume, please, that the skid marks extend from the rear of the Leonard Brothers' trailer a distance of 145 feet back along the highway, as you can see there, to the point where they began, based on those, on that assumption, can you give an opinion as to the speed of the trailer?'

When the appellee thereafter sought the witness' opinion based on the hypotheticals, the appellants objected. As to the opinion based on the first hypothetical, the appellants' objection was stated as follows:

> 'Now, I would object to that, Your Honor, that there not being a proper predicate laid for the witness to give an opinion based on merely those two photographs.'

As to the opinion based on the third hypothetical, the appellants' objection was stated as follows:

> 'I am going to make the same objection, Your Honor, that a proper predicate has not been laid for the witness to give his opinion on this.'

"The objections were overruled and the witness expressed an opinion that the speed difference between the two vehicles at the time of impact was between 40 and 60 miles per hour; that the Nat Harrison truck at that time was traveling less than 10 miles an hour, and the speed of the Leonard Brothers' trailer (apparently at the time of impact) was 51 miles an hour.

* * *

"* * * When an expert is called upon to give an opinion as to past events which he did not witness, all facts related to the event which are essential to the formation of his opinion should be submitted to the expert in the form of a hypothetical question. No other facts related to the event should be taken into consideration by the expert as a foundation for his opinion. The facts submitted to the expert in the hypothetical question propounded on direct examination must be supported by competent substantial evidence in the record at the time the question is asked or by reasonable inferences from such evidence. See Atlantic Coast Line R. Co. v. Shouse, supra; Autrey v. Carroll, Fla.1970, 240 So.2d 474; Sheehan v. Frith, Fla.App.1962, 138 So.2d 76. Adherence to this form for the direct examination of an expert prevents the expert from expressing an opinion based on unstated and perhaps unwarranted factual assumptions concerning the event; facilitates cross-examination and rebuttal; and fosters an understanding of the opinion by the trier of fact.

"Once an expert has been qualified to give opinion testimony, the sufficiency of the facts submitted to the expert to permit him to formulate an opinion must normally be decided by the witness himself, at least in the first instance. This of necessity must be the rule because, the trial judge (like an appellate judge) would not ordinarily be in a position to know whether the facts submitted to the expert were sufficient to permit the formation of the expert's opinion. See Myers v. Korbly, Fla.App.1958, 103 So.2d 215, 221. As a corollary to this proposition, deficiencies in a factual predicate submitted to an expert as a basis for an expert opinion, normally relate to the weight and not the admissibility of the opinion. Compare State Road Department v. Falcon, Inc., Fla.App.1963, 157 So.2d 563, 566, and Rimmer v. Tesla, Fla.App.1967, 201 So.2d 573. Where, however, the factual predicate submitted to the expert witness in the hypothetical question omits a fact which is so obviously necessary to the formation of an opinion that the trial judge may take note of the omission on the basis of his common knowledge, an objection founded on the inadequacy of the predicate may be sustained. Delta Rent-A-Car, Inc. v. Rihl, Fla.App. 1969, 218 So.2d 469.

"The first question which was submitted to the expert witness called for his opinion as to the difference in speed between the two vehicles at the time of the collision. The only basis for the opinion was damage to the vehicles as shown by photographs in evidence. The defendants objected to the question on the ground that the photographs were insufficient as a foundation or predicate for the opinion. This objection should have been sustained because the factual predicate was clearly lacking an essential fact, namely, the weight of the respective vehicles. That such was an essential fact was demonstrated by the testimony of the expert witness himself which led up to the asking of the hypothetical question. * * *

"With respect to the third question, it called for an opinion of the expert witness as to the speed of the Leonard Brothers' trailer (apparently at the time of the impact) based on the skid marks which were evidently developed by the trailer after the collision. The objection, based on insufficiency of predicate, was not as specific as it should have been; however, in our opinion the omission from the factual predicate submitted to the witness was so apparent that it should have been recognized even without a more specific objection. The question completely failed to submit to the expert witness any assumption with respect to the appropriate coefficient of friction which would apply to the trailer moving over the road surface in question. Without some assumption as to a proper coefficient of friction supported by competent substantial evidence, there was no basis upon which the expert could have formed an opinion as to speed solely from the length of skid marks. That such was an essential assumption is demonstrated by the answer of the witness wherein he indicated that he gratuitously assumed a coefficient of friction or 'drag factor' of .60, even though the same was neither submitted to him in the question nor based upon any evidence in the record which has been called to our attention. Such an assumption was so clearly necessary to the opinion sought that the trial judge, in our view, should have sustained the objection."

HARRIS v. SMITH, 372 F.2d 806, 810 (8th Cir.1967). "It has long been recognized in this circuit as well as most other jurisdictions that it is improper, when asking a hypothetical question of an expert witness, to incorporate within the question being asked the opinion of other expert witnesses, for opinion upon opinion diverges much too far from the plain facts upon which all proper hypothetical questions must be grounded."

ARKANSAS STATE HIGHWAY COMMISSION v. SCHELL

Court of Appeals of Arkansas, 1985.
13 Ark.App. 293, 683 S.W.2d 618.

CORBIN, JUDGE.

Appellant, Arkansas State Highway Commission, appeals from a judgment entered on a jury verdict assessing compensation in the amount of $50,000.00 for the taking of the lands of appellees, Harold D. and Bertha E. Schell. Appellant contends that the trial court erred in refusing to adopt its statement of the evidence, in refusing to grant its motion for a new trial and in refusing to allow appellant to inquire into the basis of the opinion of witness Neil Palmer. We reverse and remand.

Appellant condemned part of a forty-acre tract of appellees for construction of the Highway 71 Relocation project. Appellees raised poultry in four poultry houses located on the property. The area of taking acquired by appellant consisted of 4.44 acres and divided appellees' forty-acre tract into two parts, leaving the west residual with 27.58 acres and the east residual with 7.98 acres. Due to the construction of the controlled access facility, appellees' east residual was landlocked following the taking. The record reflects that after construction of the new highway, appellees' easternmost poultry house would be approximately 250 to 270 feet from the nearest traffic lane of the highway.

Mark Risk, an expert witness who testified at the trial for appellees, determined the amount of damages from the taking to be $61,000.00. Appellee Bertha E. Schell testified that the damages from the taking amounted to $75,000.00. Larry Dupree and Neil Palmer, expert witnesses for appellant, testified that the amount of compensation owed appellees was $20,600.00 and $25,800.00, respectively.

* * *

The issue of concern to this Court and the one which we hold constitutes reversible error is the refusal of the trial court to allow appellant to inquire into the basis of the opinion of witness Neil Palmer. Neil Palmer was a real estate appraiser for appellant and was called by appellees as their second witness.

The record reflects that Neil Palmer was asked on direct examination by counsel for appellees to tell the jury how he went about making his appraisal. He was further questioned as to whether he considered any severance damages to the property. Neil Palmer responded by stating that he was involved in a study and determined that severance damages were improper. During its questioning of the witness, counsel for appellant attempted to go into the basis of Neil Palmer's opinion that no severance damages were assigned by him to the fourth poultry house by virtue of its proximity to the highway. Counsel for appellees objected and the following exchange took place:

> MR. PEARSON (counsel for appellees): Your Honor, I,—I object. Ugh,—who he talked to is totally irrelevant, and he can't testify as to what they said. This, I believe, is for the purpose of trying to prejudice the jury without going into the parties' qualifications.
>
> THE COURT: Well, I think you're right, Mr. Pearson. I'll sustain the objection. He may testify that he talked to people he considered knowledgeable, and that's it.
>
> MR. PUTMAN (counsel for appellant): Your Honor, aren't we going to be allowed to show the nature and depth and extent of his investigation?
>
> THE COURT: Ugh,—No, because, I think you'd be,—ugh,—I think you'd be lending weight to their opinion. Ugh,—he may testify that he made an investigation—

Counsel for appellant then made the following proffer:

> MR. PUTMAN: Let the record show that if he were allowed to answer, the witness would testify that the nature of his study about whether or not there were any severance damages to the poultry house number four, or what's been referred to as poultry house number four; he consulted with a poultry expert at the University of Arkansas in the College of Agriculture; that he consulted with people who were in-

volved in the poultry industry who have, I believe, the designation of integrators, who organize and present overall poultry programs, and place poultry in certain particular locations. * * * And, also, he talked to poultry raisers; the people in the field, who raise both chickens and turkeys; that he went on site, and examined the poultry houses in which both chickens and turkeys were being raised at distances ranging from fifteen feet to two hundred and over from the highway, and determined in each case that there were no deleterious effects, and further, had the benefit of a particular study conducted by the University of South Carolina in a field called poultry hysteria, dealing specifically with the effects of noise and other such phenomena on the raising of poultry, and from all of these, determined that the proximity of the highway would have no effect whatsoever on the raising of the poultry in the house in question.

THE COURT: Well, the Court's ruling is that the witness would be permitted to testify that he talked to people he considered to be experts in the field,—ugh,—including poultry raisers and,—ugh,—including,—ugh,—people,—ugh,—who are considered expert in the area; but, if you go any further than that, you are lending weight to his conclusion. You're bringing in testimony of experts when they are not here.

MR. PUTMAN: Well, I think it's true what Your Honor says. It does lend weight to his testimony; but, I think it's the type of weight which the jury is entitled to know about.

THE COURT: I don't think so.

The questions that were asked of Neil Palmer were proper and his answers were admissible. It is well settled that an expert may base his opinion on facts learned from others despite their being hearsay. Dixon v. Ledbetter, 262 Ark. 758, 561 S.W.2d 294 (1978); Ark. State Hwy. Comm'n. v. Bradford, 252 Ark. 1037, 482 S.W.2d 107 (1972); Ark. State Hwy. Comm'n. v. Russell, 240 Ark. 21, 398 S.W.2d 201 (1966). When an expert's testimony is based on hearsay, the lack of personal knowledge on the part of the expert does not mandate the exclusion of the opinion but, rather presents a jury question as to the weight which should be assigned the opinion. Stated another way, Neil Palmer's method of gathering the data he utilized in forming his opinion should have been explained in order for the jury to weigh his opinion. The rule for admission of expert testimony does not depend on the relative certainty of the subject matter of testimony, but rather on the assistance given by the expert testimony to the trier of fact in understanding the evidence or determining a fact in issue. Ark.Unif.R.Evid. 702. Moreover, the relative weakness or strength of the factual underpinning of the expert's opinion goes to the weight and credibility, rather than admissibility. Polk v. Ford Motor Co., 529 F.2d 259 (8th Cir.), *cert. denied,* 426 U.S. 907, 96 S.Ct. 2229, 48 L.Ed.2d 832 (1976).

Ark.Unif.R.Evid. 703 provides:

Basis of opinion testimony by experts.—The facts or data in the particular case upon which an expert bases an opinion or inference may be those perceived by or made known to him at or before the

> hearing. If of a type reasonably relied upon by experts in the particular field in forming opinions or inferences upon the subject, the facts or data need not be admissible in evidence.

Under this rule an expert must be allowed to disclose to the trier of fact the basis facts for his opinion, as otherwise the opinion is left unsupported in midair with little if any means for evaluating its correctness. E. Cleary, *McCormick on Evidence* (3d ed. 1984), § 324.2, p. 910. Underlying Rule 703 is the idea that an expert is likely to understand better than a court the quality and nature of data essential to support an opinion in his own field. This rule does not, however, abdicate judicial responsibility to the expert for it leaves room for rejection of testimony if reliance on the facts or data is unreasonable. The rule directs the trial judge to accord deference to the expert's explanation of what is reasonable, but it does not require the trial judge to accept what amounts to wishful thinking, guesswork, or speculation. The reasonable reliance standard set by Rule 703 obviously points toward broad admissibility of expert testimony. D. Louisell and C. Mueller, *Federal Evidence* (1979), § 389, p. 658. Once the evidence is admitted, adequate safeguards remain to deal with this evidence such as cross-examination of the expert.

Ark.Unif.R.Evid. 705 has simplified the manner in which expert testimony may be presented by eliminating mandatory preliminary disclosure of the facts or data underlying an expert's opinion. Rule 705 provides:

> Disclosure of facts or data underlying expert opinion.—The expert may testify in terms of opinion or inference and give his reasons therefor without prior disclosure of the underlying facts or data, unless the court requires otherwise. The expert may in any event be required to disclose the underlying facts or data on cross-examination.

Requiring the jury to be informed of the basis of the expert's opinion makes sense. The opinion would be irrelevant if grounded on facts found by the trier of fact not to exist in the particular case; but obviously the trier of fact cannot assess the validity of the assumed facts without knowing what they are. J. Weinstein, *Weinstein's Evidence Commentary on Rules of Evidence for the United States Courts and State Courts* (Vol. 3 1982), § 705[1], pp. 705–4, 705–5. Emphasis is placed upon the function of cross-examination by this rule and the burden is put upon the opponent of the calling party to demonstrate that the conclusion of the expert lacks adequate support in order for the testimony to be subject to being stricken by the trial court. D. Louisell and C. Mueller, *supra,* § 400, p. 709. See, Martin v. Arkansas Arts Center, 627 F.2d 876 (8th Cir.1980); United States v. 1,014.16 Acres of Land, 558 F.Supp. 1238 (W.D.Mo.1983); Rounsaville v. Ark. State Hwy. Comm'n, 258 Ark. 642, 527 S.W.2d 922 (1975); Annot., 49 A.L.R.Fed. 363 (1980); Annot., 12 A.L.R.3d 1064 (1967). Rule 705 does not limit the disclosure of facts or data underlying an expert's opinion to cross-examination. This rule merely removes any legal requirement to develop in the beginning the basis for an expert's conclusions.

Instead, he may state his conclusions straight away. The pressures of orderly presentation will often lead to divulgence of at least some of the supporting data. J. Weinstein, supra, § 705[1], p. 705–7. An expert may be asked on direct examination to state the grounds of his opinion, i.e., the general data which form the basis of his judgment upon specific data observed by him. J. Wigmore, *Evidence in Trials at Common Law* (Vol. 2 1979), § 562, p. 759.

From our review of the record, we believe that the court's erroneous ruling on the admissibility of expert Neil Palmer's basis for his opinion unduly circumscribed appellant in its examination of the witness. Further, we believe that there is a reasonable likelihood that the limitation imposed by the court could have affected the jury's impression as to the basis of the expert testimony and the credibility of the witness. We cannot conclude that the court's erroneous limitation was harmless, and accordingly, we will remand for a new trial.

REVERSED AND REMANDED.

COOPER, J., agrees.

MAYFIELD, J., concurs.

MAYFIELD, JUDGE, concurring.

Uniform Evidence Rule 703 allows an expert witness to base an opinion or inference, under proper circumstances, upon facts or data not admissible in evidence, and I have no problem with the statement from E. Cleary, *McCormick on Evidence* § 324.2 (3d ed. 1984), relied upon in the majority opinion, that an expert must be allowed to disclose the basis for his opinion. However, I want to emphasize the following statement found in the same section of *McCormick on Evidence:*

> It does not mean that the expert becomes the sole judge of the admissibility of the basis facts: they must still be of a type reasonably relied upon by experts in the field, and they are subject to such general evidentiary principles as exclusion for prejudice or irrelevancy.

In connection with the above statement, I also want to emphasize the following statement from Saltzburg & Redden, *Federal Rules of Evidence Manual* 467 (3d ed. 1982):

> Evidence not otherwise admissible is not admitted under this Rule for its truth; it is admitted to explain the basis of the expert opinion. A limiting instruction often should be required to explain this to the jury. However, we would emphasize that Rule 403 could be used to keep such evidence out where its admission might be unfair to an opposing party. One of the things that a Court might consider in assessing the reasonableness of reliance by an expert on facts not in evidence is whether an opposing party could effectively examine the expert concerning the reasonableness, reliability, significance, strengths and weaknesses of the facts not in evidence.

Another quotation that I think worth special notice is found in 3 Louisell & Mueller, *Federal Evidence* § 389 at 663 (1979):

> While Rule 703 permits an expert witness to take into account matters which are unadmitted and inadmissible, it does not follow that such a witness may simply report such matters to the trier of fact: The Rule was not designed to enable a witness to summarize and reiterate all manner of inadmissible evidence, but rather to pave the way for whatever assistance may be provided by expertise in analyzing, explaining, and interpreting such data in the whole context of the case.

Some cases that are cited by the above authorities in support of the statements I have quoted are: United States v. Brown, 548 F.2d 1194 (5th Cir.1977); United States v. Cox, 696 F.2d 1294 (11th Cir.1983); and Northern Nat. Gas v. Beech Aircraft, 202 Neb. 300, 275 N.W.2d 77 (1979).

In *Brown* the defendant was charged with counseling, procuring and advising the preparation and filing of fraudulent income tax returns. An IRS agent was allowed to testify that between 90% and 95% of about 160 returns prepared by the defendant contained overstated itemized deductions. The opinion stated that the agent must have obtained this information through conversations with each of the taxpayers audited. The court pointed out that the defendant had no opportunity to cross-examine these taxpayers or to even adequately cross-examine the agent since she testified from memory. "Thus," the opinion states, "the jury had no way to examine the trustworthiness of [the agent's] testimony." In a footnote the opinion noted that the agent's testimony was not admissible under Rule 703 because she was not testifying as an expert but "to establish as a fact—not opinion—that defendant had committed similar acts in the past."

In *Cox* the court said: "Although certain hearsay testimony by experts is permitted, it must be based on the type of evidence 'reasonably relied upon by experts in the particular field in forming opinions or inferences upon the subject.' * * * The testimony being offered by this witness was of a historical nature." And in the *Northern Nat. Gas* case the trial court declared a recess when it became apparent that there was a problem with the admissibility of the expert's testimony. After an offer of proof in chambers, the court held that the data sought to be introduced by the expert's testimony went far beyond data reasonably relied upon by experts in his field. In affirming the trial court's action, the appellate court said:

> While under our Rules of Evidence the expert may not be required to disclose the underlying facts or data before rendering his opinion, the trial court on its own motion can require such disclosure. * * * In this case the trial court made such a requirement, and upon hearing what the expert proposed to testify, concluded that neither the record nor the apparent qualifications of the expert would justify such an opinion. A trial court is given large discretion in determining whether or not the witness' qualification to state his opinion has been established, and this discretion will not ordinarily be disturbed on appeal unless there is an abuse of that discretion.

I have called attention to the above because the question involved in this case has not been previously considered by us and I have found very little discussion of the matter. It is with reluctance that I agree to reverse this case; however, I think in fairness to all involved, an opportunity should be given for a new trial after court and counsel have been able to carefully consider the matter. It should be noted that the majority opinion is based on the record we have before us. In the event of a new trial, it seems to me that a proffer of this evidence by question and answer, out of the presence of the jury, might be helpful. In that way the real purpose of the evidence sought to be introduced could be determined and, if admissible, any limitations upon its use could be set in the calm of the court's chambers instead of the pressure of the courtroom.

I concur in the reversal and remand of this case.

UNITED STATES v. ARIAS, 678 F.2d 1202, 1206 (4th Cir.1982), cert. denied, 459 U.S. 910, 103 S.Ct. 218, 74 L.Ed.2d 173 (1982). "Error is assigned to admitting the testimony of the prosecution's expert witness. Dr. Franzosa, a forensic chemist and ballistics expert employed by the D.E.A., testified that he compared the quaaludes which were seized from the plane with a sample quaalude pill that he had received from an agent in Colombia. In his opinion, the seized quaaludes had been made by the same machine as the tablet from Colombia, and they could not have been made by any of the legitimate or illicit laboratories in the United States from which the D.E.A. had samples. The D.E.A. had samples from all legitimate laboratories in this country. Appellants protest that this testimony should not have been admitted because the government failed to establish a chain of custody for the sample sent from Colombia. In effect, they say, Dr. Franzosa's testimony was based on hearsay as to the origin of the sample tablet. Under F.R.E. Rule 703, however, an expert may base his testimony upon the type of hearsay he would normally rely upon in the course of his work. The sample pill was sent to Dr. Franzosa by a D.E.A. agent in Colombia in a heat sealed container by diplomatic pouch with the agent's identification thereupon. D.E.A. forensic scientists rely upon agents in the field to submit samples and to establish their authenticity as is shown by the fact that the pill in question was catalogued and kept for sample use by the D.E.A. Thus, Dr. Franzosa's reliance on the agent's report that the control sample was obtained in Colombia does not make his testimony inadmissible; rather, it is a factor to be considered by the jury in assessing the weight of his testimony, for it is not the fact of whether or not the sample pill came from Colombia which is at issue, the issue is whether Dr. Franzosa could use the sample pill in forming an opinion. We think its use was permissible under F.R.E. 703."

STATE v. ROLLS, 389 A.2d 824, 829–30 (Me.1978). "The scope of the phrase 'reasonably relied upon' has caused some fear that enlargement of permissible data may tend to break down unduly the rules of exclusion. See generally 3 Weinstein's Evidence, par. 703[02]; Field & Murray, Maine Evidence, § 703.2 (1976). Fairness to litigants, especially to criminal defendants, is a proper concern of courts in the application of rules of evidence to expert testimony. See State v. Williams, Me., 388 A.2d 500 (1978) (Nichols, J., concurring).

"Since we have not heretofore had occasion to apply Rule 703, we commend the following statement from Field & Murray, Maine Evidence, § 703.2, as indicative of the proper scope of the phrase:

> * * * (T)he reasonableness of the reliance is a preliminary question for the judge to decide. He is not bound by a statement of the witness that he, or experts generally, customarily uses such facts or data or finds them reliable in forming opinions. Nor is it enough to show that he relies upon such material only in preparing for litigation; he must establish that experts would act upon it for purposes other than testifying in a lawsuit. The use must be reasonable in the context of a fair administration of the judicial system.

"Before admitting the witness' testimony, the presiding justice heard evidence from which he could have found as a preliminary fact that the blood grouping surveys from which Agent Spalding drew were of a type which were reasonably relied upon by those in the field. On this record, we are unable to say that there was no proper foundation to support admission of Agent Spalding's testimony."

IN RE AIR CRASH DISASTER AT NEW ORLEANS, LA.

United States Court of Appeals, Fifth Circuit, 1986.
795 F.2d 1230.

PATRICK E. HIGGINBOTHAM, CIRCUIT JUDGE:

Pan American World Airways Flight 759 crashed on takeoff from the New Orleans airport on July 9, 1982. In this appeal, we apply the substantive law of Louisiana in reviewing judgments for three children whose parents were among the 138 passengers killed when the Boeing 727 disintegrated on impact. Pan American challenges the allowance of loss of inheritance damages; the amount of the primary damage award; and numerous rulings by the court below. We are persuaded that the evidence in support of the claimed loss of inheritance was too speculative and that the remaining awards of the jury were so excessive as to require a new trial. We reverse in part, vacate in part, and remand for a new trial.

I

When Flight 759 crashed, Ted and Margaret Eymard had three children: Ted, Jr., age 9; Natalie, age 6; and Tenille, age 3. Margaret was in her last trimester of pregnancy with a fourth child at her death.

This diversity suit against Pan American was brought on behalf of the children by Pearl Crosby Eymard, their paternal grandmother and legal guardian. Pan American conceded liability before trial and the amount of damages was the only issue before the jury. Most of the trial testimony focused on the prospects that a number of marine companies, owned and operated by Ted Eymard, Sr. and various relatives, had at the time of Eymard's death.

Sometime after the air crash, the Eymard companies entered into Chapter 11 bankruptcy. The parties disputed the amount of future income Ted Eymard, Sr. would have had available to spend on behalf of his children had he lived, and how much he would have ultimately accumulated for their inheritance. Plaintiffs' evidence tended to show that Ted Eymard was the key figure in the management of the Eymard companies, which grew under his direction from a four or five boat operation to a group of companies grossing approximately $11 million per year at the time of his death. Witnesses for the plaintiffs testified that without Ted's financial and organizational leadership, and his entrepreneurial vision, the companies were unable to weather a down cycle in the marine industry similar to others they had survived under Ted's direction in the 1970's. Witnesses for Pan American, on the other hand, contended that Ted died just before a downturn in the Louisiana marine industry more serious than those already experienced, and that an unwise purchase of an offshore business, coupled with the highly-leveraged nature of the companies, made bankruptcy inevitable even had he lived. Other testimony focused on the Eymard's relationship with the children, their spending habits and assets, the future financial needs of the children, and details of the crash.

The jury awarded the children a total of $3,600,000. Responding to global inquiries, the jury awarded each child $1,100,000 for all their damages arising out of the loss of their parents, excluding their loss of inheritance. The jury also awarded $100,000 to each child for loss of inheritance. The trial judge denied Pan American's post-trial motions for a new trial, for judgment notwithstanding the verdict, and to amend the judgment.

Pan American raises numerous issues on appeal, but we reach only two: whether an award for loss of inheritance should have been allowed, and whether the primary award was excessive.

II

* * *

–1–

Since the adoption of the Federal Rules of Evidence in 1975, we have accorded trial courts considerable discretion in determining the admissibility of opinion evidence by experts. We have said that the discretion is "broad" and that the determination of admissibility should be sustained "unless manifestly erroneous." *See United States v. Johnson,* 575 F.2d 1347, 1360 (5th Cir.1978), *cert. denied,* 440 U.S. 907, 99

S.Ct. 1214, 59 L.Ed.2d 454 (1979); *Crawford v. Worth,* 447 F.2d 738, 740–41 (5th Cir.1971). This deference reflects the superior opportunity of the trial judge to gauge both the competence of the expert and the extent to which his opinion would be helpful to the jury. Despite the seeming breadth of the language we have used to describe this deference, trial court rulings regarding the admission of expert testimony remain reviewable. We have not left all such decisionmaking to trial judges, nor should we.

Basic policy questions that affect the very nature of a trial lie behind decisions to receive expert testimony. Under the Federal Rules of Evidence, experts not only explain evidence, but are themselves sources of evidence. These two roles, though related, are quite distinct. In deciding whether *explanation* by an expert will assist the jury or judge, the superior position of the trial judge over the appellate judge is apparent. By comparison, in deciding whether *evidence* should be allowed from this source, the trial judge draws less upon the scene and the cast immediately before him, and more upon the substantive law. To the extent that the decision to allow expert testimony as a source of evidence is significantly intertwined with the underlying substantive law, we will accord it less deference, and take a much closer look.

For example, in the typical products liability case, the jury is asked to decide whether a product was defective. Stripped to essentials, jury instructions regarding defect are little more than an open-ended request to balance utility and safety. Absence of rigor in the inquiries that determine liability does not necessarily result from poor drafting of the charge; rather, the difficulty is often inherent in the underlying substantive law. This is not the occasion for an attack upon that difficulty. Our point is that the ultimate issue in such cases can too easily become whatever an expert witness says it is, and trial courts must be wary lest the expert become nothing more than an advocate of policy before the jury. Stated more directly, the trial judge ought to insist that a proffered expert bring to the jury more than the lawyers can offer in argument. Indeed, the premise of receiving expert testimony is that it "will assist the trier of fact to understand the evidence or to determine a fact in issue * * *." Fed.R.Evid. Rule 702.

Our customary deference also assumes that the trial judge actually exercised his discretion. In saying this, we recognize the temptation to answer objections to receipt of expert testimony with the shorthand remark that the jury will give it "the weight it deserves." This nigh reflexive explanation may be sound in some cases, but in others it can mask a failure by the trial judge to come to grips with an important trial decision. Trial judges must be sensitive to the qualifications of persons claiming to be experts. Because the universe of experts is defined only by the virtually infinite variety of fact questions in the trial courts, the signals of competence cannot be catalogued. Nevertheless, there are almost always signs both of competence and of the contribution such experts can make to a clear presentation of the dispute. While we leave their detection to the good sense and instincts of the trial judges, we point by way of example to two. First, many experts are members of the academic community who supplement their teaching salaries with consulting work. We know from our judicial experience that many such able persons present studies and express opinions that they might not be willing to express in an article submitted to a refereed journal of their discipline or in other contexts subject to peer review. We think that is one important signal, along with many others, that ought to be considered in deciding whether to accept expert testimony. Second, the professional expert is now commonplace. That a person spends substantially all of his time consulting with attorneys and testifying is not a disqualification. But experts whose opinions are available to the highest bidder have no place testifying in a court of law, before a jury, and with the imprimatur of the trial judge's decision that he is an "expert."

In sum, we adhere to the deferential standard for review of decisions regarding the admission of testimony by experts. Nevertheless, we take this occasion to caution that the standard leaves appellate judges with a considerable task. We will turn to that task with a sharp eye, particularly in those instances, hopefully few, where the record makes it evident that the decision to receive expert testimony was simply tossed off to the jury under a "let it all in" philosophy. Our message to our able trial colleagues: it is time to take hold of expert testimony in federal trials.

–2–

The economist in this case testified that over the life of his employment with the Eymard companies, Ted experienced an average annual salary increase of 40% per year. While conceding that Ted's salary could not continue to grow at this rate indefinitely, the economist assumed that his salary would increase by 8%, in real terms, every year until the year 2021. Despite the testimony concerning Ted Eymard's business acumen, we find an assumed 8% annual salary increase continuing over almost 40 years to be unsupported by the record and completely incredible. In reaching this figure, the economist looked solely at Ted Eymard's income in prior years, and he failed to consider either the limits on future expansion that the Eymard companies would encounter as they continued to grow in an already competitive industry; or the depressed state of the marine industry at the time of trial and its cyclical nature in general; or the future personal choices Ted Eymard might make to avoid work-related health or stress problems later in his career.

Even more incredible is a presumption that because Ted Eymard paid only 5% of his income in taxes in earlier years, this artificially low tax rate would continue throughout his career. Testimony at trial indicated that the earlier 5% rate resulted from depreciation on boats owned by the Eymard "subchapter S" companies, and from interest paid on personal debt, which Ted Eymard was able to offset against income in calculating his tax liability. Apart from its insensitivity to the ephemeral character of the tax laws, the assumption ignores the reality that in order to incur the depreciation and interest expenses necessary to maintain a 5% tax rate in 1995 when he would presumably be making approximately $1 million per year, Ted Eymard would have to incur personal debt of $2 million, and expand to a fleet of 129 boats. The company fleet would have to continue increasing by 19 boats per year at a cost of $1 million per boat to 361 ships by the year 2005.[1]

While the Eymards had virtually no savings or money in retirement plans at the time of their deaths, the economist assumed, without any objective basis for doing so, that they would begin saving in 1990 at a rate of 5% of total income, and increase their rate of savings to 20% from the year 2000 on. Furthermore, rather than attempting to calculate probable future consumption of income based on the Eymards' spending habits prior to their death, the economist relied on statistical studies showing how average families consume available income. This was inappropriate, especially in light of testimony that the Eymards' disposition of income was idiosyncratic, and evidence that suggested increasingly significant sums had been spent in previous years on gambling junkets to Las Vegas.

In sum, we find the assumptions of plaintiffs' economist so abusive of the known facts, and so removed from any area of demonstrated expertise, as to provide no reasonable basis for calculating how much of Ted Eymard's income would have found its way into assets or savings to be inherited by his children. An award for damages "cannot stand when the only evidence to support it is speculative or purely conjectural." *Marks,* 785 F.2d at 542 (quoting *Haley v. Pan American World Airways,* 746 F.2d 311 at 316 (5th Cir.1984)). We reverse the award for loss of inheritance and leave for another day the legal question of whether, on less speculative testimony, loss of inheritance damages would be allowed as a matter of Louisiana law.

* * *

REVERSED in part, VACATED in part, REMANDED for a new trial.

MERCADO v. AHMED, 756 F.Supp. 1097 (N.D.Ill.1991). "Is the testimony of an economist on the cash value of the lost pleasure of life admissible?

* * *

"It can be argued that courts ought simply to admit opinions of experts without any inquiry whether the area of expertise is a field of

1. Even assuming the market could absorb such a large fleet, there was testimony that the companies at that size would probably sell stock and become publicly owned, which would not only result in a sharp decrease in Ted's salary, but would also preclude him from deducting depreciation on the ships from his personal income.

knowledge. If the expertise is flawed it can be met with evidence that proves these flaws. For example, the prosecutor in a criminal case might counter a defense psychiatrist with another psychiatrist to testify that any psychiatrist, including the defense psychiatrist, does not know enough to testify with any degree of certainty. Courts will sometimes defend the admission of expert testimony because the other side can defend itself by calling its own expert. Sherrod v. Berry, 629 F.Supp. 159 (N.D.Ill.1985). As a principle that justifies admission of evidence, it goes too far because it would permit an astrologer to take the stand and say, 'Smith, an Aries, could not have had (or must have had) an intent to defraud on November 18.' Surely another astrologer could be found to disagree or to say that astrology is not knowledge.

* * *

"The question today is whether I ought to interpret the law to permit an economist to testify as an expert on the monetary value of the pleasure of Brian Mercado's life. Brian Mercado is about eleven years old. He has significant mental and emotional deficits. He will likely never be able to hold a job or live alone. Psychiatric treatment is likely to be a consistent necessity. Brian Mercado was in kindergarten when he went with his family to visit the Museum of Science and Industry. In the parking lot he was struck by a taxicab and was injured. The jury found the taxicab driver was negligent. Assuming that the taxicab accident caused Brian Mercado an injury which turned him from a normal child into a severely disabled one,[11] there is no question that Brian Mercado has lost a considerable degree of the pleasure of life. Assuming that Illinois law allows recovery for this lost pleasure of life [12] the jury would have to quantify the dollar value of this loss. Brian Mercado offers an economist whose testimony I heard outside the jury's presence and who is prepared to opine that this value in Brian Mercado's case lies between $1,500,000 and $2,500,000. The taxicab driver and the taxicab company say that this is not admissible.

"This kind of evidence is well described in T. Miller, Willingness to Pay Comes of Age: Will the System Survive?, 83 Nw.U.L.Rev. 876 (1989). In brief, Miller notes that economists are researching the 'ways to measure the value that individuals place upon reducing the risk of dying' by examining the markets. Id. at 878–79. They examine 'what people actually pay—in dollars, time, discomfort, and inconvenience—for small reductions in health and safety risks.' Id. at 879. Of particular significance, economists have estimated the values people place on risk reduction based on the following factors: 1) the extra wages employers pay to induce people to take risky jobs; 2) the demand and price for products—such as safer cars, smoke detectors, houses in

11. The jury did not find this to be so. There was medical testimony and testimony by Brian Mercado's kindergarten teacher that Brian Mercado's woes (and they are quite real) existed before the taxicab struck him. The jury accepted this evidence against contrary testimony of other physicians and members of Brian Mercado's family.

12. Sometimes called hedonic damages.

polluted areas, and life insurance—that enhance health and safety; 3) the tradeoffs people make among time, money, comfort, and safety—in studies involving pedestrian tunnel use, safety belt use, speed choice, and drivers' travel time; and 4) surveys that ask people about their willingness to invest money to enhance their health or safety. Id. at 880–81.

"However, there is no basic agreement among economists as to what elements ought to go into the life valuation. There is no unanimity on which studies ought to be considered. There is a lack of reliability. In fact, Smith was prepared to testify based on seventy or eighty studies; Miller relies on twenty-nine; in Sherrod v. Berry, 629 F.Supp. 159, 163 (N.D.Ill.1985), Smith testified on the basis of fifteen studies. Smith acknowledged that more studies could be done on the willingness-to-pay issue. In particular Smith noted that further studies will focus on a set of consumers to uncover when these consumers make or do not make choices for safety, and these results may help establish validity. The fact that the bottom lines of most studies (between less than $100,000 to more than $12,000,000) arguably do not wind up very far apart (by some definitions of 'very far') may be coincidence and not the result of the application of a scientific method.

"Survey of attitudes and views of others as a basis for concluding something is true is not necessarily wrong. Some science as it comes into court is the result of consensus by practitioners of some area of expertise that a certain law of nature is correct. What is wrong here is not that the evidence is founded on consensus or agreement, it is that the consensus is that of persons who are no more expert than are the jurors on the value of the lost pleasure of life. Even if reliable and valid, the evidence may fail to 'assist the trier of fact to understand the evidence or determine a fact in issue' in a way more meaningful than would occur if the jury asked a group of wise courtroom bystanders for their opinions.

"For the reasons stated here and in open court, I grant the defendants' motion to bar testimony of plaintiff's expert, Stan V. Smith, on the issue of hedonic damages."

Note

In August, 1991, the Committee on Rules of Practice and Procedure of the Judicial Conference of the United States recommended that Fed.R.Evid. 702 be amended to read as follows:

> "Testimony proving scientific, technical, or other specialized information, in the form of an opinion or otherwise, may be permitted only if (1) the information is reasonably reliable and will substantially assist the trier of fact to understand the evidence or to determine a fact in issue, and (2) the witness is qualified as an expert by knowledge, skill, experience, training or education to provide such testimony. Except with leave of court for good cause shown, the witness shall not testify on direct examination in any civil action to any opinion or inference, or reason or basis therefor, that has not been seasonably disclosed as

required by Rules 26(a)(2) and 26(e)(1) of the Federal Rules of Civil Procedure."

137 F.R.D. 53, 156. According to the Committee Notes, "This revision is intended to limit the use, but increase the utility and reliability, of party-initiated opinion testimony bearing on scientific and technical issues." Id.

UNITED STATES v. PICCINONNA

United States Court of Appeals, Eleventh Circuit, 1989.
885 F.2d 1529.

FAY, CIRCUIT JUDGE:

In this case, we revisit the issue of the admissibility at trial of polygraph expert testimony and examination evidence. Julio Piccinonna appeals his conviction on two counts of knowingly making false material statements to a Grand Jury in violation of Title IV of the Organized Crime Control Act of 1970. 18 U.S.C. 1623 (1982). * * *

I. BACKGROUND

* * *

Prior to trial, Piccinonna requested that the Government stipulate to the admission into evidence of the results of a polygraph test which would be administered subsequently. The Government refused to stipulate to the admission of any testimony regarding the polygraph test or its results. Despite the Government's refusal, George B. Slattery, a licensed polygraph examiner, tested Piccinonna on November 25, 1985. Piccinonna asserted that the expert's report left no doubt that he did not lie when he testified before the Grand Jury. (R1–38–2). On November 27, 1985, Piccinonna filed a motion with the district court requesting a hearing on the admission of the polygraph testimony. On January 6, 1986, the district court held a hearing on the defendant's motions. Due to the per se rule, which holds polygraph evidence inadmissible in this circuit, the trial judge refused to admit the evidence. * * *

Piccinonna was convicted on two counts of making false material declarations concerning a matter the Grand Jury was investigating. * * * On appeal, Piccinonna urges us to modify our per se rule excluding polygraph evidence to permit its admission in certain circumstances.

II. THE PER SE RULE

In federal courts, the admissibility of expert testimony concerning scientific tests or findings is governed by Rule 702 of the Federal Rules of Evidence. Rule 702 provides:

> If scientific, technical, or other specialized knowledge will assist the trier of fact to understand the evidence or to determine a fact in issue, a witness qualified as an expert by knowledge, skill, experience, training or education, may testify thereto in the form of an opinion or otherwise.

Fed.R.Evid. 702. Under this rule, to admit expert testimony the trial judge must determine that the expert testimony will be relevant and will be helpful to the trier of fact. In addition, courts require the proponent of the testimony to show that the principle or technique is generally accepted in the scientific community. McCormick, *McCormick on Evidence* § 203 (3rd ed. 1984).

The general acceptance requirement originated in the 1923 case of *Frye v. United States*, 293 F. 1013 (D.C.Cir.1923). *Frye* involved a murder prosecution in which the trial court refused to admit results from a systolic blood pressure test, the precursor of the polygraph. The defendant appealed, arguing that the admissibility of the scientific test results should turn only on the traditional rules of relevancy and helpfulness to the trier of fact. The court of appeals disagreed and imposed the requirement that the area of specialty in which the court receives evidence must have achieved general acceptance in the scientific community. *Id.* 293 F. at 1014. The court stated that "while courts will go a long way in admitting expert testimony deduced from a well-recognized scientific principle or discovery, the thing from which the deduction is made must be sufficiently established to have gained general acceptance in the particular field in which it belongs." *Id.* The court concluded that the systolic blood pressure test lacked the requisite "standing and scientific recognition among physiological and psychological authorities." *Id.*

Courts have applied the *Frye* standard to various types of scientific tests, including the polygraph.[4] However, the *Frye* standard has historically been invoked only selectively to other types of expert testimony, and has been applied consistently only in cases where the admissibility of polygraph evidence was at issue. *See* McCormick, *Scientific Evidence: Defining a New Approach to Admissibility,* 67 Iowa L.Rev. 879, 884 (1982).[5] Most courts had little difficulty with the desirability of excluding polygraph evidence and thus, applied the *Frye* standard with little comment. *Id.* at 885. This circuit also has consistently reaffirmed, with little discussion, the inadmissibility of polygraph evidence. *United States v. Hilton,* 772 F.2d 783, 785 (11th Cir.1985); *United States v. Rodriguez,* 765 F.2d 1546, 1558 (11th Cir.1985); *cf. United States v. Beck,* 729 F.2d 1329, 1332 (11th Cir.) (court implied that polygraph evidence may be admissible when the parties stipulate to its admissibility), *cert. denied,* 469 U.S. 981, 105 S.Ct. 383, 83 L.Ed.2d 318

4. For the next fifty years, the *Frye* holding acted as a complete bar to the admissibility of polygraph evidence. *Kaminski v. State,* 63 So.2d 339, 340 (Fla. 1952); *Boeche v. State,* 151 Neb. 368, 377, 37 N.W.2d 593, 597 (1949); *Henderson v. State,* 94 Okl.Cr. 45, 52–55, 230 P.2d 495, 502–505, *cert. denied* 342 U.S. 898, 72 S.Ct. 234, 96 L.Ed. 673 (1951). For brief history of polygraph admissibility *see State v. Valdez,* 91 Ariz. 274, 371 P.2d 894, 896 n. 4 (1962).

5. *See also* Giannelli, *The Admissibility of Novel Scientific Evidence: Frye v. United States, a Half-Century Later,* 80 Colum.L.Rev. 1197, 1219–21 (1980); *Reed v. State,* 283 Md. 374, 391 A.2d 364, 403 (1978) (Smith, J., dissenting) (*Frye* standard has generally not been relied upon for the admission of evidence such as fingerprints, ballistics, intoxication tests, and X-rays).

(1984). Our position was derived from former Fifth Circuit precedent excluding polygraph evidence, which we adopted as law in this circuit. *Bonner v. City of Prichard,* 661 F.2d 1206, 1207 (11th Cir.1981).

Recently, the application of the *Frye* standard to exclude polygraph evidence has been subject to growing criticism.[7] Since the *Frye* decision, tremendous advances have been made in polygraph instrumentation and technique.[8] Better equipment is being used by more adequately trained polygraph administrators. Further, polygraph tests are used extensively by government agencies. Field investigative agencies such as the FBI, the Secret Service, military intelligence and law enforcement agencies use the polygraph. Thus, even under a strict adherence to the traditional *Frye* standard, we believe it is no longer accurate to state categorically that polygraph testing lacks general acceptance for use in all circumstances. For this reason, we find it appropriate to reexamine the per se exclusionary rule and institute a rule more in keeping with the progress made in the polygraph field.

III. Differing Approaches to Polygraph Admissibility

Courts excluding polygraph evidence typically rely on three grounds: 1) the unreliability of the polygraph test,[9] 2) the lack of standardization of polygraph procedure,[10] and 3) undue impact on the jury.[11] Proponents of admitting polygraph evidence have attempted to

7. Commentators have consistently criticized application of the *Frye* standard. Some commentators advocate a requirement of substantial acceptance as an alternative to the general acceptance standard. J. Richardson, *Modern Scientific Evidence* § 2.5 at 24 (2d ed. 1974). Other commentators question the necessity for any special rules governing the admissibility of scientific evidence and believe that the concerns of *Frye* proponents could be met with careful application of traditional rules regarding relevancy and expert testimony. *See e.g.* Trautman, *Logical or Legal Relevancy—A Conflict in Theory,* 5 Vand.L.Rev. 385, 396 (1952). Professor McCormick agreed with this approach stating that "[g]eneral scientific acceptance is a proper condition for taking judicial notice of scientific facts, but it is not a suitable criterion for the admissibility of scientific evidence. Any relevant conclusions supported by a qualified expert witness should be received unless there are distinct reasons for exclusion. These reasons are the familiar ones of prejudicing or misleading the jury or consuming undue amounts of time." *McCormick on Evidence, supra* § 203 at 608 (footnotes omitted). Dean Wigmore concurs with McCormick's standard for admission of polygraph evidence. Wigmore, *Evidence,* § 990 (3d ed. 1940).

8. Barland, Raskin, *"Detection of Deception" Electro-Dermal Activity in Psychological Research* (1973); Barland, Raskin, *An Evaluation of Field Techniques in the Detection of Deception,* 12 Psychophysiology 321 (1975); Podlesny, Raskin, *Effectiveness of Techniques and Physiological Measurers in the Detection of Deception,* 15 Psychophysiology 344 (1978).

9. *United States v. Gloria,* 494 F.2d 477, 483 (5th Cir.), *cert. denied,* 419 U.S. 995, 95 S.Ct. 306, 42 L.Ed.2d 267 (1974); *United States v. Skeens,* 494 F.2d 1050, 1053 (D.C.Cir.1974); *People v. Anderson,* 637 P.2d 354, 358 (Col.1981); *People v. Baynes,* 88 Ill.2d 225, 230, 58 Ill.Dec. 819, 824, 430 N.E.2d 1070, 1075 (1981); *State v. Grier,* 307 N.C. 628, 300 S.E.2d 351, 360 (1983); *Fulton v. State,* 541 P.2d 871, 872 (Okla. 1975).

10. *People v. Anderson,* 637 P.2d 354, 358 (Col.1981); *People v. Baynes,* 88 Ill.2d 225, 58 Ill.Dec. 819, 824, 430 N.E.2d 1070, 1075 (1981); *State v. Grier,* 307 N.C. 628, 300 S.E.2d 351, 360 (1983); *State v. Dean,* 103 Wis.2d 228, 307 N.W.2d 628, 633 (1981); *State v. Stanislawski,* 62 Wis.2d 730, 216 N.W.2d 8 (1974).

11. *United States v. Alexander,* 526 F.2d 161 (8th Cir.1975); *United States v. Jenkins,* 470 F.2d 1061, 1064 (9th Cir.1972), *cert. denied,* 411 U.S. 920, 93 S.Ct. 1544, 36 L.Ed.2d 313 (1973); *People v. Anderson,* 637 P.2d 354, 358 (Col.1981); *People v. Baynes,*

rebut these concerns. With regard to unreliability, proponents stress the significant advances made in the field of polygraphy.[12] Professor McCormick argues that the fears of unreliability "are not sufficient to warrant a rigid exclusionary rule. A great deal of lay testimony routinely admitted is at least as unreliable and inaccurate, and other forms of scientific evidence involve risks of instrumental or judgmental error." McCormick, *supra,* § 206 at 629. Further, proponents argue that the lack of standardization is being addressed and will progressively be resolved as the polygraph establishes itself as a valid scientific test. Sevilla, *Polygraph 1984: Behind the Closed Door of Admissibility,* 16 U.West L.A.L.Rev. 5, 19 (1984).[13] Finally, proponents argue that there is no evidence that jurors are unduly influenced by polygraph evidence. *Id.* at 17. In fact, several studies refute the proposition that jurors are likely to give disproportionate weight to polygraph evidence.[14]

In the wake of new empirical evidence and scholarly opinion which have undercut many of the traditional arguments against admission of polygraph evidence, a substantial number of courts have revisited the admissibility question. Three roughly identifiable approaches to the problem have emerged. First, the traditional approach holds polygraph evidence inadmissible when offered by either party, either as substantive evidence or as relating to the credibility of a witness. McCormick, *supra,* § 206 at 628.[15] Second, a significant number of jurisdictions permit the trial court, in its discretion, to receive polygraph evidence if the parties stipulate to the evidence's admissibility before the adminis-

88 Ill.2d 225, 58 Ill.Dec. 819, 828, 430 N.E.2d 1070, 1079 (1981); *State v. Grier,* 307 N.C. 628, 300 S.E.2d 351, 360 (1983); *State v. Dean,* 103 Wis.2d 228, 307 N.W.2d 628 (1981); *State v. Stanislawski,* 62 Wis.2d 730, 216 N.W.2d 8 (1974).

12. Polygraph examiners contend that a properly administered polygraph test is a highly effective way to detect deception and cite figures between 92% and 100% for its accuracy. McCormick, *supra,* § 206 at 626. Others suggest figures in the range of 63–72%. *Id.*

13. For instance, Sevilla points out that experts in the polygraph field have developed detailed standards for administration of polygraph tests. The American Polygraph Association and state organizations have standards in their charters which members must follow as well. *See* Sevilla, *supra* at 19.

14. Carlson, Pasano & Jannunzzo, *The Effect of Lie Detector Evidence on Jury Deliberations: An Empirical Study,* 5 J.Pol.Sci. & Admin. 148; Markwart & Lynch, *The Effect of Polygraph Evidence on Mock Jury Decision-Making,* 7 J.Pol.Sci. & Admin. 324 (1979); Peters, *A Survey of Polygraph Evidence in Criminal Trials,* 68 A.B.A.J. 162, 165 (1982) (citing cases in which the jury verdict in criminal trials was at odds with the testimony of the polygraph examiner.)

15. *United States v. Brevard,* 739 F.2d 180 (4th Cir.1984); *De Vries v. St. Paul Fire & Marine Insurance Co.,* 716 F.2d 939, 945 (1st Cir.1983); *Smith v. Gonzales,* 670 F.2d 522, 528 (5th Cir.), *cert. denied,* 459 U.S. 1005, 103 S.Ct. 361, 74 L.Ed.2d 397 (1982); *United States v. Zeiger,* 475 F.2d 1280 (D.C.Cir.1972); *United States v. Bando,* 244 F.2d 833, 841 (2nd Cir.), *cert. denied,* 355 U.S. 844, 78 S.Ct. 67, 2 L.Ed.2d 53 (1957); *Pulakis v. State,* 476 P.2d 474, 479 (Alaska 1970); *People v. Anderson,* 637 P.2d 354, 358 (Colo.1981); *People v. Baynes,* 88 Ill.2d 225, 58 Ill.Dec. 819, 430 N.E.2d 1070 (1981); *Kelley v. State,* 288 Md. 298, 418 A.2d 217, 219 (1980); *State v. Mitchell,* 402 A.2d 479, 482 (Me.1979); *State v. Biddle,* 599 S.W.2d 182, 185 (Mo.1980); *State v. Steinmark,* 195 Neb. 545, 239 N.W.2d 495, 497 (1976); *Birdsong v. State,* 649 P.2d 786, 788 (Okl.Cr.1982); *State v. Frazier,* 162 W.Va. 602, 252 S.E.2d 39, 49 (1979); *State v. Dean,* 103 Wis.2d 228, 307 N.W.2d 628 (1981).

tration of the test and if certain other conditions are met.[16] Finally, some courts permit the trial judge to admit polygraph evidence even in the absence of a stipulation, but only when special circumstances exist.[17] In these jurisdictions, the issue is within the sound discretion of the trial judge.

Relying on the typical grounds to exclude polygraph evidence, the Fourth, Fifth and District of Columbia Circuits historically have adhered to the traditional approach of per se inadmissibility. *United States v. Brevard,* 739 F.2d 180 (4th Cir.1984); *United States v. Clark,* 598 F.2d 994, 995 (5th Cir.1979), vacated *en banc* 622 F.2d 917 (1980), *cert. denied,* 449 U.S. 1128, 101 S.Ct. 949, 67 L.Ed.2d 116 (1981); *United States v. Skeens,* 494 F.2d 1050, 1053 (D.C.Cir.1974). While these circuits have sometimes hinted at the possibility of adopting a more liberal approach, they have consistently returned to per se inadmissibility. *See e.g. United States v. Webster,* 639 F.2d 174, 186 (4th Cir.)

16. *Anderson v. United States,* 788 F.2d 517, 519 (8th Cir.1986) (for purposes of prosecution's duty to reveal favorable evidence to accused, review of polygraph statements in camera proper in determining whether the statements were material to guilt or punishment); *State v. Valdez,* 91 Ariz. 274, 283–84, 371 P.2d 894, 900 (1962) (In court's discretion polygraph evidence may be admitted pursuant to signed stipulation. Opposing side is entitled to broad cross-examination and limiting instruction to the jury as to the evidentiary purpose of the testimony); *State v. Bullock,* 262 Ark. 394, 557 S.W.2d 193 (1977) (where there is dispute as to existence of stipulation, polygraph evidence admissible only if parties have executed a written agreement); *People v. Trujillo,* 67 Cal.App.3d 547, 136 Cal. Rptr. 672, 676 (5th Dist.1977) (results of polygraph may be admitted pursuant to a stipulation by both parties provided that the stipulation was not entered into as a result of fraud, excusable neglect, misrepresentation, or mistake of fact, and further provided that the facts have not changed and there are no other special circumstances rendering it unjust to enforce the stipulation); *Codie v. State,* 313 So.2d 754, 756 (Fla.1975) (stipulation need not be in writing if defendant freely and voluntarily submitted to taking polygraph examination); *Pavone v. State,* 273 Ind. 162, 402 N.E.2d 976, 978–79 (1980) (even if the parties enter into a written stipulation, court still retains discretion to deny admission of polygraph results); *State v. Marti,* 290 N.W.2d 570, 586–87 (Iowa 1980) (stipulation must be agreed to by both parties, should be a matter of record, and polygraph may be admitted only in the proceeding for which stipulation was intended); *State v. Roach,* 223 Kan. 732, 576 P.2d 1082, 1086 (1978) (polygraph evidence admissible if both parties stipulate, the stipulation is a matter of record, defendant knowingly and voluntarily consents to the examination, counsel and defendant stipulate that results are to be admissible, the trial court is satisfied that the examiner is qualified and the examination is conducted under the proper conditions, and the opposing party is given adequate opportunity to cross-examine the polygraph examiner on his qualifications and the limitations of polygraph interrogation); *State v. Souel,* 53 Ohio St.2d 123, 134, 372 N.E.2d 1318, 1323–24 (1978) (adopts *Valdez* rule); *Cullin v. State,* 565 P.2d 445, 457 (Wyo.1977) (in addition to stipulation by both parties, trial court must require a showing of the reliability and acceptance of the polygraph and allow cross-examination before admitting polygraph evidence).

17. *United States v. Miller,* 874 F.2d 1255 (9th Cir.1989); *United States v. Johnson,* 816 F.2d 918, 923 (3rd Cir.1987); *Wolfel v. Holbrook,* 823 F.2d 970, 972 (6th Cir.1987), *cert. denied,* ___ U.S. ___, 108 S.Ct. 1035, 98 L.Ed.2d 999 (1988); *United States v. Hall,* 805 F.2d 1410 (10th Cir. 1986); *United States v. Webster,* 639 F.2d 174, 186 (4th Cir.) (trial judge has broad discretion to admit polygraph evidence), *cert. denied, Christian v. United States,* 454 U.S. 857, 102 S.Ct. 307, 70 L.Ed.2d 152 (1981), *modified in other respects* 669 F.2d 185, *cert. denied,* 456 U.S. 935, 102 S.Ct. 1991, 72 L.Ed.2d 455 (1982); *State v. Dorsey,* 88 N.M. 184, 539 P.2d 204 (1975) (polygraph evidence admissible if polygraph expert is qualified as an expert, the testing procedure is shown reliable as approved by authorities in the field, and the tests made on the subject are shown to be valid).

(admissibility of polygraph evidence can be within discretionary powers of trial judge), *cert. denied, Christian v. United States* (1981), *modified in other respects* 669 F.2d 185 (4th Cir.), *cert. denied,* 456 U.S. 935, 102 S.Ct. 1991, 72 L.Ed.2d 455 (1982); *United States v. Brevard,* 739 F.2d 180 (4th Cir.1984) (per se inadmissible); *United States v. Clark,* 622 F.2d 917, 917 (5th Cir.1980) (twelve concurring judges agreed that the per se rule should be reconsidered), *cert. denied,* 449 U.S. 1128, 101 S.Ct. 949, 67 L.Ed.2d 116 (1981); *Tyler v. United States,* 193 F.2d 24 (D.C.Cir.1951), *cert. denied,* 343 U.S. 908, 72 S.Ct. 639, 96 L.Ed. 1326 (1952) (not error for trial court to admit polygrapher's testimony for purpose of deciding whether the defendant's confession was voluntary); *United States v. Skeens,* 494 F.2d at 1053 (D.C.Cir.1974) (polygraph evidence per se inadmissible).

The Eighth Circuit has developed a more liberal approach which allows admission of polygraph evidence only when the parties stipulate. *Anderson v. United States,* 788 F.2d 517, 519 (8th Cir.1986); *United States v. Alexander,* 526 F.2d 161, 166 (8th Cir.1975). However, another line of Eighth Circuit cases appears to be more permissive in allowing the introduction of polygraph evidence. *United States v. Yeo,* 739 F.2d 385, 388 (8th Cir.1984); *United States v. Oliver,* 525 F.2d 731, 736 (8th Cir.1975) (a discretionary rather than a per se exclusionary rule is appropriate). Hence, while the Eighth Circuit falls within the second category, it appears to be leaning toward greater admissibility of polygraph evidence.

Finally, the Third, Sixth, Seventh, Ninth and Tenth Circuits, and the Court of Military Appeals permit admission of polygraph evidence even in the absence of a stipulation when special circumstances exist. The Third and Seventh Circuits permit polygraph evidence to be introduced for the purpose of rebutting a claim by the defendant that his confession was the result of coercion. *United States v. Johnson,* 816 F.2d 918, 923 (3rd Cir.1987); *United States v. Kampiles,* 609 F.2d 1233, 1245 (7th Cir.1979), *cert. denied,* 446 U.S. 954, 100 S.Ct. 2923, 64 L.Ed.2d 812 (1980). The Tenth Circuit has permitted the government to introduce the fact that the defendant failed a polygraph test to explain why the police detective had not conducted a more thorough investigation. *United States v. Hall,* 805 F.2d 1410 (10th Cir.1986). In its attempt to mitigate the potential problems with polygraph evidence, the Sixth Circuit has promulgated a two-step approach to admission. *Wolfel v. Holbrook,* 823 F.2d 970 (6th Cir.1987), *cert. denied,* ___ U.S. ___, 108 S.Ct. 1035, 98 L.Ed.2d 999 (1988). "First, the trial court must determine if the proffered evidence is relevant. Second, if the court concludes that the proffered evidence is relevant, it must balance the probative value of the evidence against the hazard of unfair prejudice and/or confusion which could mislead the jury." *Id.* at 972. The Ninth Circuit holds polygraph evidence admissible only in instances narrowly tailored to limit the prejudicial impact of the evidence. *United States v. Miller,* 874 F.2d 1255, 1262 (9th Cir.1989). The *Miller* court, in considering prior Ninth Circuit cases on this issue, noted that polygraph evidence might be admissible if it is "introduced for a limited purpose that is unrelated to the substantive correctness of the results of the polygraph examination." *Id.* at 1261. In *United States v. Bowen,* 857 F.2d 1337, 1341 (9th Cir.1988), the court held that if "the polygraph evidence is being introduced because it is relevant that a polygraph examination was given, regardless of the result, then it may be admissible * * *" *Id.* at 1341.

The common thread running through the various approaches taken by courts which have modified the per se rule is a recognition that while wholesale exclusion under rule 702 is unwarranted, there must be carefully constructed limitations placed upon the use of polygraph evidence in court. Absent a stipulation by the parties, we are unable to locate any case in which a court has allowed polygraph expert testimony offered as substantive proof of the truth or falsity of the statements made during the polygraph examination. The myriad of "special circumstances" and conditions that have been held to constitute appropriate scenarios for use of polygraph evidence are necessarily rough estimates by the courts of when and where the danger of unfair prejudice due to the admission of the evidence is least significant.

IV. Principles for Admissibility

There is no question that in recent years polygraph testing has gained increasingly widespread acceptance as a useful and reliable scientific tool. Because of the advances that have been achieved in the field which have led to the greater use of polygraph examination, coupled with a lack of evidence that juries are unduly swayed by polygraph evidence, we agree with those courts which have found that a per se rule disallowing polygraph evidence is no longer warranted. Of course, polygraphy is a developing and inexact science, and we continue to believe it inappropriate to allow the admission of polygraph evidence in all situations in which more proven types of expert testimony are allowed. However, as Justice Potter Stewart wrote, "any rule that impedes the discovery of truth in a court of law impedes as well the doing of justice." *Hawkins v. United States,* 358 U.S. 74, 81, 79 S.Ct. 136, 140, 3 L.Ed.2d 125 (1958) (concurring). Thus, we believe the best approach in this area is one which balances the need to admit all relevant and reliable evidence against the danger that the admission of the evidence for a given purpose will be unfairly prejudicial. Accordingly we outline two instances where polygraph evidence may be admitted at trial, which we believe achieve the necessary balance.

A. Stipulation

The first rule governing admissibility of polygraph evidence is one easily applied. Polygraph expert testimony will be admissible in this circuit when both parties stipulate in advance as to the circumstances of the test and as to the scope of its admissibility. The stipulation as to circumstances must indicate that the parties agree on material matters such as the manner in which the test is conducted, the nature of the questions asked, and the identity of the examiner administering the test. The stipulation as to scope of admissibility must indicate the purpose or purposes for which the evidence will be introduced. Where the parties agree to both of these conditions in advance of the polygraph test, evidence of the test results is admissible.

B. Impeachment or Corroboration

The second situation in which polygraph evidence may be admitted is when used to impeach or corroborate the testimony of a witness at trial. Admission of polygraph evidence for these purposes is subject to three preliminary conditions. First, the party planning to use the evidence at trial must provide adequate notice to the opposing party that the [illegible] will be offered. Second, polygraph expert testimon[illegible] posing party was given rea[illegible] expert administer a test [illegible] ailure to provide adequate [illegible] opposing side to administ[illegible] of the evidence.

Fina[illegible] the admissibility of the p[illegible] governed by the Federal [illegible] corroboration or impeach[illegible] mits the use of opinion [illegible] ility of a witness in the f[illegible] ter is admissible only aft[illegible] ulness has been attacked [illegible] vise." Thus, evidence th[illegible], used to corroborate th[illegible] admissible under Rule 60[illegible] itness were first attacked [illegible] met, admission of polygraph evidence for impeachment or corroboration purposes is left entirely to the discretion of the trial judge.

Neither of these two modifications to the per se exclusionary rule should be construed to preempt or limit in any way the trial court's discretion to exclude polygraph expert testimony on other grounds under the Federal Rules of Evidence. Our holding states merely that in the limited circumstances delineated above, the *Frye* general acceptance test does not act as a bar to admission of polygraph evidence as a matter of law. As we have stated, the chief criterion in determining whether expert testimony is appropriate is whether it will help the trier of fact to resolve the issues. Fed.R.Evid. 702; *Worsham v. A.H. Robins Co.,* 734 F.2d 676, 685 (11th Cir.1984). The expert testimony must also, of course, be relevant. Fed.R.Evid. 401; *United States v. Roark,* 753 F.2d 991, 994 (11th Cir.1985). Rule 401 defines relevant evidence as evidence "having any tendency to make the existence of any fact that is of consequence to the determination of the action more probable or less probable than it would be without the evidence." Further, Rule 403 states that even though relevant, evidence may be excluded by the trial court "if its probative value is substantially outweighed by the danger of unfair prejudice, confusion of the issues, or misleading the jury, or by consideration of undue delay, waste of time, or needless presentation of cumulative evidence." Thus, we agree with the Ninth Circuit "that polygraph evidence should not be admitted, even for limited purposes, unless the trial court has determined that 'the probative value of the polygraph evidence outweighs the potential prejudice and time consumption involved in presenting such evidence.'" *United States v. Miller,* 874 F.2d 1255 (9th Cir.1989) (*quoting Brown v. Darcy,* 783 F.2d 1389, 1397 n. 14 (9th Cir.1986)).

Thus under the Federal Rules of Evidence governing the admissibility of expert testimony, the trial court may exclude polygraph expert testimony because 1) the polygraph examiner's qualifications are unacceptable; 2) the test procedure was unfairly prejudicial or the test was poorly administered; or 3) the questions were irrelevant or improper. The trial judge has wide discretion in this area, and rulings on admissibility will not be reversed unless a clear abuse of discretion is shown. *Worsham,* 734 F.2d at 686.

V. CONCLUSION

We neither expect nor hope that today's holding will be the final word within our circuit on this increasingly important issue. The advent of new and developing technologies calls for flexibility within the legal system so that the ultimate ends of justice may be served. It is unwise to hold fast to a familiar rule when the basis for that rule ceases to be persuasive. We believe that the science of polygraphy has progressed to a level of acceptance sufficient to allow the use of polygraph evidence in limited circumstances where the danger of unfair prejudice is minimized. We proceed with caution in this area because the reliability of polygraph testing remains a subject of intense scholarly debate. As the field of polygraph testing continues to progress, it may become necessary to reexamine the rules regarding the admissibility of polygraph evidence.

The judgment of conviction is VACATED and the case is REMANDED to the district court for further proceedings consistent with this opinion.

JOHNSON, CIRCUIT JUDGE, concurring in part and dissenting in part, in which RONEY, CHIEF JUDGE, HILL and CLARK, CIRCUIT JUDGES, join:

I concur with the Court's holding that polygraph evidence should be admissible in this Circuit when both parties stipulate in advance to the circumstances of the test and to the scope of its admissibility, subject to the understanding that such stipulations may be accepted or rejected by the trial judge at his discretion.[1] I dissent, however, from

1. If the parties wish to alter the applicability of Rules 403 and 702 in their case, they should be able to do so by advance stipulation, as long as they do not interfere with any third party's interests or the adjudicatory role of the courts. *See Wigmore on Evidence* § 7a (P. Tillers rev. 1983). *But see id.* at 602 n. 35 (courts generally hold polygraph results inadmissible even where there is a stipulation). Because such a stipulation would alter the applicability of rules of evidence, however, the

the Court's finding that the polygraph has gained acceptance in the scientific community as a reliable instrument for detecting lies, and from the Court's holding that polygraph evidence is admissible under Fed.R.Evid. 608.

I. Polygraph Theory

A. Introduction

The Court's reasoning begins with the proposition that polygraph technology has reached the point where its accuracy is generally accepted by the scientific community. In fact, the scientific community remains sharply divided on the reliability of the polygraph. U.S. Congress, Office of Technology Assessment, *Scientific Validity of Polygraph Testing: A Research Review and Evaluation—A Technical Memorandum* 43 (1983) [hereinafter *OTA Memorandum*]. Many theorists question the basic assumptions underlying the polygraph: that telling lies is stressful, and that this stress manifests itself in physiological responses which can be recorded on a polygraph. *See* Ney, *Expressing Emotions and Controlling Feelings,* in *The Polygraph Test: Lies, Truth and Science* 65 (A. Gale ed. 1988) [hereinafter *The Polygraph Test*]; *Employee Polygraph Protection Act: Hearing on H.R. 208 Before the Education and Labor Comm.,* 100th Cong., 1st Sess. 51 (1987) (testimony of John F. Beary, III, M.D. on behalf of the American Medical Association) [hereinafter *H.R. Hearing*]. Moreover, Congress has sharply limited use of the polygraph in the private sector. Employee Polygraph Protection Act of 1988, P.L. 100–347, 102 Stat. 646 (codified at 29 U.S.C.A. § 2001 (West Supp.1989)).[2]

The polygraph device records the subject's physiological activities (e.g., heart rate, blood pressure, respiration, and perspiration) as he is questioned by a polygraph examiner. Bull, *What is the Lie Detection Test?* in *The Polygraph Test* 11–12. There are two major types of polygraph examinations: the "control question test" and the "concealed information test." The control question test is used most frequently in investigating specific incidents. The examiner compares the data corresponding to (a) questions relevant to the crime (b) "control" questions designed to upset the subject but not directly relevant to the crime, and (c) neutral questions. If the subject reacts more strongly to the relevant questions than to the control and neutral questions, then the examiner infers that the subject is lying. *Id.* at 13–17. There is much debate about the accuracy of control question tests in specific-incident investigations. Raskin, *Does Science Support Polygraph Testing,* in *The Polygraph Test* 98–99.

trial judge has the discretion to reject the parties' proposed stipulation. The trial judge has broad discretion on questions of the admissibility of evidence and should not be reversed unless there is a clear abuse of discretion. *United States v. Borders,* 693 F.2d 1318, 1324 (11th Cir.1982); *Scheib v. Williams–McWilliams Co.,* 628 F.2d 509, 511 (5th Cir.1980).

2. The Employee Polygraph Protection Act prohibits the use of polygraphs in pre-employment screening and sharply curtails the permissible uses of the polygraph in specific-incident investigations. 29 U.S.C.A. §§ 2002, 2006 to 2007 (West Supp. 1989).

The concealed information test focuses on the fact that only the person involved in the crime could know the answers to certain questions. The examiner presents a series of multiple choice questions concerning the crime while the polygraph machine records the subject's physiological activities. If the subject has relatively strong physiological reactions to the correct alternatives, then the examiner infers that the subject is attempting to conceal information about the crime. *Id.* at 102. The concealed information test assumes that information about the crime is protected, but in fact police often inform all suspects and even the media about the crime. *Id.*

B. The Polygraph Is Based On Questionable Assumptions

Lie detection is based on four assumptions: (1) that individuals cannot control their physiologies and behavior, (2) that specific emotions can be triggered by specific stimuli, (3) that there are specific relationships between the different aspects of behavior (such as what people say, how they behave, and how they respond physiologically), and (4) that there are no differences among people, so that most people will respond similarly.

The assumption that individuals cannot control their physiologies is subject to serious debate. Some theorists argue that individuals can learn to control their physiological responses and that by producing physiological responses at opportune times during the polygraph test these people could portray themselves as truthful when they are not. Ney, *Expressing Emotions and Controlling Feelings* at 67 ("Jet-fighter pilots learn to control their emotions (and therefore their physiology) in order to operate with maximum efficiency under extreme physical and psychological stress.") These techniques for fooling the polygraph are called countermeasures. Gudjonsson, *How to Defeat the Polygraph Tests* in *The Polygraph Test* 126. Little research has been done on the effectiveness of countermeasures in reducing detection of lies, but the results of research that has been done, while conflicting, indicate that countermeasures can be effective. *OTA Memorandum* at 100–01; Gudjonsson, *How to Defeat the Polygraph Tests* at 135 (concluding that use of physical countermeasures (e.g., pressing toes to floor) is effective when the subject has been trained in countermeasures).[3]

3. In order to fool the control question test, the subject must enhance his physiological reactions to neutral questions, and/or decrease his physiological reactions to relevant questions. Inducing physical pain or muscle tension during non-relevant questions can reduce the difference between physiological responses to relevant and neutral questions. One study found that pressing one's toes against the floor during neutral questions reduced the detection of lies from 75% to 10%. Gudjonsson, *How to Defeat the Polygraph tests,* at 129 (citing Kubis, *Studies in Lie Detection: Computer Feasibility Considerations* (Technical Report 62–205, prepared for Air Force Systems Command) (1962)). A competing study concluded that such countermeasures caused no reduction in detection of lies. *Id.* (citing More, *Polygraph Research and the University,* 14 Law and Order 73–78 (1966)). The Office of Technology Assessment reviewed the available research on this issue in 1983 and concluded that counter-measures can be effective and that further research in the area is necessary to prevent persons engaged in illicit activities from creating "false negatives" on polygraph exams and, in this way, clearing themselves of any suspicion. *OTA Memorandum* at 100–01 ("The possible ef-

Another assumption underlying the polygraph is that specific emotions will be triggered by the act of lying. Some theorists, however, do not believe that emotions are automatically triggered by the presence of such specific stimuli. These theorists see a more indirect causal chain between stimuli and emotion: a person is presented with stimuli, then appraises it, and only then reacts with an emotion, which is based on the person's cognitive appraisal of the stimuli.[4] According to this theory, people can adjust their thinking to "reappraise" the stressful stimuli and create a different emotional reaction than one might expect. Ney, *Expressing Emotions and Controlling Feelings* 68 ("tell the truth and think of something painful and the truth may appear on the polygraph as a lie").[5] Of course, there would be no way for an examiner to determine how the subject is appraising the stimuli in his mind.

The third assumption underlying the polygraph is that there are set patterns of physiological responses that reflect dishonesty: changed blood pressure, heart rate, respiration, and perspiration. There is controversy over this proposition in the scientific community. *Id.* at 70; *H.R. Hearing* at 51 (statement of John F. Beary, III, M.D.) ("there is no Pinocchio response. If you lie your nose does not grow a half inch longer or some other unique bodily response.")

The fourth assumption underlying the lie detector is that people can be expected to respond to similar stimuli in similar ways. Some researchers maintain, however, that individuals do not respond to stress similarly and that no one index can be used to measure emotions in different individuals. Ney, *Expressing Emotions and Controlling Feelings* at 71–72; Gudjonsson, *How to Defeat the Polygraph Tests* 135.

C. *Appellant's Statistics Are Misleading*

Piccinonna claims that "the relevant scientific community"[6] estimates the accuracy of the polygraph to be in the upper-eighty to mid-

fects of counter-measures are particularly significant to the extent that the polygraph is used and relied on for national security purposes * * *. [T]hose individuals who the Federal Government would most want to detect (e.g., for national security violations) may well be the most motivated and perhaps the best trained to avoid detection.")

4. This is Lazarus's cognitive appraisal theory of emotion. *See* Ney, *Expressing Emotions and Controlling Feelings* at 68 (citing Lazarus, Coyne, and Folkman, *Cognition, Emotion and Motivation: The Doctoring of Humpty–Dumpty,* in *Approaches to Emotion* (K. Scherer and P. Ekman eds. 1984)).

5. Even when the subject is not employing countermeasures, cognitive appraisal seems to affect the results of tests where the subject is accused of a nebulous crime or where the sole issue is criminal intent. In these cases, the issue is not as distinct as in cases where the subject is accused of a physical act. The issue calls for an interpretation, which may be subject to distortion or rationalization in the defendant's mind. Barland, *The Polygraph Test in the U.S.A. and Elsewhere* in *The Polygraph Test* 83–84. In the instant case, the defendant is accused of knowingly telling a falsehood when he denied knowledge of an agreement among south Florida garbage companies. The defendant could have rationalized his answers to questions on such ambiguous issues, and avoided an emotional and a physiological response to the questions.

6. Piccinonna claims that the "relevant scientific community" is "those who have done research on the techniques and/or have had training or experience in the

ninety percent range. *Appellant's En Banc Brief* at 9. This figure is misleading and subject to serious dispute. The polygraph must do two things: correctly identify liars and correctly identify those who are telling the truth.[7] *Employee Polygraph Protection Act: Hearing on S. 185 Before the Senate Committee on Labor and Human Resources,* 100th Cong., 1st Sess. (Appendix to statement of John F. Beary, III, M.D.) (1988) [Hereinafter "*S. Hearing*"]. No single figure, therefore, can fully express the accuracy of the polygraph. The Office of Technology Assessment compiled the results of six prior reviews of polygraph research, ten field studies, and fourteen analog studies that the Office of Technology Assessment determined met minimum scientific standards. All of the studies used the control question technique in specific-incident criminal investigation settings. The results were as follows:

Six prior reviews of field studies:

-average accuracy ranged from 64 to 98 percent.

Ten individual field studies:

-correct guilty detections ranged from 70.6 to 98.6 percent and averaged 86.3 percent;

-correct innocent detections ranged from 12.5 to 94.1 percent and averaged 76 percent;

-false positive rate (innocent persons found deceptive) ranged from 0 to 75 percent and averaged 19.1 percent; and

-false negative rate (guilty persons found nondeceptive) ranged from 0 to 29.4 percent and averaged 10.2 percent.

Fourteen individual analog studies:

-correct guilty detections ranged from 35.4 to 100 percent and averaged 63.7 percent;

-correct innocent detections ranged from 32 to 91 percent and averaged 57.9 percent;

techniques [of polygraph testing] * * *." *Appellant's En Banc Brief* at 9. The Office of Technology Assessment has stated, however, that "Basic polygraph research should consider the latest research from the fields of psychology, physiology, psychiatry, neuroscience, and medicine" in order to develop a stronger theoretical base for the polygraph. *OTA Memorandum* at 6. It is reasonable to argue, therefore, that experts from these fields are competent to comment on the validity of polygraph testing. Gianelli, *The Admissibility of Novel Scientific Evidence: Frye v. United States, a Half-Century Later,* 80 Colum.L.Rev. 1197, 1210 (1980) ("The purpose of the *Frye* test is defeated by an approach which allows a court to ignore the informed opinions of a substantial segment of the scientific community which stands in opposition to the process in question.' " (quoting *Reed v. State,* 283 Md. 374, 399, 391 A.2d 364, 377 (1978))). Congress has recognized that the community of experts competent to testify on the polygraph reaches beyond polygraph examiners and their proponents. For example, Dr. John F. Beary III appeared on behalf of the American Medical Association before the House Education and Labor Committee and the Senate Committee on Labor and Human Resources to oppose the use of polygraphs in the workplace. *H.R. Hearing* at 51; *S. Hearing* at 16.

7. For example, a polygraph examiner who accused every subject of lying would be 100% accurate at detecting liars. His accuracy at detecting those who are truthful, however, would be unacceptably low.

> -false positives ranged from 2 to 50.7 percent and averaged 14.1 percent; and
>
> -false negatives ranged from 0 to 28.7 percent and averaged 10.4 percent.

OTA Memorandum at 97. Note that because the question "Is the subject lying?" is a yes or no question, a random method of answering the question (e.g., a coin toss) would be correct 50% of the time. The Memorandum concluded,

> The wide variability of results from both prior research reviews and [The Office of Technology Assessment's] own review of individual studies makes it impossible to determine a specific overall quantitative measure of polygraph validity. The preponderance of research evidence does indicate that, when the control question technique is used in specific-incident criminal investigation, the polygraph detects deception at a rate better than chance, but with error rates that could be considered significant.

Id.

D. Extrinsic Factors Affect Accuracy

A number of extrinsic factors affect polygraph validity. Most important, because the examiner must formulate the questions, supplement the data with his own impression of the subject during the exam, and infer lies from a combination of the data and his impressions, the level of skill and training of the examiner will affect the reliability of the results. S.Rep. No. 284, 100th Cong., 2d Sess. 42, *reprinted in* 1988 U.S.Code Cong. & Admin.News 726, 729 [hereinafter *Senate Report*]; Barland, *The Polygraph in the USA and Elsewhere* in *The Polygraph Test* 82. Unfortunately, there are no uniform standards for the training of polygraph examiners in this country. *Senate Report* at 43, U.S.Code Cong. & Admin.News at 731; *S. Hearing* at 27 (statement of Mr. William J. Scheve, Jr., American Polygraph Association); *see* Barland, *The Polygraph in the USA and Elsewhere* at 75 (the American Polygraph Association has accredited over 30 polygraph schools with courses ranging from seven to fourteen weeks).

A quality control system that reviews the examiners' conclusions also affects the validity of polygraph results. The results of most federally administered polygraph exams are checked by quality control officers, who call for reexaminations if the data does not indicate that the examiner's conclusion was correct. Barland, *The Polygraph in the USA and Elsewhere* 87. Few police examiners work within such a system, and almost no private examiners have quality control. *Id.* at 82.

The length of a polygraph exam will also affect the validity of the results. One advocate of the polygraph has stated that an expert polygraph exam would take a minimum of several hours to complete. *Senate Report* at 43, 1988 *U.S.Code Cong. and Admin.News* at 730–31.

II. Polygraph Tests Should Be Excluded Under the Federal Rules of Evidence

Under Federal Rule of Evidence 702, expert testimony is proper if the testimony would assist the trier of fact in analyzing the evidence. Fed.R.Evid. 702 advisory committee's note (West 1989). Because the polygraph can predict whether a person is lying with accuracy that is only slightly greater than chance, it will be of little help to the trier of fact. Moreover, this slight helpfulness must be weighed against the dangers of unfair prejudice, confusion of the issues and waste of time. Fed.R.Evid. 403. The Ninth Circuit has found that polygraph evidence has an overwhelming potential for prejudicing the jury. *Brown v. Darcy,* 783 F.2d 1389, 1396 (9th Cir.1986) (citing *United States v. Alexander,* 526 F.2d 161, 168 (8th Cir.1975)); *see also* Gianelli, *The Admissibility of Novel Scientific Evidence: Frye v. United States, a Half-Century Later,* 80 Colum.L.Rev. 1197, 1237 (1980) ("The major danger of scientific evidence is its potential to mislead the jury; an aura of scientific infallibility may shroud the evidence and thus lead the jury to accept it without critical scrutiny.") The *Brown* court determined that unstipulated polygraph evidence is inadmissible under both Rule 702 and Rule 403. *Brown,* 783 F.2d at 1396 n. 13. The polygraph presents itself as being very scientific. For instance, it is said to measure "galvanic skin response," *Appellant's En Banc Brief* at 10, which merely means that it measures how much a person perspires. Bull, *What is the Lie-Detection Test?* at 11. This scientific aura tends to cloud the fact that the machine's accuracy at detecting lies is little better than chance. *Brown,* 783 F.2d at 1396 (quoting *Alexander,* 526 F.2d at 168); *OTA Memorandum* at 97.

The Ninth Circuit also found that admission of polygraph evidence had the potential of confusing the issues and wasting time. *Id.* at 1397; *see* Fed.R.Evid. 403. In the *Brown* case, for instance, the polygraph evidence consumed one fourth of the entire trial. *Brown,* 783 F.2d at 1397 (two full days of an eight-day trial). Because polygraph evidence is of little help to the trier of fact, and has great potential for prejudicing the trier of fact, confusing the issues and wasting time, it should be excluded under Federal Rule of Evidence 403.

The danger of prejudice, confusion of the issues and wasting time should also prevent courts from admitting polygraph evidence under Rule 608 for purposes of impeaching a witness. As the Court's opinion correctly states, all offers of polygraph evidence should be analyzed in light of Rule 403. *Cf. United States v. Miller,* 874 F.2d 1255, 1261 (9th Cir.1989) (even when offered for a limited purpose, polygraph evidence must go through a Rule 403 analysis). To hold that polygraph evidence is admissible under Rule 608 would create too large an exception to the rule barring polygraph evidence generally, and polygraph test results would wind up being admitted into evidence in most cases. Moreover, there is nothing special about the Rule 608 impeachment procedure that lessens the dangers of prejudice and confusion of the issues. *Cf. United States v. Toney,* 615 F.2d 277 (5th Cir.1980) ("Rule 403 is a general rule, 'designed as a guide for the handling of situations for which no specific rules have been formulated.' ")

III. CONCLUSION

The scientific community remains sharply divided over the issue of the validity of polygraph exams. Although presented as a rigorously "scientific" procedure, the polygraph test in fact relies upon a highly subjective, inexact correlation of physiological factors having only a debatable relationship to dishonesty as such. The device detects lies at a rate only somewhat better than chance. Polygraph evidence, therefore, should not be admissible under Rule 702 or under Rule 608 to impeach a witness.

In this case, the government did not stipulate to the admissibility of the defendant's polygraph evidence and did not participate in selection of the examiner or the determination of the circumstances of the test. I would therefore AFFIRM the judgment below.

UNITED STATES v. DOWNING, 753 F.2d 1224, 1234–37 (3d Cir. 1985). "Because the general acceptance standard set out in *Frye* was the dominant view within the federal courts at the time the Federal Rules of Evidence were considered and adopted, one might expect that the rules themselves would make some pronouncement about the continuing vitality of the standard. Neither the text of the Federal Rules of Evidence nor the accompanying notes of the advisory committee, however, explicitly set forth the appropriate standard by which the admissibility of novel scientific evidence is to be established. Although the commentators agree that this legislative silence is significant, they disagree about its meaning. Professors Saltzburg and Redden, for example, have stated, '[i]t would be odd if the Advisory Committee and the Congress intended to overrule the vast majority of cases excluding such evidence as lie detectors without explicitly stating so.' Saltzburg & Redden, supra, at 452. See also 1 D. Louisell & C. Mueller, supra, § 105, at 818 ('Probably the general scientific acceptance approach has survived the enactment of the Federal Rules, and will continue to be applied in determining the relevancy of such proof under Rule 401.'); Giannelli, supra, at 1228–29.

"The opposing view, espoused by Judge Weinstein, Professor Berger, and others, maintains that '[T]he silence of the rule [702] and its drafters should be regarded as tantamount to an abandonment of the general acceptance standard.' J. Weinstein & M. Berger, supra, ¶ 702[03] at 702–16. See also C. Wright & K. Graham, 22 Federal Practice and Procedure § 5168, at 86–90 (1978). Cf. State v. Williams, 388 A.2d 500, 503 (Me.1978) (interpreting Maine rules of evidence, which are patterned after the federal rules, as not incorporating *Frye*). Arguing that *Frye* is inconsistent with the policies animating the Federal Rules of Evidence, this view focuses in particular on the broad scope of relevance in the federal rules. * * * Thus, because the mere relevance of novel scientific evidence does not hinge on its 'general acceptance' in the scientific community, Rules 401 and 402, taken together, arguably create a standard of admissibility of novel scientific evidence that is inconsistent with *Frye*. See C. Wright & K. Graham, 22 Federal Practice and Procedure § 5168, at 89–90 (1978). Notwithstanding the appeal of this analysis, the notes of the advisory committee make clear that Rule 402 is limited by Fed.R.Evid. 403 and by the rules contained in Article VII of the Federal Rules of Evidence, including Rule 702. The touchstone of Rule 702, as was noted above, is the helpfulness of the expert testimony, i.e., whether it 'will assist the trier of fact to understand the evidence or to determine a fact in issue.' Fed.R.Evid. 702. Thus, the rules themselves contain a counterweight to a simple relevancy analysis.

"Although we believe that 'helpfulness' necessarily implies a quantum of reliability beyond that required to meet a standard of bare logical relevance, see discussion infra, it also seems clear to us that some scientific evidence can assist the trier of fact in reaching an accurate determination of facts in issue even though the principles underlying the evidence have not become 'generally accepted' in the field to which they belong. Moreover, we can assume that the drafters of the Federal Rules of Evidence were aware that the *Frye* test was a judicial creation, and we find nothing in the language of the rules to suggest a disapproval of such interstitial judicial rulemaking. Therefore, although the codification of the rules of evidence may counsel in favor of a re-examination of the general acceptance standard, on balance we conclude that the Federal Rules of Evidence neither incorporate nor repudiate it. Cf. Saltzburg & Redden, supra, at 452 (suggesting the decision as to the proper standard for evaluating scientific evidence will continue to be made on a case-by-case basis). We will consider, therefore, the advantages of and the problems associated with *Frye's* general acceptance standard.

* * *

"Notwithstanding the valid evidentiary concerns subsumed in the general acceptance standard, critics of the standard have cited two general problems with it: its vagueness and its conservatism. See, e.g., 1 D. Louisell & C. Mueller, supra, § 105, at 821. Professor Giannelli's excellent and comprehensive article catalogues the numerous difficulties that have arisen in applying the test. Giannelli, supra, at 1208–28. First, the vague terms included in the standard have allowed courts to manipulate the parameters of the relevant 'scientific community' and the level of agreement needed for 'general acceptance.' Thus, some courts, when they wish to admit evidence, are able to limit the impact of *Frye* by narrowing the relevant scientific community to those experts who customarily employ the technique at issue. See, e.g., People v. Williams, 164 Cal.App.2d Supp. 858, 331 P.2d 251 (App.Dep't Super.Ct.1958) (in admitting results of the Nalline test for narcotics use, the court held that the *Frye* test was satisfied upon showing of general acceptance by those who are expected to be familiar with the use of the technique, although the prosecution's own expert had conceded the lack of acceptance within the medical profession generally). Judicial interpretation of the 'general acceptance' component of the test has yielded even more disparate results. One court has described 'general acceptance' as 'widespread; prevalent; extensive though not universal,' United States v. Zeiger, 350 F.Supp. 685, 688 (D.D.C.), rev'd 475 F.2d 1280 (D.C.Cir.1972), while another has suggested that the test requires agreement by a 'substantial section of the scientific community.' United States v. Williams, 443 F.Supp. 269, 273 (S.D.N.Y.1977), aff'd, 583 F.2d 1194 (2d Cir.1978), cert. denied, 493 U.S. 1117, 99 S.Ct. 1025, 59 L.Ed.2d 77 (1979).

"Professor Giannelli and others have discussed other problems that arise in applying the *Frye* test: the selectivity among courts in determining whether evidence derives from 'novel' principles; the inadequacy of expert testimony on many scientific issues; an uncritical acceptance of prior judicial, rather than scientific, opinion as a basis for finding 'general acceptance'; and the narrow scope of review by which some appellate courts review trial court rulings. See Giannelli, supra, at 1208–21. All of these problems contribute to the 'essential vagueness' of the *Frye* test. 1 D. Louisell & C. Mueller, supra, at 821.

"Apart from these various difficulties in implementation, moreover, *Frye's* general acceptance standard has been found to be unsatisfactory in other respects. Under *Frye,* some have argued, courts may be required to exclude much probative and reliable information from the jury's consideration, thereby unnecessarily impeding the truth-seeking function of litigation. See, e.g., United States v. Sample, 378 F.Supp. 44, 53 (E.D.Pa.1974) (Frye 'precludes too much relevant evidence'); see also 1 D. Louisell & C. Mueller, supra, at 822; Lacey, 'Scientific Evidence,' 24 Jurimetrics, Journal of Law, Science, and Technology 254, 265 (1984) (Frye jurisdictions will always lag behind advances in science). But see United States v. Addison, 498 F.2d 741, 743 (D.C.Cir.1974) (consequence that *Frye* standard retards the admissibility of scientific evidence is not an 'unwarranted cost').

"In sum, the *Frye* test suffers from serious flaws. The test has proved to be too malleable to provide the method for orderly and uniform decision-making envisioned by some of its proponents. Moreover, in its pristine form the general acceptance standard reflects a conservative approach to the admissibility of scientific evidence that is at odds with the spirit, if not the precise language, of the Federal Rules of Evidence. For these reasons, we conclude that 'general acceptance in the particular field to which [a scientific technique] belongs,' *Frye,* 293 F. at 1014, should be rejected as an independent controlling standard of admissibility. Accordingly, we hold that a particular degree of acceptance of a scientific technique within the scientific community is neither a necessary nor a sufficient condition for admissibility; it is, however, one factor that a district court normally should consider in deciding whether to admit evidence based upon the technique.

"The language of Fed.R.Evid. 702, the spirit of the Federal Rules of Evidence in general, and the experience with the *Frye* test suggest the appropriateness of a more flexible approach to the admissibility of novel scientific evidence. In our view, Rule 702 requires that a district court ruling upon the admission of (novel) scientific evidence, i.e., evidence whose scientific fundaments are not suitable candidates for judicial notice, conduct a preliminary inquiry focusing on (1) the soundness and reliability of the process or technique used in generating the evidence, (2) the possibility that admitting the evidence would overwhelm, confuse, or mislead the jury, and (3) the proffered connection between the scientific research or test result to be presented, and particular disputed factual issues in the case."

REED v. STATE, 283 Md. 374, 391 A.2d 364, 369–72 (1978). "The *Frye* test has been subjected to some criticism, primarily on the grounds that it is too conservative and unduly prevents or delays the admission of relevant scientific evidence. United States v. Sample, 378 F.Supp. 44, 53 (E.D.Pa.1974); McCormick, Evidence § 203, pp. 490–491 (2d ed. 1972); cf. United States v. Baller, 519 F.2d 463, 466 (4th Cir.1975), cert. denied, 423 U.S. 1019, 96 S.Ct. 456, 46 L.Ed.2d 391 (1975). There are, however, compelling reasons which justify the *Frye* principle.

"Fairness to a litigant would seem to require that before the results of a *scientific* process can be used against him, he is entitled to a *scientific* judgment on the reliability of that process. As stated by Judge McGowan, speaking for the court in United States v. Addison, 162 U.S.App.D.C. 199, 201, 498 F.2d 741, 743–744 (1974):

> '[T]he *Frye* standard retards somewhat the admission of proof based on new methods of scientific investigation by requiring that they attain sufficient currency and status to gain the general acceptance of the relevant scientific community. This is not to say, however, that the *Frye* standard exacts an unwarranted cost. The requirement of general acceptance in the scientific community assures that those most qualified to assess the general validity of a scientific method will have the determinative voice.'

"This is an especially significant consideration with regard to those scientific techniques in which highly subjective judgments are based upon the data received from sophisticated mechanical devices. In these circumstances, the apparent objectivity of the machine may suggest a degree of certainty inconsistent with the subjective aspects of the enterprise. United States v. Addison, supra, 162 U.S.App.D.C. at 202, 498 F.2d at 744; People v. Kelly, supra. As the Supreme Court of California stated in *Kelly* (130 Cal.Rptr. at 149, 549 P.2d at 1245):

'* * * *Frye* was deliberately intended to interpose a substantial obstacle to the unrestrained admission of evidence based upon new scientific principles. * * * Several reasons founded in logic and common sense support a posture of judicial caution in this area. Lay jurors tend to give considerable weight to "scientific" evidence when presented by "experts" with impressive credentials. We have acknowledged the existence of a "* * * misleading aura of certainty which often envelops a new scientific process, obscuring its currently experimental nature." (Huntingdon v. Crowley, supra, 64 Cal.2d 647 at p. 656, 51 Cal.Rptr. 254 at p. 262, 414 P.2d 382 at p. 390; * * *.) As stated in *Addison,* supra, in the course of rejecting the admissibility of voiceprint testimony, "scientific proof may in some instances assume a posture of mystic infallibility in the eyes of a jury * * *." (United States v. Addison, supra, 498 F.2d at p. 744.)'

"In addition to the advantage of substituting scientific for lay judgment as to scientific reliability, the court in United States v. Addison, supra, 162 U.S.App.D.C. at 202, 498 F.2d at 744, pointed out that the *Frye* test

'* * * protects prosecution and defense alike by assuring that a minimal reserve of experts exists who can critically examine the validity of a scientific determination in a particular case. * * * [T]he ability to produce rebuttal experts, equally conversant with the mechanics and methods of a particular technique, may prove to be essential.'

"The dissenting opinion, however, suggests that instead we adopt the rule enunciated by McCormick, that '[a]ny relevant conclusions which are supported by a qualified expert witness should be received unless there are other reasons for exclusion.' McCormick on Evidence § 203 at 491 (2d ed. 1972). McCormick, in opposition to the great weight of judicial authority, believes that disagreement in the scientific community regarding the reliability of a scientific process should go to the weight rather than the admissibility of scientific evidence.

"This view seems to us unacceptable. It fails to recognize that laymen should not on a case by case basis resolve a dispute in the scientific community concerning the validity of a new scientific technique. When the positions of the contending factions are fixed in the scientific community, it is evident that controversies will be resolved only by further scientific analysis, studies and experiments. Juries and judges, however, cannot experiment. If a judge or jurors have no foundation, either in their experience or in the accepted principles of scientists, on which they might base an informed judgment, they will be left to follow their fancy. Thus, courts should be properly reluctant to resolve the disputes of science. 'It is not for the law to experiment but for science to do so,' State v. Cary, supra, 99 N.J.Super. at 332, 239 A.2d at 684.

"Nonetheless, under the McCormick standard, juries would be compelled to make determinations regarding the validity of experimental or novel scientific techniques. As a result, one jury might decide that a particular scientific process is reliable, while another jury might find that the identical process is not. However, the reliability of the underlying technique or process to perform as it is supposed to does not vary with different cases. Using the polygraph as an example, although particular polygraph tests may give different results under different circumstances, the basic validity of the polygraph technique in general to give the type of results which are claimed for it does not change with the facts of each case. Nevertheless, if the trier of facts is to determine the *validity* of the polygraph test on a case by case basis, one judge or jury might determine that it is reliable and convict or acquit a defendant on the basis of the test results, whereas the very next judge or jury, sitting in the same courthouse and listening to the same operator giving the same type of test results, might determine that the technique is unreliable and ignore the results. Such inconsistency concerning the validity of a given scientific technique or process would be intolerable. See Commonwealth v. Sullivan, 146 Mass. 142, 145, 15 N.E. 491 (1888) (Holmes, J.).

"Under the *Frye* test, however, this difficulty is largely avoided. As long as the scientific community remains significantly divided, results of controversial techniques will not be admitted, and all defendants will face the same burdens. If, on the other hand, a novel scientific process does achieve general acceptance in the scientific community, there will likely be as little dispute over its reliability as there is now concerning other areas of forensic science which have been deemed admissible under the *Frye* standard, such as blood tests, ballistics tests, etc.

"In addition, there is a related danger under the McCormick view. The introduction of evidence based on a scientific process, not yet generally accepted in the scientific community, is likely to distract the fact finder from its central concern, namely the rendition of a judgment on the merits of the litigation. Without the *Frye* test or something similar, the reliability of an experimental scientific technique is likely to become a central issue in each trial in which it is introduced, as long as there remains serious disagreement in the scientific community over its reliability. Again and again, the examination and cross-examination of expert witnesses will be as protracted and time-consuming as it was at the trial in the instant case, and proceedings may well degenerate into trials of the technique itself. The *Frye* test is designed to forestall this difficulty as well."

PEOPLE v. COLLINS

Supreme Court of California, 1968.
68 Cal.2d 319, 66 Cal.Rptr. 497, 438 P.2d 33.

SULLIVAN, JUSTICE.

We deal here with the novel question whether evidence of mathematical probability has been properly introduced and used by the prosecution in a criminal case. While we discern no inherent incompatibility between the disciplines of law and mathematics and intend no general disapproval or disparagement of the latter as an auxiliary in the fact-finding processes of the former, we cannot uphold the technique employed in the instant case. As we explain in detail infra, the testimony as to mathematical probability infected the case with fatal error and distorted the jury's traditional role of determining guilt or innocence according to long-settled rules. Mathematics, a veritable sorcerer in our computerized society, while assisting the trier of fact in the search for truth, must not cast a spell over him. We conclude that on the record before us defendant should not have had his guilt determined by the odds and that he is entitled to a new trial. We reverse the judgment.

A jury found defendant Malcolm Ricardo Collins and his wife defendant Janet Louise Collins guilty of second degree robbery (Pen. Code, §§ 211, 211a, 1157). Malcolm appeals from the judgment of conviction. Janet has not appealed.[1]

On June 18, 1964, about 11:30 a.m. Mrs. Juanita Brooks, who had been shopping, was walking home along an alley in the San Pedro area of the City of Los Angeles. She was pulling behind her a wicker basket carryall containing groceries and had her purse on top of the packages. She was using a cane. As she stooped down to pick up an empty carton, she was suddenly pushed to the ground by a person whom she neither saw nor heard approach. She was stunned by the fall and felt some pain. She managed to look up and saw a young woman running from the scene. According to Mrs. Brooks the latter appeared to weigh about 145 pounds, was wearing "something dark," and had hair "between a dark blond and a light blond," but lighter than the color of defendant Janet Collins' hair as it appeared at trial. Immediately after the incident, Mrs. Brooks discovered that her purse, containing between \$35 and \$40, was missing.

About the same time as the robbery, John Bass, who lived on the street at the end of the alley, was in front of his house watering his lawn. His attention was attracted by "a lot of crying and screaming" coming from the alley. As he looked in that direction, he saw a woman run out of the alley and enter a yellow automobile parked across the street from him. He was unable to give the make of the car. The car started off immediately and pulled wide around another parked vehicle so that in the narrow street it passed within six feet of Bass. The latter then saw that it was being driven by a male Negro, wearing a mustache and beard. At the trial Bass identified defendant as the driver of the yellow automobile. However, an attempt was made to impeach his identification by his admission that at the preliminary hearing he

1. Hereafter, the term "defendant" is intended to apply only to Malcolm, but the term "defendants" to Malcolm and Janet.

testified to an uncertain identification at the police lineup shortly after the attack on Mrs. Brooks, when defendant was beardless.

In his testimony Bass described the woman who ran from the alley as a Caucasian, slightly over five feet tall, of ordinary build, with her hair in a dark blond ponytail, and wearing dark clothing. He further testified that her ponytail was "just like" one which Janet had in a police photograph taken on June 22, 1964.

On the day of the robbery, Janet was employed as a housemaid in San Pedro. Her employer testified that she had arrived for work at 8:50 a.m. and that defendant had picked her up in a light yellow car [2] about 11:30 a.m. On that day, according to the witness, Janet was wearing her hair in a blonde ponytail but lighter in color than it appeared at trial.[3]

There was evidence from which it could be inferred that defendants had ample time to drive from Janet's place of employment and participate in the robbery. Defendants testified, however, that they went directly from her employer's house to the home of friends, where they remained for several hours.

In the morning of June 22, Los Angeles Police Officer Kinsey, who was investigating the robbery, went to defendants' home. He saw a yellow Lincoln automobile with an off-white top in front of the house. He talked with defendants. Janet, whose hair appeared to be a dark blonde, was wearing it in a ponytail. Malcolm did not have a beard. The officer explained to them that he was investigating a robbery specifying the time and place; that the victim had been knocked down and her purse snatched; and that the person responsible was a female Caucasian with blonde hair in a ponytail who had left the scene in a yellow car driven by a male Negro. He requested that defendants accompany him to the police station at San Pedro and they did so. There, in response to police inquiries as to defendants' activities at the time of the robbery, Janet stated, according to Officer Kinsey, that her husband had picked her up at her place of employment at 1 p.m. and that they had then visited at the home of friends in Los Angeles. Malcolm confirmed this. Defendants were detained for an hour or two, were photographed but not booked, and were eventually released and driven home by the police.

* * *

Officer Kinsey interrogated defendants separately on June 23 while they were in custody and testified to their statements over defense counsel's objections * * *. According to the officer, Malcolm stated

2. Other witnesses variously described the car as yellow, as yellow with an off-white top, and yellow with an egg-shell white top. The car was also described as being medium to large in size. Defendant drove a car at or near the times in question which was a Lincoln with a yellow body and a white top.

3. There are inferences which may be drawn from the evidence that Janet attempted to alter the appearance of her hair after June 18. Janet denies that she cut, colored or bleached her hair at any time after June 18, and a number of witnesses supported her testimony.

that he sometimes wore a beard but that he did not wear a beard on June 18 (the day of the robbery), having shaved it off on June 2, 1964.[5]
* * *

* * *

At the seven-day trial the prosecution experienced some difficulty in establishing the identities of the perpetrators of the crime. The victim could not identify Janet and had never seen defendant. The identification by the witness Bass, who observed the girl run out of the alley and get into the automobile was incomplete as to Janet and may have been weakened as to the defendant. There was also evidence, introduced by the defense, that Janet had worn light-colored clothing on the day in question, but both the victim and Bass testified that the girl they observed had worn dark clothing.

In an apparent attempt to bolster the identifications, the prosecutor called an instructor of mathematics at a state college. Through this witness he sought to establish that, assuming the robbery was committed by a Caucasian woman with a blond ponytail who left the scene accompanied by a Negro with a beard and mustache, there was an overwhelming probability that the crime was committed by any couple answering such distinctive characteristics. The witness testified, in substance, to the "product rule," which states that the probability of the joint occurrence of a number of *mutually independent* events is equal to the product of the individual probabilities that each of the events will occur.[8] *Without presenting any statistical evidence whatsoever in support of the probabilities for the factors selected,* the prosecutor then proceeded to have the witness *assume*[9] probability factors for the various characteristics which he deemed to be shared by the guilty couple and all other couples answering to such distinctive characteristics.[10]

5. Evidence as to defendant's beard and mustache is conflicting. Defense witnesses appeared to support defendant's claims that he had shaved his beard on June 2. There was testimony that on June 19 when defendant appeared in court to pay fines on another matter he was bearded. By June 22 the beard had been removed.

8. In the example employed for illustrative purposes at the trial, the probability of rolling one die and coming up with a "2" is $1/6$, that is, any one of the six faces of a die has one chance in six of landing face up on any particular roll. The probability of rolling two "2's" in succession is $1/6 \times 1/6$, or $1/36$, that is, on only one occasion out of 36 double rolls (or the roll of two dice), will the selected number land face up on each roll or die.

9. His argument to the jury was based on the same gratuitous assumptions or on similar assumptions which he invited the jury to make.

10. Although the prosecutor insisted that the factors he used were only for illustrative purposes—to demonstrate how the probability of the occurrence of mutually independent factors affected the probability that they would occur together—he nevertheless attempted to use factors which he personally related to the distinctive characteristics of defendants. In his argument to the jury he invited the jurors to apply their own factors, and asked defense counsel to suggest what the latter would deem as reasonable. The prosecutor himself proposed the individual probabilities set out in the table below. Although the transcript of the examination of the mathematics instructor and the information volunteered by the prosecutor at that time create some uncertainty as to precisely which of the characteristics the prosecutor assigned to the individual probabilities, he re-stated in his argument to the jury that they should be as follows:

Applying the product rule to his own factors the prosecutor arrived at a probability that there was but one chance in 12 million that any couple possessed the distinctive characteristics of the defendants. Accordingly, under this theory, it was to be inferred that there could be but one chance in 12 million that defendants were innocent and that another equally distinctive couple actually committed the robbery. Expanding on what he had thus purported to suggest as a hypothesis, the prosecutor offered the completely unfounded and improper testimonial assertion that in his opinion, the factors he had assigned were "conservative estimates" and that, in reality "the chances of anyone else besides these defendants being there, * * * having every similarity, * * * is somewhat like one in a billion."

Objections were timely made to the mathematician's testimony on the grounds that it was immaterial, that it invaded the province of the jury, and that it was based on unfounded assumptions. The objections were "temporarily overruled" and the evidence admitted subject to a motion to strike. When that motion was made at the conclusion of the direct examination, the court denied it, stating that the testimony had been received only for the "purpose of illustrating the mathematical probabilities of various matters, the possibilities for them occurring or re-occurring."

Both defendants took the stand in their own behalf. They denied any knowledge of or participation in the crime and stated that after Malcolm called for Janet at her employer's house they went directly to a friend's house in Los Angeles where they remained for some time. According to this testimony defendants were not near the scene of the robbery when it occurred. Defendants' friend testified to a visit by them "in the middle of June" although she could not recall the precise date. Janet further testified that certain inducements were held out to her during the July 9 interrogation on condition that she confess her participation.

Defendant makes two basic contentions before us: * * * second, that the introduction of evidence pertaining to the mathematical theory of probability and the use of the same by the prosecution during the trial was error prejudicial to defendant. We consider the latter claim first.

As we shall explain, the prosecution's introduction and use of mathematical probability statistics injected two fundamental prejudicial errors into the case: (1) The testimony itself lacked an adequate foundation both in evidence and in statistical theory; and (2) the testimony and the manner in which the prosecution used it distracted the jury from its proper and requisite function of weighing the evidence

Characteristic	Individual Probability
A. Partly yellow automobile	1/10
B. Man with mustache	1/4
C. Girl with ponytail	1/10
D. Girl with blond hair	1/3
E. Negro man with beard	1/10
F. Interracial couple in car	1/1000

In his brief on appeal defendant agrees that the foregoing appeared on a table presented in the trial court.

on the issue of guilt, encouraged the jurors to rely upon an engaging but logically irrelevant expert demonstration, foreclosed the possibility of an effective defense by an attorney apparently unschooled in mathematical refinements, and placed the jurors and defense counsel at a disadvantage in sifting relevant fact from inapplicable theory.

We initially consider the defects in the testimony itself. As we have indicated, the specific technique presented through the mathematician's testimony and advanced by the prosecutor to measure the probabilities in question suffered from two basic and pervasive defects—an inadequate evidentiary foundation and an inadequate proof of statistical independence. First, as to the foundation requirement, we find the record devoid of any evidence relating to any of the six individual probability factors used by the prosecutor and ascribed by him to the six characteristics as we have set them out in footnote 10, ante. To put it another way, the prosecution produced no evidence whatsoever showing, or from which it could be in any way inferred, that only one out of every ten cars which might have been at the scene of the robbery was partly yellow, that only one out of every four men who might have been there wore a mustache, that only one out of every ten girls who might have been there wore a ponytail, or that any of the other individual probability factors listed were even roughly accurate.[12]

The bare, inescapable fact is that the prosecution made no attempt to offer any such evidence. Instead, through leading questions having perfunctorily elicited from the witness the response that the latter could not assign a probability factor for the characteristics involved,[13] the prosecutor himself suggested what the various probabilities should be and these became the basis of the witness' testimony (see fn. 10, ante). It is a curious circumstance of this adventure in proof that the prosecutor not only made his own assertions of these factors in the hope that they were "conservative" but also in later argument to the jury invited the jurors to substitute their "estimates" should they wish to do so. We can hardly conceive of a more fatal gap in the prosecution's scheme of proof. A foundation for the admissibility of the witness' testimony was never even attempted to be laid, let alone established. His testimony was neither made to rest on his own testimonial knowledge nor presented by proper hypothetical questions based upon valid

12. We seriously doubt that such evidence could ever be compiled since no statistician could possibly determine after the fact which cars, or which individuals, "might" have been present at the scene of the robbery; certainly there is no reason to suppose that the human and automotive populations of San Pedro, California, include all potential culprits—or, conversely, that all members of these populations are proper candidates for inclusion. Thus the sample from which the relevant probabilities would have to be derived is itself undeterminable. (See generally, Yaman, Statistics, An Introductory Analysis (1964), ch. I.)

13. The prosecutor asked the mathematics instruction: "Now, let me see if you can be of some help to us with some independent factors, and you have some paper you may use. Your specialty does not equip you, I suppose, to give us some probability of such things as a yellow car as contrasted with any other kind of car, does it? * * * I appreciate the fact that you can't assign a probability for a car being yellow as contrasted to some other car, can you? A. No, I couldn't."

data in the record. (See generally: 2 Wigmore on Evidence (3d ed. 1940) §§ 478, 650–652, 657, 659, 672–684; Witkin, Cal.Evidence (2d ed. 1966) § 771; McCormick on Evidence pp. 19–20; Evidence: Admission of Mathematical Probability Statistics Held Erroneous for Want of Demonstration of Validity (1967) Duke L.J. 665, 675–678, citing People v. Risley (1915) 214 N.Y. 75, 85, 108 N.E. 200; State v. Sneed (1966) 76 N.M. 349, 414 P.2d 858). In the *Sneed* case, the court reversed a conviction based on probabilistic evidence, stating: "We hold that mathematical odds are not admissible as evidence to identify a defendant in a criminal proceeding *so long as the odds are based on estimates, the validity of which have [sic] not been demonstrated.*" (Italics added.) (414 P.2d at p. 862.)

But, as we have indicated, there was another glaring defect in the prosecution's technique, namely an inadequate proof of the statistical independence of the six factors. No proof was presented that the characteristics selected were mutually independent, even though the witness himself acknowledged that such condition was essential to the proper application of the "product rule" or "multiplication rule." (See Note, supra, Duke L.J. 665, 669–670, fn. 25.)[14] To the extent that the traits or characteristics were not mutually independent (e.g. Negroes with beards and men with mustaches obviously represent overlapping categories[15]), the "product rule" would inevitably yield a wholly erroneous and exaggerated result even if all of the individual components had been determined with precision. (Siegel, Nonparametric Statistics for the Behavioral Sciences (1956) 19; see generally Harmon, Modern Factor Analysis (1960).)

In the instant case, therefore, because of the aforementioned two defects—the inadequate evidentiary foundation and the inadequate proof of statistical independence—the technique employed by the prosecutor could only lead to wild conjecture without demonstrated relevancy to the issues presented. It acquired no redeeming quality from the prosecutor's statement that it was being used only "for illustrative purposes" since, as we shall point out, the prosecutor's subsequent utilization of the mathematical testimony was not confined within such limits.

14. It is there stated that: "A trait is said to be independent of a second trait when the occurrence or non-occurrence of one does not affect the probability of the occurrence of the other trait. The multiplication rule cannot be used without some degree of error where the traits are not independent." (Citing Huntsberger, Elements of Statistical Inference (1961) 77; Kingston & Kirk, The Use of Statistics in Criminalistics (1964) 55 J.Crim.L.C. & P.S. 516.) (Note, supra, Duke L.J. fn. 25, p. 670.)

15. Assuming *arguendo* that factors B and E (see fn. 10, ante), were correctly estimated, nevertheless it is still arguable that most Negro men with beards *also* have mustaches (exhibit 3 herein, for instance, shows defendant with both a mustache and a beard, indeed in a hirsute continuum); if so, there is no basis for multiplying 1/4 by 1/10 to estimate the proportion of Negroes who wear beards *and* mustaches. Again, the prosecution's technique could *never* be meaningfully applied, since its accurate use would call for information as to the degree of interdependence among the six individual factors. (See Yaman, op. cit. supra.) Such information cannot be compiled, however, since the relevant sample necessarily remains unknown. (See fn. 10, ante.)

We now turn to the second fundamental error caused by the probability testimony. Quite apart from our foregoing objections to the specific technique employed by the prosecution to estimate the probability in question, we think that the entire enterprise upon which the prosecution embarked, and which was directed to the objective of measuring the likelihood of a random couple possessing the characteristics allegedly distinguishing the robbers, was gravely misguided. At best, it might yield an estimate as to how infrequently bearded Negroes drive yellow cars in the company of blonde females with ponytails.

The prosecution's approach, however, could furnish the jury with absolutely no guidance on the crucial issue: *Of the admittedly few such couples, which one, if any, was guilty of committing this robbery?* Probability theory necessarily remains silent on that question, since no mathematical equation can prove beyond a reasonable doubt (1) that the guilty couple *in fact* possessed the characteristics described by the People's witnesses, or even (2) that only *one* couple possessing those distinctive characteristics could be found in the entire Los Angeles area.

As to the first inherent failing we observe that the prosecution's theory of probability rested on the assumption that the witnesses called by the People had conclusively established that the guilty couple possessed the precise characteristics relied upon by the prosecution. But no mathematical formula could ever establish beyond a reasonable doubt that the prosecution's witnesses correctly observed and accurately described the distinctive features which were employed to link defendants to the crime. (See 2 Wigmore on Evidence (3d ed. 1940) § 478.) Conceivably, for example, the guilty couple might have included a light-skinned Negress with bleached hair rather than a Caucasian blonde; or the driver of the car might have been wearing a false beard as a disguise; or the prosecution's witnesses might simply have been unreliable.[16]

The foregoing risks of error permeate the prosecution's circumstantial case. Traditionally, the jury weighs such risks in evaluating the credibility and probative value of trial testimony, but the likelihood of human error or of falsification obviously cannot be quantified; that likelihood must therefore be excluded from any effort to assign a *number* to the probability of guilt or innocence. Confronted with an equation which purports to yield a numerical index of probable guilt, few juries could resist the temptation to accord disproportionate weight to that index; only an exceptional juror, and indeed only a defense attorney schooled in mathematics, could successfully keep in mind the fact that the probability computed by the prosecution can represent, *at*

16. In the instant case, for instance, the victim could not state whether the girl had a ponytail, although the victim observed the girl as she ran away. The witness Bass, on the other hand, was sure that the girl whom he saw had a ponytail. The demonstration engaged in by the prosecutor also leaves no room for the possibility, although perhaps a small one, that the girl whom the victim and the witness observed was, in fact, the same girl.

best, the likelihood that a random couple would share the characteristics testified to by the People's witnesses—*not necessarily the characteristics of the actually guilty couple.*

As to the second inherent failing in the prosecution's approach, even assuming that the first failing could be discounted, the most a mathematical computation could *ever* yield would be a measure of the probability that a random couple would possess the distinctive features in question. In the present case, for example, the prosecution attempted to compute the probability that a random couple would include a bearded Negro, a blonde girl with a ponytail, and a partly yellow car; prosecution urged that this probability was no more than one in 12 million. Even accepting this conclusion as arithmetically accurate, however one still could not conclude that the Collinses were probably *the* guilty couple. On the contrary, as we explain in the Appendix, the prosecution's figures actually imply a likelihood of over 40 percent that the Collinses could be "duplicated" by at least *one other couple who might equally have committed the San Pedro robbery.* Urging that the Collinses be convicted on the basis of evidence which logically establishes no more than this seems as indefensible as arguing for the conviction of X on the ground that a witness saw either X or X's twin commit the crime.

Again, few defense attorneys, and certainly few jurors, could be expected to comprehend this basic flaw in the prosecution's analysis. Conceivably even the prosecutor erroneously believed that his equation established a high probability that *no* other bearded Negro in the Los Angeles area drove a yellow car accompanied by a ponytailed blonde. In any event, although his technique could demonstrate no such thing, he solemnly told the jury that he had supplied mathematical proof of guilt.

Sensing the novelty of that notion, the prosecutor told the jurors that the traditional idea of proof beyond a reasonable doubt represented "the most hackneyed, stereotyped, trite, misunderstood concept in criminal law." He sought to reconcile the jury to the risk that, under his "new math" approach to criminal jurisprudence, "on some rare occasion * * * an innocent person may be convicted." "Without taking that risk," the prosecution continued, "life would be intolerable * * * because * * * there would be immunity for the Collinses, for people who chose not to be employed to go down and push old ladies down and take their money and be immune because how could we ever be sure they are the ones who did it?"

In essence this argument of the prosecutor was calculated to persuade the jury to convict defendants whether or not they were convinced of their guilt to a moral certainty and beyond a reasonable doubt. (Pen.Code, § 1096.) Undoubtedly the jurors were unduly impressed by the mystique of the mathematical demonstration but were unable to assess its relevancy or value. Although we make no appraisal of the proper applications of mathematical techniques in the proof of facts (see People v. Jordan (1955) 45 Cal.2d 697, 707, 290 P.2d 484; People v. Trujillo (1948) 32 Cal.2d 105, 109, 194 P.2d 681; in a slightly differing context see Whitus v. State of Georgia (1967) 385 U.S. 545, 552, fn. 2, 87 S.Ct. 643, 17 L.Ed.2d 599; Finkelstein, The Application of Statistical Decision Theory to the Jury Discrimination Cases (1966) 80 Harv.L.Rev. 338, 338–340), we have strong feelings that such applications, particularly in a criminal case, must be critically examined in view of the substantial unfairness to a defendant which may result from ill conceived techniques with which the trier of fact is not technically equipped to cope. (See State v. Sneed, supra, 414 P.2d 858; Note, supra, Duke L.J. 665.) We feel that the technique employed in the case before us falls into the latter category.

We conclude that the court erred in admitting over defendant's objection the evidence pertaining to the mathematical theory of probability and in denying defendant's motion to strike such evidence. The case was apparently a close one. The jury began its deliberations at 2:46 p.m. on November 24, 1964, and retired for the night at 7:46 p.m.; the parties stipulated that a juror could be excused for illness and that a verdict could be reached by the remaining 11 jurors; the jury resumed deliberations the next morning at 8:40 a.m. and returned verdicts at 11:58 a.m. after five ballots had been taken. In the light of the closeness of the case, which as we have said was a circumstantial one, there is a reasonable likelihood that the result would have been more favorable to defendant if the prosecution had not urged the jury to render a probabilistic verdict. In any event, we think that under the circumstances the "trial by mathematics" so distorted the role of the jury and so disadvantaged counsel for the defense, as to constitute in itself a miscarriage of justice. After an examination of the entire cause, including the evidence, we are of the opinion that it is reasonably probable that a result more favorable to defendant would have been reached in the absence of the above error. (People v. Watson (1956) 46 Cal.2d 818, 836; 299 P.2d 243.) The judgment against defendant must therefore be reversed.

* * *

Note

See Broun & Kelly, Playing the Percentages and the Law of Evidence, 1970 U.Ill.L.F. 23; Charrow & Smith, A Conversation About "A Conversation About Collins," 64 Geo.L.J. 669 (1976); Fairley & Mosteller, A Conversation About Collins, 41 U.Chi.L.Rev. 242 (1974); Finkelstein & Fairley, A Bayesian Approach to Identification Evidence, 83 Harv.L.Rev. 489 (1970); Finkelstein & Fairley, A Comment on "Trial by Mathematics," 84 Harv. L.Rev. 1801 (1971); Kaye, The Laws of Probability and the Law of the Land, 47 U.Chi.L.Rev. 34 (1979); Tribe, Trial by Mathematics: Precision and Ritual in the Legal Process, 84 Harv.L.Rev. 1329 (1971).

TORRES v. COUNTY OF OAKLAND

United States Court of Appeals, Sixth Circuit, 1985.
758 F.2d 147.

CONTIE, CIRCUIT JUDGE.

Belen Torres appeals a judgment entered upon a jury verdict in favor of the defendants, County of Oakland and Oakland Community Mental Health Services Board, in this employment discrimination action brought under Title VII and 42 U.S.C. § 1981. Torres' complaint alleged discriminatory treatment based on her national origin. The defendants cross-appeal the district court's denial of attorney's fees. See 42 U.S.C. § 1988.

I.

Because Torres does not challenge the sufficiency of the evidence, the facts may be briefly stated. Torres is a Filipino by birth but has become a United States citizen. She has a Masters degree in social work and has worked for the defendants since September 1979 as a "casework supervisor."

At a meeting in February of 1980, Torres' supervisor, Norbert Birnbaum, used the term "ass" or "asshole" in reference to her. Torres offered some evidence to show that this was purely name-calling. The defendants offered evidence tending to show that, in context, the remark was that Torres would make an "ass" or "asshole" of herself if she continued to discuss subjects after the meeting's discussion had moved to other matters on the agenda.

Torres also offered evidence that her six-month evaluation was downgraded from "outstanding" to "average" in one category without consulting her. The defendants admitted that the evaluation was unilaterally downgraded, but presented evidence tending to show that the change was required by uniformly applied guidelines for attendance. The evaluation form itself reveals that in seven out of eight categories Torres did receive a rating of "outstanding"; only in the eighth category, for attendance, was she rated as "average."

In 1980, the Board decided to create a new supervisory position. Torres applied for this opening but was not promoted. The defendants did not dispute that Torres possessed the general qualifications for this position but instead presented evidence tending to show that there was a high degree of dissension in the ranks of their employees. Thus, it was advisable, in the defendants' view, to hire a new employee to fill the position rather than to promote someone from within the ranks.

II.

Torres' first argument is that the trial court erred in admitting certain testimony of Dr. Quiroga into evidence. Dr. Quiroga is the defendants' Director of Children's Services and took part in selecting the person to fill the new supervisory position. During the examination of Dr. Quiroga by the defendants, the following exchange took place:

> Q. It is true, Dr. Quiroga, that you did not believe that Ms. Torres had been discriminated against because of her national origin in that interview process?
>
> MR. KAREGA: Objection, your Honor.
>
> THE COURT: No, she may state her opinion on that.
>
> A. That is correct.

Torres argues that Dr. Quiroga's opinion testimony was not proper under Federal Rule of Evidence 701 both because it was not sufficiently based on personal perception and because it was testimony containing a legal conclusion.

Federal Rule of Evidence 701 provides:

> If the witness is not testifying as an expert, his testimony in the form of opinions or inferences is limited to those opinions or inferences which are (a) rationally based on the perception of the witness and (b) helpful to a clear understanding of his testimony or the determination of a fact and issue.

The essence of Torres' first argument is that Dr. Quiroga's testimony required her to know the intent or state of mind of Dr. Malueg, who ultimately made the decision not to promote Torres, and that an opinion on another's intent cannot be "rationally based on the perception of the witness."

The illogicality of this argument has been succinctly demonstrated by Wigmore:

> The argument has been made that, because we cannot directly see, hear, or feel the state of another person's mind, therefore testimony to another person's state of mind is based on merely conjectural and therefore inadequate data. This argument is finical enough; and it proves too much, for if valid it would forbid the jury to find a verdict upon the supposed state of a person's mind. If they are required and allowed to find such a fact, it is not too much to hear such testimony from a witness who has observed the person exhibiting in his conduct the operations of his mind.

2 J. Wigmore, *Wigmore on Evidence* § 661 (J. Chadbourn rev. 1979). Another commentator explains the requirement that a lay witness' opinion testimony must be "rationally based on the perception of the witness" as merely requiring that "the opinion or inference is one which a normal person would form on the basis of the observed facts." See 3 J. Weinstein & M. Berger, *Weinstein's Evidence* ¶ 701[03], page 701–11 (1982). Accordingly, witnesses have been allowed to give opinions on whether another person subjectively believed that he would be shot by an agressor, see John Hancock Mutual Life Insurance Co. v. Dutton, 585 F.2d 1289, 1293–94 (5th Cir.1978), and, in a civil rights action, that an arrest was "motivated by racial prejudice," see Bohan-

non v. Pegelow, 652 F.2d 729, 731–32 (7th Cir.1981). As the Fifth Circuit stated in *Dutton:*

> When, as here, the witness observes first hand the altercation in question, her opinions on the feelings of the parties are based on her personal knowledge and rational perceptions and are helpful to the jury. The Rules require nothing more for admission of the testimony.

Dutton, 585 F.2d at 1294.

The record in this case clearly establishes that Dr. Quiroga was privy to the details of Dr. Malueg's selecting the new supervisor. The foundational requirement of personal knowledge of the outward events has thus been satisfied. Since we do not believe that it is beyond the ken of an ordinary person to infer from another's outward actions what his inward feelings are regarding a third person's national origin, Dr. Quiroga's testimony was rationally based on her perceptions.

Torres' second argument rests on the last clause in Rule 701, that the opinion must be "helpful" to the jury. She argues that because Dr. Quiroga's testimony was couched as a legal conclusion, it was not helpful to the jury. We agree.

At the outset, it should be noted what we do not decide. Since Federal Rule of Evidence 704 provides that "testimony * * * otherwise admissible is not objectionable because it embraces the ultimate issue to be decided," Dr. Quiroga's testimony cannot be challenged as an improper conclusion on an ultimate fact. The Advisory Committee notes point out, however, that Rule 704 "does not lower the bars so as to admit all opinions." The effect of Rule 704 is merely to remove the proscription against opinions on "ultimate issues" and to shift the focus to whether the testimony is "otherwise admissible." See United States v. Baskes, 649 F.2d 471, 479 (7th Cir.1980), *cert. denied,* 450 U.S. 1000, 101 S.Ct. 1706, 68 L.Ed.2d 201 (1981) ("Rule 704, however, does not provide that witnesses' opinions as to the legal implications of conduct are admissible."). As the Advisory Committee note explains, certain opinions which embrace an ultimate issue will be objectionable on other grounds.

> Under Rules 701 and 702, opinions must be helpful to the trier of fact, and Rule 403 provides for exclusion of evidence which wastes time. These provisions afford ample assurances against the admission of opinions which would merely tell the jury what result to reach, somewhat in the manner of the oath-helpers of an earlier day. They also stand ready to exclude opinions phrased in terms of inadequately explored legal criteria. Thus the question, "Did T have capacity to make a will?" would be excluded, while the question "Did T have sufficient mental capacity to know the nature and extent of his property and the natural objects of his bounty and formulate a rational scheme of distribution?" would be allowed.

The problem with testimony containing a legal conclusion is in conveying the witness' unexpressed, and perhaps erroneous, legal standards to the jury. This "invade[s] the province of the court to determine the applicable law and to instruct the jury as to that law." F.A.A. v. Landy, 705 F.2d 624, 632 (2d Cir.), *cert. denied,* — U.S. —, 104 S.Ct. 243, 78 L.Ed.2d 232 (1983). See also Marx & Co. v. Diner's Club, Inc., 550 F.2d 505, 509–10 (2d Cir.), *cert. denied,* 434 U.S. 861, 98 S.Ct. 188, 54 L.Ed.2d 134 (1977) ("It is not for witnesses to instruct the jury as to applicable principles of law, but for the judge."); 3 J. Weinstein & M. Berger, supra, at ¶ 704[02], page 704–11. Although trial judges are accorded a relatively wide degree of discretion in admitting or excluding testimony which arguably contains a legal conclusion, see Stoler v. Penn Central Transportation Co., 583 F.2d 896, 899 (6th Cir.1978), that discretion is not unlimited. This discretion is appropriate because it is often difficult to determine whether a legal conclusion is implicated in the testimony. See, e.g., Owen v. Kerr–McGee Corp., 698 F.2d 236, 240 (5th Cir.1983) ("The task of separating impermissible questions which call for overbroad or legal responses from permissible questions is not a facile one."); Wade v. Haynes, 663 F.2d 778, 783–84 (8th Cir.1981), *aff'd sub nom.* Smith v. Wade, 461 U.S. 30, 103 S.Ct. 1625, 75 L.Ed.2d 632 (1983).

The best resolution of this type of problem is to determine whether the terms used by the witness have a separate, distinct and specialized meaning in the law different from that present in the vernacular. If they do, exclusion is appropriate. See United States v. Hearst, 563 F.2d 1331, 1351 (9th Cir.1977), *cert. denied,* 435 U.S. 1000, 98 S.Ct. 1656, 56 L.Ed.2d 90 (1978) (testimony is not objectionable as containing a legal conclusion where the "average layman would understand those terms and ascribe to them essentially the same meaning intended"). Thus, when a witness was asked whether certain conduct was "unlawful," the trial court properly excluded the testimony since "terms that demand an understanding of the nature and scope of the criminal law" may be properly excluded. See *Baskes,* 649 F.2d at 478. See also *Owen,* 698 F.2d at 239–40 (trial court properly excluded testimony on "cause" of the accident when there was no dispute as to the factual "cause" of the accident but only the legal "cause" of the accident); Christiansen v. National Savings and Trust Co., 683 F.2d 520, 529 (D.C.Cir.1982) (inadmissibility of conclusion that defendants held a "fiduciary" relationship to plaintiffs); Strong v. E.I. DuPont de Nemours Co., 667 F.2d 682, 685–86 (8th Cir.1981) (trial court properly excluded expert's testimony that defendant's warnings were "inadequate" and that the product was therefore "unreasonably dangerous"); *Stoler,* 583 F.2d at 898–99 (trial court properly excluded testimony that a railroad crossing was "extra hazardous," a legal term of art under governing law, since it "amounted to a legal opinion").

The precise language of the question put to Dr. Quiroga was whether "Torres had been discriminated against because of her national origin." In concluding that this question called for an improper legal conclusion, we rely on several factors. First, the question tracks almost verbatim the language of the applicable statute. Title VII makes it unlawful for an employer to "discriminate against any individual * * * because of such individual's * * * national origin." See 42 U.S.C. § 2000e–2. Second, the term "discrimination" has a specialized meaning in the law and in lay use the term has a distinctly less precise meaning. See Ward v. Westland Plastics, Inc., 651 F.2d 1266, 1271 (9th Cir.1980) (witness "incompetent to voice an opinion on whether that or any other conduct constituted *illegal* sex discrimination").

We emphasize that a more carefully phrased question could have elicited similar information and avoided the problem of testimony containing a legal conclusion. The defendants could have asked Dr. Quiroga whether she believed Torres' national origin "motivated" the hiring decision. This type of question would directly address the factual issue of Dr. Malueg's intent without implicating any legal terminology. Cf. *Bohannon,* 652 F.2d at 731–33.

Although we hold that the trial judge should not have admitted this testimony, we conclude that this error was harmless. See Fed. R.Civ.P. 61; Fed.R.Evid. 103(a). First, this error involved only one brief question out of a rather lengthy trial. Second, Torres admitted, upon being impeached by her deposition testimony, that she had previously stated that she did not feel that she had been discriminated against during the interview process. Under the circumstances, we hold that the admission of this testimony containing a legal conclusion was harmless error.

* * *

The judgment of the district court is Affirmed.

STATE v. WATSON, 243 Or. 454, 414 P.2d 337 (1966). "We may assume, without deciding, that a book might be so bad as to demonstrate on its face (a) its dominant theme, (b) its patent offensiveness, and (c) its utter lack of 'redeeming social value.' The state in this case, however, did not rely upon *res ipsa loquitur.* The prosecution called as an expert witness the then incumbent district attorney of the county. He personally had purchased the book [Lust Pad] and had signed the complaint. The district attorney was permitted to testify, over timely objection, that in his opinion the book in question satisfied all statutory requirements (as those requirements must be interpreted in light of Roth v. United States, 354 U.S. 476, 77 S.Ct. 1304, 1 L.Ed.2d 1498 (1957), and subsequent decisions of the United States Supreme Court.)

"It is manifest error to permit a witness, who has no special qualification so to testify, to tell the jury that in his opinion a crime had been committed. The witness revealed that he knew little of relevant contemporary community standards and virtually nothing of contemporary literature. (Since 1939 or 1940, he admitted, he had read no books outside his professional field, and only the Readers' Digest, religious papers, and news periodicals in other fields. Further, he said he had not read beyond the first two chapters of the book in question.)

"Since we are unable to say that the introduction of so-called expert testimony from a patently unqualified witness did not prejudice the defendant, the judgment cannot stand."

SPECHT v. JENSEN, 853 F.2d 805 (10th Cir.1988), cert. denied, 488 U.S. 1008, 109 S.Ct. 792, 102 L.Ed.2d 783 (1989). "The question considered is whether Fed.R.Evid. 702 will permit an attorney, called as an expert witness, to state his views of the law which governs the verdict and opine whether defendants' conduct violated that law. We conclude the testimony was beyond the scope of the rule and thus inadmissible.

"This case is an action for damages pursuant to 42 U.S.C. § 1983 grounded upon allegedly invalid searches of the plaintiffs' home and office. * * * [W]hether defendants' conduct involved a 'search' within the meaning of the Fourth Amendment and whether plaintiffs consented to the search were issues to be determined by the jury.

* * *

"* * * On the basis of hypothetical questions tailored to reflect plaintiffs' view of the evidence, the expert concluded there had been no consent given, and illegal searches had occurred.

* * *

"Following the advisory committee's comments, a number of federal circuits have held that an expert witness may not give an opinion on ultimate issues of law. * * *

"The courts in these decisions draw a clear line between permissible testimony on issues of fact and testimony that articulates the ultimate principles of law governing the deliberations of the jury. These courts have decried the latter kind of testimony as directing a verdict, rather than assisting the jury's understanding and weighing of the evidence. In keeping with these decisions, we conclude the expert in this case was improperly allowed to instruct the jury on how it should decide the case. The expert's testimony painstakingly developed over an entire day the conclusion that defendants violated plaintiffs' constitutional rights. He told the jury that warrantless searches are unlawful, that defendants committed a warrantless search on plaintiffs' property, and that the only applicable exception to the warrant requirement, search by consent, should not vindicate the defendants because no authorized person voluntarily consented to allow a search of the premises. He also stated that the acts of the private individual could be imputed to the accompanying police officer to constitute sufficient 'state action' for a § 1983 claim. By permitting the jury to hear this array of legal conclusions touching upon nearly every element of the plaintiffs' burden of proof under § 1983, the trial court allowed the expert to supplant both the court's duty to set forth the law and the jury's ability to apply this law to the evidence.

"Given the pervasive nature of this testimony, we cannot conclude its admission was harmless. * * *

* * *

"The line we draw here is narrow. We do not exclude all testimony regarding legal issues. We recognize that a witness may refer to the law in expressing an opinion without that reference rendering the testimony inadmissible. Indeed, a witness may properly be called upon to aid the jury in understanding the facts in evidence even though reference to those facts is couched in legal terms. For example, we have previously held that a court may permit an expert to testify that a certain weapon had to be registered with the Bureau of Alcohol, Tobacco, and Firearms. United States v. Buchanan, 787 F.2d 477, 483 (10th Cir.1986). In that case, however, the witness did not invade the court's authority by discoursing broadly over the entire range of the applicable law. Rather, the expert's opinion focused on a specific question of fact. * * *

"These cases demonstrate that an expert's testimony is proper under Rule 702 if the expert does not attempt to define the legal parameters within which the jury must exercise its fact-finding function. However, when the purpose of testimony is to direct the jury's understanding of the legal standards upon which their verdict must be based, the testimony cannot be allowed. In no instance can a witness be permitted to define the law of the case.

"Plaintiffs seek to avoid this conclusion by arguing the expert testimony here was no different from a medical expert testifying that specific conduct constitutes medical malpractice. We do not believe, however, there is an analog between the testimony of the medical expert and that of the legal expert because the former does not usurp the function of the court. The testimony of the medical expert in plaintiffs' hypothesis is more like that of the legal expert who explains a discrete point of law which is helpful to the jury's understanding of the facts."

Notes

(1) "More troubling is the System's allegation that one of the defendants' experts, Lee Pickard, a former head of the Securities and Exchange Commission's Division of Market Regulations and a lawyer, was allowed to explain the reach and meaning of § 28(a) to the jury. This was error. Explaining the law is the judge's job. Pickard's extensive law-related expert testimony allowed him to usurp the judge's place. * * * Some commentators have criticized the general rule against allowing experts to testify on the meaning of the law and have noted with approval the erosion of the rule in some courts, see, e.g., Note, 97 Harv.L.Rev. 797 (1984). We cannot agree that the trend is a good one." Police Retirement System v. Midwest Investment Advisory Service, Inc., 940 F.2d 351, 357 (8th Cir. 1991).

(2) In Harbor Ins. Co. v. Continental Bank Corp., 922 F.2d 357 (7th Cir.1990), a lawyer testified as an expert on the meaning of the word

"indemnity" as used in the charter. "The charter is ambiguous, and therefore testimony—including in suitable cases testimony by a lawyer—was a permissible aid to interpretation. * * * But the lawyer * * * based his opinion * * * on an examination of the word 'indemnity' as it is used in judicial opinions. * * * By allowing the insurance companies' witness to tell the jury what the witness's legal research had turned up on the meaning of a key term in the case, the judge allowed the jury to infer that it could look to that witness for legal guidance; and by doing this the judge impermissibly tilted the balance of power between the parties toward the insurance companies." Id. at 365–66.

UNITED STATES v. EDWARDS

United States Court of Appeals, Eleventh Circuit, 1987.
819 F.2d 262.

VANCE, CIRCUIT JUDGE:

Roland Edwards was charged with unarmed bank robbery under 18 U.S.C. § 2113(a). He pleaded not guilty by reason of insanity. After a two day trial, a jury returned a verdict of guilty. Edwards appeals, claiming that the district court allowed improper psychiatric testimony. He argues that the district court erred in permitting a government witness to give opinion testimony in violation of Fed.R.Evid. 704(b).[1] We affirm.

On April 30, 1984, Edwards entered a bank in Naples, Florida and handed a teller a note demanding that she place all "twenties, fifties, and hundreds" in a bank bag. The note was handwritten and legible. Edwards told the teller that he had worked in a bank, "knew what he was doing," and warned her "not to do anything." Edwards carried a vinyl zipper bag which contained a bulky L-shaped object. Throughout the robbery, he kept his right hand inside the bag, handling the object in such a way that the teller thought it was a gun. Edwards left the bank with $2,040. He sprinted to a pick-up truck and sped away.

A bystander thought he saw the name "Edwards Construction" on the side of the getaway vehicle. Shortly after the robbery, sheriff's deputies located Edwards' ex-wife. She contacted Edwards using a beeper that he carried. Edwards returned her call, and at his ex-wife's urging, Edwards admitted that he had "robbed a bank."

At trial Edwards did not contest his role in the bank robbery, but argued that he was insane at the time that he committed the offense. Edwards' ex-wife and an old friend testified that they believed Edwards to be incapable of criminal activity. The crux of the defense case, however, was the testimony of Doctor Adolfo Vilasuso, a board-certified psychiatrist. Doctor Vilasuso examined Edwards approximately six

1. Federal Rules of Evidence 704(b) provides: No expert witness testifying with respect to the mental state or condition of a defendant in a criminal case may state an opinion or inference as to whether the defendant did or did not have the mental state or condition constituting an element of the crime charged or of a defense thereto. Such ultimate issues are matters for the trier of fact alone.

times during October, 1985 and continued seeing Edwards once or twice a week up to the date of trial in February, 1986. Doctor Vilasuso noted that Edwards had endured a difficult past and stated that he thought Edwards was "off the wall." Doctor Vilasuso testified that he had a "very, very strong suspicion" that Edwards suffered from "manic-depressive" illness during April, 1984. The government countered with the rebuttal testimony of Doctor Albert Jaslow, another psychiatrist. Doctor Jaslow concluded from Edwards' description of events that Edwards was not in "an active manic state" at the time of the robbery because Edwards' actions were reasonably well controlled and goal directed.

The testimony at issue concerns Doctor Jaslow's analysis of Edwards' frustration with his financial problems at the time of the robbery:

> Q [by Prosecutor]:
>
> What sort of things were going on that would have depressed him?
>
> A [by Doctor Jaslow]:
>
> His inability to come to grips with his financial problems; inability to handle the relationship with the I.R.S., who were after him and who were not permitting him to, according to him, of course, to settle down sufficiently so he could gain enough monies to take care of the financial problems and so on. These were bothering him tremendously, of course.
>
> Q: Were these feelings understandable, in your opinion?
>
> Defense Counsel: Objection. It's improper. That's not a proper question for a doctor.
>
> The Court: Overruled.
>
> A: Under the circumstances of the responsibilities, the problems that he had, it was quite understandable. He would be disturbed; it was quite understandable he would be upset. It's quite understandable he would be frantically trying to find ways to modify his situation so he could get on with his life.

Edwards contends that the trial court erred in allowing this testimony because it contained a psychiatrist's opinion concerning his sanity, the ultimate issue at trial. We disagree.

"In resolving the complex issue of criminal responsibility, it is of critical importance that the defendant's entire relevant symptomatology be brought before the jury and explained." *Gordon v. United States,* 438 F.2d 858, 883 (5th Cir.) *cert. denied,* 404 U.S. 828, 92 S.Ct. 142, 30 L.Ed.2d 56 (1971). It has long been the position of our court that this is the only way a jury may become sufficiently informed so as to make a determination of a defendant's legal sanity. *See, e.g., United States v. Alexander,* 805 F.2d 1458, 1462–64 (11th Cir.1986); *Boykins v. Wainwright,* 737 F.2d 1539, 1544–45 (11th Cir.1984), *cert. denied,* 470 U.S. 1059, 105 S.Ct. 1725, 84 L.Ed.2d 834 (1985); *Blake v. United States,* 407

F.2d 908, 911 (5th Cir.1969) (en banc). This was also the attitude of Congress when it passed Rule 704(b):

> Psychiatrists, of course, must be permitted to testify fully about the defendant's diagnosis, mental state and motivation (in clinical and commonsense terms) at the time of the alleged act so as to permit the jury or judge to reach the ultimate conclusion about which they and only they are expert.

S.Rep. No. 225, 98th Cong., 1st Sess. 231 (quoting American Psychiatric Association Statement on the Insanity Defense, Dec. 1982, at 18–19), *reprinted in* 1984 U.S. Code Cong. & Admin.News 3182, 3413.

Congress did not enact Rule 704(b) so as to limit the flow of diagnostic and clinical information. Every actual fact concerning the defendant's mental condition is still as admissible after the enactment of Rule 704(b) as it was before. *See United States v. Mest,* 789 F.2d 1069, 1071–72 (4th Cir.), *cert. denied,* ___ U.S. ___, 107 S.Ct. 163, 93 L.Ed.2d 102 (1986). Rather, the Rule "changes the style of question and answer that can be used to establish both the offense and the defense thereto." *Id.* at 1071. The prohibition is directed at a narrowly and precisely defined evil:

> When, however, "ultimate issue" questions are formulated by the law and put to the expert witness who must then say "yea" or "nay," then the expert witness is required to make a leap in logic. He no longer addresses himself to medical concepts but instead must infer or intuit what is in fact unspeakable, namely, the probable relationship between medical concepts and legal or moral constructs such as free will. These impermissible leaps in logic made by expert witnesses confuse the jury.

S.Rep. No. 225, 98th Cong., 1st Sess. 231 (quoting American Psychiatric Association Statement on the Insanity Defense, Dec. 1982, at 18), *reprinted in* 1984 U.S.Code Cong. & Admin.News 3182, 3412–13. Accordingly, Rule 704(b) forbids only "conclusions as to the ultimate legal issue to be found by the trier of fact." *Id.* at 3412. *See, e.g., United States v. Hillsberg,* 812 F.2d 328, 331 (7th Cir.1987) (expert cannot state opinion as to whether defendant had the capacity to conform his conduct to the law); *United States v. Buchbinder,* 796 F.2d 910, 917 (7th Cir.1986) (expert could not testify as to whether defendant had the requisite mental state to defraud, but could testify as to the extent of defendant's depression over son's death).

The ultimate legal issue at Edwards' trial was whether Edwards "lack[ed] substantial capacity either to appreciate the wrongfulness of his conduct or to conform his conduct to the requirements of law." *Blake v. United States,* 407 F.2d 908, 916 (5th Cir.1969) (en banc). In fact, the challenged statements offer no conclusions at all about Edwards. Doctor Jaslow was simply observing that people who are not insane can nevertheless become frantic over a financial crisis.

The prosecution placed Doctor Jaslow on the stand to dispute Doctor Vilasuso's diagnosis. Using a common sense generalization,

Doctor Jaslow explained why the defendant's behavior—his frantic efforts to pay bills, his manifestations of energy, his lack of sleep, and his feelings of depression—did not necessarily indicate an active manic state. We think that the doctor played exactly the kind of role which Congress contemplated for the expert witness:

> [I]t is clear that the psychiatrist's first obligation and expertise in the courtroom is to "do psychiatry," i.e., to present medical information and opinion about the defendant's mental state and motivation and to explain in detail the reason for his medical-psychiatric conclusions.

S.Rep. No. 225, 98th Cong., 1st Sess. 231 (quoting American Psychiatric Association Statement on the Insanity Defense, Dec. 1982, at 18), *reprinted in* 1984 U.S.Code Cong. & Admin.News 3182, 3413. We conclude that the district court committed no error in permitting this testimony.

AFFIRMED.

BUCHANAN v. AMERICAN MOTORS CORP.

United States Court of Appeals, Sixth Circuit, 1983.
697 F.2d 151.

MERRITT, CIRCUIT JUDGE.

Appellant, a defendant in a federal, diversity, products liability, wrongful death action in North Carolina for injury arising from a claimed design defect in a Jeep manufactured by appellant, seeks to subpoena appellee, an expert residing in Michigan who has published a lengthy adverse research study about the safety of appellant's product. The subpoena reads in pertinent part as follows:

> To Richard G. Snyder, Highway Safety Research Institute of the University of Michigan, Ann Arbor, Michigan.
>
> You are commanded to appear at 290 City Center Building at the offices of Huron Reporting Service in the city of Ann Arbor on the 23rd day of July, 1981, at 10:00 A.M. to testify * * * at the taking of a deposition in the above-entitled action pending in the United States District Court for the Western District of North Carolina and bring with you any and all research data, memoranda, correspondence, lab notes, reports, calculations, moving pictures, photographs, slides, statements and the like pertaining to the on-road crash experience of utility vehicles study by the Highway Safety Research Institute of the University of Michigan for the Insurance Institute for Highway Safety in which you participated.

(Appendix, p. 3.) Appellee is a stranger to the North Carolina litigation and is not an expert witness or adviser to any party to that litigation under Rule 26(b)(4) of the Federal Rules of Civil Procedure or to the Court under Rule 706(a) of the Federal Rules of Evidence. Appellant states that its reason for seeking discovery from the expert is that it expects its adversary in the North Carolina litigation to use the research study as one basis for expressing an adverse expert opinion about the safety of appellant's product.

Assuming without deciding that the expert here, whose testimony and data have been subpoenaed, has neither an absolute nor qualified privilege to refuse discovery and is subject to the same general evidentiary rules requiring discovery as any other witness, it is nevertheless clear that the question of the scope of discovery addresses itself to the sound discretion of the District Court in the first instance. See Judge Friendly's opinion for the Second Circuit in Kaufman v. Edelstein, 539 F.2d 811, 822 (2d Cir.1976) (trial court's decision respecting quashing subpoena addressed to expert who is a stranger to litigation "represent[s] an exercise of discretion"). Our review of the record indicates that the District Court did not abuse its discretion in quashing the subpoena duces tecum in the instant case on grounds that it is unreasonably burdensome. Compliance with the subpoena would require the expert who has no direct connection with the litigation to spend many days testifying and disclosing all of the raw data, including thousands of documents, accumulated over the course of a long and detailed research study. Like the District Court, we note that the expert is not being called because of observations or knowledge concerning the facts of the accident and injury in litigation or because no other expert witnesses are available. Appellant wants to attempt to prove that the expert's written opinions stated in the research study are not well founded.

The District Court did not err in finding improper the practice of calling an eminent expert witness (who is a stranger to the litigation) under a burdensome subpoena duces tecum that would require him to spend a large amount of time itemizing and explaining the raw data that led him to a research opinion adverse to the interest of a party which is the author of the subpoena.

Accordingly, the judgment of the District Court quashing the subpoena in question is affirmed.

KAUFMAN v. EDELSTEIN, 539 F.2d 811, 818 (2d Cir.1976). "Article VII of the Rules deals with 'Opinions and Expert Evidence' and contains six rules, 701–706. Although the framers of the rules must have been well aware of the frequently made contention that experts enjoy some kind of privilege, neither this chapter nor the proposed rules on privilege which the framers proposed but Congress rejected contain any suggestion that an expert enjoys either an absolute or a qualified privilege against being called by a party against his will. The only reference to the need of consent by an expert is in Rule 706(a), dealing with court appointed experts. This provides in part that 'An expert witness shall not be appointed by the court unless he consents to act'—language taken verbatim from former F.R.Cr.P. 28. The situation of the court appointed expert who is expected to delve deeply into the problem and arrive at an informed and unbiased opinion differs utterly from that of an expert called by a party to state what facts he may know and what opinion he may have formed without being asked to make any further investigation. If any inference is to be drawn from the Federal Rules of Evidence, it is thus against the claim of privilege by an expert, not for it."

OLEKSIW v. WEIDENER

Supreme Court of Ohio, 1965.
2 Ohio St.2d 147, 207 N.E.2d 375.

MATTHIAS, JUDGE.

The question raised by this appeal is whether in a malpractice action expert testimony may be elicited from a physician defendant called by plaintiff "as if under cross-examination," pursuant to Section 2317.07, Revised Code.

This section provides as follows:

"At the instance of the adverse party, a party may be examined as if under cross-examination orally, by way of deposition, like any other witness * * *. The party calling for such examination shall not thereby be concluded but may rebut it by evidence."

The obvious purpose of this section is to permit the production of all pertinent evidence in order that the trier of facts might have all the facts necessary to render a just decision. Any relevant evidence is made available to the parties, even evidence in the possession of the adverse party. 56 Ohio Jurisprudence 2d 456, Witnesses, Section 21; cf. State, Use of Miles, v. Brainin, 224 Md. 156, 167 A.2d 117, 88 A.L.R.2d 1178.

* * *

Other jurisdictions which have considered the question in the instant case under a similar statute are divided. Although the modern trend is to permit the examination of the opponent as an expert, the number of jurisdictions on each side is roughly equal. Annotation, 88 A.L.R.2d 1186. Although the question has never previously been before this court, the Ninth District Court of Appeals has twice held that in an action for malpractice a plaintiff may not require expert testimony of the defendant physician called for cross-examination. Forthofer v. Arnold, 60 Ohio App. 436, 21 N.E.2d 869; Wiley v. Wharton, 68 Ohio App. 345, 351, 41 N.E.2d 255.

The cases which do not permit a party to elicit expert testimony from his opponent find that such a practice would be contrary to the purpose of the statute. See Osborn v. Carey, 24 Idaho 158, 168, 132 P. 967; Ericksen v. Wilson, 266 Minn. 401, 123 N.W.2d 687; Hunder v. Rindlaub, 61 N.D. 389, 409, 237 N.W. 915; Forthofer v. Arnold, supra, 60 Ohio App. 442, 21 N.E.2d 869. Those cases do not specify anything inherently wrong with examining the opponent as an expert and are general in their reason for finding that the statute was not intended to include such examination. The real basis seems to be that it would not be fair or sporting to allow the plaintiff to force the defendant to become his expert. See 5 Southern California Law Review 448; Ericksen v. Wilson, supra; Hull, Admr., v. Plume, 131 N.J.Law 511, 517, 37 A.2d 53.

No question of fairness should be involved in this matter. A person has no right to remain silent if he has information which is needed in a judicial proceeding. Since the withholding of relevant testimony obstructs the administration of justice, the duty to testify is owed to society not to the individual parties. The question is not whether it is fair for a party to require the adverse party to testify but whether it is fair for society to require a party to testify, where his testimony will aid his opponent. See 8 Wigmore, Evidence (1961), 70, Section 2192; State v. Antill, 176 Ohio St. 61, 64, 197 N.E.2d 548; In re Story, 159 Ohio St. 144, 148, 149, 111 N.E.2d 385, 36 A.L.R.2d 1312.

There is no analogy between a defendant in a malpractice action and a defendant in a criminal prosecution. The latter is specifically exempted from his duty to testify by constitutional protection against self-incrimination. Article V, Amendments, U.S. Constitution; Section 10, Article I, Ohio Constitution. A civil defendant has no protection against subjecting himself to liability. If his testimony will provide facts which will aid the court in arriving at a just decision, he has a duty to testify. Any loss to the sporting aspect of adversary proceedings would be outweighed by the benefit to the judicial system.

"Courts are intent upon arriving at just decisions and upon employing properly expedient means to attain such an end. If a defendant in a malpractice action may truthfully testify that his conduct conformed to the standard required, his case is, of course, substantially strengthened and, if he cannot so testify, the plaintiff's chances of recovery are unquestionably increased. In either case, the objective of the court in doing justice is achieved." McDermott v. Manhattan Eye, Ear & Throat Hospital, 15 N.Y.2d 20, 255 N.Y.S.2d 65, 72, 203 N.E.2d 469, 474.

We feel that the cases which permit the plaintiff to call the defendant physician and examine him as an expert represent the more enlightened view. * * *

In a malpractice action, expert testimony may be elicited from a physician-defendant called by plaintiff, "as if under cross-examination," pursuant to Section 2317.07, Revised Code.

Judgment reversed.

Chapter 6

AUTHENTICATION AND IDENTIFICATION *

[FED.R.EVID. ART. IX]

UNITED STATES v. JOHNSON

United States Court of Appeals, Ninth Circuit, 1980.
637 F.2d 1224.

SPENCER WILLIAMS, DISTRICT JUDGE:

Larry Burdette Johnson was convicted of one count of assault resulting in serious bodily injury in violation of 18 U.S.C. §§ 1153 and 113(f) (1976). On this appeal, Johnson raises several instances of claimed error which occurred during his trial, the most important of which was the trial court's refusal to deliver lesser included offense jury instructions. We conclude that the failure to give such instructions was reversible error.

I

Facts

Johnson, an Indian, was charged with two counts of assault resulting in serious bodily injury. The charges stemmed from an incident occurring within the boundaries of the Fort Hall Indian Reservation on or about April 23, 1978. The victim in Count I was Edwin Papse, and the victim in Count II was Richard Johnson, appellant's father. Both victims are Indians.

During the day of April 22, 1978, Johnson, the victims, and others were drinking alcoholic beverages in Blackfoot, Idaho, a short distance

* See 3 Wigmore, Evidence §§ 693–709 (Chadbourn rev. 1970); 4 id. ch. 39 (Chadbourn rev. 1972); 7 id. ch. 74 (Chadbourn rev. 1978); McCormick, Evidence chs. 21, 22 (4th ed. 1992); Alexander & Alexander, The Authentication of Documents Requirement: Barrier to Falsehood or to Truth? 10 San Diego L.Rev. 266 (1973); Risinger, Denbeaux & Saks, Exorcism of Ignorance as a Proxy for Rational Knowledge: The Lessons of Handwriting Identification "Expertise," 137 U.Pa.L.Rev. 731 (1989); Strong, Liberalizing the Authentication of Private Writings, 52 Cornell L.Q. 284 (1967).

from the Fort Hall Indian Reservation. Later that day these individuals went to Johnson's residence on the Fort Hall Reservation. In the late evening or early morning, Johnson had an argument with his wife. Afterwards, he allegedly struck Papse and Richard Johnson with the blunt end and handle of a long-handled ax. * * *

At Johnson's trial, the United States called Papse as a witness. A long-handled ax was offered into evidence during his testimony. Pursuant to a search warrant, this ax had been seized at Johnson's residence five days after the assault. Papse identified the ax, apparently with some hesitancy, as the weapon used to commit the assault on him. Over Johnson's objection that there had been insufficient foundation or authentication, the ax was admitted into evidence.

* * *

The jury returned a verdict of guilty as to Count I (assault on Papse) and not guilty as to Count II (assault on Richard Johnson). A sentence of ten years imprisonment was imposed. This appeal followed.

* * *

VI

Admissibility of the Ax

Johnson argues the ax allegedly used in the assault was admitted into evidence without first being authenticated properly. He contends Papse's testimony was inadequate as authentication because the witness failed to state specifically that he could distinguish this ax from any other, because he did not identify specific characteristics of this ax which could tie it to the incident, and because he appeared to base his identification largely on an assumption, derived from his belief that this ax was the only ax on the premises, that this ax *must* have been the weapon in question. In addition, Johnson contends the ax introduced into evidence was in a changed condition from the ax noted at the scene of the incident, and for this reason the court should have been especially cautious about its admission.[34]

Federal Rule of Evidence 901(a) provides that "[t]he requirement of authentication or identification as a condition precedent to admissibility is satisfied by evidence sufficient to support a finding that the matter in question is what its proponent claims." The terms of the Rule are thus satisfied, and the proffered evidence should ordinarily be admitted, once a prima facie case has been made on the issue. *See* 5 Weinstein's Evidence § 901(a)[01], at 901–16 (1976). At that point the matter is

34. Johnson inaccurately states in his brief that testimony revealed the ax observed at the crime scene had "blood and hair upon the blade end of it." In fact, the testimony was that Rose Edmo, a witness, had been told by Barney Dixie, another witness, only that "there was hair on the axe." Reporter's Transcript at 101. The ax admitted as an exhibit did not have hair on it. Assuming the testimony about the hair is believed, the absence of hair represents the only change in the ax's condition which was noted between the time of the alleged assault and its seizure five days later.

committed to the trier of fact to determine the evidence's credibility and probative force. *See United States v. Oaxaca,* 569 F.2d 518, 526 (9th Cir.1978), *cert. denied,* 439 U.S. 926, 99 S.Ct. 310, 58 L.Ed.2d 319 (1978).

Here, although the trial record reveals the identification of the ax made by Papse may not have been entirely free from doubt, the witness did state that he was "pretty sure" this was the weapon Johnson had used against him, that he saw the ax in Johnson's hand, and that he was personally familiar with this particular ax because he had used it in the past. Based on Papse's testimony, a reasonable juror could have found that this ax was the weapon allegedly used in the assault. Papse's ability or inability to specify particular identifying features of the ax, as well as the evidence of the ax's alleged changed condition, should then go to the question of the weight to be accorded this evidence, which is precisely what the trial court ruled. In other words, although the jury remained free to reject the government's assertion that this ax had been used in the assault, the requirements for admissibility specified in Rule 901(a) had been met.

Finally, the trial court did not abuse its discretion in failing to exclude the ax for being more prejudicial than probative under Evidence Rule 403. "District judges have wide latitude in passing on the admissibility of evidence, and admission will not be overturned on appeal absent an abuse of discretion." *United States v. Kearney,* 560 F.2d 1358, 1369 (9th Cir.1977), *cert. denied,* 434 U.S. 971, 98 S.Ct. 522, 54 L.Ed.2d 460 (1977). The ax, as the suspected assault weapon, was very relevant to the government's case and the jury was entitled to see it.

* * *

REVERSED AND REMANDED.

UNITED STATES v. OLSON, 846 F.2d 1103, 1116–17 (7th Cir. 1988), cert. denied, 488 U.S. 850, 109 S.Ct. 131, 102 L.Ed.2d 104 (1988). "Defendant next alleges that the trial court erroneously admitted certain physical evidence despite the government's failure to adequately establish a chain of custody for the items. 'A trial court's decision to admit real evidence will not be reversed unless it has abused its discretion.' United States v. Wheeler, 800 F.2d 100, 106 (7th Cir.1986). We find no abuse of discretion in this case.

"Briefly, the defendant argues that certain bullets and bullet fragments recovered from the victim's body during the autopsy were improperly admitted because the evidence at trial indicated that, after these items were brought to the Wisconsin State Crime Laboratory and sealed in containers, FBI Agent Gregory Hunter unsealed each container and wrapped the items in cotton for shipping to the FBI Laboratory in Washington, D.C. Defendant complains that, while the evidence at trial (in the form of the FBI Agent's 'Report of Activity') indicated what the agent 'did in terms of unsealing the package, [and] what he did in terms of wrapping [the items] * * * the report surely doesn't say anything about how they were replaced in the cartons or when they were replaced in the cartons or anything else.'

"The government concedes that because of the death of Agent Hunter prior to Olson's trial, there are unavoidable gaps in the chain of custody of the bullets and bullet fragments. An uninterrupted chain of custody, however, is not a prerequisite to admissibility. Gaps in the chain go to the weight of the evidence, not its admissibility. *Wheeler,* 800 F.2d at 106. 'If the trial judge is satisfied that in reasonable probability the evidence has not been altered in any material respect, he may permit its introduction.' United States v. Aviles, 623 F.2d 1192, 1198 (7th Cir.1980).

"In this case, the defendant presented no affirmative evidence of altering or tampering with the evidence. Additionally, the nature of the evidence—bullets and bullet fragments—makes alteration of the evidence unlikely. See United States v. Brown, 482 F.2d 1226, 1228 (8th Cir.1973) (considering nature of the articles (packages of heroin) as factor in determining admissibility). Finally, where the items have been in official custody and there is no affirmative evidence of tampering, a 'presumption of regularity attends official acts of public officers and the courts presume that their official duties have been discharged properly.' *Aviles,* 623 F.2d at 1198; see also United States v. Jefferson, 714 F.2d 689, 696 (7th Cir.1983). Given these factors, we find no abuse of discretion in the admission into evidence of the bullets and bullet fragments recovered from the victim's body during the autopsy.

"Olson also objects to the admission of a lead fragment that allegedly fell out of the victim's arm when his body was taken from the Wolf River. There was testimony at trial that Alex Askanet, a Tribal Police Officer, picked up the piece of lead. There was also testimony that FBI Special Agent Robert Kleinschmidt gave FBI Special Agent Richard Prokop a piece of lead, allegedly the fragment retrieved by Officer Askanet, on the same day. The chain of custody of the lead fragment from that point on is not challenged; the defendant's argument is that there was no evidence connecting the lead fragment retrieved by Tribal Police Officer Askanet with that given by Kleinschmidt to Prokop. Neither Askanet nor Kleinschmidt testified at trial; Agent Kleinschmidt had retired and Officer Askanet was deceased. As the government points out, however, Agent Prokop did testify that he sent Agent Kleinschmidt to the scene with instructions to contact the tribal authorities. Moreover, Agent Prokop testified that he recognized Agent Kleinschmidt's initials as well as 'Alex A,' an abbreviation for 'Alex Askanet,' on the container that held the lead fragment. As stated above, '[t]he trial court's discretionary ruling on identification of evidence sufficient for its admissibility is subject to reversal only for an abuse of discretion,' United States v. Bridges, 499 F.2d 179, 185 (7th Cir.), cert. denied 419 U.S. 1010, 95 S.Ct. 330, 42 L.Ed.2d 284 (1974), and

gaps in the chain of custody go to the weight of the evidence rather than its admissibility. We find no abuse of discretion in the trial court's determination that the testimony at trial established a chain of custody sufficient for admissibility; whatever deficiencies may have existed were properly a matter to be resolved by the jury in weighing the evidence."

UNITED STATES v. MANGAN

United States Court of Appeals, Second Circuit, 1978.
575 F.2d 32, cert. denied, 439 U.S. 931, 99 S.Ct. 320, 58 L.Ed.2d 324 (1978).

FRIENDLY, CIRCUIT JUDGE:

Fraud, Lord Macnaghten said, Reddaway v. Banham, [1896] A.C. 199, 211, is "infinite in variety." These appeals reveal a variety new at least to us. The fraud became possible because appellant Frank Mangan was an IRS Agent, working at the Mineola, L.I., office. According to the Government, the scheme, perpetrated by Frank and his brother Kevin, was this: Frank obtained the names and social security numbers of seven taxpayers, six named John McCarthy and the seventh Scott Murphy.[1] In January and February 1972, Frank prepared 1971 income tax returns for these taxpayers and caused them to be filed. Each was accompanied by a W–2 tax withholding form showing that the seven taxpayers had worked for Atlas Investing Co., Inc., Ace Industries, Inc. or Admiral Realty Co., Inc.,[2] and that they had withholdings ranging from $12,000 to $14,000. The returns claimed partnership losses sufficient to entitle each taxpayer to a refund in the $9,000 range and gave false addresses at rooming houses and transient hotels on the upper west side of Manhattan, where Kevin had rented rooms in the taxpayers' names. The Government mailed refund checks to six of the taxpayers at these addresses.[3] Four McCarthy checks and the Murphy check were picked up and deposited in bank accounts that Kevin had opened in their names at four different locations.[4] The proceeds were withdrawn in cash during March and April, 1972. * * *

A grand jury returned a thirteen count indictment with Count I charging conspiracy to file false claims against the United States in violation of 18 U.S.C. § 286, Counts II–VI charging use of the mails to defraud in violation of 18 U.S.C. § 1341 and Counts VII–XIII charging the filing of false and fraudulent income tax returns in violation of IRS § 7206(1). The jury convicted on all counts. * * *

* * *

1. The favor thus shown to taxpayers of Irish origin was doubtless related to the need for Kevin's renting rooms and opening bank accounts in their names.

2. Apparently, these companies were fictitious. A tax examiner from the IRS testified that she was unable to locate a telephone listing for any of them.

3. The check for one of the John McCarthys was not mailed because the return used a temporary Social Security number assigned by the IRS for internal purposes and unavailable to anyone outside the Service.

4. One of the McCarthy checks was never negotiated.

(2) *LACK OF AUTHENTICATION OF EXEMPLARS OF FRANK MANGAN'S HANDWRITING*

The Government's handwriting expert, Louis Caputo, associated with the New York City Department of Investigation, used as exemplars of Frank Mangan's handwriting the body of two of his federal income tax returns discussed above and forms contained in Frank Mangan's personnel file, which were written mostly in block capitals as were the fictitious returns. Although no witness testified that these were indeed written by Frank Mangan, the judge permitted them to be used as exemplars because of the statutory presumption, IRC § 6064, of the genuineness of the signatures on the tax returns, the similarity of these signatures to those in the IRS personnel files, the fact that the papers in the personnel file were of the sort that normally would be filled out by the employee, and the similarity of the material in block capitals on the returns and on the personnel forms. Appellant claims that this violated 28 U.S.C. § 1731,[10] is contrary to the principle announced in VII Wigmore, *supra* § 2148, and is unsupported by authority, including Federal Rule of Evidence 901. Conceding that *United States v. Liguori,* 373 F.2d 304 (2 Cir.1967), lends considerable support to the use of the income tax returns and papers in the personnel file as exemplars, appellant argues that *Liguori* "appears to depart from the mainstream" and that its precedential value is weakened by the lack of adequate briefing.

Be all that as it may, the issue is now governed by Rule 901. Subdivision (a) lays down a general test,

> (a) General provision.—The requirement of authentication or identification as a condition precedent to admissibility is satisfied by evidence sufficient to support a finding that the matter in question is what its proponent claims * * *,

and subdivision (b) gives several illustrations of sufficient authentication, one of which is

> (4) Distinctive characteristics and the like. Appearance, contents, substance, internal patterns, or other distinctive characteristics, taken in conjunction with circumstances.

Weinstein & Berger's Commentary on the Federal Rules states, ¶ 901(b)(4)[01] at 901–47, that "Wigmore's conclusion that mere contents will not suffice unless only the author would have known the details is contrary to the federal rules and unsound" (footnote omitted) and that "[T]he common law prejudice against self-authenticating documents is not carried over into the Federal Rules." Against this appellant points to the fact that the body of income tax returns is often written by someone other than the taxpayer. However, appellant advances no explanation as to who else could have written the material in his personnel files and the handwriting expert later testified, as the judge

10. This provides:

The *admitted or proved* handwriting of any person shall be admissible, for purposes of comparison, to determine genuineness of other handwriting attributed to such person. (Emphasis supplied).

was aware he would, that the lettering on these was penned by the same person as penned that in the income tax returns. We hold the exemplars were sufficiently authenticated, cf. *Scharfenberger v. Wingo,* 542 F.2d 328, 336–37 (6 Cir.1976).

* * *

The judgments of conviction are affirmed.

STATE v. FRESHWATER, 30 Utah 442, 85 P. 447, 448 (1906). "It is now urged that the court erred in permitting Delia Nance, who claimed to have seen the defendant write but once, to testify that the letter written by hand which she claimed was received by her, and the address on the envelope in which it came, was in the defendant's handwriting. The rule is well settled that writing may be proved by evidence of a witness who has seen the person write. In 1 Greenleaf on Ev. 577, it is said: 'It is held sufficient for this purpose that the witness has seen him write but once and then only his name. The proof in such case may be very light, but the jury will be permitted to weigh it.' In 2 Jones on Ev. § 559, the author says: 'But whatever degree of weight his testimony may deserve, which is a question exclusively for the jury, it is an established rule that if one has seen the person write, he will be competent to speak as to his handwriting; and this is true, although the impression on the witness may be faint and inaccurate. Thus, the testimony has been admitted although the witness has not seen the person write for many years before the trial and although he has only seen the person write on a single occasion, and even though he only saw the person write his name, or even his surname.' And again: 'It is not necessary that the witness should be an expert. These are matters affecting not the admissibility but the weight of such testimony.' McKelvey, in his work on Evidence, p. 360, says: 'It has from early times been settled that no great degree of familiarity with handwriting is required to render a witness competent to give an opinion. If he has seen the person write a single time, it has generally been held sufficient.' "

MAGGIPINTO v. REICHMAN, 481 F.Supp. 547, 551–52 (E.D.Pa. 1979), remanded in part on other grounds, 607 F.2d 621 (3d Cir.1979). "Digressing to the elementary, the basic steps to be followed in offering documentary material into evidence at a trial are clearly outlined in a typical, yet authoritative, basic trial practice textbook used in many of our region's law schools:

> The introduction of a document involves these separate steps: (1) having it marked by the reporter for identification; (2) authenticating the document by the testimony of the witness (unless it has a certifi-

> cate or other authenticating characteristics); (3) offering the document in evidence; (4) permitting adverse counsel to examine the document; (5) adverse counsel's objecting, if he so chooses; (6) submitting the document to the court for examination if the court so desires; (7) the court's ruling on its admission; and (8) if it is admitted in evidence, presenting it to the jury by reading, passing it among them, or other means.

R. Keeton, Trial Tactics and Methods, 63 (2d ed. 1973) (footnote omitted). The importance to the cause that each and every step be taken is demonstrated by the following observation:

> Frequently inexperienced counsel will have a document identified and authenticated with scrupulous care and then fail to take the all-important step of moving for the admission of the document into evidence. Such a lapse can often have serious consequence, such as undermining the evidentiary support of a favorable verdict, resulting in its reversal.

American Law Institute—American Bar Association Committee on Continuing Professional Education, Civil Trial Manual, student edition, 300 (1976) (footnote omitted). See also R. Hunter, Federal Trial Handbook, § 58.2, at 489 (1974); J. McElhaney, Effective Litigation 14 (1974)."

UNITED STATES v. VITALE

United States Court of Appeals, Eighth Circuit, 1977.

549 F.2d 71, cert. denied, 431 U.S. 907, 97 S.Ct. 1704, 52 L.Ed.2d 393 (1977).

PER CURIAM.

Defendant appeals from a jury conviction on three counts of distributing controlled substances (dilaudid, cocaine and heroin) on August 12 and 20, 1976, in violation of 21 U.S.C. § 841(a)(1). * * *

* * *

THE TELEPHONE CALL

Officer Zinselmeier testified that on August 12, 1976, he placed a telephone call to the residence of one Peggy Lindsay. A female voice answered. After the court sustained defense counsel's objection of lack of a proper foundation for testimony about the phone call, Zinselmeier testified that he had spoken with appellant on at least three occasions (two of which were face-to-face meetings), that he could identify appellant's voice, and that the voice on the other end of the phone was appellant's. The district court then overruled defense counsel's lack of foundation objection. Zinselmeier testified that the first call was followed by a second call during which the same female voice identified herself as Juanita Vitale, arranged to sell Zinselmeier dilaudid at a restaurant parking lot, and gave a physical description of herself and the car in which she would go to the parking lot. One hour later appellant, who matched the physical description given in the phone call and who was riding in the car described in the phone call, met

Zinselmeier in the designated parking lot and sold him the substance later identified as dilaudid.

Appellant alleges that evidence about the telephone conversations should have been excluded because no proper foundation was laid. The essence of this allegation is that Zinselmeier had not spoken to appellant prior to the phone call and could not identify her voice then.

Rule 901(a) of the Federal Rules of Evidence provides that the requirement of authentication is met where there is "evidence sufficient to support a finding that the matter in question is what its proponent claims." *See also United States v. Biondo,* 483 F.2d 635, 644 (8th Cir.1973). Rule 901(b)(5) allows for identification of a voice "by opinion based upon hearing the voice at any time under circumstances connecting it with the alleged speaker." In the Notes of the Advisory Committee to Rule 901(b)(5), the Committee stated: "[T]he requisite familiarity may be acquired *either before or after* the particular speaking which is the subject of the identification, * * * (emphasis added)." In the instant case, Officer Zinselmeier testified that he had spoken with appellant personally on two occasions and could identify her voice. This clearly seems to meet the standards of admissibility.

Furthermore, identity may be proven by circumstantial evidence. *United States v. Biondo, supra; United States v. Alper,* 449 F.2d 1223, 1229 (3d Cir.1971), *cert. denied,* 405 U.S. 988, 92 S.Ct. 1248, 31 L.Ed.2d 453, *rehearing denied,* 406 U.S. 911, 92 S.Ct. 1605, 31 L.Ed.2d 822 (1972); *Cwach v. United States,* 212 F.2d 520, 525 (8th Cir.1954). Appellant's presence at the parking lot designated during the second phone call, matching the physical description given on the phone, and riding in the car described on the phone is strong evidence that she is the party with whom Zinselmeier spoke.

* * *

Affirmed.

UNITED STATES v. POOL, 660 F.2d 547, 560 (5th Cir.1981). "On August 5, 1978, at 10:40 a.m. DEA Agent Starratt received a call from a person who identified himself as 'Chip,' a nickname used by appellant Loye throughout the investigation. The caller told the agent that Petrulla wanted DEA Agent Story to obtain another boat. Based on this conversation Agent Starratt identified Loye as the telephone participant charged with the § 843(b) violation in Count 9. The conversation was not recorded. Starratt never met Chip and he never made any voice comparison with Loye. The only way Starratt could identify the caller was through the caller's self-identification. Under these circumstances, Loye argues that Starratt's testimony identifying him is inadmissible because it was not authenticated, Fed.R.Evid. 901. Loye also argues that the identification was hearsay. Loye's contention that the identity of the caller was not properly authenticated finds support in our case law. Federal Rule of Evidence 901(a) states:

> The requirement of authentication or identification as a condition precedent to admissibility is satisfied by evidence sufficient to support a finding that the matter in question is what its proponent claims.

"We have previously remarked that 'a telephone call out of the blue from one who identifies himself as X may not be, in itself, sufficient authentication of the call as in fact coming from X.' United States v. Register, 496 F.2d 1072, 1077 (5th Cir.1974). We agree with the government that the standard of admissibility of voice identification testimony is *prima facie.* Id. We also agree that circumstantial evidence may be used in meeting this standard. Id. However, there is not sufficient evidence to support the conclusion that Agent Starratt actually heard Loye's voice. As noted, Starratt had never met Loye and no voice comparisons were made. Under these circumstances, Loye's use of the nickname 'Chip' does not make out a *prima facie* case that he was the caller. See United States v. Hyatt, 565 F.2d 229, 232 (2d Cir.1977). The possibility that someone else was using his nickname in this clandestine operation is too great to properly admit Agent Starratt's identification. This identification was essential to Loye's § 843(b) conviction. Accordingly, we reverse Loye's conviction for Count 9."

UNITED STATES v. HINES, 717 F.2d 1481, 1491 (4th Cir.1983), cert. denied, 467 U.S. 1214, 1219, 104 S.Ct. 2656, 2668, 81 L.Ed.2d 363, 373 (1984). "Ronald Hines claims a lack of proof as to his identity as a participant in the conspiracy because he was not identified pursuant to Fed.R.Evid. 901(b)(6). That rule allows '[b]y way of illustration only' identification of a telephone caller by evidence that the call was made to a number assigned to him. Hines claims that the proof of his identity was inadequate because 'the called party only identified himself as "Ronnie." The number * * * is not subscribed to by a Ronnie.' Hines also points out that there is no proof that he was at the residence at the time of the call. Nor was the recorded voice identified as his. His argument is completely without merit.

"Not only did the conversant identify himself as 'Ronnie,' but the phone was registered in the name of his parents and Hines was at the house when a DEA investigator visited the house. That evidence is sufficient to establish Hines's identity as the conversant."

UNITED STATES v. PORTSMOUTH PAVING CORP., 694 F.2d 312, 321–22 (4th Cir.1982). "The issue, then, is whether the record contains independent evidence demonstrating that the woman with whom Remington spoke was an agent of Saunders speaking about a matter within the scope of her employment.[12] We conclude that the record does contain such evidence.

"First, Remington testified that he 'called Mr. Saunders' office.' Not only does this testimony authenticate the occurrence of the telephone call in accordance with the standard illustrated by Rule 901(b)(6),[13] but the testimony also supports the inference that the one who answered the telephone was Saunders' agent. One would usually and properly assume upon the dialing of a business office phone number that the person who answers is employed by and has the authority to speak for the business.

"Second, Remington testified that 'the secretary' answered the call. That a businessman's secretary is an agent of the businessman for purposes of relaying messages to and from the businessman is common knowledge. Notwithstanding other testimony that casts some doubt on the accuracy of Remington's characterization of the answerer as a secretary, his description of the one with whom he spoke constitutes a portion of the necessary independent evidence.

"Finally, the two female employees in Saunders' office in 1975, the year that Remington made his call, testified that they occasionally answered the telephone and by radio relayed messages to and from Saunders. This testimony, in conjunction with that previously identified, virtually compels the conclusion that the woman to whom Remington spoke was an agent of Saunders with the authority to relay messages from Saunders to those who called his business office."

UNITED STATES v. KAIRYS

United States Court of Appeals, Seventh Circuit, 1986.
782 F.2d 1374, cert. denied, 476 U.S. 1153, 106 S.Ct. 2258, 90 L.Ed.2d 703 (1986).

CUMMINGS, CHIEF JUDGE.

The defendant, Liudas Kairys, appeals an order of the United States District Court for the Northern District of Illinois revoking his

12. The evidence necessary to establish the existence and scope of the agency relationship must be independent of the statement attributed to the agent. In other words, to avoid bootstrapping, agency must be demonstrated without the help of the statement sought to be admitted. Cf. United States v. Dockins, 659 F.2d 15, 16 (4th Cir.1981) (admissibility under 801(d)(2)(E) conditioned on evidence of conspiracy 'other than the statement itself'); Joyner v. United States, 547 F.2d 1199, 1203 (4th Cir.1977) (coconspirator rule requires evidence of conspiracy 'other than the statements in question') Thus, the secretary's quotation of Saunders may not be used to prove her status as Saunders' agent. That is not to say, however, that Remington's description of the telephone call, except for the secretary's words, may not qualify as the requisite independent evidence.

13. Rule 901(b)(6) provides that for purposes of admissibility telephone conversations may be authenticated by evidence that a call was made to the number assigned at the time by the telephone company to a particular person or business, if * * * (B) in the case of a business, the call was made to a place of business and the conversation related to business reasonably transacted over the telephone.

The Advisory Committee's Note explains that '[i]f the number is that of a place of business, the mass of authority allows an ensuing conversation if it relates to business reasonably transacted over the telephone, on the theory that the maintenance of the telephone connection is an invitation to do business without further identification.'

See United States v. Espinoza, 641 F.2d 153, 170–71 (4th Cir.), cert. denied, 454 U.S. 841, 102 S.Ct. 153, 70 L.Ed.2d 125 (1981).

citizenship pursuant to 8 U.S.C. § 1451(a). *United States v. Kairys,* 600 F.Supp. 1254 (1984). Section 1451(a) allows for revocation of citizenship that was "illegally procured" or "procured by concealment of a material fact or by willful misrepresentation." We affirm.

* * *

The main issue at trial was the defendant's identity—was Kairys the person the government claimed him to be? The defendant contends that he is Liudas Kairys born in Kuanas, Lithuania, on December 20, 1924. As a child he moved to Svilionys, Lithuania, where he completed four years of grammar school. His schooling continued in Svencionys, Lithuania, and he then completed three years of secondary education in Vilnius, Lithuania. Defendant asserts that between 1940 and 1942 he worked on a farm in Radviliskis, Lithuania, and that in 1942 he was captured and sent to the Hammerstein prisoner of war (POW) camp. The defendant claims he was a forced laborer in various locations throughout Lithuania and Poland for the remainder of the war.

The government, on the other hand, maintains that the defendant is Liudvikas Kairys born in Svilionys, then Polish, on December 24, 1920. He joined the Lithuanian army, which merged with the Russian army in 1939. The government contends that some time before March of 1940 Kairys moved to Vilnius, Lithuania, and obtained Lithuanian citizenship. During the German invasion of Poland, Kairys was captured and placed in the Hammerstein POW camp. In June of 1942 he was recruited by the Nazis and sent to training camp at Trawniki, Poland. In March of 1943 Kairys was transferred to the Treblinka labor camp in Poland to serve as a Nazi camp guard, where he remained until the camp was closed in July 1944 when the Russians advanced into Poland. At some point during his service he was promoted to *Oberwachmann* of his Nazi guard unit.

* * *

Both parties are in agreement as to what transpired after the war. Kairys worked as a farm laborer in Wiesent, Germany. In 1947 he entered the United States Army Labor Service Corps. Kairys applied for a visa in April of 1949, which was granted shortly thereafter. In May of 1949 he arrived in Chicago where he has since resided. In 1957 Kairys applied for naturalization, the petition was approved and the district court granted him citizenship later that year. From 1951 to the present Kairys has held one job in Chicago, has married and has two daughters. He is active in community and Lithuanian community affairs.

* * *

Kairys' argument focuses on the accuracy and admissibility of a *Personalbogen*, which is a German Waffen Schutzstaffel (SS) identity card. The government relied in part on the *Personalbogen* to establish its version of the defendant's identity. The district court admitted the *Personalbogen* under Federal Rule of Evidence 901(b)(8). The defendant argues that the admission of the document was error, claiming that it is a forgery fraught with inaccuracies, erasures, inconsistencies, and unexplained problems. The government counters that the defendant failed to produce any substantive evidence that the document was anything other than what it was purported to be—the defendant's Nazi SS personnel card.

A. *ADMISSIBILITY*

Federal Rule of Evidence 901(b)(8) governs the admissibility of ancient documents. The Rule states that a document is admissible if it "(A) is in such condition as to create no suspicion concerning its authenticity, (B) was in a place where it, if authentic, would likely be, and (C) has been in existence 20 years or more at the time it is offered." The question of whether evidence is suspicious and therefore inadmissible is a matter of the trial court's discretion. *United States v. Bridges,* 499 F.2d 179 (7th Cir.1974), certiorari denied, 419 U.S. 1010, 95 S.Ct. 330, 42 L.Ed.2d 284 (1974). We see no error here.

Although the Rule requires that the document be free of suspicion, that suspicion goes not to the content of the document, but rather to whether the document is what it purports to be. As Rule 901(a) states: "The requirement of authentication * * * as a condition precedent to admissibility is satisfied by evidence sufficient to support a finding that the matter in question is what its proponent claims." In other words, the issue of admissibility is whether the document is a *Personalbogen* from the German SS records located in the Soviet Union archives and is over 20 years old. Whether the contents of the document correctly identify the defendant goes to its weight and is a matter for the trier of fact; it is not relevant to the threshold determination of its admissibility. *Koziy,* 728 F.2d at 1322.

The defendant does argue that a question was raised about whether the document was actually an original *Personalbogen.* First, the defendant raises general allegations that the Soviet Union routinely disseminates forged documents as part of propaganda campaigns. Next the defendant contends that the thumbprint ink was "unusual" and that it could have been placed on the document by mechanical means. But government witnesses testified that the only likely way for the print to appear on the *Personalbogen* was from the defendant's pressing his thumb to the paper. Additionally, the defendant notes that the government failed to establish the proper chain of custody from Treblinka to the Soviet archives. However, it is not necessary to show a chain of custody for ancient documents. Rule 901(b)(8) merely requires that the document be found in a place where, if authentic, it would likely be. All that is left, then, is the vague allegation that the Soviet Union regularly releases forged documents. That is not sufficient to make the document suspicious for purposes of admissibility.

There was sufficient evidence in the record that the document was a German SS *Personalbogen.* It matched other authenticated *Personalbogens* in form, 600 F.Supp. at 1261; it was found in the Soviet Union archives, the depository for German SS documents, *id.*; and its paper fiber was consistent with that of documents more than 20 years old, *id.* at 1260. Its admission was not error.

* * *

For the reasons stated above, the district court committed no error in the proceedings. Accordingly, the order of the district court revoking the defendant's naturalization is affirmed.

FISHER v. STATE

Court of Appeals of Arkansas, 1982.
7 Ark.App. 1, 643 S.W.2d 571.

COOPER, JUDGE.

This is a criminal case in which the appellant was charged with theft of property having a value of over $100.00, but less than $2,500.00. After a trial by jury, she was found guilty and sentenced to a term of four years in the Arkansas Department of Correction and a fine of $5,000.00. The trial court suspended imposition of the four year sentence and imposed the $5,000.00 fine. On appeal, the appellant challenges the sufficiency of the evidence, and alleges that the trial court erred in ruling that certain portions of a video tape recording were properly admitted into evidence. We find no merit to either contention, and therefore we affirm.

THE FACTS

The appellant and her two daughters were employed by M & W Thriftway in Nashville, Arkansas to clean the store. On August 12, 1981, the appellant and her daughters arrived at the store for the purpose of cleaning it. The manager and owner of the store had installed a video tape camera on the premises, prior to the time that the appellant and her daughters arrived. He testified that he adjusted the camera, started it, and then left the building, leaving the camera unattended. He testified that he started the video tape camera at approximately 9:15 p.m. and that he returned at approximately midnight. He testified that he replaced the tape in the camera, since the first tape was about to run out. The manager testified that at approximately 1:30 to 2:00 a.m., he returned to get the tapes. When he arrived at the store, he found law enforcement officers on the scene, and, pursuant to their instructions, he removed the video tapes. He testified that he had safeguarded those tapes until the time of trial.

The sheriff of Howard County, Dick Wakefield, testified that he observed the appellant's daughters removing groceries in paper sacks from the back door of the store. The sheriff had the individuals arrested. He testified that the appellant indicated that she had left a check for the groceries at the store. He further testified that there was a check on top of the cash register in the amount of $29.64. The officers recovered seven bags of groceries, which the owner of the store testified were valued at $183.29. One of the appellant's daughters testified that she did help sack the groceries and that she intended to return with a check to pay for the balance of the groceries. The appellant testified that she had an agreement with the owner of the store that she could purchase groceries in the manner described above and that she did not intend to steal any groceries from the store.

THE ADMISSIBILITY OF THE VIDEO TAPE RECORDING

The appellant argues that the trial court erred in admitting in evidence a video tape recording [1], since no witness testified that the photographic evidence was a fair and accurate representation of the subject matter.

Immediately prior to the trial, the trial court conducted a hearing on the appellant's motion *in limine* which sought to preclude the State from introducing the video tapes. The trial court required the State to present the foundational facts which would support its claim that the video tapes were admissible. The manager of the store, Mr. Moore, testified that he had positioned the video tape camera on a tripod on top of an ice machine, so as to provide a view of the back door. He testified that he loaded the tape into the camera, started it, and checked to make sure that it was operating properly, prior to the time that he left the store. He testified that at the time he left the store, no one else was present in the store. He further testified that he changed the tape approximately two hours later and that he had continuous custody of the tapes, since the date of the alleged theft.

Mr. Moore further testified regarding the contents of the tapes, that the camera worked properly at all times, and that there were no gaps in the tapes. He testified that, when he returned to the store, the camera had not been moved or tampered with in any way, and that that fact could be verified, since the tapes would have shown movement had the camera been moved. He testified that in order to turn the camera off or to change the tapes, he had to pass in front of the camera and that his image appeared on the video tapes. He also testified that, once the camera had been turned on, the controls could not be approached, without a picture of that approach being made.

The trial court held that a proper foundation had been presented, and that the video tape was admissible. He found that the video tape fairly represented the situation that existed at the store, and he further

1. A video tape recording is an electronic means of recording sound and action on tape for subsequent playback in the form of a sound motion picture. 1 C. Scott, Photographic Evidence § 87 (2d ed. 1969). Video tape recordings are admissible in evidence on the same basis as sound motion picture films. 3 C. Scott, Photographic Evidence § 1294 (2d ed. Supp.1980).

noted that any question regarding the tapes went more to their credibility, rather than to admissibility. He noted it was for the jury to determine whether any criminal activity was taking place by virtue of the events which were shown on the video tape. The tape showed appellant and her daughters sacking groceries, and removing them.

The admissibility of photographic evidence is based on two different theories. One theory is the "pictorial testimony" theory. Under this theory, the photographic evidence is merely illustrative of a witness' testimony and it only becomes admissible when a sponsoring witness can testify that it is a fair and accurate representation of the subject matter, based on that witness' personal observation. Obviously, the photographic evidence in this case is not admissible under such a theory, since no person could verify that the video tape accurately represented what occurred at the store, based on personal observation. A second theory under which photographic evidence may be admissible is the "silent witness" theory. Under that theory, the photographic evidence is a "silent witness" which speaks for itself, and is substantive evidence of what it portrays independent of a sponsoring witness. *See,* 2 C. Scott, Photographic Evidence § 1021 (2d ed. Supp.1980); 3 J. Wigmore, Evidence § 790 (Chadbourn rev. 1970).

In Arkansas, photographic evidence is admissible under the "pictorial testimony" theory, when a sponsoring witness testifies that it is a fair and accurate representation of the subject matter. *Martin v. State,* 258 Ark. 529, 527 S.W.2d 903 (1975); *Ballew v. State,* 246 Ark. 1191, 441 S.W.2d 453 (1969); *Gross v. State,* 246 Ark. 909, 440 S.W.2d 543 (1969); *Lillard v. State,* 236 Ark. 74, 365 S.W.2d 144 (1963); *Hays v. State,* 230 Ark. 731, 324 S.W.2d 520 (1959); *Reaves v. State,* 229 Ark. 453, 316 S.W.2d 824 (1958), *cert. denied,* 359 U.S. 944, 79 S.Ct. 723, 3 L.Ed.2d 676 (1959); *Grays v. State,* 219 Ark. 367, 242 S.W.2d 701 (1951); *Simmons v. State,* 184 Ark. 373, 42 S.W.2d 549 (1931); *Sellers v. State,* 93 Ark. 313, 124 S.W. 770 (1910).

The question presented on this appeal has never been answered in Arkansas. A video tape recording and a film produced by an automatic camera have been admitted into evidence in two cases. However, the precise objection made in the case at bar was not raised in either case. *See, French v. State,* 271 Ark. 445, 609 S.W.2d 42 (1980); *Lunon v. State,* 264 Ark. 188, 569 S.W.2d 663 (1978).

This case presents the question of whether photographic evidence may be admitted as substantive evidence under the "silent witness" theory. We hold that the trial court correctly ruled that the video tape recording was admissible.

The Uniform Rules of Evidence, Rule 901(a), Ark.Stat.Ann. § 28–1001 (Repl.1979), provides that authentication is a condition precedent to the admissibility of evidence and that this requirement is met by a showing of evidence sufficient to support a finding that the matter in question is what its proponent claims. Section (b) lists various illustrations, showing methods of authentication or identification. The Uniform Rules of Evidence, Rule 1001(2), Ark.Stat.Ann. § 28–1001 (Repl. 1979), provides that "photographs" includes photographs, x-ray films, video tapes, and motion pictures.

X-ray films are admissible in Arkansas, subject to proper authentication. *Oxford v. Villines,* 232 Ark. 103, 334 S.W.2d 660 (1960); *Arkansas Amusement Corporation v. Ward,* 204 Ark. 130, 161 S.W.2d 178 (1942); *Prescott & N.W.R. Co. v. Franks,* 111 Ark. 83, 163 S.W. 180 (1914); *Miller v. Minturn,* 73 Ark. 183, 83 S.W. 918 (1904). Obviously, it is impossible for a witness to testify that an x-ray film is a fair and accurate representation of the subject matter, based on that witness' personal observation. Therefore, x-rays could never be admissible under the "pictorial testimony" theory. 3 C. Scott, Photographic Evidence § 1262 (2d ed. 1969). Every jurisdiction admits x-ray films as substantive evidence upon a sufficient showing of authentication, thus utilizing the "silent witness" theory, even if unintentionally.[2] We note that Rule 1001(2) treats x-rays, photographs, video tapes, and motion pictures, as one and the same.

Photographic evidence is the best available means of preserving the appearance of a scene at a given time. It is superior to eyewitness testimony in certain respects. Eyewitness testimony is subject to errors in perception, memory lapse, and a witness' problem of adequately expressing what he observed in language so that the trier of fact can understand. *See,* 1 C. Scott, Photographic Evidence § 41–54 (2d ed. 1969). Photographic evidence can observe a scene in detail without interpreting it, preserve the scene in a permanent manner, and transmit its message more clearly than the spoken word.

We hold that photographic evidence is admissible where its authenticity can be sufficiently established in view of the context in which it is sought to be admitted.[3] Obviously, the foundational requirements for the admissibility of photographic evidence under the "silent witness" theory are fundamentally different from the foundational requirements under the "pictorial testimony" theory. It is neither possible nor wise to establish specific foundational requirements for the admissibility of photographic evidence under the "silent witness" theory, since the context in which the photographic evidence was obtained and its intended use at trial will be different in virtually every case. It is enough to say, that adequate foundational facts must be presented to the trial court, so that the trial court can determine that the trier of fact can reasonably infer that the subject matter is what its proponent

2. Some jurisdictions treat x-rays as scientific evidence, and not photographic evidence. *See, Howard v. State,* 264 Ind. 275, 342 N.E.2d 604 (1976). Professor Wigmore treats the admissibility of x-rays as scientific evidence, even though admitting that the "silent witness" theory may be a "more satisfactory rationale." 3 J. Wigmore, Evidence § 795 n. 1 (Chadbourn rev. 1970).

3. Photographic evidence is subject to the same rules as other evidence. Thus, even if photographic evidence is properly authenticated, it may still be excluded because it is not relevant or because its probative value is substantially outweighed by the danger of unfair prejudice, confusion of the issues, or misleading the jury. Uniform Rules of Evidence, Rules 401, 402, 403, Ark.Stat.Ann. § 28–1001 (Repl.1979).

claims. The trial court determines the preliminary questions regarding the admissibility of evidence, and the appellate court reviews those determinations only for an abuse of discretion. Uniform Rules of Evidence, Rule 104(a), (b), Ark.Stat.Ann. § 28–1001 (Repl.1979); *Wilson v. City of Pine Bluff,* 6 Ark.App. 286, 641 S.W.2d 33 (1982). Our holding in this case in no way affects the admissibility of, or the foundational requirements for, photographic evidence used as demonstrative evidence under the "pictorial testimony" theory.

In adopting the "silent witness" theory, we join the overwhelming majority of other jurisdictions that have decided this issue. *United States v. Gordon,* 548 F.2d 743 (8th Cir.1977); *United States v. Gray,* 531 F.2d 933 (8th Cir.1976), *cert. denied,* 429 U.S. 841, 97 S.Ct. 117, 50 L.Ed.2d 110 (1976); *United States v. Stearns,* 550 F.2d 1167 (9th Cir. 1977); *United States v. Taylor,* 530 F.2d 639 (5th Cir.1976), *cert. denied,* 429 U.S. 845, 97 S.Ct. 127, 50 L.Ed.2d 117 (1976); *United States v. Pageau,* 526 F.Supp. 1221 (N.D.N.Y.1981); *Watkins v. Reinhart,* 243 Ala. 243, 9 So.2d 113 (1942); *State v. Kasold,* 110 Ariz. 558, 521 P.2d 990 (1974); *South Santa Clara Valley Water Conservation Dist. v. Johnson,* 231 Cal.App.2d 388, 41 Cal.Rptr. 846 (1965); *People v. Bowley,* 59 Cal.2d 855, 382 P.2d 591, 31 Cal.Rptr. 471 (1963); *People v. Doggett,* 83 Cal.App.2d 405, 188 P.2d 792 (1948); *Oja v. State,* 292 So.2d 71 (Fla.App. 1974); *Franklin v. State,* 69 Ga. 36, 47 Am.Rep. 748 (1882); *Bergner v. State,* 397 N.E.2d 1012 (Ind.App.1979); *State v. Holderness,* 293 N.W.2d 226 (Iowa 1980); *Cook v. Clark,* 186 N.W.2d 645 (Iowa 1971); *State v. Thompson,* 254 Iowa 331, 117 N.W.2d 514 (1962); *Franzen v. Dimock,* 251 Iowa 742, 101 N.W.2d 4 (1960); *Perry v. Eblen,* 250 Iowa 1338, 98 N.W.2d 832 (1959); *Foreman v. Heinz,* 185 Kan. 715, 347 P.2d 451 (1959); *Litton v. Commonwealth,* 597 S.W.2d 616 (Ky.1980); *State v. Young,* 303 A.2d 113 (Me.1973); *Sisk v. State,* 236 Md. 589, 204 A.2d 684 (1964); *Hartley v. A.I. Rodd Lumber Co.,* 282 Mich. 652, 276 N.W. 712 (1937); *Hancock v. State,* 209 Miss. 523, 47 So.2d 833 (1950); *State v. Withers,* 347 S.W.2d 146 (Mo.1961); *Vaca v. State,* 150 Neb. 516, 34 N.W.2d 873 (1948); *King v. State,* 108 Neb. 428, 187 N.W. 934 (1922); *People v. Byrnes,* 33 N.Y.2d 343, 308 N.E.2d 435, 352 N.Y.S.2d 913 (1974); *State v. Hunt,* 297 N.C. 447, 255 S.E.2d 182 (1979); *Dunford v. State,* 614 P.2d 1115 (Okla.Cr.App.1980); *State v. Brown,* 4 Or.App. 219, 475 P.2d 973 (1970); *State v. Goyet,* 120 Vt. 12, 132 A.2d 623 (1957); *Ferguson v. Commonwealth,* 212 Va. 745, 187 S.E.2d 189 (1972), *cert. denied,* 409 U.S. 861, 93 S.Ct. 150, 34 L.Ed.2d 108 (1972), *reh. denied,* 409 U.S. 1050, 93 S.Ct. 533, 34 L.Ed.2d 504; *State v. Dunn,* 246 S.E.2d 245 (W.Va.1978). *But see, Casson v. Nash,* 54 Ill.App.3d 783, 370 N.E.2d 564, 12 Ill.Dec. 760 (1977); *Foster v. Bilbruck,* 20 Ill.App.2d 173, 155 N.E.2d 366 (1959).

* * *

Affirmed.

STATE v. STOTTS

Supreme Court of Arizona, 1985.
144 Ariz. 72, 695 P.2d 1110.

GORDON, VICE CHIEF JUSTICE:

On July 8, 1976, appellant James Stotts, aka James Aye, pled guilty to the old-code crime of armed aggravated assault with one prior. See A.R.S. § 13–245(C) (repealed). This conviction arose from an incident in which appellant, armed with a knife, attacked a fifteen year old girl in an apparent attempted sexual assault.

The trial court suspended imposition of sentence and placed appellant on probation for fifteen years. The conditions of probation included appellant's return to the State of Washington, where appellant was wanted as a parole violator. In Washington, appellant would report to the Western State Hospital in Fort Steilacoom, Washington (hereinafter referred to as Western State) for evaluation and in-patient treatment. The court also instructed appellant to "follow all conditions required by the Probation Department."

Appellant, however, neither signed nor received any written conditions at the time probation was imposed. Nevertheless, authorities returned him to Washington to finish that state's parole. There, in late 1976, he entered into the "Sex Offender Treatment Program" at Western State.

When appellant's Washington parole was about to expire in late 1978, Arizona and Washington authorities executed an "Application for Compact Services" and an "Agreement to Return." Appellant signed both documents. The documents at once made Arizona the probation authority and made Washington the state that would supervise the probation. The "Agreement to Return" stated that appellant, in consideration of being granted probation by Arizona, would remain at Western State under the conditions of probation as fixed by either Washington or Arizona. Subsequently, in April of 1979 and July of 1981, appellant signed documents entitled "Interstate Compact—Conditions of Probation and Parole." These documents stated various conditions appellant had to follow in his interstate probation. One of the chief conditions was appellant's participation in the Sex Offender Treatment Program at Western State. Further, the 1981 conditions included successfully completing "all phases of the Western State Sexual Psychopath program."

In 1982, however, Washington authorities concluded that appellant was no longer treatable and was dangerous to be at large. Appellant's therapy group at the hospital voted him out of the program because of his lack of progress. Appellant also expressed a desire to leave the program. Based upon these circumstances, appellant's Washington Probation Officer wrote a "Violations Report" recommending revocation of appellant's probation.

Appellant was returned to Arizona, where a probation revocation hearing was held. After the presentation of evidence, the trial court determined appellant had violated his conditions of probation and ordered it revoked. After a dispositional hearing, the trial court sentenced appellant to not less than ten years and not more than life in prison, the maximum sentence for the old-code crime of armed aggravated assault with one prior. We have jurisdiction pursuant to Ariz. Const. Art. 6, § 5(3) and A.R.S. § 13–4031.

Appellant presents the following issues:

* * *

(4) Did the trial court abuse its discretion when it admitted various exhibits at the violation hearing?

* * *

Proceeding to the authentication question, however, we first note that documentary evidence offered at probation revocation hearings must be authenticated in conformance with our Rules of Evidence. According to Rule 19.3, Ariz.R.Crim.P., 17 A.R.S., "[t]he law of evidence relating to civil actions shall apply to criminal proceedings, except as otherwise provided." Nothing in the Rules of Criminal Procedure indicates that documentary evidence presented at probation revocation hearings should not be authenticated. In reviewing a trial court's decision to admit or exclude evidence, however, we will not disturb the lower court's ruling absent an abuse of discretion. *State v. Robles,* 135 Ariz. 92, 659 P.2d 645 (1983).

Appellant objected to a total of nine exhibits on authentication grounds. Exhibit 2 is a June 1976 letter purportedly from a Deputy Pima County Attorney to an Assistant Public Defender discussing a plea agreement for appellant. The prosecutor attempted to authenticate the letter by swearing to the Court that he retrieved the letter from the files of the Pima County Attorney.

Rule 901, Rules of Evidence, 17A A.R.S. governs the authentication of evidence. According to Rule 901(a) "[t]he requirement of authentication or identification as a condition precedent to admissibility is satisfied by evidence sufficient to support a finding that the matter in question is what its proponent claims." Subsection (b) sets out numerous illustrations of how to authenticate documents.

We cannot discern any 901(b) illustration applying to exhibit 2. The letter is not a public record under 901(b)(7).[2] That illustration provides for authentication of evidence qualifying as "a writing authorized by law to be recorded or filed and in fact recorded or filed in a public office, or a purported public record, report, statement, or data compilation, in any form, * * * from the public office where items of this nature are kept." The prosecutor's avowal merely established that

2. The prosecutor never made clear under which method he was attempting to authenticate this document nor indeed any other document admitted into evidence. Thus, we must assume the various potential bases for admitting the evidence.

he retrieved the letter from the files of his office. It did not establish whether the County Attorney was a public office, whether the office had the authority to keep such records, whether the record was properly kept, nor whether the prosecutor had knowledge of these facts.[3] We believe the above showings are required to admit evidence under Rule 901(b)(7). See *State v. Rhymes,* 129 Ariz. 56, 628 P.2d 939 (1981); Cleary, McCormick on Evidence, § 234 at 551 (2d ed. 1972); 5 Weinstein, Weinstein's Evidence, United States Rules § 901(b)(7)[01] (1983). We find no other basis for admitting this exhibit under Rule 901. Absent such a basis, the trial court abused its discretion in admitting exhibit 2.

The trial court also abused its discretion in admitting Exhibit 5 which is a handwritten letter purportedly from appellant to "Dear Sir" stamped "received" by the Pima County Adult Probation Department. Appellant objected to admission of Exhibit 5 based upon a lack of authentication. The prosecutor attempted to authenticate the letter through the testimony of a Pima County Adult Probation Department official. The witness stated that his department received the letter, stamped it "received", and kept it in the files of the Probation Department. The court then stated that there was no foundation that appellant actually wrote the letter. Nevertheless, the trial court admitted the evidence because "it's part of the probation file."

That the letter was part of the probation file goes to its reliability as hearsay. Being a part of the probation file, however, does not authenticate the letter. Furthermore, there was insufficient foundation for finding the letter qualified as a public record under rule 901(b)(7). The witness' testimony established that the letter came from the files of the Pima County Adult Probation Department. As with exhibit 2 above, nothing established the authority of the Department to keep the record, whether the record was properly kept, whether his office was a public office, or whether the witness had any knowledge of such facts. We see no other basis for admitting the letter. Thus, the trial court abused its discretion in admitting exhibit 5.

Exhibit 6 is a five page document. Page 1 is a "Reply by Receiving State" accepting supervision of Appellant by Washington; Pages 2–3 are an Interstate Placement Investigation report; page 4 is appellant's "Application for Compact Services;" and page 5 is appellant's "Agreement to Return" to Washington. Defense counsel objected to admission of exhibit 6 based on authentication.

As to the first page of exhibit 6, there was no authentication. No signature appears anywhere on the page, and the document did not qualify as a public record. Further, it has no apparent connection to

3. We would view with skepticism the claim that the County Attorney is a "public office" that keeps "public records" within the meaning of Rule 901(b)(7). "Public records are usually understood to include acts of legislatures, judicial records, and reports of administrative offices." Weinstein, 5 Weinstein's Evidence, United States Rules 901(b)(7)[01] (1983). The internal records of the County Attorney are not public records of a public office under rule 901(b)(7), Ariz.R.Evid., 17A A.R.S.

any other document in exhibit 6 that might have been authenticated. The trial court had no basis for admitting page one of exhibit 6, and, therefore, the trial judge abused his discretion in admitting page one.

Pages two and three consist of one page reports with a signature of a Washington State Probation Officer, Mr. Harris. Washington Probation Officer Stinson recognized the signature at the end of the report. Under Rule 901(b)(2) a party can authenticate a document by "[n]on-expert opinion as to the genuineness of handwriting, based on familiarity not acquired for purposes of the litigation." Familiarity with a person's handwriting can be attained by working with that person over a period of time. See *State v. Adamson,* 136 Ariz. 250, 665 P.2d 972 *cert. denied,* ___ U.S. ___, 104 S.Ct. 204, 78 L.Ed.2d 178 (1983).

In the instant case, Stinson stated he had worked for the Washington State Adult Probation Department for six years. He also stated that Harris was his supervisor and that he recognized his signature. This testimony established a sufficient foundation pursuant to Rule 901(b)(2). The trial court did not abuse its discretion in admitting pages two and three of exhibit 6.

Pages four and five are an Application for Compact Services and an Agreement to Return. At the probation revocation hearing, Stinson recognized both Harris' and appellant's signature at the bottom of both documents. The trial court did not abuse its discretion in admitting this portion of the exhibit. As stated, Officer Stinson was familiar with Harris' signature by virtue of a professional relationship. Furthermore, Stinson also supervised appellant at the Western State Hospital beginning in 1978, and he said he recognized appellant's signature by virtue of that supervision.

Exhibit 7 is a six page document: page one is a copy of a certification signed by Harris stating that the attached copy of the "Agreement to Return" is a true and exact copy of the original on file in Washington. The rest of the document contains the "Agreement to Return," an "Interstate Compact," and a certified "Application for Compact Services." Defense Counsel objected based on authentication.

The prosecution apparently attempted to self-authenticate the copy of the Agreement to Return under Rule 902(4), rules of Evidence, 17A A.R.S. This rule makes admissible, without further evidence of authenticity, certified copies of public records. The rule provides:

> "Extrinsic evidence of authenticity as a condition precedent to admissibility is not required with respect to the following:
>
> * * *
>
> "(4) Certified copies of public records. A copy of an official record or report or entry therein, or of a document authorized by law to be recorded or filed and actually recorded or filed in a public office, including data compilations in any form, certified as correct by the custodian or other person authorized to make the certification, by

certificate complying with Paragraph (1), (2), or (3) of this rule or complying with any applicable statute or rule."

Rule 902(2), Rules of Evidence, 17A A.R.S. provides for self-authentication of a public document not under seal when the public document bears the signature "in his official capacity of an officer or employee" of any state "if a public officer having a seal and having official duties [in the state] of the officer or employee certifies under seal that the signer has the official capacity and that the signature is genuine." See *State v. LeMaster,* 137 Ariz. 159, 669 P.2d 592 (1983).

The Agreement to Return in Exhibit 7 fails to meet the requirements of Rule 902(4) and (2). The certification in the instant case is a copy of a certification. The proffered evidence in the instant case is a copy of a certified copy. Rule 902(4), Rules of Evidence, 17A A.R.S. does not provide for self-authentication of copies of certified copies. " 'Certified copies' cannot and does not mean *copies* of certified copies." *State v. McGuire,* 113 Ariz. 372, 375, 555 P.2d 330, 333 (1976). (emphasis in the original.) We find no other authentication for this portion of Exhibit 7. The trial court's admission into evidence of the Agreement to Return in Exhibit 7 was an abuse of discretion.

Page three of exhibit 7 is an "Interstate Compact—Conditions of Probation and Parole" setting out appellant's probation conditions. Stinson recognized appellant's signature and the signature of another Washington parole officer with whom Stinson had worked, Carol Porter. Stinson had previously established his familiarity with appellant's signature, and he again stated he recognized the signature. This testimony was sufficient to authenticate the Interstate Compact under Rule 901(b)(2).

The rest of exhibit seven is an "Application for Compact Services" with an attached "certification." No foundation for admission of this portion of exhibit 7 appears in the record. The attached certification is merely a copy of a certification and therefore cannot qualify as a self-authenticating certified copy. (*See* discussion, *supra,* regarding the "Agreement to Return" portion of Exhibit 7). As no basis for admission of the "Application for Compact Services" appears in the record, the trial court abused its discretion in admitting this portion of exhibit 7.

Exhibit 8 is a second "Interstate Compact—Conditions of Probation and Parole" dated April 2, 1979. The prosecution authenticated this exhibit through Stinson's testimony that he recognized appellant's and Harris' signature. This foundation was sufficient for authentication under Rule 901(b)(2). Stinson had previously established his familiarity with both Harris' and appellant's signature, and he again stated he recognized them.

Exhibit 9 is a 1981 "Interstate Compact—Conditions of Probation and Parole" dated July 27, 1981 identical to page 3 of exhibit 7. It was authenticated through Stinson's testimony that he recognized appellant's and Carol Porter's signature. Again, as Stinson recognized appellant's and Porter's signatures, the document was properly admitted under Rule 901(b)(2).

Prejudice

Having found that the trial court abused its discretion in admitting various exhibits, we proceed to decide whether the court's errors prejudiced appellant. An error in a probation revocation hearing is non-prejudicial if it can be said that the error, by a preponderance of the evidence had no effect on the trier of fact's decision. The question, then, is whether, absent the error, this Court can say by a preponderance of the evidence that the trier of fact would have found the defendant violated his conditions of probation. See *State v. Hunter,* 136 Ariz. 45, 664 P.2d 195 (1983); *State v. Williams,* 133 Ariz. 220, 650 P.2d 1202 (1982).

In the instant case, the trial court improperly admitted the following evidence: (1) exhibit 2, (2) exhibit 5, (3) page 1 of exhibit 6; (4) the Agreement to Return in exhibit 7, (this same agreement to return, however, was properly admitted as part of exhibit 6); and (5) the "Application for Compact Services" in exhibit 7.

Properly admitted, however, were both "Interstate Compact Conditions of Probation and Parole" dated April 2, 1979 and July 27, 1981 and the Agreement to Return dated November 8, 1978. Also properly admitted were numerous documents establishing appellant's violations of these conditions. Moreover, the trial court heard substantial testimony regarding appellant's violation of his conditions of probation. Based upon this admissible evidence, we can say by a preponderance of the evidence that the trier of fact would have found appellant violated his conditions of probation.

* * *

Pursuant to A.R.S. § 13–4035, we have searched the entire record for fundamental error, and we have found none. The revocation of probation and the sentence imposed are affirmed.

STATE v. HOOPER, 145 Ariz. 538, 703 P.2d 482, 493 (1985), cert. denied, 474 U.S. 1073, 106 S.Ct. 834, 88 L.Ed.2d 805 (1986). "First, we reject defendant's claim that the documents showing his prior convictions were simply 'abstracts' of records instead of an actual copy of a record as required by Rule 902(4), Ariz.R.Evidence, 17A A.R.S. We have reviewed the record in question and believe it to qualify as a self authenticating document under Rule 902. We also reject defendant's claim that the certifications lacked trustworthiness because a judge from Cook County signed the certification 'under seal' yet no seal appeared next to his name. Rule 902(2) provides that a document can be self-authenticating if a public officer without seal signs the document so long as 'a public officer having a seal and having official duties in the district or political subdivision of the officer or employee certified under seal that the signer has the official capacity and that the signature is genuine.' In the instant case, the Clerk of the Circuit Court of Cook County, Illinois did exactly what Rule 902(2) describes."

Note

In addition to self-authentication as provided in Fed.R.Evid. 902, authentication may be obviated by admission or stipulation. See Fed.R.Civ.P. 36, 37. See also Fed.R.Civ.P. 16(3) (use of pre-trial conference "to consider * * * [t]he possibility of obtaining admissions of fact and of documents which will avoid unnecessary proof").

Chapter 7

CONTENTS OF WRITINGS, RECORDINGS, AND PHOTOGRAPHS (THE "BEST EVIDENCE RULE") *

[FED.R.EVID. ART. X]

UNITED STATES v. DUFFY

United States Court of Appeals, Fifth Circuit, 1972.
454 F.2d 809.

WISDOM, CIRCUIT JUDGE:

The defendant-appellant James H. Duffy was convicted by a jury of transporting a motor vehicle in interstate commerce from Florida to California knowing it to have been stolen in violation of 18 U.S.C.A. § 2312. He was sentenced to imprisonment for a term of two years and six months. On this appeal, Duffy complains of error in the admission of certain evidence and of prejudice resulting from members of the jury having been present during a sentencing in an unrelated case. We affirm.

At the trial, the Government established that Duffy was employed in the body shop of an automobile dealership in Homestead, Florida; that the stolen vehicle was taken by the dealership as a trade-in on the purchase of a new car; that the vehicle was sent to the body shop for repair; and that the vehicle and the defendant disappeared over the same weekend. The Government also presented testimony as to the discovery of the car in California including the testimony of 1) a witness who was found in possession of the vehicle and arrested and who testified he had received the vehicle from the defendant, 2) a San Fernando, California police officer who made the arrest and recovered the automobile, and 3) an F.B.I. agent who examined the vehicle, its contents, and the vehicle identification number. The defense stipu-

* See 4 Wigmore, Evidence (Chadbourn rev. 1972); McCormick, Evidence ch. 23 (4th ed. 1992); Cleary & Strong, The Best Evidence Rule: An Evaluation in Context, 51 Iowa L.Rev. 825 (1966).

lated to the authenticity of fingerprints, identified as Duffy's found on the rear-view mirror of the vehicle. The defense sought, through the testimony of three witnesses including the defendant, to establish that Duffy had hitchhiked to California and that, although he had worked on the stolen vehicle in the automobile dealership in Florida, he had not stolen it and had not transported it to California.

Both the local police officer and the F.B.I. agent testified that the trunk of the stolen car contained two suitcases. Found inside one of the suitcases, according to the witnesses, was a white shirt imprinted with a laundry mark reading "D–U–F". The defendant objected to the admission of testimony about the shirt and asked that the government be required to produce the shirt. The trial judge overruled the objection and admitted the testimony. This ruling is assigned as error.

The appellant argues that the admission of the testimony violated the "Best Evidence Rule". According to his conception of the "Rule", the Government should have been required to produce the shirt itself rather than testimony about the shirt. This contention misses the import of the "Best Evidence Rule". The "Rule", as it exists today, may be stated as follows:

> "[I]n proving the terms of a *writing,* where such terms are material, the original writing must be produced, unless it is shown to be unavailable for some reason other than the serious fault of the proponent. (Emphasis supplied.)"

McCormick, Evidence [560 (1972)]. See also United States v. Wood, 1840, 14 Pet. 430, 10 L.Ed. 527; 4 Wigmore, Evidence §§ 1173–1282 (3rd ed. 1940). Although the phrase "Best Evidence Rule" is frequently used in general terms, the "Rule" itself is applicable only to the proof of the contents of a writing. See 2 Wharton's Criminal Evidence 476 (1955) and cases cited therein: McCormick, Evidence [559–563 (1972)]; United States v. Waldin, 3 Cir.1958, 253 F.2d 551; Dicks v. United States, 5 Cir.1958, 253 F.2d 713; Burney v. United States, 5 Cir.1964, 339 F.2d 91. McCormick summarizes the policy-justifications for the rule preferring the original writing:

> "(1) * * * precision in presenting to the court the exact words of the writing is of more than average importance, particularly as respects operative or dispositive instruments, such as deeds, wills and contracts, since a slight variation in words may mean a great difference in rights, (2) * * * there is a substantial hazard of inaccuracy in the human process of making a copy by handwriting or typewriting, and (3) as respects oral testimony purporting to give from memory the terms of a writing, there is a special risk of error, greater than in the case of attempts at describing other situations generally. In the light of these dangers of mistransmission, accompanying the use of written copies or of recollection, largely avoided through proving the terms by presenting the writing itself, the preference for the original writing is justified."

McCormick, Evidence 410 (1954).

The "Rule" is not, by its terms or because of the policies underlying it, applicable to the instant case. The shirt with a laundry mark would not, under ordinary understanding, be considered a writing and would not, therefore, be covered by the "Best Evidence Rule". When the disputed evidence, such as the shirt in this case, is an object bearing a mark or inscription, and is, therefore, a chattel *and* a writing, the trial judge has discretion to treat the evidence as a chattel or as a writing. See 4 Wigmore, Evidence § 1182 and cases cited therein; McCormick, Evidence [562–563] and cases cited therein. In reaching his decision, the trial judge should consider the policy-consideration behind the "Rule". In the instant case, the trial judge was correct in allowing testimony about the shirt without requiring the production of the shirt. Because the writing involved in this case was simple, the inscription "D–U–F", there was little danger that the witness would inaccurately remember the terms of the "writing". Also, the terms of the "writing" were by no means central or critical to the case against Duffy. The crime charged was not possession of a certain article, where the failure to produce the article might prejudice the defense. The shirt was collateral evidence of the crime. Furthermore, it was only one piece of evidence in a substantial case against Duffy.

The appellant relies on Watson v. United States, 5 Cir.1955, 224 F.2d 910 for his contention that the testimony was inadmissible without production of the shirt. *Watson* involved a prosecution for possession of liquor without internal revenue stamps affixed to the containers in violation of what was then 26 U.S.C.A. § 2803(a). This Court held that admission of testimony that there were no revenue stamps on seized containers without requiring production of the containers was erroneous. This case, however, does not provide support for appellant's assertion. First, the only case cited in *Watson* in support of application of the "Best Evidence Rule" to an object was a 1917 Ninth Circuit case involving a writing and not an object. See Simpson v. United States, 9 Cir.1917, 245 F. 278. Second, the containers in *Watson* were critical to the proof of the crime. Possession of the containers was an element of the crime. As mentioned above, the shirt in the instant case, was not critical and possession of the shirt was not an element of the crime. Finally, *Watson,* although it has never been specifically overruled, has been distinguished into oblivion by this and other courts. See Atkins v. United States, 5 Cir.1957, 240 F.2d 849 at 852; Dicks v. United States, 5 Cir.1958, 253 F.2d 713; West v. United States, 5 Cir.1958, 259 F.2d 868; Palmquist v. United States, 5 Cir.1960, 283 F.2d 758; Chandler v. United States, 10 Cir.1963, 318 F.2d 356; United States v. Alexander, 4 Cir.1964, 326 F.2d 736; Burney v. United States, 5 Cir.1964, 339 F.2d 91; O'Neal v. United States, 5 Cir.1965, 341 F.2d 581. Where *Watson* has been followed, a writing has been involved. See Daniel v. United States, 5 Cir.1956, 234 F.2d 102; United States v. Maxwell, 2 Cir.1967, 383 F.2d 437. In *Burney,* we held that oral testimony describing the contents of two containers as distilled spirits was admissible without producing the containers or their contents.

> "The Watson decision is a minority decision on this point. As far as we are able to ascertain, the Watson case is the only case in all of the Circuits which does not confine the scope of the best evidence rule to the production of original documents or writings whenever feasible."

339 F.2d at 93.

In sum, the admission of the testimony in the instant case did not violate the "Best Evidence Rule".

* * *

Affirmed.

UNITED STATES v. GONZALES-BENITEZ

United States Court of Appeals, Ninth Circuit, 1976.
537 F.2d 1051, cert. denied, 429 U.S. 923, 97 S.Ct. 323, 50 L.Ed.2d 291 (1976).

KENNEDY, CIRCUIT JUDGE:

Aida Gonzales-Benitez and Ambrosio Hernandez-Coronel were convicted for importing and distributing heroin * * *.

* * *

THE BEST EVIDENCE ARGUMENT

Appellants contend the trial court erred in permitting testimony that related their conversations with the informers during a certain meeting in a motel room in Arizona. They claim that since the conversations were recorded on tapes, the tapes themselves, and not testimony of one of the participants, were the "best evidence" of the conversations. We are puzzled that this argument should be advanced so seriously and would not consider it if attorneys for both appellants had not argued the point so strenuously both in their briefs and in the court below. Certainly the trial court was correct in dismissing the objection out of hand.

The appellants simply misconstrue the purpose and effect of the best evidence rule. The rule does not set up an order of preferred admissibility, which must be followed to prove any fact. It is, rather, a rule applicable only when one seeks to prove the contents of documents or recordings. Fed.R.Evid. 1002. Thus, if the ultimate inquiry had been to discover what sounds were embodied on the tapes in question, the tapes themselves would have been the "best evidence."

However, the content of the tapes was not in itself a factual issue relevant to the case. The inquiry concerned the content of the conversations. The tape recordings, if intelligible,[2] would have been admissible as evidence of those conversations. But testimony by the participants was equally admissible and was sufficient to establish what was said.

2. We note that the reason the tapes were not introduced here was that the recording quality was so poor that the court translator was unable to understand and translate them.

* * *

Affirmed.

D'ANGELO v. UNITED STATES, 456 F.Supp. 127, 131 (D.Del. 1978), aff'd, 605 F.2d 1194 (3d Cir.1979). "Defendant moved to strike Atkins' testimony regarding the amount paid by Copter, Inc., for fringe benefits for D'Angelo. The basis for this objection was stated to be the Best Evidence Rule, in that written records of Copter must have been available on this point and were not produced.

"The 'best evidence' rule, embodied in Fed.R.Ev. 1002, comes into play only when the *terms* of a *writing* are being established and an attempt is made to offer secondary evidence, i.e., a copy, to prove the contents of the original writing. The rule is not applicable when a witness testifies from *personal knowledge* of the matter, even though the same information is contained in a writing.

"As an officer of Copter, Incorporated, Mr. Atkins attended directors meetings and participated in the preparation of the company's annual budget. He testified from personal knowledge that for the last several years preceding D'Angelo's death, the cost of employee benefits, specifically medical benefits, ranged between five and ten percent of the employee's base salary.

"Since Mr. Atkins testified from personal knowledge and did not purport to testify as to the contents of any document, defendant's Best Evidence objection is misdirected, even though the corporate books of Copter, Inc., would establish the same facts as he testified to. Mobilift Equipment of Florida, Inc. v. Bryan, 415 F.2d 841, 844 (5th Cir.1969).

"Defendant's motion to strike the testimony of Stuart Atkins as it related to the amounts paid by Copter, Inc., for fringe benefits for John P. D'Angelo, will be denied."

UNITED STATES v. RANGEL

United States Court of Appeals, Eighth Circuit, 1978.
585 F.2d 344.

Per Curiam.

Tiburcio A. Rangel appeals his conviction of knowingly and fraudulently demanding that a debt due from the United States be paid by virtue of a false instrument, in violation of 18 U.S.C. § 1003. We affirm the judgment of conviction.

Rangel, an employee of the United States Environmental Protection Agency, submitted three vouchers to the E.P.A. requesting reimbursement for lodging costs incurred in conjunction with three business trips. To each voucher he allegedly attached a photocopy of a duplicate, or a customers' copy of a Master Charge sales slip, as documentation for lodging expenses incurred. Photocopies of these Master Charge customer receipts submitted by Rangel were introduced into evidence with the vouchers, as were the corresponding duplicate merchant copies, which had been retained by the hotelkeepers. In each instance the photocopies submitted by Rangel showed greater lodging expenses than did the duplicate merchant copies. The invoice number on the merchant copies matched the number of the photocopied customer copies Rangel submitted to the E.P.A. The total amount Rangel received in excess of his actual lodging was approximately $53.59.

On appeal Rangel's main contention focuses on the admission of the travel authorization forms, travel vouchers and photocopied Master Charge receipts submitted to the E.P.A. Rangel contends the admission of these exhibits into evidence violated the best evidence rule and the Federal Business Records Act, 28 U.S.C. § 1732. He further urges that without this evidence the government has failed to provide sufficient evidence to sustain his guilt.

Rangel challenges the admissibility of the customer photocopies because they are not the "original" altered receipts and therefore did not constitute the "best evidence." We disagree. The government had to prove the contents of the photocopy of the altered receipt since the photocopy, not the altered receipt, was identified as the document Rangel had submitted to support his demand for payment. Thus the photocopies were admitted as originals. *See* 5 Weinstein's Evidence, ¶ 1001(3)[01] at 1001–49 (1976). However, even if the photocopies are considered to be duplicates, as xerox copies may be, *Weinstein's Evidence,* supra, ¶ 1001(4)[01] at 1001–68, they would also be admissible, since Rangel did not raise a genuine issue concerning their authenticity.

Rangel's challenge to the merchant copies is also based on the best evidence rule. These exhibits however, were admitted without objection. Therefore, their admission into evidence may only be reviewed for plain error affecting substantial rights. Fed.R.Evid. 103(a)(1), (d); United States v. Davis, 557 F.2d 1239 (8th Cir.), cert. denied, 434 U.S. 971, 98 S.Ct. 523, 54 L.Ed.2d 461 (1977). We find no such error. The merchants' copies were described by the district court as carbon copies of Master Charge sales slips, and as such were properly admitted as originals under Fed.R.Evid. 1001(3).

* * *

The judgment of conviction is affirmed.

UNITED STATES v. MARCANTONI

United States Court of Appeals, Fifth Circuit, 1979.
590 F.2d 1324, cert. denied, 441 U.S. 837, 99 S.Ct. 2063, 60 L.Ed.2d 666 (1979).

TJOFLAT, CIRCUIT JUDGE:

Charlie and Helen Suzanne Tune Marcantoni, husband and wife, were convicted in two counts of armed bank robbery and assault with a dangerous weapon during the commission thereof in violation of 18 U.S.C. §§ 2, 2113(a), (d) (1976). * * *

* * *

* * * August 9, 1976, Charlie Marcantoni consented to and assisted in a search of his Rogers Avenue residence by the Tampa police. During the search, Detective Edward Brodesser examined several hundred dollars in currency and recorded the serial numbers from the faces of the $10 bills he found, but he did not seize the bills. Later in the day separate lineups were conducted with respect to each of the Marcantonis, and they were identified as the gunman and driver involved in the robbery.

On August 13, 1976, Detective Brodesser returned to the Marcantoni residence on Rogers Avenue with a search warrant authorizing the seizure of any of the bait money that might be there. Following his August 9 search of the residence Brodesser had learned that the serial numbers he had recorded from two of the $10 bills he had uncovered during the search matched the serial numbers of two $10 bills on the Bank's list of the bait money taken in the robbery. Brodesser was unable to find these bills on August 13, however, when he returned with the search warrant. Six days later the Marcantonis were indicted.

At the trial, the Government proved its case mainly through the testimony of three Bank tellers who witnessed the robbery, two bystanders who witnessed the getaway, and Detective Brodesser and an expert from the U.S. Bureau of Printing and Engraving who, together, established that two of the $10 bills seen by Brodesser during his initial search of the Marcantoni residence were part of the bait money. * * *

* * *

The Marcantonis' alternative objection to the reception of Brodesser's testimony is that rule 1004 required the Government to introduce the two bills in evidence. Brodesser's testimony, they argue, was secondary evidence of the contents of the bills and not admissible because the Government failed to establish any of the conditions to the admissibility of secondary evidence specified by Fed.R.Evid. 1004. That rule states,

> The original is not required, and other evidence of the contents of a writing, recording, or photograph is admissible if—
>
> (1) *Originals lost or destroyed.* All originals are lost or have been destroyed, unless the proponent lost or destroyed them in bad faith; or
>
> (2) *Original not obtainable.* No original can be obtained by any available judicial process or procedure; or
>
> (3) *Original in possession of opponent.* At a time when an original was under the control of the party against whom offered, he was put on notice, by the pleadings or otherwise, that the contents would be a subject of proof at the hearing, and he does not produce the original at the hearing; or

(4) *Collateral matters.* The writing, recording, or photograph is not closely related to a controlling issue.

The Government made no formal attempt to qualify Brodesser's recital of the incriminating serial numbers as secondary evidence admissible under the rule. First, as the Government concedes, it did not undertake to show that the two bills were lost or destroyed. Second, it was not established that the Marcantonis were served notice that the contents of the bills would be a subject of proof at trial, and no process was directed to them to produce the bills in court. Finally, the Government did not, and in our opinion could not, contend that the evidence was "not closely related to a controlling issue."

There was little if anything in the argument of counsel that even addressed the qualifications of rule 1004 or, much less, whether they had been met in this instance. In overruling the Marcantonis' objection, the trial judge, quite understandably we think, gave no reasons for his decision. Consequently, we cannot determine whether the court treated Brodesser's statements about the serial numbers as secondary evidence, and, if so, which of the conditions to admissibility prescribed by the rule it found to be fulfilled.

If, in truth, the court considered Brodesser's testimony to be secondary evidence, we must assume that the court was satisfied that at least one of those conditions had been established. It should have been obvious after Detective Brodesser's return to the Marcantoni residence with a search warrant failed to produce the two $10 bills in question that the bills would not be available to the prosecution for trial. We have no difficulty in concluding that, under the circumstances of this case, the trial judge would have been authorized to find, under section (1) of the rule, that the two bills were "lost or [had] been destroyed." Surely, the Marcantonis could not have contended that the unavailability of the bills was the product of Government "bad faith." The trial judge could also have found, under section (2) of the rule, that "[n]o original [could] be obtained by any available judicial process or procedure." Even assuming that the Marcantonis were amenable to a subpoena directing the production of the bills at trial,[5] we think it unrealistic to expect that they would have readily produced the two instruments that would have made the Government's case against them complete. In short, the Government was not required to go through the motion of having a subpoena issued, served and returned unexecuted in order to establish, under section (2), that the bills were unobtainable.

As for section (3) of the rule, a legitimate argument can be made on this record that the Marcantonis were "put on notice" that the serial numbers of the two $10 bills "would be a subject of proof" at the trial,

5. We think it fairly debatable whether the Marcantonis could have been compelled, in the face of the fifth amendment privilege against self-incrimination, to produce the two $10 bills for use by the prosecution at trial. *See generally Bellis v. United States,* 417 U.S. 85, 94 S.Ct. 2179, 40 L.Ed.2d 678 (1974); *United States v. Hankins,* 565 F.2d 1344 (5th Cir.1978).

and that, having not produced them at trial, the Marcantonis could not object to the use of Brodesser's notes. In sum, although the trial judge, in overruling the Marcantonis' best evidence objection, should have announced the predicate to admissibility he found to have been established under rule 1004, his decision to receive the evidence was correct.

* * *

For the reasons we have stated, the convictions of Charlie and Helen Suzanne Tune Marcantoni are AFFIRMED.

ESTATE OF GRYDER v. C.I.R., 705 F.2d 336, 338 (8th Cir.1983), cert. denied, 464 U.S. 1008, 104 S.Ct. 525, 78 L.Ed.2d 709 (1983). "At trial, the Commissioner was unable to produce the originals of many corporate records, including journals and check-stub books. These records were destroyed by employees of the Internal Revenue Service after Cordial's criminal trial. The Tax Court's finding that these documents were destroyed negligently but not in bad faith is not clearly erroneous; thus, the Commissioner could seek to prove their contents by secondary evidence. Fed.R.Evid. 1004(1)."

FARR v. ZONING BOARD OF APPEALS OF TOWN OF MANCHESTER

Supreme Court of Errors of Connecticut, 1953.
139 Conn. 577, 95 A.2d 792.

BROWN, CHIEF JUSTICE.

This proceeding began as an appeal from the zoning board of appeals of the town of Manchester. The trial court rendered judgment for the plaintiffs sustaining the appeal. The defendants, the petitioner and the board, have appealed to this court. The question involves the board's right to grant a variance.

* * *

The brief of the defendant states that the first of the two issues on this appeal is whether the court erred in concluding that the plaintiffs are aggrieved within the meaning of § 160b of the 1951 Cumulative Supplement to the General Statutes and so are entitled to appeal. He urges that in admitting the testimony of the plaintiffs that they are Manchester taxpayers, landowners and electors the court violated the best evidence rule and so committed error. It is further claimed that this leaves the finding of these facts unsupported and that it must be stricken out. The defendant's claim overlooks the distinction which exists in a case involving ownership of land between the proof which is essential where the question of title is directly in issue and that which is essential where it is only collaterally involved. The best evidence rule "applies when the issue of title or ownership is directly involved, and not when it is collaterally involved, in which case a prima facie right of ownership may be established by parol evidence from one qualified to speak." Mathews v. Livingston, 86 Conn. 263, 273, 85 A. 529, 533; see 4 Wigmore, Evidence (3d Ed.) § 1246. As Wigmore points out, ordinarily "where the terms of a document are not in actual dispute, it is inconvenient and pedantic to insist on the production of the instrument itself." 4 Wigmore, op. cit., p. 482. Furthermore, as was observed in the Mathews case, if testimony as to ownership upon a collateral issue is disputed it can easily be contested. This the defendant made no attempt to do. The question of title was only collaterally involved in the present case, because the decision of the case would not conclusively determine whether the plaintiffs were the owners of the properties concerning which they testified. Abundant authority supports the court's ruling in allowing the testimony to prove ownership. Shanks v. Robertson, 101 Kan. 463, 464, 168 P. 316, 1 A.L.R. 1140; State ex rel. Walton v. Superior Court, 18 Wash.2d 810, 822, 140 P.2d 554; In re Mingo Drainage District, 267 Mo. 268, 281, 183 S.W. 611; Littlefield v. Bowen, 90 Wash. 286, 291, 155 P. 1053; 20 Am.Jur. 368, § 408, and see p. 258; note, 1 A.L.R. 1143; 4 Wigmore, op. cit., § 1254 and n. 1. For like reasons the court properly admitted the testimony of the plaintiffs that they were also taxpayers and electors. * * *

* * *

There is no error.

NEVILLE CONSTRUCTION CO. v. COOK PAINT & VARNISH CO.

United States Court of Appeals, Eighth Circuit, 1982.
671 F.2d 1107.

BRIGHT, CIRCUIT JUDGE.

Cook Paint and Varnish Company (Cook) appeals from a judgment entered upon a jury verdict awarding $80,000 in damages to Neville Construction Company (the Nevilles) in this action based on negligence and breach of warranty. We affirm.

* * *

1. SECONDARY EVIDENCE

Cook contends that the trial court should not have permitted Dennis Neville to testify regarding the contents of Cook's brochure describing the characteristics of Coro-foam insulation. Neville testified that the fire destroyed the brochure supplied by Kreis. The Nevilles attempted to introduce a similar brochure distributed by Cook; however, the court sustained Cook's objection to admissibility of the brochure on the ground that the exhibit had not been included on the pretrial exhibit list. Dennis Neville then testified that Kreis had given him literature on Coro-foam insulation which he had glanced through before deciding to buy the insulation. Neville testified, over objection, that the literature described Coro-foam's fire retardance.

Cook maintains that Neville's testimony was not the best evidence to prove the contents of Cook's brochure. Cook contends that because the witness had identified a brochure similar to the one destroyed in the fire it was incumbent upon the Nevilles to introduce that brochure as a duplicate.

Cook's argument lacks merit. Because Cook successfully objected to the admission of the similar brochure, it now cannot complain that that document provided the only proper evidence of the contents of the brochure destroyed in the fire. Moreover, the Federal Rules of Evidence recognize no degrees of secondary evidence to prove the contents of a writing that has been lost or destroyed. See United States v. Standing Soldier, 538 F.2d 196, 203 n. 8 (8th Cir.), *cert. denied,* 429 U.S. 1025, 97 S.Ct. 646, 50 L.Ed.2d 627 (1976); Fed.R.Evid. 1004 advisory committee note. The court, therefore, properly admitted the testimony of Dennis Neville as secondary evidence of the contents of the brochure destroyed in the fire.

* * *

Affirmed.

AMOCO PRODUCTION CO. v. UNITED STATES, 619 F.2d 1383, 1389–91 (10th Cir.1980). "The appellants offered evidence in an attempt to show that the routine practice of the FFMC was to reserve a one-half mineral interest in all property transferred during the relevant period. The court excluded this evidence on the ground that under Rule 1005 of the Federal Rules of Evidence, the availability of a properly recorded version of the 1942 deed precluded admission of any other evidence of the contents of the deed. We believe the court misinterpreted the purpose and effect of Rule 1005.

"Rule 1005 provides:

> The contents of an official record, or of a document authorized to be recorded or filed and actually recorded or filed, including data compilations in any form, if otherwise admissible, may be proved by copy, certified as correct in accordance with rule 902 or testified to be correct by a witness who has compared it with the original. If a copy which complies with the foregoing cannot be obtained by the exercise of reasonable diligence, then other evidence of the contents may be given.

"The notes of the Advisory Committee on the proposed rules of evidence help explain the purpose of this rule:

> Public records call for somewhat different treatment. Removing them from their usual place of keeping would be attended by serious inconvenience to the public and to the custodian. As a consequence judicial decisions and statutes commonly hold that no explanation need be given for failure to produce the original of a public record. * * * This blanket dispensation from producing or accounting for the origi-

nal would open the door to the introduction of every kind of secondary evidence of contents of public records were it not for the preference given certified or compared copies. Recognition of degrees of secondary evidence in this situation is an appropriate *quid pro quo* for not applying the requirement of producing the original.

"Rule 1005 authorizes the admission of certified copies of records and documents filed and stored in public offices. The purpose of the rule is to eliminate the necessity of the custodian of public records producing the originals in court. This purpose is not furthered by extending the rule to encompass documents not filed and stored in public offices.

"Rule 1005, by its terms, extends to 'a document authorized to be recorded or filed and actually recorded or filed.' This language encompasses deeds, mortgages and other documents filed in a county recorder's office. However, it is the actual record maintained by the public office which is the object of Rule 1005, not the original deed from which the record is made. If the original deed is returned to the parties after it is recorded, it is not a public record as contemplated by Rule 1005.

"Applying Rule 1005 to exclude all other evidence of the contents of a deed is especially troublesome in a case such as this one. We cannot embrace an interpretation of the Rule which would exclude all evidence of the original deed other than the recorded version when the very question in controversy is whether the original deed was correctly transcribed onto the recorded version. Rule 1004(1), which authorizes the admission of other evidence of the contents of a writing if all originals are lost or destroyed, rather than Rule 1005, is applicable to the 1942 deed.[6] Accordingly, assuming it is otherwise admissible, evidence of a routine practice of the FFMC is relevant to prove conduct under Rule 406, and is admissible in lieu of the original under Rule 1004(1). Even if the evidence is not extremely probative, as indicated by the court, Record, vol. 2, at 431 n. 2, it is sufficient to create a question of fact and render summary judgment improper. Accordingly, the case must be remanded for the district court to consider admissibility of the evidence under a proper interpretation of Rules 1004 and 1005."

UNITED STATES v. JOHNSON, 594 F.2d 1253, 1255–56 (9th Cir.1979), cert. denied sub nom. Richey v. United States, 444 U.S. 964, 100 S.Ct. 451, 62 L.Ed.2d 376 (1979). "The Government invoked Fed. R.Evid. 1006, which provides:

6. The court properly applied Rule 1005 in admitting a certified copy of the deed as recorded by the county recorder. Furthermore, because such a certified copy was available, the court should properly exclude any other proffered evidence of the contents of the recorded version of the deed. However, Rule 1005 does not preclude the admission of other evidence of the contents of the original 1942 deed. That deed is not a public record and Rule 1005 does not apply to it.

'The contents of voluminous writings, recordings, or photographs which cannot conveniently be examined in court may be presented in the form of a chart, summary, or calculation. The originals, or duplicates, shall be made available for examination or copying, or both, by other parties at reasonable time and place. The court may order that they be produced in court.'

We hold that under this Rule the proponent of the summary must establish that the underlying materials upon which the summary is based are admissible in evidence.

"The purpose of Rule 1006 is to allow the use of summaries when the volume of documents being summarized is so large as to make their use impractical or impossible; summaries may also prove more meaningful to the judge and jury. See Note of Advisory Committee on Proposed Rules, reprinted in 28 U.S.C.A. Federal Rules of Evidence at 783; S. Saltzburg & K. Redden, Federal Rules of Evidence Manual 694 (2d ed. 1977); 5 J. Weinstein & M. Berger, Weinstein's Evidence ¶ 1006[02] (1975). Such a rationale imports that instead of using a summary, the proponent of the summary could introduce the underlying documents upon which the summary is based. See United States v. Smyth, 556 F.2d 1179, 1184 & n. 11 (5th Cir.), cert. denied, 434 U.S. 862, 98 S.Ct. 190, 54 L.Ed.2d 135 (1977).

* * *

"Finally, Congress placed Rule 1006 not in the Article of the Federal Rules dealing with exceptions to the hearsay rule, Article VIII, but rather in the Article dealing with 'Contents of Writings, Recordings and Photographs,' Article X. While the Government argues that this Article X Rule abrogates the hearsay limitations of Article VIII, the Article X provisions more properly deal with the 'best evidence' problems arising from the use of materials other than originals. See Fed.R.Evid. 1002. And when Congress intended to provide an exception to the hearsay rule for materials which it also exempted from the best evidence rule in Article X, it did so by a provision in Article VIII. For example, Rule 1005 provides that public records may be proved with other than the original under some circumstances. Rules 803(8), (9), and (10), however, provide the hearsay exception for various types of public records. Similarly, Rule 1007 allows the use of secondary materials to prove the contents of testimony or a written admission of a party. But Rule 801(d)(2) provides that admissions are not subject to the hearsay rule. In claiming that Rule 1006 provides an exception from both the 'best evidence' rule for summaries and the hearsay rule for the underlying materials, the Government (and the district court) misapprehended this congressional scheme.

"Commentators and other courts have agreed that Rule 1006 requires that the proponent of a summary establish that the underlying documents are admissible in evidence. For example, Judge Weinstein and Professor Berger write:

> 'Before the chart, summary, or calculation may be admitted, it is necessary for the party offering the exhibit to lay a proper foundation for the admission of the original or duplicate materials on which the exhibit is based, or for the parties to stipulate to the admissibility of the materials. Charts, summaries, or calculations are inadmissible as evidence if, for any reason, the original or duplicate materials on which they are based are inadmissible. Thus, if the original materials contain hearsay and fail to qualify as admissible evidence under one of the exceptions to the hearsay rule, the chart, summary, or calculation based on that material is inadmissible.'

5 Weinstein on Evidence ¶ 1006[03], at 1006–5 to 1006–6 (footnotes omitted); see 2 Jones on Evidence § 7:30 (Gard rev. 1972); Federal Rules of Evidence Manual 196 (1978 Supp.)."

McALLEN STATE BANK v. LINBECK CONST. CORP., 695 S.W.2d 10, 16 (Tex.App.1985). "First, Linbeck argues that the computer printouts were inadmissible because each was 'a summary of underlying [business] records' for which 'a proper predicate for their admission had not been laid.' More specifically, Linbeck argues that, since the underlying records allegedly had never been made available to it by the Bank, the requisites for the admission of a summary of underlying business records under Duncan Development, Inc. v. Haney, 634 S.W.2d 811 (Tex.1982), were not met.

"In Duncan Development, Inc. v. Haney, the Texas Supreme Court wrote:

> A summary of business records may be admitted into evidence upon proof of an additional predicate. This includes proof (1) that the records are voluminous, (2) they have been made available to the opponent for a reasonable period of time to afford inspection and an opportunity for cross-examination, and (3) the supporting documents are themselves admissible in evidence. Black Lake Pipeline Co. v. Union Construction Co., 538 S.W.2d 80, 93–94 (Tex.1976); Cooper v. La Gloria Oil and Gas Co., 436 S.W.2d 889, 891 (Tex.1969).

Duncan Development, Inc. v. Haney, 634 S.W.2d at 812–813. However, Duncan Development, Inc. v. Haney dealt with a summary of invoices from its 'some three dozen subcontractors' that was prepared for trial purposes; whereas, here, we are dealing with two computer printout summary/breakdowns that, although each is a summary of underlying business records (labor and materials records), are themselves business records. Therefore, the computer printouts were entitled to be treated as business records, and not as a summary of business records for trial purposes. See Marquis Construction Company, Inc. v. Johnson Masonry, 665 S.W.2d 514 (Tex.App.—Houston [1st Dist.] 1983, no writ); See also Hodges v. Peden, 634 S.W.2d 8 (Tex.App.—Houston [14th Dist.] 1982, no writ); Voss v. Southwestern Bell Telephone Company, 610 S.W.2d 537 (Tex.Civ.App.—Houston [1st Dist.] 1980, writ ref'd. n.r.e.)."

SEILER v. LUCASFILM, LTD., 808 F.2d 1316, 1319–20 (9th Cir. 1986), cert. denied, 484 U.S. 826, 108 S.Ct. 92, 98 L.Ed.2d 53 (1987). "As we hold that the district court correctly concluded that the best evidence rule applies to Seiler's drawings, Seiler was required to produce his original drawings unless excused by the exceptions set forth in Rule 1004. The pertinent subsection is 1004(1), which provides:

> The original is not required, and other evidence of the contents of a writing, recording, or photograph is admissible if—
>
> > (1) Originals lost or destroyed. All originals are lost or have been destroyed, unless the proponent lost or destroyed them in bad faith * * *

"In the instant case, prior to opening statement, Seiler indicated that he planned to show to the jury reconstructions of his 'Garthian Striders' during the opening statement. The trial judge would not allow items to be shown to the jury until they were admitted in evidence. Seiler's counsel reiterated that he needed to show the reconstructions to the jury during his opening statement. Hence, the court excused the jury and held a seven-day hearing on their admissibility. At the conclusion of the hearing, the trial judge found that the reconstructions were inadmissible under the best evidence rules as the originals were lost or destroyed in bad faith. This finding is amply supported by the record.

"Seiler argues on appeal that regardless of Rule 1004(1), Rule 1008 requires a trial because a key issue would be whether the reconstructions correctly reflect the content of the originals. Rule 1008 provides:

> When the admissibility of other evidence of contents of writings, recordings, or photographs under these rules depends upon the fulfillment of a condition of fact, the question whether the condition has been fulfilled is ordinarily for the court to determine in accordance with the provisions of rule 104. However, when an issue is raised (a) whether the asserted writing ever existed, or (b) whether another writing, recording, or photograph produced at the trial is the original, or (c) whether other evidence of contents correctly reflects the contents, the issue is for the trier of facts to determine as in the case of other issues of fact.[2]

"Seiler's position confuses admissibility of the reconstructions with the weight, if any, the trier of fact should give them, after the judge has ruled that they are admissible. Rule 1008 states, in essence, that when the *admissibility* of evidence other than the original depends upon the fulfillment of a condition of fact, the trial judge generally makes the determination of that condition of fact. The notes of the Advisory

2. Lucas conceded the originals existed and Seiler conceded the items he sought to introduce were not the originals. Hence, as subsections (a) and (b) are not in issue, Seiler is arguing that 1008(c) requires that the case be submitted to the jury.

Committee are consistent with this interpretation in stating: 'Most preliminary questions of fact in connection with applying the rule preferring the original as evidence of contents are for the judge * * * [t]hus the question of * * * fulfillment of other conditions specified in Rule 1004 * * * is for the judge.' In the instant case, the condition of fact which Seiler needed to prove was that the originals were not lost or destroyed in bad faith. Had he been able to prove this, his reconstructions would have been admissible and then their accuracy would have been a question for the jury. In sum, since admissibility of the reconstructions was dependent upon a finding that the originals were not lost or destroyed in bad faith, the trial judge properly held the hearing to determine their admissibility."

Chapter 8

PRIVILEGES
[FED.R.EVID. ART. V]

SECTION 1. HUSBAND–WIFE *

STAFFORD v. STATE

Criminal Court of Appeals of Oklahoma, 1983.
665 P.2d 1205, cert. denied, 474 U.S. 865, 106 S.Ct. 188, 88 L.Ed.2d 157 (1985).

CORNISH, JUDGE:

Roger Dale Stafford was convicted on six counts of Murder in the First Degree and sentenced to death.

On July 16, 1978, Roger Stafford, his wife, Verna Stafford, and his brother, Harold Stafford, drove from Tulsa to Oklahoma City to rob the Sirloin Stockade Restaurant. The trio waited in the restaurant parking lot until all the customers had left. At around 10:00 p.m. they exited their automobile and Roger Stafford knocked on the side door of the restaurant. The manager answered the door and was greeted by Roger and Harold Stafford pointing guns at him. They forced him to take them to the cash register and the office safe.

Inside the restaurant, the manager began taunting them, saying that he could not understand why people rob others instead of working for themselves. Roger Stafford hit the manager and demanded that he call his employees to the cash register. The manager complied with the demand.

Harold and Verna Stafford held the employees at gunpoint while the appellant and the manager emptied the office safe which contained about $1290.00. After they obtained the money, the employees were ordered inside the restaurant's walk-in freezer. The appellant then asked Harold Stafford to help him in the freezer. Harold reminded the appellant that no one was to be hurt. The appellant retorted that

* See 8 Wigmore, Evidence chs. 79, 83 (McNaughton rev. 1961); McCormick, Evidence § 66, ch. 9 (4th ed. 1992).

"they are going to get what they deserve." He then shot the only black employee, and both men opened fire on the remaining employees. Verna Stafford testified that she heard a lot of gunfire and screaming.

Roger Stafford then told Verna that it was time for her to take part. He placed his gun in Verna's hand and helped her pull the trigger. All six Sirloin Stockade employees died as a result of the shootings.

* * *

V

Stafford advances that the trial court erred by allowing Verna Stafford to testify. He contends that Verna Stafford's testimony violated the husband and wife privilege under 12 O.S.1981, § 2504. Section 2504 provides in part:

> A. A communication is confidential for purposes of this section if it is made privately by any person to his spouse and is not intended for disclosure to any other person.
>
> B. An accused in a criminal proceeding has a privilege to prevent his spouse from testifying as to any confidential communication between the accused and the spouse.

Verna Stafford testified in regard to the facts and circumstances surrounding the Sirloin Stockade murders. She stated that her husband, Roger Stafford, planned the robbery and subsequently caused the death of several of the employees. Our initial inquiry is whether Verna Stafford's testimony breached any confidential communications between her and Roger Stafford.

In Lavicky v. State, 632 P.2d 1234, 1236 (Okl.Cr.1981), we stated that "[c]onfidential communications between husband and wife are those made when they're alone, or are those expressly made confidential, or are of a confidential nature induced by the marital relationship, the disclosure of which are calculated to disturb the marital relationship." In this case, the trial judge specifically limited Verna Stafford's testimony to her personal observations and conversations with her husband which were made in the presence of third persons. Clearly, the conversations between Verna and Roger Stafford in the presence of a third party were not of a confidential nature as is required under 12 O.S.1981, § 2504(A).

The evidence at trial sufficiently established that Harold Stafford was present during most of the conversations between Verna and Roger Stafford. The trial judge specifically excluded all statements made privately between Verna and Roger Stafford, therefore, we conclude that Verna's testimony did not violate the husband-wife privilege, as protected under Section 2504(B).

In a related argument, Stafford contends that the trial court erred in admitting the testimony of Linda Lewis. Ms. Lewis overheard a conversation between Roger and Verna Stafford. Stafford argues that the conversation was intended to be confidential and therefore protected under Section 2504, the husband-wife privilege.

Ms. Lewis testified that she overheard a conversation between Roger and Verna in the parking lot outside her Tulsa motel window after the homicides. She related to the jury the following events:

> Ms. Lewis: I was in my room, sir. I heard the commotion. I went to my window. I looked out, and I seen who it was. And, you know, I seen him hit her, and I opened my door—
>
> A. All right, excuse me. Just tell us, please, what you heard and saw? In the first place, are you—who was it that you saw?
>
> A. I saw Roger and Verna.
>
> Q. All right. Tell us what you first saw, please?
>
> A. I saw Roger slap Verna, and she said, "I'm calling the police." And Roger said, "Go ahead. You would be in as much trouble as I would".
>
> And she said, "I didn't kill them Roger. You did." Roger said, "You were there, and you were with us".
>
> And I heard something else, and then Verna said, "No".

The appellant, citing Seigler v. State, 54 Okl.Cr. 141, 15 P.2d 1048 (1932), argues that where a conversation between husband and wife is intended to be confidential and the parties are unaware of an eavesdropper, the conversation maintains its cloak of privilege. A plain reading of *Seigler* makes obvious the inaccuracy of the appellant's statement. In *Seigler,* this Court stated that "[t]he rule is that third parties may testify to communications had between husband and wife, overheard by such third persons." 54 Okl.Cr. at 143, 15 P.2d at 1048. We hold that irrespective of whether communications between husband and wife are intended to be confidential, third persons may testify as to conversations overheard, whether accidentally or by design. See Hilderbrandt v. State, 22 Okl.Cr. 58, 209 P. 785 (1922). Accordingly, we find that Ms. Lewis' testimony was properly admitted into evidence.

* * *

Finding no error warranting reversal or modification, the judgments and sentences are AFFIRMED.

Notes

(1) Most authorities agree that an eavesdropper unknown to either spouse may testify to an otherwise privileged marital communication, but judicial attitudes change markedly when the "eavesdropper" has been procured by the recipient spouse. See United States v. Neal, 532 F.Supp. 942, 948–49 (D.Colo.1982).

(2) "[C]onversations between husband and wife about crimes in which they are jointly participating when the conversations occur are not marital communications for the purpose of the marital privilege, and thus do not fall within the privilege's protection of confidential marital communica-

tions." United States v. Mendoza, 574 F.2d 1373, 1381 (5th Cir.1978), cert. denied, 439 U.S. 988, 99 S.Ct. 584, 58 L.Ed.2d 661 (1978).

(3) Communications made prior to the marriage are not privileged; divorce, however, does not end the protection for a communication made during coverture. See United States v. Pensinger, 549 F.2d 1150, 1152 (8th Cir.1977); McCormick, Evidence §§ 81, 85 (4th ed. 1992).

(4) On parent-child privilege, see State v. Maxon, p. 803 infra.

CONSTANCIO v. STATE

Supreme Court of Nevada, 1982.
98 Nev. 22, 639 P.2d 547.

PER CURIAM:

Appellant was convicted, upon a jury verdict, of rape (former NRS 200.363) and of two counts of the infamous crime against nature (NRS 201.190 as it then read; see 1977 Nev.Stats. ch. 598, § 17, at 1632).

A former wife of appellant was permitted to testify, over objection, that during their marriage appellant had often had difficulty achieving an erection. Appellant objected to the admission of this testimony, on the theory that sexual behavior during marriage should be classified as communication protected by the spousal privilege, citing State v. Robbins, 35 Wash.2d 389, 213 P.2d 310 (1950), in which the court concluded that all facts known to a spouse because of the marital relation should be within the privilege. We are not inclined to so extend the meaning of "communication".

The applicable statute provides that "[n]either a husband nor a wife can be examined, during the marriage or afterwards, without the consent of the other, as to any communication made by one to the other during marriage." NRS 49.295(1)(b). We have previously held that this privilege "is intended to protect confidential communications between spouses". Deutscher v. State, 95 Nev. 669, 683, 601 P.2d 407, 416 (1979). Webster's Third New International Dictionary, at 460 (1976 ed.), defines "communicate" as "to make known: inform a person of: convey the knowledge or information of". We agree that under a statute such as ours, "the privilege should be limited to *expressions* intended by one spouse to convey a meaning or message to the other." McCormick, *Evidence* § 79, at 163 (2d ed. E. Cleary 1972). See, e.g. Posner v. New York Life Ins. Co., 56 Ariz. 202, 106 P.2d 488 (1940); Tanzola v. De Rita, 45 Cal.2d 1, 285 P.2d 897 (1955). We therefore conclude that the trial court was correct in its decision to overrule appellant's objection.

* * *

The judgment of conviction and sentence are accordingly affirmed.

Notes

(1) Accord, United States v. Parker, 834 F.2d 408, 411 (4th Cir.1987), cert. denied, 485 U.S. 938, 108 S.Ct. 1118, 99 L.Ed.2d 279 (1988); United

States v. Estes, 793 F.2d 465, 467 (2d Cir.1986); State v. Hannuksela, 452 N.W.2d 668, 674–78 (Minn.1990).

(2) "Perhaps the reductio ad absurdum of the 'acts' cases is State v. Robbins [cited in *Constancio*]. There the husband was charged with automobile theft, and evidence of his former wife that when she was presenting application for license for the stolen car at the office her husband was waiting outside in an automobile was a 'communication' and privileged. The court said, 'It is obvious that he would not have waited in the automobile had he not relied on the confidence between them by reason of the marital relation.'" McCormick, Evidence § 79, at 192 n. 9 (3d ed. 1984).

STATE v. FREEMAN

Supreme Court of North Carolina, 1981.
302 N.C. 591, 276 S.E.2d 450.

COPELAND, JUSTICE.

The sole issue presented by this appeal is whether this Court should continue to adhere to the common law rule rendering spouses incompetent to testify against each other in a criminal proceeding. We believe that the common law rule no longer complies with the purposes for which it was created, therefore, we alter the rule in the manner set forth below to more closely achieve its purpose without unduly hindering the administration of criminal justice.

Defendant contends that because the common law rule preventing spouses from testifying against each other in a criminal action is codified at G.S. 8–57, this Court is without power to judicially modify the rule. G.S. 8–57 provides in pertinent part that "[n]othing herein shall render any spouse competent or compellable to give evidence against the other spouse in any criminal action or proceeding," with such exceptions as are thereinafter set forth. This Court has previously held that this provision of G.S. 8–57, and similar provisions of the previous versions of this statute, are not affirmative statements by the legislature that spouses are not competent as witnesses against each other in a criminal proceeding. G.S. 8–57 and its predecessors merely state that, aside from the exceptions listed therein, the common law rule pertaining to the competency of spouses to testify against each other remains unchanged and in full effect. State v. Alford, 274 N.C. 125, 161 S.E.2d 575 (1968); Rice v. Keith, 63 N.C. 319 (1869). See also State v. Suits, 296 N.C. 553, 251 S.E.2d 607 (1979). Absent a legislative declaration, this Court possesses the authority to alter judicially created common law when it deems it necessary in light of experience and reason. State v. Alford, supra; State v. Wiseman, 130 N.C. 726, 41 S.E. 884 (1902). See also Trammel v. United States, 445 U.S. 40, 100 S.Ct. 906, 63 L.Ed.2d 186 (1980); Hawkins v. United States, 358 U.S. 74, 79 S.Ct. 136, 3 L.Ed.2d 125 (1958). Consequently, we hold that this Court is empowered to change the common law rule at issue in this case, and defendant's allegations to the contrary are without merit.

At common law, the spouse of a defendant was incompetent to testify either for or against the defendant in a criminal proceeding. Trammel v. United States, supra; State v. Suits, supra; State v. Alford, supra; 1 Stansbury's North Carolina Evidence § 59 (Brandis Rev.1973). This rule disqualifying the testimony of a spouse arose from two long-abandoned medieval doctrines; first, that an accused was prohibited from testifying in his own behalf due to his interest in the action, and second, that husband and wife were considered to be one under the law, with the wife possessing no separate legal existence. Trammel v. United States, supra; Funk v. United States, 290 U.S. 371, 54 S.Ct. 212, 78 L.Ed. 369 (1933); State v. Alford, supra; 8 J. Wigmore, Evidence § 2227 (McNaughton Rev.1961 & Supp.1980). The portion of the common law rule preventing one spouse from testifying on behalf of the other in a criminal proceeding has long been abandoned by statute in this jurisdiction. G.S. 8–57; 1 Stansbury's North Carolina Evidence § 59 (Brandis Rev.1973). See also State v. Rice, 222 N.C. 634, 24 S.E.2d 483 (1943). The portion of the doctrine which prohibits one spouse from testifying against the other in a criminal proceeding remains in effect under the modern justification that the peace and harmony of the marriage relationship will be preserved and fostered when each spouse may rely on the other's disability to testify. It is thought that the spousal disqualification will encourage free and open communication between marriage partners. Trammel v. United States, supra; Hawkins v. United States, supra; State v. Alford, supra; State v. Brittain, 117 N.C. 783, 23 S.E. 433 (1895); State v. Jolly, 20 N.C. 108 (1838); 8 J. Wigmore, Evidence § 2228 (McNaughton Rev.1961 & Supp.1980).

When we consider the common law rule preventing spouses from testifying against each other as to *any* matter at issue in a criminal proceeding in light of its purpose to promote marital harmony, we find that the rule sweeps more broadly than its justification. In the case *sub judice,* defendant invoked the rule of spousal disqualification not to protect confidential marital communications, but to exclude evidence of criminal acts committed in a public place and in the presence of a third person. Under these circumstances, the rule is employed more to thwart the system of justice than to promote family peace. It is difficult to discern how defendant's marriage could be bolstered by excluding Mrs. Freeman's testimony indicating that defendant shot and killed her brother in her presence. In such a situation, the public interest in ascertaining the truth outweighs any policy to promote marital harmony. Trammel v. United States, supra; State v. Alford, supra. See also State v. Clark, 296 N.W.2d 372 (Minn.1980); 8 J. Wigmore, Evidence § 2332 (McNaughton Rev.1961 & Supp.1980). In the event that an application of a common law rule cannot achieve its aim, as in the case before us, then adherence to precedent is the only justification in support of the rule, and the courts are compelled to reexamine the common law doctrine. Trammel v. United States, supra; Francis v. Southern Pacific Co., 333 U.S. 445, 68 S.Ct. 611, 92 L.Ed. 798

(1948) (Black, J., dissenting); Funk v. United States, supra; State v. Alford, supra.

We hold that the common law rule at issue in this case must be modified to comply with its purpose. Henceforth, spouses shall be incompetent to testify against one another in a criminal proceeding only if the substance of the testimony concerns a "confidential communication" between the marriage partners made during the duration of their marriage.[1] This holding allows marriage partners to speak freely

1. The common law rule rendering spouses incompetent to testify against one another in criminal proceedings has been abrogated to some extent in almost every jurisdiction. However, the rule prohibiting testimony which concerns a confidential communication between spouses during the marriage has remained effective in some form in every jurisdiction.

Only six states provide that spouses are completely incompetent to testify against each other in a criminal proceeding: Hawaii Rev.Stat. § 621–18 (1976); Iowa Code Ann. § 622.7 (West 1950); Ohio Rev.Code Ann. § 2945.42 (Page 1980 Supp.); Pa.Stat. Ann. tit. 19, § 683 (Purdon 1964); Tex. Crim.Pro.Code Ann. § 38.11 (Vernon 1979); Wyo.Stat. § 1–12–104 (1977). Mississippi provides that spouses are incompetent to testify against each other, Miss.Code Ann. § 13–1–5 (1972), but the spousal disqualification may be waived if both partners consent. See Brewer v. State, 233 So.2d 779 (Miss.1970).

Five jurisdictions have altered the common law spousal disqualification by statute, providing for a privilege against adverse spousal testimony which is vested in the witness spouse alone, but have also provided by statute that spouses are incompetent to testify as to confidential communications made between them during the marriage: D.C.Code Encycl. § 14–306 (West 1966); Ky.Rev.Stat. § 421.210 (Cum. Supp.1978); Md.Cts. & Jud.Proc.Code Ann. §§ 9–101, 9–105, 9–106 (1980); Mass.Ann. Laws Ch. 233, § 20 (Law. Co-op 1974); Mo. Ann.Stat. § 546.260 (Vernon 1953).

Twelve jurisdictions provide by statute for a privilege against adverse spousal testimony which is vested in both spouses or in the accused spouse alone. This privilege extends to all testimony against the accused spouse and to any testimony concerning a confidential communication made between the spouses during the marriage: Colo.Rev.Stat. § 13–90–107 (1973); Idaho Code § 9–203 (Supp.1980); Mich. Comp.Laws Ann. § 600.2162 (1968); Minn. Stat.Ann. § 595.02 (West Cum.Supp.1980); Montana Code Ann. § 26–1–802 (1979); Neb.Rev.Stat. § 27–505 (1979); N.J.Stat. Ann. § 2A–84A–17 (West 1976); Or.Rev. Stat. § 44.040 (1979); Utah Code Ann. § 78–24–8 (1977); Va.Code § 19.2–271.2 (Cum.Supp.1980); Wash.Rev.Code Ann. § 5.60.060 (Cum.Supp.1981); W.Va.Code §§ 57–3–3, 57–3–4 (1966).

Five states entitle the witness-spouse alone to assert a privilege against adverse spousal testimony, with court decisions holding that these statutory provisions do not affect the common law privilege not to testify as to confidential communications within the marriage: Ala.Code § 12–21–227 (1975); Cal.Evid.Code §§ 970–973 (West 1966); Conn.Gen.Stat.Ann. § 54–84 (West Cum.Supp.1980); Ga.Code Ann. § 38–1604 (1981); La.Rev.Stat.Ann. § 15:461 (West 1967). See also Arnold v. State, 353 So.2d 524 (Ala.1977); People v. Delph, 94 Cal.App.3d 411, 156 Cal.Rptr. 422 (1979); Robinson v. State, 232 Ga. 123, 205 S.E.2d 210 (1974); State v. Bennett, 357 So.2d 1136 (La.1978). Rhode Island also provides for a privilege against adverse spousal testimony vested in the witness spouse. R.I.Gen.Laws § 12–17–10 (1970). This statute has been interpreted as an alteration of the common law privilege to prevent testimony involving confidential communications; this privilege is now vested in the witness spouse alone. State v. Angell, 405 A.2d 10 (R.I.1979).

Four states have abolished the spousal disqualification totally in criminal cases, but provide by statute that spouses are incompetent to testify as to confidential communications made during the marriage: Ill.Ann.Stat. ch. 38, § 155–1 (Smith-Hurd Cum.Supp.1980); Ind.Code Ann. §§ 34–1–14–4, 34–1–14–5 (Burns 1973); N.H.Rev.Stat.Ann. § 516:27 (1974); Vt. Stat.Ann. tit. 12, § 1605 (1973). Delaware and Tennessee have also abolished the spousal disqualification in criminal proceedings. Del.Code Ann. tit. 11, § 3502 (1979); Tenn.Code Ann. § 40–2404 (1975). These statutes have no effect on the common law rule in those states rendering spouses incompetent to testify as to confidential communications between them.

to each other in confidence without fear of being thereafter confronted with the confession in litigation. However, by confining the spousal disqualification to testimony involving "confidential communications" within the marriage, we prohibit the accused spouse from employing the common law rule solely to inhibit the administration of justice. In the words of Jeremy Bentham more than a century and a half ago, our holding prevents the accused in a criminal action from converting his home into "a den of thieves." Trammel v. United States, 445 U.S. at 51–52, 100 S.Ct. at 913, 63 L.Ed.2d at 195, *quoting from* 5 Rationale of Judicial Evidence 340 (1827).

Whether a particular segment of testimony includes a "confidential communication" within the meaning of the rule we adopt in this case is to be determined by the guidelines set forth in our previous decisions interpreting the term under G.S. 8–56, the statute preserving a privilege in civil actions not to testify as to "confidential communications" with one's spouse. In making such a determination, the question is whether the communication, whatever it contains, was induced by the marital relationship and prompted by the affection, confidence, and loyalty engendered by such relationship. Wright v. Wright, 281 N.C. 159, 188 S.E.2d 317 (1972); Hicks v. Hicks, 271 N.C. 204, 155 S.E.2d 799 (1967); Hagedorn v. Hagedorn, 211 N.C. 175, 189 S.E. 507 (1937); McCoy v. Justice, 199 N.C. 602, 155 S.E. 452 (1930); State v. Freeman, 197 N.C. 376, 148 S.E. 450 (1929); Whitford v. North State Life Ins. Co., 163 N.C. 223, 79 S.E. 501 (1913). When this definition is applied to the facts of the case *sub judice,* it is apparent that Mrs. Freeman's proposed testimony included no confidential communication which would render it incompetent under the rule established in this case. Mrs. Freeman stipulated that had she been allowed to testify, she would have stated that defendant parked his car in a public parking lot, approached her and her brother carrying a shotgun, asked if they wished to speak with him, and immediately discharged the shotgun, killing Mrs. Freeman's

Mole v. State, 396 A.2d 153 (Del.1978); Royston v. State, 450 S.W.2d 39 (Tenn.Cr. App.1969).

Nine jurisdictions have abolished the spousal disqualification in criminal proceedings, but also provide by statute that the accused spouse has a privilege to prevent the other spouse from testifying as to any confidential communication between them. Ariz.Rev.Stat.Ann. §§ 12–2231, 12–2232 (1956 & Supp.1980); Ark.Stat.Ann. § 28–1001, Rules 501 and 504 (1979); Fla. Stat.Ann. §§ 90:501, 90:504 (Harrison 1979); Kan.Stat.Ann. §§ 60–407, 60–428 (1976); Me.Rev.Stat.Ann., Maine Rules of Evidence, Rules 501, 504 (West Supp.1980); N.Y.Crim.Proc.Law § 60.10 (McKinney 1971), N.Y.Civ.Proc.Law §§ 4502, 4512 (McKinney 1963); N.D.Cent.Code, N.D.Rules of Evid., Rules 501, 504 (Supp. 1979); Okla.Stat.Ann. tit. 12, §§ 2103, 2501, 2504 (West 1980); S.D.Codified Laws Ann. §§ 19–13–1, 19–13–12 thru 19–13–15 (1979). New Mexico and South Carolina have abolished the spousal disqualification in criminal proceedings and provided by statute that the witness spouse alone may assert a privilege not to testify as to confidential communications between the spouses during the marriage: N.M.Stat.Ann. § 38–6–6 (1978); S.C.Code § 19–11–30 (1977). See also State v. Motes, 264 S.C. 317, 215 S.E.2d 190 (1975).

The United States Supreme Court held in Trammel v. United States, 445 U.S. 40, 100 S.Ct. 906, 63 L.Ed.2d 186 (1980), that in federal courts the privilege against adverse spousal testimony shall vest only in the witness spouse. This decision did not affect the independent rule establishing a privilege to prohibit testimony concerning a confidential marital communication. Blau v. United States, 340 U.S. 332, 71 S.Ct. 301, 95 L.Ed. 306 (1951).

brother. Such actions in a public place and in the presence of a third person could not have been a communication made in the confidence of the marital relationship or one which was induced by affection and loyalty in the marriage. See, e.g., Hicks v. Hicks, supra; State v. Freeman, supra. Consequently, Mrs. Freeman's testimony is competent and admissible under the rule adopted in this case.

For the reasons stated above, we find that although the trial court correctly followed the previous decisions of this Court in granting defendant's motion *in limine* to suppress the testimony of his wife, the suppression of Mrs. Freeman's testimony was error under the rule established in this case. Accordingly, the judgment of the trial court is

REVERSED.

Notes

(1) Where an incompetency, or a privilege held by an accused, against adverse spousal testimony is recognized, it is always subject to an exception for crimes against the person of the spouse. "And the statutes frequently go further and expressly except particular crimes (aside from crimes against the person or property of the spouse) such as bigamy, adultery, rape, crimes against the children of either or both, and abandonment and support proceedings." McCormick, Evidence § 66, at 162 n. 11 (3d ed. 1984). See also 2 Wigmore, Evidence § 488 (Chadbourn rev. 1979); 8 id. §§ 2239, 2240 (McNaughton rev. 1961).

(2) As for the duration of the testimonial incompetency or privilege (whether held by the accused or by the witness), it is generally held to apply only to testimony during the marriage. Therefore, unlike the communications privilege, it is terminated by divorce. See, e.g., United States v. Fisher, 518 F.2d 836, 840 (2d Cir.1975), cert. denied, 423 U.S. 1033, 96 S.Ct. 565, 46 L.Ed.2d 407 (1975). Whether it applies to testimony during marriage concerning events prior to the marriage has been controversial. Most older cases applied the privilege, even where the marriage was clearly motivated in part by a design to silence the witness, e.g., San Fratello v. United States, 340 F.2d 560, 566 (5th Cir.1965), unless the marriage was characterized as "fraudulent, spurious," United States v. Apodaca, 522 F.2d 568, 571 (10th Cir.1975). More recent versions usually contain an exception "as to matters occurring prior to the marriage." E.g., Haw.R.Evid. 505(c)(2); Or.R.Evid. 505(4)(b); United States v. Clark, 712 F.2d 299, 302 (7th Cir.1983).

SECTION 2. LAWYER-CLIENT *

IN RE GRAND JURY SUBPOENAS (ANDERSON)

United States Court of Appeals, Tenth Circuit, 1990.
906 F.2d 1485.

McKay, Circuit Judge.

This case involves an emergency appeal by several attorneys who were held in contempt and placed in jail because they refused to reveal

* See 8 Wigmore, Evidence ch. 82 (McNaughton rev. 1961); McCormick, Evidence ch. 10 (4th ed. 1992); Goode, Identity, Fees, and the Attorney-Client Privi-

the source of payment of their fees incurred during their representation of four defendants on drug charges.

I. FACTS

Beginning in approximately April of 1989 the grand jury in the Northern District of Oklahoma began investigating James Coltharp and the organization he controlled under a suspicion of connection with illegal drug activity. Mr. Coltharp allegedly employed a "crew" to assist him in his drug efforts. Relators represented four defendants, who were allegedly crew members in the Coltharp organization, on drug charges in the Eastern District of Oklahoma. The grand jury sought fee information from the relators under a suspicion that Mr. Coltharp may have paid the legal fees for his alleged crew members.

On October 5, 1989, the grand jury issued subpoenas to the relators. The relators' clients had been convicted at trial and at least two of the relators had filed appeals for their clients. Each of the relators filed motions to quash the subpoenas which were finally denied on November 21, 1989. The trial court ordered the relators to appear and testify before the grand jury on December 5, 1989.

On December 5, 1989, the relators appeared before the grand jury as the trial court had ordered. However, each relator refused to testify or to provide any of the documents requested in the subpoena. The trial court held each of the relators in contempt for their refusal to comply with the subpoenas and had them immediately incarcerated. Relators filed an emergency Motion to Stay Proceedings in this court. Later that same day we granted the stay and released each of the relators on their own recognizance.

Our issuance of the stay allowed us to hear oral argument on the appeal of this case a few days thereafter. Relators now challenge the contempt holding on several grounds. Relators claim that the fee information sought by the grand jury is subject to the attorney-client privilege, infringes on the sixth amendment rights of their clients, and should not be disclosed because the government failed to make the necessary showing of need. In addition, relators claim that the trial court's proceedings leading up to the contempt holding violated their due process rights and that the trial court improperly denied bail pending appeal. We will consider each of these arguments in turn.

* * *

III. ATTORNEY-CLIENT PRIVILEGE

It is well recognized in every circuit, including our own, that the identity of an attorney's client and the source of payment for legal fees are not normally protected by the attorney-client privilege. *United*

lege, 59 Geo.Wash.L.Rev. 307 (1991); Hazard, An Historical Perspective on the Attorney-Client Privilege, 66 Calif.L.Rev. 1061 (1978); Sedler & Simeone, The Realities of Attorney-Client Confidences, 24 Ohio St.L.J. 1 (1963).

States v. Hodgson, 492 F.2d 1175, 1177 (10th Cir.1974); *In re Grand Jury Subpoenas,* 803 F.2d 493, 496–98 (9th Cir.1986); *In re Shargel,* 742 F.2d 61, 62 (2d Cir.1984); *In re Grand Jury Investigation,* 723 F.2d 447, 451 (6th Cir.1983); 84 A.L.R.Fed. 852, 859 (1987). However, some circuit courts have created exceptions to this general rule for unique circumstances. The three major exceptions are known as the legal advice exception, the last link exception, and the confidential communication exception.

A. Legal Advice Exception

Several circuit courts have created an exception to the general rule that client identity and fee information are not protected by the attorney-client privilege where there is a strong probability that disclosure would implicate the client in the very criminal activity for which legal advice was sought. *United States v. Strahl,* 590 F.2d 10, 11–12 (1st Cir.1978), *cert. denied,* 440 U.S. 918, 99 S.Ct. 1237, 59 L.Ed.2d 468 (1979); *In re Grand Jury Investigation,* 631 F.2d 17, 19 (3d Cir.1980), *cert. denied,* 449 U.S. 1083, 101 S.Ct. 869, 66 L.Ed.2d 808 (1981), *later questioned by, United States v. Liebman,* 742 F.2d 807 (3d Cir.1984); *In re Special Grand Jury No. 81–1,* 676 F.2d 1005, 1009 (4th Cir.1982), *vacated when target became a fugitive,* 697 F.2d 112 (4th Cir.1982); *In re Grand Jury Proceedings in Matter of Fine,* 641 F.2d 199, 204 (5th Cir.1981); *In re Grand Jury Investigation No. 83–2–35,* 723 F.2d 447, 452 (6th Cir.1983), *cert. denied,* 467 U.S. 1246, 104 S.Ct. 3524, 82 L.Ed.2d 831 (1984); *United States v. Hodge & Zweig,* 548 F.2d 1347, 1353 (9th Cir.1977). Some of these holdings are now of questionable validity, although they have not been overruled. For example, the Ninth Circuit has more recently interpreted this exception to prohibit disclosure of the source of fees only when disclosure of the identity of the client would be in substance a disclosure of a confidential communication in the professional relationship between the client and the attorney. *See In re Grand Jury Subpoenas,* 803 F.2d 493, 497 (9th Cir.1986); *In re Osterhoudt,* 722 F.2d 591, 593 (9th Cir.1983).

We need not decide whether this exception will be adopted in this circuit because it does not apply to this case. In order for the legal advice exception to apply, the person seeking the legal advice must be the client of the attorney involved. In this case, the record before us contains no evidence that relators have made a claim that the person paying their fees was a client of any kind. At a minimum relators must assert that the fee was paid by a client.

Relators must also assert that the client sought legal advice about the very activity for which the fee information is sought. For example, in *Baird v. Koerner,* 279 F.2d 623 (9th Cir.1960), the Ninth Circuit refused to require an attorney to divulge the identity of his client when that client had consulted him regarding improperly paid taxes, and the attorney had forwarded an anonymous check to the Internal Revenue Service. The IRS sought the name of the client to allow further review of the questionable tax returns. Identifying this client would have implicated the client in the very activity for which the client consulted the attorney—income tax problems. *Id.*

The facts of this case dictate that we refuse to adopt the legal advice exception in this case for precisely the same reasons on which the Third Circuit relied in *In re Grand Jury Investigation,* 631 F.2d 17 (3d Cir.1980). "The fact of an attorney-client relationship between [attorney] and [client] has been freely admitted and no contention has been made that disclosure of the fee arrangement would further implicate [client] in the matter for which he consulted [attorney]. Furthermore, it has never been suggested that individuals who may have made payments on [client's] behalf were clients of [attorney]. Therefore, disclosure of the names of any third parties would not disrupt any other attorney-client relationship." *Id.* at 19.

B. Last Link Exception

Relators argue in this court, and in the district court, that this circuit should adopt the last link exception which has been adopted in at least two other circuits. The last link exception was largely formulated by the Fifth Circuit in two cases. *See In re Grand Jury Proceedings,* 680 F.2d 1026 (5th Cir.1982) ("*Pavlick* "), and *In re Grand Jury Proceedings,* 517 F.2d 666 (5th Cir.1975) ("*Jones* ").[1] Partially relying on the *Baird* case, the *Jones* court held that "information, not normally privileged, should also be protected when so much of the substance of the communications is already in the government's possession that additional disclosures would yield substantially probative links in an existing chain of inculpatory events or transactions." *Jones,* 517 F.2d at 674. This test was further refined in *Pavlick* in which the court stated that it "also recognized [in *Jones*] a limited and narrow exception to the general rule, one that obtains when the disclosure of the client's identity by his attorney would have supplied the last link in an existing chain of incriminating evidence likely to lead to the client's indictment." *Pavlick,* 680 F.2d at 1027.

Contrary to relators' suggestion in their brief, the last link exception has been explicitly rejected by at least one circuit and implicitly rejected by others. In *In re Grand Jury Investigation,* 723 F.2d 447 (6th Cir.1983), the Sixth Circuit explicitly rejected the last link exception as formulated by the Fifth Circuit.

> Upon careful consideration this Court concludes that, although language exists in *Baird* to support viability of *Pavlick*'s "last link" exception, the exception is simply not grounded upon the preservation

1. The test has also been adopted by the Eleventh Circuit. *See In re Grand Jury Proceedings,* 689 F.2d 1351 (11th Cir.1982). However, the Eleventh Circuit has recently interpreted the last link exception to apply only in cases where the disclosure of the client's identity would expose other privileged communications, such as motive or strategy, and when the incriminating nature of privileged communications has created in the client a reasonable expectation that the information would be kept confidential. *In re Grand Jury Proceedings,* 896 F.2d 1267 (11th Cir.1990). This very recent decision is broadly supportive of the position we adopt on the last link exception.

> of confidential *communications* and hence not justifiable to support the attorney-client privilege. Although the last link exception may promote concepts of fundamental fairness against self-incrimination, these concepts are not proper considerations to invoke the attorney-client privilege. Rather, the focus of the inquiry is whether disclosure of the identity would adversely implicate the confidentiality of communications. Accordingly, this Court rejects the last link exception as articulated in *Pavlick.*

Id. at 453–54 (footnote omitted).

The last link exception has also been implicitly rejected in the Second, Third, and Ninth Circuits. In *In re Shargel,* 742 F.2d 61 (2d Cir.1984), the court found that the purpose of the attorney-client privilege was to enable attorneys to offer informed legal advice by encouraging full disclosure by clients. The court went on to conclude that attorney disclosure of the source of fees did not impair the attorney's ability to render informed legal advice.

> It is, of course, true that payment of another person's legal fees may imply facts about a prior or present relationship with that person. However, an attorney's ability to give informed legal advice is not impaired by a rule allowing disclosure of such payments * * *. [T]he view of the privilege we adopt thus denies protection to evidence indicating payment of one person's legal fees by another.

Id. at 64–65.

The Third Circuit refused to apply the last link exception because the exception went further in sustaining the attorney-client privilege than the court had been willing to accept in the past. *United States v. Liebman,* 742 F.2d 807, 810 n. 2 (3d Cir.1984). The court did not rely on the last link exception because it found that there had been a protected communication. *Id.*

The Ninth Circuit implicitly rejected the exception when it held that "[f]ee arrangements usually fall outside the scope of the privilege simply because such information ordinarily reveals no confidential professional communication between attorney and client, and not because such information may not be incriminating." *In re Osterhoudt,* 722 F.2d 591, 593 (9th Cir.1983).

Thus, we recognize a split among the circuits over the adoption of the last link exception. This circuit has not spoken directly to this issue, contrary to the claim by amicus curiae, American Civil Liberties Union, that we adopted the last link exception in *United States v. Hodgson,* 492 F.2d 1175 (10th Cir.1974). In *Hodgson* we merely distinguished the facts of that case from the facts of another case in which the response to a summons would have revealed the identity of an unknown client. *Id.* at 1177. Merely drawing that distinction in that case cannot be construed to explicitly or implicitly adopt the last link exception.

The government argues in its brief that this circuit should reject the last link exception in this case because the clients of relators are not targets of the subpoenas. There has been some confusion throughout these proceedings whether the clients of relators are or are not targets of the grand jury investigation. We think the argument is merely a matter of semantics. The United States Attorney admitted during oral argument that relators' clients could be liable, at least for money laundering, if the information revealed to the grand jury about attorney's fees incriminated the clients. In fact, the government explained that it refused to give immunity to relators' clients precisely because it wanted to preserve the option of charging them with money laundering or other crimes. To suggest that relators' clients are not targets of the grand jury investigation in one breath, while explaining that information revealed to the grand jury may be used against them in the next, approaches intellectual dishonesty. Relators' clients are clearly "targets" of the grand jury investigation if information gathered in that investigation could be used to charge the clients with further crimes. Thus, we decline to follow the government's suggestion that we reject the last link test in this case based only on the fact that the relators' clients are not targets.

The last link exception is a very narrow one which is carefully fact based. We need not ultimately decide whether even that narrow exception should apply in this circuit because we are of the view that the facts of this case take it outside the standards of whatever is left of *Jones,* which is the principle precedential base for the exception. Unlike our case, *Jones* involved payment of fees for one client by a person who was also a client of the same attorney. This is an important distinction. There is at least a stronger arguable basis on which to invoke the attorney-client privilege to protect the identity of an actual client than there is to protect the identity of a third person who may implicate the attorney's actual client in some wrongdoing.

In addition, the most recent Fifth Circuit case clarifying the exception, *Pavlick,* explained the unique fact situation which gave rise to the test and refused to apply it in a case in which the promise of legal services was made as a fringe benefit in recruiting criminal conspirators. The *Pavlick* court explained the *Jones* decision as follows:

> [O]ur decision rested on the peculiar facts of that case and "should not be taken as any indication of how we would decide a similar question if the inculpatory value of sought-after testimony were less obvious or largely attenuated." Among those "peculiar facts" was that the six attorneys drawn before the grand jury in *Jones* represented a generous portion of the criminal law bar of the lower Rio Grande Valley area, and the project was a rather broad attempt to canvass that portion for information detrimental to certain of its clients * * *.

Pavlick, 680 F.2d at 1027 (citation omitted).[2] Thus, even the Fifth Circuit has limited the last link exception to the facts of *Jones* which

2. The Eleventh Circuit has also recently clarified the last link exception, limiting its application to cases in which the disclosure of the client's identity would result in

are very different from the facts of this case. *Jones* involved a case in which a large part of the criminal bar in a certain area was subpoenaed to testify before the grand jury. This was merely a broad search for incriminating evidence concerning fee information. In addition, the attorneys in *Jones* claimed that the fees were paid by an individual which they were currently representing professionally. In fact, the *Jones* court based its decision on the fact that the attorneys were called "for the purpose of incriminating their undisclosed clients." *Jones,* 517 F.2d at 672.

The facts of the present case are different from *Jones* in three important respects. First, a large portion of the criminal bar in a specific area was not subpoenaed and the information sought was specific and aimed at a specified third party. Second, relators do not claim that their clients' fees were paid by another of their clients. Finally, relators seek to assert the privilege for their known clients whose fees were paid. Relators have never claimed that they were asserting the privilege to protect the undisclosed source of the fees, as in the *Jones* case. Given these factual differences, we do not believe the Fifth Circuit would apply the last link exception in this case. We too reject its application on these facts.

We wish to clarify, however, that we do not reject what we consider to be the underlying principle supporting the last link exception. We believe that the Fifth Circuit's articulation of the "last link" exception fails adequately to discipline the thinking of lawyers and courts on this issue. The last link exception ultimately stems from *Baird v. Koerner,* 279 F.2d 623 (9th Cir.1960), even in the Fifth Circuit. Relying on *Baird,* several circuit courts have backed away from both the legal advice and last link exceptions. These courts have carefully applied the facts and holding of *Baird* to create what is known as the confidential communication exception. The confidential communication exception holds that an exception to the general rule that a client's identity is not privileged exists in the situation where the disclosure of the client's identity would be tantamount to disclosing an otherwise protected confidential communication. *See United States v. Strahl,* 590 F.2d 10, 11–12 (1st Cir.1978), *cert. denied,* 440 U.S. 918, 99 S.Ct. 1237, 59 L.Ed.2d 468 (1979); *In re Shargel,* 742 F.2d 61, 62–63 (2d Cir.1984); *United States v. Liebman,* 742 F.2d 807, 809 (3d Cir.1984); *NLRB v. Harvey,* 349 F.2d 900, 905 (4th Cir.1965); *In re Grand Jury Investigation No. 83–2–35,* 723 F.2d 447, 452–54 (6th Cir.1983), *cert. denied,* 467 U.S. 1246, 104 S.Ct. 3524, 82 L.Ed.2d 831 (1984); *In re Witnesses Before the Special Mar. 1980 Grand Jury,* 729 F.2d 489, 492–94 (7th Cir.1984); *In re Osterhoudt,* 722 F.2d 591, 593–94 (9th Cir.1983); *In re Grand Jury Proceedings,* 896 F.2d 1267, 1271–73 (11th Cir.1990). We believe that the confidential communication exception represents a more disciplined

disclosure of other privileged communications such as motive or strategy. *In re Grand Jury Proceedings,* 896 F.2d 1267 (11th Cir.1990). This holding is consistent with our resolution of this case.

interpretation of *Baird* than does the Fifth Circuit's last link exception. Thus, we reject the last link exception to the extent it has deviated from the holding of *Baird.*

We agree that a disciplined exception to the attorney-client privilege must mirror the facts and analysis of *Baird.* In *Baird* the mere identification of the client would have disclosed the confidential communication from the client that he had committed the crime for which he sought advice. The client in *Baird* sought advice strictly concerning the case then under investigation. We hold that in order to invoke the attorney-client privilege under similar facts in this Circuit, the advice sought must have been *Baird*-like. In other words, the advice sought must have concerned the case then under investigation and disclosure of the client's identity would now be, in substance, the disclosure of a confidential communication by the client, such as establishing the identity of the client as the perpetrator of the alleged crime at issue. This case does not involve any claim that the source of the fees was a client who sought advice on any subject. Nor is there any claim that advice was given concerning the case now under investigation. Given these facts, disclosure of the source of the fees would not disclose any confidential communication from client to attorney.

The purpose behind the attorney-client privilege is to preserve *confidential communications* between attorney and client. *In re Grand Jury Investigation,* 723 F.2d 447, 453–54 (6th Cir.1983); *In re Osterhoudt,* 722 F.2d 591, 593 (9th Cir.1983); *In re Shargel,* 742 F.2d 61, 64–65 (2d Cir.1984). Information regarding the fee arrangement is not normally part of the professional consultation and therefore it is not privileged even if it would incriminate the client in wrongdoing. *In re Osterhoudt,* 722 F.2d at 593. In other words, while payment of a fee to an attorney is necessary to obtain legal advice, disclosure of the fee arrangement does not inhibit the normal communications necessary for the attorney to act effectively in representing the client. *In re Grand Jury Subpoena Served Upon Doe,* 781 F.2d 238, 247–48 (2d Cir.1985). Absent one of those rare circumstances in which the payment of the fee itself is unlawful or where an actual client paid the fee and sought advice concerning the actual case under investigation as in *Baird,* we hold that fee arrangements are not protected by the attorney-client privilege.

In this case the subpoenas requested seven pieces of information from the relators. The subpoenas asked for the identity of the source of the fees, the amount of the fees, the manner of payment, the date of payment, the name of any others partially responsible for payment of the fee, and whether any part of the fee came from the client or his family.[3] The subpoena also requested all documents relating to the payment or acceptance of the fees, including checks, cashier's checks, deposit slips, receipts, wire transfers, fee contracts, and IRS form

3. There is no attorney-client privilege between an attorney and a member of the client's family. Thus, the attorney-client privilege does not prohibit the government from asking if a family member paid part of the client's fee.

8300's. We hold that none of these requests is protected by the attorney-client privilege and thus must be disclosed, with one exception.

We believe that disclosing the actual fee contracts has the potential for revealing confidential information along with unprotected fee information. Thus, we remand this issue to the district court for its determination of whether, in light of this opinion, the fee contracts contain any confidential communications that are protected by the attorney-client privilege. *See In re Witnesses Before Special March 1980 Grand Jury,* 729 F.2d 489, 495 (7th Cir.1984) (remanding to district court for determination of whether attorney-client privilege protected disclosure of billing sheets or time sheets); *In re Grand Jury Witnesses,* 695 F.2d 359, 362–63 (9th Cir.1982) ("*Salas*") (remanding to district court for determination of whether fee contract contained communications protected by attorney-client privilege). The decision whether to review the fee contracts *in camera* is within the discretion of the trial court. *See In re Grand Jury Proceedings,* 723 F.2d 1461, 1467 (10th Cir.1983), *cert. denied,* 469 U.S. 819, 105 S.Ct. 90, 83 L.Ed.2d 37 (1984) ("*Vargas*"). However, we believe that *in camera* review is appropriate in this case. *See In re Slaughter,* 694 F.2d 1258, 1260 n. 2 (11th Cir.1982) (referring to *in camera* review of possibly privileged documents in context of request for information relating to attorneys' fees). Nevertheless, the subpoena, with the exception noted, does not request privileged information.

* * *

VIII. Conclusion

We conclude that the attorney fee information in this case (with the exception of actual fee contracts) is not subject to the attorney-client privilege, and its disclosure does not violate relators' clients' rights to counsel. We remand to the district court the issue of whether the fee contracts contain protected information. We hold that the government is under no obligation to make a preliminary showing of need or lack of other source in order to subpoena attorney fee information. We also hold that the procedures used in this case did not violate due process and that the sentence imposed was not an abuse of discretion.

The decision of the district court is AFFIRMED except to the extent that it requires the disclosure of the fee contracts themselves. The fee contracts issue is REMANDED to the district court.

UNITED STATES v. KENDRICK, 331 F.2d 110, 111, 113–14 (4th Cir.1964). "This is an appeal from the District Court's decision denying, after hearing, the petitioner's motion under 28 U.S.C.A. § 2255 to vacate an illegal sentence on the grounds that the petitioner was incompetent to stand trial. * * *

* * *

"We do not agree with the petitioner that the testimony of his trial counsel should have been excluded at the post-conviction hearing on the basis of the attorney-client privilege.

"We need not now consider whether the assertion that he was incapable of effective communication and cooperation with trial counsel is a waiver of the attorney-client privilege on the ground that the petitioner has flung open the curtain of secrecy which otherwise would conceal his actual communications. Nor need we enter the controversy as to whether such an assertion is always so necessarily an implicit attack upon the competence of trial counsel as to amount to a waiver of the privilege to the extent necessary to enable trial counsel to defend himself and his reputation. See Gunther v. United States, 97 U.S.App. D.C. 254, 230 F.2d 222 (1956); cf. United States v. Wiggins, 184 F.Supp. 673 (D.C.1960); United States v. Bostic, 206 F.Supp. 855 (D.C.1962). We do not here consider the question of waiver on either ground, for the attorney's testimony was well within an established exception to the privilege.

"Communications made in confidence by a client to his attorney are protected by the attorney-client privilege. It is the substance of the communications which is protected, however, not the fact that there have been communications. Excluded from the privilege, also, are physical characteristics of the client, such as his complexion, his demeanor, his bearing, his sobriety and his dress. Such things are observable by anyone who talked with the client, and there is nothing, in the usual case, to suggest that the client intends his attorney's observations of such matters to be confidential.[2] In short, the privilege protects only the client's confidences, not things which, at the time, are not intended to be held in the breast of the lawyer, even though the attorney-client relation provided the occasion for the lawyer's observation of them. See generally VIII Wigmore, Evidence (McNaughton Revision) § 2306.

"Here the attorney testified to just such nonconfidential matters. Petitioner, the attorney testified, was responsive, readily supplied the attorney with his version of the facts and the names of other people involved, was logical in his conversation and his reasoning, and appeared to know and understand everything that went on before and during the trial. No mention was made of the substance of any communication by client to attorney; the witness testified only about his client's cooperativeness and awareness.

"All of the matters to which the attorney testified are objectively observable particularizations of the client's demeanor and attitude. Made at a time when neither client nor lawyer manifested any reason to suppose they were confidential, they were not within the privilege.

2. Particular circumstances may alter the rule. If the client reveals to the attorney a physical defect, usually concealed by clothing, which may be relevant to the attorney's representation of him, it well may be a confidential and protected communication.

Certainly, the client was then making no secret of his capacity, or want of capacity to communicate with his attorney and to cooperate in his defense.

"It is suggested that, in these circumstances, adequate cross-examination of attorney-witness might require the petitioner to inquire into the substance of his communications. That is speculative, however. Effective cross-examination need not go so far. And, if difficulty inheres in the situation, it is no more than if the question were the client's sobriety or inebriety at the time of an otherwise unrelated consultation. If the attorney who testifies his client's hair was blonde when she consulted him had confused her with another client, inquiry as to the substance of the communication might be the only effective means of revealing his confusion, but his testimony is not drawn within the privilege on that account."

IN RE GRAND JURY SUBPOENA (BIERMAN), 788 F.2d 1511 (11th Cir.1986). "The district court denied the government's motion to compel Bierman to answer the last grand jury question on the ground that the information sought is privileged.

* * *

"In United States v. Clemons, 676 F.2d 124, 125 (5th Cir. Unit B 1982), the court held that '[a]n attorney's message to his client concerning the date of trial is not a privileged communication.' The government argues that under *Clemons,* Bierman must disclose whether he communicated the surrender date to the client. *Clemons* does not, however, apply to this case.

"United States v. Freeman, 519 F.2d 67, 68 (9th Cir.1975) is not to the contrary. The evidence sought to be elicited from the defendant's attorney in *Freeman* was not protected under the attorney-client privilege because '[i]t simply related to whether [the attorney] had advised his client of the court's order to appear.' The challenged question here asks more than whether Bierman gave the client notice of the surrender date. The question asked: What did you say to or tell your client about the notice to surrender? It takes only a little imagination to recognize the numerous possible answers that would involve legal advice of the most sensitive nature. Communications between an attorney and his client made for the purpose of securing legal advice are protected under the attorney-client privilege. In Re Grand Jury Proceedings (Twist), 689 F.2d 1351, 1352 (11th Cir.1982).

"If the government wanted to know only whether Bierman had advised his client of the surrender date, it should have asked him that directly and precisely. We note that after the district court's ruling, the government did not call Bierman before the grand jury to answer the narrower question of whether he informed the client of the surrender date. We agree with the district court: The information sought is privileged."

CLUTCHETTE v. RUSHEN, 770 F.2d 1469, 1470–71 (9th Cir.1985), cert. denied, 475 U.S. 1088, 106 S.Ct. 1474, 89 L.Ed.2d 729 (1986). "The appellant, John Wesley Clutchette, was convicted in state court of first degree murder on the basis of evidence that his wife obtained and then turned in to the police while she worked as an investigator for Clutchette's defense counsel. Clutchette appeals from the denial of his habeas corpus petition. He asserts that he was deprived of the effective assistance of counsel guaranteed by the Sixth and Fourteenth Amendments. * * * We affirm.

* * *

"* * * Clutchette's wife contacted the Oakland and Sacramento Police Departments. She informed the police that she had served as an investigator for her husband's defense counsel. In the course of her service, she continued, the attorney had sent her to retrieve certain receipts from an individual in Los Angeles. She believed that these receipts would serve as evidence in the case against her husband. After this conversation, Mrs. Clutchette turned the receipts over to the police.

"The receipts were from an automobile upholstery shop where Clutchette had brought his car for reupholstering. The police visited the store and picked up leather seat covers which the store owner identified as those removed from Clutchette's 1976 Lincoln. With the help of a forensic serologist, the police determined that the seat covers bore tiny but tell-tale bloodstains matching the victim's blood type. * * *

"The receipts provided the cornerstone of the prosecution's case against Clutchette. Although the trial judge, relying on the attorney-client privilege, suppressed all communications about the case which Mrs. Clutchette disclosed to the police, he allowed the introduction of the receipts themselves at trial. Following a jury trial, Clutchette was convicted as charged.

* * *

"We recognize that the introduction of evidence obtained either directly or indirectly through interference with the attorney-client relationship is a paradigm example of the kind of prejudice that warrants finding a denial of the right to counsel. See, e.g., Irwin, 612 F.2d at 1186–87; see also United States v. Shapiro, 669 F.2d 593, 598 (9th Cir.1982); United States v. Bagley, 641 F.2d 1235, 1238–39 (9th Cir.), cert. denied, 454 U.S. 942, 102 S.Ct. 480, 70 L.Ed.2d 251 (1981). That is not this case, however. Clutchette's defense attorney faced a separate duty under state law to surrender the receipts to the prosecution.

"It is true, presumably, that Clutchette told his attorney where to find the receipts and that the attorney relayed that communication to Mrs. Clutchette. No doubt these communications were privileged. The receipts themselves, however, were not, once the defense attorney removed them from their original location. California law requires that a defense attorney must, after a reasonable time, turn evidence taken from its original resting place over to the prosecution. See People v. Lee, 3 Cal.App.3d 514, 526, 83 Cal.Rptr. 715, 722 (1970); see also People v. Meredith, 29 Cal.3d 682, 631 P.2d 46, 175 Cal.Rptr. 612 (1981) (when defense counsel removes or alters evidence discovered through a privileged communication, the attorney-client privilege does not bar revelation of the evidence's original location or condition). Had the attorney left the receipts in their original location, he could have claimed the privilege and refused to disclose Clutchette's communication to the authorities. Instead, he dispatched Mrs. Clutchette, his agent, to retrieve them. Once the receipts were in his constructive possession, Clutchette's attorney was obligated to give them to the state. The state's acquisition of the receipts directly from Mrs. Clutchette therefore did not prejudice the defense."

DIKE v. DIKE

Supreme Court of Washington, 1968.
75 Wash.2d 1, 448 P.2d 490.

NEILL, JUDGE.

This is an appeal from a conviction of an attorney for contempt committed in the presence of the court.

Appellant was the attorney for Robbin Angela Dike, defendant in a divorce action. On November 17, 1967, the court entered an order in the divorce action placing temporary custody of the parties' minor child with a Mr. and Mrs. McCutchin, subject to visitation rights by both parents and to the defendant mother's right of temporary custody on weekends. Appellant, as attorney for defendant, had full knowledge of the provisions of the order.

On November 29, 1967, Mrs. Dike removed the minor child from the McCutchin home and failed to return her. A motion to find defendant in contempt for violation of the custody order was served on appellant on December 8, 1967. Neither defendant nor appellant appeared at the December 15th hearing on the motion for contempt. The court thereupon directed plaintiff's counsel to prepare an order addressed to appellant requiring him to appear before the court at 11:30 a.m. on December 18, 1967, and to produce defendant or to show cause why he should not produce her. This order was served on appellant at 9:30 a.m., December 18th.

Appellant appeared as directed. He filed a special appearance, motion to quash, and motion and affidavit of prejudice for transfer to a different department of the court. All were summarily denied. He refused to answer any questions relative to his client's whereabouts. He contended that the questions were improper because his information was confidential and that disclosing this information would be in violation of the canons of professional ethics.

The court thereupon had a uniformed deputy sheriff come to the courtroom, remove appellant, handcuffed, to the county jail where he was booked, fingerprinted and "mugged". Subsequently, appellant was released on $5,000 cash bail. It was not until January 8, 1968, that, pursuant to a motion by appellant, an order in compliance with RCW 7.20.030 [1] was entered. An order was entered January 12, 1968, purging appellant of the contempt and exonerating his bond. This order recites that defendant had appeared at the trial of the divorce action on January 2d.[2]

Appellant contends that the court erred in denying his motion to transfer the action to a different department in the superior court and in overruling his special appearance and motion to quash the show cause order on the basis of lack of jurisdiction. Appellant's contention that the matter should have been transferred to another department is without merit. The trial court had properly assumed continuing jurisdiction over the minor child and had awarded temporary custody to someone other than the parents, pending a final determination of the divorce action. The primary purpose of the hearing at which appellant was ordered to appear was to investigate into the alleged violation of the court's temporary custody order and to determine the whereabouts of the child. The judge who acted in the temporary order was familiar with the facts of the case including the mother's wrongful actions. He, therefore, was the proper judge to consider appellant's refusal to disclose the whereabouts of the mother and child.

* * *

Appellant assigns error to several of the findings made by the court, but our reading of the record convinces us that the findings are supported by the evidence with one exception. The court found that "Robbin Angela Dike intermittently observed and disregarded said order until November 29, 1967 when Mrs. Dike, with the knowledge of John Simmons, her Attorney, forcibly removed the minor from the McCutchin's custody * * *." We see no support for the finding that the actions of Mrs. Dike were performed with the knowledge of her attorney. However, even striking such finding will not alter the basic issue since the wrongful act of Mrs. Dike was continuing and it is obvious that appellant became aware of her misdeed during its continuance.

1. "When a contempt is committed in the immediate view and presence of the court or officer, it may be punished summarily, for which an order must be made reciting the facts as occurring in such immediate view and presence, determining that the person proceeded against is thereby guilty of contempt, and that he be punished as therein prescribed." RCW 7.20.030.

2. It is of passing interest that the divorce trial resulted in the defendant's obtaining custody of the child.

* * *

Before turning to a discussion of the applicability of the attorney-client privilege, we should touch upon one other preliminary issue. The canons of professional ethics (CPE 1) provide in part that

> It is the duty of the lawyer to maintain towards the Courts a respectful attitude, not for the sake of the temporary incumbent of the judicial office, but for the maintenance of its supreme importance. Judges, not being wholly free to defend themselves, are peculiarly entitled to receive the support of the Bar against unjust criticism and clamor.

The attorney's duty flowing from CPE 1 has been explained as follows (Drinker, [LEGAL ETHICS (1953)] at 69):

> Although it is both the right and duty of a lawyer to protest vigorously rulings on evidence or procedure or statements in the judge's charge which he deems erroneous, nevertheless, when the ruling has been finally made, the lawyer must, for the time being, accept it and invoke his remedy by appeal to the higher court.
>
> * * *

On the basis of this principle, respondent contends that appellant's refusal to disclose the whereabouts of his client constituted contempt irrespective of whether or not the court erred in ruling that the information sought was not privileged.

In Robertson v. Commonwealth of Virginia, 181 Va. 520, 536, 25 S.E.2d 352, 358, 146 A.L.R. 966 (1943), an attorney was ordered by the trial court to produce certain evidence. The attorney refused on the ground that the evidence was within the attorney-client privilege protecting confidential communications. The trial court held the attorney in contempt and the attorney appealed. The Virginia court stated:

> A judgment, decree or order entered by a court which lacks jurisdiction of the parties or of the subject matter, or which lacks the inherent power to make or enter the particular order involved, is void. (Citing authority.)
>
> Where a court has jurisdiction of the parties and of the subject matter, and has the power to make the order or rulings complained of, but the latter is based upon a mistaken view of the law or upon the erroneous application of legal principles, it is erroneous. (Citing case.)
>
> It is, of course, well settled that disobedience of, or resistance to a void order, judgment, or decree is not contempt. (Citing authority.) This is so because a void order, judgment, or decree is a nullity and may be attacked collaterally.
>
> But there is a vast difference between a judgment which is void and one which is merely erroneous. In 31 Am.Jur., Judgments, § 401, p. 66, it is said: "* * * a void judgment should be clearly distinguished from one which is merely erroneous or voidable. There are many rights belonging to litigants—rights which a court may not properly deny, and yet if denied, they do not render the judgment void. Indeed,

it is a general principle that where a court has jurisdiction over the person and the subject matter, no error in the exercise of such jurisdiction can make the judgment void, and that a judgment rendered by a court of competent jurisdiction is not void merely because there are irregularities or errors of law in connection therewith. This is true even if there is a fundamental error of law appearing upon the face of the record. Such a judgment is, under proper circumstances, voidable, but until avoided is regarded as valid."

* * *

The rule that an order directing a witness to answer questions or to produce documentary evidence in his possession, although erroneously made or entered, until reversed, must be obeyed, is subject to these exceptions:

(1) In view of the constitutional provisions, both State and Federal, that no one shall be compelled to furnish evidence against himself, a witness can not be punished for contempt for refusing to answer questions when such answers would incriminate him. (Citing cases.)

(2) A witness can not be compelled to divulge privileged matters which have been given to him in confidence. (Citing authority.)

Appellant seeks to come within this second exception.

We have quoted extensively from *Robertson,* supra, because it succinctly sets forth the principles here involved. The court in *Rovertson* went on to hold that the trial court correctly ruled that the information sought was not a privileged communication and therefore affirmed the judgment of contempt.[3]

In State ex rel. Sowers v. Olwell, 64 Wash.2d 828, 833, 394 P.2d 681, 684 (1964), we followed the general principles set forth in *Robertson,* stating:

On the basis of the attorney-client privilege, the subpoena duces tecum issued by the coroner is defective on its face because it requires the attorney to give testimony concerning information received by him from his client in the course of their conferences. The subpoena names the client and requires his attorney to produce, in an open hearing, physical evidence allegedly received from the client. This is tantamount to requiring the attorney to testify against the client without the latter's consent. RCW 36.24.080 makes testifying in a coroner's inquest similar to testifying in a superior court, and, therefore, the attorney-client privilege should be equally applicable to witnesses at a coroner's inquest. We, therefore, hold that appellant's refusal to testify at the inquest for the first reason stated by him was not contemptuous.

* * *

Because the subpoena duces tecum in this case is invalid, since it required the attorney to testify without the client's consent regarding

3. See Ex parte Enzor, 270 Ala. 254, 117 So.2d 361 (1960), where attorney's contempt conviction was reversed on basis that the information the attorney refused to give the court was privileged.

matters arising out of the attorney-client relationship, the order of the trial court finding appellant to be in contempt and punishing him therefor is hereby reversed with directions to dismiss this proceeding.

Therefore, if we hold that the whereabouts of appellant's client was protected by the attorney-client privilege, then appellant's refusal to disclose the information to the court did not constitute contempt and we must reverse the trial court's judgment.

* * *

The attorney-client privilege, as defined in Canon 37, is not absolute; but rather is subject to recognized exceptions. Drinker, supra, p. 133.

The exceptions which have arisen are the result of a balancing process in which the courts have had to weigh the benefits of the privilege against the public interest in the criminal investigation process as discussed in *Sowers,* supra.

As the privilege may result in the exclusion of evidence which is otherwise relevant and material, contrary to the philosophy that justice can be achieved only with the fullest disclosure of the facts, the privilege cannot be treated as absolute; but rather, must be strictly limited to the purpose for which it exists. With these general guidelines in mind, we turn to the specific issue which we must decide—namely, whether the whereabouts of appellant's client was privileged information.

Although we have not had occasion to consider this question before, it appears that the general rule is as stated in Ex parte Schneider, 294 S.W. 736, at 738 (Mo.App.1927):

> [A]n address, given by a client to an attorney while consulting him in a professional capacity on a business matter, for the purpose of enabling the attorney to communicate with the client in respect thereto, is a privileged communication. (Citing authority.) If the client's residence has been concealed (as here), or if the client is in hiding for some reason or other, and the attorney knows his address only because the client has communicated it to him confidentially as his attorney for the purpose of being advised by him, and has not communicated it to the rest of the world, then the client's address is a matter of professional confidence, which the attorney may not be required to disclose. (Citing authority.)

* * *

All of the factors which have been held to be necessary prerequisites to compelling an attorney to disclose the address of his client are present in the case at bar: appellant has appeared in the action in which the address is sought; appellant's client is a party to that action and has sought the use of the courts; the action was still pending and had not gone to judgment; the attorney-client relationship still existed; the address was not sought for the purpose of pursuing the client in subsequent actions; and the information is necessary not only to protect the rights of a party adverse to the client, but also the interests of an innocent third party—the minor child. Therefore, in the instant case the address of appellant's client was not privileged information. * * *

The court is faced with the task of balancing society's interest in the free and open flow of communication between attorney and client, which the privilege promotes, against society's interest in the administration of justice by our courts on the basis of a full disclosure of the facts and with the affirmative assistance of attorneys, which the privilege discourages. On the basis of the reasoning of the authorities above discussed, we hold that under the facts hereof, appellant was not privileged to withhold his client's whereabouts from the court. The necessity for unhindered communication between attorney and client is outweighed, not so much by society's interest in having the truth disclosed as to crimes already completed, but rather by society's interest in protecting the present and future victims of the client. In other words, although we will not discard the privilege when the sole purpose in doing so is merely to punish the client for a wrong committed in the past, nevertheless we will not allow the shield of silence constructed by the privilege to aid the client in continuing his wrongdoing at the expense of other members of society.

* * *

In reaching this conclusion, we recognize that we may be imposing a Draconian rule on attorneys with respect to the attorney-client privilege. Whenever a trial court orders an attorney to disclose information which the attorney conscientiously believes to be within the protection of the privilege, the attorney has two alternatives: (1) to obey the court and disclose the information; or (2) to disobey the court and appeal the resulting contempt citation to a higher court. If the attorney chooses the first alternative when, in fact, the desired information is privileged, there is authority for the proposition that the attorney has acted improperly, if not unethically. As stated in a concurring opinion in People v. Kor, 129 Cal.App.2d 436, 447, 277 P.2d 94, 101 (1954):

> Here the attorney was compelled to testify against his client under threat of punishment for contempt. Such procedure would have been justified only in case the defendant with knowledge of his rights had waived the privilege in open court or by his statements and conduct had furnished explicit and convincing evidence that he did not understand, desire or expect that his statements to his attorney would be kept in confidence. *Defendant's attorney should have chosen to go to jail and take his chances of release by a higher court.* (Italics ours.)

On the other hand, if the attorney follows his conscience and chooses the second alternative, and *if* this court agrees that the desired information was privileged, then the contempt citation is dismissed and the attorney vindicated. But in that second "if" lies the attorney's dilemma, as the contempt citation stands if this court holds with the lower court. Such a procedure might be justified if the application of the attorney-client privilege to any set of facts were clear and definite; but certainly not when, as here, the application of the privilege is rather obscure.

However, we do not believe it is necessary to leave appellant in this position. In State v. Caffrey, 70 Wash.2d 120, 422 P.2d 307 (1966), we recognized that punishment for contempt is within the discretion of the court. We follow our usual rule regarding review of discretionary matters and in so doing are impressed with the view stated by the court in Appeal of the United States Sec. & Exch. Com'n, 226 F.2d 501, 520 (6th Cir.1955):

> An additional independent basis of our decision is that, even if appellant Timbers had been in error in his interpretation of the law and the binding effect of the Commission's rules and directives upon which he based his declination to produce the information demanded, the district judge abused his discretion in committing the attorney to imprisonment for contempt in the circumstances of the case. As was stated recently [February 11, 1955], in relation to an attorney's status "when standing upon his rights" not to divulge the contents of papers claimed to be privileged: "It is difficult to imagine the occurrence of anything beyond *pro forma* detention while the necessary steps are taken to get an appellate review." Chapman v. Goodman, 9 Cir., 219 F.2d 802, 807.
>
> In our view, the foregoing recital of the judge's own words and actions demonstrates that he abused all justifiable discretion. An attorney is entitled to consideration of a claimed privilege not to disclose information which he honestly regards as confidential and should not stand in danger of imprisonment for asserting respectfully what he considers to be lawful rights. If the attorney's position, in the opinion of the trial court, is wrong to the point of contempt, he should be so adjudged; but substantial justice would demand that he be given the benefit of counsel and an opportunity for review by an appellate court before being deprived of his liberty with the resultant ignominy.

Accordingly, both the oral order and the written order adjudging and committing appellant for contempt of court are vacated and set aside. It is directed that appellant be completely absolved from any punishment for his refusal to answer the court's inquiry.

FINLEY, C.J., HUNTER and HAMILTON, JJ., and LANGENBACH, J. pro tem., concur.

CONSOLIDATION COAL CO. v. BUCYRUS–ERIE CO.

Supreme Court of Illinois, 1982.
89 Ill.App.2d 103, 59 Ill.Dec. 666, 432 N.E.2d 250.

UNDERWOOD, JUSTICE:

Plaintiff, Consolidation Coal Company (Consolidation), brought this action in the circuit court of Cook County on January 18, 1977, to recover damages allegedly sustained on August 7, 1973, when its wheel excavator collapsed at its Pinckneyville, Illinois, coal mine. The excavator was designed, manufactured and repaired for Consolidation by defendant, Bucyrus–Erie (B–E), a Delaware corporation, licensed to do business in Illinois with its principal place of business and corporate headquarters in Wisconsin. Its attorneys are licensed to practice law in Illinois and Wisconsin. During the course of pretrial discovery, B–E refused to comply with the trial court's orders, and its attorney was held in contempt of court and fined $50. The appellate court affirmed the discovery rulings with some modification (93 Ill.App.3d 35, 48 Ill.Dec. 568, 416 N.E.2d 1090), and we allowed B–E's petition for leave to appeal to consider the scope of the attorney-client and work-product privileges in Illinois.

Consolidation commenced discovery in May of 1977 by filing a production request for all of B–E's documents relating to the design, manufacture, erection, and repair of the wheel excavator and all documents relating to the investigation of the excavator's collapse or otherwise relating to the facts in controversy, including memoranda, notes, correspondence, reports, statements, interviews, photographs, slides, films, recordings, tapes, micrographs, and metallurgical test data. B–E produced thousands of documents for inspection, but, invoking the attorney-client and work-product privileges, refused to produce a "metallurgical report" prepared by its employee, Richard Sailors, a report prepared by Tom Learmont, its director of engineering and mining machinery, and memoranda and notes of interviews with various B–E employees prepared by its in-house counsel. Following several hearings pursuant to Consolidation's motion to compel compliance, extensive briefings by the parties and an *in camera* inspection of the contested documents, the trial court ordered B–E to provide all of the documents in question, with the exception of certain deleted portions which it ruled constituted "work product" and the "Learmont Report," which the court ruled was exempt from discovery under the attorney-client privilege. No question is now raised regarding the trial court's ruling on the privileged status of the "Learmont Report."

The appellate court considered the attorney-client privilege inapplicable because there was no allegation by B–E that the disputed documents were received from members of B–E's "control group." It further held that neither Sailors' metallurgical report nor the bulk of B–E's attorneys' notes constituted work product. It found that Sailors' report contains objective and material information that does not reflect or disclose B–E's attorneys' mental impressions, theories or litigation plans and modified the trial court's order to the extent that no deletions were necessary. Similarly, the court found that the attorneys' notes, with minor exceptions, contain factual information submitted by B–E's employees and do not reveal the attorneys' mental processes in shaping litigation strategy.

* * *

The work-product doctrine in Illinois, which protects against disclosure of "the theories, mental impressions, or litigation plans of [a] party's attorney" (73 Ill.2d R. 201(b)(2)), is believed necessary to prevent complete invasion of counsel's files. (*Monier v. Chamberlain* (1966), 35 Ill.2d 351, 359, 221 N.E.2d 410; *Stimpert v. Abdnour* (1962), 24 Ill.2d 26, 31, 179 N.E.2d 602.) In the Federal courts, this material, generally referred to by commentators as "opinion" work-product (see, *e.g.*, Comment, *Discovery and the Work Product Doctrine,* 11 Loy.Chi.L.J. 863, 873 (1980)), is discoverable, if at all, only under "rare" circumstances (*Hickman v. Taylor* (1947), 329 U.S. 495, 513–14, 67 S.Ct. 385, 394–95, 91 L.Ed. 451, 463–64; see also *Upjohn Co. v. United States* (1981), 449 U.S. 383, 399–400, 101 S.Ct. 677, 687–88, 66 L.Ed.2d 584, 597–98; *United States v. Nobles* (1975), 422 U.S. 225, 244–45, 95 S.Ct. 2160, 2173, 45 L.Ed.2d 141, 157 (White, J., concurring)), because it is thought that requiring disclosure of an attorney's strategies, legal theories and mental impressions would result in inefficiency, unfairness and sharp practices which would ultimately have a "demoralizing" effect on the legal profession (*Hickman v. Taylor* (1947), 329 U.S. 495, 511, 67 S.Ct. 385, 394, 91 L.Ed. 451, 462).

In *Monier,* we distinguished between memoranda made by counsel of his impression of a prospective witness and verbatim statements of such witness in an attempt to clarify the work-product doctrine in Illinois. We consider today whether counsel's notes and memoranda of employees' or witnesses' oral statements which are not verbatim and are not reviewed, altered, corrected, or signed by these individuals are protected work-product. While our rule differs significantly from the more broadly protective Federal rule (see generally Johnston, *Discovery in Illinois and Federal Courts,* 2 J.Mar.J.Prac. & Proc. 22 (1968)), we agree with the Supreme Court that notes regarding oral statements of witnesses, whether in the form of attorney's mental impressions or memoranda, necessarily reveal in varying degrees the attorney's mental processes in evaluating the communications. See *Upjohn Co. v. United States* (1981), 449 U.S. 383, 399–400, 101 S.Ct. 677, 687–88, 66 L.Ed.2d 584, 597–98, citing *Hickman v. Taylor* (1947), 329 U.S. 495, 67 S.Ct. 385, 91 L.Ed. 451 ("what he saw fit to write down regarding witnesses' remarks"; "the statement would be his [the attorney's] language, permeated with his inferences"); see also *In re Grand Jury Investigation* (E.D.Pa.1976), 412 F.Supp. 943, 949 (notes of conversation with witnesses "are so much a product of the lawyer's thinking and so little probative of the witnesses' actual words").

Some of the disputed documents prepared by B–E's attorneys in this case are handwritten; others are typewritten in the form of memoranda. In our *in camera* inspection, it was evident that the typewritten documents, which were reduced to succinct and concise form, represent the attorneys' efforts in reviewing, analyzing and summarizing the portion of the communications with potential witnesses which the attorneys believed important in developing their theories of their client's cause. As such, they necessarily " 'reveal the shaping process by which the attorney[s] [have] arranged the available evidence for use in trial as dictated by [their] training and experience' " (*Monier v. Chamberlain* (1966), 35 Ill.2d 351, 359, 221 N.E.2d 410) and are therefore entitled to protection. The handwritten notes represent a mixture of factual material and counsel's work product in the form of his conclusions, characterizations and summaries. Concededly, some of the factual material may be relevant to the issues. In many instances, however, this material is so inextricably intertwined with the privileged material that its isolation is virtually impossible. To impose upon the trial bench of this State the burden of reviewing voluminous material of this character would be totally incompatible with the efficient disposition of litigation. Moreover, and more importantly perhaps, such a procedure would violate the spirit of *Monier* and our discovery procedures which contemplate that discovery generally proceed without judicial intervention. (*Williams v. A.E. Staley Manufacturing Co.* (1981), 83 Ill.2d 559, 564, 48 Ill.Dec. 221, 416 N.E.2d 252.) It would only serve to "increase the burden of already crowded court calendars, and thwart the efficient and expeditious administration of justice" which *Monier* sought to prevent. (*Monier v. Chamberlain* (1966), 35 Ill.2d 351, 357, 221 N.E.2d 410.) Accordingly we hold that attorneys' notes and memoranda of oral conversations with witnesses or employees are not routinely discoverable. However, because of the possibility that such notes and memoranda may, on rare occasions, constitute the only source of factual material, we believe that an exception must be made from the absolute work-product exemption. We are cognizant of the difficulty and conflict which may arise in applying any exception, which, of course, led us to reject the Federal good-cause doctrine in *Monier*. Nonetheless, we believe that a narrowly limited exception must be made and defined to permit access to such material in those rare instances. Since the exception will rarely be operable, conflicts should be minimal. We therefore hold that the attorney's notes or memoranda are discoverable only if the party seeking disclosure conclusively demonstrates the absolute impossibility of securing similar information from other sources.

There is nothing in this record to indicate any necessity that would lead us to hold the exception applicable here. Indeed, according to the affidavit of one of Consolidation's attorneys, B–E has made available for inspection "engineering records, design calculations, material specifications, correspondence and notes estimated to include tens of thousands of individual documents." In short, there is nothing which indicates that Consolidation does not already have or cannot obtain through its attorneys' efforts and depositions the same factual information that is now included in the form of B–E's attorneys' work product.

We do not believe, however, that Sailors' metallurgical report can fairly be characterized as B–E's attorneys' work product. As the appellate court noted, the report is actually a notebook that contains objective and material information consisting of mathematical computations, formulae, tables, drawings, photographs, industry specification data, and handwritten notes. It does not reflect or disclose the theories, mental impressions or litigation plans of B–E's attorneys. Nor is it the product of the attorneys' mental processes. Sailors never communicated with the legal department prior to preparing this material, nor was he advised by his superior, who had requested Sailors' help, as to what the theories or plans of the attorneys were relative to this litigation. He was simply asked to analyze pieces of the machinery and render an opinion as to what had occurred. When his report was transferred to the legal department some six months to a year after it had been made, it did not, as B–E argues, thereby become part of the attorneys' thought processes. It is therefore not entitled to protection under the work-product doctrine. (See generally Johnston, *Discovery in Illinois and Federal Courts,* 2 J.Mar.J.Prac. & Proc. 22, 48–51 (1968) (examining the possibility that an expert's report may constitute work product as defined in *Monier*).) Nor is it, in our judgment, exempt from discovery under the attorney-client privilege.

The question of who speaks for a corporation on a privileged basis has created considerable confusion and conflict in the Federal system and has frequently been the subject of law review commentaries. (*E.g.,* Burnham, *Confidentiality and the Corporate Lawyer: The Attorney-Client Privilege and "Work Product" in Illinois,* 56 Ill.B.J. 542 (1968); Weinschel, *Corporate Employee Interviews and the Attorney-Client Privilege,* 12 B.C.Ind. & Comm.L.Rev. 873 (1970); Note, *Attorney-Client Privilege for Corporate Clients: The Control Group Test,* 84 Harv.L.Rev. 424 (1970); Note, *Upjohn Co. v. United States: Death Knell for the Control Group Test and a Plea for a Policy-Oriented Standard to Corporate Discovery,* 31 Syracuse L.Rev. 1043 (1980).) B–E urges that we abandon the "control group" test first adopted in Illinois by the appellate court in *Day v. Illinois Power Co.* (1964), 50 Ill.App.2d 52, 199 N.E.2d 802, as a means of defining "client" in the corporate context. (See also *Johnson v. Frontier Ford, Inc.* (1979), 68 Ill.App.3d 315, 319, 24 Ill.Dec. 908, 386 N.E.2d 112; *Shere v. Marshall Field & Co.* (1974), 26 Ill.App.3d 728, 731–32, 327 N.E.2d 92; *Golminas v. Teitelbaum Construction Co.* (1969), 112 Ill.App.2d 445, 449, 251 N.E.2d 314.) This test was recently rejected by the Supreme Court as the governing test in the Federal courts. *Upjohn Co. v. United States* (1981), 449 U.S. 383, 101 S.Ct. 677, 66 L.Ed.2d 584.

In *Cox v. Yellow Cab Co.* (1975), 61 Ill.2d 416, 337 N.E.2d 15, this court indicated that there are many factors relevant to a determination whether a statement given by a corporate employee is protected by the attorney-client privilege, including "the purpose for which the statement was required, the understanding by its maker as to that purpose, the extent to which its confidentiality was maintained after it was made and in the course of its transmission to counsel, and others." (61 Ill.2d 416, 420, 337 N.E.2d 15.) While listing some of the requirements essential to assertion of the privilege, the court declined to articulate a particular test and expressed no opinion on the appellate court's application of the control-group test since there were insufficient facts in the record from which the existence of the privilege could be ascertained.

In the Federal system prior to *Upjohn,* three major tests had emerged. The most widely adopted control-group test was first announced in *City of Philadelphia v. Westinghouse Electric Corp.* (E.D.Pa. 1962), 210 F.Supp. 483, *petition for writ of mandamus or prohibition denied sub nom. General Electric Co. v. Kirkpatrick* (3d Cir.1962), 312 F.2d 742, *cert. denied* (1963), 372 U.S. 943, 83 S.Ct. 937, 9 L.Ed.2d 969, at a time when one Federal court had held that the attorney-client privilege was not available to corporations (*Radiant Burners, Inc. v. American Gas Association* (N.D.Ill.1962), 207 F.Supp. 771, *aff'd on reconsideration* (N.D.Ill.1962), 209 F.Supp. 321, *rev'd* (7th Cir.1963) (*en banc*), 320 F.2d 314, *cert. denied* (1963), 375 U.S. 929, 84 S.Ct. 330, 11 L.Ed.2d 262).

This test focuses on the status of the employee within the corporate hierarchy:

> "[I]f the employee making the communication, of whatever rank he may be, is in a position to control or even to take a substantial part in a decision about any action which the corporation may take upon the advice of the attorney, or if he is an authorized member of a body or group which has that authority, then, in effect, he is (or personifies) the corporation when he makes his disclosure to the lawyer and the privilege would apply. In all other cases the employee would be merely giving information to the lawyer to enable the latter to advise those in the corporation having the authority to act or refrain from acting on the advice." (*City of Philadelphia v. Westinghouse Electric Corp.* (E.D.Pa.1962), 210 F.Supp. 483, 485.)

This approach was subsequently followed by the Third, Sixth and Tenth Circuits (*In re Grand Jury Investigation* (3d Cir.1979), 599 F.2d 1224; *United States v. Upjohn Co.* (6th Cir.1979), 600 F.2d 1223, *rev'd* (1981), 449 U.S. 383, 101 S.Ct. 677, 66 L.Ed.2d 584; *Natta v. Hogan* (10th Cir.1968), 392 F.2d 686), as well as several district courts outside those circuits (*e.g., Virginia Electric & Power Co. v. Sun Shipbuilding & Dry Dock Co.* (E.D.Va.1975), 68 F.R.D. 397; *Burlington Industries v. Exxon Corp.* (D.Md.1974), 65 F.R.D. 26; *Garrison v. General Motors Corp.* (S.D.Cal.1963), 213 F.Supp. 515; see also Annot., 9 A.L.R.Fed. 685 (1971).) In addition, several States have incorporated this test in their rules of evidence. See Stern, *Attorney–Client Privilege: Supreme Court Repudiates the Control Group Test,* 67 A.B.A.J. 1142, 1144 n. 4 (1981).

The Seventh Circuit, in *Harper & Row Publishers, Inc. v. Decker* (7th Cir.1970), 423 F.2d 487, *aff'd by an equally divided court* (1971), 400 U.S. 348, 91 S.Ct. 479, 27 L.Ed.2d 433, adopted a broader approach for determining when a corporation could claim the attorney-client privilege. The *Harper & Row* test, sometimes referred to as the "subject matter" or "scope of employment" test, is said to focus on why an attorney was consulted rather than with whom he communicated. (See *Diversified Industries, Inc. v. Meredith* (8th Cir.1977), 572 F.2d 596, 609;

see also Note, *Attorney-Client Privilege Under the Newly Adopted Weinstein Subject Matter Test* (1979), 28 Drake L.Rev. 191.) Under the *Harper & Row* test, "an employee of a corporation, though not a member of its control group, is sufficiently identified with the corporation so that his communication to the corporation's attorney is privileged where the employee makes the communication at the direction of his superiors in the corporation and where the subject matter upon which the attorney's advise is sought by the corporation and dealt with in the communication is the performance by the employee of the duties of his employment." 423 F.2d 487, 491–92. See also *Hasso v. Retail Credit Co.* (E.D.Pa.1973), 58 F.R.D. 425; *cf. Duplan Corp. v. Deering Milliken, Inc.* (D.S.C.1974), 397 F.Supp. 1146 (approach combining both *Harper & Row* and an expanded control-group test).

Finally, the Eighth Circuit, in *Diversified Industries, Inc. v. Meredith* (8th Cir.1977) (*en banc*), 572 F.2d 596, responding to one of the criticisms of the subject matter test—that a corporation could protect much information by simply directing all their employees to channel business reports to corporate attorneys—announced a modified version of the *Harper & Row* test:

> "[T]he attorney-client privilege is applicable to an employee's communication if (1) the communication was made for the purpose of securing legal advice; (2) the employee making the communication did so at the direction of his corporate superior; (3) the superior made the request so that the corporation could secure legal advice; (4) the subject matter of the communication is within the scope of the employee's corporate duties; and (5) the communication is not disseminated beyond those persons who, because of the corporate structure, need to know its contents." (572 F.2d 596, 609.)

Under this modified subject matter approach, any communication in which the employee functioned merely as a "fortuitous" or "bystander" witness would not be privileged. The *Harper & Row* court had implicitly recognized this same limitation.

All of the above tests have been criticized and additional tests have been proposed. (*E.g., D.I. Chadbourne, Inc. v. Superior Court* (1964), 60 Cal.2d 723, 36 Cal.Rptr. 468, 388 P.2d 700 (11 "basic principles" should be considered); *In re Ampicillin Antitrust Litigation* (D.D.C.1978), 81 F.R.D. 377, 387 (neither control-group nor *Harper & Row* test is sufficient; focus should be subject matter of communication and context in which it is made); *Duplan Corp. v. Deering Milliken, Inc.* (D.S.C.1974), 397 F.Supp. 1146 (subject matter test a necessary corollary of control-group test; scope of control-group test expanded); *United States v. United Shoe Machinery Corp.* (D.Mass.1950), 89 F.Supp. 357 (unlimited approach—all communications furnished to the attorney "by an officer or employee" of the corporation in confidence are privileged); Simon, *The Attorney-Client Privilege as Applied to Corporations,* 65 Yale L.J. 953 (1956) (test classifying corporate employees as "managing agents," "communicating agents," and "source agents"); Note, *Evidence—Privileged Communications—The Attorney-Client Privilege in the Corporate*

Setting: A Suggested Approach, 69 Mich.L.Rev. 360 (1970) ("natural or appropriate person" approach); Comment, *The Privileged Few: The Attorney–Client Privilege as Applied to Corporations,* 20 U.C.L.A.L.Rev. 288 (1972) (an expanded control-group test—communications of employee privileged if he had the ability to direct or take substantial part in directing corporation's *business* policy).) The broader tests have been criticized as shielding too much relevant information from discovery, whereas the principal criticism of the control-group test is that it frustrates the purpose of the attorney-client privilege by failing to take into account modern "corporate realities." (See *Upjohn Co. v. United States* (1981), 449 U.S. 383, 101 S.Ct. 677, 66 L.Ed.2d 584, *Diversified Industries, Inc. v. Meredith* (8th Cir.1978) (*en banc*), 572 F.2d 596.) While the Supreme Court rejected this test as inadequate, it declined to articulate an alternative standard to govern future cases in the Federal courts.

Whether a narrow or broad test should prevail depends, it seems to us, on the value to be accorded the two competing policies. As Justice Cardozo once remarked concerning the attorney-client privilege in another context:

> "[T]he recognition of a privilege does not mean that it is without conditions or exceptions. The social policy that will prevail in many situations may run foul in others of a different social policy, competing for supremacy. It is then the function of a court to mediate between them, assigning, so far as possible, a proper value to each, and summoning to its aid all the distinctions and analogies that are the tools of the judicial process. The function is the more essential where a privilege has its origin in inveterate but vague tradition, and where no attempt has been made either in treatise or in decisions to chart its limits with precision." *Clark v. United States* (1933), 289 U.S. 1, 13, 53 S.Ct. 465, 469, 77 L.Ed. 993, 999.

The purpose of the attorney-client privilege is to encourage and promote full and frank consultation between a client and legal advisor by removing the fear of compelled disclosure of information. (See 8 Wigmore, Evidence sec. 2291 (rev. ed. 1961); see also *People v. Adam* (1972), 51 Ill.2d 46, 48, 28 N.E.2d 205 (citing Wigmore's list of the essentials for the creation and continued existence of the privilege).) Under some circumstances, however, the privilege poses an absolute bar to the discovery of relevant and material evidentiary facts, and in the corporate context, given the large number of employees, frequent dealings with lawyers and masses of documents, the "zone of silence grows large." (Simon, *The Attorney–Client Privilege as Applied to Corporations,* 65 Yale L.J. 953, 955 (1956).) That result, in our judgment, is fundamentally incompatible with this State's broad discovery policies looking to the ultimate ascertainment of the truth (*Monier v. Chamberlain* (1966), 35 Ill.2d 351, 221 N.E.2d 410; see also *Williams v. A.E. Staley Manufacturing Co.* (1981), 83 Ill.2d 559, 565, 48 Ill.Dec. 221, 416 N.E.2d 252; *Sarver v. Barrett Ace Hardware, Inc.* (1976), 63 Ill.2d 454, 459–60, 349 N.E.2d 28), which we continue to find essential to the fair disposition of a lawsuit. (See *Ostendorf v. International Harvester Co.* (1982), 89 Ill. 273, 60 Ill.Dec. 456, 433 N.E.2d 253.) Its potential to insulate so much material from the truth-seeking process convinces us that the privilege ought to be limited for the corporate client to the extent reasonably necessary to achieve its purpose. As Dean Wigmore admonished:

> "[T]he privilege remains an exception to the general duty to disclose. Its benefits are all indirect and speculative; its obstruction is plain and concrete * * *. It is worth preserving for the sake of a general policy, but it is nonetheless an obstacle to the investigation of the truth. It ought to be strictly confined within the narrowest possible limits consistent with the logic of its principle." (8 Wigmore, Evidence sec. 2291, at 554 (rev. ed. 1961).)

The control-group test appears to us to strike a reasonable balance by protecting consultations with counsel by those who are the decision-makers or who substantially influence corporate decisions and by minimizing the amount of relevant factual material which is immune from discovery. We note, too, that the burden of showing facts which give rise to the privilege rests on the one who claims the exemption. (*Cox v. Yellow Cab Co.* (1975), 61 Ill.2d 416, 419–20, 337 N.E.2d 15; *Krupp v. Chicago Transit Authority* (1956), 8 Ill.2d 37, 42, 132 N.E.2d 532.) Moreover, the claimant must show certain threshold requirements in order to avail itself of the privilege, including a showing that the communication originated in a confidence that it would not be disclosed, was made to an attorney acting in his legal capacity for the purpose of securing legal advice or services, and remained confidential. (See 8 Wigmore, Evidence sec. 2292 (rev. ed. 1961); *United States v. United Shoe Machinery Corp.* (D.Mass.1950), 89 F.Supp. 357, 358–59.) Although the control-group test has been noted for its predictability and ease of application, we believe it is necessary to elaborate on those individuals whom we believe should be considered as members of the corporate control group.

In many of the cases in which the control-group test was adopted, the party claiming the privilege either presented no evidence which indicated that the particular employee had any actual authority to make a judgment or decision (*e.g., Golminas v. Teitelbaum Construction Co.* (1969), 112 Ill.App.2d 445, 449, 251 N.E.2d 314; *Day v. Illinois Power Co.* (1964), 50 Ill.App.2d 52, 59, 199 N.E.2d 802) or, as in the present case, conceded that none of the employees whose statements were alleged to be privileged were a part of their control group. (See, *e.g., In re Grand Jury Investigation* (3d Cir.1979), 599 F.2d 1224, 1237.) Some courts have indicated that the labels or titles of the employees are not determinative; rather, the actual duties or responsibilities delegated to these individuals determine their status as decisionmakers. (See *Congoleum Industries, Inc. v. GAF Corp.* (E.D.Pa.1969), 49 F.R.D. 82, 85, *aff'd* (3d Cir.1973), 478 F.2d 1398; see also *Honeywell, Inc. v. Piper Aircraft Corp.* (M.D.Pa.1970), 50 F.R.D. 117, 120 ("persons in management may range from the lowest junior executive or executive trainee to the chairman of the board").) Nevertheless, as a practical matter, the only communications that are ordinarily held privileged under this test are those made by top management who have the ability to make a final decision (see *United States v. Upjohn Co.* (6th Cir.1979), 600 F.2d 1223, *rev'd* (1981), 449 U.S. 383, 101 S.Ct. 677, 66 L.Ed.2d 584), rather than those made by employees whose positions are merely advisory (*Congoleum Industries, Inc. v. GAF Corp.* (E.D.Pa.1969), 49 F.R.D. 82, 85). We believe that an employee whose advisory role to top management in a particular area is such that a decision would not normally be made without his advice or opinion, and whose opinion in fact forms the basis of any final decision by those with actual authority, is properly within the control group. However, the individuals upon whom he may rely for supplying information are not members of the control group. Thus, if an employee of the status described is consulted for the purpose of determining what legal action the corporation will pursue, his communication is protected from disclosure. This approach, we think, better accommodates modern corporate realities and recognizes that decisionmaking within a corporation is a process rather than a final act. See Note, *Attorney–Client Privilege for Corporate Clients: The Control Group Test,* 84 Harv.L.Rev. 424, 430.

While B–E has conceded that Richard Sailors was not a member of its control group in the usual sense, we must consider whether he qualifies for that group as we have defined it. The record indicates that he began employment with B–E in April 1974, several months after the accident from which this litigation arose. From 1974 through June 1977, he was materials development engineer and reported directly to the chief engineer; in 1977, he was appointed chief standards engineer, a position he held until August 1980, when he left B–E's employ. According to his affidavit, his duties included "(a) developing and specifying material standards to insure the production of mining and construction machinery of uniform quality; (b) providing technical assistance to the [B–E] engineering departments engaged in the metallurgical and welding aspects of the manufacture of said mining and construction machinery; (c) developing new materials (metals) as required to suit new machine models and applications; (d) conducting tests on and analyzing machinery materials which failed to function properly; and (f) recommending corrective action to remedy material malfunction or failure."

In October 1976, he was contacted by a superior and asked to examine pieces of the machine in question which were in B–E's possession and render an opinion. There is a conflict in the record as to which superior contacted him. B–E's attorney's affidavit indicated that Lennart Hansson, who was B–E's engineer in charge of overseeing technical aspects of litigation involving mining machinery, requested Sailors' assistance; Sailors stated in his deposition that he was contacted by Tom Learmont, B–E's director of engineering-mining machinery whose responsibilities included supervising several chief engineers. In our judgment, it is clear that Sailors was not a member of B–E's corporate control group. As one of several engineers within his department, he supplied information to those whose opinions were sought and relied upon by others such as Hansson who occupied an advisory role and substantially contributed to decisionmaking. It is this fact which is critical, for it seems clear that Sailors' role was one of supplying the factual bases upon which were predicated the opinions and recommendations of those who advised the decisionmakers. While those who directly advise the decisionmakers could, conceivably, come within the control group, it is evident that Sailors did not.

Accordingly, we hold that Sailors' report is not privileged and must be made available to Consolidation for inspection. The notes and memoranda of B–E's attorneys are exempt from discovery under the work-product doctrine as expressed in this opinion.

Since the attorneys' notes and memoranda are not discoverable, and the question concerning the discoverability of Sailors' report involved issues of first impression in this court, the circuit court's order imposing a fine on B–E's attorney for contempt of court will be set aside. See *Sarver v. Barrett Ace Hardware, Inc.* (1976), 63 Ill.2d 454, 462, 349 N.E.2d 28.

The judgments of the appellate and circuit courts are vacated, and the cause is remanded to the circuit court of Cook County for further proceedings consistent with this opinion.

Vacated and remanded.

MAY DEPARTMENT STORES CO. v. RYAN, 699 S.W.2d 134 (Mo.App.1985). "The underlying action is one for false imprisonment brought by Maria Sanfilippo. She was allegedly detained for investigation of shoplifting by Sharon Lutz, an employee of the May Department Stores Company, on January 29, 1983. On that same date, Lutz prepared an incident report entitled 'SECURITY CASE REPORT,' with the word 'CONFIDENTIAL' beneath the main heading. This report was transmitted to the May Company's liability insurer, Liberty Mutual Insurance Company.

"Relators objected to the plaintiff's motion to produce numerous documents, including this report. Respondent ruled that the report was subject to discovery. Relators then filed their application for a writ of prohibition in this court. They argue that the report is attorney work product and hence non-discoverable absent a showing of hardship by plaintiff, and alternatively, relators contend that the report falls under the insurer-insured/attorney-client privilege. We agree with relators on both alternatives.

* * *

"An existing insured-insurer relationship, whereby an insured is contractually obligated to report promptly covered incidents to the insurer who in turn is obligated to defend and indemnify the insured, is similar to an attorney-client relationship insofar as discovery is concerned. Any communication between insured and insurer which relates to the former's duty to report incidents and the latter's duty to defend and to indemnify falls within the attorney-client privilege and is excluded from discovery under Rule 56.01(b)(1). State ex rel. Cain v. Barker, 540 S.W.2d 50, 53 (Mo. banc 1976). The opinion in *Cain* contains a thorough explanation of the public policy considerations underlying such a conclusion, which need not be repeated here. Suffice it to say, *Cain* surrounds the insured-insurer relationship with the same cloak of privileged confidentiality that protects the communications between attorney and client from discovery. Thus, a report made by an employee to his employer concerning the details of an incident, which is transmitted to the employer's attorney or insurer, is within the confidential communication privilege and is not subject to discovery, absent a waiver.

* * *

"Respondent also challenges relators' assertion that the report was prepared in anticipation of litigation. Clearly, it was. 'A report to a liability insurer can have no purpose other than use in potential litigation.' McCormick on Evidence § 96, at 224 (3rd ed. 1984). Over 30 years ago the Missouri Supreme Court characterized as 'naive' one who failed to recognize that litigation would ensue after a serious injury. State ex rel. Terminal Railroad Association v. Flynn, 257 S.W.2d at 74. In concluding that a written report of an employee to his employer regarding an accident was made for potential use in future litigation, the Western District in Lindberg v. Safeway Stores, Inc., 525 S.W.2d at 572, referred to the 'realities of the situation.' In State ex rel. Kroger Company v. Craig, 329 S.W.2d 804, 807 (Mo.App.1959), the Southern District reached a similar conclusion. Today, in what is frequently called the most litigious society in the history of mankind, we would indeed be naive and unrealistic if we failed to agree with our brethren that a written report of an employee to his employer of any untoward incident is required because of potential litigation.

* * *

"We have not hesitated to order the production of employee prepared incident reports where the record shows such reports to have been made for purposes other than anticipated litigation, and where the transmittal of such reports to an insurance company is unrelated to the insurance coverage and the defense of a potential lawsuit. In State ex rel. Little Rock Hospital v. Gaertner, 682 S.W.2d 146 (Mo.App.1984), we held an incident report prepared by an employee and forwarded to an insurance company was subject to discovery. However, as opposed to the facts in the instant case, the report in *Little Rock Hospital,* was prepared as part of a computerized future loss prevention program, not with a view toward potential litigation. The report form expressly stated that it was 'not a notice of loss.' Rather, it was made and used in the ordinary course of the hospital's business as a means of accident prevention. Therefore, the report was neither privileged, as it was not prepared or transmitted pursuant to the insurance or indemnity agreement, nor was it work product, as it was not made in anticipation of litigation. Here, the converse is true in both respects.

"Finally, we decline respondent's suggestion that we indulge in speculation that the report may have been made or used for purposes other than anticipated litigation. The report was transmitted to the insurer and is presently in the hands of relators' defense counsel. The mere possibility that it could also be used for other purposes, such as transmittal to a prosecuting attorney for the instigation of criminal proceedings, does not destroy its protected status. Evidence that it was actually used in this or similar manner may destroy the confidentiality of the report and thus constitute a waiver of the privilege. However, there is no such evidence in this case."

IN RE GRAND JURY PROCEEDINGS (HILL), 786 F.2d 3, 6 n. 4 (1st Cir.1986). "Hill does not urge that the questions asked of her are protected by the attorney-client privilege. We assume, without deciding, that if it were shown that Hill was, in fact, a paralegal or an otherwise authorized agent of a qualified attorney, Hill could assert a claim of privilege. See e.g., Fisher v. United States, 425 U.S. 391, 402 n. 8, 96 S.Ct. 1569, 1576 n. 8, 48 L.Ed.2d 39 (1976) (attorney may raise attorney-client privilege); United States v. Kovel, 296 F.2d 918 (2d Cir.1961) (under some circumstances, attorney-client privilege may apply to employee/agent of lawyer); Dabney v. Investment Corporation of America, 82 F.R.D. 464, 465 (E.D.Pa.1979) (privilege, if applicable, applies to paralegals, among others); see generally 8 Wigmore, Evidence § 2301 (McNaughton Rev.1961)."

UNITED STATES v. SCHWIMMER, 892 F.2d 237, 243–44 (2d Cir.1989). "The attorney-client privilege generally forbids an attorney from disclosing confidential communications that pass in the course of professional employment from client to lawyer. See generally 81 Am.Jur.2d Witnesses § 172 (1976). The relationship of attorney and client, a communication by the client relating to the subject matter upon which professional advice is sought, and the confidentiality of the expression for which the protection is claimed, all must be established in order for the privilege to attach. In Re Grand Jury Subpoena Duces Tecum, 731 F.2d 1032 (2d Cir.1984). The privilege also is held to cover communications made to certain agents of an attorney, including accountants hired to assist in the rendition of legal services. United States v. Kovel, 296 F.2d 918 (2d Cir.1961). As to such agents, '[w]hat is vital to the privilege is that the communication be made *in confidence* for the purpose of obtaining *legal* advice *from the lawyer.*' *Id.* at 922 (emphasis in original). Information provided to an accountant by a client at the behest of his attorney for the purposes of interpretation and analysis is privileged to the extent that it is imparted in connection with the legal representation. Id. See generally Annotation, Applicability of Attorney–Client Privilege to Communications Made in Presence of or Solely to or by Third Person, 14 A.L.R.4th 594, 635 (1982).

"The joint defense privilege, more properly identified as the 'common interest rule,' see generally Capra, The Attorney–Client Privilege In Common Representations, 20 Trial Lawyers Quarterly, Summer 1989, at 20, has been described as 'an extension of the attorney client privilege,' Waller v. Financial Corp. of Am., 828 F.2d 579, 583 n. 7 (9th Cir.1987). It serves to protect the confidentiality of communications passing from one party to the attorney for another party where a joint defense effort or strategy has been decided upon and undertaken by the parties and their respective counsel. See United States v. Bay State Ambulance and Hosp. Rental Serv., 874 F.2d 20, 28 (1st Cir.1989). Only those communications made in the course of an ongoing common enterprise and intended to further the enterprise are protected. Eisenberg v. Gagnon, 766 F.2d 770, 787 (3d Cir.), cert. denied, 474 U.S. 946, 106 S.Ct. 342, 88 L.Ed.2d 290 (1985); Matter of Bevill, Bresler & Schulman Asset Management Corp., 805 F.2d 120 (3d Cir.1986). 'The need to protect the free flow of information from client to attorney logically exists whenever multiple clients share a common interest about a legal matter,' Capra, 20 Trial Lawyers Quarterly, at 21 (citation omitted), and it is therefore unnecessary that there be actual litigation in progress for the common interest rule of the attorney-client privilege to apply, United States v. Zolin, 809 F.2d 1411, 1417 (9th Cir.1987), vacated in part on other grounds, 842 F.2d 1135 (9th Cir.1988) (en banc), aff'd in part and vacated in part on other grounds, ___ U.S. ___, 109 S.Ct. 2619, 105 L.Ed.2d 469 (1989). Neither is it necessary for the attorney representing the communicating party to be present when the communication is made to the other party's attorney. Matter of Grand Jury Subpoena, 406 F.Supp. 381 (S.D.N.Y.1975); cf. Hunydee v. United States, 355 F.2d 183 (9th Cir.1965).

"As in all claims of privilege arising out of the attorney-client relationship, a claim resting on the common interest rule requires a showing that the communication in question was given in confidence and that the client reasonably understood it to be so given. See United States v. Keplinger, 776 F.2d 678, 701 (7th Cir.1985), cert. denied, 476 U.S. 1183, 106 S.Ct. 2919, 91 L.Ed.2d 548 (1986); Kevlik v. Goldstein, 724 F.2d 844, 849 (1st Cir.1984). The protection afforded by the privilege extends to communications made in confidence to an accountant assisting lawyers who are conducting a joint defense on behalf of the communicating clients. See United States v. Judson, 322 F.2d 460 (9th Cir.1963). It applies 'regardless of the manner in which it is sought to put the communications in evidence, whether by direct examination, cross-examination, or *indirectly as by bringing out facts brought to knowledge solely by reason of a confidential communication.*' 81 Am.Jur.2d Witnesses § 194 (emphasis added). The burden of establishing the attorney-client privilege, in all its elements, always rests upon the person asserting it. In re Horowitz, 482 F.2d 72 (2d Cir.), cert. denied, 414 U.S. 867, 94 S.Ct. 64, 38 L.Ed.2d 86 (1973); von Bulow v. von Bulow, 811 F.2d 136, 146 (2d Cir.), cert. denied, 481 U.S. 1015, 107 S.Ct. 1891, 95 L.Ed.2d 498 (1987).

"Schwimmer has carried the burden of establishing that the information he furnished to Glickman, the accountant hired by Renda's attorney to serve the joint interests of Renda and himself, was protected by the attorney-client privilege. Schwimmer was directed by his attorney, Fink, to speak freely with Glickman, who had been hired by Silverman, Renda's attorney, on behalf of both clients. The attorneys had agreed to cooperate in all matters of mutual concern relating to the investigation by the government then in progress, and Fink represented to Schwimmer that any conversations with Glickman would be privileged. The common interest rule clearly is applicable here, since the information given by Schwimmer to Glickman was imparted in confidence for the ultimate purpose of assisting attorneys who had agreed upon and undertaken a joint strategy of representation, all of which was well understood by Schwimmer."

GULF OIL CORP. v. FULLER, 695 S.W.2d 769, 774 (Tex.App.1985). "All of the Defendants are relying upon Gulf's assertion of a work product/common defense privilege. Where communications are exchanged between commonly aligned parties, such a privilege extends to those materials which further the common defense. Magnaleasing, Inc. v. Staten Island Mall, 76 F.R.D. 559 (S.D.N.Y.1977). In Duplan Corporation v. Deering Milliken, Inc., 397 F.Supp. 1146, 1172 (D.S.C.1974), the court stated:

> A community of interest exists among different persons or separate corporations where they have an identical legal interest with respect to the subject matter of a communication between an attorney and a client concerning legal advice. The third parties receiving copies of the communication and claiming a community of interest may be distinct legal entities from the client receiving the legal advice and may be a non-party to any anticipated or pending litigation. The key consideration is that the nature of the interest be identical, not similar, and be legal, not solely commercial.

The court recognized the joint defense privilege, *Duplan,* 397 F.Supp. at 1173, but concluded that it was not absolute and was relative to the precise legal interest shared."

EISENBERG v. GAGNON, 766 F.2d 770, 787–88 (3d Cir.1985), cert. denied, 474 U.S. 946, 106 S.Ct. 342, 88 L.Ed.2d 290 (1985). "We agree with the district court's ruling that the correspondence was privileged, since it is best viewed as part of an ongoing and joint effort to set up a common defense strategy between a defendant and an attorney who was responsible for coordinating a common defense position. Communications to an attorney to establish a common defense strategy are privileged even though the attorney represents another client with some adverse interests. See United States v. McPartlin, 595 F.2d 1321, 1336–37 (7th Cir.), cert. denied, 444 U.S. 833, 100 S.Ct. 65, 62 L.Ed.2d 43 (1979); Hunydee v. United States, 355 F.2d 183, 184–85 (9th Cir.1965); Continental Oil Co. v. United States, 330 F.2d 347, 349–50 (9th Cir. 1964); 2 J. Weinstein & M. Berger, Weinstein's Evidence ¶ 503(b)[06] (1982). See also id. ¶ 503(b)[07] at 503–65.

"This situation is not governed by those cases holding there is no privilege for communications with another's attorney where the parties' interests are completely adverse and it is clear that the statements were not made in the expectation that the relationship was confidential. See Government of the Virgin Islands v. Joseph, 685 F.2d 857, 862 (3d Cir.1982); United States v. Cariello, 536 F.Supp. 698, 702 (D.N.J.1982)."

UNITED STATES v. LOPEZ, 777 F.2d 543, 552–53 (10th Cir.1985). "In several cases, courts have found a confidential relationship to exist despite the presence of co-defendants and their attorneys. United States v. McPartlin, 595 F.2d 1321 (7th Cir.1979), cert. denied, 444 U.S. 833, 100 S.Ct. 65, 62 L.Ed.2d 43 (1979); Hunydee v. United States, 355 F.2d 183 (9th Cir.1965). In these cases, the courts found that the communications were among attorneys and their clients for purposes of a common defense. In other cases, courts have found confidential communications between co-defendants and one or more attorneys who had agreed to represent them. In all the cases in which a confidential relationship was found to exist, the defendants either had retained counsel who were present during the communications or the defendants had not retained counsel but were planning to join the defense team."

CLARK v. STATE

Court of Criminal Appeals of Texas, 1953.
159 Tex.Crim. 187, 261 S.W.2d 339, cert. denied, 346 U.S. 905, 74 S.Ct. 217, 98 L.Ed. 404 (1953).

MORRISON, JUDGE.

The offense is murder; the punishment, death.

The deceased secured a divorce from appellant on March 25, 1952. That night she was killed, as she lay at home in her bed, as the result of a gunshot wound. From the mattress on her bed, as well as from the bed of her daughter, were recovered bullets which were shown by a firearms expert to have been fired by a .38 special revolver having Colt characteristics. Appellant was shown to have purchased a Colt .38 Detective Special some ten months prior to the homicide.

* * *

Marjorie Bartz, a telephone operator in the City of San Angelo, testified that at 2:49 in the morning of March 26, 1952, while on duty, she received a call from the Golden Spur Hotel; that at first she thought the person placing the call was a Mr. Cox and so made out the slip; but that she then recognized appellant's voice, scratched out the word "Cox" and wrote "Clark." She stated that appellant told her he wanted to speak to his lawyer, Jimmy Martin in Dallas, and that she placed the call to him at telephone number Victor 1942 in that city and made a record thereof, which record was admitted in evidence. Miss Bartz testified that, contrary to company rules, she listened to the entire conversation that ensued, and that it went as follows:

The appellant: "Hello, Jimmy, I went to the extremes."

The voice in Dallas: "What did you do?"

The appellant: "I just went to the extremes."

The voice in Dallas: "You got to tell me what you did before I can help."

The appellant: "Well, I killed her."

The voice in Dallas: "Who did you kill; the driver?"

The appellant: "No, I killed her."

The voice in Dallas: "Did you get rid of the weapon?"

The appellant: "No, I still got the weapon."

The voice in Dallas: "Get rid of the weapon and sit tight and don't talk to anyone, and I will fly down in the morning."

It was stipulated that the Dallas telephone number of appellant's attorney was Victor 1942.

* * *

Proposition (1b) is predicated upon the contention that the court erred in admitting the testimony of the telephone operator, because the conversation related was a privileged communication between appellant and his attorney.

As a predicate to a discussion of this question, we note that the telephone operator heard this conversation through an act of eavesdropping.

In 20 Am.Jur., p. 361, we find the following:

> "Evidence procured by eavesdropping, if otherwise relevant to the issue, is not to be excluded because of the manner in which it was obtained or procured * * *"

eavesdrop evid not excluded

This Court has recently, in Schwartz v. State, supra, affirmed by the Supreme Court of the United States on December 15, 1952, 73 S.Ct.

232, authorized the introduction of evidence secured by means of a mechanical interception of a telephone conversation.

We now discuss the question of the privileged nature of the conversation. Wigmore on Evidence (Third Edition), Section 2326, reads as follows:

> "The law provides subjective freedom for the client by assuring him of exemption from its processes of disclosure against himself or the attorney or their agents of communication. This much, but not a whit more, is necessary for the maintenance of the privilege. Since the means of preserving secrecy of communication are entirely in the client's hands, and since the privilege is a derogation from the general testimonial duty and should be strictly construed, it would be improper to extend its prohibition to third persons who obtain knowledge of the communications."

The precise question here presented does not appear to have been passed upon in this or other jurisdictions.

In Hoy v. Morris, 13 Gray 519, 79 Mass. 519, a conversation between a client and his attorney was overheard by Aldrich, who was in the adjoining room. The Court therein said:

> "Aldrich was not an attorney, not in any way connected with Mr. Todd; and certainly in no situation where he was either necessary or useful to the parties to enable them to understand each other. On the contrary, he was a mere bystander, and casually overheard conversation not addressed to him nor intended for his ear, but which the client and attorney meant to have respected as private and confidential. Mr. Todd could not lawfully have revealed it. But, in consequence of a want of proper precaution, the communications between him and his client were overheard by a mere stranger. As the latter stood in no relation of confidence to either of the parties, he was clearly not within the rule of exemption from giving testimony; and he might therefore, when summoned as a witness, be compelled to testify as to what he overheard, so far as it was pertinent to the subject matter of inquiry upon the trial * * * "

In Walker v. State, 19 Tex.App. 176, we find the following:

> "Mrs. Bridges was not incompetent or disqualified because she was present and heard the confessions made by defendant, even assuming that the relation of attorney and client subsisted in fact between him and Culberson."

The above holding is in conformity with our statute, Article 713, Code Cr.Proc.

> "All other persons, except those enumerated in articles 708 and 714, whatever may be the relationship between the defendant and witness, are competent to testify, except that an attorney at law shall not disclose a communication made to him by his client during the existence of that relationship, nor disclose any other fact which came to the knowledge of such attorney by reason of such relationship." * * *

We hold that the trial court properly admitted the evidence of the telephone operator.

* * *

Finding no reversible error, the judgment of the trial court is affirmed.

ON APPELLANT'S MOTION FOR REHEARING

WOODLEY, JUDGE.

We are favored with masterful briefs and arguments in support of appellant's motion for rehearing, including amicus curiae brief by an eminent and able Texas lawyer addressed to the question of privileged communications between attorney and client.

* * *

As to the testimony of the telephone operator regarding the conversation between appellant and Mr. Martin, the conversation is set forth in full in our original opinion. Our holding as to the admissibility of the testimony of the operator is not to be considered as authority except in comparable fact situations.

* * *

It is in the interest of public justice that the client be able to make a full disclosure to his attorney of all facts that are material to his defense or that go to substantiate his claim. The purpose of the privilege is to encourage such disclosure of the facts. But the interests of public justice further require that no shield such as the protection afforded to communications between attorney and client shall be interposed to protect a person who takes counsel on how he can safely commit a crime.

We think this latter rule must extend to one who, having committed a crime, seeks or takes counsel as to how he shall escape arrest and punishment, such as advice regarding the destruction or disposition of the murder weapon or of the body following a murder.

One who knowing that an offense has been committed conceals the offender or aids him to evade arrest or trial becomes an accessory. The fact that the aider may be a member of the bar and the attorney for the offender will not prevent his becoming an accessory.

Art. 77, P.C. defining an accessory contains the exception "One who aids an offender in making or preparing his defense at law" is not an accessory.

The conversation as testified to by the telephone operator is not within the exception found in Art. 77 P.C. When the Dallas voice advised appellant to "get rid of the weapon" (which advice the evidence shows was followed) such aid cannot be said to constitute aid "in making or preparing his defense at law". It was aid to the perpetrator of the crime "in order that he may evade an arrest or trial."

Is such a conversation privileged as a communication between attorney and client?

If the adviser had been called to testify as to the conversation, would it not have been more appropriate for him to claim his privilege against self-incrimination rather than that the communication was privileged because it was between attorney and client?

Appellant, when he conversed with Mr. Martin, was not under arrest nor was he charged with a crime. He had just inflicted mortal wounds on his former wife and apparently had shot her daughter. Mr. Martin had acted as his attorney in the divorce suit which had been tried that day and had secured a satisfactory property settlement. Appellant called him and told him that he had gone to extremes and had killed "her", not "the driver". Mr. Martin appeared to understand these references and told appellant to get rid of "the weapon".

We are unwilling to subscribe to the theory that such counsel and advice should be privileged because of the attorney-client relationship which existed between the parties in the divorce suit. We think, on the other hand, that the conversation was admissible as not within the realm of legitimate professional counsel and employment.

The rule of public policy which calls for the privileged character of the communication between attorney and client, we think, demands that the rule be confined to the legitimate course of professional employment. It cannot consistent with the high purpose and policy supporting the rule be here applied.

The murder weapon was not found. The evidence indicates that appellant disposed of it as advised in the telephone conversation. Such advice or counsel was not such as merits protection because given by an attorney. It was not in the legitimate course of professional employment in making or preparing a defense at law.

Nothing is found in the record to indicate that appellant sought any advice from Mr. Martin other than that given in the conversation testified to by the telephone operator. We are not therefore dealing with a situation where the accused sought legitimate advice from his attorney in preparing his legal defense.

* * *

Appellant's motion for rehearing is overruled.

CALDWELL v. DISTRICT COURT IN AND FOR THE CITY AND COUNTY OF DENVER

Supreme Court of Colorado, 1982.
644 P.2d 26.

LOHR, JUSTICE.

In this original proceeding pursuant to C.A.R. 21, we directed the Denver District Court to show cause why the petitioners' motion to compel discovery of certain documents possessed by Bruno Weinschel, The Hertz Corporation (Hertz), and their attorney, Ronald Hill, should not be granted. We conclude that the trial court erred in summarily denying the requested discovery and so make the rule absolute.

I.

The petitioners, George and Hattie Caldwell, brought this action in Denver District Court, contending that the defendants, Hertz, Hill, and Weinschel, fraudulently concealed information and misrepresented facts in an earlier personal injury action brought by the Caldwells, with the result that summary judgment for Weinschel was improperly granted and Hertz, as Weinschel's insuror, was unjustly insulated from payment of damages for the Caldwells' injuries. The petitioners' efforts to obtain discovery of information bearing on their claim of fraud have resulted in the issues now before us. A rather detailed exposition of the facts is necessary to an understanding of the questions that we must resolve.

The present action stems from an automobile accident on December 5, 1974, in which a car carrying the Caldwells was struck by a second automobile owned by Hertz. The Hertz car had been rented by Bruno Weinschel, and was being operated by Werner Baumgart at the time of the accident. Weinschel was not in the car with Baumgart when the mishap occurred.

Baumgart and Weinschel had travelled together from the East Coast to Colorado for a skiing vacation. Weinschel had rented the Hertz car in order to provide transportation from the Denver airport to the resort community of Vail, Colorado. After arriving in Vail, it became necessary to return to Denver to pick up two women who were joining Baumgart and Weinschel for their skiing holiday. Baumgart departed alone for this purpose, picked up the women at Stapleton Airport, and was involved in the auto accident while returning to Vail on Interstate 70.

On August 14, 1975, the Caldwells brought a negligence action against Baumgart and Hertz in the Denver District Court (Action No. C–57586). Hertz retained attorney Ronald Hill to represent its interests and those of Baumgart. Shortly thereafter, the Caldwells stipulated that Hertz be dismissed as a party, without prejudice.

On January 23, 1978, with the permission of the court, the Caldwells added Bruno Weinschel as a defendant in the negligence action, claiming that Weinschel was vicariously liable for Baumgart's negligence on the theories of agency and joint enterprise. Hertz again turned to Hill, this time for representation of Weinschel. Hill filed a motion for a summary judgment dismissing Weinschel from the action. On October 17, 1978, the motion was granted.

The Caldwells proceeded with their action against Baumgart, which was set for trial on August 27, 1979. On August 22, 1979, the trial court granted Hill permission to withdraw as counsel for Baumgart due to his inability to locate Baumgart and prepare a defense. On August 30, 1979, the Caldwells obtained a judgment against Baumgart, which awarded damages of $74,989.86 to Hattie Caldwell and $20,-451.78 to George Caldwell.

As judgment creditors, the Caldwells served a writ of garnishment on Hertz, contending that Hertz was liable for their damages as Baumgart's insurer. Hertz denied any obligation to pay the judgment. In the course of the garnishment action, the Caldwells' counsel was allowed limited discovery into the files of Hertz and its attorney Hill concerning the Baumgart action. Review of these documents led the Caldwells' counsel to believe that Hertz, Weinschel, and Hill had committed fraud in defending the Caldwell personal injury action.

Consequently, a new action was filed in the Denver District Court against Hertz, Hill, and Weinschel (defendants), alleging fraud and civil conspiracy (No. 80–CV–3184). In the first claim for relief, the Caldwells alleged that the defendants knowingly made false representations and withheld material information concerning the presence of a joint venture or agency relationship between Baumgart and Weinschel at the time of the car accident in December 1974. Specifically, they alleged that in the summer of 1975 Hill and Hertz were aware of a statement by Baumgart that the purpose of Baumgart's trip to Denver was to transport two women to Vail to join Weinschel and Baumgart for their skiing vacation, and that Baumgart made this trip at Weinschel's request and with his consent. The complaint also alleged that Hertz and Hill had received letters from Baumgart stating that "[the Hertz car] was driven by me with the full consent of the lessee, Mr. Bruno Weinschel, of Gaithersburg, Maryland, for whom I am acting as an export consultant." The complaint states that awareness of the business relationship between Baumgart and Weinschel is also reflected by letters sent from Hill to Weinschel in 1977.

The complaint alleges that, notwithstanding this information, Hill submitted a motion for a summary judgment dismissing Weinschel from the Caldwell's personal injury action in which Hill stated that, at the time of the accident, Baumgart was performing a personal errand that did not involve or concern Weinschel in any way. The complaint states that, in support of the motion for summary judgment, Hill submitted an affidavit of Weinschel averring, "I [Weinschel,] did not request that [Baumgart] go to Denver, and he did not perform any errands or other functions for me. He used the automobile strictly for his own purposes." The complaint alleges these statements constituted knowing misrepresentations made with the intent to insulate Weinschel and Hertz from liability for the accident. If successful, the result would be to leave the Caldwells with a judgment against only Baumgart, who could not be located. In the second count of the Caldwells' complaint they incorporate the allegations of their first count and further assert that the alleged acts of misrepresentation and fraud were perpetrated pursuant to an agreement between the defendants constituting a civil conspiracy.

Pursuant to C.R.C.P. 34, the Caldwells filed a request for production of documents concerning the defendants' assessments of the value of Baumgart's testimony and Baumgart's potential liability to the Caldwells. The Caldwells also requested production of any correspondence between Hill and Hertz or between Hill and Weinschel during the period from December 5, 1974, to April 1, 1980. The defendants resisted discovery of these documents on the basis that they were privileged. The Caldwells filed a motion under C.R.C.P. 37 to compel production of the papers. On March 20, 1981, the trial court denied the motion, agreeing with the defendants that the requested documents were privileged.

On January 6, 1982, the Caldwells filed a petition for relief in the nature of mandamus asking us to direct the trial court to order the requested discovery. We then issued a rule to show cause why the requested relief should not be granted. Two issues are presented by this proceeding: (1) whether this is a proper case for review under C.A.R. 21; and (2) whether the trial court erred in denying the requested discovery on the basis that the documents are privileged. We address these issues in turn.

* * *

III.

Hertz and Weinschel contend that the requested documents are protected from discovery by the attorney-client privilege, which is codified in section 13–90–107(1)(b), C.R.S.1973 (1981 Supp.). It provides:

> (1) There are particular relations in which it is the policy of the law to encourage confidence and to preserve it inviolate; therefore, a person shall not be examined as a witness in the following cases:
>
> * * *
>
> (b) An attorney shall not be examined without the consent of his client as to any communication made by the client to him or his advice given thereon in the course of professional employment; * * *

Hertz and Weinschel argue that the statute does not provide for any exceptions to the privilege—that its terms are absolute and unyielding. However, such a rigid approach to the attorney-client privilege is incorrect. We have previously limited its scope where the communications between a client and his attorney are made for the purpose of aiding the commission of a future crime or a present continuing crime. A. v. District Court, 191 Colo. 10, 550 P.2d 315 (1976), *cert. denied,* 429 U.S. 1040, 97 S.Ct. 737, 50 L.Ed.2d 751 (1977); Losavio v. District Court, 188 Colo. 127, 533 P.2d 32 (1975). The reason for this exception to the privilege was explained in A. v. District Court, supra:

> The attorney-client privilege is rooted in the principle that candid and open discussion by the client to the attorney without fear of disclosure will promote the orderly administration of justice. The criminal purpose exception to the privilege grows out of a competing value of

> our society which is manifested in the rule that 'the public has the right to every man's evidence, particularly in grand jury proceedings.' Consequently, the attorney-client privilege is not absolute.

191 Colo. at 22, 550 P.2d at 324–25 (citation omitted).

Our past recognition of the "future crimes" exception, however, does not dispose of the issue in this case. The question we now address is whether that exception should be extended to communications between attorney and client for the purpose of aiding a continuing or future civil wrong. We expressly reserved that question in A. v. District Court, supra, where we stated:

> The cases seem to disagree on the breadth of the exception regarding non-criminal wrongdoings in the attorney-client relationship. As this case only involves certain alleged *criminal* conduct in the relationship, we need not address the issue of the scope of the exception in this opinion, and, of course, we do not decide it.

191 Colo. at 22, n. 11, 550 P.2d at 324, n. 11. We now hold that the exception does extend to civil fraud.

Although the exception to the attorney-client privilege created for future illegal activity was at one time limited to criminal activity, see Annot., 125 A.L.R. 508, 514 (1940), it is now well-settled that this exception is also applicable to advice or aid secured in the perpetration of a fraud. See 8 *J. Wigmore, Evidence* § 2298 (McNaughton Rev.1961 and 1981 Supp.); *McCormick, Evidence* § 95 (2d ed. 1972 and 1978 Supp.); Gardner, *The Crime or Fraud Exception to the Attorney–Client Privilege,* 47 A.B.A.J. 708 (1961) (Gardner, *The Crime or Fraud Exception*); Uniform Rules of Evidence, Rule 502(d), 13 U.L.A. 250 (Master Ed.1980); see generally Annot., 125 A.L.R. 508 (1940 and Supps.).

The rationale for excluding such communications from the attorney-client privilege is that the policies supporting the existence of that privilege are inapplicable where the advice and aid sought refers to future wrongdoing rather than prior misconduct. As stated by Wigmore:

> [The policy reasons supporting the attorney-client privilege] predicate the need of confidence on the part not only of injured persons, but also of those who, being already wrongdoers in part or all of their cause, are seeking legal advice suitable for their plight. The confidences of such persons may legitimately be protected, wrongdoers though they have been, because, as already noticed (§ 2291 supra), the element of wrong is not always found separated from an element of right; because, even when it is, a legal adviser may properly be employed to obtain the best available or lawful terms of making redress; and because the legal adviser must not habitually be placed in the position of an informer. But these reasons all cease to operate at a certain point, namely, where the desired advice refers *not to prior wrongdoing,* but to *future wrongdoing.* From that point onwards, no protection is called for by any of these considerations.

8 *J. Wigmore, Evidence,* supra, § 2298 at 573 (emphasis in original).

We follow the majority rule that an appropriate case alleging civil fraud may also require that the privilege give way.[5] The remaining question is whether this is an appropriate case for application of this exception.

In A. v. District Court, supra, we addressed the procedure to be followed in determining whether the criminal purpose exception was applicable. There we held that a judge may order disclosure of the allegedly privileged documents upon a *prima facie* showing that the future crimes exception is applicable. We stated that this *prima facie* showing is "not tantamount to proof of a prima facie case," but requires that there be a showing of "some foundation in fact" for the alleged illegal conduct. We also held that the trial court may conduct an *in camera* review of the allegedly privileged documents without first requiring a *prima facie* showing if it determines that this would aid its assessment of the privilege's applicability. The ultimate burden is upon the party asserting the exception to the privilege, and it must be demonstrated that the exception applies to each document before that document is stripped of its privilege. Id.

We believe that the procedure adopted in A. v. District Court, supra, is appropriate to the civil as well as the criminal context. The courts and commentators are generally agreed that the proponent of the crime or fraud exception must make a showing of the applicability of the exception before the privilege recedes. E.g., United States v. Hodge and Zweig, 548 F.2d 1347, 1354 (9th Cir.1977); Union Camp Corp. v. Lewis, 385 F.2d 143 (4th Cir.1967); Duplan Corp. v. Deering Milliken, Inc., 397 F.Supp. 1146, 1172, 1194 (D.S.C.1974); United Services Automobile Assn. v. Werley, 526 P.2d 28 (Alaska 1974); State ex rel. North Pacific Lumber Co. v. Unis, 282 Or. 457, 579 P.2d 1291 (1978); Note, The Future Crime or Tort Exception to Communications Privileges, 77 Harv.L.Rev. 730 (1964) (Note, *The Future Crime or Tort Exception*); Gardner, *The Crime or Fraud Exception,* supra. We recognize that there is some apparent division in authority over whether this showing must amount to a *prima facie* case or whether some lesser quantum of proof is adequate. See generally, Gardner, *The Crime or Fraud Exception,* supra. However, we believe A. v. District Court, supra, appropriately reconciled the need for protection of the attorney-client relationship and the competing need to avoid use of that relationship as a shield for the perpetration of wrongful conduct by concluding that a foundation in fact for the charge is sufficient to invoke the crime exception. Requiring a strict *prima facie* case may not be possible at the discovery stage, and would result in an overzealous protection of the attorney-client privilege in a context where the rationale for that

5. There is a division of authority over whether the crime or fraud exception extends to all form of tortious conduct. See United Services Automobile Assn. v. Werley, 526 P.2d 28, 32 (Alaska 1974); Annot., 2 A.L.R.3d 861 (1965 and 1981 Supp.); *McCormick, Evidence,* supra § 95 at 201; 8 *Wigmore, Evidence,* supra § 2298 at 573–577. Because the present case involves a claim of fraud, we need not and do not reach the question of whether this exception to the attorney-client privilege extends to other forms of tortious conduct.

privilege may be inapplicable. This intermediate burden of proof has been approved in recognition of the significant proof problems facing a proponent of the exception. See Note, *The Future Crime or Tort Exception,* supra; Gardner, *The Crime or Fraud Exception,* supra.

Further, because of those proof problems, we follow *A. v. District Court* in holding that the trial court, in its discretion and without prior establishment of a foundation in fact that the crime or fraud exception applies, may order the production of relevant documents for an *in camera* inspection to determine whether that exception is applicable. See Duplan Corp. v. Deering Milliken, Inc., supra, 397 F.Supp. at 1195. In exercising that discretion the judge should require a showing of a factual basis adequate to support a good faith belief by a reasonable person that wrongful conduct sufficient to invoke the crime or fraud exception to the attorney-client privilege has occurred. Cf. C.R.C.P. 11 ("The signature of an attorney [on a pleading] constitutes a certificate by him that he has read the pleading; that to the best of his knowledge, information, and belief there is good ground to support it * * * If a pleading * * * is signed with intent to defeat the purpose of this Rule, it may be stricken * * *").

Two additional issues which may arise in connection with further proceedings in this case are whether, in order for the crime or fraud exception to the attorney-client privilege to apply: (1) the attorney must be aware of the illegal use to which his advice is being put and (2) the client must know or reasonably should know of the unlawfulness of his conduct. In accord with the prevailing view we answer the first question in the negative and the second in the affirmative.

Whether or not the attorney is aware of the wrongful purpose for which his advice is sought, the policy considerations for recognizing an exception to the attorney-client privilege are equally applicable. Thus, his knowledge or participation is not necessary to application of the exception, and this is the general rule. E.g., 8 *Wigmore, Evidence,* supra, § 2298 at 573–77.

It is also generally accepted that the crime or fraud exception applies only when the client knows or reasonably should know that the advice is sought for a wrongful purpose. E.g., State ex rel. North Pacific Lumber Co. v. Unis, supra; *McCormick, Evidence,* supra § 95 at 199 and n. 48; Gardner, *The Crime or Fraud Exception,* supra at 710; see also United Services Automobile Assn. v. Werley, supra, at 32 (advice must be sought for a knowingly unlawful end); 8 *Wigmore, Evidence,* supra § 2298 at 573–77 (advice must be sought for a knowingly unlawful end). The reason for this limitation on the scope of the exception has been expressed as follows:

> Good-faith consultations with attorneys by clients who are uncertain about the legal implications of a proposed course of action are entitled to the protection of the privilege, even if that action should later be held improper.

State ex rel. North Pacific Lumber Co. v. Unis, supra, 282 Or. at 464, 579 P.2d at 1295.

Consequently, the trial court should determine in the course of further proceedings whether the Caldwells have made a *prima facie* showing—one that gives their assertions a foundation in fact—that the crime or fraud exception is applicable. If this showing is made, then the documents relevant to their claim of civil fraud are discoverable. In determining whether this is a proper case for application of the exception, the court, if it deems it advisable, may order a production of the documents for *in camera* review. The court must also find that these communications were sought in furtherance of an end that the client knew or reasonably should have known to be improper, but it need not find that Hill was a participant in or aware of the alleged fraud.

Because we do not have the allegedly privileged documents before us, we do not resolve whether the Caldwells have made the necessary *prima facie* showing. We do note, however, that from the limited record available the Caldwells have sufficiently substantiated their allegations to merit careful review by the district court.

IV.

In refusing to order discovery of the documents requested by the Caldwells, the trial court stated only that they were privileged. The source of that privilege was not specified. While Hertz and Weinschel have based their argument upon the attorney-client privilege, it is possible that the trial court relied in part upon the work product privilege. C.R.C.P. 26(b)(3). As we stated in A. v. District Court, supra, the work product and attorney-client privileges are related but distinct theories:

> Generally, the attorney-client privilege protects communications between the attorney and the client, and the promotion of such confidences is said to exist for the benefit of the client. On the other hand, the work-product exemption generally applies to "documents and tangible things * * * prepared in anticipation of litigation or for trial," C.R.C.P. 26(b)(3), and its goal is to insure the privacy of the attorney from opposing parties and counsel.

191 Colo. at 25, 550 P.2d at 327 (citations omitted).

Here, the Caldwells requested not only correspondence between Hill and Hertz or Weinschel, but also "memoranda, documents, notes or any other writing or item which in any way discusses or concerns any of the defendants' opinions, ideas, or comments * * * concerning the value of WERNER BAUMGART'S testimony, the value of WERNER BAUMGART as a witness, or the possibility of WERNER BAUMGART being found liable to the [Caldwells]." Some of these documents may qualify as the work product of attorney Hill.

However, the work product privilege is also subject to the crime or fraud exception. Natta v. Zletz, 418 F.2d 633 (7th Cir.1969); Hercules

Inc. v. Exxon Corp., 434 F.Supp. 136, 155 (D.Del.1977). Just as the attorney-client privilege may not be abused as a shield for ongoing or future illegal activity, so the privilege created for an attorney's work product cannot be allowed to protect the perpetration of wrongful conduct. Upholding the assertion of these privileges in that context would be a perversion of their legitimate purpose and scope.

Our rule to show cause is made absolute, and the trial court is directed to conduct further proceedings in accordance with the views expressed in this opinion.

UNITED STATES v. ZOLIN, 491 U.S. 554, 109 S.Ct. 2619, 2623, 2632, 105 L.Ed.2d 469 (1989). "The specific question presented is whether the applicability of the crime-fraud exception must be established by 'independent evidence' (i.e., without reference to the content of the contested communications themselves), or, alternatively, whether the applicability of that exception can be resolved by an *in camera* inspection of the allegedly privileged material. * * *

* * *

"In sum, we conclude that a rigid independent evidence requirement does not comport with 'reason and experience,' Fed.Rule Evid. 501, and we decline to adopt it as part of the developing federal common law of evidentiary privileges. We hold that *in camera* review may be used to determine whether allegedly privileged attorney-client communications fall within the crime-fraud exception. We further hold, however, that before a district court may engage in *in camera* review at the request of the party opposing the privilege, that party must present evidence sufficient to support a reasonable belief that *in camera* review may yield evidence that establishes the exception's applicability. Finally, we hold that the threshold showing to obtain *in camera* review may be met by using any relevant evidence, lawfully obtained, that has not been adjudicated to be privileged.

"Because the Court of Appeals employed a rigid independent-evidence requirement which categorically excluded the partial transcripts and the tapes themselves from consideration, we vacate its judgment on this issue and remand the case for further proceedings consistent with this opinion."

STEGMAN v. MILLER

Court of Appeals of Kentucky, 1974.
515 S.W.2d 244.

PALMORE, JUSTICE.

Catherine Eckel, a childless widow, died testate in September of 1969. Her will had been executed on April 9, 1968. She left a part of her estate to certain charities and the rest to her surviving brothers and sisters, including the mother of Charles Miller, the appellee in this proceeding. The appellant, executor of Mrs. Eckel's will, appeals from a judgment entered pursuant to a verdict awarding Miller $8,000 on an implied contract by which Mrs. Eckel is alleged to have been obligated to make a provision in her will for payment of the reasonable value of personal services rendered to her by Miller during her lifetime.

A principal ground for the appeal is that the evidence was not sufficient under the principles of Stewart v. Brandenburg, Ky., 383 S.W.2d 122 (1964), and other comparable decisions to support a recovery. Without a detailed exposition of the evidence, suffice it to say that what might *not* be "extraordinary" services by a close relative under some circumstances may very well be extraordinary under other circumstances, including, as in this case, the distance necessarily traveled in order to perform the services. We cannot say as a matter of law that Miller's services were not extraordinary.

We have much reluctance to reverse the judgment of the trial court, or even to consume the necessary time to write at length upon it, except that it involves an important principle of law on which some of our earlier opinions may conduce to invite misunderstanding with respect to the attorney-client privilege, KRS 421.210(4).

The applicable portion of this statute reads as follows: "No attorney shall testify concerning a communication made to him, in his professional character, by his client, or his advice thereon, without the client's consent * * *."

Though long-since codified by direct legislation, the attorney-client privilege was "unquestioned" in the latter days of Elizabeth I and is the oldest privilege for confidential communications vouchsafed to us by the common law. 8 Wigmore, Evidence § 2290 (McNaughton rev. 1961). Resting then on other policies, it survives today for the promotion of free and honest consultation between attorney and client. Id. § 2291; Model Code of Evidence, Rule 210, Comment *a* (1942). There is much to be said, and has been said, against it, but as the substantive law of evidence is generally understood to be subject to legislative prerogative we are not disposed either to prostitute or to improve upon it to suit our own inclinations.

Over objection by the executor the witness Louis Arnold, an attorney, was permitted to testify that he represented Mrs. Eckel in his professional capacity for a number of years ending some six months before her death. He said that on several occasions he visited at her home, "all through the early 1960's and more particularly in 1961 and in 1964 she talked about the will and I did keep after Mrs. Eckel because I felt she should have a will and she indicated she wanted one. I did keep after her and in fact I even wrote and advised her it was important." During these discussions of a proposed will, according to Arnold, "She said she wanted to leave some money to her nephew Charlie Miller and she explained why—I can't tell you her exact words but she said she was obligated to him or owed him for the looking after the property, taking care of the building and that he had done all her driving around and taking her places, wherever she had to go. I can't tell you the exact words but she said she was obligated or owed him and wanted to put that in the will."

As so often appears to be the case, however, Mrs. Eckel never did get around to drawing that will, and in 1968 she had another attorney prepare a will in which she did not carry out the intention theretofore communicated to Arnold.

Obviously Arnold's testimony was of great importance to Miller's case, hence its admissibility presents a vital question on this appeal. It centers on a traditional exception to the attorney-client privilege that applies to the execution and contents of a will.

As stated in Wigmore, supra, § 2314, after a testator's death the attorney who drew the will "is at liberty to disclose all that affects the execution and tenor of the will," for the reason that "it seems hardly open to dispute that they are the very facts which the testator expected and intended to be disclosed after his death." The attorney may also testify concerning the testator's mental capacity, but only because his knowledge derives from personal observation rather than confidential communication. Ibid; Bonta v. Sevier, 202 Ky. 334, 259 S.W. 703 (1924).

The exception is limited to actions between or among persons claiming under the testator. Annotation, Privilege as to communications, etc., 64 A.L.R. 184, 185 (1929). Conversely, it does not apply to an action between those claiming under the testator and third parties, or "strangers," claiming adversely. Id. at p. 191; Supplement, 66 A.L.R.2d 1302, 1307 (1959). For an excellent statement of the rule see Paley v. Superior Court, 137 Cal.App.2d 450, 290 P.2d 617, 621 (1956).

By this time, no doubt, the reader of this opinion may be asking himself what is the relevance of this discussion to the would-be drafter of a will that was never drafted, and the answer is that we are attempting to show that even if Arnold *had* drafted Mrs. Eckel's will the attorney-client privilege would bar his testimony in an action adverse to those claiming under it. *A fortiori,* the exception could not apply to a witness who never drew a will at all.

We need not determine whether Hood v. Nichol, 236 Ky. 779, 34 S.W.2d 429 (1930), was correct in holding admissible the testimony of an attorney concerning discussions incident to the preparation of a will that was later revoked. The opinion did not address the point that the paper in question never took effect as a will. In any event, the action was between parties all of whom claimed *under* and not against the deceased client's estate, a condition which is not met in this case.

In Hecht's Adm'r v. Hecht, 272 Ky. 400, 114 S.W.2d 499 (1938), although the litigation concerned the effect of an *inter vivos* transfer of stock, the conversation in which the client explained its purpose and terms related directly to the preparation of a new will which was later admitted to probate. Again, all of the parties to that controversy also were claiming under the deceased client and the exception was held applicable, "for it is the rule that the death of a client removes the pledge of secrecy previously imposed upon communications between attorney and client for the free administration of justice, because after the client's death, *where all the parties are claiming under him,* there are no reasons ordinarily why proof of such communications should not be admitted in evidence." (Emphasis added.) Id. at 114 S.W.2d 501.

More nearly applicable to the facts of this case is Doyle v. Reeves, 112 Conn. 521, 152 A. 882 (1931), an action to recover for personal services in which it was held error for the trial court to allow an attorney to introduce and testify concerning a proposed will he had drafted at the client's instructions but which had never been executed:

> "'Unless otherwise provided by statute, communications, by a client to the attorney who drafted his will, in respect to that document and transactions between them leading up to its execution, are not privileged, after the client's death, in a suit between devisees under the will and heirs at law, or other parties who all claim under him. The principal reason is that the general rule is designed for the protection of the client, and it is deemed not for the interest of the testator, in a controversy between the parties, all of whom claim under him, to have those declarations and transactions excluded which promote a proper fulfillment of his will. Also a witness to a will, although attorney for the testator, is permitted to disclose everything which he knew concerning his attestation and the circumstances surrounding and leading up to it. * * * The conditions underlying and essential to these relaxations of the general rule are not met by the situation before us. We are not dealing with a completed and executed will, but with a mere draft never executed by the decedent or even, so far as appears, read to and approved by him. Also the action is one between the testator's representative and a stranger, in legal contemplation, not claiming under him * * *. We conclude, therefore, that both the consultations between Cole and Reeves preliminary to the preparation of the new draft, Exhibit E, and the instrument itself were within the protection of the privileged communication rule, when invoked in behalf of the decedent's executor and representative.' Id. at 152 A. 883–884."

We reach the same conclusion here.

* * *

The judgment is reversed on the appeal * * * with directions for a new trial.

All concur.

COMMONWEALTH v. GOLDMAN

Supreme Judicial Court of Massachusetts, 1985.
395 Mass. 495, 480 N.E.2d 1023, cert. denied, 474 U.S. 906, 106 S.Ct. 236, 88 L.Ed.2d 237 (1985).

LIACOS, JUSTICE.

In June, 1982, a Norfolk County grand jury indicted the defendant, Lawrence Goldman, for conspiracy to murder a former Boston police officer named John Glenn. When it became apparent that the Commonwealth would call Glenn as a witness at the defendant's trial, defense counsel, Mr. Willie J. Davis, filed a motion in limine seeking a pretrial ruling on a question concerning the attorney-client privilege. Following a hearing, a Superior Court judge made certain findings of fact and ruled on the motion. She then reported to the Appeals Court four questions raised by the motion. See Mass.R.Crim.P. 34, 378 Mass. 905 (1979). This court allowed the defendant's application for direct appellate review.

We summarize the facts as found by the judge. In January, 1982, Glenn made an unsuccessful attempt to murder an individual named Leo Shorter. The Commonwealth theorizes that the defendant, a codefendant in this case named John Miskel, and others hired Glenn to kill Shorter because Shorter had cheated the defendant in a drug deal. A Norfolk County grand jury indicted Glenn for assault with intent to murder Shorter. Shortly after his arraignment in January, 1982, Glenn met with Mr. Davis concerning the possibility of Mr. Davis's representing Glenn. Glenn and Mr. Davis discussed the indictment; Glenn gave confidential information about the case to Mr. Davis. They reached no agreement, however, concerning Mr. Davis's representation of Glenn, and Mr. Davis did not represent Glenn at his trial.

Following a trial in the Superior Court in Norfolk County, Glenn was convicted. His sentencing has been continued pending his testimony in the instant case. In this case, the Commonwealth alleges that, after Glenn's unsuccessful attempt to kill Shorter, the defendant conspired with Miskel to kill Glenn, and that Miskel unsuccessfully attempted to kill Glenn.[1]

After Mr. Davis filed the motion in limine, the judge held an in camera hearing at which Mr. Davis testified as to the substance of his conversation with Glenn.[2] Based on the testimony and exhibits, the judge found that in March, 1983, after his conviction, Glenn began to cooperate with the Commonwealth concerning his association with Miskel, the defendant, and others. Glenn gave statements relative to the attempt on the life of Shorter to officers of the Quincy police department. These statements were recorded, and, later, a transcription of them was made available to Mr. Davis as counsel for the defendant. The statements Glenn made to Mr. Davis are "diametrically opposed" to those which Glenn gave to Quincy police officers. Glenn is a key prosecution witness, and his credibility will be a central issue in the upcoming trial. Glenn's statements to Mr. Davis could be viewed by a reasonable juror as seriously damaging Glenn's credibility if he should testify in accordance with his taped statements. Glenn invokes

1. The defendant and Miskel also have been indicted on charges arising out of Glenn's attempt on Shorter's life.

2. We make no comment on the propriety of such an in camera disclosure of privileged communications absent the consent of the client.

the attorney-client privilege with respect to his conversation with Mr. Davis and refuses to waive it. Glenn has indicated his continuing intention not to waive the privilege.

The judge reported the following questions:

"1. Whether a witness waives the attorney-client privilege in regard to confidential communications previously made to an attorney concerning certain events, now the subject matter of this trial, when that witness takes the stand at trial and gives testimony as to those events, but specifically refuses to waive the attorney-client privilege as to the confidential communications.

"2. If not, whether the privilege should be overridden in the interest of justice.

"3. Whether defendant's attorney, to whom the Commonwealth's witness previously made confidential communications is required to withdraw because of the conflict of interest [which would] be inherent in his (the attorney's) continued representation of the defendant.

"4. Whether the defendant can voluntarily, knowingly, and intelligently consent to the continued representation by his attorney despite the conflict of interest where, because of the attorney-client privilege, full disclosure cannot be made by counsel to the defendant." [3]

We hold that, by testifying in the instant case, Glenn does not automatically waive the attorney-client privilege concerning his conversation with Mr. Davis, and that, on this record, justice does not require that the privilege be overridden. Although a genuine conflict of interest exists which may require withdrawal by Mr. Davis, the defendant may consent to his continued representation by Mr. Davis, so long as his consent is voluntarily, knowingly, and intelligently made.

1. *Waiver of attorney-client privilege.*[4] For over a century, Massachusetts case law has been in conflict on the issue whether a witness waives the attorney-client privilege when testifying. Neitlich v. Peterson, 15 Mass.App. 622, 626, 447 N.E.2d 671 (1983). P.J. Liacos, Massachusetts Evidence 215 (5th ed. 1981). Spalding, The Uncertain State of the Law as to Waiver of Professional Privilege as to Confidential Communications, 20 Mass.L.Q. (No. 3) 16, 17 (1935). In Woburn v. Henshaw, 101 Mass. 193, 200 (1869), the source of one line of cases, this court ruled that "[t]he policy of the law will not allow the counsel himself to make disclosures of confidential communications from his client; but if the client sees fit to be a witness, he makes himself liable to full cross-examination like any other witness. This is true even as to

3. In ruling on the motion, the judge answered these questions as follows: (1) "No"; (2) "No"; (3) "Yes"; (4) "No." Consequently, she ordered that Mr. Davis withdraw as the defendant's counsel.

4. We note that Mr. Davis does not dispute that the statements made by Glenn to him in January, 1982, came within the purview of the attorney-client privilege, even though he did not become Glenn's defense counsel. See Mailer v. Mailer, 390 Mass. 371, 374, 455 N.E.2d 1211 (1983); Commonwealth v. O'Brien, 377 Mass. 772, 775, 388 N.E.2d 658 (1979); Vigoda v. Barton, 348 Mass. 478, 485–486, 204 N.E.2d 441 (1965).

defendants in criminal cases. Commonwealth v. Mullen, 97 Mass. 545 [1867]."[5]

* * *

The contrary line of cases, holding that a witness's taking the stand, by itself, does not produce a wholesale waiver of the privilege, began with Montgomery v. Pickering, 116 Mass. 227, 231 (1874). Montgomery was followed by Blount v. Kimpton, 155 Mass. 378, 380, 29 N.E. 590 (1892), and McCooe v. Dighton, Somerset, & Swansea St. Ry., 173 Mass. 117, 119, 53 N.E. 133 (1899). More recently, in Kendall v. Atkins, 374 Mass. 320, 325, 372 N.E.2d 764 (1978), we assumed, without deciding, that the plaintiff properly could claim the privilege after having testified in her own behalf.

In his argument the defendant apparently confuses two distinct scenarios. In the first, a witness testifies as to events which happen to have been a topic of a privileged communication. In the second, the witness testifies as to the specific content of an identified privileged communication. We believe that the privilege is not waived in the first example, and we decline to follow that line of cases, based on Woburn v. Henshaw, supra, which appear to be to the contrary. A waiver may be found, however, where the client testifies as to the content of a privileged communication. Neitlich v. Peterson, supra, 15 Mass.App. at 626–627, 447 N.E.2d 671. See Montgomery v. Pickering, supra. Cf. Proposed Mass.R.Evid. 510 (1980).[6]

"[T]estimony about an event * * * should not be construed as a waiver of the privilege, merely because the subject matter of the testimony may also have been discussed in the privileged communication," People v. Lynch, 23 N.Y.2d 262, 271, 296 N.Y.S.2d 327, 244 N.E.2d 29 (1968); waiver of the attorney-client privilege should not be implied from a witness's taking the stand. See People v. Shapiro, 308 N.Y. 453, 457–460, 126 N.E.2d 559 (1955). Glenn is expected to testify about certain events which took place, not about the specifics of his conversation with Mr. Davis. Such testimony cannot be considered a waiver of the attorney-client privilege.

The defendant argues, however, that, even where there is no waiver of the privilege, the interests of justice require that it be overridden. Apropos of the defendant's argument is the rule set forth in Annot., 51 A.L.R.2d 521, 528 (1957), that "where an accomplice turns state's evidence and attempts to convict others by testimony which also

5. The court in *Woburn* made an erroneous analogy to Commonwealth v. Mullen, supra, which held that, upon testifying, a criminal defendant waives the privilege against self-incrimination. *Spalding,* supra at 18.

6. Some of the cases on which the defendant relies involve testimony as to specific privileged conversations, rather than to events which were a topic of a privileged conversation. See, e.g., In re Sealed Case, 676 F.2d 793, 808–809 (D.C.Cir.1982). Another case cited by the defendant, United States v. Jones, 696 F.2d 1069, 1072 (4th Cir.1982), is inapposite for a different reason. In *Jones* the court held that a waiver occurred because the clients publicized portions of their attorney's tax law opinions in brochures, a disclosure inconsistent with maintaining the confidential nature of the attorney-client relationship.

convicts himself, he thereby waives the privilege against disclosing communications between himself and counsel." See id., cases cited. The rationale underlying this approach was described in Jones v. State, 65 Miss. 179, 184, 3 So. 379 (1887): "The reason for maintaining such privileges ceases, when one has voluntarily exposed himself by his own testimony, to the very consequences from which it was intended by the privilege to protect him. To preserve such privilege in such case would be worse than vain, for while it could not help the witness, it might, by withholding the only means of contradicting and impeaching him, operate with the greatest injustice towards the party on trial." That Glenn is the victim of, rather than accomplice to, the crime does not serve to make this rationale inapplicable; Glenn is expected to testify about events for which he has already been convicted.

Nevertheless, the policy justifications for the attorney-client privilege override the reasoning of the court in *Jones* and support the judge's conclusion that, on this record, the privilege should not yield in the interest of justice.[8] The privilege operates to protect disclosures which might not have been made absent the privilege. Fisher v. United States, 425 U.S. 391, 403, 96 S.Ct. 1569, 1577, 48 L.Ed.2d 39 (1976). It encourages clients to seek an attorney's advice and to be truthful with the attorney, which in turn allows the attorney to give informed advice; the attorney-client privilege serves the public interest and the interest of the administration of justice. Upjohn Co. v. United States, 449 U.S. 383, 389, 101 S.Ct. 677, 682, 66 L.Ed.2d 584 (1981). Matter of Colton, 201 F.Supp. 13, 15 (S.D.N.Y.1961), aff'd, 306 F.2d 633 (2d Cir.1962), cert. denied, 371 U.S. 951, 83 S.Ct. 505, 9 L.Ed.2d 499 (1963). United States v. United Shoe Mach. Corp., 89 F.Supp. 357, 358 (D.Mass.1950). We reject the rationale of *Jones*. In this case, the "social good derived from the proper performance of the functions of lawyers acting for their clients * * * outweigh[s] the harm that may come from the suppression of the evidence." United Shoe, supra, quoting Model Code of Evidence Rule 210 comment a (1942).

In conclusion, we choose to follow the rule stated in 8 J. Wigmore, Evidence § 2327, at 637 (McNaughton rev. ed. 1961): "The client's offer of his *own testimony* in the cause *at large* is not a waiver for the purpose either of cross-examining him to the communications or of calling the attorney to prove them. Otherwise the privilege of consultation would be exercised only at the penalty of closing the client's own

8. We emphasize that, absent a trial, neither we nor a trial judge can resolve the question whether the common law attorney-client privilege would have to yield to a constitutionally based claim of denial of the right of confrontation or of the right to a fair trial. See, e.g., Davis v. Alaska, 415 U.S. 308, 94 S.Ct. 1105, 39 L.Ed.2d 347 (1974) (statutory privilege as to juvenile proceedings must yield to confrontation right to cross-examine effectively as guaranteed by Sixth and Fourteenth Amendments); Commonwealth v. Ferrara, 368 Mass. 182, 330 N.E.2d 837 (1975) (same); Commonwealth v. Joyce, 382 Mass. 222, 415 N.E.2d 181 (1981) (rape-shield law, G.L. c. 233, § 21B, interpreted so as to protect confrontation right of cross-examination to show bias).

mouth on the stand." (Emphasis in original.) See Littlefield v. Superior Court, 136 Cal.App.3d 477, 483–485, 186 Cal.Rptr. 368 (1982); State v. Hollins, 184 N.W.2d 676, 678 (Iowa 1971); Dunn v. Commonwealth, 350 S.W.2d 709, 713 (Ky.1961). Accordingly, we agree with the judge that the proper answer to reported questions (1) and (2) is "No."

2. *Conflict of interest.* The defendant argues that, should we hold that Glenn does not waive the attorney-client privilege by testifying, no conflict of interest arises. He maintains that ethical considerations present themselves only if Mr. Davis testifies, and is then faced with arguing his own credibility. We disagree. Mr. Davis will face a genuine conflict of interest in his cross-examination of Glenn.

A conflict of interest arises whenever an attorney's regard for one duty leads to disregard of another. United States v. Miller, 463 F.2d 600, 602 (1st Cir.), cert. denied sub nom. Gregory v. United States, 409 U.S. 956, 93 S.Ct. 300, 34 L.Ed.2d 225 (1972). In the instant case, Mr. Davis has a clear duty to maintain the confidence of his former client Glenn. S.J.C. Rule 3:07, Canon 4, DR 4–101(B), as amended, 382 Mass. 778 (1981). Mailer v. Mailer, 390 Mass. 371, 374, 455 N.E.2d 1211 (1983). Commonwealth v. O'Brien, 377 Mass. 772, 775, 388 N.E.2d 658 (1979). Dunn v. Commonwealth, supra. A.B.A. Code of Professional Responsibility and Canons of Judicial Ethics, EC 4–6 (1969).[9] At the same time, Mr. Davis must zealously represent the defendant. S.J.C. Rule 3:07, Canon 7, as amended, 382 Mass. 784 (1981). He must avoid representing a client where the interests of another, former client may impair his independent professional judgment. S.J.C. Rule 3:07, Canon 5, as amended, 382 Mass. 779 (1981).[10]

During cross-examination of Glenn, Mr. Davis will confront a genuine conflict of interest. On behalf of the defendant, Mr. Davis will likely cross-examine Glenn in an effort to impeach his credibility. During this cross-examination, Mr. Davis must avoid using any confidential information which he may have obtained from Glenn in their

9. Although not adopted by this court, the ethical considerations appearing in the American Bar Association's Code of Professional Responsibility and Canons of Judicial Ethics may be relied on in interpreting the Canons of Ethics and Disciplinary Rules. Commonwealth v. Michel, 381 Mass. 447, 456 n. 17, 409 N.E.2d 1293 (1980).

10. Such a conflict of interest may later give rise to a claim by a criminal defendant that he received ineffective assistance of counsel. See, e.g., Commonwealth v. Cobb, 379 Mass. 456, 405 N.E.2d 97, vacated sub nom. Massachusetts v. Hurley, 449 U.S. 809, 101 S.Ct. 56, 66 L.Ed.2d 12 (1980), appeal dismissed, 382 Mass. 690, 414 N.E.2d 1006 (1981). In Commonwealth v. Hodge, 386 Mass. 165, 434 N.E.2d 1246 (1982), we refused to apply to art. 12 of the Massachusetts Declaration of Rights the requirement of Cuyler v. Sullivan, 446 U.S. 335, 100 S.Ct. 1708, 64 L.Ed.2d 333 (1980), that under the Sixth Amendment of the Constitution of the United States a criminal defendant must show that an actual conflict of interest adversely affected his lawyer's performance. We held that under art. 12, having established a genuine conflict of interest, a defendant need not prove prejudice or adverse effect. *Hodge,* supra, 386 Mass. at 170, 434 N.E.2d 1246. Where a "tenuous," as opposed to "genuine," conflict of interest appears, a defendant must establish that the conflict of interest resulted in material prejudice. Commonwealth v. Soffen, 377 Mass. 433, 435–440, 386 N.E.2d 1030 (1979).

privileged conversation of January, 1982. "The conflict [thus] engendered in the attorney's own mind may have unmeasurable adverse effects on the client's interests." Commonwealth v. Rondeau, 378 Mass. 408, 416 n. 7, 392 N.E.2d 1001 (1979). Conflicts such as the one here at issue have resulted in court-ordered substitution of counsel, in remand orders, and in successful petitions for habeas corpus. * * *

* * * We answer the third reported question: A genuine conflict of interest exists which requires that Mr. Davis withdraw, unless Glenn waives his attorney-client privilege, which the judge has found he will not, or unless the defendant waives his right to be represented by counsel who bears him undivided loyalty. We now turn to the remaining reported question.

3. *Waiver of right to an attorney with undivided loyalty.* The Superior Court judge noted that the defendant has indicated a desire to waive representation by an attorney with undivided loyalty. A defendant's right to have the effective assistance of counsel, guaranteed by the Sixth Amendment to the Constitution of the United States, contemplates that the assistance be "untrammeled and unimpaired * * * free of any conflict of interest and unrestrained by commitments to others." Commonwealth v. Davis, 376 Mass. 777, 780–781, 384 N.E.2d 181 (1978). Glasser v. United States, 315 U.S. 60, 76, 62 S.Ct. 457, 467, 86 L.Ed. 680 (1942). A defendant, however, may waive this right to an attorney "unhindered by a conflict of interests." Commonwealth v. Connor, 381 Mass. 500, 504, 410 N.E.2d 709 (1980), quoting Holloway v. Arkansas, 435 U.S. 475, 483 n. 5, 98 S.Ct. 1173, 1178 n. 5, 55 L.Ed.2d 426 (1978). The ability to waive the right to a conflict-free attorney arises from (1) a criminal defendant's right to present his defense, with its corollary right of self-representation, and (2) his right to be represented by counsel of choice. *Connor,* supra, citing Faretta v. California, 422 U.S. 806, 818, 833, 95 S.Ct. 2525, 2532, 2540, 45 L.Ed.2d 562 (1975). *Davis,* supra, 376 Mass. at 787 n. 12, 384 N.E.2d 181.

The judge ruled that, although an argument can be made that the defendant's waiver may be voluntary, the defendant cannot make a "knowing and intelligent" waiver; because the information is privileged, the defendant cannot know what the information is and, therefore, cannot know how his defense will be affected. We think that this ruling is incorrect. The defendant need not know the exact content of the privileged communication to make an informed decision. Presumably, the defendant will be informed that Glenn's anticipated testimony is "diametrically opposed" to the privileged communication, and from that basis the defendant will be able to extrapolate any effect that Mr. Davis's constrained cross-examination will have on his defense.

Before remanding the case to the Superior Court, we discuss the conditions under which a judge properly may find that a defendant has waived the right to an attorney with undivided loyalty. First, a finding of waiver of a constitutional right to counsel should not be made lightly. See Commonwealth v. Cavanaugh, 371 Mass. 46, 53, 353 N.E.2d 732 (1976). Courts should indulge " 'every reasonable presumption against waiver' of [a] fundamental constitutional right[ ] and * * * 'not presume acquiescence in the loss of [such] rights.' " Johnson v. Zerbst, 304 U.S. 458, 464, 58 S.Ct. 1019, 1023, 82 L.Ed. 1461 (1938), quoting Aetna Ins. Co. v. Kennedy, 301 U.S. 389, 393, 57 S.Ct. 809, 811, 81 L.Ed. 1177 (1937), and Ohio Bell Tel. Co. v. Public Utilities Comm'n, 301 U.S. 292, 307, 57 S.Ct. 724, 731, 81 L.Ed. 1093 (1937). The waiver must be an "intentional relinquishment or abandonment of a known right," *Zerbst,* supra, not only voluntary but also a "knowing, intelligent act[ ] done with sufficient awareness of the relevant circumstances and likely consequences." Brady v. United States, 397 U.S. 742, 748, 90 S.Ct. 1463, 1469, 25 L.Ed.2d 747 (1970).

* * *

Finally, in a rare instance, in ruling on the validity of a defendant's waiver, the trial judge may take into account, aside from the rights of the defendant, the interests of the court in the "fair and proper administration of justice." *Connor,* supra, 376 Mass. at 504, 384 N.E.2d 181. Counsel's undivided loyalty to the client is crucial to the integrity of the entire adversary system. Commonwealth v. Leslie, 376 Mass. 647, 652, 382 N.E.2d 1072 (1978), cert. denied, 441 U.S. 910, 99 S.Ct. 2006, 60 L.Ed.2d 381 (1979). See id., 376 Mass. at 656, 658, 382 N.E.2d 1072 (Liacos, J., concurring); Kabase v. Eighth Judicial Dist. Court, 96 Nev. 471, 611 P.2d 194, 195 (Nev.1980); Developments in the Law, supra at 1394. In criminal cases, the public has a substantial interest in the fairness of the process and its expeditious administration. This principle, however, cannot, in most instances, overcome the right of a defendant to choose his counsel, even if that attorney is conflict-burdened, provided the defendant's waiver is voluntary, knowing, and intelligent. Thus, we conclude that the judge erred in answering the fourth reported question, "No." We hold that the defendant can waive his right to a conflict-free counsel in the circumstances of this case. Whether he will do so on being fully advised of his rights in accordance with the procedures and principles set forth in this opinion is unclear. We express no views whether the judge should exercise her discretion to override, in the interests of the administration of justice, such a waiver should it be exercised. Accordingly, we vacate the judge's order requiring Mr. Davis to withdraw and remand this case to the Superior Court for further proceedings consistent with this opinion.

So ordered.

SECTION 3. PHYSICIAN-PATIENT AND PSYCHOTHERAPIST-PATIENT *

MILLER v. COLONIAL REFRIGERATED TRANSPORTATION INC.

United States District Court, Middle District of Pennsylvania, 1979.
81 F.R.D. 741.

HERMAN, DISTRICT JUDGE.

On October 30, 1978, the Plaintiff in the above-captioned case, Elsie Romaine Miller, filed a motion to quash a subpoena or in the alternative for a protective order pursuant to Rule 45(b) and Rule 26(c) of the Federal Rules of Civil Procedure. The subpoena in question is a subpoena duces tecum issued to Joseph G. Saxon, M.D. at the request of the Defendants and involves psychiatric records. In the motion, Plaintiff requests the Court to quash the subpoena, or in the alternative for a protective order, on the grounds that the psychiatric records contain matters that do not relate to the accident, contain matters that are privileged and contain matters personal in nature and private to Plaintiff, and to reveal such would cause harm and embarrassment to Plaintiff.

The motion to quash the subpoena will be denied, however we will issue a limited protective order.

This action arises out of a traffic accident on January 14, 1975, in which Plaintiff is alleged to have sustained, *inter alia,* mental and emotional injuries in the form of post-traumatic neurosis. Plaintiff is seeking to recover for her alleged personal injuries including the post-traumatic neurosis.

Rule 26(b)(1) of the Federal Rules of Civil Procedure provides that "Parties may obtain discovery regarding any matter, *not privileged,* which is relevant to the subject matter involved in the pending action * * *." (emphasis supplied). We believe there can be no dispute as to the relevancy of the material sought. Where compensation is sought for personal injury the health of the Plaintiff both before and after the accident may be inquired into. 4 Moore's Federal Practice ¶ 26.56[1]. This principle would seem to have equal applicability to an emotional or mental injury when that is what a Plaintiff seeks compensation for. The problem in this case revolves around the Plaintiff's assertion of her "professional privilege" as the privilege against disclosure of communications between physician and patient is applicable in discovery pro-

* See 8 Wigmore, Evidence ch. 86 (McNaughton rev. 1961); McCormick, Evidence ch. 11 (4th ed. 1992) Louisell & Sinclair, Reflections on the Law of Privileged Communications: The Psychotherapist–Patient Privilege in Perspective, 59 Calif.L.Rev. 30 (1971); Shuman & Weiner, The Privilege Study: An Empirical Examination of the Psychotherapist–Patient Privilege, 60 N.C.L.Rev. 893 (1982); Slovenko, Psychotherapist–Patient Testimonial Privilege: A Picture of Misguided Hope, 23 Cath.L.Rev. 649 (1974); Winslade & Ross, Privacy, Confidentiality and Autonomy in Psychotherapy, 64 Neb.L.Rev. 578 (1985).

ceedings. 4 Moore's Federal Practice ¶ 26.60[2]. What is privileged under the law of evidence has been taken as a measure of what is privileged from discovery, and Rule 501 of the Federal Rules of Evidence provides that on state law claims or defenses, the question of privilege is governed by state law. 4 Moore's ¶ 26.60[7].

The Plaintiff bases her objection to discovery of her psychiatric record on a privilege based in Pennsylvania statute and on a claimed constitutional right of privacy based upon both the Pennsylvania and United States Constitutions. The Plaintiff's assertion of privilege is based in large measure on the recent case from the Pennsylvania Supreme Court, In re "B", Pa., 394 A.2d 419 (1978) in which Justice Manderino, joined by one other Justice, found a constitutional right of privacy in the prevention of disclosure of information revealed in the context of the psychotherapist-patient relationship. The Manderino opinion in that case creates a novel discovery problem in that it seeks to place the confidentiality of the psychotherapist-patient relation in the realm of constitutionally protected interests.

We will examine the statutory privilege first and then the asserted constitutional privilege. In Plaintiff's motion she indicated that there are matters which do not relate to the accident in her psychiatric records. If there are matters which are truly separable from the accident and not discoverable, these should not have to be revealed, however when a person puts in question the cause and effect of her mental or emotional state it would seem difficult if not impossible to separate some information on a person's mental and emotional condition from other information.

Pennsylvania Privilege Statutes:

There are two Pennsylvania statutes that relate to the psychotherapist-patient privilege. Pennsylvania's physician-patient privilege statute, Act of June 7, 1907, codified by the Act of July 9, 1976, P.L. 586, 42 Pa.C.S.A. § 5929 (formerly 28 P.S. § 328), provides:

"§ 5929. Physicians not to disclose information

> No physician shall be allowed, in any civil matter, to disclose any information which he acquired in attending the patient in a professional capacity, and which was necessary to enable him to act in that capacity, which shall tend to blacken the character of the patient, without consent of said patient, except in civil matters brought by such patient, for damages on account of personal injuries."

Another Pennsylvania statute, Act of March 23, 1972, P.L. 136, No. 52, now codified by the Act of July 9, 1976, P.L. 586, 42 Pa.C.S.A. § 5944 (formerly 63 P.S. § 1213) provides as follows:

"§ 5944. Confidential communications to licensed psychologists

> No person who has been licensed under the act of March 23, 1972 (P.L. 136, No. 52), to practice psychology shall be, without the written consent of his client, examined in any civil or criminal matter as to any information acquired in the course of his professional services in

> behalf of such client. The confidential relations and communications between a psychologist and his client shall be on the same basis as those provided or prescribed by law between an attorney and client."

Although the physician-patient privilege statute, 42 Pa.C.S.A. § 5929 speaks in terms of "* * * any information acquired in attending the patient", it has been held that the statute is limited to "communications" received from the patient and that the act does not prevent disclosure of information learned by a doctor through examination or observation. In re "B", Pa., 394 A.2d 419 (1978); In Re Phillips Estate, 295 Pa. 349, 145 A. 437 (1929); Panko v. Consolidated Mutual Insurance Co., 423 F.2d 41 (3d Cir.1970); Woods v. National Life and Accident Insurance Co., 347 F.2d 760 (3d Cir.1965). The statute requires a privilege as to communications which tend to "blacken the character" of the patient. This requirement that disclosure of the communication would "blacken the character" has received a narrow interpretation. In Skruch v. Metropolitan Life Insurance Co., 284 Pa. 299, 131 A. 186 (1925) the Pennsylvania Supreme Court concluded that the act's prohibition applies only to communications received from the patient which indicate that the patient was suffering from some "loathsome disease". See, Soltaniak v. Metropolitan Life Insurance Co., 133 Pa.Super. 139, 2 A.2d 501 (1938). The privilege is further qualified in the statute by its provision that the physician may disclose information acquired in civil matters brought by the patient for damages on account of personal injuries. Whether or not the Plaintiff's psychiatric records could be considered to be such as would "blacken" her character, they would seem to clearly fall within the exception for civil matters brought by the patient for damages on account of personal injuries.

This narrow view of the privilege contained in 42 Pa.C.S.A. § 5929 was outlined by Justice Manderino's opinion in In re "B", Pa., 394 A.2d 419 (1978). However, Justice Roberts pointed out in a concurring opinion that the opinion of Justice Manderino does not address the scope or effect of the Act of March 23, 1972, P.L. 136, No. 52, 63 P.S. § 1213, Section 13, now codified at 42 Pa.C.S.A. § 5944 (formerly at 63 P.S. § 1213). Justice Roberts states in his concurring opinion:

> "Although this statute does not expressly apply to medical doctors engaged in the practice of psychotherapy, but rather only to those with graduate degrees in psychology, see id., § 6, 63 P.S. § 1206, it would be arbitrary to believe that the Legislature intended the scope of a patient's privilege to depend on whether the attending therapist is a medical doctor or a psychologist."

In re "B", Pa., 394 A.2d at 428. However, in recodifying this statute the Legislature specifically referred to the Act of March 23, 1972, P.L. 136, No. 52, and that statute deals only with psychologists and provides at 63 P.S. § 1203(2) that persons licensed to practice any of the healing arts in this Commonwealth shall be exempt from the provisions of the act. The resulting statutory tangle creates the incongruous result that a patient-psychologist relationship appears to retain more of a confidential privilege than a patient psychiatrist relationship.[1]

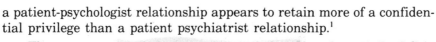

The statutory psychologist-patient privilege found at 42 Pa.C.S.A. § 5944 is not by its terms applicable to this case as this case involves the records of a psychiatrist. 42 Pa.C.S.A. § 5929, the statutory physician patient privilege, provides no privilege because the patient has brought a civil action for damages for the alleged condition which was the subject of the psychiatrist's treatment. Therefore, the Pennsylvania privilege statutes provide the Plaintiff no protection in this case. See generally, Annotation, 44 A.L.R.3d 24, "Privilege in Judicial or Quasi-Judicial Proceedings, Arising From Relationship Between Psychiatrist or Psychologist and Patient".

CONSTITUTIONAL PRIVILEGE

The Plaintiff asserts that she has a constitutional privilege to retain the confidentiality of her patient-psychiatrist relationship based on Justice Manderino's holding in In re "B", Pa., 394 A.2d 419 (1978). In that case Justice Manderino said:

> "We conclude that in Pennsylvania, an individual's interest in preventing the disclosure of information revealed in the context of a psychotherapist-patient relationship has deeper roots than the Pennsylvania doctor-patient privilege statute, and that the patient's right to prevent disclosure of such information is constitutionally based. This constitutional foundation emanates from the penumbras of the various guarantees of the Bill of Rights, Griswold v. Connecticut, supra, [381 U.S. 479, 85 S.Ct. 1678, 14 L.Ed.2d 510] as well as from the guarantees of the Constitution of this Commonwealth, see especially, Article I, Section 1 (inherent right to enjoy and defend life and liberty, to protect reputation and pursue happiness); Article I, Section 2 (all political power is inherent in the people); Article I, Sections 3 and 4 (people's right to freedom of religion); Article I, Section 7 (freedom of press and speech guaranteed to every citizen so that they may speak, write, or print freely on any subject '* * * being responsible for the abuse of that liberty.'); Article I, Section 8 (people shall be secure in their persons, houses, papers, and possessions from unreasonable search and seizures); Article I, Section 9 (an accused in a criminal proceeding cannot be compelled to give evidence against himself); Article I, Section 11 (courts are to be open to all to provide remedy for injury done to reputation); Article I, Section 20 (right of assembly); Article I, Section 23 (prohibition of the peacetime quartering of troops in any house without the consent of the owner); and Article I, Section 25 (reservation of powers in the people); and Article I, Section 26 (prohibi-

1. Justice Roberts attempts to deal with this situation in his concurring opinion in In re "B", Pa., 394 A.2d 416, at 428, n. 2 (1978), by suggesting that if there is no privilege for the psychotherapeutic relation when the therapist is a medical doctor, there would be no bar to finding such protection under the common law. In light of an earlier ruling by the Pennsylvania Supreme Court in Commonwealth v. Sykes, 353 Pa. 392, 45 A.2d 43 (1946) *cert. denied,* 328 U.S. 847, 66 S.Ct. 1021, 90 L.Ed. 1620, that no common law privilege as to communications between physician and patient existed, it would seem the better course for this Court to defer to the Pennsylvania courts for the creation of such a right.

> tion against the denial by the Commonwealth of the enjoyment of any civil right). In some respects these state constitutional rights parallel those of the Federal Constitution, see especially, Amendments 1, 3, 4, 5, and 9. In other respects our Constitution provides more rigorous and explicit protection for a person's right of privacy, e.g., Article I, Section 1, 3, 4, 7 and 11."

394 A.2d at 425.

As we have already mentioned, a threshold issue in this case is the weight to give the Pennsylvania Supreme Court's treatment of In re "B", Pa., 394 A.2d 419 (1978). The Pennsylvania Supreme Court failed to articulate a majority view on the question of a constitutional psychotherapist-patient privilege. An opinion was written by Justice Manderino, apparently joined in by Justice Larsen, arguing for the privilege. 394 A.2d at 420. Two other justices concurred in the result filing no opinions. Justice Roberts filed a concurring opinion limited to approving the result on a statutory privilege basis. 394 A.2d at 426. It can be argued that while Chief Justice Eagen dissented he recognized some form of right of privacy privilege as he stated in his dissent, "Because of the important state interest in treatment and welfare of juveniles, I do not believe the right of privacy should prevail under the circumstances of this case." 394 A.2d at 430. Justice Pomeroy, joined by Justice Nix, dissented because they felt Justice Manderino's opinion gratuitously created a constitutional question when none was presented by the parties. 394 A.2d at 430. Since less than a majority of the Pennsylvania Supreme Court held the constitutional privilege view, the opinion of Justice Manderino must be treated only as an expression of the view of a minority of the court. See, Greiner v. Volkswagenwerk Aktiengeselleschaft, 540 F.2d 85 (3d Cir.1976).

To understand the opinions in In re "B", Pa., 394 A.2d 419 (1978) it is helpful to look at the factual situation presented. *In re "B"* involved a contempt citation issued to a psychiatrist during the dispositional phase of a juvenile delinquency proceeding. As part of the state common pleas court's effort to determine proper placement for the delinquent juvenile, "B's" mother had received inpatient psychiatric treatment. Based upon this information the juvenile court's psychiatrist recommended obtaining the hospital records regarding "B's" mother and her treatment. The patient's clinic refused to release the records of "B's" mother's treatment without the patient's consent. The court held the clinic's representative in contempt and the appeal ensued. *In re "B"* presents a situation in which the patient is an interested third party to court proceedings rather than one in which a person has directly raised a claim based upon her emotional or mental condition as is presented in our case.

In Caesar v. Mountanos, 542 F.2d 1064 (9th Cir.1976), *cert. denied,* 430 U.S. 954, 97 S.Ct. 1598, 51 L.Ed.2d 804, a psychiatrist was adjudged in contempt for refusing to obey an order directing him to answer questions relating to communications with a former patient. The California Evidence Code, § 1016 provides for a psychotherapist-patient privilege, however the privilege is not an absolute one, but rather provides for several exceptions including one known as the "patient-litigant exception". The patient-litigant exception was challenged in the *Caesar* case for, *inter alia,* violating the patient's federal constitutional right of privacy. The Ninth Circuit Court of Appeals in *Caesar* followed the opinion of the Supreme Court of California in In re Lifschutz, 2 Cal.3d 415, 85 Cal.Rptr. 829, 467 P.2d 557 (1970) and upheld the validity of the California evidentiary rule against an assertion that the psychotherapist-patient privilege is an absolute one under the constitutional right to privacy.

It was averred in *Caesar* that the alleged absolute constitutional protection for communications between patients and their psychotherapists, particularly in light of the broader reach of doctor-patient privacy recognized subsequently to Griswold v. Connecticut, 381 U.S. 479, 85 S.Ct. 1678, 14 L.Ed.2d 510 (1965) in Roe v. Wade, 410 U.S. 113, 93 S.Ct. 705, 35 L.Ed.2d 147 (1973) and Doe v. Bolton, 410 U.S. 179, 93 S.Ct. 739, 35 L.Ed.2d 201 (1973), was required by the nature of the relationship which depends on a patient's confidence that what he reveals to his psychotherapist will remain totally confidential. *Caesar* went on to assume a measure of constitutional protection for the psychotherapist-patient relationship and pointed out that such protection required a compelling state interest to overcome the privilege. The compelling state interest was found in seeing that truth is ascertained in legal proceedings in the state's courts of law, and the Court also alluded to a fairness requirement by stating "Every person who brings a lawsuit under our system of jurisprudence must bear disclosure of those facts upon which his claim is based." 542 F.2d at 1068.

Proposed Rule 504 of the Federal Rules of Evidence as promulgated by the United States Supreme Court, 56 F.R.D. 183, 240–41 (1973), ultimately rejected by Congress in favor of the more general Rule 501, provided for a psychotherapist-patient privilege quite similar to the California rule. The relevant portions of the proposed Rule 504 provided:

> "(b) General rule of privilege. A patient has a privilege to refuse to disclose and to prevent any other person from disclosing confidential communications, made for the purposes of diagnosis or treatment of his mental or emotional condition, including drug addiction, among himself, his psychotherapist, or persons who are participating in the diagnosis or treatment under the direction of the psychotherapist, including members of the patient's family.
>
> * * *
>
> (d) Exceptions.
>
> * * *
>
> (3) Condition an element of claim or defense. There is no privilege under this rule as to communications relevant to an issue of the mental or emotional condition of the patient in any proceeding in which he relies upon the condition as an element of his claim or

defense, or, after the patient's death, in any proceeding in which any party relies upon the condition as an element of his claim or defense.

Advisory Committee's Note

* * *

Subdivision (d). The exceptions differ substantially from those of the attorney-client privilege, as a result of the basic differences in the relationships. While it has been argued convincingly that the nature of the psychotherapist-patient relationship demands complete security against legally coerced disclosure in all circumstances * * * the committee of psychiatrists and lawyers who drafted the Connecticut statute concluded that in three instances the need for disclosure was sufficiently great to justify the rise of possible impairment of the relationship.

* * *

(1) [commitment proceedings]

* * *

(2) [court-ordered examinations]

* * *

(3) By injecting his condition into litigation the patient must be said to waive the privilege, in fairness and to avoid abuses. * * *"

56 F.R.D. 240–244.

The United States Supreme Court has recognized that the constitutional doctrine of privacy involves at least two different kinds of interests. Whalen v. Roe, 429 U.S. 589, 599, 97 S.Ct. 869, 51 L.Ed.2d 64, 73 (1977). One involves the interest in making certain kinds of important decisions, such as those relating to marriage, procreation, contraception, family relationships, and child rearing and education. See, Paul v. Davis, 424 U.S. 693, 713, 96 S.Ct. 1155, 47 L.Ed.2d 405 (1976). The other is the individual interest in avoiding disclosure of personal matters. Whalen v. Roe, 429 U.S. 589, 599, 97 S.Ct. 869, 51 L.Ed.2d 64, 73 (1977).

The commentators have recognized a distinction between patients with physical complaints who will consult a physician regardless of whether confidentiality is guaranteed, and a person with emotional or mental problems because a psychotherapist's capacity to help his patients is completely dependent upon their willingness and ability to talk freely. See McCormick, Evidence § 99 at 213, n. 9 (Cleary, 2d ed. 1972); United States Supreme Court's Proposed Federal Rules of Evidence, Advisory Committee's Note to Rule 504, 56 F.R.D. 183, 241–42 (1973). However, if such a privilege can be said to exist, it would not be absolute. Lora v. Board of Education of the City of New York, 74 F.R.D. 565 (E.D.N.Y.). The interests of the state in seeing that truth is ascertained in legal proceedings and fairness in the adversary process justify a patient-litigant exception to confidentiality such as the one provided for in the California Evidence Code, § 1016 and the proposed

Rule 504 of the Federal Rules of Evidence. Therefore we will deny the motion to quash the subpoena.

Notes

(1) Despite opposition by most legal writers, led by Wigmore, see 8 Wigmore, Evidence § 2380a (McNaughton rev. 1961), most states now have some sort of statutory physician-patient privilege. See id. § 2380. However:

> "While many states have by statute created the privilege, the exceptions which have been found necessary in order to obtain information required by the public interest or to avoid fraud are so numerous as to leave little if any basis for the privilege. Among the exclusions from the statutory privilege, the following may be enumerated; communications not made for purposes of diagnosis and treatment; commitment and restoration proceedings; issues as to wills or otherwise between parties claiming by succession from the patient; actions on insurance policies; required reports (venereal diseases, gunshot wounds, child abuse); communications in furtherance of crime or fraud; mental or physical condition put in issue by patient (personal injury cases); malpractice actions; and some or all criminal prosecutions. California, for example, excepts cases in which the patient puts his condition in issue, all criminal proceedings, will and similar contests, malpractice cases, and disciplinary proceedings, as well as certain other situations, thus leaving virtually nothing covered by the privilege. California Evidence Code §§ 990–1007."
>
> Proposed Fed.R.Evid. 504 advisory committee note.

(2) The psychotherapist-patient privilege has found more support. See, e.g., Slovenko, Psychiatry and a Second Look at the Medical Privilege, 6 Wayne L.Rev. 175 (1960); Proposed Fed.R.Evid. 504.

(3) In certain circumstances a communication to a physician or psychotherapist that is outside the protection of either of these privileges may be protected by another, such as lawyer-client (see City & County of San Francisco v. Superior Court, 37 Cal.2d 227, 231 P.2d 26 (1951)) or self-incrimination (see Estelle v. Smith, 451 U.S. 454, 101 S.Ct. 1866, 68 L.Ed.2d 359 (1981)).

SECTION 4. GOVERNMENTAL PRIVILEGES *

UNITED STATES v. NIXON

Supreme Court of the United States, 1974.
418 U.S. 683, 94 S.Ct. 3090, 41 L.Ed.2d 1039.

MR. CHIEF JUSTICE BURGER delivered the opinion of the Court.

This litigation presents for review the denial of a motion, filed in the District Court on behalf of the President of the United States, in

* See 8 Wigmore, Evidence ch. 85 (McNaughton rev. 1961); McCormick, Evidence ch. 12 (4th ed. 1992).

the case of United States v. Mitchell et al. (D.C.Crim. No. 74–110), to quash a third-party subpoena *duces tecum* issued by the United States District Court for the District of Columbia, pursuant to Fed.Rule Crim.Proc. 17(c). The subpoena directed the President to produce certain tape recordings and documents relating to his conversations with aides and advisers. The court rejected the President's claims of absolute executive privilege, of lack of jurisdiction, and of failure to satisfy the requirements of Rule 17(c). The President appealed to the Court of Appeals. We granted both the United States' petition for certiorari before judgment (No. 73–1766), and also the President's cross-petition for certiorari before judgment (No. 73–1834), because of the public importance of the issues presented and the need for their prompt resolution 417 U.S. 927 and 960, 94 S.Ct. 2637 and 3162, 41 L.Ed.2d 231 (1974).

On March 1, 1974, a grand jury of the United States District Court for the District of Columbia returned an indictment charging seven named individuals with various offenses, including conspiracy to defraud the United States and to obstruct justice. Although he was not designated as such in the indictment, the grand jury named the President, among others, as an unindicted coconspirator. On April 18, 1974, upon motion of the Special Prosecutor, a subpoena *duces tecum* was issued pursuant to Rule 17(c) to the President by the United States District Court and made returnable on May 2, 1974. This subpoena required the production, in advance of the September 9 trial date, of certain tapes, memoranda, papers, transcripts or other writings relating to certain precisely identified meetings between the President and others. The Special Prosecutor was able to fix the time, place, and persons present at these discussions because the White House daily logs and appointment records had been delivered to him. On April 30, the President publicly released edited transcripts of 43 conversations; portions of 20 conversations subject to subpoena in the present case were included. On May 1, 1974, the President's counsel, filed a "special appearance" and a motion to quash the subpoena under Rule 17(c). This motion was accompanied by a formal claim of privilege. At a subsequent hearing, further motions to expunge the grand jury's action naming the President as an unindicted coconspirator and for protective orders against the disclosure of that information were filed or raised orally by counsel for the President.

On May 20, 1974, the District Court denied the motion to quash and the motions to expunge and for protective orders. 377 F.Supp. 1326. It further ordered "the President or any subordinate officer, official, or employee with custody or control of the documents or objects subpoenaed," id., at 1331 to deliver to the District Court, on or before May 31, 1974, the originals of all subpoenaed items, as well as an index and analysis of those items, together with tape copies of those portions of the subpoenaed recordings for which transcripts had been released to the public by the President on April 30. The District Court rejected jurisdictional challenges based on a contention that the dispute was nonjusticiable because it was between the Special Prosecutor and the Chief Executive and hence "intra-executive" in character; it also rejected the contention that the Judiciary was without authority to review an assertion of executive privilege by the President. The court's rejection of the first challenge was based on the authority and powers vested in the Special Prosecutor by the regulation promulgated by the Attorney General; the court concluded that a justiciable controversy was presented. The second challenge was held to be foreclosed by the decision in Nixon v. Sirica, 159 U.S.App.D.C. 58, 487 F.2d 700 (1973).

The District Court held that the judiciary, not the President, was the final arbiter of a claim of executive privilege. The court concluded that under the circumstances of this case the presumptive privilege was overcome by the Special Prosecutor's prima facie "demonstration of need sufficiently compelling to warrant judicial examination in chambers * * *." 377 F.Supp., at 1330. The court held, finally, that the Special Prosecutor had satisfied the requirements of Rule 17(c). The District Court stayed its order pending appellate review on condition that review was sought before 4 p.m., May 24. The court further provided that matters filed under seal remain under seal when transmitted as part of the record.

On May 24, 1974, the President filed a timely notice of appeal from the District Court order, and the certified record from the District Court was docketed in the United States Court of Appeals for the District of Columbia Circuit. On the same day, the President also filed a petition for writ of mandamus in the Court of Appeals seeking review of the District Court order.

Later on May 24, the Special Prosecutor also filed, in this Court, a petition for a writ of certiorari before judgment. On May 31, the petition was granted with an expedited briefing schedule, 417 U.S. 927, 94 S.Ct. 2637, 41 L.Ed.2d 231. On June 6, the President filed, under seal, a cross-petition for writ of certiorari before judgment. This cross-petition was granted June 15, 1974, 417 U.S. 960, 94 S.Ct. 3162, 41 L.Ed.2d 1134, and the case was set for argument on July 8, 1974. * * *

IV

THE CLAIM OF PRIVILEGE

A

Having determined that the requirements of Rule 17(c) were satisfied, we turn to the claim that the subpoena should be quashed because it demands "confidential conversations between a President and his close advisors that it would be inconsistent with the public interest to produce." App. 48a. The first contention is a broad claim that the separation of powers doctrine precludes judicial review of a President's claim of privilege. The second contention is that if he does not prevail on the claim of absolute privilege, the court should hold as a matter of constitutional law that the privilege prevails over the subpoena *duces tecum.*

In the performance of assigned constitutional duties each branch of the Government must initially interpret the Constitution, and the interpretation of its powers by any branch is due great respect from the others. The President's counsel, as we have noted, reads the Constitution as providing an absolute privilege of confidentiality for all Presidential communications. Many decisions of this Court, however, have unequivocally reaffirmed the holding of Marbury v. Madison, 1 Cranch. 137, 2 L.Ed. 60 (1803), that "[i]t is emphatically the province and duty of the judicial department to say what the law is." Id., at 177, 2 L.Ed. 60.

No holding of the Court has defined the scope of judicial power specifically relating to the enforcement of a subpoena for confidential Presidential communications for use in a criminal prosecution, but other exercises of power by the Executive Branch and the Legislative Branch have been found invalid as in conflict with the Constitution. Powell v. McCormack, 395 U.S. 486, 89 S.Ct. 1944, 23 L.Ed.2d 491 (1969); Youngstown Sheet & Tube Co. v. Sawyer, 343 U.S. 579, 72 S.Ct. 863, 96 L.Ed. 1153 (1952). In a series of cases, the Court interpreted the explicit immunity conferred by express provisions of the Constitution on Members of the House and Senate by the Speech or Debate Clause, U.S. Const. Art. I, § 6. Doe v. McMillan, 412 U.S. 306, 93 S.Ct. 2018, 36 L.Ed.2d 912 (1973); Gravel v. United States, 408 U.S. 606, 92 S.Ct. 2614, 33 L.Ed.2d 583 (1972); United States v. Brewster, 408 U.S. 501, 92 S.Ct. 2531, 33 L.Ed.2d 507 (1972); United States v. Johnson, 383 U.S. 169, 86 S.Ct. 749, 15 L.Ed.2d 681 (1966). Since this Court has consistently exercised the power to construe and delineate claims arising under express powers, it must follow that the Court has authority to interpret claims with respect to powers alleged to derive from enumerated powers.

Our system of government "requires that federal courts on occasion interpret the Constitution in a manner at variance with the construction given the document by another branch." Powell v. McCormack, supra, 395 U.S., at 549, 89 S.Ct., at 1978. And in Baker v. Carr, 369 U.S., at 211, 82 S.Ct., at 706, the Court stated:

> "[D]eciding whether a matter has in any measure been committed by the Constitution to another branch of government, or whether the action of that branch exceeds whatever authority has been committed, is itself a delicate exercise in constitutional interpretation, and is a responsibility of this Court as ultimate interpreter of the Constitution."

Notwithstanding the deference each branch must accord the others, the "judicial Power of the United States" vested in the federal courts by Art. III, § 1, of the Constitution can no more be shared with the Executive Branch than the Chief Executive, for example, can share with the Judiciary the veto power, or the Congress share with the Judiciary the power to override a Presidential veto. Any other conclusion would be contrary to the basic concept of separation of powers and the checks and balances that flow from the scheme of a tripartite government. The Federalist, No. 47, p. 313 (S. Mittell ed. 1938). We therefore reaffirm that it is the province and duty of this Court "to say what the law is" with respect to the claim of privilege presented in this case. Marbury v. Madison, supra, 1 Cranch. at 177, 2 L.Ed. 60.

B

In support of his claim of absolute privilege, the President's counsel urges two grounds, one of which is common to all governments and one of which is peculiar to our system of separation of powers. The first ground is the valid need for protection of communications between high Government officials and those who advise and assist them in the performance of their manifold duties; the importance of this confidentiality is too plain to require further discussion. Human experience teaches that those who expect public dissemination of their remarks may well temper candor with a concern for appearances and for their own interests to the detriment of the decisionmaking process.[15] Whatever the nature of the privilege of confidentiality of Presidential communications in the exercise of Art. II powers, the privilege can be said to derive from the supremacy of each branch within its own assigned area of constitutional duties. Certain powers and privileges flow from the nature of enumerated powers; the protection of the confidentiality of Presidential communications has similar constitutional underpinnings.

The second ground asserted by the President's counsel in support of the claim of absolute privilege rests on the doctrine of separation of powers. Here it is argued that the independence of the Executive Branch within its own sphere, Humphrey's Executor v. United States, 295 U.S. 602, 629–630, 55 S.Ct. 869, 874–875, 79 L.Ed. 1611 (1935); Kilbourn v. Thompson, 103 U.S. 168, 190–191, 26 L.Ed. 377 (1881), insulates a President from a judicial subpoena in an ongoing criminal prosecution, and thereby protects confidential Presidential communications.

However, neither the doctrine of separation of powers, nor the need for confidentiality of high-level communications, without more, can sustain an absolute, unqualified Presidential privilege of immunity from judicial process under all circumstances. The President's need for complete candor and objectivity from advisers calls for great deference from the courts. However, when the privilege depends solely on the broad, undifferentiated claim of public interest in the confidentiality of such conversations, a confrontation with other values arises. Absent a

15. There is nothing novel about governmental confidentiality. The meetings of the Constitutional Convention in 1787 were conducted in complete privacy. 1 M. Farrand, The Records of the Federal Convention of 1787, pp. xi-xxv (1911). Moreover, all records of those meetings were sealed for more than 30 years after the convention. See 3 Stat. 475, 15th Cong., 1st Sess., Res. 8 (1818). Most of the Framers acknowledge that without secrecy no constitution of the kind that was developed could have been written. C. Warren, The Making of the Constitution 134–139 (1937).

claim of need to protect military, diplomatic, or sensitive national security secrets, we find it difficult to accept the argument that even the very important interest in confidentiality of Presidential communications is significantly diminished by production of such material for *in camera* inspection with all the protection that a district court will be obliged to provide.

The impediment that an absolute, unqualified privilege would place in the way of the primary constitutional duty of the Judicial Branch to do justice in criminal prosecutions would plainly conflict with the function of the courts under Art. III. In designing the structure of our Government and dividing and allocating the sovereign power among three co-equal branches, the Framers of the Constitution sought to provide a comprehensive system, but the separate powers were not intended to operate with absolute independence.

> "While the Constitution diffuses power the better to secure liberty, it also contemplates that practice will integrate the dispersed powers into a workable government. It enjoins upon its branches separateness but interdependence, autonomy but reciprocity." Youngstown Sheet & Tube Co. v. Sawyer, 343 U.S., at 635, 72 S.Ct., at 870 (Jackson, J., concurring).

To read the Art. II powers of the President as providing an absolute privilege as against a subpoena essential to enforcement of criminal statutes on no more than a generalized claim of the public interest in confidentiality of nonmilitary and nondiplomatic discussions would upset the constitutional balance of "a workable government" and gravely impair the role of the courts under Art. III.

C

Since we conclude that the legitimate needs of the judicial process may outweigh Presidential privilege, it is necessary to resolve those competing interests in a manner that preserves the essential functions of each branch. The right and indeed the duty to resolve that question does not free the Judiciary from according high respect to the representations made on behalf of the President. United States v. Burr, 25 F.Cas. pp. 187, 190, 191–192 (No. 14,694) (CCVa.1807).

The expectation of a President to the confidentiality of his conversations and correspondence, like the claim of confidentiality of judicial deliberations, for example, has all the values to which we accord deference for the privacy of all citizens and, added to those values, is the necessity for protection of the public interest in candid, objective, and even blunt or harsh opinions in Presidential decisionmaking. A President and those who assist him must be free to explore alternatives in the process of shaping policies and making decisions and to do so in a way many would be unwilling to express except privately. These are the considerations justifying a presumptive privilege for Presidential communications. The privilege is fundamental to the operation of Government and inextricably rooted in the separation of powers under the Constitution.[17] In Nixon v. Sirica, 159 U.S.App.D.C. 58, 487 F.2d 700 (1973), the Court of Appeals held that such Presidential communications are "presumptively privileged," id., at 75, 487 F.2d, at 717, and this position is accepted by both parties in the present litigation. We agree with Mr. Chief Justice Marshall's observation, therefore, that "[i]n no case of this kind would a court be required to proceed against the president as against an ordinary individual." United States v. Burr, 25 F.Cas., at 192.

But this presumptive privilege must be considered in light of our historic commitment to the rule of law. This is nowhere more profoundly manifest than in our view that "the twofold aim [of criminal justice] is that guilt shall not escape or innocence suffer." Berger v. United States, 295 U.S., at 88, 55 S.Ct., at 633. We have elected to employ an adversary system of criminal justice in which the parties contest all issues before a court of law. The need to develop all relevant facts in the adversary system is both fundamental and comprehensive. The ends of criminal justice would be defeated if judgments were to be founded on a partial or speculative presentation of the facts. The very integrity of the judicial system and public confidence in the system depend on full disclosure of all the facts, within the framework of the rules of evidence. To ensure that justice is done, it is imperative to the function of courts that compulsory process be available for the production of evidence needed either by the prosecution or by the defense.

Only recently the Court restated the ancient proposition of law, albeit in the context of a grand jury inquiry rather than a trial.

> "that 'the public * * * has a right to every man's evidence,' except for those persons protected by a constitutional, common-law, or statutory privilege, United States v. Bryan, 339 U.S. [323, 331, 70 S.Ct. 724, 730 (1949)]; Blackmer v. United States, 284 U.S. 421, 438 [52 S.Ct. 252, 76 L.Ed. 375] (1932). * * * " Branzburg v. Hayes, United States, 408 U.S. 665, 688 [92 S.Ct. 2646, 33 L.Ed.2d 626] (1972).

The privileges referred to by the Court are designed to protect weighty and legitimate competing interests. Thus, the Fifth Amendment to the Constitution provides that no man "shall be compelled in any criminal case to be a witness against himself." And, generally, an attorney or a priest may not be required to disclose what has been revealed in professional confidence. These and other interests are recognized in law by privileges against forced disclosure, established in the Constitution, by statute, or at common law. Whatever their origins, these exceptions to the demand for every man's evidence are not lightly

17. "Freedom of communication vital to fulfillment of the aims of wholesome relationships is obtained only by removing the specter of compelled disclosure. * * * [G]overnment * * * needs open but protected channels for the kind of plain talk that is essential to the quality of its functioning." Carl Zeiss Stiftung v. V.E.B. Carl Zeiss, Jena, 40 F.R.D. 318, 325 (DC 1966). See Nixon v. Sirica, 159 U.S.App. D.C. 58, 71, 487 F.2d 700, 713 (1973); Kaiser Aluminum & Chem. Corp. v. United States, 141 Ct.Cl. 38, 157 F.Supp. 939 (1958) (Reed, J.); The Federalist, No. 64 (S. Mittell ed. 1938).

created nor expansively construed, for they are in derogation of the search for truth.[18]

In this case the President challenges a subpoena served on him as a third party requiring the production of materials for use in a criminal prosecution; he does so on the claim that he has a privilege against disclosure of confidential communications. He does not place his claim of privilege on the ground they are military or diplomatic secrets. As to these areas of Art. II duties the courts have traditionally shown the utmost deference to Presidential responsibilities. In C. & S. Air Lines v. Waterman S.S. Corp., 333 U.S. 103, 111, 68 S.Ct. 431, 436, 92 L.Ed. 568 (1948), dealing with Presidential authority involving foreign policy considerations, the Court said:

> "The President, both as Commander-in-Chief and as the Nation's organ for foreign affairs, has available intelligence services whose reports are not and ought not to be published to the world. It would be intolerable that courts, without the relevant information, should review and perhaps nullify actions of the Executive taken on information properly held secret."

In United States v. Reynolds, 345 U.S. 1, 73 S.Ct. 528, 97 L.Ed. 727 (1953), dealing with a claimant's demand for evidence in a Tort Claims Act case against the Government, the Court said:

> "It may be possible to satisfy the court, from all the circumstances of the case, that there is a reasonable danger that compulsion of the evidence will expose military matters which, in the interest of national security, should not be divulged. When this is the case, the occasion for the privilege is appropriate, and the court should not jeopardize the security which the privilege is meant to protect by insisting upon an examination of the evidence, even by the judge alone, in chambers." Id., at 10.

No case of the Court, however, has extended this high degree of deference to a President's generalized interest in confidentiality. Nowhere in the Constitution, as we have noted earlier, is there any explicit reference to a privilege of confidentiality, yet to the extent this interest relates to the effective discharge of a President's powers, it is constitutionally based.

The right to the production of all evidence at a criminal trial similarly has constitutional dimensions. The Sixth Amendment explicitly confers upon every defendant in a criminal trial the right "to be confronted with the witnesses against him" and "to have compulsory process" for obtaining witnesses in his favor. Moreover, the Fifth

18. Because of the key role of the testimony of witnesses in the judicial process, courts have historically been cautious about privileges. Mr. Justice Frankfurter, dissenting in Elkins v. United States, 364 U.S. 206, 234, 80 S.Ct. 1437, 1454, 4 L.Ed.2d 1669 (1960), said of this: "Limitations are properly placed upon the operation of this general principle only to the very limited extent that permitting a refusal to testify or excluding relevant evidence has a public good transcending the normally predominant principle of utilizing all rational means for ascertaining truth."

Amendment also guarantees that no person shall be deprived of liberty without due process of law. It is the manifest duty of the courts to vindicate those guarantees, and to accomplish that it is essential that all relevant and admissible evidence be produced.

In this case we must weigh the importance of the general privilege of confidentiality of Presidential communications in performance of the President's responsibilities against the inroads of such a privilege on the fair administration of criminal justice.[19] The interest in preserving confidentiality is weighty indeed and entitled to great respect. However, we cannot conclude that advisors will be moved to temper the candor of their remarks by the infrequent occasions of disclosure because of the possibility that such conversations will be called for in the context of a criminal prosecution.[20]

On the other hand, the allowance of the privilege to withhold evidence that is demonstrably relevant in a criminal trial would cut deeply into the guarantee of due process of law and gravely impair the basic function of the courts. A President's acknowledged need for confidentiality in the communications of his office is general in nature, whereas the constitutional need for production of relevant evidence in a criminal proceeding is specific and central to the fair adjudication of a particular criminal case in the administration of justice. Without access to specific facts a criminal prosecution may be totally frustrated. The President's broad interest in confidentiality of communications will not be vitiated by disclosure of a limited number of conversations preliminarily shown to have some bearing on the pending criminal cases.

We conclude that when the ground for asserting privilege as to subpoenaed materials sought for use in a criminal trial is based only on the generalized interest in confidentiality, it cannot prevail over the fundamental demands of due process of law in the fair administration

19. We are not here concerned with the balance between the President's generalized interest in confidentiality and the need for relevant evidence in civil litigation, nor with that between the confidentiality interest and congressional demands for information, nor with the President's interest in preserving state secrets. We address only the conflict between the President's assertion of a generalized privilege of confidentiality and the constitutional need for relevant evidence in criminal trials.

20. Mr. Justice Cardozo made this point in an analogous context, speaking for a unanimous Court in Clark v. United States, 289 U.S. 1, 53 S.Ct. 465, 77 L.Ed. 993 (1933), he emphasized the importance of maintaining the secrecy of the deliberations of a petit jury in a criminal case. "Freedom of debate might be stifled and independence of thought checked if jurors were made to feel that their arguments and ballots were to be freely published to the world." Id., at 13, 53 S.Ct., at 469. Nonetheless, the Court also recognized that isolated inroads on confidentiality designed to serve the paramount need of the criminal law would not vitiate the interests served by secrecy:

> "A juror of integrity and reasonable firmness will not fear to speak his mind if the confidences of debate are barred to the ears of mere impertinence or malice. He will not expect to be shielded against the disclosure of his conduct in the event that there is evidence reflecting upon his honor. The chance that now and then there may be found some timid soul who will take counsel of his fears and give way to their repressive power is too remote and shadowy to shape the course of justice." Id., at 16, 53 S.Ct., at 470.

of criminal justice. The generalized assertion of privilege must yield to the demonstrated, specific need for evidence in a pending criminal trial.

D

We have earlier determined that the District Court did not err in authorizing the issuance of the subpoena. If a President concludes that compliance with a subpoena would be injurious to the public interest he may properly, as was done here, invoke a claim of privilege on the return of the subpoena. Upon receiving a claim of privilege from the Chief Executive, it became the further duty of the District Court to treat the subpoenaed material as presumptively privileged and to require the Special Prosecutor to demonstrate that the Presidential material was "essential to the justice of the [pending criminal] case." United States v. Burr, 25 Fed.Cas., at 192. Here the District Court treated the material as presumptively privileged, proceeded to find that the Special Prosecutor had made a sufficient showing to rebut the presumption, and ordered an *in camera* examination of the subpoenaed material. On the basis of our examination of the record we are unable to conclude that the District Court erred in ordering the inspection. Accordingly we affirm the order of the District Court that subpoenaed materials be transmitted to that court. We now turn to the important question of the District Court's responsibilities in conducting the *in camera* examination of Presidential materials or communications delivered under the compulsion of the subpoena *duces tecum.*

E

Enforcement of the subpoena *duces tecum* was stayed pending this Court's resolution of the issues raised by the petitions for certiorari. Those issues now having been disposed of, the matter of implementation will rest with the District Court. "[T]he guard, furnished to [the President] to protect him from being harassed by vexatious and unnecessary subpoenas, is to be looked for in the conduct of a [district] court after those subpoenas have issued; not in any circumstance which is to precede their being issued." United States v. Burr, supra, at 34. Statements that meet the test of admissibility and relevance must be isolated; all other material must be excised. At this stage the District Court is not limited to representations of the Special Prosecutor as to the evidence sought by the subpoena; the material will be available to the District Court. It is elementary that *in camera* inspection of evidence is always a procedure calling for scrupulous protection against any release or publication of material not found by the court, at that stage, probably admissible in evidence and relevant to the issues of the trial for which it is sought. That being true of an ordinary situation, it is obvious that the District Court has a very heavy responsibility to see to it that Presidential conversations, which are either not relevant or not admissible, are accorded that high degree of respect due the President of the United States. Mr. Chief Justice Marshall, sitting as a trial judge in the *Burr* case, supra, was extraordinarily careful to point out that "[i]n no case of this kind would a court be required to proceed against the president as against an ordinary individual." at 192.

Marshall's statement cannot be read to mean in any sense that a President is above the law, but relates to the singularly unique role under Art. II of a President's communications and activities, related to the performance of duties under that Article. Moreover, a President's communications and activities encompass a vastly wider range of sensitive material than would be true of any "ordinary individual." It is therefore necessary [21] in the public interest to afford Presidential confidentiality the greatest protection consistent with the fair administration of justice. The need for confidentiality even as to idle conversations with associates in which casual reference might be made concerning political leaders within the country or foreign statesmen is too obvious to call for further treatment. We have no doubt that the District Judge will at all times accord to Presidential records that high degree of deference suggested in United States v. Burr, supra and will discharge his responsibility to see to it that until released to the Special Prosecutor no *in camera* material is revealed to anyone. This burden applies with even greater force to excised material; once the decision is made to excise, the material is restored to its privileged status and should be returned under seal to its lawful custodian.

Since this matter came before the Court during the pendency of a criminal prosecution, and on representations that time is of the essence, the mandate shall issue forthwith.

Affirmed.

MR. JUSTICE REHNQUIST took no part in the consideration or decision of these cases.

Notes

(1) See Proposed Fed.R.Evid. 509; Unif.R.Evid. 508; 8 Wigmore, Evidence §§ 2378–2379 (McNaughton rev. 1961); McCormick, Evidence §§ 107–110 (4th ed. 1992); Berger, Executive Privilege: A Constitutional Myth (1975); Cox, Executive Privilege, 122 U.Pa.L.Rev. 1383 (1974); Dorsen & Shattuck, Executive Privilege, the Congress and the Courts, 35 Ohio St.L.J. 1 (1974); Freund, Foreword: On Presidential Privilege, 88 Harv. L.Rev. 13 (1974); Gard, Executive Privilege: A Rhyme Without a Reason, 8 Ga.L.Rev. 809 (1974); Nathanson, From Watergate to Marbury v. Madison: Some Reflections on Presidential Privilege in Current Historical Perspective, 16 Ariz.L.Rev. 59 (1974); Owens, The Establishment of a Doctrine: Executive Privilege After United States v. Nixon, 4 Tex.So.U.L.Rev. 22 (1976); Rotunda, Presidents and Ex–Presidents as Witnesses: A Brief Historical Footnote, 1975 U.Ill.L.F. 1 (1975); Symposium, United States v.

21. When the subpoenaed material is delivered to the District Judge *in camera,* questions may arise as to the excising of parts, and it lies within the discretion of that court to seek the aid of the Special Prosecutor and the President's counsel for *in camera* consideration of the validity of particular excisions, whether the basis of excision is relevancy or admissibility or under such cases as United States v. Reynolds, 345 U.S. 1, 73 S.Ct. 528, 97 L.Ed. 727 (1953), or C. & S. Air Lines v. Waterman S.S. Corp., 333 U.S. 103, 68 S.Ct. 431, 92 L.Ed. 568 (1948).

Nixon, 22 U.C.L.A.L.Rev. 1 (1974); Symposium, United States v. Nixon: An Historical Perspective, 9 Loyola L.A.L.Rev. 11 (1975).

(2) See also Nixon v. Administrator of General Services, 433 U.S. 425, 97 S.Ct. 2777, 53 L.Ed.2d 867 (1977); Dellums v. Powell, 642 F.2d 1351 (D.C.Cir.1980); Nixon v. Freeman, 670 F.2d 346 (D.C.Cir.1982), cert. denied, 459 U.S. 1035, 103 S.Ct. 445, 74 L.Ed.2d 601 (1982); Halkin v. Helms, 690 F.2d 977 (D.C.Cir.1982); Jabara v. Webster, 691 F.2d 272 (6th Cir.1982), cert. denied, 464 U.S. 863, 104 S.Ct. 193, 78 L.Ed.2d 170 (1983); Ellsberg v. Mitchell, 709 F.2d 51 (D.C.Cir.1983), cert. denied sub nom. Russo v. Mitchell, 465 U.S. 1038, 104 S.Ct. 1316, 79 L.Ed.2d 712 (1984).

McCRAY v. ILLINOIS

Supreme Court of the United States, 1967.
386 U.S. 300, 87 S.Ct. 1056, 18 L.Ed.2d 62.

MR. JUSTICE STEWART delivered the opinion of the Court.

The petitioner was arrested in Chicago, Illinois, on the morning of January 16, 1964, for possession of narcotics. The Chicago police officers who made the arrest found a package containing heroin on his person and he was indicted for its unlawful possession. Prior to trial he filed a motion to suppress the heroin as evidence against him, claiming that the police had acquired it in an unlawful search and seizure in violation of the Fourth and Fourteenth Amendments. See Mapp v. Ohio, 367 U.S. 643, 81 S.Ct. 1684, 6 L.Ed.2d 1081. After a hearing, the court denied the motion, and the petitioner was subsequently convicted upon the evidence of the heroin the arresting officers had found in his possession. The judgment of conviction was affirmed by the Supreme Court of Illinois, and we granted certiorari to consider the petitioner's claim that the hearing on his motion to suppress was constitutionally defective.

The petitioner's arrest occurred near the intersection of 49th Street and Calumet Avenue at about seven in the morning. At the hearing on the motion to suppress, he testified that up until a half hour before he was arrested he had been at "a friend's house" about a block away, that after leaving the friend's house he had "walked with a lady from 48th to 48th and South Park," and that, as he approached 49th Street and Calumet Avenue, "[t]he Officers stopped me going through the alley." "The officers," he said, "did not show me a search warrant for my person or an arrest warrant for my arrest." He said the officers then searched him and found the narcotics in question. The petitioner did not identify the "friend" or the "lady," and neither of them appeared as a witness.

The arresting officers then testified. Officer Jackson stated that he and two fellow officers had had a conversation with an informant on the morning of January 16 in their unmarked police car. The officer said that the informant had told them that the petitioner, with whom Jackson was acquainted, "was selling narcotics and had narcotics on his person and that he could be found in the vicinity of 47th and Calumet at this particular time." Jackson said that he and his fellow officers drove to that vicinity in the police car and that when they spotted the petitioner, the informant pointed him out and then departed on foot. Jackson stated that the officers observed the petitioner walking with a woman, then separating from her and meeting briefly with a man, then proceeding alone, and finally, after seeing the police car, "hurriedly walk[ing] between two buildings." "At this point," Jackson testified, "my partner and myself got out of the car and informed him we had information he had narcotics on his person, placed him in the police vehicle at this point." Jackson stated that the officers then searched the petitioner and found the heroin in a cigarette package.

Jackson testified that he had been acquainted with the informant for approximately a year, that during this period the informant had supplied him with information about narcotics activities "fifteen, sixteen times at least," that the information had proved to be accurate and had resulted in numerous arrests and convictions. On cross-examination, Jackson was even more specific as to the informant's previous reliability, giving the names of people who had been convicted of narcotics violations as the result of information the informant had supplied. When Jackson was asked for the informant's name and address, counsel for the State objected, and the objection was sustained by the court.[4]

Officer Arnold gave substantially the same account of the circumstances of the petitioner's arrest and search, stating that the informant had told the officers that the petitioner "was selling narcotics and had narcotics on his person now in the vicinity of 47th and Calumet." The informant, Arnold testified, "said he had observed [the petitioner] selling narcotics to various people, meaning various addicts, in the area of 47th and Calumet." Arnold testified that he had known the informant "roughly two years," that the informant had given him information concerning narcotics "20 or 25 times," and that the information had resulted in convictions. Arnold too was asked on cross-examination for the informant's name and address, and objections to these questions were sustained by the court.

4. "Q. What is the name of this informant that gave you this information?

"Mr. Engerman: Objection, Your Honor.

"The Court: State for the record the reasons for your objection.

"Mr. Engerman: Judge, based upon the testimony of the officer so far that they had used this informant for approximately a year, he has worked with this individual, in the interest of the public, I see no reason why the officer should be forced to disclose the name of the informant, to cause harm or jeopardy to an individual who has cooperated with the police. The City of Chicago have a tremendous problem with narcotics. If the police are not able to withhold the name of the informant they will not be able to get informants. They are not willing to risk their lives if their names become known.

"In the interest of the City and the law enforcement of this community, I feel the officer should not be forced to reveal the name of the informant. And I also cite People vs. Durr.

"The Court: I will sustain that.

"Mr. Adam: Q. Where does this informant live?

"Mr. Engerman: Objection, your Honor, same basis.

"The Court: Sustained."

There can be no doubt, upon the basis of the circumstances related by Officers Jackson and Arnold, that there was probable cause to sustain the arrest and incidental search in this case. Draper v. United States, 358 U.S. 307, 79 S.Ct. 329, 3 L.Ed.2d 327. Unlike the situation in Beck v. State of Ohio, 379 U.S. 89, 85 S.Ct. 223, 13 L.Ed.2d 142, each of the officers in this case described with specificity "what the informer actually said, and why the officer thought the information was credible." 379 U.S., at 97, 85 S.Ct., at 229. The testimony of each of the officers informed the court of the "underlying circumstances from which the informant concluded that the narcotics were where he claimed they were, and some of the underlying circumstances from which the officer concluded that the informant * * * was 'credible' or his information 'reliable.'" Aguilar v. State of Texas, 378 U.S. 108, 114, 84 S.Ct. 1509, 1514, 12 L.Ed.2d 723. See United States v. Ventresca, 380 U.S. 102, 85 S.Ct. 741, 13 L.Ed.2d 684. Upon the basis of those circumstances, along with the officers' personal observations of the petitioner, the court was fully justified in holding that at the time the officers made the arrest "the facts and circumstances within their knowledge and of which they had reasonably trustworthy information were sufficient to warrant a prudent man in believing that the petitioner had committed or was committing an offense. Brinegar v. United States, 338 U.S. 160, 175–176, 69 S.Ct. 1302, 1310–1311, 93 L.Ed. 1879; Henry v. United States, 361 U.S. 98, 102, 80 S.Ct. 168, 171, 4 L.Ed.2d 134," Beck v. State of Ohio, supra, 379 U.S. at 91, 85 S.Ct. at 225. It is the petitioner's claim, however, that even though the officers' sworn testimony fully supported a finding of probable cause for the arrest and search, the state court nonetheless violated the Constitution when it sustained objections to the petitioner's questions as to the identity of the informant. We cannot agree.

In permitting the officers to withhold the informant's identity, the court was following well-settled Illinois law. When the issue is not guilt or innocence, but, as here, the question of probable cause for an arrest or search, the Illinois Supreme Court has held that police officers need not invariably be required to disclose an informant's identity if the trial judge is convinced, by evidence submitted in open court and subject to cross-examination, that the officers did rely in good faith upon credible information supplied by a reliable informant. This Illinois evidentiary rule is consistent with the law of many other States. In California, the State Legislature in 1965 enacted a statute adopting just such a rule for cases like the one before us:

> "[I]n any preliminary hearing, criminal trial, or other criminal proceeding, for violation of any provision of Division 10 (commencing with Section 11000) of the Health and Safety Code, evidence of information communicated to a peace officer by a confidential informant, who is not a material witness to the guilt or innocence of the accused of the offense charged, shall be admissible on the issue of reasonable cause to make an arrest or search without requiring that the name or identity of the informant be disclosed if the judge or magistrate is

satisfied, based upon evidence produced in open court, out of the presence of the jury, that such information was received from a reliable informant and in his discretion does not require such disclosure." California Evid.Code § 1042(c).

The reasoning of the Supreme Court of New Jersey in judicially adopting the same basic evidentiary rule was instructively expressed by Chief Justice Weintraub in State v. Burnett, 42 N.J. 377, 201 A.2d 39:

"If a defendant may insist upon disclosure of the informant in order to test the truth of the officer's statement that there is an informant or as to what the informant related or as to the informant's reliability, we can be sure that every defendant will demand disclosure. He has nothing to lose and the prize may be the suppression of damaging evidence if the State cannot afford to reveal its source, as is so often the case. And since there is no way to test the good faith of a defendant who presses the demand, we must assume the routine demand would have to be routinely granted. The result would be that the State could use the informant's information only as a lead and could search only if it could gather adequate evidence of probable cause apart from the informant's data. Perhaps that approach would sharpen investigatorial techniques, but we doubt that there would be enough talent and time to cope with crime upon that basis. Rather we accept the premise that the informer is a vital part of society's defensive arsenal. The basic rule protecting his identity rests upon that belief.

"* * *

"We must remember also that we are not dealing with the trial of the criminal charge itself. There the need for a truthful verdict outweighs society's need for the informer privilege. Here, however, the accused seeks to avoid the truth. The very purpose of a motion to suppress is to escape the inculpatory thrust of evidence in hand, not because its probative force is diluted in the least by the mode of seizure, but rather as a sanction to compel enforcement officers to respect the constitutional security of all of us under the Fourth Amendment. State v. Smith, 37 N.J. 481, 486, 181 A.2d 761 (1962). If the motion to suppress is denied, defendant will still be judged upon the untarnished truth.

"* * *

"The Fourth Amendment is served if a judicial mind passes upon the existence of probable cause. Where the issue is submitted upon an application for a warrant, the magistrate is trusted to evaluate the credibility of the affiant in an *ex parte* proceeding. As we have said, the magistrate is concerned, not with whether the informant lied, but with whether the affiant is truthful in his recitation of what he was told. If the magistrate doubts the credibility of the affiant, he may require that the informant be identified or even produced. It seems to us that the same approach is equally sufficient where the search was without a warrant, that is to say, that it should rest entirely with the judge who hears the motion to suppress to decide whether he needs such disclosure as to the informant in order to decide whether the officer is a believable witness." 42 N.J., at 385–388, 201 A.2d, at 43–45.

What Illinois and her sister States have done is no more than recognize a well-established testimonial privilege, long familiar to the law of evidence. Professor Wigmore, not known as an enthusiastic advocate of testimonial privileges generally, has described that privilege in these words:

"A genuine privilege, on * * * fundamental principle * * *, must be recognized for the *identity of persons supplying the government with information concerning the commission of crimes.* Communications of this kind ought to receive encouragement. They are discouraged if the informer's identity is disclosed. Whether an informer is motivated by good citizenship, promise of leniency or prospect of pecuniary reward, he will usually condition his cooperation on an assurance of anonymity—to protect himself and his family from harm, to preclude adverse social reactions and to avoid the risk of defamation or malicious prosecution actions against him. The government also has an interest in nondisclosure of the identity of its informers. Law enforcement officers often depend upon professional informers to furnish them with a flow of information about criminal activities. Revelation of the dual role played by such persons ends their usefulness to the government and discourages others from entering into a like relationship.

"That the government has this privilege is well established, and its soundness cannot be questioned." (Footnotes omitted.) 8 Wigmore, Evidence § 2374 (McNaughton rev. 1961).

In the federal courts the rules of evidence in criminal trials are governed "by the principles of the common law as they may be interpreted by the courts of the United States in the light of reason and experience." This Court, therefore, has the ultimate task of defining the scope to be accorded to the various common law evidentiary privileges in the trial of federal criminal cases. See Hawkins v. United States, 358 U.S. 74, 79 S.Ct. 136, 3 L.Ed.2d 125. This is a task which is quite different, of course, from the responsibility of constitutional adjudication. In the exercise of this supervisory jurisdiction the Court had occasion 10 years ago, in Roviaro v. United States, 353 U.S. 53, 77 S.Ct. 623, 1 L.Ed.2d 639, to give thorough consideration to one aspect of the informer's privilege, the privilege itself having long been recognized in the federal judicial system.

The *Roviaro* case involved the informer's privilege, not at a preliminary hearing to determine probable cause for an arrest or search, but at the trial itself where the issue was the fundamental one of innocence or guilt. The petitioner there had been brought to trial upon a two-count federal indictment charging sale and transportation of narcotics. According to the prosecution's evidence, the informer had been an active participant in the crime. He "had taken a material part in bringing about the possession of certain drugs by the accused, had been present with the accused at the occurrence of the alleged crime, and might be a material witness as to whether the accused knowingly transported the drugs as charged." 353 U.S., at 55, 77 S.Ct., at 625.

The trial court nonetheless denied a defense motion to compel the prosecution to disclose the informer's identity.

This Court held that where, in an actual trial of a federal criminal case,

> "the disclosure of an informer's identity * * * is relevant and helpful to the defense of an accused, or is essential to a fair determination of a cause, the privilege must give way. In these situations the trial court may require disclosure and, if the Government withholds the information, dismiss the action. * * *
>
> * * *
>
> "We believe that no fixed rule with respect to disclosure is justifiable. The problem is one that calls for balancing the public interest in protecting the flow of information against the individual's right to prepare his defense. Whether a proper balance renders nondisclosure erroneous must depend on the particular circumstances of each case, taking into consideration the crime charged, the possible defenses, the possible significance of the informer's testimony, and other relevant factors." 353 U.S., at 60–61, 62, 77 S.Ct., at 628. (Footnotes omitted.)

The Court's opinion then carefully reviewed the particular circumstances of Roviaro's trial, pointing out that the informer's "possible testimony was highly relevant * * *," that he "might have disclosed an entrapment * * *," "might have thrown doubt upon petitioner's identity or on the identity of the package * * *," "might have testified to petitioner's possible lack of knowledge of the contents of the package that he 'transported' * * *," and that the "informer was the sole participant, other than the accused, in the transaction charged." 353 U.S., at 63–64, 77 S.Ct., at 629–630. The Court concluded "that, under these circumstances, the trial court committed prejudicial error in permitting the Government to withhold the identity of its undercover employee in the face of repeated demands by the accused for his disclosure." 353 U.S., at 65, 77 S.Ct., at 630.

What *Roviaro* thus makes clear is that this Court was unwilling to impose any absolute rule requiring disclosure of an informer's identity even in formulating evidentiary rules for federal criminal trials. Much less has the Court ever approached the formulation of a federal evidentiary rule of compulsory disclosure where the issue is the preliminary one of probable cause, and guilt or innocence is not at stake. Indeed, we have repeatedly made clear that federal officers need *not* disclose an informer's identity in applying for an arrest or search warrant. As was said in United States v. Ventresca, 380 U.S. 102, 108, 85 S.Ct. 741, 745, 13 L.Ed.2d 684, we have "recognized that 'an affidavit may be based on hearsay information and need not reflect the direct personal observations of the affiant,' so long as the magistrate is 'informed of some of the underlying circumstances' supporting the affiant's conclusions and his belief that any informant involved '*whose identity need not be disclosed* * * * was "credible" or his information "reliable."' Aguilar v. State of Texas, supra, 378 U.S., at 114, 84 S.Ct., at 1514." (Emphasis added.) See also Jones v. United States, 362 U.S. 257, 271–272, 80 S.Ct. 725, 736–737, 4 L.Ed.2d 697; Rugendorf v. United States, 376 U.S. 528, 533, 84 S.Ct. 825, 828, 11 L.Ed.2d 887. And just this Term we have taken occasion to point out that a rule virtually prohibiting the use of informers would "severely hamper the Government" in enforcement of the narcotics laws. Lewis v. United States, 385 U.S. 206, 210, 87 S.Ct. 424, 427, 17 L.Ed.2d 312.

In sum, the Court in exercise of its power to formulate evidentiary rules for federal criminal cases has consistently declined to hold that an informer's identity need always be disclosed in a federal criminal trial, let alone in a preliminary hearing to determine probable cause for an arrest or search. Yet we are now asked to hold that the Constitution somehow compels Illinois to abolish the informer's privilege from its law of evidence and to require disclosure of the informer's identity in every such preliminary hearing where it appears that the officers made the arrest or search in reliance upon facts supplied by an informer they had reason to trust. The argument is based upon the Due Process Clause of the Fourteenth Amendment, and upon the Sixth Amendment right of confrontation, applicable to the States through the Fourteenth Amendment. Pointer v. State of Texas, 380 U.S. 400, 85 S.Ct. 1065, 13 L.Ed.2d 923. We find no support for the petitioner's position in either of those constitutional provisions.

The arresting officers in this case testified, in open court, fully and in precise detail as to what the informer told them and as to why they had reason to believe his information was trustworthy. Each officer was under oath. Each was subjected to searching cross-examination. The judge was obviously satisfied that each was telling the truth, and for that reason he exercised the discretion conferred upon him by the established law of Illinois to respect the informer's privilege.

Nothing in the Due Process Clause of the Fourteenth Amendment requires a state court judge in every such hearing to assume the arresting officers are committing perjury. "To take such a step would be quite beyond the pale of this Court's proper function in our federal system. It would be a wholly unjustifiable encroachment by this Court upon the constitutional power of States to promulgate their own rules of evidence * * * in their own state courts * * *." Spencer v. State of Texas, 385 U.S. 554, 568–569, 87 S.Ct. 648, 656, 17 L.Ed.2d 606.

The petitioner does not explain precisely how he thinks his Sixth Amendment right to confrontation and cross-examination was violated by Illinois' recognition of the informer's privilege in this case. If the claim is that the State violated the Sixth Amendment by not producing the informer to testify against the petitioner, then we need no more than repeat the Court's answer to that claim a few weeks ago in Cooper v. State of California:

> "Petitioner also presents the contention here that he was unconstitutionally deprived of the right to confront a witness against him, because the State did not produce the informant to testify against him.

This contention we consider absolutely devoid of merit." 386 U.S. 58, at 62, n. 2, 87 S.Ct. 788, at 791, 17 L.Ed.2d 730.

On the other hand, the claim may be that the petitioner was deprived of his Sixth Amendment right to cross-examine the arresting officers themselves, because their refusal to reveal the informer's identity was upheld. But it would follow from this argument that no witness on cross-examination could ever constitutionally assert a testimonial privilege, including the privilege against compulsory self-incrimination guaranteed by the Constitution itself. We have never given the Sixth Amendment such a construction, and we decline to do so now.

Affirmed.

MR. JUSTICE DOUGLAS, with whom THE CHIEF JUSTICE, MR. JUSTICE BRENNAN and MR. JUSTICE FORTAS concur, dissenting.

We have here a Fourth Amendment question concerning the validity of an arrest. If the police see a crime being committed they can of course seize the culprit. If a person is fleeing the scene of a crime, the police can stop him. And there are the cases of "hot pursuit" and other instances of probable cause when the police can make an arrest. But normally an arrest should be made only on a warrant issued by a magistrate on a showing of "probable cause, supported by Oath or affirmation," as required by the Fourth Amendment. At least since Mapp v. Ohio, 367 U.S. 643, 81 S.Ct. 1684, 6 L.Ed.2d 1081, the States are as much bound by those provisions as is the Federal Government. But for the Fourth Amendment they could fashion the rule for arrests that the Court now approves. With all deference, the requirements of the Fourth Amendment now make that conclusion unconstitutional.

No warrant for the arrest of petitioner was obtained in this case. The police, instead of going to a magistrate and making a showing of "probable cause" based on their informant's tip-off, acted on their own. They, rather than the magistrate, became the arbiters of "probable cause." The Court's approval of that process effectively rewrites the Fourth Amendment.

In Roviaro v. United States, 353 U.S. 53, 61, 77 S.Ct. 623, 628, 1 L.Ed.2d 639, we held that where a search *without a warrant* is made on the basis of communications of an informer and the Government claims the police had "probable cause," disclosure of the identity of the informant is normally required. In no other way can the defense show an absence of "probable cause." By reason of Mapp v. Ohio, supra, that rule is now applicable to the States.

In Beck v. State of Ohio, 379 U.S. 89, 96, 85 S.Ct. 223, 228, 13 L.Ed.2d 142, we said:

> "An arrest without a warrant by-passes the safeguards provided by an objective predetermination of probable cause, and substitutes instead the far less reliable procedure of an after-the-event justification

for the arrest or search, too likely to be subtly influenced by the familiar shortcomings of hindsight judgment."

For that reason we have weighted arrests with warrants more heavily than arrests without warrants. See United States v. Ventresca, 380 U.S. 102, 106, 85 S.Ct. 741, 744, 13 L.Ed.2d 684. Only through the informer's testimony can anyone other than the arresting officers determine "the persuasiveness of the facts relied on * * * to show probable cause." Aguilar v. State of Texas, 378 U.S. 108, 113, 84 S.Ct. 1509, 1513, 12 L.Ed.2d 723. Without that disclosure neither we nor the lower courts can ever know whether there was "probable cause" for the arrest. Under the present decision we leave the Fourth Amendment exclusively in the custody of the police. As stated by Mr. Justice Schaefer dissenting in People v. Durr, 28 Ill.2d 308, 318, 192 N.E.2d 379, 384, unless the identity of the informer is disclosed "the policeman himself conclusively determines the validity of his own arrest." That was the view of the Supreme Court of California in Priestly v. Superior Court, 50 Cal.2d 812, 818, 330 P.2d 39, 43:

> "Only by requiring disclosure and giving the defendant an opportunity to present contrary or impeaching evidence as to the truth of the officer's testimony and the reasonableness of his reliance on the informer can the court make a fair determination of the issue. Such a requirement does not unreasonably discourage the free flow of information to law enforcement officers or otherwise impede law enforcement. Actually its effect is to compel independent investigations to verify information given by an informer or to uncover other facts that establish reasonable cause to make an arrest or search."

There is no way to determine the reliability of Old Reliable, the informer, unless he is produced, at the trial and cross-examined. Unless he is produced, the Fourth Amendment is entrusted to the tender mercies of the police. What we do today is to encourage arrests and searches without warrants. The whole momentum of criminal law administration should be in precisely the opposite direction, if the Fourth Amendment is to remain a vital force. Except in rare and emergency cases, it requires magistrates to make the findings of "probable cause." We should be mindful of its command that a judicial mind should be interposed between the police and the citizen. We should also be mindful that "disclosure, rather than suppression, of relevant materials ordinarily promotes the proper administration of criminal justice." Dennis v. United States, 384 U.S. 855, 870, 86 S.Ct. 1840, 1849, 16 L.Ed.2d 973.

Note

See Proposed Fed.R.Evid 510; Unif.R.Evid 509; 8 Wigmore, Evidence § 2374 (McNaughton rev. 1961); McCormick, Evidence § 111 (4th ed. 1992).

SECTION 5. OTHER PRIVILEGES PROTECTING CONFIDENTIAL INFORMATION *

MATTER OF CONTEMPT OF WRIGHT

Supreme Court of Idaho, 1985.
108 Idaho 418, 700 P.2d 40.

HUNTLEY, JUSTICE.

By this appeal we are asked to determine whether there exists under the United States or the Idaho Constitution a newsperson's qualified privilege to refuse to disclose confidential sources. We hold there is such a *qualified* privilege under the First Amendment to the United States Constitution and Art. I, § 9 of the Idaho Constitution. We reverse and remand to the trial court for further proceedings consistent with this opinion.

This case arose when Jim Wright, reporter for the Moscow, Idaho, Daily Idahonian, refused to disclose the name of a confidential source he had interviewed in the course of writing an article about marijuana growing. The criminal defendant, Gary Kiss, had been charged with felony manufacture and possession of a controlled substance based solely on the word of Lewis, one of Kiss' co-defendants. The State wanted Wright to corroborate Lewis' testimony against Kiss so that the State could meet its evidentiary burden under I.C. § 19–2117, which provides:

19–2117. Testimony of accomplice—Corroboration.—

> A conviction cannot be had on the testimony of an accomplice, unless he is corroborated by other evidence, which in itself, and without the aid of the testimony of the accomplice, tends to connect the defendant with the commission of the offense; and the corroboration is not sufficient, if it merely shows the commission of the offense, or the circumstances thereof.

The district court held a hearing to receive testimony from Wright as to whether he would disclose his source. He refused, stating that he had written the article to uncover the inadequacies and falsity of police reporting in marijuana raids. He also said he had promised his source confidentiality, and that he believed he would not have gotten the information had he not promised the grower confidentiality.

The district court found no absolute or qualified privilege to excuse Wright from testifying. It found Wright in contempt, and fined him $500 a day, that fine being stayed pending this appeal.

Wright appealed, contending that compulsion of his disclosure of a confidential source without appropriate hearing to evaluate his claim of

* See 8 Wigmore, Evidence chs. 81, 87 (McNaughton rev. 1961); McCormick, Evidence §§ 75–77 (4th ed. 1992).

privilege was in violation of the First Amendment, and of his due process rights under the Fourteenth Amendment of the U.S. Constitution. Rather than an absolute privilege, Wright seeks a privilege qualified by application, in a separate hearing, of a balancing test. The test would encompass consideration of (1) the relevancy of the information compelled; (2) whether the information is critical to the State's claim, and (3) whether there are alternative sources for the information sought to be compelled. This Court accepted the appeal for plenary review.

BACKGROUND

Reporters maintain that successful investigative reporting requires the ability to maintain confidential sources. That belief has been incorporated in the American Newspaper Guild's Code of Ethics: "Newspapermen shall refuse to reveal confidences or disclose sources of confidental information in court or before judicial or investigative bodies." *See,* P. Marcus, The Reporter's Privilege: an Analysis of the Common Law, Branzburg v. Hayes and Recent Statutory Developments, 25 Arizona L.R. 815 (1983). Without confidential sources, reporters argue, many informants, sensitive to threats of exposure, would be silenced. Not only newspeople, but the public as well would suffer the resulting loss of information.

This Court, and many others, have acknowledged reporters' concerns, and more importantly, public interest in the need for effective investigative reporting. In *Marks v. Vehlow,* 105 Idaho 560, 671 P.2d 473 (1983), we noted our basic agreement with this statement from *Zerilli v. Smith,* 656 F.2d 705, 711 (D.C.Cir.1981):

> Without an unfettered press, citizens would be far less able to make informed political, social, and economic choices * * *. [T]he press' function as a vital source of information is weakened whenever the ability of journalists to gather news is impaired. Compelling a reporter to disclose the identity of a source may significantly interfere with his news gathering ability; journalists frequently depend on informants to gather news, and confidentiality is often essential to establishing a relationship with an informant. (Footnotes omitted.)

Compelling a reporter to disclose the identity of a confidential source clearly raises First Amendment considerations. The First Amendment guarantees a free press in large part because of the important role it can play as "a vital source of public information." *Grosjean v. American Press Co.,* 297 U.S. 233, 250, 56 S.Ct. 444, 449, 80 L.Ed. 660 (1936).

In his dissenting opinion in *Caldero v. Tribune Publishing Co.,* 98 Idaho 288, 562 P.2d 791 (1977), *cert. denied,* 434 U.S. 930, 98 S.Ct. 418, 54 L.Ed.2d 291 (1977), Chief Justice Donaldson asserted that every case involving an infringement of First Amendment rights raises the question of whether there is a compelling interest justifying the infringement. A First Amendment case necessarily involves the balancing between the competing interests of maintaining a strong First Amendment and the interest asserted as justifying the impairment of First Amendment freedoms. The balance, he stated, is weighted in favor of the First Amendment—the competing interest must be "compelling" or "paramount". *Caldero, supra* at 298, 562 P.2d 791.

In *Branzburg v. Hayes,* 408 U.S. 665, 92 S.Ct. 2646, 33 L.Ed.2d 626 (1972), the United States Supreme Court, in a plurality opinion, held that a journalist has no absolute privilege under the First Amendment to refuse to disclose confidential sources to a grand jury conducting a criminal investigation. The Court recognized, however, that news gathering does have some First Amendment protection, and that in certain circumstances, such as in a bad faith investigation or official harassment, a newsperson would have a qualified privilege even before a grand jury. Justice Powell, casting the deciding vote for the majority, wrote a concurring opinion which recognized that courts may determine whether a privilege exists by applying a balancing test:

> The asserted claim to privilege should be judged on its facts by the striking of a proper balance between freedom of the press and the obligation of all citizens to give relevant testimony with respect to criminal conduct. The balance of these vital constitutional and societal interests on a case-by-case basis accords with the tried and traditional way of adjudicating such questions. *Branzburg, supra,* 408 U.S. at 710, 92 S.Ct. at 2671.

Justice Powell emphasized the limited nature of the majority holding, *id.* at 725, 92 S.Ct. at 2671; in fact, the majority specifically limited its holding to the issue of "the obligation of reporters to respond to grand jury subpoenas as other citizens do and to answer questions relevant to an investigation into the commission of crime." *Id.* at 682, 92 S.Ct. at 2657.

The District of Columbia Circuit took the opportunity in *U.S. v. Liddy,* 478 F.2d 586 (1972), shortly after the *Branzburg* decision, to analyze Justice Powell's opinion. Judge Leventhal stated:

> * * * I begin with the premise that the *Branzburg* decision is controlled in the last analysis by the concurring opinion of Justice Powell (408 U.S. at 709, 92 S.Ct. at 2670) as the fifth Justice of the majority. That opinion holds, as I understand it, that there is no universal constitutional privilege of a newsman to keep confidential the identity of his sources and the content of their revelations. The assertion of that privilege may, however, come to involve a question under the First Amendment freedom of the press, and in such case there will be need for balancing that assertion against the need for the material in the interest of society, as in a case where a newsman has "reason to believe that his testimony implicates confidential source relationships without a legitimate need of law enforcement." (p. 710, 92 S.Ct. at 2671). That does not require a demonstration of either total lack of legitimacy or utter lack of any possible need, for it may be raised on a claim that the information desired of the newsman has only a "remote" relationship to the subject of the investigation. As to the conduct of the balancing test, Justice Powell made it clear that the judge is "free to balance the

competing interests on their merits in the particular case." *Id.* at 586–7.

The now widely accepted view of *Branzburg* appears to be that it was limited by the specific facts presented by the consolidated cases, and that a case-by-case analysis must be used in "balancing freedom of the press against a compelling and overriding public interest in the information sought." *Zelenka v. State,* 83 Wis.2d 601, 266 N.W.2d 279, 287 (1978). *See also, Riley v. City of Chester,* 612 F.2d 708, 714 (3rd Cir.1979); *Farr v. Pitchess,* 522 F.2d 464, 467 (9th Cir.1975) *cert. denied,* 427 U.S. 912, 96 S.Ct. 3200, 49 L.Ed.2d 1203 (1976); *State v. Siel,* 122 N.H. 254, 444 A.2d 499, 502 (1982); *State v. Sandstrom,* 224 Kan. 573, 581 P.2d 812, 814–15 (1978) *cert. denied,* 440 U.S. 929, 99 S.Ct. 1265, 59 L.Ed.2d 485 (1979); *Gadsden County Times, Inc. v. Horne,* 426 So.2d 1234 (Fla.App. 1 Dist.1983); Marcus, *supra,* at 838; Comment, The Newsman's Privilege After Branzburg, The Case for a Federal Shield Law, 24 UCLA 160, 172–74 (1976).

Courts finding a qualified privilege generally have applied a balancing test similar to one proposed by Justice Stewart in his *Branzburg* dissent. *See, e.g. United States v. Burke,* 700 F.2d 70, 77 (2nd Cir.1983) *cert. denied,* — U.S. ——, 104 S.Ct. 72, 78 L.Ed.2d 85 (1983); *Miller v. Transamerican Press, Inc.,* 621 F.2d 721 (5th Cir.1980) *cert. denied,* 450 U.S. 1041, 101 S.Ct. 1759, 68 L.Ed.2d 238 (1981); *WBAL-TV Div., Hearst Corp. v. State,* 300 Md. 233, 477 A.2d 776, 781 (1984). That test consists of the following elements:

> (1) Whether there is probable cause to believe that the newsperson has information that is clearly relevant to a specific probable violation of law;
>
> (2) Whether the information sought cannot be obtained by alternative means less destructive of First Amendment rights;
>
> (3) Whether there is demonstrated a compelling and overriding interest in the information. *Branzburg,* 408 U.S. at 744, 92 S.Ct. at 2681.

Procedural requirements for the evaluation process vary: many courts hold an in-camera hearing with a reporter and sometimes even with a source; others establish stringent burdens of proof with requirements of specific findings in the record and opportunity for immediate appeal. *See e.g., State v. Siel, supra; In re Farber,* 78 N.J. 259, 394 A.2d 330 (1978) *cert. denied,* 439 U.S. 997, 99 S.Ct. 598, 58 L.Ed.2d 670 (1978); *Wisconsin ex rel. Green Bay Newspaper v. Circuit Court,* 9 Med.Law Rptr. 1889 (1983). Our trial judges are well qualified to select the procedure to fit the circumstances, but specific findings should be provided in all cases to facilitate review.

Idaho Cases

In *Mark's, supra* we stated:

> We view this case as presenting a unique set of circumstances—a habeas corpus proceeding in which a journalist is a witness. Because

> we find a compelling and legitimate governmental interest in assuring the efficacy of the writ of habeas corpus, we hold that here there is no qualified newsman's privilege beyond the usual inquiry concerning relevance and materiality of the information sought * * *.
>
> * * *.
>
> * * * We therefore decline to establish a specific newsman's privilege with respect to such information. (Footnotes omitted.) 105 Idaho at 568–569, 671 P.2d 473.

We did not there preclude the finding in other circumstances of a qualified privilege as the result of a case-by-case balancing process. *In Sierra Life v. Magic Valley Newspapers, Inc.,* 101 Idaho 795, 623 P.2d 103 (1980) and *Caldero, supra,* the issue of a newsperson's privilege arose in the context of a libel action. We stated in *Sierra:*

> We recognize that the news media rely upon confidential sources in the preparation of many stories, particularly those involving government or large organizations. The ability to keep the identity of those sources confidential is not infrequently a prerequisite to obtaining information. This interest, while legitimate, is not so paramount that the legitimate discovery needs of a libel plaintiff must bow before it. But by the same token a trial court can be expected to exercise caution when it orders these sources to be revealed. As the Supreme Court of the United States has suggested, the first question to be answered is whether the identity of the sources is *relevant.* In *Caldero,* the very crux of the case was whether or not the "police expert" actually existed, and whether or not he said that which the newspaper published. Relevance was there established beyond quibble. *Sierra,* 101 Idaho at 801, 623 P.2d 103.

The dissenters in *Caldero* stated that the interest in compelling testimony could be balanced differently in a civil action than in a criminal matter. *Caldero,* 98 Idaho at 299, 562 P.2d 791. Commentators have pointed out that in a civil setting, courts are more reluctant to require disclosure. *See, e.g., Marcus, supra* at 850–51. An exception to that statement appears to occur in two situations:

> (1) Where a reporter is a plaintiff making allegations of wrongdoing against defendants; *see e.g. Anderson v. Nixon,* 444 F.Supp. 1195 (D.C.Cir.1978).
>
> (2) Where a newsperson, paper or publisher is the defendant in a defamation action. *See Senear v. The Daily Journal–American,* 97 Wash.2d 148, 641 P.2d 1180 (1982).

It might be noted that these situations could be viewed not as exceptions to a general rule of privilege, but as circumstances in which the balancing favors disclosure, since the source or information at issue may be so relevant and material as to be at the very heart of the claim. *See, Garland v. Torre,* 259 F.2d 545 (2d Cir.) *cert. denied,* 358 U.S. 910, 79 S.Ct. 237, 3 L.Ed.2d 231 (1958). If the source or information is also not available elsewhere, and of overriding interest to the moving party, then Justice Stewart's balancing test has been met. While *Caldero* has been read as refusing to find either an absolute or qualified privilege, it more properly can be seen as a case in which there was implicit balancing, with the result being that the need for the identity of a source there outweighed the First Amendment interest. To the extent that *Caldero* holds that under no circumstances is there a qualified newsperson's privilege in Idaho which is protected by the First Amendment of the U.S. Constitution, we decline to follow it as precedent. Since *Caldero* there has been an increasing recognition by federal and other state courts, as well as state legislatures which have passed "shield laws" (26 to date),[1] of the connection between freedom of the press and the public's right to know. A careful balancing by the courts between a First Amendment privilege, and any interest asserted which may conflict with that privilege, will serve the parties and the public most appropriately.

We hold that the elements of Justice Stewart's balancing test in *Branzburg* are the proper ones to be used. This test may be applied in both a criminal and a civil context; however, the weight given to each factor will vary depending on the type of case and the interest at issue. In a criminal matter where, for example, the defendant asserts a Sixth Amendment right to a fair trial to compel disclosure, the weight of such a constitutional interest may tip the balance in favor of disclosure. In a civil matter, disclosure will not be compelled absent a showing of a significant interest by the moving party supported by the balancing test elements.

A balancing test such as we adopt will not adversely affect a criminal or civil trial or even a grand jury process. Many states had adopted such a test by statute as early as 1971 with no apparent disruption of the investigative process. *See* Comment, The Newsman's Privilege After *Branzburg;* The Case for a Federal Shield Law, 24 U.C.L.A. L.Rev. 160, 167 (1976). Moreover, we reiterate that such a balancing test does not contemplate an absolute immunity; if the material is relevant, unavailable from other sources, and of significant interest in an investigation or case, the reporter will be compelled to divulge sources and information.

1. The following states have Shield Laws which provide a newsperson's privilege:

Alabama
Alaska
Arizona
Arkansas
California
Delaware
Illinois
Indiana
Kentucky
Louisiana
Maryland
Michigan
Minnesota
Montana
Nebraska
Nevada
New Jersey
New Mexico
New York
North Dakota
Ohio
Oklahoma
Oregon
Pennsylvania
Rhode Island
Tennessee

See, Comment, *supra,* 24 U.C.L.A.L.Rev. 160, 167 (1976).

Art. I, § 9 of the Idaho Constitution provides for protection of freedoms substantially similar to those of the First Amendment to the U.S. Constitution. Accordingly, for the reasons discussed above, we also ground this decision on the mandates of the Idaho Constitution.

We reverse and remand to the trial court for appropriate proceedings consistent with this opinion.

No attorney fees. Costs to appellant.

DONALDSON, C.J., and BAKES and BISTLINE, JJ., concur.

DONALDSON, CHIEF JUSTICE, specially concurring.

While I am in basic agreement with the majority opinion, I must express the following reservations. First, the majority grounds its decision on the United States Constitution and the Idaho Constitution. In my opinion it is error to ground the decision on the United States Constitution. After *Branzburg v. Hayes,* 408 U.S. 665, 92 S.Ct. 2646, 33 L.Ed.2d 626 (1972), the federal constitutional status of the newsperson's privilege is anything but clear. *See, e.g., Herbert v. Lando,* 441 U.S. 153, 99 S.Ct. 1635, 60 L.Ed.2d 115 (1979); *New York Times Co. v. Jascalevich,* 439 U.S. 1331, 99 S.Ct. 11, 58 L.Ed.2d 38 (1978); *New York Times Co. v. New Jersey,* 439 U.S. 997, 99 S.Ct. 598, 58 L.Ed.2d 670 (1978).

Instead, relying on the United States Supreme Court's invitation in *Branzburg* for state courts "to [respond] in their own way and [construe] their own constitutions so as to recognize a newsman's privilege, either qualified or absolute," (408 U.S. at 706, 92 S.Ct. at 2669) I would ground this decision wholly on art. 1, § 9 of the Idaho Constitution. Art. 1, § 9 provides that "[e]very person may freely speak, write and publish on all subjects, being responsible for the abuse of that liberty." * * *

* * *

My second reservation with the majority opinion concerns the procedures for determining whether the privilege applies in a given case. The newsperson in this case, Jim Wright, claims that his constitutional due process rights entitle him to a separate hearing to determine his privilege claim. The majority opines that "our trial judges are well qualified to select the procedure to fit the circumstances." Then, the majority remands the case to the trial court for appropriate proceedings consistent with the opinion leaving it unclear whether Wright is entitled to a separate hearing. My interpretation of "proceedings consistent with the opinion" is that Wright is not constitutionally entitled to a separate hearing but rather is only entitled to that procedure selected by the trial judge to fit the circumstances.

Accordingly, I concur in that part of the opinion that rests its decision on ID. CONST. art. 1, § 9 and that remands the case to the trial court to apply the test set out by the majority in a procedure selected by the trial court.

BISTLINE, JUSTICE, specially concurring.

I.

While I agree with Justice Huntley that under the United States and Idaho Constitutions there does exist a newsperson's qualified privilege not to disclose confidential sources, we need not have reached this conclusion, for there is also a common law privilege co-extensive to the constitutional privilege announced by the Court today.

It is a fundamental principle of law that when a court can decide a case on non-constitutional grounds, it should do so. *State v. Hightower,* 101 Idaho 749, 757, 620 P.2d 783, 791 (1980); *Erickson v. Amoth,* 99 Idaho 907, 910, 591 P.2d 1074, 1077 (1978). We can and should do so here.

* * *

II.

The concept of privileges arose in England in the 1600's. It developed only after witnesses could be compelled to testify. In England prior to the fifteenth century the concept of a witness was non-existent, for the jury served both as trier of fact and witness. 8 J. Wigmore, *Evidence in Trials at Common Law* § 2190, at 62 (McNaughton rev. ed. 1960). This method proved inefficient, and over time the bifurcation of witness and jury duties developed. *Id.,* pp. 63–65.

As the bifurcation of witnesses and juries occurred, new problems arose, the chief one being that there was no way for a court to require a witness to appear and give testimony. *Id.* This shortcoming was remedied by the Statute of Elizabeth in "which a penalty was imposed and a civil action was granted against any person who refused to attend (and testify) after service of process and tender of expenses." *Id.*

This statute is the source of the maxim that "the public * * * has a right to every man's evidence." *Id.,* § 2192, at 70; *see also Caldero v. Tribune Publishing Co.,* 98 Idaho 288, 291, 562 P.2d 791, 794 (1977). It was after the statute was enacted and the possibility of testimonial compulsion became a reality that the concept of privilege arose. Sherman and Weiser, *The Privilege Study: An Empirical Examination of the Psychotherapist–Patient Privilege,* 60 N.C.L.Rev. 895, 904 (1982).

Originally, the basis for a privilege was in the notion of "honor among gentlemen." 8 Wigmore, *supra,* § 2286, at 530.[1] The "honor among gentlemen" basis for privileges, however, was rejected in the 1776 case of Duchess of Kingston's Trial, 20 How.St.Trials 573 (1776), cited in *McCormick on Evidence,* § 98 at 212 (2d ed. 1972), in which the court refused to recognize a physician-patient privilege that was based simply upon the physician's honor not to divulge his confidences.[2] A

1. For example, the attorney-client privilege arose out of an attorney's honorable obligation not to disclose information confided by a client. *Id.,* at 531.

2. Mr. Chief Justice Mansfield said in part:

If a surgeon was voluntarily to reveal these secrets, to be sure, he would be guilty of a breach of honor and of great indiscretion; but to give that information in a court of justice, which by the law of the land he is bound to do, will

primary result of *Duchess of Kingston's Trial* was that the "honor among gentlemen" basis for justifying a privilege was replaced by a stricter utilitarian standard based on strong policy grounds. 8 Wigmore, *supra,* § 2286, at 531.

Based upon this stricter utilitarian standard, Professor Wigmore has formulated what he believes to be the four requirements for a privilege to be recognized at common law:

> (1) The communications must originate in a *confidence* that they will not be disclosed.
>
> (2) This element of *confidentiality must be essential* to the full and satisfactory maintenance of the relation between the parties.
>
> (3) The *relation* must be one which in the opinion of the community ought to be sedulously *fostered.*
>
> (4) The *injury* that would inure to the relation by the disclosure of the communications must be *greater than the benefit* thereby gained for the correct disposal of the litigation. *Id.* § 2285, at 527 (emphasis original).

Many courts and commentators have accepted Wigmore's test as the proper method for determining if a proposed privilege ought to be recognized. *See, e.g., Senear [v. Daily Journal–American,* 97 Wash.2d 148, 641 P.2d 1180 (1982)], 641 P.2d at 1182; *Allred v. State,* 554 P.2d 411, 417 (Alaska 1976); Slovenko, *Psychiatry and a Second Look at the Medical Privilege,* 6 Wayne L.Rev. 175, 184–99 (1960). It must always be remembered, however, that proper application of this test depends upon a correct understanding of the reason for privileges, which is "that in the balance of human liberty, more is achieved by safeguarding certain relationships from state molestation than is lost through the resulting impediment to the fact finding process." Louisell and Sinclair, *Forward: Reflections on the Law of Privileged Communications,* 59 Cal.L.Rev. 30, 53–54 (1971).

III.

Applying Wigmore's test, it is indisputable that in light of the needs of present-day society there does exist in the common law a qualified journalistic privilege.

* * *

IV.

I concur with the Washington Supreme Court's determination that, although a journalist's privilege does exist at common law, it is a qualified one that can be defeated if certain conditions are met:

> First, there must be a showing that the claim is meritorious; *i.e.,* it must not be frivolous or brought for the purpose of harassing the reporter. *Branzburg v. Hayes,* 408 U.S. 665, 710, 92 S.Ct. 2646, 2671,

never be imputed to him as any indiscretion whatever.

Id.

33 L.Ed.2d 626 (1972) (Powell, J., concurring); *Winegard v. Oxberger, supra* [258 N.W.2d 847 (Iowa 1977)].

Second, the information sought must be necessary or critical to the cause of action or the defense pleaded. It must, as was stated by Judge (later Justice) Potter Stewart, go "to the heart of the plaintiff's claim". *Garland v. Torre,* 259 F.2d 545, 550 (2d Cir.), *cert. denied,* 358 U.S. 910, 79 S.Ct. 237, 3 L.Ed.2d 231 (1958). *See also Carey v. Hume,* 492 F.2d 631, 636–37 (D.C.Cir.), *cert. dismissed,* 417 U.S. 938, 94 S.Ct. 2654, 41 L.Ed.2d 661 (1974); *Zerilli v. Smith,* 656 F.2d 705, 7 Media L.Rptr. 1121, 1127 (D.C.Cir.1981); *Baker v. F & F Inv.,* 470 F.2d 778, 783–84 (2d Cir.1972), *cert. denied,* 411 U.S. 966, 93 S.Ct. 2147, 36 L.Ed.2d 686 (1973).

Third, a reasonable effort must be made to acquire the desired information by other means. Even when the information is critical and necessary to plaintiff's case, the plaintiff must exhaust reasonably available alternative sources before a reporter is compelled to disclose.

> The values resident in the protection of the confidential sources of newsmen certainly point towards compelled disclosure from the newsman himself as normally the end, and not the beginning, of the inquiry.

Carey v. Hume, supra at 638 (concluding after balancing the interests that the reporter must disclose confidential sources); *see also Riley v. City of Chester, supra* [612 F.2d] at 717 [(3d Cir.1979)]; *Baker v. F & F Inv., supra* at 784. *City of Chester, supra* at 717; *Baker v. F & F Inv., supra* at 784. *Senear, supra,* 641 P.2d at 1183–84.

Thus, whether the privilege will attach in a particular case will depend upon the facts of that case. Determining whether the privilege will apply should be done in an in-camera hearing before the district court.

Relating to the above three factors discussed in *Senear,* it should be noted that in criminal cases [3] a *defendant's right* to a fair trial is a more compelling interest in favor of disclosure than a civil litigant's right. That is contrasted, however, to instances such as this case where it is the *state* seeking the information. While the state's interest in acquiring information concerning criminal conduct is important, it is not so important as to justify allowing it to, in effect, require private parties in all instances to do the investigatory work it has the responsibility of doing by demanding, upon threat of fine or incarceration, information acquired by private parties through private efforts. One final note, a journalist should receive greater protection if he or she is not a party to the case.

* * *

BAKES, JUSTICE, concurring specially:

3. The Washington Supreme Court in *State v. Rinaldo,* 102 Wash.2d 749, 689 P.2d 392 (1984) held that there exists a common law privilege in criminal as well as civil cases.

I concur in the result reached by the majority opinion. As I stated in a dissenting opinion in *Caldero v. Tribune Publishing Co.*, 98 Idaho 288, 562 P.2d 791 (1977), "the First Amendment to the United States Constitution affords a newsman a limited privilege against disclosure of his news sources in some cases." However, that qualified privilege exists solely by virtue of the interpretation placed upon the first amendment of the United States Constitution by the Supreme Court of the United States and other federal courts, and for no other reason. I disagree with the majority opinion in this case that such a privilege exists under Art. 1, § 9, of the Idaho Constitution, and also disagree that such a privilege existed at common law.

SHEPARD, JUSTICE, dissenting.

The Court today fashions from thin air a new evidentiary privilege which effectively allows an amorphous, undefined class of persons to refuse to testify in court. The majority does not limit the privilege or tell us its extent. The majority postulates no rationale for its decision, other than the vague assertion that it is founded in freedom of the press.

The majority finds no agreement within itself as to the basis of its holding. Huntley, J., with whom Bakes, J., concurs, surmises that the privilege grows out of the federal constitution. Donaldson, C.J., and Huntley, J. suggest that the privilege arises from Idaho's constitution. Bistline, J., plucks the privilege from the common law, where it has evidently slumbered unnoticed through the centuries.

The majority suggests that a successful assertion of the privilege will depend upon a "balancing" test, but I perceive that "balancing" as a thinly-veiled predicate for ad hoc decisions with no true legal foundation. Society and its system of criminal law will be ill-served by decisions which at bottom state, "it all depends," "that's different," or candidly, "our inability to withstand pressure has foreordained the result, hence there is no importance to how we arrive at that result."

There is only one conceivable rationale for the testimonial privilege created by the majority today, which rationale is that there is a constitutional protection of the freedom of the press; that such constitutional protection extends to the right of the press to not only disseminate news but to gather news; and that if a member of the press is required to testify in court regarding information obtained during news gathering, there will be a chilling effect on the freedom to publish news. That precise rationale was addressed and demolished by White, J., in *Branzburg v. Hayes,* 408 U.S. 665, 698–699, 92 S.Ct. 2646, 2665, 33 L.Ed.2d 626 (1972):

> "We are admonished that refusal to provide a First Amendment reporter's privilege will undermine the freedom of the press to collect and disseminate news. But this is not the lesson history teaches us. As noted previously, the common law recognized no such privilege, and the constitutional argument was not even asserted until 1958. From the beginning of our country the press has operated without constitu-

tional protection for press informants, and the press has flourished. The existing constitutional rules have not been a serious obstacle to either the development or retention of confidential news sources by the press."

The Court went on to say, 408 U.S. at 702–703, 92 S.Ct. at 2667–2668:

"If newsmen's confidential sources are as sensitive as they are claimed to be, the prospect of being unmasked whenever a judge determines the situation justifies it is hardly a satisfactory solution to the problem. For them, it would appear that only an absolute privilege would suffice.

"We are unwilling to embark the judiciary on a long and difficult journey to such an uncertain destination."

The problem of exactly who constitutes the "press" and to whom the testimonial privilege will be extended was also pointed out in *Branzburg* as a factor requiring the rejection of the asserted privilege. The Court stated, 408 U.S. at 703–704, 92 S.Ct. at 2668:

"The administration of a constitutional newsman's privilege would present practical and conceptual difficulties of a high order. Sooner or later, it would be necessary to define those categories of newsmen who qualified for the privilege, a questionable procedure in light of the traditional doctrine that liberty of the press is the right of the lonely pamphleteer who uses carbon paper or a mimeograph just as much as of the large metropolitan publisher who utilizes the latest photo composition methods."

The Oregon Supreme Court in *State v. Buchanan,* 250 Or. 244, 436 P.2d 729, 731–732 (1968), put it as follows:

"Apart from the definitional difficulties in attempting to give constitutional status to a privilege for qualified news gatherers which presumably would be denied to less favored classes, there is another objection to discrimination between news gatherers and other persons. Such a practice would be potentially destructive of the very freedom that is sought to be preserved by this appeal. After the lessons of colonial times, the First Amendment required the federal government to resist the normal temptation of rulers to regulate, license, or otherwise pass upon the credentials of those claiming to be authors and publishers. An invitation to the government to grant a special privilege to a special class of 'news gatherers' necessarily draws after it an invitation to the government to define the membership of that class. We doubt that all news writers would want the government to pass on the qualifications of those seeking to enter their field.

* * *

"Assuming that legislators are free to experiment with such definitions, it would be dangerous business for courts, asserting constitutional grounds, to extend to an employe of a 'respectable' newspaper a privilege which would be denied to an employe of a disreputable newspaper; or to an episodic pamphleteer; or to a free-lance writer seeking a story to sell on the open market; or, indeed, to a shaggy nonconformist who wishes only to write out his message and nail it to a tree. If the claimed privilege is to be found in the Constitution, its benefits cannot be limited to those whose credentials may, from time to time, satisfy the government."

Simply stated, there is no coherent or reasonable rationale for the decision of the majority. The majority's creation of a new privilege is fraught with danger and uncertainty as to what persons will be permitted to assert the privilege and under what circumstances the assertion of the privilege will be sustained. As will be discussed below, there is no basis in the federal constitution, the State constitution, or the common law for the creation of such a privilege. Hence, I dissent. Our courts do not belong to the judges, the lawyers, the press, or any other class, but rather they belong to the people and serve as a forum wherein truth can be learned and rights can be vindicated. It is truly a sad day when, in the name of "the people's right to know," a barrier is erected which will prevent the people and its courts from learning the truth.

The majority finds support for its creation of a qualified federal constitutional privilege in *Branzburg v. Hayes,* 408 U.S. 665, 92 S.Ct. 2646, 33 L.Ed.2d 626 (1972). No matter how one may attempt to interpret *Branzburg,* the opinion of the Court of four Justices, specially concurred in by a fifth, states, 408 U.S. at 689–690, 92 S.Ct. at 2661:

"Until now the only testimonial privilege for unofficial witnesses that is rooted in the Federal Constitution is the Fifth Amendment privilege against compelled self-incrimination. We are asked to create another by interpreting the First Amendment to grant newsmen a testimonial privilege that other citizens do not enjoy. *This we decline to do.*"

However much my brethren might wish that *Branzburg* had created the privilege asserted by the majority today, *Branzburg* simply does not do so. *See also United States v. Nixon,* 418 U.S. 683, 94 S.Ct. 3090, 41 L.Ed.2d 1039 (1974), in which the Court held that every citizen, including the President of the United States, has a duty to appear and testify in the courts of the people.

As stated by Judge Sirica in *United States v. Liddy,* 354 F.Supp. 208, 214 (D.D.C.1972):

"There can be little dispute that the common law recognized no privilege which would support a newspaper or reporter in refusing, upon proper demand, to disclose information received in confidence. Such a privilege, if it exists, must grow out of the First Amendment free press guarantee. Quite appropriately, in this Court's view, the Supreme Court has recognized as component parts of that guarantee the freedom to publish without prior governmental approval, a right of circulation, freedom to distribute literature, and the right to receive printed matter. And most recently with the Supreme Court's decision in *Branzburg,* it may be said that a right to gather news has been explicitly acknowledged. While acknowledging this corollary right, however, the Court rejected the claim that such a right implies a privilege to protect the identity of news sources. After citing numer-

> ous cases in which restrictions on the right to gather news have been sustained, the Court classified the requirement to answer subpoenas and disclose sources as another instance of permissible restriction."

Accord Tofani v. State, 297 Md. 165, 465 A.2d 413 (1983); *Georgia Communications Corp. v. Horne,* 164 Ga.App. 227, 294 S.E.2d 725 (1982); *Com. v. Corsetti,* 387 Mass. 1, 438 N.E.2d 805 (1982); *Newburn v. Howard Hughes Med. Inst.,* 95 Nev. 368, 594 P.2d 1146 (1979); *Matter of Farber,* 78 N.J. 259, 394 A.2d 330, *cert. denied,* 439 U.S. 997, 99 S.Ct. 598, 58 L.Ed.2d 670 (1978); *Ammerman v. Hubbard Broadcasting, Inc.,* 91 N.M. 250, 572 P.2d 1258 (App.1977), *cert. denied,* 436 U.S. 906, 98 S.Ct. 2237, 56 L.Ed.2d 404 (1978); *Caldero v. Tribune Pub. Co.,* 98 Idaho 288, 562 P.2d 791, *cert. denied,* 434 U.S. 930, 98 S.Ct. 418, 54 L.Ed.2d 291 (1977). *See also Gagnon v. Dist. Court In & For Cty. of Fremont,* 632 P.2d 567 (Colo.1981) (treating the issue of whether newsgatherer's source should be compelled disclosed as a question of relevance under civil procedure Rule 26(b)(1)).

I turn now to the assertion by two members of the majority that the Idaho Constitution provides a bulwark behind which certain persons may hide and refuse to testify in court. Those two members of the Court do not inform us as to why a different result follows when viewing the Idaho Constitution than that which is reached in interpreting the federal constitution. My only conclusion is that they view the decisions of the United States Supreme Court as foreclosing the federal constitution as a source of a privilege, but since the result is foreordained, they seize upon the Idaho Constitution as a convenient vehicle by which to obtain the desired result. Such, of course, ignores the previous decisions of this Court.

In *Caldero v. Tribune Pub. Co.,* 98 Idaho 288, 562 P.2d 791, *cert. denied,* 434 U.S. 930, 98 S.Ct. 418, 54 L.Ed.2d 291 (1977), the Court held that no privilege in an absolute or qualified form existed by reason of either the federal or the Idaho Constitution. The Court stated, 98 Idaho at 294, 562 P.2d at 797:

> "[O]ur reading of *Branzburg v. Hayes* * * * is to the effect that no newsman's privilege against disclosure of confidential sources founded on the First Amendment exists in an absolute or qualified version. The only restrictions against compelled disclosure appear to be in those cases where it is demonstrably intended to unnecessarily harass members of the news media on a broad scale by means having an unnecessary impact on protected rights of speech, press or association."

That language of *Caldero* was couched in the context of a civil libel case. Its language is even more compelling when viewed in the context of today's case, *i.e.,* a *Branzburg* type criminal proceeding in which the rights of society are sought to be vindicated and pursued by the enforcement of criminal sanctions for the violation of statutes enacted by the people.

The result of *Caldero* was affirmed in *Sierra Life Ins. v. Magic Valley Newspapers,* 101 Idaho 795, 623 P.2d 103 (1981), a decision wherein Bistline, J., writing for the majority, stated, 101 Idaho at 800, 623 P.2d at 108, "[T]he holding in *Caldero* and its application to the facts of this case [are] of concern. The debate over the validity of *Caldero* was apparently put to rest by the United States Supreme Court in *Herbert v. Lando,* 441 U.S. 153, 99 S.Ct. 1635, 60 L.Ed.2d 115 (1979)." In *Sierra Life,* a newspaper libel defendant had asserted "that the initial error here was in the trial court's order directing the defendants to reveal their confidential sources, and that a correct ruling at that point would have avoided placing the court in the ensuing situation which resulted in the imposition of sanctions." 101 Idaho at 800, 623 P.2d at 108. Thus, the Court in *Sierra Life,* although reversing for what it perceived to be overly harsh sanctions, did not modify *Caldero.*

Most recently, in *Marks v. Vehlow,* 105 Idaho 560, 671 P.2d 473 (1983), the Court drew a parallel to *Branzburg* and rejected the assertion of a newsman's privilege to refuse to appear and testify. That opinion was cast in the context of a newsman's refusal to supply information pertinent to the location of a kidnapped child. Donaldson, C.J., writing for the majority, stated:

> "Because we find a compelling and legitimate governmental interest in assuring the efficacy of the writ of habeas corpus, we hold that here there is no qualified newsman's privilege beyond the usual inquiry concerning relevance and materiality of the information sought. Furthermore, we believe that the obligation to attend and to give testimony in a habeas corpus proceeding wherein liberty interests are determined is at least as compelling as the duty to appear before a grand jury, *Branzburg v. Hayes,* 408 U.S. 665, 92 S.Ct. 2646, 33 L.Ed.2d 626 (1972); cf. *Matter of Farber,* 78 N.J. 259, 394 A.2d 330, 334 (obligation to appear on behalf of a criminal defendant as compelling as duty to appear before a grand jury), cert. denied, 439 U.S. 997, 99 S.Ct. 598, 58 L.Ed.2d 670 (1978). The concealing of information or the identities of informants which could lead to the discovery of a person sought by means of habeas corpus proceedings should be discouraged. We therefore decline to establish a specific newsman's privilege with respect to such information." 105 Idaho at 568–569, 671 P.2d at 481–482.

The majority postulates no rationale why it departs from the previous decisions of this Court. As the press is viewed from a national perspective in *Branzburg,* so also I view the press in Idaho. I do not find the press in this State to have been in the past the craven tool of government, of the courts, or of special interests groups. I do not find that its vigor, assertiveness, or dedication to the public's right to know has in any way been diminished or hamstrung by the previous decisions of this Court. Under our constitution, as it has been interpreted, the press within the State of Idaho may be many things. At times it is accused of being arrogant, abrasive, and overly intrusive. At other times its critics suggest bias in its reporting of the news or outrageousness in its editorial opinion. Whatever its virtues or its faults, no one appears to argue its dedication and ability to inform the public. Nor do any of its critics suggest that the press in Idaho lies supine under the heel of authority. Simply put, the assertions of the majority of dangers to the press are overblown, non-existent, and ignorant of the teachings of history.

Appellant also argues, and Bistline, J., apparently agrees, that this Court should exercise its authority to create a common law privilege which insulates certain persons from the usual mandate of the law to appear and give evidence in the courts on the grounds that "it is indisputable that in light of present day society there does exist in the common law a qualified journalistic privilege." To suggest, as does Bistline, J., that the common law is dynamic and capable of growth, evolution, and adaptation is only to posit that such privilege has not existed in the common law, and that the common law should be changed to accommodate the need for such a privilege. The whole basis of the common law is its effort to resolve disputes by determining where the truth might lie.

Privileged communications during the past hundreds of years have been recognized, but each has been bottomed on a clearly enunciated and understood rationale. At common law, a privilege was recognized for communications between spouses during marriage,[1] for disclosures by clients to their attorneys,[2] and for military and diplomatic government secrets.[3] There appears to have been no privilege at common law as to information obtained as a result of a physician-patient relationship,[4] and while priest-penitent privilege was discussed in early cases, Wigmore has concluded that the privilege was not established or accepted by common law.[5]

Beyond those enunciated testimonial privileges, judicial creation of other privileges is disfavored because such evidentiary privileges preclude reliable evidence from being placed before the court, and the search for truth is thereby obstructed. *Caldero v. Tribune Pub. Co.,* 98 Idaho 288, 562 P.2d 791, *cert. denied,* 434 U.S. 930, 98 S.Ct. 418, 54 L.Ed.2d 291 (1977).

1. Marital communications privilege: *See* 8 Wigmore on Evidence §§ 2227–2243 (McNaughton Rev.1961); McCormick on Evidence, Chapter 9 (3d ed. 1984); Bell, Handbook of Evidence for the Idaho Lawyer, pp. 73–75 (2d ed. 1972). *See also Shields v. Ruddy,* 3 Idaho 148, 28 P. 405 (1891) (marital privilege recognized by statute).

2. Attorney-client privilege: *See Later v. Haywood,* 12 Idaho 78, 85 P. 494 (1906); *State v. Perry,* 4 Idaho 224, 38 P. 655 (1894); 8 Wigmore on Evidence §§ 2290–2329 (McNaughton Rev.1961); McCormick on Evidence, Chapter 10 (3d ed. 1984); Bell, Handbook of Evidence for the Idaho Lawyer, pp. 71–73 (2d ed. 1972).

3. Government secrets: *See* 8 Wigmore on Evidence §§ 2367–2379 (McNaughton Rev.1961); McCormick on Evidence, Chapter 12 (3d ed. 1984); *Penn Mutual Life Ins. Co. v. Ireton,* 57 Idaho 466, 65 P.2d 1032 (1937).

4. Doctor-patient privilege: *See* Bell, Handbook of Evidence for the Idaho Lawyer, pp. 75–76 (2d ed. 1972); 8 Wigmore on Evidence §§ 2380–2391 (McNaughton Rev. 1961); McCormick on Evidence, Chapter 11 (3d ed. 1984).

5. Priest-penitent privilege: *See Angleton v. Angleton,* 84 Idaho 184, 370 P.2d 788 (1962) (decided on the basis of I.C. § 9–203); 8 Wigmore on Evidence §§ 2394–2396 (McNaughton Rev.1961); McCormick on Evidence, p. 184 (3d ed. 1984); Bell, Handbook of Evidence for the Idaho Lawyer, p. 78 (2d ed. 1972).

Beyond judge-made privileges, legislative enactments have created, recognized, or defined certain privileges. *See, e.g.*, I.C. § 9–203(1) (interspousal communications); I.C. § 9–203(2) (attorney-client communications); I.C. § 9–203(3) (confessions made to clergy); I.C. § 9–203(4) (information acquired by virtue of the doctor-patient relationship); I.C. § 9–203(5) (official confidences made to a public officer); I.C. § 9–203(6) (communications between school counselor and student); I.C. § 9–203(7) (parent-child communications); I.C. § 54–2314 (psychologist-client secrets); I.C. § 54–3410 (1982) (disclosures between professional counselor and client); I.C. § 54–3213 (consultations with social workers); I.C. § 39–1392b (hospital records). Those privileges have presumably been debated and resolved in the hard light of legislative policy decisions wherein duly elected representatives of the public, selected for their ability to make policy decisions, considered the pros and cons.

As noted by the majority opinion, some states have enacted statutes which, to varying extents and under certain circumstances, insulate the press from testimonial requirements. Our legislature has not seen fit to enact such a statutory privilege. Indeed, there appears substantial debate among the membership of the press as to the desirability of enactment of such "shield laws." Substantial numbers of the press hold to the view that such shield legislation is a subjugation of the press to the legislative branch of government, and that what the legislature giveth, it may at another day take away. Most thoughtful members of the press suggest that disclosure or nondisclosure is and should be a matter of individual conscience. Others suggest that it is within the realm of ethics of a profession. Those who argue ethics, of course, are also among the first to argue that the membership of the press is not restricted to any orthodox or recognizable class, nor is it to be licensed by the government as are doctors or lawyers. Hence, there can be enforced no journalistic code of ethics, nor can a breach thereof be punished, since no authority exists over members of the so-called class. When one views the need for adaptation of the common law to create the asserted privilege, it appears that the inability to fashion extents and limits, the failure to demonstrate otherwise adverse results, and the need of society to discover truth in its court proceedings, all militate against the creation of the asserted privilege.

Our rules of civil procedure and our retention of sanction powers traditionally exercised by our courts adequately shield witnesses, including reporters, from undue harassment and vexation. Limitation or termination of examinations conducted in bad faith is authorized, I.R.C.P. 30(d), as are protective orders to prevent annoyance, embarrassment or oppression of any person during court proceedings, I.R.C.P. 26(c).

The instant case is cast in terms of a criminal prosecution. Information is being withheld which is allegedly of assistance to that prosecution. The alleged crime is not perhaps the most important, but it nevertheless involves proscribed criminal behavior. Society has a substantial interest in, and a right to, enforcement of its criminal statutes. Although Bistline, J., asserts a difference between the right of a defendant to secure information for his defense, and the right of society to secure information for effective prosecution, I disagree that such a distinction should be made. Today's case involves a prosecution whose purposes and methods may be offensive to certain members of the press. Hence, there is a refusal to testify. Tomorrow's case may involve the withholding of information potentially beneficial to a criminal defendant whose views or conduct may be equally offensive to certain members of the press. I respectfully suggest that there is no difference in the two cases, and that this Court, having created the privilege, must be equally willing to enforce it in either case, however distasteful the result.

Valid efforts to reduce violence and enforce statutes proscribing unlawful activity should not be thwarted by stretching of the common law or of the constitution solely to accommodate the special interests of criminal informants. At bottom, an orderly society depends upon vindication of its rights in the courts. The rights of individuals and society cannot be determined and protected by the courts, unless those courts are allowed to undiscriminatingly and fairly pursue the truth. I view today's decision as an unnecessary and unjustified intrusion into our judiciary's search for truth.

STATE v. MAXON, 110 Wash.2d 564, 756 P.2d 1297, 1298–99 (1988). "The federal and state constitutions afford no basis for a parent-child privilege, and neither does the weight of common law. As we perceive it, public policy also disfavors creation of such a privilege by judicial fiat.

* * *

"* * * While this issue is one of first impression in this state, it has received considerable attention from courts and legislatures across the country over the past decade. The majority of state courts that have considered the issue have declined to recognize a parent-child privilege.[8] Likewise, most federal courts which have considered the issue have refused to recognize a parent-child privilege.[9]

"Thus far only one federal court, a trial court, has recognized a

8. See, e.g., In re Terry W., 59 Cal. App.3d 745, 130 Cal.Rptr. 913 (1976); State v. Gilroy, 313 N.W.2d 513 (Iowa 1981); Three Juveniles v. Commonwealth, 390 Mass. 357, 455 N.E.2d 1203 (1983), cert. denied, 465 U.S. 1068, 104 S.Ct. 1421, 79 L.Ed.2d 746 (1984); People v. Dixon, 161 Mich.App. 388, 411 N.W.2d 760 (1987); State v. Bruce, 655 S.W.2d 66 (Mo.Ct.App. 1983); In re Gail D., 217 N.J.Super. 226, 525 A.2d 337 (1987).

9. See, e.g., United States v. Jones, 683 F.2d 817 (4th Cir.1982); Port v. Heard, 764 F.2d 423 (5th Cir.1985); United States v. Ismail, 756 F.2d 1253 (6th Cir.1985); United States v. Davies, 768 F.2d 893 (7th Cir.), cert. denied, 474 U.S. 1008, 106 S.Ct. 533, 88 L.Ed.2d 464 (1985); United States v. Penn, 647 F.2d 876 (9th Cir.), cert. denied, 449 U.S. 903, 101 S.Ct. 276, 66 L.Ed.2d 134 (1980); In re Grand Jury Subpoena of Santarelli, 740 F.2d 816, reh'g denied, 749 F.2d 733 (11th Cir.1984).

parent-child privilege.[10] Similarly, only New York has judicially adopted such a privilege.[11] The legislatures of three states have enacted statutes granting limited parent-child privileges.[12] There appears, however, to be considerable support for such a privilege among legal commentators.[13]"

Notes

(1) On the clergy-communicant privilege, see Proposed Fed.R.Evid. 506; Unif.R.Evid. 505; 8 Wigmore, Evidence ch. 87 (McNaughton rev. 1961); McCormick, Evidence § 76.2 (4th ed. 1992); Callahan, Historical Inquiry into the Priest-Penitent Privilege, 36 Jurist 328 (1976); Kuhlman, Communications to Clergymen—When Are They Privileged?, 2 Val.U.L.Rev. 265 (1968); Mitchell, Must Clergy Tell? Child Abuse Reporting Requirements Versus the Clergy Privilege and Free Exercise of Religion, 71 Minn.L.Rev. 723 (1987); Reece, Confidential Communications to the Clergy, 24 Ohio St.L.J. 55 (1963); Smith, The Pastor on the Witness Stand: Toward a Religious Privilege in the Courts, 29 Cath.Law. 1 (1984); Stoyles, The Dilemma of the Constitutionality of the Priest-Penitent Privilege—The Application of the Religion Clauses, 29 U.Pitt.L.Rev. 27 (1967); Yellin, The History and Current Status of the Clergy-Penitent Privilege, 23 Santa Clara L.Rev. 95 (1983).

(2) Other privileges sporadically created by statutes or, more rarely, by judicial decisions are described in 8 Wigmore, Evidence § 2286 (McNaughton rev. 1961) and McCormick, Evidence § 76.2 (4th ed. 1992).

SECTION 6. SELF-INCRIMINATION *

CARTER v. KENTUCKY

Supreme Court of the United States, 1981.
450 U.S. 288, 101 S.Ct. 1112, 67 L.Ed.2d 241.

JUSTICE STEWART delivered the opinion of the Court.

In this case a Kentucky criminal trial judge refused a defendant's request to give the following jury instruction: "The defendant is not

10. See In re Agosto, 553 F.Supp. 1298 (D.Nev.1983).

11. See In re A & M, 61 A.D.2d 426, 403 N.Y.S.2d 375, 6 A.L.R.4th 532 (1978); People v. Fitzgerald, 101 Misc.2d 712, 422 N.Y.S.2d 309 (1979).

12. See Idaho Code § 9-203(7) (1979 & Supp.1986); Mass.Gen.Laws Ann. ch. 233, § 20 (West Supp.1988); Minn.Stat. § 595.-02(1)(i) (1986 & Supp.1987).

13. See, e.g., Coburn, Child-Parent Communications: Spare the Privilege and Spoil the Child, 74 Dick.L.Rev. 599 (1970); Stanton, Child-Parent Privilege for Confidential Communications: An Examination and Proposal, 16 Fam.L.Q. 1 (1982). But see Schlueter, The Parent-Child Privilege: A Response to Calls for Adoption, 19 St. Mary's L.J. 35 (1987) (includes a critique of proposed ABA Model Parent-Child Privileges Statute); Comment, Parent-Child Privilege: Constitutional Right or Specious Analogy?, 3 U. Puget Sound L.Rev. 177 (1979).

* See 8 Wigmore, Evidence ch. 80 (McNaughton rev. 1961); McCormick, Evidence ch. 13 (4th ed. 1992); Levy, Origins of the Fifth Amendment (1968); Dolinko, Is There a Rationale for the Privilege Against Self-Incrimination?, 33 U.C.L.A. L.Rev. 1063 (1986); Heidt, The Conjurer's Circle—The Fifth Amendment Privilege in Civil Cases, 91 Yale L.J. 1062 (1982); Heidt, The Fifth Amendment Privilege and Documents—Cutting Fisher's Tangled Line, 49 Mo.L.Rev. 439 (1984); Pittman, The Colonial and Constitutional History of the Privilege Against Self-Incrimination in America, 21 Va.L.Rev. 763 (1935); Ritchie, Compulsion that Violates the Fifth Amendment: The Burger Court's Definition, 61 Minn.L.Rev. 383 (1977); Saltzburg, The Re-

compelled to testify and the fact that he does not cannot be used as an inference of guilt and should not prejudice him in any way." The Supreme Court of Kentucky found no error. We granted certiorari to consider the petitioner's contention that a defendant, upon request, has a right to such an instruction under the Fifth and Fourteenth Amendments of the Constitution. 449 U.S. 819, 101 S.Ct. 71, 66 L.Ed.2d 21.[2]

* * *

II

A

The constitutional question presented by this case is one the Court has specifically anticipated and reserved, first in Griffin v. California, 380 U.S. 609, 615, n. 6, 85 S.Ct. 1229, 1233, n. 6, 14 L.Ed.2d 106, and more recently in Lakeside v. Oregon, 435 U.S. 333, 337, 98 S.Ct. 1091, 1093, 55 L.Ed.2d 319. But, as a question of federal statutory law, it was resolved by a unanimous Court over 40 years ago in Bruno v. United States, 308 U.S. 287, 60 S.Ct. 198, 84 L.Ed. 451. The petitioner in *Bruno* was a defendant in a federal criminal trial who had requested a jury instruction similar to the one requested by the petitioner in this case. The Court, addressing the question whether *Bruno* "had the indefeasible right" that his proffered instruction be given to the jury, decided that a federal statute, which prohibits the creation of any presumption from a defendant's failure to testify, required that the "substance of the denied request should have been granted * * *." Id., at 294,[9] 60 S.Ct., at 200.

quired Records Doctrine: Its Lessons for the Privilege Against Self-Incrimination, 53 U.Chi.L.Rev. 6 (1986).

2. Kentucky is one of at least five States that prohibit giving such an instruction to the jury. Others are Minnesota, see *State v. Sandve,* 279 Minn. 229, 232–234, 156 N.W.2d 230, 233–234, but see *State v. Grey,* Minn., 256 N.W.2d 74, 77–78 (the instruction may be necessary in some cases to prevent manifest injustice); Nevada, see *Jackson v. State,* 84 Nev. 203, 208, 438 P.2d 795, 798, Nev.Rev.Stat. § 175.181 (1979); Oklahoma, see *Brannin v. State,* 375 P.2d 276, 279–280 (Crim.App.); *Hanf v. State,* 560 P.2d 207, 212 (Crim.App.); and Wyoming, see *Kinney v. State,* 36 Wyo. 466, 472, 256 P. 1040, 1042. A few States have a statutory requirement that such an instruction be given to the jury unless the defendant objects. See *e.g.,* Conn.Gen.Stat. § 54–84 (1958). The majority of the States, by judicial pronouncement, require that a defense request for such a jury instruction be honored. See, *e.g., Woodard v. State,* 234 Ga. 901, 218 S.E.2d 629.

9. At common law, defendants in criminal trials could not be compelled to furnish evidence against themselves, but they were also not permitted to testify. In the context of the original enactment of the federal statute found dispositive in the *Bruno* case, this Court commented on the alteration of this common-law rule: "This rule, while affording great protection to the accused against unfounded accusation, in many cases deprived him from explaining [incriminating] circumstances * * *. To relieve him from this embarrassment the law was passed * * *. [H]e is by the act in question permitted * * * to testify. * * *" Wilson v. United States, 149 U.S. 60, 65–66, 13 S.Ct. 765, 766, 37 L.Ed. 650. Following enactment of the federal statute, the States followed suit with similar laws. See Dills, The Permissibility of Comment on the Defendant's Failure to Testify in His Own Behalf in Criminal Proceedings, 3 Wash.L.Rev. 161, 164–165 (1928); 8 J. Wigmore, Evidence § 2272, p. 427 (J. McNaughton rev. 1961).

The issue in *Wilson,* supra, was whether it was error for the prosecutor to comment

The *Griffin* case came here shortly after the Court had held that the Fifth Amendment command that no person "shall be compelled in any criminal case to be a witness against himself" is applicable against the States through the Fourteenth Amendment. Malloy v. Hogan, 378 U.S. 1, 84 S.Ct. 1489, 12 L.Ed.2d 653. In *Griffin,* the Court considered the question whether it is a violation of the Fifth and Fourteenth Amendments to invite a jury in a state criminal trial to draw an unfavorable inference from a defendant's failure to testify. The trial judge had there instructed the jury that "a defendant has a constitutional right not to testify," and that the defendant's exercise of that right "does not create a presumption of guilt or by itself warrant an inference of guilt" nor "relieve the prosecution of any of its burden of proof." But the instruction additionally permitted the jury to "take that failure into consideration as tending to indicate the truth of [the State's] evidence and as indicating that among the inferences that may be reasonably drawn therefrom those unfavorable to the defendant are the more probable." 380 U.S., at 610, 85 S.Ct., at 1230.

This Court set aside Griffin's conviction because "the Fifth Amendment * * * forbids either comment by the prosecution on the accused's silence or instructions by the court that such silence is evidence of guilt." Id., at 615, 85 S.Ct., at 1233. It condemned adverse comment on a defendant's failure to testify as reminiscent of the " 'inquisitorial system of criminal justice,' " id., at 614, 85 S.Ct., at 1232, quoting Murphy v. Waterfront Comm'n, 378 U.S. 52, 55, 84 S.Ct. 1594, 1596, 12 L.Ed.2d 678, and concluded that such comment effected a court-imposed penalty upon the defendant that was unacceptable because "[i]t cuts down on the privilege by making its assertion costly." 380 U.S., at 614, 85 S.Ct., at 1232.

The Court returned to a consideration of the Fifth Amendment and jury instructions in Lakeside v. Oregon, 435 U.S. 333, 98 S.Ct. 1091, 55 L.Ed.2d 319, where the question was whether the giving of a "no-inference" instruction over defense objection violates the Constitution. Despite trial counsel's complaint that his strategy was to avoid any mention of his client's failure to testify, a no-inference instruction was given by the trial judge. The petitioner contended that when a trial judge in any way draws the jury's attention to a defendant's failure to testify, unless the defendant acquiesces, the court invades the defendant's privilege against compulsory self-incrimination. This argument was rejected.

The *Lakeside* Court reasoned that the Fifth and Fourteenth Amendments bar only *adverse* comment on a defendant's failure to testify, and that "a judge's instruction that the jury must draw *no* adverse inferences of any kind from the defendant's exercise of his

adversely on the defendant's failure to testify. The Court unanimously held that it was, observing that "[n]othing could have been more effective with the jury to induce them to disregard entirely the presumption of innocence to which by the law he was entitled. * * *" 149 U.S., at 66, 13 S.Ct., at 766. As later in *Bruno,* however, the Court did not reach any Fifth Amendment issue.

privilege not to testify is 'comment' of an entirely different order." Id., at 339, 98 S.Ct., at 1094. The purpose of such an instruction, the Court stated, "is to remove from the jury's deliberations any influence of unspoken adverse inferences," and "cannot provide the pressure on a defendant found impermissible in *Griffin.*" Ibid.

The Court observed in *Lakeside* that the petitioner's argument there rested on "two very doubtful assumptions:"

> First, that the jurors have not noticed that the defendant did not testify and will not, therefore, draw adverse inferences on their own. Second, that the jurors will totally disregard the instruction, and affirmatively give weight to what they have been told not to consider at all. Federal constitutional law cannot rest on speculative assumptions so dubious as these." Id., at 340, 98 S.Ct., at 1095 (footnote omitted).

Finally, the Court stressed that "[t]he very purpose" of a jury instruction is to direct the jurors' attention to important legal concepts "that must not be misunderstood, such as reasonable doubt and burden of proof," and emphasized that instruction "in the meaning of the privilege against compulsory self-incrimination is no different." Ibid.

B

The inclusion of the privilege against compulsory self-incrimination in the Fifth Amendment

> "reflects many of our fundamental values and most noble aspirations: our unwillingness to subject those suspected of crime to the cruel trilemma of self-accusation, perjury or contempt; * * * our fear that self-incriminating statements will be elicited by inhumane treatment and abuses; our sense of fair play which dictates 'a fair state-individual balance by requiring the government * * *, in its contest with the individual to shoulder the entire load,' * * *; our distrust of self-deprecatory statements; and our realization that the privilege, while sometimes 'a shelter to the guilty,' is often 'a protection to the innocent.'" Murphy v. Waterfront Comm'n, supra, at 55, 84 S.Ct., at 1596.[15]

The principles enunciated in our cases construing this privilege, against both statutory and constitutional backdrops, lead unmistakably to the conclusion that the Fifth Amendment requires that a criminal trial

15. The Court has recognized that there are many reasons unrelated to guilt or innocence for declining to testify:

"It is not every one who can safely venture on the witness stand though entirely innocent of the charge against him. Excessive timidity, nervousness when facing others and attempting to explain transactions of a suspicious character, and offences charged against him, will often confuse and embarrass him to such a degree as to increase rather than remove prejudices against him. It is not every one, however honest, who would, therefore, willingly be placed on the witness stand." *Wilson v. United States,* 149 U.S., at 66, 13 S.Ct., at 766. Other reasons include the fear of impeachment by prior convictions (the petitioner's fear in the present case), or by other damaging information not necessarily relevant to the charge being tried, *Griffin,* 380 U.S., at 615, 85 S.Ct., at 1233, and reluctance to "incriminate others whom [defendants] either love or fear," *Lakeside,* 435 U.S., at 344, n. 2, 98 S.Ct., at 1097 n. 2 (dissenting opinion).

judge must give a "no-adverse-inference" jury instruction when requested by a defendant to do so.

In *Bruno,* the Court declared that the failure to instruct as requested was not a mere "technical erro[r] * * * which do[es] not affect * * * substantial rights * * *." It stated that the "right of an accused to insist on" the privilege to remain silent is "[o]f a very different order of importance * * *" from the "mere etiquette of trials and * * * the formalities and minutiae of procedure." 308 U.S., at 293–294, 60 S.Ct., at 200. Thus, while the *Bruno* Court relied on the authority of a federal statute, it is plain that its opinion was influenced by the absolute constitutional guarantee against compulsory self-incrimination.

The *Griffin* case stands for the proposition that a defendant must pay no court-imposed price for the exercise of his constitutional privilege not to testify. The penalty was exacted in *Griffin* by adverse comment on the defendant's silence; the penalty may be just as severe when there is no adverse comment, but when the jury is left to roam at large with only its untutored instincts to guide it, to draw from the defendant's silence broad inferences of guilt. Even without adverse comment, the members of a jury, unless instructed otherwise, may well draw adverse inferences from a defendant's silence.

The significance of a cautionary instruction was forcefully acknowledged in *Lakeside,* where the Court found no constitutional error even when a no-inference instruction was given over a defendant's objection. The salutary purpose of the instruction, "to remove from the jury's deliberations any influence of unspoken adverse inferences," was deemed so important that it there outweighed the defendant's own preferred tactics.[18]

* * *

A trial judge has a powerful tool at his disposal to protect the constitutional privilege—the jury instruction—and he has an affirmative constitutional obligation to use that tool when a defendant seeks its employment. No judge can prevent jurors from speculating about why a defendant stands mute in the face of a criminal accusation, but a judge can, and must, if requested to do so, use the unique power of the jury instruction to reduce that speculation to a minimum.

C

The only state interest advanced by Kentucky in refusing a request for such a jury instruction is protection of the defendant: "the request-

18. It has been almost universally thought that juries notice a defendant's failure to testify. "[T]he jury will, of course, realize this quite evident fact, even though the choice goes unmentioned. * * * [It is] a fact inescapably impressed on the jury's consciousness." *Griffin,* supra, at 621, 622, 85 S.Ct., at 1237 (dissenting opinion). In *Lakeside* the Court cited an acknowledged authority's statement that " '[t]he layman's natural first suggestion would probably be that the resort to privilege in each instance is a clear confession of crime.' " 435 U.S., at 340, n. 10, 85 S.Ct., at 1095, n. 10, quoting 8 J. Wigmore, Evidence § 2272, p. 426 (J. McNaughton rev. 1961).

ed 'no inference' instruction * * * would have been a direct 'comment' by the court and would have emphasized the fact that the accused had not testified in his own behalf." Green v. Commonwealth, Ky., 488 S.W.2d, at 341. This purported justification was specifically rejected in the *Lakeside* case, where the Court noted that "[i]t would be strange indeed to conclude that this cautionary instruction violates the very constitutional provision it is intended to protect." 435 U.S., at 339, 98 S.Ct., at 1094.

Kentucky also argues that in the circumstances of this case the jurors knew they could not make adverse inferences from the petitioner's election to remain silent because they were instructed to determine guilt "from the evidence alone," and because failure to testify is not evidence. The Commonwealth's argument is unpersuasive. Jurors are not lawyers; they do not know the technical meaning of "evidence." They can be expected to notice a defendant's failure to testify, and, without limiting instruction, to speculate about incriminating inferences from a defendant's silence.

* * *

III

The freedom of a defendant in a criminal trial to remain silent "unless he chooses to speak in the unfettered exercise of his own will" is guaranteed by the Fifth Amendment and made applicable to state criminal proceedings through the Fourteenth. Malloy v. Hogan, 378 U.S., at 8, 84 S.Ct., at 1493. And the Constitution further guarantees that no adverse inferences are to be drawn from the exercise of that privilege. Griffin v. California, 380 U.S. 609, 85 S.Ct. 1229, 14 L.Ed.2d 106. Just as adverse comment on a defendant's silence "cuts down on the privilege by making its assertion costly," id., at 614, 85 S.Ct., at 1232, the failure to limit the jurors' speculation on the meaning of that silence, when the defendant makes a timely request that a prophylactic instruction be given, exacts an impermissible toll on the full and free exercise of the privilege. Accordingly, we hold that a state trial judge has the constitutional obligation, upon proper request, to minimize the danger that the jury will give evidentiary weight to a defendant's failure to testify.

For the reasons stated, the judgment is reversed, and the case is remanded to the Supreme Court of Kentucky for further proceedings not inconsistent with this opinion.

It is so ordered.

JUSTICE POWELL, concurring.

* * *

The one person who usually knows most about the critical facts is the accused. For reasons deeply rooted in the history we share with England, the Bill of Rights included the Self-Incrimination Clause, which enables a defendant in a criminal trial to elect to make no contribution to the fact-finding process. But nothing in the Clause requires that jurors not draw logical inferences when a defendant chooses not to explain incriminating circumstances. Jurors have been instructed that the defendant is presumed to be innocent and that this presumption can be overridden only by evidence beyond a reasonable doubt. California Chief Justice Traynor commented that judges and prosecutors should be able to explain that "a jury [may] draw unfavorable inferences from the defendant's failure to explain or refute evidence when he could reasonably be expected to do so. Such comment would not be evidence and would do no more than make clear to the jury the extent of its freedom in drawing inferences." Traynor, The Devils of Due Process in Criminal Detection, Detention, and Trial, 33 U.Chi. L.Rev. 657, 677 (1966); accord, Schaefer, Police Interrogation and the Privilege Against Self–Incrimination, 61 Nw.U.L.Rev. 506, 520 (1966).

I therefore would have joined Justices Stewart and White in dissent in *Griffin.* But *Griffin* is now the law, and based on that case the present petitioner was entitled to the jury instruction that he requested. I therefore join the opinion of the Court.

JUSTICE STEVENS, with whom JUSTICE BRENNAN joins, concurring.

While I join the Court's opinion, I add this comment to emphasize that today's holding is limited to cases in which the defendant has requested that the jury be instructed not to draw an inference of guilt from the defendant's failure to testify. I remain convinced that the question whether such an instruction should be given in any specific case—like the question whether the defendant should testify on his own behalf—should be answered by the defendant and his lawyer, not by the State. See Lakeside v. Oregon, 435 U.S. 333, 343–348, 98 S.Ct. 1091, 1096–1099, 53 L.Ed.2d 319 (1978) (Stevens, J., dissenting).

JUSTICE REHNQUIST, dissenting.

* * *

If we begin with the relevant provisions of the Constitution, which is where an unsophisticated lawyer or layman would probably think we should begin, we find the provision in the Fifth Amendment stating that "[n]o person * * * shall be compelled in any criminal case to be a witness against himself * * *." Until the mysterious process of transmogrification by which this Amendment was held to be "incorporated" and made applicable to the States by the Fourteenth Amendment in Malloy v. Hogan, 378 U.S. 1, 84 S.Ct. 1489, 12 L.Ed.2d 653 (1964), the provision itself would not have regulated the conduct of criminal trials in Kentucky. But even if it did, no one here claims that the defendant was forced to take the stand against his will or to testify against himself inconsistently with the provisions of the Fifth Amendment. The claim is rather that in Griffin v. California, supra, the Court, building on the language of the Constitution itself and on *Malloy,* supra, held that a charge to the effect that any evidence or facts adduced against the defendant which he could be reasonably expected to deny or explain could be taken into consideration by the jury violated the constitutional privilege against compulsory self-incrimination. The author of the present opinion dissented from that holding, stating:

> "The formulation of procedural rules to govern the administration of criminal justice in the various States is properly a matter of local concern. We are charged with no general supervisory power over such matters; our only legitimate function is to prevent violations of the Constitution's commands." 380 U.S., at 623, 85 S.Ct., at 1237.

But even *Griffin,* supra, did not go as far as the present opinion, for as that opinion makes clear it left open the question of whether a state-court defendant was entitled as a matter of right to a charge that his refusal to take the stand should not be taken into consideration against him by the jury. The Court now decides that he is entitled to such a charge, and, I believe, in doing so, wholly retreats from the statement in the *Griffin* dissent that "[t]he formulation of procedural rules to govern the administration of criminal justice in the various States is properly a matter of local concern."

The Court's opinion states that "[t]he *Griffin* case stands for the proposition that a defendant must pay no court-imposed price for the exercise of his constitutional privilege not to testify." Such Thomistic reasoning is now carried from the constitutional provision itself, to the *Griffin* case, to the present case, and where it will stop no one can know. The concept of "burdens" and "penalties" is such a vague one that the Court's decision allows a criminal defendant in a state proceeding virtually to take from the trial judge any control over the instructions to be given to the jury in the case being tried. I can find no more apt words with which to conclude this dissent than those stated by Justice Harlan, concurring in the Court's opinion in *Griffin*:

> "Although compelled to concur in this decision, I am free to express the hope that the Court will eventually return to constitutional paths which, until recently, it has followed throughout its history." 380 U.S., at 617, 85 S.Ct., at 1234.

PENFIELD v. VENUTI

United States District Court, Connecticut, 1984.
589 F.Supp. 250.

Ruling on Pending Motions

José A. Cabranes, District Judge:

In this diversity action, plaintiff alleges that late in the evening of June 6, 1979, while operating his motorcycle on Route 17 in Middletown, Connecticut, he was struck and seriously injured by a motor vehicle owned by defendant Joseph Venuti. Plaintiff contends that his injuries resulted from the negligent operation of that vehicle by Joseph Venuti, or by his son, defendant Scott Venuti, or by their agent, servant or employee. *See* Complaint ¶¶ 2–7 (filed May 5, 1981). Defendants maintain that they were both at home asleep when the incident occurred and thus deny all liability.

On March 1, 1984, defendants filed a motion *in limine* seeking the exclusion of evidence * * * that Scott Venuti invoked his Fifth Amendment privilege against self-incrimination at a deposition held September 10, 1979 in a substantially identical state court action. * * *

* * *

The Fifth Amendment secures a right "to remain silent unless [a witness] chooses to speak in the unfettered exercise of his own will, and to suffer no penalty * * * for such silence." *Spevack v. Klein,* 385 U.S. 511, 514–515, 87 S.Ct. 625, 627–628, 17 L.Ed.2d 574 (1967). However, "the Fifth Amendment does not forbid adverse inferences against parties to civil actions when they refuse to testify in response to probative evidence offered against them * * *." *Baxter v. Palmigiano,* 425 U.S. 308, 318, 96 S.Ct. 1551, 1558, 47 L.Ed.2d 810 (1976), *citing* 8 J. Wigmore, *Evidence* § 2272, at 439 (J. McNaughton rev. ed. 1961); *id.* at 335, 96 S.Ct. at 1566 (Brennan, J., concurring in part and dissenting in part); *Lefkowitz v. Cunningham,* 431 U.S. 801, 808 n. 5, 97 S.Ct. 2132, 2137 n. 5, 53 L.Ed.2d 1 (1977); *see National Acceptance Co. v. Bathalter,* 705 F.2d 924, 929–931 (7th Cir.1983) ("*Baxter* established that the drawing of an adverse inference from privileged silence in a civil case does not make the exercise of the privilege sufficiently 'costly' to amount to compulsion when there is other evidence of the fact"). Connecticut decisions are in accord with this "prevailing rule." *See Olin Corp. v. Castells,* 180 Conn. 49, 53–54, 428 A.2d 319, 321 (1980).[2]

At a deposition held September 10, 1979, Scott Venuti refused to answer any questions concerning his whereabouts the evening plaintiff was injured or otherwise pertaining to his involvement in or knowledge of the incident, invoking his Fifth Amendment privilege. There is no doubt that the privilege against compelled self-incrimination may be invoked in a pretrial proceeding such as a deposition. *E.F. Hutton & Co. v. Juniper Development Corp.,* 91 F.R.D. 110, 114 (S.D.N.Y.1981); *see In re Folding Carton Antitrust Litigation,* 609 F.2d 867 (7th Cir.1979). It is equally clear, however, that a refusal to answer questions upon assertion of the privilege is relevant evidence from which the trier of fact in a civil action may draw whatever inference is reasonable in the circumstances. *Brinks, Inc. v. City of New York,* 539 F.Supp. 1139, 1140–1141 (S.D.N.Y.1982) (Weinfeld, J.), *aff'd,* 717 F.2d 700, 710 (2d Cir.1983); *see also Young Sik Woo v. Glantz,* 99 F.R.D. 651, 652–653 (D.R.I.1983); *Davis v. Northside Realty Associates, Inc.,* 95 F.R.D. 39, 45 (N.D.Ga.1982); *E.H. Boerth Co. v. LAD Properties,* 82 F.R.D. 635, 644 (D.Minn.1979).

The fact that Scott Venuti's assertion of the privilege did not occur in open court does not alter this result. At a deposition,

2. The court has previously determined that questions in this case concerning evidentiary privileges are to be resolved in accordance with Connecticut law. *Penfield v. Venuti, supra,* 93 F.R.D. at 366; *see* Rule 501, Fed.R.Evid.; 10 *Moore's Federal Practice* § 501.06 (2d ed. 1982).

> [t]he invoking statement is uttered in the course of a formal proceeding, after the party and his counsel have had an opportunity to consider their response. It is a sufficiently grave admission that parties who resort to it are likely to have reviewed and reflected on their actions beforehand.

Heidt, *The Conjurer's Circle: The Fifth Amendment Privilege in Civil Cases,* 91 Yale L.J. 1062, 1118–1119 (1982); *see United States v. Local 560, International Brotherhood of Teamsters,* 581 F.Supp. 279, 305–306 (D.N.J.1984); *cf.* C. McCormick, *supra,* § 263, at 632 ("when a man speaks against his own interest it is to be supposed that he has made an adequate investigation").

Permitting an adverse inference to be drawn against a party who invokes the Fifth Amendment privilege during discovery prevents use of the privilege as a weapon in civil litigation. Invocation of the privilege as a defense strategy

> clearly cripples plaintiff's effort to conduct meaningful discovery and to marshal proof in an expeditious fashion, if at all.

SEC v. Musella, 578 F.Supp. 425, 428 (S.D.N.Y.1984); *see SEC v. Gilbert,* 79 F.R.D. 683, 686 (S.D.N.Y.1978) (Lasker, J.). The arguable harshness of the practice, *see Lionti v. Lloyd's Insurance Co.,* 709 F.2d 237, 245–246 (3d Cir.) (Stern, J., dissenting), *cert. denied,* ___ U.S. ___, 104 S.Ct. 490, 78 L.Ed.2d 685 (1983), is mitigated by the ability of the person invoking the privilege to explain why he did so or "to show by other evidence that his response would not have incriminated him." Heidt, *supra,* 91 Yale L.J. at 1119 & n. 212.

The conclusion that Scott Venuti's invocation of the privilege is relevant does not end the inquiry. The court must also consider whether the probative value of such evidence is "substantially outweighed by the danger of unfair prejudice." Rule 403, Fed.R.Evid.; *Brinks, supra,* 539 F.Supp. at 1141; *see Farace v. Independent Fire Insurance Co.,* 699 F.2d 204, 210–211 (5th Cir.1983); 5 J. Weinstein & M. Berger, *Weinstein's Evidence* ¶ 403[03] (1983).

When Scott Venuti invoked his Fifth Amendment privilege at the September 10, 1979 deposition, he did so on the advice of Joseph Bransfield, an attorney appointed by the Superior Court to represent his interests in connection with the then-pending divorce proceeding between his parents. He was sixteen years old at the time. Counsel representing him in the instant case and the related state litigation were not present at the deposition, assertedly because they were given inadequate notice and because plaintiff's counsel declined to postpone the deposition. *See* Motion in Limine (filed Mar. 1, 1984) at 2. *But see* Deposition of Scott Venuti (dated Sept. 10, 1979) at 3, No. 30597 (Conn.Super.Ct.). Why Scott Venuti's counsel, including one of Connecticut's largest law firms, nevertheless permitted their minor client to be deposed in their absence is difficult to fathom.

The probative value of Scott Venuti's invocation of the privilege is apparent. His actions on the night of June 6, 1979 are obviously "of consequence" to plaintiff's claims, and his involvement in the collision which injured Gary Penfield is certainly made "more probable" by a permissible inference flowing from his assertions of the privilege in response to questions regarding his activities that evening. *See Brinks, supra,* 539 F.Supp. at 1140; Rule 401, Fed.R.Evid. Neither Scott Venuti's age nor his representation by counsel possibly unacquainted with the state court tort action nor his willingness to respond to similar lines of questioning at a second deposition two years later significantly diminish the probative value of his refusal to answer. He was not directed to remain silent at the deposition, but invoked the privilege of his own volition based on the advice of counsel that answering the questions might tend to incriminate him. Deposition of Scott Venuti (dated Dec. 23, 1981) at 67–74. Moreover, as Scott Venuti himself pointed out, he was enrolled at the time "in a class on law and the Constitution" in which he studied the Fifth Amendment "pretty thoroughly." *Id.* at 66. He was not a child blindly obeying instructions with no comprehension of their significance. Scott Venuti was represented at the deposition only by court-appointed counsel because his regular counsel in this and the related state case decided not to attend, for reasons best known to themselves. That decision cannot now be employed to escape the consequences of Scott Venuti's invocation of the Fifth Amendment privilege. Finally, Scott Venuti's willingness to answer questions at a second deposition does not necessarily demonstrate that his invocation of the privilege at the first deposition was the result of purported procedural irregularities. A trier of fact could also infer that his later responses were a more recent fabrication.

Rule 403 provides that evidence which is probative "may be excluded if its probative value is substantially outweighed by the danger of unfair prejudice * * *." The rule does not contemplate exclusion of evidence which is prejudicial merely in the sense that it is damning; the prejudice must be "unfair." *See Brinks, supra,* 717 F.2d at 710; *United States v. Cirillo,* 468 F.2d 1233, 1234 (2d Cir.1972), *cert. denied,* 410 U.S. 989, 93 S.Ct. 1501, 36 L.Ed.2d 188 (1973). Evidence is unfairly prejudicial for purposes of Rule 403 only if it tends to have some adverse effect on the party against whom it is offered beyond the tendency to prove the fact which justifies its admission into evidence. *United States v. Figueroa,* 618 F.2d 934, 943 (2d Cir.1980); *see Brinks, supra,* 717 F.2d at 710; *United States v. DeLillo,* 620 F.2d 939, 947 n. 2 (2d Cir.), *cert. denied,* 449 U.S. 835, 101 S.Ct. 107, 66 L.Ed.2d 41 (1980); 22 C. Wright & K. Graham, *Federal Practice and Procedure: Evidence* § 5215, at 274–275 (1978).

It has been suggested that because "assertion of the privilege, particularly on the advice of counsel, is an ambiguous response" and because there is a danger that jurors will regard any party invoking the privilege as "a criminal who has probably eluded justice," the admission in a civil case of a party's refusal to answer on Fifth Amendment grounds may constitute unfair prejudice. *Farace, supra,* 669 F.2d at 210–211. In *Brinks,* however, Judge Weinfeld held that evidence of an invocation of the privilege is not unfairly prejudicial if it is probative of an issue in the litigation; it is " 'hardly the equivalent' of passing a bloody shirt among the jury or introducing a dying accusation of poisoning." 539 F.Supp. at 1141, *citing United States v. Leonard,* 524 F.2d 1076, 1091 (2d Cir.1975) (Friendly, J.), *cert. denied,* 425 U.S. 958, 96 S.Ct. 1737, 48 L.Ed.2d 202 (1976); *see Brinks, supra,* 717 F.2d at 710.

Accordingly, defendants' motion *in limine* with respect to evidence of Scott Venuti's invocation of his Fifth Amendment privilege against compelled self-incrimination is denied. Plaintiff's counsel will be permitted to read to the jury the questions which Scott Venuti refused to answer at the September 10, 1979 deposition. The court will then instruct the jury that it may, but need not, draw an adverse inference against Scott Venuti based on his refusal to answer, if such an inference is "warranted by the facts surrounding [the] case." *Baxter v. Palmigiano, supra,* 425 U.S. at 317, 96 S.Ct. at 1557.

* * *

It is so ordered.

HOFFMAN v. UNITED STATES, 341 U.S. 479, 486–88, 71 S.Ct. 814, 818–19, 95 L.Ed. 1118 (1951). "The privilege afforded not only extends to answers that would in themselves support a conviction under a federal criminal statute but likewise embraces those which would furnish a link in the chain of evidence needed to prosecute the claimant for a federal crime. (Patricia) Blau v. United States, 1950, 340 U.S. 159, 71 S.Ct. 232. But this protection must be confined to instances where the witness has reasonable cause to apprehend danger from a direct answer. Mason v. United States, 1917, 244 U.S. 362, 365, 37 S.Ct. 621, 622, 61 L.Ed. 1198, and cases cited. The witness is not exonerated from answering merely because he declares that in so doing he would incriminate himself—his say-so does not of itself establish the hazard of incrimination. It is for the court to say whether his silence is justified, Rogers v. United States, 1951, 340 U.S. 367, 71 S.Ct. 438, and to require him to answer if 'it clearly appears to the court that he is mistaken.' Temple v. Commonwealth, 1880, 75 Va. 892, 899. However, if the witness, upon interposing his claim, were required to prove the hazard in the sense in which a claim is usually required to be established in court, he would be compelled to surrender the very protection which the privilege is designed to guarantee. To sustain the privilege, it need only be evident from the implications of the question, in the setting in which it is asked, that a responsive answer to the question or an explanation of why it cannot be answered might be dangerous because injurious disclosure could result. The trial judge in appraising the claim 'must be governed as much by his personal perception of the peculiarities of the case as by the facts actually in evidence.' See Taft, J., in Ex parte Irvine, C.C.S.D.Ohio, 1896, 74 F. 954, 960.

* * *

"In this setting it was not '*perfectly clear,* from a careful consideration of all the circumstances in the case, that the witness is mistaken, and that the answer[s] *cannot possibly* have such tendency' to incriminate. Temple v. Commonwealth, 1880, 75 Va. 892, 898, cited with approval in Counselman v. Hitchcock, 1892, 142 U.S. 547, 579–580, 12 S.Ct. 195, 204, 35 L.Ed. 1110."

ALLEN v. ILLINOIS, 478 U.S. 364, 365, 368–70, 372–73, 106 S.Ct. 2988, 2990–94, 92 L.Ed.2d 296 (1986). "The question presented by this case is whether the proceedings under the Illinois Sexually Dangerous Persons Act (Act), Ill.Rev.Stat., ch. 38, ¶ 105–1.01 et seq. (1985), are 'criminal' within the meaning of the Fifth Amendment's guarantee against compulsory self-incrimination.

* * *

"The Self–Incrimination Clause of the Fifth Amendment, which applies to the States through the Fourteenth Amendment, Malloy v. Hogan, 378 U.S. 1, 84 S.Ct. 1489, 12 L.Ed.2d 653 (1964), provides that no person 'shall be compelled in any criminal case to be a witness against himself.' This Court has long held that the privilege against self-incrimination 'not only permits a person to refuse to testify against himself at a criminal trial in which he is a defendant, but also "privileges him not to answer official questions put to him in any other proceeding, civil or criminal, formal or informal, where the answers might incriminate him in future criminal proceedings." ' Minnesota v. Murphy, 465 U.S. 420, 426, 104 S.Ct. 1136, 1141, 79 L.Ed.2d 409 (1984) (quoting Lefkowitz v. Turley, 414 U.S. 70, 77, 94 S.Ct. 316, 322, 38 L.Ed.2d 274 (1973)); McCarthy v. Arndstein, 266 U.S. 34, 40, 45 S.Ct. 16, 17, 69 L.Ed. 158 (1924). In this case the Illinois Supreme Court ruled that a person whom the State attempts to commit under the Act is protected from use of his compelled answers in any subsequent criminal case in which he is the defendant. What we have here, then, is not a claim that petitioner's statements to the psychiatrists might be used to incriminate him in some future criminal proceeding, but instead his claim that because the sexually-dangerous-person proceeding is itself 'criminal,' he was entitled to refuse to answer any questions at all.

"The question whether a particular proceeding is criminal for the purposes of the Self–Incrimination Clause is first of all a question of statutory construction. See United States v. Ward, 448 U.S. 242, 248, 100 S.Ct. 2636, 2641, 65 L.Ed.2d 742 (1980); One Lot Emerald Cut Stones and One Ring v. United States, 409 U.S. 232, 236–237, 93 S.Ct. 489, 492–493, 34 L.Ed.2d 438 (1972). Here, Illinois has expressly provided that proceedings under the Act 'shall be civil in nature,' ¶ 105–3.01, indicating that when it files a petition against a person under the Act it intends to proceed in a nonpunitive, noncriminal manner, 'without regard to the procedural protections and restrictions available in criminal prosecutions.' Ward, supra, at 249, 100 S.Ct., at

2641. As petitioner correctly points out, however, the civil label is not always dispositive. Where a defendant has provided 'the clearest proof' that 'the statutory scheme [is] so punitive either in purpose or effect as to negate [the State's] intention' that the proceeding be civil, it must be considered criminal and the privilege against self-incrimination must be applied. 448 U.S., at 248–249, 100 S.Ct., at 2641. We think that petitioner has failed to provide such proof in this case.

"The Illinois Supreme Court reviewed the Act and its own case law and concluded that these proceedings, while similar to criminal proceedings in that they are accompanied by strict procedural safeguards, are essentially civil in nature. 107 Ill.2d, at 100–102, 89 Ill.Dec., at 851–852, 481 N.E.2d, at 694–695. We are unpersuaded by petitioner's efforts to challenge this conclusion. Under the Act, the State has a statutory obligation to provide 'care and treatment for [persons adjudged sexually dangerous] designed to effect recovery,' ¶ 105–8, in a facility set aside to provide psychiatric care, ibid. And '[i]f the patient is found to be no longer dangerous, the court shall order that he be discharged.' ¶ 105–9. While the committed person has the burden of showing that he is no longer dangerous, he may apply for release at any time. Ibid. In short, the State has disavowed any interest in punishment, provided for the treatment of those it commits, and established a system under which committed persons may be released after the briefest time in confinement. The Act thus does not appear to promote either of 'the traditional aims of punishment—retribution and deterrence.' Kennedy v. Mendoza–Martinez, 372 U.S. 144, 168, 83 S.Ct. 554, 567, 9 L.Ed.2d 644 (1963). Cf. Addington v. Texas, 441 U.S. 418, 428, 99 S.Ct. 1804, 1810, 60 L.Ed.2d 323 (1979) (in Texas 'civil commitment state power is not exercised in a punitive sense'); French v. Blackburn, 428 F.Supp. 1351, 1358–1359 (MDNC 1977), summarily aff'd, 443 U.S. 901, 99 S.Ct. 3091, 61 L.Ed.2d 869 (1979) (State need not accord privilege against self-incrimination in civil commitment proceeding).

* * *

"Relying chiefly on In re Gault, 387 U.S. 1, 87 S.Ct. 1428, 18 L.Ed.2d 527 (1967), petitioner also urges that the proceedings in question are 'criminal' because a person adjudged sexually dangerous under the Act is committed for an indeterminate period to the Menard Psychiatric Center, a maximum-security institution that is run by the Illinois Department of Corrections and that houses convicts needing psychiatric care as well as sexually dangerous persons. Whatever its label and whatever the State's alleged purpose, petitioner argues, such commitment is the sort of punishment—total deprivation of liberty in a criminal setting—that *Gault* teaches cannot be imposed absent application of the privilege against self-incrimination. We believe that *Gault* is readily distinguishable.

"First, *Gault*'s sweeping statement that 'our Constitution guarantees that no person shall be "compelled" to be a witness against himself when he is threatened with deprivation of his liberty,' id., at 50, 87

S.Ct., at 1455, is plainly not good law. Although the fact that incarceration may result is relevant to the question whether the privilege against self-incrimination applies, *Addington* demonstrates that involuntary commitment does not itself trigger the entire range of criminal procedural protections. Indeed, petitioner apparently concedes that traditional civil commitment does not require application of the privilege. Only two Terms ago, in Minnesota v. Murphy, 465 U.S. at 435, n. 7, 104 S.Ct., at 1147, n. 7, this Court stated that a person may not claim the privilege merely because his answer might result in revocation of his probationary status. Cf. Middendorf v. Henry, 425 U.S. 25, 37, 96 S.Ct. 1281, 1288, 47 L.Ed.2d 556 (1976) ('[F]act that a proceeding will result in loss of liberty does not *ipso facto* mean that the proceeding is a "criminal prosecution" for purposes of the Sixth Amendment').

"The Court in *Gault* was obviously persuaded that the State intended to *punish* its juvenile offenders, observing that in many States juveniles may be placed in 'adult penal institutions' for conduct that if committed by an adult would be a crime. 387 U.S., at 49–50, 87 S.Ct., at 1455. Here, by contrast, the State serves its purpose of *treating* rather than punishing sexually dangerous persons by committing them to an institution expressly designed to provide psychiatric care and treatment."

UNITED STATES v. HEARST

United States Court of Appeals, Ninth Circuit, 1977.
563 F.2d 1331, cert. denied, 435 U.S. 1000, 98 S.Ct. 1656, 56 L.Ed.2d 90 (1978).

PER CURIAM:

Appellant was tried under a two-count indictment charging her with armed robbery of a San Francisco bank in violation of 18 U.S.C. §§ 2113(a), (d) and 924(c)(1). The government introduced photographs and testimony descriptive of appellant's role in the robbery. Appellant raised the defense of duress, contending her co-participants compelled her to engage in the criminal activity. * * *

* * *

During the trial appellant elected to testify in her own behalf. She described in exhaustive detail the events immediately following her kidnapping of February 4, 1974. These included physical and sexual abuses by members of the Symbionese Liberation Army (SLA), extensive interrogations, forced tape recordings and written communications designed to convince her family that she had become a revolutionary, and training in guerrilla warfare. She next described how the SLA compelled her under threat of death to participate in the robbery of the Hibernia Bank on April 15, 1974, and to identify herself by reading a revolutionary speech. She explained that by the time the group moved to Los Angeles, the SLA had convinced her that they would kill her if she tried to escape and that the Federal Bureau of Investigation also desired to murder her. Appellant added that the SLA required her to make various post-robbery admissions about her voluntary role in the crime.

Appellant's story continued by describing her participation one month after the robbery in the disturbance at Mel's Sporting Goods Store. She claimed that her reaction in firing at the store resulted from fear of the SLA, as did her admission to Thomas Matthews of complicity in the bank robbery. She then told how she, the Harrises, and Jack Scott traveled from Los Angeles to Berkeley, then to New York, to Pennsylvania, and finally to Las Vegas in September of 1974. Again, she emphasized that she was an unwilling companion of the group. After mentioning her arrival in Las Vegas, her testimony jumped a year to the time of her arrest in San Francisco on September 18, 1975.

On cross-examination, appellant refused to answer most questions concerning the period between her arrival in Las Vegas and her arrest in San Francisco. In response to questions about her activities, residences, and association with other suspected members of the SLA during this year, she invoked the Fifth Amendment privilege against self-incrimination 42 times.

Prior to government questioning, appellant had moved for an order limiting the scope of the cross-examination so as to avoid the necessity of invoking the Fifth Amendment in response to questions implicating her in other crimes for which she was not on trial. Finding that appellant had waived her privilege against self-incrimination as to all relevant matters by testifying in her own behalf, the court denied this motion and allowed the government to ask her questions which resulted in her assertion of the Fifth Amendment. *United States v. Hearst,* 412 F.Supp. 885 (N.D.Cal.1976). Appellant now offers five separate grounds for finding that the court committed reversible error in making this ruling.

1. The Fifth Amendment provides that "[n]o person * * * shall be compelled in any criminal case to be a witness against himself." But it is also true, as the trial court stressed, that a defendant who testifies in his own behalf waives his privilege against self-incrimination with respect to the relevant matters covered by his direct testimony and subjects himself to cross-examination by the government. *Brown v. United States,* 356 U.S. 148, 154–55, 78 S.Ct. 622, 2 L.Ed.2d 589 (1958). Appellant contends that she "did not voluntarily waive her Fifth Amendment privilege by testifying because her testimony was compelled by the introduction of certain evidence, i.e., post-crime conduct, which was challenged as inadmissible and highly prejudicial." Reply Brief for Appellant at 7. She pleads that she was caught between the "rock and the whirlpool" when forced to decide whether to testify or allow the evidence to stand unrebutted.

The validity of this argument depends largely on appellant's assumption that evidence of her post-robbery behavior was admitted erroneously, and that she had no choice but to respond to this inadmissible evidence. We have concluded previously, however, that the trial court determined correctly that this evidence was relevant and admissible. Thus, appellant's attempt to compare her situation to that involved in *Harrison v. United States,* 392 U.S. 219, 88 S.Ct. 2008, 20 L.Ed.2d 1047 (1968), where the defendant had to testify in order to overcome the impact of prior confessions which had been illegally obtained and introduced, is unconvincing. In the present case, neither the trial court nor we found that any illegal, inadmissible evidence forced appellant to testify.

Appellant also suggests it is sufficient that she *thought* she was being compelled to testify in response to the admission of evidence which she *perceived* as prejudicial, inadmissible, and damaging to her defense. We refuse to hold that a defendant's subjective impressions of what he is "forced" to do during his trial are enough to render his testimony involuntary. A defendant often will view evidence as incriminating and inadmissible, and feel that he must take the witness stand in order to save his case. This is an inherent feature of our criminal justice system, however:

> The defendant in a criminal trial is frequently forced to testify himself and to call other witnesses in an effort to reduce the risk of conviction. When he presents his witnesses, he must reveal their identity and submit them to cross-examination which in itself may prove incriminating or which may furnish the State with leads to incriminating rebuttal evidence. That the defendant faces such a dilemma demanding a choice between complete silence and presenting a defense has never been thought an invasion of the privilege against compelled self-incrimination.

Williams v. Florida, 399 U.S. 78, 83–84, 90 S.Ct. 1893, 1897, 26 L.Ed.2d 446 (1970). In *Williams,* the Supreme Court found that the defendant had a free choice between giving notice of his alibi defense, as required by a Florida statute, and refraining from presenting this defense. Similarly, in our case, we find that appellant freely elected to testify in her own behalf.

2. Appellant also argues that she did not waive her privilege against self-incrimination because her testimony was limited to the collateral issue of the voluntarincss of certain statements (i.e., the admissions of willing participation in the bank robbery) made by her and introduced into evidence over her objection. She contends that since her testimony did not address the merits of the case, the government should not have been allowed to ask questions which attempted to prove her guilt. She refers us to *Calloway v. Wainwright,* 409 F.2d 59, 66 (5th Cir.), *cert. denied,* 395 U.S. 909, 89 S.Ct. 1752, 23 L.Ed.2d 222 (1969), which stated: "[t]hat appellant took the stand for the sole purpose of testifying upon the credibility of the voluntariness of his [earlier] confession should not be taken as a complete waiver of his constitutional privilege against self-incrimination."

Appellant's assumption about the nature of her testimony is completely erroneous. The central theme of her lengthy testimony was that from the moment of her kidnapping to the time of her arrest she was an unwilling victim of the SLA who acted under continual threats of death. She tried to show, not merely that she made her admissions involuntarily, but that she acted under duress in robbing the Hibernia Bank, firing at the sporting goods store, and traveling with the Harrises for over one year. She disputed the main element of the government's case: that she had the necessary criminal intent when she participated in the bank robbery. Thus, her reliance on *Calloway* is misplaced, for that case dealt with the much narrower situation in which a defendant takes the witness stand solely to deny the voluntariness of his confession. *Calloway v. Wainwright, supra,* 409 F.2d at 66.

3. Appellant next claims that even if she did waive her privilege against self-incrimination by testifying in her own behalf, the waiver did not extend to the period between her arrival in Las Vegas and her arrest in San Francisco. She argues that since she did not testify concerning her activities during this "lost year," the government had no right or reason to ask any questions about it. She would confine the proper scope of cross-examination to the events which she specifically discussed during her direct testimony.

We find that appellant misinterprets the controlling case law on waiver and the permissible limits of the cross-examination of a testifying defendant. The Supreme Court has stated that when a defendant takes the witness stand, "his credibility may be impeached and his testimony assailed like that of any other witness, and the breadth of his waiver is determined by the scope of relevant cross-examination." *Brown v. United States, supra,* 356 U.S. at 154–55, 78 S.Ct. at 626. "[A] defendant who takes the stand in his own behalf cannot then claim the privilege against cross-examination on matters reasonably related to the subject matter of his direct examination." *McGautha v. California,* 402 U.S. 183, 215, 91 S.Ct. 1454, 1471, 28 L.Ed.2d 711 (1971). This rule is premised on basic goals of fairness and ascertainment of the truth:

> The witness himself, certainly if he is a party, determines the area of disclosure and therefore of inquiry. Such witness has the choice, after weighing the advantage of the privilege against self-incrimination against the advantage of putting forward his version of the facts and his reliability as a witness, not to testify at all. He cannot reasonably claim that the Fifth Amendment gives him not only this choice but, if he elects to testify, an immunity from cross-examination on the matters he has himself put in dispute.

Brown v. United States, supra, 356 U.S. at 155–56, 78 S.Ct. at 627. Nowhere in this rule is there even a suggestion that the waiver and the permissible cross-examination are to be determined by what the defendant actually discussed during his direct testimony. Rather, the focus is on whether the government's questions are "reasonably related" to the subjects covered by the defendant's testimony.

Applying this principle to the present case, we conclude that the trial court did not abuse its broad discretion, *United States v. Higginbotham,* 539 F.2d 17, 24 (9th Cir.1976), in allowing the government to ask questions about the year which appellant failed to cover in her direct testimony. As we have already concluded, appellant's testimony was not limited to disputing the voluntariness of her post-robbery admissions. Instead, she attempted to show that from her kidnapping until her arrest she acted exactly as her captors directed. She tried to persuade the jury that her post-robbery conduct and feelings of fear, dependence, and obedience proved that she had also acted involuntarily and without criminal intent in robbing the Hibernia Bank.

We agree with the trial court's conclusion that appellant's testimony placed in issue her behavior during the entire period from abduction to arrest, and gave the government a right to question her about the "lost year." *See United States v. Hearst, supra,* 412 F.Supp. at 887. Although appellant did not discuss this year, the natural inference from her other testimony, if believed, was that she had acted involuntarily during this period. Having offered selective evidence of the nature of her behavior for the whole period, appellant had no valid objection to the government's attempt to show that her conduct during the omitted year belied her story and proved that she was a willing member of the SLA. Since appellant's direct testimony raised an issue about the nature of her conduct during the entire one and one-half years prior to her arrest, the government's questions about her activities, associations, and residences during the interim year were more than "reasonably related" to the subject matter of her prior testimony. That answers to these questions might have implicated appellant in crimes for which she was not on trial had no bearing on the questions' relevancy or relationship to her direct testimony.

4. Appellant argues that even if she had no right to refuse to answer the government's questions, the court erred in allowing the prosecution to continue to ask questions which it knew would elicit repeated assertions of the privilege against self-incrimination. We find that appellant's authorities do not support her proposition. Her cases involve situations in which the government or the defendant questioned a witness or a co-defendant, knowing that a valid, unwaived Fifth Amendment privilege would be asserted. *E.g., United States v. Roberts,* 503 F.2d 598 (9th Cir.1974), *cert. denied,* 419 U.S. 1113, 95 S.Ct. 791, 42 L.Ed.2d 811 (1975); *United States v. Beye,* 445 F.2d 1037 (9th Cir.1971); *Sanders v. United States,* 373 F.2d 735 (9th Cir.1967). She fails to offer support relating to the very different problem, present in our case, in which the government attempts to cross-examine a witness-defendant who has previously waived his privilege against self-incrimination.

In determining whether it is improper for the government to ask a defendant questions which will result in an assertion of the privilege against self-incrimination, the central consideration is whether the defendant has waived his privilege as to the propounded questions. When a witness or a defendant has a valid Fifth Amendment privilege, government questions designed to elicit this privilege present to the jury information that is misleading, irrelevant to the issue of the witness's or the defendant's credibility, and not subject to examination by defense counsel. *See Namet v. United States,* 373 U.S. 179, 186–87, 83 S.Ct. 1151, 10 L.Ed.2d 278 (1963). Therefore, we do not allow this form of questioning.

But when a defendant has voluntarily waived his Fifth Amendment privilege by testifying in his own behalf, the rationale for prohibiting privilege-invoking queries on cross-examination does not apply. The defendant has chosen to make an issue of his credibility; he has elected to take his case to the jury in the most direct fashion. The government, accordingly, has a right to challenge the defendant's story on cross-examination. *Brown v. United States, supra,* 356 U.S. at 154–56, 78 S.Ct. 622. The government may impeach the defendant by developing inconsistencies in his testimony; the government may also successfully impeach him by asking questions which he refuses to answer. If the refusals could not be put before the jury, the defendant would have the unusual and grossly unfair ability to insulate himself from challenges merely by declining to answer embarrassing questions. He alone could control the presentation of evidence to the jury.

Our view finds support in decisions construing the propriety of judicial and prosecutorial comment upon a defendant's refusal to testify. *Griffin v. California,* 380 U.S. 609, 615, 85 S.Ct. 1229, 14 L.Ed.2d 106 (1965), held that neither the government nor the court may comment on an accused's exercise of his Fifth Amendment privilege by refusing to testify. But it has long been established that comment is allowed when a defendant fails to explain evidence against him after first waiving his privilege by taking the witness stand. *Caminetti v. United States,* 242 U.S. 470, 492–95, 37 S.Ct. 192, 61 L.Ed. 442 (1917).[7] Since the offering of questions designed to elicit invocations of the Fifth Amendment is really only a form of comment upon the defendant's failure to testify, intended to present to the jury the government's interpretation of his credibility, we believe that the rule of *Caminetti* should apply to the present case.

We have concluded that appellant waived her privilege against self-incrimination with respect to her activities during the interval between her arrival in Las Vegas and her arrest in San Francisco. Therefore, it was permissible for the government to ask questions about this period, even though they led to 42 assertions of the Fifth Amendment.

* * *

Affirmed.

7. The indication in *Brown v. United States, supra,* 356 U.S. at 154–55, 78 S.Ct. 622, that a defendant retains a privilege against self-incrimination as to subjects not related to his direct testimony suggests that the prosecution may not comment upon the defendant's silence on matters beyond the scope of his direct examination.

DOE v. UNITED STATES

Supreme Court of the United States, 1988.
487 U.S. 201, 108 S.Ct. 2341, 101 L.Ed.2d 184.

JUSTICE BLACKMUN delivered the opinion of the Court.

This case presents the question whether a court order compelling a target of a grand jury investigation to authorize foreign banks to disclose records of his accounts, without identifying those documents or acknowledging their existence, violates the target's Fifth Amendment privilege against self-incrimination.

I

Petitioner, named here as John Doe, is the target of a federal grand jury investigation into possible federal offenses arising from suspected fraudulent manipulation of oil cargoes and receipt of unreported income. Doe appeared before the grand jury pursuant to a subpoena that directed him to produce records of transactions in accounts at three named banks in the Cayman Islands and Bermuda. Doe produced some bank records and testified that no additional records responsive to the subpoena were in his possession or control. When questioned about the existence or location of additional records, Doe invoked the Fifth Amendment privilege against self-incrimination.

The United States branches of the three foreign banks also were served with subpoenas commanding them to produce records of accounts over which Doe had signatory authority. Citing their governments' bank-secrecy laws, which prohibit the disclosure of account records without the customer's consent, the banks refused to comply. See App. to Pet. for Cert. 17a, n. 2. The Government then filed a motion with the United States District Court for the Southern District of Texas that the court order Doe to sign 12 forms consenting to disclosure of any bank records respectively relating to 12 foreign bank accounts over which the Government knew or suspected that Doe had control. The forms indicated the account numbers and described the documents that the Government wished the banks to produce.

The District Court denied the motion, reasoning that by signing the consent forms, Doe would necessarily be admitting the existence of the accounts. The District Court believed, moreover, that if the banks delivered records pursuant to the consent forms, those forms would constitute "an admission that [Doe] exercised signatory authority over such accounts." App. to Pet. for Cert. 20a. The court speculated that the Government in a subsequent proceeding then could argue that Doe must have guilty knowledge of the contents of the accounts. Thus, in the court's view, compelling Doe to sign the forms was compelling him "to perform a testimonial act that would entail admission of knowledge of the contents of potentially incriminating documents," *id.*, at 20a, n. 6, and such compulsion was prohibited by the Fifth Amendment. The District Court also noted that Doe had not been indicted, and that his signing of the forms might provide the Government with the incriminating link necessary to obtain an indictment, the kind of "fishing expedition" that the Fifth Amendment was designed to prevent. *Id.,* at 21a.

The Government sought reconsideration. Along with its motion, it submitted to the court a revised proposed consent directive that was substantially the same as that approved by the Eleventh Circuit in *United States v. Ghidoni,* 732 F.2d 814, cert. denied, 469 U.S. 932, 105 S.Ct. 328, 83 L.Ed.2d 264 (1984). The form purported to apply to any and all accounts over which Doe had a right of withdrawal, without acknowledging the existence of any such account. The District Court denied this motion also, reasoning that compelling execution of the consent directive might lead to the uncovering and linking of Doe to accounts that the grand jury did not know were in existence. The court concluded that execution of the proposed form would "admit signatory authority over the speculative accounts [and] would implicitly authenticate any records of the speculative accounts provided by the banks pursuant to the consent." App. to Pet. for Cert. 13a, n. 7.

The Court of Appeals for the Fifth Circuit reversed in an unpublished *per curiam* opinion. Relying on its intervening decision in *In re United States Grand Jury Proceedings (Cid),* 767 F.2d 1131 (1985), the court held that Doe could not assert his Fifth Amendment privilege as a basis for refusing to sign the consent directive, because the form "did not have testimonial significance" and therefore its compelled execution would not violate Doe's Fifth Amendment rights. App. to Pet. for Cert. 7a.

On remand, the District Court ordered petitioner to execute the consent directive. He refused. The District Court accordingly found petitioner in civil contempt and ordered that he be confined until he complied with the order. App. to Pet. for Cert. 2a. The court stayed imposition of sanction pending appeal and application for writ of certiorari. *Id.,* at 2a–3a.

The Fifth Circuit affirmed the contempt order, again in an unpublished *per curiam,* concluding that its prior ruling constituted the "law of the case" and was dispositive of Doe's appeal. *Id.,* at 3a. We granted certiorari, ___ U.S. ___, 108 S.Ct. 64, 98 L.Ed.2d 28 (1987), to resolve a conflict among the Courts of Appeals as to whether the compelled execution of a consent form directing the disclosure of foreign bank records is inconsistent with the Fifth Amendment. We conclude that a court order compelling the execution of such a directive as is at issue here does not implicate the Amendment. *

II

It is undisputed that the contents of the foreign bank records sought by the Government are not privileged under the Fifth Amendment. See *Braswell v. United States,* ___ U.S. ___, ___, 108 S.Ct. 2284, 2290, 99 L.Ed.2d ___ (1988); *United States v. Doe,* 465 U.S. 605, 104 S.Ct. 1237, 79 L.Ed.2d 552 (1984); *Fisher v. United States,* 425 U.S. 391, 96 S.Ct. 1569, 48 L.Ed.2d 39 (1976). There also is no question that the foreign banks cannot invoke the Fifth Amendment in declining to produce the documents; the privilege does not extend to such artificial entities. See *Braswell v. United States,* ___ U.S., at ___, 108 S.Ct., at 2287; *Bellis v. United States,* 417 U.S. 85, 89–90, 94 S.Ct. 2179, 2183–2184, 40 L.Ed.2d 678 (1974). Similarly, petitioner asserts no Fifth Amendment right to prevent the banks from disclosing the account records, for the Constitution "necessarily does not proscribe incriminating statements elicited from another." *Couch v. United States,* 409 U.S. 322, 328, 93 S.Ct. 611, 616, 34 L.Ed.2d 548 (1973). Petitioner's sole claim is that his execution of the consent forms directing the banks to release records as to which the banks believe he has the right of withdrawal has independent testimonial significance that will incriminate him, and that the Fifth Amendment prohibits governmental compulsion of that act.

The Self-Incrimination Clause of the Fifth Amendment reads: "No person * * * shall be compelled in any criminal case to be a witness against himself." This Court has explained that "the privilege protects a person only against being incriminated by his own compelled testimonial communications." *Fisher v. United States,* 425 U.S., at 409, 96 S.Ct., at 1580, citing *Schmerber v. California,* 384 U.S. 757, 86 S.Ct. 1826, 16 L.Ed.2d 908 (1966); *United States v. Wade,* 388 U.S. 218, 87 S.Ct. 1926, 18 L.Ed.2d 1149 (1967); and *Gilbert v. California,* 388 U.S. 263, 87 S.Ct. 1951, 18 L.Ed.2d 1178 (1967). The execution of the consent directive at issue in this case obviously would be compelled, and we may assume that its execution would have an incriminating effect. The question on which this case turns is whether the act of executing the form is a "testimonial communication." The parties disagree about both the meaning of "testimonial" and whether the consent directive fits the proposed definitions.

A

Petitioner contends that a compelled statement is testimonial if the Government could use the content of the speech or writing, as opposed to its physical characteristics, to further a criminal investigation of the witness. The second half of petitioner's "testimonial" test is that the statement must be incriminating, which is, of course, already a separate requirement for invoking the privilege. Thus, Doe contends, in essence, that every written and oral statement significant for its content is necessarily testimonial for purposes of the Fifth Amendment.[6]

6. Petitioner's blanket assertion that a statement is testimonial for Fifth Amendment purposes if its content can be used to obtain evidence confuses the requirement that the compelled communication be "testimonial" with the separate requirement that the communication be "incriminating." If a compelled statement is "not testimonial and for that reason not protected by the privilege, it cannot become so because it will lead to incriminating evidence." *In re Grand Jury Subpoena,* 826 F.2d, at 1172, n. 2 (concurring opinion).

Petitioner's heavy reliance on this Court's decision in *Kastigar v. United States,* 406 U.S. 441, 92 S.Ct. 1653, 32 L.Ed.2d 212 (1972), for a contrary proposition is misguided. *Kastigar* affirmed the constitutionality of 18 U.S.C. §§ 6002 and 6003, which permit the Government to compel testimony as long as the witness is immunized against the use in any criminal case of the "testimony or other information" provided. In holding that the immunity provided by the statute is coextensive with the Fifth Amendment privilege, the

Under this view, the consent directive is testimonial because it is a declarative statement of consent made by Doe to the foreign banks, a statement that the Government will use to persuade the banks to produce potentially incriminating account records that would otherwise be unavailable to the grand jury.

The Government, on the other hand, suggests that a compelled statement is not testimonial for purposes of the privilege, unless it implicitly or explicitly relates a factual assertion or otherwise conveys information to the Government. It argues that, under this view, the consent directive is not testimonial because neither the directive itself nor Doe's execution of the form discloses or communicates facts or information. Petitioner disagrees.

The Government's view of the privilege, apparently accepted by the Courts of Appeals that have considered compelled consent forms, is derived largely from this Court's decisions in *Fisher* and *Doe.* The issue presented in those cases was whether the act of producing subpoenaed documents, not itself the making of a statement, might nonetheless have some protected testimonial aspects. The Court concluded that the act of production could constitute protected testimonial communication because it might entail implicit statements of fact: by producing documents in compliance with a subpoena, the witness would admit that the papers existed, were in his possession or control, and were authentic. *Doe,* 465 U.S., at 613, and n. 11, 104 S.Ct., at 1242, and n. 11; *Fisher,* 425 U.S., at 409–410, 96 S.Ct., at 1580; *id.,* at 428, 432, 96 S.Ct., at 1589, 1591 (concurring opinions). See *Braswell v. United States,* ___ U.S., at ___, 108 S.Ct., at 2288; *id.,* at ___, 108 S.Ct., at 2297 (dissenting opinion). Thus, the Court made clear that the Fifth Amendment privilege against self-incrimination applies to acts that imply assertions of fact.

We reject petitioner's argument that this test does not control the determination as to when the privilege applies to oral or written statements. While the Court in *Fisher* and *Doe* did not purport to announce a universal test for determining the scope of the privilege, it also did not purport to establish a more narrow boundary applicable to acts alone. To the contrary, the Court applied basic Fifth Amendment principles. An examination of the Court's application of these principles in other cases indicates the Court's recognition that, in order to be testimonial, an accused's communication must itself, explicitly or im-

Court implicitly concluded that the privilege prohibits "the use of compelled testimony, as well as evidence derived directly and indirectly therefrom." 406 U.S., at 453, 92 S.Ct., at 1661. The prohibition of derivative use is an implementation of the "link in the chain of evidence" theory for invocation of the privilege, pursuant to which the "compelled testimony" need not itself be incriminating if it would lead to the discovery of incriminating evidence. See *Hoffman v. United States,* 341 U.S. 479, 486, 71 S.Ct. 814, 818, 95 L.Ed. 1118 (1951). See also *Murphy v. Waterfront Comm'n,* 378 U.S. 52, 79, 84 S.Ct. 1594, 1609, 12 L.Ed.2d 678 (1964); 8 J. Wigmore, Evidence § 2260 (McNaughton rev. 1961) (Wigmore). This prohibition, however, assumes that the suspect's initial compelled communication is testimonial.

plicitly, relate a factual assertion or disclose information.[9] Only then is a person compelled to be a "witness" against himself.

This understanding is perhaps most clearly revealed in those cases in which the Court has held that certain acts, though incriminating, are not within the privilege. Thus, a suspect may be compelled to furnish a blood sample, *Schmerber v. California,* 384 U.S., at 765, 86 S.Ct., at 1832; to provide a handwriting exemplar, *Gilbert v. California,* 388 U.S., at 266–267, 87 S.Ct., at 1953 or a voice exemplar, *United States v. Dionisio,* 410 U.S. 1, 7, 93 S.Ct. 764, 768, 35 L.Ed.2d 67 (1973); to stand in a lineup, *United States v. Wade,* 388 U.S., at 221–222, 87 S.Ct., at 1929; and to wear particular clothing, *Holt v. United States,* 218 U.S. 245, 252–253, 31 S.Ct. 2, 6, 54 L.Ed. 1021 (1910). These decisions are grounded on the proposition that "the privilege protects an accused only from being compelled to testify against himself, or otherwise provide the State with evidence of a testimonial or communicative nature." *Schmerber,* 384 U.S., at 761, 86 S.Ct., at 1830. The Court accordingly held that the privilege was not implicated in each of those cases, because the suspect was not required "to disclose any knowledge he might have," or "to speak his guilt," *Wade,* 388 U.S., at 222–223, 87 S.Ct., at 1929–1930. See *Dionisio,* 410 U.S., at 7, 93 S.Ct., at 768; *Gilbert,* 388 U.S., at 266–267, 87 S.Ct., at 1953. It is the "extortion of information from the accused," *Couch v. United States,* 409 U.S., at 328, 93 S.Ct., at 616; the attempt to force him "to disclose the contents of his own mind," *Curcio v. United States,* 354 U.S. 118, 128, 77 S.Ct. 1145, 1151, 1 L.Ed.2d 1225 (1957), that implicates the Self–Incrimination Clause. See also *Kastigar v. United States,* 406 U.S. 441, 445, 92 S.Ct. 1653, 1656, 32 L.Ed.2d 212 (1972) (the privilege "protects against any *disclosures* that the witness reasonably believes could be used in a criminal prosecution or could lead to other evidence that might be so used") (emphasis added). "Unless some attempt is made to secure a communication—written, oral or otherwise—upon which reliance is to be placed as involving [the accused's] consciousness of the facts and the operations of his mind in expressing it, the demand made upon him is not a testimonial one." 8 J. Wigmore, Evidence § 2265, p. 386 (McNaughton rev. 1961).

It is consistent with the history of and the policies underlying the Self–Incrimination Clause to hold that the privilege may be asserted only to resist compelled explicit or implicit disclosures of incriminating information. Historically, the privilege was intended to prevent the use of legal compulsion to extract from the accused a sworn communication of facts which would incriminate him. Such was the process of the ecclesiastical courts and the Star Chamber—the inquisitorial meth-

9. We do not disagree with the dissent that "[t]he expression of the contents of an individual's mind" is testimonial communication for purposes of the Fifth Amendment. We simply disagree with the dissent's conclusion that the execution of the consent directive at issue here forced petitioner to express the contents of his mind. In our view, such compulsion is more like "be[ing] forced to surrender a key to a strong box containing incriminating documents," than it is like "be[ing] compelled to reveal the combination to [petitioner's] wall safe."

od of putting the accused upon his oath and compelling him to answer questions designed to uncover uncharged offenses, without evidence from another source. See *Andresen v. Maryland,* 427 U.S. 463, 470–471, 96 S.Ct. 2737, 2743–2744, 49 L.Ed.2d 627 (1976); 8 Wigmore § 2250; E. Griswold, The Fifth Amendment Today 2–3 (1955). The major thrust of the policies undergirding the privilege is to prevent such compulsion. The Self–Incrimination Clause reflects " 'a judgment * * * that the prosecution should [not] be free to build up a criminal case, in whole or in part, with the assistance of enforced *disclosures* by the accused' " (emphasis added). *Ullmann v. United States,* 350 U.S. 422, 427, 76 S.Ct. 497, 501, 100 L.Ed. 511 (1956), quoting *Maffie v. United States,* 209 F.2d 225, 227 (CA1 1954). The Court in *Murphy v. Waterfront Comm'n,* 378 U.S. 52, 84 S.Ct. 1594, 12 L.Ed.2d 678 (1964), explained that the privilege is founded on

> "our unwillingness to subject those suspected of crime to the cruel trilemma of self-accusation, perjury or contempt; our preference for an accusatorial rather than an inquisitorial system of criminal justice; our fear that self-incriminating statements will be elicited by inhumane treatment and abuses; our sense of fair play which dictates 'a fair state-individual balance by requiring the government to leave the individual alone until good cause is shown for disturbing him and by requiring the government in its contest with the individual to shoulder the entire load,' * * *; our respect for the inviolability of the human personality and of the right of each individual 'to a private enclave where he may lead a private life,' * * * ; our distrust of self-deprecatory statements; and our realization that the privilege, while sometimes 'a shelter to the guilty,' is often 'a protection to the innocent.' " *Id.,* at 55, 84 S.Ct., at 1596–1597 (citations omitted).

These policies are served when the privilege is asserted to spare the accused from having to reveal, directly or indirectly, his knowledge of facts relating him to the offense or from having to share his thoughts and beliefs with the Government.

We are not persuaded by petitioner's arguments that our articulation of the privilege fundamentally alters the power of the Government to compel an accused to assist in his prosecution. There are very few instances in which a verbal statement, either oral or written, will not convey information or assert facts. The vast majority of verbal statements thus will be testimonial and, to that extent at least, will fall within the privilege.[12] Furthermore, it should be remembered that

12. In particular, we do not agree that our articulation cuts back on the Court's explanation in *Miranda v. Arizona,* 384 U.S. 436, 86 S.Ct. 1602, 16 L.Ed.2d 694 (1966), that "the privilege is fulfilled only when the person is guaranteed the right 'to remain silent unless he chooses to speak in the unfettered exercise of his own will.' " *Id.,* at 460, 86 S.Ct., at 1620, quoting *Malloy v. Hogan,* 378 U.S. 1, 8, 84 S.Ct. 1489, 1493, 12 L.Ed.2d 653 (1964). In *Miranda,* the Court addressed a suspect's Fifth Amendment privilege in the face of custodial interrogation by the Government. Our test for when a communication is "testimonial" does not authorize law enforcement officials to make an unwilling suspect speak in this context. It is clear that the accused in a criminal case is exempt from giving answers altogether, for (at least on the prosecution's assumption) they

there are many restrictions on the Government's prosecutorial practices in addition to the Self–Incrimination Clause. Indeed, there are other protections against governmental efforts to compel an unwilling suspect to cooperate in an investigation, including efforts to obtain information from him. We are confident that these provisions, together with the Self–Incrimination Clause, will continue to prevent abusive investigative techniques.

B

The difficult question whether a compelled communication is testimonial for purposes of applying the Fifth Amendment often depends on the facts and circumstances of the particular case. *Fisher,* 425 U.S., at 410, 96 S.Ct., at 1581. This case is no exception. We turn, then, to consider whether Doe's execution of the consent directive at issue here would have testimonial significance. We agree with the Court of Appeals that it would not, because neither the form, nor its execution, communicates any factual assertions, implicit or explicit, or conveys any information to the Government.

The consent directive itself is not "testimonial." It is carefully drafted not to make reference to a specific account, but only to speak in the hypothetical. Thus, the form does not acknowledge that an account in a foreign financial institution is in existence or that it is controlled by petitioner. Nor does the form indicate whether documents or any other information relating to petitioner are present at the foreign bank, assuming that such an account does exist. Cf. *United States v. Ghidoni,* 732 F.2d, at 818; *In re Grand Jury Proceedings (Ranauro),* 814 F.2d 791, 793 (CA1 1987); *In re Grand Jury Subpoena,* 826 F.2d 1166, 1170 (CA2 1987), cert. pending, No. 87–517; *In re Grand Jury Proceedings (Cid),* 767 F.2d, at 1132. The form does not even identify the relevant bank. Although the executed form allows the Government access to a potential source of evidence, the directive itself does not point the Government toward hidden accounts or otherwise provide information that will assist the prosecution in uncovering evidence. The Government must locate that evidence " 'by the independent labor of its officers,' " *Estelle v. Smith,* 451 U.S. 454, 462, 101 S.Ct. 1866, 1872, 68 L.Ed.2d 359 (1981), quoting *Culombe v. Connecticut,* 367 U.S. 568, 582, 81 S.Ct. 1860, 1867, 6 L.Ed.2d 1037 (1961) (opinion announcing the judgment). As in *Fisher,* the Government is not relying upon the " 'truthtelling' " of Doe's directive to show the existence of, or his control over, foreign bank account records. See 425 U.S., at 411, 96 S.Ct. at 1581, quoting 8 Wigmore § 2264, p. 380.

Given the consent directive's phraseology, petitioner's compelled act of executing the form has no testimonial significance either. By

will disclose incriminating information that the suspect harbors.

To the extent petitioner attempts to construe *Miranda* as establishing an absolute right against being compelled to speak, that understanding is refuted by the Court's decision in *United States v. Dionisio,* 410 U.S. 1, 93 S.Ct. 764, 35 L.Ed.2d 67 (1973), in which the Court held that a suspect may not invoke the privilege in refusing to speak for purposes of providing a voice exemplar.

signing the form, Doe makes no statement, explicit or implicit, regarding the existence of a foreign bank account or his control over any such account. Nor would his execution of the form admit the authenticity of any records produced by the bank. Cf. *United States v. Ghidoni,* 732 F.2d, at 818–819; *In re Grand Jury Subpoena,* 826 F.2d, at 1170. Not only does the directive express no view on the issue, but because petitioner did not prepare the document, any statement by Doe to the effect that it is authentic would not establish that the records are genuine. Cf. *Fisher,* 425 U.S., at 413, 96 S.Ct., at 1582. Authentication evidence would have to be provided by bank officials.

Finally, we cannot agree with petitioner's contention that his execution of the directive admits or asserts Doe's consent. The form does not state that Doe "consents" to the release of bank records. Instead, it states that the directive "shall be construed as consent" with respect to Cayman Islands and Bermuda bank-secrecy laws. Because the directive explicitly indicates that it was signed pursuant to a court order, Doe's compelled execution of the form sheds no light on his actual intent or state of mind.[14] The form does "direct" the bank to disclose account information and release any records that "may" exist and for which Doe "may" be a relevant principal. But directing the recipient of a communication to do something is not an assertion of fact or, at least in this context, a disclosure of information. In its testimonial significance, the execution of such a directive is analogous to the production of a handwriting sample or voice exemplar: it is a nontestimonial act. In neither case is the suspect's action compelled to obtain "any knowledge he might have." *Wade,* 388 U.S., at 222, 87 S.Ct., at 1930.[15]

14. The consent directive at issue here differs from the form at issue in *Ranauro* which suggested that the witness, in fact, had consented: "I, [witness], consent to the production to the [District Court and Grand Jury] of any and all records related to any accounts held by, or banking transactions engaged in with, [bank X], which are in the name of, or on behalf of: [witness], if any such records exist." 814 F.2d, at 796. Further, the *Ranauro* form, unlike the directive here, did not indicate that it was executed under court order. *Id.,* at 795. It is true that the First Circuit made clear that its conclusion that the *Ranauro* form was testimonial did not turn on these distinctions, *ibid.,* but we are not sanguine that the differences are irrelevant. Even if the Self-Incrimination Clause was not implicated, it might be argued that the compelled signing of such a "consent" form raises due process concerns. Cf. *In re Grand Jury Subpoena,* 826 F.2d, at 1171 (finding no due process violation where directive clearly states that witness is signing under compulsion of court order); *United States v. Ghidoni,* 732 F.2d, at 818, n. 7 (same). Neither issue, of course, is presented by this case, and we take no position on whether such compulsion in fact would violate Fifth Amendment or due process principles.

15. Petitioner apparently maintains that the performance of every compelled act carries with it an implied assertion that the act has been performed by the person who was compelled, and therefore the performance of the act is subject to the privilege. In *Wade, Gilbert,* and *Dionisio,* the Court implicitly rejected this argument. It could be said in those cases that the suspect, by providing his handwriting or voice exemplar, implicitly "acknowledged" that the writing or voice sample was his. But as the holdings make clear, this kind of simple acknowledgement—that the suspect in fact performed the compelled act—is not "sufficiently testimonial for purposes of the privilege." *Fisher,* 425 U.S., at 411, 96 S.Ct., at 1581. Similarly, the acknowledgement that Doe directed the bank to disclose any records the bank thinks are Doe's—an acknowledgement im-

We read the directive as equivalent to a statement by Doe that, although he expresses no opinion about the existence of, or his control over, any such account, he is authorizing the bank to disclose information relating to accounts over which, in the bank's opinion, Doe can exercise the right of withdrawal. Cf. *Ghidoni,* 732 F.2d, at 818, n. 8 (similarly interpreting a nearly identical consent directive). When forwarded to the bank along with a subpoena, the executed directive, if effective under local law,[16] will simply make it possible for the recipient bank to comply with the Government's request to produce such records. As a result, if the Government obtains bank records after Doe signs the directive, the only factual statement made by anyone will be the *bank's* implicit declaration, by its act of production in response to the subpoena, that *it* believes the accounts to be petitioner's. Cf. *Fisher,* 425 U.S., at 410, 412–413, 96 S.Ct., at 1581–1582. The fact that the bank's customer has directed the disclosure of his records "would say nothing about the correctness of the bank's representations." Brief for United States 21–22. Indeed, the Second and Eleventh Circuits have concluded that consent directives virtually identical to the one here are inadmissible as an admission by the signator of either control or existence. *In re Grand Jury Subpoena,* 826 F.2d, at 1171; *Ghidoni,* 732 F.2d, at 818, and n. 9.

III

Because the consent directive is not testimonial in nature, we conclude that the District Court's order compelling petitioner to sign the directive does not violate his Fifth Amendment privilege against

plicit in Doe's placing his signature on the consent directive—is not sufficiently testimonial for purposes of the privilege.

The dissent apparently disagrees with us on this point, although the basis for its disagreement is unclear. Surely, the fact that the executed form creates "a new piece of evidence that may be used against petitioner" is not relevant to whether the execution has testimonial significance, for the same could be said about the voice and writing exemplars the Court found were not testimonial in nature. Similarly irrelevant to the issue presented here is the dissent's invocation of the First Circuit's hypothetical of how the Government might use the directive to link petitioner to whatever documents the banks produce. That hypothetical, as the First Circuit indicated, *Ranauro,* 814 F.2d, at 793, goes only to showing that the directive may be *incriminating,* an issue not presented in this case. It has no bearing on whether the compelled execution of the directive is *testimonial.*

16. The Government of the Cayman Islands maintains that a compelled consent, such as the one at issue in this case, is not sufficient to authorize the release of confidential financial records protected by Cayman law. Brief for Government of Cayman Islands as *Amicus Curiae* 9–11. The Grand Court of the Cayman Islands has held expressly that a consent directive signed pursuant to an order of a United States court and at the risk of contempt sanctions, could not constitute "consent" under the Cayman confidentiality law. See *In re ABC Ltd.,* 1984 C.I.L.R. 130 (1984) (reviewing the consent directive at issue in *Ghidoni*). Respondent observes that the cited decision has not been appealed and argues accordingly that Cayman law on the point has not been definitely settled.

The effectiveness of the directive under foreign law has no bearing on the constitutional issue in this case. Nevertheless, we are not unaware of the international comity questions implicated by the Government's attempts to overcome protections afforded by the laws of another nation. We are not called upon to address those questions here.

self-incrimination. Accordingly, the judgment of the Court of Appeals is affirmed.

It is so ordered.

JUSTICE STEVENS, dissenting.

A defendant can be compelled to produce material evidence that is incriminating. Fingerprints, blood samples, voice exemplars, handwriting specimens or other items of physical evidence may be extracted from a defendant against his will. But can he be compelled to use his mind to assist the prosecution in convicting him of a crime? I think not. He may in some cases be forced to surrender a key to a strong box containing incriminating documents, but I do not believe he can be compelled to reveal the combination to his wall safe—by word or deed.

The document the Government seeks to extract from John Doe purports to order third parties to take action that will lead to the discovery of incriminating evidence. The directive itself may not betray any knowledge petitioner may have about the circumstances of the offenses being investigated by the Grand Jury, but it nevertheless purports to evidence a reasoned decision by Doe to authorize action by others. The forced execution of this document differs from the forced production of physical evidence just as human beings differ from other animals.[1]

1. The forced production of physical evidence, which we have condoned, see *Gilbert v. California,* 388 U.S. 263, 87 S.Ct. 1951, 18 L.Ed.2d 1178 (1967) (handwriting exemplar); *United States v. Wade,* 388 U.S. 218, 87 S.Ct. 1951, 18 L.Ed.2d 1178 (1967) (voice exemplar); *Schmerber v. California,* 384 U.S. 757, 87 S.Ct. 1951, 18 L.Ed.2d 1178 (1966) (blood test); *Holt v. United States,* 218 U.S. 245, 31 S.Ct. 2, 54 L.Ed. 1021 (1910) (line-up), involves no intrusion upon the contents of the mind of the accused. See *Schmerber,* 384 U.S., at 765, 86 S.Ct., at 1832 (forced blood test permissible because it does not involve "even a shadow of testimonial compulsion upon or enforced communication by the accused"). The forced execution of a document that purports to convey the signer's authority, however, does invade the dignity of the human mind; it purports to communicate a deliberate command. The intrusion on the dignity of the individual is not diminished by the fact that the document does not reflect the true state of the signer's mind. Indeed, that the assertions petitioner is forced to utter by executing the document are false causes an even greater violation of human dignity. For the same reason a person cannot be forced to sign a document purporting to authorize the entry of judgment against himself, cf. *Brady v. United States,* 397 U.S. 742, 748, 90 S.Ct. 1463, 25 L.Ed.2d 747 (1970), I do not believe he can be forced to sign a document purporting to authorize the disclosure of incriminating evidence. In both cases the accused is being compelled "to be a witness against himself"; indeed, here he is being compelled to bear false witness against himself.

The expression of the contents of an individual's mind falls squarely within the protection of the Fifth Amendment. *Boyd v. United States,* 116 U.S. 616, 633–635, 6 S.Ct. 524, 533–535, 29 L.Ed. 746 (1886); *Fisher v. United States,* 425 U.S. 391, 420, 96 S.Ct. 1569, 1585, 48 L.Ed.2d 39 (1976). Justice Holmes' observation that "the prohibition of compelling a man in a criminal court to be witness against himself is a prohibition of the use of physical or moral compulsion to extort communications from him," *Holt v. United States,* 218 U.S., at 252–253, 31 S.Ct., at 6, manifests a recognition that virtually any communication reveals the contents of the mind of the speaker. Thus the Fifth Amendment privilege is fulfilled only when the person is guaranteed the right " 'to remain silent unless he chooses to speak in the unfettered exercise of his own will.' " *Miranda v. Arizona,* 384 U.S. 436, 460, 86 S.Ct. 1602, 1620, 16 L.Ed.2d 694 (1966) (quoting *Malloy v. Hogan,* 378 U.S. 1, 8, 84 S.Ct. 1489, 1493, 12 L.Ed.2d 653 (1964)). The deviation from this principle can only lead to mischievous abuse of the dignity the Fifth Amendment

If John Doe can be compelled to use his mind to assist the Government in developing its case, I think he will be forced "to be a witness against himself." The fundamental purpose of the Fifth Amendment was to mark the line between the kind of inquisition conducted by the Star Chamber and what we proudly describe as our accusatorial system of justice. It reflects "our respect for the inviability of the human personality," *Murphy v. Waterfront Comm'n of New York Harbor,* 378 U.S. 52, 55, 84 S.Ct. 1594, 1597, 12 L.Ed.2d 678 (1964). "[I]t is an explicit right of a natural person, protecting the realm of human thought and expression." *Braswell v. United States, ante,* ___ U.S., at ___, 108 S.Ct., at 2286 (Kennedy, J., dissenting) [slip op. at 1]. In my opinion that protection gives John Doe the right to refuse to sign the directive authorizing access to the records of any bank account that he may control. Accordingly, I respectfully dissent.

BRASWELL v. UNITED STATES

Supreme Court of the United States, 1988.
487 U.S. 99, 108 S.Ct. 2284, 101 L.Ed.2d 98.

CHIEF JUSTICE REHNQUIST delivered the opinion of the Court.

This case presents the question whether the custodian of corporate records may resist a subpoena for such records on the ground that the act of production would incriminate him in violation of the Fifth Amendment. We conclude that he may not.

From 1965 to 1980, petitioner Randy Braswell operated his business—which comprises the sale and purchase of equipment, land, timber, and oil and gas interests—as a sole proprietorship. In 1980, he incorporated Worldwide Machinery Sales, Inc., a Mississippi corporation, and began conducting the business through that entity. In 1981, he formed a second Mississippi corporation, Worldwide Purchasing, Inc., and funded that corporation with the 100 percent interest he held in Worldwide Machinery. Petitioner was and is the sole shareholder of Worldwide Purchasing, Inc.

Both companies are active corporations, maintaining their current status with the State of Mississippi, filing corporate tax returns, and keeping current corporate books and records. In compliance with Mississippi law, both corporations have three directors, petitioner, his wife, and his mother. Although his wife and mother are secretary-treasurer and vice-president of the corporations, respectively, neither has any authority over the business affairs of either corporation.

In August 1986, a federal grand jury issued a subpoena to "Randy Braswell, President Worldwide Machinery, Inc. [and] Worldwide Pur-

commands the Government afford its citizens. Cf. *Schmerber v. California,* 384 U.S., at 764, 86 S.Ct., at 1832. The instant case is illustrative. In allowing the Government to compel petitioner to execute the directive, the Court permits the Government to compel petitioner to speak against his will in answer to the question "Do you consent to the release of these documents." Beyond this affront, however, the Government is being permitted also to demand that the answer be "yes."

chasing, Inc.," App. 6, requiring petitioner to produce the books and records of the two corporations. The subpoena provided that petitioner could deliver the records to the agent serving the subpoena, and did not require petitioner to testify. Petitioner moved to quash the subpoena, arguing that the act of producing the records would incriminate him in violation of his Fifth Amendment privilege against self-incrimination. The District Court denied the motion to quash, ruling that the "collective entity doctrine" prevented petitioner from asserting that his act of producing the corporations' records was protected by the Fifth Amendment. The court rejected petitioner's argument that the collective entity doctrine does not apply when a corporation is so small that it constitutes nothing more than the individual's alter ego.

The United States Court of Appeals for the Fifth Circuit affirmed, citing *Bellis v. United States,* 417 U.S. 85, 88, 94 S.Ct. 2179, 2182, 40 L.Ed.2d 678 (1974), for the proposition that a corporation's records custodian may not claim a Fifth Amendment privilege no matter how small the corporation may be. The Court of Appeals declared that *Bellis* retained vitality following *United States v. Doe,* 465 U.S. 605, 104 S.Ct. 1237, 79 L.Ed.2d 552 (1984), and therefore, "Braswell, as custodian of corporate documents, has no act of production privilege under the fifth amendment regarding corporate documents." *In re Grand Jury Proceedings,* 814 F.2d 190, 193 (CA5 1987). We granted certiorari to resolve a conflict among the Courts of Appeals. 484 U.S. ___, 108 S.Ct. 64, 98 L.Ed.2d 28 (1987). We now affirm.

There is no question but that the contents of the subpoenaed business records are not privileged. See *Doe, supra; Fisher v. United States,* 425 U.S. 391, 96 S.Ct. 1569, 48 L.Ed.2d 39 (1976). Similarly, petitioner asserts no self-incrimination claim on behalf of the corporations; it is well established that such artificial entities are not protected by the Fifth Amendment. *Bellis, supra.* Petitioner instead relies solely upon the argument that his act of producing the documents has independent testimonial significance, which would incriminate him individually, and that the Fifth Amendment prohibits government compulsion of that act. The bases for this argument are extrapolated from the decisions of this Court in *Fisher, supra,* and *Doe, supra.*

In *Fisher,* the Court was presented with the question whether an attorney may resist a subpoena demanding that he produce tax records which had been entrusted to him by his client. The records in question had been prepared by the client's accountants. In analyzing the Fifth Amendment claim forwarded by the attorney, the Court considered whether the client-taxpayer would have had a valid Fifth Amendment claim had he retained the records and the subpoena been issued to him. After explaining that the Fifth Amendment prohibits "compelling a person to give 'testimony' that incriminates him," 425 U.S., at 409, 96 S.Ct., at 1580, the Court rejected the argument that the contents of the records were protected. The Court, however, went on to observe:

> "The act of producing evidence in response to a subpoena nevertheless has communicative aspects of its own, wholly aside from the contents of the papers produced. Compliance with the subpoena tacitly concedes the existence of the papers demanded and their possession or control by the taxpayer. It also would indicate the taxpayer's belief that the papers are those described in the subpoena. *Curcio v. United States,* 354 U.S. 118, 125 [77 S.Ct. 1145, 1150, 1 L.Ed.2d 1225] (1957). The elements of compulsion are clearly present, but the more difficult issues are whether the tacit averments of the taxpayer are both 'testimonial' and 'incriminating' for purposes of applying the Fifth Amendment. These questions perhaps do not lend themselves to categorical answers; their resolution may instead depend on the facts and circumstances of particular cases or classes thereof." *Id.,* at 410, 96 S.Ct., at 1581.

The Court concluded that under the "facts and circumstances" there presented, the act of producing the accountants' papers would not "involve testimonial self-incrimination." *Id.,* at 411, 96 S.Ct., at 1581.[3]

Eight years later, in *United States v. Doe, supra,* the Court revisited the question, this time in the context of a claim by a sole proprietor that the compelled production of business records would run afoul of the Fifth Amendment. After rejecting the contention that the contents of the records were themselves protected, the Court proceeded to address whether respondent's act of producing the records would constitute protected testimonial incrimination. The Court concluded that respondent had established a valid Fifth Amendment claim. It deferred to the lower courts, which had found that enforcing the subpoenas at issue would provide the Government valuable information: By producing the records, respondent would admit that the records existed, were in his possession, and were authentic. 465 U.S., at 613, n. 11, 104 S.Ct. 1242, n. 11.

Had petitioner conducted his business as a sole proprietorship, *Doe* would require that he be provided the opportunity to show that his act of production would entail testimonial self-incrimination. But petitioner has operated his business through the corporate form, and we have long recognized that for purposes of the Fifth Amendment, corporations and other collective entities are treated differently from individuals. This doctrine—known as the collective entity rule—has a lengthy and distinguished pedigree.

The rule was first articulated by the Court in the case of *Hale v. Henkel,* 201 U.S. 43, 26 S.Ct. 370, 50 L.Ed. 652 (1906). Hale, a corporate officer, had been served with a subpoena ordering him to produce corporate records and to testify concerning certain corporate transac-

3. After observing that the papers in question had been prepared by the taxpayer's accountants, the Court noted: "The existence and location of the papers are a foregone conclusion and the taxpayer adds little or nothing to the sum total of the Government's information by conceding that he in fact has the papers." 425 U.S., at 411, 96 S.Ct., at 1581. Nor would the taxpayer's production of the papers serve to authenticate or vouch for the accuracy of the accountants' work. *Id.,* at 413, 96 S.Ct., at 1582.

tions. Although Hale was protected by personal immunity, he sought to resist the demand for the records by interposing a Fifth Amendment privilege on behalf of the corporation. The Court rejected that argument: "[W]e are of the opinion that there is a clear distinction * * * between an individual and a corporation, and * * * the latter has no right to refuse to submit its books and papers for an examination at the suit of the State." *Id.*, at 74, 26 S.Ct., at 379. The Court explained that the corporation "is a creature of the State," *ibid.*, with powers limited by the State. As such, the State may, in the exercise of its right to oversee the corporation, demand the production of corporate records. *Id.*, at 75, 26 S.Ct., at 379.

The ruling in *Hale* represented a limitation on the prior holding in *Boyd v. United States*, 116 U.S. 616, 6 S.Ct. 524, 29 L.Ed. 746 (1886), which involved a court order directing partners to produce an invoice received by the partnership. The partners had produced the invoice, but steadfastly maintained that the court order ran afoul of the Fifth Amendment. This Court agreed. After concluding that the order transgressed the Fourth Amendment, the Court declared: "[A] compulsory production of the *private* books and papers of the owner of goods sought to be forfeited * * * is compelling him to be a witness against himself, within the meaning of the Fifth Amendment to the Constitution * * *." *Id.*, at 634–635, 6 S.Ct., at 534 (emphasis added). *Hale* carved an exception out of *Boyd* by establishing that corporate books and records are not "private papers" protected by the Fifth Amendment.

Although *Hale* settled that a corporation has no Fifth Amendment privilege, the Court did not address whether a corporate officer could resist a subpoena for corporate records by invoking his personal privilege—Hale had been protected by immunity. In *Wilson v. United States*, 221 U.S. 361, 31 S.Ct. 538, 55 L.Ed. 771 (1911), the Court answered that question in the negative. There, a grand jury investigating Wilson had issued a subpoena to a corporation demanding the production of corporate letter press copy books, which Wilson, the corporation's president, possessed. Wilson refused to produce the books, arguing that the Fifth Amendment prohibited compulsory production of personally incriminating books that he held and controlled. The Court rejected this argument, observing first that the records sought were not private or personal, but rather belonged to the corporation. * * *

In a companion case, *Dreier v. United States*, 221 U.S. 394, 31 S.Ct. 550, 55 L.Ed. 784 (1911), the Court applied the holding in *Wilson* to a Fifth Amendment attack on a subpoena addressed to the corporate custodian. Although the subpoena in *Wilson* had been addressed to the corporation, the Court found the distinction irrelevant: "Dreier was not entitled to refuse the production of the corporate records. By virtue of the fact that they were the documents of the corporation in his custody, and not his private papers, he was under the obligation to produce them when called for by proper process." 221 U.S., at 400, 31 S.Ct., at 550.

The next significant step in the development of the collective entity rule occurred in *United States v. White,* 322 U.S. 694, 64 S.Ct. 1248, 88 L.Ed. 1542 (1944), in which the Court held that a labor union is a collective entity unprotected by the Fifth Amendment. There, a grand jury had issued a subpoena addressed to a union requiring the production of certain union records. White, an assistant supervisor of the union, appeared before the grand jury and declined to produce the documents " 'upon the ground that they might tend to incriminate [the union], myself as an officer thereof, or individually.' " *Id.,* at 696, 64 S.Ct., at 1250.

We upheld an order of contempt against White, reasoning first that the Fifth Amendment privilege applies only to natural individuals and protects only private papers. Representatives of a "collective group" act as agents "[a]nd the official records and documents of the organization that are held by them in a representative rather than in a personal capacity cannot be the subject of the personal privilege against self-incrimination, even though production of the papers might tend to incriminate them personally." *Id.,* at 699, 64 S.Ct., at 1251. * * * In applying the collective entity rule to unincorporated associations such as unions, the Court jettisoned reliance on the visitatorial powers of the State over corporations owing their existence to the State—one of the bases for earlier decisions. See *id.,* at 700–701, 64 S.Ct., at 1252.

The frontiers of the collective entity rule were expanded even further in *Bellis v. United States,* 417 U.S. 85, 94 S.Ct. 2179, 40 L.Ed.2d 678 (1974), in which the Court ruled that a partner in a small partnership could not properly refuse to produce partnership records. Bellis, one of the members of a three-person law firm that had previously been dissolved, was served with a subpoena directing him to produce partnership records he possessed. The District Court held Bellis in contempt when he refused to produce the partnership's financial books and records. We upheld the contempt order. * * *

The plain mandate of these decisions is that without regard to whether the subpoena is addressed to the corporation, or as here, to the individual in his capacity as a custodian, see *Dreier, supra; Bellis, supra,* a corporate custodian such as petitioner may not resist a subpoena for corporate records on Fifth Amendment grounds. Petitioner argues, however, that this rule falls in the wake of *Fisher v. United States,* 425 U.S. 391, 96 S.Ct. 1569, 48 L.Ed.2d 39 (1976), and *United States v. Doe,* 465 U.S. 605, 104 S.Ct. 1237, 79 L.Ed.2d 552 (1984). In essence, petitioner's argument is as follows: In response to *Boyd v. United States,* 116 U.S. 616, 6 S.Ct. 524, 29 L.Ed. 746 (1886), with its privacy rationale shielding personal books and records, the Court developed the collective entity rule, which declares simply that corporate records are not private and therefore are not protected by the Fifth Amendment. The collective entity decisions were concerned with the contents of the documents subpoenaed, however, and not with the act of production. In *Fisher* and *Doe,* the Court moved away from the privacy based collective entity rule, replacing it with a compelled testimony standard under which the contents of business documents are never privileged but the act of producing the documents may be. Under this new regime, the act of production privilege is available without regard to the entity whose records are being sought. See *In re Grand Jury Matter (Brown),* 768 F.2d 525, 528 (CA 3 1985) (en banc) ("[*Fisher* and *Doe*] make the significant factor, for the privilege against self-incrimination, neither the nature of entity which owns the documents, nor the contents of documents, but rather the communicative or noncommunicative nature of the arguably incriminating disclosures sought to be compelled").

To be sure, the holding in *Fisher*—later reaffirmed in *Doe*—embarked upon a new course of Fifth Amendment analysis. See *Fisher, supra,* 425 U.S., at 409, 96 S.Ct., at 1580. We cannot agree, however, that it rendered the collective entity rule obsolete. The agency rationale undergirding the collective entity decisions, in which custodians asserted that production of entity records would incriminate them personally, survives. From *Wilson* forward, the Court has consistently recognized that the custodian of corporate or entity records holds those documents in a representative rather than a personal capacity. Artificial entities such as corporations may act only through their agents, *Bellis, supra,* 417 U.S., at 90, 94 S.Ct., at 2184, and a custodian's assumption of his representative capacity leads to certain obligations, including the duty to produce corporate records on proper demand by the Government. Under those circumstances, the custodian's act of production is not deemed a personal act, but rather an act of the corporation. Any claim of Fifth Amendment privilege asserted by the agent would be tantamount to a claim of privilege by the corporation—which of course possesses no such privilege.

* * *

Indeed, the opinion in *Fisher*—upon which petitioner places primary reliance [5]—indicates that the custodian of corporate records may not interpose a Fifth Amendment objection to the compelled production of corporate records, even though the act of production may prove personally incriminating. The *Fisher* court cited the collective entity decisions with approval and offered those decisions to support the conclusion that the production of the accountant's workpapers would "not * * * involve testimonial self-incrimination." 425 U.S., at 411, 96

5. Petitioner also offers *United States v. Doe,* 465 U.S. 605, 104 S.Ct. 1237, 79 L.Ed.2d 552 (1984), as support for his position, but that decision is plainly inapposite. The *Doe* opinion begins by explaining that the question presented for review is "whether, and to what extent, the Fifth Amendment privilege against compelled self-incrimination applies to the business records of a *sole proprietorship.*" *Id.,* at 606, 104 S.Ct., at 1239 (emphasis added). A sole proprietor does not hold records in a representative capacity. Thus, the absence of any discussion of the collective entity rule can in no way be thought a suggestion that the status of the holder of the records is irrelevant.

S.Ct., at 1581. The Court observed: "This Court has * * * time and again allowed subpoenas against the custodian of corporate documents or those belonging to other collective entities such as unions and partnerships and those of bankrupt businesses over claims that the documents will incriminate the custodian despite the fact that producing the documents tacitly admits their existence and their location in the hands of their possessor." *Id.*, at 411–412, 96 S.Ct., at 1581. The Court later noted that "in *Wilson, Dreier, White, Bellis,* and *In re Harris,* [221 U.S. 274, 31 S.Ct. 557, 55 L.Ed. 73 (1911)], the custodian of corporate, union, or partnership books or those of a bankrupt business was ordered to respond to a subpoena for the business' books even though doing so involved a 'representation that the documents produced are those demanded by the subpoena,' *Curcio v. United States,* 354 U.S., at 125 [77 S.Ct., at 115]." *Id.*, at 413, 96 S.Ct., at 1582 (citations omitted). In a footnote, the Court explained: "In these cases compliance with the subpoena is required even though the books have been kept by the person subpoenaed and his producing them would itself be sufficient authentication to permit their introduction against him." *Id.,* at 413, n. 14, 96 S.Ct., at 1582, n. 14. The Court thus reaffirmed the obligation of a corporate custodian to comply with a subpoena addressed to him.

* * *

Petitioner also attempts to extract support for his contention from *Curcio v. United States,* 354 U.S. 118, 77 S.Ct. 1145, 1 L.Ed.2d 1225 (1957). But rather than bolstering petitioner's argument, we think *Curcio* substantiates the Government's position. Curcio had been served with two subpoenas addressed to him in his capacity as secretary-treasurer of a local union, which was under investigation. One subpoena required that he produce union books, the other that he testify. Curcio appeared before the grand jury, stated that the books were not in his possession, and refused to answer any questions as to their whereabouts. Curcio was held in contempt for refusing to answer the questions propounded. We reversed the contempt citation, rejecting the Government's argument "that the representative duty which required the production of union records in the *White* case requires the giving of oral testimony by the custodian." *Id.*, at 123, 77 S.Ct., at 1149.

Petitioner asserts that our *Curcio* decision stands for the proposition that although the contents of a collective entity's records are unprivileged, a representative of a collective entity cannot be required to provide testimony about those records. It follows, according to petitioner, that because *Fisher* recognizes that the act of production is potentially testimonial, such an act may not be compelled if it would tend to incriminate the representative personally. We find this reading of *Curcio* flawed.

The *Curcio* Court made clear that with respect to a custodian of a collective entity's records, the line drawn was between oral testimony and other forms of incrimination. "A custodian, by assuming the duties of his office, undertakes the obligation to produce the books of which he is custodian in response to a rightful exercise of the State's visitorial [*sic*] powers. But he cannot lawfully be compelled, in the absence of a grant of adequate immunity from prosecution, to condemn himself by his own *oral testimony.*" 354 U.S., at 123–24, 77 S.Ct., at 1149 (emphasis added).

In distinguishing those cases in which a corporate officer was required to produce corporate records and merely identify them by oral testimony, the Court showed that it understood the testimonial nature of the act of production: "The custodian's act of producing books or records in response to a subpoena *duces tecum* is itself a representation that the documents produced are those demanded by the subpoena. Requiring the custodian to identify or authenticate the documents for admission in evidence merely makes explicit what is implicit in the production itself." *Id.,* at 125, 77 S.Ct., at 1150. In the face of this recognition, the Court nonetheless noted: "In this case petitioner might have been proceeded against for his failure to produce the records demanded by the subpoena *duces tecum.*" [7] *Id.,* at 127, n. 7, 77 S.Ct., at 1151 n. 7. As Justice Brennan later observed in his concurrence in *Fisher:* "The Court in *Curcio,* however, apparently did not note any self-incrimination problem [with the testimonial significance of the act of production] because of the undertaking by the custodian with respect to the documents." 425 U.S., at 430, n. 9, 96 S.Ct., at 1590, n. 9.

We note further that recognizing a Fifth Amendment privilege on behalf of the records custodians of collective entities would have a detrimental impact on the Government's efforts to prosecute "white-collar crime," one of the most serious problems confronting law enforcement authorities. "The greater portion of evidence of wrongdoing by an organization or its representatives is usually found in the official records and documents of that organization. Were the cloak of the privilege to be thrown around these impersonal records and documents, effective enforcement of many federal and state laws would be impossible." *White,* 322 U.S., at 700, 64 S.Ct., at 1252. If custodians could assert a privilege, authorities would be stymied not only in their enforcement efforts against those individuals but also in their prosecutions of organizations. In *Bellis,* the Court observed: "In view of the inescapable fact that an artificial entity can only act to produce its records through its individual officers or agents, recognition of the individual's claim of privilege with respect to the financial records of

7. The dissent's suggestion that we have extracted from *Curcio* a distinction between oral testimony and act of production testimony that is nowhere found in the *Curcio* opinion simply ignores this part of *Curcio.* Similarly, the dissent pays mere lip service to the agency rationale supporting an unbroken chain of collective entity decisions. We have consistently held that for Fifth Amendment purposes a corporate custodian acts in a representative capacity when he produces corporate documents under the compulsion of a subpoena. The dissent's failure to recognize this principle and its suggestion that petitioner was not called upon to act in his capacity as an agent of the corporations cannot be squared with our previous decisions.

the organization would substantially undermine the unchallenged rule that the organization itself is not entitled to claim any Fifth Amendment privilege, and largely frustrate legitimate governmental regulation of such organizations." 417 U.S., at 90, 94 S.Ct., at 2184.

Petitioner suggests, however, that these concerns can be minimized by the simple expedient of either granting the custodian statutory immunity as to the act of production, 18 U.S.C. §§ 6002, 6003, or addressing the subpoena to the corporation and allowing it to choose an agent to produce the records who can do so without incriminating himself. We think neither proposal satisfactorily addresses these concerns. Taking the last first, it is no doubt true that if a subpoena is addressed to a corporation, the corporation "must find some means by which to comply because no Fifth Amendment defense is available to it." *In re Sealed Case,* 266 U.S.App.D.C. 30, 44, n. 9, 832 F.2d 1268, 1282, n. 9 (1987). The means most commonly used to comply is the appointment of an alternate custodian. See, *e.g., In re Two Grand Jury Subpoenae Duces Tecum,* 769 F.2d 52, 57 (CA2 1985); *United States v. Lang,* 792 F.2d 1235, 1240–1241 (CA4), cert. denied, 479 U.S. ___, 107 S.Ct. 574, 93 L.Ed.2d 578 (1986); *In re Grand Jury No. 86–3 (Will Roberts Corp.),* 816 F.2d 569, 573 (CA11 1987). But petitioner insists he cannot be required to aid the appointed custodian in his search for the demanded records, for any statement to the surrogate would itself be testimonial and incriminating. If this is correct, then petitioner's "solution" is a chimera. In situations such as this—where the corporate custodian is likely the only person with knowledge about the demanded documents—the appointment of a surrogate will simply not ensure that the documents sought will ever reach the grand jury room; the appointed custodian will essentially be sent on an unguided search.

This problem is eliminated if the Government grants the subpoenaed custodian statutory immunity for the testimonial aspects of his act of production. But that "solution" also entails a significant drawback. All of the evidence obtained under a grant of immunity to the custodian may of course be used freely against the corporation, but if the Government has any thought of prosecuting the custodian, a grant of act of production immunity can have serious consequences. Testimony obtained pursuant to a grant of statutory use immunity may be used neither directly nor derivatively. 18 U.S.C. § 6002; *Kastigar v. United States,* 406 U.S. 441, 92 S.Ct. 1653, 32 L.Ed.2d 212 (1972). And "[o]ne raising a claim under [the federal immunity] statute need only show that he testified under a grant of immunity in order to shift to the government the heavy burden of proving that all of the evidence it proposes to use was derived from legitimate independent sources." *Id.,* at 461–462, 92 S.Ct., at 1665. Even in cases where the Government does not employ the immunized testimony for any purpose—direct or derivative—against the witness, the Government's inability to meet the "heavy burden" it bears may result in the preclusion of crucial evidence that was obtained legitimately.

Although a corporate custodian is not entitled to resist a subpoena on the ground that his act of production will be personally incriminating, we do think certain consequences flow from the fact that the custodian's act of production is one in his representative rather than personal capacity. Because the custodian acts as a representative, the act is deemed one of the corporation and not the individual. Therefore, the Government concedes, as it must, that it may make no evidentiary use of the "individual act" against the individual. For example, in a criminal prosecution against the custodian, the Government may not introduce into evidence before the jury the fact that the subpoena was served upon and the corporation's documents were delivered by one particular individual, the custodian. The Government has the right, however, to use the corporation's act of production against the custodian. The Government may offer testimony—for example, from the process server who delivered the subpoena and from the individual who received the records—establishing that the corporation produced the records subpoenaed. The jury may draw from the corporation's act of production the conclusion that the records in question are authentic corporate records, which the corporation possessed, and which it produced in response to the subpoena. And if the defendant held a prominent position within the corporation that produced the records, the jury may, just as it would had someone else produced the documents, reasonably infer that he had possession of the documents or knowledge of their contents. Because the jury is not told that the defendant produced the records, any nexus between the defendant and the documents results solely from the corporation's act of production and other evidence in the case.[11]

Consistent with our precedent, the United States Court of Appeals for the Fifth Circuit ruled that petitioner could not resist the subpoena for corporate documents on the ground that the act of production might tend to incriminate him. The judgment is therefore

Affirmed.

JUSTICE KENNEDY, with whom JUSTICE BRENNAN, JUSTICE MARSHALL, and JUSTICE SCALIA join, dissenting.

* * *

I

There is some common ground in this case. All accept the longstanding rule that labor unions, corporations, partnerships, and other

11. We reject the suggestion that the limitation on the evidentiary use of the custodian's act of production is the equivalent of constructive use immunity barred under our decision in *Doe,* 465 U.S., at 616–617, 104 S.Ct., at 1244. Rather, the limitation is a necessary concomitant of the notion that a corporate custodian acts as an agent and not an individual when he produces corporate records in response to a subpoena addressed to him in his representative capacity.

We leave open the question whether the agency rationale supports compelling a custodian to produce corporate records when the custodian is able to establish, by showing for example that he is the sole employee and officer of the corporation, that the jury would inevitably conclude that he produced the records.

collective entities have no Fifth Amendment self-incrimination privilege; that a natural person cannot assert such a privilege on their behalf; and that the contents of business records prepared without compulsion can be used to incriminate even a natural person without implicating Fifth Amendment concerns. Further, all appear to concede or at least submit the case to us on the assumption that the act of producing the subpoenaed documents will effect personal incrimination of Randy Braswell, the individual to whom the subpoena is directed.

The petitioner's assertion of the Fifth Amendment privilege against the forced production of documents is based not on any contention that their contents will incriminate him but instead upon the unchallenged premise that the act of production will do so. When the case is presented on this assumption, there exists no historical or logical relation between the so-called collective entity rule and the individual's claim of privilege. A brief review of the foundational elements of the Self-Incrimination Clause and of our cases respecting collective entities is a necessary starting point.

A

In *Boyd v. United States,* 116 U.S. 616, 6 S.Ct. 524, 29 L.Ed. 746 (1886), we held that the compelled disclosure of the contents of "private papers" (which in *Boyd* was a business invoice), *id.,* at 622, 6 S.Ct., at 528, was prohibited not only by the Fifth Amendment but by the Fourth Amendment as well. The decision in *Boyd* generated nearly a century of doctrinal ambiguity as we explored its rationale and sought to define its protection for the contents of business records under the Fifth Amendment.

That effort was not always successful. As we recently recognized, *Boyd's* reasoning is in many respects inconsistent with our present understanding of the Fourth and Fifth Amendments, and "[s]everal of *Boyd's* express or implicit declarations have not stood the test of time." *Fisher v. United States,* 425 U.S. 391, 407, 96 S.Ct. 1569, 1579, 48 L.Ed.2d 39 (1976). Its essential premise was rejected four years ago, when we held that the contents of business records produced by subpoena are not privileged under the Fifth Amendment, absent some showing that the documents were prepared under compulsion. *United States v. Doe,* 465 U.S. 605, 610–611, n. 8, 104 S.Ct. 1237, 1240–41, n. 8, 79 L.Ed.2d 552 (1984) (*Doe I*). Our holding followed from a straightforward reading of the Fifth Amendment privilege. We held that unless the Government has somehow compelled the preparation of a business document, nothing in the Fifth Amendment prohibits the use of the writing in a criminal investigation or prosecution. *Id.,* at 610–612, 104 S.Ct., at 1240–42.

A subpoena does not, however, seek to compel creation of a document; it compels its production. We recognized this distinction in *Fisher,* holding that the act of producing documents itself may communicate information separate from the documents' contents and that such communication, in some circumstances, is compelled testimony.

An individual who produces documents may be asserting that they satisfy the general description in the subpoena, or that they were in his possession or under his control. Those assertions can convey information about that individual's knowledge and state of mind as effectively as spoken statements, and the Fifth Amendment protects individuals from having such assertions compelled by their own acts.

This is well-settled law, or so I had assumed. In *Doe I,* for example, when we reviewed a claim of Fifth Amendment privilege asserted by a sole proprietor in response to a Government subpoena for his business records, our opinion announced two principal holdings. First, we unequivocally rejected the notion, derived from *Boyd,* that any protection attached to their contents. 465 U.S., at 612, 104 S.Ct., at 1242. Second, in reliance on the findings of the District Court that production would be testimonial and self-incriminating, we upheld the claim that the act of producing these documents was privileged. *Id.,* at 613–614, 104 S.Ct., at 1242–43. Our second holding did not depend on who owned the papers, how they were created, or what they said; instead, we rested on the fact that "the act of producing the documents would involve testimonial self-incrimination." *Id.,* at 613, 104 S.Ct., at 1242. That principle ought to be sufficient to resolve the case before us.

The majority does not challenge the assumption that compliance with the subpoena here would require acts of testimonial self-incrimination from Braswell; indeed, the Government itself made this assumption in submitting its argument. Tr. of Oral Arg. 26, 36. The question presented, therefore, is whether an individual may be compelled, simply by virtue of his status as a corporate custodian, to perform a testimonial act which will incriminate him personally. The majority relies entirely on the collective entity rule in holding that such compulsion is constitutional.

B

The collective entity rule provides no support for the majority's holding. The rule, as the majority chooses to call it, actually comprises three distinct propositions, none of which is relevant to the claim in this case. First, since *Hale v. Henkel,* 201 U.S. 43, 26 S.Ct. 370, 50 L.Ed. 652 (1906), it has been understood that a corporation has no Fifth Amendment privilege and cannot resist compelled production of its documents on grounds that it will be incriminated by their release. Second, our subsequent opinions show the collective entity principle is not confined to corporations, and we apply it as well to labor unions, *United States v. White,* 322 U.S. 694, 64 S.Ct. 1248, 88 L.Ed. 1542 (1944), and partnerships, *Bellis v. United States,* 417 U.S. 85, 94 S.Ct. 2179, 40 L.Ed.2d 678 (1974). Finally, in *Wilson v. United States,* 221 U.S. 361, 31 S.Ct. 538, 55 L.Ed. 771 (1911), we extended the rule beyond the collective entity itself and rejected an assertion of privilege by a corporate custodian who had claimed that the disclosure of the contents of subpoenaed corporate documents would incriminate him. *Id.,* at 363, 31 S.Ct., at 538. In none of the collective entity cases cited by the majority, and in none that I have found, were we presented with a claim that the custodian would be incriminated by the act of production, in contrast to the contents of the documents.

The distinction is central. Our holding in *Wilson* was premised squarely on the fact that the custodian's claim rested on the potential for incrimination in the documents' contents, and we reasoned that the State's visitatorial powers over corporations included the authority to inspect corporate books. * * * *Fisher* put to rest the notion that a privilege may be claimed with respect to the contents of business records that were voluntarily prepared.

The act of producing documents stands on an altogether different footing. While a custodian has no necessary relation to the contents of documents within his control, the act of production is inescapably his own. Production is the precise act compelled by the subpoena, and obedience, in some cases, will require the custodian's own testimonial assertions. That was the basis of our recognition of the privilege in *Doe I.* The entity possessing the documents in *Doe I* was, as the majority points out, a sole proprietorship, not a corporation, partnership, or labor union. But the potential for self-incrimination inheres in the act demanded of the individual, and as a consequence the nature of the entity is irrelevant to determining whether there is ground for the privilege.

* * *

C

The testimonial act demanded of petitioner in this case must be analyzed under the same principles applicable to other forms of compelled testimony. In *Curcio v. United States,* 354 U.S. 118, 77 S.Ct. 1145, 1 L.Ed.2d 1225 (1957), we reviewed a judgment holding a union custodian in criminal contempt for failing to give oral testimony regarding the location and possession of books and records he had been ordered to produce. *White* had already established that a labor union was as much a collective entity for Fifth Amendment purposes as a corporation, and the Government argued in *Curcio* that the custodian could not claim a personal privilege because he was performing only a "representative duty" on behalf of the collective entity to which he belonged. Brief for United States in *Curcio v. United States,* O.T.1956, No. 260, p. 17. We rejected that argument and reversed the judgment below. We stated:

> "[F]orcing the custodian to testify orally as to the whereabouts of nonproduced records requires him to disclose the contents of his own mind. He might be compelled to convict himself out of his own mouth. That is contrary to the spirit and letter of the Fifth Amendment." *Curcio,* 354 U.S., at 128, 77 S.Ct., at 1151–52.

We confront the same Fifth Amendment claim here. The majority is able to distinguish *Curcio* only by giving much apparent weight to the words "out of his own mouth," reading *Curcio* to stand for the proposition that the Constitution treats oral testimony differently than it does other forms of assertion. There is no basis in the text or history of the Fifth Amendment for such a distinction. The self-incrimination clause speaks of compelled "testimony," and has always been understood to apply to testimony in all its forms. *Doe v. United States*, ___ U.S. ___, ___, n. 8, 108 S.Ct. 2341, 2347, n. 8, 99 L.Ed.2d ___ (1988) (*Doe II*). Physical acts will constitute testimony if they probe the state of mind, memory, perception, or cognition of the witness. The Court should not retreat from the plain implications of this rule and hold that such testimony may be compelled, even when self-incriminating, simply because it is not spoken.

The distinction established by *Curcio* is not, of course, between oral and other forms of testimony; rather it is between a subpoena which compels a person to "disclose the contents of his own mind," through words or actions, and one which does not. *Ibid.* A custodian who is incriminated simply by the contents of the documents he has physically transmitted has not been compelled to disclose his memory or perception or cognition. A custodian who is incriminated by the personal knowledge he communicates in locating and selecting the document demanded in a Government subpoena has been compelled to testify in the most elemental, constitutional sense.

D

* * *

The majority gives the corporate agent fiction a weight it simply cannot bear. In a peculiar attempt to mitigate the force of its own holding, it impinges upon its own analysis by concluding that, while the Government may compel a named individual to produce records, in any later proceeding against the person it cannot divulge that he performed the act. But if that is so, it is because the Fifth Amendment protects the person without regard to his status as a corporate employee; and once this be admitted, the necessary support for the majority's case has collapsed.

Perhaps the Court makes this concession out of some vague sense of fairness, but the source of its authority to do so remains unexplained. It cannot rest on the Fifth Amendment, for the privilege against self-incrimination does not permit balancing the convenience of the Government against the rights of a witness, and the majority has in any case determined that the Fifth Amendment is inapplicable. If Braswell by his actions reveals information about his state of mind that is relevant to a jury in a criminal proceeding, there are no grounds of which I am aware for declaring the information inadmissible, unless it be the Fifth Amendment.

In *Doe I* we declined expressly to do what the Court does today. Noting that there might well be testimonial assertions attendant upon the production of documents, we rejected the argument that compelled production necessarily carried with it a grant of constructive immunity. We held that immunity may be granted only by appropriate statutory proceedings. The Government must make a formal request for statutory use immunity under 18 U.S.C. §§ 6002, 6003 if it seeks access to records in exchange for its agreement not to use testimonial acts against the individual. 465 U.S., at 614–617, 104 S.Ct., at 1243–44. Rather than beginning the practice of establishing new judicially created evidentiary rules, conferring upon individuals some partial use immunity to avoid results the Court finds constitutionally intolerable, I submit our precedents require the Government to use the only mechanism yet sanctioned for compelling testimony that is privileged: a request for immunity as provided by statute.

II

The majority's abiding concern is that if a corporate officer who is the target of a subpoena is allowed to assert the privilege, it will impede the Government's power to investigate corporations, unions, and partnerships, to uncover and prosecute white collar crimes, and otherwise to enforce its visitatorial powers. There are at least two answers to this. The first, and most fundamental, is that the text of the Fifth Amendment does not authorize exceptions premised on such rationales. Second, even if it were proper to invent such exceptions, the dangers prophesied by the majority are overstated.

Recognition of the right to assert a privilege does not mean it will exist in many cases. In many instances, the production of documents may implicate no testimonial assertions at all. In *Fisher,* for example, we held that the specific acts required by the subpoena before us "would not itself involve testimonial self-incrimination" because, in that case, "the existence and location of the papers [were] a foregone conclusion and the taxpayer adds little or nothing to the sum total of the Government's information by conceding that he in fact has the papers." 425 U.S., at 411, 96 S.Ct., at 1581. Whether a particular act is testimonial and self-incriminating is largely a factual issue to be decided in each case. *Doe II, supra.* In the case before us, the Government has made its submission on the assumption that the subpoena would result in incriminating testimony. The existence of a privilege in future cases, however, is not an automatic result.

Further, to the extent testimonial assertions are being compelled, use immunity can be granted without impeding the investigation. Where the privilege is applicable, immunity will be needed for only one individual, and solely with respect to evidence derived from the act of production itself. The Government would not be denied access to the records it seeks, it would be free to use the contents of the records against everyone, and it would be free to use any testimonial act implicit in production against all but the custodian it selects. In appropriate cases the Government will be able to establish authenticity, possession, and control by means other than compelling assertions about them from a suspect.

* * *

Chapter 9

PRESUMPTIONS *

[FED.R.EVID. ART. III]

LEGILLE v. DANN

United States Court of Appeals, District of Columbia Circuit, 1976.
544 F.2d 1.

SPOTTSWOOD W. ROBINSON, III, CIRCUIT JUDGE:

An application for a United States patent filed within twelve months after filing of an application for a foreign patent on the same invention is statutorily accorded the filing date of the foreign application and the effect thereof. If, however, the interval between the filings exceeds twelve months, patent protection in the United States may not be available. The practice of the Patent Office, unchallenged in this litigation, is to file the duplicating United States application upon receipt.

This appeal, by the Commissioner of Patents, brings to this court a controversy as to the filing date properly to be given four applications domestically mailed to the Patent Office in time for normal delivery

* See 9 Wigmore, Evidence chs. 89–90 (Chadbourn rev. 1981); McCormick, Evidence ch. 36 (4th ed. 1992); Allen, Structuring Jury Decisionmaking in Criminal Cases: A Unified Constitutional Approach to Evidentiary Devices, 94 Harv.L.Rev. 321 (1980); Allen, More on Constitutional Process-of-Proof Problems in Criminal Cases, 94 Harv.L.Rev. 1795 (1981); Allen, Presumptions in Civil Actions Reconsidered, 66 Iowa L.Rev. 844 (1981); Allen, Presumptions, Inferences and Burden of Proof in Federal Civil Actions—An Anatomy of Unnecessary Ambiguity and a Proposal for Reform, 76 Nw.U.L.Rev. 892 (1983); Cleary, Presuming and Pleading: An Essay in Juristic Immaturity, 12 Stan.L.Rev. 5 (1959); Gausewitz, Presumptions in a One–Rule World, 5 Vand.L.Rev. 324 (1952); Jeffries & Stephan, Defenses, Presumptions and Burden of Proof in the Criminal Law, 88 Yale L.J. 1325 (1979); Ladd, Presumptions in Civil Actions, 1977 Ariz.St. L.J. 275; Louisell, Construing Rule 301: Instructing the Jury on Presumptions in Civil Actions and Proceedings, 63 Va. L.Rev. 281 (1977); McBaine, Burden of Proof: Presumptions, 2 U.C.L.A.L.Rev. 13 (1954); McNaughton, Burden of Production of Evidence: A Function of the Burden of Persuasion, 68 Harv.L.Rev. 1382 (1955); Morgan, Some Observations Concerning Presumptions, 44 Harv.L.Rev. 906 (1931); Morgan, Presumptions, 12 Wash.L.Rev. 255 (1937); Nesson, Rationality, Presumptions and Judicial Comment: A Response to Professor Allen, 94 Harv.L.Rev. 1574 (1981).

before expiration of the twelve-month period but allegedly received thereafter. On cross-motions for summary judgment, the District Court, utilizing the familiar presumption of regularity of the mails, ruled in favor of the applicants. Our examination of the record, however, discloses potential evidence capable of dispelling the presumption and generating an issue of fact as to the date on which the applications arrived. We accordingly reverse the judgment and remand the case for trial.

I

From affidavits submitted in support of the motions for summary judgment, we reconstruct the facts apparently undisputed. On March 1, 1973, appellees' attorney mailed from East Hartford, Connecticut, to the Patent Office in Washington, D.C., a package containing four patent applications. Each of the applications had previously been filed in the Grand Duchy of Luxembourg, three on March 6, 1972, and the fourth on the following August 11. The package was marked "Airmail," bore sufficient airmail postage and was properly addressed. Delivery of air mail from East Hartford to Washington at that time was normally two days.

The applications were date-stamped "March 8, 1973," by the Patent Office. Each of the four applications was assigned that filing date on the ground that the stamped date was the date of receipt by the Patent Office. If the action of the Patent Office is to stand, three of appellees' applications, on which Luxembourg patents had been granted, fail in this country.

Appellees petitioned the Commissioner of Patents to reassign the filing date. The petition was denied. Appellees then sued in the District Court for a judgment directing the Commissioner to accord the applications a filing date not later than March 6, 1973. Both sides moved for summary judgment on the basis of the pleadings and affidavits respectively submitted. Not surprisingly, none of the affidavits reflected any direct evidence of the date on which the applications were actually delivered to the Patent Office.

The District Court correctly identified the central issue: "whether there exists a genuine issue of fact as to when these applications were received by the Patent Office." By the court's appraisal, appellees' suit was "predicated upon the legal presumption that postal employees discharge their duties in a proper manner and that properly addressed, stamped and deposited mail is presumed to reach the addressee in due course and without unusual delay, unless evidence to the contrary is proven." The court believed, however, that the Commissioner's position rested "primarily upon a presumption of procedural regularity based upon the normal manner, custom, practice and habit established for the handling of incoming mail at the Patent Office and upon the absence of evidence showing that the subject applications were not handled routinely in accordance with those established procedures." On this analysis, the court "concluded that the presumption relied upon by the [Commissioner] is insufficient to overcome the strong presumption that mails, properly addressed, having fully prepaid postage, and deposited in the proper receptacles, will be received by the addressee in the ordinary course of the mails." "This latter presumption," the court held, "can only be rebutted by proof of specific facts and not by invoking another presumption"; "the negative evidence in this case detailing the manner, custom, practice and habit of handling incoming mail by the Patent Office fails to overcome or rebut the strong presumption that the applications were timely delivered in the regular course of the mails to the Patent Office." In sum,

> [appellees] rely upon the strong presumption of the regularity of the mails to show that, in the normal course of postal business, these applications would be delivered within two days from March 1, 1973. [The Commissioner] does not show nor offer to show by way of any positive evidence that the presumption is inapplicable in this case. On the contrary, he relies on negative evidence as to custom, habit and usual procedure to create a conflicting presumption that the agency's business and procedure were followed in this case. Under the circumstances of this case, this Court holds, as a matter of law, that this presumption is insufficient to rebut or overcome the presumption of the regularity of the mails.

II

Proof that mail matter is properly addressed, stamped and deposited in an appropriate receptacle has long been accepted as evidence of delivery to the addressee. On proof of the foundation facts, innumerable cases recognize a presumption to that effect. Some presume more specifically that the delivery occurred in due course of the mails. The cases concede, however, that the presumption is rebuttable. We think the District Court erred in adhering to the presumption in the face of the evidentiary showing which the Commissioner was prepared to make.

Rebuttable presumptions [24] are rules of law attaching to proven evidentiary facts certain procedural consequences as to the opponent's duty to come forward with other evidence. In the instant case, the presumption would normally mean no more than that proof of proper airmailing of appellees' applications required a finding, in the absence of countervailing evidence, that they arrived at the Patent Office

24. We distinguish the presumption "of law"—the procedural rule dictating a factual conclusion in the absence of contrary evidence—from the presumption "of fact," which in reality is not a presumption at all, see 9 J. Wigmore, Evidence § 2491 at 288–289 (3d ed. 1940), and from the "conclusive" presumption, which is actually a substantive rule of law. See 9 J. Wigmore, Evidence § 2492 (3d ed. 1940); C. McCormick, Evidence § 342 at 804 (2d ed. 1972). We also differentiate presumptions from inferences, a dissimilarity which "is subtle, but not unreal. A presumption, sometimes called a presumption of law, is an inference which the law directs the [trier of fact] to draw if it finds a given set of facts; an inference is a conclusion which the [trier of fact] is *permitted,* but not compelled, to draw from the facts." Bray v. United States, 113 U.S.App.D.C. 136, 140, 306 F.2d 743, 747 (1962) (emphasis in original). See also Pendergrast v. United States, 135 U.S.App.D.C. 20, 32 n. 72, 416 F.2d 776, 788 n. 72, *cert. denied,* 395 U.S. 926, 89 S.Ct. 1782, 23 L.Ed.2d 243 (1969).

within the usual delivery time. There is abundant authority undergirding the proposition that, as a presumption, it did not remain viable in the face of antithetical evidence. As Dean Wigmore has explained, "the peculiar effect of a presumption 'of law' (that is, the real presumption) is merely to invoke a rule of law compelling the [trier of fact] to reach a conclusion in the absence of evidence to the contrary from the opponent. If the opponent does offer evidence to the contrary (sufficient to satisfy the judge's requirement of some evidence), the presumption disappears as a rule of law, and the case is in the [factfinder's] hands free from any rule." [29] As more poetically the explanation has been put, "[p]resumptions * * * may be looked on as the bats of the law, flitting in the twilight, but disappearing in the sunshine of actual facts." [30]

We are aware of the fact that this view of presumptions—the so-called "bursting bubble' theory [31]—has not won universal acclaim.[32] Nonetheless, it is the prevailing view, to which jurists preponderantly have subscribed; [33] it is the view of the Supreme Court,[34] and of this

29. 9 J. Wigmore, Evidence § 2491 at 289 (3d ed. 1940).

30. Stumpf v. Montgomery, 101 Okl. 257, 226 P. 65, 69, 32 A.L.R. 1490 (1924), quoting Mackowik v. Kansas City, St. J. & C.B.R.R., 196 Mo. 550, 94 S.W. 256, 262 (1906).

31. See, e.g., C. McCormick, Evidence § 345 at 821–826 (2d ed. 1972).

32. See, e.g., Morgan & McGuire, Looking Backward and Forward at Evidence, 50 Harv.L.Rev. 909, 913 (1937); Morgan, Instructing the Jury Upon Presumptions and Burden of Proof, 47 Harv.L.Rev. 59, 82–83 (1933); Gausewitz, Presumptions in a One-Rule World, 5 Vand.L.Rev. 324 (1952). Contra, Laughlin, In Support of the Thayer Theory of Presumptions, 52 Mich.L.Rev. 195 (1953). See also the discussion in C. McCormick, Evidence § 345 at 821–829 (2d ed. 1972).

33. See * * * cases collected at 9 J. Wigmore, Evidence §§ 2419 at 290–292 n. 6, 2519 at 431–432 n. 2 (3d ed. 1940), Supp. 1975 at 102–108, 197–198.

34. New York Life Ins. Co. v. Gamer, 303 U.S. 161, 170, 171, 58 S.Ct. 500, 503, 82 L.Ed. 726, 730, 731 (1938) (presumption of death by accident rather than by suicide "is not evidence and ceases upon the introduction of substantial proof to the contrary. * * * The presumption is not evidence and may not be given weight as evidence."); Del Vecchio v. Bowers, 296 U.S. 280, 286–287, 56 S.Ct. 190, 193, 80 L.Ed. 229, 233 (1935) (as to statute presuming, in absence of contrary evidence, that injury to employee was not occasioned by wilful intention to injure or kill himself, "[o]nce the employer has carried his burden by offering testimony sufficient to justify a finding of suicide, the presumption falls out of the case. It never had and cannot acquire the attribute of evidence in the claimant's favor [footnote omitted]. Its only office is to control the result where there is an entire lack of competent evidence. If the employer alone adduces evidence which tends to support the theory of suicide, the case must be decided upon that evidence. Where the claimant offers substantial evidence in opposition, * * * the issue must be resolved upon the whole body of proof pro and con [footnote omitted] * * *"); Mobile J. & K.C.R.R. v. Turnipseed, 219 U.S. 35, 42, 43, 31 S.Ct. 136, 137, 55 L.Ed. 78, 80 (1910) (effect of state statute, providing that proof of injury inflicted by operation of locomotives or cars by railroad shall be "*prima facie* evidence of the want of reasonable skill and care on the part of the servants of the company in reference to such injury," was "to provide that evidence of an injury arising from the actual operation of trains shall create an inference of negligence * * *. The only legal effect of this inference is to cast upon the railroad company the duty of producing some evidence to the contrary. When that is done the inference is at an end, and the question of negligence is one for the jury upon all of the evidence."); Lincoln v. French, 105 U.S. 614, 617, 26 L.Ed. 1189, 1190 (1881) ("[p]resumptions are indulged to supply the place of facts; they are never allowed against ascertained and established facts. When these appear, presumptions disappear.") See also Western &

court as well.[35] It is also the approach taken by the Model Code of Evidence [36] and, very importantly, by the newly-adopted Federal Rules of Evidence.[37] These considerations hardly leave us free to assume a contrary position. Beyond that, we perceive no legal or practical justification for preferring either of the two involved presumptions over the other.[39] In light of the Commissioner's showing on the motions for

A.R.R. v. Henderson, 279 U.S. 639, 49 S.Ct. 445, 73 L.Ed. 884 (1929).

35. Harlem Taxicab Ass'n v. Nemesh, 89 U.S.App.D.C. 123, 124, 191 F.2d 459, 461 (1951) ("[a]n association's name and insignia raise a presumption that it owns or controls a cab on which they appear, but this is decisive only in the absence of contrary evidence [citations omitted]. * * * When substantial evidence contrary to a presumption is introduced, the underlying facts that originally raised the presumption may or may not retain some degree of probative force as evidence but they no longer have any artificial or technical force; in other words, 'the presumption falls out of the case * * *' " [quoting Del Vecchio v. Bowers, supra note 34, 296 U.S. at 286, 56 S.Ct. at 193, 80 L.Ed. at 233]); Stone v. Stone, 78 U.S.App.D.C. 5, 7, 136 F.2d 761, 763 (1943) ("[i]n an action which challenges the conduct of a public officer, a presumption of law is indulged in his favor that his official duties were properly performed. Like other such presumptions, it disappears so soon as substantial countervailing evidence is introduced [footnote omitted]."); Rosenberg v. Murray, 73 App. D.C. 67, 68, 116 F.2d 552, 553 (1940) (statutory presumption that vehicle was driven with owner's consent "continues until there is credible evidence to the contrary, and ceases when there is uncontradicted proof that the automobile was not at the time being used with the owner's permission.").

36. American Law Institute, Model Code of Evidence, Rule 704(2) (1942).

37. "In all civil actions and proceedings not otherwise provided for by Act of Congress or by these rules, a presumption imposes on the party against whom it is directed the burden of going forward with evidence to rebut or meet the presumption, but does not shift to such party the burden of proof in the sense of the risk of nonpersuasion, which remains throughout the trial upon the party on whom it was originally cast." Fed.R.Evid. 301. The history of this provision portrays a fluctuating evolution. As originally proposed by the Supreme Court, the presumptions governed were given the effect of placing on the opposing party the burden of establishing the nonexistence of the presumed fact, and "[t]he so-called 'bursting bubble' theory, under which a presumption vanishes upon the introduction of evidence which would support a finding of the nonexistence of the presumed fact, even though not believed, [was] rejected as according presumptions too 'slight and evanescent' an effect." Advisory Committee's Note to original Rule 301. The House Committee on the Judiciary agreed, but substituted a shift in the burden of going forward in place of a shift of the burden of proof, and conferred evidentiary value on the presumption. H.R.Rep. No. 93–650, 93d Cong., 1st Sess. 7 (1973), U.S.Code Cong. & Admin.News 1974, p. 7075. The Senate Committee on the Judiciary felt, however, that "the House amendment is ill-advised. * * * 'Presumptions are not evidence, but ways of dealing with evidence.' [footnote omitted]. This treatment requires juries to perform the task of considering 'as evidence' facts upon which they have no direct evidence and which may confuse them in performance of their duties." S.Rep. No. 93–1277, 93d Cong., 2d Sess. 9–10 (1974), first quoting *Hearings on H.R. 2463 Before the Senate Committee on Judiciary,* 93d Cong., 2d Sess. 96 (1974) U.S.Code Cong. & Admin.News 1974, pp. 7051, 7056. The Senate Committee accordingly modified Rule 301 to its present form, and the Conference Committee adopted the Senate version. H.R.Rep. No. 93–1597, 93d Cong., 2d Sess. 5–6 (1974) U.S.Code Cong. & Admin.News 1974, p. 7098.

The District Court rendered its decision in the instant case long prior to the effective date of the Rules of Evidence, and prior to emergence of the final text. We do not reach the question whether, now that the Rules are operative, we should give Rule 301 per se application on this appeal. It is enough for present purposes simply to point to the anomaly of rendering a judicial decision on an approach that has become a thing of the past.

39. The presumption of due delivery of the mails is predicated upon the fixed methods and systematic operation of the postal service. 1 J. Wigmore, Evidence § 94 at 524 (3d ed. 1940). The presumption of regularity of the Patent Office's

summary judgment, then, we conclude that the District Court should have declined a summary disposition in favor of a trial.

III

Conservatively estimated, the Patent Office receives through the mails an average of at least 100,000 items per month. The procedures utilized for the handling of that volume of mail were meticulously described in an affidavit by an official of the Patent Office, whose principal duties included superintendence of incoming mail. Ordinary mail—other than special delivery, registered and certified—arrives at the Patent Office in bags, which are date-marked if the items contained were placed by the postal service in the Patent Office pouch earlier than the date of delivery of the bags. A number of readers open the wrappers, compare the contents against any included listing—such as a letter of transmittal or a return postcard—and note any discrepancy, and apply to at least the principal included paper a stamp recording thereon the receipt date and the reader's identification number. Another employee then applies to the separate papers the official mailroom stamp, which likewise records the date; the two stamps are used in order to minimize the chance of error. The date recorded in each instance is the date on which the Patent Office actually receives the particular bag of mail, or a previous date when the bag is so marked. From every indication, the affidavit avers, appellees' applications were not delivered to the Patent Office until March 8, 1973.

We cannot agree with the District Court that an evidentiary presentation of this caliber would do no more than raise "a presumption of procedural regularity" in the Patent Office. Certainly it would accomplish that much; it would cast upon appellees the burden of producing contradictory evidence, but its effect would not be exhausted at that point. The facts giving rise to the presumption would also have evidentiary force, and as evidence would command the respect normally accorded proof of any fact. In other words, the evidence reflected by the affidavit, beyond creation of a presumption of regularity in date-stamping incoming mail, would have probative value on the issue of date of receipt of appellees' applications; and even if the presumption were dispelled, that evidence would be entitled to consideration, along with appellees' own evidence, when a resolution of the issue is undertaken. And, clearly, a fact-finder convinced of the integrity of the Patent Office's mail-handling procedures would inexorably be led to the conclusion that appellees' applications simply did not arrive until the date which was stamped on them.

handling of incoming mail, text infra at note 50, rests on exactly the same phenomena. In sum, both presumptions have a common origin in regularity of action. Id. § 92; see C. McCormick, Evidence § 343 at 807–808 (2d ed. 1972). We see nothing suggesting that the methodology buttressing the one is any more or less foolproof than that underpinning the other. We are mindful that some presumptions are founded in part upon exceptionally strong and visible policies, which have been said to persist despite proof rebutting the factual basis for the presumption. See, e.g., C. McCormick, Evidence § 345 at 822–823 (2d ed. 1972). The answer here is that from aught that appears the policy reflections are in equilibrium.

In the final analysis, the District Court's misstep was the treatment of the parties' opposing affidavits as a contest postulating a question of law as to the relative strength of the two presumptions rather than as a prelude to conflicting evidence necessitating a trial. Viewed as the mere procedural devices we hold that they are, presumptions are incapable of waging war among themselves.[58] Even more importantly, the court's disposition of the case on a legal ruling disregarded the divergent inferences which the evidentiary tenders warranted, and consequently the inappropriateness of a resolution of the opposing claims by summary judgment. As only recently we said, "[t]he court's function is not to resolve any factual issue, but to ascertain whether any exists, and all doubts in that regard must be resolved against summary judgment." [60] Here the District Court was presented with an issue of material fact as to the date on which appellees' applications were received by the Patent Office, and summary judgment was not in order.

The judgment appealed from is accordingly reversed, and the case is remanded to the District Court for further proceedings. The cross-motions for summary judgment will be denied, and the case will be set down for trial on the merits in regular course.

So ordered.

FAHY, SENIOR CIRCUIT JUDGE (dissenting):

I am in essential agreement with Judge Waddy of the District Court. The evidence reflected in the affidavit relied upon by the Patent Office in my opinion is not sufficient to overcome the strong presumption arising from the evidence reflected in the affidavits filed by appellee—a presumption of law that the applications were received by the Patent Office in regular course of the mails, that is, not later than March 6, 1973:

> Where, as in this case, matter is transmitted by the United States mails, properly addressed and postage fully prepaid, there is a strong presumption that it will be received by the addressee in the ordinary course of the mails. Henderson v. Carbondale Coal & Coke Co., 140 U.S. 25, 11 S.Ct. 691, 35 L.Ed. 332 * * *; Crude Oil Corp. v. Commissioner, 10 Cir., 161 F.2d 809, 810. While the presumption is a rebut-

58. "[P]resumptions do not conflict. The evidentiary facts, free from any rule of law as to the duty of producing evidence, may tend to opposite inferences, which may be said to conflict. But the rule of law which prescribes this duty of production either is or is not at a given time upon a given party. If it is, and he removes it by producing contrary evidence, then that presumption, as a rule of law, is satisfied and disappears; he may then by his evidence succeed in creating another presumption which now puts the same duty upon the other party, who may in turn be able to dispose of it satisfactorily. But the same duty cannot at the same time exist for both parties, and thus in strictness the presumptions raising the duty cannot conflict. There may be successive shiftings of the duty, by means of presumptions successively invoked by each; but it is not the one presumption that overturns the other, for the mere introduction of sufficient evidence would have the same effect in stopping the operation of the presumption as a rule of law." 9 J. Wigmore, Evidence § 2493 at 292 (3d ed. 1940).

60. Bouchard v. Washington, 168 U.S.App.D.C. 402, 405, 514 F.2d 824, 827 (1975). * * *

table one it is a very strong presumption and can only be rebutted by specific facts and not by invoking another presumption.

Arkansas Motor Coaches v. Commissioner of Internal Revenue, 198 F.2d 189, 191 (8th Cir.1952). * * *

E.L. CHEENEY CO. v. GATES, 346 F.2d 197, 202 (5th Cir.1965). "In Houston News Company v. Shavers, supra, many times expressly approved, Judge, later Justice Alexander for the Court of Civil Appeals described this presumption as 'a mere rule of procedure.' And, the Court went on, 'the presumption vanishes when positive evidence to the contrary is introduced.' Judge Alexander then reduced it to terms which all lawyers, certainly those artificers who labor in the courtroom, would understand with pained recollections. 'The effect of the rule is to "smoke out" the defendant and to compel him to disclose the true facts within his knowledge. When, however, he discloses the true facts within his possession and such evidence is positive to the effect that the servant was not engaged in the master's business at the time of the injury, the presumption is nullified and the burden is then upon the plaintiff to produce other evidence or his cause fails.' 64 S.W.2d 384, 386."

CHARLESTON NATIONAL BANK v. HENNESSY, 404 F.2d 539, 543 (5th Cir.1968). "The presumption of negligence arising from a rear-end collision was applicable, even though both automobiles were moving. Stephens v. Dichtenmueller, 207 So.2d 718 (Fla.Dist.Ct.App.1968); see also Shaw v. York, 187 So.2d 397 (Fla.D.C.App.1966); Busbee v. Quarrier, 172 So.2d 17 (Fla.Dist.Ct.App.1965); Rianhard v. Rice, 119 So.2d 730 (Fla.Dist.Ct.App.1960). Once the presumption came into existence the plaintiff had satisfied his burden of non-persuasion of the jury. The obligation was then cast upon the defendant to produce 'evidence which fairly and reasonably tends to show that the real fact [i.e., negligence of Samples] is not as presumed.' If the defendant did so the impact of the presumption was dissipated. Whether the defendant had produced such evidence was for the court, a matter of satisfying the judge (though not with a preponderance), not a matter of persuading the jury. The appellant did not produce evidence 'fairly and reasonably tending to show' that Samples was not negligent as presumed. The defense of heart attack, or some other unexpected, unforeseen, and unidentified physical or mental catastrophe, never arose above a scintilla at most, conjecture and speculation at least. The trial court should have instructed the jury that the presumption of negligence required a verdict for the plaintiff."

RYAN v. METROPOLITAN LIFE INS. CO., 206 Minn. 562, 289 N.W. 557, 560–61 (1939). "There is authority that presumptions are evidence. Annot., 103 A.L.R. 185, 191. But the weight of judicial conclusion is the other way. Idem. We deny probative weight for the presumption against suicide. Scott v. Prudential Ins. Co., 203 Minn. 547, 282 N.W. 467.

"The function of a presumption, as shown first by Thayer and then by Wigmore, (Thayer, Preliminary Treatise on Evidence, 339; 5 Wigmore, Evidence, 2 ed. §§ 2490, 2491) is solely to control decision on a group of unopposed facts. Given death from violence, without more, decision must be that it was accidental. So also an unexplained and otherwise unexplainable absence for seven years compels decision that the person is dead. In such cases there is nothing for the jury. Decision is controlled by a rule of law. That is the true and limited function of a presumption. It controls rather than permits, decision.

"With us a presumption does not shift the burden of proof. McAlpine v. Fidelity & Casualty Co., 134 Minn. 192, 158 N.W. 967; Topinka v. Minnesota Mutual Life Ins. Co., 189 Minn. 75, 248 N.W. 660, 95 A.L.R. 739. This seems to be the point at which Mr. Morgan disagrees with the Thayer–Wigmore doctrine. His conclusion is that there should be a general rule, by 'uniform statute' if need be, 'that the sole effect of every presumption shall be to place upon the opponent the burden of persuading the trier of fact of the nonexistence of the presumed fact.' Morgan & Maguire, 'Looking Backward and Forward at Evidence.' 50 Harv.L.Rev. 909, 913.

"A presumption may and frequently does shift the burden of going on with the evidence. That is to say only that it makes a prima facie case. If the trial stops there, without further evidence opposing the case so made, there is nothing for the jury. By nonsuit or directed verdict, the judge decides the issue as one of law. If, however, the prima facie case is met by adequate evidence, the case goes to the jury with the burden of proof where it was in the beginning. So the presumption is properly appraised as a mere 'procedural device' for allocation of the burden of going on with evidence. Where no further evidence is forthcoming, it requires decision as matter of law for the unopposed prima facie case. That view has long been widely held. It has the support of preponderant authority. Note, 114 A.L.R. 1226. * * *

"It follows that if the case is one for the jurors the presumption should not be submitted as something to which they may attach probative force. The weight of the evidence is for them, to be ascertained on the scales of their experience and their judgment, rather than those of the judge. It would be an intrusion into their field to suggest that they substitute for any real evidence, or any reasonable inference therefrom, the assumed weight of something which is not evidence. A presumption not being evidence, it should be no more subject for such an instruction than any other non-evidentiary factor.

* * *

"Being unable to find any legitimate purpose to be served by an instruction allowing the jury to give weight to a presumption as of law, in addition to the facts on which it is based, we hold such direction improper. The jury gets all the facts. Theirs is the exclusive function of reasonable inference therefrom. In addition they should not get, ready made from the court, a deduction to which they are authorized to attach independent probative value. To allow that would be to assign evidentiary value to that which is not evidence."

EDMUND M. MORGAN, PRESUMPTIONS, 12 Wash.L.Rev. 255, 257 (1937). "* * * [D]ifferent considerations call different presumptions into existence. (1) Some are designed to expedite the trial by relieving a party from introducing evidence upon issues which may not be litigated. For example, why does a court which put upon the prosecution the burden of proving a defendant's sanity beyond a reasonable doubt, at the same time give the prosecution the benefit of a presumption of sanity? Simply to avoid the waste of time and effort required to take evidence on an issue which, aside from statute, is raised by the plea of not guilty but in most cases will not be raised by evidence. The defendant must at least show that the question raised by the pleadings is to be litigated in the evidence. (2) In some cases a presumption may be necessary to avoid a procedural impasse. Where a court has a fund to be distributed, and the determination of the rights of conflicting claimants depends upon the date of the death of X, it may be established that X disappeared more than seven years before action was brought; this raises a presumption of his death, but by the orthodox view raises no presumption as to the date of death. If he died soon after his disappearance, A will take. If he died between four and six years after his disappearance, B will take; if later, C will take. In the absence of evidence and of any presumption as to date of death, the court simply cannot decide the case. This has led some courts to raise a presumption of death on the last instant of the seventh year. (3) Some presumptions are based upon a preponderance of probability. Indeed, Mr. Justice Holmes once said that all true presumptions have such a foundation. To save time, it is well for the court to compel the trier of fact to assume the usual and to require the party relying upon the unusual to show that he has at least enough evidence to make its existence reasonably probable. (4) In some instances there will be the added element of difficulty in securing legally competent evidence in cases of the particular class. This is exemplified in the common law rule that a long continued exercise of what would be a right if properly originated raises a presumption of a legally created right. (5) Another group of presumptions owe their origin to the fact that one of the parties has peculiar means of access to the evidence or peculiar knowledge of the facts. For example, at common law, where freight is delivered in good order to an initial carrier and is delivered in bad order to the consignee by the terminal carrier, although it may have been transported over the lines of several connecting carriers, the presumption is that the damage was done by the terminal carrier. Here, there is no procedural convenience or preponderance of probability or general inaccessibility of evidence to call forth the presumption, but as between consignee and carrier, the last carrier has peculiar means of access to the facts. (6) Again, many presumptions express the result that the courts creating them deem them socially desirable. This causes such courts to require the trier to assume the existence of that result in the absence of any showing to the contrary. The stock illustration has already been given, namely, that a right enjoyed by usage for a long period is presumed to have had a legal origin. That the judicial conviction of social desirability was the chief reason for this presumption is shown by its evolution from a mere inference through a presumption to a hard and fast rule of law which gives to adverse possession for the prescribed period the effect of creating a new title. (7) Finally, many, if not most, of the generally recognized presumptions are supported by two or more of the foregoing. The presumption that a child born in wedlock is the legitimate child of the husband, for instance, is supported by a heavy preponderance of probability, by the consideration of difficulty in producing legally competent evidence of the paternity of a child born to a married woman, and by considerations of policy predicated upon a society in which the family is the fundamental unit, the institution by which the devolution of property is determined, and as to the intimate aspects of which accepted notions of decency and propriety demand a discreet secrecy."

MATTER OF ESTATE OF McGOWAN

Supreme Court of Nebraska, 1977.
197 Neb. 596, 250 N.W.2d 234.

McCown, Justice.

This is an action to contest the admission of a will to probate on the grounds of lack of testamentary capacity and undue influence * * *.

* * *

The jury found in favor of the proponent and against the contestants upon the issues of mental competency and undue influence. The District Court entered judgment affirming the order of the county court admitting the will to probate.

The contentions of the contestants on this appeal rest on the assertion that the instructions to the jury erroneously placed the burden on the contestants to prove undue influence. The argument is grounded on the assumption that the evidence was sufficient to establish a presumption of undue influence, and that under the provisions of section 27–301, R.R.S.1943, the establishment of the presumption shifted the burden of proof from the contestants to the proponent and the instructions were therefore erroneous. The critical issues involve the effect of section 27–301, R.R.S.1984, and whether it applies to a "presumption" of undue influence in the making and execution of a will.

Section 27–301, R.R.S.1943, is a part of the Nebraska Evidence Rules adopted by the Legislature in 1975, and is effective as to all trials commenced after December 31, 1975. That section provides: "In all cases not otherwise provided for by statute or by these rules a presumption imposes on the party against whom it is directed the burden of proving that the nonexistence of the presumed fact is more probable than its existence."

Prior to the effective date of section 27–301, R.R.S.1943, the effect of a presumption in Nebraska was only to shift the burden of going forward with the evidence, and the burden of proof or persuasion did not shift. When evidence was introduced to rebut the presumption, the presumption disappeared. The presumption was not evidence itself but only sustained the burden of proof until evidence rebutting the presumption was introduced. In re Estate of Goist, 146 Neb. 1, 18 N.W.2d 513; Loomis v. Estate of Davenport, 192 Neb. 461, 222 N.W.2d 369.

The Nebraska Evidence Rules, including section 27–301, R.R.S.1943, were essentially the same as the then *proposed* Federal Rules of Evidence, but were adopted by the Nebraska Legislature prior to the final adoption of the federal rules by Congress. When Congress finally adopted the federal rules later in the same year, Rule 301 was completely changed. Instead of the language of section 27–301, R.R.S.1943, Rule 301 of Public Law 93–595 reads: "In all civil actions and proceedings not otherwise provided for by Act of Congress or by these rules, a presumption imposes on the party against whom it is directed the burden of going forward with evidence to rebut or meet the presumption, but does not shift to such party the burden of proof in the sense of the risk of nonpersuasion, which remains throughout the trial upon the party on whom it was originally cast." In essence, the new federal rule is the former Nebraska rule. Although the Nebraska Legislature adopted the proposed version of federal Rule 301, it did not adopt the special section on the procedural effect of that rule. Neither the Nebraska rules nor the federal rules define or prescribe what constitutes a presumption within the meaning of Rule 301.

A presumption is a standardized practice under which certain facts are held to call for uniform treatment with respect to their effect as proof of other facts. McCormick on Evidence (2d ed.), § 342, p. 802. The same authority suggests that "presumption" is the slipperiest member of the family of legal terms, except its first cousin, "burden of proof." Reasons for the creation of presumptions are numerous and the treatment of presumptions also differs widely. There are at least eight senses in which the term has been used by courts. The former Nebraska approach to presumptions is ordinarily referred to as the "bursting bubble" theory. Under that approach when evidence was introduced to rebut the presumption, the presumption disappeared and the burden of proof or persuasion did not shift. Under such a rule whether a particular set of basic facts gave rise to the dignity of a presumption was ordinarily not critical in the matter of instructing a jury after trial. What was many times referred to as a "presumption" was often merely a permissible or probable inference, or was a method of indicating that the evidence was sufficient to withstand a motion for a directed verdict or to constitute a prima facie case. In terms of instructions to the jury the new rule poses far greater problems. An additional problem is posed in a case such as this because the presumed fact of undue influence is also the ultimate fact to be determined by the jury.

Ordinarily the basic facts which give rise to a true presumption are specific and definite. They can be readily determined and uniformly applied. That is not the case with the so-called presumption of undue influence in Nebraska. An analysis of the Nebraska cases demonstrates that the basic facts which have been held to give rise to a presumption of undue influence in the making of a will have not been specific nor definite nor uniform. Instead the basic facts have themselves varied, and have been formulated from the facts and circumstances of each particular case. Almost without exception we have used the term "presumption" in connection with undue influence to mean that the evidence was sufficient to constitute a prima facie case or to withstand a motion for a directed verdict. In most instances the term "presumption" seems to have been intended to mean a permissible or probable inference when used in undue influence cases.

The Report of the Committee on Practice and Procedure in connection with the proposed Nebraska Rules of Evidence confirms the conclusion that this court can place the burden of proof in the first place, or hold that a particular set of basic facts does not rise to the dignity of a presumption under the rule. It is also obvious that situations which have previously been referred to as presumptions when only permissible or probable inference was meant, or those where the term "presumption" was used to indicate that the basic facts were sufficient to constitute a prima facie case or to withstand a motion for directed verdict, are cases which may be excluded from the operation of the rule. See Proposed Nebraska Rules of Evidence, Article III, Presumptions, p. 35 (1973).

We therefore hold that under Nebraska law a so-called "presumption of undue influence" is not a presumption within the ambit and meaning of section 27–301, R.R.S.1943.

The policy considerations which support the right of a competent testator to dispose of his property at death by a duly executed will also demand that the burden of proof on the issue of undue influence be placed upon the party contesting the will. We therefore hold that in a will contest the burden of proof or the risk of nonpersuasion on the issue of undue influence is on the contestant and remains there throughout the trial.

* * *

AFFIRMED.

Note

Compare In re Estate of Malnar, 73 Wis.2d 192, 243 N.W.2d 435 (1976).

CHARLES T. McCORMICK, CHARGES ON PRESUMPTIONS AND BURDEN OF PROOF, 5 N.C.L.Rev. 291, 295 (1927). "What is the effect of a 'presumption' upon this process of whipping up the respective parties to produce evidence, this 'duty' which shifts from one side to the other like a tennis ball in play? * * * A presumption is a standardized practice, under which certain oft-recurring fact-groupings are held to call for uniform treatment whenever they occur, with respect to their effect as proof to support issues. Admittedly, as we have seen, proof of one class of type-situation (e.g., delivery of a shipment in good condition to a carrier, and its delivery by the carrier at destination in a damaged state) may by a rule of practice, be recognized as calling for a ruling that the producer of the proof has gone forward far enough to 'get to the jury' on the inference (damage by acts of the carrier) which is desired. Every judge in every case should so rule, and he is relieved of the usual necessity of critically considering the rational permissibility of the inference. But we have also seen that in another class of fact-groupings (e.g., the facts of the mailing of a letter properly stamped and addressed offered to show receipt by the addressee) the standardized practice to be automatically applied by the judge is to rule that the proof of the particular recognized group of facts is *conclusive,* that is, the inference is not to be weighed by judge or jury, but if the circumstantial facts are undisputed, or if disputed are found to be true, the conclusion follows as a matter of law provided no counter-proof is offered. Does a 'presumption' give its beneficiary the right to the first of these rulings, the *permission* to the jury to infer, or to the second, the *compulsion* to find (in the absence of contrary proof) without weighing the inference? Very few of the decisions discuss this distinction, because very seldom does the adversary fail to produce some counterproof, so that the effect of the stark fact-groups, standing alone, seldom comes in issue. Thayer, Wigmore, and Chamberlayne, the great triumvirate of law-writers on Evidence, unite in attributing to the 'presumption' the (provisionally) *compulsory* effect. Many judicial definitions are in accord. On the other hand, many decisions which hold merely that the group of facts considered was *sufficient* to warrant the desired inference, describe the result as a 'presumption'. In this latter sense a presumption is the same as a 'prima facie case.' Probably the best practical treatment of the problem of nomenclature is to recognize the word 'presumption' as a collective term embracing both varieties of procedural rules, but to distinguish the two as *permissive* presumptions, and *mandatory* presumptions. The recognition of permissive presumptions as true presumptions is a departure from the language of the textbooks, but accords with actual judicial usage."

TRUJILLO v. CHAVEZ

Court of Appeals of New Mexico, 1979.
93 N.M. 626, 603 P.2d 736.

LOPEZ, JUDGE.

This action was brought in the District Court of Bernalillo County to recover damages resulting from an automobile accident. After a jury trial, a verdict was returned denying recovery both on plaintiff Leonella Trujillo's complaint and defendant Virginia Chavez' counterclaim. Chavez is the executrix of the estate of A.T. Montoya; Montoya died in the accident. * * *

* * *

CHAVEZ APPEAL

Chavez argues that the court erred in submitting two instructions to the jury concerning the presumption arising from ownership of an automobile. These instructions were numbered 25 and 26 and read:

> 25. If after considering the evidence, you are unable to determine based upon credible and substantial evidence who was driving the automobile at the time of the accident, then the law provides that the owner is presumed to be the operator of the vehicle. Therefore, if you are unable to decide that there is sufficient evidence to allow a reasonable mind to accept is [sic] adequate to support a conclusion concerning who was driving the vehicle, you may accept the legal presumption that the Defendant, decedent, being the owner of the vehicle was the driver of the vehicle.
>
> 26. The presumption referred to in the last instruction disappears and ceases to exist if you find credible and substantial evidence which would support a contrary finding.

Until the adoption of the Rules of Evidence in 1973, the law in New Mexico was that a presumption ceases to exist upon the introduction of evidence which would support a finding of its nonexistence. Hartford Fire Insurance Co. v. Horne, 65 N.M. 440, 338 P.2d 1067 (1959); Morrison v. Rodey, 65 N.M. 474, 340 P.2d 409 (1959); Morris v. Cartwright, 57 N.M. 328, 258 P.2d 719 (1953); Payne v. Tuozzoli, 80 N.M. 214, 453 P.2d 384 (Ct.App.1969). This theory of presumptions, known as the "bursting bubble" theory, is not proper under the Rules of Evidence adopted by the New Mexico Supreme Court. According to the Commentary to Rule 301 of the Advisory Committee which prepared and submitted the proposed federal rule of evidence (which New Mexico adopted), the "bursting bubble" theory is inconsistent with Federal Rule of Evidence 301.

> The so-called "bursting bubble theory, under which a presumption vanishes upon the introduction of evidence which would support a

finding of the nonexistence of the presumed fact, even though not believed, is rejected as according presumptions too "slight and evanescent" an effect.

"The disappearance of the presumption upon the presentation of contrary evidence was eliminated, however, when the 1973 Rules of Evidence were adopted." State Farm Mutual Automobile Insurance Co. v. Duran, No. 3678, 93 N.M. 489, 601 P.2d 722 (Ct.App.1979). The cases listed above, to the extent they are contrary to Evidence Rule 301, are no longer applicable.

Instruction 26 directs the jury that the presumption disappears if there is credible and substantial evidence to support its nonexistence. This is a proper formulation of the "bursting bubble" theory of presumptions. Since this theory is no longer applicable in New Mexico, the instruction is erroneous.

N.M.R.Evid. 301, N.M.S.A.1978 states:

> In all cases not otherwise provided for by statute or by these rules, a presumption imposes on the party against whom it is directed the burden of proving that the nonexistence of the presumed fact is more probable than its existence.

The effect, then, of Evidence Rule 301 is to shift the burden of persuasion.

> Presumptions governed by this rule are given the effect of placing upon the opposing party the burden of establishing the nonexistence of the presumed fact, once the party invoking the presumption establishes the basic facts giving rise to it.

Advisory Committee's Note to Federal Evidence Rule 301.

Although New Mexico Evidence Rule 301 is silent on whether the jury is to be instructed concerning presumptions, it is logical that the jury should be informed who has the burden of persuasion, as it is in other instances where presumptions are not involved. This is also the opinion of the draftsmen of the New Jersey Evidence Code, which contains a rule similar to our Rule 301 giving presumptions the effect of shifting the burden of persuasion. The New Jersey Committee suggests that "the instructions would be phrased entirely in terms of assuming facts and burden of proof." New Jersey Supreme Court Committee on Evidence 51 (1963), *quoted in* 1 Weinstein, Evidence, ¶ 301[02], at 301–32 (1978).

The jury must also be informed of the presumption, if it is to give the presumption any effect. Insofar as evidence against a presumed fact must be weighed for its credibility, the jury must be informed of the presumption in order that it may be given effect if it rejects the evidence in question. Annot., 5 A.L.R.3d 19 at 45 (1966). However, to avoid unduly influencing the jury, the word "presumption" should be avoided.

> [T]he specific instruction should avoid using the word "presumption" because of the danger that the jury will mistakenly attribute effects to

> this term other than those described by the judge and prescribed by Rule 301.

Weinstein, supra, 301–34.

This does not mean that a reversal is warranted because a court mentions the dreaded word "presumption." Weinstein, supra, at 301–28. The complaining party would still have to demonstrate prejudice by use of the word. However, because "presumption" is such a technical term, the better practice is to describe the presumption in terms of assumed facts and burden of proof.

In civil cases the effect of a presumption that is not rebutted is disputed. The states are split on whether, once evidence establishing the presumption has been introduced, and in the absence of persuasive evidence to the contrary, the jury *must,* or *may,* find the presumed fact true. The view in New Mexico is that the jury must find the presumed fact true if evidence to the contrary has not been introduced. *Hartford Insurance Co.,* supra.

Rule 301 does not change the requirement that the jury must find the presumed fact true, in certain circumstances. It merely changes the circumstances in which this finding must be made. Formerly, the jury was required to find the presumed fact true only when no credible and substantial evidence which would support a contrary finding was introduced. *Hartford,* supra. Under Evidence Rule 301, the jury is required to so find, only when the party against whom the presumption operates fails to persuade the jury that the nonexistence of the presumed fact is more probable than its existence.

The view that the jury should be required to find the presumed fact, if sufficient evidence to the contrary is not adduced, is implicit in the jury instructions suggested by the New Jersey Supreme Court Committee on Evidence.

> Where the existence of the basic facts is to be determined by the jury, "the judge must instruct that if the jury finds the basic fact, they *must* also find the presumed fact unless persuaded by the evidence that its nonexistence is more probable than its existence" Morgan, supra at 42 * * *. (Emphasis added.)

Quoted in Weinstein, supra at 301–32. This view is also implicit in the instructions suggested by Weinstein and Prof. Morgan. See generally, Weinstein, supra; Morgan, Instructing the Jury upon Presumptions and Burden of Proof, 47 Harv.L.Rev. 59 (1933). There is no constitutional infirmity in requiring the jury, in civil cases, to find the presumed fact true if it has not been controverted by a showing that its nonexistence is more probable than its existence. Dick v. New York Life Insurance Co., 359 U.S. 437, 79 S.Ct. 921, 3 L.Ed.2d 935 (1959).

From this discussion, four considerations emerge. (1) The effect of a presumption, under Evidence Rule 301, is to place the burden of proof on the party against whom the presumption operates. The jury should be instructed where the burden of proof lies. (2) The failure of the party on whom the burden of proof has fallen to show that it is *more probable than not* that the presumed fact does *not* exist results in the presumption becoming effective. The jury is the body that weighs the evidence and decides if this party has met his burden. (3) The use of the word "presumption" is to be avoided as it is more likely to confuse than to aid the jury. (4) The jury must find the presumed fact true if, (a) the jury is persuaded of the existence of the basic fact from which the presumed fact is inferred, and (b) the party against whom the presumption operates has failed to show that the nonexistence of the presumed fact is more probable than its existence.

Instruction 25 does not properly instruct on presumptions under Evidence Rule 301. It fails to explain that the burden of proof is on Chavez to show that it is more probable than not that Montoya, the undisputed owner of the car, was not driving at the time of the accident; and it does not clearly inform the jury of the consequences of Chavez' failure to show this. Also, the jury was instructed that it *might* find the presumption to be true, whereas the law in civil cases in New Mexico is that the jury *must* find the presumption true if the party opposing the presumption has not met his burden of proof. Instructions 25 and 26 were erroneous. A better instruction for this case would have been:

> Because the evidence is undisputed that Montoya was the owner of the car in which he was riding at the time of the accident, you must find that Montoya was the driver unless Montoya's estate has proved that it is more probable that he was not driving than that he was driving. The proof required of Montoya's estate in this instruction is in addition to the burden of proof placed on the parties in other instructions.

Chavez also contends that the trial court erred in admitting testimony concerning a statement made by an unknown bystander. This statement was offered to prove that Montoya was driving at the time of the accident. Chavez claims that the statement was hearsay and not admissible under any of the exceptions to the hearsay rule. She argues that the court, in admitting this testimony, committed reversible error. We agree.

* * *

Based upon the foregoing, we reverse the judgment and order of the court denying Chavez' motion for a new trial, and we remand this cause for a new trial.

IT IS SO ORDERED.

WOOD, CHIEF JUDGE (specially concurring).

I concur in Judge Lopez's opinion. This special concurrence goes only to Evidence Rule 301 and its practical effect.

1. The Estate appealed, challenging the propriety of the presumption instructions. It relied on the New Mexico law prior to the adoption of Evidence Rule 301. Under that prior law, the instructions

should not have been given because there was credible and substantial evidence which would have supported a finding that Montoya was not driving the car. With this evidence, the presumption disappeared. Hartford Fire Insurance Company v. Horne, 65 N.M. 440, 338 P.2d 1067 (1959). Evidence Rule 301, however, changed the law. Under Evidence Rule 301, the Estate had a burden of persuasion which it did not have prior to adoption of the evidence rule. The Estate is in no position to complain of the instructions given because those instructions imposed less of a burden on the Estate than should have been imposed pursuant to Evidence Rule 301. Significantly, Judge Lopez does not hold that the erroneous instructions amounted to reversible error.

2. Judge Lopez's opinion points out that the fact finder, in this case the jury, must decide whether the party against whom the presumption is directed has proved that the nonexistence of the presumed fact is more probable than its existence. Evidence Rule 301. This rule does not change the trial judge's function of deciding whether there is sufficient evidence for the jury to determine whether this burden has been met. The standard for determining whether the evidence is sufficient to raise a jury issue is the same standard used in determining whether a verdict should be directed. 1 Weinstein's Evidence (1978) ¶ 301[02], page 301–30. Thus, if there are conflicts in the evidence going to the probability of the nonexistence of the presumed fact, it is for the jury to determine whether the burden has been met. See Hayes v. Reeves, 91 N.M. 174, 571 P.2d 1177 (1977); Skyhook Corp. v. Jasper, 90 N.M. 143, 560 P.2d 934 (1977).

3. In this case the evidence that Montoya owned the car was uncontradicted. In a case where the evidence of ownership was conflicting, a factual determination of ownership would have to be made. Until it was determined as a fact that an occupant of the car was the owner, the presumption would not be applicable. Where the evidence of ownership is conflicting, the jury must be instructed that the presumption (or assumed fact) does not exist until the basic fact of the presumption has been found to exist. Since such an instruction would go only to a part of the case, will the jury be confused in applying it?

4. In this case, the "burden" of Evidence Rule 301 does not add to the Estate's problems of persuasion because the Estate counterclaimed. Under the counterclaim, the Estate was required to prove that Trujillo was the driver. But what if there were no counterclaim and no affirmative defense which involved the question of who was the driver? The defense would have a burden of proof under Evidence Rule 301, and the jury instructions would have to distinguish between the burdens on plaintiff and defendant. No matter how carefully instructed, the allocation of different burdens has the potential for confusing the jury, particularly so when one of the burdens involves proof of the probability of a negative.

5. Another problem, settled in New Mexico concerning the presumption of validity of marriage, see Panzer v. Panzer, 87 N.M. 29, 528

P.2d 888 (1974), involves conflicting presumptions. If other conflicting presumptions should arise, and I suspect they will, see Wood, *The Community Property Law of New Mexico* (1954) § 27 and Myers v. Kapnison, 93 N.M. 215, 598 P.2d 1175 (Ct.App.1978) how are they to be handled under Evidence Rule 301? Weinstein, supra, ¶ 301[03] suggests the question is an open one.

6. Evidence Rule 301 was not discussed in Archibeque v. Homrich, 88 N.M. 527, 543 P.2d 820 (1975). Compare opinion of Judge Hernandez in the same case, 87 N.M. 265, 531 P.2d 1238 (Ct.App.1975). The facts of *Archibeque* suggest a case for application of the presumption involved in this case; however, res ipsa loquitur was involved. Gausewitz, Presumptions in a One–Rule World, 5 Vand.L.Rev. 324 at 333 (1952) states: "Since a presumption is by definition mandatory, a verdict must be directed that the presumed fact exists if the presumption is not rebutted. One instance of a departure may be the case of *res ipsa loquitur.*" Is the res ipsa doctrine an exception to Evidence Rule 301? The rule does not state any exceptions.

7. New Mexico appellate decisions have recognized the change effected by the adoption of Evidence Rule 301. Panzer v. Panzer, supra; State Farm Mutual Automobile Ins. Co. v. Duran, 93 N.M. 489, 601 P.2d 722 (Ct.App.1979). However, compare Garmond v. Kinney, 91 N.M. 646, 579 P.2d 178 (1978). Although a burden of persuasion approach is the "rule" in New Mexico, alongside that rule is a decision giving evidentiary effect to the presumption of insanity. State v. Wilson, 85 N.M. 552, 514 P.2d 603 (1973). See State v. Santillanes, 91 N.M. 721, 580 P.2d 489 (Ct.App.1978) where this special evidentiary effect was recognized, but where the presumption rule for criminal cases, Evidence Rule 303, was not discussed. Compare Trefzer v. Stiles, 56 N.M. 296, 243 P.2d 605 (1952) with Hartford Fire Insurance Company v. Horne, supra. Weinstein, supra, page 301–5 indicates that giving a presumption an evidentiary effect is "obvious nonsense." My point in this paragraph, simply, is that Evidence Rule 301 may not be "*the* rule" where the presumption of insanity is involved.

8. Eminent writers have supported the burden of persuasion approach adopted in Evidence Rule 301. I, of course, must apply that rule. Alexander v. Delgado, 84 N.M. 717, 507 P.2d 778 (1973). Paragraphs 3 through 7 raise, for me, the question of whether the logic of the various writers, see Weinstein, supra, pages 300–1 to 301–17, has led to the adoption of a rule which causes more problems than it solves, which has the potential of causing the most careful trial judge to err in the instructions given, and which has the potential to confuse a jury. New Mexico adopted, as its rule, the wording proposed by the drafting committee. Both Houses of Congress rejected the same language. See Weinstein, supra, pages 301–1 to 301–13. The evidence rule enacted by Congress follows the bursting bubble approach; that is, the approach used in New Mexico prior to the adoption of Evidence Rule 301, Rule 301, 28 U.S.C.A. (1975) page 66.

9. Evidence Rule 301 may have been improvidently adopted; at least, it should be reconsidered. Compare State v. Howell, 93 N.M. 64, 596 P.2d 277 (Ct.App.1979).

CHARLES T. McCORMICK, WHAT SHALL THE TRIAL JUDGE TELL THE JURY ABOUT PRESUMPTIONS?, 13 Wash.L.Rev. 185, 187–192 (1938). "Moreover, it seems that as to some presumptions, the custom of informing the jury in some fashion of the rule of presumption, is well-nigh universal. *Res ipsa loquitur,* and the presumption of receipt of a letter from due mailing are instances. In criminal cases, this is especially true of those presumptions which look to a general rather than to a specific inference, and might be called 'hortatory' presumptions, such as the presumption of innocence, the presumption that one intended the consequences of his acts, and the presumption against one who suppresses evidence, that it would have made against him. * * *

"It seems to me that the practice is wise and indeed almost necessary. In most of our states, the trial judge has lost his common law power of summing up the testimony orally and informally in language the jury can understand, and advising them as to the way of judging the credibility of conflicting witnesses and the persuasiveness of rival inferences from the facts. Instead, he must often, as in Washington, give his charge in writing, and as a practical matter he must use abstract language, preferably culled from appellate opinions in past cases, so as to avoid the danger that, in fitting the instructions to the particular case, he may be held to have violated the prohibition against commenting on the evidence. Instructions upon presumptions, whether permissive or mandatory, since they announce judicial custom crystallized into rules, escape the imputation of being the judge's individual opinion or comment.

"They can give the jury substantial aid in avoiding mistakes in difficult cases. A presumption is a rule which has the effect that from certain circumstances a certain inference may be drawn. Persons unaccustomed to weighing evidence and particularly persons of limited intelligence are notoriously suspicious of circumstantial inferences. Such persons, on the other hand, are prone to be overcredulous of direct testimony. If a party having the burden of persuasion, then, must rest upon circumstantial evidence to prove an issuable fact, there is danger that the jury reading the burden-of-proof charge will mistakenly suppose that the circumstantial inference, especially if countered by direct testimony, could not be 'a preponderance of the evidence.' If the counsel can find a presumption upon which to rely, and can secure a charge upon it, he can use it in his argument as a basis for an explanation which may prevent the case from being decided upon this mistaken notion. Such an argument will be especially effective in states which, like Washington, require the judge to give instructions to the jury before the argument.

"* * * We must face, then, a second and more difficult question: What is to be the form and purport of such an instruction? What shall the jury be told about the presumption, and their use of it? I assume that some standard approach, good for all presumptions except for occasional deviation, should be sought. * * *

"The baffling nature of the presumption as a tool for the art of thinking bewilders one who searches for a form of phrasing with which to present the notion to a jury. In a matter where intuition and conjecture play so large a part, it is dangerous to be dogmatic, but certain formulas seem likely to be of little use to the jury. For example, judges have occasionally contented themselves with a statement in the instructions of the terms of the presumption, without more. This leaves the jury in the air, or implies too much. * * * More attractive theoretically, is the suggestion that the judge instruct the jury that the presumption is to stand accepted, unless they find that the facts upon which the presumed inference rests are met by evidence of equal weight, or in other words, unless the contrary evidence leaves their minds in equipoise, in which event they should decide against the party having the burden of persuasion upon the issue. It is hard to phrase such an instruction without conveying the impression that the presumption itself is 'evidence' which must be 'met' or 'balanced.' The over-riding objection, however, in my mind is the impression of futility that it conveys. It prescribes a difficult metaphysical task for the jury, which they would only attempt to perform if they were hesitant and doubtful as to how to proceed, and having performed it, if the doubt remains, the reward is the instruction to disregard the presumption. It seems to me that it is more calculated to mystify than to help the average jury.

"There are some forms of instruction that might give genuine aid toward an intelligent consideration of the issue. Usually, where a presumption is faced with adverse circumstantial evidence, if there is an issue to go to the jury at all, it is because the facts on which the presumption rests create a general probability that the presumed fact exists. The judge might mention these foundation facts, and point out the general probability of the circumstantial inference, as one of the factors to be considered by the jury. * * *

* * *

"* * * [T]he custom has persisted in many states, with surprisingly tough resistance to the criticisms of the text-writers, of charging the jury as to certain presumptions having a substantial backing of probability, that the presumption stands until overcome in the jury's mind by a preponderance of evidence to the contrary. In other words, the presumption is a 'working' hypothesis which works by shifting the burden to the party against whom it operates of satisfying the jury that the presumed inference is untrue. This often gives a more satisfactory apportionment of the burden of persuasion on a particular issue than can be given by the general rule that the pleader has the burden. One looks rather to the ultimate goal, the case or defense as a whole, the other to a particular fact-problem within the case. Moreover, an instruction that the presumption stands until the jury are persuaded to the contrary, has the advantage that it seems to make sense, and so far as we may judge by the other forms thus far invented of instructions on presumptions by that name, I think we can say that it is almost the only one that does."

SANDERLIN v. MARTIN, 373 F.2d 447, 449 (4th Cir.1967) (Haynsworth, C.J., dissenting). "I applaud the move by the Virginia Supreme Court of Appeals to eliminate the practice in Virginia of instructing juries in negligence cases as to the burden of persuasion in terms of a presumption of due care, but I cannot join my brothers in concluding that the District Court's charge, considered as a whole, was prejudicial in any way to the plaintiff.

"In the hands of the court, presumptions are useful things in fixing and shifting the burden of going forward with evidence. Some presumptions serve other offices. Such presumptions as that of death after seven years of unexplained absence mandate the drawing of an ultimate inference from the circumstantial evidence in the absence of direct testimonial contradiction of the ultimate fact in issue. I have long shared Professor Wigmore's opinion, however, that rarely, if ever, should a jury be instructed in terms of presumptions or their effects. A problem sometimes arises in explaining to a jury that it may permissively draw reasonable inferences from circumstantial proof despite direct testimonial contradiction of the ultimate fact, but use of the word 'presumption' in a charge is so likely to carry with it an implication of artificial evidentiary value that it ought to be avoided, as I have had occasion to say before."

Note

On instructions about presumptions, see also Louisell, Construing Rule 301: Instructing the Jury on Presumptions in Civil Actions and Proceedings, 63 Va.L.Rev. 281 (1977); Mueller, Instructing the Jury Upon Presumptions in Civil Cases: Comparing Federal Rule 301 with Uniform Rule 301, 12 Land & Water L.Rev. 219 (1977).

COUNTY COURT OF ULSTER COUNTY v. ALLEN

Supreme Court of the United States, 1979.
442 U.S. 140, 99 S.Ct. 2213, 60 L.Ed.2d 777.

MR. JUSTICE STEVENS delivered the opinion of the Court.

A New York statute provides that, with certain exceptions, the presence of a firearm in an automobile is presumptive evidence of its illegal possession by all persons then occupying the vehicle.[1] The United States Court of Appeals for the Second Circuit held that respondents may challenge the constitutionality of this statute in a federal habeas corpus proceeding and that the statute is "unconstitutional on its face." 568 F.2d 998, 1009. We granted certiorari to review these holdings and also to consider whether the statute is constitutional in its application to respondents.

Four persons, three adult males (respondents) and a 16–year–old girl (Jane Doe, who is not a respondent here), were jointly tried on charges that they possessed two loaded handguns, a loaded machinegun, and over a pound of heroin found in a Chevrolet in which they were riding when it was stopped for speeding on the New York Thruway shortly after noon on March 28, 1973. The two large-caliber handguns, which together with their ammunition weighed approximately six pounds, were seen through the window of the car by the investigating police officer. They were positioned crosswise in an open handbag on either the front floor or the front seat of the car on the passenger side where Jane Doe was sitting. Jane Doe admitted that the handbag was hers.[2] The machinegun and the heroin were discovered in the trunk after the police pried it open. The car had been borrowed from the driver's brother earlier that day; the key to the trunk could not be found in the car or on the person of any of its occupants, although there was testimony that two of the occupants had

1. New York Penal Law § 265.15(3):

"The presence in an automobile, other than a stolen one or a public omnibus, of any firearm, defaced firearm, firearm silencer, bomb, bombshell, gravity knife, switchblade knife, dagger, dirk, stiletto, billy, blackjack, metal knuckles, sandbag, sandclub or slungshot is presumptive evidence of its possession by all persons occupying such automobile at the time such weapon, instrument or appliance is found, except under the following circumstances:

"(a) * * * if such weapon, instrument or appliance is found upon the person of one of the occupants therein;

"(b) if such weapon, instrument or appliance is found in an automobile which is being operated for hire by a duly licensed driver in the due, lawful and proper pursuit of his trade, then such presumption shall not apply to the driver; or

"(c) if the weapon so found is a pistol or revolver and one of the occupants, not present under duress, has in his possession a valid license to have and carry concealed the same."

In addition to the three exceptions delineated in §§ 265.15(3)(a)–(c) above as well as the stolen-vehicle and public-omnibus exception in § 265.15(3) itself, § 265.20 contains various exceptions that apply when weapons are present in an automobile pursuant to certain military, law enforcement, recreational, and commercial endeavors.

2. The arrest was made by two state troopers. One officer approached the driver, advised him that he was going to issue a ticket for speeding, requested identification and returned to the patrol car. After a radio check indicated that the driver was wanted in Michigan on a weapons charge, the second officer returned to the vehicle and placed the driver under arrest. Thereafter, he went around to the right side of the car and, in "open view," saw a portion of a .45 automatic pistol protruding from the open purse on the floor or the seat. 40 N.Y.2d 505, 508–509, 354 N.E.2d 836, 838–839 (1976). He opened the car door, removed that gun and saw a .38 caliber revolver in the same handbag. He testified that the crosswise position of one or both of the guns kept the handbag from closing. After the weapons were secured, the two remaining male passengers, who had been sitting in the rear seat, and Jane Doe were arrested and frisked. A subsequent search at the police station disclosed a pocketknife and marihuana concealed on Jane Doe's person.

placed something in the trunk before embarking in the borrowed car.[3] The jury convicted all four of possession of the handguns and acquitted them of possession of the contents of the trunk.

Counsel for all four defendants objected to the introduction into evidence of the two handguns, the machinegun, and the drugs, arguing that the State had not adequately demonstrated a connection between their clients and the contraband. The trial court overruled the objection, relying on the presumption of possession created by the New York statute. Because that presumption does not apply if a weapon is found "upon the person" of one of the occupants of the car, see n. 1, supra, the three male defendants also moved to dismiss the charges relating to the handguns on the ground that the guns were found on the person of Jane Doe. Respondents made this motion both at the close of the prosecution's case and at the close of all evidence. The trial judge twice denied it, concluding that the applicability of the "on the person" exception was a question of fact for the jury.

At the close of the trial, the judge instructed the jurors that they were entitled to infer possession from the defendants' presence in the car. He did not make any reference to the "upon the person" exception in his explanation of the statutory presumption, nor did any of the defendants object to this omission or request alternative or additional instructions on the subject.

Defendants filed a post-trial motion in which they challenged the constitutionality of the New York statute as applied in this case. The challenge was made in support of their argument that the evidence, apart from the presumption, was insufficient to sustain the convictions. The motion was denied, and the convictions were affirmed by the Appellate Division without opinion. 49 App.Div.2d 639, 370 N.Y.S.2d 243 (1975).

The New York Court of Appeals also affirmed. It rejected the argument that as a matter of law the guns were on Jane Doe's person because they were in her pocketbook. Although the court recognized that in some circumstances the evidence could only lead to the conclusion that the weapons were in one person's sole possession, it held that this record presented a jury question on that issue. Since the defendants had not asked the trial judge to submit the question to the jury, the Court of Appeals treated the case as though the jury had resolved this fact question in the prosecution's favor. It therefore concluded that the presumption did apply and that there was sufficient evidence to support the convictions. 40 N.Y.2d 505, 509–512, 354 N.E.2d 836,

3. Early that morning the four defendants had arrived at the Rochester, N.Y. home of the driver's sister in a Cadillac. Using her telephone, the driver called their brother, advised him that "his car ran hot" on the way there from Detroit and asked to borrow the Chevrolet so that the four could continue on to New York City. The brother brought the Chevrolet to the sister's home. He testified that he had recently cleaned out the trunk and had seen no weapons or drugs. The sister also testified, stating that she saw two of the defendants transfer some unidentified item or items from the trunk of one vehicle to the trunk of the other while both cars were parked in her driveway.

839–841 (1976). It also summarily rejected the argument that the presumption was unconstitutional as applied in this case.

Respondents filed a petition for a writ of habeas corpus in the United States District Court for the Southern District of New York contending that they were denied due process of law by the application of the statutory presumption of possession. The District Court issued the writ, holding that respondents had not "deliberately bypassed" their federal claim by their actions at trial and that the mere presence of two guns in a woman's handbag in a car could not reasonably give rise to the inference that they were in the possession of three other persons in the car.

The Court of Appeals for the Second Circuit affirmed, but for different reasons. First, the entire panel concluded that the New York Court of Appeals had decided respondents' constitutional claim on its merits rather than on any independent state procedural ground that might have barred collateral relief. Then, the majority of the court, without deciding whether the presumption was constitutional as applied in this case, concluded that the statute is unconstitutional on its face because the "presumption obviously sweeps within its compass (1) many occupants who may not know they are riding with a gun (which may be out of their sight), and (2) many who may be aware of the presence of the gun but not permitted access to it."[4] Concurring separately, Judge Timbers agreed with the District Court that the statute was unconstitutional as applied but considered it improper to reach the issue of the statute's facial constitutionality. 568 F.2d at 1011–1012.

The State's petition for a writ of certiorari presented three questions: (1) whether the District Court had jurisdiction to entertain respondents' claim that the presumption is unconstitutional; (2) whether it was proper for the Court of Appeals to decide the facial constitutionality issue; and (3) whether the application of the presumption in this case is unconstitutional. We answer the first question in the affirmative, the second two in the negative. We accordingly reverse.

* * *

II

Although § 2254 authorizes the federal courts to entertain respondents' claim that they are being held in custody in violation of the Constitution, it is not a grant of power to decide constitutional questions not necessarily subsumed within that claim. Federal courts are courts of limited jurisdiction. They have the authority to adjudicate specific controversies between adverse litigants over which and over

4. The majority continued:

"Nothing about a gun, which may be only a few inches in length (e.g., a Baretta or Derringer) and concealed under a seat in a glove compartment or beyond the reach of all but one of the car's occupants, assures that its presence is known to occupants who may be hitchhikers or other casual passengers, much less that they have any dominion or control over it." 568 F.2d, at 1007.

whom they have jurisdiction. In the exercise of that authority, they have a duty to decide constitutional questions when necessary to dispose of the litigation before them. But they have an equally strong duty to avoid constitutional issues that need not be resolved in order to determine the rights of the parties to the case under consideration. E.g., New York Transit Authority v. Beazer, 440 U.S. 568, 99 S.Ct. 1355, 59 L.Ed.2d 587.

A party has standing to challenge the constitutionality of a statute only insofar as it has an adverse impact on his own rights. As a general rule, if there is no constitutional defect in the application of the statute to a litigant, he does not have standing to argue that it would be unconstitutional if applied to third parties in hypothetical situations. Broadrick v. Oklahoma, 413 U.S. 601, 610, 93 S.Ct. 2908, 2914, 37 L.Ed.2d 830 (and cases cited). A limited exception has been recognized for statutes that broadly prohibit speech protected by the First Amendment. Id., at 611–616, 93 S.Ct., at 2915–2918. This exception has been justified by the overriding interest in removing illegal deterrents to the exercise of the right of free speech. E.g., Gooding v. Wilson, 405 U.S. 518, 520, 92 S.Ct. 1103, 1105, 31 L.Ed.2d 408; Dombrowski v. Pfister, 380 U.S. 479, 486, 85 S.Ct. 1116, 1120, 14 L.Ed.2d 22. That justification, of course, has no application to a statute that enhances the legal risks associated with riding in vehicles containing dangerous weapons.

In this case the Court of Appeals undertook the task of deciding the constitutionality of the New York statute "on its face." Its conclusion that the statutory presumption was arbitrary rested entirely on its view of the fairness of applying the presumption in hypothetical situations—situations, indeed, in which it is improbable that a jury would return a conviction,[14] or that a prosecution would ever be instituted.[15] We must accordingly inquire whether these respondents had standing to advance the arguments that the Court of Appeals considered decisive. An

14. Indeed, in this very case the permissive presumptions in § 265.15(3) and its companion drug statute, N.Y.Pen.L. § 220.-25(1), were insufficient to persuade the jury to convict the defendants of possession of the loaded machinegun and heroin in the trunk of the car notwithstanding the supporting testimony that at least two of them had been seen transferring something into the trunk that morning. See n. 3, supra.

The hypothetical, even implausible, nature of the situations relied upon by the Court of Appeals is illustrated by the fact that there are no reported cases in which the presumption led to convictions in circumstances even remotely similar to the posited situations. In those occasional cases in which a jury has reached a guilty verdict on the basis of evidence insufficient to justify an inference of possession from presence, the New York appellate courts have not hesitated to reverse. E.g., People v. Scott, 53 App.Div.2d 703, 384 N.Y.S.2d 878 (1976); People v. Garcia, 41 App.Div.2d 560, 340 N.Y.S.2d 35 (1973).

In light of the improbable character of the situations hypothesized by the Court of Appeals, its facial analysis would still be unconvincing even were that type of analysis appropriate. This Court has never required that a presumption be accurate in every imaginable case. See Leary v. United States, 395 U.S. 6, 53, 89 S.Ct. 1532, 1557, 23 L.Ed.2d 57.

15. See n. 4, supra, and text accompanying. Thus, the assumption that it would be unconstitutional to apply the statutory presumption to a hitchhiker in a car containing a concealed weapon does not necessarily advance the constitutional claim of the driver of a car in which a gun was found on the front seat, or of other defendants in entirely different situations.

analysis of our prior cases indicates that the answer to this inquiry depends on the type of presumption that is involved in the case.

Inferences and presumptions are a staple of our adversarial system of factfinding. It is often necessary for the trier of fact to determine the existence of an element of the crime—that is, an "ultimate" or "elemental" fact—from the existence of one or more "evidentiary" or "basic" facts. E.g., Barnes v. United States, 412 U.S. 837, 843–844, 93 S.Ct. 2357, 2361–2362, 37 L.Ed.2d 380; Tot v. United States, 319 U.S. 463, 467, 63 S.Ct. 1241, 1244, 87 L.Ed.2d 1519; Mobile, J. & K.C.R. Co. v. Turnipseed, 219 U.S. 35, 42, 31 S.Ct. 136, 137, 55 L.Ed. 78. The value of these evidentiary devices, and their validity under the Due Process Clause, vary from case to case, however, depending on the strength of the connection between the particular basic and elemental facts involved and on the degree to which the device curtails the factfinder's freedom to assess the evidence independently. Nonetheless, in criminal cases, the ultimate test of any device's constitutional validity in a given case remains constant: the device must not undermine the factfinder's responsibility at trial, based on evidence adduced by the State, to find the ultimate facts beyond a reasonable doubt. See In re Winship, 397 U.S. 358, 364, 90 S.Ct. 1068, 1072, 25 L.Ed.2d 368; Mullaney v. Wilbur, 421 U.S. 684, 702–703 n. 31, 95 S.Ct. 1881, 1891–1892 n. 31, 44 L.Ed.2d 508.

The most common evidentiary device is the entirely permissive inference or presumption, which allows—but does not require—the trier of fact to infer the elemental fact from proof by the prosecutor of the basic one and that places no burden of any kind on the defendant. See, e.g., Barnes v. United States, 412 U.S., at 840 n. 3, 93 S.Ct., at 2360 n. 3. In that situation the basic fact may constitute prima facie evidence of the elemental fact. See, e.g., Turner v. United States, 396 U.S. 398, 402 n. 2, 90 S.Ct. 642, 645, n. 2, 24 L.Ed.2d 610. When reviewing this type of device, the Court has required the party challenging it to demonstrate its invalidity as applied to him. E.g., Barnes v. United States, supra, 412 U.S. at 845, 93 S.Ct., at 2362; Turner v. United States, supra, 396 U.S., at 419–424, 90 S.Ct., at 653–656. See also United States v. Gainey, 380 U.S. 63, 67–68, 69–70, 85 S.Ct. 754, 757–758, 758–759, 13 L.Ed.2d 658. Because this permissive presumption leaves the trier of fact free to credit or reject the inference and does not shift the burden of proof, it affects the application of the "beyond a reasonable doubt" standard only if, under the facts of the case, there is no rational way the trier could make the connection permitted by the inference. For only in that situation is there any risk that an explanation of the permissible inference to a jury, or its use by a jury, has caused the presumptively rational factfinder to make an erroneous factual determination.

A mandatory presumption is a far more troublesome evidentiary device. For it may affect not only the strength of the "no reasonable doubt" burden but also the placement of that burden; it tells the trier that he or they *must* find the elemental fact upon proof of the basic fact, at least unless the defendant has come forward with some evidence to rebut the presumed connection between the two facts. E.g., Turner v. United States, supra, 396 U.S., at 401–402, and n. 1, 90 S.Ct., at 644–645, and n. 1; Leary v. United States, 395 U.S. 6, 30, 89 S.Ct. 1532, 1545, 23 L.Ed.2d 57; United States v. Romano, 382 U.S. 136, 137, and n. 4, 138, 143, 86 S.Ct. 279, 280, and n. 4, 281, 283, 15 L.Ed.2d 210; Tot v. United States, supra, 319 U.S., at 469, 63 S.Ct., at 1245.[16] In this situation, the Court has generally examined the presumption ~~on its~~ face

16. This class of more or less mandatory presumptions can be subdivided into two parts: presumptions that merely shift the burden of production to the defendant, following the satisfaction of which the ultimate burden of persuasion returns to the prosecution; and presumptions that entirely shift the burden of proof to the defendant. The mandatory presumptions examined by our cases have almost uniformly fit into the former subclass, in that they never totally removed the ultimate burden of proof beyond a reasonable doubt from the prosecution. E.g., Tot v. United States, supra, at 469, 63 S.Ct., at 1245. See Roviaro v. United States, 353 U.S. 53, 63, 77 S.Ct. 623, 629, 1 L.Ed.2d 639 describing the operation of the presumption involved in *Turner, Leary,* and *Romano.*

To the extent that a presumption imposes an extremely low burden of production—e.g., being satisfied by "any" evidence—it may well be that its impact is no greater than that of a permissive inference and it may be proper to analyze it as such. See generally, Mullaney v. Wilbur, supra, at 703 n. 31, 95 S.Ct., at 1892 n. 31.

In deciding what type of inference or presumption is involved in a case, the jury instructions will generally be controlling, although their interpretation may require recourse to the statute involved and the cases decided under it. Turner v. United States, supra, provides a useful illustration of the different types of presumptions. It analyzes the constitutionality of two different presumption statutes (one mandatory and one permissive) as they apply to the basic fact of possession of both heroin and cocaine, and the presumed facts of importation and distribution of narcotic drugs. The jury was charged essentially in the terms of the two statutes.

The importance of focusing attention on the precise presentation of the presumption to the jury and the scope of that presumption is illustrated by a comparison of United States v. Gainey, 380 U.S. 63, 85 S.Ct. 754, 13 L.Ed.2d 658, with United States v. Romano, 382 U.S. 136, 86 S.Ct. 279, 15 L.Ed.2d 210. Both cases involved statutory presumptions based on proof that the defendant was present at the site of an illegal still. In *Gainey* the Court sustained a conviction "for carrying on" the business of the distillery in violation of 26 U.S.C.A. § 5601(a)(4), whereas in *Romano,* the Court set aside a conviction for being in "possession, custody, and * * * control" of such a distillery in violation of § 5601(a)(1). The difference in outcome was attributable to two important differences between the cases. Because the statute involved in *Gainey* was a sweeping prohibition of almost any activity associated with the still, whereas the *Romano* statute involved only one narrow aspect of the total undertaking, there was a much higher probability that mere presence could support an inference of guilt in the former case than in the latter.

Of perhaps greater importance, however, was the difference between the trial judge's instructions to the jury in the two cases. In *Gainey* the judge had explained that the presumption was permissive; it did not require the jury to convict the defendant even if it was convinced that he was present at the site. On the contrary, the instructions made it clear that presence was only "a circumstance to be considered along with all the other circumstances in the case." As we emphasized, the "jury was thus told that the statutory presumption was not conclusive." 380 U.S., at 69–70, 85 S.Ct., at 758–759. In *Romano* the trial judge told the jury that the defendant's presence at the still "shall be deemed sufficient evidence to authorize conviction." 382 U.S., at 182, 86 S.Ct., at 281. Although there was other evidence of guilt, that instruction authorized conviction even if the jury disbelieved all of the testimony except the proof of presence at the site. This Court's holding that the statutory presumption could not support the *Romano* conviction was thus dependent, in part, on the specific instructions given by the trial judge. Under those instructions it was necessary to decide whether, regardless of the specific circumstances of the particular case, the statutory presumption adequately supported the guilty verdict.

to determine the extent to which the basic and elemental facts coincide. E.g., Turner v. United States, supra, 396 U.S. at 408–418, 90 S.Ct., at 648–653; Leary v. United States, supra, 395 U.S., at 45–52, 89 S.Ct., at 1552–1553; United States v. Romano, supra, 382 U.S., at 140–141, 86 S.Ct., at 281–282; Tot v. United States, supra, 319 U.S., at 468, 63 S.Ct., at 1245. To the extent that the trier of fact is forced to abide by the presumption, and may not reject it based on an independent evaluation of the particular facts presented by the State, the analysis of the presumption's constitutional validity is logically divorced from those facts and based on the presumption's accuracy in the run of cases.[17] It is for this reason that the Court has held it irrelevant in analyzing a mandatory presumption, but not in analyzing a purely permissive one, that there is ample evidence in the record other than the presumption to support a conviction. E.g., Turner v. United States, supra, 396 U.S., at 407, 90 S.Ct., at 647; Leary v. United States, supra, 395 U.S., at 31–32, 89 S.Ct., at 1545–1546; United States v. Romano, supra, 382 U.S., at 138–139, 86 S.Ct., at 280–281.

Without determining whether the presumption in this case was mandatory, the Court of Appeals analyzed it on its face as if it were. In fact, it was not, as the New York Court of Appeals had earlier pointed out. 40 N.Y.2d at 510–511, 387 N.Y.S.2d, at 100, 354 N.E.2d, at 840.

The trial judge's instructions make it clear that the presumption was merely a part of the prosecution's case,[19] that it gave rise to a

17. In addition to the discussion of *Romano* in n. 16, supra, this point is illustrated by Leary v. United States, supra. In that case, Dr. Timothy Leary, a professor at Harvard University was stopped by customs inspectors in Laredo, Texas as he was returning from the Mexican side of the international border. Marihuana seeds and a silver snuff box filled with semirefined marihuana and three partially smoked marihuana cigarettes were discovered in his car. He was convicted of having knowingly transported marihuana which he knew had been illegally imported into this country in violation of 21 U.S.C.A. § 176a. That statute includes a mandatory presumption: "possession shall be deemed sufficient evidence to authorize conviction [for importation] unless the defendant explains his possession to the satisfaction of the jury." Leary admitted possession of the marihuana and claimed that he had carried it from New York to Mexico and then back.

Justice Harlan for the Court noted that under one theory of the case, the jury could have found direct proof of all of the necessary elements of the offense without recourse to the presumption. But he deemed that insufficient reason to affirm the conviction because under another theory the jury might have found knowledge of importation on the basis of either direct evidence or the presumption, and there was accordingly no certainty that the jury had not relied on the presumption. 395 U.S., at 31–32, 89 S.Ct., at 1545–1546. The Court therefore found it necessary to test the presumption against the Due Process Clause. Its analysis was facial. Despite the fact that the defendant was well educated and had recently traveled to a country that is a major exporter of marihuana to this country, the Court found the presumption of knowledge of importation from possession irrational. It did so not because Dr. Leary was unlikely to know the source of the marihuana but instead because "a majority of possessors" were unlikely to have such knowledge. Id., at 53, 89 S.Ct., at 1557. Because the jury had been instructed to rely on the presumption even if it did not believe the Government's direct evidence of knowledge of importation (unless, of course, the defendant met his burden of "satisfying" the jury to the contrary), the Court reversed the conviction.

19. "It is your duty to consider all the testimony in this case, to weigh it carefully and assess the credit to be given to a witness by his apparent intention to speak the truth and by the accuracy of his memory to reconcile, if possible, conflicting state-

permissive inference available only in certain circumstances, rather than a mandatory conclusion of possession, and that it could be ignored by the jury even if there was no affirmative proof offered by defendants in rebuttal.[20] The judge explained that possession could be actual or constructive, but that constructive possession could not exist without the intent and ability to exercise control or dominion over the weapons.[21] He also carefully instructed the jury that there is a mandatory presumption of innocence in favor of the defendants that controls unless it, as the exclusive trier of fact, is satisfied beyond a reasonable doubt that the defendants possessed the handguns in the manner described by the judge.[22] In short, the instructions plainly directed the jury to consider all the circumstances tending to support or contradict the inference that all four occupants of the car had possession of the two loaded handguns and to decide the matter for itself without regard

ments as to material facts and in such ways to try and get at the truth and to reach a verdict upon the evidence.

"To establish the unlawful possession of the weapons, again the People relied upon the presumption and, in addition thereto, the testimony of Anderson and Lemmons who testified in their case in chief.

"Accordingly, you would be warranted in returning a verdict of guilt against the defendants or defendant if you find the defendants or defendant was in possession of a machine gun and the other weapons and that the fact of possession was proven to you by the People beyond a reasonable doubt, and an element of such proof is the reasonable presumption of illegal possession of a machine gun or the presumption of illegal possession of firearms, as I have just before explained to you."

20. "Our Penal Law also provides that the presence in an automobile of any machine gun or of any handgun or firearm which is loaded is presumptive evidence of their unlawful possession.

"In other words, these presumptions or this latter presumption upon proof of the presence of the machine gun and the hand weapons, you may infer and draw conclusions that such prohibitive weapon was possessed by each of the defendants who occupied the automobile at the time when such instruments were found. The presumption or presumptions is effective only so long as there is no substantial evidence contradicting the conclusion flowing from the presumption, and the presumption is said to disappear when such contradictory evidence is adduced.

"The presumption or presumptions which I discussed with the jury relative to the drugs or weapons in this case need not be rebutted by affirmative proof or affirmative evidence but may be rebutted by an evidence or lack of evidence in the case."

21. "As so defined, possession means actual physical possession, just as having the drugs or weapons in one's hand, in one's home, or other place under one's exclusive control, or constructive possession which may exist without personal dominion over the drugs or weapons but with the intent and ability to retain such control or dominion."

22. "[Y]ou are the exclusive judge of all the questions of fact in this case. That means that you are the sole judges as to the weight to be given to the evidence and to the weight and probative value to be given to the testimony of each particular witness and to the credibility of any witness.

"Under our law, every defendant in a criminal trial starts the trial with the presumption in his favor that he is innocent, and this presumption follows him throughout the entire trial and remains with him until such time as you, by your verdict find him or her guilty beyond a reasonable doubt or innocent of the charge. If you find him or her not guilty, then, of course, this presumption ripens into an established fact. On the other hand, if you find him or her guilty then this presumption has been overcome and is destroyed.

"Now, in order to find any of the defendants guilty of the unlawful possession of the weapons, the machine gun, the .45 and the .38, you must be satisfied beyond a reasonable doubt that the defendants possessed the machine gun and the .45 and the .38, possessed it as I defined it to you before."

to how much evidence the defendants introduced.[23]

Our cases considering the validity of permissive statutory presumptions such as the one involved here have rested on an evaluation of the presumption as applied to the record before the Court. None suggests that a court should pass on the constitutionality of this kind of statute "on its face." It was error for the Court of Appeals to make such a determination in this case.

III

As applied to the facts of this case, the presumption of possession is entirely rational. Notwithstanding the Court of Appeals' analysis, respondents were not "hitch-hikers or other casual passengers," and the guns were neither "a few inches in length" nor "out of [respondents'] sight." See n. 4, supra, and text accompanying. The argument against possession by any of the respondents was predicated solely on the fact that the guns were in Jane Doe's pocketbook. But several circumstances—which, not surprisingly, her counsel repeatedly emphasized in his questions and his argument—made it highly improbable that she was the sole custodian of those weapons.

Even if it was reasonable to conclude that she had placed the guns in her purse before the car was stopped by police, the facts strongly suggest that Jane Doe was not the only person able to exercise dominion over them. The two guns were too large to be concealed in her handbag. The bag was consequently open, and part of one of the guns was in plain view, within easy access of the driver of the car and even, perhaps, of the other two respondents who were riding in the rear seat.

Moreover, it is highly improbable that the loaded guns belonged to Jane Doe or that she was solely responsible for their being in her purse. As a 16–year–old girl in the company of three adult men she was the least likely of the four to be carrying one, let alone two, heavy handguns. It is far more probable that she relied on the pocketknife found in her brassiere for any necessary self-protection. Under these circumstances, it was not unreasonable for her counsel to argue and for the jury to infer that when the car was halted for speeding, the other passengers in the car anticipated the risk of a search and attempted to conceal their weapons in a pocketbook in the front seat. The inference is surely more likely than the notion that these weapons were the sole property of the 16–year–old girl.

Under these circumstances, the jury would have been entirely reasonable in rejecting the suggestion—which, incidentally, defense

23. The verdict announced by the jury, clearly indicates that it understood its duty to evaluate the presumption independently and to reject it if it was not supported in the record. Despite receiving almost identical instructions on the applicability of the presumption of possession to the contraband found in the front seat and in the trunk, the jury convicted all four defendants of possession of the former but acquitted all of them of possession of the latter. See n. 14, supra.

counsel did not even advance in their closing arguments to the jury[26]—that the handguns were in the sole possession of Jane Doe. Assuming that the jury did reject it, the case is tantamount to one in which the guns were lying on the floor or the seat of the car in the plain view of the three other occupants of the automobile. In such a case it is surely rational to infer that each of the respondents was fully aware of the presence of the guns and had both the ability and the intent to exercise dominion and control over the weapons. The application of the statutory presumption in this case therefore comports with the standard laid down in Tot v. United States, 319 U.S. 463, 467, 63 S.Ct. 1241, 1244, 87 L.Ed.2d 1519, and restated in Leary v. United States, supra, 395 U.S., at 36, 89 S.Ct., at 1548. For there is a "rational connection" between the basic facts that the prosecution proved and the ultimate fact presumed, and the latter is "more likely than not to flow from" the former.[27]

26. Indeed, counsel for two of the respondents virtually invited the jury to find to the contrary:

> "One more thing. You know, different people live in different cultures and different societies. You may think that the way [respondent] Hardrick has his hair done up is unusual; it may seem strange to you. People live differently * * *. For example, if you were living under their times and conditions and you traveled from a big city, Detroit, to a bigger city, New York City, *it is not unusual for people to carry guns, small arms to protect themselves, is it?* There are places in New York City policemen fear to go. But you have got to understand; you are sitting here as jurors. These are people, live flesh and blood, the same as you, different motives, different objectives." (emphasis added).

It is important in this regard that respondents passed up the opportunity to have the jury instructed not to apply the presumption if it determined that the handguns were "upon the person" of Jane Doe.

27. The New York Court of Appeals first upheld the constitutionality of the presumption involved in this case in People v. Russo, 303 N.Y. 673, 102 N.E.2d 834 (1951). That decision relied upon the earlier case of People v. Terra, 303 N.Y. 332, 335–336, 102 N.E.2d 576, 578–579 (1951), which upheld the constitutionality of another New York statute that allowed a jury to presume that the occupants of a room in which a firearm was located possessed the weapon. The analysis in *Terra,* which this Court affirmed summarily, 342 U.S. 938, 72 S.Ct. 561, 96 L.Ed. 698, is persuasive:

> "There can be no doubt about the 'sinister significance' of proof of a machine gun in a room occupied by an accused or about the reasonableness of the connection between its illegal possession and occupancy of the room where it is kept. Persons who occupy a room, who either reside in it or use it in the conduct and operation of a business or other venture—and that is what in its present context the statutory term 'occupying' signifies * * *—normally know what is in it; and, certainly, when the object is as large and uncommon as a machine gun, it is neither unreasonable nor unfair to presume that the room's occupants are aware of its presence. That being so, the legislature may not be considered arbitrary if it acts upon the presumption and erects it into evidence of a possession that is 'conscious and knowing'."

See also Controlled Substances, Dangerous Unless Used as Directed, N.Y.Leg.Doc. No. 10, at 69 (1972), in which the drafters of the analogous automobile/narcotics presumption in N.Y.Pen.L. § 220.25, explained the basis for that presumption:

> "We believe, and find, that it is rational and logical to presume that all occupants of a vehicle are aware of, and culpably involved in, possession of dangerous drugs found abandoned or secreted in a vehicle when the quantity of the drug is such that it would be extremely unlikely for an occupant to be unaware of its presence. * * *
>
> "We do not believe that persons transporting dealership quantities of contraband are likely to go driving around with innocent friends or that they are likely to pick up strangers. We do not doubt that this can and does in fact occasional-

Respondents argue, however, that the validity of the New York presumption must be judged by a "reasonable doubt" test rather than the "more likely than not" standard employed in *Leary*.[28] Under the more stringent test, it is argued that a statutory presumption must be rejected unless the evidence necessary to invoke the inference is sufficient for a rational jury to find the inferred fact beyond a reasonable doubt. See Barnes v. United States, 412 U.S. 837, 842–843, 93 S.Ct. 2357, 2361–2362, 37 L.Ed.2d 380. Respondents' argument again overlooks the distinction between a permissive presumption on which the prosecution is entitled to rely as one not-necessarily-sufficient part of its proof and a mandatory presumption which the jury must accept even if it is the sole evidence of an element of the offense.[29]

In the latter situation, since the prosecution bears the burden of establishing guilt, it may not rest its case entirely on a presumption unless the fact proved is sufficient to support the inference of guilt beyond a reasonable doubt. But in the former situation, the prosecution may rely on all of the evidence in the record to meet the reasonable doubt standard. There is no more reason to require a permissive statutory presumption to meet a reasonable doubt standard before it may be permitted to play any part in a trial than there is to require that degree of probative force for other relevant evidence before it may be admitted. As long as it is clear that the presumption is not the sole and sufficient basis for a finding of guilt, it need only satisfy the test described in *Leary*.

The permissive presumption, as used in this case, satisfied the *Leary* test. And, as already noted, the New York Court of Appeals has concluded that the record as a whole was sufficient to establish guilt beyond a reasonable doubt.

The judgment is reversed.

Mr. Chief Justice Burger, concurring.

ly happen, but because we find it more reasonable to believe that the bare presence in the vehicle is culpable, we think it reasonable to presume culpability in the direction which the proven facts already point. Since the presumption is an evidentiary one, it may be offset by any evidence including the testimony of the defendant, which would negate the defendant's culpable involvement."

Legislative judgments such as this one deserve respect in assessing the constitutionality of evidentiary presumptions. E.g., Leary v. United States, supra, 395 U.S., at 39, 89 S.Ct., at 1549; United States v. Gainey, supra, 380 U.S., at 67, 85 S.Ct., at 757.

28. "The upshot of *Tot, Gainey,* and *Romano* is, we think, that a criminal statutory presumption must be regarded as 'irrational' or 'arbitrary,' and hence unconstitutional, unless it can at least be said with substantial assurance that the presumed fact is more likely than not to flow from the proved fact on which it is made to depend." 395 U.S., at 36.

29. The dissenting argument rests on the assumption that "the jury [may have] rejected all of the prosecution's evidence concerning the location and origin of the guns." Even if that assumption were plausible, the jury was plainly told that it was free to disregard the presumption. But the dissent's assumption is not plausible; for if the jury rejected the testimony describing where the guns were found, it would necessarily also have rejected the only evidence in the record proving that the guns were found in the car. The conclusion that the jury attached significance to the particular location of the handguns follows inexorably from the acquittal on the charge of possession of the machineguns and heroin in the trunk.

I join fully in the Court's opinion reversing the judgment under review. In the necessarily detailed step-by-step analysis of the legal issues, the central and controlling facts of a case often can become lost. The "underbrush" of finely tuned legal analysis of complex issues tends to bury the facts.

On this record, the jury could readily have reached the same result without benefit of the challenged statutory presumption; here it reached what was rather obviously a compromise verdict. Even without relying on evidence that two people had been seen placing something in the car trunk shortly before respondents occupied it, and that two machineguns and a package of heroin were soon after found in that trunk, the jury apparently decided that it was enough to hold the passengers to knowledge of the two pistols which were in such plain view that the officer could see them from outside the car. Reasonable jurors could reasonably find that what the officer could see from outside, the passengers within the car could hardly miss seeing. Courts have long held that in the practical business of deciding cases the factfinders, not unlike negotiators, are permitted the luxury of verdicts reached by compromise.

MR. JUSTICE POWELL, with whom MR. JUSTICE BRENNAN, MR. JUSTICE STEWART, and MR. JUSTICE MARSHALL join dissenting.

I agree with the Court that there is no procedural bar to our considering the underlying constitutional question presented by this case. I am not in agreement, however, with the Court's conclusion that the presumption as charged to the jury in this case meets the constitutional requirements of due process as set forth in our prior decisions. On the contrary, an individual's mere presence in an automobile where there is a handgun does not even make it "more likely than not" that the individual possesses the weapon.

I

In the criminal law presumptions are used to encourage the jury to find certain facts, with respect to which no direct evidence is presented, solely because other facts have been proved.[1] See, e.g., Barnes v. United States, 412 U.S. 837, 840 n. 3, 93 S.Ct. 2357, 2360 n. 3, 37 L.Ed.2d 380 (1973); United States v. Romano, 382 U.S. 136, 138, 86 S.Ct. 279, 280, 15 L.Ed.2d 210 (1965). The purpose of such presumptions is plain: Like certain other jury instructions, they provide guidance for jurors' thinking in considering the evidence laid before them. Once in the juryroom, jurors necessarily draw inferences from the evidence—both direct and circumstantial. Through the use of presumptions, certain inferences are commended to the attention of jurors by legislatures or courts.

1. Such encouragement can be provided either by statutory presumptions, see, e.g., 18 U.S.C.A. § 1201(b), or by presumptions created in the common law. See, e.g., Barnes v. United States, 412 U.S. 837, 93 S.Ct. 2357, 37 L.Ed.2d 380 (1973). Unless otherwise specified, "presumption" will be used herein to refer to "permissible inferences," as well as to "true" presumptions. See F. James, Civil Procedure § 7.9 (1965).

Legitimate guidance of a jury's deliberations is an indispensible part of our criminal justice system. Nonetheless, the use of presumptions in criminal cases poses at least two distinct perils for defendants' constitutional rights. The Court accurately identifies the first of these as being the danger of interference with "the factfinder's responsibility at trial, based on evidence adduced by the State, to find the ultimate facts beyond a reasonable doubt." If the jury is instructed that it must infer some ultimate fact (that is, some element of the offense) from proof of other facts unless the defendant disproves the ultimate fact by a preponderance of the evidence, then the presumption shifts the burden of proof to the defendant concerning the element thus inferred.[2]

But I do not agree with the Court's conclusion that the only constitutional difficulty with presumptions lies in the danger of lessening the burden of proof the prosecution must bear. As the Court notes, the presumptions thus far reviewed by the Court have not shifted the burden of persuasion; instead, they either have required only that the defendant produce some evidence to rebut the inference suggested by the prosecution's evidence, see Tot v. United States, 319 U.S. 463, 63 S.Ct. 1241, 87 L.Ed.2d 1519 (1943), or merely have been suggestions to the jury that it would be sensible to draw certain conclusions on the basis of the evidence presented.[3] See Barnes v. United States, supra, 412 U.S. at 840 n. 3, 93 S.Ct., at 2360 n. 3. Evolving from our decisions, therefore, is a second standard for judging the constitutionality of criminal presumptions which is based—not on the constitutional requirement that the State be put to its proof—but rather on the due process rule that when the jury is encouraged to make factual inferences, those inferences must reflect some valid general observation about the natural connection between events as they occur in our society.

This due process rule was first articulated by the Court in Tot v. United States, supra, in which the Court reviewed the constitutionality of § 2(f) of the Federal Firearms Act. That statute provided in part that "possession of a firearm or ammunition by any * * * person [who has been convicted of a crime of violence] shall be presumptive evidence that such firearm or ammunition was shipped or transported [in inter-

2. The Court suggests that presumptions that shift the burden of persuasion to the defendant in this way can be upheld provided that "the fact proved is sufficient to support the inference of guilt beyond a reasonable doubt." As the present case involves no shifting of the burden of persuasion, the constitutional restrictions on such presumptions are not before us, and I express no views on them.

It may well be that even those presumptions that do not shift the burden of persuasion cannot be used to prove an element of the offense, if the facts proved would not permit a reasonable mind to find the presumed fact beyond a reasonable doubt. My conclusion in Part II, infra, makes it unnecessary for me to address this concern here.

3. The Court suggests as the touchstone for its analysis a distinction between "mandatory" and "permissive" presumptions. For general discussions of the various forms of presumptions, see Jeffries & Stephan, Defenses, Presumptions and Burden of Proof in the Criminal Law, 88 Yale L.J. 1325 (1979); F. James Civil Procedure § 7.9 (1965). I have found no recognition in the Court's prior decisions that this distinction is important in analyzing presumptions used in criminal cases. Cf. F. James, Civil Procedure, ibid (distinguishing true "presumptions" from "permissible inferences").

state or foreign commerce]." As the Court interpreted the presumption, it placed upon a defendant only the obligation of presenting some exculpatory evidence concerning the origins of a firearm or ammunition, once the Government proved that the defendant had possessed the weapon and had been convicted of a crime of violence. Noting that juries must be permitted to infer from one fact the existence of another essential to guilt, "if reason and experience support the inference," id., at 467, 63 S.Ct., at 1244, the Court concluded that under some circumstances juries may be guided in making these inferences by legislative or common-law presumptions, even though they may be based "upon a view of relation broader than that a jury might take in a specific case," 319 U.S., at 468, 63 S.Ct., at 1245. To provide due process, however, there must be at least "a rational connection between the facts proved and the fact presumed"—a connection grounded in "common experience." Id., at 467, 63 S.Ct., at 1245. In *Tot,* the Court found that connection to be lacking.[4]

Subsequently, in Leary v. United States, 395 U.S. 6, 89 S.Ct. 1532, 23 L.Ed.2d 57 (1969), the Court reaffirmed and refined the due process requirement of *Tot* that inferences specifically commended to the attention of jurors must reflect generally accepted connections between related events. At issue in *Leary* was the constitutionality of a federal statute making it a crime to receive, conceal, buy, or sell marihuana illegally brought into the United States, knowing it to have been illegally imported. The statute provided that mere possession of marihuana "shall be deemed sufficient evidence to authorize conviction unless the defendant explains his possession to the satisfaction of the jury." After reviewing the Court's decisions in Tot v. United States, supra, and other criminal presumption cases, Mr. Justice Harlan, writing for the Court, concluded "that a criminal statutory presumption must be regarded as 'irrational' or 'arbitrary,' and hence unconstitutional, unless it can be said with substantial assurance that the presumed fact is more likely than not to flow from the proved fact on which it is made to depend." 395 U.S., at 36, 89 S.Ct., at 1548 (footnote omitted). The Court invalidated the statute, finding there to be insufficient basis in fact for the conclusion that those who possess marihuana are more likely than not to know that it was imported illegally.[5]

Most recently, in Barnes v. United States, supra, we considered the constitutionality of a quite different sort of presumption—one that suggested to the jury that "[p]ossession of recently stolen property, if

4. The analysis of Tot v. United States, 319 U.S. 463, 63 S.Ct. 1241, 87 L.Ed.2d 1519 (1943), was used by the Court in United States v. Gainey, 380 U.S. 63, 85 S.Ct. 754, 13 L.Ed.2d 658 (1965), and United States v. Romano, 382 U.S. 136, 86 S.Ct. 279, 15 L.Ed.2d 210 (1965).

5. Because the statute in Leary v. United States, 395 U.S. 6, 89 S.Ct. 1532, 23 L.Ed.2d 57 (1969), was found to be unconstitutional under the "more likely than not" standard, the Court explicitly declined to consider whether criminal presumptions also must follow "beyond a reasonable doubt" from their premises, if an essential element of the crime depends upon the presumption's use. Id., at 36 n. 64, 89 S.Ct., at 1548 n. 64. The Court similarly avoided this question in Turner v. United States, 396 U.S. 398, 416, 90 S.Ct. 642, 652, 24 L.Ed.2d 610 (1970).

not satisfactorily explained, is ordinarily a circumstance from which you may reasonably draw the inference * * * that the person in possession knew the property had been stolen." Id., 412 U.S. at 840 n. 3, 93 S.Ct., at 2360 n. 3. After reviewing the various formulations used by the Court to articulate the constitutionally required basis for a criminal presumption, we once again found it unnecessary to choose among them. As for the presumption suggested to the jury in *Barnes,* we found that it was well founded in history, common sense, and experience, and therefore upheld it as being "clearly sufficient to enable the jury to find beyond a reasonable doubt" that those in the unexplained possession of recently stolen property know it to have been stolen. Id., at 845, 93 S.Ct., at 2363.

In sum, our decisions uniformly have recognized that due process requires more than merely that the prosecution be put to its proof.[6] In addition, the Constitution restricts the court in its charge to the jury by requiring that, when particular factual inferences are recommended to the jury, those factual inferences be accurate reflections of what history, common sense, and experience tell us about the relations between events in our society. Generally this due process rule has been articulated as requiring that the truth of the inferred fact be more likely than not whenever the premise for the inference is true. Thus, to be constitutional a presumption must be at least more likely than not true.

II

In the present case, the jury was told that,

> "Our Penal Law also provides that the presence in an automobile of any machine gun or of any handgun or firearm which is loaded is presumptive evidence of their unlawful possession. In other words, [under] these presumptions or this latter presumption upon proof of the presence of the machine gun and the hand weapons, you may infer and draw a conclusion that such prohibited weapon was possessed by each of the defendants who occupied the automobile at the time when such instruments were found. The presumption or presumptions is effective only so long as there is no substantial evidence contradicting the conclusion flowing from the presumption, and the presumption is said to disappear when such contradictory evidence is adduced."

Undeniably, the presumption charged in this case encouraged the jury to draw a particular factual inference regardless of any other evidence presented: to infer that respondents possessed the weapons found in the automobile "upon proof of the presence of the machine gun and the hand weapon" and proof that respondents "occupied the automobile at the time such instruments were found." I believe that the presumption thus charged was unconstitutional because it did not fairly reflect what common sense and experience tell us about passen-

6. The Court apparently disagrees, contending that "the factfinder's responsibility * * * to find the ultimate facts beyond a reasonable doubt" is the only constitutional restraint upon the use of criminal presumptions at trial.

gers in automobiles and the possession of handguns. People present in automobiles where there are weapons simply are not "more likely than not" the possessors of those weapons.

Under New York law, "to possess" is "to have physical possession or otherwise to exercise dominion or control over tangible property." N.Y.Penal Law § 10.00(8). Plainly the mere presence of an individual in an automobile—without more—does not indicate that he exercises "dominion or control over" everything within it. As the Court of Appeals noted, there are countless situations in which individuals are invited as guests into vehicles the contents of which they know nothing about, much less have control over. Similarly, those who invite others into their automobile do not generally search them to determine what they may have on their person; nor do they insist that any handguns be identified and placed within reach of the occupants of the automobile. Indeed, handguns are particularly susceptible to concealment and therefore are less likely than are other objects to be observed by those in an automobile.

In another context, this Court has been particularly hesitant to infer possession from mere presence in a location, noting that "[p]resence is relevant and admissible evidence in a trial on a possession charge; but absent some showing of the defendant's function at [the illegal] still, its connection with possession is too tenuous to permit a reasonable inference of guilt—'the inference of the one from proof of the other is arbitrary * * *.' Tot v. United States, 319 U.S. 463, 467, 63 S.Ct. 1241, 1245, 87 L.Ed.2d 1519." United States v. Romano, 382 U.S. 136, 141, 86 S.Ct. 279, 282, 15 L.Ed.2d 210 (1965). We should be even more hesitant to uphold the inference of possession of a handgun from mere presence in an automobile, in light of common experience concerning automobiles and handguns. Because the specific factual inference recommended to the jury in this case is not one that is supported by the general experience of our society, I cannot say that the presumption charged is "more likely than not" to be true. Accordingly, respondents' due process rights were violated by the presumption's use.

As I understand it, the Court today does not contend that in general those who are present in automobiles are more likely than not to possess any gun contained within their vehicles. It argues, however, that the nature of the presumption here involved requires that we look, not only to the immediate facts upon which the jury was encouraged to base its inference, but to the other facts "proved" by the prosecution as well. The Court suggests that this is the proper approach when reviewing what it calls "permissive" presumptions because the jury was urged "to consider all the circumstances tending to support or contradict the inference."

It seems to me that the Court mischaracterizes the function of the presumption charged in this case. As it acknowledges was the case in *Romano,* supra, the "instruction authorized conviction even if the jury disbelieved all of the testimony except the proof of presence" in the automobile.[7] The Court nevertheless relies on all of the evidence introduced by the prosecution and argues that the "permissive" presumption could not have prejudiced defendants. The possibility that the jury disbelieved all of this evidence, and relied on the presumption, is simply ignored.

I agree that the circumstances relied upon by the Court in determining the plausibility of the presumption charged in this case would have made it reasonable for the jury to "infer that each of the respondents was fully aware of the presence of the guns and had both the ability and the intent to exercise dominion and control over the weapons." But the jury was told that it could conclude that respondents possessed the weapons found therein from proof of the mere fact of respondents' presence in the automobile. For all we know, the jury rejected all of the prosecution's evidence concerning the location and origin of the guns, and based its conclusion that respondents possessed the weapons solely upon its belief that respondents had been present in the automobile.[8] For the purposes of reviewing the constitutionality of the presumption at issue here, we must assume that this was the case. See Bollenbach v. United States, 326 U.S. 607, 613, 66 S.Ct. 402, 405, 90 L.Ed. 350 (1946); cf. Leary v. United States, 395 U.S. 6, 31, 89 S.Ct. 1532, 1545, 23 L.Ed.2d 57 (1969).

The Court's novel approach in this case appears to contradict prior decisions of this Court reviewing such presumptions. Under the Court's analysis, whenever it is determined that an inference is "permissive," the only question is whether, in light of all of the evidence adduced at trial, the inference recommended to the jury is a reasonable one. The Court has never suggested that the inquiry into the rational basis of a permissible inference may be circumvented in this manner. Quite the contrary, the Court has required that the "evidence *necessary to invoke the inference* [be] sufficient for a rational juror to find the

7. In commending the presumption to the jury, the court gave no instruction that would have required a finding of possession to be based on anything more than mere presence in the automobile. Thus, the jury was not instructed that it should infer that respondents possessed the handguns only if it found that the guns were too large to be concealed in Jane Doe's handbag, that the guns accordingly were in the plain view of respondents, that the weapons were within "easy access of the driver of the car and even, perhaps, of the other two respondents who were riding in the rear seat"; that it was unlikely that Jane Doe was solely responsible for the placement of the weapons in her purse; or that the case was "tantamount to one in which the guns were lying on the floor or the seat of the car in the plain view of the three other occupants of the automobile."

8. The Court is therefore mistaken in its conclusion that, because "respondents were not 'hitchhikers or other casual passengers,' and the guns were neither 'a few inches in length' nor 'out of [respondents'] sight,' " reference to these possibilities is inappropriate in considering the constitutionality of the presumption as charged in this case. To be sure, respondents' challenge is to the presumption as charged to the jury in this case. But in assessing its application here, we are not free, as the Court apparently believes, to disregard the possibility that the jury may have disbelieved all other evidence supporting an inference of possession. The jury may have concluded that respondents—like hitchhikers—had only an incidental relationship to the auto in which they were traveling, or that, contrary to some of the testimony at trial, the weapons were indeed out of respondents' sight.

inferred fact * * *." Barnes v. United States, 412 U.S. 843, 93 S.Ct. 2357, 37 L.Ed.2d 380 (1973) (emphasis supplied). See Turner v. United States, 396 U.S. 398, 407, 90 S.Ct. 642, 647, 24 L.Ed.2d 610 (1970). Under the presumption charged in this case, the only evidence necessary to invoke the inference was the presence of the weapons in the automobile with respondents—an inference that is plainly irrational.

In sum, it seems to me that the Court today ignores the teaching of our prior decisions. By speculating about what the jury may have done with the factual inference thrust upon it, the Court in effect assumes away the inference altogether, constructing a rule that permits the use of any inference—no matter how irrational in itself—provided that otherwise there is sufficient evidence in the record to support a finding of guilt. Applying this novel analysis to the present case, the Court upholds the use of a presumption that it makes no effort to defend in isolation. In substance, the Court—applying an unarticulated harmless error standard—simply finds that the respondents were guilty as charged. They may well have been but rather than acknowledging this rationale, the Court seems to have made new law with respect to presumptions that could seriously jeopardize a defendant's right to a fair trial. Accordingly, I dissent.

FRANCIS v. FRANKLIN

Supreme Court of the United States, 1985.
471 U.S. 307, 105 S.Ct. 1965, 85 L.Ed.2d 344.

Justice Brennan delivered the opinion of the Court.

This case requires that we decide whether certain jury instructions in a criminal prosecution in which intent is an element of the crime charged and the only contested issue at trial satisfy the principles of Sandstrom v. Montana, 442 U.S. 510, 99 S.Ct. 2450, 61 L.Ed.2d 39 (1979). Specifically, we must evaluate jury instructions stating that: (1) "[t]he acts of a person of sound mind and discretion are presumed to be the product of a person's will, but the presumption may be rebutted" and (2) "[a] person of sound mind and discretion is presumed to intend the natural and probable consequences of his acts, but the presumption may be rebutted." App. 8a–9a. The question is whether these instructions, when read in the context of the jury charge as a whole, violate the Fourteenth Amendment's requirement that the State prove every element of a criminal offense beyond a reasonable doubt. See *Sandstrom,* supra; In re Winship, 397 U.S. 358, 364, 90 S.Ct. 1068, 1072, 25 L.Ed.2d 368 (1970).

I

Respondent Raymond Lee Franklin, then 21 years old and imprisoned for offenses unrelated to this case, sought to escape custody on January 17, 1979, while he and three other prisoners were receiving dental care at a local dentist's office. The four prisoners were secured by handcuffs to the same 8–foot length of chain as they sat in the dentist's waiting room. At some point Franklin was released from the chain, taken into the dentist's office and given preliminary treatment, and then escorted back to the waiting room. As another prisoner was being released, Franklin, who had not been reshackled, seized a pistol from one of the two officers and managed to escape. He forced the dentist's assistant to accompany him as a hostage.

In the parking lot Franklin found the dentist's automobile, the keys to which he had taken before escaping, but was unable to unlock the door. He then fled with the dental assistant after refusing her request to be set free. The two set out across an open clearing and came upon a local resident. Franklin demanded this resident's car. When the resident responded that he did not own one, Franklin made no effort to harm him but continued with the dental assistant until they came to the home of the victim, one Collie. Franklin pounded on the heavy wooden front door of the home and Collie, a retired 72–year-old carpenter, answered. Franklin was pointing the stolen pistol at the door when Collie arrived. As Franklin demanded his car keys, Collie slammed the door. At this moment Franklin's gun went off. The bullet traveled through the wooden door and into Collie's chest killing him. Seconds later the gun fired again. The second bullet traveled upward through the door and into the ceiling of the residence.

Hearing the shots, the victim's wife entered the front room. In the confusion accompanying the shooting, the dental assistant fled and Franklin did not attempt to stop her. Franklin entered the house, demanded the car keys from the victim's wife, and added the threat "I might as well kill you." When she did not provide the keys, however, he made no effort to thwart her escape. Franklin then stepped outside and encountered the victim's adult daughter. He repeated his demand for car keys but made no effort to stop the daughter when she refused the demand and fled. Failing to obtain a car, Franklin left and remained at large until nightfall.

Shortly after being captured, Franklin made a formal statement to the authorities in which he admitted that he had shot the victim but emphatically denied that he did so voluntarily or intentionally. He claimed that the shots were fired in accidental response to the slamming of the door. He was tried in the Superior Court of Bibb County, Georgia, on charges of malice murder [1]—a capital offense in Georgia—and kidnaping. His sole defense to the malice murder charge was a lack of the requisite intent to kill. To support his version of the events Franklin offered substantial circumstantial evidence tending to show a lack of intent. He claimed that the circumstances surrounding the firing of the gun, particularly the slamming of the door and the

1. The malice murder statute at the time in question provided:

"A person commits murder when he unlawfully and with malice aforethought, either express or implied, causes the death of another human being. * * * Malice shall be implied where no considerable provocation appears and where all the circumstances of the killing show an abandoned and malignant heart." Ga.Code Ann. § 26–1101(a) (1978).

trajectory of the second bullet, supported the hypothesis of accident, and that his immediate confession to that effect buttressed the assertion. He also argued that his treatment of every other person encountered during the escape indicated a lack of disposition to use force.

On the dispositive issue of intent, the trial judge instructed the jury as follows:

> "A crime is a violation of a statute of this State in which there shall be a union of joint operation of act or omission to act, and intention or criminal negligence. A person shall not be found guilty of any crime committed by misfortune or accident where it satisfactorily appears there was no criminal scheme or undertaking or intention or criminal negligence. The acts of a person of sound mind and discretion are presumed to be the product of the person's will, but the presumption may be rebutted. A person of sound mind and discretion is presumed to intend the natural and probable consequences of his acts, but the presumption may be rebutted. A person will not be presumed to act with criminal intention but the trier of facts, that is, the Jury, may find criminal intention upon a consideration of the words, conduct, demeanor, motive and all other circumstances connected with the act for which the accused is prosecuted." App. 8a–9a.

Approximately one hour after the jury had received the charge and retired for deliberation, it returned to the courtroom and requested reinstruction on the element of intent and the definition of accident. Id., at 13a–14a. Upon receiving the requested reinstruction, the jury deliberated 10 more minutes and returned a verdict of guilty. The next day Franklin was sentenced to death for the murder conviction.

Franklin unsuccessfully appealed the conviction and sentence to the Georgia Supreme Court. Franklin v. State, 245 Ga. 141, 263 S.E.2d 666, cert. denied, 447 U.S. 930, 100 S.Ct. 3029, 65 L.Ed.2d 1124 (1980). He then unsuccessfully sought state post-conviction relief. See Franklin v. Zant, Habeas Corpus File No. 5025 (Super.Ct. Butts Cty., Ga., Sept. 10, 1981), cert. denied, 456 U.S. 938, 102 S.Ct. 1995, 72 L.Ed.2d 458 (1982). Having exhausted state postconviction remedies, Franklin sought federal habeas corpus relief, pursuant to 28 U.S.C. § 2254, in the United States District Court for the Middle District of Georgia on May 14, 1982. That court denied the application without an evidentiary hearing. App. 16a.

Franklin appealed to the United States Court of Appeals for the Eleventh Circuit. The Court of Appeals reversed the District Court and ordered that the writ issue. The court held that the jury charge on the dispositive issue of intent could have been interpreted by a reasonable juror as a mandatory presumption that shifted to the defendant a burden of persuasion on the intent element of the offense. For this reason the court held that the jury charge ran afoul of fundamental Fourteenth Amendment due process guarantees as explicated in Sandstrom v. Montana, 442 U.S. 510, 99 S.Ct. 2450, 61 L.Ed.2d 39 (1979). See 720 F.2d 1206, 1208–1212 (1983). In denying petitioner Francis' subsequent petition for rehearing, the panel elaborated its earlier holding to make clear that the effect of the presumption at issue had been considered in the context of the jury charge as a whole. See 723 F.2d 770, 771–772 (1984) (*per curiam*).

We granted certiorari. 467 U.S. ——, 104 S.Ct. 2677, 81 L.Ed.2d 873 (1984). We affirm.

II

The Due Process Clause of the Fourteenth Amendment "protects the accused against conviction except upon proof beyond a reasonable doubt of every fact necessary to constitute the crime with which he is charged." In re Winship, 397 U.S. 358, 364, 90 S.Ct. 1068, 1073, 25 L.Ed.2d 368 (1970). This "bedrock, 'axiomatic and elementary' " [constitutional] principle, id., at 363, 90 S.Ct., at 1072, prohibits the State from using evidentiary presumptions in a jury charge that have the effect of relieving the State of its burden of persuasion beyond a reasonable doubt of every essential element of a crime. Sandstrom v. Montana, supra, at 520–524, 99 S.Ct., at 2457–2459; Patterson v. New York, 432 U.S. 197, 210, 215, 97 S.Ct. 2319, 53 L.Ed.2d 281 (1977); Mullaney v. Wilbur, 421 U.S. 684, 698–701, 95 S.Ct. 1881, 1889–1890, 44 L.Ed.2d 508 (1975); see also Morissette v. United States, 342 U.S. 246, 274–275, 72 S.Ct. 240, 255, 96 L.Ed. 288 (1952). The prohibition protects the "fundamental value determination of our society," given voice in Justice Harlan's concurrence in *Winship,* "that it is far worse to convict an innocent man than to let a guilty man go free." 397 U.S. at 372, 90 S.Ct., at 1077. See Speiser v. Randall, 357 U.S. 513, 525–526, 78 S.Ct. 1332, 1341–1342, 2 L.Ed.2d 1460 (1958). The question before the Court in this case is almost identical to that before the Court in *Sandstrom:* "whether the challenged jury instruction had the effect of relieving the State of the burden of proof enunciated in *Winship* on the critical question of * * * state of mind," 442 U.S., at 521, 99 S.Ct., at 2458, by creating a mandatory presumption of intent upon proof by the State of other elements of the offense.

The analysis is straightforward. "The threshold inquiry in ascertaining the constitutional analysis applicable to this kind of jury instruction is to determine the nature of the presumption it describes." *Id.,* at 514, 99 S.Ct., at 2454. The court must determine whether the challenged portion of the instruction creates a mandatory presumption, see id., at 520–524, 99 S.Ct., at 2457–2459, or merely a permissive inference, see Ulster County Court v. Allen, 442 U.S. 140, 157–163, 99 S.Ct. 2213, 2224–2227, 60 L.Ed.2d 777 (1979). A mandatory presumption instructs the jury that it must infer the presumed fact if the State proves certain predicate facts.[2] A permissive inference suggests to the

2. A mandatory presumption may be either conclusive or rebuttable. A conclusive presumption removes the presumed element from the case once the State has proven the predicate facts giving rise to the presumption. A rebuttable presumption does not remove the presumed element from the case but nevertheless requires the jury to find the presumed element unless the defendant persuades the jury that such a finding is unwarranted. See Sandstrom v. Montana, 442 U.S. 510, 517–518, 99 S.Ct. 2450, 2455–2456, 61 L.Ed.2d 39 (1979).

jury a possible conclusion to be drawn if the State proves predicate facts, but does not require the jury to draw that conclusion.

Mandatory presumptions must be measured against the standards of *Winship* as elucidated in *Sandstrom*. Such presumptions violate the Due Process Clause if they relieve the State of the burden of persuasion on an element of an offense. Patterson v. New York, supra, 432 U.S., at 215, 97 S.Ct., at 2329 ("a State must prove every ingredient of an offense beyond a reasonable doubt and * * * may not shift the burden of proof to the defendant by presuming that ingredient upon proof of the other elements of the offense"). See also *Sandstrom*, supra, 442 U.S., at 520–524, 99 S.Ct., at 2457–2459; Mullaney v. Wilbur, supra, 421 U.S., at 698–701, 95 S.Ct., at 1889–1890.[3] A permissive inference does not relieve the State of its burden of persuasion because it still requires the State to convince the jury that the suggested conclusion should be inferred based on the predicate facts proven. Such inferences do not necessarily implicate the concerns of *Sandstrom*. A permissive inference violates the Due Process Clause only if the suggested conclusion is not one that reason and common sense justify in light of the proven facts before the jury. *Ulster County Court*, supra, 442 U.S., at 157–163, 99 S.Ct., at 2224–2227.

Analysis must focus initially on the specific language challenged, but the inquiry does not end there. If a specific portion of the jury charge, considered in isolation, could reasonably have been understood as creating a presumption that relieves the State of its burden of persuasion on an element of an offense, the potentially offending words must be considered in the context of the charge as a whole. Other instructions might explain the particular infirm language to the extent that a reasonable juror could not have considered the charge to have created an unconstitutional presumption. Cupp v. Naughton, 414 U.S. 141, 147, 94 S.Ct. 396, 400, 38 L.Ed.2d 368 (1973). This analysis "requires careful attention to the words actually spoken to the jury * * *, for whether a defendant has been accorded his constitutional rights depends upon the way in which a reasonable juror could have interpreted the instruction." *Sandstrom*, supra, 442 U.S., at 514, 99 S.Ct., at 2454.

A

Franklin levels his constitutional attack at the following two sentences in the jury charge: "The acts of a person of sound mind and discretion are presumed to be the product of a person's will, but the presumption may be rebutted. A person of sound mind and discretion is presumed to intend the natural and probable consequences of his acts, but the presumption may be rebutted." App. 8a–9a.[4] The Geor-

presumption

3. We are not required to decide in this case whether a mandatory presumption that shifts only a burden of production to the defendant is consistent with the Due Process Clause, and we express no opinion on that question.

4. Intent to kill is an element of the offense of malice murder in Georgia. See Patterson v. State, 239 Ga. 409, 416–417, 238 S.E.2d 2, 8 (1977).

gia Supreme Court has interpreted this language as creating no more than a permissive inference that comports with the constitutional standards of Ulster County Court v. Allen, supra. See Skrine v. State, 244 Ga. 520, 521, 260 S.E.2d 900 (1979). The question, however, is not what the State Supreme Court declares the meaning of the charge to be, but rather what a reasonable juror could have understood the charge as meaning. *Sandstrom,* 442 U.S., at 516–517, 99 S.Ct., at 2455 (state court "is not the final authority on the interpretation which a jury could have given the instruction"). The federal constitutional question is whether a reasonable juror could have understood the two sentences as a mandatory presumption that shifted to the defendant the burden of persuasion on the element of intent once the State had proved the predicate acts.

The challenged sentences are cast in the language of command. They instruct the jury that "acts of a person of sound mind and discretion *are presumed* to be the product of the person's will," and that a person "*is presumed* to intend the natural and probable consequences of his acts," App. 8a–9a (emphasis added). These words carry precisely the message of the language condemned in *Sandstrom,* supra, at 515, 99 S.Ct., at 2454 ("'[t]he law presumes that a person intends the ordinary consequences of his voluntary acts'"). The jurors "were not told that they had a choice, or that they *might* infer that conclusion; they were told only that the law presumed it. It is clear that a reasonable juror could easily have viewed such an instruction as mandatory." 442 U.S., at 515, 99 S.Ct., at 2454 (emphasis added). The portion of the jury charge challenged in this case directs the jury to presume an essential element of the offense—intent to kill—upon proof of other elements of the offense—the act of slaying another. In this way the instructions "undermine the factfinder's responsibility at trial, based on evidence adduced by the State, to *find* the ultimate facts beyond a reasonable doubt." Ulster County Court v. Allen, supra, 442 U.S., at 156, 99 S.Ct., at 2224 (emphasis added).

The language challenged here differs from *Sandstrom,* of course, in that the jury in this case was explicitly informed that the presumptions "may be rebutted." App. 8a–9a. The State makes much of this additional aspect of the instruction in seeking to differentiate the present case from *Sandstrom.* This distinction does not suffice, however, to cure the infirmity in the charge. Though the Court in *Sandstrom* acknowledged that the instructions there challenged could have been reasonably understood as creating an irrebuttable presumption, 442 U.S., at 517, 99 S.Ct., at 2455, it was not on this basis alone that the instructions were invalidated. Had the jury reasonably understood the instructions as creating a mandatory *rebuttable* presumption the instructions would have been no less constitutionally infirm. Id., at 520–524, 99 S.Ct., at 2457–2459.

An irrebuttable or conclusive presumption relieves the State of its burden of persuasion by removing the presumed element from the case entirely if the State proves the predicate facts. A mandatory rebuttable presumption does not remove the presumed element from the case if the State proves the predicate facts, but it nonetheless relieves the State of the affirmative burden of persuasion on the presumed element by instructing the jury that it must find the presumed element unless the defendant persuades the jury not to make such a finding. A mandatory rebuttable presumption is perhaps less onerous from the defendant's perspective, but it is no less unconstitutional. Our cases make clear that "[s]uch shifting of the burden of persuasion with respect to a fact which the State deems so important that it must be either proved or presumed is impermissible under the Due Process Clause." Patterson v. New York, 432 U.S., at 215, 97 S.Ct., at 2329. In *Mullaney v. Wilbur* we explicitly held unconstitutional a mandatory rebuttable presumption that shifted to the defendant a burden of persuasion on the question of intent. 421 U.S., at 698–701, 95 S.Ct., at 1889–1890. And in *Sandstrom* we similarly held that instructions that might reasonably have been understood by the jury as creating a mandatory rebuttable presumption were unconstitutional. 442 U.S., at 524, 99 S.Ct., at 2459.[5]

When combined with the immediately preceding mandatory language, the instruction that the presumptions "may be rebutted" could reasonably be read as telling the jury that it was required to infer intent to kill as the natural and probable consequence of the act of firing the gun unless the defendant persuaded the jury that such an inference was unwarranted. The very statement that the presumption "may be rebutted" could have indicated to a reasonable juror that the defendant bore an affirmative burden of persuasion once the State proved the underlying act giving rise to the presumption. Standing alone, the challenged language undeniably created an unconstitutional burden-shifting presumption with respect to the element of intent.

5. The dissent's suggestion that our holding with respect to the constitutionality of mandatory rebuttable presumptions "extends" prior law is simply inaccurate. In *Sandstrom v. Montana* our holding rested on equally valid alternative rationales: "the question before this Court is whether the challenged jury instruction had the effect of relieving the State of the burden of proof enunciated in *Winship* on the critical question of petitioner's state of mind. We conclude that *under either of the two possible interpretations of the instruction set out above*, precisely that effect would result, and that the instruction therefore represents constitutional error." 442 U.S., at 521, 99 S.Ct., at 2458 (emphasis added). In any event, the principle that mandatory rebuttable presumptions violate due process had been definitively established prior to *Sandstrom*. In *Mullaney v. Wilbur*, it was a mandatory *rebuttable* presumption that we held unconstitutional. 421 U.S., at 698–701, 95 S.Ct., at 1889–1890. As we explained in *Patterson v. New York:*

> "*Mullaney* surely held that a State * * * may not shift the burden of proof to the defendant by presuming that ingredient upon proof of the other elements of the offense. * * * Such shifting of the burden of persuasion with respect to a fact which the State deems so important that it must be either proved or presumed is impermissible under the Due Process Clause." 432 U.S., at 215, 97 S.Ct., at 2329.

An *irrebuttable* presumption, of course, does not shift any burden to the defendant; it eliminates an element from the case if the State proves the requisite predicate facts. Thus the Court in *Patterson* could only have been referring to a mandatory *rebuttable* presumption when it stated that "such *shifting* of the burden of persuasion * * * is impermissible." Ibid. (emphasis added).

B

The jury, of course, did not hear only the two challenged sentences. The jury charge taken as a whole might have explained the proper allocation of burdens with sufficient clarity that any ambiguity in the particular language challenged could not have been understood by a reasonable juror as shifting the burden of persuasion. See Cupp v. Naughton, 414 U.S. 141, 94 S.Ct. 396, 38 L.Ed.2d 368 (1973). The State argues that sufficient clarifying language exists in this case. In particular, the State relies on an earlier portion of the charge instructing the jurors that the defendant was presumed innocent and that the State was required to prove every element of the offense beyond a reasonable doubt.[6] The State also points to the sentence immediately following the challenged portion of the charge, which reads: "[a] person will not be presumed to act with criminal intention. * * * " App. 9a.

As we explained in *Sandstrom,* general instructions on the State's burden of persuasion and the defendant's presumption of innocence are not "rhetorically inconsistent with a conclusive or burden-shifting presumption," because "[t]he jury could have interpreted the two sets of instructions as indicating that the presumption was a means by which proof beyond a reasonable doubt as to intent could be satisfied." 442 U.S., at 518–519, n. 7, 99 S.Ct., at 2456, n. 7. In light of the instructions on intent given in this case, a reasonable juror could thus have thought that, although intent must be proved beyond a reasonable doubt, proof of the firing of the gun and its ordinary consequences constituted proof of intent beyond a reasonable doubt unless the defendant persuaded the jury otherwise. Cf. Mullaney v. Wilbur, 421 U.S., at 703, n. 31, 95 S.Ct., at 1891, n. 31. These general instructions as to the prosecution's burden and the defendant's presumption of innocence do not dissipate the error in the challenged portion of the instructions.

Nor does the more specific instruction following the challenged sentences—"A person will not be presumed to act with criminal intention but the trier of facts, that is, the Jury, may find criminal intention upon a consideration of the words, conduct, demeanor, motive and all other circumstances connected with the act for which the accused is prosecuted," App. 9a—provide a sufficient corrective. It may well be that this "*criminal* intention" instruction was not directed to the element of intent at all, but to another element of the Georgia crime of malice murder. The statutory definition of capital murder in Georgia requires malice aforethought. Ga.Code Ann. § 16–5–1 (1984) (formerly Ga.Code Ann. § 26–1101(a) (1978)). Under state law malice aforethought comprises two elements: intent to kill and the absence of

6. These portions of the instructions read:

"* * * I charge you that before the State is entitled to a verdict of conviction of this defendant at your hands * * * the burden is upon the State of proving the defendant's guilt as charged * * * beyond a reasonable doubt." App. 4a.

"Now * * * the defendant enters upon his trial with the presumption of innocence in his favor and this presumption * * * remains with him throughout the trial, unless it is overcome by evidence sufficiently strong to satisfy you of his guilt * * * beyond a reasonable doubt." Id., at 5a.

provocation or justification. See Patterson v. State, 239 Ga. 409, 416–417, 238 S.E.2d 2, 8 (1977); Lamb v. Jernigan, 683 F.2d 1332, 1337 (CA11 1982) (interpreting Ga.Code Ann. § 16–5–1), cert. denied, 460 U.S. 1024, 103 S.Ct. 1276, 75 L.Ed.2d 496 (1983). At another point in the charge in this case, the trial court, consistently with this understanding of Georgia law, instructed the jury that malice is "the unlawful, deliberate intention to kill a human being without justification or mitigation or excuse." App. 10a.

The statement "*criminal* intention may not be presumed" may well have been intended to instruct the jurors that they were not permitted to presume the absence of provocation or justification but that they could infer this conclusion from circumstantial evidence. Whatever the court's motivation in giving the instruction, the jury could certainly have understood it this way. A reasonable juror trying to make sense of the juxtaposition of an instruction that "a person of sound mind and discretion is presumed to intend the natural and probable consequences of his acts," App. 8a–9a and an instruction that "[a] person will not be presumed to act with criminal intention," App. 9a, may well have thought that the instructions related to different elements of the crime and were therefore not contradictory—that he could presume intent to kill but not the absence of justification or provocation.[7]

7. Because the jurors heard the divergent intent instructions before they heard the instructions about absence of justification, the dissent argues that no reasonable juror could have understood the criminal intent instruction as referring to the absence of justification. The dissent reproves the Court for reading the instructions "as a 'looking-glass charge' which, when held to a mirror, reads more clearly in the opposite direction." A reasonable juror, however, would have sought to make sense of the conflicting intent instructions not only at the initial moment of hearing them but also later in the jury room after having heard the entire charge. One would expect most of the juror's reflection about the meaning of the instructions to occur during this subsequent deliberative stage of the process. Under these circumstances, it is certainly reasonable to expect a juror to attempt to make sense of a confusing earlier portion of the instruction by reference to a later portion of the instruction. The dissent obviously accepts this proposition because much of the language the dissent marshals to argue that the jury would not have misunderstood the intent instruction appears several paragraphs after the conflicting sentences about intent. Indeed much of this purportedly clarifying language appears *after* the portion of the charge concerning the element of absence of justification.

It is puzzling that the dissent thinks it "defies belief" to suggest that a reasonable juror would have related the contradictory intent instructions to the later instructions about the element of malice. As the portion of the charge quoted in the dissent makes clear, the later malice instructions specifically spoke of intent: "Malice * * * is the unlawful, deliberate intention to kill a human being without justification or mitigation or excuse, which intention must exist at the time of the killing." App. 10a. A reasonable juror might well have sought to understand this language by reference to the earlier instruction referring to criminal intent.

Finally, the dissent's representation of the language in this part of the charge as a clarifying "express statement[ ] * * * that there was no burden on the defendant to disprove malice" is misleading. The relevant portion of the charge reads: "it is not required of the accused to prove an absence of malice, if the evidence for the State shows facts which may excuse or justify the homicide." App. 10a. This language is most naturally read as implying that if the State's evidence *does not* show mitigating facts the defendant *does* have the burden to prove absence of malice. Thus, if anything, this portion of the charge exacerbates the potential for an unconstitutional shifting of the burden to the defendant.

Even if a reasonable juror could have understood the prohibition of presuming "criminal intention" as applying to the element of intent, that instruction did no more than contradict the instruction in the immediately preceding sentence. A reasonable juror could easily have resolved the contradiction in the instruction by choosing to abide by the mandatory presumption and ignore the prohibition of presumption. Nothing in these specific sentences or in the charge as a whole makes clear to the jury that one of these contradictory instructions carries more weight than the other. Language that merely contradicts and does not explain a constitutionally infirm instruction will not suffice to absolve the infirmity. A reviewing court has no way of knowing which of the two irreconcilable instructions the jurors applied in reaching their verdict.[8] Had the instruction "[a] person * * * is presumed to intend the natural and probable consequences of his acts," App. 8a–9a, been followed by the instruction "*this means that* a person will not be

8. The dissent would hold a jury instruction invalid only when "it is at least likely" that a reasonable juror would have understood the charge unconstitutionally to shift a burden of persuasion. Apparently this "at least likely" test would not be met even when there exists a reasonable possibility that a juror would have understood the instructions unconstitutionally, so long as the instructions admitted of a "more 'reasonable'" constitutional interpretation. Apart from suggesting that application of the "at least likely" standard would lead to the opposite result in the present case, the dissent leaves its proposed alternative distressingly undefined. Even when faced with clearly contradictory instructions respecting allocation of the burden of persuasion on a crucial element of an offense, a reviewing court apparently would be required to intuit, based on its sense of the "tone" of the jury instructions as a whole, see Ibid., whether a reasonable juror was more likely to have reached a constitutional understanding of the instructions than an unconstitutional understanding of the instructions.

This proposed alternative standard provides no sound basis for appellate review of jury instructions. Its malleability will certainly generate inconsistent appellate results and thereby compound the confusion that has plagued this area of the law. Perhaps more importantly, the suggested approach provides no incentive for trial courts to weed out potentially infirm language from jury instructions; in every case, the "presumption of innocence" boilerplate in the instructions will supply a basis from which to argue that the "tone" of the charge as a whole is not unconstitutional. For these reasons, the proposed standard promises reviewing courts, including this Court, an unending stream of cases in which ad hoc decisions will have to be made about the "tone" of jury instructions as a whole.

Most importantly, the dissent's proposed standard is irreconcilable with bedrock due process principles. The Court today holds that contradictory instructions as to intent—one of which imparts to the jury an unconstitutional understanding of the allocation of burdens of persuasion—create a reasonable likelihood that a juror understood the instructions in an unconstitutional manner, unless other language in the charge *explains* the infirm language sufficiently to eliminate this possibility. If such a reasonable possibility of an unconstitutional understanding exists, "we have no way of knowing that [the defendant] was not convicted on the basis of the unconstitutional instruction." *Sandstrom,* 442 U.S., at 526, 99 S.Ct., at 2460. For this reason, it has been settled law since Stromburg v. California, 283 U.S. 359, 51 S.Ct. 532, 75 L.Ed. 1117 (1931), that when there exists a reasonable possibility that the jury relied on an unconstitutional understanding of the law in reaching a guilty verdict, that verdict must be set aside. See Leary v. United States, 395 U.S. 6, 31–32, 89 S.Ct. 1532, 1545–1546, 23 L.Ed.2d 57 (1969); Bachellar v. Maryland, 397 U.S. 564, 571, 90 S.Ct. 1312, 1316, 25 L.Ed.2d 570 (1970). The dissent's proposed alternative cannot be squared with this principle; notwithstanding a substantial doubt as to whether the jury decided the State proved intent beyond a reasonable doubt, the dissent would uphold this conviction based on an impressionistic and intuitive judgment that it was *more* likely that the jury understood the charge in a constitutional manner than in an unconstitutional manner.

presumed to act with criminal intention but the jury may find criminal intention upon consideration of all circumstances connected with the act for which the accused is prosecuted," a somewhat stronger argument might be made that a reasonable juror could not have understood the challenged language as shifting the burden of persuasion to the defendant. Cf. *Sandstrom,* 442 U.S., at 517, 99 S.Ct., at 2455 ("given the lack of qualifying instructions as to the legal effect of the presumption, we cannot discount the possibility that the jury may have interpreted the instruction" in an unconstitutional manner). See also Corn v. Zant, 708 F.2d 549, 559 (CA11 1983), cert. denied, 467 U.S. ___, 104 S.Ct. 2670, 81 L.Ed.2d 375 (1984). Whether or not such explanatory language might have been sufficient, however, no such language is present in this jury charge. If a juror thought the "criminal intention" instruction pertained to the element of intent, the juror was left in a quandary as to whether to follow that instruction or the immediately preceding one it contradicted.[9]

Because a reasonable juror could have understood the challenged portions of the jury instruction in this case as creating a mandatory presumption that shifted to the defendant the burden of persuasion on the crucial element of intent, and because the charge read as a whole

9. Rejecting this conclusion, the dissent "simply do[es] not believe" that a reasonable juror would have paid sufficiently close attention to the particular language of the jury instructions to have been perplexed by the contradictory intent instructions. See also Sandstrom v. Montana, 442 U.S., at 528, 99 S.Ct., at 2461 (Rehnquist, J., concurring) ("I continue to have doubts as to whether this particular jury was so attentively attuned to the instructions of the trial court that it divined the difference recognized by lawyers between 'infer' and 'presume' "). Apparently the dissent would have the degree of attention a juror is presumed to pay to particular jury instructions vary with whether a presumption of attentiveness would help or harm the criminal defendant. See, e.g., Parker v. Randolph, 442 U.S. 62, 73, 99 S.Ct. 2132, 2139, 60 L.Ed.2d 713 (1979) (opinion of Rehnquist, J.) ("A crucial assumption underlying that system [of trial by jury] is that juries will follow the instructions given them by the trial judge. Were this not so, it would be pointless for a trial court to instruct a jury, and even more pointless for an appellate court to reverse a criminal conviction because the jury was improperly instructed. * * * [A]n instruction directing the jury to consider a codefendant's extrajudicial statement only against its source has been found sufficient to avoid offending the confrontation right of the implicated defendant"); see also id., at 75, n. 7, 99 S.Ct., at 2140, n. 7 ("The 'rule'—indeed, the premise upon which the system of jury trials functions under the American system judicial system—is that juries can be trusted to follow the trial court's instructions"). Cf. Wainwright v. Witt, 469 U.S. ___, 105 S.Ct. 844, 83 L.Ed.2d 841 (1985).

The Court presumes that jurors, conscious of the gravity of their task, attend closely the particular language of the trial court's instructions in a criminal case and strive to understand, make sense of, and follow the instructions given them. Cases may arise in which the risk of prejudice inhering in material put before the jury may be so great that even a limiting instruction will not adequately protect a criminal defendant's constitutional rights. E.g., Bruton v. United States, 391 U.S. 123, 88 S.Ct. 1620, 20 L.Ed.2d 476 (1968); Jackson v. Denno, 378 U.S. 368, 84 S.Ct. 1774, 12 L.Ed.2d 908 (1964). Absent such extraordinary situations, however, we adhere to the crucial assumption underlying our constitutional system of trial by jury that jurors carefully follow instructions. As Chief Justice Traynor has said, "we must assume that juries for the most part understand and faithfully follow instructions. The concept of a fair trial encompasses a decision by a tribunal that has understood and applied the law to all material issues in the case." Quoted in Connecticut v. Johnson, 460 U.S. 73, 85, n. 14, 103 S.Ct. 969, 977, n. 14, 74 L.Ed.2d 823 (1983) (opinion of Blackmun, J.).

does not explain or cure the error, we hold that the jury charge does not comport with the requirements of the Due Process Clause.

* * *

Affirmed.

JUSTICE POWELL, dissenting.

* * *

Together, I believe that the instructions on reasonable doubt and the presumption of innocence, the instruction that "criminal intention" cannot be presumed, and the instructions governing the interpretation of circumstantial evidence removed any danger that a reasonable juror could have believed that the two suspect sentences placed on the defendant the burden of persuasion on intent. When viewed as a whole, the jury instructions did not violate due process. I accordingly dissent.

JUSTICE REHNQUIST, with whom THE CHIEF JUSTICE and JUSTICE O'CONNOR join, dissenting.

* * *

I see no meaningful distinction between *Cupp* and the case at bar. Here the jury was instructed no less than four times that the State bore the burden of proof beyond a reasonable doubt. This language was accompanied early in the charge by a detailed discussion indicating that the jurors were the judges of their own reasonable doubt, that this doubt could arise after taking into account all the circumstances surrounding the incident at issue, and that where such doubt existed it was the jurors' duty to acquit. Four sentences prior to the offending language identified by the Court the jury was explicitly charged that "there is no burden on the defendant to prove anything." Immediately following that language the jury was charged that a person "will not be presumed to act with criminal intention," but that the jury could find such intention based upon the circumstances surrounding the act. The jury was then charged on Georgia's definition of malice, an essential element of murder which includes (1) deliberate intent to kill (2) without justification or mitigation or excuse. Again, the jury was explicitly charged that "it is not incumbent upon the accused to prove an absence of malice, if the evidence for the prosecution shows facts which may excuse or justify the homicide."

The Court nevertheless concludes, upon reading the charge in its entirety, that a "reasonable juror" could have understood the instruction to mean (1) that the State had satisfied its burden of proving intent to kill by introducing evidence of the defendant's acts—drawing, aiming and firing the gun—the "natural and probable consequences" of which were the death in question; (2) that upon proof of these acts the burden shifted to the defendant to disprove that he had acted with intent to kill; and (3) that if the defendant introduced no evidence or the jury was unconvinced by his evidence, the jury was *required* to find that the State had proved intent to kill even if the State's proof did not convince them of the defendant's intent.

The reasoning which leads to this conclusion would appeal only to a lawyer, and it is indeed difficult to believe that "reasonable jurors" would have arrived at it on their own. * * *

Chapter 10

JUDICIAL NOTICE *
[FED.R.EVID. ART. II]

VARCOE v. LEE

Supreme Court of California, 1919.
180 Cal. 338, 181 P. 223.

OLNEY, J.

This is an action by a father to recover damages suffered through the death of his child, resulting from her being run over by an automobile of the defendant Lee, driven at the time by the other defendant, Nichols, the chauffeur of Lee. The automobile was going south on Mission street in San Francisco, and was approaching the crossing of Twenty–First street, when the child, in an endeavor to cross the street, was run over and killed. The cause was tried before a jury, which returned a verdict of $5,000 for the plaintiff. From the judgment upon this verdict, the defendants appeal.

The alleged negligence, upon which plaintiff's right to recover is predicated, consisted in the speed at which it is claimed the automobile was proceeding. * * *

* * *

* * * When he came to charge the jury, the trial judge instructed them that, if they found that the defendant Nichols was running the automobile along Mission street at the time of the accident at a greater speed than 15 miles an hour, he was violating the city ordinance, and also the state Motor Vehicle Act, and that such speed was negligence in itself. The trial judge then read to the jury the portion of subdivision

* See 9 Wigmore, Evidence ch. 92 (Chadbourn rev. 1981); McCormick, Evidence ch. 35 (4th ed. 1992); Maguire, Evidence—Common Sense and Common Law 166–75 (1947); Davis, Judicial Notice, 1969 Law & Soc.Ord. 513; Mansfield, Jury Notice, 74 Geo.L.J. 395 (1985); McNaughton, Judicial Notice—Excerpts Relating to the Morgan–Wigmore Controversy, 14 Vand.L.Rev. 779 (1961); Morgan, Judicial Notice, 57 Harv. L.Rev. 269 (1944); Roberts, Preliminary Notes Toward a Study of Judicial Notice, 52 Cornell L.Q. 210 (1967); Turner, Judicial Notice and Federal Rule of Evidence 201—A Rule Ready for Change, 45 U.Pitt. L.Rev. 181 (1983).

"b" of section 22 of the Motor Vehicle Act (St.1913, p. 639), which provides that it shall be unlawful to operate a motor "in the business district" of any incorporated city or town at a greater speed than 15 miles an hour, and defines (see section 1) a business district as "territory * * * contiguous to a public highway, which is at that point mainly built up with structures devoted to business." Having read this definition, the court proceeded with its charge as follows:

> "That is the situation on Mission street between Twentieth and Twenty-Second streets, where this accident happened, so that is a business district and the maximum legal rate of speed on that street at the time of the happening of this accident was 15 miles an hour." * * *

So far as the record itself goes, there is little to show what the character of Mission street between Twentieth and Twenty-Second streets is. The defendant Nichols himself refers to it in his testimony as part of the "downtown district," undoubtedly meaning thereby part of the business district of the city. The evidence shows incidentally that at the scene of the accident there was a drug store, a barber shop, a haberdashery, and a saloon. If there had been any issue or question as to the character of the district, the record in this meager condition would not justify the taking of the question from the jury, as was undoubtedly done by the instruction complained of.

The actual fact of the matter is, however, that Mission street, between Twentieth and Twenty-Second streets, is a business district, within the definition of the Motor Vehicle Act, beyond any possibility of question. It has been such for years. Not only this, but its character is known as a matter of common knowledge by any one at all familiar with San Francisco. Mission street, from its downtown beginning at the water front to and beyond the district of the city known as the Mission, is second in importance and prominence as a business street only to Market street. The probabilities are that every person in the courtroom at the trial, including judge, jury, counsel, witnesses, parties and officers of the court, knew perfectly well what the character of the location was. It was not a matter about which there could be any dispute or question. If the court had left the matter to the determination of the jury, and they for some inconceivable reason had found that it was not a business district, it would have been the duty of the court to set aside the verdict. We are asked now to reverse the judgment, because the court assumed, without submitting to the jury, what could not be disputed, and what he and practically every resident in the county for which the court was sitting knew to be a fact. If error there was, it is clear that, upon the actual fact, there was no prejudice to the defendants.

It would have been much better if counsel for the plaintiff or the trial judge himself had inquired of defendants' counsel, before the case went to the jury, whether there was any dispute as to the locality being a business district within the meaning of the state law. There could have been but one reasonable answer, and, if any other were given, the matter could have been easily settled beyond any possibility of question. But this was not done, and we are now confronted by the question whether either this court or the trial court can take judicial notice of the real fact.

An appellate court can properly take judicial notice of any matter of which the court of original jurisdiction may properly take notice. Pennington v. Gibson, 16 How. 65, 14 L.Ed. 847; Salt Lake City v. Robinson, 39 Utah 260, 116 P. 442, 35 L.R.A., N.S., 610, Ann.Cas.1913E, 61; 15 Ruling Case Law, 1063.

In fact, a particularly salutary use of the principle of judicial notice is to sustain on appeal, a judgment clearly in favor of the right party, but as to which there is in the evidence an omission of some necessary fact which is yet indisputable and a matter of common knowledge, and was probably assumed without strict proof for that very reason. Campbell v. Wood, 116 Mo. 196, 22 S.W. 796.

The question, therefore, is: Was the superior court for the city and county of San Francisco, whose judge and talesmen were necessarily residents of the city, entitled to take judicial notice of the character of one of the most important and best-known streets in the city? If it were, the court was authorized to charge the jury as it did. Section 2102, Code Civ.Proc.

It should perhaps be noted that the fact that the trial judge knew what the actual fact was, and that it was indisputable would not of itself justify him in recognizing it. Nor would the fact that the character of the street was a matter of common knowledge and notoriety justify him in taking the question from the jury, if there were any possibility of dispute as to whether or not that character was such as to constitute it a business district within the definition of the statute applicable. If such question could exist, the fact involved—whether the well-known character of the street was sufficient to make it a business district—was one for determination by the jury. But we have in this case a combination of two circumstances. In the first place, the fact is indisputable and beyond question. In the second place, it is a matter of common knowledge throughout the jurisdiction in and for which the court is sitting.

* * *

It is truly said that the power of judicial notice is, as to matters claimed to be matters of general knowledge, one to be used with caution. If there is any doubt whatever, either as to the fact itself or as to its being a matter of common knowledge, evidence should be required; but, if the court is of the certain opinion that these requirements exist, there can properly be no hesitation. In such a case there is, on the one hand, no danger of a wrong conclusion as to the fact—and such danger is the reason for the caution in dispensing with the evidence—and, on the other hand, purely formal and useless proceedings will be avoided.

Little assistance can be had by a search of the authorities for exactly similar cases. The one perhaps nearest to it that we have found is State v. Ruth, 14 Mo.App. 226. What may be a proper subject of judicial notice at one time or place may not be at another. It would be wholly unreasonable to require proof, if the fact became material, as to the general location in the city of San Francisco of its city hall before a judge and jury made up of residents of that city and actually sitting in the building. But before a judge and jury in another county proof should be made. The difference lies in the fact being one of common knowledge in one jurisdiction and not in the other. Similarly it has been held repeatedly that courts will judicially notice the general doctrines of any religious denomination prevalent within its jurisdiction, and yet it was held by an Ohio court, and properly held, in the early days of Christian Science, that notice would not be taken of the doctrines of that sect. Evans v. State, 9 Ohio St.C.Pl.Dec. 222, 6 Ohio N.P. 129. Now that the sect has grown to large numbers, and its general doctrines are a matter of common knowledge, it is as proper to notice them as to notice those of older denominations. As is well said by Wigmore, 4 Wigmore on Ev. § 2580:

> "Applying the general principle (ante, section 2565), especially in regard to the element of notoriousness, courts are found noticing, from time to time, a varied array of unquestionable facts, ranging throughout the data of commerce, industry, history, and natural science. It is unprofitable, as well as impracticable, to seek to connect them by generalities and distinctions; for the notoriousness of a truth varies much with differences of period and of place. It is even erroneous, in many, if not in most instances, to regard them as precedents. It is the spirit and example of the rulings, rather than their precise tenor, that is to be useful in guidance."

The test, therefore, in any particular case where it is sought to avoid or excuse the production of evidence because the fact to be proven is one of general knowledge and notoriety, is: (1) Is the fact one of common, everyday knowledge in that jurisdiction, which every one of average intelligence and knowledge of things about him can be presumed to know? and (2) is it certain and indisputable? If it is, it is a proper case for dispensing with evidence, for its production cannot add or aid. On the other hand, we may well repeat, if there is any reasonable question whatever as to either point, proof should be required. Only so can the danger involved in dispensing with proof be avoided. Even if the matter be one of judicial cognizance, there is still no error or impropriety in requiring evidence.

Applying this test to the facts of the case, the matter is not in doubt. The character of Mission street is as well known to San Franciscans as the character of Spring street to residents of Los Angeles, or of State street to residents of Chicago, or of Forty-Second street to residents of New York, or of F street to residents of Washington. It is a matter of their everyday common information and experience, and one about which there can be no dispute.

The conclusion follows that the charge of the trial court that Mission street, between Twentieth and Twenty-Second streets, was a business district, was not error. That judgment is therefore affirmed.

UNITED KLANS OF AMERICA v. McGOVERN, 453 F.Supp. 836, 839 (N.D.Ala.1978), aff'd, 621 F.2d 152 (5th Cir.1980). "Alternatively, the court makes this determination pursuant to Rule 201 of the Federal Rules of Evidence which, in pertinent part, states that the court can take judicial notice of a fact 'generally known within the territorial jurisdiction of the trial court or * * * capable of accurate and ready determination by resort to sources whose accuracy cannot reasonably be questioned.' The United Klans has been and continues to be a 'white supremacy' organization whose purposes and policies are implemented by acts of terror and intimidation. U.S. v. Crenshaw County Unit of the United Klans of America, 290 F.Supp. 181 (M.D.Ala.1968), footnote 2; U.S. v. Original Knights of the KKK, 250 F.Supp. 330 (E.D.La.1965). 'This court would not hesitate to judicially notice the historical reputation of the Klan as a whole concerning its purposes and methods.' U.S. v. Crenshaw County Unit of the United Klans of America, supra, footnote 1.

"It is plain and generally publicly known within this district that said organization is a white hate group. The court judicially notices this fact."

LASTER v. CELOTEX CORP.

United States District Court, Southern District of Ohio, 1984.
587 F.Supp. 542.

ORDER DENYING MOTIONS TO TAKE JUDICIAL NOTICE

CARL B. RUBIN, CHIEF JUDGE.

This matter is before the Court pursuant to plaintiffs' pretrial Motion to Take Judicial Notice of Asbestosis (doc. no. 28) and Motion to Take Judicial Notice of Mesothelioma (doc. no. 29). For the reasons that follow, the motions are denied.

Plaintiff Laster alleges that Chester Laster contracted pleural mesothelioma as a result of his exposure to and inhalation of asbestos dust and fibers while he was employed at the Philip-Carey/Celotex Plant from 1929 through 1970. The plaintiffs have moved under Rule 201, Federal Rules of Evidence, that the Court take judicial notice "of the fact that asbestosis is a disease which is caused by the inhalation of asbestos dust and fibers." (Doc. No. 28). A bibliography as well as a proposed jury instruction were attached. The instruction stated "that inhalation of asbestos fibers and asbestos dust is the cause of the medical condition known as asbestosis." (Id.).

Rule 201 provides in pertinent part:

(a) This rule governs only judicial notice of adjudicative facts.

(b) A judicially noted fact must be one not subject to reasonable dispute in that it is either (1) generally known within the territorial jurisdiction of the trial court or (2) capable of accurate and ready determination by resort to sources whose accuracy cannot reasonably be questioned.

* * *

(d) A court shall take judicial notice if requested by a party and supplied with the necessary information.

Fed.R.Evid. 201. At the outset it is acknowledged that federal not state law is applicable to this inquiry. Gallup v. Caldwell, 120 F.2d 90, 94 (3d Cir.1941); Baltimore & O.R. Co. v. Reaux, 59 F.Supp. 969, 975 (N.D.Ohio 1945). In this particular context, "Rule 201 relates to medical facts not subject to reasonable dispute." Hardy v. Johns-Manville Sales Corp., 681 F.2d 334, 347 (5th Cir.1982). Clearly, the facts pertaining to whether asbestosis and mesothelioma are caused by exposure to asbestos are "adjudicative facts" under Rule 201. See United States v. Gould, 536 F.2d 216, 219 (8th Cir.1976). Because the physical, chemical and physiological properties of asbestos fibers and dust are not "generally known" within the territorial jurisdiction of this Court, subsection (b)(1) of Rule 201 is inapplicable.

The defendant challenges the accuracy of the statement as phrased by the plaintiff because its implication that asbestos causes asbestosis regardless of the physical characteristics of the fiber and the length of exposure. This point is well taken. There are a number of conditions that must be evaluated before it can be stated with any degree of medical certainty that asbestosis will be induced by the inhalation of asbestos fibers and dust. See e.g., Frank, *Asbestosis,* 4A Attorneys' Textbook of Medicine § 205C–13 (R. Gray ed., 3d ed. 1984) (asbestos "dust particles must be less than 100 micra in size" to be inhaled); Califano, Appendix to *Asbestos Law: Victim's Rights and Industry Reaction,* 330 Annals N.Y.Acad.Sci. 266, 268 (1979) ("[t]he Surgeon General advises me that clinical experience indicates a person who smokes and has been exposed to asbestos faces a greater risk of developing asbestosis and of dying from a respiratory ailment that [sic] an asbestos exposed individual who does not smoke."); Irwig, *Risk of Asbestosis in Crocidolite and Amosite Mines in South Africa,* id. at 43–45 ("The prevalence of parenchymal abnormality is not predicted by race or asbestos type but, in addition to age and duration of exposure, is predicted by the fiber concentration to which workers are exposed. This prediction applies to short fibers and less significantly to long fibers."); Anderson, *Asbestosis Among Household Contacts of Asbestos Factory Workers,* id. at 397. "It is important to note that many people exposed to asbestos—perhaps a majority—suffer no apparent ill effects." Richmond, 330 Annals N.Y.Acad.Sci. at 270.

The Court finds that the conditions under which a person may contract asbestosis are subject to reasonable dispute and not capable of accurate and ready determination by resort to sources whose accuracy cannot reasonably be questioned. Taking judicial notice that the inhalation of asbestos *may* cause asbestosis under certain conditions would have no appreciable impact on the length of expert testimony in this case.

Turning to the next issue, the plaintiff requests that the Court take judicial notice of "the fact that mesothelioma is a disease which is caused by the inhalation of asbestos dust and fibers." (Doc. No. 29). Attached to the memorandum are a bibliography and a proposed jury instruction, which states "that inhalation of asbestos fibers and asbestos dust is the cause of the medical condition known as mesothelioma." (Id.).

In *Non-Asbestos Related Malignant Mesothelioma: A Review,* the authors acknowledge that while there have been reports finding a link between asbestos inhalation and mesothelioma, there have been other "excellent review articles that indicate a less clear association between asbestos exposure and mesothelioma." (Doc. No. 32, Exhibit 1 at 2). Other hypothesized agents for the induction of mesothelioma include fibrous glass, plastics, thorium dioxide and other chemicals, radioactivity, viruses and nickel. (Id. at 11); Frank at § 205C–20 ("Zeolites have been associated with the development of mesotheliomas in man. Changes in the pleura caused by asbestos * * * have not been found useful to date as predicators of the development of mesothelioma."). "[S]ufficient evidence exists to suggest that non-asbestos agents can induce malignant mesotheliomas in man." (Doc. No. 32, Exhibit 1 at 1).

Because there is no consensus on the etiology of mesothelioma, the Court finds that the proposed fact, "asbestos is the cause of mesothelioma," is subject to reasonable dispute by the medical community and is not capable of accurate and ready determination by resort to sources whose accuracy cannot reasonably be questioned. This holding is consistent with the decision of *Hardy,* wherein the Court found judicial notice of the fact that asbestos causes cancer inappropriate because the facts were subject to reasonable dispute. 681 F.2d at 347–48 ("[t]he proposition that asbestos causes cancer, because it is inextricably linked to a host of disputed issues—e.g., can mesothelioma arise without exposure to asbestos * * *."). Accordingly, the plaintiffs' Motion to Take Judicial Notice of Mesothelioma (doc. no. 29) is **DENIED.**

The plaintiffs' Motion to Take Judicial Notice of Asbestosis (doc. no. 28) and Motion to Take Judicial Notice of Mesothelioma (doc. no. 29) are each **DENIED.**

IT IS SO ORDERED.

COUNTRY CLUB HILLS HOMEOWNERS ASS'N v. JEFFERSON METROPOLITAN HOUSING AUTHORITY, 5 Ohio App.3d 77, 449

N.E.2d 460, 463–64 (1981). "There is no evidence in the record of this case that proves that plaintiffs were property owners and taxpayers of Jefferson County. When defense counsel called this fact to the attention of the trial court, counsel for plaintiffs asked the trial court, pursuant to Evid.R. 201(D), to take judicial notice that the plaintiffs are property owners pursuant to Evid.R. 201(B), which provides as follows:

'A judicially noticed fact must be one not subject to reasonable dispute in that it is either (1) generally known within the territorial jurisdiction of the trial court or (2) capable of accurate and ready determination by resort to sources whose accuracy cannot reasonably be questioned.'

"Counsel for plaintiffs argued that the question whether plaintiffs were property owners and taxpayers of Jefferson County could be readily determined at the county recorder's office in the courthouse.

"The trial court in its 'Findings of Fact' found that plaintiffs were property owners and taxpayers of the city of Steubenville and the Indian Creek School District but did not state the basis of such finding.

"We hold that placing the burden on the trial judge to check the records of the county recorder's office to determine whether plaintiffs were property owners and taxpayers is not 'capable of * * * ready determination' within the meaning of Evid.R. 201(B). The burden of proof is on the plaintiffs and not on the trial judge. All that was necessary was for some plaintiffs to testify that they were property owners and taxpayers.

"Therefore, we hold that the trial judge could not take judicial notice that plaintiffs were property owners and taxpayers under the facts of this case."

HADLAND v. SCHROEDER, 326 N.W.2d 709, 713 (N.D.1982). "In the instant case, the district court took judicial notice *sua sponte* as is proper under Rule 201(c), N.D.R.Ev. The Explanatory Note to Rule 201, North Dakota Rules of Court '81 Pamph., West, states in pertinent part:

> 'Whenever a judge contemplates taking judicial notice of a fact on his own motion, he should clearly inform the parties of his intention and provide an opportunity for hearing of the issue. If the court fails to give prior notification, it must provide an opportunity for objection after judicial notice has been taken.
>
> 'The object of this subdivision [Rule 201(e)] is to achieve procedural fairness. No special form of notice is required nor is there a need for a formal hearing. If the parties, in fact, are given notice and an opportunity to be heard, the requirements of this subdivision will have been satisfied.'

"Even though there is no indication in the record that the parties were informed of the district court's intention to take judicial notice, both parties were present when the court delivered its memorandum decision and, therefore, had an opportunity to object when the court took judicial notice of the fact that a man who has undergone a successful vasectomy cannot father a child. Therefore, the court did not commit error when it took judicial notice in the instant case."

PRESTIGE HOMES, INC. v. LEGOUFFE

Supreme Court of Colorado, 1983.
658 P.2d 850.

LOHR, JUSTICE.

This case arises from a workmen's compensation claim filed by the respondent, Guy Y. Legouffe, for a permanent disability suffered as a result of a heart attack allegedly precipitated by an industrial accident. The Industrial Commission (commission) denied benefits, affirming a referee's finding that Legouffe had not established a causal connection between the accident and the injury. The Colorado Court of Appeals reversed and remanded the case to the commission for further proceedings to determine the amount of benefits due the respondent. Legouffe v. Prestige Homes, Inc., 634 P.2d 1010 (Colo.App.1981). We granted certiorari to review the court of appeals' judgment and now reverse that judgment and direct that the case be remanded to the commission for further proceedings.

The industrial accident giving rise to the present controversy occurred on September 8, 1976, while Legouffe was carrying out his regular duties as a construction superintendent for the petitoner, Prestige Homes, Inc. At that time, Legouffe was thirty-three years old and had been working for the company for approximately five years. His duties included field supervision of construction of single family residences as well as some manual labor as a carpenter.

On the day of the accident, Legouffe proceeded to connect an air compressor unit on the back of his pickup truck to a temporary electric supply at the job site. After plugging one end of a cable into the electric supply, Legouffe connected the other end to the air compressor and suddenly received a shock of 220 volts. The claimant testified that he felt the shock enter one hand and travel through his arm and chest and out the other arm. He fell to the ground and experienced chest pain and difficulty in breathing. A co-worker took him to the hospital where the attending physician, Dr. Lissauer, diagnosed the problem as myocardial infarction (heart attack). Tests performed on November 10, 1976, revealed that Legouffe suffers from coronary artery disease and a ventricular aneurysm, which significantly impair his circulation and the proper functioning of his heart.

The employer filed an accident report and the insurance carrier filed a general admission of liability with the workmen's compensation section of the State Department of Labor and Employment. Thereafter, Dr. Lissauer filed a supplemental medical report stating his opinion that Legouffe is permanently disabled due to heart disease, and Legouffe filed a claim for workmen's compensation benefits for a permanent disability. The insurance carrier requested that the claimant undergo an additional medical examination by Dr. Mutz, who subsequently filed reports in which he concluded that neither the claimant's heart attack nor his heart disease was causally related to the electric shock. The insurance carrier then filed a denial of liability and requested reimbursement for payments already made to Legouffe pursuant to the earlier general admission of liability. Evidentiary hearings on the issues of causation and extent of disability were held before a Department of Labor and Employment referee.

The expert testimony at the hearings on the issue of causation was in conflict. Dr. Lissauer testified for the claimant. The doctor stated his opinion that the electric shock was the precipitating cause of the heart attack, but that an after-the-fact attempt to ascertain the specific manner in which the shock caused the heart attack would be conjectural. The doctor testified that the cause of the claimant's left ventricular aneurysm was definitely the heart attack, but that he could not express an opinion as to whether the coronary artery disease was preexisting because the testing method used for diagnosing the disease does not give any indication of the cause. Dr. Lissauer did agree, however, that such disease is usually a long-standing condition.

Dr. Mutz testified for the employer and gave his opinion that the claimant had serious preexisting coronary artery disease, that he was predisposed to having myocardial infarction, and that there was no causal connection between the electric shock and the heart attack.[2] The doctor based his opinion on the facts that coronary artery disease is a long-term degenerative condition which is often asymptomatic until the time of infarction, and that a shock of 220 volts is not severe enough to cause a heart attack of the type experienced by the respondent.[3] One indication of the lack of severity of the shock, he testified, is that the claimant did not suffer any external burns on his body.

2. The doctor also stated his opinion in his medical reports and testimony that Legouffe may not have received a shock. He speculated that the trauma of the heart attack itself could have given the claimant the impression that he had suffered a shock, especially because he was holding electric wires at the time of the heart attack. However, the question of whether or not Legouffe received a shock is not at issue because the employer stipulated at the commencement of the hearings that the occurrence of an industrial accident is not disputed. Counsel for the claimant did not object to the portions of Dr. Mutz' medical reports and testimony admitted into evidence that refer to his opinion concerning the nonoccurrence of a shock. While this evidence is irrelevant, the referee's and commission's orders indicate that this evidence was disregarded, and appropriate findings were made that Legouffe did suffer an electric shock within the course and scope of his employment. On remand, the referee should disregard evidence that Legouffe may not have experienced an electric shock.

3. Dr. Mutz testified that a less severe electric shock could result in ventricular fibrillation, which will cause unconsciousness and can damage the heart if not promptly corrected, but the claimant's continued consciousness after the shock reflected that he had not experienced ventricular fibrillation.

The referee issued an order denying the claim for compensation, finding that a causal connection between the electric shock and Legouffe's heart attack had not been shown. Upon the claimant's petition for review, the referee issued a supplemental order, which summarized the evidence and concluded that the claim should be denied. The commission reviewed the record and adopted and affirmed the referee's findings, conclusions and decision.

On appeal, the Colorado Court of Appeals reversed the commission's final order and remanded the case for further proceedings to determine the amount of benefits to which the claimant is entitled. The court first addressed the issue of whether Legouffe was required to prove that "unusual exertion" caused his heart attack as suggested by section 8–41–108(2.5), C.R.S.1973 (1982 Supp.), and concluded that such proof is not required in cases where a preexisting heart disease is aggravated by job-related trauma. The court then held that the proper standard of proof on the issue of causation is whether such causal connection is established with reasonable probability rather than reasonable medical certainty, noting that the referee's findings indicate confusion over the proper standard to apply. Finally, the court took judicial notice of certain scientific propositions found in medical treatises and concluded that Dr. Mutz' testimony was based upon an erroneous assumption of scientific fact and therefore could not serve as a basis for the referee's conclusion that no causal connection had been shown. We first address the judicial notice issue and conclude that the court of appeals' judgment should be reversed because of its erroneous application of the judicial notice rule, C.R.E. 201. We agree with the court of appeals' conclusion that the referee's findings indicate confusion in the application of the "unusual exertion" requirement and in the standard of proof the claimant was required to satisfy, and accordingly remand the case for further findings applying appropriate standards.

I.

In reversing the commission's order denying benefits to the claimant, the court of appeals disregarded the referee's factual finding, based on Dr. Mutz' testimony, that the heart attack was not caused by the electric shock. It did so on the ground that the finding was based upon an assumption contrary to certain propositions of scientific fact of which the court took judicial notice pursuant to Colorado Rule of Evidence 201. We conclude that the court of appeals erred in applying the judicial notice rule to disregard the referee's factual finding; therefore, reversal of that court's judgment is required.

Facts subject to the judicial notice rule are those "not subject to reasonable dispute" and must be either "generally known within the territorial jurisdiction of the trial court" or "capable of accurate and ready determination by resort to sources whose accuracy cannot reasonably be questioned." C.R.E. 201(b). Appellate courts, as well as trial courts, may make use of this rule. C.R.E. 201(f). The rule is a codification of existing case law, Larsen v. Archdiocese of Denver, 631

P.2d 1163 (Colo.App.1981), and has traditionally been used cautiously in keeping with its purpose to bypass the usual fact finding process only when the facts are of such common knowledge that they cannot reasonably be disputed. See Anderson v. Lett, 150 Colo. 478, 374 P.2d 355 (1962) (conclusions reached by application of mathematical principles cannot be judicially noticed unless such conclusions are irrefutable); Winterberg v. Thomas, 126 Colo. 60, 246 P.2d 1058 (1952) (unquestioned laws of mathematics are judicially noticeable); Sierra Mining Co. v. Lucero, 118 Colo. 180, 194 P.2d 302 (1948) (calendar days and dates are subject to judicial notice); People ex rel. Flanders v. Neary, 113 Colo. 12, 154 P.2d 48 (1944) (the fact that a term of public office was due to expire in a short time was judicially noticed); see also Federal Rules of Evidence, Note to Subdivision (b) of Rule 201, Notes of Advisory Committee on Proposed Rules.

The court of appeals relied on medical treatises not offered or admitted into evidence, and not cited by either Dr. Lissauer or Dr. Mutz, for its finding that an electric shock caused by contact with a 220 volt power line can cause serious injury without leaving a visible burn mark. The court in effect assumed the role of an expert medical witness by discrediting the opinion of Dr. Mutz based on independent research and interpretation of medical texts which properly should be interpreted only by experts in the appropriate field. See Sayers v. Gardner, 380 F.2d 940 (6th Cir.1967); Ross v. Gardner, 365 F.2d 554 (6th Cir.1966). To accept the court's substitution of its own fact findings for those of the referee in this instance would expand the judicial notice rule far beyond its intended scope. The court compared the type of facts judicially noticed here with the simple mathematical calculations based on distance and speed in Winterberg v. Thomas, supra. The conclusions to be drawn from the scientific propositions cited by the court of appeals, however, are clearly not indisputable, as shown by the conflicting testimony in the present case. Dr. Lissauer and Dr. Mutz, both certified as experts in the field of cardiology, had different opinions about the effects of a 220 volt shock on the human body. Dr. Lissauer stated that, although he could not express an opinion as to the significance of external burns, in his experience he had observed a patient with severe heart damage from electrocution without external burns. Dr. Mutz, on the other hand, expressed his opinion, without citing specific cases, that the lack of visible burn marks on the hands reflects that the shock did not directly damage Legouffe's heart.[4]

Even if the proposition that a 220 volt shock could cause serious injury without burn marks were widely recognized within the relevant community, the fact that two medical experts have a reasonable dispute over the conclusion to be reached from that proposition—namely,

4. The two opinions are not necessarily inconsistent. As previously noted, Dr. Mutz testified that a less severe shock, which would not cause burns, could result in heart damage through ventricular fibrillation, but the claimant's symptoms were inconsistent with such a diagnosis. See note 3, supra.

whether Legouffe's heart attack was caused by the shock in this case—makes the court of appeals' disregard of the referee's findings clearly erroneous. As we stated in Anderson v. Lett, supra:

> Courts cannot indulge in arbitrary deductions from scientific laws as applied to evidence except where the conclusions reached are so irrefutable that no room is left for the entertainment by reasonable minds of any other conclusion. [Citation omitted.]

150 Colo. at 481–82, 374 P.2d at 357. Dr. Mutz' medical conclusion that Legouffe's heart attack could not have been caused by the shock is entirely consistent with the factual proposition stated by the court of appeals that "serious injury" can result from a 220 volt shock without external burns.[5] The court of appeals has supplied its own conclusion from a scientific proposition that does not compel that conclusion.

* * *

UNITED STATES v. GOULD

United States Court of Appeals, Eighth Circuit, 1976.
536 F.2d 216.

Gibson, Chief Judge.

Defendants, Charles Gould and Joseph Carey, were convicted of conspiring to import (Count I) and actually importing (Count II) cocaine from Colombia, South America, into the United States in violation of the Controlled Substances Import and Export Act. 21 U.S.C. § 951 et seq. (1970). * * *

* * *

Defendants do not challenge the sufficiency of the evidence but contend that the District Court erred in (1) improperly taking judicial notice and instructing the jury that cocaine hydrochloride is a schedule II controlled substance * * *.

As to the first issue, defendants contend that evidence should have been presented on the subject of what controlled substances fit within schedule II for the purpose of establishing a foundation that cocaine hydrochloride was actually within that schedule. Schedule II controlled substances, for the purpose of the Controlled Substances Import and Export Act, conclude the following:

> (a) Unless specifically excepted or unless listed in another schedule, any of the following substances whether produced directly or indirectly by extraction from substances of vegetable origin, or inde-

5. See notes 3 and 4, supra. Additionally we note that the court of appeals has mischaracterized the bases of Dr. Mutz' conclusion that there was no causal connection between the accident and the injury. Our reading of his testimony indicates that the doctor's opinion was based only in part on the lack of external burn marks and that other factors, including the nature and extent of Legouffe's preexisting disease, influenced his conclusion. Thus, even if we accept the court of appeals' use of judicial notice, the facts noticed are not sufficient to undercut the doctor's opinion and the referee's conclusions drawn from the evidence as a whole.

pendently by means of chemical synthesis, or by a combination of extraction and chemical synthesis:

* * *

(4) Coca leaves and any salt, compound, derivative, or preparation of coca leaves, and any salt, compound, derivative, or preparation thereof which is chemically equivalent or identical with any of these substances, except that the substances shall not include decocainized coca leaves or extraction of coca leaves, which extractions do not contain cocaine or ecgonine.

21 U.S.C. § 812 (1970); see 21 C.F.R. § 1308.12 (1975).

At trial, two expert witnesses for the Government testified as to the composition of the powdered substance removed from Ms. Kenworthy's platform shoes at the Miami airport. One expert testified that the substance was comprised of approximately 60 percent cocaine hydrochloride. The other witness stated that the white powder consisted of 53 percent cocaine.[3] There was no direct evidence to indicate that cocaine hydrochloride is a derivative of coca leaves. In its instructions to the jury, the District Court stated:

> If you find the substance was cocaine hydrochloride, you are instructed that cocaine hydrochloride is a schedule II controlled substance under the laws of the United States.

Our inquiry on this first assignment of error is twofold. We must first determine whether it was error for the District Court to take judicial notice of the fact that cocaine hydrochloride is a schedule II controlled substance. Secondly, if we conclude that it was permissible to judicially notice this fact, we must then determine whether the District Court erred in instructing the jury that it must accept this fact as conclusive.

The first aspect of this inquiry merits little discussion. In Hughes v. United States, 253 F. 543, 545 (8th Cir.1918), cert. denied, 249 U.S. 610, 39 S.Ct. 291, 63 L.Ed. 801 (1919), this court stated:

> It is also urged that there was no evidence that morphine, heroin, and cocaine are derivatives of opium and coca leaves. We think that is a matter of which notice may be taken. In a sense the question is one of the definition or meaning of words long in common use, about which there is no obscurity, controversy, or dispute, and of which the imperfectly informed can gain complete knowledge by resort to dictionaries within reach of everybody. * * * Common knowledge, or the common means of knowledge, of the settled, undisputed, things of life, need not always be laid aside on entering a courtroom.

It is apparent that courts may take judicial notice of any fact which is "capable of such instant and unquestionable demonstration, if desired, that no party would think of imposing a falsity on the tribunal in the

3. It is not significant that one expert witness testified that the substance contained cocaine hydrochloride and the other testified that it was comprised in part of cocaine. The fact that cocaine hydrochloride contains cocaine is common knowledge. United States v. Sims, 529 F.2d 10, 11 (8th Cir.1976).

face of an intelligent adversary." IX J. Wigmore, *Evidence* § 2571, at 548 (1940). The fact that cocaine hydrochloride is derived from coca leaves is, if not common knowledge, at least a matter which is capable of certain, easily accessible and indisputably accurate verification. See *Webster's Third New International Dictionary* 434 (1961). Therefore, it was proper for the District Court to judicially notice this fact. Our conclusion on this matter is amply supported by the weight of judicial authority. United States v. Mills, 149 U.S.App.D.C. 345, 463 F.2d 291, 296 n. 27 (D.C.Cir.1972); Padilla v. United States, 278 F.2d 188, 190 (5th Cir.1960); United States v. Amidzich, 396 F.Supp. 1140, 1148 (E.D.Wis. 1975); see United States v. Sims, 529 F.2d 10, 11 (8th Cir.1976); United States v. Pisano, 193 F.2d 355, 359 (7th Cir.1971).

Our second inquiry involves the propriety of the District Court's instruction to the jurors that this judicially noticed fact must be accepted as conclusive by them. Defendants, relying upon Fed.R.Ev. 201(g), urge that the jury should have been instructed that it could discretionarily accept or reject this fact. Rule 201(g) provides:

> In a civil action or proceeding, the court shall instruct the jury to accept as conclusive any fact judicially noticed. In a criminal case, the court shall instruct the jury that it may, but is not required to, accept as conclusive any fact judicially noticed.[4]

It is clear that the reach of rule 201 extends only to adjudicative, not legislative, facts. Fed.R.Ev. 201(a). Consequently, the viability of defendants' argument is dependent upon our characterization of the fact judicially noticed by the District Court as adjudicative, thus invoking the provisions of rule 201(g). In undertaking this analysis, we note at the outset that rule 201 is not all-encompassing. "Rule 201 * * * was deliberately drafted to cover only a small fraction of material usually subsumed under the concept of 'judicial notice.'" 1 J. Weinstein, *Evidence* ¶ 201[01] (1975).

The precise line of demarcation between adjudicative facts and legislative facts is not always easily identified. Adjudicative facts have been described as follows:

> When a court * * * finds facts concerning the immediate parties—who did what, where, when, how, and with what motive or intent—the court * * * is performing an adjudicative function, and the facts are conveniently called adjudicative facts. * * *

4. In the proposed federal Rules of Evidence, forwarded by the Supreme Court of the United States to Congress on February 5, 1973, rule 201(g) did not draw this distinction between civil and criminal cases. The proposed rule 201(g) provided that "[t]he judge shall instruct the jury to accept as established any facts judicially noticed." Congress disagreed with this unqualified rule requiring mandatory instructions in all cases. It was feared that requiring the jury to accept a judicially noticed adjudicative fact in a criminal case might infringe upon the defendants' Sixth Amendment right to a trial by jury. H.Rep. No. 93–650, 93d Cong., 1st Sess. 6–7 (1973), reprinted in 4 U.S.Code Cong. & Admin.News pp. 7075, 7080 (1974). Consequently, Congress adopted the present text of rule 201(g) which requires a mandatory instruction in civil cases but a discretionary instruction in criminal cases.

> Stated in other terms, the adjudicative facts are those to which the law is applied in the process of adjudication. They are the facts that normally go to the jury in a jury case. They relate to the parties, their activities, their properties, their businesses.

2 K. Davis, *Administrative Law Treatise* § 15.03, at 353 (1958).

Legislative facts, on the other hand, do not relate specifically to the activities or characteristics of the litigants. A court generally relies upon legislative facts when it purports to develop a particular law or policy and thus considers material wholly unrelated to the activities of the parties.

> Legislative facts are ordinarily general and do not concern the immediate parties. In the great mass of cases decided by courts * * *, the legislative element is either absent or unimportant or interstitial, because in most cases the applicable law and policy have been previously established. But whenever a tribunal engages in the creation of law or of policy, it may need to resort to legislative facts, whether or not those facts have been developed on the record.

2 K. Davis, *Administrative Law Treatise,* supra at § 15.03.[5]

Legislative facts are established truths, facts or pronouncements that do not change from case to case but apply universally, while adjudicative facts are those developed in a particular case.

Applying these general definitions, we think it is clear that the District Court in the present case was judicially noticing a legislative fact rather than an adjudicative fact. Whether cocaine hydrochloride is or is not a derivative of the coca leaf is a question of scientific fact applicable to the administration of the Comprehensive Drug Abuse Prevention and Control Act of 1970. 21 U.S.C. § 801 et seq. (1970). The District Court reviewed the schedule II classifications contained in 21 U.S.C. § 812, construed the language in a manner which comports with common knowledge and understanding, and instructed the jury as to the proper law so interpreted. It is undisputed that the trial judge is required to fully and accurately instruct the jury as to the law to be applied in a case. Bird v. United States, 180 U.S. 356, 361, 21 S.Ct. 403, 405, 45 L.Ed. 570, 573 (1901). When a court attempts to ascertain the governing law in a case for the purpose of instructing the jury, it must necessarily rely upon facts which are unrelated to the activities of the immediate parties. These extraneous, yet necessary, facts fit within the definition of legislative facts and are an indispensable tool used by judges when discerning the applicable law through interpretation.[6]

5. For a further discussion on the distinction between legislative and adjudicative facts, see Marshall v. Sawyer, 365 F.2d 105, 111–12 (9th Cir.1966), *cert. denied,* 385 U.S. 1006, 87 S.Ct. 713, 17 L.Ed.2d 545 (1967); State v. Freeman, 440 P.2d 744, 757–58 (Okla.1968); C. McCormick *Law of Evidence* §§ 328, 331 (2d ed. 1972); Fed. R.Ev. 201, Notes of Advisory Committee; Davis, Judicial Notice, 55 Colum.L.Rev. 945, 952–59 (1955).

6. The Notes of the Advisory Committee to rule 201 offer support for the proposition that courts utilize legislative facts when they interpret a statute.

While judges use judicial notice of "propositions of generalized knowledge" in a variety of situations: *determining the va-*

The District Court, therefore, was judicially noticing such a legislative fact when it recognized that cocaine hydrochloride is derived from coca leaves and is a schedule II controlled substance within the meaning of § 812.

Through similar reasoning, this judicially noticed fact simply cannot be appropriately categorized as an adjudicative fact. It does not relate to "who did what, where, when, how, and with what motive or intent," nor is it a fact which would traditionally go to the jury. See 2 K. Davis, *Administrative Law Treatise,* supra at § 15.03. The fact that cocaine hydrochloride is a derivative of coca leaves is a universal fact that is unrelated to the activities of the parties to this litigation. There was no preemption of the jury function to determine what substance was actually seized from Ms. Kenworthy at the Miami airport. The jury was instructed that, if it found that the confiscated substance was cocaine hydrochloride, the applicable law classified the substance as a schedule II controlled substance.

It is clear to us that the District Court took judicial notice of a legislative, rather than an adjudicative, fact in the present case and rule 201(g) is inapplicable. The District Court was not obligated to inform the jury that it could disregard the judicially noticed fact. In fact, to do so would be preposterous, thus permitting juries to make conflicting findings on what constitutes controlled substances under federal law.[7]

* * *

The judgment of conviction is affirmed.

DAWSON v. VANCE, 329 F.Supp. 1320, 1322 (S.D.Tex.1971). "The state statute in question, Article 524, Texas Penal Code, forbids and condemns the practice of sodomy. Sodomy is an act upon or concerning the physical being of a person. It is an act of immemorial anathema both at common law, wherein it was punishable by death, 81 C.J.S. Sodomy § 1, p. 370, and in ancient times. Genesis 19:1–29. It is clearly an offense involving moral turpitude whether defined by common law or by statute. The practice is inherently inimical to the

> *lidity and meaning of statutes,* formulating common law rules, deciding whether evidence should be admitted, assessing the sufficiency and effect of evidence, *all are essentially nonadjudicative in nature.* (Emphasis added.)

See State v. Freeman, 440 P.2d 744, 757 (Okl.1968); C. McCormick, *Law of Evidence* § 328, at 759 (2d ed. 1972); 1 J. Weinstein, *Evidence* ¶ 201[01] (1975).

7. Common sense dictates that the construction urged upon us by defendants is not well-taken. The fact that cocaine hydrochloride is derived from coca leaves is scientifically and pharmacologically unimpeachable. It would be incongruous to instruct the jurors on this irrefutable fact and then inform them that they may disregard it at their whim. It would be similarly illogical if we were to conclude that trial judges could rely upon generally accepted, undisputed facts in interpreting the applicable statutory law, yet obligate them to instruct the jury that it could disregard the factual underpinnings of the interpretation in its discretion.

general integrity of the human person. This is a postulate not of dogma but of common knowledge. It warrants the dignity of judicial knowledge. The primary authority and responsibility of the several states to forbid and control otherwise natural libidinal vice could scarcely be questioned. Their primary power over aberrational libidinal vice is no less sure. Sodomy is, therefore, in the general sense a crime the control of which is clearly within the reserved and police powers of the several states."

UNITED STATES v. JONES

United States Court of Appeals, Sixth Circuit, 1978.
580 F.2d 219.

ENGEL, CIRCUIT JUDGE.

Appellee William Allen Jones, Jr. was convicted by a district court jury of illegally intercepting telephone conversations of his estranged wife and of using the contents of the intercepted communications, in violation of 18 U.S.C. §§ 2511(1)(a) and (d) (1976). The proofs at trial showed only that the telephone which Jones had tapped was furnished by South Central Bell Telephone Company. Other than this fact, the government offered no evidence to show that South Central Bell was at the time a "person engaged as a common carrier in providing or operating * * * facilities for the transmission of interstate or foreign communications." 18 U.S.C. § 2510(1). See also 18 U.S.C. § 2510(10) and 47 U.S.C. § 153(h), defining common carrier.

Following the jury verdict of guilty on three of the five counts of the indictment, Jones' counsel moved the court for a new trial on the ground that the government had altogether failed to prove that the wire communication which the defendant tapped came within the definition of Section 2510. Upon a careful review of the evidence, United States District Judge Frank Wilson agreed and entered a judgment of acquittal. The government has appealed.

It is not seriously disputed that an essential element of the crimes charged, and one which the government was obligated to prove beyond a reasonable doubt, was that the conversation which was tapped was a "wire communication" as defined in the Act. Instead, the issue is whether the abbreviated proof offered by the government was minimally sufficient for the *prima facie* case which the government was obligated to place before the jury. In other words, was the proof that the tapped telephone was installed and furnished by "South Central Bell Telephone Company," without more, sufficient to enable the jury to find as a matter of fact that South Central Bell was a common carrier which provided facilities for the transmission of interstate or foreign communications? The government contends that, construing that evidence in the light most favorable to it, these facts could be permissibly inferred by the jury without any other proof.

The government's argument is essentially twofold. First, it urges that South Central Bell's status may reasonably be characterized as a fact within the common knowledge of the jury and that no further record evidence was necessary. Failing that, the government urges that such a fact is the proper subject of judicial notice which may be taken at any stage of the proceeding, including appeal, under Federal Rule of Evidence 201(f).

The government's first argument finds some support in Wigmore. 9 Wigmore on Evidence § 2570 at 542–43 (3d ed. 1940). Similarly, the legislative history of the Federal Rules of Evidence indicates that, even in criminal cases, "matters falling within the common fund of information supposed to be possessed by jurors need not be proved." Advisory Committee Note to Federal Rule of Evidence 201(g) (1969 draft), quoted, 1 Weinstein's Evidence 201–2 (1977). As that Note further indicates, however, such matters "are not, properly speaking, adjudicative facts but an aspect of legal reasoning." Id. Thus, while the jury may properly rely upon its own knowledge and experience in evaluating evidence and drawing inferences from that evidence, there must be sufficient record evidence to permit the jury to consult its general knowledge in deciding the existence of the fact.

While Wigmore notes that "[t]he range of [a jury's] general knowledge is not precisely definable," *Wigmore,* supra, § 2570 at 546, "the scope of this doctrine is narrow; it is strictly limited to a few matters of elemental experience in human nature, commercial affairs, and everyday life." Id. at 544. This category of fact is not so much a matter of noticing facts outside the record as it is a matter of the communication value of the words used, which can only be understood in the light of the common experience of those who employ them. See generally K. Davis, Administrative Law Text § 15.06 at 305 (3d ed. 1972).

While the issue is not without difficulty, we are satisfied that South Central Bell's status as a "common carrier * * * providing * * * facilities for the transmission of interstate * * * communications" is a fact which, if to be established without direct or circumstantial proof, must be governed by the judicial notice provisions of the Federal Rules of Evidence.

The government did not at any time during the jury trial specifically request the district court to take judicial notice of the status of South Central Bell. Nevertheless, it relies upon the provisions of Rule 201(f) which state that "[j]udicial notice may be taken at any stage of the proceeding." It is true that the Advisory Committee Note to 201(f) indicates that judicial notice is appropriate "in the trial court *or on appeal.*" (Emphasis added). See 1 Weinstein's Evidence ¶ 201[06] (1976). It is also true that the language of 201(f) does not distinguish between judicial notice in civil or criminal cases. There is, however, a critical difference in the manner in which the judicially noticed fact is to be submitted to the jury in civil and criminal proceedings:

> Instructing jury. In a civil action or proceeding, the court shall instruct the jury to accept as conclusive any fact judicially noticed. In a criminal case, the court shall instruct the jury that it may, but is not required to, accept as conclusive any fact judicially noticed.

Fed.R.Evid. 201(g). Thus under subsection (g) judicial notice of a fact in a civil case is conclusive while in a criminal trial the jury is not bound to accept the judicially noticed fact and may disregard it if it so chooses.

It is apparent from the legislative history that the congressional choice of language in Rule 201 was deliberate. In adopting the present language, Congress rejected a draft of subsection (g) proposed by the Supreme Court, which read:

> The judge shall instruct the jury to accept as established any facts judicially noticed.

The House Report explained its reason for the change:

> Rule 201(g) as received from the Supreme Court provided that when judicial notice of a fact is taken, the court shall instruct the jury to accept that fact as established. Being of the view that mandatory instruction to a jury in a criminal case to accept as conclusive any fact judicially noticed is inappropriate because contrary to the spirit of the Sixth Amendment right to a jury trial, the Committee adopted the 1969 Advisory Committee draft of this subsection, allowing a mandatory instruction in civil actions and proceedings and a discretionary instruction in criminal cases.

H.Rep. No. 93–650, 93d Cong., 1st Sess. 6–7 (1973), U.S.Code Cong. & Admin.News 7075, 7080 (1974). Congress intended to preserve the jury's traditional prerogative to ignore even uncontroverted facts in reaching a verdict. The legislature was concerned that the Supreme Court's rule violated the spirit, if not the letter, of the constitutional right to a jury trial by effectively permitting a partial directed verdict as to facts in a criminal case.[8]

As enacted by Congress, Rule 201(g) plainly contemplates that the jury in a criminal case shall pass upon facts which are judicially noticed. This it could not do if this notice were taken for the first time after it had been discharged and the case was on appeal. We, therefore, hold that Rule 201(f), authorizing judicial notice at the appellate level, must yield in the face of the express congressional intent manifested in 201(g) for criminal jury trials. To the extent that the earlier practice may have been otherwise, we conceive that is has been altered by the enactment of Rule 201.

Accordingly, the judgment of the district court is affirmed.

8. The Supreme Court of Utah expressed a similar concern in State v. Lawrence, 120 Utah 323, 234 P.2d 600 (1951):

> If a court can take one important element of an offense from the jury and determine the facts for them because such fact seems plain enough to him, then which element cannot be similarly taken away, and where would the process stop?

234 P.2d at 603.

ATKINS v. HUMES, 110 So.2d 663, 666 (Fla.1959). "But jurors of ordinary intelligence, sense and judgment are, in many cases, capable of reaching a conclusion, without the aid of expert testimony, in a malpractice case involving a charge of negligence in the application or administration of an approved medical treatment. For example, in the exercise of only common sense and ordinary judgment, a jury would have the right to conclude that it is negligence to permit a wound to heal superficially with nearly half a yard of gauze deeply imbedded in the flesh, Walker Hospital v. Pulley, 74 Ind.App. 659, 127 N.E. 559, 128 N.E. 933; to fail to sterilize surgical instruments before performing an operation, Lanier v. Trammell, 1944, 207 Ark. 372, 180 S.W.2d 818; to cut off part of a patient's tongue in removing adenoids, Evans v. Roberts, 172 Iowa 653, 154 N.W. 923; to perforate the urethra in performing an operation in which it was necessary to use care not to do so, Goodwin v. Hertzberg, 1952, 91 U.S.App.D.C. 385, 201 F.2d 204. Many other examples are cited in the annotation in 141 A.L.R. at pp. 12 et seq.; and see the cases cited in Montgomery v. Stary, supra, 84 So.2d [34] at page 40."

LANE v. SARGENT

United States Court of Appeals, First Circuit, 1914.
217 Fed. 237.

BINGHAM, CIRCUIT JUDGE.

The plaintiff, Sargent, a citizen of the state of New Hampshire, brings this action against the defendant, Lane, a citizen of the commonwealth of Massachusetts, in the District Court of the United States for the District of New Hampshire, to recover damages for injuries received on August 4, 1912, by being run into by an automobile operated by the defendant. The accident took place while the plaintiff was crossing Main street, in Salisbury, Mass. There was a trial by jury and a verdict for the plaintiff. The case is now here on defendant's bill of exceptions, and the errors assigned are to the exclusion of certain evidence offered by the defendant and the refusal of the judge to give certain requests for rulings.

The accident having occurred in Massachusetts, and the law of the road of that state being a material point in the case, the defendant offered to show what the law of Massachusetts on that subject was by introducing in evidence three decisions of the Massachusetts Supreme Judicial Court, as reported in Galbraith v. West End St. Ry. Co., 165 Mass. 581, 43 N.E. 501, Scannell v. Boston Elevated Ry. Co., 176 Mass. 173, 57 N.E. 341, and Commonwealth v. Horsfall, 213 Mass. 232, 100 N.E. 362, Ann.Cas. 1914A, 682. The evidence was excluded, and the defendant excepted. The trial court, in excluding the evidence, made the following ruling:

> "I think this question is a question of law for the court to pass upon, and the court is very glad to have any citation of Massachusetts law submitted to the court, and the court will instruct the jury upon what the Massachusetts law is. Upon that assumption, with this view of the law, the court will not allow the opinions of the Massachusetts court which have been called to its attention to be read to the jury."

The defendant contends that the law of Massachusetts, where the accident occurred, is the law of a foreign jurisdiction, and must be proved as a fact; that the court could not take judicial cognizance of it. This contention cannot be sustained. In Mills v. Green, 159 U.S. 651, 657, 16 S.Ct. 132, 134, 40 L.Ed. 293, Mr. Justice Gray, in delivering the opinion of the court, said:

> "The lower courts of the United States, and this court, on appeal from their decisions, take judicial notice of the Constitution and public laws of each state of the Union." * * *

And in Hanley v. Donoghue, 116 U.S. 1, 6, 6 S.Ct. 242, 245, 29 L.Ed. 535, the same Justice, in speaking for the court, said:

> "In the exercise of its general appellate jurisdiction from a lower court of the United States, this court takes judicial notice of the laws of every state of the Union, because those laws are known to the court below as laws alone, needing no averment or proof. * * *
>
> "But on a writ of error to the highest court of a state, in which the revisory power of this court is limited to determining whether a question of law depending upon the Constitution, laws, or treaties of the United States has been erroneously decided by the state court upon the facts before it—while the law of that state, being known to its courts as law, is of course within the judicial notice of this court at the hearing on error—yet, as in the state court the laws of another state are but facts, requiring to be proved in order to be considered, this court does not take judicial notice of them, unless made part of the record sent up, as in Green v. Van Buskirk, 7 Wall. 139 [19 L.Ed. 109]. * * *
>
> "Where by the local law of a state (as in Tennessee, Hobbs v. Memphis & Charleston Railroad, 9 Heisk. 873) its highest court takes judicial notice of the laws of other states, this court also, on writ of error, might take judicial notice of them."

See Martin v. Baltimore & Ohio Railroad, 151 U.S. 673, 678, 14 S.Ct. 533, 38 L.Ed. 311.

The Pawashick, 2 Low. 142, Fed.Cas. No. 10,851, a case relied upon by the defendant in support of his contention, is not in point. There the question was whether a federal court would take judicial notice of the law of a foreign country or it should be proved as a fact.

* * *

The judgment of the District Court is affirmed, and the defendant in error recovers his costs on appeal.

BOSWELL v. RIO DE ORO URANIUM MINES, INC., 68 N.M. 457, 362 P.2d 991, 994 (1961). "Appellant urges for the first time by its reply brief that this transaction is governed by the Oklahoma Statute of Frauds. The Oklahoma statute was not pleaded nor does it appear that it was called to the attention of the trial court. We have heretofore said that in the absence of pleading and proof to the contrary, the law of a sister state is presumed to be the same as the law of the forum. Carron v. Abounador, 28 N.M. 491, 214 P. 772; Norment v. Turley, 31 N.M. 400, 246 P. 748. However, we are cognizant of our subsequent Rule of Civil Procedure 44(d) (§ 21–1–1(44) N.M.S.A.1953 Comp.) which reads in part:

> "The courts of the state of New Mexico shall take judicial notice of the following facts:
>
> * * *
>
> '(3) * * * the laws of the several states and territories of the United States, and the interpretation thereof by the highest courts of appellate jurisdiction of such states and territories.'

"While the rule has not been construed in this jurisdiction, it is almost identical in language and clearly has the same intent and meaning as the Uniform Judicial Notice of Foreign Law Act. 9A U.L.A. p. 318. Those states adopting the Uniform Act and which have construed it, generally hold that the judicial notice required merely relieves the making of formal proof of foreign laws but that it was not intended to remove the necessity of at least informing the court of such foreign law or statute and of presenting it when relied upon for recovery or defense. Revlett v. Louisville & N.R. Co., 114 Ind.App. 187, 51 N.E.2d 95, 500; Kingston v. Quimby, Fla., 80 So.2d 455; Bates v. Equitable Life Assur. Soc., 27 Tenn.App. 17, 177 S.W.2d 360; Annotation 23 A.L.R.2d 1437 §§ 10, 13. Compare, Scott v. Scott, 153 Neb. 906, 46 N.W.2d 627, 23 A.L.R.2d 1431.

"While we are authorized under the rule to take judicial notice of the statutes of other states and their construction by the highest courts of appellate jurisdiction we will do so only where such statute has been presented to the trial court and where error is asserted because the trial court failed to judicially notice or follow such foreign statute, or where it is necessary for us to take judicial notice of the statute of another state upon which a decision of that state, relied upon, is predicated. Furthermore, appellant has not pointed out any essential difference between the English Statute of Frauds and the Oklahoma statute which would require a construction different than under our law."

Notes

(1) See also Roden v. Connecticut Co., 113 Conn. 408, 155 A. 721, 723–24 (1931) (judicial notice of administrative regulations); General Motors

Corp. v. Fair Employment Practices Div., 574 S.W.2d 394, 399–400 (Mo. 1978) (judicial notice of municipal ordinances); In re K.B.I.D., 417 S.W.2d 702, 704 (Mo.App.1967) (judicial notice of the records of another case).

(2) On proof of foreign law, see Fed.R.Civ.P. 44.1; Fed.R.Crim.P. 26.1; 2 Wright, Federal Practice and Procedure: Criminal §§ 431, 432 (2d ed. 1982); 9 Wright & Miller, Federal Practice and Procedure: Civil §§ 2441–2447 (1971); Baade, Proving Foreign and International Law in Domestic Tribunals, 17 Va.J.Int.L. 619 (1978).

*

INDEX

References are to Pages

References are to Pages

References are to Pages

References are to Pages

References are to Pages

†